T0396649

The Palgrave Handbook of the Anthropology of Technology

"This extraordinarily ambitious and comprehensive volume shows how many things we might have previously considered merely the context for studying technologies are themselves technologies. Through this perspective, we come to learn how technologies facilitate the creation of moral norms, social orders, infrastructures and power. Examples range from datafication and energy to committees, knowledge, gender, authenticity, food and many forms of classification. Such a holistic sensibility is surely apt for the discipline of anthropology, continuing a tradition that recognises that technologies are as much concerned with making people as with making things."

—Daniel Miller, *University College London, co-author of The Global Smartphone*

"Whether you take up this *Handbook* as an introduction or a review, these writings expand and update our conceptual framework for thinking with anthropology about technology. Technologies, in these writings, are inseparable from the knowledge practices, collectives, controversies and infrastructures that configure them and render their significance. Framed as technological, socio-material relations have been incorporated into histories and political economies specific to colonial and instrumentalist logics of development and progress. Locating technology as one among the many tropes, processes and practices that conjoin matter and meaning, this collection opens lines of analysis able to generate radically different stories."

—Lucy Suchman, *Lancaster University, author of Human-Machine Reconfigurations*

"A monument to the unison of hand, book and tool, this ambitious compendium offers resounding proof that the anthropology of technology has come of age. In their sheer richness and diversity, the volume's many contributions show that researching technology, far from a narrow specialism, seeks nothing less than to place human being and becoming in a world undergoing unprecedented, and potentially cataclysmic transformation. From the climate emergency, through the energy transition and public health, to race and inequality, these studies address some of the most pressing questions of our time. Authoritative, wide-ranging and forward-looking, the *Handbook* will be an indispensable source for years to come."

—Tim Ingold, *University of Aberdeen, author of Imagining for Real*

"This is a handbook in the best sense of the word, a convincing expansion of anthropological approaches to technical systems to dozens of contemporary hot topics: energy transition, robotics, digital culture, issues of discrimination, welfare austerity, emerging technologies. The articles analyzing the body, gestures, and objects will provide the reader with excellent theoretical and methodological syntheses, and scores of up-to-date references."

—Pierre Lemonnier, *The French National Centre for Scientific Research (CNRS), author of Mundane Objects*

Maja Hojer Bruun • Ayo Wahlberg
Rachel Douglas-Jones
Cathrine Hasse • Klaus Hoeyer
Dorthe Brogård Kristensen
Brit Ross Winthereik
Editors

The Palgrave Handbook of the Anthropology of Technology

palgrave
macmillan

Editors
Maja Hojer Bruun
Department of Educational
Anthropology
Aarhus University
Aarhus, Denmark

Rachel Douglas-Jones
Department of Business IT
IT University of Copenhagen
Copenhagen, Denmark

Klaus Hoeyer
Center for Medical Science &
Technology Studies
University of Copenhagen
Copenhagen, Denmark

Brit Ross Winthereik
Department of Business IT
IT University of Copenhagen
Copenhagen, Denmark

Ayo Wahlberg
Department of Anthropology
University of Copenhagen
Copenhagen, Denmark

Cathrine Hasse
Department of Educational
Anthropology
Aarhus University
Aarhus, Denmark

Dorthe Brogård Kristensen
Department of Business and
Management
University of Southern Denmark
Odense, Denmark

ISBN 978-981-16-7083-1   ISBN 978-981-16-7084-8   (eBook)
https://doi.org/10.1007/978-981-16-7084-8

PREFACE

How did this book come into being? In the spring of 2017, we submitted an application to the Independent Research Fund Denmark for a research network on 'The Anthropology of Technology: future technologies, culture, and human practices' following Maja Hojer Bruun's vision to bring together anthropologists widely dispersed across Denmark's universities and other institutions, often working in interdisciplinary research environments. What united us was a common empirical interest in the ways in which technologies (re-)shape political economies, societies, cultures, and identities in different parts of the world. The network kicked off at Aarhus University in May 2018 and has come together on a regular basis for seminars and conferences hosted at each of our respective universities ever since.

Working across robotics, drones, biomedicine, energy, digital data, and infrastructures, our ambitions grew as we received positive feedback from those who took part in our many events, furthering anthropological conversations focused on technology. We determined that one way to further boost the study of technology in anthropology, not just in Denmark but internationally, would be by publishing a Handbook. Why did such an exciting sub-field of anthropology not have its own Handbook? We immediately realised the obligating implications of such an enunciation, not least at a moment when massive societal challenges of climate change, energy transitions, rising healthcare needs, welfare austerity, inequality, discrimination, and political unrest loomed large.

With contributions from no less than 46 scholars from around the world, we are proud to present this *Handbook of the Anthropology of Technology*. The obstacles inherent to a global pandemic have imposed an increased workload and emotional pressure on academics worldwide, the authors in this volume being no exception. Yet, despite immense challenges to upholding writing routines and daily life, they have contributed a diverse and rich set of chapters highlighting different aspects of the anthropology of technology. We thank each one of them for their efforts. There is no doubt that the insights presented will be of great value to future generations of anthropologists.

As anyone who has ever been involved in bringing together a Handbook will attest, doing so is no small task but, rather, one involving countless editorial meetings to design and debate content and structure, globally disseminating invitations to contribute chapters, preparation of a book proposal, meetings with potential publishers, requests for peer reviews of chapter drafts, preparation of feedback, and more. We are eternally grateful to all the contributors and peer reviewers for finding the time to work on, complete, and review the 39 chapters that make up this *Handbook of the Anthropology of Technology*. We are appreciative of your commitment to this collective project and of the result.

We thank the Independent Research Fund Denmark for funding the research network, seminars, and conferences (funding ID: DFF-7023-00101), and Aarhus University Research Foundation for supporting the editorial process (funding ID: AUFF-E-2020-4-32). We would also like to thank our editor at Palgrave, Joshua Pitt, for believing in this project from very early on and for his guidance throughout the editorial process. Thanks also go to our student assistant Mette Trans Ebbekær Jensen, copy editor Marie-Louise Karttunen, and indexer Donald Howes who have been invaluable in realising this book project.

Aarhus, Denmark   Maja Hojer Bruun
Copenhagen, Denmark   Dorthe Brogård Kristensen
Odense, Denmark   Rachel Douglas-Jones
                                                              Klaus Hoeyer
                                                          Cathrine Hasse
                                                          Ayo Wahlberg
                                                  Brit Ross Winthereik

CONTENTS

NOTES ON CONTRIBUTORS

Simone Abram is Professor of Anthropology at Durham University, UK, and co-director of the Durham Energy Institute. She is a co-investigator at the National Centre for Energy Systems Integration (2016–2021) and co-investigator at the Centre for Inclusive Decarbonisation led by Tanja Winther at Oslo University. Recent publications include *Electrifying Anthropology: Perspectives on electric practices and infrastructures (2019)* (with Brit Ross Winthereik and Thomas Yarrow), 'Our Lives with Electric Things' (2017) (with Jamie Cross, Lea Schick, and Mike Anusas), and *Ethnographies of Power (2021)* (with Tristan Loloum and Nathalie Ortar).

Astrid Oberborbeck Andersen holds a PhD in Social Anthropology from the University of Copenhagen. She is Associate Professor of Techno-anthropology at Aalborg University. Her research centres on human–environment relations, specialising in anthropological perspectives on climatic change and environmental crises with a focus on water politics in Peru and Latin America, and wildlife and ecosystems management in Greenland. The cross-disciplinary politics of knowledge and collaboration on technological and environmental issues are central in Astrid's research. She is currently co-principal investigator of the research project 'Muskox Pathways: Resources and Ecologies in Greenland', and co-leads an environmental humanities research network.

Anne Beaulieu is Associate Professor of Science and Technology Studies and director of the Data Research Centre, University of Groningen, where she leads the research group 'Knowledge Infrastructures for Sustainability' and has developed the minor 'Data Wise: Data Science in Society' (with Gert Stulp). Beaulieu's work focuses on diversity and complexity in knowledge infrastructures. She is co-author of *Virtual Knowledge: Experimenting in the Humanities and the Social Sciences* and of *Data and Society: A Critical Introduction* (2021). Since September 2018, she has been co-coordinator of the national PhD training network of the Netherlands Graduate Research School of Science, Technology, and Modern Culture (WTMC).

Mikkel Bille holds a PhD in Social Anthropology from University College London. He is an associate professor at Roskilde University, leading the project 'Living with Nordic Lighting' (Velux Foundation). His research focuses on the materiality, atmospheres, and social uses of lighting, particularly in Scandinavia and the Middle East. His most recent books include *Living with Light* (2019), *Being Bedouin around Petra* (2019), and *Elements of Architecture* (co-edited with Tim Flohr Sørensen).

Cal Biruk is Associate Professor of Anthropology at McMaster University and the author of *Cooking Data: Culture and Politics in an African Research World* (2018). Biruk's research interests lie at the intersection of medical anthropology, critical data studies, global health studies, and queer studies. Biruk's projects focus on the sociotechnical infrastructures that produce and quantify 'key populations' in Malawi as objects of knowledge, investment, and affect, on the racialised politics of aid economies and audit cultures in southern Africa, and on fitness wearables as technologies that harbour queer potential.

Francesca Bray is an anthropologist and historian of science, technology, and medicine in East Asia, with a particular focus on how technologies serve to weave gender principles into the very fabric of states and government; see, for instance, *Technology, Gender and History in Imperial China* (2013). She is co-editor of the forthcoming *Cambridge History of Technology*, and Emerita Professor of Social Anthropology at the University of Edinburgh.

Maja Hojer Bruun is Associate Professor in the Department of Educational Anthropology, Aarhus University, and convenor of the Danish research network for the Anthropology of Technology (AnTech). Her research centres on emerging digital technologies, spanning robots, drones, urban living labs, and data encryption infrastructures, and in her work she explores collaborative, interventionist, and experimental ethnographic methods. In her current research project she is interested in the forms of knowledge, organisation, and government through which cities are turned into living labs and sites of experimentation, and how people, data infrastructures, and digital devices are enrolled in processes of urban planning.

Mikkel Bunkenborg is Associate Professor of China Studies in the Department of Cross-Cultural and Regional Studies, University of Copenhagen. Working at the intersection of China studies and anthropology, his research has focused on bodies and medicine, on politics and popular religion in rural North China, and on Chinese globalisation as it unfolds through infrastructure construction, resource extraction, and trade in Mongolia and Mozambique. He is currently the primary investigator of a collaborative ethnographic project entitled 'Moral Economies of Food in Contemporary China'.

Stephanie Bunn is Senior Lecturer in Social Anthropology at the University of St Andrews. She has conducted research into Central Asian felt textiles and basketry worldwide and curated numerous exhibitions, including the first-ever

British Museum exhibition of Kyrgyz felt textiles. She is author of *Nomadic Felt*, editor of *Anthropology and Beauty (2010)*, and co-editor with Victoria Mitchell of *The Material Culture of Basketry (2020)*. She coordinated the Woven Communities Project, on Scottish basketry heritage, and is currently collaborating with educational mathematician Professor Ricardo Nemirovsky, Professor Cathrine Hasse, and three basket makers on the Royal Society-funded 'Forces in Translation', researching the relationship between basket work and mathematics.

Alison Cool is Assistant Professor of Anthropology at the University of Colorado. She is a cultural anthropologist whose research focuses on digital technologies, data ethics, and how people think about privacy and surveillance. Her current project, based on fieldwork in Sweden, is an ethnographic study of how experts, professionals, and activists go about the ethical and pragmatic work of protecting and sharing personal data. She also researches and writes about how behavioural economists see the world, and the role of twins as scientific and medical research subjects.

Ludovic Coupaye is Associate Professor of Anthropology at University College London. His research focuses on four interrelated topics: material and visual culture in Oceania; art and aesthetics among the 'Abelam' communities of Papua New Guinea; anthropology of techniques, skills, and materiality; and anthropology of technology and Modernity. His most recent interests are the relationships between 'technology' and 'society' from the angle of technical activities, technical objects, and technical systems. He is the author of *Growing Artefacts, Displaying Relationships: Yams, Art and Technology Amongst the Nyamikum Abelam of Papua New Guinea* (2013).

Mie S. Dam is Assistant Professor at the University of Copenhagen. Her research explores the development of new medical treatments at the intersection between laboratory and clinic. She takes a special interest in how researchers navigate scientific and moral responsibilities as they work to translate science into better human lives. In her current research, she explores personalised modelling and patient selection in cancer genomics. This project is part of the 'MeInWe' project. Her PhD was conducted as part of the LifeWorth project and concerned translation across animal model and human patient in experimental neonatology.

Rachel Douglas-Jones is Associate Professor at the IT University of Copenhagen, where she heads the Technologies in Practice research group and co-directs the ETHOS Lab. She conducts research on questions of ethics and the governance of science and technology, and is currently the principal investigator of 'Moving Data-Moving People', a study of emergent social credit systems in China through the lens of trust. Her recent publications include 'Committee as Witness' (the *Cambridge Journal of Anthropology*, 2021) and 'Bodies of Data' (*Journal of the Royal Anthropological Institute* (JRAI), 2021).

She is the editor (with Antonia Walford and Nick Seaver) of 'Towards an Anthropology of Data' (JRAI, 2021).

Joseph Dumit is an anthropologist of passions, performance, brains, games, bodies, drugs, and facts. Chair of Performance Studies and Professor of Anthropology and Science & Technology Studies at the University of California, he is author of *Picturing Personhood: Brain Scans and Biomedical America* (2004) and *Drugs for Life: How Pharmaceutical Companies Define Our Health* (2012). He works with neuroscientists, artists, and improvisers in Denmark, Germany, and France on multimedia installations for social learning and togetherness.

Christina Dunbar-Hester is the author of *Hacking Diversity: The Politics of Inclusion in Open Technology Cultures* (2020) and *Low Power to the People: Pirates, Protest, and Politics in FM Radio Activism* (2014). She is a faculty member at the Annenberg School of Communication at the University of Southern California in Los Angeles, and she holds a PhD in Science & Technology Studies from Cornell University, USA. Her writing and research centres on the politics of technology in culture, especially media and tech activisms, infrastructures, and envirotechnical assemblages.

Vaike Fors is Associate Professor at the School of Information Technology at Halmstad University, Sweden. Her area of expertise lies in the fields of visual, sensory, and design ethnography. In her pursuit to contribute to further understandings of contemporary conditions for learning, she has studied people's interaction with new and emerging technologies in various research projects. Fors is an experienced project leader of international scientific, applied, and collaborative research projects. Recent publications include the book *Imagining Personal Data: Experiences of Self-Tracking* (2020).

Iben M. Gjødsbøl is Assistant Professor at the University of Copenhagen. Her research explores how medical technologies and clinical practices shape our understandings and experiences of health and illness. As part of the 'MeInWe' project, her current research explores how precision medicine is being developed and consolidated within the field of cardiology. Her PhD was conducted as part of the LifeWorth project and concerned how life's worth is practised and experienced at the end of life when people age into dementia.

Gökçe Günel is Assistant Professor of Anthropology at Rice University. Her latest book, *Spaceship in the Desert: Energy, Climate Change, and Urban Design in Abu Dhabi* (2019), focuses on the construction of renewable energy and clean technology infrastructures in the United Arab Emirates, more specifically concentrating on the Masdar City project. Her articles have been published and are forthcoming in *Public Culture*, *Anthropological Quarterly*, *Engineering Studies*, *South Atlantic Quarterly*, *Log*, *e-flux*, and *PoLAR*, among others. Currently, she is working on a book on electricity production in Ghana, provisionally titled *Energy Accumulation*.

Cathrine Hasse is Professor in the Department of Educational Anthropology, Aarhus University, and programme manager of the research programme 'Future Technologies, Culture, and Learning'. She is the author of *Posthumanist Learning* (2020) and *An Anthropology of Learning* (Springer 2015). She has been coordinator of several EU projects (e.g. REELER—Responsible and Ethical Learning in Robotics) as well as Danish projects exploring processes of learning with technology. She holds a PhD in cultural learning processes in physics from Copenhagen University (2000). Her writing centres on learning as a conceptual-material change of environments.

Mette M. High is Reader in Social Anthropology and Director of the Centre for Energy Ethics at the University of St Andrews. She is author of *Fear and Fortune: Spirit Worlds and Emerging Economies in the Mongolian Gold Rush* (2017) and co-editor of 'Energy and Ethics?' (JRAI Special Issue, 2019). Her current project examines money, oil, and climate change in global energy markets.

Klaus Hoeyer is Professor of Medical Science and Technology Studies, Department of Public Health, University of Copenhagen. He is a social anthropologist whose work focuses on the interaction between patients, health professionals, and larger organisational and regulatory processes when new medical technologies are being introduced. His research focuses on the drivers for and implications of intensified data sourcing in healthcare.

Linda F. Hogle is an anthropologist of science, technology, and medicine, and Professor Emerita at the University of Wisconsin-Madison School of Medicine and Public Health. Her research on emerging biomedical technologies spans stem cell research, tissue engineering, enhancement technologies, medical data use and privacy, and digital surrogates for humans, focusing largely on how novel entities adapt to or resist standardisation. She currently examines authentication practices in cell, food, and health information technologies as efforts to stabilise ambiguous entities and their infrastructures.

Alvaro Jarrín is Associate Professor of Anthropology at the College of the Holy Cross, Massachusetts. His research explores the imbrication of medicine, the body, and inequality in Brazil, with focuses on plastic surgery, genomics, and gender nonconforming activism. He is the author of *The Biopolitics of Beauty: Cosmetic Citizenship and Affective Capital in Brazil (2017)*, co-editor of *Remaking the Human: Cosmetic Technologies of Body Repair, Reshaping and Replacement (2021)*, and co-editor of *Precarious Democracy: Ethnographies of Hope, Despair and Resistance in Brazil (2021)*.

Hannah Knox is Associate Professor of Anthropology at University College London and her work focuses on the relationship between technical infrastructures and social life through ethnographic studies of projects of technical transformation. Her recent work includes research on the social imaginaries and effects of road construction in Latin America, and the governmental challenges of climate change in the UK and Europe. Knox is editor of the *Journal of the Royal Anthropological Institute*, and her recent books include *Roads: An Anthropology of Infrastructure and Expertise (2015)* (with Penny Harvey), *Ethnography for a Data Saturated World (2018)* (with Dawn Nafus), and *Thinking Like a Climate: Governing a City in Times of Environmental Change (2020).*

Emma Kowal is Professor of Anthropology at the Alfred Deakin Institute at Deakin University. She is a cultural and medical anthropologist who previously worked as a medical doctor and public health researcher in Indigenous health. Her research interests lie at the intersection of science and technology studies (STS) and Indigenous studies and have recently focused on the many iterations and resonances of 'Indigenous DNA'. She has authored over 100 publications including the monograph *Trapped in the Gap: Doing Good in Indigenous Australia (2015)* and the collection *Cryopolitics: Frozen Life in a Melting World (2017)*. Her current book project is entitled *Haunting Biology: Science and Indigeneity in Australia.*

Jakob Krause-Jensen is Associate Professor in the Department of Educational Anthropology, Aarhus University. He is interested in how anthropological research strategies, theories, and methodologies can be used to study contemporary organisations and work life, and in particular how notions of culture are used in management practices. He is editor of the Anthropology at Work book series, and his current research focuses on the shipping industry in Denmark, in particular on the interplay between digital technologies and the green transition.

Dorthe Brogård Kristensen is Associate Professor of Consumption Studies at the University of Southern Denmark. Her current interests include self-tracking technologies, algorithmic culture, health, and consumption. She has published in *New Media and Society*, the *Journal of Consumer Culture*, *Critical Health Communication*, *Health*, *Appetite* and the *Journal of Marketing Management.*

Merete Lie is Professor Emeritus and former head of the Centre for Gender Research at the Norwegian University of Science and Technology. She is a social anthropologist and her field of research is feminist technoscience, including ICTs, assisted reproductive technologies, medical imaging and bioart, as well as research on gender and change in China and Southeast Asia. Her books include the edited/co-edited volumes *Making Technology Our Own? Domesticating Technology Into Everyday Life* (1996); *He, She and IT Revisited: New Perspectives on Gender in the Information Society* (2003); *The Social Meaning of Children and Fertility Change in Europe* (2013); and *Assisted Reproduction Across Borders: Feminist Perspectives on Normalizations, Disruptions and Transmissions* (2017).

Thomas Lindgren is an industrial PhD researcher at Volvo Cars and Halmstad University, Sweden. He has an MSc in Interaction Engineering from the Lulea University of Technology and has a long background in Human Machine Interaction and User Experience Research & Development within the automotive industry since 1999. His PhD research is on anticipatory user experiences of emerging technologies related to the automotive industry and, over the past three years, he has been conducting ethnographic research on online communities, following families at home and on their car commutes to understand how digitalisation, electrification, and automation change how people experience cars.

Amade M'charek, is Professor of Anthropology of Science at the Department of Anthropology, University of Amsterdam. As the principal investigator of the 'RaceFaceID' project, an ERC-consolidator project on forensic identification and the making of face and race, her focus is on genetic diversity, population genetics, and forensic DNA practices. She emphasises the ir/relevance of race in such practices, highlighting the relation between the individual and the collective. She has published widely on these topics in various academic journals. Her most recent research on forensics addresses the issue of death in the Mediterranean and the forensic identification of dead migrants.

Anders Kristian Munk is Associate Professor at the Aalborg University in Copenhagen, director of the Techno-Anthropological Laboratory (TANTlab), and a co-founder of the Public Data Lab. He holds a D.Phil. in Geography from the University of Oxford and has worked as a visiting research fellow at the Sciences Po médialab. His research focuses on digital methods for controversy mapping and computational anthropology more broadly.

Laura E. Navne is a senior researcher at the Danish Centre for Social Science Research and a postdoctoral researcher at the University of Copenhagen in the research project 'MeInWe' where she examines practices and experiences of relatedness and naming emerging with precision medicine in clinical genetics and diabetes care. In her PhD research, she investigated practices and experiences of a life worth living at the beginning of life in a Neonatal Intensive Care Unit as part of the research project 'LifeWorth'.

Katalin Osz is a UX Strategy and Design Researcher at Volvo Cars and an affiliated design researcher at the School of Information Technology at Halmstad University, Sweden. Previously, she worked as a postdoctoral researcher on various international projects related to sustainable energy consumption in Sweden and in the UK. She has a mixed background in cultural anthropology and design and holds an MSc in Culture and Society from the London School of Economics and Political Science and a PhD in Built Environment from Loughborough University.

Sarah Pink is Professor and Director of the Emerging Technologies Research Lab at Monash University, Australia. She is International Guest Professor at the

School of Information Technology at Halmstad University, Sweden, and Visiting Professor at the Design School at Loughborough University, UK.

Lindsay Poirier is Assistant Professor of Statistical and Data Sciences at Smith College. As a cultural anthropologist working within the field of data studies, Poirier examines data infrastructure design work and the politics of representation emerging from data practices. She is also the Lead Platform Architect for the Platform for Experimental Collaborative Ethnography (PECE).

Kaspar Raats received a BSc in Computer Science from Tallinn University of Technology in Estonia followed by an MSc in Interaction Design from Chalmers University of Technology in Sweden. He is an industrial PhD candidate at Volvo Cars and Halmstad University Sweden and a visiting researcher at the Emerging Technologies Research Lab in Australia. At Volvo Cars he is working with User Experience research in future-oriented technology projects. In his PhD research he investigates how trust in intelligent technologies develops in people's real-life, complex social encounters and contingent situations, and how this can inform the development of intelligent technologies and services.

Jennifer Robertson is Professor Emerita of Anthropology and the History of Art at the University of Michigan, Ann Arbor. She is also an affiliate professor of Anthropology and Japan Studies at the University of Washington, Seattle. Among her seven books are *Native and Newcomer: Making and Remaking a Japanese City* (1991), *Takarazuka: Sexual Politics and Popular Culture in Modern Japan* (1998; Japanese translation, 2000), and *Robo Sapiens Japanicus: Robots, Gender, Family, and the Japanese Nation* (2018).

Minna Ruckenstein is Associate Professor at the Centre for Consumer Society Research and the Helsinki Centre for Digital Humanities at the University of Helsinki. She directs a research team that explores economic, social, emotional, and imaginary aspects of data practices and datafication. Recently funded projects focus on algorithmic culture and rehumanising automated decision-making.

Emilia Sanabria is a French-Colombian anthropologist trained in the UK and working in Brazil for over fifteen years. She was Assistant Professor at ENS Lyon for seven years before joining the CNRS in 2018 where she is a member of the CERMES3. Her research is situated at the crossroads of medical anthropology and STS. Her book *Plastic Bodies: Sex hormones and menstrual suppression in Brazil* was published by Duke University Press and awarded the Rosaldo and Forsythe prizes. She has published on nutrition and food justice, evidence-based medicine, and the anthropology of pharmaceuticals, and is Principal Investigator of the ERC project 'Healing Encounters' (2018–2024).

Sunniva Sandbukt is a PhD fellow in the Technologies in Practice research group at the IT University of Copenhagen, Denmark. Her work examines social infrastructures, mobility, and the circulation of value, focusing on how these infrastructures impact socio-economic relationships by generating new or maintaining existing inequalities, and how people navigate within and appropriate these technologies to meet their own needs. Her research draws on extensive fieldwork related to mobilities, transport, and digital payments in Indonesia.

Christo Sims is an associate professor in the Department of Communication, and an affiliated faculty member in Science Studies, Ethnic Studies, and the Design Lab, at the University of California, San Diego. His first solo-authored book, *Disruptive Fixation: School Reform and the Pitfalls of Techno-Idealism* (2017), won the 2018 Best Book Award from the Communication, Information Technologies, and Media Sociology section of the American Sociological Association. He is currently a member of the Institute for Advanced Study in Princeton, New Jersey, where he is working on a book project about how monopolistic technology corporations are deploying avant-garde architecture as a political technology.

Mette N. Svendsen is Professor of Medical Anthropology at the University of Copenhagen. She has headed several research projects, including 'LifeWorth', which explores the worth of life across species, and 'MeInWe', which investigates the relationship between person and collectivity in the field of precision medicine. She is the author of *Near Human: Border Zones of Life, Species, and Belonging (2021).*

Susanna Trnka is an associate professor at the University of Auckland. Her work examines embodiment through a variety of lenses including pain, political violence, respiratory health, movement, and youth wellbeing. She has contributed to new theories of collective responsibility through her co-edited book *Competing responsibilities* (2017), and her monograph on asthma, *One blue child: Asthma, responsibility, and the politics of global health* (2017). She is currently the principal investigator on a Royal Society of New Zealand project examining youth mental health and digital technology use. Her most recent book, *Traversing: Embodied Lifeworlds in the Czech Republic* (2020), is a phenomenological examination of movement.

Irene van Oorschot, PhD, is a Marie Curie IF postdoctoral researcher at the Life Sciences and Society Lab, KU Leuven, Belgium. Drawing on ethnography and postcolonial STS, she has published on a variety of topics, ranging from the production of facts and accounts in legal settings, to the performativity of social-scientific technologies of measurement, and the agency of case files, to the making and unmaking of racial difference in forensic and legal practices. Her monograph on the production of knowledge and judgement in sociological and legal settings, *The Law Multiple: Judgment and Knowledge in Practice*, was recently published by Cambridge University Press.

Ayo Wahlberg is Professor MSO in the Department of Anthropology, University of Copenhagen. Working broadly within the field of social studies of (bio)medicine, his research has focused on the modernisation of traditional herbal medicine (in Vietnam and the United Kingdom), the routinisation of reproductive technologies (in China), and the shaping of chronic living in the everyday lives of millions of people who live with (multiple) chronic conditions. Ayo is the author of *Good Quality—the Routinization of Sperm Banking in China (2018)*, co-editor of *Southern Medicine for Southern People—Vietnamese Medicine in the Making (2012)*, and editor of the journal *BioSocieties* (Palgrave Macmillan).

Brit Ross Winthereik is Professor of Science and Technology Studies and Ethnography at the IT University of Copenhagen where she is head of the Center for Digital Welfare. She has published widely on information infrastructures and transformations of the welfare state based on studies of development aid, renewable energy, and public governance. She is co-author of *Monitoring Movements in Development Aid: Recursive Infrastructures and Partnerships* (2013, with Casper Bruun Jensen), and co-editor of *Electrifying Anthropology: Exploring Electrical Practices and Infrastructures* (2019, with Simone Abram and Thomas Yarrow), *Experimenting with Ethnography: A Companion to Analysis* (2021, with Andrea Ballestero), and *Energy Worlds in Experiments* (2021, with James Maguire and Laura Watts).

List of Figures

CHAPTER 1

The Anthropology of Technology: The Formation of a Field

Introduction

Maja Hojer Bruun and Ayo Wahlberg

Technology, defined anthropologically, is not material culture but rather a *total social phenomenon* in the sense used by Mauss, a phenomenon that marries the material, the social and the symbolic in a complex web of associations.
—Bryan Pfaffenberger, *Fetishised Objects and Humanised Nature: Towards an Anthropology of Technology*, 1988, p. 249

Technology embraces all aspects of the process of action upon matter, whether it is scratching one's nose, planting sweet potatoes, or making jumbo jets … technologies are—like myths, marriage prohibitions, or exchange systems—social productions in themselves.
—Pierre Lemonnier, *Elements for an Anthropology of Technology*, 1992, pp. 1–2, 11

The shift from the classical concept of *tekhné* to the modern concept of technology has brought about a profound change in the way we think about the relation between human beings and their activity. The image of the artisan, immersed with the whole of his being in a sensuous engagement with the material, has given way to that of the operative whose job it is to set in motion an exterior system of productive forces, according to principles of mechanical functioning that are entirely indifferent to particular human aptitudes and sensibilities.
—Tim Ingold, *Eight themes in the Anthropology of Technology*, 1997, pp. 130–131

M. H. Bruun (✉)
Department of Educational Anthropology, Aarhus University, Aarhus, Denmark
e-mail: mhbruun@edu.au.dk

A. Wahlberg
Department of Anthropology, University of Copenhagen, Copenhagen, Denmark
e-mail: ayo.wahlberg@anthro.ku.dk

M. H. Bruun et al. (eds.), *The Palgrave Handbook of the Anthropology of Technology*, https://doi.org/10.1007/978-981-16-7084-8_1

1

Once seen as producing worldwide homogenization and generalized acculturation, cosmopolitan science and technology are now viewed in terms of their real
or potential contribution to the formation of hybrid cultures and to processes of
self-affirmation of their selective and partially autonomous adoption. ... [N]ew
languages are needed that allow different groups of people (experts, social movements, citizens' groups) to reorient the dominant understanding of technology.
—Arturo Escobar, *Welcome to Cyberia: Notes on the Anthropology
of Cyberculture*, 1994, pp. 215, 221

Anthropos and *techne* are inseparable when it comes to the study of humans and
their societies. From its very origins as a discipline, anthropology has recorded
and researched human-technology interfaces in efforts to account for and
understand forms of social organisation and practice as well as systems of belief
and meaning throughout the world. Whether approached in terms of the tools
and dexterous capabilities that were seen to separate humans from other species or the technical systems that allowed for subsistence and the reproduction
of society, human ingenuity and practice involving the development and use of
various kinds of technologies has been a definitive object of ethnographic
inquiry.

Today, two decades into the twenty-first century, anthropological approaches
to studying technology are thriving. In this Handbook, we have brought
together 39 chapters to demonstrate that while there is no single 'anthropology of technology', there is a set of approaches that constitutes a field of
enquiry. This field is informed by just over a century of anthropological
thought, the history of which illuminates as much the changing landscapes of
technological advance as it does the anthropological theories that have been
used to make sense of technologies in development and use. We begin this
chapter by cataloguing a plethora of definitions of technology, each of which
has informed this collection in different ways. From there, we provide readers
with a historical exposé that takes us from early evolutionary studies of technology via critiques of it by those who championed diffusionist understandings to
more contemporary notions of socio-technical systems and infrastructures.
With the advantage of digital search technologies and global journals, our view
of the history of the place of technology in the discipline is shaped by technology itself. Once we have situated the anthropology of technology historically,
we move on to explain the logic of how we have structured the chapters that
follow. Finally, we end this introduction by recapitulating why it remains so
relevant and important to mobilise anthropological studies of technology at
the present time.

The Handbook is organised around what we see as some of the most important characteristics of anthropological studies of technology, often in dialogue
with work in archaeology, sociology, history, political science, and, not least,
science and technology studies (STS). Our four thematic sections are dedicated
to: (1) the diverse knowledge practices that technologies involve and on which
they depend; (2) the communities, collectives, and categories that emerge

around technologies; (3) anthropology's contribution to proliferating debates on ethics, values, and morality in relation to technology; and (4) infrastructures that highlight how all technologies are embedded in broader political economies and socio-historical processes that shape and often reinforce inequality and discrimination while also generating diversity. Importantly, all sections and chapters share a commitment to fieldwork, perhaps not always in a conventional sense but always with a focused attention to experiences, embodiments, practices, and materialities in the daily lives of those people and institutions involved in the development, manufacturing, deployment, and/or use of particular technologies. While the Handbook's four thematic sections all have separate introductions, in this opening chapter the perspectives, fields, and approaches covered in the Handbook's first section are woven into our account of the gradual formation of 'anthropology of technology' as a field of enquiry.

TECHNOLOGY AND TECHNIQUES

Colloquially, technologies are understood as artefacts. This foregrounds their material existence, origin, creation, and use. In classic ethnographies of the introduction and adoption of new or 'foreign' technologies in new settings (e.g. Sharp 1968[1952]; Godelier and Garanger 1979), artefacts like stone and steel axes are singled out and described, at times in deterministic, evolutionary ways. To this day, in popular accounts, technologies are often disembedded from the social and from human bodies, as they come to 'stand out' materially. Perhaps this is because there are still too few narrative repertoires that allow for the weaving together of technology and social relations into integrated wholes, since it would require us to abandon modernity's divide between technology and society (cf. Latour 1993). Or is it because there *is* something immanent in technologies that either lends them special, magic powers (Gell 1992), or makes them disappear, like Heidegger's (1973[1927]) ready-to-hand hammer, which only appears when it breaks down, Merleau-Ponty's (2002[1945]) blind stick or invisible infrastructures (Star and Ruhleder 1996)?

While sociologists or historians of technology usually study the development of a product or innovation in modern science or engineering (e.g. Bijker et al. 1987; Bijker and Law 1992; Bijker 1995; Hughes 1983), and most technical sciences do not consider anything else as technology, anthropologists have worked according to a wider concept. This breadth is reflected in our Handbook, with chapters covering basket-weaving techniques, reproductive technologies, technologies of beauty, and technologies of government. Anthropologists and archaeologists have always shared an interest in the most mundane and taken-for-granted *things* of everyday life, and studied these as technology or material culture: typically baskets, pots, hoes, arrows, or other tools, not to forget pipettes, smart phones, and cars. At the same time, however, anthropologists have recorded a multiplicity of contemporary human technological practices involving all kinds of ephemeral activities and perishable materials that do not leave traces for archaeological excavation. What counts as technology in particular contexts and for whom are some of the open questions that are brought to various fields of study and fieldwork sites.

Anthropologists have provided several useful definitions of technology that emphasise that if we are to understand technologies, we must go beyond the artefacts and include human bodies, skills, traditions, practices, processes, and socio-technical systems when conceptualising them. We selected four contrasting quotes to open this volume for the distinct perspectives on technology that they offer, founded in three distinct anthropological traditions in France, the United Kingdom, and the United States. These distinctions can be partially understood through the way the terms 'technique' and 'technology' are used in French and English.

In his 1994 encyclopaedia entry on technology, François Sigaut discusses the terms systematically and defines techniques (the preferred term in French anthropology) by referring to Marcel Mauss's proposition: 'We call techniques an ensemble of movements or actions, in general and for the most part manual, which are organized and traditional, and which work together towards the achievement of a goal known to be physical or chemical or organic' (Mauss 2006[1941/1948], p. 149). Those aspects of technology that relate to bodily movements and material actions implicated in techniques often escape the attention of Anglo-American scholars because of the modernist connotations of 'technology' in English (Sigaut 1994; cf. Schlanger 2006). Here, the concept of technology usually refers to the achievements of modern engineering, 'in short, those techniques that are informed by a relatively scientific content and methods' (Sigaut 1994, p. 422).[1] This understanding of technology, as Nathan Schlanger (2006) points out, leads to a hierarchical, or hierarchising, difference between the 'technical' and the 'technological'. In this hierarchy, 'techniques' and 'technical' skills apply to phenomena that are traditional, small-scale, or tacit, while 'technology' refers to phenomena deemed modern, complex, and sophisticated. In this sense, 'technology' did not exist in so-called pre-modern societies, only 'tools' and technical skills. Think, for example, of the difference between basketry techniques and ballistic technology.

Mauss was the first to suggest that there is something fundamentally non-technical about technology. He argued that technology needed to be put back on the research agenda of the social sciences after its confinement to a marginal position during the formation of the modern sciences of the social (Schlanger 2006). Although Mauss had already in his work on religion and magic compared magic and techniques, both of which are *actes traditionelles efficaces* (Mauss 1903; passim in Schlanger 2006, p. 15), it was only after his personal experiences as a soldier during the First World War, and the general recognition of the powers of modern war technologies that followed from the war, that he formulated an explicit programme for the social study of technology. His essay on techniques of the body (2007[1935]) remains the most widely known. Here his point was that there are techniques which do not require extra-somatic instruments, while they always require the body: 'The body is man's first and most natural instrument' (2007[1935], p. 56). Just as importantly, however, as

Sigaut noted, Mauss pointed out that techniques are an ensemble of move-ments or actions that are organised (sometimes translated as 'effective') and traditional, which here means that they must be learned, taught, and transmit-ted in collective contexts, either as habitus or through oral transmission. Moreover, techniques are goal oriented, and 'they are felt by the author as *actions of a mechanical, physical, or psycho-chemical order* and … they are pur-sued with that aim in view' (2007[1935], p. 56). This is the Maussian legacy on which the French anthropologist Pierre Lemonnier (1992, 1993, 2012) builds in his anthropological theories of technology. He argues that techniques *as material actions* are always themselves social phenomena and are always sys-temic in that all techniques involve the five interacting elements of matter, energy, objects, gestures, and knowledge. This in turn obliges the ethnogra-pher to follow and document the material and social processes that form, for example, through gardening, hunting, farming, building eel-traps, canoes, or smartphones (Lemonnier 2012).

Somewhat in contrast, Tim Ingold has argued that, rather than techniques of the individual body, anthropologists should empirically foreground *skills* through an 'ecological approach, which situates the practitioner … in the con-text of an active engagement with the constituents of his or her surroundings' (Ingold 1997, p. 110). For Ingold, skills involve the qualities of care, judge-ment, and dexterity. Hence, he argues that we must attend, conceptually and methodologically, not to techniques (of the body) but to 'making'. A mix of improvisation and imitation, making arises within the form-generating poten-tials of complex processes of skilled movement. At the same time, as we saw in one of the epigraphs to this introduction, like Sigaut and Schlanger, Ingold too affirms that 'technology' has come to denote modern society's control over nature, adding that to use the term technology is not only to denote a thing but to make a claim: 'technology [is] the means by which a rational under-standing of [the] external world is turned to account for the benefit of society' (2000, p. 312). He points out that the images invoked by contemporary uses of the concept of technology—of operators rather than artisans and of exterior mechanisms rather than embodied skills—impact profoundly on the way we allow ourselves to think about technology and technology's role in society (see also Bunn this volume).

Coming from American cultural anthropology, and with an Anglo-Saxon understanding of technology as operative systems, Bryan Pfaffenberger (1988) has argued that anthropologists should focus on interwoven socio-technical systems and systems of meaning. In his 1992 *Annual Review of Anthropology* article on the anthropology of technology, Pfaffenberger introduces the then 'emergent field known as science and technology studies (STS)' (1992a, p. 493) to a broader anthropological audience. In doing so, he draws a parallel between Mauss's 'total social phenomena' and Thomas Hughes's 'sociotechni-cal system' (1987). While Hughes and other Social Construction of Technological Systems (SCOT) scholars (see Bijker et al. 1987) had already showed that a successful technological innovation depends on the 'seamless' (i.e. indissolubly linked) integration of technical, social, economic, and political aspects, Pfaffenberger argued that socio-technical systems are *also* embedded in culture, in ritual and mythic narratives. In this view, 'to construct a technology is not merely to deploy materials and techniques; it is also to construct social and economic alliances, to invent new legal principles for social relations, and to provide powerful new vehicles for culturally-provided myths' (Pfaffenberger 1992a, p. 249).While Pfaffenberger formulated a programme for a new STS-inspired anthropology of technology, others would in a sense invert this programme when taking anthropology to STS, generating a string of post-structural analyses of emerging technologies (e.g. Escobar 1994; Martin 1994; Rabinow 1996; Franklin 1997; Downey and Dumit 1997a). In the 1960s to 1970s, the interdisciplinary field of science and technology studies was dominated by the history, philosophy, and sociology of science. However, by the late 1970s and throughout the 1980s, two turns in STS brought this field together with anthropological studies of technology. A series of ethnographic studies of and in laboratories (Knorr 1977; Latour and Woolgar 1979; Traweek 1988), introduced anthropological methods to STS, along with methodological approaches to the cultures, practices, and social relations in the making of scientific facts that have gained influence over the years to form a 'practice turn' or 'empirical turn' in STS (e.g. Mol 2002). In the same period, a 'turn to technology' occurred in STS (Pinch and Bijker 1984; MacKenzie and Wajcman 1985; Akrich 1992; De Laet and Mol 2000) that also drew anthropologists interested in technology (e.g. Pfaffenberger 1988, 1992a). As the chapters in this handbook show, many scholars working with different anthropologies of technology are equally committed to both anthropology and STS, and many debates and research environments overlap.

Working at the intersections of anthropology and STS, Arturo Escobar went on to reformulate anthropological definitions of technology when arguing 'that human and social reality is as much a product of machines as of human activity, that we should grant agency to machines, and that the proper task for an anthropology of science and technology is to examine ethnographically how technology serves as agent of social and cultural production', while at the same time insisting that anthropologists 'start paying attention to Third World technological innovation' (Escobar 1994, pp. 216, 221). Finally, Pfaffenberger's notion of a socio-technical system would also, as we will see, go on to inform anthropological conceptualisations of infrastructure systems (Larkin 2013; Harvey et al. 2017; Anand et al. 2018; Abram et al. 2019).

These different anthropological approaches to conceptualising technology are often seen as in contradistinction to each other. However, it is our contention that it is exactly this multiplicity of approaches that has contributed to the thriving anthropologies of technology that are on display in the chapters that follow. What these approaches to the anthropological study of technology enable is a kind of analytical and methodological scaling on the part of the ethnographer, who can choose to focus on the embodied skills, on the practices/material actions, or on the larger socio-technical systems which *together* make up technologies in different parts of the world. Let us now turn to a historical account of how anthropological understandings and ethnographic studies of technology have changed over the past century.

EVOLUTION VERSUS DIFFUSION

Any history of the way anthropologists have studied technologies must grapple with its colonial and racist legacy, not least since technology was given a specific marking role in the early evolutionary theories developed by nineteenth-century anthropologists. In *Ancient Society*, Lewis Henry Morgan (1877) shows how material technologies were considered both engine and marker of civilisation when he posits a 'natural as well as necessary sequence of progress' through a savage (subdivided into lower, middle, and upper), a barbarian (also subdivided into lower, middle, and upper), and finally a civilised stage. Distinguishing each of these stages, he argued, was an evolving complexity in discoveries, inventions, and arts of subsistence, starting with 'knowledge of the use of fire', through 'the invention of the Bow and Arrow', 'the cultivation of maize and plants by Irrigation', and 'the invention of the process of Smelting Iron', culminating in 'the invention of a Phonetic Alphabet' (Morgan 1877, p. 3, 12; see Ingold 1997). Throughout the nineteenth century, European and American natural historians, archaeologists, and anthropologists endeavoured to 'divide mankind into large families and subdivisions [in order] … to establish a description of them, in as concise terms as the Botanist, when he examines the plants of a certain region' (Ethnological Society of London 1848, p. 3; see Blumenbach 1865; Lubbock 1875; Ratzel 1896), not least by collecting and cataloguing the 'material culture' they encountered during their travels in the form of artefacts, tools, and decorative objects. The classificatory principle underlying such cataloguing suggested development from simple artefacts towards more and more complex technologies. Perhaps most famously, British archaeologist and anthropologist Augustus Pitt Rivers would apply this evolutionary 'doctrine of development of species' in his extensive 'development-series' museum collection displays of 'implements, appliances, and products of human life, such as boats, looms, dress, musical instruments, magical and religious symbols, artistic decoration, and writing' (Tyler 1901, p. 269).

While dominant and pervasive, the evolutionary schema of the late nineteenth and early twentieth centuries did not go unchallenged in its own time. As early as 1885, Haitian anthropologist Anténor Firmin firmly rejected its overtly racist premises when setting out his vision for a 'positivist anthropology' in *The Equality of the Human Races*. Marking an 'epistemological break' in anthropological thought and laying the groundwork for modern ethnography, Firmin argued that 'all men are endowed with the same qualities and the same faults, without distinction of color or anatomical form', thus defining anthropology as 'the study of Man in his physical, intellectual and moral dimensions as he is found in any of the different races which constitute the human species' (Firmin 2000[1885], p. 405, cited in Fluehr-Lobban 2000, pp. 449,

451). Firmin received his legal training in Haiti, only moving to France following political unrest in 1883 where he became a member of the Société d'Anthropologie de Paris. While his rejection of evolutionary thought was initially silenced by colleagues at the Société (see Magloire-Danton 2005, pp. 194–195), by 1902, in a lecture on the history of religions, fellow anthropologist Marcel Mauss would publicly concur, stating that 'there are no uncivilized peoples, only peoples with different civilizations' (1902, p. 43).

In the United States, German-born anthropologist Franz Boas would likewise reject evolutionary theory, arguing that 'articulate language, the use of implements, and the power of reasoning belong to all members of the human species as opposed to the higher animals' (Boas 1921, p. 247). He based this claim on anthropological studies among Inuit groups on Baffin Island (1883–1884) and the Kwakiutl people (1886–1890) of the Pacific Northwest Coast in Canada. And finally, in Britain, Cambridge neurologist William H.R. Rivers, who famously stumbled into anthropology upon accepting Alfred C. Haddon's invitation to join his Torres Strait Islands expedition in 1893, also ended up rejecting evolutionary theory halfway through writing his two-volume analysis of Melanesian society. Rivers pointed out that he had travelled to Melanesia 'as a firm adherent of the current English school, being almost exclusively interested in the evolution of belief, custom and institution, paying little attention to the complexity of individual cultures ... [until] at a definite point in my argument, I was led to see that Melanesian society is complex' (Rivers 1914, pp. 1–2). And so, by the early twentieth century, the task of Euro-American socio-cultural anthropology was no longer to hierarchise different human societies according to 'growing intelligence through inventions and discoveries' (Morgan 1877, p. 12); rather, it was to describe ethnographically the *different* 'modes of life' that could be found in societies throughout the world, all of which were complex in their own ways.

How then could differences and similarities in the modes of subsistence, artefacts, techniques, religions, or kinship systems that were observed be accounted for? If technologies formed an index that organised and represented evolutionary logics, as evolutionary theory lost credibility, new theories were required to account for differences and similarities. Morgan had already acknowledged partial resemblances between cultures at the turn of the century, but Rivers went further, arguing that resemblances were much more a matter of *diffusion* than of *evolution*. Following travels in Melanesia, Polynesia, Egypt, and India, he had learned, not only that supposedly 'simple' societies were in fact complex, as he had put it, but also that 'the transitions which have been taken to be evidence of independent processes of evolution' can instead be 'ascribed to the mixture of cultures and of peoples' through travel and contact that led to 'direct transmission from one people to another' (Rivers 1914, pp. 388, 387). Likewise, Franz Boas argued that similarities in the fishhooks, food pounders, and chisels found along the Pacific coast region 'from Costa Rica to Alaska', as well as in 'Hawaii and other sections of marginal Polynesia ranging even to New Zealand', suggested that 'from time-to-time small groups of Polynesians and possibly other Pacific Islanders deliberately or accidentally reached our shores and were effectually absorbed in the native Indian population' (Boas 1938, pp. 211–212). Hence, a novel classificatory principle was required which pointed to the modes of contact between different societies facilitated by political alliances, forms of transportation, or exchange of goods leading to the diffusion of various technologies, ideas, and social and cultural institutions.[2]

FROM ARTEFACTS TO PROCESSES

As modern fieldwork methods took hold in the early twentieth century, ethnography not only provided the impetus to revise evolutionary theory but also shifted attention from artefacts to the social processes and broader systems that gave rise to them. Perhaps most famously, in his study of the Kula exchange system in Melanesia, Bronislaw Malinowski describes the complex operations and craftsmanship that go into the building of *masawa* (sea-going canoes) as a key technology allowing for interaction and exchange between peoples in the Trobriand Islands. Malinowski focused, however, on the association of canoe-making with magic and broader systems of economic exchange and belief, as he regarded technologies in a holistic fashion as much more than technical effort (Bubandt and Otto 2010). For Malinowski and his British contemporaries, it was important to study human societies as whole systems; as he wrote, 'an Ethnographer who sets out to study only religion, or only technology, or only social organisation cuts out an artificial field for inquiry, and he will be seriously handicapped in his work' (Malinowski 1922, p. 17). These observations notwithstanding, artefacts and technologies would meld into the background as systems of kinship, economic exchange, religious belief, or political authority were brought to the fore in structural-functionalist analysis.

In distinct contrast, a French tradition that took its point of departure in the body took hold, as already noted, following the publication of Mauss's influential 1935 essay on 'The Techniques of the Body' in which he argued, 'man's first and most natural technical object, and at the same time technical means, is his body' (Mauss 2007[1935], p. 56). Drawing on ethnographic examples from different parts of the world covering everyday practices of swimming, digging, or walking, Mauss invokes the 'social nature of the "habitus"', arguing that 'a manual knack can only be learnt slowly. Every technique properly so-called has its own form [and] each society has its own special habits' (Mauss 2007[1935], p. 52). In *Gesture and Speech*, French archaeologist and anthropologist André Leroi-Gourhan would, consequently, link such body techniques to material instruments such as potter's wheels, wood lathes, and carts. In bringing social, biological, and archaeological anthropology together, Leroi-Gourhan proposed a set of 'fundamental criteria of humanity', the most important of which were 'erect posture, a short face and a free hand during locomotion' (1993[1964], p. 19). From these, he goes on to argue that 'freedom of the hand almost necessarily implies a technical activity different from that of apes, and a hand that is free during locomotion, together with a short face and the absence of fangs, commands the use of artificial organs, that is, of implements' (1993[1964], p. 20). These implements or tools, in turn, are 'only a testimony of the exteriorisation of an efficient gesture … it is the materialization of the interaction of matter with the means to transform it', leading Leroi-Gourhan to propose the notion of an operational sequence (*chaîne opératoire*) (Leroi-Gourhan 1943, 1945, 1993, cited in Audouze 2002, pp. 287–288; see Coupaye this volume). While Leroi-Gourhan's *longue-durée* evolutionary analysis in *Gesture and Speech* also included a third section on what he called 'values and rhythms' focusing on speech, writing, memory, and art, it was especially Mauss's, Haudricourt's, and Leroi-Gourhan's approach to studying *manual action in technical activities* that was continued at the Centre National de la Recherche Scientifique (CNRS) under the auspices of Hélène Balfet and Robert Cresswell and, later, Pierre Lemonnier and, since 1976, through the French journal *Techniques et Culture*.

From the late 1960s to the 1980s, processual perspectives on technology were also taken up as part of the debates around cultural ecology, cultural materialism, and the anthropological neo-Marxism of the time. While the founding figures of cultural ecology, Julian Steward (1955) and Leslie White (1959), had in some ways receded into the past, a new generation of scholars expanded upon Marxist materialism. They produced analyses that illustrated the significance of economic, material, and technological relations in determining social structures, and the dialectic between social relations and technical forces of production in the forming of different modes of production (primitive-communal or pre-capitalist, feudal, capitalist, communist, and so on). These studies had a comparative and historical sweep, and the issues at stake were the origins of the state (e.g. Goody 1971), the technological foundations of war, despotism and slavery, and the connection between technology, land use, and population growth. To take just two influential examples that tied technology and power together, Karl August Wittfogel (1957; see also Fei 1992[1947]) argued that the need to manage water led to hydraulic despotism, and Ester Boserup, in her studies of agrarian change (1965), identified a correlation in increased population density with the shift from the hoe to the plough. To mention a few scholars from this generation, the structural Marxism of Maurice Godelier (1975, 1986[1982]) sought to understand the relations between the environment, technology, and society by studying the power of Baruya Great Men through their control of warring, hunting, shamanism, and rites of initiation. Marshall Sahlins (1972), among others, discussed 'the domestic mode of production' of households in so-called primitive societies where kinship, culture, and religion are ingrained in economic and technological forces. Finally, Marvin Harris (1979) coined the term 'cultural materialism' and argued that culture is essentially a product of material forces, claiming, for example, that religious taboos prohibiting eating cattle in India have a material basis in that cattle are reserved for agricultural production.

While artefacts have long joined the interests of anthropologists with those of archaeologists, we can see a shift in terminology during the twentieth century from 'technology' through to the conceptualisation of 'material culture'. Malinowski had condemned what he called 'the purely *technological* enthusiasm of material culture ethnologists' and, with the emergence of fieldwork-based anthropology, the study of technology and material culture fell out of fashion and was relegated to museums (Pfaffenberger 1992a, p. 491). This coincided with the increasing dematerialisation of the concept of culture in American cultural anthropology where 'what is culture is the *idea* behind the artifact' (Kroeber & Kluckhohn cited in Pfaffenberger 1992a, p. 492). Writing from his work with the vast Pitt Rivers Museum, British archaeologist Dan Hicks (2010) has observed that while archaeologists maintained an interest in material objects and 'technology', the invention during the early twentieth century of the idea of 'material culture' in anthropology, as a separate interest, marks a shift in mainstream anthropology away from technologies (see also Bille this volume).

An increase in attention towards material culture in the UK during the late 1970s and early 1980s, however, created something of a rapprochement between the disciplines of archaeology and social anthropology, not least as the interdisciplinary *Journal of Material Culture* was established in the wake of a shared material-cultural turn focused on 'the relationship between people and things irrespective of time and space' (Miller and Tilley 1996, p. 5). Ethno-archaeology (Hodder 1982) developed as a comparative form of archaeological study to understand the past through contemporary material practices and ethnographic methods, bringing anthropologists and archaeologists together. Daniel Miller, himself a trained ethnoarchaeologist, conveyed the significance of objects and materials in everyday social life as he examined the social symbolism of material culture in the contemporary world through several extensive studies (e.g. Miller 1997, 1998, 2005). While cultural materialists had focused on different modes of production, Miller focused his theories on *consumption* (1987), arguing that consumption is one of the processes of objectification whereby things gain meaning in modern everyday life. For example, in Miller's theory of shopping (1998), consumption is not to be understood as destruction but as a creative process and the transformation or enrolment of commodities into social relations, so that shopping is viewed as a 'technology of love', a way to show care and concern (Miller 2006, p. 350). *Both* production and consumption thus came to be seen as technological processes.

In these ways, far from the invention and artefact-oriented conceptualisations of technology that underpinned evolutionary ideas about stages of civilisational development in the nineteenth century, twentieth-century ethnographers had recast technologies into important elements within the processes and systems that undergirded *different* societies.

1980s AND 1990s: PROGRAMMES FOR AN ANTHROPOLOGY OF TECHNOLOGY

By the 1980s and into the 1990s, as mass production, transportation, global communication, and migration intensified (Douglas and Isherwood 1979; Appadurai 1986, 1996; Hannerz 1996; Tsing 2000), efforts to theorise a new anthropology of technology for an age of globalisation took hold. Several initiatives emerged as different clusters of anthropologists began organising seminars, formulating programmes, and putting forth publications aimed at promoting the project (Lemonnier 1986, 1992; Pfaffenberger 1988, 1992a; Gell 1988, 1992; Gibson and Ingold 1993; Escobar 1994; Ingold 1997; Harvey 1997; Downey and Dumit 1997a; Schiffer 2001). Each of these initiatives would further distance itself from the determinist evolutionary theories that still haunted discussions of technology, tackling the legacy of divides between 'modern' and 'pre-modern' that had seeped into public discourse. The classic anthropological themes of tools and tool use were taken up again, in re-evaluations of the role and notion of 'the material', embedding materials thoroughly in the social and inserting new connections and new roles into anthropological conceptualisations of technology. In hindsight, we can see how anthropological interest in technology in fact waxed and waned throughout the twentieth century.

This interest notwithstanding, technologies have regularly been seen to occupy a secondary or peripheral status within anthropology, and scholars have sought to diagnose reasons for its 'neglect' (Sigaut 1994, p. 420) and 'underdevelopment' (Ingold 1997, p. 106) as an anthropological field of study. As we saw earlier, according to Ingold, it had to do with modernity's general cutting loose of technology from society and culture, thereby placing it *outside* society (Ingold 2000). One of the key reasons these commentators could duly complain about technology's relative neglect was the absence of a thriving subfield: technology was rarely included as a core component of curricula, in contrast to, say, kinship, medicine, religion, economic exchange, or political systems. Indeed, Bryan Pfaffenberger decried a 'lack of interest in technology' (Pfaffenberger 1988, p. 237), suggesting that the peripheral status of the study of technology and material culture in anthropology was due to modernist anthropology's immaterial understanding of culture. Pfaffenberger attributed this in part to Malinowski's quest for the professionalisation of the discipline. In response to his desire to shift anthropology away from decontextualised amateur collections set up to compare material objects, socio-cultural anthropology increasingly separated itself from archaeology and material culture studies. Much can be explained by the isolation of the French *Techniques et Culture* school (see Coupaye this volume), the splitting off of material culture studies as a rather independent interdisciplinary field (see Bille this volume) and the discontinuities and distinctions in the use of the concepts of technology and techniques we discussed earlier. All of this, however, would change, as a flurry of lectures, symposiums, and seminars were organised in the closing decades of the twentieth century resulting in a number of publications central to anthropology of technology.

Between 1983 and 1986, building on his series of lectures ('The Ethnology of Technology') delivered as Chargé de Conférence at the Ecole des Hautes Etudes en Sciences Sociales in Paris, Pierre Lemonnier suggested that 'a veritable anthropology of technology is ... taking shape' (1986, p. 147). That these lectures were delivered in Paris was no coincidence as, ever since the early 1970s, as noted earlier, Lemonnier had been part of a cluster of researchers at the Centre National de la Recherche Scientifique (CNRS) who were engaged in the study of techniques. Lemonnier formulated an empirically demanding programme for a comparative anthropology of technology based on the concepts of material actions, technological systems, and technological choices (1986, 1992, 1993, 2012). 'Technological choices', a concept gleaned from Lévi-Strauss, addresses questions that arise from the observation that many techniques are far from 'rational', 'efficient', or the 'best possible' and that, among several technological possibilities, societies seize, adopt, or develop only some features while dismissing others (Lemonnier 1993). Building on the French tradition of Mauss, Haudricourt and Leroi-Gourhan, Bruno Latour and Pierre Lemonnier (1994) endeavoured to integrate the various paradigms of technology at an interdisciplinary symposium in the early 1990s alongside primatologists, archaeologists, ethnologists, philosophers, and science studies scholars. While Latour went on to develop actor-network theory (Latour 2005), Lemonnier continued Mauss's programme and summarised and refined his work in the field of *technologie culturelle* in *Mundane Objects: Materiality and Non-Verbal Communication* (2012), emphasising that material actions and mundane artefacts are at the very core of human existence. It is through close ethnographic attention to material techniques, Lemonnier posits, that anthropologists can understand basic human logics, social relationships, and societies.[3]

Across the Atlantic in the United States, anthropologists looked to philosophy to bring together the material and operational aspects of technology. Drawing on both German philosopher Martin Heidegger's (1977[1953]) essay on 'the Question Concerning Technology' as well as French historian and philosopher Michel Foucault's (1990[1976]) writings on the emergence of technologies and rationalities of government, anthropologists were tackling technology anew. Heidegger had highlighted what he called an 'instrumental and anthropological definition of technology' which suggested:

> Technology is a means to an end ..., a human activity. ... The manufacture and utilization of equipment, tools, and machines, the manufactured and used things themselves, and the needs and ends that they serve, all belong to what technology is. The whole complex of these contrivances is technology. Technology itself is a contrivance, or, in Latin, an *instrumentum*. (Heidegger 1977[1953], pp. 4–5)

It was at the University of California, Berkeley, that the exegesis of Heidegger's writings by American philosopher, Professor Hubert Dreyfus (1995), went on to have a big impact on the way his concepts and critique of technology were received and understood by North American scholars (see Dreyfus and Rabinow 1982). It was also Berkeley where Foucault would spend time in the 1980s, conceptualising what he famously called 'biopower'. Diagnosing the emergence of novel technologies and techniques of government in eighteenth- and nineteenth-century Europe, he sought to describe 'endeavours to administer, optimize, and multiply [life], subjecting it to precise controls and comprehensive regulations' (Foucault 1990, p. 137). As we will see, Foucault's concepts went on to shape those anthropologies of technology that have focused on biomedicine and biotechnology, not least as developed by Paul Rabinow (Rabinow 1996; see Escobar 1994; Wahlberg this volume).

By the end of the 1980s, a series of influential articles would be published, each emerging from distinct theoretical traditions and each leaving a significant imprint on how anthropological studies of technology would proceed from that point. Firstly, as seen in one of the opening epigraphs of our introduction, Pfaffenberger's 1988 article, 'Fetishised Objects and Humanised Nature: Towards an Anthropology of Technology', introduced a definition of technology in terms of a *total* socio-technical system understood as 'humanised nature':

> any behaviour that is technological is also, and at the same time, political, social and symbolic. It has a legal dimension, it has a history, it entails a set of social relationships and it has a meaning. (Pfaffenberger 1988, p. 244)

With this definition, Pfaffenberger—a Berkeley anthropology graduate working at the School of Engineering and Applied Science at the University of Virginia—sought to bring STS and anthropology into dialogue, not just anthropology's fieldwork methodology but also anthropological theory, adapting, for example, Victor Turner's (1974) concept of social dramas as technological dramas. More than material actions, technological activities 'bring to life a deeply desired vision of social life, often with a degree of fervor that can only be termed millenarian' (Pfaffenberger 1992b, p. 506).

Secondly, in his article on "Technology and Magic" (also published in 1988), Alfred Gell (1988, 1992), based at the London School of Economics, built on the work of Malinowski in arguing that technologies do not only pertain to material production and reproduction, but also to magic, enchantment, and art. With this approach to technology, Gell clearly departs from the Maussian approach where techniques are always physical actions on the material world. For Gell, 'technologies of enchantment' comprise 'all those technical strategies, especially art, music, dances, rhetoric, gifts, etc. which human beings employ in order to secure the acquiescence of other people in their intentions or projects' (Gell 1988, p. 7). Gell suggests that magic haunts technical activity like a shadow and that magical technology is the reverse side of productive technology (Gell 1992). Although it is rare to see magic discussed explicitly in relation to modern technology, magical thinking and magical ideas are always concomitant with the production of modern technology, for example, in the apotheosis of 'innovation' or the mythologies created through advertisements that serve to entice consumers to buy the products of new technology (Gell 1988, p. 9). In a similar vein, Peter Pels (2010) has noted how frequently the term magic is applied in relation to computer technologies and finds that folk theories of the magic of computers reflect a fetishised way of looking at the world. It is not just that computers are seen as magical machines, but programming is turned into a magical activity, and computer programmers and hackers are often described as magicians or 'wizards' (e.g. Hafner and Lyon 1996). In their conceptualisation of 'technologies of the imagination', Sneath et al. (2009) draw on Gell's 'technologies of enchantment' (1992), and Ingold's (1997) processes of 'exaptation', to examine the imaginative efficacy of technology: for example, when 'avatar' personae that internet users create in chat rooms give rise to particular ethical notions of the users' selves (Humphrey 2009).

Thirdly, and also in 1988, feminist science studies scholar Donna Haraway published her landmark essay, 'Situated Knowledges: The Science Question in Feminism and the Privilege of Partial Perspective', in which she rejected the notion of 'objectivity' in 'scientific and technological, late-industrial, militarized, racist, and male-dominant societies' in favour of 'a doctrine of embodied objectivity that accommodates paradoxical and critical feminist science projects: Feminist objectivity means quite simply situated knowledges' (Haraway 1988, p. 581). Building on Haraway's work in particular, Gary Downey, Joseph Dumit, and a number of like-minded American anthropologists doing ethnography at the intersections of anthropology and STS began organising panel sessions on 'Science and Technology' at the annual conferences of the American Anthropological Association. These sessions led to the formation of CASTAC (The Committee for the Anthropology of Science, Technology & Computing) and culminated in a weeklong seminar organised by Downey and Dumit at the School of American Research in Santa Fe, New Mexico, in October 1993, with contributions from Donna Haraway, Emily Martin, Paul Rabinow, Rayna Rapp, Sharon Traweek, Deborah Heath, David Hess, and Sarah Williams. In the introduction to the resulting publication, *Cyborgs & Citadels: Anthropological Interventions in Emerging Sciences and Technologies*, Downey and Dumit (1997b) argue for 'new ways of locating and intervening in emerging sciences, technologies and medicines through cultural perspectives and ethnographic fieldwork' given the ubiquity of biomedical, information, and communication technologies in everyday lives (pp. 5–8).

In this iteration of an anthropology of technology, ethnographic engagements with techniques and embodied skills like gardening, canoe-making, or weaving (see Bunn this volume) were supplemented with ethnographic interest in the 'hi-tech' worlds of, for example, genomic sequencing, cancer clinical trials, fertility treatment, prenatal screening, robotics, engineering, or digital finance. Downey and Dumit point to an urgency in the anthropological study of emerging technologies since, 'We cannot say No to the experience of science, technology, and medicine collectively as a disciplining center that polices other meanings and orders power relations in contemporary life' (Downey and Dumit 1997b, p. 5; see also Escobar 1994). On the one hand, this requires ethnographies in the 'Citadel', which is to say the laboratories, clinics, and workspaces of bioscientists, physicists, computer programmers, engineers, and biomedical doctors (cf. Latour and Woolgar 1979), while on the other (and in keeping with 'classic' ethnographic interest in everyday lives), it requires that the resulting technologies (e.g. DNA testing, reproductive treatments, water meters, robots, or surveillance algorithms) be followed as they come to be routinised, taken up, and (re)appropriated in daily use. Indeed, Emily Martin (1994), Paul Rabinow (1996), Sarah Franklin (1997), and Rayna Rapp (1999) had all been carrying out forms of assemblage ethnography (see Wahlberg this volume) at and across these intersections in their respective ethnographic studies of immunity, genomic sequencing, assisted reproduction, and prenatal testing technologies throughout the 1990s, showing how scientific knowledge, laws, regulations, media reporting, biomedical technologies, and the people developing, practicing, and using them were all imbricated in the making of these phenomena. As feminist technoscience studies (see Lie this volume), many of these ethnographies empirically demonstrated that 'there is no such thing as a pure and politically innocent "basic" science that can be transformed into technological applications to be "applied" in "good" or "bad" ways at a comfortable distance from the "clean" hands of the researcher engaged in the former'; rather science and technology are always 'entangled in societal interests' (Åsberg and Lykke 2010, p. 299), as Pfaffenberger had also insisted. Indeed, anthropological and STS studies showed how different technologies and technological activities are gendered and coded and re-coded in different ways according to gender stereotypes in different contexts and during different times in history (e.g. Cowan 1983; Wajcman 2000; Hicks 2017; Bray 2007, see also Bray this volume).

Fourthly, taking his point of departure in a phenomenology of the body in the early 1990s, Tim Ingold would bring tools and skills back to the fore in his efforts to (re)define the anthropology of technology. Together with Kathleen Gibson, Ingold convened a Wenner Gren Symposium on 'Tools, Language and Intelligence: Evolutionary Implications', resulting in the publication of their edited volume, *Tools, Language and Cognition in Human Evolution* (1993), which was, however, dominated by contributions from the fields of archaeology, biological anthropology, cognitive psychology, and neurophysiology. While cognitive scientists were interested in how technology was related to evolving language and intelligence in different cultures, drawing on the ecological psychology of James Gibson and the phenomenology of Merleau-Ponty, Ingold insisted that what was needed was a theorisation of skill and craft. These themes were subsequently taken up in a seminar series on *Technology as Skilled Practice* held at the University of Manchester from 1994 to 1996 that brought together anthropologists (including, among others, Penelope Harvey, Tim Ingold, Bryan Pfaffenberger, and Marilyn Strathern), psychologists, and historians of technology, resulting in a special issue of *Social Analysis* (Harvey 1997). For this group of scholars, anthropology must continue to pay empirical attention to the skills and tools that people need and use in their everyday lives wherever they might be (Ingold 1997, 2001).

Finally, alongside feminist studies of science and technology, postcolonial theory would also significantly shape the now burgeoning field of anthropology of technology during the 1990s, as scholars demonstrated how the development of modern science and technology was inextricably bound up with colonial histories (Prakash 1999). As already noted, anthropologist Arturo Escobar was quick to point out that most of the ethnographic studies of so-called emerging technologies by Haraway-inspired anthropologists were being carried out in countries of the Global North and, consequently, 'the effect of cosmopolitan technologies on Third World groups remains insufficiently understood' (Escobar 1995a, p. 410). Invoking Arjun Appadurai's notion of technoscapes and ethnoscapes (Appadurai 1990), and as seen in one of the opening epigraphs of our introduction, Escobar argued that 'once seen as producing worldwide homogenization and generalized acculturation, cosmopolitan science and technology are now viewed in terms of their real or potential contribution to the formation of hybrid cultures and to processes of self-affirmation through selective and partially autonomous adoption of modern technologies' (Escobar 1995a, p. 410). His call would not go unheeded as ethnographers began studying the uptake and development of, for example, mobile phones in Jamaica, assisted reproductive technologies in India, or agricultural machinery in Thailand (Horst 2006; Bharadwaj 2016; Morita 2013). These are all examples of the 'sciences from below'—which Sandra Harding and colleagues suggested should receive greater attention—which is to say, 'any and every culture's institutions and systematic empirical and theoretical practices of coming to understand how the world around us works' (Harding 2008, p. 16). The decolonisation of knowledge and technology has, in recent years, been bolstered by insights from indigenous knowledge (e.g. TallBear 2013; de la Cadena 2015) and critical race theory (e.g. Benjamin 2016, 2019) and these forms of critique have subsequently been brought into areas of study, such as design (Escobar 2018), which have otherwise more often than not been limited to western contexts. At the same time though, anthropologists have also shown how a globalising bioscience continues to reify, for example, biologised notions of race, despite promises to end its use as a proxy for genetic difference (Kowal this volume; see also Anderson 2006; Fullwiley 2008).

It is little wonder, then, that by the turn of the millennium Michael Brian Schiffer (2001) was noting that 'sociocultural anthropologists of the late twentieth century are avidly investigating technology, developing theories and case studies, and their works are beginning to influence practitioners in other disciplines' (Schiffer 2001, p. 1). Schiffer had brought together Bryan Pfaffenberger,

Tim Ingold, Lucy Suchman, and other colleagues for a seminar on the 'Anthropology of Technology' at the Amerind Foundation in Arizona (11–16 October 1998) leading to an edited volume outlining *Anthropological Perspectives on Technology* (Schiffer 2001). In his introduction, Schiffer points to the numerous definitions of technology that were then circulating among anthropologists ranging from those focusing on the manufacturing and use of artefacts to those which understood technologies in terms of instrumental means to achieve goals.

And so, with foundations in the nineteenth-century origins of the anthropological discipline, and developed through the twentieth century, we might well say that by the turn of the millennium an anthropology of technology had 'finally' established itself as a subfield in anthropology, but one that supplements rather than substitutes for other fields of anthropology, such as medical anthropology, environmental anthropology, political anthropology, and more, as these fields have themselves come to be dominated by 'new' technologies. Now, as the chapters in this *Handbook of the Anthropology of Technology* so clearly attest, it is no coincidence that such a subfield has taken root in a globalised twenty-first-century world where forms of individual experience, life-worlds, systems of meaning, and forms of social organisation are in profound ways being shaped by and through technoscapes (Appadurai 1996; Kearney 1995), technocracies (Ferguson 1990; Escobar 1995b), technoscientific knowledge production (Marcus 1995a; Fujimura 1996; Haraway 1997; Rapp 1999), 'emerging technologies' (Martin 1994; Rabinow 1996; Downey and Dumit 1997a; Pink et al. this volume), technocapitalist frictions (Tsing 2005), and global assemblages (Collier and Ong 2005), all of which connect multiple sites and scales at one and the same time (Marcus 1995b; Schiffer 2001). It is these multiple sites that anthropologists of technology continue to engage to this day.

THE EARLY 2000S: INTERDISCIPLINARY COLLABORATION AND METHODOLOGICAL INNOVATION

In the first two decades of the twenty-first century, anthropologists around the world have continued to reinvigorate research into the ways in which technologies are shaped by and come to shape daily lives in a host of different settings. One landmark publication was the volume, *Global Assemblages* (Ong and Collier 2005), that included such influential contributions and conceptualisations as those on 'therapeutic citizenship' (Nguyen 2005), 'biological citizenship' (Rose and Novas 2005), biopolitics (Collier 2005) and, of course, assemblage (Collier and Ong 2005; see also Wahlberg this volume), among many others. New empirical fields of study have arisen together with new technical developments (e.g. anthropological studies of algorithms (Seaver 2017, 2018)), data (Douglas-Jones et al. 2021), datafication (Hoeyer 2019), new interlocutors, such as data scientists and programmers (Kelty 2008; Knox and Nafus 2018; Seaver 2017, 2018) and hackers (Coleman 2013, 2014; Nova and

Bloch 2020), and revived concepts, such as infrastructure (Larkin 2013; Harvey et al. 2017; Anand et al. 2018; see Part V this volume).

In this last section of our historical account of the formation of today's anthropologies of technology, we emphasise two tendencies that we suggest have in particular characterised the first two decades of the twenty-first century. First, anthropologists are increasingly being called upon to participate in interdisciplinary collaborations that are centred in and around the so-called emerging technologies that drive the contemporary global economy, enjoying enormous corporate and state investment at the forefront of technological innovation. Emerging technologies range from health and medical technologies to biotechnology, artificial intelligence, and robotics, 'green' technologies, energy infrastructures, information and communication technologies, as well as big data and financial technologies.

Much has been written and said of the 'collaborative turn' in social studies of science and technology, not least within anthropology (see Marcus 2000; Lassiter 2005; Prainsack et al. 2010; Stavrianakis 2015; Fitzgerald and Callard 2015; Hastrup 2018). As noted above, beginning in the 1980s, anthropologists had entered the 'citadel' to study the practices of biomedical scientists, computer engineers, physicists, and more. Partly as a consequence, they were eventually asked to participate in collaborative research applications, not least those focusing on the ethical, legal, and social implications (ELSI) of 'emerging technologies'. This was because epistemic partners from the technical, medical, and natural sciences feared the public's concerns and possible rejection or lack of confidence in new technologies, as was the case with genetically modified organisms (Wynne 2001), while also hoping to gain socially robust knowledge and products (Nowotny et al. 2001). Ever since the large investments in the Human Genome Project that provided fertile grounds for anthropological studies (cf. Lindee et al. 2003; Pálsson 2007; Kowal this volume), funding agencies have increasingly included demands for interdisciplinarity that combines social science and humanities perspectives in their calls. From the very outset, however, these collaborations have entailed frictions due to more or less explicit disciplinary hierarchies and less than reciprocal commitments to 'inter-literacy' between the disciplines (see e.g. Frickel et al. 2016). Nevertheless, anthropologists of technology have steadily entered into collaborations on the strength of those insights that can be gained through fieldwork focused on the daily lives of people and institutions involved in the development, manufacturing, deployment, and/or use of particular technologies. Interdisciplinary engagements with emerging technologies, such as the development of humanoid robots (Hasse this volume), spur perennial questions for anthropology about what it means to be human and how human relationships and sociality with other humans, animals, plants, and other animate or inanimate non-human objects are enacted in different places and at different times.

One such field of interdisciplinary engagement and collaboration worth noting in regard to anthropology of technology is design (e.g. Clarke 2011; Blomberg and Karasti 2013; Smith et al. 2016; Murphy and Wilf 2021), where anthropologists within and beyond academia have collaborated with designers, software engineers, and other technicians. In design anthropology, a new wave of future-oriented researchers is urging anthropologists to take on active interventionist roles in collaborations with industry actors and to take responsibility not only for their interventions during fieldwork but also for new inventions that may come out of these collaborations outside academia (Salazar et al. 2017; Pink et al. this volume).

A second tendency that has characterised the first two decades of twenty-first-century anthropologies of technology has been anthropologists' quests for methodological innovation when studying technology, sometimes studying technologies by means of the technologies under study, such as in the case of digital and computational technologies (Coleman 2010; Horst and Miller 2012; Fortun et al. 2014; Pink et al. 2015; Knox and Nafus 2018; Geismar and Knox 2021; see also Munk and Winthereik this volume). Whether engaged in ethnographic studies of Internet use in different social contexts (Miller and Slater 2000) or in virtual ethnography from inside the Internet as a site of interaction (Hine 2000; Boellstorff 2008), the field of digital ethnography has contributed to the development of a range of methodological innovations as new possibilities for online ethnography are explored—not least during the COVID-19 pandemic when in-person interactions were impossible (Lupton 2020; Breslin et al. 2020).

While classic fieldwork with participant observation is still a core modality (not least in the chapters of this handbook), 'anthropology by means of design' (Gatt and Ingold 2013) and design methods, such as prototyping (Corsín Jiménez and Estalella 2016), are on the increase. Indeed, the very idea of anthropological fieldwork as a design process and the field as constructed, designed, or curated has been gaining ground since the critique of 'Malinowskian' fieldwork in *Writing Culture* and *Anthropology as Cultural Critique* in the 1980s (Clifford and Marcus 1986; Marcus and Fischer 1986). Today, and especially in fieldwork related to technology, research participants are often engaged as 'epistemic partners' in conceptualising the research through carefully staged events, or para-sites, such as workshops and seminars (Faubion and Marcus 2009), or experimental collaborations (Estalella and Criado 2018).

We are faced with methodological challenges when we want to capture the complex flows of digitalised information and communication (Waltorp 2021; Waltorp and Bruun forthcoming), technology-mediated sociality on social media or gaming platforms (Burrell 2012; Nardi 2009; Boellstorff 2008; Boellstorff et al. 2012), or the opaque work practices of people working in front of screens (Messeri 2021). Multimodal research methods (Collins et al. 2017), from drawing (Douglas-Jones 2021), mapping, filming, and photographing to utilising Facebook, Instagram, Twitter, or other platforms for 'life fieldnoting' (Wang 2012), 'appnography' (Cousineau et al. 2019), or 'sending private messages from the field' (Abidin and Seta 2020), are helpful in these endeavours. Perhaps more than ever before ethnographic research methods have become flexible and pliable.

A HANDBOOK OF THE ANTHROPOLOGY OF TECHNOLOGY
FOR THE TWENTY-FIRST CENTURY

Two decades into the twenty-first century, we now have both a vantage point on the diverse ways in which technology has been conceptualised within anthropology, and a sense of urgency about the relevance of what has become a firmly established field in different parts of the world, namely the anthropology of technology. In the sections and chapters that follow, a host of different approaches and empirical fields of study are presented. All chapters contain both a review of the key literature in relation to their topics and advance an ethnographic case through which the particular theme and take on technology is unfolded empirically, in keeping with anthropological mores. While diverse, there are nonetheless certain characteristics that we suggest tie most anthropological studies of technology together, characteristics which are directly linked to the anthropological conceptualisations of technology we have discussed in this Introduction. Firstly, through its commitment to fieldwork, an anthropology of technology tends to focus on embodiment, skills, and/or materialities in the daily lives of those people involved in the development, manufacturing, deployment, and/or use of particular technologies, whether in the form of a power grid, a kitchen blender, or assisted reproduction. Forms of design anthropology, ethnographic studies of tools and skills, STS-inspired laboratory ethnographies, or ethnographic studies of how, for example, water meters or water pipe infrastructures are tampered with and appropriated by people living in slums or shanty towns, each aim to bring to light the everyday practices that emerge when specific technologies are (co-)produced and become routinised parts of embodied daily practices.

A second distinctive feature of the different anthropologies of technology covered in this Handbook is that they 'stay with the trouble' (Haraway 2016) when empirically identifying those conundrums and ethical issues that very often emerge alongside new technological opportunities, as well as the (un) intended social consequences of, for example, algorithms or industrial food production technologies. By attending to practices and material actions, ethnographers often map out and bring to the fore the situated ways in which particular technologies generate ethical dilemmas and problems as much as they provide 'solutions' to particular challenges. Indeed, as noted above, anthropologists are increasingly invited into interdisciplinary collaborations for this very reason.

Finally, in locating particular technologies within broader political economies, socio-technical systems, and infrastructures, anthropological approaches to the study of technology often highlight how particular technologies are always embedded within socio-historical processes that shape access and often reinforce inequalities and forms of discrimination. The production of techno-science, as well as the diffusion or routinisation of specific technologies throughout the world, cannot be detached from the entrenched stratifications that continue to underpin global technocapitalism.

These distinctive features of the subfield of anthropology are clearly discernible within the chapters that make up this Handbook. Without pretending to be fully exhaustive, we cover a total of nine perspectives, approaches, and fields in the anthropological study of technology that, as we have shown, have crystallised over the past three decades. What makes a perspective, an approach, or a field is not always clear-cut, however. Indeed, part of the diversity found within the anthropology of technology relates exactly to the ways in which ethnographers can mobilise insights from across the differences in analytical foci, methodologies, and empirical settings that we cover through the chapters in the handbook's first section: first, *technique*, technical activity, and the *chaîne opératoire* (Coupaye this volume); second, *skill*, skilled practice, and tool use (Bunn this volume); third, *materiality* and material culture studies (Bille this volume); fourth, *feminism* and in particular feminist technoscience (Lie this volume); fifth, *post-structuralism*, with its focus on assemblages, socio-technical systems, and infrastructures (Wahlberg this volume); sixth, *posthumanism* (Hasse this volume); seventh, *biopolitics* and biotechnology in postcolonial studies (Kowall this volume); eighth, *design* anthropology (Pink et al. this volume); and finally, ninth, *digital* and experimental anthropologies (Winthereik and Munk this volume).

These overarching perspectives, approaches, and fields that have coalesced within the anthropology of technology over the past decades, we suggest, remain so important given that technology—and ideas about what technological solutions can accomplish (cf. Morozov 2013)—seems to be the 'big narrative' of the twenty-first century. Regardless of whether you see climate change, global health problems, economic inequality, poverty, racial discrimination, or the ageing of populations as the major problem of our time, throughout the world, governments, companies, non-governmental organisations, and grassroots social movements look towards possible technological solutions as a way to comprehend, present, and address these societal challenges. 'Change the world one app at a time', as one slogan goes. At the same time, however, technologies are also recurrently portrayed as inherently troubling, whether in the form of the carbon emissions and toxic pollution for which they are responsible; the 'tampering with nature' view of the genetic modification of plants, animals, and humans; the disturbing possibilities for surveillance, control, and discrimination they are seen to hold; or the divisive and polarising effects for which social media are held culpable. As such, technologies can be said to incarnate our best hopes and worst fears (cf. Bijker and Law 1992). As several commentators have noted (e.g. Dijck et al. 2018), the political landscape is changing too, as big tech companies and their digital platforms are not only competing with states to be the most powerful governing bodies, but it is also through them and their services that people take their bearings and look for the fulfilment of their needs, from medical services to food, education, finance, and transport.

Technologies do not only play a supporting role in people's lives. Rather, as anthropologists have insisted, technologies have always been co-extensive with humans: lending humans agency, empowerment, and new identities, as attested to by the everyday use of hearing aids and prostheses, the ubiquity of smartphones, watches, and other computing devices, biotechnological vaccine development, and intensifying efforts to produce 'green energy'. We live in a world where human-technology configurations can tinker with human lives in unseen ways, reaching new heights as gene-editing CRISPR technology, big data, and digital devices come together in new forms of surveillance, and human's technological activities anthropogenically impact not only our near surroundings but also the Earth's ecosystem and geology. We are all cyborgs, or biological-machinic-digital amalgams, and there is no easy way to draw a line between nature, culture, technology, and humans (see Suchman 2007; Hogle this volume). Indeed, discussions about, and critiques of, anthropocentrism, humanism and posthumanism, and the agency of materials and objects continue to drive debates about the anthropology of technology forward (see Latour 1993; de la Cadena 2015; Escobar 2018; Hornborg 2019, 2021; Hasse this volume).

It is the multiscalar perspectives found within the anthropology of technology that make it so well equipped to help address these many urgent challenges. The embodied skills required to play a musical instrument or culture cells in a laboratory are always located within larger socio-technical systems. Conversely, the political economies and material actions that shape water infrastructures or algorithm development are always tied to intimate moments in stratified and discriminatory ways as human (and non-human) lives are affected. It is the role of anthropology and anthropologists to cultivate and provide empirically informed, critical analyses of technology in a multiplicity of ways. Some anthropologists make it their contribution to speak up for those whose voices are otherwise silenced, discriminated against, or overlooked in discussions about the development, uses, and (unintended) consequences of specific technologies (e.g. prenatal screening, digital payment infrastructures, or electricity meters). Others see an important role in tempering the 'hype' that can surround 'emerging technologies', such as self-driving cars or personalised medicine, by focusing on the many trade-offs and often damaging effects that they unavoidably generate. And still others insist on historically and ethnographically situating that which has come to be taken for granted—such as the routinised prescription of pharmaceuticals or proliferating use of biometric identification—as a way of demonstrating that things could be otherwise. These different forms of critique do not amount to a rejection of technology, which would be futile in any case given the inseparability of *anthropos* and *techne*. Rather what they enable are more nuanced and sophisticated understandings of how and why technologies come to take the shapes and generate the kinds of effects they do in and among those people whose everyday lives are unavoidably touched by them. We hope that this handbook, at this particular moment, will be a vehicle for asking new questions and opening new research agendas.

Acknowledgements We would like to thank Tim Ingold, Pierre Lemonnier, and Daniel Miller for their insightful comments both on the history and on the substance of the anthropology of technology; their suggestions have been invaluable. We would also like to thank Palgrave Macmillan's anonymous reviewers of the Handbook in general and our Introduction specifically for excellent feedback and comments that have considerably improved our chapter. And finally we would like to thank Rachel Douglas-Jones, Klaus Hoeyer, and the team of Handbook co-editors for their careful reading and their comments.

NOTES

1. Indeed, Mauss makes a case that 'technology' should be formalised into the science of techniques: 'Technology is to technics what every other science is or would be to its objects, what linguistics is to language, for instance, or ethology to behaviour' (Sigaut 1994, p. 422).The question of whether we understand technology as the study of techniques (as biology is the study of organisms) or as an operative system built into the machinery of production (as we sometimes talk of the 'biology' of the body) has been hugely influential for the divergent ways in which the anthropologies of technology have developed, for example, in Francophone and Anglophone countries, and it also lies behind many misunderstandings (Ingold, personal communication; cf. Canguilhem 2009).
2. Disputes between evolutionism and diffusionism partly continued within anthropology, for example through Julian Steward's (1955) cultural ecology as the study of human adaptation to the environment and Leslie White's (1959) neo-evolutionary studies of technology, even though they were gradually marginalised from mainstream socio-cultural anthropology.
3. An interesting debate about questions of technology's materiality (or not) was set in motion following a book symposium on Lemonnier's *Mundane Objects: Materiality and Non-Verbal Communication* (Latour 2014; Lemonnier 2014; Ingold 2014).

REFERENCES

Abidin, C., & Seta, G. d. (2020). Private messages from the field: Confessions on digital ethnography and its discomforts. *Journal of Digital Social Research, 2*(1), 1–19.

Abram, S., Winthereik, B. R., & Yarrow, T. (Eds.) (2019). *Electrifying anthropology: Exploring Electrical practices and infrastructures*. London: Taylor & Francis Group.

Akrich, M. (1992). The De-scription of Technical Objects. In W. E. Bijker & J. Law (Eds.), *Shaping Technology/Building Societies* (pp. 205–224). Cambridge: MIT Press.

Appadurai, A. (Ed.) (1986). *The social life of things. Commodities in cultural perspective*. Cambridge: Cambridge University Press.

Appadurai, A. (1990). Disjuncture and difference in the global cultural economy. *Theory, Culture & Society, 7*(2–3), 295–310.

Appadurai, A. (1996). *Modernity at large: cultural dimensions of globalization*. Minneapolis: University of Minnesota Press.

Anand, N., Gupta, A., & Appel, H. (Eds.) (2018). *The promise of infrastructure*. Durham: Duke University Press.

Anderson, W. (2006). *Colonial pathologies: American tropical medicine, race, and hygiene in the Philippines*. Durham: Duke University Press.

Audouze, F. (2002). Leroi-Gourhan, a philosopher of technique and evolution. *Journal of Archaeological Research, 10*(4), 277–306.

Benjamin, R. (2016). Catching our breath: Critical race STS and the carceral imagination. *Engaging Science, Technology, and Society, 2*, 145–156.

Benjamin, R. (2019). *Race after technology: Abolitionist tools for the new Jim code*. Cambridge, England: Polity Press.

Bharadwaj, A. (2016). *Conceptions: Infertility and procreative technologies in India*. Oxford: Berghahn Books.

Bijker, W. E. (1995). *Of Bicycles, Bakelites, and Bulbs. Toward a Theory of Sociotechnical Change*. Cambridge, MA: The MIT Press.

Bijker, W. E., Hughes, T. P., & Pinch, T. J. (Eds.) (1987). *The Social Construction of Technological Systems. New directions in the sociology and history of technology*. Cambridge, MA: The MIT Press.

Bijker, W. E., & Law, J. (Eds.) (1992). *Shaping Technology/Building Societies*. Cambridge, MA: The MIT Press.

Blomberg, J., & Karasti, H. (2013). Ethnography: positioning Ethnography within Participatory Design. In J. Simonsen & T. Robertsen (Eds.), *Routledge International Handbook of Participatory Design* (pp. 86–116). New York & London: Routledge.

Blumenbach, J. F. (1865). On the Natural Variety of Mankind. In *The Anthropological Treatises of Blumenbach*. London: Longman, Green, Longman, Roberts & Green.

Boas, F. (1921). *The Mind of Primitive Man*. New York: The Macmillan Company.

Boas, F. (Ed.) (1938). *General Anthropology*. Washington, DC: D.C. Heath and Company.

Boellstorff, T. (2008). *Coming of Age in Second Life: An Anthropologist Explores the Virtually Human*. Princeton University Press.

Boellstorff, T., Nardi, B. A., Pearce, C., & Taylor, T. L. (2012). *Ethnography and virtual worlds: a handbook of method*. Princeton: Princeton University Press.

Boserup, E. (1965). *The conditions of agricultural growth: The economics of agrarian change under population pressure*. London: Allen & Unwin.

Bray, F. (2007). Gender and Technology. *Annual Review of Anthropology, 36*, 37–53.

Breslin, S. D., Enggaard, T. R., Blok, A., Gårdhus, T., & Pedersen, M. A. (2020). *How We Tweet About Coronavirus, and Why: A Computational Anthropological Mapping of Political Attention on Danish Twitter during the COVID-19 Pandemic*. http://somatosphere.net/forumpost/covid19-danish-twitter-computational-map/. Accessed 21 June 2021.

Bubandt, N., & Otto, T. (2010). Anthropology and the Predicaments of Holism. In T. Otto & N. Bubandt (Eds.), *Experiments in Holism. Theory and Practice in Contemporary Anthropology* (pp. 1–15). Chichester: Wiley-Blackwell.

Burrell, J. (2012). *Invisible users: youth in the Internet cafes of urban Ghana*. Cambridge, MA: The MIT Press.

Canguilhem, G. 2009. *Knowledge of Life*. New York: Fordham University Press.

Clifford, J., & Marcus, G. E. (1986). *Writing culture: the poetics and politics of ethnography*. London: University of California Press.

Clarke, A. J. (2011). *Design anthropology: object culture in the 21st century*. Wien: Springer.

Coleman, E. G. (2010). Ethnographic Approaches to Digital Media. *Annual Review of Anthropology, 39*, 487–505.

Coleman, E. G. (2013). *Coding freedom: the ethics and aesthetics of hacking*. Princeton: Princeton University Press.

Coleman, G. (2014). *Hacker, hoaxer, whistleblower, spy: the many faces of anonymous*. London: Verso.

Collier, S. J. (2005). Budgets and Biopolitics. In *Global Assemblages. Technology, Politics, and Ethics as Anthropological Problems* (pp. 373–390). Oxford: Blackwell Publishers

Collier, S. J., & Ong, A. (2005). Global Assemblages, Anthropological Problems. In A. Ong & S. J. Collier (Eds.), *Global Assemblages. Technology, Politics, and Ethics as Anthropological Problems*. Oxford: Blackwell Publishers.

Collins, S. G., Durington, M., & Gill, H. (2017). Multimodality: An Invitation. *American Anthropologist, 119*(1), 142–146.

Corsín Jiménez, A., & Estalella, A. (2016). Ethnography: A Prototype. *Ethnos, 82*(5), 846–866. https://doi.org/10.1080/00141844.2015.1133688.

Cousineau, L. S., Oakes, H., & Johnson, C. W. (2019). Appnography: Modifying ethnography for app-based culture. In D.C. Parry, C.W. Johnson, & S. Fullagar (Eds.), *Digital Dilemmas: Transforming gender identities and power relations in everyday life* (pp. 95–117). Basingstoke: Palgrave Press.

Cowan, R. S. (1983). *More Work for Mother: The Ironies of Household Technology from the Open Hearth to the Microwave*. Basic Books.

De Laet, M., & Mol, A. (2000). The Zimbabwe Bush Pump: Mechanics of a Fluid Technology. *Social Studies of Science, 30*(2), 225–263.

de la Cadena, M. (2015). *Earth beings: ecologies of practice across Andean worlds*. Durham: Duke University Press.

Dijck, J. v., Poell, T., & Waal, M. d. (2018). *The platform society*. New York: Oxford University Press.

Douglas, M., & Isherwood, B. (1979). *The world of goods: towards an anthropology of consumption*. London: Allen Lane.

Douglas-Jones, R. (2021). Drawing as Analysis: Thinking in Images, Writing in Words. In A. Ballestero & B. R. Winthereik (Eds.), *Experimenting with Ethnography. A Companion to Analysis*. Durham: Duke University Press.

Douglas-Jones, R., Walford, A., & Seaver, N. (2021). Introduction: Towards an anthropology of data. *Journal of the Royal Anthropological Institute, 27*(S1), 9–25. https://doi.org/10.1111/1467-9655.13477.

Downey, G. L., & Dumit, J. (1997a). Locating and Intervening. An introduction. In G. L. Downey & J. Dumit (Eds.), *Cyborgs & citadels: anthropological interventions in emerging sciences and technologies* (pp. 5–29). Santa Fe, NM: School of American Research Press.

Downey, G. L., & Dumit, J. (Eds.) (1997b). *Cyborgs & citadels: anthropological interventions in emerging sciences and technologies*. Santa Fe, NM: School of American Research Press.

Dreyfus, H. (1995). Heidegger on Gaining a Free Relation to Technology. In A. Feenburg & A. Hannay (Eds.), *Technology and the Politics of Knowledge* (pp. 25–33). Bloomington: Indiana University Press.

Dreyfus, H. L., & Rabinow, P. (1982). *Michel Foucault: Beyond structuralism and hermeneutics*. University of Chicago Press.

Escobar, A. (1994). Welcome to Cyberia: Notes on the Anthropology of Cyberculture. *Current Anthropology, 35*(3), 211–223.

Escobar, A. (1995a). Anthropology and the future: New technologies and the reinvention of culture. *Futures, 27*(4), 409–421.

Escobar, A. (1995b). *Encountering Development*. Princeton: Princeton University Press.

Escobar, A. (2018). *Designs for the Pluriverse. Radical Interdependence, Autonomy, and the Making of Worlds*. Durham, NC: Duke University Press.

Estalella, A., & Criado, T. S. (Eds.) (2018). *Experimental Collaborations. Ethnography through Fieldwork Devices*. Oxford: Berghahn Books.

Ethnological Society of London (1848). *Journal of the Ethnological Society of London, Vol. 1*. Edinburgh: Neill and Company, Printers, Old Fishmarket.

Faubion, J. D., & Marcus, G. E. (Eds.) (2009). *Fieldwork is not what it used to be: learning anthropology's method in a time of transition*. Ithaca, NY: Cornell University Press.

Fei, X. (1992[1947]). *From the Soil: The foundations of Chinese society* (trans: Hamilton, G., & Zheng, W.). Berkley: University of California Press.

Ferguson, J. (1990). *The anti-politics machine: "development", depoliticization, and bureaucratic power in Lesotho* (8. printing. ed.). Cambridge: Cambridge University Press.

Firmin, J. A. (2000[1885]). *The Equality of the Human Races*. New York: Garland Publishing, Inc.

Fitzgerald, D., & Callard, F. (2015). *Rethinking interdisciplinarity across the social sciences and neurosciences*. Springer Nature.

Fluehr-Lobban, C. (2000). Anténor Firmin: Haitian pioneer of anthropology. *American Anthropologist, 102*(3), 449–466.

Fortun, K., Fortun, M., Bigras, E., Saheb, T., Costelloe-Kuehn, B., Crowder, J., et al. (2014). Experimental Ethnography Online: The asthma files. *Cultural studies, 28*(4), 632–642.

Foucault, M. (1990[1976]). *The history of sexuality, Vol. 1*. New York: Vintage Books.

Franklin, S. (1997). *Embodied Progress: A Cultural Account of Assisted Conception*. London: Routledge.

Frickel, S., Albert, M., & Prainsack, B. (Eds.) (2016). *Investigating Interdisciplinary Collaboration. Theory and Practice across Disciplines*. New Brunswick, New Jersey & London: Rutgers University Press.

Fujimura, J. H. (1996). *Crafting science: a sociohistory of the quest for the genetics of cancer*. Cambridge, MA: Harvard University Press.

Fullwiley, D. (2008). The Biologistical Construction of Race: 'Admixture' Technology and the New Genetic Medicine. *Social Studies of Science, 38*(5), 695–735.

Gatt, C., & Ingold, T. (2013). From Description to Correspondence: Anthropology in Real Time. In W. Gunn, T. Otto, & R. C. Smith (Eds.), *Design Anthropology. Theory and Practice*. London: Bloomsbury.

Geismar, H., & Knox, H. (Eds.) (2021). *Digital Anthropology* (2nd edition). Abingdon, Oxon: Routledge.

Gell, A. (1988). Technology and Magic. *Anthropology Today, 4*(2), 6–9.

Gell, A. (1992). The Technology of Enchantment and the Enchantment of Technology. In J. Coote & A. Shelton (Eds.), *Anthropology, Art and Aesthetics*. Oxford: Oxford University Press.

Gibson, K. R., & Ingold, T. (Eds.) (1993). *Tools, language and cognition in human evolution*. Cambridge: Cambridge University Press.

Godelier, M. (1975). Modes of production, kinship, and demographic structures. In M. Bloch (Ed.), *Marxist Analyses and Social Anthropology* (pp. 3–27). London: Malaby Press.

Godelier, M. (1986[1982]). *The making of great men: male domination and power among the New Guinea Baruya*. Cambridge: Cambridge University Press.

Godelier, M., & Garanger, J. (1979). Stone tools and steel tools among the Baruya of New Guinea. Some ethnographic and quantitative data. *Social Science Information,* *18*(4–5), 633–678.

Goody, J. (1971). *Technology, tradition, and the state in Africa.* Oxford: Oxford University Press.

Hafner, K., & Lyon, M. (1996). *Where wizards stay up late: the origins of the Internet.* New York: Simon & Schuster.

Hannerz, U. (1996). *Transnational Connections: Cultures, People, Places.* New York: Routledge.

Haraway, D. (1988). Situated Knowledges: The Science Question in Feminism and the Privilege of Partial Perspective. *Feminist Studies, 14*(3), 575–599. https://doi. org/10.2307/3178066.

Haraway, D. J. (1997). *ModestWitness@SecondMillennium.FemaleManMeetsOncoMouse: feminism and technoscience.* New York: Routledge.

Haraway, D. (2016). *Staying with the Trouble. Making Kin in the Chthulucene.* Durham & London: Duke University Press.

Harding, S. (2008). *Sciences from below: Feminisms, postcolonialities, and modernities.* Durham & London: Duke University Press.

Harris, M. (1979). *Cultural materialism: the struggle for a science of culture.* New York: Random House.

Harvey, P. (1997). Introduction: Technology as Skilled Practice: approaches from Anthropology, History and Psychology. *Social Analysis, 41*(1), 3–14.

Harvey, P., Jensen, C. B., & Morita, A. (Eds.) (2017). *Infrastructures and social complexity: a companion.* Abingdon, Oxon: Routledge.

Hastrup, K. (2018). Collaborative Moments. Expanding the Anthropological Field through Cross-Disciplinary Practice. *Ethnos, 83*(2), 316–334. https://doi.org/1 0.1080/00141844.2016.1270343.

Heidegger, M. (1973[1927]). *Being and time.* Oxford: Basil Blackwell.

Heidegger, M. (1977[1953]). The question concerning technology (trans: Lovitt, W.). In *The Question Concerning Technology and Other Essays* (pp. 3–35). New York: Harper Torchbooks.

Hicks, D. (2010). Material-Cultural Turn. Event and Effect. In D. Hicks & M. C. Beaudry (Eds.), *The Oxford handbook of material culture studies.* Oxford: Oxford University Press.

Hicks, M. (2017). *Programmed inequality: how Britain discarded women technologists and lost its edge in computing.* Cambridge, MA: The MIT Press.

Hine, C. (2000). *Virtual ethnography.* London: Sage Publications.

Hodder, I. (1982). *Symbols in action: ethnoarchaeological studies of material culture.* Cambridge: Cambridge University Press.

Hoeyer, K. (2019). Data as promise: Reconfiguring Danish public health through personalized medicine. *Social studies of science, 49*(4), 531–555.

Hornborg, A. (2019). *Nature, Society, and Justice in the Anthropocene: Un-raveling the Money-Energy-Technology Complex.* Cambridge: Cambridge University Press.

Hornborg, A. (2021). Objects Don't Have Desires: Toward an Anthropology of Technology beyond Anthropomorphism. *American Anthropologist, n/a*(n/a).

Horst, H. A. (2006). The blessings and burdens of communication: cell phones in Jamaican transnational social fields. *Global Networks, 6*(2), 143–159.

Horst, H. A., & Miller, D. (Eds.) (2012). *Digital anthropology.* London: Berg.

Hughes, T. P. (1983). *Networks of Power: Electrification in Western Society, 1880–1930*. London: The John Hopkins University Press.

Hughes, T. P. (1987). The Evolution of Large Technological Systems. In W. E. Bijker, T. P. Hughes, & T. J. Pinch (Eds.), *The Social Construction of Technological Systems. New Directions in the Sociology and History of Technology* (pp. 51–82). Cambridge, MA: The MIT Press.

Humphrey, C. (2009). The Mask and the Face: Imagination and Social Life in Russian Chat Rooms and Beyond. *Ethnos, 74*(1), 31—50.

Ingold, T. (1997). Eight Themes in the Anthropology of Technology. *Social Analysis, 41*(1), 106–138.

Ingold, T. (2000). Society, nature and the concept of technology. In T. Ingold (Ed.), *The Perception of the Environment* (pp. 312–322). London: Routledge.

Ingold, T. (2001). Beyond Art and Technology: The Anthropology of Skill. In M. B. Schiffer (Ed.), *Anthropological Perspectives on Technology* (pp. 17–31). Albuquerque: University of New Mexico Press.

Ingold, T. (2014). Resonators uncased. Mundane objects or bundles of affect? *HAU: Journal of Ethnographic Theory, 4*(1), 517–521.

Kearney, M. (1995). The local and the global: The anthropology of globalization and transnationalism. *Annual Review of Anthropology, 24*(1), 547–565.

Kelty, C. M. (2008). *Two Bits. The Cultural Significance of Free Software*. Durham: Duke University Press.

Knorr, K. D. (1977). Producing and reproducing knowledge: descriptive or constructive? Toward a model of research production. *Social Science Information, 16*(6), 669–696.

Knox, H., & Nafus, D. (Eds.) (2018). *Ethnography for a data-world*. Manchester: Manchester University Press.

Larkin, B. (2013). The Politics and Poetics of Infrastructure. *Annual Review of Anthropology, 42*, 327–343.

Lassiter, L. E. (2005). Collaborative Ethnography and Public Anthropology. *Current Anthropology, 46*(1), 83–106. https://doi.org/10.1086/425658.

Latour, B. (1993). *We have never been modern*. Cambridge, MA: Harvard University Press.

Latour, B. (2005). *Reassembling the Social. An Introduction to Actor-Network-Theory*. Oxford: Oxford University Press.

Latour, B. (2014). Technical does not mean material. *Hau, 4*(1), 507–510.

Latour, B., & Lemonnier, P. (Eds.) (1994). *De la préhistoire aux missiles balistiques: L'intelligence sociale des techniques*. Paris: La Découverte.

Latour, B., & Woolgar, S. (1979). *Laboratory Life: The Construction of Scientific Facts*. London: Sage Publications.

Lemonnier, P. (1986). The study of material culture today: Toward an anthropology of technical systems. *Journal of Anthropological Archaeology, 5*(2), 147–186. https://doi.org/10.1016/0278-4165(86)90012-7.

Lemonnier, P. (1992). *Elements for an Anthropology of Technology*. Ann Arbor: University of Michigan, Museum of Anthropology.

Lemonnier, P. (Ed.) (1993). *Technological Choices: Transformation in Material Cultures since the Neolithic*. London: Routledge.

Lemonnier, P. (2012). *Mundane objects: materiality and non-verbal communication*. Walnut Creek, CA: Left Coast Press.

Lemonnier, P. (2014). The blending power of things. *HAU: Journal of Ethnographic Theory, 4*(1), 537–548.

Leroi-Gourhan, A. (1943). Evolution et Techniques I—L'Homme et la Matière, Paris: Albin Michel.

Leroi-Gourhan, A. (1945). Evolution et Techniques II—Milieu et Techniques, Paris: Albin Michel.

Leroi-Gourhan, A. (1993[1964]). *Gesture and Speech*. Cambridge, MA.: The MIT Press

Lindee, M. S., Goodman, A. H., & Heath, D. (2003). Anthropology in the Age of Genetics. Practice, Discourse, and Critique. In A. H. Goodman, D. Heath, & M. S. Lindee (Eds.), *Genetic Nature/Culture: Anthropology and Science Beyond the Two Culture Divide* (pp. 1–19). Berkeley: University of California Press.

Lubbock, J. (1875). *The Origin of Civilisation and the Primitive Condition of Man*. London: Longmans, Green & Co.

Lupton, D. (Ed.) (2020). *Doing fieldwork in a pandemic* (crowd-sourced document). Available at: https://docs.google.com/document/d/1clGjGABB2h2qbduTgfqribHmog9B6P0NvMgVuiHZCl8/edit?ts=5e88ae0a#. Accessed 21 June 2021.

MacKenzie, D. A., & Wajcman, J. (1985). *The social shaping of technology: how the refrigerator got its hum*. Milton Keynes: Open University Press.

Magloire-Danton, G. (2005). Anténor Firmin and Jean Price-Mars: Revolution, Memory, Humanism. *Small Axe, 9*(2), 150–170.

Malinowski, B. (1922). *Argonauts of the Western Pacific: An account of native enterprise and adventure in the archipelagoes of Melanesian New Guinea*. London: Routledge & Kegan Paul Ltd.

Marcus, G. E. (Ed.) (1995a). *Technoscientific Imaginaries. Conversations, Profiles, and Memoirs*. Chicago & London: University of Chicago Press.

Marcus, G. E. (1995b). Ethnography in/of the World System: The Emergence of Multi-Sited Ethnography. *Annual Review of Anthropology, 24*, 95–117.

Marcus, G. (2000). *Para-Sites: A Casebook against Cynical Reason*. Chicago: University of Chicago Press.

Marcus, G. E., & Fischer, M. M. J. (1986). *Anthropology as cultural critique: an experimental moment in the human sciences*. Chicago: University of Chicago Press.

Martin, E. (1994). *Flexible bodies: Tracking immunity in American culture from the days of polio to the age of AIDS*. Boston: Beacon Press.

Mauss, M. (1902). L'enseignement de l'histoire des religions des peuples non-civilisés à l'école des hautes études. *Revue de l'histoire des religions, 45*, 36–55.

Mauss, M. (1903). Esquisse d'une théorie générale de la magie (with H. Hubert). *Année sociologique, 7*, 1–146.

Mauss, M. (2006[1941/1948]). Techniques and Technology. In N. Schlanger (Ed.), *Techniques, technology and civilization* (pp. 147–153). New York & Oxford: Berghahn Books.

Mauss, M. (2007[1935]). Techniques of the body. In M. Lock & J. Farquhar (Eds.), *Beyond the Body Proper. Reading the Anthropology of Material Life* (pp. 50–68). Durham: Duke University Press.

Merleau-Ponty, M. (2002[1945]). *The Phenomenology of Perception*. London: Routledge.

Messeri, L. (2021). Realities of illusion: tracing an anthropology of the unreal from Torres Strait to virtual reality. *Journal of the Royal Anthropological Institute*, (n/a).

Miller, D. (1987). *Material culture and mass consumption*. Oxford: Basil Blackwell.

Miller, D. (Ed.) (1997). *Material cultures. Why some things matter*. London: UCL Press.

Miller, D. (1998). *A Theory of Shopping*. Cambridge: Polity Press.

Miller, D. (2005). Materiality: An introduction. In D. Miller (Ed.), *Materiality*. Durham: Duke University Press.

Miller, D. (2006). Consumption. In C. Tilley, W. Keane, S. Küchler, M. Rowlands, & P. Spyer (Eds.), *Handbook of Material Culture* (pp. 341–354). London: Sage.

Miller, D., & Slater, D. (2000). *The Internet: An ethnographic approach.* Oxford: Berg.

Miller, D., & Tilley, C. (1996). Editorial. *Journal of Material Culture, 1*(1), 4–15.

Morgan, L. H. (1877). *Ancient Society or Researches in the Lines of Human Progress From Savagery, Through Barbarism to Civilization.* New York: Henry Holt and Company

Mol, A. (2002). *The Body Multiple. Ontology in Medical Practice.* Durham: Duke University Press.

Morita, A. (2013). Traveling engineers, machines, and comparisons: intersecting imaginations and journeys in the Thai Local Engineering Industry. *East Asian Science, Technology and Society, 7*(2), 221–241.

Morozov, E. (2013). *To save everything, click here: technology, solutionism, and the urge to fix problems that don't exist.* London: Allen Lane.

Murphy, K. M., & Wilf, E. Y. (Eds.) (2021). *Designs and Anthropologies. Frictions and Affinities.* Santa Fe: School for Advanced Research Press.

Nardi, B. A. (2009). *My Life as a Night Elf Priest. An Anthropological Account of World of Warcraft.* Ann Arbor: University of Michigan Press.

Nguyen, V.-K. (2005). Antiretroviral Globalism, Biopolitics, and Therapeutic Citizenship. In A. Ong & S. J. Collier (Eds.), *Global Assemblages* (pp. 124–144). Oxford: Blackwell Publishers.

Nova, N., & Bloch, A. (2020). *Dr. Smartphones: an ethnography of mobile phone repair shops.* Morges: IDPURE éditions.

Nowotny, H., Scott, P., & Gibbons, M. (2001). *Re-Thinking Science: Knowledge and the Public in an Age of Uncertainty.* Cambridge: Polity.

Ong, A., & Collier, S. J. (Eds.) (2005). *Global assemblages: technology, politics, and ethics as anthropological problems.* Oxford: Blackwell Publishers.

Pálsson, G. (2007). *Anthropology and the new genetics.* Cambridge: Cambridge University Press.

Pels, P. (2010). Magical Things: On Fetishes, Commodities, and Computers. In D. Hicks & M. C. Beaudry (Eds.), *The Oxford handbook of material culture studies*. Oxford: Oxford University Press.

Pfaffenberger, B. (1988). Fetishised Objects and Humanised Nature: Towards an Anthropology of Technology. *Man, 23*(2), 236–252. https://doi.org/10.2307/2802804.

Pfaffenberger, B. (1992a). Social Anthropology of Technology. *Annual Review of Anthropology, 21,* 491–516.

Pfaffenberger, B. (1992b). Technological Dramas. *Science, Technology & Human Values, 17*(3), 282–312.

Pinch, T. J., & Bijker, W. E. (1984). The Social Construction of Facts and Artefacts: Or How the Sociology of Science and the Sociology of Technology Might Benefit Each Other. *Social Studies of Science, 14*(3), 399–441.

Pink, S., Horst, H., Postill, J., Hjorth, L., Lewis, T., & Tacchi, J. (Eds.) (2015). *Digital Ethnography. Principle and Practice.* Los Angeles & London: Sage.

Prainsack, B., Svendsen, M. N., Koch, L., & Ehrich, K. (2010). How do we collaborate? Social science researchers' experience of multidisciplinarity in biomedical settings. *BioSocieties, 5*(2), 278–286.

Prakash, G. (1999). *Another reason: Science and the imagination of modern India.* Princeton: Princeton University Press.

Rabinow, P. (1996). *Making PCR: a story of biotechnology.* Chicago: University of Chicago Press.

Rapp, R. (1999). *Testing women, testing the fetus: The social impact of amniocentesis in America.* New York: Psychology Press.

Ratzel, J. (1896) *The History of Mankind. 3 Volumes.* London: Macmillan & Co., Ltd.

Rivers, W.H.R. (1914). *The History of Melanesian Society, Vol. 2.* London: Cambridge University Press.

Rose, N., & Novas, C. (2005). Biological Citizenship. In S. J. Collier & A. Ong (Eds.), *Global Assemblages. Technology, Politics, and Ethics as Anthropological Problems* (pp. 439–463). Oxford: Blackwell Publishers.

Sahlins, M. (1972). *Stone Age Economics.* New York: Aldine de Gruyter.

Salazar, J. F., Pink, S., Irving, A., & Sjöberg, J. (Eds.) (2017). *Anthropologies and Futures. Researching Emerging and Uncertain Worlds.* London: Bloomsbury.

Schiffer, M. B. (Ed.) (2001). *Anthropological Perspectives on Technology.* Albuquerque: University of New Mexico Press.

Schlanger, N. (2006). Introduction. Technological Commitments: Marcel Mauss and the Study of Techniques in the French Social Sciences. In M. Mauss (Ed.), *Techniques, technology and civilization, edited and introduced by Nathan Schlanger.* New York & Oxford: Berghahn Books.

Seaver, N. (2017). Algorithms as culture: Some tactics for the ethnography of algorithmic systems. *Big Data & Society, 4*(2), 1–12. https://doi.org/10.1177/2053951717738104.

Seaver, N. (2018). What Should an Anthropology of Algorithms Do? *Cultural Anthropology, 33*(3), 375–385. https://doi.org/10.14506/ca33.3.04.

Sharp, L. (1968[1952]). Steel Axes for Stone-Age Australians. In Y. A. Cohen (Ed.), *Man in Adaption. The Cultural Present.* Chicago: Aldine.

Sigaut, F. (1994). Technology. In T. Ingold (Ed.), *Companion Encyclopedia of Anthropology* (pp. 420–459). London & New York: Routledge.

Smith, R. C., Vangkilde, K. T., Kjærsgaard, M. G., Otto, T., Halse, J., & Binder, T. (Eds.) (2016). *Design anthropological futures.* London: Bloomsbury Academic.

Sneath, D., Holbraad, M., & Pedersen, M. A. (2009). Technologies of the Imagination: An Introduction. *Ethnos, 74*(1), 5–30.

Star, S. L., & Ruhleder, K. (1996). Steps Toward an Ecology of Infrastructure: Design and Access for Large Information Spaces. *Information Systems Research, 7*(1), 5–134.

Stavrianakis, A. (2015). From anthropologist to actant (and back to anthropology): Position, Impasse, and Observation in Sociotechnical Collaboration. *Cultural Anthropology, 30*(1), 169–189.

Steward, J. H. (1955). *Theory of culture change: the methodology of multilinear evolution.* Urbana: University of Illinois Press.

Suchman, L. (2007). *Human-Machine Reconfigurations: Plans and Situated Actions* (2nd edition). Cambridge: Cambridge University Press.

TallBear, K. (2013). *Native American DNA: tribal belonging and the false promise of genetic science.* Minneapolis: University of Minnesota Press.

Traweek, S. (1988). *Beamtimes and lifetimes: the world of high energy physicists.* Cambridge, MA: Harvard University Press.

Tsing, A. (2000). The Global Situation. *Cultural Anthropology, 15*(3), 327–360.

Tsing, A. L. (2005). *Friction. An Ethnography of Global Connection*. Princeton & Oxford: Princeton University Press.

Tyler, E. (1901). Pitt-Rivers. In L. Stephen (Ed.), *Dictionary of national biography, Vol. 3*. London: Smith, Elder, & co.

Turner, V. W. (1974). *Dramas, Fields and Metaphors: Symbolic Action in Human Society*. Ithaca & London: Cornell University Press.

Wajcman, J. (2000). Reflections on Gender and Technology Studies: What State is the Art? *Social Studies of Science, 30*(3), 447–464.

Waltorp, K. (2021). Multimodal Sorting: The Flow of Images across Social Media and Anthropological Analysis. In A. Ballestero & B. R. Winthereik (Eds.), *Experimenting with Ethnography. A Companion to Analysis*. Durham: Duke University Press.

Waltorp, K., & Bruun, M. H. (forthcoming). Flying Drones and the Flow of Images: A Gendered Issue of Concern. In D. Lanzeni, K. Waltorp, S. Pink, & R. C. Smith (Eds.), *An Anthropology of Futures and Technologies*. London: Routledge.

Wang, P. (2012, August 12). Writing Live Fieldnotes: Towards a More Open Ethnography. *Ethnography Matters*.

White, L. A. (1959). *The evolution of culture: the development of civilization to the fall of Rome*. New York: McGraw-Hill.

Wittfogel, K. A. (1957). *Oriental despotism a comparative study of total power*. New Haven: Yale University Press.

Wynne, B. (2001). Creating Public Alienation: Expert Cultures of Risk and Ethics on GMOs. *Science as Culture, 10*(4), 445–481.

Åsberg, C., & Lykke, N. (2010). Feminist technoscience studies. *European Journal of Women's Studies* 17(4): 299–305.

PART I

Perspectives, Fields, and Approaches

CHAPTER 2

Making 'Technology' Visible: Technical Activities and the Chaîne Opératoire

Technique

Ludovic Coupaye

'Technology' is a problematic category for social and historical sciences. As authors such as Ruth Oldenziel (1999, pp. 19–50), Leo Marx (2010), or, more recently, Eric Schatzberg (2018) have shown, the term emerged out of a complex history of mistranslations and confusions, leading to the merging together of heterogeneous meanings and phenomena, such as practices, knowledge, devices, and large organisations, within a masculinist and colonial frame. Beyond issues of semantics (Sigaut 1985), this epistemologically biased confusion allowed it to become a pervasive trope in public, media, and corporate discourses, as 'an ostensibly discrete entity—one capable of becoming a virtually autonomous, all-encompassing agent of change' (Marx 2010 [1997], p. 564).

The combination of conceptual black-boxing, pervasiveness, and suggestions of rational linear determinism is perhaps the reason why, unlike history, philosophy, or sociology, anthropology has hesitated to make technology an explicit topic of investigation—as it did with religion, kinship, politics, art, and even nature itself—although subjects such as subsistence modes and techniques were part of early ethnographies and museum analyses (see Blackwood 1970; Pitt-Rivers 1906). Indeed, anthropologists, especially those working in the English language, seemed to have been reluctant to make it a proper and

L. Coupaye (✉)
University College London, London, UK
e-mail: l.coupaye@ucl.ac.uk

© The Author(s), under exclusive license to Springer Nature Singapore Pte Ltd. 2022
M. H. Bruun et al. (eds.), *The Palgrave Handbook of the Anthropology of Technology*, https://doi.org/10.1007/978-981-16-7084-8_2

identified topic of enquiry, in spite of a few calls to develop an actual 'Anthropology of Technology' (Lemonnier 1992; Pfaffenberger 1992; Ingold 1997; Sigaut 2002 [1994]; Eglash 2006), making the present volume even more exceptional.

Yet, despite its absence as an identified subdiscipline, the phenomena to which 'technology' refers are an important part of both anthropology and material culture studies. Several manifestations have been carefully investigated, although in different settings, under different terminologies, and following different paradigms, from the anthropology of skills and making to, more recently, the anthropology of infrastructure.[1] In parallel, over the last three decades, the expansion of organisational forms, industrial, digital, or otherwise, and new types of devices and 'objects', such as robots, software, algorithms, and AI, have attracted renewed anthropological scrutiny, as the present volume exemplifies. In particular, approaches associated with constructivism have done much to challenge and unpack the unquestioned ontological blackboxing of 'technology' and its association with linear determinisms, revealing the co-construction of people *with* artefacts, devices, and systems (e.g. Bijker et al. 1987; Latour 1991).

Scholars in sociology and philosophy have suggested that 'technology' usually refers to three orders of phenomena (see Winner 1985 [1977], pp. 11–12; Matthewman 2011, pp. 8–20): (1) devices and/or equipment, contraptions, and artefacts; (2) ways of making and doing things, which includes skills and knowledge; and (3) large organisational forms, such as infrastructures and supply chains, as well as the complex socio-technical networks of research, development, and commercial organisations. In a nutshell, practices and objects unfold together in the first two orders and are always ensconced within the third order, be it a household, a small workshop, or a multinational company; all three vary in size, extent, and scale.

The second order, which deals with actual practices, skills, and creativity, has a long and rich tradition within the discipline of anthropology, because it lends itself the most to close-up empirical ethnographic investigation. I therefore use it to discuss a method developed in previous anthropological traditions, with the intent to put it to work in relation to contemporary analytical discussions on 'technology'. In this chapter, I (re)introduce the *chaîne opératoire* (Fr.; 'operational chain', more generally translated into English as 'operational sequence') as an *ethnographically driven method* particularly fitted to challenging the invisibility of 'technology', and revelative of the fundamental relationality of artefacts, practices, and networks. It is a method that can give empirical grounding to contemporary analytical concepts such as 'agency', 'affordances', 'network', 'materiality', and 'subjectification' (Gell 1998; Knappett 2004; Latour 2005; Miller 2005; Warnier 2007), as well as creating the space to resort to cognitive or phenomenological investigations (Hutchins 1996; Ingold 2013; Malafouris 2013).

Designed purposefully as a descriptive and interpretative tool, the chaîne opératoire aims at *graphically revealing* the sequential and structural dimensions of technical activities (Cresswell 2011 [1976]; Lemonnier 1992). It helps *make visible* their fundamental material, social, and cultural heterogeneity, relational intricacy, and the interweaving of causalities, choices, and contingencies, whilst also evaluating the concrete and precise weight of each actor, human and non-human, in the whole process (Coupaye 2015a, 2015b, 2016). It allows consideration of the place of objects enrolled in the process and how simple activities reveal the localised effects of larger structural settings and infrastructures.

I start this chapter with a general presentation of the chaîne opératoire method and then unpack my preferred use of 'technical' as an analytical category. If not more descriptive, it is at least less loaded with contemporary vernacular associations with, and assumptions of, progress and determinism than 'technology' and, moreover, allows me to emphasise the performative dimensions of technical processes. I then situate these *technical activities* within a broad picture of how material culture studies have dealt with their processual dimensions. In the following section, I discuss some methodological aspects of the use of the chaîne opératoire in order to prevent some misconceptions about its potential and limits. In the final section, I discuss its application in two ethnographic cases—using a laptop computer in France and shifting cultivation in Papua New Guinea—to illustrate the analytical potential of the chaîne opératoire in two different settings.

THE CHAÎNE OPÉRATOIRE: DEFINITIONS, TRAJECTORIES, AND ISSUES

Marcel Mauss, in the wake of his writings and teaching on *technology* (as 'the study of technics'), was one of the first to insist on the temporal and sequential nature of material activities (2007 [1947], pp. 67–68). Remarking, in a rather Durkheimian way, that collective cultural norms were also found in mundane daily bodily activities (such as walking, swimming, or digging with a spade—even in having sex) through the *habitus* (Mauss 1973 [1935], p. 75), Mauss also suggested that these could be found in the making of artefacts. As a result, analysing artefacts in terms of finished products was no longer enough, and instead required the documentation and analysis of the actual process of manufacture, from the original material to the end result. He particularly insisted on the importance of tracing the 'organic chain' (*l'enchaînement organique*, 2007 [1947], p. 67[2]) of operations, including their different steps, changes from one form or state to another, as well as types of gestures and movements involved. This idea of organic unfolding was a way to foreground, analytically, how the different stages and elements composing the operation were temporally and spatially related to one another and context-dependent.

His student, André Leroi-Gourhan, a prehistorian and archaeologist, gave the chaîne opératoire its name and its first definition by specifying that '[a] technique is made of both gesture and tool, organised in a *chain* by a true syntax, which gives operational sequences both their fixity and flexibility'[3] (1993 [1964], p. 114, my emphasis). At a time when structuralism was the main paradigm, the use of the concept of 'syntax' aimed at describing this organic, temporal, relational, and unfolding structure of the operational sequence, the performance of which was equated with the performance of language: something common to a group but each time performed by an individual.[4]

Leroi-Gourhan's use of the term of chaîne opératoire originally referred to both human and animal procedural knowledge. This operational memory manifests itself at three different levels of consciousness: that which is automatic and present in all animal species (human infants and their hand grip; a foal that stands 30 minutes after its birth); processes learned and embodied through education and experience, the performance of which requires little intervention of language or conscious thinking (skills, see Sennet 2008; Ingold 2010; Marchand 2010); and the highest level of awareness at which language and self-reflection play an important role, either to correct a mistake or to create new sequences (Leroi-Gourhan 1993 [1964], p. 230). All three levels pointed out the cognitive dimensions of technical activities, but the second and third were essential to move the notion of 'style' towards behavioural dimensions and 'ways of making/doing' (see also Lechtman 1977; Dietler and Herbich 1998).

From then on, the chaîne opératoire became less of a theory of procedural knowledge and more of a method which followed two main disciplinary paths (see Schlanger 2005). One was in archaeology, prompted by Leroi-Gourhan's and his students' work on prehistory (Pélegrin 1990). In large part connected to experimental archaeology and ethno-archaeology, it made its way into British archaeology at the end of the 1980s through the publication of a special issue of the *Archaeological Review from Cambridge* (Sinclair and Schlanger 1990), among other media.[5] The second path was in anthropology, notably through the work of the French research unit, 'Techniques & Culture]', in the 1970s, with the work of Robert Cresswell (2011 [1976]), Hélène Balfet (1991), Marie-Claude Mahias (1993), and others, including Pierre Lemonnier, better known in English-speaking academia (1986, 1992, 2012). Against a background of Marxism, materialism, and structuralism, this trend was resolutely empirical, using the chaîne opératoire method to produce detailed ethnographies of the technical activities of both Western and indigenous communities (Balfet 1991; Bartholeyns et al. 2011). It was then hoped that the method would produce ethnographies that allowed for the examination of the 'more physical side of the relations between productive forces and social relations of productions' (Lemonnier 2012, p. 16) in an objective and scientific way. This project proved a dead end because, on the one hand, there was a lack of interest among the more Marxist anthropologists in paying proper attention to objects, techniques, and know-how, and, on the other, understanding of the method was limited to the production of stereotypic sequences of actions that sought to find the actual 'language' of techniques—its 'technems' (e.g.

Koechlin 1975). Neither ethnographic trend ever really made its way into studies of material culture in American or British anthropology, both of which had taken a turn towards topics such as exchange, consumption, discourse, and the politics of culture (Buchli 2002; Carroll et al. 2020).

It is perhaps Nathan Schlanger who best gives definitions of the chaîne opératoire which reflect both archaeological and anthropological trajectories. In archaeology it can refer to 'a generalised model or pattern of technical behaviour inferred from archaeological and experimental studies (e.g. the "Acheulean hand axe *chaîne opératoire*")' (Schlanger 2005, p. 25; italics in original). This archaeological definition became a way to infer a template from existing material which, in turn, could be used to interrogate materials and artefacts in terms of sequences, providing them with hypotheses about the mental and cognitive process of the actor (Gowlett 1990; Digard 2004). It enabled the conceptualisation of a generalised model aiming at reconstituting past processes, based solely on their material results, whether whole artefacts or the traces left by the manufacturing process. In anthropology, by contrast, it 'designate[s] a concrete occurrence of some particular technical process' (Schlanger 2005, p. 25) (e.g. the weaving of a piece of textile or the moulding of a pot).

In both disciplines, the main contribution of the chaîne opératoire was to draw attention away from the finished product and, instead, to focus it on processes. For archaeologists, it became the main concept enabling the reconstitution of past technical processes based on the type of material analysed (lithic material or pottery; see Soressi and Geneste 2011 for an overview). By contrast, for anthropologists, Schlanger's definition pointed to its role in providing the ethnographic data required to analyse the relational complexity of human technical activities. It became an empirical method aimed at documenting the succession of operations included in a particular observed task, not only leading to the making of artefacts, such as pottery or textiles, but also of 'techniques of acquisition', such as hunting, agriculture, fishing, and mining, and 'techniques of consumption' (such as exchange and food; see Leroi-Gourhan 1971, 1973). It helped provide the actual and concrete evidence required to investigate the internal organic logic of a technical process, the respective roles of the different 'actors' (humans and/or non-humans), the variations and decisions made during the process, and the relations between the documented process and other domains such as kinship, gender, politics, and religion. Because of this profoundly empirical grounding, the chaîne opératoire, instead of the purely theoretical model it became for archaeologists, is also, at its core, a rigorous ethnographic method.

Related to its definition as a method aimed at documenting technical processes, the term mostly refers to a specific analytical object: a chaîne opératoire is the transcription of ethnographic notes into a *diagrammatic or graphic form* (Lemonnier 1992, pp. 37–44; Djindjian 2013). As such, it should not pretend to be anything other than an *analytical representation*, a specific way of visualising the heterogeneity and complexity of the particular, related technical process. It remains oriented towards the unveiling of the vernacular nature of the logics at play in the actors' ways of doing and making things. Accordingly, the chaîne opératoire has been used to analyse the deeply social and cultural nature of technical activities: by identifying 'strategic operations'—steps which 'cannot be (1) delayed, (2) cancelled, or (3) replaced without jeopardizing the whole process or its final result' (Lemonnier 1992, p. 22)—the chaîne opératoire made visible contrasting operations that were dependent on individual or local choices and variations.

It is important to note that the quality of the result often also depends on *vernacular conceptions of appropriateness.* For instance, a question that I ask students is whether, when making tea in a cup, they add the milk *before or after* the boiling water and whether they can taste the difference; many claim that their way is the proper way and that the other does not result in 'proper tea'. By comparison, non-strategic operations are those that present variations and choices across actors, times, and places as 'technical choices' (Lemonnier 1992, 1993; van der Leeuw 1993; Sillar and Tite 2000). The combination of both categories of operations thus allows the analyst to consider, in a non-restrictive way, both technical imperatives and historical, cultural, and personal inclinations and circumstances.

'Technical' as an Analytical Category: From 'Technical Acts' to 'Technical Activities'

At its most empirical level, the chaîne opératoire method focuses on technical activities as they are performed by actors. This empiricism finds its source in Mauss's pragmatic approach to sociality as transparent in his original definition of 'technique':

> I call technique an action which is *effective* and *traditional* (and you will see that in this it is no different from a magical, religious or symbolic action). It has to be effective and traditional. There is no technique and no transmission in the absence of tradition. (Mauss 1973 [1935], p. 75, original emphasis)

To be analytically useful, the two emphasised terms require precision. 'Traditional', in Mauss's terms, referred to the acquired nature of skills (following appropriate, recognised, and shared forms of performance and practices, including improvisation). It also included both the socio-cultural context of transmission and historical dynamics that incorporate changes and innovations.

'Effective', referring to efficacy *according to the actor* (see also Mauss 2003 [1909], p. 52; Warnier 2009; Coupaye 2013, pp. 257–246, 2018, pp. 6–9), occupies a central role in the study of technical processes. Indeed, on the one hand, this *vernacular* efficacy takes into account all acts considered appropriate by the actor, whether they are aimed at matter or at intangible entities or substances. Thus, importantly, it operates as an analytical category which can reflect the 'emic' or vernacular values ('Modern' or 'Non-Modern', to reuse

Bruno Latour's terminology 1993 [1991]) attributed to the performance of action, sometimes regardless of the empirical result or effect on its objects—whether clay, the self, divinities, or whole institutions such as the government or the environment. On the other hand, the important analytical consequences of Mauss's 'formula' (Sigaut 2003) are that, from a vernacular perspective, technical, ritual (such as praying), and aesthetic acts (e.g. painting, but also songs or dances) and their effects can often be totally undifferentiated by the actors.

This definition of 'technical acts' not only offers us guidelines for what we should attend to when studying technical activities, it also helps by-pass the conceptual confusion associated with 'technology', or its adjectival form 'technological', by analytically decentring it. As Latour recognised, the adjective 'technical' is indeed able to resonate with many phenomena encompassed within the loose analytical category of 'materiality' (Latour 2014, p. 508), as well as affording an (analytical) escape route from Euro-American understandings of 'matter'. As analytical category, 'technical' can thus be extended to the two other orders of phenomena which are also part of what 'technology' is used to refer to.

Thus, 'technical objects' include things (in a broad sense, including a stone to be thrown, or a ritual image) that are made or enrolled in a process of performing efficacious actions (which is different to qualifying these objects as efficacious *in themselves*); these 'objects' are 'traditional' because their design is often part of longer historical dynamics of progressive and transmitted changes, improvements, or innovations (see Kubler 1962; Simondon 2017 [1958]). This category includes what we define as 'physical' tools and instruments, as well as machines, and can also be extended to less tangible entities such as algorithms, software, or prayer (see Coupaye 2013, pp. 98–99, 2021a).

'Technical systems' can refer, then, to the systemic relations between technical objects and technical activities, as well as their relations with other phenomena, such as religion or politics (Lemonnier 1992, pp. 7–11). Yet the term can also denote how these two orders can themselves be part of larger-scale sociotechnical organisations (Bijker et al. 1987) or industrial and digital infrastructures, which contain 'messy, complex, problem-solving components' (Hughes 1986, p. 50), often emerging from longer historical processes. 'Technical systems'—or networks—cannot be experienced directly, their effects instead being 'encountered' in the course of processes wherein other forms of agency are experienced besides that emanating from the agents directly involved (see Coupaye 2021b).

As I hinted in the introduction, whilst not always directly associated with the category of 'technology', what I describe as 'technical activities' are far from being a new topic in studies of material culture. In recent decades, the study of object/subject relations has seen the re-emergence of interest in ways of 'making' and 'doing' and the revitalisation of the study of modes of production (Douny and Naji 2009). Whether associated with the notion of crafts (Sennet 2008), with skills (e.g. Ingold 2010), or examined through their relation with knowledge (Marchand 2010), cognition (e.g. Malafouris 2013), or their cultural or socialising dimensions (Lechtman 1977; Warnier 2001, 2007; Mohan and Douny 2020), the ways in which people physically make (*poiesis*) and do (*praxis*) things are each time distinguished as the point of convergence between a body, what is acted upon, and a socio-cultural whole (Mauss 1973 [1935]). Stemming from this diversity, a series of concepts have become recurrent in such analyses, such as 'agency', 'affordance', 'network', 'materiality', and 'ontology'.

Such diversity of domains, approaches, and theories is undoubtedly the mark of a vibrant vitality within material, visual, and now digital culture studies, often resulting in vigorous debates (e.g. Ingold 2007), which should not, however, distract attention from one fundamental characteristic of all processes as experienced by actors: all are complex, messy, multi-layered, and multiscalar flows. Technical processes can unfold in one or several spaces (workshop or hunting territory; see Balfet 1991, p. 15); they can involve a small group of people, such as a craftsman and his apprentices, or several related institutions or corporations; they can be at times smooth or jerky, with different rhythms and velocities, intended and unintended breaks. In other words, *processes are fundamentally heterogeneous and reticulated.*

Revealing such heterogeneity has arguably been the main project sustaining Science and Technology Studies (STS) and Actor-Network Theory (ANT) (Law 2009; Latour 2005). As pragmatic and empirical approaches, they have aimed at mapping out the network of relationships from which specific 'objects' (e.g. the camera, transport systems, science, and law) emerged. However, some critiques have pointed out several issues pertaining to these approaches, including an implied idea of concatenation of discrete elements or a form of political flatness which does not, perhaps, pay enough attention to the context (e.g. Ingold 2008; Tsing 2010). More importantly, 'network' (or 'meshwork'; Knappett 2011) can come to be used as an analytical black box, qualifying a whole set of relations without actually specifying what forms they take (though such an attitude was less prevalent in early examples published by Michel Callon, Bruno Latour, or John Law; see Law 2009). As a result, the effects of the weight of the different elements on the relations, as well as the asperities, the effects of irregularities, or the symbolic content of what makes the network/meshwork, can appear underplayed. Once again, analytical categories end up overwriting vernacular ones and 'networks' themselves can come close to transcendental entities, acting more as an explanatory model rather than a descriptive one.

By contrast, an ethnography of technical activities should be able to open these black boxes and empirically investigate what they are made of. It should enable examination of the process, the flow, and its rhythms and breaks, revealing its temporality and spatiality, as well as describing its fundamental (cultural, material, *and* social) heterogeneity. Doing so should not lead to qualifying processes as concatenations of discrete elements, but instead to the *exposure of the relations* that articulate humans, things, gestures, imaginations, and logics—and their qualifications. It means paying attention to the reticulated, relational, situated, *and* sequential nature of ways of doing and making things.

These technical activities are fundamentally lived, enacted, and situated practices and experiences. As such, from an ethnographic perspective, they are as much about explicit verbal representations and images, as they are about implicit—yet realised when performed—assumptions about the world and its inhabitants (material or not, visible or not, present or remote) and steeped in affects. They are thus a privileged way to investigate how these assumptions and affects manifest themselves through actual practices and choices, which at times can also take verbal forms. As material culture studies have demonstrated, approaches to designs, crafts, arts, knowledge, or skills—whether grounded in phenomenology, pragmatism, or cognition—have re-examined how bodies, materials, devices, and memory are crucial to the construction of subjects, imagination, and identity. The non-verbal nature of such practices can make them more difficult to observe and then analyse and convey in written, verbal form, yet the quality is ethnographically decisive (Pierre Lemonnier 2012). Through participation, one can gain access to these implicit assumptions and understandings, the verbal rationale of which is unnecessary, impossible, or at times not recommended. The chaîne opératoire thus offers an ethnographic method able to unveil the logic nested within, and manifested in, technical activities as they unfold through time and space.

TAMING THE ANALYTICAL: METHODOLOGICAL CONSIDERATIONS

While its empirical versatility and analytical affordances constitute the chaîne opératoire's main strengths, a narrow reading of Leroi-Gourhan's cognitive model and the collapse of the ethnographic method into those of ethno-archaeology and experimental archaeology can lead to a confusion between a general model of technical processes and its actualisation by actors. As a result, the chaîne opératoire can become confused with a theory about actors' ways of making and doing (see Ingold 2013, p. 26). But, from an ethnographic perspective, the chaîne opératoire should not be mistaken for a theory: it has to remain firmly a *method* of documenting technical activities in the field, resulting in their rendition as an ethnographic document. However, it is not completely neutral and requires that two specificities of technical activities be kept in mind.

Firstly, as François Sigaut reminds us, we do not see people doing techniques, much less chaînes opératoires; we only see people doing and/or making things (2002 [1994], p. 424). This means remembering that, heeding Pierre Bourdieu's warning, the model of reality should not be confused with the reality of the model (1990 [1980], p. 39). The actual chaîne opératoire is the product of the ethnographer her/himself, as indicated by its diagrammatic form (Balfet 1991; Djindjian 2013); it is the product of an encounter between the ethnographer and actual actors in action. Whilst actors might indeed possess what Leroi-Gourhan called an 'operational memory' (Leroi-Gourhan

1993 [1964], pp. 230–234)—skills that she/he can perform automatically—the chaîne opératoire can only refer metaphorically to the performance inasmuch as it points to a subject's internalised schemas or practices.

Indeed, actors experience most technical activities as continuums or flows precisely because apprenticeship and training inscribe skills so deeply into their body and cognition that they become a form of non-verbal procedural knowledge (Warnier 2007, pp. 8–9; Sennet 2008, pp. 179–193) or 'operational memory' which does not mobilise language or the full consciousness (Leroi-Gourhan 1993 [1964], p. 232; see also Marchand 2010; Ingold 2010; Malafouris 2013). The process itself might become a conscious object of enquiry only when something goes wrong and the actor must solve the problem. The chaîne opératoire itself is thus nothing more (and nothing less) than the visual transcription of the performance itself. It is an 'artefact' produced by the ethnographer in order to visualise, in another form than a written narrative or a film, the succession of events comprising a process, their sequential unfolding, and what intervenes at which moment. In the examples I have provided later, 'chaîne opératoire' thus refers to the four diagrams, not to my own ethnographic notes, even less to what the actors were doing.

Secondly, not all technical activities have a visible or empirical *material* result. Indeed, the ethnographer has to keep in mind Jean-Pierre Warnier's critique of the ways the *Techniques & Culture* approach (2009) was restricted to action on matter, eschewing two central points in Mauss's formula of technical acts as 'traditional' and 'effective'. As I signalled earlier, deciding what to include in the chaîne opératoire requires suspending Euro-American assumptions on material ('rational') efficacy and avoiding confusion with 'efficiency', an input/output ratio. This leads indeed to the inclusion of operations such as those usually qualified as rituals, or whose effects might be invisible or imagined but incorporated by the actors.

This means that, methodologically speaking, the descriptors used must be critically examined. Lemonnier aptly defined five 'components' of technical activities: tools, matter, gestures, knowledge, and energies (*cf.* Lemonnier 1992, pp. 5–6). These only have a heuristic role; their direct application to a particular process might, at times, be problematic (see Coupaye 2013, pp. 98–100, 159–163), as they can end up overwriting vernacular categories, which, for the actors, may play a crucial role in the whole process. Whatever the analytical purchase these 'components' might present, the ethnographer must be ready to criticise and, when necessary, discard them. This reflexive moment, through which every anthropologist should go, can then invite her/him to let the ethnography challenge the anthropologist's own analytical categories (e.g. does *mana* intervene as an energy or an actual actor? [see Coupaye 2018, pp. 6–9]; do ancestors help in the carving of a ceremonial bowl? [see Revolon 2018]). In my own research on Abulës-Speakers' ('Abelam') yam cultivation (see Fig. 2.3), the Jëwaai, an invisible substance contained in scent and many other bodily fluids, is said to be crucial to plant growth, making it one of the major 'components' of the technical process, without my being able to qualify it clearly as a substance or an energy. It became a 'component'/'actor' in itself.

In addition, the chaîne opératoire method itself is only valid as long as the ethnographer takes into account the scale of the phenomenon observed, the means of observation available (writing, photographs, or videos), and, crucially, the research question (Martinelli 1991, pp. 65–67). Not every analysis of a given process requires the minute and precise transcription of each detail of an action—at times it is sufficient simply to think of a chaîne opératoire in a similar way as the concept of the biography of things (Kopytoff 1986; Drazin 2021)—but questioning what each affords can, in itself, be sufficient to attract attention to potential evidence.

The importance of the research question is reflected in the scale of observation, the scale of analysis, and the scale of visualisation. This is perhaps where the chaîne opératoire might be confused with a general template, even though the actual phenomenon can present some regularities across its different iterations. On a very broad scale, my own ethnographic recording of Abulës-Speakers' swidden horticulture follows the same pattern as many other ethnographic cases from the same region (see Fig. 2.3), and 'loses' its validity as a 'concrete occurrence'. But putting together the elements I have actually witnessed and moving away from the scale of actual actions (on materials and subjects) can yield some hints about the articulation of local logics with material requirements, the intricacy of agencies and decisions, and the heterogeneity of actors and collectives (Fig. 2.4).

In the end, the aim is to make processes—this elusive although pervasive analytical category—visible.

Making Processes Visible

Making a chaîne opératoire starts with ethnographic observations and transcriptions (Lemonnier 1992, pp. 25–50), first in a written form, then transposed into a graphic representation of what can be understood from the actors' actions (Practical Sheets, *Techniques & Culture*, 2019). It also means adjusting the scale of observation in relation to the research question (and to the contingencies in the field), depending, for instance, on whether one wants to reveal how the 'minutely adaptable exercise of embodied skills precisely requires an openness to and awareness of the specifics of a situation' (Sutton 2008, p. 49); to document the organisation of the different steps of a specific ceremony which takes several days; or to map out the actual biography of a thing (Kopytoff 1986) and how its processes of transformation operate.

Alongside the capacity to make visible the flowing nature of making and doing things, and the complexity of engaging with materials, the chaîne opératoire can also be used to follow the transformation of a single material (from supply chain to recycling), or the particular trajectory of recruitment and mobilisation of human and/or non-human actors from wider immanent collectives, such as the 'environment', kinship relations, interest groups, or ancestors. 'Collectives', another analytical category, appear then as immanent in prototypic categories, only realised through actual processes as actors recruit elements that they evaluate as required for the achievement of the task (Coupaye 2013, pp. 179–206). By indicating their respective weight, agency, conflicts, and tensions, the method might be able to give a topographical (and topological) view of the 'network', which will no longer be flat, thus providing an empirical response to some of the critiques made of ANT.

The four chaînes opératoires I present here concretely illustrate some of these points based on two ethnographic examples. Whilst adding photographs or videos of specific moments is usually the best way to make a process visible, in these examples I only present the diagrams. The first example (Figs. 2.1 and 2.2) deals with an actor starting to write while visiting friends in France with a UK laptop; the second (Figs. 2.3 and 2.4) comes from research I conducted in Nyamikum, an Abulës-speaking village in the Sepik Province of Papua New Guinea, between 2001–2003 and 2014. I have not tried in this chapter to simplify the diagrams. In order to demonstrate the intricacy, heterogeneity, and complexity of the processes documented, I present them here as a taste of what can be done with the method, along with some details and the analytical points that emerged.

The first two figures represent the organic relations between the different stages leading to commencing work on the computer. Figure 2.1 is a representation of the sequence of events from the moment the actor awakes to the moment she/he starts to write. It is less detailed, instead illustrating the actual,

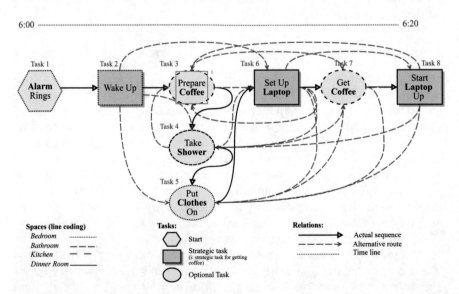

Fig. 2.1 Chaîne Opératoire of the writer's morning, representing the relations between alternative sequences, strategic tasks (which, for the writer, includes getting coffee), and the actual sequence

overall unfolding of the morning, as well as a whole series of alternate sequences which could have led to the same moment (including one in which she/he starts working without having put any clothes on!). These make visible what Lemonnier calls 'strategic operations': for instance, one cannot start typing on the computer effectively without having turned it on first (in Figs. 3.3 and 3.4: one cannot plant the crops before having burnt the remains of the opening of the garden; one cannot make a tea without grabbing a cup/bowl/recipient from which to drink it). All other operations and their sequence are thus either contingent, accidental, or derive from personal taste.

Figure 2.2 details the period between the actor's turning on the laptop to realise she/he has forgotten a UK/Fr adaptor and the beginning of actual writing. It also represents in more detail the role and timing of non-humans, such as the cables, the laptop, the codes and algorithms in its hard drive that activate the operating system and the software, and the external hard drive in which the document is saved (not as a piece of paper, but as a set of 'bits' forming instructions which the word processing program will actualise on the screen). Their agencies and affordances (Gibson 1986) are multiple: their mobility (being a laptop); their physical resistance (the need for a protective case); their capacity to become entangled and disentangled; and their encoding and decoding to become actual words or images on a computer screen. The absence of an adaptor in the bag (which is itself the result of the actor's fatigue or perhaps distraction) makes infrastructures and their differences crucial, giving the network or the system—here, electricity supply—actual visibility. But then interpersonal and historical relationships between the actor and her/his hosts are revealed by the fact that she/he had left an adapter in their care, foreseeing a future visit, and that she/he feels comfortable enough to rummage for it in their kitchen. Choices and personal inclinations are also revealed: the need for coffee, the decision to use a mouse instead of the now-pervasive touchpad which requires different manual skills.

Then, other agencies—this time not completely analytical and more literal—unfold, also manifesting themselves as automatic processes escaping the actor's direct experience and agency: electricity flows through cables and then wires to activate the motherboard, the processor, the magnetic memory devices (all hidden inside the machine), and the screen and fans. The electric current (coming from the local power grid, not from the battery, and in the form of electrons) circulates through the CPU's microscopic circuit (made of silicate and magnesium or germanium), which 'opens' or 'closes' according to the instructions coded as '1' and '0' contained within the hard drive, stored in temporary memory slots. This coding (still as electric impulses) then travels back into the hard drive, through the motherboard, and is 'translated' into sets of instructions, which are sent through the graphic card, the screen, the keyboard, the USB ports, and so on, to 'execute' other processes (launching software or translating physical hits on the keyboard into letters or numbers on the screen). The downloading of the encoded email message on the machine mobilises an

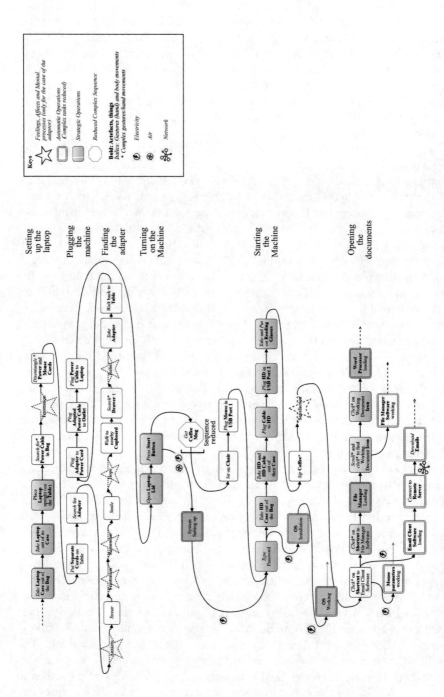

Fig. 2.2 Chaîne Opératoire at a closer scale of the steps between Fig. 2.1's Task 6 and Task 8 of the writer's morning. Here, affects, human and non-human agencies, and processes have been taken into account to show the heterogeneity of the whole process

entire invisible infrastructure of wireless signal and local provider, as well as satellites or servers located somewhere where the 'inbox' (another set of bits instructions) is stored.

Skills unfold, some below the level of consciousness, mobilising embodied knowledge, cognitive processes, and mental states: walking and typing (in a different language than the actor's native one and on a keyboard where letters are organised differently) join other more conscious activities, such as measuring out the coffee, disentangling the cables, and searching for the adaptor. All these are interwoven with mental processes (thinking, remembering), affects, and feelings, which can be reactions or operators in how the sequence unfolds. Anxiety, concentration, and satisfaction, although not fitting the original definition of the chaîne opératoire, contribute to the course of the task and have their own effects on the result. Had another human actor been involved, then social relations would have been materialised more directly (in relation to their age, gender, and racial identity, or their social status, perhaps).

Figures 2.3 and 2.4 refer to the cultivation of long yams among the Abulës-Speakers (cf. Coupaye 2013, 2018). While, elsewhere, I have documented minute gestures and actual occurrences at length, here I created these chaînes opératoires to show the role of vernacular efficacy and logics, as well as to make visible the network of relationships and collectives involved in the process. Each step in both figures could be developed into its own sequence, each demonstrating the same level of complexity, although at a magnified scale.

I start with the general sequence of gardening (Fig. 2.3), to give a general idea of its main steps, including those that Nyamikum people considered were *required* for the success of food production, such as the Waapi Saaki ceremony which marks the transition from one cycle ('a sun') to the next. The visualisation, although apparently linear, in fact contains several paces, spaces, and rhythms: the different places where operations occur, for example, and the cyclical and recursive dimensions of the process. Labels also give some information about the content of steps.

Figure 2.4 starts with vernacular explanations for organising a Long Yam ceremony, called Waapi Saaki in Nyamikum: 'the Waapi Saaki is meant to celebrate and please the long yam (*waapi*), so that they will come back the following year. And as *waapi* open the road to all food that comes out of the garden, if you don't harvest *waapi*, you will die of hunger' (Tepmanyëgy, in a discussion with me in 2002; see Coupaye 2013, p. 106).

This statement reveals that, first, the ritual itself was conceived as a necessary step—a vernacular strategic operation—in the whole process of food production and, second, that long yam cultivation, although physically separated from other gardening activities, could only be understood in relation to food cultivation and to other types of ritual activities. Practices such as the Yakët, a set of behavioural prescriptions and proscriptions, and intangible bodily substances

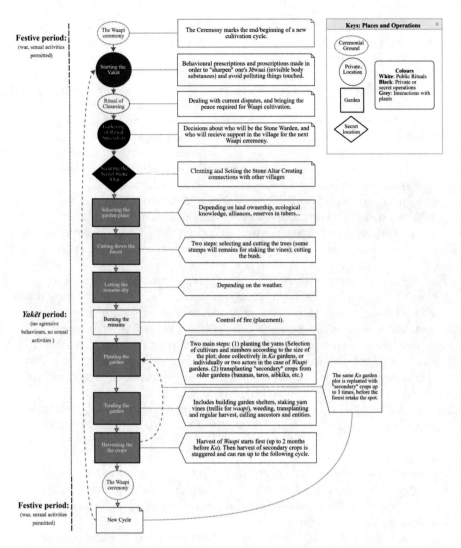

Fig. 2.3 Chaîne Opératoire of the long yam cycle, starting with the ceremony (etic model). Notable elements of the different stages (defined by the ethnographer) are indicated on the right

such as the Jëwaai had to be approached in relation to the role they played in the whole meshwork, alongside the complex sets of skills, knowledge (about the plants, their stage and behaviours, the state of the forest, the land), and ecological and social relations (between kin, with other descent groups and other villages, with entities living in the landscape such as spirits, animals, as well as with plants themselves).

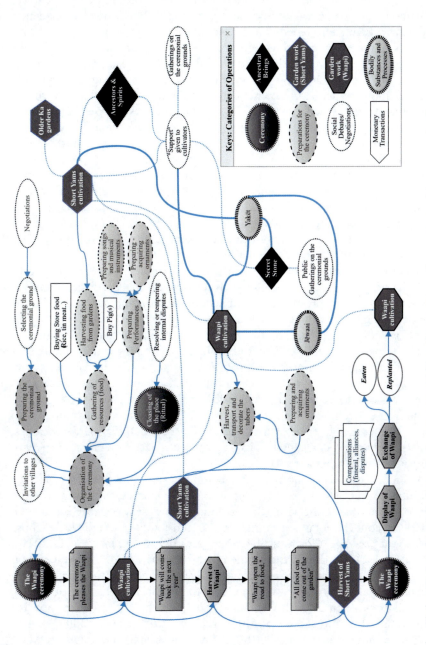

Fig. 2.4 Chaîne Opératoire of the large, long yam network, based on a vernacular account of the yam cycle, illustrating the relational heterogeneity of operations, actors, tasks, and places

Conclusion: Making Concepts Visible

All 'components' or elements encountered in the recording of the technical activities I have described unfold not as 'context', but instead immanently emerge as actual heterogeneous collectives of humans and non-humans, living beings or not, emerging through different spatial arrangements and temporalities—not as discrete entities, but, rather, defined by their relations with neighbouring and surrounding ones. All four chaînes opératoires (again, as graphic representations of actual experiences and/or observations) differ in form, as each aims to reveal specific characteristics of the processes analysed. They intersect with practices or effects, evoking, more or less directly, wider issues such as those of knowledge, secrecy, gender, economics, kinship, religion, and politics, which must be unpacked through a full textual analysis.

In the case of yam cultivation, while some of these collectives might be present in Nyamikum people's imagination, all emerged as the cultivation process recruited them and made them coalesce, often temporarily, into active participants or components of the whole (see Coupaye 2013, 2016, 2018). In the case of the writing session, socio-technical systems, infrastructures, and ANT's networks of 'actants' appear to emerge as the trajectory of the whole process mobilises or encounters them, and to manifest as *effects* of reticulated relations.

Both these technical activities took the form of one particular temporal (sequential) journey through a landscape populated by landmarks and bifurcations, crossing paths with other beings and encountering events, some of which the actor had planned and provoked, some totally unexpected or initiated by others, human or otherwise. The four chaînes opératoires are thus not like flat maps of a geographical area, but *recordings of particular itineraries within reticulated worlds.* It is this analogy which made me compare the chaîne opératoire to a transect (see Buckland et al. 2001), an ecological method of sampling through an environment such as a dense forest which records encounters with a heterogeneous sequence of trees, plants, bushes, but also barrows, rocks, rivulets, and living beings, materialising a chosen trajectory among a variety of alternative paths (Coupaye 2015a).

As a method, it is not, however, a skeleton key and cannot pretend to reveal *everything* about processes, including processes of making. Not only does the chaîne opératoire coexist with other 'technographic' methods (see Buob et al. 2019), its contributions and limits are also constantly re-examined by those who use it (see the 'Practical Sheets' in *Techniques & Culture*, 71, 2019). Echoing its other critiques, the chaîne opératoire—as a graphic representation and through its rendition of techniques—bears the mark of the 'grammatisation of flows as a process of discretization—for example, of the flow of speech, or the flow of gestures of the worker's body', which 'is what makes possible their technical reproducibility and thus their control' (Stiegler 2009, p. 40). Yet, by 'taming the analytical', the chaîne opératoire—not unlike writing, another form of linear representation—makes possible the visualisation of time and of complexity, making them available for thinking through and analysis.

Unlike linear representations of evolution or corporate planning, and the narrow teleological, utilitarian, and ethnocentric narratives these contain, it leaves room for the inclusion of forms of vernacular (emic) teleology, without simplifying the rendition into a purely deterministic or purely relativistic model. As only one form of documentation, all chaînes opératoires should be complemented by thicker descriptions (Geertz 1997 [1973], pp. 3–30), whether in academic, literary, or poetic forms of writing, as well as audio-visual documents. It cannot work by itself as an explanatory model, as the last section demonstrated.

As with all ethnographic accounts—and no two ethnographers will produce identical descriptions of their experience and observations of the same phenomenon unless, perhaps, at the upper scale of general process—there are no two identical chaînes opératoires. It is perhaps this very versatility of domains, extending to rituals, designs, meetings, gaming, recycling practices, or making bark cloth, which gives the chaîne opératoire its analytical potential (Coupaye 2015a, 2015b).[6] Its limits depend on the anthropological methodological awareness (the reflexive moment during which one reflects on what one's method shows and what it conceals, one's epistemological assumptions, and the position of empiricism within one's practice) underlying the analytical move. But giving matter to concepts ('network', 'agency', 'affordances', 'relations', 'ontology', 'politics'), as well as *taking the actor's categories seriously*, might also require the acknowledgement that more often than not, not every 'process' flows smoothly or homogeneously.

It is, after all, one of the ways to make 'technology' visible.

Acknowledgements This chapter owes much to students enrolled in the course, *Anthropology of Techniques and Technology*, or who followed sessions on the 'ChOp', for their contributions and critiques, and crucially for their experiments with the method in too many different contexts to list here. Thanks to the people of Nyamikum village in Papua New Guinea for their trust and patience, as well as to Rosalie Allain for her critical reading of various drafts, and to the two anonymous reviewers for their feedback. Thanks to Alexandra Fanghanel, Philippe Minvielle, and Stephanie Lécuyer for their constant support. Finally, thanks to the editors for their help with the whole text.

NOTES

1. A very broad range of authors have addressed these phenomena, which have been and are still at the heart of many debates. Along with others quoted in this chapter, the most frequently recurring references include Kopytoff (1986), Gell (1998), Knappett (2004), Ingold (2010, 2013), Marchand (2010), Larkin (2013), Malafouris (2013). See also Tilley et al. (2006) and Warnier (2007).
2. The English translation unfortunately uses the term 'concatenation'; for obvious reasons, I personally prefer to keep the less mechanistic and more relational term of 'chain'.
3. '*La technique est à la fois geste et outil, organisés en chaîne par une véritable syntaxe qui donne aux séries opératoires à la fois leur fixité et leur souplesse.*'

4. Beyond Leroi-Gourhan's initial formulation, definitions of the chaîne opératoire vary according to the theoretical and methodological premises of the author. Robert Cresswell defined it as 'a series of operations which transforms a raw material into a product, be it an object for consumption or a tool' (Cresswell 2011 [1976], p. 26, my translation), while Lemonnier simplifies it as 'the series of operations involved in any transformation of matter (including our own body) by human beings' (1992, p. 26).

5. Interestingly, archaeologist Michael B. Schiffer developed a methodological concept independently of the chaîne opératoire in his text on 'behavioral chain analysis' (1975).

6. For examples on recycling, see Fanchette (2016). Other graphs made by students are available online: http://www.materialworldblog.com/2015/07/unleashing-the-chaine-operatoire-students-experimentation-with-an-old-methodology/. In addition, whilst I have no space to expand further on this relation, there are methodological similarities with methods used in digital design, in particular UX mapping and customer experience journey maps. But arguably the analytical aims differ.

REFERENCES

Balfet, H. (Ed.) (1991). *Observer l'action technique. Des chaînes opératoires, pour quoi faire?* Paris: Editions du CNRS.

Bartholeyns, G., Govoroff, N., and Joulian, F. (Eds.) (2011). Cultures Matérielles. Anthologie raisonnée de 'Techniques & Culture'. *Techniques & Culture*, 54–55.

Bijker, W., Hughes, T. P., and Pinch, T. (Eds.) (1987). *The Social Construction of Technological Systems: New Directions in the Sociology and History of Technology.* Cambridge, MA: The MIT Press.

Blackwood, B. (1970). *The Classification of Artefacts in the Pitt Rivers Museum Oxford.* Occasional Papers on Technology no 11. Oxford: Pitt Rivers Museum.

Bourdieu, P. (1990 [1980]). *The Logic of Practice* (trans: R. Nice). Cambridge: Polity Press.

Buchli, V. (2002). *The Material Culture Reader.* Oxford & New York: Berg.

Buckland, S. T., Anderson, D. R., Burnham, K. P., Laake, J. L., Borchers, D. L., and Thomas, L. (Eds.) (2001). *Introduction to Distance Sampling.* Oxford: Oxford University Press.

Buob, B., Chevallier, D., and Gosselain, O. (2019). Technographies: Dans la trousse à outils de celles et ceux qui travaillent sur la technique. *Techniques & Culture*, *71*, 10–25.

Carroll, T., Walford, A., and Walton, S. (2020). *Lineages and Advancements in the Anthropology of Material Culture.* London: UCL Press.

Coupaye, L. (2013). *Growing Artefacts, Displaying Relationships: Yams, Art and Technology Amongst the Nyamikum Abelam of Papua New Guinea.* Oxford & New York: Berghahn Books.

Coupaye, L. (2015a). Chaîne opératoire, transects et théories: quelques réflexions et suggestions sur le parcours d'une méthode classique'. In P. Soulier (Ed.), *André Leroi-Gourhan 'l'homme tout simplement'* (pp. 69–84). Paris: Éditions de Boccard - Travaux de la MAE - Maison de l'Archéologie et de l'Ethnologie, René-Ginouvès.

Coupaye, L. (2015b). Unleashing the Chaîne Opératoire: Students' experimentation with an old methodology. *Material World blog.* http://www.materialworldblog.com/2015/07/unleashing-the-chaine-operatoire-students-experimentation-with-an-old-methodology/. Accessed 27 August 2020.

Coupaye, L. (2016). Yams as Vernacular Methodology? Approaching Vital Processes Through Technical Processes. In P. Pitrou, L. Coupaye, and F. Provost (Eds.), *Des êtres vivants et des artefacts.* Paris: musée du Quai Branly, Les actes. http://actes-branly.revues.org/673. Accessed 23 August 2020.

Coupaye, L. (2018). 'Yams Have No Ears!': *Tekhne*, Life and Images in Oceania. *Oceania, 88*(1), 13–30.

Coupaye, L. (2021a). 'Things Ain't the Same Anymore': Towards an Anthropology of Technical Objects (or 'When Simondon Meets MVC'). In T. Carroll, A. Walford, and S. Walton (Eds.), *Lineages and Advancements in the Anthropology of Material Culture* (pp. 46–60). London: UCL Press.

Coupaye, L. (2021b). Technology. In L. A. De Cunzo and C. Dann Roeber (Eds.), *Cambridge Handbook of Material Culture.* Cambridge: Cambridge University Press.

Cresswell, R. (2011[1976]). Techniques et Cultures. Les bases d'un programme de travail. *Techniques & Culture, 54–55*, 20–45.

Dietler, M., and Herbich, I. (1998). Habitus, Techniques, Style: An Integrated Approach to the Social Understanding of Material Culture and Boundaries. In M. T. Stark (Ed.), *The Archaeology of Social Boundaries* (pp. 232–263). Washington, DC: Smithsonian Press.

Digard, J.-P. (2004). Anthropologie des techniques et anthropologie cognitive. *Études rurales, 169–170*, 253–267.

Djindjian, F. (2013). Us et abus du concept de "chaîne opératoire" en archéologie. In S. Krausz, A. Colin, K. Gruel, I. Ralston, and T. Dechezlepetre (Eds.), *L'Age du Fer en Europe. Mélanges offerts à Olivier Buchsenchütz* (pp. 93–107). Bordeaux: Editions Ausonius.

Douny, L., and Naji, M. (2009). Editorial. *Journal of Material Culture, 14*(4), 411–432.

Drazin, A. (2021). The Object Biography. In T. Carroll, A. Walford, and S. Walton (Eds.), *Lineages and Advancements in the Anthropology of Material Culture.* London: UCL Press.

Eglash, R. (2006). Technology as Material Culture. In C. Tilley, K. Webb, S. Kuechler, M. Rowlands, and P. Spyer (Eds.), *Handbook of Material Culture* (pp. 327–340). London & New York: SAGE Publications.

Fanchette, S. (2016). Papeterie et recyclage dans les villages de métier. *Techniques & Culture, 65–66*, 198–201. http://journals.openedition.org/tc/7954. Accessed 26 August 2020.

Geertz, C. (1997 [1973]). *The Interpretation of Cultures.* London: Fontana Press.

Gell, A. (1998). *Art and Agency.* Oxford Clarendon Press.

Gibson, J. J. (1986). *The Ecological Approach to Visual Perception.* Hillsdale, NJ: Lawrence Erlbaum Associates.

Gowlett, J. J. (1990). Technology, Skill and the Psychological Sector in the Long term of Human Evolution. *Archaeological Review from Cambridge, 9*(1), 82–103.

Hughes, T. P. (1986). The Evolution of Large Technological System. In W. Bijker, T. P. Hughes, and T. Pinch (Eds.), *The Social Construction of Technological Systems* (pp. 51–82). Cambridge, MA & London: The MIT Press.

Hutchins, E. (1996). *Cognition in the Wild.* Cambridge, MA & London: The MIT Press.

Ingold, T. (1997). Eight Themes in the Anthropology of Technology. *Social Analysis, 41*(1), 106–138.

Ingold, T. (2007). Materials Against Materiality. *Archaeological Dialogues, 14*(1), 1–16.

Ingold, T. (2008). When ANT Meets SPIDER: Social Theory for Arthropods. In C. Knapett, and L. Malafouris (Eds.), *Material Agency. Towards a Non-Anthropocentric Approach* (pp. 209–215). New York: Springer.

Ingold, T. (2010). The Textility of Making. *Cambridge Journal of Economics, 34,* 91–102.

Ingold, T. (2013). *Making: Anthropology, Archaeology, Art and Architecture.* London & New York: Routledge.

Knappett, C. (2004). The Affordances of Things: A Post Gibsonian Perspective on the Relationality of Mind and Matter. In E. DeMarrais, C. Gosden, and A. C. Renfrew (Eds.), *Rethinking Materiality: The Engagement of Mind with the Material World* (pp. 43–51). Cambridge: McDonald Institute for Archaeological Research.

Knappett, C. (2011). Networks of Objects, Meshworks of Things. In T. Ingold (Ed.), *Redrawing Anthropology: Materials, Movements, Lines* (pp. 45–64). London: Ashgate.

Koechlin, B. (1975). *Les Vezo du Sud-Ouest de Madagascar. Contributions à l'étude de l'écosystème de semi-nomades marins.* Paris & La Haye: Mouton.

Kopytoff, I. (1986). The Cultural Biography of Things: Commoditization as Process. In A. Appadurai (Ed.), *The Social Life of Things: Commodities in Cultural Perspective* (pp. 65–91). Cambridge: Cambridge University Press.

Kubler, G. (1962). *The Shape of Time.* New Haven, CT: Yale University Press.

Larkin, B. (2013). The Politics and Poetics of Infrastructure. *Annual Review of Anthropology, 42,* 327–343.

Latour, B. (1991). Technology Is Society Made Durable. In J. Law (Ed.), *A Sociology of Monsters? Essays on Power, Technology and Domination* (pp. 103–131). London: Routledge.

Latour, B. (1993 [1991]). *We Have Never Been Modern* (trans: C. Porter). London: Harvester Wheatsheaf.

Latour, B. (2005). *Reassembling the Social: An Introduction to Actor-Network-Theory.* Oxford: Oxford University Press.

Latour, B. (2014). Technical Does Not Mean Material. Comment on Lemonnier, P. (2012). *Mundane Objects: Materiality and Non-verbal Communication.* Walnut Creek, CA: Left Coast Press. *Hau: Journal of Ethnographic Theory, 4*(1), 507–510.

Law, J. (2009). Actor Network Theory and Material Semiotics. In B. S. Turner (Ed.), *The New Blackwell Companion to Social Theory* (pp. 141–158). Malden, MA, & Oxford: Wiley-Blackwell.

Lechtman, H. (1977). Style in Technology—Some Early Thoughts. In H. Lechtman and R. Merrill (Eds.), *Material Culture: Styles, Organization, and Dynamics of Technology* (pp. 3–20). St Paul: Xest.

Lemonnier, P. (1986). The Study of Material Culture Today: Toward an Anthropology of Technical Systems. *Journal of Anthropological Archaeology, 5*(2), 147–186.

Lemonnier, P. (1992). *Elements for an Anthropology of Technology.* Ann Arbor: University of Michigan Press.

Lemonnier, P. (Ed.) (1993). *Technological Choices: Transformation in Material Culture Since the Neolithic.* London & New York: Routledge.

Lemonnier, P. (2012). *Mundane Objects: Materiality and Non-Verbal Communication.* Walnut Creek, CA: Left Coast Press.

Leroi-Gourhan, A. (1971). *L'Homme et la Matière (Evolution et Techniques I)*. Paris: Albin Michel.

Leroi-Gourhan, A. (1973). *Milieu et techniques (Evolution et Techniques II)*. Paris: Albin Michel.

Leroi-Gourhan, A. (1993 [1964]). *Gesture and Speech* (trans: A. Bostock Berger). Cambridge, MA & London: The MIT Press.

Mahias, M.-C. (1993). Pottery Techniques in India: Technical Variant and Social Choice. In P. Lemonnier (Ed.), *Technological Choices: Transformation in Material Culture Since the Neolithic* (pp. 157–180). London & New York: Routledge.

Malafouris, L. (2013). *How Things Shape the Mind: A Theory of Material Engagement*. Cambridge, MA & London: The MIT Press.

Marchand, T. H. J. (2010). Making Knowledge: Exploration of the Indissoluble Relation Between Minds, Bodies, and Environment. *Journal of the Royal Anthropological Institute (N.S.), 16*, S1–S21.

Martinelli, B. (1991). Une chaîne opératoire halieutique au Togo. Réflexion sur la méthode. In H. Balfet (Ed.), *Observer l'action technique. Des chaînes opératoires, pour quoi faire?* (pp. 65–86). Paris: Editions du CNRS.

Marx, L. (2010 [1997]). 'Technology': The Emergence of a Hazardous Concept. *Technology and Culture, 51*(3), 561–677.

Matthewman, S. (2011). *Technology and Social Theory*. New York: Palgrave Macmillan.

Mauss, M. (1973 [1935]). Techniques of the Body. *Economy and Society, 2*(1), 70–88.

Mauss, M. (2007 [1947]). *Manual of Ethnography* (trans: D. Lussier). New York & Oxford: Berghahn Books.

Mauss, M. (2003 [1909]). On Prayer (trans. S. Leslie). New York & Oxford: Durkheim Press & Berghahn Books.

Miller, D. (2005). *Materiality*. Durham & London: Duke University Press.

Mohan, U., and Douny, L. (Eds.) (2020). *The Material Subject: Rethinking Bodies and Objects in Motion*. London: Bloomsbury.

Oldenziel, R. (1999). *Making Technology Masculine: Men, Women, and Modern Machines in America, 1870–1945*. Amsterdam: Amsterdam University Press.

Pélegrin, J. (1990). Prehistoric Lithic Technology: Some aspect of Research. *Archaeological Review from Cambridge, 9*(1), 116–125.

Pfaffenberger, B. (1992). Social Anthropology of Technology. *Annual Review of Anthropology, 21*, 491–516.

Pitt-Rivers, A. H. L. F. (1906). *The Evolution of Culture and Other Essays*. Clarendon Press Oxford UK.

'Practical Sheets 1-5'. (2019). *Techniques & Culture*, 71 (Special issue 'Technographies'): https://journals.openedition.org/tc/. Accessed 27 August 2020.

Revolon, S. (2018). Iridescence as Affordance: On Artefacts and Light Interference in the Renewal of Life Among the Owa (Eastern Solomon Islands). *Oceania, 88*(1), 31–40.

Schatzberg, E. (2018). *Technology: Critical History of a Concept*. Chicago & London: The University of Chicago Press.

Schiffer, M. B. (1975). Behavioral Chain Analysis: Activities, Organization, and the Use of Space, Chapters in the Prehistory of Eastern Arizona, IV. *Fieldiana: Anthropology, 65*, 103–119.

Schlanger, N. (2005). The Chaîne Opératoire. In C. Renfrew and P. Bahn (Eds.), *Archaeology. The Key Concepts* (pp. 25–31). London & New York: Routledge.

Sennet, R. (2008). *The Craftsman*. New Haven & London: Yale University Press.

Sigaut, F. (1985). More (and Enough) on Technology! *History and Technology,* *2*, 115–132.

Sigaut, F. (2002 [1994]). Technology. In T. Ingold (Ed.), *Companion Encyclopedia of Anthropology* (pp. 420–459). London: Routledge.

Sigaut, F. (2003). La formule de Mauss. *Techniques & Culture, 40*, 153–168.

Sillar, B., and Tite. M. S. (2000). The Challenge of 'Technological Choice' for Materials Science Approaches in Archaeology. *Archaeometry, 42*(1), 2–20.

Simondon, G. (2017 [1958]). *On the Mode of Existence of Technical Objects* (trans: C. Malaspina and J. Rogove). Minneapolis: Univocal Publishing.

Sinclair, A., and Schlanger, N. (1990). Technology in the Humanities. *Archaeological Review from Cambridge, 9*(1), 3–157.

Soressi, M., and Geneste, J.-M. (2011). The History and Efficacy of the Chaîne Opératoire Approach to Lithic Analysis: Studying Techniques to Reveal Past Societies in an Evolutionary Perspective. *PaleoAnthropology, 63*, 334–350.

Stiegler, B. (2009). Teleologics of the snail: The Errant Self Wired to a WiMax Network. *Theory, Culture & Society, 26*(2–3), 23–45.

Sutton, J. (2008). Material Agency, Skills and History: Distributed Cognition and the Archaeology of Memory. In C. Knapett and L. Malafouris (Eds.), *Material Agency: Towards a Non-Anthropocentric Approach* (pp. 37–55). New York: Springer.

Tilley, C., Webb, K., Kuechler, S., Rowlands, M., and Spyer, P. (2006). *Handbook of Material Culture*. London & New York: SAGE Publications.

Tsing, A. (2010). Worlding the Matsutake Diaspora: Or, Can Actor–Network Theory Experiment With Holism? In T. Otto and N. Bubandt (Eds.), *Experiments in Holism: Theory and Practice in Contemporary Anthropology* (pp. 47–66). Oxford: Wiley-Blackwell.

van der Leeuw, S. E. (1993). Giving the Potter a Choice: Conceptual Aspects of Pottery Techniques. In P. Lemonnier (Ed.), *Technological Choices: Transformation in material culture since the Neolithic* (pp. 238–288). London & New York: Routledge.

Warnier, J.-P. (2001). A Praxeological Approach to Subjectivation in a Material World. *Journal of Material Culture, 6*(1), 5–24.

Warnier, J.-P. (2007). *The Pot-King: The Body and Technologies of Power*. Leiden & Boston, MA: Brill.

Warnier, J.-P. (2009). Technology as Efficacious Action on Objects… and Subjects. *Journal of Material Culture, 14*(4), 459–470.

Winner, L. (1985 [1977]). *Autonomous Technology: Technics-Out-of-Control as a Theme in Political Thought*. Cambridge: The MIT Press.

CHAPTER 3

Technology as Skill in Handwork and Craft: Basketwork and Handweaving

Skill

Stephanie Bunn

From so simple a beginning, endless forms so beautiful and most wonderful have been, and are being, evolved
—Charles Darwin, On the Origin of Species.

What can basketry teach us about technology?[1] Baskets—creaky, rustling, interlaced, handheld containers—are a form of textile constructed by makers using a range of basketry techniques: weaving, twining, plaiting, coiling, and looping with plant materials. But is basketry a technology, or just a handicraft? And is there a difference? The answers lie, I suggest, in how we think about technology and crafts, and also about activities such as making, work, skilfulness, and production. In this chapter, I draw upon basket weaving to explore technology as a process which emerges through, and is entirely grounded in, skilled human engagement with the environment to make artefacts which in themselves can also become forms of technology through their use. I contrast this with cloth weaving to discuss how apparently more or less 'mechanised'

S. Bunn (✉)
University of St Andrews, St Andrews, UK
e-mail: sjb20@st-andrews.ac.uk

© The Author(s), under exclusive license to Springer Nature Singapore Pte Ltd. 2022
M. H. Bruun et al. (eds.), *The Palgrave Handbook of the Anthropology of Technology*, https://doi.org/10.1007/978-981-16-7084-8_3

61

craft practices, from basketry to weaving on a loom, can illustrate how craft skills combine bodily techniques and tools to act as forms of technology.

In respect to technology as skilful production, I am closely aligned with Tim Ingold's approach (2000). Ingold argues that technology does not simply embrace a post-eighteenth century, machine-age notion of making practices, along with an assumed, ever-increasing separation of human involvement from the 'technological domain'. Rather, he proposes, technology also includes tool use in all manner of societies, along with the skilled human practice involved in using these tools, and the whole circuit of the process, from maker to artefact (Ingold 2000, pp. 294–311). Thus, an exploration of developing craft skills and tool use is an exploration of technology, with human skill having a rightful creative and social role within such technological practices. Understanding how human bodily, cognitive, and social practices are embedded in technological development can, thus, enable us to 're-humanise' technology.

This human element in 'skill as technology' is revealed in the dynamic between practitioners, tools, and materials in craft, where tools and other devices can develop and complement handskills through enhancing strength, accuracy, and changes of attention. Skilled practice can unite mind and body through movement, stimulating human intelligence by evoking behaviours such as problem-solving, patience, and intuitive responses to serendipity. At the same time, skilled embodied work such as basketry elicits pleasure, judgement, and creativity through engagement with materials, focused attention, and the rhythm of work. Thus, handskills are inextricably bound up with human cognitive and creative development.

The above terms—'textile', 'technique', 'technology', from the ancient Greek *tekhné* (art, skill, craftmanship) or Latin *texere* (to weave)—reveal a longstanding relationship between skill and technology, linking the integrity of woven fabric in 'textile' with craft and skill. However, this Old (European) World terminology gives us just one perspective. Weaving is 'the prototype act of creation' in the Andes, tied to production more broadly in communities (Harris 2007, p. 143). The Andean science of weaving, Denise Arnold proposes, emphasises the integration of communities through collective work, which is honoured among Andean peoples as a way of continually committing energy between humans and deities and making the earth fruitful (Arnold 2015, pp. 22–23; Harris 2007, pp. 141–148). In contrast, in Ancient Greece, handcraft became seen as a form of work akin to slavery because makers were subject to necessity rather than masters of it (Harris 2007, pp. 138–143).

Herein, Ingold argues, lies the source of the perceived separation between humans and technology. He proposes that, on the one hand, human skills have become increasingly externalised in machines as technology has developed and humans have ceased to guide technical movement at the 'point of action' (2000, p. 301); yet, on the other, this development goes hand-in-hand with the economics of industrial capitalism (Ingold 2000, p. 309), resulting in both machine and employer commanding the labour power of the worker at the expense of their skill. Thus, our contemporary Eurocentric notions of technology and skill are quite bound up with our approach to work, and will likely consider the purpose of technology to be to separate humans from work, especially handwork, and be 'labour-saving', whatever the wishes of the worker. This is accompanied by an almost inevitable and progressive deskilling of humans, as they accept, as Ingold describes, a process 'in which human beings, to an ever increasing extent, have become authors of their own dehumanisation' (2000, p. 311).

Thus, I argue that the view that human development entails an increasing separation from technology, whereby humans become subservient to machines (whether a factory production line or an Amazon warehouse), is tied more to economic and power relations than to necessity. The dynamic of the relationship between humans and technology is, therefore, an ethical and moral one. What is also of concern is that in assuming that handwork is not relevant in this post-modern age, humans cease to employ embodied cognitive skills, or to build upon them, potentially undermining critical pathways for potential development of our human intelligence.

Baskets and Basketry

Baskets and related artefacts are generally made from plant materials, ranging from soft materials such as rush or pandanus to hard materials such as willow, spruce roots, or rattan. These materials may be processed into flat strips, such as birch bark or split bamboo, or used as filaments like willow or sedge roots. Contemporary makers may also use recycled materials, such as cut-up tetrapaks, telephone wire, or plastic packing tape.

Basketry techniques are hand techniques, since basket making still cannot be replicated by machine, which places basketry in a unique position for the exploration of handskills as technology. These handskills employ dextrous strokes, twists, and folds, which arguably developed through simple playful acts of trial and error—twiddling, twisting grass, twining rush, leaves, or other fibres, plaiting hair—employing bodily rhythms through acts of curiosity and care (Bunn 1999, 2009; Kimmerer 2013). From these rhythmic engagements with materials have emerged classic basketry techniques including weaving, coiling, plaiting, looping, twining, and knotting.[2] These techniques incorporate a range of forces, including tension, friction, compression, and stretch, into materials to create structural integrity. None of these techniques, however, involves physically joining. Instead it is the force generated at the crossing point of the interlaced materials which creates the structural integrity which holds the basket together.

Basketry is most often used to make containers. Indeed the English term 'basketry' incorporates both the form (basket) and technique of the craft. The use of containers for moving and transporting goods is possibly a uniquely human development, a 'technological first' in the animal kingdom. But mats, rope, screens, thatch, walls, huts, even houses are also constructed using basketry techniques, which provide essential knowhow for other technological

Fig. 3.1 Close up of different basketry techniques and structures. Top left: simple weaving; Top centre: twining; Top right: coiling; Bottom: plaiting

developments: cordage for lashing handaxes and spears, traps for hunting, nets for fishing, and shelter.[3] Thus, basketry is a technique for making baskets and so much more, since the artefacts produced, from containers to cordage, may be technological forms in themselves (Fig. 3.1).

TECHNOLOGY AS SKILL AND TOOL USE: A PHENOMENOLOGICAL APPROACH

To explore basketry skill and tool use as technology, we must draw on qualitative research of skilled practitioners in action. This is a phenomenological approach, in that by exploring work through the 'grain' of human skill in action we focus on experience and consider technology as a process, revealing subtleties and nuances of human-material-tool-machine-artefact interface. It is also a holistic approach, traversing the process from plant to basket, from husbanding and gathering materials, through processing them, to working with them to create the outcome—the basket—and continuing through the basket's life story into use, where it may become an element of other technologies. Pfaffenberger's approach marries that of Ingold, positing that technology is social, a part of human life (even though we often treat it as a separate and autonomous force), yet it also entails an interaction between people and the environment, drawing on both collective skills and the earth's resources, which become known as 'materials' (Ingold 2000; Pfaffenberger 1988).

By considering the human-skill-material-technology interface, we can see that people, their bodies, and materials play reciprocating roles in the mechanics of production. We have, effectively, as Ingold discusses, a 'kinematic chain' of maker, skill, and artefact, as each element of a basket's construction plays multiple roles interchangeably (see Reuleaux 1876; Ingold 2000, pp. 304–306). The maker acts as creator, as provider of strength, but also as lever and tool through bodily techniques. The material acts as both force and fabric, creating strength through the textile structure and building the substance of the artefact at the same time. The artefact, the basket, provides both the form or structure and the technology or frame around which the weaving takes place, and is thus entwined into this reciprocal technological process.

From a more social perspective, Pfaffenberger's critique of two discourses of technology—'technological somnambulism' (where we see technology as morally and ethically neutral) and 'technological determinism' (where technology is considered to dictate the pattern of human social and cultural life) (Pfaffenberger 1988, pp. 238–239)—claims that these discourses are both predicated on alienating, de-socialised notions of technology and argues for its re-socialising. Through both these aspects of technology—practical engagement with materials and the environment, and social interaction with it—we come to know the world skilfully, enhancing our understanding of its workings further and building upon our capacity for human growth and development.

To explore these themes, I draw on the anthropology of learning, skill, and cognition, and of craft and textiles, along with philosophical approaches to human experience. But I also consider history, ethnographies, and ethnomathematics to address how knowledge, skill, and science can be embedded in specific cultural forms and practices which may not be considered 'technological'. Some basket makers also learn their skills autodidactically, from 'how-to' books, diagrams, or YouTube videos, and we could even consider whether such approaches to learning could be phenomenological.

Gathering Basketry Knowledge

Basketry was probably one of the earliest forms of textile technology (Emery 1966; Seiler-Baldinger 1979; Wendrich 1999), preceding the use of the weaving loom. Ironically, despite its ephemeral, biodegradable nature, so unlike our contemporary image of technology as powerful and enduring, basketry and cordage may well have preceded more durable human innovations such as flint axe and arrow-head making; although baskets' perishable composition makes this difficult to prove (Hurcombe 2014; Wendrich 1999). This degradable, ephemeral aspect of basketry may contribute to the low value often attributed to baskets by historians.[4] Yet Wendrich's phenomenological approach, insisting on practice-based methods in the study of baskets, reveals the complexities of learning and skill entailed in their making. The ubiquity of baskets also reflects how they have been significant, yet understated fabrics of society for millennia, essential elements for all manner of human activity and industry: from collecting food to cooking, from farming to fishing, from measuring to carrying, from factory production to migration (Hurcombe 2014; Wendrich 1999). Thus, they have multiple associations with human origins, and human narratives of origin.[5]

Until recently, in line with their rather undervalued status, much early writing about basketry was by basket makers themselves. Thus George Wharton-James, founder of the American Basket Fraternity, wrote both ethnographic studies of indigenous American basketry (1903) and 'how-to' basketry books. Similarly, much early UK basketry literature was written by two esteemed members of the Ancient and Worshipful Company of Basketmakers: Thomas Okey, who wrote the first 'how-to' book of British basketry (1915), and H.H. Bobart who wrote *Basketry through the Ages* (1936).

While today, 'how-to' books may seem more relevant for hobbyists than for scholarly study, they are also distillations of many years of practice and experience, and are full of drawings and diagrams: visualisations of 'how to' make a stake-and-strand basket or a shopper, work with rush or willow, do a 'three rod wale' border, and so on. Aimed at the handicraft practitioner, such books are helpful to the learner, but also provide a record, a guide, and a means to reflect upon how basket makers depict how they learn, and the role of the visual in communicating basketry practice.

In some ways, basketry structure itself provides the full evidence of 'how to' make a basket, since its interwoven form contains all the elements of its construction. Many diagrams in 'how-to' books reflect this, and reproduce these elements in their instruction. But anyone who has tried to make a basket from a diagram will tell you it is not always that easy, although a skilfully drawn diagram can help. The movements and forces in the maker's hands are not simple to convey, however; crossing or pulling an element in the 'wrong' way can change everything. Nevertheless, the diagram as a visualisation of the process can be both a part of the technology of basketry and a guide. It acts as a 'summary' of the making process but can also be traced or visually followed to explore how the elements are interlaced. Thus, as a means of communicating skill, even 'how-to books' can contribute to the rich picture of basketry technology (Fig. 3.2).

Among the first scholars to take basketry seriously as technology was Otis Mason (1895), an early curator of the Smithsonian Institution, who put basketry at the heart of his review of cultural and technological evolution. It was he who first noted that baskets cannot be made by machine. Anthropologist Franz Boas conducted research on the string figures (1888) and basketry of the US Northwest Coast (1893, 1928), and members of the Torres Straits expedition followed this interest, collecting material on basketry and related subjects including string figures, banana leaf skirts, wattle house structures, and plaitwork (Rivers and Haddon 1902; Hingston Quiggin 1912; Wilkin and Haddon 1912). Later, Deacon and Wedgewood (1934) showed how sand drawings (a

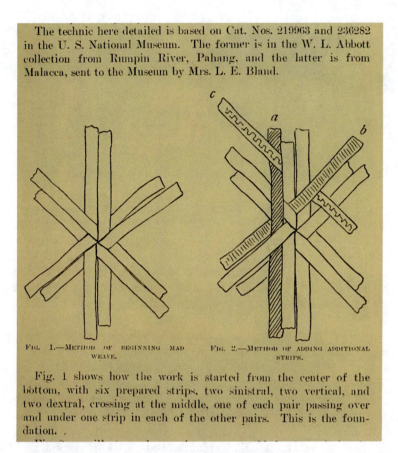

The technic here detailed is based on Cat. Nos. 219963 and 236282 in the U. S. National Museum. The former is in the W. L. Abbott collection from Rumpin River, Pahang, and the latter is from Malacca, sent to the Museum by Mrs. L. E. Bland.

FIG. 1.—METHOD OF BEGINNING MAD WEAVE.

FIG. 2.—METHOD OF ADDING ADDITIONAL STRIPS.

Fig. 1 shows how the work is started from the center of the bottom, with six prepared strips, two sinistral, two vertical, and two dextral, crossing at the middle, one of each pair passing over and under one strip in each of the other pairs. This is the foundation.

Fig. 3.2 *Anyam gila* (mad weave) instructions by Otis Mason

drawn interlacing technique from Vanuatu/Malekula) reflected significant geometric comprehension, incorporating both artefact and visualised diagram into one form. All these 'knowledge technologies' exemplify what Küchler (2001) describes as an 'externalisation of spatial cognition', extending geometry beyond the Euclidean. She notes that the early interest in such forms was such that, in the first half of the twentieth century, more academic papers were published on string figures, for example, than on any other ethnographic museum artefact (Küchler 2001, p. 60).

The focus on the spatial aspect of such technologies declined as interest in linguistic anthropological models grew in the 1950s (Küchler 2001). Yet there were occasional monographs, such as Griaule's *Conversations with Ogotommêli* on Dogon origins (1965), Pinxten's study of Navajo geometry (1987), and Guss's *To Weave and Sing* on Amazonian Yekuana basketry (1989), which discussed how, in these societies, baskets were perceived as microcosms, aspects of an unfolding universe from body, to basket, to house, to cosmos. These studies

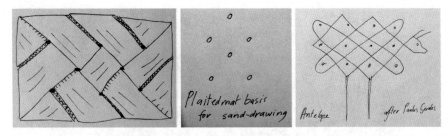

Fig. 3.3 Drawings to depict the relationship between a plaited basketry weave (left) and the guide lines for sand drawings (centre and right). After Paulus Gerdes

may focus more on cultural and symbolic concerns than technology per se, but as ethnomathematicians such as Gerdes (1999, 2010), Verran (2001), and the Ascher and Ascher (1981) have shown, the divide between culture and science has not always been clearly articulated in small-scale societies. Gerdes, in particular, demonstrated that African plaited basketry contains multiple tacit mathematical insights. These may include, he suggested, understanding of symmetry, tessellation, and two and three-dimensional geometric forms, from tetrahedrons to hexagons; he also showed how plaited basketry mats could provide algorithms, or templates—effectively kinds of grid—for constructing related forms such as sand drawings (Gerdes 1999, p. 164) (Fig. 3.3).

It is perhaps Küchler who has most comprehensively argued that interlaced textiles creatively synthesise practical, social, and geometric aspects of cultural life through her research into Pacific binding and knotting. In her discussion of the negative space in knotted *malanggan* carvings of New Ireland, twine covered Tahitian idols (*to'o*), and the braided sacred cords (*aha*) of Hawaiian kings, she proposes that interlacings such as knots and twining are a kind of knowledge of the 'linking of things, material and mental' (Küchler 2001, pp. 71–73). These textile processes, she says, connect social bonds and ties within a decentred, topological system of spatial cognition that acts as a reference point for actions linking the social and the sacred, independent of particular points of view. The Hawaiian king's title, *haku*, meaning 'ruler', 'weaver', 'order-maker', and 'composer of chants' (Küchler 2001), illustrates how weaving, knotting, and binding bridge these different realms of experience in this region, interweaving and reproducing the relationship between kin relations, spatial relations, and the sacred through interweaving cords and chants.

BASKETRY 'KNOWING HOW'

In recent years, anthropologists have returned to studying craft, and have been particularly concerned with 'knowing how', in terms of learning and skill. There are two related, but distinct approaches. Leroi-Gourhan's, and subsequently Pierre Lemonnier's, notion of *chaîne opératoire* offers one starting point for studying craft knowhow (Leroi-Gourhan 1964; Lemonnier 1992, see also Coupaye, this volume). This approach to craft is aimed at breaking down skill into a series of key methodological stages that can be reproduced. While useful when exploring questions of intangible heritage, it has its limitations, and is based on a rather mechanistic model. Basketry *does* involve stages: first gathering materials, then drying them, then sorting, soaking, and mellowing them, and then making the basket. This latter stage might consist of making the base, then the sides, then border and handle. Yet, while all these processes do constitute a 'chain of basketry production', in perceiving the process purely as a 'chain' we are left us with a somewhat stilted timeline rather than a rich texture of skill, materials, movements and rhythms, communications between people, and problems to be solved. In a sense, the *chaîne opératoire* provides a different kind of 'diagram'—a temporal, externalised sequence of production that can omit the texture and reciprocal and dynamic quality of the process.

An alternative approach is provided by anthropologists of learning and apprenticeship theory, and phenomenological thinkers such as John Dewey. The apprenticeship approach to learning skill involves learning through practice, 'on the job', from other, more skilled practitioners, and imitating them. It often takes place without having the making process distilled as a helpful summary by a teacher or knowing the 'rules' in advance. Dewey (1997 [1938]), François Sigaut (1993), and Gislii Palsson (1994) all challenge the notion of skill as a body of condensed knowledge which can easily be broken down into stages or parcels and passed from one head to another. 'Experience does not go on simply inside a person', writes Dewey (1997 [1938], p. 39). It can never, Sigaut observes, be purely condensed and communicated through a book, it must be learned through doing. Furthermore, as Lave and Wenger (1991) propose, learning is 'situated'—it takes place within a context and is communicated between people who constitute a 'community of practice'.

Ingold further argues that this learning process is improvisatory, not a defined series of events, but instead 'a particular gathering together or interweaving of materials in movement' (2010, p. 96). 'Every step is a development of the one before and a preparation for the one following. ... The force, amplitude, speed and torque varies ... as does the posture of the body ... not merely reproducing the same gesture [or] the repetitive execution of a single step in the operational sequence (*chaîne opératoire*). [Rather, a maker] follows the materials, responds to its singularities ... brings the many concurrent variables with which he must engage more or less into phase with one another' (2010, p. 98). This is how the basketweaver works.

Learning a skill is, then, above all, a sensory and kinaesthetic process, and attention is key. Parallels can be drawn between learning basketwork and how to dance or to play a musical instrument.[6] Caroline Potter (2008) describes the development of attention in a dancer as the dancer 'direct[s] attention inwards, towards the workings of one's own body', fine-tuning its movements, sense of gravity, and balance, and also paying attention 'outwards, towards an audience with whom one attempts to relate', balancing 'the internal connection with the external (desire to perform)' (p. 453). Here, the senses extend into movement, and working with one's 'sense of movement', or kinaesthesia, is essential (Potter 2008, p. 453).

In craft, attention also extends between inside and out, through the maker's hands, fingers, and arms into the materials. This provides a classic illustration of Bateson's notion of 'mind in environment' (1972), where the practitioner's embodied circuit of mind extends beyond the body, into tools and materials. Here we also see the conjoining of sensing with motor skills, since the hands both feel (sense) the material and create the emerging form (Gibson 1966; Bunn 1999).

Materials constitute a particular gap in technology literature, 'the action, the physical engagement of maker with materials, is usually overlooked' (Bunn 1999, p. 15). Yet one aspect of technological expertise is to be able to feel the potential within the material through one's hands and through tools. With basketry, this entails subtle nuances of the pressure needed to bend rather than kink, to fold rather than split, and to interweave materials to develop form. Beyond this intimate engagement, makers must also learn plant life-cycles and management, nurturing shoots, weeding, and harvesting.

In this era of the anthropological 'plant turn' we have learned that as people engage with plant materials, plant materials also engage people, drawing practitioners into intimate knowledge about subtleties of variation and properties (Peri and Paterson 1976; Kimmerer 2013). Thus, the skilled basket maker is provoked by their engagement to keep learning, to increase their knowledge, to learn about plant varieties. They grow to love the colour of certain bark, the subtle variations of flexibility between different willow stems or sedge roots; scans the landscape for sites of rush growth (which they keep secret); wants to plant more, to harvest correctly, and familiarise themselves with plant knowledge and lore (Bunn 2014, 2021; see also Kneebone on expertise, 2020).

Much of this learning is tactile and, as skill develops, it becomes tacit (Polanyi 1967). The techniques have become, as Heidegger describes, 'ready to hand' (1927). In a professional basket makers' workshop, apprentices endlessly practice and repeat certain strokes until they have mastered them. They begin with the most simple, and gradually progress to more challenging techniques, moving towards becoming skilful. The embeddedness of such skills is such that, even in old age, when other memories fail, when presented with the tools of their trade, retired fishermen, for example, can still mend a net, and teach others to do so (Brown 2012; see also Kneebone 2020). Makers have a repertoire of these techniques, and their knowledge, much of it non-verbal, is backed up by sayings and phrases which mimic the actions: 'in-front-of-two, behind-one, and out-to-the-front-again'; 'no-overtaking'; 'tip-to-tip and butt-to-butt', and so on. Making and rhythmic speaking act in conjunction as the rhythm of the technique becomes established. The two processes, doing and speaking, work in dialogue with each other, bringing the action in and out of conscious articulation as the rhythm of the technique becomes established. Some techniques, such as knotting and string figures, are even accompanied by stories during their tying.

Fig. 3.4 Shetland man, probably from Fair Isle, weaving a *flakkie*, extending his skill into the materials. NE 03226. © Shetland Museum and Archive

In basketry, therefore, hands and fingers work dextrously, extending sensation outwards into the materials, moving and sensing different fibres and their strengths, yet also transforming them. Within this embrace, the basket maker seems quite still, sitting in one place, often the basket maker's plank. The movement is focused at one point of action, where the hand touches materials. Here, all the force of the maker's skill, strength, and technique, all the movement in engaging with the materials, are held in check by the basketry strokes, which whether through tension or friction, are interwoven to make a strong and sturdy basket (Fig. 3.4).

Basketry, Skill, and Machines

However skilful the maker, craft is not simply a case of mechanically reproducing an artefact from an image one has in mind. Every act of skilful making is, as David Pye (1968) says, the 'workmanship of risk', where the 'quality of the result is continuously at risk during the process of making' (p. 20). The basket maker continually exercises 'judgement, dexterity and care', especially care, even if habitual and unconscious, but they can never fully control the outcome

(Pye 1968, p. 7). To achieve that integration of mind and body essential for 'flow', makers have to lose the will to control (Bunn 1999). It is this very step into the unknown which allows the synthesis of attention and action which enables quality work to emerge.

The opposite of the 'workmanship of risk' is, according to Pye, the 'workmanship of certainty'. This move towards 'production by certainty' is often achieved through standardisation and mechanisation, linked to a perceived need for speed and accuracy, often reflecting economic aims of fast, effective production (1968, p. 22). Yet, as discussed above, it has not yet been possible to create an algorithm for basketry skills so they can be replicated by machine. While a 3-D printer may make a basket-like artefact, it is not held together by the same forces as a handmade basket. This is partly explained by the basket's three-dimensional structure, which acts as both the technology—the loom or frame on which the basket is made—and at the same time, as weaving progresses, it is built up to become the form of the basket itself. This is compounded by the variation of natural materials in basket making which, not being standard, require continued adjustment and varying pressure in the making. Such processes are, as Pfaffenberger describes, 'resistant to codification' (1988, p. 241).

There are, however, all manner of labour-saving devices, aspects of the technology which basket makers have developed themselves over millennia, such as clamps, jigs, and ties, along with a variety of customised tools: cutters, knives, bodkins, dollies, and rapping irons. These assist in the basket's creation, either by extending the skill of the maker, or by acting as an 'extra pair of hands', freeing the maker's attention for other tasks, rather than externalising the creative process. In this case, human skill in conjunction with tools forms a total basketry technology.

This explains why basketry is such a valuable illustration of technology as craft-in-action. The maker, as Albers (1943) describes for craft in general, 'is the coordinator of all the forces affecting his [or her] product' (p. 4). Basketry is an example of a 'whole' technology, one which resists specialisation. The basket must be made in one process, rather than from components which can be assembled, and it is this holistic, integrated process which, while using tools and other devices with skill, allows baskets to 'embody the many forces that took part in their making' (Albers 1943, p. 5). This is also another reason why they are so emblematic of technology at its most human.

It must be emphasised that machines can also be employed like tools, in a skilful and embodied way. Palsson (1994), talking of Icelandic fishing technology, shows how, even when using sophisticated sonar equipment in a fishing fleet, some skippers can still use the technology to 'fish by skill', understanding how the actions of birds and the surface of the water indicate the presence of a potential catch and using the technology as simply a part of their toolkit. He describes how the sonar and other electronic equipment becomes a part of the skipper's person as he learns to 'think like a fish', finding fish by 'some kind of whisper'. Those who rely purely on the machines, however, are described as those who 'fish by force'.

On this theme, Heather Paxson (2016), talking of artisanal cheesemaking, describes the contradictory restraints of working with organic material full of bacterial and fungal matter and the demand for a safe product with consistent taste. Makers may take up this craft because they enjoy its natural variation and material integrity, but they are also interested in milk chemistry and science, and try to develop a balance. The process is time consuming and there are devices such as mechanical stirrers to speed it up. Yet makers also enjoy the more direct interaction of hands-on stirring which enables a more personal kind of cheese management; it is part of the 'beauty' of what they are doing (Paxson 2011, 2014, 2016). Basketmakers, too, are subject to the economic necessity of speed and will often say they will not make a specific basketry form until they can make it quickly enough for it to pay, but they still have to make it by hand. In such cases, as Venkatesan describes for makers in India, work becomes labour, and makers often do not consider the process one of pleasure.

Contrasting Hand and Loom Weaving

Although basketry is not mechanisable, by comparing basket-weaving techniques with cloth weaving, we can explore the divergent pathways that link weaving today either with hand or machine technology. As a textile technology, basket-weaving differs from cloth weaving because it does not use a loom. In both kinds of weaving, there are, however, two sets of fibres set at right angles—warp and weft. These are interlaced, usually by weaving the weft, or 'strands' in basketry, so that they go in and out of the warp or 'stakes', which are held still and in tension. This tension is a key feature of all kinds of weaving, and is why both woven baskets and woven cloth are so strong.

One key difference is that basket-weaving materials are usually short, whereas loom weaving works with long pre-spun threads for both warp and weft. This enables the warp to be held in tension by the loom as a series of parallel threads, while the weft is woven forwards and back between them. In contrast, the thicker, stronger plant fibre stakes of a woven basket are usually tied loosely together to keep them in place. This balance between the strength of these and the finer strands or weft must constantly be factored into basket weaving, and because basketry strands are short, new ones must frequently be introduced. The maker is constantly making decisions about which to add, adjusting spaces with their fingers to accommodate different lengths and uneven strength in the materials to keep the tension even. As Ingold says, such materials have a vitality, 'properties which are not necessarily predisposed to fall into the shape required of them' (2010, pp. 93–94) (Fig. 3.5).

A critical development in loom weaving came with the invention of the 'shed stick' and heddle. Inserting the shed stick between alternate warp threads creates a 'shed' or gap through which the weft can be woven, enabling it to go across between the warp all in one movement. To create a counter-shed for

Fig. 3.5 John White tying stakes, illustrating the variability of materials. Photograph by Ian Whitaker, 1959 (BV111_7d_3828). ©School of Scottish Studies Archives, University of Edinburgh

alternate rows is achieved by a second rod, the heddle. Development of these two devices significantly enhanced the efficiency and speed of loom weaving, and provided the potential for further development. Basketry's three-dimensional forms and use of short materials means that these devices could not generally be used.

The ultimate development of the heddle into multiple shafts enabled ever-more complex patterns such as twills to be woven, and additional features, such as the treadle and foot loom, enabled weaving to become systematically mechanised and powered, paving the way for sophisticated developments such as the Jacquard loom,[7] which allows for very fine changes of shed and patterns. The loom's potential for mechanisation is exactly why Annie Albers, the famous Bauhaus weaver, considered that cloth weaving has been developed to a more sophisticated and industrialised form than any other textile technology and, indeed, why it was at the forefront of the Industrial Revolution (Albers 1965, pp. 30–36).

While the heddle paved the way for innovation, the mechanical shed can also be restrictive. 'Each step towards the mechanical perfection of the loom, in common with all machines, in its degree, lessens the freedom of the weaver, and his control of the design in working' (Hooper 1920 in Albers 1943, p. 7). This is because the weaver is then limited in their engagement with the threads of warp and weft and the outcome becomes more pre-set from the start, leaving less potential for improvisation. The highly complex developments in Andean weaving, done on a back-strap loom, and in Salish weaving of the Pacific Northwest Coast, done on a simple frame or warp-weighted loom, often with no heddle, illustrate the innovative moves that can be performed if weavers are able, for example, to manipulate warp threads (Arnold 2018; Tepper et al. 2017). Kneebone highlights how, in many crafts, mechanisation can enhance efficiency and what can be achieved, while at the same time, it may restrict or blunt it (Kneebone 2020, p. 105).

Thus, while basketry's generally unmechanisable character may appear to have limited its technological development, basket makers can be extremely attentive to the process and engagement with materials in ways that loom weavers may no longer be. Such resourcefulness within material limitations, along with the opportunity for improvisation, can be a prerequisite for producing innovation, in design historian Wilhelm Flusser's view, 'representing design on the edge of feasibility, where nothing could be done but somehow the possibility of something emerging through human understanding remained' (Pawley 1999). Makers such as Alison Martin and Patrick Dougherty, in pushing the material and technique to its limits, show in very different ways the architectural potential of their work, and its material resonance with forms of flight, for example (Martin 2015) (Fig. 3.6).

Skill and Knowledge

It is tempting to set up oppositions between skill and the kinds of knowledge we think can be extracted or condensed from a craft process and transferred into a diagram for a novice learner, for example, or into the workings of a machine. While Ingold shows that the difference between skill, knowhow, and knowledge is never absolute (Ingold 2000, pp. 299–300), at the same time, as Albers says, the progressive restrictions upon improvisation and the human creative endeavour that machines may delimit suggests that there are elements in skilful practices which are omitted with mechanisation.

The skill and knowledge incorporated into basketry and hand-loom weaving have certainly led them along very different paths, the basket almost to obsolescence with the advent of the plastic bag, and the loom to form a centrepiece of industrialisation. Yet both forms are cited as exemplifying specific kinds of mathematical and technological intelligence which suggests that both are integrated within human technical understanding. The spatial moves in basket weaving and plaiting have brought them to the attention of geometers, ethnomathematicians, and computer modellers. In knotting, the projection of the three-dimensional form of knots into two dimensions on computer screens has helped expand the whole topological branch of mathematics. For cloth

Fig. 3.6   Alison Martin. The mathematical inevitability of natural form

weaving, the link between Jacquard weaving and early calculating machines, along with parallels between drafting weave notations and computer coding, have been taken up by programmers and coders. The overlapping processes of these techniques would appear to be fundamentally bound up with embodied insights about both numbers and space.

Thus, Gerdes (1999) shows how simple hexagonal plaiting can assist in the comprehension of creating changes of surface, from planes to curved and undulating forms. In a similar vein, Phil Ayres explores how hexagonal plaiting can be modelled on a computer to help predict or visualise the creation of large-scale bamboo structures (Ayres et al. 2018). Implicit in both these approaches, however, is the assumption that basketry patterning simply serves to confirm more abstract forms of technical and mathematical knowledge— Ayres, for example, developing patterns woven from imagined infinitely long strips of straight metal to allow for a level of abstraction which makes the materials invisible. Both scholars bypass the practical knowledge of the maker and the idiosyncrasies of materials and process.

In regard to loom weaving, and challenging the overwhelming focus on the Jacquard loom as a precursor to early computers, Harlizius-Klück (2017) suggests we should rather address how the very basis of the weaving process, moving thread in and out of alternate sheds even on a hand-loom, demonstrates that practical weaving has always been a binary art (embedded within activity). One could argue much the same point for woven basketry. Further, plaited basketry techniques, whether two-directional interlacing or triaxial hexagonal and 'mad weaves', are also, in themselves, acts of intelligence, from symmetrical understanding to angular creations of surface curvature. Knots too *are* topological crossings, rather than mere illustrations of these qualities.

Mathematical educationalists, such as Nemirovsky (2012) and De Freitas, have shown how the body should not be 'demoted as the vehicle of the mental or the ideal, but taken to be the generative force of mathematical concepts' (De Freitas 2016, p. 658). For anthropologist Trevor Marchand, qualities such as symmetry, balance, proportion, scale, three-dimensional forms, and spatial relationships are first and foremost circulated through the senses and the body in motion. 'Numbers, formulae and equations are material devices … in any creative activity of any kind, conceptual thinking and embodied forms of cognition are inseparable' (Marchand 2018, pp. 299–300). Thus basketry 'knowing how' is a kind of mathematics in action. It is the very gestural moves used in craft, including basketwork, that articulate the physical rhythm of bodily learning which embody our understandings of spatial relationships, proportions, and forces in the material world (Nemirovsky 2012) (Fig. 3.7).

THE HUMAN IN THE WEAVING

At the beginning of this chapter, I proposed that a definition of technology must include human skill and tool use, and also include human interactions with the materials and forces involved. Technology is not divorced from human action; it is a part of it. Craft as technology, technology as craft, are a part of a single intelligent process. From this perspective, basketry is not simply a 'handicraft' soon to be obsolete. Similarly, printing presses and computers are tools, not devices developed to bypass human involvement.

I have also shown that there can be more to a skilful process than the act of making, since learning a skill changes people as they become skilful in action and, when it goes well, can also be an act of pleasure, even joy. Further, as the basket-maker (and the hand-loom cloth weaver) move with their materials in

Fig. 3.7   Joanna Gilmour. Darwin's baskets

the making, and join in its rhythm, they are at the same time honing, perfecting, and adding new combinations of ideas to their understanding of the material world, its spatial relations, and the forces that hold structures together. These practices are significant and valuable kinds of technological knowledge. They allow us to build on old knowledge, produce innovative work, and make associations of ideas, a factor not encountered in machines. At the same time, they are also embedded in social relations.

By interweaving fibres to create form and fabric, technologies of interlacing interlink the material and mental, the social and scientific, as Küchler describes above. Skilled practice also resonates with the interweaving of community and kin, the social and the sacred. In weaving a basket, all these aspects of life are condensed into one activity. Yet, just as Pfaffenberger argues that the *social* is an invisible aspect of technology (1988, p. 241), so aspects of human skill in technical processes are also, to a degree, unknown, invisible, and difficult to define—'below the line' or 'taken for granted' as Dormer (1970) and Mitchell describe (1997, p. 324). The mystery is in the middle, in the doing. Thus, even if basket making could be coded and mechanised, any code, plan, or draft would not be the whole story of the means of achievement.

Stuart Brand (1994) describes the gap between the plans of a building and the building itself as a 'kink' (p. 2). For anthropologist Alfred Gell (1992), the knowledge in that kink is a 'technology of enchantment' where the skill of the maker is so incomprehensible to the viewer that the artefact appears to be made by magic. This magic is David Pye's workmanship of risk, letting go of what is known and becoming one with the work (1968). Finnish thinker Juhani Palassmaa (2009) describes the gap between the artist and their drawing as a process of 'touching' what is being drawn with the eyes and making it alive, visible on paper to the viewer. Sheets-Johnstone (2015) similarly describes the experience for dance:

> Something alive and vibrant is happening ... we too are alive and vibrant ... Judgements, beliefs, interpretations are suspended; our experience ... is free of any manner of reflection. We are spontaneously and wholly intent upon the continuously emerging form which appears before us, thoroughly engrossed in its unfolding. (p. 1)

These scholars tell of the *experience* of skilfulness that makes technology work. Within that experience is an intelligence released by the activity, attention, and engagement that is fundamental to how humans develop and innovate.

As Tomasello (2009) discusses, a remarkable feature of human development is that through our capacity to build on past experience, we accumulate and grow our intelligence further, becoming capable of new invention through acts of engagement, cooperation, and altruistic teaching. I therefore propose there is a need for a continued valuation of knowledgeable, intelligent bodies at the heart of technology. Basketry and other hand skills are holistic, following processes in their entirety. These skills are magical, astonishing, enchanting because they enable us to learn through our bodies about the spatial, tangible, sometimes apparently unknowable aspects of the world, not because they are mystical and unattainable. If we follow the view that mechanisation externalises the human from the technology, then the practical capacity for humans to tap into this means of innovative thinking and intelligent understanding, which help us develop such technologies, is diminished. In that humans are a part of technology, we can consider how it develops, and include all its necessary aspects, handmade and mechanistic, according to our requirements.

NOTES

1. I am very grateful to Joanna Gilmour for directing me to this quotation.
2. W. Wendrich, *Who is afraid of basketry: a guide to recording basketry and cordage for archaeologists and ethnographers,* Leiden University, Centre for Non-Western Studies, 1991; R. Ellen, 'A modular approach to understanding the transmission

of technical knowledge: Nuaulu basket-making from Seram, eastern Indonesia', in *Journal of Material Culture*, 2009, pp. 243–76.

3. K. Von Frisch, *Animal Architecture*, Harcourt, 1974; M. Hansell, *Animal Architecture*, Oxford University Press, 2005

4. In a similar vein, Heather Paxson's work on artisanal cheese (2014) and the AA special issue on comestibles also reveal how the more organic and material aspects of technology have been neglected (Heath and Meneley 2007).

5. The Yakutat Tlingit origin story, for example, how the human wife of the Sun one day 'took some roots and idly began to plait them together in the shape of a basket'. Her husband increased its size and 'lowered her and her children to their homeland the earth. Their great basket settled near Yakutat on the Alesk River and that is the reason that the first baskets in south-eastern Alaska were made by the Yakutat women' (Petkau 2002, p. 25). See also Marcel Griaule's (1965) account of Dogon creation, where the primordial Nummo brought plant fibres to earth, modelling the granary, itself a model of the cosmos, on a woven basket.

6. See also Mitchell (2020) for a discussion on the relationship between braiding and dancing.

7. This provided a model system for early computers.

REFERENCES

Albers, A. (1943) *On Designing*. Middletown, CT.: Wesleyan University Press

Albers, A. (1965). *On Weaving*. Dover: New York

Arnold, D. (2015). *The Andean Science of Weaving: Structures and Techniques of Warp-faced Weaves*. London: Routledge

Arnold, D. (2018). Making textiles into persons: Gestural sequences and relationality in communities of weaving practice of the south-central Andes. *Journal of Material Culture*, 23(2), 239–260.

Ascher, M., & Ascher, R. (1981). *Code of the Quipu: a study in media mathematics and culture*. Ann Arbor: University of Michigan Press.

Ayres, P., Martin, A.G., & Zwierzycki, M. (2018). Beyond the basket case. In L. Hesselgren, A. Kilian, S. Malek, K-G. Olsson, O. Sorkine-Hornung, & C. Williams (Eds.), *AAG 2018: Advances in Architectural Geometry* (pp. 72–93). Chalmers University of Technology.

Bateson, G. (1972). Form, Substance and Difference. In *Steps to an Ecology of Mind* (pp. 423–44). London: Paladin.

Boas, F. (1893). Basketry Designs of the Salish Indians. In *Memoirs of the American Museum of Natural History: the Jesup North Pacific Expedition*. Leiden: Brill.

Boas, F. (1888). The Game of Cat's Cradle. *International Archiv für Ethnographie, 1*, 229.

Boas, F. (1928). *Coiled Basketry in British Columbia and Surrounding Region*. Washington: GPO.

Bobart, H. H. (1936). *Basketwork through the Ages*. London: Oxford University Press

Brand, S. (1994). *How Buildings Learn: What Happens to Them After They're Built*. London: Penguin.

Brown, P. (2012). Hand memories in basketwork and net-making among people with dementia in Uist and Lewis, told through life-moment stories and associated images.

In S. Bunn and V. Mitchell (Eds.), *The Material Culture of Basketry* (pp. 179–184). London: Bloomsbury.

Bunn, S. J. (1999). The importance of materials. *Journal of Museum Ethnography,* (11), 15–28.

Bunn, S. J. (2009). Transformations. In W. Gunn (Ed.), *Fieldnotes and Sketchbooks: Challenging the Boundaries between Descriptions and Processes of Describing.* Denmark: Peter Lang.

Bunn, S. (2014). Making plants and growing baskets. In T. Ingold & E. Hallam (Eds.), *Making and Growing.* London: Ashgate.

Bunn, S. J. (2021). Introduction. In S. Bunn & V. Mitchell (Eds.), *The Material Culture of Basketry.* London: Bloomsbury.

Bunn, S., & V. Mitchell (Eds.) (2021). *The Material Culture of Basketry.* London: Bloomsbury.

Deacon, A. B., & Wedgewood, C. H. (1934). Geometric drawings from Malekula and Other islands of the New Hebrides. *JRAI,* 64, 129–175.

De Freitas, E. (2016). Number, sense and the calculating child: Measure, multiplicity and mathematical monsters. *Discourse: Studies of the Cultural Politics of Education, 37*(5), 650–661.

Dewey, J. (1997 [1938]). *Experience and Education.* New York: Touchstone

Dormer, P. (1970). *The Meanings of Modern Design.* London: Thames and Hudson.

Emery, I. (1966). *The Primary Structure of Fabrics.* Washington: The Textile Museum.

Gell, A. (1992) The technology of enchantment and the enchantment of technology. In J. Coote and A. Shelton (Eds.), *Anthropology, Art and Aesthetics.* London: Clarendon.

Gerdes, P. (1999). *Geometry from Africa: Mathematical and Educational Explorations.* USA: The Mathematical Association of America.

Gerdes, P. (2010). *Otthava: Making Baskets and Doing Geometry in the Makhuwa Culture in the Northeast of Mozambique.* Maputo: Centre for Mozambican Studies and Ethnoscience.

Gibson, J. (1966). *The Senses Considered as Perceptual Systems.* George Allen and Unwin.

Griaule, M. (1965). *Conversations with Ogotommeli.* Oxford: Oxford University Press.

Guss, D. (1989). To *Weave and Sing: Art, Symbol, and Narrative in the South American Rainforest.* Berkeley: University of California Press.

Harlizius-Klück, E. (2017). Weaving as Binary Art and the Algebra of Patterns. *Textile: Cloth and Culture,* 15(2), 176–197.

Harris, O. (2007) What makes people work? In R. Astuti, J. Parry, & C. Stafford (Eds.), *Questions of Anthropology* (pp. 147–165). London: Berg.

Heath, D., & Meneley, A. (2007). Techne, Technoscience, and the Circulation of Comestible Commodities. *American Anthropologist,* 109(4), 593–602.

Heidegger, M. (1927). *Being and Time.* New York: Harper.

Hingston Quiggin, A. (1912). Textiles. In *Reports of the Cambridge Anthropological Expedition to Torres Straits. Vol. IV.* Cambridge: The University Press.

Hurcombe, L. (2014). *Perishable Material Culture in Prehistory.* Routledge: London.

Ingold, T. (2000). *The Perception of the Environment.* London: Routledge.

Ingold, T. (2010). The textility of making. *Cambridge Journal of Economics, 34,* 91–102.

Kimmerer, R.W. (2013). *Braiding sweetgrass: indigenous wisdom, scientific knowledge, and the teachings of plants.* Minneapolis: Milkweed Editions.

Kneebone, R. (2020). *Expert: Understanding the Path to Mastery.* London: Penguin.

Küchler, S. (2001). Why knot? Towards a theory of art and mathematics. In C. Pinney & N. Thomas, *Beyond Aesthetics: Art and the Technologies of Enchantment.* Oxford: Berg.

Lave, J., & Wenger, E. (1991). *Situated learning.* Cambridge: Cambridge University Press.

Lemonnier, P. (1992). Elements for an Anthropology of Technology. *Anthropological Papers 88.* Ann Arbor, MI.: Museum of Anthropology.

Leroi-Gourhan, A. (1964). *Gesture and Speech.* Cambridge, MA.: The MIT Press.

Marchand, T. H. J. (2018). Towards an anthropology of mathematizing. *Interdisciplinary science reviews, 43*(3–4), 295–316.

Martin, A. G. (2015). A basketmaker's approach to structural morphology. In *Future Visions: Proceedings of the International Association for Shell and Spatial Structures Symposium.*

Mason, O.T. (1895). *The Origins of Invention.* London: Walter Scott Ltd.

Mitchell, V. (1997). Text, Textile, Techné. In T. Harrod (Ed.), *Obscure Objects of Desire,* Conference Proceedings. London: Crafts Council Publication.

Mitchell, V. (2020). Braiding and Dancing: Rhythmic Interlacing and Patterns of Interaction. S.J. Bunn & V. Mitchell (Eds.), *The Material Culture of basketry.* London: Bloomsbury.

Nemirovsky, R. (2012). Modalities of bodily engagement in mathematics activity and learning. *Journal of the Learning Sciences, 21*(2), 207–215.

Okey, T. (1915). *An Introduction to the Art of Basket-making.* London: Pitman.

Palassmaa, J. (2009). *The Thinking Hand.* London: Wiley.

Palsson, G. (1994). Enskilment at Sea, *Man, 29*(4), 901–927 .

Pawley, M. (1999). Introduction. In W. Flusser (Ed.), *The Shape of Things.* Reaktion Books.

Paxson, H. (2011). The 'art' and 'science' of handcrafting cheese in the United States. *Endeavour, 35*(2–3), 116–124.

Paxson, H. (2014). The perils and promises of microbial abundance: Novel natures and model ecosystems, from artisanal cheese to alien seas. *Social Studies of Science 2014, 44*(20), 165–193.

Paxson, H. (2016). Craftsmanship and quality in artisanal cheesemaking. In S. L. Martin McAuliffe (Ed.), *Food and architecture: at the table.* London: Bloomsbury.

Peri, D., & Paterson, S. (1976).The Basket is in the Roots, That's Where it Begins. *Journal of California Anthropology, 3*(2), 17–32.

Pfaffenberger, B. (1988). Fetishized objects and humanized nature: towards an anthropology of technology. *Man, 23,* 236–252.

Petkau, K. (2002). *Baskets carrying a culture: the distinctive regional styles of basket-making nations in the Pacific north-west.* Unpublished Thesis White Rock Museum, BC, Canada.

Pinxten, R. (1987). *Towards a Navajo Indian Geometry.* Ghent: Kultuur, Kennis en Integratie v.z.ww.

Polanyi, M. (1967). *The Tacit Dimension.* London: Routledge & Kegan Paul.

Potter, C. (2008). Senses of Motion, Senses of Self: Becoming a Dancer'. *Ethnos, 73*(4), 444–465.

Pye, D. (1968). *The Nature and the Art of Workmanship.* London: Bloomsbury Academic.

Reuleaux, F. (1876). *The kinematics of machinery: outlines of a theory of machines.* London: Macmillan.

Rivers, W. H. R., & Haddon, A. C. (1902). 109 A Method of Recording String Figures and Tricks. *Man, 2,* 146–153. https://doi.org/10.2307/2840498.

Seiler-Baldinger, A. (1979). *Classification of Textile Techniques.* Ahmedabad: The Calico Museum.

Sheets-Johnstone. (2015). The *Phenomenology of Dance.* Philadelphia: Temple University Press.

Sigaut, F. (1993). Learning, Teaching and Apprenticeship. *New Literary History, 24,* 105–114.

Tepper, L. H., George, J., & Joseph W. (2017). *Salish Blankets: Robes of Protection and Transformation, Symbols of Wealth.* Lincoln & London: University of Nebraska Press.

Tomasello, M. (2009). *Why we cooperate.* Cambridge, MA.: The MIT Press

Verran, H. (2001). *Science and an African Logic.* London: University of Chicago Press.

Wendrich, W. (1999). *The World According to Basketry.* Leiden University: Center of Non-Western Studies.

Wharton-James, G. (1903). *Indian Basketry.* New York: Henry Malkan.

Wilkin, A., & Haddon, A.C. (1912). Houses. In *Reports of the Cambridge Anthropological Expedition to Torres Straits. Vol. IV.* Cambridge: The University Press.

CHAPTER 4

Material Culture Studies: Objectification, Agency, and Intangibility

Materiality

Mikkel Bille

All technologies require some sort of material: from a stone axe or clockwork to a fighter jet or smartphone app. They are made by people, using particular techniques and materials that may differ in origins, efficacy, or aesthetic value, but are nonetheless material. What materials are then used, and why? How do the makers—or users—develop, use, and make sense of a technology and its material qualities? What kind of (global) social life is entangled in its production and consumption? And what role do the technologies have in constituting social identities? Questions like these are characteristic of material culture studies. They attend to the qualities of the socio-material relations through which technologies come into existence and (dis)use. The material qualities matter to people: whether made of plastic, metal, or wood; recycled, new, or recyclable; homemade or imported from the UK or China; whether the object or material has the ability to convey either physical or spiritual powers or carries social meanings of prestige, exclusivity, or throw-away culture. Even in the most reductionist understanding of technology as an exclusively mechanic or electronic *object*—rather than technology as a *process* of applying skills, knowledge, materials, and energy for practical purposes (see Lemonnier and Pfaffenberger 1989; Pfaffenberger 1988)—the materials may be central for the use, value, or function of a technology.

M. Bille (✉)
Roskilde University, Roskilde, Denmark
e-mail: mikkelbille@ruc.dk

M. H. Bruun et al. (eds.), *The Palgrave Handbook of the Anthropology of Technology*, https://doi.org/10.1007/978-981-16-7084-8_4

Since its earliest days, anthropology has explored objects and technologies as lenses onto to human culture with various degrees of interest. Since the 1980s, however, the multidisciplinary field of *material culture studies* has focused on things, highlighting their active and constitutive role in human lives (Buchli 2002b; Hicks and Beaudry 2010; Tilley et al. 2006; Woodward 2007). Material forms like phones, freezers, knives, and so on are more than merely a backdrop representation of human life or a one-way projection of prior mental ideas onto things. Rather, things are imbedded in the networks of relations or dialectical processes through which people shape things and things shape people (Appadurai 1986; Hodder 1982, 1989; Latour 2005; Miller 1997, 2005, 2008; Miller and Tilley 1996). This perspective has evolved into a 'material turn' in the social sciences, and may unfold in studies of an *individual* object, such as a potsherd, coat, or toothbrush (Drazin 2021; Holtorf 2002; Stallybrass 1998), a *class* of objects such as radios or amulets (Hill 2007; Skuse 2005), a *type* of material such as aluminium, water, or stone (Arregui 2015; Strang 2005; Tilley 2004), *artistic* objects (Geismar 2004; Gell 1992, 1998; Küchler 1987), *religious* forms (Engelke 2005; Meyer 2008; Morgan 1998), the *politics* of museum and heritage objects (Harrison 2019; Macdonald 2006), or the *networks* of societal infrastructure (Larkin 2013; Shove et al. 2014), to name a few.

The focus on material culture opens up an enormous range of things to study, many of which, however, do not normally fall into the category of 'technology' (see Bruun & Wahlberg, this volume). For instance, most of the examples above would not normally be seen as 'technologies', and yet the precise difference between technology and material culture is not clear cut. The title of Ron Eglash's (2006) review of anthropology and technology is perhaps most telling of the interlinked fields of technology and material culture studies: 'Technology as material culture'. Technology is material culture, but material culture is also much more. And there is not only *one* material culture approach to technology. One could thus say that writing an article on technology from a material culture perspective is futile, since it is a broader category of object investigations (Candlin and Guins 2009) that *may* include studies of technologies in the narrow understanding of mechanic, electronic, or digital objects.

Nonetheless, it is the contention here that material culture studies have contributed to the anthropology of technology by paying attention to the important role of things in human lives, and thus the field warrants attention. For instance, a lesson from material culture studies is that most objects and technologies work in subtle ways to form human lives through what Daniel Miller has called 'the humility of things' (1987, pp. 85–108). Most technologies do not stand out as items of adoration, like the longest bridge, newest smartphone, or spaceship to the moon. Rather, Miller notes, 'Objects don't shout at you like teachers, or throw chalk at you like mine did, but they help you gently to learn how to act appropriately' (2010, p. 53). To Miller this illustrates 'processes of objectification' through which humans shape, and are shaped by, things.

The constitutive role of technologies in social lives is reminiscent of central points of Science and Technology Studies. As Phillip Vannini notes (2009), 'to study material culture is to study the technological underpinnings of culture, and to study technology is to study the material character of everyday life and its processes of objectification' (p. 3). While narrowing 'material culture studies' to processes of objectification is a gross simplification, coming at the expense of, for instance, influential semiotic or phenomenological explorations (Keane 2005; Preucel 2006; Tilley 1994, 2004), I pick on three related themes here where material culture studies have shaped studies of technology: objectification, agency, and materiality.

In the following I first present the development of material culture studies in the twentieth century. Then I turn to the implication of a subtle shift in wording, from 'material culture' to 'materiality'. This shift in term, it is argued, focuses attention more on the constituting webs of relations that objects make possible, and thus ties material culture studies closer to science and technology studies in a broader 'material turn'. In large part I refer to studies and people in British anthropology, particularly those connected to University College London, but it is important to acknowledge how other milieus and people have also shaped this material turn, as represented elsewhere in this volume. The chapter exemplifies the implications of a material culture approach to technology through the case of lighting as a material phenomenon that makes spaces stand out and take shape through merging tangible and intangible qualities. It ends with a brief discussion of some current themes in material culture studies in relation to technology.

Technology and Material Culture

Archaeologist Dan Hicks (2010) has shown that the use of terms like 'technology' and 'material culture' largely took shape in a context of disciplinary developments between archaeology and anthropology, at least in Britain. He notes that the term 'material culture' was actually not current in British anthropology and archaeology until the interwar period in the twentieth century, and instead the preoccupation with objects had mainly been through terms like 'technology'. While objects under the heading of 'technology' continued to be the main focus in archaeology, the term fell largely into the background in anthropology in the interwar years. Part of this, Hicks argues, may rest in the researchers' careful attention to minute detail as part of a salvage paradigm of ethnographic objects in the wake of industrialisation in the late nineteenth century. This work was particularly delegated to the museum, but went out of fashion in mainstream anthropology at the expense of studying 'social' aspects of society such as rituals, kinship, and socio-economic models (see also Lofgren 1997). In the interwar period, Hicks argues, a shift from 'technology' to 'material culture' occurred which was desirable for both fieldwork-oriented and museum anthropologists. The term 'material culture' would mark a shift from the technological determinism that had earlier pervaded the evolutionary field of anthropology, and for the museum anthropologists it would simultaneously mark out museum collections as 'more than simply assemblages of objects' (Hicks 2010, p. 37).

In mainstream anthropology, studying technologies and material culture, however, soon went out of fashion. There are exemptions, of course, such as studies where things are mostly treated in structural analyses as categories to *think with*, rather than individual objects of exploration (cf. Bourdieu 1970, 1984; Douglas and Isherwood 1979; Glassie 1975), or in neo-evolutionary or cultural materialist writings by, for instance, Leslie White and Marvin Harris. Generally, it is within other fields and disciplines, however, that studies of technology and material objects are in focus, such as museums studies, archaeology, history, and sociology of science and technology in the mid-twentieth century. Bryan Pfaffenberger's (1988) call for an *anthropology of technology* in the late 1980s (see Bruun & Wahlberg, this volume) was in parallel with the development of a more dedicated view on material culture at the intersection between archaeology and anthropology (Hodder 1982, 1989; Miller 1985, 1987; Munn 1983; Shanks and Tilley 1987). It reflected a renewed cross-disciplinary interest in the material aspects of human lives, which gained prominence in solving the long-standing problems of the relationship between the social and the material, and sharp divisions between object and subject.

The very term material *culture* illustrates a duality in offering a material understanding of culture, and a cultural understanding of material objects. It was particularly in the works of archaeologist Ian Hodder in Cambridge and his inspiration in postmodern theory that focus was put on the meanings of things and the practices in which they were entangled, as well as the subjectivity of the researcher. The central feature of material culture studies is the way 'artefacts are implicated in the construction, maintenance and transformation of social identities' (Miller and Tilley 1996, p. 5). Take, for instance, Nicolas Govoroff's (1993) study of hunting in the Haute Provence region of southern France in the second half of the twentieth century. When the male hunter is learning to shoot, the calibre of the weapon increases with growing skill. It seems like a logical development. However, Govoroff then shows that, when reaching a certain level, the male hunter starts downscaling again, using smaller and less efficient weapon technology, such as that associated with female hunters, and compensating for the reduced firepower with their advanced skills, knowledge, and aim.

Material culture studies have in particular focused on themes like 'commodities' and 'consumption' of things, rather than technology per se. The focus on commodities has yielded insights into how objects, like people, have 'social lives', to follow Appadurai (1986) and 'biographies' in the words of Kopytoff (1986), which have proved no less relevant when it comes to understanding technologies. In their exchange and reappropriation, they come to shape social identities and themselves take shape. Breaking from the previous focus on *production*, Daniel Miller has been particularly prominent in highlighting the productive aspects of *consumption*, showing, for instance, how the very act of consumption helps shape social identities. Miller's theory of objectification (1987) exemplifies this, as he has shown in studies of the home, rituals, or the process of buying things (Miller 1993, 2001b, 2004), as well as technologies ranging from the Internet, Facebook, and cars, to mobile phones (Clarke 1998; Horst and Miller 2006; Miller 2001a, 2011; Miller and Slater 2000). Discussing the unfulfilled desires of people in Trinidad that the Internet helps alleviate, he notes that it is not 'that Trinidadians use the Internet, or that the Internet creates Trinidadians. It's more that the Trinidadian Internet is something distinct from all other Internets and makes the Trinidadian who uses the Internet something beyond previous forms of being Trinidadian' (2010, p. 118). Thus, rather than seeing objects as *representations* of social identities, he presents a dialectical theory of material culture that shows how 'objects make us, as part of the very process by which we make them' (2010, p. 60). To Miller, this implies that there ultimately is no separation between subject and object. Even if material culture studies have also taken other theoretical routes, the theory of objectification as a way of understanding the conflation of material and social, subject and object, form and content is still at the core of material culture studies, and has shown relevance in areas such as digital ethnography, as discussed later.

By the 1990s material culture studies had become much more consolidated, with the emergence of both dedicated journals and specialised education theorising material culture. The implication of the short historical overview above is, then, that talking about material culture *of* technology omits the history and interconnectedness of the terms. And also that material culture studies cover many themes that do not normally fall into the category of technology studies. Furthermore, while there are other positions in material culture studies that contribute to understanding technology, a basic lesson from Miller's approach is to understand how technologies are actively entangled in shaping social identities and life through local processes of objectification.

From Material Culture to Materiality

At the turn of the twenty-first century a slight shift in terminology occurred again, with the word 'materiality' rather than 'material culture' becoming dominant; Robert Preucel, for instance, distinguishes material culture as 'the manifestation of culture through material fabrication'. Material culture is about things, whereas 'materiality, or material agency, can be defined as the social constitution of self and society by means of the object world' (ibid., 2006, pp. 4–5). The terminological shift between material culture and materiality facilitates taking up another distinction that has been highlighted in social science theory, namely, that between materiality and immateriality. As Miller and colleagues illustrate in an edited volume on materiality (Miller 2005), there is no way to escape the process of objectification. Regardless of how much people may want to avoid materiality, they simply pay even more attention to the specificity of the selected range of objects that they do live with.

Christopher Tilley notes, 'the concept of materiality is one that needfully addresses the "social lives" of [things] in relation to the social lives of persons' (2007, p. 17). Yet one may initially find it hard to see how the focus on 'materiality' distinguishes itself from Miller's earlier version of material culture studies that actively points to the central place of things in the constitution of social identities. However, the terminology does indicate a shift to more pronounced focus on the *relationships* and *processes* between people and things. As Victor Buchli notes, 'looking at what happens before and after the artefact is more significant than the artefact itself; that is, the terms of materiality rather than material culture itself and the differential ability of individuals to participate in these processes is more important' (2002a, p. 19).

A recent volume on the material culture of failure (Carroll et al. 2017) takes the distinction as point of departure. It highlights how objects actually play a crucial role when things (technological or political visions, for instance) do not go as planned. The distinction between material culture and materiality is 'between the constitutive substances of the failure and the analytical frame of investigation' (Carroll et al. 2017, p. 5). Material failure is when the objects fail to do as they 'should'. On the other hand, a fruitful lens onto failures is supplied by looking at the materials involved, which may not in themselves *not* do as they should, but either act to escalate a calamitous spiral or become the material evidence for such failure. This is what Carroll et al. (2017) call 'the materiality of failure'. The key point is that 'failure' is not simply a 'social', 'mental', or 'immaterial' phenomenon, but a material one as well. This is important when looking at technology from a material culture perspective. A technology may fail—a spaceship or a nuclear plant may burst into flames—but the materiality of the technological failure may also express itself in the broader environment, and perhaps even escalate because of the material surroundings.

Materials and Materiality

While it can be claimed that scholars did explore issues of material processes and relations before it became central to define distinctions between the terms 'material culture' and 'materiality', the shift in terms leaves us in another predicament. If we focus on the role of material culture/technology in people's life, what have we actually said about materials? Buchli claims in the extract quoted above that the artefact in itself is of less importance than the processes of materialisation; that is, have we only talked about the life *around* the material objects—the relations—and not the materials *as such*?

To exemplify, another prominent figure in material culture studies, Tim Ingold (2007) argues that the preoccupation with 'materiality' may see a building or book but has lost track of the plaster or ink that makes up these objects, which he sees as better understood through the lens of Gibson's notion of medium, substances, and surfaces. The materials are still there, but if we talk about the materiality of the text there is a danger of never getting to the ink. The properties of materials, he argues, are always relational and processual since no-*thing* lasts forever (for a critique of this work, see the commentaries on the article in the same issue by Miller, Tilley, Knappett, and others). Discussions like these have fruitfully developed material culture studies to the point that they embrace, not only what things represent, mean, do, and the variety of roles they play in their lifespan, but also what the actual material qualities and 'affordances' (Knappett 2004) have to offer in specific contexts.

Christopher Tilley, for instance, directs our attention to the bodily and phenomenological aspects of the material qualities of objects, showing how bodily engagements with landscapes and stones *in place* constitute senses of self and society (2004). In a paper on protective technologies against malevolent spiritual forces, I have also shown how among the Bedouin in Jordan some materials quite literally are seen to decompose when absorbing evil, while other objects with Islamic inscriptions, equally tangible, are seen as *less* material, even immaterial due to their spiritual and affective abilities (Bille 2010). The shift from material culture to materiality, in other words, emphasises *relations* between the social and material, but Tilley, Ingold, and others remind us that it is equally important to engage with the sensuous, affective, and, indeed, material qualities as well.

Regardless of how technology is approached from material culture perspectives (material culture, materiality, materials), recent decades have shown the relevance of engaging with the active webs of material and social lives. Whether we catalogue research under the heading of material culture studies or not, it is evident that the success of the material turn (including New materialism, 'Thing theory', and STS studies) has made technologies central in contemporary ethnographic analysis. This is witnessed in many recent publications that not only explore the social life constituted *around* an object or technology, or the impact of technologies *on* said social life, but also the role of the very materials in human lives. The range of materials studied is expanding rapidly as exemplified by studies of homes made of trash (Harkness 2011), the techno-politics of mining aluminium (Arregui 2015), the social implications of environmental science of water and rocks (Green 2020), the very soil under our feet (Lyons 2020), and other resources (Bakker and Bridge 2006), all of which are entangled in the use and development of technologies.

Agency

The implication of studying the active role of technologies in society is to understand that things *do* something. With 'material agency', Preucel above refers to a term that became popular in the late 1990s and in many ways also marks a characteristic feature of material culture studies (Gell 1998; Latour 2005): the need to think of causation as a central aspect of the relationship between human and object. The notion that things actually infringe and shape social lives has long been recognised, yet within anthropology it is with Alfred Gell (1998) and his studies of art that we see a more theorised version of what that actually entails: *the agency of things*. In Gell's version of agency, it is not merely people who produce it and are agents; so too are things, even if there is no will or intention in inanimate objects. Human intentionality is distributed into objects, most famously argued by Gell in terms of the agency of the land-mine, where the mine is the agent, but intentions are distributed into it: from the soldier placing it, the leadership ordering it, and engineers constructing it.

Material culture studies that home in on technologies often explore questions of what, how, and when things do what they do, some explicitly in terms of agency (Bille and Sørensen 2007; Corsín Jiménez and Nahum-Claudel 2019; Dickson 2018; Rice 2010; Seaver 2019). The argument is not that objects inherently 'have' agency, but that agency is *produced* at certain points by particular objects causing events to happen, thus emphasising ethnographic context. The notion of object or material agency is still critically discussed (see also Coupaye 2021; Knappett and Malafouris 2008; Lindstrøm 2015; Ribeiro 2016; Sørensen 2016), yet such discussions highlight the active role of things in social life and the untenability of clear distinctions between subject and object, the argument being that when something 'happens', it is a combination of material and human agency. To emphasise the close relationship between material culture studies and sociology of technology, here we see relations with parallel discussions in Bruno Latour's work and subsequent ANT and Post-ANT approaches.

The Essence and Absence of Things

This material turn also relates to the somewhat recent discussion in anthropology about 'ontology'—that is the essence of things (Henare et al. 2007; Holbraad and Pedersen 2016)—which in large part also further integrates the perspectives from material culture studies and STS wherein parallel discussions occurred (e.g. Law and Singleton 2005; Mol 2002). As the central feature of material culture studies is figuring out how distinctions between subject and object, materiality and immateriality, and technologies and their material properties are tied up in social worlds, then the very question of the nature of objects in these relations in specific ethnographic settings is pivotal. Studies within the ontological turn thus also effectively address how things—from powder (Holbraad 2007) and cigarettes (Reed 2007) to fire burning cotton (Harman 2009, p. 113) and heroine clinics (Schepelern Johansen and Schepelern Johansen 2014)—are material and have a materiality that may radically differ from other contexts and thus aid in theoretical development of understanding technology. The argument goes that what a thing *is*, is in this sense not given but unfolds through the multiple ontologies in which people perform and engage. There are no *a priori* distinctions between material and immaterial, thoughts and things, subject and object.

It is tempting to focus on tangible things when dealing with material culture studies of technology. Yet this is ill-advised. The absent technologies may play central role as well—the next iPhone, the lost car, or the explicit rejection of technologies (Bille et al. 2010). Furthermore, many technologies are inherently caught up in intangible forces. For instance, the point of a hot air balloon is not the basket and the enveloping fabric, but how it is handled in relation to the heat from the ignited flame and the wind. The wind, heat, and the balloon's air may not be 'made' by people like the basket and the balloon's structure; nonetheless, what matters is how they, even as intangible material forms, are taken in, moulded with the flame that in itself is a product of material relations, only to become part of human lives, not merely as consequences of social life, but as actively constituting it (McCormack 2018). Material culture studies of technologies are in this sense not only concerned with the tangible object and its relation to social lives. The intangible, the absent, and the local ontologies of what indeed *is* material and immaterial are equally important. Light, as we shall see, is a case in point.

CASE STUDY: ATMOSPHERIC TECHNOLOGIES

Of all the senses, vision has held a central position in human life. Yet in order to see, there needs to be light. Anthropologists have explored the human sensorium extensively, in particular vision, but often at the expense of the technologies that shape that sensation. A material culture study of lighting technologies turns this around and shows how aspects of social life are conditioned by the selected technologies (Bille 2019; for more on the anthropology of luminosity see Bille and Sørensen 2007). In the following I use lighting to show how a focus on materiality and the technologies related to it invites discussion of blurred categories, materiality as both nature and culture, and the role of the material in a specific technology.

One should not just oppose light with darkness but engage with how features of things appear remarkably different depending on the very material qualities of light (shadows, glare, colour, contrasts, dimming, distribution, etc.). A space may seem fundamentally different depending on the colour temperature (*kelvin*), colour reproduction (*ra*), and amount (*lumen*) of the light source, not to speak of the effect of the location of the light source(s). As electromagnetic energy, light is a remarkable physical phenomenon that, depending on wavelength, is visible to the human eye. Or rather, as Ingold points out, we do not see light, but see *in* light as it embraces the surfaces of our material surroundings (Ingold 2000, 2011, p. 134). At least phenomenologically speaking, we can say that light changes the material qualities of the objects on which it is cast. To exemplify, the material quality of light is used for crime prevention in urban space when fluorescent pink lighting, so-called zit bulbs, are used in urban areas where teenagers congregate, working to shame them as it exposes their acne more than normal street lighting (Walsh 2008, p. 125), or when fluorescent blue light is used to deter drug injection in public washrooms (Crabtree et al. 2013). In essence, how things—including one's own body—appear to a human eye is shaped by the quality of lighting that shines upon it. To talk about light and lighting technologies as material culture is to engage with the role of vision and the luminous qualities of lighting technologies in human lives.

Lighting technologies have been fundamental in developing modern society as they have enabled states and commercial interests to conquer the night and extend the day in urban areas (Nye 2018; Schivelbusch 1988; Schulte-Römer 2019; Shaw 2018; Sneath 2009). Large investments are currently being made in exchanging old lighting technologies with new more energy-saving ones and smart city solutions. This has had great impact on how urban spaces look in terms of 'colder' light or more glare, and it is evident that politics are strongly implicated when it comes to deciding which areas should be replaced first and what technologies and design to use, not to mentioned the mixed responses of the public (Ebbensgaard 2019a). The new technologies have gained increasing attention from social sciences due to the new possibilities for lighting urban scenes, whether in terms of basic street lighting, festivals, pleasure gardens, and nightlife or the downsides of lighting pollution and social exclusion (Brandi and Geissmar-Brandi 2006; Ebbensgaard 2019a, 2019b; Edensor 2015; Edensor and Bille 2017; Entwistle and Slater 2019; Meier et al. 2014; Shaw 2014). Such studies clearly show how human values are materialised, but also how local forces shape responses and uses. In other words, beyond recognising how the material qualities of lighting change the appearance of other materials, focus is on the kinds of social worlds these technologies are part and product of. To relate to the theory of objectification, you could say that the desire to illuminate the night is shaping human lives in a dialectical process.

Going beyond questions of the perception of materials and the social and political life of lighting, there is remarkable cultural variation in this fundamental material element. From the use of candle, gas, or electricity and the implied infrastructure of parts, sockets, and distribution net, to the way natural lighting falls through fenestrations during the day and night, lighting is not just lighting. It is embedded in cultural meanings, practices, and bodily norms that, beyond *seeing*, are about *feeling* in particular ways: that is material culture studies of lighting technologies may be concerned with the practices and cultural appreciation of how the world appears, beyond the symbolic powers of light. The literature on lighting practices and cultures now includes examples from Japan (Daniels 2015; Hui 2020), Sweden (Garnert 1994; Gerhardsson et al. 2020), Denmark (Bille 2019; Genus and Jensen 2017; Hauge 2015), England (Ebbensgaard 2019a; Edensor 2017), India (Cross 2019; Kumar 2015), Tanzania (Winther 2008), Australia (Pink et al. 2015; Pink and Sumartojo 2018; Sumartojo and Pink 2018), China (Wu 2009), Canada (Vannini and Taggart 2013), Greece (Petrova 2018), from past societies (Papadopoulos and Moyes 2022), and many others. Here, the central feature is to understand socio-material entanglements and cultural variation through exploring lighting technologies.

I have, for instance, examined the appreciation of bright, energy-saving light among the settled Bedouin in Jordan, the sharp glare of a fluorescent bulb reflected from white walls painted with shining acrylic paint in their almost empty reception rooms. This preference for shininess was more than simply an imitation of the sharp natural light from the sun; it also materialised important values of hospitality and formality with all the notions of honour and prestige this entails among the Bedouin (Bille 2017). It was not so much the white—and in my personal impression as a Dane 'cold'—light that instigated my interest in the phenomenon. Rather, it was the fact that many houses at the time had installed green toned windows that bathed the domestic spaces in a green verdant haze as the sun shone in. This was just seen as 'good light'. The bodily normalisation of a green embrace, wrapping itself around every object and body in the room, so different from my own norms, highlighted the need to understand material and sensory norms—in this case as they relate to attuning oneself to spiritual protection against evil forces in a context of Islamic revivalism, where many previous techniques were deemed un-Islamic. Lighting acts as medium for bodily attunement. While it clearly makes sense to see this as a process of objectification, there is also a more phenomenological approach, inspired by Ingold (2011) and Tilley's work (1994, 2004), to lighting technologies that emphasises the bodily emplacement and spatial atmosphere that determines the implementation of some—rather than other—technologies.

Jordanian lighting was in stark contrast to my native upbringing in Denmark where the lighting is characterised by dimmed and dispersed notes, often supplemented with candlelight. Here the point is not formality, but rather the opposite: the informal sense of cosy comfort where a lack of hierarchy and the encouragement to relax is the point—what in local terms is called *hygge* or cosiness (see Bille 2019). By 2012 incandescent light bulbs were banned from production (unless for professional lighting), thus enmeshing a technology that had lit the twentieth century in the political and commercial interests of lowering energy consumption. It was precisely this appreciation of cosy light that meant that, unlike the Bedouin who had easily adopted white light from the energy-saving light bulb into their aesthetics of hospitality, Danes were highly critical as the colour temperature was seen as 'cold' and the bulbs often could not be dimmed. In Danish homes, more than simply turning lights on and off, there is a day-long process of manipulating the home to offer a particular atmosphere by varying the distribution of light, dimming it, or lighting candles. As interlocutors pointed out, in many ways light is something you *do*. It may have objectified desires for less energy consumption, but not the bodily sensation of cosiness.

This example highlights that when observing technologies from a material culture perspective they are not simply seen as *signs* of social status or identities. One can approach them as processes of objectification which aid in constituting identities: for instance, the role played by light in achieving hospitality or cosiness, or in producing agency by scaring off a potential burglar, drug addict, or evil spirits. But more centrally, their very material qualities matter. Lighting, like many other technologies, has affective potentials and stirs emotions. Light may work as an atmospheric tool to produce spaces that make people feel safe, relaxed, unwelcome, or sleepy, by highlighting the textures and material qualities of other objects in a space—in recent literature termed the *atmosphere* (Bille et al. 2015; Ingold 2012; Schroer and Schmitt 2018; Sumartojo and Pink 2019). Much of this literature follows phenomenologist Gernot Böhme's notion that atmospheres are characteristic manifestations of the co-presence of subject and object (1998, p. 114). As he explains,

> atmospheres are indeterminate above all as regards their ontological status. We are not sure whether we should attribute them to the objects or environments from which they proceed or to the subjects who experience them. We are also unsure where they are. They seem to fill the space with a certain tone or feeling like a haze. (1993, p. 114)

A focus on atmospheres marks a shift in attention from what an object represents or does, to how they are present, even if we cannot point out the exact location of the affective quality. To a material culture study of technology, it may thus not necessarily be the clear ontological status as tangible material objects—or intangible in the case of light—that is at stake, nor the 'immaterial' meanings and values or their dialectical processes. Rather it may be their atmospheric qualities of making spaces and people *feel* particular ways (see also Navaro-Yashin 2012). While a material culture study of technology may be inclined to focus on the wax dripping from a candle, what it *does*, or how the light bulb symbolises Modernity, it also includes more phenomenologically inspired studies of the affective impact a technology has on other material objects and people within its reach.

Looking Ahead

A lesson from the above is that the breadth of material culture studies is so encompassing that there is no single material culture approach to technology, although Miller's and Ingold's perspectives have been particularly fruitful and dominating. Material culture studies offer a very broad entry to understanding technologies, with theories also deriving from studies of art and consumption, and museum and religious studies. Given the new virtual technologies and advanced, even extra-terrestrial, technical devices that have become objects of attention for material culture studies, we are at a time, I would claim, where distinctions between a multidisciplinary field of material culture studies and Science and Technology Studies are not necessarily clear cut (e.g. illustrated by Buchli 2016, 2021; Eglash 1999; Knox 2021; Knox and Nafus 2018; Küchler 2008; Miller 2011; Walford 2021). This is also evident in light of studies that increasingly explore digital technologies through the very premise of questioning distinctions between the material and immaterial (e.g. Geismar 2018, 2021; Knox and Nafus 2018; Miller 2011). Even in digital anthropology, Horst and Miller (2012) note, the materiality of the digital world is neither more nor less material than the worlds preceding it: it is not the social media platforms that produce content, it is the users. And it is they who make sense of these technologies. Yet digital devices are not only subject to interpretation, but also '*produce* their own ways of seeing and knowing' (Knox 2021, p. 102) that force one to go beyond modes of analysis such as agency or objectification to embrace them as 'empirical or knowledge-producing entities' (Knox 2021, p. 102; see also Rheinberger 1997).

Currently we are seeing areas such as data science increasingly becoming fields of critical anthropological investigation. Even things like 'data' viewed, simplistically, as being 'out there' and simply collected, are actually made through human-technological processes. Or, as Antonia Walford notes (2021), there may be an aesthetics of data, where the ability to create accurate data, 'is a result of a process of delicate and committed crafting, of eliciting qualities, forms, patterns, and intensities, and managing their relationship to other forms of social relations' (p. 206). Such an analysis rests in some part on theories from material culture studies, such as Gell's agency, but it is also reminiscent of STS approaches, demonstrating the close contemporary links between the fields when it comes to understanding technology. Thus, despite the increasing interest in immaterial, digital, and virtual worlds, along with the kind of data that new technologies produce, use, and make available, there is still the basic feature that all technologies entail some sort of material element or representation, which warrants some sort of attention.

REFERENCES

Appadurai, A. (1986). *The Social Life of Things: Commodities in Cultural Perspective.* Cambridge: Cambridge University Press.

Arregui, A. (2015). Amazonian quilombolas and the technopolitics of aluminum. *Journal of Material Culture, 20*(3), 249–272.

Bakker, K., & Bridge, G. (2006). Material worlds? Resource geographies and the 'matter of nature'. *Progress in Human Geography, 30*(1), 5–27.

Bille, M. (2010). Seeking Providence Through Things. The Words of God versus Black Cumin. In M. Bille, F. Hastrup & T. F. Sørensen (Eds.), *An Anthropology of Absence. Materializations of Transcendence and Loss* (pp. 167–184). New York: Springer Press.

Bille, M. (2017). Ecstatic things : The power of light in shaping Bedouin homes. *Home Cultures, 14*(1), 25–49.

Bille, M. (2019). *Homely atmospheres and lighting technologies in Denmark. Living with Light.* London: Bloomsbury.

Bille, M., Bjerregaard, P., & Sørensen, T. F. F. (2015). Staging Atmospheres. Materiality, Culture and the texture of the in-between. *Emotion, Space & Society, 15*, 31–38.

Bille, M., Hastrup, F., & Sørensen, T. F. (2010). Introduction: An Anthropology of Absence. In M. Bille, F. Hastrup & T. F. Sørensen (Eds.), *An Anthropology of Absence: Materializations of Transcendence and Loss* (pp. 3–22). New York: Springer.

Bille, M., & Sørensen, T. F. (2007). An Anthropology of Luminosity. The agency of light. *Journal of Material Culture, 12*(3), 263–284.

Böhme, G. (1993). Atmosphere as the Fundamental Concept of a New Aesthetics. *Thesis Eleven, 36*, 113–126.

Böhme, G. (1998). Atmosphere as an aesthetic concept. *Daidalos, 68*, 112–115.

Bourdieu, P. (1970). The Berber house or the world reversed. *Social Science Information*, *9*(2), 151–170.

Bourdieu, P. (1984). *Distinction: A Social Critique of the Judgement of Taste*. Cambridge, MA.: Harvard University Press.

Brandi, U., & Geissmar-Brandi, C. (2006). *Light for Cities : Lighting Design for Urban Spaces. A Handbook*. Walter de Gruyter.

Buchli, V. (2002a). Introduction. In V. Buchli (Ed.), *The Material Culture Reader* (pp. 1–22). Oxford: Berg.

Buchli, V. (2002b). *The Material Culture Reader*. Oxford: Berg.

Buchli, V. (2016). *An archaeology of the immaterial*. London: Routledge.

Buchli, V. (2021). Extra-terrestrial methods: toward an ethnography of the ISS. In T. Carroll, A. Walford & S. Walton (Eds.), *Lineages and Advancements in Material Culture Studies Perspectives from UCL Anthropology*. London & New York: Routledge.

Candlin, F., & Guins, R. (Eds.) (2009). *The Object Reader*. New York: Routledge.

Carroll, T, Jeevendrampillai, D., & Parkhurst, A. (2017). Introduction. In T. Carroll, D. Jeevendrampillai, A. Parkhurst & J. Shackelford (Eds.), *The material culture of failure* (pp. 1–20). London: Bloomsbury.

Clarke, A. (1998). Window shopping at home: classifieds, catalogues and new consumer skills. In D. Miller (Ed.), *Material Cultures: Why some things matter*. Chicago: University of Chicago Press.

Corsín Jiménez, A., & Nahum-Claudel, C. (2019). The anthropology of traps: Concrete technologies and theoretical interfaces. *Journal of Material Culture*, *24*(4), 383–400.

Coupaye, L. (2021). 'Things ain't the same anymore' Towards an anthropology of technical objects (or 'When Leroi- Gourhan and Simondon meet MCS'). In T. Carroll, A. Walford & S. Walton (Eds.), *Lineages and Advancements in Material Culture Studies*. London: Routledge.

Crabtree, A., Mercer, G., Horan, R., Grant, S., Tan, T., & Buxton, J. A. (2013). A qualitative study of the perceived effects of blue lights in washrooms on people who use injection drugs. *Harm Reduction Journal*, *10*(1).

Cross, J. (2019). No Current: Electricity and Disconnection in Rural India. In S. Abram, B. R. Winthereik & T. Yarrow (Eds.), *Electrifying anthropology. Exploring electrical practices and infrastructures* (pp. 65–82). London: Bloomsbury.

Daniels, I. (2015). Feeling at home in contemporary Japan: Space, atmosphere and intimacy. *Emotion, Space and Society*, *15*, 47–55.

Dickson, J. (2018). Warfarin as a materially and digitally informed drug. *Journal of Material Culture*, *23*(3), 312–327.

Douglas, M., & Isherwood, B. C. (1979). *The world of goods: towards an anthropology of consumption*. London: Allen Lane.

Drazin, A. (2021). The object biography. In T. Carroll, A. Walford & Shireen Walton (Eds.), *Lineages and Advancements in Material Culture Studies* (pp. 61–74). London: Routledge.

Ebbensgaard, C. L. (2019a). Making sense of diodes and sodium: Vision, visuality and the everyday experience of infrastructural change. *Geoforum*, *103*, 95–104.

Ebbensgaard, C. L. (2019b). Standardised difference: Challenging uniform lighting through standards and regulation. *Urban Studies*.

Edensor, T. (2015). Light design and atmosphere. *Visual Communication*, *14*(3).

Edensor, T. (2017). *From Light to Dark: Daylight, Illumination and Gloom*. Minneapolis & London: University of Minnesota Press.

Edensor, T., & Bille, M. (2017). 'Always like never before': Learning from the lumito-pia of Tivoli Gardens. *Social & Cultural Geography*.

Eglash, R. (1999). *African fractals: Modern computing and indigenous design*. Rutgers University Press.

Eglash, R. (2006). Technology as material culture. In C. Tilley, W. Keane, S. Küchler, M. Rowlands & P. Spyer (Eds.), *Handbook of Material Culture*. London: Sage.

Engelke, M. (2005). Sticky Subjects and sticky objects. The substance of African Christian Healing. In D. Miller (Ed.), *Materiality* (pp. 118–139). Durham & London: Duke University Press.

Entwistle, J., & Slater, D. (2019). Making space for 'the social': connecting sociology and professional practices in urban lighting design 1. *British Journal of Sociology*, *0*(0), 1–22.

Garnert, J. (1994). Seize the Day. Ethnological perspectives on light and darkness. *Ethnologia Scandinavica*, *24*, 38–59.

Geismar, H. (2004). The Materiality of Contemporary Art in Vanuatu. *Journal of Material Culture*, *9*, 43–58.

Geismar, H. (2018). *Museum Object Lessons for the Digital Age*. London: UCL Press.

Geismar, H. (2021). A new instrumentalism? In T. Carroll, A. Walford & S. Walton (Eds.), *Lineages and Advancements in Material Culture Studies* (pp. 75–88). London: Routledge.

Gell, A. (1992). The technology of enchantment and the enchantment of technology. In J. Coote & A. Shelton (Eds.), *Anthropology, Art and Aesthetics* (pp. 40–63). Oxford: Clarendon Press.

Gell, A. (1998). *Art and Agency: An Anthropological Theory*. Oxford: Oxford University Press.

Genus, A., & Jensen, C. (2017). Beyond 'behaviour': The institutionalisation of prac-tice and the case of energy-efficient lighting in Denmark. *Journal of Consumer Culture*, *19*(3), 340-358.

Gerhardsson, K. M., Laike, T., & Johansson, M. (2020). Leaving lights on – A con-scious choice or wasted light? Use of indoor lighting in Swedish homes. *Indoor and Built Environment*, *0*(0).

Glassie, H. H. (1975). *Folk Housing in Middle Virginia: A Structural Analysis of Historic Artifacts*. Knoxville: University of Tennessee Press.

Govoroff, N. C. (1993). The hunter and his gun in Haute-Provence. In P. Lemonnier (Ed.), *Technological choices: transformation in material cultures since the Neolithic*. London: Routledge.

Green, L. (2020). *ROCK | WATER | LIFE*. Durham & London: Duke University Press.

Harkness, R. (2011). Earthships: The Homes That Trash Built. *Anthropology Now*, *3*(1), 54–65.

Harman, G. (Ed.) (2009). *Prince of Networks Bruno Latour and Metaphysics*. Melbourne: repress.

Harrison, R. (2019). NEW MATERIALITIES AND THE ENACTMENT On Heritage Ontologies: Rethinking the Material World of Heritage, *91*(4), 1365–1384.

Hauge, B. (2015). Lives under the sun: The sensory qualities of daylight in designing the everyday. *Senses and Society*, *10*(1), 71–91.

Henare, A, Holbraad, M., & Wastell, S. (2007). *Thinking Through Things. Theorising artefacts ethnographically*. London & New York: Routledge.

Hicks, D. (2010). The Material-Cultural Turn: event and effect. In D. Hicks & M. C. Beaudry (Eds.), *Oxford Handbook of Material Culture Studies* (pp. 25–98). Oxford: Oxford University Press.

Hicks, D., & Beaudry, M. C. (Eds.) (2010). *Oxford Handbook of Material Culture Studies*. Oxford: Oxford University Press.

Hill, J. (2007). The Story of the Amulet: Locating the Enchantment of Collections. *Journal of Material Culture, 12*, 65–87.

Hodder, I. (1982). *Symbols in Action: Ethnoarchaeological studies of material culture.* Cambridge: Cambridge University Press

Hodder, I. (1989). *The Meanings of Things: Material Culture and Symbolic Expression.* London: Unwin Hyman.

Holbraad, M. (2007). The Power of Powder: multiplicity and motion in the divinatory cosmology of Cuban Ifa (or mana, again). In A. Henare, M. Holbraad & S. Wastell (Eds.), *Thinking Through Things. Theorising artefacts ethnographically* (pp. 189–225). London: Routledge.

Holbraad, M., & Pedersen, M. A. (2016). *The Ontological Turn: An Anthropological Exposition*. Cambridge: Cambridge University Press.

Holtorf, C. (2002). Notes on the life history of a pot sherd. *Journal of Material Culture, 7*, 49–71.

Horst, H. A., & Miller, D. (2006). *Cell phone: an anthropology of communication.* Oxford: Berg.

Horst, H. A., & Miller, D. (2012). *Digital Anthropology*. London: Bloomsbury.

Hui, L. H. (2020). A light burden: cultural discourse of light in Japan. *Asian Education and Development Studies, ahead-of-p.*

Ingold, T. (2000). Stop, look and listen! Vision, hearing and human movement. In T. Ingold (Ed.), *The Perception of the Environment: Essays on Livelihood, Dwelling and Skill* (pp. 243–287). London: Routledge.

Ingold, T. (2007). Materials against materiality. *Archaeological Dialogues, 14*(1), 1–16.

Ingold, T. (2011). *Being alive. Essays on movement, knowledge and description*. London: Routledge.

Ingold, T. (2012). The atmosphere. *Chiasmi International, 14*, 75–87.

Keane, W. (2005). Signs are not the garb of meaning: On the social analysis of material things. In D. Miller (Ed.), *Materiality* (pp. 182–205). London: Duke.

Knappett, C. (2004). The Affordances of Things: a Post-Gibsonian Perspective on the Relationality of Mind and Matter. In E. Demarrais, C. Gosden & C. Renfrew (Eds.), *Rethinking Materiality: The Engagement of Mind with the Material World* (pp. 43–51). Cambridge: McDonald Institute for Archaeological Research.

Knappett, C., & Malafouris, L. (2008). *Material Agency*. New York: Springer

Knox, H. (2021). Digital Devices: Knowing Material Culture. In T. Carroll, A. Walford & S. Walton (Eds.), *Lineages and Advancements in Material Culture Studies Perspectives from UCL Anthropology*. London & New York: Routledge.

Knox, H., & Nafus, D. (Eds.) (2018). *Ethnography for a data-saturated world*. Manchester: Manchester University Press.

Kopytoff, I. (1986). The Cultural biography of things: commoditization as process. In A. Appadurai (Ed.), *The Social Life of Things: Commodities in Cultural Perspective* (pp. 64–91). Cambridge: Cambridge University Press.

Küchler, S. (1987). Malangan: Art and Memory in a Melanesian Society. *Man, New Series, 22*(2), 238–255.

Küchler, S. (2008). Technological Materiality: Beyond the Dualist Paradigm. *Theory, Culture & Society*, *25*(1), 101–120.

Kumar, A. (2015). Cultures of lights. *Geoforum*, *65*, 59–68.

Larkin, B. (2013). The Politics and Poetics of Infrastructure. *Annual Review of Anthropology*, *42*, 327–347.

Latour, B. (2005). *Reassembling the Social*. Oxford: Oxford University Press.

Law, J., & Singleton, V. (2005). Object lessons. *Organization*, *12*(3), 331–355.

Lemonnier, P., & Pfaffenberger, B. (1989). Towards an Anthropology of Technology. *Man*, *24*, 526–527.

Lindstrøm, T. C. (2015). Agency 'in itself'. A discussion of inanimate, animal and human agency. *Archaeological Dialogues*, *22*(2), 207–238.

Lofgren, O. (1997). Scenes From a Troubled Marriage: Swedish Ethnology and Material Culture Studies. *Journal of Material Culture*, *2*, 95–113.

Lyons, K. M. (2020). *Vital decomposition. Soil practitioners and life politics*. Durham & London: Duke University Press.

Macdonald, S. (2006). Words in Stone?: Agency and Identity in a Nazi Landscape. *Journal of Material Culture*, *11*, 105–126.

McCormack, D. P. (2018). *Atmospheric Things*. London: Duke University Press.

Meier, J., Hasenöhrl, U., Krause, K., & Pottharst, M. (Eds.) (2014). *Urban lighting, light pollution and society*. London: Routledge.

Meyer, B. (2008). Materializing Religion. *Material Religion: The Journal of Objects, Art and Belief*, *4*, 227.

Miller, D. (1985). *Artefacts as categories: a study of ceramic variability in Central India*. Cambridge: Cambridge University Press.

Miller, D. (1987). *Material Culture and Mass Consumption*. Oxford: Blackwell.

Miller, D. (1993). *Unwrapping Christmas*. Oxford: Clarendon Press.

Miller, D. (1997). Why some things matter. In D. Miller (Ed.), *Why some things matter* (pp. 3–21). London: UCL Press.

Miller, D. (2001a). *Car cultures*. Oxford: Berg.

Miller, D. (Ed.) (2001b). *Home Possessions*. Oxford: Berg.

Miller, D. (2004). Making love in supermarkets. In A. Amin & N. Thrift (Eds.), *The Blackwell Cultural Economy Reader*. New Jersey: Wiley-Blackwell.

Miller, D. (2005). Materiality: An Introduction. In D. Miller (Ed.), *Materiality* (pp. 1–50). Durham: Duke University Press.

Miller, D. (2008). *Comfort of things*. Cambridge: Polity Press.

Miller, D. (2010). *Stuff*. Cambridge: Polity.

Miller, D. (2011). *Tales from Facebook*. Cambridge: Polity.

Miller, D., & Slater, D. (2000). *The Internet: an ethnographic approach*. London: Routledge.

Miller, D., & Tilley, C. (1996). Editorial. *Journal of Material Culture*, *1*(1), 5–14.

Mol, A. (2002). *The Body Multiple. Ontology in medical practice*. Durham & London: Duke University Press.

Morgan, D. (1998). *Visual piety: a history and theory of popular religious images*. Berkeley: University of California Press.

Munn, N. (1983). *The fame of GAwa*. Cambridge: Cambridge University Press.

Navaro-Yashin, Y. (2012). *The Make-Believe Space. Affective geography in a post war polity*. Durham & London: Duke University Press.

Nye, D. (2018). *American Illuminations. Urban Lighting, 1800–1920*. Cambridge, MA.: The MIT Press.

Papadopoulos, C., & Moyes, H. (Eds.) (2022). *Oxford Handbook of Light in Archaeology.* Oxford: Oxford University Press.

Petrova, S. (2018). Illuminating austerity: Lighting poverty as an agent and signifier of the Greek crisis. *European Urban and Regional Studies, 25*(4), 360–372.

Pfaffenberger, B. (1988). Fetishised Objects and Humanised Nature: Towards an Anthropology of Technology. *Man, 23*(2), 236–252.

Pink, S., Mackley, K. L., & Morosanu, R. (2015). Researching in atmospheres: video and the 'feel' of the mundane. *Visual Communication, 14*(3), 351–369.

Pink, S., & Sumartojo, S. (2018). The lit world: living with everyday urban automation. *Social and Cultural Geography, 19*(7).

Preucel, R. (2006). *Archaeological Semiotics.* New Jersey: Wiley-Blackwell.

Reed, A. (2007). 'Smuk is king': the action of cigarettes in a Papua New Guinea Prison. In A. Henare, M. Holbraad & S. Wastell (Eds.), *Thinking through Things. Theorising artefacts ethnographically.* New York: Routledge.

Rheinberger, H-J. (1997). *Toward a History of Epistemic Things: Synthesizing Proteins in the Test Tube.* Stanford: Stanford University Press.

Ribeiro, A. (2016). Against object agency. A counterreaction to Sørensen's 'Hammers and nails'. *Archaeological Dialogues, 23*(02), 229–235.

Rice, T. (2010). 'The hallmark of a doctor': The stethoscope and the making of medical identity. *Journal of Material Culture, 15*(3), 287–301.

Schepelern Johansen, B., & Schepelern Johansen, K. (2014). Heroin: From Drug to Ambivalent Medicine. *Culture, Medicine, and Psychiatry, 39*(1), 75–91.

Schivelbusch, W. (1988). *Disenchanted Night: The Industrialization of Light in the Nineteenth Century.* Berkeley: The University of California Press.

Schroer, S. A., & Schmitt, S. B. (Eds.) (2018). *Exploring Atmospheres Ethnographically.* London: Routledge.

Schulte-Römer, N. (2019). Research in the Dark. *Nature and Culture, 14*(2), 215–227.

Seaver, N. (2019). Captivating algorithms: Recommender systems as traps. *Journal of Material Culture, 24*(4), 421–436.

Shanks, M., & Tilley, C. (1987). Social Theory and Archaeology. Oxford: Polity Press

Shaw, R. (2014). Streetlighting in England and Wales: New technologies and uncertainty in the assemblage of streetlighting infrastructure. *Environment and Planning A, 46*(9).

Shaw, R. (2018). *The Nocturnal City.* London: Routledge.

Shove, E., Walker, G., & Brown, S. (2014). Material culture, room temperature and the social organisation of thermal energy. *Journal of Material Culture, 19*(2), 113–124.

Skuse, A. (2005). Enlivened objects: The social life, death and rebirth of radio as commodity in Afghanistan. *Journal of Material Culture, 10*(2), 123–137.

Sneath, D. (2009). Reading the signs by Lenin's light: Development, divination and metonymic fields in Mongolia. *Ethnos, 74*(1), 72–90.

Sørensen, T. F. (2016). Hammers and nails. A response to Lindstrøm and to Olsen and Witmore. *Archaeological Dialogues, 23*(01), 115–127.

Stallybrass, P. (1998). Marx's Coat. In P. Spyer (Ed.), *Border Fetishisms: Material Objects in Unstable Spaces* (pp. 183–207). London: Routledge.

Strang, V. (2005). Common Senses: Water, Sensory Experience and the Generation of Meaning. *Journal of Material Culture, 10*, 92–120.

Sumartojo, S., & Pink, S. (2018). Moving Through the Lit World: The Emergent Experience of Urban Paths. *Space and Culture, 21*(4).

Sumartojo, S., & Pink, S. (2019). *Atmospheres and the Experiential World*. London: Routledge.

Tilley, C. (1994). *A Phenomenology of Landscape: Places, Paths and Monuments*. Oxford: Berg.

Tilley, C. (2004). *The Materiality of Stone: Explorations in Landscape Phenomenology*. London: Routledge.

Tilley, C. (2007). Materiality in materials. *Archaeological Dialogues, 14*(1), 16–20.

Tilley, C., Keane, W., Küchler, S., Rowlands, M., & Spyer, P. (2006). *Handbook of Material Culture*. London: Sage.

Vannini, P. (2009). Introduction. In P. Vannini (Ed.), *Material Culture and technology in everyday life* (pp. 1–14). New York: Peter Lang.

Vannini, P., & Taggart, J. (2013). Domestic lighting and the off-grid quest for visual comfort. *Environment and Planning D: Society and Space, 31*(6), 1076–1090.

Walford, A. (2021). Data aesthetics. In T. Carroll, A. Walford & S. Walton (Eds.), *Lineages and Advancements in Material Culture Studies Perspectives from UCL Anthropology*. New York & London: Routledge.

Walsh, C. (2008). The mosquito: A repellent response. *Youth Justice, 8*(2), 122–133.

Winther, T. (2008). *The impact of electricity: development, desires and dilemmas*. New York & Oxford: Berghahn Books.

Woodward, I. D. (2007). *Understanding material culture*. London: Sage.

Wu, X. (2009). *Ein Jahrhundert Licht: eine technikethnologische Studie zur Beleuchtung im chinesischen ländlichen Alltag*. Wiesbaden: Otto Harrassowitz Verlag.

CHAPTER 5

Feminist Technoscience and New Imaginaries of Human Reproduction

Feminism

Merete Lie

A Sidestep on the Power of Materiality: The Gender of Things

Science and technology have long been associated with objectivity and hard facts. 'Do artefacts have gender?' is a question paraphrasing Langdon Winner's (1985) title 'Do artefacts have politics?' Technology has been characterised as frozen culture,[1] and as such it embeds not only particular designs but also social relations of power, most visible in the structures of workplaces. But, technology 'resists' a place among objects of culture and is generally understood as a product based on functionality and efficiency. In order to make visible that there is more to the technical objects we are using in everyday life than appears at first glance, we organised a set of exhibitions entitled 'The Gender of Things'.[2] The artefacts displayed were objects such as kitchen gear, watches, and bicycles. One aim was to reveal how everyday life is made up of gadgets that confirm the content of the categories of masculine and feminine and thus contribute to making them evident and self-confirming. Another

M. Lie (✉)
Norwegian University of Science and Technology, Trondheim, Norway
e-mail: merete.lie@ntnu.no

© The Author(s), under exclusive license to Springer Nature Singapore
Pte Ltd. 2022
M. H. Bruun et al. (eds.), *The Palgrave Handbook of the Anthropology of Technology*, https://doi.org/10.1007/978-981-16-7084-8_5

aim was to make visitors aware of the way artefacts are shaped with a user in mind, sometimes unacknowledged. Theoretically, leaning on the concept of 'script', this means that, 'like a film script, technical objects define a framework of action together with the actors and the space in which they are supposed to act' (Akrich 1992, p. 208). We wanted to draw attention to how technology is designed in ways that predict the interests, skills, and behaviour of future users and—by shifting the perspective—demonstrate that the artefacts accordingly distribute skills, agency, and responsibilities to the users. Yet we also wanted to communicate that technologies are open to different interpretations and usage, reflecting the ways in which they are domesticated by users. Thus, the second exhibition offered texts that were more open and questioning, presenting the artefacts as things 'to think with'. By participating in interpreting the technologies at the exhibition, visitors might experience for themselves that technologies are not 'given' but may be understood and used in various ways. Even more important was to emphasise how new technologies may be catalysts of cultural change. Hence, in a feminist technoscience perspective, 'gendered artifacts may constitute the glue that sometimes keeps gender relations stable, sometimes on the move' (Berg and Lie 1995, p. 346). In other words, while the materiality of technical artefacts has power over given user directions, these are not resistant to change.

The term 'feminist technoscience' includes an epistemology of the interweaving of science, technology, and cultural processes. A feminist perspective implies not taking gender as an established phenomenon that you can 'add and stir' but, rather, studying how the cultures of science and its products are gendered. Taking as a point of departure that gender is implicated within the practices and content of technoscience means radically questioning the production of science and technologies and looking out for the politics behind them. This aligns with science and technology studies (STS) in the study of science and technology in the making. Both STS and feminist studies include ethics and social justice as vital aspects of this making. Where STS has benefited from feminist studies is in questioning binaries, most essentially that of nature and culture, and maintaining more diversity in the recruitment to science and technology and more diversity in technical innovation (Subramaniam and Wiley 2017).[3] Over time, intersectional studies including distinctions of race, class, and sexualities have broadened feminist technoscience research. Feminist questions to technosciences concern what they will change and whether they are oppressive or liberating; thus, the aim of feminist studies is to get beyond 'science as usual' and look out for alternatives to explore.

STS and feminist theory are both interdisciplinary academic endeavours. Where does anthropology make its mark in the field of feminist technoscience? Ethnographic fieldwork has been influential in STS, particularly in laboratory studies where scientists are followed within their material and social relationships in the actions of doing science. For feminists, Sharon Traweek's anthropological study of the male-dominated field of nuclear physics is exemplary for the way in which it outlines a 'culture of no culture' (Traweek 1988). To the nuclear physicists, their work is one of pure science and based on technologies that give precise, numerical data—thus a field of science that claims to be cultureless. As ethnographic fieldwork became influential within STS, anthropologists studying science and technology realised that this often led away from bounded field sites (Downey and Dumit 1997). More often, the researcher is led from the laboratory to society at large, to activists and legislators, the media, and so on, as with the call of Actor-Network Theory to follow the actors (Latour 1987). In line with anthropological perspectives on the human scale (Barth 1978), this involves ethnographically following how laypeople make novel technoscience and everyday technologies meaningful in the contexts where they meet them (Lie and Sørensen 1996; Oudshoorn and Pinch 2003).

Thematically, the cultures of science, including their metaphors, symbols, and language, are important fields of study for anthropologists. Here, Emily Martin and colleagues have pioneered field work that dismantles the citadel of science by including sites and voices inside and outside of science on equal levels, resulting in complex patterns woven together of the various actors' theories on the reproductive body, illness, and the immune system (e.g. Martin 1987, 1994). When it comes to studies of the body and the biomedical sciences and their technologies, feminist anthropologists have been at the forefront. This is noticeable, for instance, in their central place in Downey and Dumit's (1997) *Cyborgs and Citadels. Anthropological Interventions in Emerging Sciences and Technologies* (with contributions from, for instance, Deborah Heath, Emily Martin, and Rayna Rapp) and the volume *Remaking Life and Death. Toward an Anthropology of the Biosciences* (Franklin and Lock 2003). Consequently, biomedical technology and changing cultural perceptions of reproduction and the body will be a central theme of this chapter.

For anthropology as a profession, feminist research on biosciences, particularly assisted reproduction, has meant a revitalisation of kinship studies (Carsten 2004). Kinship studies used to be a central part of the profession—studied as the organising principle of so-called stateless societies—today recognised in its multifaceted organising of social relations in contemporary societies worldwide. Starting out with reproduction as a central theme in any society, and one undergoing radical change, Marilyn Strathern and others revitalised classical anthropological theories by studying how people reflected on reproductive technologies within their idioms of kinship and filiation, biology and 'facts of nature', and ethics and religion (Franklin 1997, 2013; Ginsburg and Rapp 1995; Melhuus 2012; Strathern 1992a, b). Within this field of study, feminist anthropologists have to different degrees drawn on, and re-thought, anthropological classics (Strathern 1992a), broader cultural analysis (Martin 1987), Foucauldian analysis of biopolitics and power (Lock and Nguyen 2010), and postcolonialism (Vora 2013).

This chapter outlines the main ideas and concepts of feminist technoscience throughout its history as an interdisciplinary field. The field is broad, including studies of gender in science, the gendering of science and its institutions, and the gendering of technologies. In addition to this endeavour is an interlude on 'the gender of things', emphasising a materialist bend in studies of technology as well as the materialisation of gender in sociocultural environments. The chapter begins with a section on the development of feminist technoscience with its feminist critique of the epistemological foundations of science and its search for alternatives. This has primarily been the work of philosophers and science historians—who often have a background in the natural sciences—but with substantial contributions from anthropologists such as Emily Martin and Sharon Traweek. These studies have questioned doxas within the natural sciences, revealing how they are stabilised through language and metaphors, and particularly troubling the distinction of nature as a stable category and object of science. The aim of these studies is to provide better and more exact models of science, thereby contributing to changing science communities and the relationship of science to society and laypeople.

From this section on feminist technoscience as an interdisciplinary endeavour with a basis in philosophy of science, the chapter proceeds to examine some of the main contributions that have come from anthropology. This section has an emphasis on innovative studies of the biomedical sciences, including science's gaze on women's bodies in terms of changes in biomedicine and assisted reproduction. Assisted reproductive technologies (ARTs) are an exemplary case of the intertwining of gender and technoscience in the sense that the research rests on a basic gender difference in reproduction while at the same time challenging this very fact. Thus, ARTs have generated studies on the cultural meaning-making taking place when perceptions of human bodies, gender, and kinship are affected. Assisted reproduction comes with a naturalisation of technologies (as helping hands to natural processes) and a culturisation of the process of reproduction (after all, it is not only natural) pointing towards the age 'after nature' (Strathern 1992b; Franklin 2013).

The final part of the chapter presents a case that illustrates the lines of analysis addressed in this chapter: a study of medical visualising technologies used in assisted reproduction. Today, egg and sperm cells have become the protagonists in human reproduction, and same-sex as well as single parenthood has become feasible. For these biomedical processes to succeed, additional cultural meaning-making processes are necessary to reconfigure the process of releasing gametes from human bodies, reuniting them in the laboratories, and ultimately coming to understand this as a slightly modified version of 'the most natural process of all'.

The thread running through these sections is the scrutiny of the basic cultural distinction of nature and culture. Feminist anthropology of technoscience—with fieldwork in biomedicine and biotechnology—has studied the implosion of nature and culture in contrast to the basic ideas that keep them apart. The chapter will explore how feminist anthropology of the emerging biosciences empirically reveal ways in which we are living in and with new naturecultures.

FROM THE WOMAN QUESTION TO THE STUDY OF SCIENCE CULTURES

Among the themes of gender and technoscience, the underrepresentation of women in science has gained the most attention—underpinned as it is by structural discrimination, informal practices, and the masculine connotations of the field. A re-direction was proposed by philosopher Sandra Harding when she re-conceptualised the field, inverting it from 'the woman problem in science', that is, the missing women, to *The Science Question in Feminism* (1986). Harding argued for a change in the ontology and epistemology of science with the aim of releasing the sciences from a history in the service of sexist, racist, homophobic, and classist social projects (Harding 1986, p. 21). This project required a new understanding of subjectivity and objectivity, of reason as antithetical to emotions, and the scientist as the privileged knowing subject. What was needed was a re-direction of attention from women to the content, politics, and power games of science. Anthropologists (and others) have carried out such studies through ethnographic fieldwork among scientists, observing their interactions in daily work life, or what in STS has been labelled 'laboratory studies'.

A pioneer in the field of feminist technoscience is Evelyn Fox Keller, who was trained as a physicist but devoted her academic life to the history and philosophy of science, with a particular focus on gender.[4] Her research on gender in science was founded on the realisation that nature, as the object of science, is perceived in feminine terms. How to become a scientist when you in fact are perceived as the object to be 'discovered, unveiled and penetrated' by the scientific gaze? Fox Keller's work has revealed the impact of deeply rooted tropes and metaphors of science, like those mentioned above, while her biography of the early geneticist and Nobel Prize winner Barbara McClintock represents one way of searching for, doing, and seeing science differently. With the title, *A Feeling for the Organism*, Fox Keller explores how McClintock re-described genetics, moving it from an understanding of the linear and deterministic to one of the processual and responsive (Keller 1983).

Anthropologist Emily Martin explores the cultures of science by drawing three different images: the citadel, the rhizome, and the string figure (Martin 1998). The traditional image of science as a citadel, securely closed off from laypeople's knowledge, is easily discarded in light of the many examples of leakages in both directions: common knowledge affects scientists' paths to knowledge, and science catalyses new ways of reasoning about nature, bodies, and society. The image of the rhizome (from Deleuze 1993) depicts science as more inventive, like a rhizome whose growth is nonlinear and unpredictive of its directions and the connections made. Still, the third image, the game of cat's cradle (from Haraway 1994), is the one that best catches the processual way of doing science. A string figure is taken over from one pair of hands to the next and transformed into new figures along the way. The metaphor of science as string figures depicts science as an ensemble of culturally informed, collaborative practices. The metaphor includes practice, process, and collaboration, and points out the unexpected, fractured, moving, and changing processes of science.

In these moves towards new images of science, a vital reconceptualisation of science as well as technology was launched by historian of science Donna Haraway's *Cyborg Manifesto* (1991). As a manifesto, it urged feminists to turn their attention to so-called hard science and peak technology in order not to leave these vital matters in the hands of men. Haraway asked for responsibility in a time when technology was implicated in the lives of everyone, all being hybrids of bios and techne. The cyborg has been a figure with a broad and lasting impact in feminist research. In the beginning, it was mainly an inspiration for studies of technology, but over time its scope has broadened to science, technology, and nature. In a more recent volume (Haraway 2016), ecology is more urgent than technology. Her call is to realise the connections between all sorts of species, making them kin with 'tentacular thinking'. 'Making-with' as well as 'thinking-with' the non-human is the strategy for alternative futures living on a damaged or troubled planet.[5]

The notion of 'figurations' is a key concept in Haraway's cultural studies of technoscience. It represents a way of inventing new modes of describing both present and future, either by new inventions or by revitalising old figures such as the cyborg.[6] Haraway's figures are inclusive and transgress set borders, thus challenging all sorts of dichotomies grounded in the fundamental one of nature and culture. As she observes, 'Figures must involve at least some kind of displacement that can trouble identifications and certainties' (Haraway 1997, p. 11). The aim is to trigger associations and emotions and to acknowledge the potential for change in the emerging technosciences. Figuration is an illustration of her analytical approach of material-semiotics, which, again, aims to untie a dichotomy and take materiality seriously as (also) semiotics.

The notion of new materialism often refers to feminist theorist Karen Barad (2007) and her analytical approach to materiality. It is particularly her concept of 'intra-action' that has been taken up by feminist researchers. The notion of the co-production of gender, science, and technology was a well-established analytical tool but was criticised by Barad for presupposing prior, independent, identifiable entities. Her posthuman notion of agency displaces the priority of humans, teleology, and stabilisation. Instead, intra-action draws attention to how matter comes into being through mutual entanglements; a figure exemplifying this theory is the way ultrasound technology produces matter perceived as a foetus but which is actually an object that comes into being only through an agential intra-action with technology (Barad 2007).[7]

The interdisciplinary endeavours have provided some common perspectives and conceptualisations of feminist technoscience studies likewise employed by anthropologists. Epistemologically, feminist science studies have explored notions of objectivity and understandings of nature as objects of science. In these efforts, intersectional perspectives of differentiation, whether based on race, gender, or sexualities, have uncovered science cultures' tacit models of unquestionable natural facts. Here, Critical Race Studies have contributed importantly with studies of the use of genetic tests as proof of biological sameness and difference and how DNA testing has affected a genomic articulation of identity (Benjamin 2016; Reardon and TallBear 2012).

Over time, feminist technoscience studies have constituted a continuous effort against naturalisation by opening the black boxes of science of established natural facts. Empirically, this has paved the way for studies of the naturecultures of gendered bodies and human reproduction.

FEMINIST ANTHROPOLOGY OF BIOMEDICINE AND REPRODUCTION

The biomedical sciences have been of special interest to feminist anthropologists, on a par with the feminist critique of a long tradition of biomedicine being in the hands of men and women serving as objects of study and therapy. To this end, Emily Martin's classic study entitled *The Woman in the Body* (1987), based on multi-sited fieldwork, explored the plurality of understandings of women's bodies and the process of reproduction. A strength of the study is that it does not only expose the ways the body is perceived in bioscience in contrast to among laypeople but also contrasts the understanding of bodies and reproduction among women across differences of race, class, and age. Martin pointed out how scientific metaphors of reproduction are based on those of production; hence the enthusiasm for the enormous production of sperm versus the slow production of eggs and the description of menstruation as the body's 'failure' to conceive. The gendered language in medical textbooks is vividly presented as a story of conception in which the sperm is active and competitive while the egg lies modestly in waiting (Martin 1991). She did find, however, research that acknowledges a more active role for the egg cell, prompting the question of why researchers do not use a more dynamic and interactive model. Most important is the questioning of this use of gendered cultural models at all, the danger lying in the ways they appear so 'natural' in biomedicine. Thus, the feminist challenge is to 'wake up the sleeping metaphors' hidden in the gendered language of biomedicine about fertility, menstruation, and menopause (Martin 1991, p. 501).

Assisted reproductive technologies have provided a new lens through which to examine biology versus cultural understandings of reproduction, as well as a vital source of new angles and new conceptualisations. This is an emerging field in which anthropological studies have laid the groundwork by questioning the givenness of 'natural facts' and 'the facts of life', and asking how new technologies for the reproduction of life reconfigure the very conception of the human (Strathern 1992b; Franklin 2013). Sarah Franklin (1997) has provided a thorough scrutiny of the way in which anthropologists have interpreted and discussed conception as a universal natural fact with varying cultural interpretations.[8] David Schneider's (1968) book on American kinship attempts to dissolve this nature/culture dichotomy by identifying a symbolic structure based on biological reproduction. Schneider posed heterosexual intercourse as a core symbol in American culture, a symbol of the creation of a 'blood relationship'. Consequently, the social relationship of marriage is transformed and understood as a biological relationship through the creation of a child. Schneider's study was important within a general critique of anthropological studies of kinship as embedded in folk theories of reproduction in the West—understood as natural facts. Feminist researchers added to this critique by pointing out how gender has been an implicit and tacit core element in the concepts and analyses of kinship (e.g. Yanagisako and Delaney 1995). Today, assisted reproductive technologies, and the life sciences more generally, have paved the way for 'culturing nature' and radically confusing distinctions of nature and culture. Franklin (2013) presents the new human as 'relatively biological' and asks how genetic engineering and synthetic biology make for a porous border between life and non-life.

Field studies of fertility clinics have become a rich empirical field for exploration of new understandings of the biological process of reproduction and 'relatively biological' kinship. Who are the mother and father of a child when the gametes may be donated and the person who gives birth may not be genetically related to the baby? As Charis Thompson (2005) notes, reproduction not only makes babies but also makes parents. Meanwhile, the innovative concept of ontological choreography captures the dynamics by which ontologically different matters are coordinated in the lab: science and technology, kinship and emotions, legal, political, and financial matters—all shaped together in new ways in the material structure of labs and clinics. The choreography includes a naturalisation strategy, resulting in a family with only one pair of parents to their offspring, with just a little helping hand in the natural processes. The choreography assigns appropriate gender roles to the intended parents as a repairment of their failed reproduction, which is associated with a failure of femininity and masculinity. At the same time, new possibilities for same-sex parenthood pose another challenge to traditional conceptions of kinship and represent fertile ground for wider studies of the notions of kinship, filiation, families, and community (Golombok 2018; Smietana 2017).

Anthropological fieldwork has also been important in studies of the global assemblages of egg, sperm, and wombs in a borderless fertility industry (e.g.

Almeling 2011; Inhorn 2003, 2012; Lie and Lykke 2017). Surrogacy has particularly attracted attention, mainly from a North-South perspective of commissioning parents from the North and surrogates from the South (e.g. Majumdar 2017; Pande 2010).[9] In the global traffic of reproduction, race, class, and sexuality position people differently. Vora and Iyengar (2017) link the North-South trade of surrogacy to a history of commodification of human bodies in the slave trade. The trade in gametes is likewise highly racialised, with fertility clinics offering a pay-scale ranging from high to low based on racial characteristics, which, as Deomampo (2019) points out, reproduces not only a racial hierarchy but, more basically, the idea of race as a biological and genetically inheritable fact.

The global exchange that today includes traffic in organs, embryos, eggs, and sperm has triggered novel approaches whereby ontologically different matters like money, ethics, bodies, and religions demand multi-sited and multi-perspectival analyses (e.g. Scheper-Hughes and Wacquant 2002). A particular anthropological focus in the matters of bodies, biomedicine, and the new life sciences has been the cultural production of meaning, including ways in which power relations affect this meaning-making and the need for intersectional analyses of race, class, and unequal global relations. How are new biotechnologies included in perceptions of functions and processes of human bodies? How can new processes of reproduction, filiation, and kinship be conceptualised? And what changes are needed in theories of globalisation and North-South relations when including traffic in the material substances of the body?

Thus, anthropologists study how the new biosciences are contributing to a radical troubling of nature-culture distinctions of gender as well as race, but also draw attention to how what is traditionally perceived as nature still functions as a model for understanding the emerging biosciences and human reproduction.

A FEMINIST TECHNOSCIENCE STUDY OF MEDICAL IMAGING TECHNOLOGIES

Within science studies, the development of medical visualisation technologies has attracted anthropologists to study the ways in which biological matter is transformed to appear on a screen and the effects of rendering the body on a molecular scale (Dumit 2004; Kelly 2008; Myers 2015a). The progress of medical visualisation technologies has been one of the prerequisites for the rapid development of assisted reproduction. In order to perform practices such as retrieving egg cells and uniting egg and sperm outside of the body, the gametes must be visible. As a result, photo-like depictions of egg and sperm cells have become available not only in the fertility clinics, but to everyone, on the Internet and media in general. Such micrographs are, however, constructions based on digital data from microscopy, whereas the real matter depicted is too tiny to be visible to the eye—in line with Barad's concept of agential intra-action referred to earlier.

The new practices, tools, and techniques used in science visualisation overlap with those used in art, popular culture, and photography generally. Science imaging builds on traditions from photography and other forms of depictions in art which contribute to animating them and making them familiar and recognisable (Kemp 2006; Jones and Galison 1998). Leaning on the authority of science, images of the interior body are given credibility as real depictions of the natural body and its miniscule parts, supported by popular science's invitations to take a look inside the body.

Previously, the attention of the public has been captured by images of the human foetus, seemingly within the womb, such as those produced by the Swedish photographer Lennart Nilsson from the 1960s onwards (Nilsson and Hamberger 1990). Feminist research has pointed out that the use of ultrasound encouraged a cultural imaginary of the foetus as a separate individual dissociated from the female body (Duden 1993). Rapid development within medical visualisation technologies has spurred this process whereby 3D technology and colours make depictions of the foetus look like a baby, that is, an independent being from a very early stage of growing within the womb.

Norwegian anthropologist Tord Larsen (2010) has identified a general social trend in which something inchoate emerges as a thing, a unit, or a category resulting in externalisation and autonomisation. He calls these processes acts of *entification* (from the Latin word *ens*, literally 'something being') whereby social phenomena increasingly get a name, a label, often in terms of a new diagnosis. 'That which bears no essential relation to our being, can be *outsourced*, managed by others and further removed from ourselves in a continuous process of entification' (Larsen 2010, p. 156).

Here, I analyse the contribution of the phenomenon of 'cellular portraits' to a process of entification in which something inchoate gains cultural significance and materialises as an autonomous entity. My argument is that the distribution of images of egg and sperm cells is conducive to a cultural process whereby the imaginary of human reproduction is shifting from heterosexual intercourse to the unification of two cells. Moreover, this contributes to a domestication process that presents 'un-assisted' and assisted reproduction as similar and normal procedures to get pregnant (Lie 2015).

With new visualisation techniques, cellular images have left the laboratories and become available in colourful versions on the internet, in popular science magazines, and in the media more broadly, where they are used as illustrations to articles on medical developments. The small samples presented below are produced by gynaecologist and photographer Yorgos Nikas, who produces visual material for fertility clinics but also reworks science images for commercial photo galleries.

Figure 5.1 is an image of an egg cell. It is perfectly circular, yellow in colour, and surrounded by the *corona radiata*, here depicted as particularly radiant, that the sperm cells must pass in order to penetrate the egg cell. The colours and radiance are, however, products of photo techniques and the preparation of the sample in the laboratory.

Figure 5.2 is an illustration of the way fertilisation takes place. The image apparently depicts 'real life' at the moment when sperm cells are in the process of penetrating the egg cell. In this illustration, the 'egg' is the yellow colour of an egg yolk whereas the sperm cells have the masculine tagging of blue. The surface of the egg cell seems apt for penetration with its many holes. What has been taken away in this image, however, are the *cumulus cells* and the *corona radiata* that surrounds the egg cell, as illustrated in Figs. 5.1 and 5.3.

As one can see from this small sample of images, with the use of microscope and photography techniques the same type of cell can be depicted in very different ways. It is a choice which colours to stain the sample, what matters to detach, and what matter to draw attention to. After lengthy preparation of samples, a single cell can be identified by employing a scanning electron microscope and will then reappear in the media as a micrograph. The colours,

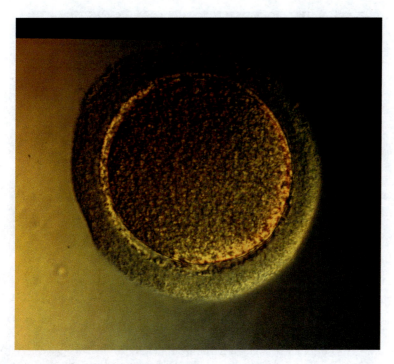

Fig. 5.1   Egg cell. (Credit: Yorgos Nikas)

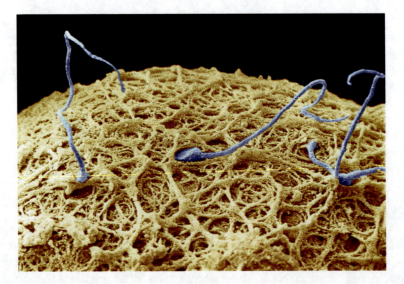

Fig. 5.2   Sperm fertilising egg. (Credit: Yorgos Nikas)

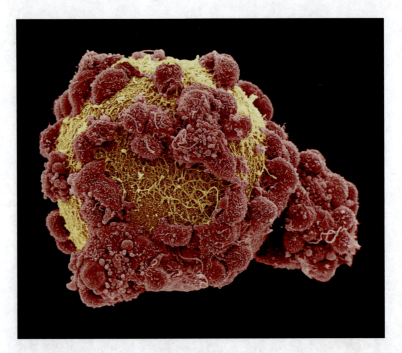

Fig. 5.3   A false colour scanning electron micrograph of a human egg cell (gold) sur-rounded by cumulus cells (orange). Cumulus cells are specialised cells that nourish the large egg cell while it grows in the ovarian follicle. (Credit: Yorgos Nikas)

background, size, and cropping are chosen by the photographer. In popular science, such images are often accompanied by humorous texts. Sometimes, the captions indicate that the cells are moving, even acting, and assign them human-like characteristics. The attribution of power, speed, and motivation to the sperm cells in contrast to the size, weight, and immobility of the egg cells contributes to anthropomorphising through associations with the well-known story of 'boy meets girl'—exactly in accordance with what Emily Martin found in her analysis of the presentation of reproduction in medical textbooks (Martin 1991). The way cell images individualise the cells and assign them particular and gendered qualities is reflected in the way people speak about them, as well as in the political debates of assisted reproduction where cells have taken the leading roles as stand-ins for men and women (Spilker and Lie 2007).

Cell images are used in popular science and the media generally, to illustrate basic research, medical practice, and illnesses such as cancer and Alzheimer's disease, thus contributing to the inclusion of cells in cultural imaginaries of the body. Cell images blur the distinctions between science, fantasy, and emotions, with even the small sample of images above revealing how the processes taking place inside the body are presented both as transparent and as a wonder hard to imagine. Visualisation is a means of cultural transformation whereby cells are transformed from an abstract concept of science into identifiable material objects. Donna Haraway's concept of material-semiotics points out that the products of science are only seemingly a result of the technical apparatus. The materialisation process is a result of the combination of social, cultural, and technical processes in which objects gain a shape recognisable within the cultural repertoire of a particular cultural context. The images of egg and sperm cells illustrate, however, the degree to which depictions of one and the same type of cell can vary; they also demonstrate the role played in the depictions by aesthetic norms and strategies which contribute to the magic surrounding egg and sperm cells and their potentiality for new life. The magic is strengthened by lifting the cells out of context, depicting them against a neutral background, and thereby presenting them as autonomous. This parallels other processes of entification wherein previously abstract and complex phenomena are made to appear detached and objectified.

In this material and cultural transformation, cells shift from elements in a theory of the composition of organic material to reappear as autonomous, material entities. The transformation serves as one precondition for making gametes commodities for research laboratories and a global fertility industry, reproducing them as private property that one can freeze for later use or donate to a global market. Human cells, more generally, are transformed into material entities to be used independently of their bodily origin parallel to other developments within biotechnical science, such as the culturing of cell lines for the production of new organs.

CONCLUSION

Coming back to key feminist questions about technosciences: are they liberating, helpful, women-friendly? These are difficult to answer given the diversity of technologies. Technology can be hero or villain, helpful or destructive, even both (cf. Lie and Sørensen 1996). Household technologies such as washing machines and dishwashers have been welcomed. This was actually what Ruth Schwartz Cowan asked for in her historical study of household technologies—why do we have technologies to send men to the moon whereas we do not have technologies to take care of the housework? (Cowan 1983). The answer was that technologies are social products embedded in social and cultural traditions; thus, more than technical change was needed as long as femininity was closely associated with home and hearth.

The biosciences marked a radical turn in technoscience by transgressing the border of bios and techne, and feminist research on biomedicine, biotechnologies, and reproduction has revitalised classical anthropological debates on the nature-culture distinction (Franklin et al. 2000; Franklin and Lock 2003; Lock 2013). On the one hand, dichotomous perceptions of nature and culture are destabilised by novel biosciences interfering with what was previously perceived as natural processes; on the other, the belief that genes are the ultimate proof of 'who you are' in terms of gender, ancestry, and race may work in the opposite direction. A call is therefore out for anthropologists to do (more) research on bioscience, in the anthropological vein of contextualising it in the specific historical, socio/political, and environmental realities of lived experience (Lock 2013, p. 291). This is exactly where feminist technoscience has proved its vitality: challenging non-contextual understandings of science and scrutinising tacit perceptions of nature and natural processes that underpin such research, as in the 'culture of no culture'.

In terms of grasping the new inventions and expanding the scope for new perspectives, the field of bioart is promising and demonstrates how novel technosciences are good to think with. Bioartists are intervening in science by using the technologies and lab procedures of science to create art (e.g. Myers 2015b; da Costa and Kavita 2008): experimenting with nature, as in the work below, with life processes and reproduction and, thereby, questioning cultural perceptions of what a natural fact and a natural process are and what they might be. To end with one mind-opening example, I have chosen the work of Japanese artist Ai Hasegawa, *I Wanna Deliver a Dolphin*, with her own text to follow. This work challenges the naturalness of human reproduction by linking reproduction to matters of other cultural categories, such as food and the extinction of endangered species, and by dissolving the boundary between humans and other creatures. In such ways bioart may transgress the limits of science and point out alternative futures—thus widening the scope of technoscience and feminist future visions (Fig. 5.4).

This project approaches the problem of human reproduction in an age of overcrowding, overdevelopment, and environmental crisis. With potential

Fig. 5.4 *I Wanna Deliver a Dolphin*. (Credit: Ai Hasegawa)

food shortages and a population of nearly seven billion people, would a woman consider incubating and giving birth to an endangered species such as a shark, tuna, or dolphin? This project introduces the argument for giving birth to our food to satisfy our demands for nutrition and childbirth and discusses some of the technical details of how this might be possible.[10]

Notes

1. Historian of technology, David Noble, presented technology as 'frozen fragments of human and social endeavour' in Noble 1986, *Forces of Production: A Social History of Industrial Automation*. New York: Oxford University Press.
2. This exhibition was firstly designed and displayed in The Netherlands; later a different version was made in Norway. See Oudshoorn et al. (2002) and Lie (2010).
3. The reference is to the editorial of a special issue of the journal *Catalyst*. Since 2014 the field of feminist technoscience has an academic journal: *Catalyst. Feminism, Theory, Technoscience*.
4. Of her many books, for example, the edited volume, with Helen Longino, *Feminism and Science* (Keller and Longino 1996).
5. See also Anna Tsing et al. (2017). *Arts of Living on a Damaged Planet*.
6. Cyborg is a short term for cybernetic and organism, launched in 1960.

7. Barad's radical ontoepistemology, based in examples from physics, has been embraced as well as criticised by feminist scholars. For critique, see, for example, a summing up in Braunmühl (2018).
8. The point of departure is the 'virgin birth debate' following Malinowski's claim that Australian aborigines as well as Trobriand Islanders were ignorant of biological paternity. This laid the ground for a dual model of kinship with, on the one hand, kinship as social organisation and, on the other, kinship as biological facts, with the two not necessarily overlapping.
9. A different anthropological approach is Teman's (2010) study from Israel of the bodily and relational experience of being a surrogate.
10. https://aihasegawa.info/i-wanna-deliver-a-dolphin. Accessed 20 September 2020.

References

Akrich, M. (1992). The de-scription of technical objects. In W. Bijker & J. Law (Eds.), *Shaping technology/building society: Studies in sociotechnical change* (pp. 205–244). Cambridge, MA: The MIT Press.

Almeling, R. (2011). *Sex cells: The medical market for eggs and sperm*. Berkeley: University of California Press.

Barad, K. (2007). *Meeting the universe halfway: Quantum physics and the entanglement of matter and meaning*. Durham: Duke University Press.

Barth, F. (1978). *Scale and social organization*. Oslo: Scandinavian University Press

Benjamin, R. (2016). Catching our breath: Critical race STS and the carceral imagination. *Engaging Science, Technology, and Society, 2*, 145–156.

Berg, A-J., & Lie, M. (1995). Feminism and constructivism: Do artifacts have gender? *Science, Technology & Human Values, 20*(3), 332–351.

Braunmühl, C. (2018). Beyond hierarchical oppositions: A feminist critique of Karen Barad's agential realism. *Feminist Theory, 19*(2), 223–240.

Carsten, J. (2004). *After kinship*. Cambridge: Cambridge University Press.

da Costa, B., & Kavita, P. (2008). *Tactical biopolitics: Art, activism, and technoscience*. Cambridge, MA: The MIT Press.

Cowan, R. S. (1983). *More work for mother: The ironies of household technology from the open hearth to the microwave*. London: Free Association Books.

Deleuze, G. (1993). Rhizome versus trees. In C. V. Boundas (Ed.), *The Deleuze reader* (pp. 27–36). New York: Columbia University Press.

Deomampo, D. (2019) Racialized commodities: Race and value in human egg donation. *Medical Anthropology, 38*(7), 620–633.

Downey, G. L., & Dumit, J. (1997). *Cyborgs and citadels. Anthropological interventions in emerging sciences and technologies*. Santa Fe: School of American Research Press.

Duden, B. (1993). *Disembodying women*. Cambridge, MA and London: Harvard University Press.

Dumit, J. (2004). *Picturing personhood: Brain scans and biomedical identity*. Princeton: Princeton University Press.

Franklin, S. (1997). *Embodied progress. A cultural account of assisted conception*. London and New York: Routledge.

Franklin, S. (2013). *Biological relatives. IVF, stem cells, and the future of kinship*. Durham and London: Duke University Press.

Franklin, S., & Lock, M. (2003). *Remaking life and death. Toward an anthropology of the biosciences*. Santa Fe: School for Advanced Research Press.

Franklin, S., Lury, C., & Stacey, J. (2000). *Global nature, global culture*. London: Sage.

Ginsburg, F. D., & Rapp, R. (Eds.) (1995). *Conceiving the new world order. The global politics of reproduction*. Berkeley: University of California Press.

Golombok, S. (2018). Research on assisted reproduction families: A historical perspective. In G. Kovacs, P. Brinsden & A. DeCherney (Eds.), *In vitro fertilization and assisted reproduction: A history* (pp. 240–247). Cambridge: Cambridge University Press.

Haraway, D. (1991 [1985]). A cyborg manifesto. In *Simians, cyborgs, and women: The reinvention of nature* (pp. 149–182). London: Free Association Books.

Haraway, D. (1994). A game of cat's cradle: Science studies, feminist theory, cultural studies. *Configurations, 2*(1), 59–71.

Haraway, D. (1997). *Modest_Witness@Second_Millenium. Feminism and technoscience*. New York and London: Routledge.

Haraway, D. (2016). *Staying with the trouble. Making kin in the Chthulucene*. Durham and London: Duke University Press.

Harding, S. (1986). *The science question in feminism*. Ithaca and London: Cornell University Press.

Inhorn, M. C. (2003). *Local babies, global science: Gender, religion, and In Vitro fertilization in Egypt*. New York and London: Routledge.

Inhorn, M. (2012) *Islam and assisted reproductive technologies: Sunni and Shia perspectives*. New York and Oxford: Berghahn.

Jones, C. A., & Galison, P. (1998). *Picturing science. Producing art*. New York and London: Routledge.

Keller, E. F. (1983). *A feeling for the organism. The life and work of Barbara McClintock*. San Francisco: W.H. Freeman.

Keller, E. F., & Longino, H. (Eds.) (1996). *Feminism and science*. Oxford: Oxford University Press.

Kelly, J. (2008). *Magnetic appeal: MRI and the myth of transparency*. Ithaca, NY: Cornell University Press.

Kemp, M. (2006). *Seen/unseen: Art, science and intuition from Leonardo to the Hubble telescope*. Oxford: Oxford University Press.

Larsen, T. (2010). Acts of entification. The emergence of thinghood in social life. In N. Rapport (Ed.), *Human nature as capacity. Transcending discourse and classification* (pp. 154–178). New York and Oxford: Berghahn.

Latour, B. (1987) *Science in action: How to follow scientists and engineers through society*. Milton Keynes: Open University Press.

Lie, M. (2010). Tingenes kjønn. En utstilling av gjenstander og teknologi (The gender of things. An exhibition of objects and technologies). In A. B. Amundsen & B. Rogan (Eds.), *Samling og museum. Kapitler av museenes historie, praksis og ideologi* (pp. 151–166). Oslo: Novus.

Lie, M. (2015). Reproduction inside/outside. Medical imaging and the domestication of assisted reproductive technologies. *European Journal of Women's Studies, 22*(1), 53–69.

Lie, M., & Lykke, N. (2017). *Assisted reproduction across borders. Feminist perspectives on normalizations, disruptions and transmissions*. London and New York: Routledge.

Lie, M., & Sørensen, K. H. (Eds.) (1996). *Making technology our own? Domesticating technology into everyday life*. Oslo: Scandinavian University Press.

Lock, M. (2013). The epigenome and nature/nurture reunification: A challenge for anthropology. *Medical Anthropology, 32*(4), 291–308.

Lock, M., & Nguyen, V-K. (2010). *An anthropology of biomedicine*. Chichester: Wiley-Blackwell.

Majumdar, A. (2017). *Transnational commercial surrogacy and the (un)making of kin in India*. Oxford: Oxford University Press.

Martin, E. (1987). *The woman in the body. A cultural analysis of reproduction*. Boston: Beacon Press.

Martin, E. (1991). The egg and the sperm. How science has constructed a romance based on stereotypical male-female roles. *Signs: Journal of Women in Culture and Society, 16*(3), 485–501.

Martin, E. (1994). *Flexible bodies: Tracking immunity in American culture from the days of polio to the age of AIDS*. Boston: Beacon Press.

Martin, E. (1998). Anthropology and the cultural study of science. *Science, Technology & Human Values, 23*(1), 24–44.

Melhuus, M. (2012). *Problems of conception. Issues of law, biotechnology, individuals and kinship*. New York and Oxford: Berghahn.

Myers, N. (2015). *Rendering life molecular: Models, modelers, and excitable matter*. Durham and London: Duke University Press.

Myers, W. (2015). *Bio art. Altered realities*. New York: Thames & Hudson.

Nilsson, L., & Hamberger, L. (1990 [1965]). *A child is born* (4th edition). London: Faber & Faber.

Oudshoorn, N., & Pinch, T. (2003). *How users matter. The co-construction of users and technology*. Cambridge, MA: The MIT Press.

Oudshoorn, N., Sætnan, A. R., & Lie, M. (2002). On gender and things. Reflections on an exhibition of gendered artifacts. *Womens' Studies International Forum, 25*(4), 471–483.

Pande, A. (2010). Commercial surrogacy in India: Manufacturing a perfect mother-worker. *Signs: Journal of Women in Culture and Society, 35*(4), 969–992.

Reardon, J., & TallBear, K. (2012). "Your DNA is *our* history". Genomics, anthropology, and the construction of whiteness as property. *Current Anthropology, 53*(Supplement 5), 233–245.

Scheper-Hughes, N., & Wacquant, L.J.D. (Eds.) (2002). *Commodifying bodies*. London: Sage.

Schneider, D. (1968). *American kinship. A cultural account*. Englewood Cliffs, NJ: Prentice-Hall.

Smietana, M. (2017). "Families like we'd always known"? Spanish gay fathers' normalization narratives in transnational surrogacy. In M. Lie & N. Lykke (Eds.), *Assisted reproduction across borders. Feminist perspectives on normalizations, disruptions and transmissions* (pp. 49–60). London and New York: Routledge.

Spilker, K., & Lie, M. (2007). Gender and bioethics intertwined—Egg donation within the context of equal opportunities. *European Journal of Women's Studies, 14*(4), 327–340.

Strathern, M. (1992a). *Reproducing the future: Essays on anthropology, kinship and the new reproductive technologies*. Manchester: Manchester University Press.

Strathern, M. (1992b). *After nature: English kinship in the late twentieth century*. Cambridge: Cambridge University Press.

Subramaniam, B., & Wiley, A. (2017). Introduction: Feminism's sciences. *Catalyst. Feminism, Theory, Technoscience, 3*(1), 1–23.

Teman, E. (2010). *Birthing a mother. The surrogate body and the pregnant self.* University of California Press.

Thompson, C. (2005). *Making parents: The ontological choreography of reproductive technologies.* Cambridge, MA: The MIT Press.

Traweek, S. (1988). *Beamtimes and lifetimes. The world of high energy physicists.* Cambridge, MA: Harvard University Press.

Tsing, A. L., Swanson, H. A., Gan, E., & Bubandt, N. (Eds.) (2017). *Arts of living on a damaged planet.* Minneapolis: University of Minnesota Press.

Vora, K. (2013). Potential, risk, and return in transnational Indian gestational surrogacy. *Current Anthropology, 54*(S7), 97–106.

Vora, K., & Iyengar, M. M. (2017). Citizen, subject, property: Indian surrogacy and the global fertility market. In M. Lie & N. Lykke (Eds.), *Assisted reproduction across borders. Feminist perspectives on normalizations, disruptions and transmissions* (pp. 25–36). London and New York: Routledge.

Winner, L. (1985). Do artifacts have politics? In D. MacKenzie & J. Wajcman (Eds.), *The social shaping of technology* (pp. 26–38). Milton Keynes: Open University Press.

Yanagisako, S., & Delaney, C. (1995). *Naturalizing power: Essays in feminist cultural analysis.* New York: Routledge.

CHAPTER 6

Assemblage Ethnography: Configurations Across Scales, Sites, and Practices

Post-Structuralism

Ayo Wahlberg

The question of how human societies are organised has been central to the discipline of anthropology from its very beginnings in the nineteenth century:

> The anthropologist compares Man to the other animals in order to separate the subject of his study from all of the surrounding subjects. ... Man is programmed for social life, which he ultimately achieves by making his own history ... [shaped by] the reasoned consistency with which Man works at constructing a society. (Firmin 2000[1885], p. 12, p. 7)

Indeed, one of the distinguishing characteristics of *anthropos*, as Fei Xiaotong observed in his examination of the rural foundations of Chinese society, is that 'with frequent and repeated interaction occurring over a long period of time ... distinctive patterns of human relationships form. ... All social groups are organized in some fashion' (Fei 1992[1947], pp. 41–42, p. 80; see also 1953). For Fei, it was 'the soil' and the technologies used to tend to it that were foundational for the patterns of social life observable in rural China as 'people live together in the same place so that they can be close to their fields ... [and] where irrigation is required, people must work together as a group' (1992[1947], p. 40; cf. Wittfogel 1957). Across the Pacific waters, on Aotearoa (New Zealand), Mākereti argued that it was patterns related to descendants

A. Wahlberg (✉)
Department of Anthropology, University of Copenhagen, Copenhagen, Denmark
e-mail: ayo.wahlberg@anthro.ku.dk

© The Author(s), under exclusive license to Springer Nature Singapore Pte Ltd. 2022
M. H. Bruun et al. (eds.), *The Palgrave Handbook of the Anthropology of Technology*, https://doi.org/10.1007/978-981-16-7084-8_6

and ancestors that were fundamental for a 'communal' Maori society where 'every Maori … knew his or her genealogy and exact relationship to every relative' and 'every member of the community, no matter what his rank, joined in the work which was to be done' (Makereti 1938, pp. 37–38). Also within this communal society, technologies were central to social organisation as 'self-controlled' family units were responsible for daily tasks that included 'collecting of firewood, preparing of the *hangi* (ovens), the making of baskets and plates, cloaks, and floor-mats' while they also 'used the *ko* (digging stick) in agriculture, felled trees and built houses and canoes, made paddles and weapons, nets, eel-baskets, etc., and did the hunting, fishing, and snaring' (Makereti 1938, p. 38).

As such, Firmin's, Mākereti's, and Fei's studies, alongside numerous cotemporaneous twentieth-century ethnographic studies from different parts of the world (Malinowski 1922; Fortes and Evans-Pritchard 1940; Radcliffe-Brown and Forde 1950), were empirically concerned with the technologically underpinned construction of human societies in terms of distinctive patterns—most often characterised as *systems*—of subsistence, kinship, healing, belief, economic exchange, political authority, and more. In China, Fei contrasted a rural 'differential mode of association (*chaxugeju*) composed of distinctive networks spreading out from each individual's personal connections [as] quite different from the modern … organizational mode of association (*tuantigeju*) [where] personal relationships depend on a common structure' (Fei 1992, p. 71). Moreover, he was specifically concerned about emerging tensions between these modes of association since China, as was the case in many other parts of the world, had entered 'a scientific era' in which 'people plan their actions according to a known relationship between means and ends' in efforts to industrialise and develop (Fei 1992, p. 139; Fei 1953).

It is against this twentieth-century backdrop of a specifically *social* anthropology that, over the past three decades, a new style of ethnography has developed out of, in particular, post-structuralist engagements with social phenomena and the modes of problematisation that surround them, whether in the empirical fields of medicine, migration, family planning, social services, or development in a globalising world. In this chapter, I show how the emergence of 'assemblage ethnography' (Wahlberg 2014a, 2014b, 2018) has, since the 1990s, involved a shift away from the study of 'societies' or 'people' as such, and towards the study of infrastructures, assemblages, complexes, or what Michel Foucault (1980) conceptualised as *dispositifs*. As we will see, it is an approach that has notably been mobilised for the purposes of cartographically tracing out and understanding social phenomena as they form *across scales, sites,* and *practices.* Thus, assemblage ethnography should be seen as a methodological response to *new* forms of technologically underpinned social organisation that are constantly emerging in a globalising world, which cut across and connect the kinds of villages, communities, tribes, and groups that Mākereti, Fei, Malinowski, and Evans-Pritchard studied. Within the anthropology of technology more specifically, it has emerged as a particular response to the complex question of *where*—to which sites—anthropologists should go to study technology.

What links assemblage ethnography to the participatory fieldwork methods that were developed and refined throughout the twentieth century is a continued interest in distinctive patterns of social organisation; however, as noted, these patterns are not sought within a rural village or a particular geographically/temporally circumscribed 'human society'. Instead, assemblage ethnography seeks to map out the *configurations* found within the *dispositifs* that coalesce around and thereby shape particular social 'problems' such as 'over population', 'poverty', 'crime', 'migration', 'infertility', or 'disease' (see Rabinow 2003). The notion of *configurations* indexes the patterns of knowledge-practice that render social problems intelligible within particular *dispositifs*, understood as assemblages of scientific expertise, laws, regulations, devices, buildings, material equipment, moral propositions put forth in news media, and more. Such *dispositifs*, in turn, grid habituated regimes and routines of practices around, for example, 'lifestyle disease prevention', thereby shaping daily lives. It is these regimes of practice that often serve as an empirical point of departure for assemblage ethnography (Wahlberg 2018).

In what follows, I present a genealogy of assemblage ethnography from when it took form in the 1990s until the present through (so far) three iterations. First, I expand on how Foucault's notion of a *dispositif* (often translated into English as 'apparatus') was mobilised as an object of study by anthropologists who set out to account for the construction and stabilisation of an international 'development apparatus' (Ferguson 1990) as a way of critiquing inbuilt self-evidence when it came to ideas about progress and improvement. Described as 'institutional ethnography' (Escobar 1995), these studies analysed technocratic plans, programmes, and projects—conceived, implemented, and monitored by international development organisations in the so-called Third World—as 'technologies of government' that required a combination of archival and interview methods to map. Secondly, I show how biotechnology became a primary empirical field where anthropologists have studied the contingently assembled practices of, for example, genetic, reproductive, and pharmaceutical technologies, particularly by adopting what George Marcus (1995) famously called 'multi-sited' ethnography. A number of scholars working at the nexus of science and technology studies (STS) and anthropology have deployed ethnographic methods to explore how health-related efforts to improve, optimise, and administer life itself are being shaped through 'new' bioscience technologies (Martin 1994; Rabinow 1996a; Franklin 1997). Finally, I show how, most recently, Deleuze and Guattari's (1988) conceptualisation of assemblages as lines rather than *dispositifs* has been mobilised to account for the unpredictable, ephemeral, and rhizome-like ways social phenomena are assembled, disassembled, and reassembled across macro, meso, and micro scales (Gale and Wyatt 2013; Zigon 2015, 2019; Youdell and McGimpsey 2015; Lameu 2016; Ghoddousi and Page 2020). I conclude by arguing that assemblage ethnography has emerged as a key approach within anthropology generally, and the anthropology of technology specifically, because of its ability to locate sited ethnographies within the broader complexes that are characteristic of a globalising world where technoscience, laws, regulations, institutions, and forms of expertise simultaneously seek to redress and are constitutive of a host of 'social problems'.

CONTEXTUALISING PREDICAMENTS

Contrasting 'traditional' with 'modern' patterns of social interaction has been a mainstay of social theory since the nineteenth century, as seen, for example, in Ferdinand Tönnies' (2002[1887]) distinction between *gemeinschaft* and *gesellschaft*, Emile Durkheim's (1984[1893]) between mechanical and organic solidarity, or Fei's between *chaxugeju* and *tuantigeju*. At the level of the episteme, we might likewise add Foucault's positing of a rupture between European 'classical thought' and 'modern thought' (and their respective regimes of truth and practice) around the time of the Enlightenment in Europe, which he archaeologically and genealogically identified in the empirical fields of madness, medicine, punishment, and sexuality (Foucault 1989): the very same time that Haitian anthropologist Anténor Firmin argued 'anthropology as a discipline [was] born' (2000[1885], p. 3). Common to each of these distinctions is a suggestion that one of the key characteristics of 'modern' society—wherever we might find ourselves in the world—has been its organisation around rationalities and practices arising from scientific disciplines, technologies, contractual laws, and regulations within nation states.

While throughout the twentieth-century anthropologists studied forms of social organisation, human relationships, lived experiences, and lifeworlds among the people where they carried out fieldwork, we can say that, in an important sense, what has come to be known as assemblage ethnography emerged out of attempts to 'contextualise' these more intimate modes of life. Following the 'modern … discovery that society can be planned' (Fei 1992, p. 134; Rabinow 1989), scholars have shown how colonial modernising processes and the reach (however incomplete) of resulting forms of government have, in profound and often devastating ways, transformed people into objects of intervention in efforts to discipline bodies, regulate populations, and 'dictate who may live and who must die' (Mbembé and Meintjes 2003, p. 11; Fanon 2003; Foucault and Ewald 2003).

Precursors to assemblage ethnography may be found in the work of anthropologists who were keen to show how the everyday lives of people were in formidable ways constrained by the colonially structured 'world system' that surrounded them. Aihwa Ong's *Spirits of Resistance and Capitalist Discipline: Factory Women in Malaysia* (1987) is exemplary. Ong sought, through ethnography, to locate the young factory women with whom she had spent time in rural Malaysia in 'the different phases of their encounter with and incorporation within the world capitalist system' (Ong 1987, p. 10). She does so in an analysis of how, 'in the labor process, young women are being reconstituted as instruments of labor and as new sexual personalities' (Ong 1987, p. 8). According to George Marcus, studies such as Ong's mobilised macrotheorists like Foucault 'as a mode of contextualizing portraiture in terms of which the predicaments of local subjects are described and analyzed' (1995, p. 96). Marcus contrasts this first iteration with 'multi-sited ethnographies' which he argued trace 'cultural formations ... across and within multiple sites of activity that destabilize the distinction between, for example, lifeworld and system' (Marcus 1995, p. 96; see also Faubion and Marcus 2009).

While Marcus' articulation of a multi-sited ethnography has certainly played an important role, the emergence of assemblage ethnography from the 1990s onwards can be located at the *nexus* of governmentality studies (focused on technologies of government), STS (the social study of interrelated knowledge production processes and technoscientific practice), and multi-sited methodological strategies (of following people, things, metaphors, and contestations). What changes in assemblage ethnography is the analytical focus: away from 'cultural formation in the world system' (Marcus 1995, p. 99) and towards the *configurations*—understood as heavy accumulations of patterned knowledges and practices—that are found within certain assemblages, complexes, or apparatuses (Wahlberg 2018, p. 10). The Foucauldian influence is clear; indeed, we can say that assemblage ethnography has as its object of study the *dispositif*:

> a thoroughly heterogeneous ensemble consisting of discourses, institutions, architectural forms, regulatory decisions, laws, administrative measures, scientific statements, philosophical, moral and philanthropic propositions. ... Such are the elements of the apparatus. The apparatus itself is the system of relations that can be established between these elements. (Foucault 1980, p. 194)

As already discussed, social theory had long distinguished between two types of societies: on the one hand, the rural societies that early twentieth-century social anthropologists characterised in terms of forms of subsistence, political systems, exchange systems, and kinship systems; on the other, the modern societies that sociologists described in terms of an organic division of labour, a spirit of capitalist production, and urban modes of mental life. With the notion of an assembled *dispositif*, ethnographers (and other scholars) were provided with a conceptual tool to train their analytical sights away from 'society' as such (whether modern or traditional) (see also Latour 2005) and focus instead on how certain modes of problematisation could form around and shape particular 'aggregate' social problems, processes that were indeed constitutive of the very 'societies' in which such problems were seen to be located (Rabinow 2003). Thus, it is no longer 'patterns of human relationships' in each society that are the primary object of study; rather, it is the power/knowledge patterns or configurations that can be discerned within a given apparatus.

APPARATUS AS ETHNOGRAPHIC OBJECT

While not named as such, there is a case to be made that James Ferguson's *The Anti-Politics Machine* (1990) is the first assemblage ethnography in the sense proposed in this chapter. In the introduction to his monograph, Ferguson makes the ethnographically uncharacteristic clarification that:

> Unlike many anthropological works on 'development', this one takes as its primary object not the people to be 'developed', but the apparatus that is to do the 'developing'. This is not a book about the Basotho people, or even about Lesotho; it is principally a book about the operation of the international 'development' apparatus in a particular setting. (1990, p. 17)

Primarily, Ferguson deploys archival methods coupled with interviews in Lesotho, amassing a collection of documents and technocratic reports focused on the conceptualisation, planning, and implementation of the Thaba-Tseka livestock and range management development project as a way to gain broader insights into the operations of 'development', not as a neocolonial ideology, but as an apparatus. Technologies were central to the Thaba-Tseka project which involved 'the construction of an all-weather road ..., a "regional centre" ... comprising office buildings, staff housing, warehouse and workshop facilities, and a "Farmers' Training Centre" equipped with electricity and a piped water system' (Ferguson 1990, p. 109). Through his analysis, Ferguson shows how development relies on processes of 'depoliticisation', observing that 'a "development" project can end up performing extremely sensitive political operations involving the entrenchment and expansion of institutional state power almost invisibly, under the cover of a neutral, technical mission to which no one can object' (Ferguson 1990, p. 256). While sited in Lesotho, these findings are equally relevant in any other country or region where a 'development apparatus' has been formed.

According to Ferguson, as well as numerous other scholars like Nikolas Rose and Andrew Barry who contributed to the elaboration of an analytic of governmentality through the 1990s (Burchell et al. 1991; Rose and Miller 1992; Dean 1995; Barry et al. 1996; see Villadsen and Wahlberg 2015), planned social interventions such as the Thaba-Tseka livestock and range management development project could be analysed as 'technologies of government'. While technologies are often conceived of in material terms (see Bruun & Wahlberg, this volume), the concept of 'technology' also has a broader meaning as Foucault explained in an early 1980s interview with Paul Rabinow:

> [W]hat interests me more is to focus on what the Greeks called the *techne*, that is to say, a practical rationality governed by a conscious goal. ... The disadvantage of this word *techne*, I realize, is its relation to the word 'technology,' which has a very specific meaning. A very narrow meaning is given to 'technology': one thinks of hard technology, the technology of wood, of fire, of electricity. Whereas government is also a function of technology: the government of individuals, the

government of souls, the government of the self by the self, the government of families, the government of children, and so on. (Foucault in Rabinow 1984, pp. 255–256)

Deploying such an understanding of technologies within the field of international development aid, Arturo Escobar continued where Ferguson had left off in his classic monograph *Encountering Development: The Making and Unmaking of the Third World*. In this book, Escobar argues that 'turning the apparatus itself into an anthropological object involves an institutional ethnography that moves from the textual and work practices of institutions to the effects of those practices in the world' (Escobar 1995, p. 107). Like Ferguson's work, Escobar's ethnography was based primarily on the collection of technocratic reports and documents which could then be analysed as 'a corpus of rational techniques—planning, methods of measurement and assessment, professional knowledges, institutional practices, and the like' in an effort to draw the 'cartographies ... or maps of the configurations of knowledge and power that define the post-World War II period' (Escobar 1995, pp. 18, 10).

While Escobar described *Encountering Development* as an 'institutional ethnography', his and Ferguson's analytical move to trace out knowledge-power configurations ethnographically within what they conceptualised as the 'development apparatus' is what leads me to suggest that theirs are among the first assemblage ethnographies. Indeed, their approach continues to resonate. For example, in *Just One Child: Science and Policy in Deng's China*, Susan Greenhalgh (2008) proposes, by bringing a governmentality analytic together with STS in an 'anthropology of science and policy', to answer ethnographically the question, 'how did the bizarre idea of limiting all couples in a country of one billion to one child become *thinkable?*' (p. 38). She does so by combining archival work, extensive interviews with government officials and scientists, and participant observation in various state institutions in order to map out the contingent ways in which policy problematisations, policy assemblages, and a micropolitics of science making and policymaking gave rise to China's infamous 'one-child policy'. Greenhalgh shows how, within China's family planning apparatus, the 'policy work of scientists and science "beyond the state"', especially in the field of cybernetics where a series of population projections contributed to a sense of urgency and even fear, cannot be detached from the policymaking of government officials (2008, p. 308).

In a similar vein, Gregory Feldman (2011b) has described his study of the European Union's 'migration apparatus' as 'nonlocal ethnography'. This multi-sited approach allowed him to map out linkages between border checkpoints, biometrics, technologies for tracking people, international regulations, and more, which together 'manage, channel, and regulate global circulations of people and objects' (Feldman 2011a, p. 380, 2011b; see also Brady 2011; Riles 2011; Davies 2012). Much like the development apparatus that Ferguson and Escobar studied, the migration apparatus, Feldman argues, 'activates and proliferates without central coordination, without tight networks among its technicians, and without a detailed master plan, all of which render it an evasive object of empiricist field research' (Feldman 2011a, p. 378). This condition calls for movement across sites, interviewing of experts, collection of reports, and observations on the part of the ethnographer. Whether in the field of development, family planning, or migration, policies and the technocracies that shape them become important empirical objects in assemblage ethnography. And, as Cris Shore and Susan Wright argued in their call for an anthropology of policy:

> [B]y focusing on policy, the field of study changes. It is no longer a question of studying a local community or 'a people'; rather, the anthropologist is seeking a method for analysing connections between levels and forms of social process and action, and exploring how those processes work in different sites—local, national and global'. (Shore and Wright 2003, p. 11; see also Prainsack and Wahlberg 2013; Brady 2014)

The ethnographies discussed in this section have each sought to map out 'configurations of knowledge and power' by choosing a particular apparatus, and not a 'society', a 'culture', a 'people', or certain 'lifeworlds', as their object. This analytical move towards configurations within apparatuses—rather than more intimate patterns of human relationships and experience—has relied on a 'broadened' notion of technology that allows ethnographers to track 'technologies of government' through what Escobar called an 'institutional ethnography' and Feldman a 'nonlocal ethnography'. Their common emphasis has been on the *technocracies* (made up of experts, techniques of assessment, planning methods, devices, laws, regulations, etc.) found within an apparatus. To be sure, this move has not been without its critics, perhaps unsurprisingly so given anthropology's methodological imperatives of 'closeness' and 'immersion'. Scholars have highlighted how the resulting methodological 'detachment' from the people with whom anthropologists have always worked so closely—through ethnographic fieldwork—and concurrent focus on mentalities or rationalities of government inevitably misses out on the 'messiness of human practices' (Stenson 1998, p. 350; see also Anand 2017) and the frictions that global connections generate (Tsing 2005), as well as various forms of resistance to governmental programmes (which Aihwa Ong had foregrounded; see also Nuijten 2004; Escobar 2008; Zhan 2009). All of this at the 'risk [of] delegitimating their subject matter's human conditions' (Kleinman and Kleinman 1991, p. 276).

A Bio-turn

In his landmark *Annual Review of Anthropology* article, George Marcus credited the works of Emily Martin, Sarah Franklin, and Paul Rabinow, all of whom straddled anthropology and STS, as some of the 'most fully achieved' multisited ethnographies (Marcus 1995, p. 108). Marcus highlighted how, respectively, they ethnographically traced the cultural formation of immunity, assisted reproductive technology, and polymerase chain reaction (a technique that made large scale genomics possible) by moving across multiple sites spanning science laboratories, scientific conferences, corporations, clinics, regulations, patient organisations, media reporting, and more. Indeed, the burgeoning social study of biotechnology by anthropologists through the 1990s and 2000s helped constitute biomedical technologies as one of the most productive empirical fields for emergent forms of assemblage ethnography. The production of knowledge through scientific disciplines (not least biology) was of course central to Foucault's conceptualisation of both the modern *episteme* and associated *dispositifs* that had formed around, for example, punishment or medicine in eighteenth-century Europe. And, just as STS had benefited from the co-option of ethnographic methods in its early days (Latour and Woolgar 1979; see Hess 2001), so too would anthropology benefit from the insights that STS scholars had generated concerning the social shaping of knowledge in (co-)production processes. While technocracies had been the focus of the first assemblage ethnographies, starting in the 1990s a generation of anthropologists moved into bioscientific and biomedical sites to carry out ethnographic research, giving rise to a veritable bio-turn within social studies of medicine (see Downey and Dumit 1997; Lock and Nguyen 2010; Wahlberg 2017).

Just as Ferguson felt compelled to clarify the object of his ethnography in the opening pages of *The Anti-Politics Machine*, so too did Emily Martin and Paul Rabinow in their pioneering ethnographies of immunity and genetic biotechnology. Emily Martin explains in the first chapter of *Flexible Bodies* (1994) that, in order to get to grips with how immunity came to be conceptualised in contemporary American society in a time of HIV/AIDS, she had to 'deliberately cross back and forth across the borders between the institutions in which scientists produce knowledge (an immunology research laboratory, clinical settings) and the wider society (neighborhoods, places of work)', prompting one of her colleagues to quip, 'don't you know how to stay put!?' (Martin 1994, p. 33). This tacking back and forth was necessary for Martin and her collaborators to see how knowledge of the body co-emerges out of certain *configurations* ('clusters of ways of thinking and ways of acting') in scientific settings, on the one hand, and 'lay understandings' of 'how people in a variety of social settings talk about health, illness, and the makeup of their bodies' on the other (Martin 1994, p. 43; see also Lock 1993; Sharp 2006).

Paul Rabinow, however, focused his ethnography more exclusively on the making of a specific biotechnology (polymerase chain reaction) within a bioscientific arena. Yet he too is compelled to move across sites in order to provide an ethnographic account of that making. In the very opening pages of his monograph, Rabinow explains how:

> *Making PCR* is an ethnographic account of the invention of PCR, the polymerase chain reaction (arguably the exemplary biotechnological invention to date), the *milieu* on which that invention took place (Cetus Corporation during

the 1980s), and the key actors (scientists, technicians, and business people) who shaped the technology and the milieu and who were, in turn, shaped by them. ... Th[e] book focuses on the emergence of biotechnology, circa 1980, as a distinctive configuration of scientific, technical, cultural, social, economic, political, and legal elements, each of which had its own separate trajectory over the preceding decades. ... In sum, it shows how a contingently assembled practice emerged, composed of distinctive *subjects*, the *site* in which they worked and the *object* they invented. (Rabinow 1996a, pp. 1–2)

Here we see the outlines of a more explicitly articulated assemblage ethnography which takes as its object 'a distinctive configuration' that allowed for the emergence of a biotechnology like PCR. Rabinow would later reflect on this work, suggesting that 'the kind of anthropology I am undertaking does not make ethnic groups its primary objects of study. Rather ... it concerns a different range of objects (problematisations, apparatuses, assemblages) ... given that what I am seeking to understand, and establish a specific kind of relationship to, are events, in a hypercomplex world' (Rabinow 2003, pp. 76–79). It is no coincidence that biotechnologies in particular have constituted some of the most prominent field sites in the development of assemblage ethnography, given Foucault's argument that one of the defining features of modern forms of governmentality has been a biopower that 'endeavors to administer, optimize, and multiply [life], subjecting it to precise controls and comprehensive regulations' (Foucault 1990, p. 137; Rabinow and Rose 2006). Indeed, assemblage ethnography has been an important part of the aforementioned bio-turn within social studies of medicine, generating a host of bio-concepts, from bio-capital to bio-value, bio-sociality and biological citizenship in the process (see Birch 2017).

Reproductive science, and the technoscientific practices that have formed around it, have constituted a particularly salient sub-field within which anthropologists have cartographically traced efforts to optimise and administer life across multiple scales and sites. In *Embodied Progress: A Cultural Account of Assisted Conception*, Sarah Franklin uses her introduction to explain how hers is not a 'conventional' ethnography of infertility treatment as, in true multi-sited fashion she,

moves from the history of anthropological theory, to the enterprise culture of Thatcherism, to the media representation of 'desperate' infertile couples, to parliamentary debate of human fertilisation and embryology, to the IVF clinic and into the private sitting rooms of a group of IVF clients [aiming] ... to reconnect culture, social organisation and individual experience along reconfigured dimensions of scale, perspective and system [and thereby] make visible the accumulated practices, assumptions and constraints which inform most contemporary assessment and discussion of new reproductive and genetic technologies. (Franklin 1997, pp. 37–39)

In a similar vein, Rayna Rapp explains how the object in her ethnographic exploration of the social impact of amniocentesis (a prenatal screening technology) in America across genetic counselling sessions, disability advocacy organisations, scientific laboratories, and prenatal clinics 'differs considerably from the usual objects of anthropological investigation', as she traces 'the intersection of multiple constituencies, contexts, and conflicts in which a ... developing reproductive technology is constituted' (Rapp 1999, p. 12).

In 2005, Aihwa Ong and Stephen Collier brought together Rabinow, Franklin, Greenhalgh, and numerous other likeminded ethnographers in their influential edited volume, *Global Assemblages: Technology, Politics, and Ethics as Anthropological Problems* (2005). In this they argue that the global assemblages which can form in and around

> technoscience, circuits of licit and illicit exchange, systems of administration or governance, and regimes of ethics or values ... are abstractable, mobile, and dynamic, moving across and reconstituting 'society,' 'culture,' and 'economy,' [through] specific technical infrastructures, administrative apparatuses, or value regimes. (Collier and Ong 2005, pp. 4, 11; see also Marcus and Saka 2006)

Global assemblages, by definition, called for the kinds of multi-sited ethnography (often across continents) that had been under development since the early 1990s. Andrew Lakoff's *Pharmaceutical Reason: Knowledge and Value in Global Psychiatry* was a case in point, as he ethnographically traced linkages between Paris and Buenos Aires in a study examining 'the encounter between a globalising apparatus for understanding and intervening in mental illness according to the norms of biomedicine, and a distinctive epistemic milieu, the Argentine *mundo-psi*' (Lakoff 2006, p. 4). In a similar fashion, Adriana Petryna's 'global ethnography', *When Experiments Travel: Clinical Trials and the Global Search for Human Subjects*, required her to crisscross the Atlantic to show how, as infrastructures,

> clinical trials are part of charged social and political landscapes that link diverse participants—researchers, trial subjects, health professionals, corporate executives, regulators, policy makers, patient-consumers, and shareholders—to a host of calculable and incalculable hopes, benefits, profits, and risks. (Petryna 2009, p. 9; see also Andersen et al. 2020; Bell 2019; Caduff 2015; MacPhail 2015; Peterson 2014; Whyte et al. 2002)

By 2012, in *Drugs for Life: How Pharmaceutical Companies Define Our Health*, Joseph Dumit no longer excuses himself for not having carried out a 'conventional' ethnography. Instead, Dumit straightforwardly explains that 'my book studies the ... naturalized logics of clinical trials and risk treatment in American culture. Using a combination of ethnography, interviewing, and media analysis, I focus on how these logics are produced, maintained, and embodied'

(2012, p. 19). While Dumit did not refer to *Drugs for Life* as an assemblage ethnography, in my review of it I suggested that it was exactly this:

> Dumit over the course of eight years has attempted to discern the logics of mass health among its producers, prescribers and users: at pharma-conferences, through pharmaceutical advertisements and clinic trials data as well as through interviews with general practitioners and patients. This is assemblage (rather than multi-sited) methodology. (Wahlberg 2014b, p. 231)

Dumit's Canguilhem-inspired focus on logics points to another important aspect of those assemblage ethnographies that were being carried out in the biotechnological field, namely, a particular empirical interest in 'following concepts', such as 'immunity', 'genetic variant', or 'health', as these are formed in scientific settings yet often leave the lab to circulate in policy, healthcare settings, media discourses, and homes (Canguilhem 1989; Latour 1987; Rabinow 1996b).

This was the same methodological approach I had adopted in China as I embarked on an ethnographic project (2007–2014) that aimed to account for the extraordinary rise of assisted reproductive technologies in 'one-child policy' China by exploring how they came to be configured and routinised as 'legitimate' components within China's restrictive reproductive complex (Wahlberg 2018; see also Franklin and Roberts 2006; Hoeyer 2013; Inhorn 2015; Kroløkke 2018). The version of assemblage ethnography that I went on to articulate in *Good Quality: the Routinization of Sperm Banking in China* (2018) was one that brought together the technocratic focus of Escobar's, Ferguson's, and Greenhalgh's institutional ethnography (as I focused on the laws, regulations, and institutions that shaped China's reproductive complex); the technoscience focus of Rabinow's, Franklin's, and Rapp's multi-sited ethnographies of specific biotechnologies (as I focused on sperm banking at China's oldest and largest sperm bank and fertility clinic in Changsha, Hunan province); Lakoff's and Petryna's following of scientific expertise and technique (as I focused on reproductive laboratory science); Dumit's focus on concepts of health (as I focused on the concept of 'quality'); and Martin's focus on 'how people in a variety of social settings talk about health, illness, and the makeup of their bodies' (1994, p. 4) (as I focused on what donors and recipient couples thought about male infertility and sperm donation). It is an approach that insists on firmly locating certain patterned ways of knowing and doing (e.g., sperm banking) within particular juridical, medical, social, economic, cultural, and institutional configurations (e.g., China's reproductive complex) (Wahlberg 2018, pp. 19–24).

LINES AND RHIZOMES

Most recently, yet another iteration of assemblage ethnography (Gale and Wyatt 2013; Youdell and McGimpsey 2015; Lameu 2016; Ghoddousi and Page 2020) or assemblic ethnography (Zigon 2015, 2019) has taken form, indebted to the theoretical work of Gilles Deleuze and Felix Guattari (1988), who have conceptualised assemblages as 'lines', rather than the systems of relations that Foucault argued make up a *dispositif* (for a helpful discussion of how the two relate see Legg 2011; also Marcus and Saka 2006). As noted earlier, studies that have adopted a governmentality analytic, with its focus on rationalities and technologies of government, have been critiqued for being 'too neat', for missing out on the messiness, leakages, and gaps that inevitably emerge as programmes and interventions are rolled out and routinised (see Anand 2017). Partly to address such critiques, while also broadening empirical focus away from biotechnology, scholars like Jarett Zigon, Deborah Youdell, and Ian McGimpsey have sought inspiration in Deleuze and Guattari's emphasis on the rhizome-like fluidity and unpredictability of assemblages in their ethnographic explorations of 'how diverse elements come together in productive relations to form apparently whole but mobile social entities' (Youdell and McGimpsey 2015, p. 119).

In his 'assemblic ethnography' of 'the war on drugs', Jarett Zigon argues for an approach that 'chases and traces a situation through its continual process of assembling across different global scales and its temporally differential localisation in diverse places' (2015, p. 515, 2019; see also Blok 2011). For Zigon, the *dispositif* is much too rigid since 'our worlds are nothing other than densely intertwined knots of several much more widely diffused and nontotalizable assemblages that constantly flow together and slip apart in a potentially infinite number of combinations' (Zigon 2015, p. 505). The drug war, Zigon insists, is not simply located in South American jungles, along the Mexican-American border, or in American prisons; 'rather, the drug war emerges—at times but not always—in all of these locales and beyond. Notice, however, that these locales are not always and only caught up in the drug war situation' (p. 506). It is these, at times fleeting, connections across different scales that Zigon wants to trace using multi-sited assemblic ethnography.

Similarly, Youdell and McGimpsey (2015) argue that their form of assemblage ethnography seeks to investigate how economic, structural, spatial, temporal, discursive, subjective, and affective orders 'play out at macro, meso and micro scales' (p. 120). Like Zigon, they argue that the 'youth services assemblage' they have studied in the United Kingdom is constantly being assembled, disassembled, and reassembled, creating a methodological need to 'follow named "lines" as "ways in" to the map of the assemblage, to see what happens, what changes, what hits a dead end, and what sense of the assemblage emerges not from a centre but from multiple positions' (Youdell and McGimpsey 2015, p. 120). Youth services have been configured for 'early intervention' as a means of 'preventing offending' at the cost of, for example, provision of cultural and leisure services. Through their research, Youdell and McGimpsey identify numerous 'lines'—including money, expert knowledge, time, specialist interventions, and youth workers—each of which is one of the constantly changing components within the youth services assemblage.

Finally, utilising a 'collaborative assemblage approach' Karen Fog Olwig, Perle Møhl, Kristina Grünenberg, and Anja Simonsen (2019) innovatively divided up various components of the European 'biometric border world assemblage' they set out to study collectively. While akin to Feldman's work on the European Union's 'migration apparatus', these scholars use the concept of 'assemblage' as a critical tool that makes it possible to conceptualise the biometric border world as composed of partially connected elements that shift constantly. Made up of four ethnographies—which focus, respectively, on border control, the development of personal identification technologies (e.g., face recognition), migrants attempting to gain entry into Europe, and families in Europe seeking reunification who must submit to DNA testing—their study shows how 'legal frameworks, physical obstacles, bodily features, social connections, time perspectives and more interweave and interact and can hardly be isolated, as the connections and mutual influences between them shift constantly' (Olwig et al. 2019, p. 7). In doing so, Olwig and colleagues draw not only on Deleuze and Guattari's notion of assemblages as shifting lines, but also on Bruno Latour's idea of actor-networks taking their ethnographic fieldwork 'from science labs to biometric and border conferences, standardization forums, associational meetings and vendor fairs' (Olwig et al. 2019, p. 29; see also Blok 2011, 2018; Zhan 2009).

What these studies of drug war, youth services, and biometric border world assemblages have in common is their suggestion that such assemblages are, unlike *dispositifs*, unstable, and that they transcend scales: from the micro experiences of drug addicts, youth, or migrants to the laws, regulations, policies, and carceral institutions of nation states. In conceptualising assemblages as lines, this form of assemblage or assemblic ethnography allows scholars to connect localised, nontotalisable situations to broader political economies, helping to nuance some of the more 'rigid' emphases that a focus on *dispositifs* has generated. As recently summarised by Pooya Ghoddousi and Sam Page (2020), 'the contribution of assemblage analysis is not the descriptive explanations of phenomena that offer generalised claims to truth (i.e. reified representations), but concepts that explain processes and patterns emerging in an ever-changing world' (2020, p. 5; see also Gale and Wyatt 2013).

CONCLUSION

In the closing months of 2013, I was preparing a grant application that proposed to explore how 'living with disease' has come to be the object of novel forms of knowledge, expertise, measurement, and management. To do so, I argued for a need to stitch together a methodology that allows us to 'follow "quality of life" around [using] a combination of situational mapping, participatory methodologies, interviews and detective-like tracking of paper trails—what we might call assemblage ethnography' (Wahlberg 2014a, p. 4, 2017). As I have shown in this chapter, this was not a novel methodology as such; rather, giving it a name helped bring together the various methodological and analytical approaches that over the past thirty years have sought to study what Rabinow called 'hypercomplex' social phenomena in a globalising world where science, technologies, laws, regulations, experts, media reports, and more (*dispositifs*) are constitutive of those social 'problems' that become matters of concern (Latour 2004). It is an approach that has empirically focused on the technologies of government identifiable within various forms of *technocratic organisation* (governments, ministries, commissions, institutions, corporations, non-governmental organisations, etc.); on the *technoscientific knowledge practices* aimed at the government of life (e.g., in the fields of international development, family planning, migration, biotechnology, reproductive technology, pharmaceutical treatment, social services, drug rehabilitation, and more)—following these across macro, meso, and micro *scales* (spanning political economies, laws, routinised organisational practices, and everyday lived experiences) and across multiple *sites* (across nation states, [non-]governmental institutions, laboratories, media reports, social movements, homes, and more).

Assemblage ethnographies are *ethnographic* due to their fieldwork in those (multiple) institutions where the people involved in social practices of legislating, administering, and governing (and the documents they produce) are to be found; in those laboratories and organisations where people involved in the development and use of scientific expertise and technologies are housed; and in the homes, neighbourhoods, and communities where people's lives are intimately interwoven with family relations, health, illness, work, schooling, and so much more (whether technologically mediated or not). Yet they distinguish themselves from those forms of ethnography which have focused on what Fei conceptualised as village-level 'accumulations of a group's common experiences ... perpetuated by a symbolic system', on the one hand, and 'transmitted patterns of social organization [that emerge] with frequent and repeated interaction occurring over a long period of time', on the other (Fei 1992, pp. 55, 42). Instead, assemblage ethnographies aim to study and locate complex social phenomena within the discernible configurations that organise an assemblage, complex, or *dispositif*. As such, we can say that the emergence of assemblage ethnography has been a methodological response to a globalising world where technocratic organisation and technoscientific expertise continue to impact on and shape the lives of people everywhere in the world. However, far from 'inauthenticating local moral worlds [or] making illegitimate the defeats and victories, the desperation and aspiration of individuals and groups', as some critics claim (Kleinman and Kleinman 1991, p. 293), assemblage ethnographies aim to contribute to an understanding of the complex ways in which the lived experiences of individuals, groups, and communities come to be profoundly shaped by the socio-historical processes of which they are unavoidably a part, with the aim of demonstrating the contingency of these processes and hence the possibility that lives could be otherwise.

Acknowledgements This chapter has benefited immensely from discussions I have had through the years with so many colleagues and collaborators. In particular I would like to thank Barbara Prainsack, Anders Blok, Maja Hojer Bruun, Brit Winthereik, Klaus Hoeyer, and two anonymous reviewers whom I have learned so much from. I would like to acknowledge the European Research Council (ERC) under the European Union's Horizon 2020 research and innovation programme for funding the VITAL project (grant agreement No ERC-2014-STG-639275) that has allowed me to contribute to the development of assemblage ethnography as a methodological approach.

References

Anand, N. (2017). *Hydraulic City: Water and the Infrastructures of Citizenship in Mumbai.* Durham, NC.: Duke University Press.

Andersen, S. L., Andersen, O., Petersen, J., & Wahlberg, A. (2020). Traveling health-promoting infrastructures: A meta-ethnographic analysis. *Health, 24*(5), 606–622.

Barry, A., Osborne, T., & Rose, N. (Eds.) (1996). *Foucault and Political Reason: liberalism, neo-liberalism and the rationalities of government.* Chicago: University of Chicago Press.

Bell, S. E. (2019). Interpreter assemblages: Caring for immigrant and refugee patients in US hospitals. *Social Science & Medicine, 226,* 29–36.

Birch, K. (2017). The problem of bio-concepts: biopolitics, bio-economy and the political economy of nothing. *Cultural Studies of Science Education, 12*(4), 915–927.

Blok, A. (2011). War of the whales: post-sovereign science and agonistic cosmopolitics in Japanese-global whaling assemblages. *Science, Technology, & Human Values, 36*(1), 55–81.

Blok, A. (2018). Planning ecologies: issue publics and the reassembling of urban green trajectories. In *Relational Planning: Tracing Artefacts, Agency and Practices* (pp. 259–282). Cham: Palgrave Macmillan.

Brady, M. (2011). Researching governmentalities through ethnography: the case of Australian welfare reforms and programs for single parents. *Critical Policy Studies, 5*(3), 264–282.

Brady, M. (2014). Ethnographies of neoliberal governmentalities: From the neoliberal apparatus to neoliberalism and governmental assemblages. *Foucault Studies, 18,* 11–33.

Burchell, G., Gordon, C., & Miller, P. (Eds.). (1991). *The Foucault effect: Studies in governmentality.* Chicago: University of Chicago Press.

Caduff, C. (2015). *The Pandemic Perhaps: Dramatic events in a public culture of danger.* Berkley: University of California Press.

Canguilhem, G. (1989). *The Normal and the Pathological.* New York: Zone Books.

Collier, S., & Ong, A. (2005). Global assemblages, anthropological problems. In Ong, A. and Collier, S. (Eds.) *Global Assemblages: Technology, politics and ethics as anthropological problems.* Oxford: Blackwell.

Davies, A. D. (2012). Assemblage and social movements: Tibet Support Groups and the spatialities of political organisation. *Transactions of the Institute of British Geographers, 37*(2), 273–286.

Dean, M. (1995). Governing the unemployed self in an active society, *Economy and Society, 24*(4), 559–583.

Deleuze, G., & Guattari, F. (1988). *A Thousand Plateaus: Capitalism and Schizophrenia*. London: Bloomsbury Publishing.

Downey, G. L., & Dumit, J. (Eds.) (1997). *Cyborgs & Citadels: Anthropological Interventions in Emerging Sciences and Technologies*. Santa Fe: School of American Research Press.

Dumit, J. (2012). *Drugs for Life: how pharmaceutical companies define our health*. Durham, NC: Duke University Press.

Durkheim, É. (1984[1893]). *The Division of Labour in Society*. London: Macmillan

Escobar, A. (1995) *Encountering Development*. Princeton, NJ.: Princeton University Press

Escobar, A. (2008). *Territories of Difference: Place, Movements, Life*. Durham, NC: Duke University Press.

Fanon, F. (2003). *Wretched of the Earth*. New York: Grove Press.

Faubion, J. D., & Marcus, G. E. (2009). *Fieldwork is Not What it Used to Be: Learning Anthropology's Method in a Time of Transition*. Ithaca: Cornell University Press.

Fei, X. (1953). *China's Gentry: Essays on Rural-Urban Relations*. Chicago: University of Chicago Press.

Fei, X. (1992[1947]). *From the Soil: The foundations of Chinese society* (trans: Hamilton, G., & Zheng, W.). Berkley: University of California Press.

Feldman, G. (2011a). If ethnography is more than participant-observation, then relations are more than connections: The case for nonlocal ethnography in a world of apparatuses. *Anthropological Theory, 11*(4), 375–395.

Feldman, G. (2011b). *The Migration Apparatus: Security, labor, and policymaking in the European Union*. Stanford University Press.

Ferguson, J. (1990). *The Anti-politics Machine: 'development', depoliticization and bureaucratic power in Lesotho*. Cambridge: Cambridge University Press.

Firmin, J.A. (2000[1885]). *The Equality of the Human Races*. New York: Garland Publishing, Inc.

Fortes, M. & Evans-Pritchard, E.E. (1940). *African Political Systems*. London: Oxford University Press

Foucault, M. (1980). *Power/Knowledge: Selected Interviews & Other Writings 1972–1977*. New York: Pantheon Books

Foucault, M. (1989). *The Order of Things. An Archaeology of the Human Sciences*. London: Routledge.

Foucault, M. (1990). *The History of Sexuality: An introduction, Vol. 1*. New York: Vintage, 95.

Foucault, M., & Ewald, F. (2003). *'Society Must Be Defended': Lectures at the Collège de France, 1975–1976, Vol. 1*. London: Macmillan.

Franklin, S. (1997). *Embodied Progress: A Cultural Account of Assisted Conception*. London: Routledge.

Franklin, S., & Roberts, C. (2006). *Born and Made: An Ethnography of Preimplantation Genetic Diagnosis*. Princeton, NJ.: Princeton University Press.

Gale, K., & Wyatt, J. (2013). Assemblage/ethnography: Troubling constructions of self in the play of materiality and representation. In *Contemporary British Autoethnography* (pp. 139–155). Rotterdam: Brill Sense.

Ghoddousi, P., & Page, S. (2020). Using ethnography and assemblage theory in political geography. *Geography Compass, 14*(10). https://doi.org/10.1111/gec3.12533.

Greenhalgh, S. (2008). *Just One Child: Science and policy in Deng's China*. Berkley: University of California Press.

Hess, D. (2001). Ethnography and the development of science and technology studies. In P. Atkinson, A. Coffey, S. Delamont, J. Lofland, & L. Lofland, (Eds.), *Handbook of Ethnography* (pp. 234–245). London: Sage.

Hoeyer, K. (2013). *Exchanging Human Bodily Material: Rethinking bodies and markets*. Dordrecht: Springer.

Inhorn, M. C. (2015). *Cosmopolitan Conceptions: IVF Sojourns in Global Dubai*. Durham, NC.: Duke University Press.

Kleinman, A., & Kleinman, J. (1991). Suffering and its professional transformation: Toward an ethnography of interpersonal experience. *Culture, Medicine and Psychiatry, 15*(3), 275–275.

Kroløkke, C. (2018). *Global Fluids: The Cultural Politics of Reproductive Waste and Value*. Oxford: Berghahn Books.

Lakoff, A. (2006). *Pharmaceutical Reason: Knowledge and Value in Global Psychiatry*. Cambridge: Cambridge University Press.

Lameu, P. (2016). Assemblage Ethnography: an inclusive approach for Social Sciences. Poster presented at conference on *Researching Social Inequality Across the Social Sciences: Contemporary Sociological Analyses of Power and Exclusion*, University of Birmingham. https://doi.org/10.13140/RG.2.1.2747.6083.

Legg, S. (2011). Assemblage/apparatus: using Deleuze and Foucault. *Area, 43*(2), 128–133.

Latour, B. (1987). *Science in Action: How to follow scientists and engineers through society*. Boston: Harvard University Press.

Latour, B. (2004). Why has critique run out of steam? From matters of fact to matters of concern. *Critical Inquiry, 30*(2), 225–248.

Latour, B. (2005). *Reassembling the Social. An Introduction to Actor-Network-Theory*. Oxford: Oxford University Press

Latour, B., & Woolgar, S. (1979). *Laboratory Life: The Construction of Scientific Facts*. London: Sage Publications.

Lock, M.M. (1993). *Encounters with Aging: Mythologies of Menopause in Japan and North America*. Berkley: University of California Press.

Lock, M. M., & Nguyen, V. K. (2010). *An Anthropology of Biomedicine*. Chichester: John Wiley & Sons.

MacPhail, T. (2015). *The Viral Network: a Pathography of the H1N1 Influenza Pandemic*. Ithaca: Cornell University Press.

Malinowski, B. (1922). *Argonauts of the Western Pacific: An account of native enterprise and adventure in the archipelagoes of Melanesian New Guinea*. London: Routledge & Kegan Paul Ltd.

Makereti. (1938). *The Old-time Maori*. London: Victor Gollancz Ltd.

Marcus, G. E. (1995). Ethnography in/of the world system: The emergence of multi-sited ethnography. *Annual Review of Anthropology, 24*(1), 95–117.

Marcus, G. E., & Saka, E. (2006). Assemblage. *Theory, Culture & Society, 23*(2–3), 101–106.

Martin, E. (1994). *Flexible Bodies: Tracking immunity in American culture from the days of polio to the age of AIDS*. Boston: Beacon Press.

Mbembé, J. A., & Meintjes, L. (2003). Necropolitics. *Public Culture, 15*(1), 11–40.

Nuijten, M. (2004). Between fear and fantasy: governmentality and the working of power in Mexico. *Critique of Anthropology, 24*(2), 209–230.

Olwig, K. F., Grünenberg, K., Møhl, P., & Simonsen, A. (2019). *The Biometric Border World: Technology, Bodies and Identities on the Move.* London: Routledge.

Ong, A. (1987). *Spirits of resistance and capitalist discipline: Factory women in Malaysia.* Albany: SUNY Press.

Ong, A., & Collier, S. (2005). *Global assemblages. Technology, Politics, and Ethics as Anthropological Problems.* Oxford: Blackwell.

Peterson, K. (2014). *Speculative Markets: Drug Circuits and Derivative Life in Nigeria.* Durham: Duke University Press.

Petryna, A. (2009). *When Experiments Travel: Clinical Trials and the Global Search for Human Subjects.* Princeton University Press.

Prainsack, B., & Wahlberg, A. (2013). Situated bio-regulation: Ethnographic sensibility at the interface of STS, policy studies and the social studies of medicine. *BioSocieties,* 8(3), 336–359.

Rabinow, P. (Ed.) (1984). *The Foucault Reader.* New York: Pantheon Books

Rabinow, P. (1989). *French Modern: Norms and Forms of the Social Environment.* Cambridge, MA.: The MIT Press.

Rabinow, P. (1996a). *Making PCR: A Story of Biotechnology.* Chicago: University of Chicago Press.

Rabinow, P. (1996b). Artificiality and Enlightenment: From Sociobiology to Biosociality. In *Essays on the Anthropology of Reason* (pp. 91–111). Princeton, NJ.: Princeton University Press

Rabinow, P. (2003). *Anthropos today: Reflections on modern equipment.* Princeton University Press.

Rabinow, P., & Rose, N. (2006). Biopower today. *BioSocieties, 1*(2), 195–217

Radcliffe-Brown, A. R., & Forde, D. (1950). *African Systems of Kinship & Marriage.* London: Oxford University Press.

Rapp, R. (1999). *Testing Women, Testing the Fetus: The social impact of amniocentesis in America.* London: Routledge.

Riles, A. (2011). *Collateral Knowledge: Legal Reasoning in the Global Financial Markets.* Chicago: University of Chicago Press.

Rose, N., & Miller, P. (1992). Political power beyond the state: Problematics of government. *British Journal of Sociology, 43*(2), 173–205.

Sharp, L. A. (2006). *Strange Harvest: Organ Transplants, Denatured Bodies, and the Transformed Self.* Berkley: University of California Press.

Shore, C., & Wright, S. (Eds.) (2003). *Anthropology of Policy: Perspectives on governance and power.* London: Routledge.

Stenson, K. (1998). Beyond Histories of the Present. *Economy and Society, 27*(4), 333–352.

Tönnies, F. (2002). *Community and Society.* Mineola, NY.: Dover Publications, Inc.

Tsing, A. L. (2005). *Friction: An Ethnography of Global Connection.* Princeton, NJ.: Princeton University Press.

Villadsen, K., & Wahlberg, A. (2015). The government of life: managing populations, health and scarcity. *Economy and Society, 44*(1), 1–17.

Wahlberg, A. (2014a). *The Vitality of Disease – Quality of Life in the Making (VITAL).* ERC Starting Grant 2014 Research proposal. European Research Council. Grant no. ERC-2014-STG-639275

Wahlberg, A. (2014b). Book review of Dumit, Joseph. 2012. Drugs for life: how pharmaceutical companies define our health. Durham, NC.: Duke University Press. *Social Anthropology, 22*(2), 230–232.

Wahlberg, A. (2017). The Vitality of Disease. In M. Meloni, J. Cromby, D. Fitzgerald, & S. Lloyd (Eds.), *Handbook of Biology and Society* (pp. 727–748). London: Palgrave Macmillan.

Wahlberg, A. (2018). *Good Quality: The Routinization of Sperm Banking in China*. Berkley: University of California Press.

Whyte, S. R., Van der Geest, S., & Hardon, A. (2002). *Social Lives of Medicines*. Cambridge: Cambridge University Press.

Wittfogel, K. (1957). *Oriental Despotism*. New Haven: Yale University Press.

Youdell, D., & McGimpsey, I. (2015). Assembling, disassembling and reassembling 'youth services' in Austerity Britain. *Critical Studies in Education*, 56(1), 116–130.

Zhan, M. (2009). *Other-Worldly: Making Chinese Medicine through Transnational Frames*. Durham, NC.: Duke University Press.

Zigon, J. (2015). What is a situation?: An assemblic ethnography of the drug war. *Cultural Anthropology*, 30(3), 501–524.

Zigon, J. (2019). *A war on people: Drug user politics and a new ethics of community*. Berkley: University of California Press.

CHAPTER 7

Humanism, Posthumanism, and New Humanism: How Robots Challenge the Anthropological Object

Posthumanism

Cathrine Hasse

What is humanism? What is posthumanism? What significance do these concepts have for anthropologists working with technology? In this chapter I explain the concepts and their relations within and outside an anthropological context, argue that posthumanism can be seen as the fertile ground from which a new view of humans is emerging in anthropology, and advocate three connected points:

1. In anthropology, posthumanism confronts a humanism which privileged human perspectives.[1] Although anthropology has been better than most disciplines at seeing human life as embedded in what Cheryl Mattingly and Thomas Wentzer have named 'its sociocultural and ecological situatedness' (2018, 144), humans are still often depicted as a determinate measuring stick and central concern in anthropologies.
2. Posthumanism can be seen as an intermediate station on the way to a new and better conceptualisation of humanism in anthropology, one in which being human is not just about relations but processes of relations.
3. Studies of technology, as well as technology as material artefacts, plays a crucial role in the development of this new concept, which is changing our

C. Hasse (✉)
Department of Educational Anthropology, Aarhus University, Aarhus, Denmark
e-mail: caha@edu.au.dk

© The Author(s), under exclusive license to Springer Nature Singapore
Pte Ltd. 2022
M. H. Bruun et al. (eds.), *The Palgrave Handbook of the Anthropology of Technology*, https://doi.org/10.1007/978-981-16-7084-8_7

understanding of humans in anthropology as more than human. New technologies can help expand our notions of humans and at the same time also show that there are limits to what counts as 'to human' (Ingold 2013).

The new humanism (Wentzer and Mattingly 2018) places people and their diverse bodily experiences together with non-humans in the middle of the comprehensible world, neither outside, above, nor below the world they inhabit. Unlike the previous humanism, these humans are not the measuring stick of everything else, but appear to be completely infiltrated by both each other and non-human beings. Humans and non-humans (understood as 'things, or objects, or beasts', Latour 1993, p. 13) merge, to the extent that the distinction may seem superfluous. This is what makes it possible for anthropologists to take on the perspectives of jaguars, forests, elephants, and mushrooms, and learn from humans with different perspectives on the world. In this new humanism, perspectivism (or perspectivalism) and ontology merge in ontogeny (i.e., the world is both the same and different as persons and environment transform each other).

Although technology is not necessarily part of this processual, relational ontology, it is not least by virtue of the creation of new technological equipment that anthropologists realise how non-humans and humans merge. However, it is the argument in this chapter that, while humans may seem limitless in their entanglements, careful anthropology can explore the boundaries to what it means to be recognised as human. Humanoid robots are a good example. When we look at human-machine relations as a process, humanoid robots do not so much show us what we are as humans, as what we are not. They show us limits to processes of what it means 'to human' (Ingold 2013).

To illustrate this last point, I present fieldwork on how children envision humanoid robots in terms of likeness or difference from themselves (Hasse 2020c). In this study we find that, although children expect robots to be mirror versions of themselves, meeting real robots rather becomes an 'inverted mirror' that shows us the boundaries of what we accept as human-like. In this, and a number of other Danish studies of humanoid robots engaging with people over time (e.g., Bruun et al. 2015; Nickelsen 2018; Blond 2019; Blond and Olesen 2020; Hasse 2018), it seems techno-animism is an ontogenetic process (Ingold 2016a, p. 303) rather than a stable relation.

In conclusion, I argue, as do Wentzer and Mattingly (2018), that although posthumanism is an important step to take along the way, it is only a transitional phase towards a 'philosophy with people in' (Ingold 1992, p. 696). Herein also lies the hope of a future that is not haunted by postmodern ghosts, the fundamental diversity of cultural relativism, frontier-bound ontologies, fixed dichotomies, or tech colonialism, but a place where people learn from non-humans and each other in a world where boundaries are constantly on the move.

CONSTRUCTING HUMANS

What is a human being? If anything, one would think that this basic question has defined anthropology as a discipline, which is, after all, named with a reference to Anthropos, but if one is to believe the anthropologist Tim Ingold this is by no means the case. Anthropology has made many studies of human practice (including scientific practice) without explicitly addressing the question of what humans are (Ingold 2004). Parts of anthropology have explicitly emphasised what man is *not*: here it is especially the poststructuralist-inspired anthropology that, following Michel Foucault, has written off modern Man as a historical category. As Foucault famously underlined, Man as a construction could be: 'erased, like a face drawn in sand at the edge of the sea' (1970, p. 422). The anthropologist Paul Rabinow found that this modern Man was one of many contained by the concept of *Anthropos,* and suggested that anthropology should not invest in further search of the true (hu) man:

> We can see more clearly today that Foucault's Man was only one instantiation of the figure of Anthropos. However, the one thing we should not be doing is attempting to find a new, hidden, deeper, unifying rationality or ontology. The alternative is not chaos. Rather, using the concept of problematization, and the topic of anthropos, we can direct our efforts toward inventing means of observing and analyzing how various logoi are currently being assembled into contingent forms. (Rabinow 2005, p. 41)

'*Anthropos*' is a construction which refers to 'the specific formation of the human sciences: anthropologies, logoi, of humans as biological and social beings' (Collier and Ong 2005, p. 69). Anthropos is, like 'the human', a contested category (Bauer and Wahlberg 2009).

In humanist anthropology the humans always had shifting boundaries in relation to the technological tools and animals in people's diverse lives (e.g., ulu-knives, seals, and caribou in Briggs 1970), but the focus was on humans as the protagonists. However, where in humanist anthropology the focus was on *human* values (e.g., Wulff 2019) some fieldwork also investigated the values of non-humans (especially animals)—such as Tim Ingold, among others, in his study of both people and reindeer in the Skolt Saami community (2013), and Viveiros De Castro (1998), who emphasises both animal and spirit subjectivities. From such studies emerge not just cultural relativism but a claim of different 'human' ontologies (De Castro 1998; Kohn 2007).

According to Descola (2013), naturalism is one of four ontologies, and is found mostly in the West, whereas animism is found outside of the West.[2] As alleged naturalists, Westerners may be said to view animals as resembling machines, and 'devoid of all the inner qualities typical of the human being' (Zuppi 2017, p. 131). How this idea of ontological diversity proposed by Descola (referring to differences in worlds not world views) can be brought forth by anthropologists has been less debated. If ontologies are tied to groups, it seems the ontological turn is back to making 'wholes' of cultures and social groups which are miraculously accessible to anthropologists. In the well-argued anthology *Thinking through things: theorising artefacts ethnographically* (Henare et al. 2007) different authors explore ontologies embedded in different worlds which are accessed by anthropologists through thinking, while employing 'to human' as a verb moves this discussion from ontology and relations to processes of relations (Hasse 2020b). In both approaches a dualist ontology is denied but in the first the emphasis is on relations, and in the second, on processes: for instance, anthropology as a process of education (Ingold 2018). The problem with the older category of 'the human' in anthropology was always a question of a dualistic ontology (West-the rest, us-them, nature-culture), although it was assumed we lived in the same world. The latter was challenged by the ontological turn (for debates see for instance De Castro 1998; Kohn 2007, 2009; Descola 2013, 2016). Moving towards ontogenetics (Ingold 2016a, 2016b) we can again live in the same world, just as we inhabit climate zones on the same planet. In Ingold's words: '[T]hat we all inhabit one world is, for me, a core principle of the discipline of anthropology. All too often, it seems to me, this principle has been neglected, along with the challenges and responsibilities it entails, in favour of a facile appeal to plurality' (Ingold 2016a, p. 303). If we assume that we live in the same world, whose world will it be?

It increasingly becomes clear that the interest in posthumanism is connected to our acknowledgement of how humans, however we define them, affect the globe in irreversible ways. This has brought back a new focus on how humans, however defined as *Anthropos,* engage with non-humans. Even if anthropologists paid attention to non-humans all along, their experiences with non-humans somehow did not always enter explicitly anthropological writings, as argued by Marianne Lien and Gisli Pálsson (2019). They recount an interview with the Norwegian anthropologist Frederik Barth, who is asked about his most enjoyable fieldwork experience. He recounts, smiling, how he, like the nomads he studied in Southern Persia, carried new born lambs that could not yet move with the herd in a sack around his neck, and how he felt the soft skin and the lamb's beating heart against his neck. Yet, in his writings, these experiences of being close to animals are not mentioned at all. Lien and Pálsson ask, what became of the animals and his clearly affective relation to them in his writings? (Lien and Pálsson 2019, p. 3). Such questions mark the shift away from the predominantly humanist agenda in anthropology towards a more-than-human posthumanism.

An interest in this new more-than-human has gained traction in anthropology while geologists who follow the development of the climate crisis have chosen to describe our geological age as '*the Anthropocene*'. Gisli Pálsson and colleagues have emphasised that anthropology needs to help conceptualise this human being that can destroy the environment on the planet: 'The larger conceptual task remains to reframe Anthropos for the modern context' (Pálsson et al. 2013, p. 4). In this perspective it seems problematic to reduce worlds to basic ontological perspectivism and ontological plurality. The *Anthropocene* has made it clear that humanist anthropology needs to change, and we may try to focus on processes of relations in an ever changing environment.

Expanding the Boundaries

The anthropological move towards posthumanism follows a more general trend. Where eighteenth-century humanism turned out, in the nineteenth century, to have been racist and sexist in its exclusion of certain groups from recognition as humans, the humanism of the twentieth century has turned out to be speciesist—privileging a human perspective over those of the non-humans (Wolfe 2010). 'To be posthumanist, anthropology must reject anthropocentrism, the assumption that everything revolves around us humans' (see Smart and Smart 2017, p. 4).

The humanistic understanding, which, for instance, was expressed in interpretive anthropology, had an anthropocentric focus understood as a less inclusive analysis: not granting stuff like technology or animals agency (unless mentioned by local humans); prone to dualistic thinking (separating nature and culture, humans from humans, or humans from non-humans); and problems with a recognition of the biases and baggage of Western humanist worldviews. It mainly focused on humans, their ontology, organisations, and agency and overlooked theoretically all material and non-human becoming with the humans. In the wake of post-structuralism and postmodernism came a new vocabulary in the humanities pointing in the direction of the posthuman, where 'emergence replaces teleology; reflexive epistemology replaces objectivism; distributed cognition replaces autonomous will; embodiment replaces a body seen as a support system for the mind' (Hayles 1999, p. 288).

Today the field of posthumanism constitutes a number of connected, yet sometimes contradictory, directions which may be roughly grouped under two headings: 'singularist' and 'spinozist' (Hasse 2020a, pp. 110–113). The first approach can be termed 'singularist' following the work of Google engineer Ray Kurzweil, who envisions a singular moment in history when humans cease to exist and are replaced by hyper intelligent AI and robotic machines (Kurzweil 2005). Flesh and blood humans need to disappear as a result of technological enhancement (e.g., More and Vita-More 2013) which will transcend human capabilities by improvements (e.g., through AI) to the extent that we become a new race (sometimes referred to as posthumanism, sometimes transhumanism). This singularist, posthuman/transhumanist machine is an engineered triumph understood as a stand-alone figure capable of rational, creative thinking, and having autonomous agency that is free to attach and influence a surrounding world. The singularist wish is to transform human bodies and minds (Kurzweil 2012) in ways that will ensure human intelligence supremacy.[3] New technologies like robots, artificial intelligence (AI), prosthetic limbs, and virtual reality (VR) have all played a part in transhumanist fantasies about the transformations of humans (e.g., More and Vita-More 2013) in which posthumanism becomes equivalent with transhumanism.

The apparently dethroned liberal humanist subject, which thought it could technologically exploit nature for its own good, is resurrected by the singularists in the forceful image of the Vitruvian Man drawn by Leonardo da Vinci around 1490. He (and it is a 'he') was formed after the perfect proportions designated by the Roman architect Vitruvius and placed right in the middle with the unquestioned right (and intelligent ability) to maintain order and use technology to form natural resources and non-humans as he pleases. This master of the universe will use technology to enhance all kinds of feeble biology through engineered devices, thereby emphasising engineers' right to transform Earth intelligently.

It has increasingly been acknowledged that, although it was originally expected that the new vocabulary of emergence, reflexive epistemology, distributed cognition, and embodiment could replace 'the liberal humanist subject's manifest destiny to dominate and control nature', while going hand in hand with a 'dynamic partnership between humans and intelligent machines' (Hayles 1999, p. 288), this was rather naive. The figure of the Vitruvian singularist posthuman basically becomes a term for a kind of technology-merged cyborgian figure, which prioritises the technologically enhanced super human. As this posthuman has no feeble body, all signs of race, ethnicity, class, and gender are also erased as it promises global enhancements—an example of what the anthropologist Sareeta Amrute has named 'Tech Colonialism Today' (Amrute 2019).

Another approach can be termed 'spinozist' (Hasse 2020a, p. 110) as at its base it often refers to the seventeenth-century philosopher Baruch Spinoza, whose thoughts resonate throughout posthumanist theories in feminist studies, science and STS, literary studies, philosophy, and anthropology (e.g., Rosi Braidotti, Karen Barad, Jane Bennett, Bruno Latour, Tim Ingold, Stefan Helmreich, Don Ihde, Robert Rosenberger, Peter-Paul Verbeek, Rosi Braidotti, Donna Haraway, and Kathrine Hayles). This conceptual and theoretical approach expands what it may mean to be human and wants us to acknowledge our humble position on planet Earth.[4] On the theoretical and conceptual side, we find a showdown with Vitruvian humanism and tech colonialism. Many strong movements in New Feminist Materialism, philosophy, and STS oppose Renaissance humanism and move towards anti-humanist and posthumanist stances (e.g., Wolfe 2010; Braidotti 2013; Barad 2007).[5] The posthumanism which emerges forms a new direction for studies of humans, with a renewed focus on non-humans (e.g., Latour 1992). Although some, like Haraway (1991), also praised the cyborg, the meaning of this figure was not about enhancement but the evaporation of boundaries: for instance, between nature and culture (which become nature-culture), machine and flesh, reality and fiction, body and mind.

The spinozists are mainly concerned with understanding humans in a humble way as entangled with the non-human world. They question human exceptionalism and our right to destroy life conditions for humans and non-humans, as well as questioning the Vitruvian normative and bounded conceptions of intelligent humans. In this perspective 'the world and humans are not dualistic entities structured according to principles of internal or external opposition' (Braidotti 2013, p. 56). This posthumanism questions the inherent dichotomies tied to 'autonomy', 'intelligence', and 'rationality', and opens up a new creative material vitality that crosses all kinds of human boundaries (Hasse 2020a, pp. 100–113).

The posthuman is, in the spinozist version, a new, post-anthropocentric, many-faceted theoretical framework that decentres humans in a world of distributed forces and pressures, which renders the wilful agency of the humanist approach a long-gone fairy tale.

The posthuman is thus a concept with two contradictory meanings: on the one hand, it refers to a transhumanist enhancement of humans that will eventually lead to a technically formed posthuman. On the other, there is a variety of new ways to understand humans as already implicated and entangled with non-humans. Taking the two together, the posthuman, in other words, needs to 'cope with an urgency for the integral redefinition of the notion of the human, following the onto-epistemological as well as scientific and bio-technological developments of the twentieth and twenty-first centuries' (Ferrando 2013, p. 26).

There is no sharp demarcation line between these directions, as the conceptual and physical transformations of humans constantly engage. Both of these directions have an impact on an anthropology of technology. Both seek an expansion of what it means 'to human'.

ACKNOWLEDGING TECHNOLOGICAL BOUNDARY MAKING

The Vitruvian singularist posthumanism shares, with anthropology and STS studies, an interest in dissolving fixed borders of what it means 'to human' through technology. In anthropology we lean towards the spinozist posthumanism as we reconceptualise Anthropos together with concepts like 'more-than-human', beyond the human, or multi-species ethnography (e.g., Kirksey and Helmreich 2010; Lien and Pálsson 2019). There are debates about the terms. Some absolutely hate the term posthuman (often because it is conflated with enhancement theories), others embrace it (often in the spinozist version). Other terms like multi-species ethnography (Kirksey and Helmreich 2010) are also criticised as they imply a universal, species-being humanity: 'For only in the purview of a universal humanity—that is, from the perspective of species-being—does the world of living things appear as a catalogue of biodiversity, as a plurality of species' (Ingold 2013, p. 19).

In the posthumanist process of acknowledging entanglements and dependencies, what it means to be human seems to endlessly expand. Studies of how we merge and become with all kinds of non-humans, from mushrooms, bacteria, implants to Petri dishes, proliferate (e.g., Franklin 2013; Tsing 2010;

Kirksey and Helmreich 2010; Suchman 2008). The ethnographers put themselves in the place of not just 'other humans' but also our 'kins' among plants and animals (e.g., Tsing 2012). These anthropologies challenge our sense of boundaries, in a healthy way, and confuse our self-evident understanding of traditional ways to conceptualise kinship, gender, and ethnicity. They also question whether this human with new boundaries has a right to do what the Vitruvian posthuman takes for granted.

It is no longer about different ontologies, animism, trans-species relations, or even humans learning with animals or plants and regarding them as kin; it is about saving the planet by siting with animals and plants rather than humans. The traditional advocacy of anthropologists protecting marginalised humans can in this posthuman perspective lead to an advocacy of prioritising animals' rights—like the elephants in Helen Kopnina's posthuman ethnography—even if this threatens the livelihood of indigenous people like poachers (e.g., Kopnina 2012). Moving towards posthuman anthropology not only means a greater awareness that Man is not always at the centre of anthropological studies, it is a development that is almost unthinkable without the technologies humans have invented; indeed, new anthropological studies of how we human with bacteria and animals are facilitated by commercial, human-made technologies.

When we extend our understanding of what it means 'to human' and look for kinship with bacteria, cells, mushrooms, and elephants, these explorations are to some extent connected to man-made technologies (GPS, microscopes, AI, internet) which set the new boundaries for what we can perceive and discuss. These mediating devices become the invisible means that make us dissolve borders, often without recognising the politics and power structures embedded in these technologies.[6] The seemingly endlessly expanding boundaries of what it means to human are partly engineered, partly a global cultural force promoted by certain technologies developed by humans in power. Posthumanist anthropology seems cut down the middle: either it studies non-human animals and plants (often helped by technologies)—or it studies technologies as designed cyborgian devices, such as AI or robots. An anthropology of technology may pay particular attention to what anthropology has to offer these debates in relation to a critical perspective on commercial technology, as it has been done in human kinship research, for example (e.g., Franklin 2013).

The mapping of the Human Genome Project studied by, among others, the anthropologists Rabinow and Gisli Pálsson (e.g., 1999), and fertility studies (Franklin 2013) involved many new technologies: petri dishes, decoding databases, sequencing machines, data analysis software, computer hardware. Advanced APS (Anti-Poaching System), and GPS equipment is often used to track poachers shooting endangered species such as rhinos, elephants, and tigers (Kamminga et al. 2018). Our nascent posthuman awareness of the planet's miserable condition and human impact on it is due to a sea of new technologies, from drilling ice cores in Greenland, to surveillance technologies, seismographs, and more. All of these technologies profoundly affect anthropology whether this is recognised or not.

Although many technologies do 'invisible work' (Star and Strauss 1999), anthropological STS scholars have increasingly focused on the technologies themselves and how they transform what it means to be human (e.g., the new technologies which enable posthuman studies of animals, bacteria, virus, and cells). The philosopher of technology, Don Ihde, has, for instance, emphasised that technologies deeply affect us in a relational ontology: 'When we humans use technologies, both what the technology "is" or may be, and we, as users undergo an embodying process—we invent our technologies, but, in use, they re-invent us as well' (Ihde 2007, p. 243).

Trying to understand new technologies highlights the power play between the disciplines in academia, between anthropologists, the engineering architects of the techno-culture, and people outside of academia engaged in many other mundane practices. This again points to the ontogenetic diversity in which we continuously become humans in processes involving, among other things, commercially made technologies. Some create new technologies (like the invention of plastic) while others experience technology as a new environment they must learn to live with. Our ontogenetic becoming involves different experiences of environmental changes following the agency of humans and non-humans.

If human ontologies are transformed when our environments are transformed (some for the better and some for the worse) how can we identify who can address the Anthropocene and ensure sustainability? If we live in the same world, should we accept the extinction of humans as a species to ensure the survival of non-humans? Should anthropologists' side with elephants rather than poachers? Are people (regardless of ontogenesis) still a priority in anthropology (e.g., over trees, elephants, and other non-humans)? Will singularist technology become tech colonialism? Are we already so entangled that it makes no sense to uphold differences between people, animals, things, material, and immaterial?

In this conundrum we may call for a new less philosophical and more empirically based humanism (Wentzer and Mattingly 2018) and this is where studies of the humanoid robots and other technology may help us. In the new humanism we may reject the idea of a fixed speciesist humanity while acknowledging that humans are learners in ways robots never can be—and that ontogenetic processes dissolve what first appear as different ontologies. All humans can learn, but anthropological studies of humanoid robots claiming to be a mirror of human existence show that there are boundaries to how humans can learn to merge seamlessly with commercial technology.

Humaning Humanoids

'It's looking right at me! Look, it's winking at me!' Ida's voice is almost in the high pitch. Along with 22 classmates aged 8–9, she sits on the floor in front of a new 'teacher'. The robot NAO stands on a high stool and 'looks' kindly towards the children. Its round eyes occasionally change colour, it moves and turns its head, and it seems to be breathing ever so slightly. It does not say anything, but when the children are sometimes silent you can hear a faint breathing. 'Is it alive?' Anders asks.

The Danish school class first met NAO together with a group of anthropologists from Aarhus University, Denmark, in 2015.[7] We studied how children envisioned a future with robots and how children expected humans to engage with robots. As part of the study, we wanted to learn more about 'children's culture' and how it encompassed robots. As in other studies we undertook (Sorenson et al. 2019; Hasse and Søndergaard 2020) on how adults envision robots in healthcare and schools, we found that the children initially perceived robots as a kind of 'mirror' existence. We asked the children to draw robots for us and in their drawings the lively robots were almost all humanoid and did everything the children did themselves: dance, watch television, eat ice-cream, go fishing with their fathers, play and fall in love—and some also carried guns and dropped bombs like adult humans.

Robots are envisioned by all, apart from a small group of children, to be mostly friendly humanoids capable of being in the world as if they were humans. So, when we introduce them to the humanoid robot NAO, it is the first time that many of them have met a real robot; their expectations stem from encounters with robots in movies and on the internet. They were clearly fascinated and did all they could to make contact. The children shared, with politicians, journalists, movie-makers, philosophers, and a few engineers in our research, a vision of robots as so human-like that it does not seem farfetched when some politicians envision a future where robots should be granted rights as humans (e.g., Robertson 2014). This emphasis on robots as human-like has not just been promoted in movies and videos but has also been reinforced by government politics in, for instance, Denmark (Hasse 2013) and Japan (Robertson, this handbook). In Japan a robotic future politically entails companionship with humanoid robots, for example, in our family life (e.g., Robertson 2010, and this handbook).

Politicians and children who live in heavily industrialised countries like Japan, Denmark, South Korea, USA, and in Europe have already formed expectations of this future with humanoid robots from politics and media. In movies like *Star Wars*, *Ex Machina*, as well as in 'demonstration' videos of 'real humanoids' on YouTube, robots are 'represented by media people, some of whom are hired by robot developers and makers' (Sorenson et al. 2019, p. 18).

Granting robots rights as if they were humans (e.g., Robertson 2014) could be said to be in line with a wider posthuman approach to dissolving human-material boundaries. There is a new movement, in and beyond anthropology, to grant animals, trees, and rivers rights as if they were humans (e.g., Alley 2019).[8] This is not animism and ontology, but an acknowledgement that humans are not the only existence on Earth with rights. In the spinozist posthumanism there is no nature separate from culture. Therefore, there is no distinction between commercial non-humans created by humans to make money (and fame), and non-humans like rivers, elephants, and trees. It is, therefore, in line with the posthumanist turn not to question recent demands for robot rights although, contrary to rights granted to rivers, elephants, and trees (e.g., Alley 2019; Kopnina 2012), these rights seem to hinge on how much humanoid robots actually are accepted as human-like.

Most anthropological studies of these humanoid robots have been media-based studies or studies made in the laboratories where the humanoids are forged (e.g., Atanasoski and Vora 2020; Kemiksiz 2020; Lindegaard 2020; Richardson 2015; Suchman 2011; Leeson 2017). Many anthropologists have been particularly interested in studying humanoid robots together with their creators in Japan and USA. From USA we have, for example, studies by Richardson (2015) and Suchman (2011), and in Japan there are several studies of the laboratory of the Japanese robot designer Hiroshi Ishiguro, where the 'human model is incorporated into the robot's machinery in order for it to assume its character and presence, thus becoming not so much a representation as an extension of Professor Ishiguro himself' (Leeson 2017, p. 64).

The engineers' attempt to mimic humans in robots has been explained by Kathleen Richardson as a creation of 'Otherness'. The making of robots 'is a mimetic process, whereby robotic scientists act out human behaviours to embed them in the machines they create. The making of robots can be understood as a practice in alterity as Otherness' (Richardson 2010, p. 75). The same point has been made by Lucy Suchman; humans create posthuman 'others' through self-imagery (Suchman 2011).

When engineers mimic humans, they project their (gendered) selves into their anthropomorphic robots; consequently, anthropologists find countless ways humans are mirrored in humanoids: through gender, sexism, family and kinship, and ethnicity (e.g., Robertson 2010; Richardson 2010; Suchman 2011). Exactly the same patterns are found in the Danish children's drawings of robots; male robots carry weapons and female robots have bows. While posthumanist anthropologists, such as those associated with STS, have made an effort to break down dichotomies between male and female, self and other, nature and culture (e.g., Latour 1993) such dichotomies are prevalent in the creation of humanoids. The real humanoid robots seem to anchor all the gender stereotypes found in media robots (e.g., Atanasoski and Vora 2020).

What happens then, when the children meet a real robot-like NAO? Even if they keep trying to make contact, NAO never responds like the robots in their drawings and, eventually, they grow tired of it. When they realise how much work and effort it takes to make NAO respond they give it up and the fascination wears off.

This is what happens when imaginaries of a posthuman future meet reality. Over the last ten years a number of my colleagues and I have studied experiments of moving humanoid robots from robot laboratories into people's everyday lives (Krause-Jensen et al. 2020; Sorenson et al. 2019; Blond 2019; Wallace 2019; Bruun et al. 2015; Nickelsen 2018; Hasse 2013, 2015a, 2018). Many of these studies show robots as very active protagonists that change the life of the humans in their surroundings. Humans' willingness to stretch their sociality seems an important part of what constitutes the human-like sociality of robots (e.g., Hasse 2015a), which follows findings in other studies, particularly from the USA and Korea, that also show humans are necessary co-creators if imaginaries of human-like robots are to be maintained (e.g., Šabanović 2014; Alač et al. 2011; Jeon et al. 2020). But the Danish (and Finnish) studies (e.g., Blond 2019; Hasse 2018) also show that it takes hard work to maintain a belief that these robots mirror humans and that over time such efforts often fail. Although engineers build their own conceptions of humans into their anthropomorphic machines, humans in general seem to grow tired of working so hard to project human liveliness onto robots when engaging with machines in social spaces.

While robots may look like humans, and even to some extent respond like humans, they are not capable of what we, inspired by the anthropologist Tim Ingold, could call 'humaning'.

To be human does not refer to a fixed category. To human is a process; it is a verb (Ingold 2013, p. 19) in which animals and stuff can be included as we attend to each other in ongoing processes. As Tim Ingold puts it in his Westermarck Memorial Lecture to the Finnish Anthropological Society, he became almost affiliated with reindeers, whom he began to consider on the same terms as human beings, as sentient and responsive creatures—just like the Skolt Saami with whom he lived: 'I began to talk about reindeer as if they were people—as if they existed in communities of their own, with their own social organisation, and made their own decisions on matters affecting their lives including, most crucially, how to respond to the presence and demands of humans' (Ingold 2013, p. 6). The same kind of relational ontology is present in many older and newer anthropologies, although not always recognised as such (e.g., Lien and Pálsson 2019).

Yet to our surprise neither children nor adults in the Danish context seemed to remain convinced of the human-like qualities of humanoids when they engaged with them over time; thus, even the most humanoid robots do not qualify to be considered human-like. Why is it that these robots in Denmark do not always practice the verb 'to human'? This calls for a deeper understanding of the processes involved in creating robots and humans—and in the end, rather than discarding the notion of humans, it calls for a renewed humanism (Wentzer and Mattingly 2018). One way of moving beyond the posthuman towards a new humanism could be to follow processes of learning. Something seems to happen when real robots leave the lab and learn to mingle with people in their messy lives.

Ontogenesis

The question becomes whether these humanoids are convincingly animated once they leave the labs and move into mundane messy life? For a long time, studies of animism in anthropology were reserved for personifications of nature (Richardson 2016, p. 110). Recently a new type of animism has inspired anthropologists to coin the term techno-animism or technological animism (Jensen and Blok 2013; Richardson 2016). However, Danish studies differ from other anthropological analysis of techno-animism: for instance, Paro, a baby-like harp seal robot, seems to be accepted as part of a family in Japan (Jensen and Blok 2013, p. 101), whereas in Denmark it is rejected over time (Hasse 2013). Are these findings really a confirmation that in Denmark people try to uphold the asymmetrical nature-culture distinction Latour and others try to dissolve (Latour 1993)? Are they a confirmation of different ontologies (Descola 2013)?

What speaks against these assumptions is that the Danish studies show a process of really hard work on the human part of the relation to accept and include the humanoid robots. In none of the studies are the robots rejected up front. On the contrary, the Danes even go to extremes to uphold the idea of the humanoids as human-like (maybe most prevalent in the studies by Christina Leeson [2017] and Lasse Blond [2019]); however, the Danes learn that, as time passes, their perceptions of robots change. Over time they begin to see robots as most engineers in our studies do (albeit not those in Ishiguru's lab)— as mere machines (Sorenson et al. 2019; Hansen 2018; Sorenson 2018); even when they make humanoids, they are aware that the actual machinery is more or less the same as in coffee machines, for example. 'Because the coffee machine in the bar is a robot, actually, because it has some sensors, it elaborates on flow and heat data, and it enacts some activity on the basis of this data. So actually, yeah, there are a lot of robots in my life' (Victor, robot designer and engineer, in Hasse 2020a, p. 25).

The same acknowledgement of robots as machines seems to emerge when we explore how children learn about robots. The more time children spend with robots, and especially when they build them themselves, the more they begin to draw robots without an innate liveliness controlled by nuts and bolts. The children with hands-on experiences with robots like NAO or LEGO Mindstorm seem to go through a learning process which changes how they perceive robots as less life-like and more technical humanoids in their drawings (Hasse 2020a, Chapters 1 and 2). Thus, if humans can differ in their views of technology over time, but robots remain fixed in their representations of humans, this can challenge the debate on ontologies and techno-animism. Robots seems to be in a stable representational relation with the world (a fixed ontology), whereas humans go through ontogenetic material-conceptual processes rather than relying on a fixed ontology.

Following Ingold, 'If we must have a "turn", let it not be ontological but ontogenetic! Ontological multiplicity gives us many worlds, all but closed to one another. Ontogenetic multiplicity, by contrast, traces open-ended pathways of becoming within one world of nevertheless continuous variation' (Ingold 2016a, p. 303). This process, creating diversity in an onto-epistemological process, is what I have termed 'cultural learning processes', which materialise the world differently as we move through it and learn from humans and non-humans (Hasse 2020b). This is the very process which makes anthropology possible (Hasse 2015b) but also begs questions of how anthropology is done in different parts of the world (e.g., Denmark and Japan). It reminds us that no matter what we call the anthropologists debating different ontologies it would not be entirely wrong to call them humans that learn in different ways. For the very same reason Cheryl Mattingly and Thomas Wentzer call for a new humanism:

> No matter where one lands in this debate [on ontology and the same world debate, red.], the primary point we are making here is that even a posthuman ontology does not free itself from consideration of the human. In fact, one could argue that it actually highlights the need to revisit a concept of the human in light of the ontological possibility to conceive of nonhuman agency and nonhuman agent. (Wentzer and Mattingly 2018, p. 148)

Ontology neither develops nor is changed without processes of learning involving all kinds of humans and non-humans.

Contrary to animals, humans have a division between those who make the technologies (supported by state-politics) and those who use them. Here our empirical studies indicate that processes of ontogeny in building robots also change how we perceive them. It is no longer just about relations (e.g., Šabanović 2020), but studies of relations with materials over time. Engineers are more prone to expect humanoids to be machines than people with no previous experience with robots. Humanoid robots sold by commercial laboratories and a media industry promise limitless entanglements, but meet boundaries when entangled over time with the messy lives of humans.

CONCLUSION

We increasingly become aware that, while non-humans were always present in anthropology, they are now distinctly recognised as an ethnography beyond the human takes form (Lien and Pálsson 2019). Humanism focused on humans—whereas posthumanism focuses on either non-humans or human and non-human entanglements. In this world, we (humans and non-humans) most certainly do not share an evenly distributed responsibility for making room for, or destroying, diversity—yet it is a world where we share a de facto common interest in maintaining a habitat.

Humans are present, even when left out of anthropological analysis, in all of these entanglements as anthropologists and technology made by humans. Even when we believe we look solely at non-humans there is, often invisibly, a technology present which at some point was made by humans which has enabled both the study and questions we ask. And it is humans, however defined, asking the questions. Humans who, like anthropologists, care to divide the world into humans, non-humans, and posthumans. Humans who create the Anthropocene or try to work against it. All these apparatuses are political and ethical as well as ontoepistemic (Barad 2007).[9]

Humanoid robots can help us understand what humans share, and maybe share with some animals as well (an ability to learn to ontogenise and to human), and where we differ (in entanglements with non-humans). It literally matters whether anthropologists solely refer to humanoids in media or include studies of robots implemented to engage with humans in their everyday lives in Japan or Denmark over time. Although humans should be thought of, and treated as, participants in larger assemblages, anthropology in particular has a significant role to play in providing theoretical tools for understanding how *Anthropocene* occurs in a world of inequality. This entails a focus where we no longer privilege fixed human perspectives, but are open to studies of processes of relational ontogenetic transformations with tech colonialism. Posthumanism made an important step in that direction by decentring humans, but new humanism, aided by and critical towards studies of technologies, points us in new directions that find hope in learning processes, which continuously dissolve relativisms, boundaries, and what we took to be fixed categories and ontologies, to create new ones. We need this 'new humanism' with people in it (Wentzer and Mattingly 2018) to move beyond the old humanism and enhancement posthumanism towards a deeper study of ontogenetics in ecologically messy lives made by humans and non-humans.

It may seem self-evident that perceptions and attentions change ontogenetically when we learn through hands-on experiences, but this process of learning with non-humans has ontogenetic implications which reach far beyond playing with robots. It shows us that 'to human' has boundaries set by the human and non-human entanglements *over time*. Anthropologists are, contrary to robots, like other humans able to learn about other people's relational transformations with their environment. This may be something robots can teach us: we are all learners (Hasse 2015b). We may have a propensity towards confirming our fixed categories of relations (dualist ontologies which separate human from non-humans), but we are also able to learn new ones. This moves our anthropological attention on what it means to human with technology from relations to processes of relations.

Notes

1. 'Humanistic anthropology involves the recognition that professional inquiry takes places in a context of human value. The humanistic orientation is particularly concerned with the personal, ethical, and political choices facing humans' (Wulff 2019, p. 1).
2. The four ontologies differ in terms of similar and dissimilar interiorities versus physicality. They are found in different parts of the world, and apart from animism and naturalism we also find totemism and analogism (Descola 2013). Ingold and Descola have had a hot debate on whether Descola sees these ontologies as framed within a naturalist framework or not (Ingold 2016a, 2016b; Descola 2016).

3. Singularity is a term from physics which Ray Kurzweil uses to explain what happens when our merging with machines make us so intelligent that we are no longer humans. This point is singular and changes everything (Kurzweil 2005).
4. There are also a few anti-humanists calls for 'doing away' with the human race altogether because we destroy life on planet Earth.
5. Francesca Ferrando does a good job in explaining the differences between various theoretical positions and the different meanings of these terms in '*Posthumanism, transhumanism, antihumanism, metahumanism,* and *new materialisms*' (Ferrando 2013).
6. Moreover, 'mediation' is a contested term. Here it refers to the man-made instruments which transform perceptions when we have learned to use them (Aagaard et al. 2018).
7. The children participated in the project 'The Robot is Present' conducted with the help of Danish schools and a Danish local museum, 'Museum', in the town of Skive in 2015 (see Hasse 2020a, pp. 167–199 and Hasse 2020c).
8. For examples of rights granted to a river considered human-like, rights for trees attributed with human-like characteristics, and rights for animals considered to be like humans. However, some also emphasise that animals, trees, and rivers should have rights of their own (if modelled on human rights), for example Alley 2019 and Kopnina 2012.
9. Barad talks of ethics, ontology, and epistemology as inseparable, coining the term 'ethico-onto-epistem-ology' (Barad 2007, p. 90).

References

Aagaard, J., Friis, J. K. B., Sorenson, J., Tafdrup, O. A., & *Hasse*, C. (Eds.) (2018). *Postphenomenological Methodologies: New Ways in Mediating Techno-Human Relationships.* (Postphenomenology and the Philosophy of Technology). New York: Lexington Books

Alač, M., Movellan, J., & Tanaka, F. (2011). When a Robot Is Social: Spatial Arrangements and Multimodal Semiotic Engagement in the Practice of Social Robotics. *Social Studies of Science, 41*(6), 893–926. https://doi.org/10.1177/0306312711420565.

Alley, K. D. (2019). *River Goddesses, Personhood and Rights of Nature: Implications for Spiritual Ecology. Religions, 10.* https://doi.org/10.3390/rel10090502.

Amrute, S. (2019). Tech Colonialism Today. Sareeta Amrute's keynote talk at EPIC2019. https://www.epicpeople.org/amrute-tech-colonialism-today/. Accessed 14 June 2021.

Atanasoski, N., & Vora, K. (2020). Why the Sex Robot becomes the Killer Robot. Reproduction, Care, and the Limits of Refusal. *Spheres: Journal for Digital Cultures. #6 Politics of Reproduction, 6,* 1–16. https://doi.org/10.25969/mediarep/13850.

Barad, K. (2007). *Meeting the universe halfway: Quantum physics and the entanglement of matter and meaning.* Durham, NC.: Duke University Press.

Bauer, S., & Wahlberg, A. (2009). Introduction: categories of life. In S. *Bauer & A. Wahlberg (Ed.), Contested Categories: 4 (Theory, Technology and Society)* (pp. 1–14). Aldershot: Ashgate.

Blond, L. (2019). *Dances with robots: Understanding social robots in practice.* Research Output. PhD thesis. Aarhus: Aarhus University.

Blond, L., & Olesen, F. (2020). Unpacking the cultural baggage of travelling robots: How socially assistive robots are integrated in practice. In C. Hasse, & D. M. Søndergaard (Eds.), *Designing Robots—Designing Humans*. New York & London: Routledge.

Braidotti, R. (2013). *The Posthuman*. Cambridge: Polity Press.

Bruun, M., Hasse, C., & Hanghøj, S. (2015). Studying social robots in practiced places. *Techne: Research in Philosophy and Technology, 19*(2), 143–165.

Briggs, J. (1970). *Never in Anger: Portrait of an Eskimo Family*. Cambridge: President and Fellows of Harvard College.

Collier, S. J., & Ong, A. (2005). Global assemblages, anthropological problems. In A. Ong & S. J. Collier (Eds.), *Global Assemblages. Technology, Politics, and Ethics as Anthropological Problems* (pp. 3–21). Malden, Oxford & Carlton: Blackwell Publishing.

De Castro, E. V. (1998). Cosmological deixis and Amerindian perspectivism. *Journal of the Royal Anthropological Institute, 4*(3), 469–488.

Descola, P. (2013). *Beyond Nature and Culture*. (trans: Lloyd, J.). Chicago: University of Chicago Press.

Descola, P. (2016). Biolatry: A surrender of understanding. Response to Ingold's "A naturalist abroad in the museum of ontology". *Anthropological Forum, 26*, 321–328.

Ferrando, F. (2013). Posthumanism, transhumanism, antihumanism, metahumanism, and new materialisms: differences and relations. *Existenz, 8*(2), 26–32.

Foucault, M. (1970). *The Order of Things: An Archaeology of the Human Sciences*. New York: Pantheon.

Franklin, S. (2013). In *vitro anthropos*: New conception models for a recursive anthropology? *Cambridge Anthropology, 31*(1), 3–32.

Hansen, S. (2018). *If we had a specific idea of the product 12 months ago, it would never be what we have today! A study in situational pragmatic actions and strategies in everyday technological development*. (REELER Working Paper Series no. 3). Aarhus University, Copenhagen, Denmark.

Haraway, D. (1991) A Cyborg Manifesto: Science, Technology, and Socialist Feminism in the Late Twentieth Century. In *Simians, Cyborgs and Women: The Reinvention of Nature* (pp. 149–181). New York: Routledge.

Hasse, C., & D. M. Søndergaard (Eds.) (2020). *Designing Robots—Designing Humans*. New York & London: Routledge.

Hasse, C. (2013). Artefacts that talk: Mediating technologies as multistable signs and tools. *Subjectivity, 6*(1), 79–100.

Hasse, C. (2015a). Multistable roboethics. In J. K. B. O. Friis & R. P. Crease (Eds.). *Technoscience and Postphenomenology: The Manhattan Papers* (pp. 169–188). Lanham, MD.: Rowman & Littlefield Publishers.

Hasse, C. (2015b) *An Anthropology of Learning*. Dordrecht: Springer

Hasse, C. (2018). How robots challenge institutional practices. *Learning, Culture and Social Interaction, 26*. https://doi.org/10.1016/j.lcsi.2018.04.003.

Hasse, C. (2020a) *Posthumanist Learning*. London: Routledge.

Hasse, C. (2020b). Material hermeneutics as cultural learning: from relations to processes of relations. *AI & Soc*. https://doi.org/10.1007/s00146-021-01171-7.

Hasse, C. (2020c) Material Concept Formation. In C. Hasse & D. M. Søndergaard (Eds.), *Designing Robots—Designing Humans* (pp. 88–110). New York & London: Routledge. https://doi.org/10.4324/9781315227207-7.

Hayles, K. (1999). *How We Became Posthuman; Virtual Bodies in Cybernetics, Literature, and Informatics*. Chicago: The University of Chicago Press.

Henare, A., Holbraad, M., & Wastell, S. (Eds.) (2007). *Thinking through things: theorising artefacts ethnographically*. London: Routledge

Ihde, I. (2007). *Listening and voice: phenomenologies of sound*. State University of New York Press.

Ingold, T. (1992). Editorial. *Man* (N.S.), *27*(4), 693–696.

Ingold, T. (2004). Anthropology after Darwin. *Social Anthropology, 12*, 177–179.

Ingold, T. (2013). Anthropology beyond humanity Edward Westermarck Memorial Lecture, May 2013. Suomen Antropologi: *Journal of the Finnish Anthropological Society, 38*(3), 5–23.

Ingold, T. (2016a). A Naturalist Abroad in the Museum of Ontology: Philippe Descola's Beyond Nature and Culture, *Anthropological Forum, 26*(3), 301–320. https://doi.org/10.1080/00664677.2015.1136591.

Ingold, T. (2016b). Rejoinder to Descola's 'Biolatry: a surrender of understanding. *Anthropological Forum, 26*(3), 329–332. https://doi.org/10.1080/00664677.2016.1212532.

Ingold, T. (2018). *Anthropology and/as Education*. London: Routledge

Jensen, C. B., & Blok, A. (2013). Techno-animism in Japan: Shinto cosmograms, actor-network theory, and the enabling powers of non-human agencies. *Theory, Culture & Society, 30*(2), 84–115. https://doi.org/10.1177/0263276412456564.

Jeon, C. Shin, H., Kim, S., & Jeong, H. (2020) Talking over the robot. A field study of strained collaboration in a dementia-prevention robot class. *Interaction Studies, 21*(1), 85–110. https://doi.org/10.1075/is.18054.jeo.

Kamminga, J., Ayele, E., Meratnia, N., & Havinga, P. (2018). Poaching detection technologies—a survey. *Sensors, 18*(5).

Kemiksiz, A. (2020). *An Ethnography of Robotics: Potentials and Challenges in Making Robots More Human*. Osaka: Osaka University.

Kohn, E. (2007). How dogs dream: Amazonian natures and the politics of transspecies engagement, *American Ethnologist, 34*(1), 3–24.

Kohn, E. (2009). A Conversation with Philippe Descola. *Tipití: Journal of the Society for the Anthropology of Lowland South America, 7*(2), 135–150

Kopnina, H. (2012). Toward conservational anthropology: addressing anthropocentric bias in anthropology. *Dialectical Anthropology, 36*(1–2), 127–46.

Leeson, C. (2017). *Anthropomorphic Robots on the Move. A Transformative Trajectory from Japan to Danish Healthcare*. Research output. PhD thesis. Copenhagen: Copenhagen University.

Lindegaard, J. F. (2020). *Parallax Machines: An Ethnography on Artificial Life in the Real World*. PhD thesis. Copenhagen: IT University of Copenhagen.

Krause-Jensen, J. Hansen, S., & Skårup, B. (2020) *Robotten/Teknologien som 'kollega'. Et bidrag til en bedre udvikling og anvendelse af teknologier om bord på skibe.* (The Robot/Technology as a 'colleague'. A contribution to the better development and use of technologies on board ships). Research Report. Aarhus Universitet. https://dpu.au.dk/fileadmin/ingen_mappe_valgt/Robotten_teknologien_som_kollega_Aarhus_Universitet_Maj2020_FINAL.pdf. Accessed 14 June 2021.

Kirksey, E., & Helmreich, S. (2010). The Emergence of Multispecies Ethnography. *Cultural Anthropology, 25*(4), 545–76.

Kurzweil, R. (2005). *The singularity is near: when humans transcend biology*. New York: Viking

Kurzweil, R. (2012). *How to Create a Mind: The Secret of Human Thought Revealed.* New York: Viking

Latour, B. (1992). Where are the missing masses? The sociology of a few mundane artifacts. In W. Bijker & J. Law (Eds.), *Shaping Technology/Building Society: Studies in Sociotechnical Change* (pp. 225–258). Cambridge, MA.: The MIT Press.

Latour, B. (1993). *We have never been modern.* Cambridge, MA.: Harvard University Press

Lien, M. E., & Pálsson, G. (2019). Ethnography Beyond the Human: The 'Other-than-Human' in Ethnographic Work. *Ethnos, 86*(1), 1–20. https://doi.org/10.108 0/00141844.2019.1628796.

More, M., & Vita-More, N. (Eds.) (2013). *The Transhumanist Reader: Classical and Contemporary Essays on the Science, Technology, and Philosophy of the Human Future.* New Jersey: Wiley-Blackwell.

Nickelsen, N. C. M. (2018). *Feeding assistive robotics, socio-technological imaginaries, and care: The case of Bestic.* (REELER Working Paper Series no. 2). Aarhus University, Copenhagen, Denmark.

Pálsson, G., & Rabinow, P. (1999). Iceland: The Case of a National *Human Genome* Project. *Anthropology Today, 15*(5), 14–18.

Pálsson, G., Szerszynski, B., Sörlin, S., Marks, J., Avril, B., & Crumley, C. (2013). Reconceptualizing the 'Anthropos' in the Anthropocene: Integrating the social sciences and humanities in global environmental change research. *Environmental Science & Policy, 28,* 3–13.

Rabinow, P. (2005). Midst Anthropology's Problems. In A. Ong & S. J. Collier (Eds.), *Global Assemblages. Technology, Politics, and Ethics as Anthropological Problems* (pp. 40–53). Malden, Oxford & Carlton: Blackwell Publishing.

Richardson, K. (2010). *Disabling as Mimesis and Alterity. Making Humanoid Robots* at the *Massachusetts Institute of Technology. Etnofoor, 22*(1), 75–90.

Richardson, K. (2015). *An Anthropology of Robots and AI. Annihilation Anxiety and Machines.* New York: Routledge.

Richardson, K. (2016). Technological animism: the uncanny personhood of humanoid machines. Special issue: animism beyond the soul: ontology, reflexivity and the making of anthropological knowledge. *Social Analysis, 60*(1), 110–28.

Robertson, J. (2010). Gendering Humanoid Robots: Robo-sexism in Japan. *Body & Society, 16*(2), 1–36. https://doi.org/10.1177/1357034X10364767.

Robertson, J. (2014). Human rights vs. robot rights: Forecasts from Japan. *Critical Asian Studies, 46*(4), 571–598. https://doi.org/10.1080/14672715.2014.960707 .

Šabanović, S. (2014). Inventing Japan's 'robotics culture': The repeated assembly of science, technology, and culture in social robotics. *Social Studies of Science, 44*(3), 342–367. https://doi.org/10.1177/0306312713509704.

Šabanović, S. (2020). *Designing "Companion Artifacts": The Relational Construction of Culture and Technology in Social Robotics* (Frontiers in Artificial Intelligence and Applications (pp. 3–4). E-book volume 335: Culturally Sustainable Social Robotics. https://doi.org/10.3233/FAIA200889.

Smart, A., & Smart, J. (2017). *Posthumanism: Anthropological insights.* Toronto: University of Toronto Press.

Sorenson, J., Zawieska, K., Vermeulen, B., Madsen, S., Trentemøller, S., & Pyka, A. (2019) *Perspectives on Robots*. https://responsiblerobotics.eu/research/perspectives-on-robots/. Accessed 23 June 2021.

Sorenson, J. (2018). *Decisions and Values: Engineering Design as a Pragmatic and Sociomaterial Negotiation Process*. (REELER Working Paper Series no. 4). Aarhus University, Copenhagen, Denmark.

Star, S. L., & Strauss, A. (1999). Layers of silence, arenas of voice: the ecology of visible and invisible work. *Computer Supported Cooperative Work, 8*, 9–30.

Suchman, L. (2008). Feminist STS and the Sciences of the Artificial. In J. Hackett (Ed)., *The Handbook of Science and Technology Studies* (pp. 139–163). Cambridge, MA.: The MIT Press.

Suchman, L. (2011). Subject Objects. *Feminist Theory, 12*(2), 119–145.

Tsing, A. (2010). Arts of Inclusion, or How to Love a Mushroom. *Manoa, 22*(2), 191–203.

Tsing, A. (2012). *Unruly Edges: Mushrooms As Companion Species,"* *Environmental Humanities, 1*(1), 141–154.

Wallace, J. (2019). *Ethics* and *inscription* in *social robot design. Paladyn, 10*(1), 66–76.

Wentzer, T. S., & Mattingly, C. (2018). Toward a New Humanism. An approach from philosophical anthropology. Introduction to Special Section. *HAU: Journal of Ethnographic Theory, 8*(1/2), 144–157. https://doi.org/10.1086/698361.

Wolfe, C. (2010). *What is Posthumanism?* Minneapolis: University of Minnesota Press.

Wulff, H. (2019). Why Humanistic Anthropology Matters. *Anthropology News.* https://doi.org/10.1111/AN.1098.

Zuppi, A. (2017). Naturalism and the representation of animals in the Southern French Pyrenees. *ANUAC, 6*(2), 129–154.

CHAPTER 8

Structuring Race into the Machine: The Spoiled Promise of Postgenomic Sequencing Technologies

Biopolitics

Emma Kowal

Every technology is a social product and a social force. They reflect and reproduce dominant social forms, and sometimes change them. Consider the humble spirometer, a machine to measure lung capacity and other aspects of lung function. In her book *Breathing Race into the Machine*, historian and biochemist Lundy Braun analyses the long history of the spirometer, revealing how racial differences, primarily between white Americans and African Americans, were incorporated into the design of the machine (Braun 2014). Most physicians and scientists shared the belief that black people had, on average, smaller lungs than white people, backed up by a plethora of studies. Scientists produced tables to allow clinicians to 'correct' their results for race, and later, these correction factors were built into the machine. All it took was the flick of a switch to shift the measurement frame from 'white' to 'black'. This correction factor had real consequences for African Americans, preventing many from accessing employer compensation for asbestos-related lung disease because their lungs were judged to be not diseased, but 'naturally' small.

The use of race in spirometry was little known before Braun published her study, as the measurement of lung function is not a topic that often grabs the

E. Kowal (✉)
Deakin University, Melbourne, VIC, Australia
e-mail: emma.kowal@deakin.edu.au

© The Author(s), under exclusive license to Springer Nature Singapore Pte Ltd. 2022
M. H. Bruun et al. (eds.), *The Palgrave Handbook of the Anthropology of Technology*, https://doi.org/10.1007/978-981-16-7084-8_8

public's attention. In contrast, this chapter discusses the persistence of race within a field of science and technology that is often in the headlines: gene sequencing. As I will explore, the ambitious international project to sequence the human genome in the 1990s was explicitly framed by its organisers as a critique of discredited notions of biological race. When Bill Clinton, the then President of the United States, stood next to scientists Francis Collins and Craig Venter to announce the completion of the project in 2000, he foregrounded the finding that all humans had nearly identical DNA: 'one of the great truths to emerge from this triumphant expedition inside the human genome is that in genetic terms, all human beings, regardless of race, are more than 99.9 percent the same' (National Human Genome Research Institute 2012). Many believed the 'postgenomic age'—a term used by social scientists to refer to the time after the sequencing of the human genome and the proliferation of whole genome sequencing technologies—would herald the end of race as a meaningful biological concept (Richardson and Stevens 2015; Reardon 2017). As we will see, however, concepts of racial, ethnic, or national difference persist in the construction of twenty-first-century postgenomic sequencing technologies.

Before embarking on the story of gene sequencing and its spoiled promises of transcending racial difference, I consider the place of genetic technologies within the anthropology of technology. Since Langdon Winner's (1980) call to recognise the social and economic contexts in which technologies are embedded while remaining attentive to the material qualities of technologies 'themselves', scholars have examined a range of technologies to decipher the social relations inhered within them (e.g. Cowan 1985; Latour 1988; Grosz 2001; Adas 1989; Haraway 1989). Few of these early studies of technology were authored by anthropologists, a phenomenon Ingold attributes to the discipline's assumption that technology is a separate domain from culture and therefore beyond their purview (Ingold 1997). In the early 1990s, Pfaffenberger challenged anthropologists to study technologies as sociotechnical systems that create, express, reinforce, or change human social structures; verbal and nonverbal communication; and the organisation of labour through assemblages of humans and non-human actors (Pfaffenberger 1992).

Studies of genetic technologies have formed a consistent thread of work within the anthropology of technology. Although the structure of DNA was discerned in 1953, it took decades longer for the technologies of molecular biology, such as polymerase chain reaction (PCR) and gene sequencing, to accelerate genetic science and its applications in genetic testing for inherited diseases, including prenatal testing. Two classic studies in the 1990s—Troy Duster's *Backdoor to Eugenics* (Duster 1990) and Nelkin and Lindee's *The DNA Mystique: The Gene as a Cultural Icon* (Nelkin and Lindee 2004 [1995])—heralded a wave of social science scholarship on what was then called the 'new genetics' (Keller 2000; Petersen and Bunton 2002; Palsson 2007; Franklin 2000; Rabinow 1996; Strathern 1992). In the current century, ever-accelerating technological advances in the wake of the Human Genome Project have turned the study of genes—genetics—into the study of the whole genome—genomics—and expanded the applications of human genomics to include genetic ancestry testing, ancient DNA research, forensic genetics, and precision medicine.

This diversity of scientific fields and realms of life touched by genetics—from reproduction to criminal justice—is reflected in the wide range of anthropological analyses of genetics that span health and disability (Tutton and Prainsack 2011; Taussig et al. 2003; Rapp 1999), identity (Foster 2016; Nelson 2008), forensics (M'Charek et al. 2014; Jasanoff 1999), kinship (Franklin and Lock 2003), race and nation (Fullwiley 2011; Montoya 2011; Wade 2014), and history (Sommer 2010; Reardon and TallBear 2012). The social study of genetic technologies thus facilitates a powerful conversation across the varied domains in which genetics operates. In all of these domains, genetic technologies and the knowledge they produce are often at the centre of fierce debates about who we are, who we should include and exclude from our polities, and whose lives are worth living. These questions of identity and justice are perhaps most urgent when we consider the genetic discernment of 'race'.

ANTHROPOLOGIES OF RACE ITSELF

'Race'—taken here to mean the shifting, biosocial, and material-semiotic divisions between human groups recognised by a varied range of actors through space and time—is a social formation (Omi and Winant 1994) that has long been entangled with technology. An account of the technologies that have produced 'race' over time might start with the amassing of skull collections and the use of measuring devices to analyse them by racial origin (Roque 2010). Eighteenth- and early nineteenth-century thinkers Carl Linnaeus, Comte de Buffon, Johann Blumenbach, and Georges Cuvier devised racial hierarchies on the basis of craniometric measurements. Subsequent generations of scholars added all kinds of measurements to the epistemology of racial difference, comparing noses, femurs, languages, and economic structures to argue for a hierarchy of discrete races (Farber 2000).

In the early twentieth century, many scientists interested in racial differences felt optimistic that the new discovery of human blood groups would create a more objective measurement of race (Bangham 2014). Other emerging sciences at the time, such as physiology, serology, and biochemistry, were soon applied to the 'race question'. Measurements of basal metabolic rate, lung capacity, and a host of other physical and serological measurements were recorded across the world and results in different regions, countries, race, and ethnic groups were compared (Heggie 2019; Radin 2017; Anderson 2002; Braun 2014; Kowal forthcoming). From the late nineteenth century, these tools and findings contributed to the rise of eugenics in many countries, seen at the time as the progressive social application of science to improve the health of national populations (Kevles 1985).

Many of these research programmes were interrupted after the revelations of National Socialism that took the principles of eugenics to a genocidal extreme (Weindling 1989). Although critiques of racial science had gradually gathered pace since the early twentieth century, the post-war UNESCO Statements on Race (1952) are the paradigmatic sign of the fall from grace of scientific concepts of race (UNESCO 1952; Barkan 1992; Stocking 1968; Stepan 1982). These critiques continued through the 1980s and 1990s, perhaps the most famous being Stephen Jay Gould's *The Mismeasure of Man* that debunked the research findings of leading nineteenth-century craniometrists (Gould 1981; see also Duster 1990; Lewontin et al. 1984; Kevles 1985; Marks 1995; Goodman 2000).[1] However, rather than ending research on 'race' altogether, these critiques led to an uneven and incomplete shift from 'race' to 'population' (Caspari 2003; Lipphardt 2012).

With the development of direct DNA methods in the 1980s, the field of population genetics—that had previously used only indirect measures of genetic make-up—was invigorated by the chance to find health-related genetic differences and unlock the secrets of ancient migrations of human populations (Reardon 2005; Lindee and Ventura Santos 2012). When the Human Genome Project, an ambitious effort to sequence the human genome, was devised in the 1990s, leading population geneticists saw the potential for their field to benefit from global DNA hype. Professor Luca Cavalli-Sforza of Stanford University steered an international research project to run in parallel with the Human Genome Project, called the Human Genome *Diversity* Project (HGDP) (Cavalli-Sforza et al. 1991). It aimed to sample genetic diversity from Indigenous populations around the world, groups referred to by the technical population genetics term 'Isolates of Historical Interest'.

Indigenous communities around the world reacted with anger at the prospect of population geneticists sampling and analysing their genes, actions Indigenous people saw as a continuation of scientific racism. The HGDP was dubbed 'The Vampire Project' by many Indigenous groups who refused to participate (Reardon 2005; Cunningham 1998; Dodson and Williamson 1999; Marks 2005). Scientists in other fields of genetics, particularly related to health and medicine, moved to distance themselves from the maligned HGDP, arguing that genetic concepts of race were only 'a crude surrogate for genetic or other biological variability' that would 'wither away' when more accurate measures of individual genetic sequence were readily available (Kahn 2013, p. 164).

When the Human Genome Project was completed in 2000, initial concern about the much smaller Human Genome Diversity Project had died down, and the completion was hailed as proving the 'great truth' of the genetic similarity of all humans ('June 2000 White House Event', 2000). However, even at this high point of optimism about the universal sameness of the human genome, some social scientists were sceptical that biological race was gone for good. As early as 2001, Skinner and Rosen warned that the increased activity in genetic research that would inevitably result from the Human Genome Project could result in a resurgence of racialised genetics (Skinner and Rosen 2001). Troy

Duster argued that biological race had been 'buried alive' after WWII and was in danger of returning as research into racial differences between populations continued and intensified (Duster 2003).

Since the turn of the twenty-first century, numerous authors have raised questions and concerns about the continuing use of racial differences in medical, scientific, and technological applications, from ethnic-specific medications to laboratory procedures to direct-to-consumer genetic ancestry products (Reardon 2005; M'Charek 2014; Fullwiley 2007; Benjamin 2009; TallBear 2013; Kowal et al. 2013; Fujimura and Rajagopalan 2011; Bolnick et al. 2007; Nelson 2016; Pollock 2012; Kahn 2013; Bliss 2012; Hammonds and Herzig 2009; El-Haj 2007; Gannett 2014; Marks 2013; Rajagopalan and Fujimura 2018). In many of these critiques, however, widespread and accessible full genome sequencing is assumed to be the panacea for racialised genetic research. When each person's full gene sequence can be known, the argument goes, there will be no need to use the imprecise 'proxy' of self-identified race or ancestry to predict a patient's risk of disease or response to pharmaceuticals (Rajagopalan and Fujimura 2012; Rotimi and Jorde 2010). This is the vision of genome-based medicine—known variously by the adjectives 'precision', 'personalised', or 'individualised'—when health providers can make decisions about diagnoses, treatment, and prevention that are tailored to the individual genetic makeup of their patient.

Social studies of race and genomics in the years since the sequencing of the Human Genome Project have troubled the promise that the postgenomic era would leave race behind. Duana Fullwiley's ethnographic research with pharmacogenetics labs in the early 2000s provided a fine-grained analysis of how race gets into the lab despite the overwhelming sameness of all human genomes. She shows that the 0.01% of SNPs—those 1 in 1000 points on the genome where some people have a different nucleotide to others—were consistently categorised by the self-identified race of their donor. Drawing on Nikolas Rose's concept of the molecularisation of life, Fullwiley shows how race 'becomes molecular' in the pharmacogenetics lab (Rose 2006).

Scientists used the United States Office for Management and Budget (OMB) racial categories to classify samples, even as they struggled to make genetic sense of social categories both in the lab and in their self-narratives. Although inconsistencies in the classification of genotypes (e.g. as 'African' or 'Caucasian') across different genetic data sets raised questions for scientists about the scientific rigour of the sample collection process, they did not question the use of racial categories themselves. Similarly, non-white scientists' personal struggles to reconcile their own identities with the blunt and rigid racial categories did not spill over into questioning the use of those categories in the lab (Fullwiley 2007).

Scholarly analysis of the first 'ethnic drug' provides another example of what Anne Pollock calls the 'durability' of race in science (Pollock 2012; Kahn 2012). Bidil was a drug for lowering blood pressure that was the first ever to be patented and licensed for use only in a specific 'racial' group, in this case, self-identified African Americans. Its emergence in the market surprised those scientists and social scientists alike who believed that the 'crude surrogate' of race as a proxy for genetics would recede after the sequencing of the human genome (Kahn 2013, p. 164). Taking the example of genetic predictors of the individualised dose of warfarin (a blood thinning drug) required by patients, Kahn shows that far from withering away, racial descriptors paradoxically proliferated as scientific knowledge of the specific gene variants involved in warfarin response increased.[2]

In the last five years, full genome sequencing has become a reality for many people in countries where advanced health care is available. While costs of sequencing and analysis in a clinical setting are somewhat more than the commonly seen claims of the '$1000 genome', they are reducing rapidly (Schwarze et al. 2020). Genomic sequencing is routinely used to diagnose inherited disorders (e.g. rare diseases and inherited cancers), and other clinical applications are continually developing. According to the vision of genomic sameness expressed at the completion of the Human Genome Project in 2000, this shift to full genome sequencing might be expected to reduce, or even end altogether, the use of racial or ethnic descriptors in genetic research. But as I explore in the remainder of this chapter, the technology of 'full genome sequencing' has remained thoroughly racialised. In a variation of the molecularisation of race that Fullwiley described, race has re-emerged as a 'structural' feature of genome sequencing. Improved scientific understanding of 'structural variation' in the genome (described below) has led many countries to develop 'ethnically-specific' reference genomes they believe are required for more accurate genome sequencing of their national populations. In the field of gene sequencing, the concept of structural variation has been the 'back door' through which racial, ethnic, and national categories have found a new niche in the postgenomic age (Duster 1990).

Structural Variation and Ethnicity-Specific Reference Genomes

When the sequencing of the human genome was completed in 2000, a commonly cited metaphor for this achievement was that the genetic 'code'—a long string of three billion base pairs of DNA molecules called nucleotides (either C, T, A, or G) divided into 23 pairs of chromosomes—had been 'cracked'. At 99.9% of these points on the genome, every human has identical nucleotides. At the remaining 0.1% of these points on the genome, people differ in their nucleotides: some might have C, others might have A. These differences are known as Single Nucleotide Polymorphisms, or SNPs. Within this logic, genome sequencing is a matter of reading all the nucleotides along the 3 billion base pairs in a human genome to determine the sequence of As, Cs, Ts, and Gs.

This vision of a common genomic structure with variation only in some SNPs is the basis of the dominant method of sequencing human genomes, variously called 'second-generation', 'shotgun', or 'short-read' sequencing. This method uses a universal reference genome as the scaffold: an international resource called the Genome Reference Consortium—Human (known as GRCh), currently in its 38th iteration.[3] The reference genome acts like the frame for a jigsaw puzzle. Shotgun sequencing produces millions of short genome sequences known as 'short reads', like millions of overlapping puzzle pieces. These are assembled onto the reference genome to read the full sequence. In this analogy, the puzzle pieces are nucleotides. Although the colour (nucleotide) of a paricular puzzle piece might vary between people—some have blue (A), some have red (C)—the structure of the jigsaw puzzle does not change.

At the same time that genome sequencing technologies have advanced in the last two decades since the completion of the Human Genome Project, other genetic researchers have learnt more about 'structural variations' in the genome.[4] This knowledge has undermined the idea of a universal template for the human genome, varying at 0.1% of nucleotides but otherwise the same. There are many other kinds of differences between genomes beyond SNPs. In relation to the universal reference genome, small sections of someone's genome can be missing (known as deletions), repeated (known as duplications), added in (known as insertions), moved to different parts of the genome (known as translocations), or backwards (known as inversions) (Feuk et al. 2006). These differences make it impossible to directly compare the genomes of two people using the same reference frame. Some genomes will have additional sections, and some will lack some sections that most other people have. These differences, comprising up to 10% of the genome, will be missed if short-read sequencing and the universal reference genome are used (Ballouz et al. 2019).

To capture structural variation, a sequencing method is needed that makes up a new jigsaw puzzle based on an individual human genome, rather than using the universal frame. This is known as 'long-read' sequencing. Instead of many short pieces of sequence that are fitted together onto a pre-existing jigsaw frame, long-read sequencing produces much longer stretches of genome sequencing. The method of de novo *assembly* then assembles these longer pieces into a full genome sequence without using the reference genome.

These newer sequencing methods, which are much more expensive than standard sequencing, are better able to capture structure variation, but whether this is an important goal is uncertain. Existing research indicates that structural variation between *individuals* contributes to risk of disorders including obesity, diabetes, Alzheimer's disease, autism, and schizophrenia (see Kowal and Llamas 2019). However, the question of whether structural variation is systematically different in different *populations*—and, thus, whether one's ethnic or racial group would provide useful information for predicting and interpreting structural variation—is unclear (Sudmant et al. 2015; Audano et al. 2019; Chaisson et al. 2019). Despite the current lack of evidence for systematic population differences in structural variation, in the last five years a number of nations have supported projects to build their own 'ethnicity-specific' reference genomes that purport to account for population-level differences in structural variation.

In 2016, Chinese researchers created the first ethnicity-specific reference genome, the 'Chinese' reference genome, using long-read sequencing and de novo assembly on a sample from one anonymous donor (Shi et al. 2016).[5] Ethnicity-specific reference genomes followed in Korea, Sweden, Denmark, Japan, and Vietnam, each using samples from a small number of individuals who were judged by scientists to best reflect their national ancestry (Shi et al. 2016; Ameur et al. 2018; Seo et al. 2016; Maretty et al. 2017; Thanh et al. 2015). In the justifications for these projects, the 'universal' reference genome (GRCh) is seen as lacking specificity and accuracy, an 'off-the-shelf' product that does not reflect national genomic makeup. An ethnic-specific reference genome is presented as a crucial technology for citizens to benefit from accurate diagnosis, treatment, and prevention in the coming age of precision medicine (e.g. Cho et al. 2016).

The technology of ethnicity-specific reference genomes recapitulates many of the problematic aspects of earlier forms of racialised genomics. Similar to the HapMap project of the early 2000s, ethnicity-specific reference genomes take a small number of people, and sometimes a single person, to stand in for the genome of an entire nation, with all the reductionism and homogenisation this implies (Reardon 2007). The distinction between *individual*-level and *population*-level variation is eroded or ignored altogether. Despite the lack of evidence that structural differences vary by *population*, the structural variation of an individual citizen or citizens (e.g. a Chinese person) are extrapolated to a national scale (the 'Chinese genome'). The fallacy, or at least prematurity, of this view is made clear in a study reporting long-read sequencing of two 'Swedish' genomes. Half of the novel structural differences found in a previously reported 'Chinese' genome were also found in the 'Swedish' genomes (Ameur et al. 2018). Similarly, the authors of the Korean reference genome describe the difficulty they experienced in identifying 'Korean' or 'Asian' structural variation because the patterns of structural variation did not follow racial lines: much structural variation was shared between a 'Chinese' and an 'African' genome (Cho et al. 2016; see also Mai et al. 2019).

Notwithstanding these signs that structural variation is not easily segregated into national or racial categories, many researchers remain committed to national reference genome projects. The Korean Reference Genome (KOREF) project authors, for example, report their difficulty classifying structural variation into ethnic categories (as explained above) but also state that '[t]he Korean population is regarded as a homogeneous ethnic group in East Asia' that has corresponding meaningful biological differences (Cho et al. 2016). The contradictions that Fullwiley observed in pharmacogenetic laboratories are apparent here; despite the practical difficulties of using race as a genomic category, these scientists remain steadfast that ethnoracial classifiers are valid. Like Fullwiley's pharmacogenetic scientists, researchers creating ethnicity-specific reference genomes perform *work*—what Benjamin calls 'strategic calibration' (see below)—to maintain race and nation as meaningful genomic categories (Fullwiley 2007; Benjamin 2009). These investments of labour in a racialised technology are best understood from a social, rather than a scientific, perspective.

Joan Fujimura and Ramya Rajagopalan have powerfully described the work of 'genome geographies' that map biological difference onto specific territory or populations (Fujimura and Rajagopalan 2011; Nash 2012). The concept of 'race' can be seen as an outcome of this work of tethering identity, place, and genomics (Gannett 2014). While for some national reference genome projects a biologised, national ideal is implicit, it is easily discernible in others. The 2017 project website for the Korean Reference Genome Project outlined its argument for the 'Korean genome' as a distinct biological entity based on mitochondrial DNA (mtDNA) and Y-chromosome haplogroups.[6] The single donor whose genome was sequenced had the most common Y-chromosome haplogroup (known as the 'proto-Korean' haplogroup) and the most common mitochondrial DNA (mtDNA) haplogroup found in previous studies of Korean populations. The website authors conclude, 'Thus KOREF can be considered as the direct descendant of proto-Koreans of the Y-chromosome and mtDNA founders' (cited in Kowal and Llamas 2019, p. 102). Although the genotypes that make up the mtDNA and Y chromosome make up just a tiny proportion of the complete genome, and although many Koreans will have different mtDNA and Y-chromosome haplogroups, these particular haplogroups function here as racial markers of the nation. The explicitly biologised account of Korean nationhood is also highlighted by science studies scholar Sandra Soo-Jin Lee. She cites the chairman of a biotech company closely involved with Korean genome projects for whom KOREF's goal is to 'decode the biological definition of the word "Korean"'. Lee interprets this as a claim that 'in genes resides an elusive essence of Korean identity that is critical to understanding and treating the Korean body' (Lee 2010).

Ruha Benjamin's term 'genomic sovereignty' is useful for understanding some aspects of this commitment to a notion of a national genomic identity. She describes how scientists and politicians create 'new biopolitical entities, "Mexican DNA" and "Indian DNA" among others, strategically calibrating socio-political categories (i.e. nationality and race-ethnicity) with scientifically produced ones (i.e. genotypes)' (Benjamin 2009, p. 341). In an effort to stimulate domestic economies, protect national patrimony, and not be 'left out' of global genome science and precision medicine, national actors calibrate uncertain science with their ideals of (biological) nationhood (Fullwiley and Gibbon 2018; Fullwiley 2011; see also Tamarkin 2020). Although Benjamin referred to national projects to collate genetic diversity within populations, the same argument may apply to ethnicity-specific reference genomes.[7] Any failures of logic or gaps in evidence, like the significance of population (rather than individual) structural variation, are papered over to produce a coherent genomic nationhood. Accounting for structural variation has been racialised, confounding the promised and hoped-for genomic universalism of the postge-nomic age.

BUILDING GENOMIC ORDER

In this concluding section, I wish to consider why ethnicity-specific reference genomes should matter to social scientists. If countries like Denmark, Sweden, Korea, China, and Vietnam wish to fund ethnicity-specific reference genome projects, even if they are based on questionable scientific assumptions, why should social scientists mount critiques or objections?

Decades of scholarship has shown that the structure of a technology influences how it can be used. For scientific instruments, their construction determines what kind of questions can be asked and, correspondingly, which lines of inquiry are obscured. The full range of possibilities for understanding some object or phenomenon are ordered and narrowed by the technologies we use to engage with it. As Winner puts it, '[T]he things we call 'technologies' are ways of building order in our world' (Winner 1980, p. 128). The order that a particular technology builds is never neutral and can have devastating consequences for some people and populations. Technologies that draw on the science of biological variation between populations have been implicated in much social harm, from racial hierarchies that justified colonialism to eugenics and the Holocaust. It is prudent, then, for social scientists to look closely at the assumptions and implications of racialising technologies.

As ethnicity-specific reference genomes are only just emerging, it is not yet clear what their consequences might be. However, as Winner notes, it is precisely at the point of emergence of a technology, when the greatest opportunity for intervention exists, that humanities and social science scholars should be asking difficult questions (Winner 1980). Once a technology is established, the organisation of labour, identities, and knowledge congeals and is difficult to shift. An example is Robert Kohler's classic history of Drosophila (fruit fly) research that illustrates how an established technology shapes the kinds of scientific problems that can be posed. In the first decade of the twentieth century, the 'standard' experimental fruit fly was literally constructed (through decades of breeding in the lab) to address the problem of genetic linkage. When this model organism was subsequently used to investigate developmental and evolutionary genetics in the 1920s and 1930s, it produced results that were difficult to interpret. Scientists ended up reporting on results relevant to genetic linkage, results that were incidental to their experiments on development and evolution, but were easier for them to interpret, and therefore easier to publish. The construction of Drosophila, plus the imperative to publish results to advance academic careers, 'operated to cause deviant practices to revert to the mainstream' (Kohler 1994, p. 181). It was only when fruit flies were redesigned as a scientific tool—most prominently, through Theodosius Dhobzhansky's innovation of collecting wild flies and mapping their genetic differences against environmental factors in the late 1930s—that new questions could be asked. In Dhobzhansky's case, this led eventually to the formulation of the modern evolutionary synthesis.

Lundy Braun notes the inertia of established technologies in her study of the spirometer (mentioned in the opening of this chapter). Braun first became aware of the issue of 'race correction' in spirometry in 1999 when she saw a newspaper article about a legal battle between the insulation manufacturer Owens Corning and former employees who suffered from asbestos-related lung disease. Lawyers for the company argued that African Americans who worked for them had to demonstrate a higher level of disability—that is, lower results on lung function tests—to access compensation. The reason behind this, she found, was over a century of scientific measurements showing that 'black lungs' are smaller than 'white lungs'. Statistical formulas for 'race correction' of spirometry results were developed in the 1970s and subsequently built into spirometry machines. With a flick of a switch on the office spirometer, race is 'corrected', potentially excluding African Americans from accessing workers' compensation. The moment 'the spirometer was applied to race', Braun tells us, 'it made the idea of racial difference difficult to contest and dislodge' (Braun 2014, p. xxix). Left unchecked, science, society, and technology will reinforce long-held notions, such as biological race, in an infinite feedback loop.

Lundy's analysis shows us that once race is built into the machine, it is difficult to take it out again. However, a focus on emerging technologies, such as long-read genome sequencing, offers an opportunity to change the script. Anthropologists have successfully formed multidisciplinary collaborations between geneticists, bioethicists, legal scholars, biological anthropologists, and others to make far-reaching critical interventions in areas such as direct-to-consumer genetic ancestry testing (Bolnick et al. 2007) and the use of racial signifiers in genetic research (Royal et al. 2010). The same kind of intervention is needed for gene sequencing and reference genomes, enabling new possibilities for conceptualising and measuring difference and diversity. Scholars of race and digital technology provide an example when they advocate for developing technologies that have less harmful consequences for non-white people. Like race in spirometry and genome sequencing, digital constructions of race have a long history, but each new iteration offers an opportunity to do things differently (Nakamura and Chow-White 2012; Benjamin 2019).

Genome scientists are debating how well the universal reference genome serves the sequencing community and how it could be improved: suggestions include a pan-genome, a consensus genome, or an ancestral genome (Ballouz et al. 2019; Sherman and Salzberg 2020). Any of these options could either invoke or reject biologised notions of race, ethnicity, and nation, depending on how the technologies are conceived of and built. To date, scientific publications on alternatives to the current universal reference genome do not mention the history of racialised technologies or the potential risks to minority groups. Expanding the conversation to include anthropologists, historians, and other scholars could help to anticipate more or less harmful ways of representing genome variation. As Duana Fullwiley puts it, a less-racialised version of genomic research would understand genetic differences 'physiologically, evolutionarily, environmentally and historically, rather than strictly "racially"' (Fullwiley 2007, p. 25).

While it is important to engage in transdisciplinary discussions, it is equally true that the most careful planning and execution may not prevent the harm of race in the machine. Some scholars argue that inequities are baked not into just individual technologies, but into our very concepts. If a concept is founded in racism, sexism, or other lines of inequality, then any new technology based on this concept may replicate its inherent injustice. Drawing on an analysis of the emergence of the science of heredity in the Middle Ages, historian Staffan Müller-Wille makes just this argument for heredity and its twentieth- and twenty-first-century iterations, principally genetics. 'Concepts of human race persist to this day', he argues, 'because they have been indelibly inscribed in the conceptual architecture that has supported, and continues to support, all attempts at describing and controlling human variation on a global scale since the early modern period' (Müller-Wille 2014, p. 218). If we are persuaded by Müller-Wille's argument that there is no possibility of a concept of human variation that escapes race, it is no surprise that every new generation of genome technology will recapitulate biologised racial difference.

Richardson and Stevens argue that just as scientists have transformed their tools in the postgenomic age, social scientists need to retool our analyses of postgenomic technologies (Richardson and Stevens 2015, p. 3). But as I have shown in this chapter, it is just as important to learn from the past. Before we move further towards structuring race in the genome, we need to heed the lessons of the spirometer and continue to ask questions about the best ways to account for difference and to order our world.

Notes

1. It should be noted that prominent defences of race science in various forms continued to be published alongside the critiques (e.g. Coon 1962; Herrnstein and Murray 1994).
2. He argues that, in the case of predicting drug responses, the 'space for race' is maintained by the unknown variability that genetics can never fully capture (Kahn 2013).
3. https://www.ncbi.nlm.nih.gov/assembly/GCF_000001405.39
4. For a detailed explanation of gene sequencing and structural variation, see Kowal and Llamas (2019).
5. A project a year earlier had produced a Danish 'national pan-genome', a similar idea to an ethnicity-specific reference genome, but this used a combination of older technologies rather than the newer long-read sequencing methods (Besenbacher et al. 2015).
6. Mitochondrial DNA is the DNA of mitochondria, small organelles within a cell that are passed on exclusively from your biological mother's egg. The DNA of your mitochondria can be classified into a haplogroup that represents your direct

maternal ancestral line. Y-chromosome DNA is inherited exclusively from fathers to sons and represents the direct paternal ancestral line.

7. On genomic sovereignty and national 'branding' in other jurisdictions, see Tupasela (2017), Schwartz-Marín and Restrepo (2013), Fortun (2008), and Sunder Rajan (2006).

References

Adas, M. (1989). *Machines as the Measure of Men: Science, Technology and Ideologies of Western Dominance*. Ithaca: Cornell University Press.

Ameur, A., Che, H., Martin, M., Bunikis, I., Dahlberg, J., Höijer, I., et al. (2018). De novo assembly of two Swedish genomes reveals missing segments from the human GRCh38 reference and improves variant calling of population-scale sequencing data. *Genes, 9*(10). https://doi.org/10.3390/genes9100486.

Anderson, W. (2002). *The Cultivation of Whiteness: Science, Health and Racial Destiny in Australia*. Melbourne: Melbourne University Press.

Audano, P. A., Sulovari, A., Graves-Lindsay, T. A., Cantsilieris, S., Sorensen, M., Welch, A. M. E., et al. (2019). Characterizing the Major Structural Variant Alleles of the Human Genome. *Cell, 176*(3), 663–675.

Ballouz, S., Dobin, A., & Gillis, J. A. (2019). Is it time to change the reference genome? *Genome Biology, 20*(159), 1–9.

Bangham, J. (2014). Blood groups and human groups: Collecting and calibrating genetic data after World War Two. *Studies in History and Philosophy of Science Part C: Studies in History and Philosophy of Biological and Biomedical Sciences, 47*(0), 74–86. https://doi.org/10.1016/j.shpsc.2014.05.008.

Barkan, E. (1992). *The Retreat of Scientific Racism: Changing Concepts of Race in Britain and the United States between the Two World Wars*. Cambridge: Cambridge University Press.

Benjamin, R. (2009). A Lab of Their Own: Genomic Sovereignty as Postcolonial Science Policy." *Policy and Society, 28*(4), 341–355.

Benjamin, R. (2019). *Race After Technology: Abolitionist Tools for the New Jim Code*. Cambridge: Polity Press.

Besenbacher, S., Liu, S., Izarzugaza, J. M. G., Grove, J., Belling, K., Bork-Jensen, J., et al. (2015). Novel variation and de novo mutation rates in population-wide de novo assembled Danish trios. *Nature Communications 6*(5969), 1–9.

Bliss, C. (2012). *Race Decoded: The Genomic Fight for Social Justice*. Stanford: Stanford University Press.

Bolnick, D., Fullwiley, D., Duster, T., Cooper, R., Fujimura, J., Kahn, J., et al. (2007). The Science and Business of Genetic Ancestry Testing. *Science, 318*(399), 400.

Braun, L. (2014). *Breathing Race into the Machine: The Surprising Career of the Spirometer from Plantation to Genetics*. Minneapolis: University of Minnesota Press.

Caspari, R. (2003). From Types to Populations: A Century of Race, Physical Anthropology, and the American Anthropological Association. *American Anthropologist, 105*(1), 65–76.

Cavalli-Sforza, L. L., Wilson, A. C., Cantor, C. R., Cook-Deegan, R. M., & King, M. (1991). Call for a worldwide survey of human genetic diversity: a vanishing opportunity for the Human Genome Project. *Genomics, 11*, 490–491

Chaisson, M. J. P., Sanders, A. D., Zhao, X., Malhotra, A., Porubsky, D., Rausch, T., et al. (2019). Multi-platform discovery of haplotype-resolved structural variation in human genomes. *Nature Communications, 10*(1). https://doi.org/10.1038/s41467-018-08148-z.

Cho, Y. S., Kim, H., Kim, H. M., Jho, S., Jun, J., Lee, Y. J., et al. (2016). An ethnically relevant consensus Korean reference genome is a step towards personal reference genomes. *Nature Communications, 7.* https://doi.org/10.1038/ncomms13637.

Coon, C. (1962). *The Origin of Races.* New York: Knopf.

Cowan, R. S. (1985). How the refrigerator got its hum. In D. A. MacKenzie & J. Wajcman (Eds.), *The Social shaping of technology: how the refrigerator got its hum* (pp. 202–218). Philadelphia Open University Press.

Cunningham, H. (1998). Colonial Encounters in Postcolonial Contexts: Patenting Indigenous DNA and the Human Genome Diversity Project. *Critique of Anthropology, 18*(2), 205–233.

Dodson, M., & Williamson, R. (1999). Indigenous peoples and the morality of the Human Genome Diversity Project. *Journal of Medical Ethics, 25*(2), 204–208.

Duster, T. (1990). *Backdoor to eugenics.* New York: Routledge.

Duster, T. 2003. Buried Alive: the concept of race in science. In A. H. Goodman, D. Heath, &M. S. Lindee (Eds.), *Genetic Nature/Culture: Anthropology and Science Beyond the Two-Culture Divide* (pp. 258–277). Berkeley: University of California Press.

El-Haj, N. A. (2007). The Genetic Reinscription of Race. *Annual Review of Anthropology, 36*, 283–300.

Farber, P. (2000). *Finding Order in Nature: The Naturalist Tradition from Linnaeus to E.O. Wilson.* Baltimore, MD.: Johns Hopkins University Press.

Feuk L., Carson A. R., & Scherer S.W. (2006). Structural variation in the human genome. *Nature Reviews Genetics, 7*, 85–97.

Fortun, M. (2008). *Promising Genomics: Iceland and deCODE Genetics in a World of Speculation.* Berkeley: University of California Press.

Foster, L. A. (2016). A Postapartheid Genome: Genetic Ancestry Testing and Belonging in South Africa. *Science, Technology, & Human Values, 41*(6), 1015–1036. https://doi.org/10.1177/0162243916658771.

Franklin, S., & Lock, M. (Eds.) (2003). *Remaking Life and Death: Toward an Anthropology of the Biosciences.* Santa Fe: School of American Research Press.

Franklin, S. (2000). Life Itself: Global Nature and the Genetic Imaginary. In S. Franklin, C. Lurie, & J. Stacey (Eds.), *Global Nature/Global Culture* (pp. 188–227). London: Sage.

Fujimura, J. H., & Rajagopalan, R. (2011). Different differences: The use of 'genetic ancestry' versus race in biomedical human genetic research. *Social Studies of Science, 41*(1), 5–30.

Fullwiley, D. (2007). The Molecularization of Race: Institutionalizing Human Difference in Pharmacogenetics Practice. *Science as Culture, 16*(1), 1–30.

Fullwiley, D. (2011). *The Enculturated Gene: Sickle Cell Health Politics and Biological Difference in West Africa.* Princeton: Princeton University Press.

Fullwiley, D., & Gibbon, S. (2018). Genomics in Emerging and Developing Economies. S. Gibbon, B. Prainsack, S. Hilgartner, & J. Lamoreaux (Eds.), In *Routledge Handbook of Genomics, Health and Society* (pp. 228–237). London & New York: Routledge.

Gannett, L. (2014). Biogeographical ancestry and race. *Studies in History and Philosophy of Science Part C: Studies in History and Philosophy of Biological and Biomedical Sciences, 47*(0), 173–184. https://doi.org/10.1016/j.shpsc.2014.05.017.

Goodman, A. H. (2000). Why genes don't count (for racial differences in health). *American Journal of Public Health, 90*(11), 1699–1702.

Gould, S. J. (1981). *The Mismeasure of Man.* New York: W.W. Norton.

Grosz, E. (2001). *Architecture from the outside: Essays on Virtual and Real Space.* Minnesota: The MIT Press.

Hammonds, E. M., & Herzig, R. (2009). *The Nature of Difference: Sciences of Race in the United States from Jefferson to Genomics.* Cambridge, MA.: MIT Press.

Haraway, D. (1989). *Primate Visions: Gender, Race, and Nature in the World of Modern Science.* New York & London: Routledge.

Heggie, V. (2019). Blood, race and indigenous peoples in twentieth century extreme physiology. *History and Philosophy of the Life Sciences, 41*(2), 26. https://doi.org/10.1007/s40656-019-0264-z.

Herrnstein, R. J., & Murray, C. (1994). *The Bell Curve: Intelligence and Class Structure in American Life.* New York: Simon & Schuster.

Ingold, T. (1997). Eight Themes in the Anthropology of Technology. *Social Analysis: The International Journal of Social and Cultural Practice, 41*(1), 106–138.

Jasanoff, S. (1999). The Eye of Everyman: Witnessing DNA in the Simpson Trial. *Social Studies of Science, 28*(5–6), 713–740.

Kahn, J. (2012). *Race in a Bottle: the Story of BiDil and Racialized Medicine in a Post-Genomic Age.* New York: Columbia University Press.

Kahn, J. (2013). *Race in a Bottle: the Story of BiDil and Racialized Medicine in a Post-Genomic Age.* New York: Columbia University Press.

Keller, E. (2000). *The Century of the Gene.* Cambridge, MA.: Harvard University Press.

Kevles, D. (1985). *In the Name of Eugenics: Genetics and the Uses of Human Heredity.* New York: Knopf.

Kohler, R. (1994). *Lords of the fly: Drosophila genetics and the experimental life.* Chicago: University of Chicago Press.

Kowal, E. (forthcoming). *Haunting Biology: Science and Indigeneity in Australia.* Durham: Duke University Press.

Kowal, E., & Llamas, B. (2019). Race in a genome: long read sequencing, ethnicity-specific reference genomes and the shifting horizon of race. *Journal of Anthropological Sciences, 97*, 91–106.

Kowal, E., Radin, J., & Reardon, J. (2013). Indigenous Body Parts, Mutating Temporalities, and the Half-Lives of Postcolonial Technoscience. *Social Studies of Science, 43*(4), 465–483.

Latour, B. (1988). Mixing Humans and Nonhumans Together: The Sociology of a Door-Closer. *Social Problems, 35*(3), 298–310.

Lee S. S.-J. (2010) The Asian Genome: Racing in an Age of Pharmacogenomics. In M. Sleeboom-Faulkner (Ed.), *Frameworks of Choice: Predictive & Genetic Testing in Asia* (pp. 211–222). Amsterdam: Amsterdam University Press.

Lewontin, R., Rose, S., & Kamin, L. (1984). *Not in Our Genes: Biology, Ideology and Human Nature.* New York: Pantheon Books.

Lindee, S., & Ventura Santos, R. (2012). The Biological Anthropology of Living Human Populations: World Histories, National Styles, and International Networks. *Current Anthropology, 53*(S5), S3–S16. https://doi.org/10.1086/663335.

Lipphardt, V. (2012). Isolates and Crosses in Human Population Genetics; or, A Contextualization of German Race Science. *Current Anthropology, 53*(S5), S69–S82.

M'Charek, A. (2014). Race, Time and Folded Objects: The HeLa Error. *Theory, Culture and Society, 31*(6), 29–56.

M'Charek, A., Schramm, K., & Skinner, D. (2014). Topologies of Race: Doing territory, population and identity in Europe. *Science, Technology & Human Values.*

Mai, Z., Liu, W., Ding, W., & Zhang, G. (2019). Misassembly of long reads undermines de novo-assembled ethnicity-specific genomes: validation in a Chinese Han population. *Human Genetics, 138*(7), 757–769. https://doi.org/10.1007/s00439-019-02032-6.

Maretty, L., Jensen, J. M., Petersen, B., Sibbesen, J. A.., Liu, S., Villesen, P., et al., (2017). Sequencing and de novo assembly of 150 genomes from Denmark as a population reference. *Nature, 548*(7665), 87–91. https://doi.org/10.1038/nature23264.

Marks, J. (1995). *Human Biodiversity: Genes, race, and history, Foundations of Human Behavior.* New York: Aldine de Gruyter.

Marks, J. (2005). Your body, my property: The problem of colonial genetics in a postcolonial world. In L. Meskel & P. Pels (Eds.), *Embedding Ethics* (pp. 29–45). Oxford: Berg.

Marks, J. (2013). The Nature/Culture of Genetic Facts. *Annual Review of Anthropology, 42*, 247–267.

Montoya, M. J. (2011). *Making the Mexican Diabetic: Race, Science, and the Genetics of Inequality.* Berkeley: University of California Press.

Müller-Wille, S. (2014). Reproducing difference: Race and heredity from a longue durée perspective. In S. Lettow (Ed.), *Race, Gender and Reproduction: Philosophy and the Early Life Sciences in Context* (pp. 217–235). New York: SUNY Press.

Nakamura, L., & Chow-White, P. (Eds.) (2012). *Race After the Internet.* London: Routledge.

Nash, C. (2012). Genetics, race, and relatedness: Human mobility and human diversity in the genographic project. *Annals of the Association of American Geographers, 102*(3), 667–684.

National Human Genome Research Institute (2012). June 2000 White House Event. Bethesda, MA: National Human Genome Research Institute. https://www.genome.gov/10001356/june-2000-white-house-event. Accessed 28 June 2021.

Nelkin, D., & Lindee, M. S. (2004[1995]). *The DNA Mystique: The Gene as a Cultural Icon.* Ann Arbor: University of Michigan Press.

Nelson, A. (2008). Bio Science: Genetic Genealogy Testing and the Pursuit of African Ancestry." *Social Studies of Science, 38*, 759–783.

Nelson, A. (2016). *The Social Life of DNA: Race, Reparations, and Reconciliation After the Genome.* Boston, MA.: Beacon Press.

Omi, M., & Winant, H. (1994). *Racial Formation in the United States: From the 1960s to the 1990s.* New York: Routledge.

Palsson, G. (2007). *Anthropology and the New Genetics.* Cambridge: Cambridge University Press.

Petersen, A., & Bunton, R. (2002). *The New Genetics and the Public's Health.* London & New York: Routledge.

Pfaffenberger, B. (1992). Social Anthropology of Technology. *Annual Review of Anthropology, 21(1)*, 491–516.

Pollock, A. (2012). *Medicating Race: Heart Disease and Durable Preoccupations with Difference*. Durham, N.C.: Duke University Press.

Rabinow, P. (1996). *Making PCR: A Story of Biotechnology*. Chicago: Chicago University Press.

Radin, J. (2017). *Life on Ice: A History of New Uses for Cold Blood*. Chicago: University of Chicago Press.

Rajagopalan, R., & Fujimura, J. H. (2012). Will personalized medicine challenge or reify categories of race and ethnicity? *Virtual Mentor, 14*(8), 657–63. https://doi.org/10.1001/virtualmentor.2012.14.8.msoc1-1208.

Rajagopalan, R., & Fujimura, J. (2018). Variations on a Chip: Technologies of Difference in Human Genetics Research. *Journal of the History of Biology, 51*(4), 841–873.

Rapp, R. (1999). *Testing Women, Testing the Fetus: The Social Impact of Amniocentesis in America*. New York: Routledge.

Reardon, J. (2005). *Race to the Finish: Identity and Governance in an Age of Genomics*. Princeton, N.J.: Princeton University Press.

Reardon, J. (2007). Democratic Mis-haps: The Problem of Democratization in a Time of Biopolitics. *BioSocieties, 2*(2), 239–256.

Reardon, J. (2017). *The Postgenomic Condition: Ethics, Justice, and Knowledge After the Genome*. Chicago: University of Chicago Press.

Reardon, J., & TallBear, K. (2012). "Your DNA is our history". *Current Anthropology, 53*(5), S233–S245.

Richardson, S. S., & Stevens, H. (Eds.) (2015). *Postgenomics: Perspectives on Biology after the Genome*: Duke University Press.

Roque, R. (2010). *Headhunting and Colonialism: Anthropology and the Circulation of Human Skulls in the Portuguese Empire, 1870–1930*. Hampshire: Palgrave Macmillan

Rose, N. (2006). *The Politics of Life Itself: Biomedicine, Power and Subjectivity*. Princeton: Princeton University Press.

Rotimi, C., & Jorde, L. (2010). Ancestry and Disease in the Age of Genomic Medicine. *New England Journal of Medicine, 363*(16), 1551–1558.

Royal, C. D., Novembre, J., Fullerton, S. M., Goldstein, D. B., Long, J. C., Bamshad, M. J., & Clark, A. G. (2010). Inferring Genetic Ancestry: Opportunities, Challenges, and Implications. *American Journal of Human Genetics, 86*(5), 661–673.

Schwartz-Marín, E., & Restrepo, E. (2013). Biocoloniality, Governance, and the Protection of 'Genetic Identities' in Mexico and Colombia. *Sociology, 47*(5), 993–1010. https://doi.org/10.1177/0038038513494506.

Schwarze, K., Buchanan, J., Fermont, J. M., Dreau, H., Tilley, M. W., Taylor J. M., et al. (2020). The complete costs of genome sequencing: a microcosting study in cancer and rare diseases from a single center in the United Kingdom. *Genetics in Medicine, 22*(1), 85–94.

Seo, J. S., Rhie, A., Kim, J., Lee, S., Sohn, M. H., Kim, C. U., et al. (2016). De novo assembly and phasing of a Korean human genome. *Nature, 538*(7624), 243–247. https://doi.org/10.1038/nature20098.

Sherman, R. M., & Salzberg, S. L. (2020). Pan-genomics in the human genome era. *Nature Reviews Genetics, 21*, 243–254.

Shi, L., Guo, Y., Dong, C., Huddleston, J., Yang, H., Han, X., et al. (2016). Long-read sequencing and de novo assembly of a Chinese genome. *Nature Communications, 7*. https://doi.org/10.1038/ncomms12065.

Skinner, D., & Rosen, P. (2001). Opening the White Box: The Politics of Racialised Science and Technology. *Science as Culture, 10*(3), 285–300.

Sommer, M. (2010). DNA and cultures of remembrance: Anthropological genetics, biohistories and biosocialities. *BioSocieties, 5*(3), 366–390. https://doi.org/10.1057/biosoc.2010.19.

Stepan, N. L. (1982). *The Idea of Race in Science: Great Britain 1800–1960*. London: Macmillan.

Stocking, G. W. (1968). *Race, Culture and Evolution: Essays in the History of Anthropology*. New York: The Free Press.

Strathern, M. (1992). *Reproducing the Future: Essays on Anthropology, Kinship and the New Reproductive Technologies*. Manchester, U.K.: Manchester University Press.

Sudmant, P. H., Mallick, S., Nelson B. J., Hormozdiari, F., Krumm, N., Huddleston, J., Coe, B. P., et al. (2015). Global diversity, population stratification, and selection of human copy-number variation. *Science, 349*(6253), 1–8.

Sunder Rajan, K. (2006). *Biocapital: The Constitution of Postgenomic Life*. Durham: Duke University Press.

TallBear, K. (2013). *Native American DNA: Tribal Belonging and the False Promise of Genetic Science*: University of Minnesota Press.

Tamarkin, N. (2020). *Genetic Afterlives: Black Jewish Indigeneity in South Africa*. Durham, N.C.: Duke University Press.

Taussig, K. S., Rapp, R., & Heath, D. (2003). Flexible Eugenics: Technologies of the Self in the Age of Genetics. In A. H. Goodman, D. Heath, & M. S. Lindee (Eds.), *Genetic Nature/Culture: Anthropology and Science Beyond the Two-Culture Divide* (pp. 58–76). Berkeley: University of California Press.

Thanh, N. D., Trang, P. T. M., Hai, D. T., Tuan, N. H. A., Quang, L. S., Minh, B. Q., Minh, D. Q., Son, P. B., & Vinh, L. S. (2015). Building Population-Specific Reference Genomes: A Case Study of Vietnamese Reference Genome. *Annals of Translational Medicine, 3*(2).

Tupasela, A. (2017). Populations as brands in medical research: placing genes on the global genetic atlas. *BioSocieties, 12*(1), 47–65. https://doi.org/10.1057/s41292-016-0029-9.

Tutton, R., & Prainsack, B. (2011). Enterprising or altruistic selves? Making up research subjects in genetics research. *Sociology of Health and Illness, 33*(7), 1081–1095.

UNESCO. (1952). *The Race Concept: Results of an Inquiry Paris: UNESCO*.

Wade, P., (Ed.) (2014). *Mestizo Genomics: Race Mixture, Nation, and Science in Latin America*. Durham, N.C.: Duke University Press.

Weindling, P. (1989). *Health, Race and German Politics Between National Unification and Nazism, 1870–1945*. London: Cambridge University Press.

Winner, L. (1980). Do Technologies have Politics? *Daedalus, 109*(1), 121–136.

CHAPTER 9

An Interventional Design Anthropology of Emerging Technologies: Working Through an Interdisciplinary Field

Design

Sarah Pink, Kaspar Raats, Thomas Lindgren, Katalin Osz, and Vaike Fors

In this chapter, by reflecting on the example of the autonomous driving (AD) car, we outline the role of the anthropology of emerging technologies as a critical and interventional voice in interdisciplinary scholarship and public debate. Emerging technologies are commonly understood as new, digital, data-driven, intelligent, or automated technological innovations either in development or at the cusp of being launched into a market. However, they might remain emerging technologies for undefined periods. The AD car is an ideal example since, in business media, AD cars were considered the most hyped emerging

S. Pink (✉)
Monash University, Melbourne, VIC, Australia
e-mail: sarah.pink@monash.edu

K. Raats • T. Lindgren • K. Osz
Volvo Cars Corporation, Gothenburg, Sweden

Halmstad University, Halmstad, Sweden
e-mail: kaspar.raats@hh.se; thomas.lindgren@hh.se; katalin.osz@volvocars.com

V. Fors
Halmstad University, Halmstad, Sweden
e-mail: vaike.fors@hh.se

© The Author(s), under exclusive license to Springer Nature Singapore
Pte Ltd. 2022
M. H. Bruun et al. (eds.), *The Palgrave Handbook of the Anthropology of Technology*, https://doi.org/10.1007/978-981-16-7084-8_9

technology in 2015 (Fortune 2015), and in 2020 they are still listed as amongst the '7 biggest technology trends' that must be prepared for (Forbes 2020). While anthropologists of technology and media have consistently studied the socio-technical relationships that come about as new digital technologies become part of everyday life, the anthropology of emerging technologies is distinct in its concern with the experience of technologies in possible futures. Such experiences cannot be explained through the conventional anthropological focus on the present and the past, or researched through traditional ethnographic methods. There is also a significant history of anthropological engagement in technology design in industry. Examples include Lucy Suchman's early work in Silicon Valley (e.g. Suchman 1998), Genevieve Bell's research leadership at Intel (e.g. Dourish and Bell 2011), and, in the AD car field, Melissa Cefkin's research at Nissan (Vinkhuyzen and Cefkin 2016; see also Cefkin 2009). However, we now need a new wave of anthropological intervention in the field of emerging technologies that goes beyond embedding applied anthropologists in the sites where technology is designed in industry, to involve sustained collaboration between academia and industry—that is, 'an interventional anthropology of emerging technologies' (Pink 2021).

In this chapter we present emerging technologies as an anthropological category, demonstrating through the example of AD cars how an anthropological approach differs from, but can usefully engage with, those of cognate disciplines of Science and Technology Studies (STS) (Marres 2018; Stilgoe 2018) and human geography, selected because they have also investigated AD cars (Bissell et al. 2018; Bissell 2018; Ash 2017). Our discussion takes into account two key themes in contemporary interdisciplinary debates about emerging technologies: ethics and trust. Through the example of AD cars, we show how the anthropology of emerging technologies can revise these categories of ethics and trust to contest technological determinist narratives in ways that accompany but extend STS and human geography approaches.

In developing this discussion we draw on our own ethnographic research, which involves using visual, sensory, and design ethnographic techniques to put human experience and imagination at the centre of discussions about the future of emerging technologies. Our work evolves in an interdisciplinary and international space where research, findings, and interventions are not the domain of the lone anthropologist but are shared, bringing together critical scholarship and collaborative practice. In doing so we draw together our existing scholarship and research, spanning projects we have developed since 2016 through collaboration across Sweden and Australia, between our universities, and Volvo Cars.

DESIGN ANTHROPOLOGY AND EMERGING TECHNOLOGIES

The anthropology of emerging technologies is not necessarily a pure academic anthropology, but, rather, a future-oriented theoretical and engaged practice (Pink and Salazar 2017). It is focused on futures and on engagement outside academia and, as demonstrated by this chapter, its scholarly contribution tends to be one of scaffolding new ideas onto directly relevant theory and ethnography rather than excavating trajectories of anthropological debates and ideas. Anthropologists have researched many facets of emerging technologies and critically analysed how they are engaged socially and politically. Examples include drone warfare (Gusterson 2016), the ontologies of drones (Fish 2019), how blockchain futures are imagined by finance professionals (Maurer 2016), cryptomining (Calvão 2019), and studies of media technologies situated in digital anthropology (Geismar and Knox 2021). These works make important interventions in fields of political, economic, and media anthropology and provide relevant opportunities to learn within specific fields, but are dispersed rather than constituting a united field of anthropology as such.

Our work is, moreover, not strictly applied anthropology. Following the pioneering work of Lucy Suchman (1998), embedded applied anthropologists have long since worked in technology industries; our particular practice, however, involves working across academia and industry to design and undertake research, publish academically, and mutually produce creative translation materials (Pink et al. 2020). Straddling academic and applied research, we situate our work as a mode of design anthropology, while learning from anthropologies of technology design practices and imaginaries, particularly how futures are articulated within them (Lanzeni 2016; Özden-Schilling 2015).

There are three waves in design anthropology (Pink et al. 2017). Lucy Suchman's ethnomethodological work in human-computer-interaction research (Suchman 1998) led the first wave and was an important step in understanding human interaction with technologies in interdisciplinary contexts ethnographically. It influenced subsequent design anthropological studies of social and interactional elements of AD, discussed below. A second wave in material culture studies (e.g. Clarke 2017) has a greater focus on object design and bears a relation to Daniel Miller and Heather Horst's (2012) material culture approach to digital technologies. A third wave is associated with Tim Ingold's phenomenological anthropology and Danish design anthropology, which acknowledges the sensory, creative, and improvisatory dimensions of design as the practice of both experts and everyday practitioners (Ingold 2013; Gunn et al. 2013; Smith et al. 2016). Rather than understanding relations as interactional or centring materiality, this wave emphasises the entangled, emergent, and processual dimensions of lives, things, and environments (Smith and Otto 2016). Our work aligns with this third wave and engages with the revisionary stance of futures anthropology, its emphasis on contingency and on the unknowability of futures (Pink and Salazar 2017; Irving 2017), and the uncertainty of the present and future (Akama et al. 2018). Therefore, we acknowledge that technologies are inextricable from their relations with humans, but rather than taking an interactional approach that focuses on human-technology relations, we situate humans and technologies as part of ongoingly changing environments. Likewise, while we account for the materiality and object-ness of digital technologies, we understand them as unfinished and as coming into being and experienced within and in relation to other things and processes, rather than as finished products. With Smith and Otto (2016), our emphasis is on how technologies might be understood as being part of ongoingly emergent worlds, and subsequently how emerging technologies might be seen not as completed products landing in a world already made, but as emerging into a world-in-progress, one with which they will continue to emerge.

EMERGING TECHNOLOGIES

The notion of an Interventional Anthropology of Emerging Technologies was coined by Sarah Pink (2021) to denote an anthropological practice that critiques dominant narratives that predict the impact of emerging technologies on futures, through attention to people's sensory, emotional, and practical experiences of imaginaries and materialities of possible future technologies. It responds to business and policy narratives where emerging technologies are understood as not having yet reached or achieved their potential in markets, and where it is expected that, when they do, they will bring benefit to society through disruptive change. Their predicted impact has a sense of urgency to understanding future waves of change across different stakeholder sectors. For instance, in the business consulting community it is stressed that '[i]t is no longer sufficient to embrace innovations and trends that are already underway. To stay ahead, companies must work methodically to sense new possibilities that exist far beyond the digital frontier' (Deloitte 2019). In 2019 AlgorithmWatch, a non-profit research and advocacy organisation, produced its 'Automating Society Report' on automated decision-making (ADM) systems, in which it posed the questions, 'Do we need new laws? Do we need new oversight institutions? Who do we fund to develop answers to the challenges ahead? Where should we invest? How do we enable citizens—patients, employees, consumers—to deal with this?' (AlgorithmWatch 2019)—thus, emphasising the need for preparedness in relation to the launch of emerging technologies.

There are many lists of top emerging technologies, also called breakthrough technologies, revised annually and published in online media by influential organisations such as the MIT Technology Review.[1] Recent examples include social robots, blockchain, drone technologies, and autonomous vehicles, as well as various medical and environmental technologies. Artificial Intelligence (AI) and automated decision-making (ADM) are often features or capabilities invested in (some) emerging technologies. Indeed, there is no circumscribable list of specific technologies defined as emerging; to crystalize in time something that is by nature continually emerging would be contrary to our argument. Instead, emerging technologies are a category of thing involved in relations with humans and other things and processes with which they share possible future environments. Rather than having a clear trajectory within a predictable future, they can be seen as inhabiting what Akama, Pink, and Sumartojo see as the inevitably uncertain sphere of the possible (Akama et al.

2018). This definition contests how emerging technologies are defined in dominant narratives and how their future impact on society is understood. Two examples demonstrate the tendencies of such narratives:

First, *Scientific American*'s online publication, which produces an annual list of emerging technologies, outlined the criteria that its Steering Group used to determine their 'Top 10 Emerging Technologies of 2019':

> Do the suggested technologies have the potential to provide major benefits to societies and economies? Could they alter established ways of doing things? Are they still in early stages of development but attracting a lot of interest from research labs, companies or investors? Are they likely to make significant inroads in the next several years? (*Scientific American* 2019).

Second, the World Economic Forum's (WEF) narrative, published on its website, resonates with that of *Scientific American*, asking, 'Which of today's technologies will shape tomorrow's world?' Answering its own question, it states, 'The emerging technologies must positively disrupt the existing order, be attractive to investors and researchers, and expect to achieve considerable scale within the coming 5 years.' The WEF website primes readers for a report that 'reveals some of the breakthrough innovations that are expected to radically impact the global social and economic order', citing the words of WEF's Chief Technology Officer, Jeremy Jurgens, 'From income inequality to climate change, technology will play a critical role in finding solutions to all the challenges our world faces today ... This year's emerging technologies demonstrate the rapid pace of human innovation and offer a glimpse into what a sustainable, inclusive future will look like' (World Economic Forum 2019).

In such narratives emerging technologies have 'not yet' impacted on the world; rather, they are represented as if poised to play a key problem-solving role in securing a better future through major disruptions to the current state of affairs. Thus, emerging technologies appear to be imagined as complete products that will be launched into society when regulation, infrastructure, and other aspects allow. Their ambitions are commendable, since they invite us to imagine sustainable futures shaped by technology. Yet these technologically determinist narratives neglect to address how intelligent and automated technologies may become part of future everyday human worlds.

The merits of taking an alternative approach are already evident. The 2019 AlgorithmWatch report cited above focused on how existing forms of ADM are already being used in society and what we might learn from these regarding prepare for the future. Therefore, demonstrating the point that emerging technologies tend to emerge slowly, often in mundane and inconspicuous ways, rather than making dramatic entrances leading to disruptive social, economic, or other changes. Maurer's (2016) discussion of blockchain accounts for how it was part of the imaginaries of the finance professionals who participated in his research, warning that this might not actually come about. AD cars present another prominent example. Fully AD cars are not currently in circulation in consumer markets. Instead, we witness gradually increasing modes of automation, represented in a series of automated features available in cars currently on the market. For instance, AD features such as automated braking, assisted cruise control, and automated parking are slowly entering individual lives and public roads. Rather than landing in society in full autonomous mode to subsequently solve societal problems, AD is already present in 'incomplete' or still developing forms (in relation to predicted future impacts) and used by people in response to their personal everyday circumstances. Thus, narratives that define emerging technologies as disruptive and problem-solving miss two key points: technologies may be slowly introduced into society as they evolve, rather than landing as fully formed solutions to problems, and people participate in determining what technologies are used for. As anthropologists know, and as is represented in critiques of such 'solutionism' (Morozov 2013), technologies do not simply impact on people and society or solve challenges.

EMERGING TECHNOLOGIES AND PROBLEM-SOLUTION NARRATIVES

A more detailed look at AD cars exemplifies how emerging technologies become implicated in problem-solution narratives of innovation agendas and how different academic disciplines approach them critically. It highlights two questions that are being asked about emerging technologies by most academic, industry, and policy stakeholders (although from different perspectives): Will people trust them? And what are their ethical implications? AD cars are particularly pertinent because they were the most hyped emerging technology in 2015. They featured amongst MIT Technology Review's Top 10 Emerging Technologies in 2015, 2016, and 2017, and are reviewed, debated, and discussed across multiple policy, industry, technology design, and public media narratives daily. Optimists hope they will contribute to solving societal problems by increasing road safety by eliminating human error (Winkle 2016), improving quality of life by freeing up driving time for infotainment or work (Kun et al. 2016), and increasing energy efficiency (Davila and Nombela 2012).

Social science and humanities scholars are critical of this technologically determinist agenda for research and design of AD. For STS scholars it neglects how AD will integrate with changing wider socio-technical systems and the new problems that this will give rise to (Stilgoe 2018; Marres 2018). STS scholars define self-driving cars as an experiment, arguing that modes of 'social learning' should be developed around them to inform their governance and policy (Stilgoe 2018), and, furthermore, that experimental methodologies should be used to investigate societal innovation during street trials (Marres 2018). Sociologists and geographers critique technologically determinist positions, arguing for investigations that further situate AD in society and its materiality (Bissell et al. 2018; Bissell 2018; Ash 2017). Previous industry-focused anthropological AD research has concentrated on human-machine interactions: what people's 'interactions look like with different aspects of the car, its spaces, technologies, and tools, and other people inside or outside the car' (Wasson et al. 2014, p. 3), the interaction involved in driving as a social and technological skill (Vinkhuyzen and Cefkin 2016, p. 524), 'socially acceptable autonomous driving' (Vinkhuyzen and Cefkin 2016, p. 522), and 'social practices of road use' (Vinkhuyzen and Cefkin 2016, p. 523). These studies usefully shift the focus away from the car itself; however, we propose going beyond the social and interactional focus to examine wider environmental and technological ecologies, and the human sensory and affective experiences and anticipatory modes that situate how people engage with existing AD car features and how future AD possibilities are imagined (Pink et al. 2017, 2018a). This agenda can be extended to any emerging technology with which people will potentially engage in their future everyday lives. Analysis guided by the anthropology of emerging technologies de-centres the technology and acknowledges that the experience of it cannot be isolated from the circumstances in which it is encountered or imagined. Recent interdisciplinary debates relating to human trust in AD and the ethics of AD car accident scenarios demonstrate why this is important by revealing how attention to sensory, affective, and anticipatory human engagement with AD cars can shift the debate. These are discussed in the next section.

Accidents, Trust, and Emerging Technologies

As new automated and intelligent technologies come onto the horizon, concerns regarding whether people will trust them have emerged for government and industry stakeholders. AD is a good example, represented as offering the technological possibility of a considerably safer transport system by eliminating human error. However, this is not without its complexities, not least due to the question of the ethics of AD cars, and the capacity they will have for ADM in different accident scenarios. This is often represented in a dystopian and sensationalised narrative in media articles, which ask if future self-driving cars will kill us.[2] Moreover, a 2018 global survey suggests 'almost half of consumers in most markets' doubt the safety of AD,[3] while in 2019 the AAA in the US found that 'Seven in ten (71 percent) U.S. drivers would be afraid to ride in a fully self-driving vehicle'.[4] It is now widely accepted internationally—across governments[5] and industry, and in science and technology media[6]—that generating human trust in future AD cars constitutes a key challenge for both automotive industry and policy stakeholders who hope that these benefits will come about. Thus, significant funds are being invested in technologically driven research agendas seeking to engender trust in and acceptance of AD.

Created in response to academic and public media discussions about the decisions an AD car might take in such accident scenarios, the Moral Machine at MIT Media Lab (http://moralmachine.mit.edu/) presents its users with a series of moral questions regarding whom an AD car might kill in an accident. The MIT experiment is an iteration of the Trolley Problem, which is frequently discussed with reference to AD cars. The Trolley Problem originates from the example of a trolley driver whose vehicle's brakes fail when going down a valley (see Ash 2017). The driver is faced with the dilemma of either crashing into five workmen who are repairing the track or turning to crash into only one workman. In the case of AD, it is used to describe and debate a situation where the car loses control and will either kill pedestrians of different categories or swerve into a wall to kill the driver, as in the MIT Moral Machine example. The Trolley Problem asks us to confront abstract but affective scenarios that are thought to reveal both human values and their relation to possible future machine decision-making.

The MIT Moral Machine website offers different combinations of persons as drivers and pedestrians who might be saved. It sought to crowd-source information about and discussion of how people respond to such moral dilemmas. The platform collected '40 million decisions in ten languages from millions of people in 233 countries and territories' (Awad et al. 2018, p. 59). Those involved in its design believed that 'Before we allow our cars to make ethical decisions, we need to have a global conversation to express our preferences to the companies that will design moral algorithms, and to the policymakers that will regulate them' (Awad et al. 2018, p. 63). They saw the Moral Machine as initiating this process, reporting,

> Our data helped us to identify three strong preferences that can serve as building blocks for discussions of universal machine ethics, even if they are not ultimately endorsed by policymakers: the preference for sparing human lives, the preference for sparing more lives, and the preference for sparing young lives. (Awad et al. 2018, p. 60)

The authors acknowledge that the scientific limitations of such an experiment are many. However, as with ethnographic practice, ethics are processual, contingent, and situated (Pink 2017). The MIT experiment investigated how rational decision-making, detected at the surface level of what people report, should happen when presented with a moral dilemma on a website. As such it reveals surface values, expressed in such moments, but cannot capture the phenomenological, environmental, and situated meanings involved in how people make decisions within the complexities of everyday worlds. Such experiments can neither engage with the very fundamental anthropological premise that people do not always do what they think or say they do, nor with the principle that our action and experience is inextricable from sensation and affect, not only representational knowledge. Yet such an experiment has enormous popular and media appeal. It is, moreover, aligned to the solutionist narratives outlined above. Awad's Ted Talk (http://moralmachine.mit.edu/) suggests that for AD cars to solve the societal problem of road accident deaths by making road travel safer for the majority, the moral dilemmas associated with road accidents need to be solved in ways that reflect human preferences; this, in turn, would encourage people to use AD cars and understand the trade-offs associated with their regulation.

As the geographer James Ash points out, the problem with utilitarian approaches to ethics in AD cars is that they focus on design and testing, and do not account for the contingencies of actual accidents. Ash argues for an ethics based on understanding 'the particular situation of the accident, rather than focus[ing] on what the vehicles were programmed or designed to do in advance of these situations' (Ash 2017, p. 158). When applied to AD cars, the Trolley Problem is associated with a societal problem, yet it is detached from realistic understandings of people and society, and derived from a limited disciplinary perspective. Contrastingly, Ash's analysis of two existing reported accidents involving cars with AD features concludes that they were the outcome of how things aligned 'in such a way that failed to disclose important qualities of objects that were necessary for the continuing homeostasis of the driver and vehicle', including 'the contingency of other drivers' (2017, p. 161). Ash insists that for AD cars,

> no matter how many hours of test-driving or simulation data a designer uses to programme a vehicle, the designer can never anticipate the contingency of [the objects they sense] because objects always have the potential to be perturbed in a way not envisaged by their designers and thus can disclose qualities (and in turn spatio-temporal relations) that exceed a smart object's ability to sense them. (Ash 2017, pp. 167–168)

Focusing on the politics of automation, the geographer David Bissell also examines the consequences of an AD accident in the US. Bissell demonstrates how 'the accident subtly reshaped the terrain of the politics of autonomous vehicles through diverse materialities' which occurred at different sites, 'through images; through the words and tenor of eyewitness testimony and newscasters; through the police reports; through the communications between city councils; and through encounters with drivers' (2018, p. 65). This, he suggests, led to a series of transformations across these different sites.

Ash's and Bissell's after-the-event analyses of the AD accident emphasise the contingent circumstances of AD and the wider ecologies within which they participate. They reveal the limitations of the Moral Machine experiment for understanding the relationships that constitute and are effected by accidents. However, there is a further anthropological step needed to comprehend the circumstances in which people might trust AD cars, which accounts for how future mobilities might be experienced within the sensory and affective routines of everyday life, memory, and imagination, and what it means to ask how people might trust AD within those circumstances.

The dominant assumption and hopeful narrative that AD cars will save lives if only people would trust and subsequently accept them is complicated by the work of social scientists and critical Human Computer Interaction (HCI) researchers. Anthropological research has demonstrated that trust is not necessarily a rational or cognitive sentiment (e.g. Evans-Pritchard 1937; Douglas 1970; Corsin 2011). While quantitative methods, such as survey studies and technological testing, treat trust as measurable, in the social sciences and humanities trust is widely regarded as 'created and reproduced through interactive processes' (Jagd and Fuglsang 2016, p. 3) and thus continuously experienced and modified within everyday life, making it difficult to measure. Survey and technological testing do not interrogate the crucial qualitative questions of how trust actually comes about in the complex configurations of everyday life as it is lived. Critical voices within the HCI community have also proposed more situated approaches to trust by attending to human experience (Norman 2007), observing 'what computers and people do together at large' (Harper 2014, p. 5), and taking 'a user-centred approach that accounts for the modes of trust that all different stakeholders need to engage in' (Sas and Khairuddin 2015, p. 341). Harper proposes a contextual approach to trust as a concept 'in the normal traffic of living' (2014, p. 9), arguing that attention to 'what happens when trust does occur', should replace the existing focus on '*mistrust*' (Harper 2014, p. 10, original italics). Collectively these literatures indicate that we need to account for trust as a qualitative, fluid, and changing experience, and to study the everyday life circumstances in which it emerges.

Trust in Emerging Technologies from an Anthropological Perspective

Within the social sciences and humanities, trust is understood as the action of stepping forward into an uncertain situation, involving some degree of risk (Luhmann 1988; Misztal 2011). Philosophers of trust propose that for trust to occur, a person must have feelings of sufficient confidence based on the degree of familiarity they feel in a given situation (Fredricksen 2016), and social scientists propose that 'trust is created and reproduced through the formation of social interaction processes which are repeated over time' (Jagd and Fuglsang 2016, p. 7). In contrast to an emphasis on trust as a cognitive category in psychological and sociological approaches (Corsin 2011, p. 178), anthropologists emphasise the embodied, sensory, and affective experience of trust, how trust is 'felt' rather than 'thought out', and locally and culturally specific dimensions of trust. Drawing on Rane Willerselv's ethnography with Yukaghir hunters in Siberia, anthropologist Alberto Corsin describes how their hunting entails relationships between humans, animals, and spirits, where modes of showing and deceit create a different economy of trust. He proposes a focus on 'what kind of work the notion [of trust] does', and attention to the materiality and intersubjectivity it may entail (2011, p. 179). The implication for trust in emerging technologies is that we should investigate what other 'things', relationships, and processes are involved in generating sufficient familiarity and confidence for people to trust using technologies within specific circumstances, rather than simply focusing on human-machine relations.

Anthropological research further suggests that trust emerges within contexts of repeated activity. Since the 1930s, it has been understood that people cope with ontological uncertainty through beliefs in witchcraft and oracle consolidated in repeated ritual processes (Evans-Pritchard 1937; Douglas 1970). Research into digital data anxieties suggests that through repeated everyday routine activities, feelings of trust emerge: people trusted that their digital data would not be lost—even when they saved it using technologies that cannot guarantee its safety—because they followed familiar personal saving routines (Pink et al. 2018b). Therefore the 'things' involved in generating trust go beyond other people and objects to include processes such as routines or rituals.

A design anthropological approach to trust in technology (Pink et al. 2018b) has engaged concepts of improvisation and contingency to situate trust within how people improvise to 'find ways of keeping on going' (Gunn and Clausen 2013, p. 174) in the continually changing (emergent) circumstances of everyday life. The idea that humans *improvise with* technologies—rather than technologies *impacting on* humans—is articulated through Ingold and Hallam's argument that improvisation is 'a necessary condition because there is no existing template that instructs us in how to deal with the continually changing contingencies of life' (Ingold and Hallam 2007, p. 2). Ingold and Hallam see improvisation as being 'inseparable from our performative engagements with the materials that surround us' (Ingold and Hallam 2007, p. 3). This is useful for understanding how people encounter new technologies in everyday life, since, following the design anthropological principle, everyday life circumstances are continually emergent (Smith and Otto 2016). Then, 'attending to how people improvise to fill in the gaps between what they think they know and the inevitable uncertainties that actions entail' (Pink et al. 2018b) offers a prism through which to consider those moments where trust is performed, felt, and experienced, but not necessarily visibly or verbally articulated, and as such not observable. Therefore, the implication is that if trust is constituted beyond our interactions with singular entities and always in contingent circumstances, then trust is neither rational nor a fixed state or relationship, but a sense of familiarity in changing environments which can change in accordance with our immediate circumstances. We demonstrate these points through examples from our research into the experience of driving and AD technologies.

ETHNOGRAPHIES OF EMERGING TECHNOLOGIES IN PRACTICE

To investigate the experience of driving and how trust came about within a team-based, industry-partnered project undertaken in Sweden, we developed interventional visual and sensory ethnography methods. Different from traditional long-term anthropological fieldwork, these methods are designed to create intensive encounters with research participants in which we collaborated with them to provide ways of surfacing and knowing their experiences of driving and of autonomous features (Pink et al. 2017). This involved sharing meals, conversations, and drives with participants in our research, during which they enacted, visualised, and discussed their experiences of driving while we video recorded. The examples we discuss demonstrate how participants' feelings of trust—that is, of having a sense of familiarity and confidence—when using a technology are not necessarily only or directly related to the technology itself or the person's interaction with that technology, but are, rather, contingent on sometimes hidden knowledge or circumstances.

Hakan drove Sarah and Vaike along his usual commute to work, as Sarah video recorded, we noticed a small toy hanging from the side of his steering wheel and asked about it. He told us his kids were given it in a burger restaurant about ten years ago, and he believed it brought him luck. He explained how 'I don't believe in myths but for some reason I still believe in this guy … for some reason … I've been so close to hitting so many times but I never hit them but I don't know why.' In fact, he told us, a particularly intense experience occurred just after they got the toy:

> My son got sick when he was 3 months old and we were really out in … we had like 300K to the hospital and we had to drive because he was getting problems breathing … I was speeding definitely because we really had to rush to the hospital, and then the moon disappeared behind me, and I realised that if I would have been one tenth later I would have hit the moose. Because the moose almost ran into the car, and this has happened to me several times … then for some reason I connected this incident to that incident, … I thought, OK, trust this guy.

Hakan's story expresses the uncertainty associated with driving and how people cope with it. He did not trust the toy itself in an interactional sense. Rather, it had become part of his car and driving experience, which invoked and symbolised a feeling of familiarity and safety. Likewise, having particular things with them in their cars enabled similar feelings for participants in other studies. For instance, in Sweden and Brazil, Pink and colleagues' (Pink et al. 2018a, c) participants found it hard to even imagine driving without their phones or would return home for them if they were forgotten. The car-smartphone configuration, and the affordances and relationships to which this extended, was integral to the constitution of a driving situation in which they could trust. Indeed, people take many things in their cars, to feel relaxed and enjoy driving. For instance, Anneli in Sweden discussed how she had things in the car that were never or rarely used, showing Thomas a fire extinguisher, snow shovel, candles, blankets, and umbrella, and explaining, 'I am [a] safety addict, one extra-large first aid with candles, jump cables and all. It's from If [insurance company] with everything.' Rather than trusting technologies to keep them safe, our ethnographic research suggests that people create situations in which they feel safe by bringing together certain objects, processes, and relationships: the toy, smartphones, and the multiple items in the last example all do this in different ways. Thus, rather than asking if people will trust emerging technologies like AD, we might better investigate how feelings of familiarity and confidence are configured through particular combinations of things and processes. Our research with five families who participated in Volvo Cars' DriveMe experiment demonstrated this in practice.

Each family was given a Volvo XC90 car with a number of high-level driving assistance systems to use for period of one and a half years on an everyday basis, accumulating experience of the car and developing routines of using it over time. The early stages of our study with these families suggest participants' feelings of trust and confidence in the automated features of the car were contingent on specific circumstances and were not constant. For example, the husband in one couple explained how he initially learned about and gradually got to know the research car by understanding what it could and could not do in everyday traffic environments. He felt comfortable using the driver assist feature during a certain stretch of his commute to work, as it meant that he did not have to cope with 'the feeling of stress and annoyance about queuing in traffic ... you put that [driver assist] on and ... you don't look so much to the road and you trust it ... and you're already in the tunnel'. However, this feeling of trust did not endure in all circumstances throughout his route. For instance, when he used driver assist and it drove at 70 km/h, he felt that 'everyone's passing you, then its stressful ... you see everyone driving by you ... the heart beat goes up'. He explained this by saying, 'There's a rhythm and flow in the traffic and if you're not in it ... when it's too slow ... it's so annoying to keep track of it, [so] it's very relaxing, very good to let the car take care of that; but when they are driving [at] 90, then it's the other way again, very stressed, ... you are not in the flow.' Similarly, the feelings of trust could shift as the road environment changed. For example, on certain parts of his commute route, he was relaxed and felt he trusted the car; in other instances, the couple felt uncomfortable with how the car drove on a particularly curvy stretch of road. Here, the husband commented that he would have liked the car to 'remember how I used to drive and then try not to take the curve ... even though I put it at 70 it's a bit sharp, 55–60 is a good feeling'. Thus, participants' feelings of confidence and familiarity that the experience of driving engendered in them were contingent and varied according to the different elements and processes that configured each different set of circumstances. Their degree of trust is not fixed and cannot be measured, but, rather, it is flexible and refined in each situation. Again, the implication is that it is not emerging technologies in which people will trust, but rather the way in which these technologies are embedded in particular and contingent material and social circumstances.

These brief ethnographic scenarios have implications for how we might understand emerging technologies anthropologically. For scholars in geography and STS a critical theory of the positioning of the AD car calls for attention to what happens around the car, the socio-technical systems in which it participates, and the wider environments it exists in and impacts on. Their focus on the AD car itself inevitably leads to a critique of the focus on the AD car itself, yet such centring of the car in the analysis has simultaneously sustained academic discussion about AD and ironically maintains the central status of the

AD car in the debate. Our ethnographic examples indicate that to the conceptual and analytical categories needed to understand how people will feel with AD cars require a focus not directly on the car itself, but on how its materiality and future imaginaries become entangled with the intricacies of everyday life materialities, logistics, and experience. Therefore, we should focus theoretical and methodological interest in emerging technologies not only on the technologies themselves but on the present and possible future lives and worlds in and with which they will be engaged. The case of AD also demonstrates compelling practical reasons for this. Emerging technologies, such as AD cars, do not emerge in isolation; they are accompanied by other emerging technologies, business models, material and sensory environments, and social practices. These entangled, or contiguous, processes of change need to be accounted for.

CONCLUSION: INSIGHTS FOR THE ANTHROPOLOGY OF EMERGING TECHNOLOGIES

In this chapter we have argued, and demonstrated through the example of AD cars, that anthropologists have a scholarly and interventional role to play in existing definitions of emerging technologies as a category, as well as in interdisciplinary explorations of specific emerging technologies. Through the example of trust in self-driving cars, we have revealed how academic, industry, and policy approaches to AD cars are bound up in a solutionist innovation narrative that is technologically determinist. We have shown how an engineering-led survey study of AD ethics framed people as rational decision-makers. By attending to critiques of such approaches within our cognate disciplines of human geography and sociology, we have shown how their commentaries and arguments unsettle the assumptions that underpin technologically determinist approaches. Instead, they alert us to the need to attend to the emergent everyday circumstances within which trust in AD might come about. Turning to anthropologies of trust we showed that existing literature in this field has paved the way to understanding trust as situated, contextual, and emergent, rather than as transactional or interactional. This approach aligns with the design anthropological approach we introduced at the beginning of this chapter. Our ethnographies of AD were interventional in that they went beyond observational ethnography and long-term fieldwork to engage with people in re-enactments, set-up situations such as meals, and in using AD features. Our ethnographic findings contributed to academic publications as well as to the production of ethnographic translation materials, which are used to question and probe in industry and policy contexts, discussed elsewhere (Pink et al. 2020).

Thus, we have outlined the basis for shaping an agenda for the anthropology of emerging technologies, rooted in anthropology, but engaged with other disciplines and across multiple sectors. Anthropological perspectives rooted in ethnographies of everyday experience account for the sensory, affective, and anticipatory. They thus extend and situate the theoretical and methodological work of cognate disciplines through uniquely anthropological dialogues between ethnography and theory =. Therefore, the anthropology of emerging technologies should be nurtured within interdisciplinary academic research contexts, as a theoretically and methodologically strong and convincing mode of understanding. However, to advance an anthropology of emerging technologies we need to be engaged both in the academy and to work collaboratively in the sites of their emergence. This involves participating in and commenting on public debates, engagement with industry research partners through actions including co-research, creating and working with ethnographic translation materials, and inviting an international community of scholars and researchers to collectively develop this field.

Acknowledgements The fieldwork discussed here was undertaken within the 'Human Expectations and Experiences of Autonomous Driving' (HEAD) project funded by Vinnova, Sweden, 2016–18, award number: 2016-02515. We thank our research participants, colleagues at Volvo Cars and the HEAD research team for their inspiration and collegiality.

NOTES

1. https://www.technologyreview.com/lists/technologies/2019/. Accessed 8 July 2021.
2. https://onezero.medium.com/how-should-self-driving-cars-choose-who-not-to-kill-442f2a5a1b59. Accessed 8 July 2021.
3. https://www2.deloitte.com/us/en/insights/industry/automotive/advanced-vehicle-technologies-autonomous-electric-vehicles.html. Accessed 14 July 2021.
4. https://newsroom.aaa.com/tag/autonomous-vehicles/. Accessed 14 July 2021.
5. https://www.aph.gov.au/Parliamentary_Business/Committees/House/Industry_Innovation_Science_and_Resources/Driverless_vehicles/Report (accessed 14 July 2021) and see, for example, Cohen et al. (2017, p. 28).
6. https://www.sciencemag.org/news/2017/12/people-don-t-trust-driverless-cars-researchers-are-trying-change. Accessed 14 July 2021.

REFERENCES

Akama, Y., Pink, S., & Sumartojo, S. (2018). *Uncertainty and Possibility*. London: Bloomsbury.

AlgorithmWatch. (2019). *AUTOMATING SOCIETY—TAKING STOCK OF AUTOMATED DECISION-MAKING IN THE EU. A report by AlgorithmWatch in cooperation with Bertelsmann Stiftung, supported by the Open Society Foundations.* Retrieved from https://algorithmwatch.org/en/automating-society/. Accessed 20 November 2020.

Ash, J. (2017). *Phase Media: Space, Time and the Politics of Smart Objects*. London: Bloomsbury.

Awad, E., Dsouza, S., Kim, R., Schulz, J., Henrifh, J., Shariff, A., Bonnefon, J-F., & Rahwan, I. (2018). The Moral Machine experiment. *Nature, 563,* 59–64.

Bissell, D. (2018). Automation interrupted: How autonomous vehicle accidents transform the material politics of automation. *Political Geography, 65*, 57–66.

Bissell, D., Birtchell, T., Elliot, A., & Hsu, E. L. (2018). Autonomous automobilities: The social impacts of driverless vehicles. *Current Sociology, 68*(1), 116–134.

Calvão, F. (2019) Crypto-miners: Digital labor and the power of blockchain technology. *Economic Anthropology, 6*, 123–134.

Cefkin, M. (Ed.) (2009). *Ethnography and the Corporate Encounter. Reflections on Research in and of Corporations.* New York & Oxford: Berghahn.

Clarke, A. (2017). *Design Anthropology Object Cultures in Transition.* London: Bloomsbury.

Cohen, T., Jones, P., & Cavoli, C. (2017). *Social and behavioural questions associated with automated vehicles.* Scoping study by UCL Transport Institute. Final report. London: Department for Transport.

Corsin, A. (2011). Trust in anthropology. *Anthropological Theory, 11*(2), 177–196.

Davila, A., & Nombela, M. (2012). Platooning—Safe and EcoFriendly Mobility. In *SAE 2012 World Congress & Exhibition.* Detroit, MI.: SAE International.

Deloitte. (2019). Beyond the Digital Frontier. Retrieved from https://www2.deloitte.com/insights/us/en/focus/tech-trends/2019/tech-trends-introduction.html. Accessed 20 November 2020.

Douglas, M. (1970). *Witchcraft Confessions and Accusations.* London: Tavistock Publications.

Dourish, P., & Bell, G. (2011). *Divining a digital future: mess and mythology in ubiquitous computing.* Cambridge, MA.: The MIT Press.

Evans-Pritchard, E. E. (1937). *Witchcraft, oracles and magic among the Azande.* Oxford: Clarendon Press.

Fish, A. (2019). Drones at the Edge of Naturecultures. *Media Fields Journal, 14.* Retrieved from http://www.research.lancs.ac.uk/portal/en/people/adam-fish(10a5067e-a828-497b-95ae-e35ed07f9ba1).html. Accessed 20 November 2020.

Forbes. (2020). The 7 Biggest Technology Trends In 2020 Everyone Must Get Ready For Now. Retrieved from https://www.forbes.com/sites/bernard-marr/2019/09/30/the-7-biggest-technology-trends-in-2020-everyone-must-get-ready-for-now/#778aba672261. Accessed 20 November 2020.

Fortune. (2015). The most hyped emerging technology of 2015. Retrieved from http://fortune.com/2015/08/20/self-driving-car-hype/. Accessed 20 November 2020.

Fredricksen, M. (2016). Divided uncertainty: A phenomenology of trust, risk and confidence. In S. Jagd, L. Fuglsang (Eds.), *Trust, Organisations and Social Interaction.* Cheltenham: Edward Elgar Publishers.

Geismar, H., & Knox, H. (Eds.) (2021). *Digital Ethnography* (2nd ed.). Oxford: Routledge.

Gunn, W., & Clausen, C. (2013). Conceptions of Innovation and Practice: Designing Indoor Climate. In W. Gunn, T. Otto, & R. C. Smith (Eds.), *Design Anthropology: Theory and Practice* (pp. 159–179). London: Bloomsbury Academic.

Gunn, W., Otto, T., & Smith, R.C. (Eds.) (2013). *Design Anthropology: Theory and Practice.* London: Bloomsbury Academic.

Gusterson, H. (2016). *Drone: Remote Control Warfare.* Cambridge, MA.: The MIT Press.

Harper, R. H. R. (2014). *Trust, Computing and Society.* Cambridge: Cambridge University Press.

Ingold, T., & Hallam, E. (2007). Creativity and cultural improvisation: an introduction. In T. Ingold & E. Hallam (Eds.), *Creativity and cultural improvisation* (pp. 1–24). Berg: Oxford.

Ingold, T. (2013). *Making*. Oxford: Routledge.

Irving, A. (2017). The art of turning left and right. In J. Salazar, S. Pink, A. Irving, & J. Sjoberg (Eds.), *Anthropologies and Futures*. London: Bloomsbury.

Jagd, S., & Fuglsang, L. (2016). Studying trust as process within and between organisations. In S. Jagd & L. Fuglsang (Eds.), *Trust, Organisations and Social Interaction*. Cheltenham: Edward Elgar Publishers.

Kun, A. L., Boll, S., & Schmidt, A. (2016) Shirting gears: User interfaces in the age of autonomous driving. *IEEE Pervasive Computing, 15*(1), 32–37.

Lanzeni, D. (2016). Smart Global Futures: designing affordable materialities for a better life. In S. Pink, E. Ardevol, & D. Lanzeni (Eds.), *Digital Materialities*. London: Bloomsbury.

Luhmann, N. (1988). Trust: Making and Breaking Cooperative Relations. In D. Gambetta (Ed.), *Familiarity, Confidence, Trust: Problems and Alternatives* (pp. 94–107). Basil Blackwell: New York.

Marres, N. (2018). What if nothing happens? Street trials of intelligent cars as experiments in participation. In S. Maassen, S. Dickel, & C. H. Schneider (Eds.), *TechnoScience in Society, Sociology of Knowledge Yearbook*. Niimegen: Springer/Kluwer.

Maurer, B. (2016). Re-risking in Realtime. On Possible Futures for Finance after the Blockchain. *BEHEMOTH A Journal on Civilisation, 9*(2), 82–96.

Morozov, E. (2013). *To Save Everything, Click Here: Technology, Solutionism, and the Urge to Fix Problems that Don't Exist*. London: Penguin Books.

Miller, D., & Horst, H. (2012). The Digital and Human: A Prospectus for Digital Anthropology. In H. Horst & D. Miller (Eds.), *Digital Anthropology* (pp. 3–35). London: Bloomsbury.

Misztal, B. (2011). Trust: Acceptance of, Precaution Against and Cause of Vulnerability. *Comparative Sociology, 10*(3), 358–379.

Norman, D. (2007). *The Design of Future Things*. New York: Basic Books.

Özden-Schilling, C. (2015). Economy Electric. *Cultural Anthropology, 30*(4), 578–88.

Pink, S. (2017). Ethics in a changing world. In S. Pink, V. Fors, & T. O'Dell (Eds.), *Theoretical Scholarship and Applied practice*. Oxford: Berghahn.

Pink, S., Fors, V., & Glöss, M. (2017). Automated Futures and the Mobile Present: in-car video ethnographies. *Ethnography, 20*(1), 88–107.

Pink, S. & Salazar, J. F. (2017). Anthropologies and Futures: setting the agenda. In J. Salazar, S. Pink, A. Irving & J. Sjoberg (Eds.), *Anthropologies and Futures*. Oxford: Bloomsbury.

Pink, S., Fors, V., & Glöss, M. (2018a). The contingent futures of the mobile present: beyond automation as innovation. *Mobilities, 13*(5), 615–631.

Pink, S., Lanzeni, D. & Horst, H. (2018b). Data Anxieties: finding trust and hope in digital mess. *Big Data and Society*, 5(1). https://doi.org/10.1177/2053951718756685.

Pink, S., Gomes, A., Zilse, R., Lucena, R., Pinto, J., Porto, A., Caminha, C., de Siqueira, G.M., & Duarte de Oliveira, M. (2018c). Automated and Connected?: Smartphones and Automobility through the Global South. *Applied Mobilities*. https://doi.org/10.1080/23800127.2018.1505263.

Pink, S., Osz, K., Raats, K., Lindgren, T., & Fors, V. (2020). Design Anthropology for Emerging Technologies: trust and sharing in Autonomous Driving futures. *Design Studies.* https://doi.org/10.1016/j.destud.2020.04.002.

Pink, S. (2021). Anthropology in an Uncertain World. In D. Podjed, M. Gorup, P. Borecky, & C. G. Montero (Eds.), *Why the World Needs Anthropologists* (pp. 56–70). Oxford: Routledge.

Sas, C., & Khairuddin, I. E. (2015). Exploring Trust in Bitcoin Technology: A Framework for HCI Research. In Proceedings of the Annual Meeting of the Australian Special Interest Group for Computer Human Interaction (OzCHI '15). Association for Computing Machinery, New York, NY, USA, 338–342. https://doi.org/10.1145/2838739.2838821.

Scientific American. (2019). Top 10 Emerging Technologies of 2019: Introduction. Retrieved from https://www.scientificamerican.com/article/top-10-emerging-technologies-of-2019-introduction/. Accessed 20 November 2020.

Smith, R. C., & Otto, T. (2016). Cultures of the Future: Emergence and Intervention in Design Anthropology. In R. C. Smith, K. T. Vangkilde, M. G. Kjærsgaard, T. Otto, J. Halse, & T. Binder (Eds.), *Design Anthropological Futures* (pp 19–36). London: Bloomsbury Academic.

Smith, R. C., Vangkilde, K. T., Kjærsgaard, M. G., Otto, T., Halse, J., & Binder, T. (Eds.) (2016). *Design Anthropological Futures* (pp 19–36). London: Bloomsbury Academic.

Stilgoe, J. (2018). Seeing like a Tesla—How can we anticipate self-driving worlds? Glocalism, 3. https://doi.org/10.12893/gjcpi.2017.3.2.

Suchman, L. (1998). Human/machine Reconsidered. *Cognitive Studies, 5*(1), 5–13.

Vinkhuyzen, E., & Cefkin, M. (2016). Developing socially acceptable autonomous vehicles. In *Ethnographic Praxis in Industry Conference Proceedings,* Minneapolis, US, 29 August–1 September 2016, pp. 522–534.

Wasson, C. et al. (2014). *The Social Life of the Car.* Retrieved from https://www.slideshare.net/ChrisFerrell7/the-social-life-of-the-car-72339802.   Accessed   20 November 2020.

Winkle, T. (2016). Safety benefits of Automated Vehicles. In M. Maurer, J. C. Gerdes, B. Lenz, & H. Winner (Eds.), *Autonomous Driving. Technical, Legal, and Social Aspects* (pp. 335–364). Berlin: Springer.

World Economic Forum. (2019). These are the top 10 emerging technologies of 2019. Retrieved from https://www.weforum.org/agenda/2019/07/these-are-the-top-10-emerging-technologies-of-2019/. Accessed 20 November 2020.

CHAPTER 10

Computational Ethnography: A Case of COVID-19's Methodological Consequences

Digital

Anders Kristian Munk and Brit Ross Winthereik

Anthropology has a computational past. As early as the 1960s, ethnoscience was seriously pursuing a formalist and computationally enabled analysis of culture with the aim of discovering what were essentially 'cultural algorithms' or rules that a stranger would need to follow in order to pass for a native (Hymes 1965; see also Seaver 2015). Yet, as ethnoscience was excluded from the ethnographic canon (see, for example, the scathing critique in Geertz 1973), so was—for a while at least—the ambition to work computationally in anthropology (Seaver 2018).

Recently, however, the anthropological interest in computation (Fortun et al. 2017), big social data (Manovich 2011), and digital methods for pattern recognition in large datasets (Munk and Jensen 2015) has been rekindled. On the heels of this renewed interest in computers for the analysis of ethnographic materials comes the question of how it challenges what ethnography is. What, if anything, changes in how anthropologists generate and analyse empirical material and with what effects? With this question, we do not mean to imply that an anthropological interest in all things digital will automatically lead to a

A. K. Munk (✉)
Aalborg University, Aalborg, Denmark
e-mail: anderskm@hum.aau.dk

B. R. Winthereik
Department of Business IT, IT University of Copenhagen, Copenhagen, Denmark
e-mail: brwi@itu.dk

201

M. H. Bruun et al. (eds.), *The Palgrave Handbook of the Anthropology of Technology*, https://doi.org/10.1007/978-981-16-7084-8_10

change in methods and methodology. Lots of ethnography has been conducted in digital environments using broadly familiar and established methods. When anthropologists study data scientists, for example, it can happen in ways that are fully within the comfort zone of participant observation and long-term engagement with informants (Boellstorff 2013; Wilf et al. 2013; Grommé et al. 2018; Lowrie 2018). Similarly, the anthropology of digital culture has produced significant literature on both virtual worlds (Dalsgaard 2008; Nardi 2010; Pearce 2011; Boellstorff 2015) and social media in everyday contexts (Miller 2011, 2016; Birkbak 2012; Barassi 2015; Albris 2018) through the adaptation of participant observation and in-depth interviewing to new and mediated contexts. We can thus distinguish between ethnographic studies of how people use digital devices in their everyday lives and 'netnographic' studies of social life in online environments. Nonetheless, they both represent situations where conventional techniques like participant observation and in-depth interviews have been adapted to new methodological needs.

Indeed, one could argue that a key feature of ethnography is that ethnographers always tend to adopt methods that facilitate seeing the world from the standpoint of its social relations. People and places matter, and if people and places are online, this is where ethnographers should be. In drawing on methods from many quarters, including the natural sciences, ethnography is experimental at its core. And, as ethnography has always sought to include material forms and artefacts as part of its methods, computation is a natural addition to kinship diagrams, index cards, tape recorders, and all the other instruments ethnographers use as methodological and analytical proxies and extensions of their bodies.

However, anthropologists' applications of computational techniques to generate and computationally analyse large volumes of data as part of their ethnographic practice are still relatively few and far between. This does not necessarily reflect an aversion to quantitative methods, although that surely is part of it in some cases, but could also be reflective of a settlement in which data science provides insights at scale about patterns and trends (big data), while ethnography provides stories (thick data) for making sense of such insights (Wang 2013; Boyd and Crawford 2012). This is a division of labour, which is nevertheless problematised when informants' use of big data and digital platforms requires anthropologists to observe and make sense of data and digital practices (Walford 2017; Douglas-Jones et al. 2021; Waltorp 2020).

Some of the first anthropologists to study hyperlink practices as the intentional authoring of online sociality argued that computational techniques for data capture and analysis are necessary if one is intent on following actors across the vast and distributed socio-technical systems that are characteristic of the world wide web (Beaulieu and Simakova 2006). When Beaulieu, in later work, talks about 'computational ethnography', she thus explicitly gives prominence to practices of coding and computing as alternatives to face-to-face interaction premised on the value of 'being there' (Beaulieu 2017) (other examples of coding and computing as part of ethnographic practices include Anderson et al. 2009; Blok et al. 2017; Flora and Andersen 2016; Geiger and Ribes 2011; Hsu 2014; Munk and Ellern 2015; Shadoan and Dudek 2013).

For computational ethnography, then, the methodological experiment is not so much about whether or how field relations can be properly maintained and rapport established with informants in mediated settings (one of the foundational questions posed in virtual ethnography [Hine 2000]). Rather, it is about becoming familiar with, and intervening in, the narrative proposed by the digital setting, in order to create an account of the social in the digital that is both mediated and situated:

> Computational ethnography focuses not on the mediation via the digital, but on the informational dimension of internet settings, big data and digital tools. As such, computational ethnography stands in tension not so much with the analogue, but rather with the narrative, the unfolding of events, which is central to ethnographic practice and accounts. (Beaulieu 2017, p. 34)

Digital methods (Marres 2017; Rogers 2013), which is the name of an interdisciplinary approach involving scholars from science and technology studies, media studies, anthropology, sociology, and human geography, are pursuing the idea of 'online grounding' (Rogers 2009). Online grounding is an approach to digital data that traces online interactions in order to make claims about sociocultural phenomena that are not isolated to the internet, but which begin there, in an online environment. In contrast to the modes of doing ethnography, where offline phenomena are being followed into online environments, this approach appropriates digital media as its empirical material and uses computational techniques for gathering and analysing this material, while also maintaining an ambition to understand social groups.

Digital methods are making use of natural language processing, network analysis, and various forms of machine learning in order to make sense of often very large and complicated datasets, and have developed a methodological apparatus that foregrounds the need to study both the web itself and happenings and events 'on' it. 'Interface methods' (Marres and Gerlitz 2016) or 'redistributed methods' (Marres 2012) reflect the idea that digital media are always, and already, methods in their own right. They have emic ways of making sense of the interaction that they host and facilitate, and these emic ways, expressed for example in linking practices, recommender systems, news feeds, or hashtags, are even performative of that interaction.

There is something quintessentially ethnographic in the claim that one must know one's field and its languages, economies, norms, and values in order to provide an empirically grounded analysis (see also Munk 2013). Our point of departure, therefore, is that introducing digital and computational methods can be interesting as a way of problematising the perceived boundaries between the digital as environment and unfolding social relations, as well as between data collection and analysis (Ballestero and Winthereik 2021; Geismar and Knox 2021).

Even though anthropologists have often driven the collaborations, a large part of these methodological experiments with computation are carried out across disciplines, some of which fall under the rubric of what has been termed 'complementary quali-quantitative approaches' (Blok and Pedersen 2014; Munk 2019; Breslin et al. 2020). The idea, in short, is to find patterns computationally in data already curated via online sources (Munk and Ellern 2015) or mobile devices (Blok et al. 2017; Flora and Andersen 2016). These data sources will then guide ethnographic interviewing and participant observation, and are perhaps even brought into the field to elicit feedback (Nafus 2018). Sarah Pink, founder of the Future Anthropologies Network, conceptualises interdisciplinary collaborative formats as 'blended practice', thus referring to ways of working that surpass the disciplinary conventions of practice and theory (Pink and Salazar 2020). She considers how the making of the very artefacts that one seeks to understand is core to the research. In defence of methods that are technologically mediated, Pink argues that what is at stake is less a matter of how the field site and its interlocutors are 'found' and more a matter of how 'the ethnographic place' is established. Taking a photograph involves the participation of both human and technological actors; the question is how mediated action forms part of defining what counts as a field site.

One way to make sense of contemporary engagements with the digital within anthropology could be to distinguish between the digital as field and the digital as method (Rogers 2015). In Fig. 10.1 we position some of the traditions outlined above in relation to the digital as field and method. Towards the right side of the diagram, emphasis on the digital as method increases. Towards the top of the diagram, on the other side, the digital as a field site gains emphasis.

The crucial point seems to be that regardless of whether your research focuses on the digital as method or the digital as field, it has methodological implications. Towards the right side of the diagram the implication is that you replace or supplement offline ethnographic methods with computational alternatives; towards the top of the diagram the implication is that you work in a field that cannot be understood without appreciating the role of digital technologies in performing the very phenomena you are seeking to understand. Sometimes, the two can live relatively separate lives, such as when a set of interviews and field notes are loaded into CAQDAS software like NVivo or ATLAS.ti and subjected to auto coding (a computational alternative to doing it by hand) or when a netnographer hangs out in an online gaming environment and takes field notes (presumably also about the role of a digital technology in performing this sociality). More often than not, however, the digital as method and the digital as field co-exist. Can you, for instance, make claims based on computational analysis of large volumes of social media data without taking an interest in the people, processes, and circumstances that produced these data? Or can you claim to have studied an online phenomenon ethnographically without at least considering the complementary use of digital techniques for charting the territory and extent of that phenomenon?

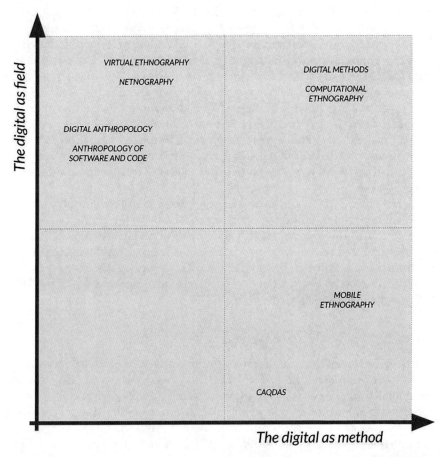

Fig. 10.1 The digital as method and/or field. Following Rogers (2015) we distinguish between research practices where the digital figures primarily as the object of inquiry, for example, virtual ethnography or the anthropology of software, and practices where it plays a role as a new set of methods, for example, mobile ethnography

IN THIS CHAPTER

After this brief survey of various instantiations of computational methods in anthropology, we now present the purpose of this chapter, which is to argue for a renewed anthropological methodology paying special attention to its experimental and collaborative dimensions. We present a case of computational ethnography, where the digital as method—scanning and analysing signals from social media—was intertwined with our efforts to construct the digital as field. As a result of our case work, a couple of insights have emerged.

First, while in some projects the qualitative and the quantitative must be actively 'stitched together' to perform analysis (Blok et al. 2017), in our example, what would precisely count as qualitative or quantitative was emergent and hard to determine. We observed that methods that are usually organised in 'silos', according to Blok et al., were not, as such, easy to categorise separately as either quantitative or qualitative. The second finding presented in this chapter is that computational ethnography is always experimental, because doing it involves (1) tinkering with tools and methods that make available the kinds of empirical material in which one is interested and (2) adhering to strict processes that monitor and adjust these tools and methods in ways that allow for accountability in the process. Computational ethnography is thus experimental both as trial-and-error and as rigorous process. Thirdly, computational ethnography is collaborative in the sense that it requires rethinking what it means to form relations with research participants, fellow researchers, and material technologies.

Overall this chapter argues that things digital transform anthropological experiences of doing ethnographic research. Future anthropologies therefore need to learn how to grapple with the challenges related to the digital, the experimental, and the collaborative, that is, of research distributed and partially connected in and through the digital. We will now provide an example of how such distribution and partial connection happened in our research of the 2020 lockdown in Denmark.

The Ethnographic Archive

In March 2020, as Denmark, like many other countries in the world, was going into lockdown in response to the COVID-19 pandemic, we set out to study the digitalisation of everyday life that was taking place as a consequence of the social distancing measures imposed by the government. Drawing on the works of anthropologist Chris Kelty and geographer Sarah Whatmore, we hypothesised that this was a situation where the 'grammar of participation' (Kelty 2017) in digitalisation processes, and in societal life in general, was changing, forcing people to fix their 'broken' everyday routines through ad-hoc and impromptu digitalisation, thus becoming differently engaged and digitally socialised in the process. We thought of the situation as affording an 'ontological disturbance in which the things on which we rely as unexamined parts of the material fabric of our everyday lives become molten and make their agential force felt' (Whatmore 2009, p. 587).

How should ontological disturbances be ethnographically studied and analysed in a situation where no one is allowed to travel or visit each other? And should the situation be documented in ways that would be valuable to a variety of emerging questions? Given the urgency of the situation we decided to study the effects of the lockdown by creating an ethnographic archive. We managed to raise funding for establishing a 'task force' of people trained in ethnography and digital methods. Reminding ourselves constantly that 'archivization produces as much as it records' (Derrida 1996), we set out to both document and produce a reality which we hoped would also become an ethnographic place, that is, a locus of serendipitous surprise.

To collect the ethnographic material of the everyday experiences of digitalisation of our interlocutors during the lockdown, a team of 15 ethnographers worked in concerted effort for three months. The team conducted 222 interviews, observed 89 virtual events, and had participants create 84 diaries collected through an app on their smart phones. Thus, field relations had to be solicited with a suite of digital methods for tracing and analysing online interaction. Due to social distancing measures, the establishment of field relations depended on digital tools. Moreover, data generation relied on computational techniques (1) to ensure broad representation beyond the ethnographers' own networks, (2) for preliminary identification of themes in the material, and (3) to establish the possibility of navigating through the material in the archive.

Regarding who to engage in the study, the question that imposed itself very quickly was who to interview and which events to participate in. We realised that as mostly Copenhagen-based academics, who had been given the order to work from home and were part of largely the same social media circles, we were likely to develop very myopic ideas about the ways in which everyday lives had been disturbed and the digital coping strategies that people adopted as a consequence. To ensure broad representation, we identified a set of core areas of Danish society where the everyday would logically have been disrupted: care homes, schools, work places, urban spaces, shops, and so on. That approach quickly fell short, however, as we realised that we were in the process of prematurely, and without empirical evidence, answering the research question that the ethnographic archive was meant to help us explore, namely how everyday life in Denmark was disturbed and digitally reordered during the pandemic. In order to generate material that would allow us to explore the breadth of possible answers to that question, we would need a much more open approach to the sampling of informants and events.

We therefore decided to organise the project around four methodological 'protocols' instead. One was an interview guide, another consisted of guidelines for online participant observation, and one was a set of instructions for how to encourage interlocutors to use a mobile ethnographic diary as an ethnographic prompt. The fourth protocol described how to use digital traces found online as a way of 'listening in' on tendencies and trends. We conceptualised this method as comparable to a seismograph being used to detect geological tremors. This method would assist us in detecting hot spots on the internet, that is, sites of increased activity within a single social media platform or across these platforms.

'Listening in' on the internet to create a pathway for interviews, observations, and ethnographic prompts for participants to take photos of their everyday lives, which was the purpose of using mobile diaries, was a way of creating an archive with as broad a representation as possible. But more than that, working this way somehow 'undid' the expectation that working across 'big data' (thousands of data traces) and 'thick data' (individual narrative) would be difficult. There was no issue of the two needing to be 'stitched together', because they were not conceived as different ways of working from the get-go.

A critic may argue that this was because the interviews were 'quantified', but even though the interviews happened online, it was not the case that the digital medium instrumentalised them. Much to the surprise of many of us, the shared experience of social isolation created forms of intimacy in the interviewer-interviewee relation.

Detecting social tremor online happened, for example, through the identification of activity around specific hashtags on twitter. The ethnographers responsible for the digital methods protocol thus used these hashtags as a way of identifying virtual events in order to suggest that ethnographers responsible for other protocols participate in these events. A secondary purpose was to make contact with people or groups who had made their identities and activities known online. The protocol would, for example, scan Facebook for events hosted on digital platforms like Zoom, Teams, or Twitch, and vet them manually to see if they were organised in response to the pandemic disturbance. It could be a sports club organising online races, where runners would take part in a competition, but run individually rather than in a large group; wine tasting, where participants would order similar brands of wine and drink them together online; or a yoga or therapy session in a group that could no longer meet physically. The ethnographers responsible for the digital methods protocol would compile a short qualitative story based on what was available online to contextualise the suggestion for the other researchers and entice them to dig deeper.

Another approach we used was to collect Corona-related talk from platforms like Twitter, Reddit, or Instagram and use network analysis to spot changes in the conversation. Sometimes these patterns reflected emergent concerns that could be followed up with ethnographic fieldwork, such as when high school students began to take a more politically active stance to ensure that social activities would be available for their age group online. Monitoring changes in the Corona-related discourse was a shared responsibility across the task force and the ethnographers met online twice a week for the duration of data collection to share experiences, debrief, and iteratively and collaboratively adjust the research design and the protocols. Interestingly, the online space served as an 'equaliser' that would flatten hierarchies between qualitative and quantitative methods and put senior and junior participants on a more equal footing. As with the relations between ethnographers and interlocutors, the fact that we were all under lockdown as a consequence of a global crisis created a sense of community in the group. We were, by necessity, a 'we' that was experimenting digitally and collaboratively. This became even clearer as the data collection came to a close and we began working our way through the material.

Navigating for Serendipity

Taken together, the transcribed interviews, diaries, and field notes comprised 1,396,332 words, corresponding to 3070 normal pages or, as one of the research assistants pointed out, almost three times the length of the entire Lord of the Rings trilogy. The question, therefore, became how any researcher intent on analysing this behemoth data body would practically go about it. Given the collaborative nature of the project, no single ethnographer had been involved in generating all or even a majority of the empirical material. The task had been distributed across the team, most of whom were no longer working together. Therefore, the collective memory on the material was limited. How should we explore what kind of narratives could be pursued? How should we use the archive? The size of the data body made it unlikely, to our minds, that it could be left to our intuition, imagination, or memory to figure out where to begin or end. Nevertheless, our ambition was to open the archived material to analysis by other researchers.

The question that arose was: What will a user who is unfamiliar with the material do in order to begin analysing? And immediately following from this a concern was raised that the archive was now already stale. How should it be kept alive? How could we avoid the death of a large dataset? Could we create a tool that would not only allow researchers to search the archive, but also add to it? In the experimental spirit of the data collection phase, we (the authors) initiated the construction of a navigation tool, a so-called datascape, which is essentially an online user interface. The navigation tool was to allow users of the archive to both search for words in the transcribed and pseudonymised materials, but also add themes to it to enable others to search. Search terms would then progressively be added to the material as part of the search process. As the analysis progressed, users would be able to use the developing codebook as an alternative way to search the archive. Rather than retrieve quotes on the basis of a search for terms in the archive, users would be able to search for other search terms and get inspired by them. To make the archive searchable, one of the research assistants ran all 13,084 text segments (paragraphs in field notes or answers in interviews) through a semantic analysis that tagged them with named entities such as technologies or toponyms. These machine-generated tags were made available as an alternative filter for the users who were navigating the archive. These tags and the search topics generated by human users would live side by side in the archive and it would be clear if a tag was generated by machine or human user. The idea was to propose alternative ways to search the archive derived from the material itself, in addition to the analytical ideas brought to the material by the researchers using the archive.

Machine tagging is naturally focused on that which is explicitly named in the text. It is relatively unproblematic to create a form of navigation that nudges a user searching the archive to think about the material as being about things like social media platforms, schools, grandparents, the prime minister, or work. These are things that are mentioned explicitly and have been automatically tagged using named entity recognition. Whereas they do constitute an alternative to the researchers' preconceived ideas about everyday pandemic digitalisation, they can also constitute some equally preconceived algorithmic ideas about what constitutes relevant information in a piece of text. To balance this 'bias' we developed a design concept that we called 'navigating for serendipity', which was a way of searching the archive laterally across sources. Using a doc2vec model (another technique in natural language processing) we measured the semantic similarity between all text segments and mapped them as a vector space. This allowed us to identify entire text segments that were related in the sense of roughly belonging to the same semantic space. To exemplify this, there would be a distinct possibility that a user would like to read across segments to learn about 'grandparents', then being inspired to addressing other topics like 'children' or 'family', 'conflict' or 'home-schooling'. The navigation tool allows for such a reading across while leaving traces for others to use. We needed the navigation to support the users' ability to be productively surprised about emergent topics in the material and realms they would not have known interested them.

COMPUTATIONAL ETHNOGRAPHY FOR FUTURE ANTHROPOLOGIES

We began this chapter by referring to a problematisation of computational ethnography, which is the difficulty of establishing a narrative in ethnographic materials that are generated in a digitally mediated space. We have discussed an attempt to deal with this issue, arguing that as anthropological methods are digitised they inevitably become experimental and collaborative in the process. We showed how people's experiences during the pandemic lockdown could be aggregated, disaggregated, and made navigable. We used natural language processing and our own experiences with ethnographic analysis, specifically our need to be surprised by our field relations and ethnographic materials as we exchange perspectives (Latour et al. 2012; Munk 2019). Rather than treating quantitative and qualitative analysis as two separate analytical levels that deal with two separate forms of empirical material, we could not allow ourselves to discriminate between the two approaches due to the digital environment and the situation that we as researchers could also not leave our homes. To end, we suggest making a virtue out of necessity by further exploring different avenues for anthropology generated by seeing digitalised research as collaborative and experimental (Estalella and Criado 2018; Marcus and Fischer 2014).

Computational ethnography follows in the wake of a long tradition of experiments in anthropology, at least since the 1960s. The ethnographic filmmaker Jean Rouch, for example, edited and produced films together with his informants in what he called 'shared ciné-anthropology':

> Finally then, the observer has left the ivory tower; his camera, tape recorder, and projector have driven him, by a strange road of initiation, to the heart of knowledge itself. And for the first time, the work is not judged by a thesis committee

but by the very people the anthropologist went out to observe. (Rouch 1975, p. 43)

This experimental approach to participation resonates with science philosopher Isabell Stengers' notion of experimental constructivism and the researcher's need to 'think in the presence of her victims' (Stengers 2005, p. 997). Indeed, this version of experimental constructivism has recently found traction at the interface between design research and anthropology (Gaspar 2018). However, to the extent that the archival project we introduced above can be seen as a form of experimental construction, it is not through any conventional involvement of informants in a participatory process.

Participatory involvement in our case amounts to something entirely different. It is not about making one's voice heard as much as it is about informants co-labouring with the researcher to make sense of a situation that is new to both, such as establishing relations while physically apart behind separate screens. If we consider the case as an experiment in establishing rapport, we should highlight the advantage that both researchers and informants encountered during the lockdown. It was an immediate advantage, for example in interviews, to begin by exercising care or sharing experiences of being 'grounded'. Similar sharing of 'digital context' can arguably be found in ethnographic studies in/of online worlds like Second Life (Boellstorff 2015) or World of Warcraft (Nardi 2010), but have so far been considered as secondary to participant observation and interviews in terms of establishing rapport. What this points to is a need for re-thinking what 'ethnographically experiencing' means. We propose future anthropologies think through digitally mediated collaboration as a social vector for bodily redistribution that stands in contrast to the ideal and practice of a single-bodied ethnographer who can sense and make sense of happenings in the field. Not only does it mark a difference between the ethnographer-individual and the ethnographer-collective, it also points to a need for rethinking classic divisions between the ethnographer as in-dividual, that is, a bounded body on the one hand and the ethnographer as dividual, that is as a distributed entity online, on the other (Strathern 1988). We hope future work will allow for such explorations and that the occasion will be less dramatic than a global pandemic.

References

Albris, K. (2018). The switchboard mechanism: How social media connected citizens during the 2013 floods in Dresden. *Journal of Contingencies and Crisis Management*, *26*(3), 350–357.

Anderson, K., Nafus, D., Rattenbury, T., & Aipperspach, R. (2009). Numbers have qualities too: Experiences with ethno-mining. *Ethnographic Praxis in Industry Conference Proceedings*, *2009*(1), 123–140.

Ballestero, A., & Winthereik, B. R. (2021). *Experimenting with ethnography: A companion to analysis*. Durham & London: Duke University Press.

Barassi, V. (2015). *Activism on the web: Everyday struggles against digital capitalism.* Abingdon: Routledge.

Beaulieu, A. (2017). Vectors for fieldwork. *The Routledge Companion to Digital Ethnography,* 29. Routledge.

Beaulieu, A., & Simakova, E. (2006). Textured connectivity: An ethnographic approach to understanding the timescape of hyperlinks. *Cybermetrics: International Journal of Scientometrics, Informetrics and Bibliometrics, 10*(1). https://dialnet.unirioja.es/servlet/articulo?codigo=1448764.

Birkbak, A. (2012). Crystallizations in the Blizzard: Contrasting informal emergency collaboration in Facebook groups. *Proceedings of the 7th Nordic Conference on Human-Computer Interaction: Making Sense Through Design,* 428–437.

Blok, A., Carlsen, H. B., Jørgensen, T. B., Madsen, M. M., Ralund, S., & Pedersen, M. A. (2017). Stitching together the heterogeneous party: A complementary social data science experiment. *Big Data & Society, 4*(2). https://doi.org/10.1177/2053951717736337.

Blok, A., & Pedersen, M. A. (2014). Complementary social science? Quali-quantitative experiments in a Big Data world. *Big Data & Society, 1*(2). https://doi.org/10.1177/2053951714543908.

Boellstorff, T. (2013). Making big data, in theory. *First Monday, 18*(10), 1–17.

Boellstorff, T. (2015). *Coming of age in Second Life: An anthropologist explores the virtually human.* Princeton, NJ.: Princeton University Press.

Boyd, D., & Crawford, K. (2012). Critical questions for big data: Provocations for a cultural, technological, and scholarly phenomenon. *Information, Communication & Society, 15*(5), 662–679.

Breslin, S. D., Enggaard, T. R., Blok, A., Gaardhus, T., & Pedersen, M. A. (2020). How We Tweet About Coronavirus, and Why: A Computational Anthropological Mapping of Political Attention on Danish Twitter during the COVID-19 Pandemic. *The COVID-19 Forum III. University of St. Andrews.*

Dalsgaard, S. (2008). Facework on Facebook: The presentation of self in virtual life and its role in the US elections. *Anthropology Today, 24*(6), 8–12.

Derrida, J. (1996). *Archive fever: A Freudian impression.* Chicago, IL: University of Chicago Press.

Douglas-Jones, R., Walford, A., & Seaver, N. (2021). Introduction: Towards an anthropology of data. *Journal of the Royal Anthropological Institute, 27*(S1), 9–25.

Estalella, A., & Criado, T. S. (2018). *Experimental Collaborations: Ethnography through Fieldwork Devices.* New York: Berghahn Books.

Flora, J., & Andersen, A. O. (2016). Whose Track Is It Anyway?: An Anthropological Perspective on Collaboration with Biologists and Hunters in Thule, Northwest Greenland. *Collaborative Anthropologies, 9*(1), 79–116.

Fortun, M., Fortun, K., & Marcus, G. E. (2017). Computers in/and Anthropology. *The Routledge Companion to Digital Ethnography,* 11. Routledge.

Gaspar, A. (2018). Idiotic Encounters: Experimenting with Collaborations Between Ethnography and Design. In A. Estalella & T. S. Criado (Eds.), *Experimental Collaborations: Ethnography through Fieldwork Devices* (pp. 34–94). New York: Berghahn.

Geertz, C. (1973). *The interpretation of cultures* (Vol. 5019). New York: Basic books.

Geiger, R. S., & Ribes, D. (2011). Trace ethnography: Following coordination through documentary practices. *2011 44th Hawaii International Conference on System Sciences,* 1–10.

Geismar, H., & Knox, H. (2021). *Digital Anthropology.* Abingdon: Routledge.

Grommé, F., Ruppert, E., & Cakici, B. (2018). Data scientists: A new faction of the transnational field of statistics. In H. Knox & D. Nafus (Eds.), *Ethnography for a data-saturated world* (pp. 33–61). Manchester: Manchester University Press.

Hine, C. (2000). *Virtual ethnography.* London; Thousand Oaks, Calif: SAGE.

Hsu, W. F. (2014). Digital ethnography toward augmented empiricism: A new methodological framework. *Journal of Digital Humanities, 3*(1), 42–64.

Hymes, D. H. (1965). *The use of computers in anthropology, Vol. 2.* The Hague: The Hague.

Kelty, C. M. (2017). Too much democracy in all the wrong places: Toward a grammar of participation. *Current Anthropology, 58*(S15), S77–S90.

Latour, B., Jensen, P., Venturini, T., Grauwin, S., & Boullier, D. (2012). 'The whole is always smaller than its parts'–a digital test of G abriel T ardes' monads. *The British Journal of Sociology, 63*(4), 590–615.

Lowrie, I. (2018). Algorithms and automation: An introduction. *Cultural Anthropology, 33*(3), 349–359.

Manovich, L. (2011). Trending: The promises and the challenges of big social data. *Debates in the Digital Humanities, 2*(1), 460–475.

Marcus, G. E., & Fischer, M. M. J. (2014). *Anthropology as Cultural Critique: An Experimental Moment in the Human Sciences.* Chicago: University of Chicago Press.

Marres, N. (2012). The redistribution of methods: On intervention in digital social research, broadly conceived. *The Sociological Review, 60,* 139–165.

Marres, N. (2017). *Digital sociology: The reinvention of social research.* Hoboken: John Wiley & Sons.

Marres, N., & Gerlitz, C. (2016). Interface methods: Renegotiating relations between digital social research, STS and sociology. *The Sociological Review, 64*(1), 21–46.

Miller, D. (2011). *Tales from facebook.* Oxford: Polity.

Miller, D. (2016). *Social media in an English village.* London: UCL Press.

Munk, A. K. (2013). Techno-anthropology and the digital natives. *What Is Techno-Anthropology,* 287–310. Aalborg University Press.

Munk, A. K. (2019). Four Styles of Quali-Quantitative Analysis: Making sense of the new Nordic food movement on the web. *Nordicom Review, 40*(s1), 159–176. https://doi.org/10.2478/nor-2019-0020.

Munk, A. K., & Ellern, A. B. (2015). Mapping the New Nordic issuescape: How to navigate a diffuse controversy with digital methods. *Tourism Encounters and Controversies: Ontological Politics of Tourism Development.* London: Routledge.

Munk, A. K., & Jensen, T. E. (2015). Revisiting the histories of mapping. *Ethnologia Europaea, Special Issue: European Ethnology Revisited, 44*(2), 31–47. https://doi.org/10.16995/ee.1125

Nafus, D. (2018). Working ethnographically with sensor data. In H. Knox & D. Nafus (Eds.), *Ethnography for a data-saturated world* (pp. 233–251). Manchester: Manchester University Press.

Nardi, B. (2010). *My life as a night elf priest: An anthropological account of World of Warcraft.* Ann Arbor: University of Michigan Press.

Pearce, C. (2011). *Communities of play: Emergent cultures in multiplayer games and virtual worlds.* Cambridge, MA.: The MIT Press.

Pink, S., & Salazar, J. F. (2020). Anthropologies and futures: Setting the agenda. In J. F. Salazar, S. Pink, A. Irving, & J. Sjöberg (Eds.), *Anthropologies and futures. Researching Emerging and Uncertain Worlds* (pp. 3–22). Abingdon: Routledge.

Rogers, R. (2009). *The end of the virtual: Digital methods* (Vol. 339). Amsterdam University Press.

Rogers, R. (2013). *Digital Methods*. Cambridge, MA.: The MIT Press.

Rogers, R. (2015). Digital Methods for Web Research. In R. A. Scott, S. M. Kosslyn, & M. Buchmann (Eds.), Emerging Trends in the *Social and Behavioral Sciences* (pp. 1–22). American Cancer Society. https://doi.org/10.1002/9781118900772. etrds0076.

Rouch, J. (1975). The camera and man. *Principles of Visual Anthropology, 1*. Mouton.

Seaver, N. (2015). Bastard algebra. *Data, Now Bigger and Better*, 27–46. Prickly Paradigm Press.

Seaver, N. (2018). What should an anthropology of algorithms do? *Cultural Anthropology, 33*(3), 375–385.

Shadoan, R., & Dudek, A. (2013). Plant Wars Player Patterns: Visualization as Scaffolding for Ethnographic Insight. *Ethnography Matters (Prístup 31. Marca 2014)*.

Stengers, I. (2005). The cosmopolitical proposal. *Making Things Public: Atmospheres of Democracy, 994*, 994. MIT Press.

Strathern, M. (1988). *The gender of the gift: Problems with women and problems with society in Melanesia*. Berkeley, CA.: University of California Press.

Walford, A. (2017). Raw Data: Making Relations Matter. *Social Analysis, 61*(2), 65–80.

Waltorp, K. (2020). Digital technologies, dreams and disconcertment in anthropological worldmaking. In J. F. Salazar, S. Pink, A. Irving, & J. Sjöberg (Eds.), *Anthropologies and futures. Researching Emerging and Uncertain Worlds* (pp. 101–116). Abingdon: Routledge.

Wang, T. (2013). Big data needs thick data. *Ethnography Matters, 13*.

Whatmore, S. J. (2009). Mapping knowledge controversies: Science, democracy and the redistribution of expertise. *Progress in Human Geography, 33*(5), 587–598.

Wilf, E., Cheney-Lippold, J., Duranti, A., Eisenlohr, P., Gershon, I., Mackenzie, A., Malaby, T. M., Seaver, N., Boellstorff, T., & Wilf, E. (2013). Toward an anthropology of computer-mediated, algorithmic forms of sociality. *Current Anthropology, 54*(6), 716–739.

PART II

Knowing, Unknowing, and Re-knowing

CHAPTER 11

Knowing, Unknowing, and Re-knowing

Introduction

Klaus Hoeyer and Brit Ross Winthereik

Most technologies are knowledge-intensive, and contemporary knowledge production is often technology-intensive. Hence, knowledge practices are a central theme for a handbook for the anthropology of technology. Consider the role of technology-mediated knowledge practices in some of the most pressing global issues of today, such as the COVID-19 pandemic, the climate crisis, and digitalised surveillance. In the case of COVID-19, the pandemic as such is knowable only through governments' use of models, statistics, and other monitoring technologies: an individual can experience illness, but not a pandemic. Similarly, a virus cannot be identified and characterised as an object of knowledge without mediating technology. In the case of the climate crisis, our understanding of it is an effect of technologically mediated knowledge practices (Edwards 2010). Moreover, attempts at handling the effects of climate change, whether as activists or government, also hinge on engagement with scientific knowledge making and on communication via digital media (Blok 2020). Digitalised surveillance, also an example of a knowledge practice, gets constituted by the use of algorithmic sorting and prediction based on indicators such as likes and reshares on social media platforms (Zuboff 2019).

K. Hoeyer (✉)
Center for Medical Science & Technology Studies, University of Copenhagen, Copenhagen, Denmark
e-mail: klho@sund.ku.dk

B. R. Winthereik
Department of Business IT, IT University of Copenhagen, Copenhagen, Denmark
e-mail: brwi@itu.dk

© The Author(s) 2022
M. H. Bruun et al. (eds.), *The Palgrave Handbook of the Anthropology of Technology*, https://doi.org/10.1007/978-981-16-7084-8_11

Digital surveillance also interacts with governmental understandings of security and reconfigures understandings of privacy, human rights, and safety (Snowden 2019; Andrejevic 2005). All these challenges are thus global phenomena constituted through knowledge practices that are mediated by technology. The same can be said about the tools for economic modelling and governance that undergird an escalating economic inequality (Murphy 2017). Knowledge and tools for knowing are intertwined. By exploring the technological mediation of knowledge practices, anthropologists can problematise them and open them up for scrutiny. There is an important task for the anthropology of technology in questioning knowledge practices.

When you hang out with policymakers and scientists, as have the authors of this section introduction, you will often hear them talk about science and technology as a cumulative process that delivers prosperity and optimisation. Sometimes the pursuit of knowledge is framed almost like a Kuhnian conquest: 'new knowledge' wins over and replaces 'old mistakes'. Anthropological narratives about technoscientific knowledge practices are very different. In contrast to notions of knowledge as a successful epistemic conquest, anthropological accounts often foreground unintended or unwarranted implications of technologies and knowledge practices. Anthropologists explore socio-economic contexts, the distributed agency of technology, and political issues related to unequal power relations. They may describe how some forms of knowledge 'work better' for some people, and why certain types of knowledge are advantageous in reaching certain goals, but mostly they do so while also considering inequality and loss. Prosperity and optimisation are typically situated gains. Not all stakeholders gain equally, changes are not improvements for all; the labour that goes into the production of certain types of knowing always involves elements of unknowing. It is therefore an important task to recover the perspectives and experiences that have been lost. Hence, as anthropologists study knowledge as technology-mediated practices, they sometimes become agents of 're-knowing'. We therefore name this section 'knowing, unknowing, and re-knowing'.

Anthropological Takes on Knowledge Practices

Traditionally, knowledge about knowing has been considered primarily a branch of philosophy or, alternatively, of theology (Zagzebski 2012). In the late nineteenth century, William James tried to claim knowledge as a phenomenon belonging to the emerging discipline of psychology—as a human capacity (James 1950). Right from the inception of the social sciences in the course of the nineteenth century, scholars like Auguste Comte and later Émile Durkheim suggested studying how humans know the world they live in as a socially constituted phenomenon (Comte 1988; Durkheim 1973, 2008). They created a research field by looking at the *social dynamics* of knowing, in contrast to seeing knowledge as an individual achievement.

The study of knowledge practices is likewise part of the foundation of the anthropological discipline. Comte was influenced by classic philosophical perceptions of epistemology portraying scientific progress from 'pre-modern' knowledge practices through 'mere speculation'. It was what he associated with *artistic* expressions and individual *reflection*. Enlightenment was seen as finally delivering 'modernity' with structured *observations* and systematic *experimentation* (Lévy-Bruhl 2018). This narrative of progress and its underlying distinction between so-called primitive and civilised thought has since been challenged in multiple ways. Lévi-Strauss, in particular, challenged the distinction between primitive and civilised, and pointed out how the societies that used to be described as 'primitive' gave rise to 'the great arts of civilization—of pottery, weaving, agriculture, and the domestication of animals' (Lévi-Strauss 1966, p. 13). They did so through techniques building on 'centuries of active and methodological observation, of bold hypotheses tested by means of endlessly repeated experiments' (p. 14). People living in societies seen by early anthropologists as 'primitive' did deploy mythical thinking. This thinking, however, also exhibited a preference for 'classification' and 'rational ordering' comparable to modern forms of science (Lévi-Strauss 1966, p. 15; see also Latour 1990). Tylor, similarly, spoke of the 'the tendency of mankind to classify out the universe' (Tylor 1899). What is more, Lévi-Strauss pointed to the 'bricoleur' as a contemporary example of primitive thought. The bricoleur is 'someone who works with his hands and uses devious means compared to those of a craftsman' (Lévi-Strauss 1966, p. 16–17). The bricoleur 'speaks not only *with* things …, but also through the medium of things' (p. 21). Knowing has, from this perspective, always been technologically mediated, and it continues to represent a human search for meaning.

After Lévi-Strauss, anthropology has continued to highlight and make visible diverse knowledge practices and treat them with the same curiosity and respect as accorded to, for example, natural scientists (Viveiros de Castro 2003; de la Cadena 2015; Escobar 1998; de la Cadena and Blaser 2018). Prominently among the authors referenced here is a political project of ensuring 'conceptual self-determination' for the people with whom anthropologists work. Viveiros de Castro reflects on relations between early structuralism and contemporary Brazilian anthropologists stating, '[F]or us the expression "la pensée sauvage" did not signify "the savage mind". To us it meant untamed thought, unsubdued thought, wild thought' (Viveiros de Castro 2003). To study knowledge practices is to both know and unknow. To know from another position can involve learning to ignore particular knowledge regimes and uncover what they have silenced.

Another way anthropologists have challenged hierarchies of thought has been by placing emphasis on socially engrained bodily forms of knowing (Martin 2013; Ingold 2011). As one of the early founding fathers of Marxism, Engels argued for the need to acknowledge the labour of the hand, not just of the mind, in relation to knowledge production (Engels 2007). Anthropologists have built a strong tradition for articulating tacit, bodily aspects of human experience that scientific data does not elucidate (Hastrup 1994). De la Cadena, in her work on Andean Indigenous knowledge practices, describes the collective labour of hand and thought as co-labouring and her interlocutors as co-labourers (de la Cadena 2015).

Classic fieldwork facilitated the study of material knowledge practices. These forms are, however, rarely adequate for studying contemporary, technology-intensive knowledge practices. As a consequence, anthropologists have often had to invent new ways of studying knowledge. Ethnography was reinvented to explore the material practices of knowledge making in laboratory settings (Latour and Woolgar 1979; Knorr-Cetina 1981, 1983). Drawing on the ethnographic tradition, Science and Technology Studies (STS) has sought to bring forth the hidden labour of knowledge production, such as in laboratory work (Fujimura 1996). Presence, being there, opens up the opportunity to notice the tacit dimensions of knowledge practices (Korsby and Stavrianakis 2018), aspects, and sensations that scientists or knowledge workers would not themselves articulate (Polanyi 1966; Law and Ruppert 2016).

Anthropology has also traced master narratives across contexts and sought to give voice to the lives lived in their shadow as a way to re-know truths that matter to some of these people (Last 1981; de la Cadena 2010). Yet another anthropological take on knowledge practices describes how the establishment of clinical trials in medical research in Kenya and Ghana depends on active neglect of particular facts, such as the role of economic incentives in enrolling participants in research, that do not align with ethical demands and protocols (Geissler 2013). This neglect is an effect of social processes and 'neither false consciousness nor conscious falseness' (p. 28). Rather, it is a form of productive 'unknowing': 'Unknowing is, then, not the opposite of knowing; the pair of terms helps, instead, to describe the work invested in, and the effects engendered by, maintaining this politically salient division' (Geissler 2013, p. 15).

Indeed, within healthcare, unknowing comes in many forms, as when health professionals game bureaucratic reporting systems (Sullivan 2017; Hunt et al. 2017; Erikson 2012), patients 'filter' their experiences before reporting to doctors (Torenholt et al. 2020), or research assistants 'clean up' data before handing it over to scientists (Biruk 2018; Kingori 2013). Unknowing is integral to how systems work when organisations use global indicators to hide local diversity (Storeng and Behage 2017; Merry 2016) or produce reports and other documents to deflect criticism (Strathern 2006); it is also integral to technological systems when citizens need to hack their payment systems to gain access to infrastructures (von Schnitzler 2013). Unknowing is vital for the political expediency of any knowledge project, not as a strategic impetus to ignore, but rather as a way of being in the world that allows it to be messy, incoherent, and imperfect. Today, technology mediates each of these dynamics.

To those scientific disciplines that anthropologists have turned into objects of study, the ethnographic approach to questions of knowledge may seem overly relativist. As Poirier points out in her contribution to this section, however, plain relativism—where no claim to truth stands above any other—no longer seems feasible. Climate science, and science more generally, is under attack by powerful groups, who are spreading misinformation to undermine the authority of scientific research. When former US President Trump dismissed scientific evidence as fake news, even anthropologists took to the streets and demonstrated *for* science. Few anthropologists were *against* science in the first place; they just worked to expand what is seen as worth knowing. Donna Haraway coined the term 'strong objectivity' to account for knowledge practices that ignore contextual—social and political—factors in processes of scientific knowledge production (Haraway 1991). The type of relativism that informs the anthropological study of technologically mediated knowledge practices is rarely anti-realist. Rather, it is attuned to the ways in which scientific practices can create more or less robust products that work well for some purposes and less well for others. Many anthropologists want to avoid totalising narratives about Truth. They insist on retaining room for different modes of knowing (Geertz 1984), which themselves are a concrete experience for many ethnographers. In the course of fieldwork, ethnographers often learn how the practices they study look very different from different perspectives. They continuously revise their own understanding, or as Hirsch (2008) notes in a manner that resonates well with this chapter's title, 'Knowing, not knowing, and knowing anew might be how best to describe this kind of anthropological inevitability' (p. 34).

In sum, anthropology does not replace knowledge forms through conquest, but highlights the multiplicity of a world that evades singular forms of knowing (Mol 2002; Gad et al. 2015). To study knowing is always also to explore forms of unknowing or 'ignorance' (Mair et al. 2012). As the contributions to this section of the handbook show, attention to the processes through which knowledge is made, unmade, and re-made involves engaging with the technologies that mediate the practices through which we know, unknow, and re-know contemporary social problems. This handbook section continues a long tradition of studying the production of knowledge as socially embedded and materially entrenched, and it expands the focus from human labour to include attention to the agency of technology. Anthropological studies stay open to multiple modes of knowing the world. Observation and experimentation did not replace human reflection and artistic sensation, as the Comteian tradition suggested; rather, different modes of knowing co-exist and have come to mingle in a multitude of ways with various technological instruments including survey methodologies, registries, and tools of accounting.

THE CHAPTERS IN THIS SECTION

Conceptually, the seven chapters in this section all deal with the intertwined processes of technologically mediated knowing and unknowing, and each in its own way illustrates the anthropological capacity for re-knowing. The first four chapters can be read as contemporary takes on the four forms of human engagement with the world outlined above as part of the Comteian conceptualisation: *artistic expression, reflection, observation,* and *experimentation.* The subsequent three chapters explore particular instantiations of three canonical technologies of knowing: the *survey*, the *registry*, and *accounting*. They illustrate very different ways in which people get enrolled into knowledge production. None of the seven chapters are written to illustrate one particular mode of knowing; on the contrary, modes of knowing overlap and co-exist, as do the technologies that mediate knowing and unknowing. Several chapters share key elements (e.g. attention to the construction of measurements) and technologies (e.g. digital processing), but they foreground different experiences and uncover different forms of lost knowledge: bodily, Indigenous, or otherwise. Thus, all chapters illustrate the co-existence of multiple forms of knowing and show how these forms interact with each other and with the socio-economic and political context where knowledge production unfolds.

Hannah Knox explores *artistic expression* as a way into studying the destabilisation of the interface between technology and knowledge. Reflecting on the technological phenomena of hyper-complex climate models, global data gathering, the environmental impacts of systems like bitcoin, and the complexity of digital algorithms, Knox suggests that contemporary technology appears to have brought us to what she terms 'the end of knowledge'. This poses a challenge for the anthropology of technology—a challenge which Knox suggests is being effectively and creatively addressed by artists who have sought to deconstruct the opposition between technology as a tool of knowing and environment as the context for knowledge production. To explore these issues Knox's chapter describes an art exhibition that worked to collapse the distinction between technology, media, and environment. In doing so, Knox shows how art can serve as a method for what we call 're-knowing' in relation to those aspects that scientific knowledge practices cannot enact.

Anthropologists have long studied artistic modes of knowing. For example, studies have explored how stage art can involve particular forms of bodily knowledge (Royce 1977; Hastrup 1998) and how poetry can embody politics (Abu-Lughod 1986). Knox, in contrast, foregrounds the role of digital technology in producing art and, furthermore, points to the agency of the artwork: it works on/with the observer. Recall Gell's classic work on the agency of technology as a form of enchantment exerting agency through material presence (Gell 1992). Similar to Gell's point, in Knox' case, knowledge is not a purely epistemic product, but a way of being in the world—as a technologically mediated form of consciousness (see also Hasse, this volume). With art, knowledge returns to a bodily experience of being situated in a larger milieu or environment. The anthropologist can engage with art by unpacking—through infrastructural designs—the ways in which bodily modes of knowing operate (Winthereik et al. 2019).

Minna Ruckenstein's chapter focuses on self-tracking. The knowledge practice that Ruckenstein observes is a contemporary, technologically mediated way of knowing the self, a form of socially embedded and technologically mediated *reflection*. Based on fieldwork in Finland among people who use tracking devices to know (and intervene in) their bodies and everyday lives, Ruckenstein explores what it means for people to act on one's body and self through technology. Self-tracking can be seen as an intervention that allows particular forms of technologically mediated work on one's body to emerge, and Ruckenstein provides insights into the experiences it entails. Moreover, she brings in sociality as she emphasises the enduring hermeneutic element of making sense of data in the company of others: data does not speak for itself.

Knowledge practices of the self have a long history and have taken many other forms: religious, psychological, and philosophical. Although often framed as speculative and inner-worldly, such knowledge practices have often been technologically mediated in one way or another. They depend on books, for example, which is a technological mediation of sorts, or they depend on rituals using material artefacts, as shown in the anthropology of religion (Evans-Pritchard 1976). Foucault famously framed such work as technologies of the self (Foucault 1986, 1997). With Ruckenstein, we see how interpretations of the body are both socially and technologically mediated. Other scholars studying datafication have argued that the act of interpretation is often silenced to enhance the power of data (Merry 2016, 2019). Such uses—and abuses—of data by those in power have engaged many anthropologists (Adams and Biehl 2016; Adams 2016; Erikson 2012; Murphy 2017; Hunt et al. 2017). Ruckenstein adds to this work by tuning in on the people making the interpretations for themselves. How others, companies for example, might use this data, as in the types of surveillance mentioned above, is not the focus in this chapter. Still, it helps us reflect upon the differences between using data to enact change in your own life and to monitor objects of governance.

With Lindsay Poirier's chapter on monitoring environmental change, we turn to practices of *observation* as they can unfold in a governmental setting. Poirier explores the knowledge practices through which pollution and air quality emerge as phenomena in need of political action in the US; these revolve around intricate socio-technological infrastructures for observation (Daston 1992). Poirier describes the many ways in which observation both knows and unknows the phenomena of air quality, thereby reflecting Ruckenstein's interest in the hermeneutics of translating data, with increased emphasis on the political choices involved in the selection of data points. Anthropology and STS have tended to criticise the natural and physical sciences for concealing these choices (Downey and Dumit 1997; Haraway 1989), and Poirier carefully balances critique with support of science that seeks to understand the challenges of pollution and the climate crisis. By uncovering the choices, she reopens the politics involved and adds to an important tradition of studying those technologically mediated forms of knowing through which states exert authority.

Historically, the urge to map the world through observation interacted with colonial and economic forms of power. In the process, a particular mode of disentangling aspects of the world as assets to be bartered and controlled was created (Parry 2004). Observation came to serve as the cornerstone of what Comte's contemporaries saw as 'modern' scientific practices, with botanist Carl von Linné's taxonomies, Friederich von Humboldt's biogeographies, and medical bedside observations such as those of William Osler. As Foucault insisted, knowledge and power are interconnected in discursive formations that have real-world effects (Foucault 1973, 1991, 2002). The anthropological work of opening the politics of knowledge making for ethnographic scrutiny involves attending to, for example, the standards used for observation (Busch 2011; Hogle 1995) and the infrastructures through which data points circulate (Star and Bowker 2002; Star and Ruhleder 1996; Bowker and Star 1999; see also the section on infrastructures). By moving closer to the establishment of measurements and infrastructures for data collection, new types of politics and governance are enacted (Essén and Sauder 2017; Douglas-Jones 2017; Winthereik, van der Ploeg, and Berg 2007; Hoeyer and Bødker 2020).

Joseph Dumit and Emilia Sanabria's chapter addresses knowledge practices revolving around a prototypical *experiment*, the randomised clinical trial (RCT). Dumit and Sanabria explore recent instantiations of this method, enacted to qualify the effects of *ayahuasca* as they are becoming financialised. They compare this with urban ritual healing and Indigenous practices that engage with, and fight the commercialisation. Dumit and Sanabria unfold an argument around the contrast between imagining healing as the identification of magic bullets or as producing container technologies. They analyse the RCT as a technologically mediated epistemic attempt to disentangle substances from their context in order to produce and market them as magic bullets. This epistemic move is interwoven with economic and political interests and embodies the ongoing practices of colonial extraction, decontextualisation, and control. Borrowing the metaphor of container technology, they invite readers to recognise substance, context, political economy, and environment as inherently entangled.

Anthropology has a long tradition of studying bricoleurs experimenting with the world around them. Healing rituals have attracted ethnographic attention as sites of knowledge production, where ritual objects, artefacts, and performances play a significant role in the making of insight (Schieffelin 1985; Port 2005; Sjørslev 2013). There is also a strong tradition for questioning the universal and decontextualised claims of biomedicine (Lambert 2006; Kleinman and Kleinman 2007). Other approaches have involved recontextualising biomedicine to show how ostensibly universal epistemic claims take on local forms (Lock 2002; Taussig 2009; Hogle 1999) or, rather, are reinvented locally (Lakoff 2005; Wahlberg 2018; Rabinow 1999). Some strains of anthropology have focused on the political economy of medical experiments (Petryna 2002, 2009) and the interaction between experimental biomedical knowledge and clinical practice (Kaufman 2015), while others focus on the role of patient activism (Epstein 1996). Some have made their own anthropological experiments, where the purpose has been to construct collaborative sites for anthropological knowledge making (Rabinow 1996, 1999). These strains articulate context, in contrast to the classic laboratory studies by Latour and colleagues, mentioned above, where context was seen as a mythical magical meta-actor (Asdal and Moser 2012). As Strathern has pointed out, context is never given; it is an analytical construct (Strathern 2004). The chapter by Dumit and

Sanabria thus invites readers to engage with a flourishing field of anthropological inquiry and it should inspire us to contemplate the political, economic, and even spiritual implications of the choices we make when construing context.

The last three chapters in this section exemplify particular technologies of knowing. Cal Biruk provides a fascinating insight into the work involved when researchers use *survey* methodology to quantify disease burden in Malawi. The survey methodology features in several of the other chapters too, but in contrast to, for example, Poirier's chapter, Biruk studies a setting where authorities do not have the means to collect the data they desire. It is also a setting where lead researchers do not always visit the sites of data production; they are placed in high-income countries, and the research promotes careers far from the suffering and social realities that the scientific methodology, which they use, aims to document. Global inequalities run through all knowledge practices. Biruk carefully describes the practices through which local research assistants on the ground create data and follow those who are collecting it, thereby providing insights into the actual work that goes into the construction of a population as a knowledge product. Biruk also invites readers to contemplate the colonial traces that 'haunt' contemporary knowledge practices (Karkazis and Jordan-Young 2020). Rather than negating the value of the survey, however, she makes these values thinkable so that others can ponder the political forces at play.

A number of studies of data collection and the representation of populations have demonstrated that the data work involved in surveys is performative: it shapes the phenomena it is said to describe by selecting and deselecting what is seen as part of a population (Grommé and Ruppert 2020; Ruppert 2012). The survey thereby constitutes a particular way of 'seeing' a population (Law 2009; Scott 1998). Other governance instruments such as evaluations, for example, share a family resemblance to surveys. As Helen Verran has demonstrated, there is a particular anthropological task in describing the calculative technologies through which social worlds are made. This includes describing the epistemic logics through which numbers, aggregate and otherwise, emerge and come to matter (Verran 2001).

The next chapter in the section, by Alison Cool, dives into knowledge practices that build on *registries*. Cool's research focuses on the use of registries in Sweden to conduct twin research to determine patterns of heredity, building on fieldwork in a country where every member of the population can be tracked via their identity numbers throughout their life course and across all governmental sectors; similar systems are in place in the other Nordic countries (Sætnan, Lommel, and Hammer 2011; Bauer 2014; Hoeyer 2019; Pálsson and Rabinow 1999; Winthereik 2003). The Nordic countries are valued for their registry data because the registries contain what is today often termed 'real-world-data' that is curated and stored by authorities—validated and certified by professionals (unlike responses to a survey). Cool explores what researchers think they can do with registries as they use statistics to tell stories about who people are (Marks 2001). Cool's chapter explores the scientists' reasoning on heredity, which she posits as akin to what Fleck termed a particular 'thought style' (Fleck 1979). In the course of fieldwork, Cool encounters an interesting phenomenon: her interlocutors are eager to act as anthropologists. They give explanations of why people accept pervasive tracking by referencing 'Swedish culture'. Cool thereby illustrates how the people that anthropologists study also reflect on, and seek to influence, the anthropological project of studying culture.

Cool's analysis of registry-mediated knowledge practices about heredity reaches back into a classical realm of anthropology, namely studies of kinship and relatedness (Franklin 2007; Franklin and McKinnon 2001; Carsten 2000). Furthermore, the chapter reminds us that the registry is as much an archetypical 'memory practice' (Bowker 2005) as a tool for knowledge making (Desrosiéres 1998). Like surveys, archives have performative effects (Derrida 1995), not least as a key element in establishing bureaucratic authority through documentation (Weber 1947). Often registry data is a by-product of governance, which is used for research at later stages. Cool thereby adds to an anthropological tradition of studying the technologically mediated power dynamics of research participation and knowledge making (Kingori 2013; Svendsen and Koch 2008; Sheikh and Jensen 2019; Lappé 2014). She also adds to studies of how to understand registrations. Despite professional validation, there are many sources of error in registry data, studies of which show that there is a continued role for anthropology in explicating the hermeneutics of data analysis (Biruk 2018; Erikson 2016, 2018), bringing to light the choices that have become silenced in other modes of knowledge production—as is also pointed out in this section's chapters by Ruckenstein and Biruk.

In the final chapter of this section, Anne Beaulieu analyses the dynamics of *accounting*, which here involves maintenance, expansion, and innovation in the infrastructures created to monitor degrees of achievement of the Sustainable Development Goals (SDGs). Beaulieu problematises the processes through which data-intensive practices create novel (un)certainties. With the SDGs, Beaulieu describes how infrastructures are being developed to ensure that different actors can contribute with the 'right' kind of data. Data is imagined to create the knowledge of 'how things are' that is deemed necessary for the SDGs to become a matter of political concern. Accounting is needed to make the SDGs actionable, but as Beaulieu shows, doing so on a global scale involves a shift from a focus on population and the kind of accountability that dominated at the end of the twentieth century, based on system-level relations and access to data on public service delivery, to a different kind that is more distributed.

Accounting is knowledge produced within organisations, small or of global range, to monitor and control the achievement of goals (Jensen and Winthereik 2013). Accounting is knowledge as governance. It has also been studied anthropologically in relation to phenomena as diverse as finance (Riles 2011), agriculture (Silverstein 2018), and ethics regulation (Jacob and Riles 2007; Douglas-Jones 2012; Hoeyer 2005). While the New Public Management era of accounting in public institutions was characterised by a firm belief that documentation, monitoring, and evaluation would lead to actionable insights that could be accounted for, the era of big data suggests more distributed forms of governance characterised by links between public and private actors (Fishenden and Thompson 2012). Hope, speculation, and the strategic formation of networks seem to have replaced the controlled feedback loops of former modes of accounting (Miyazaki 2006; Hockenhull and Cohn 2021). Co-design, co-creation, and governance networks are the social and organisational technologies of today. As anthropological research shows, quantitative digital data has become ubiquitous in governance today.

CONCLUSION

Anthropological studies of technologically mediated knowledge practices have shown that as something comes to be known, something else becomes unknown. There is always a task for anthropology in recovering lost knowledge and in articulating the types of knowledge that science cannot measure, or measures in ways that leave out important insights for those who are affected by the measurement. There is likewise a long tradition of questioning anthropological forms of knowing. The discipline has, again and again throughout its history, challenged and reinvented its own knowledge practices and presumptions. The aim has been to build more inclusive ways of knowing and move beyond, for example, colonial thinking, injustice, or prejudice. Anthropology has also learned to know, unknow, and re-know in its own disciplinary development and, indeed, will continue to do so. Unknowing and re-knowing in anthropology is typically associated with the discipline's multiple 'turns'. They exemplify how it has been necessary to unknow earlier anthropological insights (Clifford 1986) and then later re-know them from new analytical vantage points, with new forms of technological mediation. Marisol de la Cadena, for example, describes how, in her study of peasant politics in the Andes, her scholarly knowledge was insufficient. To understand peasants' struggle for political influence, she had to be able to not know, or ignore, all that her training had taught her about 'culture' and 'belief systems' (de la Cadena 2015, 2021). With her, some anthropologists have turned to ontology as yet another way of figuring out knowledge practices—other people's as well as anthropologists' own (Holbraad, Pedersen, and Viveiros de Castro 2014; Holbraad and Pedersen 2017).

When acknowledging the similarities between the anthropological history of knowing, unknowing, and re-knowing, and the work described above on the knowledge practices anthropologists study, we believe the potential antagonism between anthropology and technoscience can dissolve—or, at least, take productive forms. No knowledge form can claim superiority for all purposes. A genuine engagement with complementary knowledge forms that exemplify different blind spots and shifting moral and political orientations should stimulate the reflective capacity that has long been the hallmark of anthropological knowledge practices. It does not mean working towards the same goals as the scientists, engineers, or doctors that we study, nor does it imply accepting a role as servant to (or slave of) more mighty disciplines (Linder 2004). Rather, it means understanding the differences and using them productively. We hope the seven chapters that follow will inspire readers to find their own ways towards that goal.

If technoscience typically works from the data scientists compile using authoritative methods, anthropologists must often invent methods as they go along. They must reflect on, and work with, empirical material on any type of experience that matters to people. Those anthropologies of technology that work with knowledge practices often find themselves doing what they study: making knowledge about knowledge making, using technology to understand technology. It involves an enduring potential for making one's own practices into a source of experience that can inform what we see in the field. We therefore wish to end on a note of invitation, asking readers to find methodological inspiration in these great chapters and also to reflect on their own intimate knowledge practices. Anthropology is a discipline that works from human experience in all its diversity, and it refuses to reduce knowledge to the data that a given disciplinarily sanctioned method may grant. Anthropologists can never simply ignore an experience just because established methods do not capture it (Favret-Saada 1980). Anthropological methods are flexible; they rarely follow strict protocols (although sometimes they can experience through protocols and even experiment with them [Ballestero and Winthereik 2021]). As anthropological technologies of knowing evolve in dialogue with the fields under study, quantitative, qualitative, survey, digital data mining, or auto-experimentation methodologies are never just dull instruments, but exciting experimental possibilities. Ethnography is the hallmark of anthropology and strongly represented in the chapters that follow, yet we see in them something else as well which is equally important: playfulness. There is no certain path to follow, and often routes go through unknowing one's own assumptions in creative ways.

This is the point with playfulness: to dare to leave the path you know—as well as to dare to return to 'old' insights, those that are no longer in fashion, when they can help us approach a problem from a new, or a forgotten, angle. Anthropology's technologies of knowing can support curiosity. They can provide the courage to know forms of life that are unaccounted for, difficult to access, or subjugated. As anthropologists also develop ways of accounting for algorithmic governance (Besteman and Gusterson 2019; Peeters and Schuilenburg 2021) and digital data work (Walford 2017; Munk and Winthereik, this volume), and as they begin to explore Artificial Intelligence (AI) as emerging 'post-human' forms of knowledge and creativity (Amoore 2019; Wilf 2013), once again they will challenge methodological dogma and disciplinary assumptions. Sometimes, the surprising angle will come from recovering lost knowledge rather than an announcement of disruption. AI involves new forms of knowing, but perhaps knowledge never rested in the human mind alone. Lévi-Strauss pointed to the materially engrained ways of knowing already established in Neolithic times, and the heralded cyborg figure suggested by Haraway (2004) should invite reflections on continuity as much as change. Still, each new technologically mediated knowledge practice poses new concrete and situated challenges to the societies in which it emerges. In societies permeated by science and technology, there is always more to be done.

Acknowledgements We would like to thank our contributors, reviewers, and the rest of the editorial board for comments and suggestions to previous drafts. Klaus Hoeyer would also like to acknowledge funding from the European Research Council (ERC) under the European Union's Horizon 2020 research and innovation programme (grant agreement number 682110). Brit Ross Winthereik would like to acknowledge funding from the Velux Foundations (funding ID 12823).

References

Abu-Lughod, L. (1986). *Veiled Sentiments. Honor and Poetry in a Bedouin Society.* Berkeley, CA.: University of California Press.

Adams, V. (2016). Introduction. In: V. Adams (Ed.), *Metrics. What counts in global health* (pp. 1–17). Durham: Duke University Press.

Adams, V., & Biehl, J. (2016). The work of evidence in critical global health. *Medicine Anthropology Theory, 3*(2), 123–126.

Amoore, L. (2019). Doubt and the Algorithm: On the Partial Accounts of Machine Learning *Theory, Culture & Society, 36*(6), 147–169.

Andrejevic, M. (2005). The work of watching one another: Lateral surveillance, risk, and governance. *Surveillance & Society, 2*(4), 479–497.

Asdal, K., & Moser, I. (2012). Experiments in context and contexting. *Science, Technology, & Human Values, 37*(4), 291–306.

Ballestero, A., & Winthereik, B. R. (Eds.) (2021). *Experimenting with ethnography: A companion to analysis.* Durham: Duke University Press.

Bauer, S. (2014). From administrative infrastructure to biomedical resource: Danish population registries, the "Scandinavian laboratory," and the "epidemiologist's dream". *Science in Context, 27*(S02), 187–213.

Besteman C., & Gusterson, H. (Eds.) (2019). *Life by Algorithms. How Roboprocesses Are Remaking Our World.* Chicago & London: The University of Chicago Press.

Biruk, C. (2018). *Cooking data. Culture and politics in an African research world.* Durham: Duke University Press.

Blok, A. (2020). Climate risk communities. In M. Krogh (Ed.), *Connectedness. An incomplete encyclopedia of the Anthropocene* (pp. 114–117). Copenhagen: Strandberg Publishing.

Bowker, G. C. (2005). *Memory practices in the sciences.* Cambridge, MA.: The MIT Press.

Bowker, G. C., & Star, S. L. (1999). *Sorting things out—Classification and its consequences.* Cambridge, MA.: The MIT Press.

Busch, L. (2011). *Standards recipes for reality.* Cambridge, MA.: The MIT Press.

Carsten, J. (2000). Introduction: Cultures of relatedness. In J. Carsten (Ed.), *Cultures of relatedness. New approaches to the study of kinship* (pp. 1–36). Cambridge: Cambridge University Press.

Clifford, J. (1986). On ethnographic allegory. In J. Clifford & G. E. Marcus (Eds.), *Writing culture. The poetics and politics of ethnography* (pp. 98–121). London: University of California Press.

Comte, A. (1988). *Introduction to positive philosophy*. Indianapolis: Hackett Publishing Company, Inc.

Daston, L. (1992). Objectivity and the escape from perspective. *Social Studies of Science, 22,* 597–618.

de la Cadena, M. (2010). Indigenous cosmopolitics in the Andes: Conceptual reflections beyond 'politics'. *Cultural Anthropology, 25*(2), 334–370.

de la Cadena, M. (2015). *Earth beings: Ecologies of practice across Andean worlds.* Durham: Duke University Press.

de la Cadena, M. (2021). Not knowing: In the presence of …. In: A. Ballestero & B.R. Winthereik (Eds.), *Experimenting with ethnography: A companion to analysis* (pp. 246–256). Durham: Duke University Press.

de la Cadena, M., & Blaser, M. (2018). *A world of many worlds.* Durham: Duke University Press.

Derrida, J. (1995). Archive fever: A Freudian impression. *Diacritics, 25*(2), 9–63.

Desrosiéres, A. (1998). *The politics of large numbers. A history of statistical reasoning.* Cambridge, MA.: Harvard University Press.

Douglas-Jones, R. (2012). A single broken thread: Integrity, trust and accountability in Asian ethics review committees. *Durham Anthropology Journal, 18*(2), 13–27.

Douglas-Jones, R. (2017). Making room for ethics: Spaces, surveys and standards in the Asia-Pacific region. *Science & Technology Studies, 30*(3), 13–34.

Downey, G. L. & Dumit, J. (1997). *Cyborgs & citadels: anthropological interventions in emerging sciences and technologies.* Santa Fe: School of American Research Press. Seattle, WA: Distributed by the University of Washington Press.

Durkheim, E. (1973). *The dualism of human nature and its social conditions. On morality and society.* London: University of Chicago Press.

Durkheim, E. (2008). *The elementary forms of the religious life.* Mineola, New York: Dover.

Edwards, P. N. (2010). *A vast machine: Computer models, climate data, and the politics of global warming.* Cambridge, MA.: The MIT Press.

Engels, F. (2007). On the part played by labor in the transition from ape to man. In M. Lock & J. Farquhar (Eds.), *Beyond the body proper: Reading the anthropology of maternal life* (pp. 25–29). Durham & London: Duke University Press.

Epstein, S. (1996). *Impure science: AIDS, activism, and the politics of knowledge.* Berkeley: University of California Press.

Erikson, S. L. (2012). Global health business: The production and performativity of statistics in Sierra Leone and Germany. *Medical Anthropology, 31*(4), 367–384.

Erikson, S. L. (2016). Metrics and market logics of global health. In V. Adams (Ed.), *Metrics. What counts in global health* (pp. 147–162). Durham: Duke University Press.

Erikson, S. L. (2018). Cell phones ≠ Self and other problems with big data detection and containment during epidemics. *Medical Anthropology Quarterly, 32*(3), 315–339.

Escobar, A. (1998). Whose knowledge, whose nature? Biodiversity, conservation, and the political ecology of social movements. *Journal of Political Ecology, 5*(1), 53–82.

Essén, A., & Sauder, M. (2017). The evolution of weak standards: the case of the Swedish rheumatology quality registry. *Sociology of Health & Illness, 39*(4), 513–531.

Evans-Pritchard, E. E. (1976). *Witchcraft, oracles, and magic among the Azande.* Oxford: Oxford University Press.

Favret-Saada, J. (1980). *Deadly words: Witchcraft in the Bocage.* New York: Cambridge University Press.

Fishenden, J., & Thompson, M. (2012). Digital government, open architecture, and innovation: Why public sector IT will never be the same again. *Journal of Public Administration Research and Theory, 23*, 977–1004.

Fleck, L. (1979). *Genesis and development of a scientific fact.* Chicago: The University of Chicago Press.

Foucault, M. (1973). *The birth of the clinic—An archaeology of medical perception.* New York: Vintage Books.

Foucault, M. (1986). *The care of the self.* London: Penguin Books.

Foucault, M. (1991). Governmentality. In G. Burchell, C. Gordon, & P. Miller (Eds.), *The Foucault effect: Studies in Governmentality* (pp. 87–104). Chicago: The University of Chicago Press.

Foucault, M. (1997). On the genealogy of ethics: An overview of work in progress. In P. Rabinow (Ed.), *Ethics. Essential works of Foucault 1954–1984, Vol. 1* (pp. 253–280). London: Penguin.

Foucault, M. (2002). *Overvågning og straf. Fængslets fødsel [Discipline and punish. The birth of the prison].* Copenhagen: Det Lille Forlag.

Franklin, S. (2007). *Dolly mixtures: The remaking of genealogy.* Durham & London: Duke University Press.

Franklin, S., & McKinnon, S. (2001). Introduction. In S. Franklin & S. McKinnon (Eds.), *Relative Values: Reconfiguring kinship studies* (pp. 1–25). Durham: Duke University Press.

Fujimura, J. (1996). Crafting science: Standardized packages, boundary objects, and "translation". In A. Pickering (Ed.), *Science as Culture and Practice* (pp. 168–214). Chicago: University of Chicago Press.

Gad, C., Jensen, C. B., & Winthereik, B. R. (2015). Practical ontology: Worlds in STS and anthropology. *Nature Culture, 3*, 67–86.

Geertz, C. (1984). Distinguished lecture: anti anti-relativism. *American Anthropologist, 86*(2), 263–278.

Geissler, P. W. (2013). Public secrets in public health: Knowing not to know while making scientific knowledge. *American Ethnologist, 40*(1), 13–34.

Gell, A. (1992). The technology of enchantment and the enchantment of technology. In J. Coote & A. Shelton (Eds.), *Anthropology, art and aesthetics* (pp. 40–63). Oxford: Clarendon Press.

Grommé, F., & Ruppert, E. (2020). Population geometries of Europe: The topologies of data cubes and grids. *Science, Technology & Human Values, 45*(2), 235–261.

Haraway, D. J. (1989). *Primate visions: Gender, race, and nature in the world of modern science.* New York: Routledge.

Haraway, D. (1991). Situated knowledges. The science question in feminism and the privilege of partial perspective. In D. Haraway (Ed.), *Simians, cyborgs and women: The reinvention of nature* (pp. 183–201). New York: Routledge.

Haraway, D. (2004). A Manifesto for Cyborgs: Science, Technology, and Socialist Feminism in the 1980s. In *The Haraway Reader* (pp. 7–45). London: Routledge.

Hastrup, K. (1994). Anthropological knowledge incorporated. Discussion. In K. Hastrup & P.- Hervik (Eds.), *Social experience and anthropological knowledge* (pp. 224–240). London: Routledge.

Hastrup, K. (1998). Theatre as a site of passage. In F. Hughes-Freeland (Ed.), *Ritual, performance, media,* (pp. 29–45). London & New York: Routledge.

Hirsch, E. (2008). Knowing, not knowing, knowing anew. In N. Halstead, E. Hirsch, & J. Okely (Eds.), *Knowing how to know: Fieldwork and the ethnographic present* (pp. 21–37). Oxford: Berghahn Books.

Hockenhull, M., & Cohn, M. L. (2021). Hot air and corporate sociotechnical imaginaries: Performing and translating digital futures in the Danish tech scene. *New Media & Society, 23*(2), 302–321.

Hoeyer, K. (2005). Studying ethics as policy: The naming and framing of moral problems in genetic research. *Current Anthropology, 46*, 71–90.

Hoeyer, K. (2019). Data as promise: Reconfiguring Danish public health through personalized medicine. *Social Studies of Science, 49*(4), 531–555.

Hoeyer, K., & Bødker, M. (2020). Weak data: The social biography of a measurement instrument and how it failed to ensure accountability in home care. *Medical Anthropology Quarterly, 0*(0), 1–18.

Hogle, L. F. (1995). Standardization across non-standard domains: The case of organ procurement. *Science, Technology, & Human Values, 20*(4), 482–500.

Hogle, L. F. (1999). *Recovering the nation's body*. New Brunswick, New Jersey, & London: Rutgers University Press.

Holbraad, M., & Pedersen, M. A. (2017). The ontological turn: An anthropological exposition. *New Departures in Anthropology*. Cambridge: Cambridge University Press.

Holbraad, M., Pedersen, M. A., & Viveiros de Castro, E. (2014). The politics of ontology: Anthropological positions. Theorizing the contemporary. *Cultural Anthropology, January 13*.

Hunt, L. M., Bell, H. S., Baker, A. M., & Howard, H. A. (2017). Electronic health records and the disappearing patient. *Medical Anthropology Quarterly, 31*(3), 403–421.

Ingold, T. (2011). *Being alive: Essays on movement, knowledge and description*. Taylor & Francis.

Jacob, M-A., & Riles, A. (2007). The new bureaucracies of virtue: Introduction. *PoLAR: Political and Legal Anthropology Review, 30*(2), 181–191.

James, W. (1950). *The principles of psychology*. New York: Dover Publications, Inc.

Jensen, C. B., & Winthereik, B. R. (2013). *Monitoring movements in development aid: Recursive partnerships and infrastructures*. Cambridge, MA.: The MIT Press.

Karkazis, K., & Jordan-Young, R. (2020). Sensing race as a ghost variable in science, technology, and medicine. *Science, Technology & Human Values, 45*(5), 763–778.

Kaufman, S. R. (2015). *Ordinary medicine. Extraordinary treatments, longer lives, and where to draw the line*. Durham: Duke University Press.

Kingori, P. (2013). Experience everyday ethics in context: Frontline data collectors perspectives and practices of bioethics. *Social Science and Medicine, 98*, 361–370.

Kleinman, A., & Kleinman, J. (2007). Somatization: The interconnections in Chinese society among culture, depressive experiences, and the meanings of pain. In M. Lock & J. Farquhar (Eds.), *Beyond the body proper: Reading the anthropology of maternal life* (pp. 469–474). Durham & London: Duke University Press.

Knorr-Cetina, K. (1981). *The manufacture of knowledge: An essay on the constructivist and contextual nature of science*. Oxford: Pergamon Press.

Knorr-Cetina, K. D. (1983). The ethnographic study of scientific work: Towards a constructivist interpretation of science. In K. D. Knorr-Cetina & M. J. Mulkay (Eds.), *Science observed: Perspectives on the social study of science* (pp. 115–140). London: Sage.

Korsby, T. M., & Stavrianakis, A. (2018). Moments in collaboration: Experiments in concept work. *Ethnos, 82*, 1–19.

Lakoff, A. (2005). *Pharmaceutical reason: Knowledge and value in global psychiatry*. Cambridge: Cambridge University Press.

Lambert, H. (2006). Accounting for EBM: Notions of evidence in medicine. *Social Science and Medicine, 62*, 2633–2645.

Lappé, M. D. (2014). Taking care: Anticipation, extraction and the politics of temporality in autism science. *BioSocieties, 9*, 304–328.

Last, M. (1981). The importance of knowing about not knowing. *Social Science and Medicine, 15B*, 387–392.

Latour, B. (1990). Drawing things together. In M. Lynch & S. Woolgar (Eds.), *Representation in scientific practice* (pp. 19–68). Cambridge & London: The MIT Press.

Latour, B., & Woolgar, S. (1979). *Laboratory life: The social construction of scientific facts*. Beverly Hills: Sage Publications.

Law, J. (2009). Seeing like a survey. *Cultural Sociology, 3*(2), 239–256.

Law, J., & Ruppert, E. (2016). *Modes of knowing: Resources from the baroque*. Manchester: Mattering Press.

Lévy-Bruhl, L. (2018). *Revival: How natives think (1926)*. Routledge.

Lévi-Strauss, C. (1966). *The savage mind*. Chicago: University of Chicago Press.

Linder, F. (2004). Slave ethics and imagining critically applied anthropology in public health research. *Medical Anthropology, 23*, 329–358.

Lock, M. (2002). *Twice dead. Organ transplants and the reinvention of death*. Berkley: University of California Press.

Mair, J., Kelly, A. & High, C. (2012). Introduction: Making ignorance an ethnographic object. In C. High, A. Kelly & J. Mair (Eds.), *The anthropology of ignorance. An ethnographic approach* (pp. 1–32). New York: Palgrave Macmillan.

Marks, J. (2001). 'We're going to tell these people who they really are': Science and relatedness. In S. Franklin & S. McKinnon (Eds.), *Relative values. Reconfiguring kinship studies* (pp. 355–383). Durham & London: Duke University Press.

Martin, E. (2013). The Potentiality of Ethnography and the Limits of Affect Theory. *Current Anthropology, 54*(S7), 149–158.

Merry, S. E. (2016). *The seductions of quantification. Measuring human rights, gender violence, and sex trafficking*. Chicago: University of Chicago Press.

Merry, S. E. (2019). Controlling numbers: How quantification shapes the world. In C. Besteman & H. Gusterson (Eds.), *Life by algorithms. How roboprocesses are remaking our world* (pp. 145–163). Chicago & London: The University of Chicago Press.

Miyazaki, H. (2006). Economy of dreams: Hope in global capitalism and its critiques. *Cultural Anthropology, 21*(2), 147–172.

Mol, A. (2002). *The body multiple: Ontology in medical practice*. London: Duke University Press.

Murphy, M. (2017). *The Economization of life*. Brightleaf: The Duke University Press.

Pálsson, G. & Rabinow, P. (1999). Iceland. The case of the national human genome project. *Anthropology Today, 15*(5), 14–18.

Parry, B. (2004). *Trading the genome. Investigating the commodification of bio-information*. New York: Columbia University Press.

Peeters R., & Schuilenburg M. (Eds.) (2021). *The algorithmic society. Technology, power, and knowledge*. London: Routledge.

Petryna, A. (2002). *Life exposed. Biological citizens after Chernobyl*. Princeton, New Jersey: Princeton University Press.

Petryna, A. (2009). *When experiments travel: Clinical trials and the global search for human subjects*. Princeton & Oxford: Princeton University Press.

Polanyi, M. (1966). *The Tacit Dimension*. Chicago: University of Chicago Press.

Port, M. V. D. (2005). Circling around the really real: Spirit possession ceremonies and the search for authenticity in Bahian Candomblé. *Ethos, 33*(2), 149–179.

Rabinow, P. (1996). *Making PCR. A story of biotechnology*. Chicago: University of Chicago Press.

Rabinow, P. (1999). *French DNA. Trouble in purgatory*. Chicago: University of Chicago Press.

Riles, A. (2011). *Collateral knowledge: Legal reasoning in the global financial markets*. Chicago: University of Chicago Press.

Royce, A. P. (1977). *The anthropology of dance*. Indiana University Press Bloomington.

Ruppert, E. (2012). The governmental topologies of database devices. *Theory, Culture & Society 29*(4–5), 116–136.

Sætnan, A. R., Lommel, H. M., & Hammer, S. (2011). Introduction. By the very act of counting—The mutual construction of statistics and society. In A. R. Sætnan, H. M. Lomell, & S. Hammer (Eds.), *The mutual construction statistics and society* (pp. 1–21). New York: Routledge Taylor & Francis Group.

Schieffelin, E. L. (1985). Performance and the cultural construction of reality. *American Ethnologist, 12*(4), 707–724.

Scott, J. C. (1998). *Seeing like a state: How certain schemes to improve the human condition have failed*. New Haven, CT.: Yale University Press.

Sheikh, Z. A., & Jensen, A. M. B. (2019). Channelling hope: An ethnographic study of how research encounters become meaningful for families suffering from genetic disease in Pakistan. *Social Science & Medicine, 228*, 103–110.

Silverstein, B. (2018). Commensuration, performativity, and the reform of statistics in Turkey. *American Ethnologist, 45*(3), 330–340.

Sjørslev, I. (2013). Boredom, rhythm, and the temporality of ritual: Recurring fieldwork in the Brazilian Candomblé. *Social Analysis, 57*(1), 95–109.

Snowden, E. (2019). *Permanent record*. London: Macmillan.

Star, S. L., & Bowker, G. C. (2002). How to infrastructure. In L. A. Lievrouw & S. Livingstone (Eds.), *Handbook of new media. Social shaping and consequences of ICTs* (pp. 151–162). London: SAGE Publications Ltd.

Star, S. L., & Ruhleder, K. (1996). Steps toward an ecology of infrastructure: Design and access for large information spaces. *Information Systems Research, 7*(1), 111–134.

Storeng, K. T., & Behage, D. P. (2017). 'Guilty until proven innocent': The contested use of maternal mortality indicators in global health. *Critical Public Health, 27*(2), 163–176.

Strathern, M. (2004). Global and local context. In L. Kalinoe & J. Leach (Eds.), *Rationales of ownership. Transactions and claims to ownership in contemporary Papua New Guinea* (pp.107–127). Wantage: Sean Kingston Publishing.

Strathern, M. (2006). Bullet-proofing. In A. Riles (Ed.), *Documents* (pp.181–205). Ann Arbor: The University of Michigan Press.

Sullivan, N. (2017). Multiple accountabilities: Development cooperation, transparency, and the politics of unknowing in Tanzania's health sector. *Critical Public Health, 27*(2), 193–204.

Svendsen, M. N., & Koch, L. (2008). Between neutrality and engagement: A case study of recruitment to pharmacogenomics research in Denmark. *BioSocieties, 3*, 399–418.

Taussig, K-S. (2009). *Ordinary genomes: Science, citizenship, and genetic identities*. Durham & London: Duke University Press.

Torenholt, R., Saltbæk, L. & Langstrup, H. (2020). Patient data work: Filtering and sensing patient-reported outcomes. *Sociology of Health & Illness, 42*(6), 1379–1393.

Tylor, E. B. (1899). Remarks on totemism with especial reference to some modern theories concerning it. *Journal of the Royal Anthropological Institute, 25*(3), 138–148.

Verran, H. (2001). *Science and an African logic.* Chicago: University of Chicago Press.

Viveiros de Castro, E. B. (2003). After-dinner speech given at Anthropology and Science, the 5th Decennial Conference of the Association of Social Anthropologists of the UK and Commonwealth, 14th of July 2003. Department of Social Anthropology, University of Manchester.

von Schnitzler, A. (2013). Traveling technologies: Infrastructure, ethical regimes, and the materiality of politics in South Africa. *Cultural Anthropology, 28*(4), 670–693.

Wahlberg, A. (2018). *Good quality. The routinization of sperm banking in China.* Oakland: University of California Press.

Walford, A. (2017). Raw data: making relations matter. *Social Analysis, 61*(2), 65–80.

Weber, M. (1947). Science as vocation. In H. H. Gerth & C. W. Mills (Eds.), *From Max Weber: Essays in sociology* (pp. 129–156). Oxford: Oxford University Press.

Wilf, E. (2013). Toward an anthropology of computer-mediated, algorithmic forms of sociality. *Current Anthropology, 54*(6), 716–739.

Winthereik, B. R. (2003). 'We fill in our working understanding': On codes, classifications and the production of accurate data. *Methods of Information in Medicine, 42*(4), 489–496.

Winthereik, B. R., Maguire, J. & Watts, J. (2019) The energy walk: Infrastructuring the imagination. In J. Vertesi & D. Ribes (Eds.), *DigitalSTS: A field guide for science & technology Studies* (pp.349–364). Princeton & Oxford: Princeton University Press.

Winthereik, B. R., van der Ploeg, I. & Berg, M. (2007). The electronic patient record as a meaningful audit tool. Accountability and autonomy in general practitioner work. *Science, Technology, & Human Values, 32*(1), 6–25.

Zagzebski, L. T. (2012). *Epistemic authority: A theory of trust, authority, and autonomy in belief.* New York: Oxford University Press.

Zuboff, S. (2019). *The age of surveillance capitalism. The fight for a human future at the new frontier of power.* New York City: Public Affairs.

CHAPTER 12

Technology, Environment, and the Ends of Knowledge

Art

Hannah Knox

There is something there, we can feel it, but what we see is not it. Something else powerful and mysterious lurks below the surface, entangled in the wires behind your black box. (Fish 2018)

In 2018, artist James Bridle published a treatise on our digital times, casting them not as an age of enlightenment but rather a 'new dark age' where opaque and unwieldy infrastructures of algorithmic organisation, machine learning, and data proliferation are shaping social worlds in unpredictable and unfathomable ways (Bridle 2018). This chapter explores what happens when technology produces not knowledge, but the ends of knowledge, and considers what resources we might draw on as anthropologists to respond to this situation. What can we learn about technology by paying attention to the way it is implicated in the limits of modern forms of understanding, and how might this signal new and more expansive horizons for our studies of technological systems?

To examine these issues, a specific focus is directed at the challenges that digital infrastructures, as a form of contemporary technology, pose for modern ways of knowing—including the ways of knowing that anthropology as a modern discipline itself deploys. Centrally, this chapter argues that the interdisciplinary work on digital infrastructures taking place across anthropology, STS, media studies, and art has repeatedly brought to the surface the unknowability

H. Knox (✉)
University College London, London, UK
e-mail: h.knox@ucl.ac.uk

M. H. Bruun et al. (eds.), *The Palgrave Handbook of the Anthropology of Technology*, https://doi.org/10.1007/978-981-16-7084-8_12

of digital infrastructures. It also argues that this interdisciplinary nexus offers us new ways of engaging these processes as critical aspects of contemporary social life and, in doing so, new directions for an anthropology of technology.

UNKNOWING TECHNOLOGY

In anthropology and associated disciplines, there has been something of a turn in recent years away from technology as a locus of study and towards the study of infrastructure (Anand et al. 2018; Harvey et al. 2017; Larkin 2013). Where digital infrastructures are concerned, this approach has drawn the attention of scholars to the geographies of globally distributed networks of cables (Starosielski 2015), to the way that the social might be found embedded deep in algorithmic code (Seaver 2018), and to the slipperiness of digital platforms and digital communications, with their tendency to constantly morph and develop in ways that sometimes surprise even the designers of such systems (boyd and Crawford 2012). As digital technologies are increasingly recognised for their infrastructural dynamics, the capacity to know them has become ever more challenging. How, for example, can we trace networks of cables that lie out of view, understand the interplay of layers of code and statistical reasoning of which no one person has a grasp, or keep track of mutating digital forms? The more that we are aware that digital infrastructures are affecting social worlds—changing our politics, altering our relations with money, amplifying the power and control of corporations, manipulating our minds, reorganising labour, and relocating the site of governmentality—the less amenable they seem to techniques of objectification and description. Digital infrastructures have thus begun to raise some profound questions for anthropologists of technology about the way in which we approach what technology is as a focus of anthropological study.

That digital infrastructures are posing a challenge to modern ways of knowing is, however, rather ironic. For the same technical infrastructures that are challenging our capacity to understand them, have emerged from precisely those systems—from the archive to cybernetics—that for most of the twentieth century have been at the foundation of promises about knowledge and its capacity to control (Gandy 2005; Halpern 2015). If we take, for example, the advent of big data, we see in this organisation of wires, code, programmers, data inputters, customers, and data analysts a long-running promise that technologies beget information, which in turn begets knowledge (Knox et al. 2010). For all the hype about the potential of new forms of tracking technologies to effect new repositories of data which promise to have world-changing effects, the foundation of such systems lies in a longer history of state surveillance, enumeration, data collection, and social control. This is a field that has long interested anthropologists of technology who have sought to explore how technologies and techniques frame knowledge and, in doing so, constitute relations of power (Gupta 2012; Hull 2012). Whether studying how states come to gain power over populations by imposing modern 'ways of seeing' on other ways of living (Scott 1998) or analysing the way that technologies, like new reproductive technologies, carry with them powerful imaginaries of what it means to relate (Strathern 1999), anthropologists have long recognised that technical artefacts play a crucial part in framing how worlds can be imagined and made in practice. It is partly for this reason that technology has emerged as an important focus for many contemporary anthropologists, who have seen in the study of technical artefacts an important route to understanding how human social worlds are made via relations, not only between people but also between people and things (Pfaffenberger 1992). In 'modern' understandings of social relations—as instantiated both in social analysis and in social life in Euro-American settings—'technology' has emerged as a particular category of thing that is understood to have the capacity both to make social worlds and to make them amenable to understanding (Marx 2010).

However, as I began to outline above, a consensus seemed to exist between anthropologists and their interlocutors that technologies have the capacity to make and describe worlds. This, however, has been fractured on both sides by the theoretical and practical realisation that systems of inscription, ordering, and control seem to be escaping their containment qua technologies, and refiguring themselves as systems of autonomous interpretation, exhibiting disordering tendencies, and becoming implicated in the production of a world that feels increasingly out of control. Examples of this might include algorithmic biases which emerge as side effects of computational systems whose logic forces them into making category errors which unintentionally but disturbingly transgress social norms. These produce in their wake things like racist image recognition software that has no interpretive agency,[1] or the sexist job selection algorithm that is sexist only on the basis of the unforeseen side effects of a calculative technique.[2] Another example might be the appearance of blockchain-based technologies that seek to resolve ethical problems with exchange by implementing regimes of anonymity and transparency, whilst simultaneously hiding the material conditions of their functioning that make the self-same distributed ledger technologies some of the biggest consumers of electricity. This has implications for another terrain of ethics oriented to questions of how to achieve sustainable environmental futures.[3] Plastics promise sterile food but also leach into water sources and pollute oceans, whilst even seemingly ethical technologies like wind power or solar electricity promise green futures for some, but a new form of technological imperialism for others (Howe and Boyer 2016). Indeed, even as tools of knowledge production, technologies are under strain. While government policies, from climate change to pandemic control, continue to be informed by predictive models that seek to place politics in the service of an apparently unambiguous and rhetorically powerful 'science', the foundations of these models are proving rocky. Indeed, their predictive promise is often questioned even by the very modellers who are most intimate with them (Thompson and Smith 2019).

Thus, despite ongoing claims that technology is capable of delivering the answers to the major global and national problems of our age, many people are sensing that there is something amiss with this view. Returning specifically to digital infrastructures: as people have begun to try and trace digital systems empirically and ethnographically, they have often found themselves confronted with a nagging feeling that 'something is lurking beneath the surface', that some form of code, or organisation, or logic is at play that is affecting our interactions with objects and with one another but which cannot be seen, felt, or known. However, attempting to know where this sense comes from or how it can be understood leaves us, as anthropologists, challenged. No longer are we confronted as social analysts with the 'standard view of technology' (Pfaffenberger 1992): that is, technology as artefact or tool that can be studied in-situ with techniques of material culture analysis to understand its instrumental value within a particular set of social relations. Nor even is it enough to highlight the role of technology as a stabilising and framing device that results in situated truths (Akrich 1992; Latour and Woolgar 1979; Scott 1998). Instead, what confronts us is technology as an unstable nexus of relations whose very shape or form is difficult to discern, its location ambiguous and its effects only detectable through partial networks of sensors and limited data (Gabrys 2016; Marres 2009). This is not just technology conceived of as a socio-technical system—a 'black box' that can be opened up for inspection (Latour 1987), but technology as a more insidious, mutating, unstable phenomenon of whose existence we can only hope to illuminate moments. In being felt but not known, sensed but not located, digital infrastructures cast us into what James Bridle has recently termed 'a new dark age' (Bridle 2018) or what philosopher Timothy Morten has called 'the end of the world' (Morton 2013).

In some respects, anthropology should be well placed to deal with technological infrastructures pulling the rug out from under its own ways of knowing. Anthropology has long been challenged by its own subject matter, not least by recent debates regarding the question of how to deal with multiple or alternative 'ontologies'. Here anthropologists have similarly had to grapple with the question of what anthropology can do when confronted with ontological conditions (and other ways of engaging those ontologies) that undercut the discipline of anthropology's own claims to descriptive control of the worlds that it seeks to represent (Holbraad and Pedersen 2017). Marisol de la Cadena's description of her extended conversation with her Andean friend and interlocutor Mauricio, for example, reveals to us the limits of anthropological frames of knowledge that rest on an ontological separation between thought and matter (de la Cadena 2015). Similarly the contributions of anthropologists of Amerindian societies to philosophical discussions about the ontological basis of claims to agency and personhood in Amazonia versus those made within post-enlightenment science have demanded anthropologists look again at the basis upon which their own claims to knowledge rest (Descola 2013; Latour 2009; Viveiros de Castro 1998, 2004).

For anthropologists involved in these debates, the limits of knowledge have been framed not by the exhaustion of a technological mode of seeing and understanding the world, but through a confrontation with 'other' worldviews that do not appear to fit the analytical frameworks of contemporary anthropology. Within discussions about technology, the challenge for anthropology and the social sciences manifests less in terms of a question of empirical equivalence between different ways of knowing, or cultural relativism; rather, it is embodied in questions such as how to describe such distributed systems (is ethnography adequate for describing global processes?), how we should approach them empirically (do distributed systems call for distributed methods?), and what we should do about the insights we gain about the way such systems operate (see recent arguments for a speculative design anthropology) (Akama et al. 2015)? Confronted with the end of the idea of technologies as things amenable to contained empirical description, what should we do?

Some of the most interesting answers to this question are emerging not within the anthropology of technology but at the intersections of anthropology and art. Thus, to consider what anthropology might do as it confronts the ends of knowing technology, I turn in the next section to consider some examples of artistic engagements with the ontological challenges of technologies recast as infrastructural systems that collapse the distinction between technology, on the one hand, and environment, on the other hand. The section is centred around an immersive art exhibition that was shown in the summer of 2019 as part of the Manchester International Festival, Rafael Lozano-Hemmer's *Atmospheric Memory*. Drawing on the way that artists have approached the challenges of distributed and seemingly unknowable digital infrastructures, I seek out answers to how, as anthropologists, we too might rethink technology as a subject of anthropological study. What emerges from these examples is a rethinking of technology less as artefact and more as environment, a realisation that I argue opens up new methodological and conceptual avenues for continued anthropological study of technology.

ATMOSPHERIC MEMORY

To enter Rafael Lozano-Hemmer's 2019 artwork *Atmospheric Memory*, the visitor must walk along a tunnel of sound and light. From the ceiling of the tunnel hang 3000 speakers, each programmed to play an individual sound: an excerpt of bird song, the sound of a cricket, the rustle of leaves. On each of the speakers there are white LEDs which light up when the sound plays. Stepping into the tunnel, an arc of these lights sweeps slowly from the distance towards you, approaching like a wave, the sound from the illuminated microphones coming nearer and getting louder as the lights approach. As the wave passes overhead threads of individual sounds become audible as voices, a tweet here, a rustle there, before the sound and light continue their movement along the tunnel reassembling into the white noise reminiscent of water crashing on a beach.

Lozano-Hemmer's artwork, developed for and displayed at the 2019 Manchester International Festival, offers a contemporary cultural commentary on the experience of living in a world reconceived as media infrastructure. According to the artist, the *Atmospheric Memory* exhibition, of which the tunnel is a part, was inspired by a line taken from an 1837 text by Charles Babbage, inventor of the analytical engine, a proto-computer powered by steam that Babbage envisaged would be able to automate the performance of programmed calculations. At one point in his text, Babbage speculates that the atmosphere might be conceived of as a library, the movements of air containing material traces of every word ever spoken:

> The air itself is one vast library on whose pages are for ever written that all man has ever said or even whispered. There in their mutable but unerring characters, mixed with the earliest, as well as the latest signs of mortality, stand for ever recorded vows unredeemed, promises unfulfilled, perpetuating in the united movements of each particle, the testimony of man's changeful will. (Babbage, 1837, p. 113)

Babbage's text goes on to imagine a computer so advanced that it might calculate the movement of air particles, tracing them back to their origin point so as to construct an atmospheric archaeology of the entire history of human voice. *Atmospheric Memory* takes this conceit as a provocation to explore the relationship between voice, media, digital technologies, and environment. If Babbage's ideas were possible, the exhibition catalogue asks, 'whose voices would we want to hear? Loved ones long gone? Languages and songs now extinct? Oral histories never transcribed? Perhaps we could find evidence of criminal acts and send old injustices for a retrial.' By evoking Babbage, the exhibition draws the visitor's attention to a moment in the history of computational technology which is fascinating for our purposes in this chapter for it appears to signal nothing less than the birth of the conceit that technology could bring about the inscription of matter, and that in doing so technology begets knowledge. By proposing to create a machine that could trace the patterns in the air, atmosphere is reconceived here as media, albeit a media which, as the opening tunnel installation implies, is experienced as noise that hints at the potential for comprehension but whose meaning nonetheless remains fleeting and just out of reach.

The preoccupations of *Atmospheric Memory* might seem at first far removed from contemporary discussions of artificial intelligence (AI), peer-to-peer trading, blockchain, drones, the internet of things, or any other digital infrastructure that is constituting social relations and shaping social worlds today. But I want to suggest that *Atmospheric Memory* articulates in artistic form many of the central themes emerging from recent anthropological reflections on digital infrastructures and the challenges that they pose to anthropological reflection.

ART AS ENVIRONMENTAL MEDIA

Atmospheric Memory is located in a huge chamber constructed within the grounds of the Manchester Museum of Science and Industry. Walking into the chamber, the walls of what looks from the outside like a solid metal structure dissipate into swirling clouds; meanwhile, water vapour from one of the installations creeps and curls around the ankles of exhibition visitors. On one wall, the words of Charles Babbage and Ada Lovelace are being projected, but the stability of these words is weak. As warm human bodies walk past the light projection, the heat from the bodies is detected, processed by algorithms, and translated into a thermodynamic flow that interferes with the projection, becoming visualised as a swirling cloud of watery heat that rises up from visitors' silhouettes, lifting, as it does so, the projected letters from the wall like leaves on a windy day and casting them upwards towards the clouds. It is unclear how the algorithm works or what the exact relationship is here between bodies and images and words. There is some kind of computational relationship at play, but no explanation of what this is for the visitor. We are asked to engage not by understanding these relations but by experiencing the effect of their digital presence in the space.

This display of algorithmic processes and the invitation to play with the effects of such processes is reminiscent of the work of other artists also grappling with the unknowability of digital systems. Crawford and Joler's (2018) anatomy of an AI system, offers us another example of a contemporary interdisciplinary approach to digital infrastructures informed by art practice and by sociology, visualising in their case the socio-technical relations and infrastructures of the Amazon Echo and Alexa systems. Crawford and Joler engage with the question of the politics and sociality of digital infrastructure through the creation of a map that takes the form of both an artistic rendering of the network of relations that constitute the Amazon Echo—from the mining of elements used in the chips that power the devices to the labour relations in sites of production—and an essay which elaborates these relations in narrative form.

Maps are of course contentious, and much ink has been spilled on the positionality, politics, and silences that maps carry in their designs (Ingold 2007; Pickles 2004). Heather Houser has recently described a fetish for such infrastructural mapping—in her case environmental visualisations—as a form of 'infogasm', warning that mapping of this kind can offer a sense of misplaced mastery and sidestep the challenges of uncertainty and misinformation (Houser 2014). However, cautioning against the idea that the map they have produced is a singular or ultimate description of this digital infrastructure, Crawford and Joler (2018) write:

> The ecological price of transformation of elements and income disparities is just one of the possible ways of representing a deep systemic inequality. We have both researched different forms of 'black boxes' understood as algorithmic processes, but this map points to another form of opacity: the very processes of creating,

> training and operating a device like an Amazon Echo is itself a kind of black box, very hard to examine and track in toto given the multiple layers of contractors, distributors, and downstream logistical partners around the world. (Crawford and Joler 2018, n.p.)

The map seems at first sight to constitute an act of unpacking the black box of a technological system, approached within the frame of critical art practice. Yet Crawford and Joler here aim to deploy maps not as revelatory technologies that can describe the Amazon Echo in all its complexity, but rather as a way of *re-scaling* technology—disaggregating it from an object to be found in space and time—to create in its place 'an exploded view of a planetary system across three stages of birth, life and death' (Crawford and Joler 2018, n.p.). The artwork is an invitation for both the public and the companies represented in the artwork to consider and attempt to traverse these scales with the artists. The difficulty of doing so, the blocks to movement, and the appearance of spaces of invisibility are all part of the experience that the artists are attempting to provoke. Like other projects of digital infrastructural mapping—such as Dodge and Kitchin's early Atlas of Cyberspace (Dodge and Kitchin 2001), or Jay Springett and Andrew Brown's 'Stacktivism'[4]—the anatomy of the AI is an attempt not just to reveal the empirical reality of the object of technology through descriptive mapping but, more radically, to rethink technology as no longer an object at all but, rather, a 'planetary system'. This rescales our understanding of technology by relocating it in global networks of labour, materiality, and sociality.

A similar re-rendering of technology through mapping can be seen in other attempts to trace and map distributed digital infrastructures. Another artwork, entitled *Black Shoals Stock Market Planetarium*, by Joshua Portway and Lisa Autogena, uses the figure of the planetarium as a mechanism to engage audiences in the hidden realities of global stock markets,[5] projecting stock market trades as star-like dots on the surface of the planetarium ceiling. Using algorithms that calculate the correlation between the stock market prices of different companies, the artwork shifts and morphs over time, creating 'galaxies' of industries that index clusters of trades. These are then represented by agglomerations of stars on the curved ceiling. About the artwork, the artists write:

> Within this environment, a complex ecology of glowing amoeba-like 'artificial life' creatures emerge. The creatures live in a world composed entirely of money and they feed on trading activity. Whenever a stock is traded its' [sic] equivalent star produces food for the creatures—the bigger the trade, the more food is produced. For these creatures the heaves and surges of the world economy are like Earths' tectonic plates.[6]

The mapping of technical systems in this artwork presents digital systems as a planetary environment, evoking the digital not as object but rather as a set of relations that exhibit ecological qualities. The mutating clusters of star-like dots effect a digital sublime (Mosco 2004) captured inside a Slotterdijkian 'atmo-sphere' of the whole planet conjured up within the walls of a single room.[7] Here, as with the opening corridor to *Atmospheric Memory*, we find art practice creating not only a map but also an affective engagement with technology rei-magined as a more ecological set of relations.

If mapping has been one response to the material opacity of digital systems, the more affective, sensorially informed, dwelling approach generated by art-works like *Black Shoals* has been another. In *Atmospheric Memory* one of the explicit aims was to render text and language not only informational but also material and experiential. We see this in the exhibits that I have already described above, but this affective embodied quality of informational media is perhaps most compellingly captured in another installation at the *Atmospheric Memory* exhibition, entitled *Last Breath*. On one of the walls of the chamber, what looks like an artefact from a hospital ward is mounted on a grey background. At one end is a ventilation machine, which is slowly moving in and out, while at the other end, attached to a long white tube, is a brown paper bag. The description of the exhibit explains that the entire contraption contains a breath from the modern classical music composer Pauline Oliveros, captured before her death in 2016. Below the pump is a digital counter, clocking up the mechanical inhalations and exhalations as Oliveros' breath continues to slowly pump in and out. Words, meaning, air, and matter here collapse into one, demanding that the viewer consider what it might mean for a spoken word to be captured in the form of air and to be retained through time in the hope that something of the person whence it came might one day be reconstructed.

Lozano-Hemmer is not alone in considering the environmental qualities of information and media through an attention to bodies and affect. Adam Fish's recent research, for example, uses drones as research tools to draw out the eco-logical dimensions of internet infrastructure. Combining drone footage with sound, visuals, and text, Fish sets out to explore, critically, the media affor-dances of drones themselves as an emergent technological form and the possi-bilities that they open up for re-seeing the information infrastructure's environmental embeddedness. As a critical media theorist, Fish's experiments with drones range from their use in visualising environmental protests over the Dakota Pipeline Project—as a mode of counter-surveillance in a site of attempted environmental justice—to an analysis of the use of drones by the Indonesian Government for sensing particulate matter from an Indonesian vol-cano. In Fish's film, *Points of Presence*, drone footage is used to collapse the divide between environment and technology, tracing the internet by following cables in and out of buildings, juxtaposing servers and waterfalls, and delving in and out of holes in the ground. In one shot, a concrete manhole cover is removed from a yellow plastic protrusion sticking out of a field of grass. As the cover is removed, the drone taking the footage is reflected in the dark pool of water that sits within. Just as the viewer catches a glimpse of the drone's reflec-tion, the footage begins to zoom up and out, revealing the landscape in which the drain is located. In this moment, settled distinctions between hidden and seen, foreground and background, media and environment are destabilised. What emerges from this research is a realisation that media technologies (both as the object of the research and the tools through which such research is conducted) are inherently material, environmental entities, and that their very materiality conditions the forms of representation that they enable (Fish 2018).

TECHNOLOGY AS ENVIRONMENTAL RELATION

Sociologist Jennifer Gabrys has also begun to explore various forms of digital infrastructure as sites of sensory perception and alternative modes of environmental dwelling. Here her attention turns to an infrastructure of remote sensing involving transformations in environmental perception. In *Program Earth: Environmental Sensing Technology and the Making of a Computational Planet* (2016), Gabrys describes how digital sensors are both making environments visible in new ways, and reframing understandings of environments as themselves relational, sensorial realms. Blurring sociology, art, and activism, Gabrys evokes a digital infrastructure that is environmental both in its design (sensing trees, visualising moss, and using animals as sensors) and in its governmental effects (smart cities and planetary computerisation). One again we see a conceptual dismantling of the boundaries between the realm of technology and the realm of nature. As Gabrys writes elsewhere,

> environments are not then simply a map of a territory but are a field of resonance and relation that can be drawn into and materialized in the experience of subjects, whether those subjects are citizen sensors, soil sensors, moss cams, migrating storks, marine debris in sensor mapped ocean currents, air-pollution-sensing devices, smart buildings, digital infrastructure or any of the many other actual computational concretizations of environmental sensing subject-superjects. (Gabrys 2014, p. 269)

In its attention to sensors, surveillance, bodies, and care, the anthropology of technology here meets the anthropology of the environment head on. Anthropologists who have centred their work on infrastructures—cities, canals, waterways, roads, and railways—have begun to find themselves turning to the body, incorporating questions of sensory perception and material affects into their descriptions of how technologies unfold in social worlds (Knox 2017; Weston 2017). At the same time, environmental anthropologists have found attention to the body has begun to draw them to the place of technological devices—prostheses, standards, regulations, RFID chips, and climate models—in the making and remaking of environmental perception (Adams et al. 2009; Kirksey 2015; Tsing 2015).

If mapping has been deployed as a means of engaging people anew in the scalar and materially distributive effects of digital systems, while attention to affective and sensory engagement with and through technologies seeks to understand the experience of being caught within the interstices of such systems, a third and final approach is one that goes even further in treating these techno-environmental hybrids not as things, or even systems, but rather as means of making and remaking worlds.

The day before I visit the *Atmospheric Memory* exhibition, I attend a symposium where Lozano-Hemmer describes another of his artworks, *Vicious Circular Breathing*. Here, as with the installation based on the projection of text on the wall described above, visitors are invited to interact with the artwork, and in doing so to change it. However, in *Vicious Circular Breathing* there is a twist. The installation is a closed system of circulating air, and visitors are invited to step inside and add their breath to it; in doing so, however, they are also required to breathe the air of those who have gone before them. The more people who enter the exhibit, the more contaminated the air becomes, with participation changing both the future of the artwork and the health of participants through their interaction in it. Here Lozano-Hemmer pushes the logic of participation and the virtues of intellectual reflection to their limits, demanding of the visitor that they no longer see the installation as something to be observed or contemplated, but instead recasting this technical artefact as an analogue of the polluted atmospheres in which we all increasingly live.

Attention to the collapse of the distinction between technology and environment returns us finally to Babbage's eternal machine, a machine which, it might be argued, marked the origin of the separation between the environment and technology. When Babbage came up with the idea of an analytical engine, the machine was proposed as a way of making sense of the complexity of 'Nature'. Babbage's contemporaries had argued that there was a conceit and hubris to the idea that man could step, god-like, outside nature and profess to understand its internal mechanics. Responding to his critics, Babbage retorted that his analytical engine, and his associated idea of the traceability of all utterances through time, was, far from stepping outside of the natural world, a part of that very world that the machine would serve to represent. The machine itself, as part of nature, would leave its own traces in the materiality of all things. For Babbage, the inventor of the analytical engine—the original computational technology—there was, in a sense, still no 'technology' to speak of, only different organisations of environmental relations.

But since then technology has done what his critics worried it would do, claiming to be god-like in its power, gaining agency all of its own. Returning to the origins of this concern is salutary for it reminds us that, however much people embrace the story of technology's autonomy, its material continuity with the world remains. As Babbage suggested, technology can never be the illuminating transformative entity it is meant to be for it remains part of the mystery of the universe, at the same time that it professes to rise above it and describe it.

Anthropology of Technology at the End of Knowledge

In this chapter I have argued that the sense of living in a new dark age—experienced both by those of us confronted by distributed digital infrastructures in our everyday lives and by scholars studying these self-same phenomena—has the effect of opening up the double life of technology: on the one hand, as a means to an external world through techniques of knowing and, on the other, as a figuration of environmental relations themselves. By holding these two versions of technology in view simultaneously, technology enacts a double presence, first as figuratively separated from the environment as context and second as ontologically environmental. The juxtaposition of these two modes of technological being, I have argued, demands that we reposition the autonomous view of technology as a powerful but ultimately limited story; yet doing so has profound consequences for anthropology's own claims to knowledge. Drawing on art practice I have suggested various ways in which technology might be productively approached through alternative techniques that strive less for the fixing of stabilised forms of knowledge and rather seek to open up new avenues for scholars and publics to ask reflexive questions about the social and cultural relations that both sustain a belief in autonomous machines and encourage the continued fetishisation of technology as the answer to society's problems.

Acknowledging the limits of technology, and the challenge that recent ways of tracing digital infrastructures pose to modern ways of knowing, demands reconsideration of the methods that we use as anthropologists to make our knowledge claims. It also requires us to reflect on how our own claims about the world that we seek to describe have been generated by a representational move that bears close relation to a technological way of being in the world. This suggests that a revision of the anthropological stance towards technology might offer something back to long-running anthropological concerns with translation between an anthropological world view and other ways of being that exceed or sit in awkward relation to our own ways of describing and holding the world still. Here we find ourselves with an anthropology of digital infrastructure that—through techniques such as mapping, dwelling, and making, rendered through the ambitions of art rather than science—aims not to carve out a modern claim to knowledge, but rather create a means to proceed with others through techno-environmental materialities that for the time being remain predominantly imagined as a world filled with technological objects.

Notes

1. https://www.theguardian.com/technology/2015/jul/01/google-sorry-racist-auto-tag-photo-app. Accessed 8 July 2021.
2. https://www.theguardian.com/technology/2018/oct/10/amazon-hiring-ai-gender-bias-recruiting-engine. Accessed 8 July 2021.
3. https://www.theguardian.com/technology/2018/mar/10/blockchain-music-imogen-heap-provenance-finance-voting-amir-taaki. Accessed 8 July 2021.

4. https://stacktivism.com Accessed 31 May 2020.
5. http://www.blackshoals.net/#home-section Accessed 31 May 2020.
6. http://www.blackshoals.net/the-project-1 Accessed 31 May 2020.
7. In a parallel way, Christian Borch (2017) analyses the use of algorithms in Financial Trading using an animalistic framing that he derives from Roger Callois' theory of mimesis. Borsch argues that under conditions of automation and digitisation, algorithms come to operate less as Foucauldian systems of governmentality power and more as relational plays of imitation, camouflage, and defence such as that found in interactions between living creatures.

References

Adams, V., Murphy, M., & Clarke, A. E. (2009). Anticipation: Technoscience, life, affect, temporality. Subjectivity. *Subjectivity, 28,* 246-265. https://doi.org/10.1057/sub.2009.18.

Akama, Y., Pink, S., & Fergusson, A. (2015). *Design+ Ethnography+ Futures: Surrendering in Uncertainty.* Paper presented at the CHI 2015: Crossings.

Akrich, M. (1992). The De-Sciption of Technical Objects. In W. Bijker & L. J. (Eds.), *Shaping Technology / Building Society* (pp. 205-222). Cambridge, MA.: The MIT Press.

Anand, N., Gupta, A., & Appel, H. (2018). *The promise of infrastructure.* Durham: Duke University Press.

Borch, C. (2017). Algorithmic Finance and (Limits to) Governmentality: On Foucault and High-Frequency Trading. *Le Foucaldien, 3*(1), 6. http://doi.org/10.16995/.

boyd, D., & Crawford, K. (2012). CRITICAL QUESTIONS FOR BIG DATA Provocations for a cultural, technological, and scholarly phenomenon. *Information, Communication & Society: Special Issue: A decade in Internet time: the dynamics of the Internet and society, 15*(5), 662–679.

Bridle, J. (2018). *New Dark Age: Technology and the End of the Future:* Verso.

Crawford, K., & Joler, V. (2018). Anatomy of an AI System: The Amazon Echo as An Anatomical Map of Human Labor, Data and Planetary Resources. *AI Now Institute and Share Lab,* (September 7, 2018) https://anatomyof.ai.

de la Cadena, M. d. l. (2015). *Earth beings: ecologies of practice across Andean worlds.* Durham: Duke University Press.

Descola, P. (2013). *Beyond nature and culture* (trans: Lloyd, J.). Chicago and London: The University of Chicago Press.

Dodge, M., & Kitchin, R. (2001). *The atlas of cyberspace.* Harlow: Addison-Wesley.

Fish, A. (2018). Points of Presence. Retrieved from screenworks.org.uk/archive/digital-ecologies-and-the-anthropocene/points-of-presence. https://doi.org/10.37186/swrks/8.2/6.

Gabrys, J. (2014). Programming environments: environmentality and citizen sensing in the smart city. *Environment and planning D, 32*(1), 30-48.

Gabrys, J. (2016). *Program earth: Environmental sensing technology and the making of a computational planet.* Minneapolis, MN.: University of Minnesota Press.

Gandy, M. (2005). Cyborg Urbanization: Complexity and Monstrosity in the Contemporary City. *29*(1), 26-49. https://doi.org/10.1111/j.1468-2427.2005.00568.x

Gupta, A. (2012). *Red tape: bureaucracy, structural violence, and poverty in India.* Durham: Duke University Press.

Halpern, O. (2015). *Beautiful data: A history of vision and reason since 1945*. Duke University Press.

Harvey, P., Jensen, C. B., & Morita, A. (2017). *Infrastructures and social complexity: a companion*. London & New York: Routledge, Taylor & Francis Group.

Holbraad, M., & Pedersen, M. A. (2017). *The ontological turn: an anthropological exposition*. Cambridge: Cambridge University Press.

Houser, H. (2014). The Aesthetics of Environmental Visualizations: More Than Information Ecstasy? *Public Culture, 26*(2(73)), 319-337. https://doi.org/10.121 5/08992363-2392084.

Howe, C., & Boyer, D. (2016). Aeolian Extractivism and Community Wind in Southern Mexico. *Public Culture, 28*(2), 215-236.

Hull, M. S. (2012). *Government of paper: the materiality of bureaucracy in urban Pakistan*. Berkeley: University of California Press.

Ingold, T. (2007). *Lines: a brief history*. London: Routledge.

Kirksey, E. (2015). *Emergent ecologies*. Durham: Duke University Press.

Knox, H. (2017). Affective Infrastructures and the Political Imagination. *Public Culture, 29*(2), 363-384.

Knox, H., O'Doherty, D., Vurdubakis, T., & Westrup, C. (2010). The Devil and Customer Relationship Management. *Journal of Cultural Economy, 3*(3), 339-359.

Larkin, B. (2013). The Politics and Poetics of Infrastructure. *Annual review of anthropology, 42*, 327.

Latour, B. (1987). *Science in Action: How to Follow Scientists and Engineers through Society*. Cambridge: Harvard University Press.

Latour, B. (2009). Perspectivism: Type or Bomb? . *Anthropology Today, 25*(2), 21-22.

Latour, B., & Woolgar, S. (1979). *Laboratory Life: The Social Construction of Scientific Fact*. London: Sage.

Marres, N. (2009). Testing Powers of Engagement: Green Living Experiments, the Ontological Turn and the Undoability of Involvement. *European Journal of Social Theory, 12*, 117-134.

Marx, L. (2010). Technology: The emergence of a hazardous concept. *Technology and Culture, 51*(3), 561-577.

Morton, T. (2013). *Hyperobjects: philosophy and ecology after the end of the world*. Minneapolis, MN.: University of Minnesota Press.

Mosco, V. (2004). *The digital sublime: myth, power, and cyberspace*. Cambridge, MA.: The MIT Press.

Pfaffenberger, B. (1992). The Social Anthropology of Technology. *Annual review of anthropology, 21*, 491-516.

Pickles, J. (2004). *A history of spaces: cartographic reason, mapping and the geo-coded world*. London & New York: Routledge.

Scott, J. C. (1998). *Seeing like a state: how certain schemes to improve the human condition have failed*. New Haven, CT. & London: Yale University Press c1998.

Seaver, N. (2018). Captivating algorithms: Recommender systems as traps. *Journal of Material Culture*. https://doi.org/10.1177/1359183518820366.

Starosielski, N. (2015). *The undersea network*. Durham: Duke University Press.

Strathern, M. (1999). *Property, substance and effect: anthropological essays on persons and things*. London: Athlone Press.

Thompson, E. L., & Smith, L. A. (2019). Escape from model-land. *Economics: The Open-Access, Open-Assessment E-Journal, 13*(40), 1-17.

Tsing, A. L. (2015). *The mushroom at the end of the world: on the possibility of life in capitalist ruins*. Princeton: Princeton University Press.

Viveiros de Castro, E. (1998). Cosmological deixis and Amerindian perspectivism. *Journal of the Royal Anthropological Institute, 4*(3), 469-488.

Viveiros de Castro, E. (2004). Exchanging Perspectives: The Transformation of Objects into Subjects in Amerindian Ontologies. *Common Knowledge, 10*(3), 463-484.

Weston, K. (2017). *Animate planet: making visceral sense of living in a high-tech ecologically damaged world*. Durham: Duke University Press.

CHAPTER 13

Charting the Unknown: Tracking the Self, Experimenting with the Digital

Reflection

Minna Ruckenstein

We sit in a circle in a comfortable meeting room—five of the participants in our self-tracking study, two researchers, and a coach—with paper reports in our hands, studying charts of stress and recovery based on our heart-rate variability data. The reports include visualisations in which stress is marked in red and recovery in green. I tell the others that my chart has green recovery bars at exactly the same time each working day: the moment I enter the day-care centre to pick up my daughter. A younger woman observes a red bar indicating stress when she opens her emails in the morning. Another comments that her stress peak, according to the chart, appears to be connected to her excessive beer drinking. We start laughing. The reports have made our bodily behaviours oddly visible. We can discuss everyday events by way of material proofs of physiological reactions. The stress and recovery charts serve as mediators and translators as they bring bodily insights to the surface to be shared with others.

The heart-rate variability measurement device used in our study is one of tens of thousands of devices and applications that have been designed for tracking physiological responses and everyday behaviours. With smart phones and watches, the tracking and measuring of aspects of lived lives, commonly referred to as self-tracking, has become an everyday practice: people use their devices to check on steps taken, hours slept, and distances travelled, a new area of activity

M. Ruckenstein (✉)
University of Helsinki, Helsinki, Finland
e-mail: minna.ruckenstein@helsinki.fi

M. H. Bruun et al. (eds.), *The Palgrave Handbook of the Anthropology of Technology*, https://doi.org/10.1007/978-981-16-7084-8_13

that has also become a vibrant area of interdisciplinary inquiry. Self-tracking can be defined as the utilisation of computational devices that track personal data about physiologies and everyday behaviours in the quest for self-knowledge. In the course of this, people are 'confronted with [their] own personal information', thereby 'engaging in self-surveillance' (Lupton 2016a, p. 103).

We ventured into the study of self-tracking with a participatory research design that shares features with the 'ethno-mining' used for cultural analysis (Anderson et al. 2009), combining the collection and analysis of quantitative data with qualitative data in an iterative framework. Building on earlier collaborative research with Mika Pantzar and Veera Mustonen (Ruckenstein and Pantzar 2015; Pantzar et al. 2017), we documented how self-tracking transforms physiologies into information and feeds it back to people in visual format, enabling, promoting, and intensifying sensory and informational attachments. By following how people discussed their newly visible physiologies, we could demonstrate how, once visualised, the data triggers new kinds of ties between people and their measured actions and reactions (Ruckenstein 2014).

Self-tracking practices are associated with a wide range of activities, including weight measurements, following likes on Instagram, sharing cycling rounds in communities like Strava, observing music-listening habits in Spotify, and engaging in lifelogging practices as art performances. Following our findings, the focus on self-tracking in this chapter mostly concerns the tracking of everyday practices, such as walking, eating, sleeping, and breathing, highlighting active and deliberate, rather than passive and pushed forms of tracking (Lupton 2016a). While passive forms of tracking are at least as important to study as those that are more reflexive, they raise different kinds of research questions. Concomitantly, the practices described in our research would feature other aspects of self-tracking if they were studied in the context of chronic diseases, workplaces, social media, or insurance, underlining the importance of careful analyses of where, how, and on whose initiative tracking takes place.

Research on self-tracking advances the study of the reproduction of everyday techno-relations, highlighting the need to engage empirically with the situational and processual ways in which people and technologies co-construct their everyday conditions and possible futures (Edwards et al. 2010). From this perspective, such exploration speaks to an established theme in anthropology, energising questions of how people make technologies and are made by them, and highlighting the coupling and mutual re-tuning of human subjects and their technological companions (Ingold 2000, pp. 289–419). Self-tracking devices belong to the same cultural universe as weight scales, calendars, diaries, and self-help books, resonating with the quest for self-knowledge and self-improvement, and interpreting and evaluating traces and aspects of the self in relation to categorisations of life-related phenomenon. Yet, despite obvious similarities between earlier self-knowledge techniques and current forms of digital self-tracking—they both promote self-reflection and educate people about who they are and who they should become—the technological mediation offered by self-tracking devices introduces novel features that call for careful analysis. As people are invited to allow self-tracking devices to scan and record their lives, the device, in its materiality, participates in how physiologies and related intimate experiences are perceived.

Anthropological studies have explored engagements with personal data in formats as diverse as CCT scans, reports on heart-rate variability, genetic tests, food diaries, and mood charts (Cohn 2010; Martin 2009; Rapp 2004). Academic research is not immune to being influenced by what is seen as 'new' and 'fashionable', and researchers tend to engage with the most recent data formats available. Emerging technologies, rather than broken and failing ones or those requiring dismantling, thus become a focus of scholarly attention (Jackson 2014); this means that the resulting studies tend to remain ahistorical and at least partly speculative, as has also been the case with work on self-tracking (Swan 2012). Self-tracking has been treated as emblematic of a wider political-economic trend of 'datafication' (van Dijck 2014; Ruckenstein and Schüll 2017), referring to the capacity to gather, store, and analyse large quantities of personal data automatically, and providing the power to transform everyday domains from health and education to advertising and public policy. In this scenario, self-tracking is a clearly defined research object, with users of self-tracking devices serving agendas that benefit corporations and governments by performing unpaid and invisible forms of data labour. Self-tracking practices aid the data-gathering efforts of consumer technology companies that then share or sell the data sets to analytics companies; these, in turn, sort behavioural traces and group users in order to benefit from the insights gained for commercial, political, or societal purposes (Crawford et al. 2015).

Anthropologists have adopted findings from research on datafication, but also pushed back on universalising tendencies, allowing better recognition of which problematic data practices are already in place, which are in the realm of possibility, and which are merely reactions to techno-deterministic hype. The company with which we collaborated in our self-tracking study did not share personal data with third parties, nor did it have an advertising-based business model, reminding us that businesses differ radically in their approaches to datafication. In order to explore a wider range of the agencies and aims at stake, anthropological work on self-tracking benefits from research conducted in the fields of critical data studies, science and technology studies, media and communication, human-computer interaction, post-phenomenology, philosophy of technology, and feminist new materialism. The goal of this chapter is to broaden the research agenda on self-tracking to the point of asking whether it even makes sense to talk about a field of 'self-tracking research'. The alignments of technologies and lived lives call for research engagements that treat 'the self-tracker' not as a stable point of reference but, like life itself, subject to constant change and contestation. Self-tracking studies benefit from a loosening of methodological and theoretical commitments in order to explore self-tracking as 'an unknown' (Dyer 2016) rather than a pre-defined research object or ideological project. One of the strengths of the anthropology of technology is its multi-stability, a quality that facilitates the exploration of the phenomenon under study from contradictory and complementary perspectives. In line with this insight, research into the field of self-tracking will maintain its originality if it finds ways to engage with the different registers and scales that are at play in processes of datafication and everyday techno-engagements.

Towards the Informatics-Behavioural

Self-tracking research highlights how, by engaging with self-tracking devices, the self-tracker is converted into 'a human in the loop'. The data that users generate are processed and fed back to them in digitally mediated feedback loops, with the goal of modelling their conduct. In studying how the self-tracker becomes modified within the human-device loop, researchers have adopted a Foucauldian perspective, emphasising that self-tracking complies with self-optimisation, a form of neoliberal subjectification (Lupton 2016b). As the narrative of neoliberal forces working their way into the inner spheres of life with the aid of self-tracking devices has consolidated in self-tracking research initiatives, anthropologists have witnessed methodologies in the field narrowing into an 'add Foucault and stir' approach. This suggests that the desire to self-optimise is all about urging individuals to govern themselves and increase their entrepreneurial potentialities. Self-tracking devices are marketed as unapologetically neoliberal in their aims: they offer individual productivity and reduction of uncertainty, and treat visibility as a necessity, with not-seeing and not-knowing as states to be avoided and overcome. This identification of bio-political tendencies, coupled with the distillation of neoliberal forces, can limit the scope of research to the degree that studies start to replicate, producing parallel findings (Pols et al. 2019). It does not matter if self-trackers are adolescent girls or senior citizens, they all confirm neoliberal values, including self-responsibilisation, risk-assumption, and a quest for personal productivity.

Importantly, however, the self-responsibilisation thesis fails to address crucial shifts in the way the everyday is made legible and accessible to intervention by means of self-tracking (Lindner 2020). Diverse fields of expertise, from statistics and public health to behavioural economics, social psychology, and sociology, are interested in quantifying aspects of people's lives, often with quite different models and expectations of how life is or should be lived. Moreover, assumptions about behavioural aspects of life are made in fields such as service design and human-computer interaction that aim to respond to individual pursuits of getting value out of personal data encounters. Thus, the vision of life modification promoted by self-tracking operates within a much larger regime than the somatic, a regime defined by Schüll (2016a) as an informatics-behavioural register that is occupied with 'bits of data about the conduct of life'. The imperative of modification is broken down into 'small steps'—termed 'micronudges' (Schüll 2016a) or 'micropractices' (Fotopoulou and O'Riordan 2017)—that involve processes of technological mediation. The 'machine' is in charge of the modification process, while a new vista of the behavioural is provided that can be used as a routine compass to navigate the everyday.

Thus, self-tracking practices incorporate various kinds of processes of objectification and subjectification, framing new possibilities for knowledge formation as well as imperatives for self-exploration and self-improvement (Foucault 1988; Schüll 2019); this roots them in the externalisation of 'nature' as something that people can observe and then transform. With the aid of sensors and devices, people can cast a critical eye over their flawed lives and bodies, and work towards eliminating unwanted or excessive everyday practices and overflowing body parts through diet and exercise. As Viseu and Suchman (2010, p. 163) argue, 'the greater visibility of bodily information implies an associated responsibility to act'. Numbers, typically offered as percentages and charts, are instrumental in transforming personal data into consumable information. Figures make risk estimates seem reliable and actionable as they pin down prescriptive regimes covering nutrition, sleep cycles, genes, and stress and recovery (Ruckenstein 2017).

Yet, while self-tracking amplifies self-surveillance, its punitive dimension is not absolute; people can—and do—end self-initiated self-tracking practices when they feel too invasive. Indeed, focusing on the starting and stopping of device-use provides a way to problematise linear self-tracking effects. Neoliberal goals of self-tracking are rarely fully realised, because the alignment of the body, technology, and everyday aims and experience is neither automatic nor mechanical; rather, it requires care and adjustment (Schwennesen 2019; Will et al. 2020). In taking into account the agentic qualities of devices and algorithms, research can attend to the technical and sensory forces associated with self-tracking that call for engaging with the materialities of data and devices and how they are addressed (Berson 2015; Schwennesen 2019). Devices that operate at the intersections of the body and daily lives are too diverse to posit a degree of internal coherence, calling for a careful assessment of the various ways in which personal data and metrics are learned and inhabited (Fors et al. 2020).

Learning with Quantified Self

In studying engagements with personal data, the Quantified Self (QS) community has served as a learning forum not only for its members but also for ethnographers interested in insights gained through quantification and data analysis (Greenfield 2016; Nafus and Sherman 2014; Sharon 2017; Sharon and Zandbergen 2017). The focus on learning at the QS meetups—exercised rigorously with 'show-and-tell presentations' during which self-trackers narrate their experiments in ten-minute time slots, recounting what they did, how they did it, and what they learned—suggests that data and metrics are never an aim in themselves. Research on QS describes how personal experiences are narrated with 'the companion medium' of data (Smith and Vonthethoff 2017, p. 12).

For their presentations, QS participants count calories and steps, but also tears, smiles, headaches, and pages of novels read, engaging with numbers and charts in an inquiring and open-ended way. Data renders aspects of a 'somewhat inaccessible world of feelings and problems more tangible and comparable' (Sharon and Zandbergen 2017, p. 1705). Narrated numbers and data practices offer a shared language with promises of datasociality, while devices enable 'connective kinwork' (Meneley 2019, p. 147) that brings family members together.

Quantified Self is a 'fringe-group' phenomenon that offers a perspective onto self-tracking that is not directly generalisable to everyday contexts (Didžiokaitė et al. 2018; Pink and Fors 2017); however, the ethnographic work that focuses on 'the exceptional' does offer entry points for thinking about cultural and societal developments, characterised by intense human-technology interactions (Schüll 2019). QS is instructive for exploring how consumer devices and services participate in defining and organising lives in the shorter or longer term (Schüll 2016a), as it queries how devices become or fail to become participants in processes of self-making (Kristensen and Ruckenstein 2018). In light of QS, self-tracking retains creative qualities; it is described as an aesthetic practice in which bits of the self, extracted and abstracted, become material for seeing and experiencing the self in other ways (Sherman 2016). As a temporal experience, self-tracking frees trackers from a sense of fixed identity and opens room for a more emergent 'time-series self' (Schüll 2016b); ultimately QS meetings become safe spaces to exercise 'soft politics' for escaping the commercial and surveillant framings created by the industry (Nafus and Sherman 2014). As Gary Wolf (2016, p. 72), one of the founders of QS, puts it, 'Against BiomedicalTechnoServiceComplex, Inc, the Quantified Self counters with an imitation game, matching—in a kind of handcrafted forgery, and of course at an infinitely slower pace—both internal machines of biology and psychology and external machines of administration and surveillance.'

The notion of mechanical objectivity—a scientific ideal that attained dominance in the mid-nineteenth century and is associated with 'seeing tools' such as cameras or microscopes—has proved fruitful for discussing technologically mediated confrontations with personal data (Daston and Galison 2010; Pantzar and Ruckenstein 2017). Self-tracking devices promote mechanical objectivity by transforming life, in all its ambiguity and messiness, into a 'lived syntax' (Schüll 2019, p. 919): numbers and charts provide a stable frame of reference, detached from subjective forces of knowledge formation. The lived syntax refers to 'the patterns and rhythms' that could 'remain uncertain forces below the threshold of perception' (Schüll 2019, p. 919) without the aid of self-tracking devices. Much like photography, self-tracking devices displace human agency in the production of images of life: visualising heart-rate variability at the exact moment when emails are opened in the morning, for example. In compliance with the notion of mechanical objectivity, personal data converts into results that are seen as accurate, consistent, and dependable. The goal of self-tracking is to obtain automated evidence that is 'uncontaminated by interpretation' (Daston and Galison 2010, p. 139): numbers are meant to offer 'pure' and 'authentic' views of daily behaviours.

Whereas the critique of self-tracking practices can emphasise the reductive and decontextualising effects of quantification—the flattening of the self—ethnographic studies demonstrate that mechanical objectivity is a valued starting point. Mechanical objectivity plays a crucial role in how self-tracking renders bodies and day-to-day life knowable, as people are encouraged to confront their bodies and health states 'predominantly via quantified calculations, predictions and comparisons' (Lupton 2015, p. 449). Yet, once the calculations and comparisons are contextualised in relation to everyday aims, they are evaluated in specific contexts. Nafus and Sherman describe how self-trackers 'traverse between what is inside and outside the body' and 'put things out in the world (software, reminders, routines, and sensors) in order to reflect on, and reorder, what is inside the body (the sensation of energy, mood, or productivity)' (2014, p. 1789).

In some cases, such as when diabetics are measuring blood glucose levels, the accuracy of results is vital. In the everyday, however, it is typically sufficient to have results that are 'accurate enough'. Consequently, we developed the notion of 'situated objectivity' (Pantzar and Ruckenstein 2017) to capture how mechanical objectivity melts in the everyday when knowledge is combined in a selective manner. Self-tracking practices are less occupied with 'facts of life' than with translating and transforming life based on earlier experiences, cultural understandings, and shared expectations. The same numbers and charts are interpreted and exercised in different ways, depending on their personal, social, political, and economic value, and, in some cases, the data revalorise underappreciated and neglected aspects of lived lives (Ruckenstein 2014; Sharon 2015). For instance, in our study we found that some participants reevaluated household tasks, such as ironing and vacuuming, as they realised their beneficial effects in terms of physiological recovery.

In contrast to QS meetings, self-tracking in the everyday tends to lose its status as a distinct practice or a practice that would even matter on its own (Didžiokaitė et al. 2018); tracking and monitoring happen in the background and people often only engage with them episodically or sporadically (Gorm and Shklovski 2019; Pink and Fors 2017). As is typical of many technologies, people do not necessarily use tracking devices and data in the way designers or website developers imagine or intend. They may tinker with devices, use them as tools, tutors, or playful gadgets (Lyall and Robards 2018). They might follow the numbers more eagerly when the charts are developing in the desired direction or, alternatively, downplay or actively ignore them if they fail to conform with intended aims. Research that addresses mundane self-tracking practices and people's inconsistent and ambivalent relationships with the data that devices generate reaches beyond 'avant-garde number crunchers' (Pols et al. 2019, p. 100) and standalone case studies of technology uses, thereby offering contextualisations and comparisons of self-tracking-related practices and lived lives more broadly (Fors et al. 2020). Yet self-tracking might still be a lively and provocative experience. Numbers 'act back', leading to effects and frictions in people's lives (Pols et al. 2019); in light of the numbers they generate, bodies can appear unruly and out of control, while numbers might make no sense at all. Tracking devices are participants and companions of lived lives as long as they are needed and feel competent; otherwise, they are forgotten, broken, or lost.

Cultivating Metric Awareness

Self-tracking devices operate as 'epistemology engines' (Van Den Eede 2015, p. 151) that transport machinic classifications of human ways of categorising, knowing, and responding into lived life. This means that specific monitoring devices and the data they generate shape assumptions of knowing, further linking to research on how various kinds of data are used in the construction of knowledge forms and knowledge spaces (Ruppert et al. 2013). Self-tracking, in all its variations, can be seen as an infinite source of raw material for governments and companies, but also as a counter-movement that aims to know and make visible the uses, purposes, and politics of data (Klauser and Albrechtslund 2014; Ruckenstein and Pantzar 2017). In order to query data uses, research on self-tracking calls for including the data that the devices produce in the ethnographic mix. Undoubtedly, the methodological strength of our own study lay in the self-tracking practices that taught us how metrics open up everyday activities for observation. We could engage first hand with the data visualisations that offered a format to discuss the lived syntax of daily lives.

Individual self-tracking data can be further aggregated to discuss processes beyond the individual: to identify collective patterns that have to do with health, everyday mobilities, time use, and environmental exposure (Nafus 2019). Inspired by rhythm analysis, we focused on collective rhythms of the heart, noting that the 'heart' and the 'mouth' disagreed about the experience of stress and recovery (Pantzar et al. 2017). By combining computational and ethnographic approaches, anthropologists can bring what are often treated as opposites into productive tension: objectifying life with metrics and carefully navigating social worlds by means of ethnographic inquiry (Blok and Pedersen 2014; Pretnar and Podjed 2018; Munk 2019). An influential aspect of the data generated by self-tracking devices is the possibility they offer to transcend and bypass familiar ways of approaching bodies and lives; technologies can become a resource for 'data feminism', for example, raising inspection issues related to various inequalities (D'Ignazio and Klein 2020). By actively using personal data streams as part of research designs, anthropologists can contrast and move between human and machine categorisations, experiment with quantitative and qualitative approaches, learn to mix them with care, and overcome the preset and the normative in order to learn new ways to conceptualise familiar existences (Blok and Pedersen 2014; Ruckenstein 2019). For instance, this can allow areas of life that are typically not included in the health field, such as spending money or loneliness, to be tracked, with the data validating the health-generating qualities of such investigation.

Using self-tracking data in research design can mean that researchers need to collaborate with technology companies, as was the case in our study. Reflexive and critical accounts of researchers' involvements with device manufacture and data analytics companies continue to be of great interest for research on self-tracking because they can highlight the social, commercial, and political underpinnings of technology development. They also promote down-to-earth perspectives on how technology companies—in the course of affecting and shaping people's daily lives and futures—interpret, design, and aim to transform those lives (Cefkin 2010). In order to unpack how norms and assumptions regarding gender, age, or ethnicity get encoded into data technology, self-tracking research has examined how designers and design processes imagine potential users and work to modify and intervene in their behaviour (Lupton 2015; Viseu and Suchman 2010). Drawing on research conducted among technology developers and marketers of personal health technology, Schüll (2016a) considers how they design algorithmic care into their products in order to assist and reinforce chosen behaviours. She detects a thermostat-like logic in their designs, which actively regulate users via automated prompts such as taps and buzzes to make the recommended daily choices. Similarly, Berg (2017, p. 6) observes how designers of wearables approach users 'as vulnerable beings in need of assistance, advice, and actionable guidance'. With research uncovering the designer assumption that human senses alone cannot handle the insecurities of daily lives, we get a view of how algorithmic practices aim for the interpenetration of technological and human forces and agencies. Digital devices seek an insider position; rather than remaining at the borders they enter the everyday, scouting and browsing it: 'the market sees you from within, measuring your body and emotional states, and watching as you move around your house, the office, or the mall,' as Fourcade and Healy (2017, p. 23) express it. Schüll (2018), on the other hand, presents a vision of 'frictionless living' that guides technology designers in their aims 'to gratify us before we know our desires'. She argues that such closeness with commercial devices can corrode our self-critical capacities and individualise us to the degree that the social becomes decomposed.

Cultivating a metrics-aware attitude includes discussing the limitations of metrics and countermeasures on the grounds of negative and unintended consequences. The study of measurers and their defining and predictive logics is not new—think of audit culture (Strathern 2000)—but it is an increasingly timely undertaking. Credit scoring, hiring practices, allocation of social benefits, social media engagement, health care diagnostics, and student evaluations now rely on algorithmic logics. Algorithmic sorting culture leans on predefined categories and controls, with limited possibilities for those measured to review and challenge them (DuFault and Schouten 2020). Findings from self-tracking research that focus on its voluntary and reflective forms can be contrasted and compared with self-tracking practices, adopted as tools of utilitarian health promotion at schools or in workplaces, and used to pressure or shame overweight workers or inactive pupils (Depper and Howe 2017). The diverse tracking contexts underline that metrics do not speak of or to the same life; on the one hand, tracking applications can approach people as though they are Pavlov's dogs or human cattle, yet other uses open reflexive spaces that not only encourage people to share aspects of their lives but allow more profound epistemological questioning. In the mental health field, for instance, participatory therapeutic interventions can allow the formulation of individual aims: young people set their own goals and choose what they track, if anything.

Self-tracking research emphasises the importance of carefully following the contextual uses of digital data and data analytics and casts doubt on universal claims about technologised futures. With their sensitivity to the liminal and in-between, ethnographers are well equipped to grasp the deep ambiguities of numbers and metrics. Metrics operate between technology and life, and by exploring situational and processual practices, ethnographers can trace the work of algorithmic powers but also reach beyond them. With a focus on questions of value and related transformations and conversions, rehearsed in the context of self-tracking, ethnographers can continue to uncover partial, selective, and indecisive ways in which metrics are put to use. Having liveable relations with algorithmic systems and metrics suggests that we need to know them as intimately as dedicated self-trackers do.

Knowing and Sensing Devices

By taking a heart-rate variability monitoring device as the centrepiece of our research, we had to take the demands and operations of the monitoring device for granted, not only recognising but also obeying its agentic qualities. Due to the nature of the device, our research participants had to be in good health, with no chronic illnesses or regular medication use. For instance, with asthma medication, the device might not analyse the heart-rate variability data correctly, suggesting that the device had a role in selecting medication-free study participants. Since we had no access to the technical features of the proprietary algorithms used for tracking the research participants' physiologies and classifying and sorting information for visualisations of stress and recovery, we had to accept the algorithmic models underlying the data gathering and analysis. This kind of 'black boxed' (Pasquale 2015) engagement, one of not knowing the kind of information with which we were dealing, emphasised our outsider position. We could not explore how technology was algorithmically reorganising the organic (Stiegler 1998, p. 85), but merely follow its aftermath.

As we discussed the reports compiled from the charts of physiological stress and recovery, we made clear to our research participants that we could not evaluate the scientific accuracy or truthfulness of the heart-rate variability data and that we were as clueless as they were when the device failed to record and analyse the data. With one of the participants, the data were so inaccurate and lacking that it made no sense to include him in the group discussion about the results of the tracking period; it was a very uncomfortable moment to have to exclude a participant because of the unsuccessful operations of a technological device. Later, we discovered that data gathering had probably failed because of the participant's hairy chest; the sensors could not read the measurements because the electrodes were not in contact with his skin.

We know from other studies that self-monitoring devices and mobile health applications and services, including the data that they generate, often fail to engage people (Lazar et al. 2015). In our study, however, the device-centric research design ensured dedicated participation, as the device promised to respond to participants' questions and expectations. They were after a device-specific view of their lives and were energised and moved by the agentic qualities of the device. For them, the device and the data that it generates represented a potential change-agent; some openly yearned for an external motivator that would persuade and nudge them. Schüll (2016a, p. 328) defines the nudge as a 'curious mechanism' that both presupposes and pushes against personal autonomy: 'it assumes a choosing subject, but one who is constitutionally ill equipped to make rational, healthy choices.' Our research participants were eager to be pushed and nudged, to learn about the temporalities and rhythms of their lives in order to be persuaded to sleep, work, and exercise better. Indeed, at times their questions were unrealistically precise: one of the participants wanted to learn about the physiological effects of a certain recovery drink which he consumed after sessions of vigorous exercise.

By using the heart-rate variability monitoring device, our research participants not only agreed to the translation of their physiologies into data and visualisations, they also expected the materialisations of their physiological processes to act on them by interrupting their unreflexive and routinised practices. Their goals aligned—at least initially—with the goals of the device. As Pols, Willems, and Aanestad (2019, p. 101) argue, this kind of alignment is crucial for frictionless engagement with devices, as it provides tools for 'self-induced nudging into self-prioritised activities'. The limitations of self-induced nudging might, however, become obvious in the course of practising self-tracking. One of the participants of our study realised that technologies are persuasive only if those who use them can respond to such persuasion: she concluded that she was not one of them.

The mutual constitution of the knowing self and the agentic qualities of the device underline how subjective feelings and communicative possibilities emerge in connection with the use of digital technologies (Lomborg and Frandsen 2016). The tracked phenomenon, whether sleep, exercise, or stress, is guided and formatted according to the classificatory and procedural logic of the device. Most digital pedometers are programmed with a daily target of 10,000 steps, suggesting novel walking practices that centre on that particular step count. As expectations of normality and health are inscribed in tracking devices' target numbers, scores, and incentives, a 'numerical ontology' (Oxlund 2012, p. 53) shapes everyday practices and bodily relations. Pedometer users can cherish the steps taken and develop a more affective relationship to step counts. The monitoring of the quality of sleep through heart-rate variability measurements can deepen caring relations with one's sleeping body. When tracked, sleeping becomes an activity, even a competence, that people can feel that they are good at. Technologies assist in increasing the consciousness of one's agentic capabilities and heighten awareness of mundane everyday doings (Kristensen and Ruckenstein 2018), meaning that self-tracking might be a way to learn what one already knows, but in an embodied and unreflective manner (Fors et al. 2020).

Devices offer sensing support, but they might also engender sensory experiences. With its look of a medical device, the design of the hearth-rate variability monitor used in our study appeared somewhat outdated in relation to the most cutting-edge consumer devices. Indeed, one of the participants mentioned that the two electrodes taped on to the skin of the chest made her feel as if she had escaped from a hospital, although her awareness soon shifted to the sensing of her everyday doings they provided. In their ethnography of hypoglycaemia, Mol and Law (2004, p. 48) discuss how the uses of measurement devices 'train inner sensitivity' to blood glucose levels, promoting what they call 'introsensing' that links certain figures to bodily sensing of levels that are too high or low. 'The data', Neff and Nafus (2016, p. 75) argue, 'become a "prosthetic of feeling", something to help us sense our bodies or the world around us.' Pink and Fors (2017, p. 376) note that self-tracking mediates 'people's tacit ways of being in the world', promoting an awareness of mind-body in the environment. The increased responsiveness in terms of sensory impact—the felt effects of eating, stress, or exercise—can generate 'sharpening of the senses' or the 'production of new senses' (Kristensen and Ruckenstein 2018, p. 9).

Fuzzy Data Doubles

When describing processes that abstract and slice 'the self' into various kinds of data flows with which people can engage, I have suggested that self-tracking enables the making of 'data doubles' that can give rise to reflection and be used for the purposes of knowledge formation (Ruckenstein 2014). The widely acknowledged definition of the data double originates from the field of surveillance studies: Haggerty and Ericson (2000, p. 606) refer to operations that first abstract human bodies by separating them into various data flows or streams and then reassemble them into data doubles to be analysed and targeted for intervention. In line with this earlier research, the data accumulated through self-tracking devices create a double that mirrors, reflects, and mediates aspects of the everyday. Pols et al. (2019) suggest that data doubles are 'look-alikes of the selves collecting them … selves turned into numbers that specify, intensify, moralise and attempt to make predictable' (p. 110). My goal was to use the concept to illustrate how technologies offer partial vistas of people's lives, 'slices of life' that become part of processes of knowledge formation; the visualisation that I particularly had in mind when thinking about data doubles was the chart presented to study participants illustrating their heart-rate variability data. The data double makes tangible what heart-rate variability says about stress and recovery.

Bode and Kristensen (2015) rightly point out the problems with using the notion of data double in a fuzzy metaphorical way, equating it with an artefact, data, or visualisation without a clear definition. They note that it can lead to the assumption that the reassembled data and its visualisation have qualities irrespective of the engagement with the person as the data source. The reification of the concept of data double leads to an analytical failure to address the relationality that is crucial to it: data doubles are part of the person as well as of the process of creating the double. Thus, research on self-tracking has corrected the epistemological flattening of the data double by paying attention to the co-evolution of people, data, and their devices (Kristensen and Ruckenstein 2018). Exploring forms of agencies that are generated in human-nonhuman assemblages offers further support for thinking about the intra-action that characterises engagements with personal data (Lupton 2019).

It is still useful, however, to think of how decorporealised data streams participate in processes of knowledge formation. As people contemplate the value they supply to the charts and figures depicting physiological reactions to various stimuli, they learn 'things' of which they may have been previously unaware. Even if personal data are produced and felt in human-device assemblages, users reflect on the potentialities, challenges, and limitations of the devices themselves as they live with and through them. Self-tracking amplifies certain aspects of the self, rather than others, reminding us of the biases and limitations inscribed into technological mediations. Long-term ethnographic engagements are particularly well-suited to exploring lively and shifting self-tracking practices, underlining that data encounters are emergent and unstable in their goals, and characterised by diffuse processes of power and affective entanglements. Experiences of self-tracking are shaped by how aware people are—or become—of ways in which tracking devices encourage or discourage them to perform in certain modes. They experiment with applications and devices, start somewhere, explore themselves from a new perspective, and come out of the experience with some lessons learned. Over time, self-tracking can either develop into a less remarkable part of everyday routine or become associated with alienation, frustration, and time-wasting. Consequently, some devices are abandoned, while others support newly formed or prevailing habits and routines.

Beyond Self-Tracking

Self-tracking research has served as an entry point to studying ways in which advanced technologies are enabling and pushing forward developments that merge people and technologies, both in the present and in imagined futures. The studies reviewed in this chapter are instructive of how a research topic dismantles itself: it should be obvious by now that self-tracking involves many different kinds of practices and that it should not be treated as a pre-defined or unified category. Walking, cycling, sleeping, and breathing are recorded by technologies attached to the body, but they point in different directions in terms of how they matter in the everyday. As digital devices latch onto people's bodies and minds and follow their daily reactions, the line between the organic and the non-organic is permanently blurred. Algorithmic processes do not treat the everyday evenly; rather, they focus on those aspects of lived lives that can be computationally addressed. Some aspects of the self and daily comportment are accentuated and amplified, while others are reduced and restricted. Research with avant-garde number crunchers suggests that a certain kind of expansion of life is possible for those who have access to self-tracking technology and can use it in a way that enables them to flourish. The intertwining of advanced technology with daily lives suggests the advent of an everyday cyborg, with the skills to manipulate and become inspired by life and its conditions of existence (Scheldeman 2010). Yet, without appropriate resources, skills, or aims, technologies can incapacitate, disable, and even make us less human: instead of the reflective self-tracker, we witness the reduced human, 'a human algorithm', controlled by machinic classifications.

Current research has some obvious gaps that call for more investigation. Studies have mainly focused on the affluent and educated, and more work needs to be done on lower-income and culturally marginalised individuals and communities (Peake 2015). Widening the geographical frame would also challenge device-centric and individualistic studies of self-tracking by offering insights into tracking-related practices more broadly, while contextualising practices that tracking devices tend to isolate. As Meneley (2019) argues, reflecting on her own walking practices in Palestine, 'Fitbit does not really care where you take these steps' (p. 134). We need more studies that query how people live, or do not live, with metrics; for example, forms of self-surveillance for the sake of self-discovery, wellness, and personal achievement are not equally available, or even rational to all, and self-tracking can appear absurd, irrelevant, or even dangerous in some places.

Within the interdisciplinary field of research on self-tracking, anthropologists have a key role in expanding the future research agenda and opening new paths forward. The range and variety of potential research directions underline that self-tracking devices transform everyday practices that have to do with health, education, insurance, personal finances, and media use. Research engagements with self-tracking can focus on the patterned nature of everyday practices; explore conceptualisations of physiologies and body parts in digital culture; raise questions about the tendency of technologies to decompose the social; demonstrate the emotional, social, and political value of data; illustrate attempts to control and optimise uncertainties in life; and study the ecological wastefulness of consumer technologies, among many other topics. Ultimately, self-tracking-related research deals with the long-standing question: What and how is human? Technologies shape assumptions and promises of life, connecting anthropological research to ways in which specific devices and algorithms are part of processes whereby the human is extended, reduced, inspired, and overpowered. Rather than promising unambiguous and direct answers, the anthropology of technology offers empirical and methodological support for mapping fields that are complex, uncertain, and constantly on the move, while its approaches provide a site for epistemic work aimed at developing concepts, modes of interaction, and directions for future research into the impact of technology on the human lifeworld.

Acknowledgements My self-tracking research has been deeply influenced by collaboration with Dorthe Brogård Kristensen, Mika Pantzar, and Natasha Dow Schüll. I am grateful to have had such brilliant scholars as companions in this journey. The research network on self-tracking and autonomised bodies with Martin Berg, Vaike Fors, Deborah Lupton, and Sarah Pink has offered further inspiration and valuable ideas on how to expand the scope of self-tracking research.

REFERENCES

Anderson, K., Nafus, D., Rattenbury, T., & Aipperspach, R. (2009). Numbers have qualities too: Experiences with ethno-mining. *Ethnographic Praxis in Industry Conference Proceedings, 1,* 123–140. https://doi.org/10.1111/j.1559-8918.2009.tb00133.x.

Berg, M. (2017). Making sense with sensors: Self-tracking and the temporalities of wellbeing. *Digital Health, 3,* 1–11. https://doi.org/10.1177/2055207617699767.

Berson, J. (2015). *Computable Bodies: Instrumented Life and the Human Somatic Niche.* London: Bloomsbury Academic.

Blok, A., & Pedersen, M. A. (2014). Complementary social science? Quali-quantitative experiments in a Big Data world. *Big Data & Society 1*(2), 1–6. https://doi.org/10.1177/2053951714543908.

Bode, M., & Kristensen, D. B. (2015). The digital doppelgänger within: A study on self-tracking and the quantified self movement. In R. Canniford, & D. Bajde (Eds.), *Assembling Consumption* (pp. 119–134). London: Routledge.

Cefkin, M. (Ed.) (2010). *Ethnography and the Corporate Encounter: Reflections on Research in and of Corporations.* Studies in Public and Applied Anthropology. Vol. 5. Brooklyn, NY: Berghahn Books.

Cohn, S. (2010). Picturing the brain inside, revealing the illness outside: A comparison of the different meanings attributed to brain scans by scientists and patients. In J. Edwards, P. Harvey, and P. Wade (Eds.), *Technologized Images, Technologized Bodies* (pp. 65–84). Brooklyn, NY: Berghahn Books.

Crawford, K., Lingel, J., & Karppi, T. (2015). Our metrics, ourselves: A hundred years of self-tracking from the weight scale to the wrist wearable device. *European Journal of Cultural Studies, 18*(4–5), 479–496. https://doi.org/10.1177/1367549415584857.

Daston, L., & Galison, P. (2010). *Objectivity.* Brooklyn, NY: Zone Books.

Depper, A., & Howe, P. D. (2017). Are we fit yet? English adolescent girls' experiences of health and fitness apps. *Health Sociology Review 26*(1), 98–112. https://doi.org/10.1080/14461242.2016.1196599.

Didžiokaitė, G., Saukko, P., & Greiffenhagen, C. (2018). The mundane experience of everyday calorie trackers: Beyond the metaphor of Quantified Self. *New Media & Society, 20*(4), 1470–1487. https://doi.org/10.1177/1461444817698478.

D'Ignazio, C., & Klein, L. F. (2020). *Data feminism.* Cambridge, MA: The MIT Press.

DuFault, B. L., & Schouten, J. W. (2020). Self-quantification and the datapreneurial consumer identity. *Consumption Markets & Culture, 23*(3), 290–316. https://doi.org/10.1080/10253866.2018.1519489.

Dyer, J. (2016) Quantified bodies: A design practice. *Digital Culture & Society. 2*(1), 161-168.

Edwards, J., Harvey, P., & Wade, P. (2010). Technologized images, technologized bodies. In J. Edwards, P. Harvey, & P. Wade (Eds.), *Technologized Images, technologized bodies* (pp. 1–35). Brooklyn, NY: Berghahn Books.

Fors, V., Pink, S., Berg, M., & O'Dell, T. (2020). *Imagining Personal Data: Experiences of Self-Tracking.* London: Routledge.

Fotopoulou, A., & O'Riordan, K. (2017). Training to self-care: fitness tracking, biopedagogy and the healthy consumer. *Health Sociology Review, 26*(1), 54–68. https://doi.org/10.1080/14461242.2016.1184582.

Foucault, M. (1988). Technologies of the Self. In L. H. Martin, H. Gutman, & P. H. Hutton (Eds.), *Technologies of the Self: A Seminar with Michel Foucault* (pp. 16–49). Amherst, MA: University of Massachusetts Press.

Fourcade, M., & Healy, K. (2017). Seeing like a market. *Socio-Economic Review, 15*(1), 9–29. https://doi.org/10.1093/ser/mww033.

Gorm, N., & Shklovski, I. (2019). Episodic use: Practices of care in self-tracking. *New Media & Society, 21*(11–12), 2505–2521. https://doi.org/10.1177/1461444819851239.

Greenfield, D. (2016). Deep Data: Notes on the n of 1. In D. Nafus (Ed.), *Quantified: Biosensing Technologies in Everyday Life* (pp. 123–146). Cambridge, MA: The MIT Press.

Haggerty, K. D., & Ericson, R. V. (2000). The surveillant assemblage. *British Journal of Sociology, 51*(4), 605–622. https://doi.org/10.1080/00071310020015280.

Ingold, T. (2000). *The Perception of the Environment: Essays on Livelihood, Dwelling and Skill.* London: Routledge.

Jackson, S. J. (2014). Rethinking repair. In T. Gillespie, P. J. Boczkowski, & K. A. Foot (Eds.), *Media Technologies: Essays on Communication, Materiality, and Society* (pp. 221–240). Cambridge, MA: The MIT Press.

Klauser, F. R., & Albrechtslund, A. (2014). From self-tracking to smart urban infrastructures: Towards an interdisciplinary research agenda on Big Data. *Surveillance & Society, 12*(2), 273–86. https://doi.org/10.24908/ss.v12i2.4605.

Kristensen, D. B., & Ruckenstein, M. (2018). Co-evolving with self-tracking technologies. *New Media & Society, 20*(10), 3624–3640. https://doi.org/10.1177/1461444818755650.

Lazar, A., Koehler, C., Tanenbaum, J., & Nguyen, D. H. (2015). Why we use and abandon smart devices. Conference paper. *Proceedings of the 2015 ACM International Joint Conference on Pervasive and Ubiquitous Computing* (pp. 635–646).

Lindner, P. (2020). Molecular Politics, Wearables, and the Aretaic Shift in Biopolitical Governance. *Theory, Culture & Society, 37*(3), 71–96. https://doi.org/10.1177/0263276419894053.

Lomborg, S. & Frandsen, K. (2016). Self-tracking as communication. *Information, Communication & Society, 19*(7), 1015–1027. https://doi.org/10.1080/1369118X.2015.1067710.

Lupton, D. (2015). Quantified sex: a critical analysis of sexual and reproductive self-tracking using apps. *Culture, Health & Sexuality, 17*(4), 440–453. https://doi.org/10.1080/13691058.2014.920528.

Lupton, D. (2016a). The diverse domains of quantified selves: self-tracking modes and dataveillance. *Economy and Society, 45*(1), 101–122.

Lupton, D. (2016b). *The Quantified Self: A Sociology of Self-Tracking*. Cambridge, MA: Polity Press.

Lupton, D. (2019). *Data selves: More-than-human perspectives*. Cambridge, MA: Polity Press.

Lyall, B., & Robards, B. (2018). Tool, toy and tutor: Subjective experiences of digital self-tracking. *Journal of Sociology, 54*(1), 108–124. https://doi.org/10.1177/1440783317722854.

Martin, E. (2009). *Bipolar Expeditions: Mania and Depression in American Culture*. Princeton, NJ: Princeton University Press.

Meneley, A. (2019). Walk This Way: Fitbit and Other Kinds of Walking in Palestine. *Cultural Anthropology, 34*(1), 130–154. https://doi.org/10.14506/ca34.1.11.

Mol, A., & Law, J. (2004). Embodied Action, Enacted Bodies: The Example of Hypoglycaemia. *Body & Society, 10*(2–3), 43–62. https://doi.org/10.1177/1357034X04042932.

Munk, A. K. (2019). Four styles of quali-quantitative analysis: Making sense of the new Nordic food movement on the web. *Nordicom Review, 40*(s1), 159–176. https://doi.org/10.2478/nor-2019-0020.

Nafus, D., & Sherman, J. (2014). This One Does Not Go Up to 11: The Quantified Self Movement as an Alternative Big Data Practice. *International Journal of Communication, 8*, 1784–1794.

Nafus, D. (2019). Data Aggregation as Social Relations: Making Datasets from Self-Tracking Data. European Review, *27*(3), 440–454.

Neff, G., & Nafus, D. (2016). *Self-tracking*. Cambridge, MA: The MIT Press.

Oxlund, B. (2012). Living by numbers: The dynamic interplay of asymptomatic conditions and low cost measurement technologies in the cases of two women in the Danish provinces. *Suomen Antropologi, 37*(3), 42–56.

Pantzar, M., & Ruckenstein, M. (2017). Living the metrics: Self-tracking and situated objectivity. *Digital Health, 3*, 1–10. https://doi.org/10.1177/2055207617712590.

Pantzar, M., Ruckenstein, M., & Mustonen, V. (2017). Social rhythms of the heart. *Health Sociology Review, 26*(1), 22–37. https://doi.org/10.1080/1446124 2.2016.1184580.

Pasquale, F. (2015). *The Black Box Society: The Secret Algorithms That Control Money and Information*. Cambridge, MA: Harvard University Press.

Peake, B. (2015, April 21). Decolonizing design anthropology with Tinn. *The CASTAC blog*. http://blog.castac.org/2015/04/designing-tinn/. Accessed 17 September 2020.

Pink, S., & Fors, V. (2017). Being in a mediated world: self-tracking and the mind–body–environment. *Cultural Geographies, 24*(3), 375–388. https://doi.org/10.1177/1474474016684127.

Pols, J., Willems, D., & Aanestad, M. (2019). Making sense with numbers. Unravelling ethico-psychological subjects in practices of self-quantification. *Sociology of Health & Illness, 41*(S1), 98–115. https://doi.org/10.1111/1467-9566.12894.

Pretnar, A., & Podjed, D. (2018). Data Mining Workspace Sensors: A New Approach to Anthropology. Conference paper. Conference on Language Technologies & Digital Humanities Ljubljana (pp. 227–233). https://e-knjige.ff.uni-lj.si/

znanstvena-zalozba/catalog/download/120/214/3104- 1?inline=1. Accessed 17 September 2020.

Rapp, R. (2004). *Testing Women, Testing the Fetus: The Social Impact of Amniocentesis in America*. London: Routledge.

Ruckenstein, M. (2014). Visualized and Interacted Life: Personal Analytics and Engagements with Data Doubles. *Societies, 4*(1), 68–84. https://doi.org/10.3390/soc4010068.

Ruckenstein, M. (2017). Keeping data alive: Talking DTC genetic testing. *Information, Communication & Society*, 20(7), 1024–1039. https://doi.org/10.1080/1369118X.2016.1203975.

Ruckenstein, M. (2019). Tracing medicinal agencies: Antidepressants and life-effects. *Social Science & Medicine*, 235, 112368. https://doi.org/10.1016/j.socscimed.2019.112368.

Ruckenstein, M., & Pantzar, M. (2015). Datafied Life: Techno-Anthropology as a Site for Exploration and Experimentation. *Techné: Research in Philosophy and Technology*, 19(2), 191–210. https://doi.org/10.5840/techne20159935.

Ruckenstein, M., & Pantzar, M. (2017). Beyond the Quantified Self: Thematic exploration of a dataistic paradigm. *New Media & Society*, 19(3), 401–418. https://doi.org/10.1177/1461444815609081.

Ruckenstein, M., & Schüll, N. D. (2017). The Datafication of Health. *Annual Review of Anthropology*, 46, 261–278. https://doi.org/10.1146/annurev-anthro-102116-041244.

Ruppert, E., Law, J., & Savage, M. (2013). Reassembling Social Science Methods: The Challenge of Digital Devices. *Theory, Culture & Society*, 30(4), 22–46. https://doi.org/10.1177/0263276413484941.

Scheldeman, G. (2010). Technokids? Insulin pumps incorporated in young people's bodies and lives. In J. Edwards, P. Harvey, & P. Wade (Eds.), *Technologized Images, Technologized Bodies* (pp. 137–160). Brooklyn, NY: Berghahn Books.

Schüll, N. D. (2016a). Data for life: Wearable technology and the design of self-care. *BioSocieties, 11*(3), 317–333. https://doi.org/10.1057/biosoc.2015.47.

Schüll, N. D. (2016b). Sensor technology and the time-series self. *Continent, 5*(1), 24–29.

Schüll, N. D. (2018, October 31). The Sense Mother. Theorizing the Contemporary. *Fieldsights*. https://culanth.org/fieldsights/the-sense-mother. Accessed 17 September 2020.

Schüll, N.D. (2019) The data-based self: Self-quantification and the data-driven (good) life. *Social Research, 86(4)*, 909–930.

Schwennesen, N. (2019). Algorithmic assemblages of care: imaginaries, epistemologies and repair work. *Sociology of Health & Illness*, 41(S1), 176–192. https://doi.org/10.1111/1467-9566.12900.

Sharon, T. (2015). Healthy citizenship beyond autonomy and discipline: Tactical engagements with genetic testing. *BioSocieties, 10*(3), 295–316. https://doi.org/10.1057/biosoc.2014.29.

Sharon, T. (2017). Self-Tracking for Health and the Quantified Self: Re-Articulating Autonomy, Solidarity, and Authenticity in an Age of Personalized Healthcare. *Philosophy & Technology*, 30(1), 93–121. https://doi.org/10.1007/s13347-016-0215-5.

Sharon, T., & Zandbergen, D. (2017). From data fetishism to quantifying selves: Self-tracking practices and the other values of data. *New Media & Society*, 19(11), 1695–1709. https://doi.org/10.1177/1461444816636090.

Sherman, J. (2016). Data in the Age of Digital Reproduction: Reading the Quantified Self through Walter Benjamin. In D. Nafus (Ed.), *Quantified: Biosensing Technologies in Everyday Life* (pp. 27–42). Cambridge, MA: The MIT Press.

Smith, G. J. D., & Vonthethoff, B. (2017). Health by numbers? Exploring the practice and experience of datafied health. *Health Sociology Review, 26*(1), 6–21. https://doi.org/10.1080/14461242.2016.1196600.

Stiegler, B. (1998). *Technics and Time, 1: The Fault of Epimetheus.* Stanford, CA: Stanford University Press.

Strathern, M. (Ed.) (2000). *Audit Cultures. Anthropological Studies in Accountability, Ethics and the Academy.* London: Routledge.

Swan, M. (2012). Sensor mania! The Internet of Things, Wearable Computing, Objective Metrics, and the Quantified Self 2.0. *Journal of Sensor and Actuator Networks, 1*(3), 217–253. https://doi.org/10.3390/jsan1030217.

Van Den Eede, Y. (2015). Tracing the Tracker: A Postphenomenological Inquiry into Self-Tracking Technologies. In R. Rosenberger & P. P. Verbeek (Eds.), *Postphenomenological Investigations: Essays on Human–Technology Relations* (pp. 143–158). Lanham, MD: Lexington Books.

van Dijck, J. (2014). Datafication, dataism and dataveillance: Big Data between scientific paradigm and ideology. *Surveillance & Society, 12*(2), 197–208. https://doi.org/10.24908/ss.v12i2.4776.

Viseu, A., & Suchman, L. (2010). Wearable augmentations: Imaginaries of the informed body. In J. Edwards, P. Harvey, & P. Wade (Eds.), *Technologized Images, Technologized Bodies* (pp. 161–184). Brooklyn, NY: Berghahn Books.

Will, C. M., Henwood, F., Weiner, K., & Williams, R. (2020). Negotiating the practical ethics of 'self-tracking' in intimate relationships: Looking for care in healthy living. *Social Science & Medicine, 266*, 113301. https://doi.org/10.1016/j.socscimed.2020.113301.

Wolf, G. (2016). The Quantified Self: Reverse Engineering. In D. Nafus (Ed.), *Quantified: Biosensing Technologies in Everyday Life* (pp. 67–78). Cambridge, MA: The MIT Press.

CHAPTER 14

Data, Knowledge Practices, and Naturecultural Worlds: Vehicle Emissions in the Anthropocene

Observation

Lindsay Poirier

Standing at the heart of the US capital city amidst a sea of March for Science protesters on 22 April 2017, the rain had soaked through my jacket. For a protest with over 100,000 people in attendance, it was an oddly anti-social (though not dispassionate) event; looking towards the speaker stage, I could see little more than rows of soaked hoods and iPhones emerging above multi-coloured umbrellas, trying to snap photos of scientific superstars like Dr Michael Mann and Bill Nye. I was attending the march with my cousin Robert—a geologist—and his family. We both care deeply about the preservation of climate data and evidence-based decision making. Robert studies climate variability and sea-level change over thousands of years by examining rock sediments and fossil corals from deep in the Earth. As an anthropologist of data infrastructure and culture, prior to the event I had been getting involved to the extent that I could with the Environmental Data Governance Initiative (EDGI)—a group of researchers, practitioners, and activists convening to plan and execute guerrilla archiving efforts to safeguard environmental data from deletion by the Trump administration.

As a diverse array of speakers shared thoughts on the importance of advancing and advocating on behalf of science, it became clear that the stakes for generating and disseminating robust data about environmental health were

L. Poirier (✉)
Smith College, Northampton, MA, USA
e-mail: lpoirier@smith.edu

M. H. Bruun et al. (eds.), *The Palgrave Handbook of the Anthropology of Technology*, https://doi.org/10.1007/978-981-16-7084-8_14

high. I got emotional as Dr Mona Hanna-Attisha—the paediatrician who exposed heightened blood lead levels in children after they had been poisoned by lead-contaminated drinking water in Flint, MI, in 2015—described how 'science spoke truth to power'. I was starstruck as Dr Mann detailed his work devising the hockey stick graph in the 1990s. I *also* felt unsettled by rhetoric that data alone should drive environmental regulation. It was not only the re-appropriation of derogatory memes such as were seen in protest signs exclaiming 'Grab 'em by the data';[1] it was also the counterpoising of data against partisanship, of empiricism against bias. Encountering protest signs stating, 'We want scientific data, not alternative facts', I did not disagree but grimaced, a signal of how my own relationship with environmental governance data can be best characterised as ambivalent. Quantitative data about our anthropogenic world are indispensable; they are also at least partially mediated by cultural forces that prioritise profit and technological progress over environmental health equity.

Over a decade after Chris Anderson (2008) claimed that 'the data deluge makes the scientific method obsolete', there has been bubbling scepticism in many governance communities over the hype of big data in knowledge production and decision making.[2] In the environmental health domain—a domain that has been 'informating' (Fortun 2004) since the 1980s—widespread expert recognition of how uncertainty and estimation figure centrally in the measurement of natural worlds predates Anderson's claims. In environmental health, researchers and policy makers time and again confront how anthropogenic history is being rewritten through new data and revised models, and how (much like the ecological systems constantly transforming under human feet, and around and through human bodies) the knowledge we have about our anthropogenic worlds is also constantly transforming in response to scientific advancements, political turnover, and industrial pressures. In constructing technologies for making sense of something as spectacular and incomprehensible as the Anthropocene, researchers and policy makers in environmental health have been forced to consider how to enforce environmental regulation when they cannot solely rely on a 'trust in numbers' (Porter 1996), and when they have to manage what they cannot (at least comprehensively) measure.

In this chapter, I detail various techno-cultural assemblages from which data collected to model and measure anthropogenic worlds emerge, arguing that data-based technologies both represent and co-produce the Anthropocene. Drawing on a case study of how vehicle emissions are measured and regulated in the US, I examine how US environmental health researchers and regulators grapple with the meaning of evidence and the basis for regulatory decisions as they confront the limits of automated data-collecting and modelling technologies. Finally, I meditate on the role of data-based technologies in mediating the environments we inhabit and the knowledge through which we perceive them.

DATA INFRASTRUCTURE AND KNOWLEDGE PRACTICES IN THE ANTHROPOCENE

Scholarship emerging at the intersection of science and technology studies (STS) and information studies (IS) has demonstrated that data infrastructure and data modelling (and the expertise and advocacy that emerge around both) are important nodes within the anthropogenic assemblages that shape history (Edwards 2017). The large-scale data infrastructures and models that enable us to visualise and make sense of the Anthropocene emerge from a series of localised practices of defining, classifying, and counting, wherein recognition, belonging, and uncertainty are continually being renegotiated. For instance, Bowker (1998) articulates how devising the neat boxes into which observations get classified involves negotiating the messiness of natural experience, navigating power struggles, and temporarily stabilising perpetually evolving worlds. Similarly, Martin and Lynch (2009) argue that counting, while seemingly trivial, does involve not only numerical operations but also discernments of what counts, calling for categorical judgements of identity and difference. Indeed, producing (ac)counts of natural observations is an embodied practice, demanding attunement to sensory experiences and eliciting emotions that style measurements and inscriptions (Calvillo 2018; Garnett 2016; Lorimer 2008).

Scholars in STS and IS have also characterised how practices of naming, classifying, and structuring data have become sites of collaboration, conflict, and politics. Standards for describing and storing data—often designed to network data across disciplinary, geographic, and temporal borders—emerge and transform in the face of capitalist, regulatory, and activist pressures (Bowker and Star 1999; Lampland and Star 2008; Ottinger 2010; Timmermans and Epstein 2010). This research has shown how, as data migrate across time and space, representations of anthropogenic worlds evolve alongside iterations in data semiotics (Bowker 2005). For example, Waterton (2002) shows how, as classification systems concerned with vegetation and natural habitats mutate in the face of controversy and instability, they come to reflect the dynamism and fluidity of the cultural systems within which they operate more than the contexts of their production.

Cultural practices of classifying and counting shape how identities form through data and how problems become both discernible and governable. Citing Hacking (2006), Kitchin and Lauriault (2014) argue that practices of counting and classifying are both contentious and consequential, 'making up people' and at least temporarily stabilising certain social and natural orders. Asdal (2008) demonstrates how nature-wholes are enacted—rendered real— through political methods of quantification and accounting designed to produce governable spaces. Kirksey (2015) demonstrates how species come into being through their entangled intra-actions with taxonomists and their technologies of classification: a dance of recognition, differentiation, and stabilisation on which many organisms depend to avert extinction. Similarly, Hepler-Smith (2019, p. 552) shows how toxic chemicals are identifiable in US regulatory structures through information practices that encode them on a molecule-by-molecule basis, a result of a 'molecular bureaucracy' in which 'law, administration, and politics meet empirical measurement and the material world'. Contemporary environmental problems receive public attention and enter debates through community engagement in environmental sense-making and the technologies they leverage. For example, Fortun et al. (2016) document how public pollution problems emerge as critical data designers couple skill in data visualisation with a hermeneutic sensibility to read the social, cultural, and political conditions that have eclipsed those problems. Other scholars have shown how research is left 'undone' because expert data systems—designed in ignorance of certain socio-cultural histories—preclude it (Frickel et al. 2010; Frickel and Vincent 2007; Nafus 2018).

Since different communities produce and consume data in different ways and with a diversity of ascribed meanings, it can be difficult to integrate data produced in different settings. Edwards et al. (2011) summarise this set of issues as 'data friction': the abrasive contact of the differing technologies, standards, and worldviews that represent and consume data. Scholars in this field have gone on to characterise how scientists address data friction in a cultural practice that involves attempts to cleanse data of their cultural influences. For instance, drawing on research in biology laboratories, Leonelli (2010) describes how, in order to facilitate the re-interpretation of data in new settings, data managers have had to learn to package data for travel, a practice that involves attempting to strip from data the personality and nuance of the contexts in which they were produced, meanwhile documenting their provenance so that others may re-contextualise the data for their own purposes. Since the contexts of data production and dissemination are often amorphous, power-laden, and unequal, Lampland and Star (2008) argue that translating data through various means of establishing common ground is always a political practice, one privileging certain semiotic orders over others.

As data move through complex and distributed socio-technical assemblages, frictional data practices call attention to their context-dependence and areas where they are incomplete or uncertain. Studies of the history and practices of data modelling have examined the ways in which such technologies mediate how knowledge is legitimised in the face of uncertainty. Oreskes (2000) argues that global data models have emerged to represent natural systems in instances when scientists lack complete access to the phenomena they are studying. Building upon this work, Knox (2018) ethnographically demonstrates how models serve as 'baseline data' against which messy and inconsistent observational data can be compared, enabling local-level administrative decision making in the face of missing data and other observational limits. However, Edwards (1999) shows that models themselves are also unstable, controversial, and constantly evolving, often in response to data frictions and inconsistencies with locally derived observational data. The movement of data across borders, scales, classification systems, and models troubles the local/global data binary. While Loukissas (2019) argues that 'all data are local'—that is all data are situated in a particular time and place—scholarship on practices and politics of data modelling demonstrates that data are also always more than local, the products of a 'cultural heterogenisation' of people, technologies, capital, media, and ideologies that propagate data flows, integrations, and disjuncture (Appadurai 1990). Through this scholarship we can see that, resonating with anthropologists' arguments that globalisation is not seamless and totalising (Ferguson 2006), global data infrastructuring is not moving us towards a mono-cultural data world. Data modelling and integration can divide the sciences and the representations they produce just as much as they bring them together.

Settings where scientists and policy makers grapple with the ambiguity and uncertainty woven through data practices and environmental sense-making are prominent sites for assessing shifting cultures of science and environmental regulation. Work in STS has documented how uncertainty can cripple scientific authority in policy making (Jasanoff 1987). For instance, Murphy (2006) has noted that, in the 1980s, the purposeful promotion of studies that furthered scientific uncertainty became a tool for anti-regulation at the US Environmental Protection Agency (EPA). However, other work in STS has shown that some scientific communities have responded to the limits of data, the complexity of environmental problems, and the extent of the unknown with 'humility and ambition'. Fortun and Fortun (2005), for instance, have described the culture of toxicology as shifting towards one that privileges experimentalism, wherein research is not necessarily designed to confirm what is already known but to generate new knowledge. In such communities, uncertainty is not seen as debilitating, and the knowledge produced through data systems and applied science is not the only knowledge useful in advancing regulation.

In summary, scholarship examining knowledge practices for characterising the natural world has demonstrated that technologies designed to measure and model the impact of human (and more-than-human) activity on earth systems are profoundly animated by the very human (and more-than-human) activities they attempt to measure. While dominant metaphors equate data with natural resources to be controlled or extracted, formulated in claims such as 'data is the new oil', or that we can be 'flooded with data' (Puschmann and Burgess 2014), scholars in critical data studies (e.g. see Gitelman 2013) often echo Bowker's (2000) claim that the term 'raw data is an oxymoron'. Suggestions that data could emerge from or return to a 'pure' or uncooked state mirror the blundering calls to return nature to its pure state. Data (and the worlds they inhabit) are always naturecultural (Haraway 2003; Subramaniam 2014). Anthropological attention to the materialities and mutability of data-producing technologies, along with the cultures and politics that shape them, can help to unpack how expertise operates, how knowledge is legitimised, and the way both have styled our experience of the Anthropocene.

Technologies for Counting and Estimating Vehicle Emissions in the US

What does it mean for environmental policies to be enacted 'based on' scientific data that are at times contested, always context-dependent, and modelled to measure things to which researchers do not have direct access? I explore this question in the following case study as I archaeologically trace select lineages of annual vehicle emissions estimates in the US to the moment when cars are first counted on federal highways. Rather than providing a holistic picture of how vehicle emissions estimates come into being, I ethnographically describe the data-collecting technologies involved in specific moments of their production in order to characterise environmental air quality regulation as a technologically mediated knowledge practice. In looking 'under the hood' at the configuration of a subset of technologies for measuring vehicle emissions, I elaborate on the diverse techno-cultural assemblages that animate systems of anthropogenic knowledge production and demonstrate the inextricable ties between the Anthropocene and the tools developed to understand it. Following Peter-Paul Verbeek's (2016) scholarship on 'technological mediation', I examine how technologies of data production mediate relationships between humans and the natural world, style everyday environments, and shape perception around what constitutes an empirical foundation for scientific claims.

Techno-Cultural Mediations of Emissions Standards

The US Clean Air Act, first signed into law in 1963 and updated several times since, was the first US policy to legislate air pollution control at the federal level.[3] A significant fortification of the federal government's role in air pollution control came with the 1970 amendments, which authorised the newly formed EPA to set National Ambient Air Quality Standards (NAAQS), and required each state to submit a periodical State Implementation Plan to the EPA outlining the policies and programmes they would enact to attain or maintain the standards.[4] NAAQS have been the subject of contentious debate and continuous evolution since the 1970s, with activists pressuring the EPA to strengthen regulation, corporations suing the EPA over the standards' stringency, and successive administrations revisiting the standards' review process, loosening or tightening the role of EPA staff in recommending policy options. Debates around the technical feasibility of implementing the standards have always been at the forefront of controversy. As a result, standards have emerged from a discursive space where technology, both available and speculative, tends to be positioned as a privileged signifier, in turn provoking changes in technological landscapes.

Responding to growing environmental concerns about smog, in 1970, Congress' amendments to the Clean Air Act mandated a 90% reduction in vehicle tailpipe emissions (including hydrocarbons, CO, and NOx) for passenger vehicles within five years (Gerard and Lave 2005). At the time, there had been no major improvements to the internal combustion engine in 20 years, and with little incentive for manufacturers to design technologies to reduce emissions, the new standard was considered 'technology-forcing' and designed to provoke innovation (Gerard and Lave 2005). For every car sold that did not meet the standards within the designated timeframe, automakers would face a $10,000 fine, double the average cost of a vehicle at the time (Gerard and Lave 2005). While the reductions were not achieved by the 1975 deadline, this regulatory pressure to innovate did lead to the introduction of the catalytic converter in 1975 and the three-way catalyst in 1981, both of which control tailpipe emissions through a chemical conversion process.

This technology-driving standard did not only spur innovation for emission control technologies but also helped motivate innovation around the chemicals that interfered with them. Until the 1970s, oil refiners had been adding lead to gasoline in order to raise the temperature and pressure at which engine knocking (or a premature ignition) occurs. At the time, lead in gasoline made up approximately 90% of airborne lead pollution, and there was growing concern about the threats the pollutant posed to public health (Stikkers 2002). Further, the combustion by-products of lead in gasoline can 'poison' catalytic converters by coating the metals responsible for converting exhaust chemicals (Stikkers 2002). As it was becoming increasingly clear that catalytic converters would be the primary means of reducing tailpipe emissions in the 1970s, the EPA began to introduce rules demanding the sale of unleaded gasoline. In culmination, the 1990 amendments to the Clean Air Act banned all leaded gasoline by 1996.

The year 1990 marked a historic change for the Clean Air Act for a number of reasons, but perhaps most notably for the way the US Congress further centred technology in standards-setting. When the Clean Air Act was first implemented in 1970, emissions standards for a number of pollutants were to be set based solely on what is requisite to protect public health (Bachmann 2007). However, as it became increasingly clear that scientific uncertainty about exposure risks would continuously immobilise the promulgation of standards, Congress pivoted the Act to require that standards be set based on the best currently available emission control technologies (or technologies available in the foreseeable future) (Flatt 2007; McCubbin 2003). Residual health risks would be assessed eight years after each standard was set. As a result, technical feasibility was increasingly privileged in standards-setting over the normative end goal of protecting health.

Approximately once a decade since the 1990 amendments, the EPA has introduced increasingly stringent standards on vehicle emissions. While in the 1990s emissions standards applied primarily to passenger vehicles, in the 2000s the same standards were extended to medium-duty passenger vehicles such as SUVs and passenger vans, and in the 2010s the standards were further extended to some heavier-duty vehicles such as cargo trucks (box vans). Successive standards also required reductions of sulphur and eventually ethanol in gasoline. Innovations such as hybrid vehicles and clean diesel engines emerged in the wake of these changes. While the EPA has been sued almost every step of the way, courts have reacted favourably to technology-forcing standards. Responding to a petition from automakers to block regulations requiring a 30% reduction in greenhouse gas emissions by 2016, Judge William Sessions III wrote in his ruling, 'History suggests that the ingenuity of the industry, once put in gear, responds admirably to most technological challenges' (Freeman 2007).

Regulators' discursive privileging of technology in connection with emissions standards has provoked shifts in technological, environmental, regulatory, and health landscapes in the US. These technology-driving standards have also, however, mediated the empirical foundation of scientific knowledge production around vehicle emissions. To calculate estimates of annual vehicle emissions, the EPA coordinates a number of scientific studies examining emissions from vehicles *meeting current standards*, along with how they fluctuate with changes in factors such as fuel additives, speed, and outdoor temperature conditions at start-up (US EPA Office of Transportation and Air Quality 2015). The EPA then estimates how many vehicles in the US meet these standards by analysing data about car sales and certifications in model years before, during, and after the phase-in of new standards. In other words, vehicle emissions standards, which emerge in a balance of what is technologically feasible and what can incentivise technological change, delimit how evidence regarding current and future vehicle emissions gets generated, in turn shaping how, when, and where environmental policies get enacted, the future prospects for transportation and energy industries, and the air we eventually breathe.

While this provides estimates of the emissions properties of certified vehicles, it does not offer information on when, where, the speed at which, and the duration of time these vehicles are actually operating. To calculate this, the EPA leverages data collection programmes that count vehicles on roads throughout the US, to which I turn next.

Vehicle-Counting Data Collection Technologies

One of the most important inputs for air emission models is the count of vehicles on federal highways each year, along with the number of miles they have travelled, a measure referred to as Vehicle Miles Travelled. Most US states have several hundred permanent traffic counters installed in or on roadways to produce continuous traffic counts. Inductive road loop counters, for instance, are coiled wires installed underneath or into the surface of roadways that can electromagnetically detect when a vehicle has passed over them. While inductive loop counts are widely considered to be accurate, the technology is expensive to install, even more expensive to maintain, and causes disruptions to traffic, roadway resurfacing, and utility repairs (The Vehicle Detector Clearinghouse 2007). Further, inductive loop counters are susceptible to fluctuations in weather conditions with freezing and thawing causing the loops to break. Thus, continuous traffic count programmes are mainly instituted to collect data regarding overall traffic trends across the state versus counts on *every* highway.

To ensure traffic is accounted for across every highway, state departments of transportation (DOTs) also manage short-term traffic count programmes. The most common method of producing these counts for a given highway is to hire consultants to lay a set of temporary pneumatic tubes on a road segment, a dangerous job that involves managing multiple lane closures (The Vehicle Detector Clearinghouse 2007). Each time a tyre passes over the rubber tubes, a signal is sent to a counter. Pneumatic road tubes are typically left in place for a few days, and then state DOTs calculate the Average Annual Daily Traffic for a roadway segment by averaging daily traffic on the days the tubes were placed and then multiplying the figure by 365. Multiplying the result by the length of the segment yields Vehicle Miles Travelled.

The daily traffic on a given highway can, however, vary drastically over the course of a week, month, or year. In order to plan for and amend these fluctuations in counts when determining annual average traffic, data collectors at state DOTs have become attuned to the cultural contexts of roadways. As a representative from a state traffic monitoring programme described in a 2016 interview with me,

> we collect 72-hour counts, but [...] you can't count before Monday at 6 AM and [after] Friday at noon. It has to fall in there. So we consider Monday say to be a typical day, [and] Tuesday, Wednesday, Thursday, Friday morning to be typical. Friday afternoons, a lot of times, I look at the [highway] or something, and everybody's heading north for the weekend [...] so we don't collect Friday afternoons.

Discerning what constitutes a 'typical' traffic day becomes more complicated when zooming out to the span of a year. In the interview, the representative discussed another situation where the DOT recognised numerical contingencies and considered options for normalising the count:

> We were looking at traffic counts [in] some real part of [the state] right near a college, ... The two previous [counts] were in the 2000s for [average daily traffic]. And the current one we were looking at was 300 and something. But then you look at the dates, and the two previous ones were taken during college. The [third] one was taken in the summer when college wasn't in session. So if it was made in a rural area, colleges—they make a huge difference in the volume of traffic, right?

This anecdote demonstrates one of many ways in which traffic counters account for cultural patterns of migration and vehicle use. Unsuitable for snowy conditions, road tubes are typically not placed down in the winter in regions where there may be snow, and seasonal adjustments must be made so as not to overestimate winter traffic. Dips and spikes in the counts from year to year can signal legitimate changes in traffic conditions or, alternatively, faulty counting equipment. On busy highways, the rubber tubes can wear down, compromising the accuracy of the count (The Vehicle Detector Clearinghouse 2007), while in areas where there is often stop-and-go traffic, it is difficult for the system to distinguish one vehicle from the next (The Vehicle Detector Clearinghouse 2007). State DOTs will use overall trends identified by continuous traffic counters, along with cultural competency, to assess the quality of short-term highway counts and make necessary adjustments.

Notably, the data collection programmes responsible for producing a calculation of Vehicle Miles Travelled are not maintained by the EPA, but by the Federal Highway Administration (FHWA), and their initial purpose was not to measure vehicle emissions but to support transportation planning and to direct the allocation of federal highway aid (Federal Highway Administration, Office of Highway Policy Information 2019). The FHWA classifies counted vehicles into 13 categories (e.g. motorcycles, buses, and combination trucks), information that is important for pavement and bridge designers when considering how to maintain highway infrastructure. Responding to the affordances of road tubes and other vehicle classifying technologies in the 1980s, the boundaries dividing one vehicle class from the next are not determined visually, but by the vehicle classifiers' detecting and calculating the spacing between a vehicle's axles (Federal Highway Administration 2014). When the FHWA first proposed these classifications, the length of the wheelbase could readily differentiate a passenger vehicle from other two-axle, four-tyre vehicles (such as a pick-up truck or van). However, as SUVs and PT Cruisers gained popularity as passenger vehicles in the US, the logic dividing these categories became increasingly fuzzy. To better represent the data that they were actually collecting, in 2007 the FHWA changed the category of passenger vehicle to *light-duty, short wheelbase vehicle*, and the other two-axle, four-tyre category *to light-duty, long wheelbase vehicle*.[5]

The EPA does not regulate vehicle emissions based on wheelbase, however, but on the vehicle's gross weight. Having designed their emissions modelling systems around the inputs available through the FHWA, the EPA had to devise new algorithms for determining what percentage of long wheelbase vehicles were actually passenger carriers rather than commercial trucks (vans) in order to model emissions (US EPA, Office of Transportation and Air Quality 2016). One strategy for this involved analysing the composition of private and commercial truck (van) fleets in the US based on the results of the Census Bureau's Vehicle Inventory and Use Survey, a paper questionnaire mailed to and then collected from US-registered truck (van) owners every five years that gathers data about vehicle use. Megan Beardsley, team leader for the EPA's vehicle emissions model MOVES (to which I turn next), acknowledged this method to be limited since the survey was last taken in 2002.

Counting cars on US highways is not simply a numerical operation. It involves an array of networked people, institutions, calibrations, technologies, and data systems. Producing an 'accurate' count rarely involves relying on vehicle counting technologies alone, but also integrates cultural expertise attuned to when and why driving habits and vehicle purchases change, and is prepared to adjust counts accordingly. State DOTs must balance counting costs against numerical accuracy in the mix of diminishing infrastructure budgets, expensive equipment, and federal air quality regulations. Counting cars is a practice that poses risks to human safety while being designed to improve highway (and air) safety conditions, one that reacts to climatic fluctuations and detection limits as it becomes an input for knowledge systems measuring anthropogenic impacts on our air and climate. In other words, vehicle counts designed to measure and model human impacts on natural worlds are also a product of naturecultural worlds.

Technologies for Modelling Vehicle Emissions

In order to model annual pollution emissions from motor vehicles for their State Implementation Plans, all states (except California)[6] must leverage the EPA's Motor Vehicle Emissions Simulator (MOVES), a computer technology developed and maintained in the EPA's Office of Transportation and Air Quality. In preparing their plans, states input data about Vehicle Miles Travelled, weather conditions, and local demographics into MOVES. The system then calculates estimated emissions of criteria air pollutants, greenhouse gases, and air toxics based on data curated from millions of scientific emissions tests. MOVES is designed to predict future vehicle emissions conditions by ordering data about past and present conditions, along with estimations of how they might change.

The first version of MOVES was released in 1978 as MOBILE and has gone through at least ten major revisions since then 'to reflect improved data, changes in vehicle, engine, and emission control system technologies, changes in applicable regulations and emission standards and test procedures, and improved understanding of in-use emission levels and the factors that influence them' (US EPA 2016). For the MOVES team, designing an all-inclusive model of vehicle emissions, one that can comprehensively account for the array of natural (and more-than-natural) forces impacting emissions, is always a pursuit, that is, always open to further improvement. As improved strategies become available for estimating emissions from different mobile sources (such as from boats, lawnmowers, snowmobiles, and other agricultural equipment), the MOVES team seeks to incorporate the inputs into the modelling technology. As mechanisms become available for more accurately tracking the speed of vehicles on highways and the times highways are most populated (such as satellites and cell phone tracking), the MOVES team seeks to incorporate the inputs into the modelling technology. In October 2016, Megan Beardsley, team leader for the MOVES model, told me that the MOVES team maintains a 'huge laundry list of stuff that [they]'d like to the model to do better'. For example, as manufacturers began improving emissions from already warmed-up vehicles, the MOVES team began diverting their attention to producing better models of the time, place, and quantity of start-up emissions, and how they vary based on fluctuations in outdoor temperatures. In the early 2010s, when the EPA promulgated stricter standards for vehicle emissions and a new standard for gasoline sulphur, the MOVES team adjusted the models to account for cleaner vehicles and fuels on the road. Thus, the knowledge MOVES models are both cumulative and iterative alongside changes in technology and regulation. MOVES inputs are meticulously curated from the expansive corpus of factors impacting emissions. At any given moment, the evidence MOVES produces is acknowledged to be both robust and, to a certain degree, partial. While the MOVES team is judicious in incorporating the latest scientific research regarding vehicle emissions into the models, the selection of inputs is still mediated by what is currently possible to quantify, what is considered a priority for inclusion, and the capacity of the MOVES team (comprising about 20 individuals, many of whom as of 2016 do not work on the project full-time) to make the revisions.

Each time a revised version of the technology is applied in modelling, the quantified history of vehicle emissions in a given region slightly morphs, as does the understanding of present and future air quality conditions. Yet the pacing of revisions to the computer technology is tempered, not only by the timing of technological innovations and scientific advancements, but also by the bureaucratic pacing of research funding, peer review, and EPA rule-making processes. Years can pass from the introduction of new emissions standards until their benefits are understood through scientific research; the same applies to the period from when scientific data becomes available until a new version of the modelling technology is released. While the Clean Air Act requires State Implementation Plans to be prepared based on the most current information and models, the plans are sometimes prepared months to years before they are approved. This means that by the time the EPA approves a State Implementation Plan, there may already be swaths of new evidence repainting the picture of past, present, and future emissions in that state. To make progress towards emissions reductions, the EPA often must make governance decisions based on admittedly outdated estimations.

For example, in the early 2000s, the Sierra Club, one of the oldest and most influential environmental organisations in the US, filed a complaint with the US DC District Court regarding the EPA's conditional decision to approve components of Washington DC's State Implementation Plan (SIP). Since 1991, Washington DC had been classified as an area of 'serious', and at times even 'severe', non-attainment of NAAQS, requiring that it submit a Rate of Progress Plan with its State Implementation Plan that demonstrated 3% reductions in emissions each year leading up to their attainment deadline. The dispute was based, in part, on Washington DC's use of MOBILE5 (an earlier version of MOVES) in measuring the rate of progress towards attainment from 1996 to 1999. While MOBILE5 had been the most recent vehicle emission model available at the time the plan was created, just a month before the plan was submitted, MOBILE6 had become available. It took the EPA another year to approve the plan. The Sierra Club contested the EPA's decision to accept a

Rate of Progress Plan that had not been based on the latest data models. The Court responded:

> Indeed, as its name suggests, MOBILE5 is the fifth generation of this particular model; MOBILE6 is sixth. To require states to revise completed plans every time a new model is announced would lead to significant costs and potentially endless delays in the approval processes. EPA's decision to reject that course, and to accept the use of MOBILE5 in this case, was neither arbitrary nor capricious. (Sierra Club v USA EPA 2004, p. 19)

While this demonstrates the politics of the model's diachronicity, battles of evidence and rival claims over what constitutes sound experimental design can underlie the data inputs that inform MOVES' emissions calculations even in moments of temporary stability. For example, in 2015, the State of Kansas, the State of Nebraska, the Energy Future Coalition, and the Urban Air Initiative filed a suit with the DC Court of Appeals, asking them to review MOVES 2014 in light of a 'flawed fuel effects study' called EPAct/V2/E-89, conducted to test the effect of ethanol on particulate emissions (State of Kansas et al. v US EPA Brief for Respondents 2015). The petitioners argued that in the study the EPA used a method of blending ethanol with gasoline called a Match Blend, while most car manufacturers use a Splash Blend method. With a Splash Blend method, 10% ethanol is simply added to gasoline. In Match Blending, however, aromatic hydrocarbons are added to the mixture in order to ensure the gasoline meets a certain boiling point. These hydrocarbons, the petitioners argued, increase the toxicity of the mixture when emissions tests are run, while simply adding ethanol should reduce the toxicity of the mixture. In MOVES2014, ethanol gets modelled according to the results of this study, and increased ethanol volumes are shown to increase toxic emissions.

The petitioners argued that the inclusion of consultants from the petroleum industry in the design of EPAct/V2/E-89 had biased the study and that the use of the computer technology for modelling emissions would injure Kansas and Nebraska by categorising them as areas of non-attainment of air quality standards, depressing ethanol prices, and imposing detrimental effects on tax revenues. In their response, the EPA defended the study, justifying the team involved in the study design and endorsing their own expertise to carry out the research effectively. They also argued that the petition lacked standing because the MOVES technology was non-binding. While the states were required to use it in preparing their State Implementation Plans, MOVES was not a legislative tool, and the EPA could consider the quality of the model's outputs on a case-by-case basis. As they argued, 'applying the model in a particular agency action requires flexibility and the exercise of judgment' (State of Kansas et al. v US EPA Brief for Petitioners 2015, p. 12). The Court dismissed the petition for lack of standing.

In this response, we see how technology can mediate the meaning of evidence-based regulation and what emissions estimates are understood to be 'based on'. While the Clean Air Act specifies that attainment decisions are to be made based on the latest data models, this case reveals that what counts as empirical evidence can shift in response to a number of political, cultural, and judiciary pressures, particularly when data are contested and technological limits on representing and measuring future emissions are recognised. Still, Beardsley acknowledged in our interview that, for the MOVES team, 'there's a real desire to do the best stuff we can', because they always face the risk of a lawsuit when the legitimacy of MOVES as an evidence-producing technology is called into question. Notably, the possibility that the EPA might be sued over their work creates incentives for slowing down the modelling technology's development to allow for more careful study design and more thorough peer review, in turn widening the liminal gap between when new evidence becomes available and when it gets incorporated into the model. In other words, the knowledge about annual vehicle emissions produced through MOVES is both cumulative and co-constitutive of the conditions, cultures, and technologies of knowledge production.

Conclusion

The arguments presented in this case study echo decades of scholarship in the anthropology of technology arguing that naturecultural worlds are co-produced with technology (Downey and Dumit 1997). Data-based representations of nature emerge from situated and routinised human engagements with technologies of data collection and analysis, helping to render complex, pervasive, yet local issues like air pollution a national (and thus, in the US, federally regulable) concern. Decisions about how to calibrate data collection technologies, what inputs to include in data modelling technologies, and how to account for various sources of technological error are made in the face of political, economic, and cultural competencies and pressures, responding to the limits to knowing the world through technologically mediated apparatuses. Corporate interest, environmental activism, and human labour are thus all represented in data about natural worlds—interlaced through standards, measurements, and estimations as data flow between different people, technologies, and institutions. These technological configurations in turn mediate how the air we breathe, the worlds we inhabit, and the technologies available for mediating them come into being and evolve. Thus, for researchers and regulators, environmental decision making often demands critical judgement beyond what automated data collection and modelling technologies can produce and what can be quantitatively measured.

Ethnographically examining technologies of data collection and modelling 'under the hood' reveals far more than merely how they work and the phenomena they are designed to represent. Ethnographies of data-producing technologies provide a unique lens into complex cultures of knowledge production and environmental regulation, along with their technological mediation. They foreground how diverse stakeholders value (in multiple senses of the word) the environment, human health, and technological innovation, how regulators learn how to manage and mitigate pollution in light of acknowledged limitations to its measurement, and how the meaning of empirical evidence gets negotiated. In other words, the anthropology of technologies of data collection and modelling can highlight what makes natural worlds, and the data through which we present them, so human.

Acknowledgements Early versions of this chapter were developed and honed in the context of *The Asthma Files* (https://theasthmafiles.org/) research project, led by Kim Fortun and Mike Fortun.

Notes

1. This was a pithy reference to a 2005 videotape in which Donald Trump, while making a number of vulgar comments about women, told US television personality Billy Bush to 'Grab 'em by the pussy'.
2. I have lost count of the number of times when, in conversation with data analysts in municipal, state, and federal governments about the dangers of an overreliance on data systems and models, I have been surprised to find them nodding in agreement and referencing Cathy O'Neil's (2016) *Weapons of Math Destruction*. Part of this abmivalence has emerged from experience; many experts and policy makers can cite several examples where over-dependence on data-based systems of governance has prevented sound decision making.
3. Federal regulation of air pollution responded to two interrelated concerns: first, that as states compete for new jobs and industry, they have incentives to side-line environmental regulations; and second, that regardless of an individual state's degree of regulation, air does not know state boundaries.
4. Once approved by the EPA, the control strategies outlined in the plan became enforceable at both state and federal levels, and failure to comply with the plans would permit the federal government to take over enforcement.
5. For example, see https://www.fhwa.dot.gov/policyinformation/statistics/2007/vm1.cfm.
6. California, with the worst traffic conditions in the country, has much more stringent air quality regulations and is thus exempt from several federal policies.

References

Anderson, C. (2008, June 23). *The End of Theory: The Data Deluge Makes the Scientific Method Obsolete*. WIRED. http://archive.wired.com/science/discoveries/magazine/16-07/pb_theory.

Appadurai, A. (1990). Disjuncture and Difference in the Global Cultural Economy. *Public Culture, 2*, 1–23.

Aryn, Martin Michael, Lynch (2009). Counting Things and People: The Practices and Politics of Counting. *Social Problems 56*(2) 243–266. https://doi.org/10.1525/sp.2009.56.2.243.

Asdal, K. (2008). Enacting things through numbers: Taking nature into account/ing. *Geoforum, 39*(1), 123–132. https://doi.org/10.1016/j.geoforum.2006.11.004.

Bachmann, J. (2007). Will the Circle Be Unbroken: A History of the U.S. National Ambient Air Quality Standards. *Journal of the Air & Waste Management Association, 57*(6), 652–697. https://doi.org/10.3155/1047-3289.57.6.652.

Bowker, G. C. (1998). The Kindness of Strangers: Kinds and Politics in Classification Systems. *Library Trends, 47*(2), 255–292. https://www.ideals.illinois.edu/handle/2142/8207.

Bowker, G. C. (2005). *Memory Practices in the Sciences.* Cambridge, MA: The MIT Press.

Bowker, G. C., & Star, S. L. (1999). *Sorting Things Out: Classification and Its Consequences.* Cambridge, MA: The MIT Press.

Calvillo, N. (2018). Political airs: From monitoring to attuned sensing air pollution. *Social Studies of Science, 48*(3), 372–388. https://doi.org/10.1177/0306312718784656.

Downey, G. L., & Dumit, J. (1997). *Cyborgs & citadels: Anthropological interventions in emerging sciences and technologies.* Santa Fe: School of American Research Press.

Edwards, P., Mayernik, M. S., Batcheller, A., Bowker, G., & Borgman, C. (2011). Science Friction: Data, Metadata, and Collaboration. *Social Studies of Science, 41*(5), 667–690. https://doi.org/10.1177/0306312711413314.

Edwards, P. N. (2017). Knowledge infrastructures for the Anthropocene. *The Anthropocene Review, 4*(1), 34–43. https://doi.org/10.1177/2053019616679854.

Evan, Hepler-Smith (2019). Molecular Bureaucracy: Toxicological Information and Environmental Protection. *Environmental History 24*(3) 534–560. https://doi.org/10.1093/envhis/emy134

Federal Highway Administration. (2014). *Verification, Refinement, and Applicability of Long-Term Pavement Performance Vehicle Classification Rules* (FHWA-HRT-13-091). https://www.fhwa.dot.gov/publications/research/infrastructure/pavements/ltpp/13091/13091.pdf. Accessed 15 October 2019.

Federal Highway Administration, Office of Highway Policy Information. (2019, April 1). *About Highway Performance Monitoring System (HPMS).* https://www.fhwa.dot.gov/policyinformation/hpms/abouthpms.cfm. Accessed 15 October 2019.

Ferguson, J. (2006). *Global Shadows: Africa in the Neoliberal World Order.* Duke University Press.

Flatt, V. B. (2007). Gasping for Breath: The Administrative Flaws of the Federal Hazardous Air Pollutant Program. *Ecology Law Quarterly, 34*(107), 107–174.

Fortun, K. (2004). From Bhopal to the Informating of Environmentalism: Risk Communication in Historical Perspective. *Osiris, 19,* 283–296.

Fortun, K., & Fortun, M. (2005). Scientific Imaginaries and Ethical Plateaus in Contemporary U.S. Toxicology. *American Anthropologist, 107*(1), 43–54. https://doi.org/10.1525/aa.2005.107.1.043.

Fortun, K., Poirier, L., Morgan, A., Costelloe-Kuehn, B., & Fortun, M. (2016). Pushback: Critical data designers and pollution politics. *Big Data & Society, 3*(2), 1–14. https://doi.org/10.1177/2053951716668903.

Freeman, S. (2007, September 13). Carmakers Defeated On Emissions Rules. *Washington Post.* http://www.washingtonpost.com/wp-dyn/content/article/2007/09/12/AR2007091202391.html.

Frickel, S., Gibbon, S., Howard, J., Kempner, J., Ottinger, G., & Hess, D. J. (2010). Undone Science: Charting Social Movement and Civil Society Challenges to Research Agenda Setting. *Science, Technology & Human Values, 35*(4), 444–473. https://doi.org/10.1177/0162243909345836.

Frickel, S., & Vincent, M. B. (2007). Hurricane Katrina, contamination, and the unintended organization of ignorance. *Technology in Society, 29*(2), 181–188. https://doi.org/10.1016/j.techsoc.2007.01.007.

Garnett, E. (2016). Developing a feeling for error: Practices of monitoring and modelling air pollution data. *Big Data & Society, 3*(2), 1–12. https://doi.org/10.1177/2053951716658061.

Geoffrey C., Bowker (2000). *Biodiversity Datadiversity. Social Studies of Science 30*(5) 643–683. https://doi.org/10.1177/030631200030005001

Gerard, D., & Lave, L. B. (2005). Implementing technology-forcing policies: The 1970 Clean Air Act Amendments and the introduction of advanced automotive emissions controls in the United States. *Technological Forecasting and Social Change, 72*(7), 761–778. https://doi.org/10.1016/j.techfore.2004.08.003.

Gitelman L. (2013). *Raw Data Is an Oxymoron*. MIT Press.

Hacking I. (2006). Making Up People. *London Review of Books 28*(16).

Haraway, D. (2003). *The Companion Species Manifesto: Dogs, People, and Significant Otherness* (M. Begelke, Ed.). Chicago, IL: Prickly Paradigm Press.

Jasanoff, S. S. (1987). Contested Boundaries in Policy-Relevant Science. *Social Studies of Science, 17*(2), 195–230. https://doi.org/10.1177/030631287017002001.

Kirksey, E. (2015). Species: A praxiographic study. *Journal of the Royal Anthropological Institute, 21*(4), 758–780. https://doi.org/10.1111/1467-9655.12286.

Kitchin R. & Lauriault T. (2014). Towards Critical Data Studies: Charting and Unpacking Data Assemblages and Their Work. *Social Science Research Network*. Available at: https://papers.ssrn.com/abstract=2474112 (accessed 6 November 2017).

Knox, H. (2018). Baseless data?: Modelling, ethnography and the challenge of the anthropocene. In H. Knox & D. Nafus (Eds.), *Ethnography for a Data-Saturated World* (pp. 128–150). Manchester: Manchester University Press. https://doi.org/10.7765/9781526127600.00014.

Lampland, M., & Star, S. L. (Eds.) (2008). *Standards and Their Stories: How Quantifying, Classifying, and Formalizing Practices Shape Everyday Life* (1st ed.). Ithaca, NY: Cornell University Press.

Leonelli, S. (2010). Packaging Small Fact for Re-use: Databases in Model Organism Biology. In P. Howlett & M. S. Morgan (Eds.), *How Well Do Facts Travel?: The Dissemination of Reliable Knowledge* (pp. 325–348). Cambridge, England: Cambridge University Press.

Lorimer, J. (2008). Counting Corncrakes: The Affective Science of the UK Corncrake Census. *Social Studies of Science, 38*(3), 377–405. https://doi.org/10.1177/0306312707084396.

Loukissas Y. A. (2019). *All Data Are Local: Thinking Critically in a Data-Driven Society*. Cambridge, Massachusetts: The MIT Press.

McCubbin, P. R. (2003). Amending the Clean Air Act to Establish Democratic Legitimacy for the Residual Risk Program. *Virginia Environmental Law Journal, 22*(1), 1–52.

Murphy, M. (2006). *Sick Building Syndrome and the Problem of Uncertainty: Environmental Politics, Technoscience, and Women Workers*. Durham, NC: Duke University Press.

Nafus, D. (2018). Exploration or Algorithm? The Undone Science Before the Algorithms. *Cultural Anthropology, 33*(3), 368–374. https://doi.org/10.14506/ca33.3.03.

O'Neil, C. (2016). *Weapons of Math Destruction: How Big Data Increases Inequality and Threatens Democracy*. (1st ed.). New York City: Crown.

Oreskes, N. (2000). Why Believe a Computer? Models, Measures, and Meaning in the Natural World. In J. Schneiderman (Ed.), *The Earth Around Us: Maintaining a Livable Planet*. W. H. Freeman & Co Ltd. https://doi.org/10.4324/9780429496653-8.

Ottinger, G. (2010). Buckets of Resistance: Standards and the Effectiveness of Citizen Science. *Science, Technology, & Human Values, 35*(2), 244–270. https://doi.org/10.1177/0162243909337121.

Paul N., Edwards (1999). Global climate science uncertainty and politics: Data-laden models model-filtered data. *Science as Culture 8*(4) 437–472 https://doi.org/10.1080/09505439909526558

Porter, T. M. (1996). *Trust in Numbers: The Pursuit of Objectivity in Science and Public Life*. Princeton, NJ: Princeton University Press.

Puschmann, C., & Burgess, J. (2014). Metaphors of Big Data. *International Journal of Communication, 8*(0), 1690–1709.

Sierra Club v US EPA Petitions for Review of Final Actions of the Environmental Protection Agency, DC Cir. No. 03-1084 (United States Court of Appeals, DC Circuit 2004).

State of Kansas, State of Nebraska, Energy Future Coalition, and Urban Air Initiative, Inc., v US EPA Brief for Petitioners, DC Cir. No. 14-1268 (United States Court of Appeals, DC Circuit 2015).

Stikkers, D. E. (2002). Octane and the environment. *Science of the Total Environment, 299*(1–3), 37–56. https://doi.org/10.1016/S0048-9697(02)00271-1.

Subramaniam, B. (2014). *Ghost Stories for Darwin: The Science of Variation and the Politics of Diversity* (1st ed.). University of Illinois Press.

The Vehicle Detector Clearinghouse. (2007). *A Summary of Vehicle Detection and Surveillance Technologies used in Intelligent Transportation Systems*. Federal Highway Administration's (FHWA) Intelligent Transportation Systems Program Office. https://www.fhwa.dot.gov/policyinformation/pubs/vdstits2007/vdstits2007.pdf. Accessed 17 November 2020.

Timmermans, S., & Epstein, S. (2010). A World of Standards but not a Standard World: Toward a Sociology of Standards and Standardization. *Annual Review of Sociology, 36*(1), 69–89. https://doi.org/10.1146/annurev.soc.012809.102629.

US EPA Office of Transportation and Air Quality. (2015). *Exhaust Emission Rates for Light-Duty On-road Vehicles in MOVES2014* (EPA-420-R-15-005). US EPA.

US EPA, Office of Transportation and Air Quality. (2016). *Population and Activity of On-road Vehicles in MOVES2014* (EPA-420-R-16-003). https://nepis.epa.gov/Exe/ZyPDF.cgi?Dockey=P100O7VJ.pdf.

Verbeek, P.-P. (2016). Toward a Theory of Technological Mediation: A Program for Postphenomenological Research. In J. Kyrre Berg, O. Friis, & R. P. Crease (Eds.), *Technoscience and Postphenomenology: The Manhattan Papers* (pp. 189–204). Lexington Books. https://research.utwente.nl/en/publications/toward-a-theory-of-technological-mediation-a-program-for-postphen.

Waterton, C. (2002). From Field to Fantasy: Classifying Nature, Constructing Europe. *Social Studies of Science, 32*(2), 177–204. https://doi.org/10.1177/0306312702032002001.

CHAPTER 15

Set, Setting, and Clinical Trials: Colonial Technologies and Psychedelics

Experiment

Joseph Dumit and Emilia Sanabria

This chapter critically engages with the model of evidence-based medicine (EBM) by analysing the tensions besieging randomised controlled trials (RCTs) as they encompass phenomena that challenge their capacity for universalisation, standardisation, and metrification. We bring together ethnographic work on technologies of healing and associated modes of knowing deployed in RCTs and psychedelic clinical trials, and ceremonial uses of the Amazonian herbal brew ayahuasca in urban Brazil. Building on a review of anthropological work on clinical trials, we argue that RCTs, even psychedelic ones, have been captured by the pharmaceutical industry in its quest to grow profits rather than reduce illness. Drawing on feminist and decolonial work, we question the use of technology as a category for thinking about health, recognising with la paperson (2017, p. 17) that as they mutate, they become 'technologies of alienation, separation, conversion of land into property and of people into targets of subjection'.

We do not engage with anthropology of technology literature that distinguishes 'non-industrialised' indigenous practices from Euro-American ones as

J. Dumit (✉)
Department of Anthropology, University of California, Davis, Davis, CA, USA
e-mail: dumit@ucdavis.edu

E. Sanabria
Université de Paris, CNRS, CERMES3, Paris, France
e-mail: emilia.sanabria@cnrs.fr

291

M. H. Bruun et al. (eds.), *The Palgrave Handbook of the Anthropology of Technology*, https://doi.org/10.1007/978-981-16-7084-8_15

if there were a metric that could make sense of it.[1] We are interested in the role that the category of technology plays in continued industrialised colonial, genocidal, and dispossessive violence. This includes the institutions of intellectual property, EBM, RCTs, pharmaceuticals, drugs, active ingredients, industrial medicine, diagnostic standards, investment capital, and treatment sovereignty.

Following la paperson (2017, pp. 24–25), we call these *colonial technologies*, because they continue patterns of erasure, unequal killing and letting die, of denying the ability to speak, sing, or learn from plants, the sovereignty to live on and with lands, and to decide presents, futures, and pasts. The use of the category of technology, with regard to medicine, continues to make a world divided into knowledge as a domain separate from belief, people who know more or less, things that appear to be neutral, and a world in which the ongoing arrangements, inequalities, and violence of people are separated from both knowledge and things.

It is not only biomedicine as a 'technology' that is colonial, but EBM and RCTs are also capitalising and individualising technologies that produce pharmaceuticals and other treatments in a 'magic bullet' form. This narrative form presumes and produces diseases and treatments as individual and technical, as the domain of experts, and often as a market. The frame of technology (as 'applied science') hinders or erases the ways in which relations of power preselect which problems are 'health-related' and which are 'political' (see Nelson 2013).[2] One of the main ways that technology does this is by distracting analysis away from structural relations that hold up power and onto supposed self-possessed actors, or Heroes.

It is difficult, notes science-fiction writer Ursula K. Le Guin (1989), to tell a tale where the action is not directly imputable to a Hero. The narrative form, Le Guin laments, has been colonised by victorious, triumphant, aggressive Promethean tales. With characteristic wit, Le Guin proposes that the problem goes back to a shift that took place when restless hunters took off, bringing back epic tales along with the added calories. Originally, she jokes, humans made do very well as gatherers. But it is 'hard to tell a really gripping tale of how I wrestled a wild-oat seed from its husk, and then another, and then another, and then another, and then another' (Le Guin 1989, p. 165). Le Guin states that we urgently need stories about the container for the thing contained. To get at this story we have to get over the killer story with Action and Heroes.

We have been inspired by Le Guin and STS scholars who take up her concern with world-making as we think through the question of technology, EBM, pharmaceuticals, and non-white healing modalities. We find it useful to analyse pharmaceutical clinical trials and psychedelic medicine experimentations through the feminist critique of the distinction between tools and containers. For Zoë Sofia (2000), foregrounding 'container technologies' requires attention to labour. Building on the heuristic contrast between tool and container, we think of the rise of the RCT and its specialised focus on magic bullets as a kind of fantasy mammoth hunt that obviates other less dramatic and heroic processes which are foundational to healing. Containers perform their functions in different ways, using modes of encounter that can be described as actively cultivated passivity. Using the idea of container technologies, we anchor our historical discussion of pharmaceutical clinical trials with a particular attention to how they claim to discover or prove a magic bullet experimentally by controlling for environmental factors.

EBM stems from at least three facets of the rise of statistical medicine in the mid-twentieth century. The first relates to the need to create a new standard of proof for the statistical causation of emphysema through smoking. Tobacco company obfuscation of facts prevented strong trends from being legally provable (Proctor 2012). The technology invented in response was the consensus report in which the state established a means for unifying competing theories of knowledge, which led to the development of clinical guidelines that would give rise to EBM (Brandt 2007). The second concerns the creation of experimental statistical medicine through RCTs. Decisions about the relative effectiveness of two drugs for acute conditions could be settled by giving randomised groups of sufferers one of the two drugs and tracking which group got better overall. This was seen as a better way to learn than polling experienced doctors about their observations regarding the two drugs. Historian Harry Marks (2000) notes that in the case of acute diseases and treatments like antibiotics, for which endpoints and improvement were easier to define, trials worked quite well. In these cases, neither the diagnosis of who has the disease nor the effectiveness of the treatment was contested. This relatively limited set of 'magic bullet' cases is not the norm in medicine, however. For chronic diseases, there were a host of difficulties: 'the strategy of collecting more and more data in the course of a study ran the risk of producing more, not less, controversy' (Marks 2000, p. 161). The third aspect of statistical health involved large-scale prospective clinical studies. The 1950s Framingham Heart Study included over 5000 members of one small city who were carefully monitored over generations. It discovered connections between smoking and biomarkers like cholesterol and future events like heart attacks and death. The study produced the notion of risk factors like elevated cholesterol levels, hypertension, and smoking. It, too, approached illnesses collectively, even if they were not spread like infectious diseases. Indeed, according to historian Jeremy Greene, by 1961 it was evident to the pharmaceutical industry that drugs could be expanded almost indefinitely (Greene 2007).

Combinations of these three technologies have led to the contemporary evidence-based clinical trial in which risk factors become seen as diseases (or pre-diseases) and in which biomarkers become the measurable outcome of the trial. Succeeding in moving a biomarker in a population in an RCT then takes the place of showing that the treatment works. Described as a 'double shift' by Greene (2007), illness began to be seen in an entirely new way. Diseases previously regarded as incurable came to be seen as chronic conditions requiring surveillance and chronic treatment (Dumit 2012).

RCTs succeeded in part because they fit a model of bureaucratic rationality that privileged metrics over experience (Strathern 2000; Adams 2016; Dumit 2010). Lost in their ascendance was their requirement for ideal experimental conditions that are heavily controlled, with real-world noise methodologically purified out. It is this final form of large-scale RCT that has, under the practices that mark the regime of Global Health, become the foundation of evidence-based medicine (Brives et al. 2016). One way in which medical anthropology critiques this growing prevalence of RCTs is through attacking the reductive-ness of its magic bullet approach, or what Richard Degrandpre (2006) calls 'pharmacologicalism'; this is founded on the supposition that it is the drug's chemical structure that determines the drug's action in the body and not the environment of the treatment or the experience of the patient (so-called non-pharmacological factors). In this sense, the hero of the RCT story is the magic bullet, the active arrow of action. RCTs strip or purify the agency of the com-plexity of the intervention to ascribe all the credit to the single molecule, gen-erating spectacular profit margins in the process (Dumit 2012; Sunder Rajan 2017).

PSYCHEDELICS AS CRITIQUES OF MAGIC BULLETS

The case of the rise, demise, and contemporary 'renaissance' of psychedelic clinical trials (Chambers 2014; Sessa 2012; Tupper et al. 2015) directly chal-lenges RCTs in this regard. Psychedelics (from the Greek *psyche*, or mind, and *delos*, to reveal) like LSD were among the first drugs ever to be used in psychia-try in the 1950s and 1960s. Psychiatrist Charles Savage, at the 1955 LSD Research roundtable of the annual meeting of the American Psychiatric Association, first proposed the idea that 'set and setting' were not environmen-tal variables to be eliminated but an inseparable part of psychedelic experience and efficacy (Oram 2018, p. 35).[3] The 'container', in other words, was seen to be part of the drug. Set and setting went on to be popularised by Timothy Leary and colleagues in *The Psychedelic Experience* (Leary et al. 1964), becom-ing canonical in the field of psychedelic exploration and acquiring a more explicit notion of intention and design of appropriate conditions, spaces, and expectations to guide psychedelic experiences.

The popularity of the idea of set and setting in the field of psychedelics emerges from its function as a kind of boundary object, being at once specific and simultaneously nebulous (everything that is not the substance is potentially the set and setting). Accounting for the synergistic biological and setting effects of psychedelics in RCTs proved a huge challenge from the outset, as psycho-pharmacology was becoming 'oriented toward magic bullet treatments' (Oram 2018, p. 211). In psychedelic clinical trials, there is a huge signal (vs a small, diffused signal rendered statistically relevant by the apparatus of the randomised controlled trial). Psychedelic clinicians are often unsure how to make sense of these changes within the grammar of cause and effect, dose and outcome mea-sure. Psychedelic medicine thus ends up being a critique of pharmacologicalism, insisting that the container of set and setting is critical to accounting for efficacy, whilst paradoxically trying to validate its efficacy through the apparatus of the RCT.

The therapeutic model at work here is somewhat orthogonal to current psychotropic medication use in psychiatry, in which antidepressants and anti-psychotics are given in standardised doses over long periods of time (often years, and unsupervised). By contrast, psychedelic-assisted therapies make use of a few—or even one—drug or dosing sessions that are always supervised, generally preceded by preliminary psychotherapeutic sessions, and always fol-lowed by integration sessions in which sense is made of the experience along-side a health provider. It is the unique combination of the substance and this context, which is modelled on traditional ritual contexts, that is understood by advocates of this method to be such a powerful modality. This is to say, that the effects of psychedelic substances are dependent on the social dynamics and subjective intentions that play out during the dosing session; they are medi-cines in context. They have also been described as 'amplifiers' of wider pro-cesses (Talin and Sanabria 2017; Langlitz 2012; Winkelman and Roberts 2007).

While we find Degrandpre and Oram to be insightful in their critiques of RCTs and the magic bullet through emphasising the importance of set and set-ting, we also want to notice how the idea of set and setting does not by itself disrupt the magic bullet metaphor. Many contemporary approaches to psyche-delics still approach the drug as the critical variable and increasingly attempt to pin down experimentally the precise dosage constellation of set and setting needed to obtain optimal clinical results. In other words, even though these clinical trials give unprecedented attention to the setting of the pharmacologi-cal intervention, our sense is that they still operate within an underlying phar-macological ideology in which the new magic bullet is the molecule in a particular container. As investors continue to move in, it is interesting to observe how the psychedelic 'revolution' in mental health is being swept up by the broader tendency for innovative health solutions to be instrumentalised within capitalist frameworks of growth.

Capitalising on Medicine

Under imperatives of corporate growth, the primary purpose of RCTs for phar-maceutical companies has become that of creating the proof that a treatment works, separate from knowing what it actually does. RCTs thus became per-verted in their aims: turning from technologies for evidence of the best treat-ment, to technologies for generating the largest profit (Dumit 2012; Greene 2007). Anthropologists, STS scholars, and other critical researchers have shown that the pharmaceutical industry is extremely aware of contexts, of set and setting, precisely in order to control and then deny them so as to sustain the ideology of direct biological action and continue to overshadow the com-plex and uncertain feedback systems through which pharmaceuticals are rendered efficacious in lived bodies (Light et al. 2013; Healy 2012; Hardon and Sanabria 2017).

In other words, pharmaceutical company RCTs are also set and setting containers in their own right, in which all forms of care are identified as keenly as possible, in order to exclude them. Researchers work diligently to create specific contexts in which their molecules can shine. It turns out to be incredibly hard to keep the individual differences between providers, and how they care for patients, out of the RCT. It is also nigh on impossible to keep the caring that an experiment conveys in a world increasingly devoid of health care from infecting patients with hope or income (Fisher 2020; Le Marcis 2015; Pollock 2019). Most placebo research can be understood as the refusal to recognise care as a therapeutic force because it cannot be monetised by the company doing the study. Placebo response involves a complex of histories and approaches too large to review in this chapter. Here we focus on the fact that the market-oriented RCT is often controlled precisely in order to show that the drug is effective through comparison with those patients not receiving the drug, those in the placebo arm of the trial. Those patients need to be comparable and, therefore, they are often given a placebo, a pill that looks like the real one but lacks the active ingredient or magic bullet. Here a problem arises. Many patients in these arms of the trials experience statistically significant and biologically measurable improvement on the placebo. This is known as the placebo response. Indeed, simply being in a therapeutic system of any kind triggers endogenous processes which positively inflect therapeutic outcomes (Walach 2015, p. 132). The use of placebo controls in contemporary corporate RCTs can be read as an attempt to contain the effects of care providers and holding space.

Placebo is a critical and expensive problem for pharmaceutical companies. As anthropologist Lakoff puts it, the RCT is not about testing whether a drug works; the magic bullet is already assumed by the time the trial is run. The question is whether or not the context—the diversity of patients, doctors, environments, and so on—can be stabilised enough to prove the drug's efficacy to regulators.

> This can be seen in drug developers' use of the term 'signal detection' to refer to the goal of the trial. Here the drug is already presumed to have targeted efficacy—that is, a signal to transmit—and the problem is how to pick up the signal. From the perspective of drug developers, when trials fail, it is not that the drug does not work but that 'noise' has crept into the process. (Lakoff 2007, p. 65)

In other words, pharmaceutical companies do care about set and setting, precisely in order to prove that they do not matter. As Lakoff discovered, they strive in the most impressive ways to outsmart context. Among other things, companies try to figure out if there are some types of people who are helped more by the context than others; such placebo responders might then be excluded from the trials. The caregivers might be too caring, and so the protocol can be sanitised so that the drug is the only form of care. Lakoff found that clinical trial consultants take this to a strangely logical limit, and was told by a trial methodology specialist that identifying and excluding trial 'non-specific supportive contact' responders (such as 'overly' sensitive patients who respond to tasks like filling in forms) was necessary to improve trial results (Montgomery cited in Lakoff 2007).

From the perspective of patients and public health, this is evil; one should want to include any and all parts of care and context that promote health (Dumit 2018). If reassurance helps a patient recover faster, then why exclude it? Why even distinguish between specific and placebo effects, given that these are additive and synergistic (Walach 2015, p. 115)? Wahlberg (2008b) has shown how medical anthropology itself played a crucial role here by legitimising the notion of symbolic efficacy, leading to a need for RCTs to demonstrate efficacy beyond the placebo. Pharmaceutical companies recognise all of this and smuggle positive synergies in whenever possible, for profit not health. As Caspi points out in a roundtable:

> It is no longer a secret, and the pharmaceutical industry knows this, that in any international multicenter trial, the pharmaceutical industry typically has more site candidates than it needs, and that it selects those sites that have in the past performed well for it in terms of showing an effect of its drugs. (Ritenbaugh et al. 2010, p. 136; see also Petryna 2009)

The challenge that psychedelic clinical trials pose to mass pharmaceutical RCTs is that they reveal the degree to which context matters. The Johns Hopkins psychedelic clinical trials on smoking cessation and existential anxiety in patients with life-threatening cancer were landmark interventions, because they showed an incredible size of effect compared with all previous treatments, and they did so thanks to the extensive preparation given to patients, psychotherapy for mindset, and the meticulous production of a caring setting (Johnson et al. 2017). The deeper challenge within psychedelic research communities is whether this can remain in the service of well-being and a more equitable world. In 2018, over 100 researchers signed a 'Statement on Open Science and Open Praxis with Psilocybin, MDMA, and Similar Substances'. The statement recognised,

> From generations of practitioners and researchers before us, we have received knowledge about these substances, their risks, and ways to use them constructively. In turn, we accept the call to use that knowledge for the common good and to share freely whatever related knowledge we may discover or develop. (https://files.csp.org/open.pdf)

The signatories committed to placing 'the common good above private gain, and [to working] for the welfare of the individuals and communities served'. They engaged not to withhold 'materials or knowledge (experiences, observations, discoveries, methods, best practices, or the like) for commercial advantage', and to place 'discoveries into the public domain, for the benefit of all'. They stated that where patents must be held, these should only be used to cover 'ordinary administrative costs'. The recognition of mutual generosity in this statement suggests a vision of a different arrangement of politics, medicine, and healing, one not organised as a market but as a self-reflexive commons. But at a recent conference 2020 conference on investment opportunities in the burgeoning field of psychedelic medicine, we found this vision to be very much contested.

> *Fieldnotes:*[4] The event began with a self-identified 'serial investor' explaining that he had set up his psychedelic biotech startup after his first encounter with aya-huasca as he was 'backpacking through the Amazon'. 'This is going to be bigger than cannabis', another investment expert promised, 'but it will take longer to get there. This is an *exceptionally complicated space*, with a very high level of entry. But those who have the potential to bring these substances to market will see a huge return on investment.'
>
> The conference marks a transition in the so-called psychedelic 'renaissance', which seeks to reinstate demonised psychedelic substances as medicines by show-ing their surprising efficacy in treating addiction, PTSD, or depression through clinical trials. Initially led by non-profit and philanthropic organisations, the 'renaissance' has recently been marked by capitalisation and attempts to stake out intellectual property claims. As psychedelics move into Phase 3 of drug develop-ment, their potential to be 'bigger than cannabis' is becoming clearer. Panellists repeatedly emphasised how central the RCT is to delivering this promise. Another psychedelic start-up CEO described how 'the way to scale psychedelic medicines is through the FDA and the FDA values data'. Data, here, refers to solid empirical evidence of the kind produced through RCTs.

The tension inherent among the signatories is that while they agree that medi-cine needs to change in the long term, in the short term they also want to use clinical trials to generate international acceptance of psychedelic-assisted ther-apy. In adopting the RCT model actors of the psychedelic revival reinforce the idea of the magic bullet, one that is reduced to a market notion of technology. Many of the newer psychedelic RCTs in turn try to contain and then exclude not just the held space of care, but also all notions of community, place, and the immaterial and transcendental realms. Some of the signers of the statement have betrayed their pledge and are withholding materials and knowledge for commercial advantage. When we have posed questions about the distinction between non- and for-profit to investors and actors in this field, we are often told that this is a 'fake problem', and one investor described the issue as one of 'accelerating access', reinforcing the assumption that only patents can deliver investment and thereby access.

'Ayahuasca'/Listening to Plants

Ayahuasca is the generic Quechua name that has been globalised to refer to the different herbal brews widespread among indigenous groups in the Upper Amazon region where it is used in shamanic settings (Dobkin de Rios 1984; Labate and Cavnar 2014). In this context, it is understood to have a foundational cosmological significance as a 'plant teacher', imparting crucial knowledge through a peculiar form of trans-species communication. Euro-American societies have approached ayahuasca essentially in molecular terms, classifying the brew as a psychedelic, given that they identify N,N-Dimethyltryptamine (DMT) as its main active ingredient. DMT has a similar profile to LSD or psilocybin, operating through the serotonergic activation of 5-HT2A receptor agonism (dos Santos et al. 2016).

In the early twentieth century, along the rubber-tapping frontier, ayahuasca shamanic practices syncretised with Christian and Afro-Brazilian religious practices, giving rise to several Christian religions that consecrate ayahuasca, each with its own specific cult and doctrine (Dawson 2013; Labate and MacRae 2010). In the last decade, ayahuasca use has undergone unprecedented global expansion. Regular ayahuasca rituals now take place in over forty countries including Australia, New Zealand, South Africa, Israel, India, Japan, Russia, and twenty-two European countries (Labate and Loures de Assis 2017).

The spectacular diversity of ritual forms that have mushroomed globally as ayahuasca is taken up for a wide array of purposes from healing to self-awareness, experiential curiosity, boosting creativity, communing with Jesus, or neo-shamanic soul retrieval, is such that no single account will ever exhaust the potentialities people are actualising in their myriad uses of the brew. In what follows, we focus specifically on practices that have been qualified as neo-ayahuasca (Labate 2000), to refer to the fact that they are neither Indigenous nor entirely bound by the doctrines of the Ayahuasca churches. These often blend Spiritist, New Age, and Indigenous elements and have a strong psycho-spiritual dimension. What interests us in these specific ritual formations, in the context of the argument we are making here about container technologies, is the way they actively refuse to know what the problem is ahead of the encounter with the plant spirit. This can be read as a rejection of the epistemology and model of the magic bullet.

Isabel Santana de Rose (2006) provides an ethnographic analysis of a Brazilian spiritual healing centre that makes use of ayahuasca and counts a significant number of medical professionals in its congregation. In the particular centre she studies, a 'shamanic cure' was developed whereby medical doctors, who are part of the congregation and commonly give orientation on managing psychiatric diagnosis and dosage of the brew, have developed a specific ritual form of working with people. Here, health professionals-as-ritual-leaders and patients drink ayahuasca *together* to 'work' on a specific ailment or issue (the Portuguese term for performing an ayahuasca ritual is often 'doing a work' for this is considered labour, not recreation). One of these leaders tells De Rose that what will transpire during the ritual is 'unpredictable' because the aya-huasca is the one who decides what has to be done, not the therapist: 'the *Daime* [name commonly given to ayahuasca] is the surgeon and I am the scal-pel. It is it [ayahuasca] that is going to say what needs to be done, and I will execute that' (de Rose 2006, our translation). Their choice of words is particu-larly interesting, as they describe ayahuasca as being the intelligent agent in the encounter and themselves as the tool or technology. The doctors-as-facilitators create oracular conditions for the ritual, holding space for it. But once the encounter begins, the plant is the one directing the spiritual cure, using them as a (mere) scalpel. The choice of referring to a medical professional through the inert technology of the scalpel suggests a critique of the notion of active ingredient to which agency without intelligence is ascribed.

Let us now turn to a case study which reveals something of the complexity of how ayahuasca, its context, the group that comes together to hold ritual, and a person's own atemporal journey through healing are entangled. Larissa has a history of sexual abuse and explains that when she was fourteen, her mother suffered a sudden and untimely heart attack and died. Larissa devel-oped a profound fear of also dying of a heart attack, becoming overwhelmed at night with tachycardia and feeling as though she was *morendo do coração* (dying of the heart). Her broken heart became the locus of her pain. She learned to live with her nightly panic attacks, to quell her terrified heart with alcohol, and to dissociate from her body. She lived in anxiety, overwhelmed by the obsessive attention to her heart's broken rhythm. She stumbled upon ayahuasca acciden-tally two years ago, thinking it would be just another *barato* (high). But her life changed dramatically after this first encounter. She approached Sanabria after a collective ritual during which the ethnographic study had been presented, to share her story.

She explained that in a recent *trabalho* (work) a concentrated form of aya-huasca known as *estrela* (star) had been served. This was so strong that it awoke her tachycardia. It was so overbearing that she almost could not stand it. '*Me fui solicitado fazer uma limpeza* [I was asked to make a cleansing, i.e. to vomit]. And I was told it would be a process.' As the *limpeza* (cleansing) was happen-ing, she expunged layer upon layer of fear. As she cleansed, she understood the nature of this fear and the effect it continued to have on her. For several months, in the ceremonies she attended, she worked with this fear every time she partook in a ritual. It was difficult, but the group facilitators, with whom she had discussed her process, supported her and she received encouragement to stay with it. As she blended the insights of the ceremonies into her daily life, she gradually came to experience a new understanding of how the fear had taken root, quite materially, in her physical being, that before being physical, fear was energy. In her last session, she explained, she was able to go further than ever into the fear. During the session, her heart began beating so fast she became convinced that she was dying. She smiled inwardly to herself, feeling gratitude for the insights she had achieved, and opened herself peacefully to what was. This brought her to a place of pure aliveness. As she reclined, she felt *beijaflors* (hummingbirds) of light hovering around her heart, their little beaks weaving, removing, re-doing, cleaning, and placing good things into her heart. When they were finished, they sealed it and flew over to work on the next person. Since this experience, she has the deep conviction that she has cured herself of 'the future [heart] attack that my fear was programming me to have'.

Larissa is describing her own version of evidence-based medicine. As Larissa's story reveals, the healing efficacy at work in such ceremonial use cannot be reduced to any linearly progressing or predetermined outcome measures. It is not straightforwardly attributable to the molecular properties of ayahuasca, nor to Larissa's intention, nor to that of any of the facilitators holding space for her process. If anything, in this particular spiritist-inflected context, efficacy would be attributed first and foremost to the agency of invisible beings, all of whom fall entirely outside the remit of RCT outcome measures.

There is an inherent tension in the current move to pass psychedelic-assisted interventions through the randomised control trial machine, given its complete incapacity to render the entangled, multifold textures of healing to which such narratives allude. In the Brazilian neo-ayahuasqueiro circles where we have worked, neither illness nor healing is treated as settled categories that can be known in the absolute, outside of a carefully built-up understanding of the specificity of each person's particular circumstances (see Talin and Sanabria 2017). While in clinical trials the intervention needs to be calibrated across all study subjects to enable comparison, and the subjects calibrated as equally suffering, in these circles it is often assumed that no two situations are ever the same and that nothing about a person's process can be known from the outside. Facilitators are trained to provide non-invasive supervision of the experience in order for each participant's process to be held without either intrusiveness or neglect. Their role is characterised by a deep presence but minimal physical and verbal contact. For many people we speak with, the experience of this kind of non-directive care was, in and of itself, deeply transformative (Talin and Sanabria 2017). In both Larissa's story and in de Rose's account, the encounter with ayahuasca is experienced as neither heroic technology nor magic bullet; rather, it is the source of understanding the situation, the healer or guide for the individual and the collective. Instead of Western science knowing that there is a medical problem to be solved by a treatment, the encounter itself is experienced as that which allows the problem to emerge as well as guiding the healing trajectory. The ethnographic work we are conducting among groups holding ceremonial ayahuasca work reveals that what matters here is how the work gathers whole communities in the telling. The very concept of technology that we, as analysts tied to the conceptual apparatus of Western analytics, find so hard to evade perpetually returns us to the intrepid Hero, the magic bullet, or the tools of motion and spatial extension, often obfuscating more unobtrusive forms of containment, rendering them invisible.

Ayahuasca Is Not a Psychedelic

The voices of Indigenous peoples are eloquent in this regard. They tirelessly remind Western enthusiasts that the stories of ayahuasca and plant medicines are indissociable from the histories of extractivism, colonialism, missionarisation, and epistemicide. They explain that trying to understand ayahuasca within the frame of biomedicine is an ongoing appropriative, colonial, and violent practice. In a declaration on cultural appropriation published in 2019, the Union of Indigenous Yagé Medics of the Colombian Amazon (UMIYAC) reaffirmed:

> Today we are still suffering from colonization and invasion. Armed groups, drug-traffickers, land grabbers, mining and hydrocarbons multinationals, timber traffickers and cattle ranchers continue to threaten the survival of our people, guardians of Amazonian ecosystems; which serve as the vital organs for life throughout the planet. The spiritual authorities of the indigenous peoples of the Amazon basin are the people responsible for preserving the spiritual traditions and knowledge of the sacred medicine of the yagé (ayahuasca). Through the practice of yagé medicine we have managed to resist the invasion and protect our autonomy. With yagé we also heal the illnesses of community members, protect our territories and protect the lives of our leaders. Thanks to the sacred yagé plant since childhood, communicating with the spirits of Mother Earth we have cultivated wisdom, and have learned which medicinal plants are useful for curing diseases. Yagé is not a hallucinogen and is not a psychedelic plant. Yagé is a plant that has a living spirit and teaches us how to live in peace and harmony with Mother Earth. (UMIYAC 2019)

The Declaration of the Third Indigenous Ayahuasca Conference, held in October 2019 on Ashaninka territory, also reminds the Western publics engaging with ayahuasca that it is impossible to dissociate the protection of sacred plants from the protection of territories, traditional knowledge, and spirituality. The declaration powerfully articulates the need for international and state-level mechanisms of environmental protection, forest regeneration, ecological management of plants and animals, and food sovereignty, and calls on state and supranational agencies to denounce and halt the illegal actions of loggers, hunters, drug traffickers, agro-industrial businesses, miners, and infrastructural projects such as dams and roads in Indigenous and protected territories.[5]

Addressing the Psychedelic Liberty Summit in May 2020, artist, activist, and scholar Daiara Tukano of the Tukano Yé'pá Mahsã Nation of the Alto Rio Negro (Brazilian Amazon) gave a powerful presentation on Indigenous concerns over the globalisation of ayahuasca. She explained that ayahuasca, for Indigenous peoples, is not 'just a medicine'. Rather, it is 'a fountain, the origin of all other knowledge'. Keepers of the knowledge of ayahuasca are much more than healers, she told an online assembly of North American and European psychonauts.[6] They are 'responsible for the continuity of the culture, the nation'. Voicing the concerns Indigenous people have with the misuse and cultural appropriation of ayahuasca, she explained that it is very challenging to see the rise of non-Indigenous use of ayahuasca given that, for her people, those who are entrusted with this knowledge and the authority to conduct ritual need to be deserving, dedicated, and have impeccable ethics. Only those who have deserved the transmission, have undergone an intense process of learning through *Dieta* (an ongoing practice of isolation, study, and meticulous obedience to ritual behavioural and alimentary proscriptions), and shown themselves to be moved by a deep community ethic (where the well-being of the entire community is central to their practice) become entrusted with the knowledge.

Daiara Tukano's intervention is extremely important as it explicitly repositions the contemporary boom of ayahuasca (itself intricately tied to the Euro-American psychedelic renaissance) within the ongoing history of colonialism. Speaking candidly of her grandfather's, father's, and uncle's deep surprise at the uptake of ayahuasca by the whites, she repositions the story of this medicine's expansion from the perspective of her Elders who were banned and demonised for expressing their culture, torn from their communities to be educated in Portuguese mission schools, and assimilated, who experienced the military dictatorship and led the fight for cultural, civic, and territorial Indigenous rights. The current move to capitalise on psychedelics does more than ignore this history, it erases the ongoing dispossession of land and language and health in the Amazon while profiting from the unequal relations of power and access, as well as intentionally excising community, plant, and planetary ethics from the ethics of clinical trial design and approval.

Indigenous scholar Ibã Dua Bake from the Huni Kuin people of Brazil foregrounds the intensely colonial relations of the rubber estate which his people endured until the early 1980s and under which ayahuasca rituals (or speaking one's language) were prohibited. Ibã was handed down the corpus of chants that accompany the *Nixi pae* ritual (Huni Kuin term for ayahuasca) from his father, Txana Tuin, who had received them from his grandfather and generations immemorial before him. What Ibã tells us is that this corpus came to his ancestors from a mythic being, Yube Inu, to whom he sometimes refers as the Spirit of the Forest. When Ibã recorded and transcribed the chants of which his father was the keeper, he carried out what he calls a first translation, a translation between Hatxa Kuin (an oral human language) into its written form (a neo-colonial artefact, a codification in writing that emerged in the context of the bilingual education programmes in which he was trained). This first transcription into the written form was met with numerous requests to translate from written Hatxa Kuin into Portuguese. Jokingly, Ibã often says he had to respond, 'Now *that* would be impossible! That was going too far into realms of incommensurability' (see also Mattos and Huni Kuin 2017).

We read this engaging resistance to submitting the corpus of sacred ayahuasca chants to translation as a refusal to allow the entangled trans-species assemblage of plant-territory-ancestors to be colonised and captured by a logic of plant-as-molecules plus set and setting. Ibã's refusal echoes the refusals of

Native American authors (Tuck and Yang 2014; Simpson 2017). The forest, its spirit beings, the village and *kupixawa* (ritual house), the stars, moon, and astral beings, the waters and winds, the living territory are not reducible here to concepts such as the 'environment' or the 'setting' of the experience. Ayahuasca is not a technology, but it has much to teach.

Conclusion

While psychedelic-assisted clinical trials are container technologies, they are modelled after traditional plant medicine settings that hold space for what needs to emerge. These settings are explicitly anti-causal, unpredictable, and deeply paradoxical encounters in which what matters (including the problem) is not knowable ahead of time. They are first and foremost concerned with providing a space for a process to unfold, where what unfolds is not reducible or attributable to the isolated actions or intentions of either healer or client. When space is held in this way, it enables something to happen without humans or things being the cause of it. In this sense it is not reducible to action, intention, or even to the act of containing. These processes have very different and emergent qualities from magic bullet trials. Holding space takes the risk of letting something occur, of surrendering to a level of unknown that may exceed the experimental boundaries and call the community to account, a process that nevertheless receives meticulous preparation.

By contrast, biomedical technologies—of the kind that are validated under our current regime of RCTs—are concerned with risk aversion and aim to circumscribe the unknown, to leave as little as possible to chance, attributing agency to a substance controlled and owned by the experimenters, and assumed to act solely at the level of a disease suffered by an individual, not a mutual transformation of all those engaged in the encounter. Starting with technology as a frame for analysis, we found it implicitly reinforces colonial orders and inequalities by implying that 'we' already know the problems and the ways in which solutions can be explored or experimented with. We are drawn to the frame of 'holding space' for different collective futures to come into being.

In this chapter, we highlighted the ways in which the RCTs we study (BigPharma and psychedelic RCTs) have built a tight coupling of heroic narratives of progress and science within an assumed context of market evaluation and institutionalised deference to regimes of intellectual property. We observe the way the market gets assumed and positioned as the source of value, deeply reorienting the utopian field of psychedelic research despite many psychedelic clinicians' stated values of openness and distrust of BigPharma. We are concerned that even their initial commitment to open-source research and benefit-sharing still maintains a frame in which they know what a medical problem looks like, and are not open to questioning psychiatric definitions of problems cast as individual issues rather than as socially or structurally unjust. We find it useful to attend to the frames of technology through the question of how they implicitly or explicitly reinforce colonial orders by pre-defining what counts as the problem and, therefore, the kinds of solutions that can legitimately be explored. Without throwing out the notion of technology altogether, we conclude by turning again to la paperson's analysis of property law as a settler-colonial technology:

> The weapons that enforce it, the knowledge institutions that legitimize it, the financial institutions that operationalize it, are also technologies. [...] Instead of settler colonialism as an ideology, or as a history, *you might consider settler colonialism as a set of technologies*—a frame that could help you to forecast colonial next operations and to plot decolonial directions'. (la paperson 2017, p. 21, emphasis added)

We read magic bullets as one pinnacle of a process of alienation that begins with the recasting of lands and nonhumans as extractable property. Factoring in setting experimentally is a potentially helpful first step for the de-individualising of mental health, but only a first step. RCTs need not always be described as colonial technologies, given that there are many different forms of colonialism and of inclusions of plant remedies into the logics of RCT (Foster 2016; Wahlberg 2008a), but in the case we are describing it is important to heed the histories and problems Indigenous peoples are raising about this process. The frame of container technology begins to get us further, but does not overcome the way Indigenous knowledge and practices are often tokenised in psychedelic events, while approaching ayahuasca and other Indigenous medicines as psychedelics contributes to the erasure of the ongoing destruction of Indigenous communities and territories and extraction/perversion of their knowledge systems. We should be ever more careful how the very frame of technology contains some worlds and delegitimates others. If set and setting are ever to have any real-world value, then they would have to include not just structural determinants of health and inequality, but spirits, community, time, the forest and equitable forms of inhabiting the world, for humans and more-than-humans.

Acknowledgements This research was made possible by generous support from the ERC Starting Grant n°757589 'Healing Encounters: reinventing an indigenous medicine in the clinic and beyond' based at CERMES3 (Université de Paris, EHESS, CNRS). The authors acknowledge invaluable feedback from the Oxidate Writing Group, as well as by the editors and anonymous reviewers of this Handbook.

Notes

1. Arguing for a better definition of technology does not change the ongoing effect of the category of the standard view of technology. Collaborations between Indigenous actors and colonial states or pharmaceutical companies are important in their successes and failures (Wahlberg 2008a), but they do not change the ongoing effects of state, colonial, and capitalist violence on communities conducted under the banner of medical and technological development.

2. COVID-19 has brought some (but only some) of these structural inequalities in medicine to the fore, but not essentially changed them (Metzl et al. 2020).
3. Medical historian Oram argues that Savage's experiments with LSD to treat depressed and psychotic patients were not only the first to make use of a control group in LSD research, but one of the earliest examples of controlled experimentality in psychiatry (Oram 2018, p. 29).
4. These are summary notes taken by the authors attending a virtual conference. Speakers have been anonymised as per the IRB.
5. An English version of the text is available here: https://chacruna.net/declaration-of-the-3rd-brazilian-indigenous-conference-on-ayahuasca/.   Accessed   3 November 2020.
6. On 'healers, but not only', see de la Cadena (2015).

REFERENCES

Adams, V. (2016). *Metrics: What Counts in Global Health.* Duke University Press.

Brandt, A. M. (2007). *The Cigarette Century: The Rise, Fall, and Deadly Persistence of the Product That Defined America.* Basic Books.

Brives, C., Le Marcis, F., & Sanabria, E. (2016). What's in a Context? Tenses and Tensions in Evidence-Based Medicine. *Medical Anthropology: Cross-Cultural Studies in Health and Illness, 35*(5). https://doi.org/10.1080/01459740.2016.1160089.

Chambers, T. (2014). Editor's Introduction: Psychedelic Resurgence—Research and Therapeutic Uses, Past and Present. *Journal of Psychoactive Drugs, 46*(1), 1–2. https://doi.org/10.1080/02791072.2014.874243.

Chacrunanet. (2020). Declaration of the 3rd Brazilian Indigenous Conference on Ayahuasca. *Chacruna.* https://chacruna.net/declaration-of-the-3rd-brazilian-indigenous-conference-on-ayahuasca/. Accessed 8 July 2021.

Dawson, A. (2013). *Santo Daime: A New World Religion.* Bloomsbury. https://doi.org/10.5040/9781472552617.

de la Cadena, M. (2015). *Earth beings: Ecologies of practice across Andean worlds.* Duke University Press.

Degrandpre, R. (2006). *The Cult of Pharmacology: How America Became the World's Most Troubled Drug Culture.* Duke University Press.

Dobkin de Rios, M. (1984). *Visionary vine: Hallucinogenic healing in the Peruvian Amazon.* Waveland Press.

dos Santos, R. G., Osorio, F. L., Crippa, J. A. S., Riba, J., Zuardi, A. W., & Hallak, J. E. C. (2016). Antidepressive, anxiolytic, and antiaddictive effects of ayahuasca, psilocybin and lysergic acid diethylamide (LSD): A systematic review of clinical trials published in the last 25 years: Antidepressive effects of ayahuasca, psilocybin and LSD. *Therapeutic Advances in Psychopharmacology*, 193–213. https://doi.org/10.1177/2045125316638008.

Dumit, J. (2010). Inter-pill-ation and the instrumentalization of compliance. *Anthropology & Medicine, 17*(2), 245–247.

Dumit, J. (2012). *Drugs for Life: How Pharmaceutical Companies Define Our Health.* Duke University Press.

Dumit, J. (2018). The Infernal Alternatives of Corporate Pharmaceutical Research: Abandoning Psychiatry. *Medical Anthropology, 37*(1), 59–74, https://doi.org/10.1080/01459740.2017.1360877.

Fisher, J. (2020). *Adverse Events: Race, Inequality, and the Testing of New Pharmaceuticals.* New York University Press.

Foster, L. (2016). The Making and Unmaking of Patent Ownership: Technicalities, Materialities, and Subjectivities. *POLAR Political and Legal Anthropology Review, 39*(1), 127–143.

Greene, J. (2007). *Prescribing by Numbers: Drugs and the Definition of Disease.* Johns Hopkins University Press.

Hardon, A., & Sanabria, E. (2017). Fluid drugs: Revisiting the anthropology of pharmaceuticals. *Annual Review of Anthropology, 46,* 117–132. https://doi.org/10.1146/annurev-anthro-102116-041539.

Healy, D. (2012). *Pharmageddon.* University of California Press.

Johnson, M. W., Garcia-Romeu, A., & Griffiths, R. R. (2017). Long-term follow-up of psilocybin-facilitated smoking cessation. *The American Journal of Drug and Alcohol Abuse, 43*(1), 55–60. https://doi.org/10.3109/00952990.2016.1170135.

Labate, B. (2000). *A reinvenção do uso da ayahuasca nos centros urbanos* [Universidade Estadual de Campinas, Instituto de Filosofia e Ciencias Humanas]. http://www.repositorio.unicamp.br/handle/REPOSIP/279073. Accessed 8 July 2021.

Labate, B., & Cavnar, C. (2014). *Ayahuasca Shamanism in the Amazon and Beyond.* Oxford University Press.

Labate, B., & Loures de Assis, G. (2017). The religion of the forest: Reflections on the international expansion of a Brazilian ayahuasca religion. In B. Labate, C. Cavnar, & A. Gearin (Eds.), *The World Ayahuasca Diaspora: Reinventions and Controversies* (pp. 57–78). Routledge.

Labate, B., & MacRae, E. (2010). *Ayahuasca, ritual and religion in Brazil.* Routledge.

Lakoff, A. (2007). The Right Patients for the Drug: Managing the Placebo Effect in Antidepressant Trials. *BioSocieties, 2*(1), 57–71. https://doi.org/10.1017/S1745855207005054.

Langlitz, N. (2012). *Neuropsychedelia: The revival of hallucinogen research since the decade of the brain.* University of California Press.

Le Guin, U. K. (1989). *Dancing at the Edge of the World.* Grove Press.

Le Marcis, F. (2015). Life promises and 'failed' family ties: Expectations and disappointment within a clinical trial (Ivory Coast). *Anthropology & Medicine, 22*(3), 295–308. https://doi.org/10.1080/13648470.2015.1081671.

Leary, T., Metzner, R., & Alpert, R. (1964). *The Psychedelic Experience: A Manual Based on The Tibetan Book of the Dead.* University Books.

Light, D., Lexchin, J., & Darrow, J. (2013). Institutional Corruption of Pharmaceuticals and the Myth of Safe and Effective Drugs. *The Journal of Law, Medicine & Ethics, 41*(3), 590–600. https://doi.org/10.1111/jlme.12068.

Marks, H. (2000). *The Progress of Experiment Science and Therapeutic Reform in the United States, 1900–1990.* Cambridge University Press.

Mattos, A. P. de, & Huni Kuin, I. (2017). Por que canta o MAHKU – Movimento dos Artistas Huni Kuin? *GIS - Gesto, Imagem e Som - Revista de Antropologia, 2*(1). https://doi.org/10.11606/issn.2525-3123.gis.2017.128974.

Metzl, J. M., Maybank, A., & De Maio, F. (2020). Responding to the COVID-19 Pandemic: The Need for a Structurally Competent Health Care System. *JAMA, 324*(3), 231–232. https://doi.org/10.1001/jama.2020.9289.

Nelson, A. (2013). *Body and soul: The Black Panther Party and the fight against medical discrimination.* University of Minnesota Press.

Oram, M. (2018). *The Trials of Psychedelic Therapy: LSD Psychotherapy in America.* Johns Hopkins University Press.

paperson, la. (2017). *A Third University Is Possible.* University of Minnesota Press.

Petryna, A. (2009). *When Experiments Travel: Clinical Trials and the Global Search for Human Subjects*. Princeton University Press.

Pollock, A. (2019). *Synthesizing Hope: Matter, Knowledge, and Place in South African Drug Discovery*. Chicago University Press.

Proctor, R. (2012). *Golden Holocaust: Origins of the Cigarette Catastrophe and the Case for Abolition*. University of California Press.

Ritenbaugh, C., Aickin, M., Bradley, R., Caspi, O., Grimsgaard, S., & Musial, F. (2010). Whole Systems Research Becomes Real: New Results and Next Steps. *The Journal of Alternative and Complementary Medicine, 16*(1), 131–137. https://doi.org/10.1089/acm.2009.0650.

Rose, I. S. de (2006). Repensando as Fronteiras entre Espiritualidade e Terapia: Reflexões sobre a 'cura' no Santo Daime. *CAMPOS - Revista de Antropologia Social, 7*(1). https://doi.org/10.5380/cam.v7i1.5450.

Sessa, B. (2012). Shaping the renaissance of psychedelic research. *The Lancet, 380*(9838), 200–201. https://doi.org/10.1016/S0140-6736(12)60600-X.

Simpson, A. (2017). The ruse of consent and the anatomy of 'refusal': Cases from indigenous North America and Australia. *Postcolonial Studies, 20*(1), 18–33. https://doi.org/10.1080/13688790.2017.1334283.

Sofia, Z. (2000). Container Technologies. *Hypatoa, 15*(2), 181–201.

Strathern, M. (2000). *Audit Cultures: Anthropological Studies in Accountability, Ethics and the Academy*. Routledge.

Sunder Rajan, K. (2017). *Pharmocracy: Trials of Global Biomedicine*. Duke University Press.

Talin, P., & Sanabria, E. (2017). Ayahuasca's entwined efficacy: An ethnographic study of ritual healing from 'addiction'. *International Journal of Drug Policy, 44*, 23–30. https://doi.org/10.1016/j.drugpo.2017.02.017.

Tuck, E., & Yang, K. W. (2014). R-words: Refusing research. In D. Paris & M. T. Winn (Eds.), *Humanizing Research: Decolonizing Qualitative Inquiry with Youth and Communities* (pp. 223–248). SAGE Publications, Inc. https://doi.org/10.4135/9781544329611.

Tupper, K. W., Wood, E., Yensen, R., Johnson, M. W., & Wood, E. (2015). *Psychedelic medicine: A re-emerging therapeutic paradigm. 187*(14), 1054–1059.

UMIYAC (The Union of Indigenous Yagé Medics of the Colombian Amazon). (2019). *Declaration about cultural appropriation from the spiritual authorities, representatives and indigenous organizations of the amazon region* [Declaration]. https://umiyac.org/2019/11/01/declaration-about-cultural-appropriation-from-the-spiritual-authorities-representatives-and-indigenous-organizations-of-the-amazon-region/?lang=en. Accessed 8 July 2021.

Wahlberg, A. (2008a). Pathways to Plausibility: When Herbs Become Pills. *BioSocieties, 3*(1), 37–56. https://doi.org/10.1017/S1745855208005942.

Wahlberg, A. (2008b). Above and beyond superstition—Western herbal medicine and the decriminalizing of placebo: *History of the Human Sciences, 21*(1), 77–101. https://doi.org/10.1177/0952695107086153.

Walach, H. (2015). Reconstructing the Meaning Effect: The Capacity to Self-Heal Emerges From the Placebo Concept. *Tidsskrift for Forskning i Sygdom og Samfund, 23*, 111–139.

Winkelman, M., & Roberts, T. (Eds.) (2007). *Psychedelic Medicine: New Evidence for Hallucinogenic Substances as Treatments*. Praeger Publisher.

CHAPTER 16

Assembling Population Data in the Field: The Labour, Technologies, and Materialities of Quantification

Survey

Cal Biruk

...this is an empire that ought to be more self reliant because it is so self contained.... It has every climate in its gigantic sweep; it has alternating seasons—while you have summer here, we in the southern hemisphere have winter there and vice versa; and in the middle of that is a great belt of tropical country over which the British flag happily flies in so many lands which abound in fertility and productive power the whole year round. There is an unbroken continuity of production and supply... the British empire is a whole world in itself. ('The British Empire Exhibit', 1920)

These words appear in a booklet, produced in 1920, that touted the prospect of a British Empire Exhibition, a spectacle that eventually became reality in a London suburb in 1924–1925.[1] The Exhibition took the form of a leisure park—featuring national pavilions, an amusement park, cinemas, and so on—that celebrated the empire's contributions to British war efforts and conjured a bright imperial future articulated in the rhetoric of a 'family of nations'. It included displays of local distinctiveness ('national gifts' ranging from artistic creations such as pottery and weaving through local foodstuffs and crops to curios and dioramic representations of humans engaged in 'native' pursuits)

C. Biruk (✉)
McMaster University, Hamilton, ON, Canada
e-mail: birukc@mcmaster.ca

© The Author(s), under exclusive license to Springer Nature Singapore Pte Ltd. 2022
M. H. Bruun et al. (eds.), *The Palgrave Handbook of the Anthropology of Technology*, https://doi.org/10.1007/978-981-16-7084-8_16

put together by dominions, colonies, industries, and private bodies in collaboration with the authorities. Meant to act as an 'object-lesson for every part of the Empire', the display reflected the ideal of a 'self contained', 'self reliant', and 'unbroken' British world that held within its boundaries—neatly containerised and secure from messy exteriors in a post-war world—people, resources, and labour that could be optimised towards imperial profit. As the Rt. Hon. L.S. Avery, M.P, put it, in response to a lecture delivered by Major Belcher on the advantages of the British Empire exhibit to the Royal Society for the Encouragement of Arts, Manufactures and Commerce on 6 March 1923, 'Development demand[s] the proper co-operation and mutual adjustment of three things, namely, *population, capital, and markets*' (Belcher 1923, p. 395, my emphasis). The Exhibition, thus, imparted to audiences their membership in a population that stretched far beyond national borders. Yet it also sought to engender support for the 'adjustment' or manipulation of relations between population and economy, intervening in the qualities, pathologies, and deviances of life itself for the good of this family of nations (Foucault 2008).[2] In imperial communications, the economy was rendered a 'container for life, surrounding it and setting its conditions of possibility' (Murphy 2017, p. 10). Indeed, the booklet optimistically celebrates the abundance of 'fertility' and 'productive power' in the Empire, casting them as latent values that require investment in the form of development. The double entendre of these words—as characteristics lying in wait to be exploited in land and natural resources, and characteristics inherent to imperial subjects who labour in two senses (production and re-production)—belies the conflation of bodies and landscape in the colonial imagination (Vaughan 1991, p. 35). Not long after the Exhibition, Britain passed the Colonial Development and Welfare Act (1940), legislation that would become central to the imperial government's provision of financial aid to dependent colonies. As Helen Tilley (2011) argues, this legislation ushered in an era of research and scientific expertise as components of a development plan, turning far-flung locations in Africa into laboratories in which imperial science could quantify and measure—and subsequently tinker with and manipulate—dimensions pertaining to resources, revenue, and production (see also Constantine 1984; Bonneuil 2000).

My chapter deliberately begins with one of the greatest colonial spectacles of all time, interested as it is in considering the role of material practices and technologies in the theatricalised, almost magical, production of a term and knowledge object ('population') that motivates ambitious projects of control and management across time and space. In the British Empire, for example, a new interest in 'development' called for statistics that could represent the numbers of people (populations)—and the problems that plagued them—across the globe. Counting entities ranging from people and diseases to arable land and mosquitos within the set borders of numerous nations became an imperative whose fundamental logics and interests resonate with those of postcolonial projects likewise invested in development, global health, and family planning. Focusing on Africa, and Malawi in particular, this chapter aims to capture the role that materialities and technologies of demographic field research (often glossed as fieldwork) play in the production of the idea and knowledge object of 'population'. This chapter recalls my long-term fieldwork with demographic research projects, based in American population studies centres, that were collecting health data in one corner of postcolonial Africa. These projects administered questionnaires (and collected other data, including, in some cases, HIV tests and anthropomorphic details) to thousands of rural households in 2007–2008, about 80 years after the imperial discussions of population and economy highlighted above.

As an anthropologist among the demographers, I traced the social lives of quantitative data collected, stored, analysed, and circulated by these projects, participating in all aspects of research including survey design, survey piloting, household-level data collection, attendance at national and international conferences centred on population science, and so on. The bulk of my time in Malawi was spent with a cohort of hundreds of Malawian research fieldworkers who took on roles as field supervisors, data collectors, and data entry clerks. On a daily basis, I accompanied fieldworkers as they navigated the complex physical, social, ethical, and power relations that congeal in the epistemological entity termed 'the field'. I observed encounters between fieldworkers and research participants, checked countless surveys for completeness and accuracy, and generally learned the ropes of being a fieldworker on longitudinal survey projects in rural areas. My interest was in showcasing the complex relations, transactions, technologies, and practices that materialise quantitative data that become the basis for claims about morbidity, mortality, marriage and reproduction, health and sickness, and economic behaviour. My work also included collecting the data points by which these phenomena can be known and captured, projects that effectively invented and stabilised 'population' as a site and container of knowledge production and management (Biruk 2018). Demographers, I show, are engaged in a set of knowing practices that take form as material engagements that reconfigure the world(s) they study (Barad 2007, p. 91).

There are significant differences between British imperial modes of knowing and counting subjects of empire and the contemporary iteration of American population science that preoccupies me here. Yet continuities in their designs and ambitions to improve, develop, and modernise 'other' people and places foreground how colonial and contemporary projects require the creation of experimental sites across the globe, including laboratories and fields (Oudshoorn 1997, p. 42). Notably, such sites do not emerge whole cloth, but are often repurposed or reconfigured for new uses as temporalities layer on top of one another: a colonial tuberculosis sanatorium in India becomes a government hospital in the present (Venkat 2019) or a Soviet-funded hospital in colonial Kenya becomes the present-day home of research co-sponsored by USAID, for example (Prince 2020). These spaces, in addition to being sites of knowledge-making and storage, also act as reservoirs of affects, memory, nostalgia, and social connections, even long after they close down operations, as Geissler et al.

(2016) show for medical research sites in Africa, and Heggie (2016) for high altitude field stations in the Alps, Antarctica, and the Himalayas. Taking as a starting point Foucault's suggestion that 'population' designates a field of objects amenable to being brought into the 'realm of explicit calculation' through some shared sameness, this chapter maps the contours of one such 'field of objects' in Malawi. In examining the material practices and technologies of quantification and coordination that characterise efforts to enumerate people, places, and things in Africa, this chapter reviews important concepts, drawn from anthropological and science studies literatures, that have animated and enhanced the anthropology of technology and technoscience as it intersects the broad concept of 'population'. The chapter is organised around two areas of inquiry crucial to understanding and analysing the production and circulation of population as an epistemic artefact: ethnographies of counting and classification and the rise of the field sciences. Before I turn to each of these, I provide a brief summary of population as a project and epistemological tool for demographers and others.

Population as Knowledge Object

The projects in which I spent time in Malawi are one node in a vast network of population activities whose logics and intentions can be traced back to nineteenth-century debates about birth control that produced twentieth-century international family planning campaigns. Demographic orthodoxy suggested that Global South societies would see declines in fertility, predicted by a demographic transition theory that linked increasing modernisation (from a Western beholder's point of view) to decreased fertility. This justified a host of development projects and interventions into reproductive processes and intimacies across the globe, particularly amid post-World War II anxieties about a 'population bomb'. A global infrastructure of family planning NGOs and projects became the platform for later clinical trials and research that continue to bring bodily material and data surrendered by Southern populations into economic circuits of biovalue reliant on embodied and clinical labour disproportionately outsourced to vulnerable populations (Petryna 2009; Murphy 2012, p. 16; Cooper and Waldby 2014; Rajan 2017).

Demography is a field that has built relevance around the study of fertility and population growth; its expertise aligned with US foreign policy needs during the Cold War and promoted family planning to solve 'third world' problems, in the process becoming strongly oriented towards policymaking and reliant on donor funds (Szreter 1993; Sharpless 1995; Sasser 2018). Greenhalgh (1996, p. 35) illuminates the roots of the field in the US in a set of anxieties around birth control, immigration, and eugenics—'activist' agendas from which demography as a field would later seek to distance itself via anxious 'scientism' invested in pure evidence and inquiry. With the rise of internationalism and new transnational institutions, the market for demographic research emerged with what we have come to know as development, a project infused with assumptions of linear progress and undergirded by investments in the goal of lowered fertility in the Global South. The latter was exacerbated by fears of being outnumbered and the security threats posed by the imaginary of entire swaths of the 'developing world' as communist breeding grounds (Murphy 2012, p. 13). In its golden years (1960s–1970s), demography became institutionalised via centres of demographic training and population science. These were funded through action grants, donors, and private foundations such as Rockefeller, Mellon, Hewlett, USAID, World Bank, UNFPA, and Ford (some of which likewise provided funds to the survey projects in Malawi), for their embrace of the family planning agenda (Harkavy 1995, pp. 41–58).

Demographers construct population through identifying common characteristics that bring different individuals into sameness (e.g., 'women of reproductive age'), in the process delinking parts of individuals from other parts of themselves and from their social context(s) (Cruz 2016). The scientific activity of comparison relies on categories and metrics that sort people into groups, a technique that relies on entanglements of people, things, and places (Merry 2011; Adams 2016). The materialities of such engagements are what make metrics portable carriers of expedient information in a larger development apparatus. For example, population scientists take the 'household' as a key unit of counting in population science (Randall et al. 2011); yet, the 'thinginess' of the household only materialises through the everyday practices of the fieldworkers who must first identify it, and then list its members onto a questionnaire's roster. This labour entails trudging through mud, getting lost, or relying on local scouts to provide them with directions and introduce them to local chiefs. It also requires that demographers invest time and resources in intensive training for data collectors that seeks to align their writing practices with standards and expectations associated with high-quality data that is accurate, valid, and ethically collected (Biruk 2012). Anthropologists have argued that modes of counting at the core of demography obscure cultural and other complexity when they convert people and processes into data points. Bledsoe (2002, p. 95), in her work on fertility in the Gambia, shows how population scientists' interpretations of their numbers fundamentally misread the local landscape: she illustrates how what appeared to be good uptake of birth control actually reflected Gambian women's efforts to rest their bodies between births, a kind of birth spacing rather than birth prevention (see also Johnson-Hanks 2007 on self-reported versus demographically attributed intentions in African countries).

Critiques of demography have illuminated it as one genre of Western science and technology that facilitates colonisation and development, a project that has in reality furthered underdevelopment or maldevelopment (Rodney 1972; Escobar 1994). Indeed, the very assumptions built into modernisation theory, which lies at the core of development projects, are grounded in racial and gendered stereotypes (Greenhalgh 1995), including those of black hypersexuality or promiscuity and pathological motherhood. Betsy Hartmann (2016, p. 10), among others, debunks such stereotypes and crude culturalist attributions, showing instead how high birth rates are often a distress signal that people's survival is endangered, not that they are endangering their own survival by having too many kids—the racialisation of sexualised tropes is evident in figures like the oversexed African woman and the US welfare mom alike. Attributing overpopulation to individual behaviours, rather than to complex structural factors, facilitates the authority of facile assumptions that capital, science, and/or technology will do away with poverty and depress birth rates. These build on long-standing discourses that uphold the 'entrepreneurial citizen' and, more recently, extol technologies produced through ethical design as minimalist forms of care (Redfield 2012; Irani 2019).

As many have documented, quantitative population data have long been used 'against' populations (as in extending military control, eradicating so-called harmful cultural practices and traditions, resettlement, and taxation). Producing population as a category of knowledge inevitably creates and reinforces taxonomies of race and culture, reifying entire groups of people as 'natives' and complex congeries of practices as 'culture' so they can be easily targeted by civilising projects rooted in logics of conversion and eradication (Mamdani 2012). Africa has long been a site of oscillating concerns between over and under population (Ittman 2010, p. 59). In 1928, F. Dixey (1928, p. 290), the government geologist of Nyasaland, cited a census report to support his claims about the water supply and the 'highly congested' native population in the 'European towns' of Blantyre and Limbe; the report mobilised rhetoric to blame water shortages on the natives who 'denuded the land of trees' such that streams dried up. The natives' supposed 'ruthless destruction of forest' is an 'evil' (p. 275) to be remedied or 'fixed', likely through resettlement or development initiatives that would facilitate the interests of Malawi's small settler population (see also Mulwafu 2011). Population becomes, as well, a moralising discourse that embeds colonial desires to make 'natives' and their practices manageable, the latter tending towards the normalisation and purification of populations.

In colonial Massachusetts, for example, witch hunts operated as a form of surveillance alongside censuses, eliminating people who posed challenges to increasing birth rates through technologies of contraception, abortion, and infanticide (Farrell 2019, pp. 657–658). In apartheid South Africa, the double entendre of the term 'population control' was driven home by immigration, mortality, and birth control policies that manifested differentially depending on the racialised or socioeconomic group targeted; birth control policies often folded in, for example, anxieties about the 'black peril' (Brown 1987, p. 262). In Uganda, meanwhile, administrations sought to acquire taxpaying subjects and a labour force; fears that STDs, particularly syphilis, were decimating the native population in the 1920s prompted an 'attempted comprehensive reconstruction of the African population' (Summers 1991, p. 807). Colonial officials often borrowed narratives that circulated in the metropole about the lower classes, repurposing, for example, accusations of 'failed motherhood' as a cause for infant mortality in the colonies (Allman 1994, p. 25). Medina-Doménach (2009) meanwhile documents how blood testing, intelligence measures, fingerprinting, and other technologies mobilised by technoscientific projects turned Equatorial Guinea into an experimental laboratory where bodily data and census counts were roped into projects of detribalisation and Hispanicisation with goals of a unified Spanish identity.

While population discourses shifted away from the nefarious language of population control in the latter half of the twentieth century, their logics and designs persist in more palatable forms (Bhatia et al. 2019). Borrowing Angus and Butler's (2011) rendering of populationism as the attribution of social and ecological ills to human numbers, Bhatia et al. (2019, p. 12) document new forms of populationism—including interventions to produce optimal population size and composition, space making and mobility control, and technological modifications of individual bodies—that seek to achieve an 'idealized human-environment, human-economy, or human-space... equilibrium', interests amplified by the climate crisis (Sasser 2018). Hoeyer (2019, p. 549) draws important attention to how personalised ('tailor-made') medicine—rather than signalling a shift from population to individual—generates 'new ways of inscribing the population in the individual'. As Gammeltoft (2008, p. 583) shows in a study of how the 'anomalous fetus' becomes an 'embodiment of national vulnerability' that can potentially be treated through technologies of prenatal diagnosis, symbolic figures attain material form and political presence amid anxieties around poverty, dependency, and crises that always index a moralised imbalance in 'population'. The rise of big data and finance, too, brings new tactics and technologies to the management and governance of populations, tactics often justified via recourse to crisis and humanitarian rhetoric (Bohon 2018; Erikson 2019a).

Permeating anthropological engagements which have population as the object of study is the effort to show how, like all knowledge objects, it is socially constructed, contingent, and malleable, reflective of the political, social, and historical context of those who create and use it. Anthropology has applied the insights that knowledge is never value-free, neutral, or pure, but validated in processes entangled with social, cultural, and political contexts (Lambek 1993; Latour and Woolgar 1979). Population science is a cultural endeavour (Halfon 2006); Mason (2018, p. 210) demonstrates, for example, that even as quantitative population health scientists aim to maintain a 'firewall' between moral purpose and scientific rigour, they nonetheless find themselves attempting to 'take care of populations they care... about' in their intimacy with statistical data. In its focus on everyday practices, transactions, and processes, ethnography holds the potential to denaturalise archives and memory practices in the sciences long after they have been settled (Bowker 2005); for example, tracking the life course of quantitative health data can capture in fine-grained detail how population—as concept, material reality, and project—is made. Following Barad (2003, p. 206), I foreground the ontological inseparability of intra-acting agencies that are distributed across human and non-human forms in research cultures focused on enumerating people or phenomena.

ETHNOGRAPHIES OF COUNTING AND CLASSIFYING

Quantification requires categories: births, deaths, HIV prevalence, and age, for example, are disarticulated from local context and treated as seams into the concept of 'population'. Any counting exercise requires a line in the sand that marks off the sameness that is being counted. Of course, this determines what can be counted, seen, and measured, with many anthropologists nicely showing how a focus on individual knowledge, behaviours, and practices (including motivation or 'attitudes' or 'beliefs') has distracted from how power and political economy impact phenomena. The translation of social difference into standard population measures and categories is a double-edged sword that can promote social justice by demonstrating negative health outcomes to a 'population' as a problem to be solved, but can also act to separate difference from other aspects of social experience in the name of simplification (Cruz 2016). Questionnaires may prompt people to objectify their culture, as Cohn shows for the British colonial census, which provided a realm for 'Indians to ask questions about themselves' (1998, p. 230; see also Appadurai 1993). Indian enumerators, then, placed themselves relative to new regimes of legibility, and later understanding of caste built upon this lexicon and its mutations.

Categories seem to freeze people in place: a fieldworker records a response onto a page, and then that etching becomes the truth that stands in for a moment in time (Bowker and Star 1999). Inscriptions in the medium of paperwork constitute all kinds of things like disease (Mol 2002), food safety protocols (Cavanagh 2016), biosecurity (Frankfurter 2019), and infrastructures (Anand 2011). Documents and writing practices are central technologies in how bureaucratic objects come to matter as real things in everyday practices (Callon 2002; Mol 2002; Riles 2006; Hull 2012). Yet people also 'turn categories around' while they are inside them (Stoler and Cooper 1997, p. 7). Slippages, play, and faking—as in the case of individuals who assumed another person's identity during apartheid population registration exercises in the Eastern Cape of South Africa (a phenomenon called 'impersonation' by magistrates and native commissioners)—permeate cultures of quantification (Rizzo 2014, p. 243). But acts of faking such as these belie the inadequacies of the categories in the first place, which themselves facilitate the 'fabrication of multiple, mimetic subjectivities' (p. 245, see also Biruk 2019; Erikson 2019b; Kingori and Gerrets 2019b).

While anthropologists have shown very effectively that numbers get things wrong (or capture only partial truths) most of the time, numbers also do a lot on the ground, bringing into being new material, social, and political realities, and making new things 'count' in the process (Benton and Sangaramoorthy 2012). As Tichenor (2017, p. 444) shows, data are key to funding and supporting public health programmes in Senegal, even if those who are closest to them and collect them know they are not actually representative of local health realities. In my own work, for example, demographers were anxious about the prospect of Malawian fieldworkers cooking data, fabricating or sullying its purity by filling in surveys willy-nilly without asking the questions of respondents, or through poor adherence to standards for data collection (Biruk 2018, see also True et al. 2011; Kingori and Gerrets 2016). These racialised anxieties overlooked, however, that it was the inventive and innovative tinkering with fieldwork standards and adaptability to field interactions that made fieldworkers crucial to the production of high-quality data (rather than a liability in the process).

Much of my time in rural Malawi was spent with Malawian fieldworkers, hired by foreign demographers to collect the information that would go on to become quantitative data. In my work, I paid close attention to the everyday labour and knowledge work of these individuals—often cast as replaceable, unskilled cogs in a larger machine of knowledge production. Yet fieldworkers and the technologies they employ in the field play a key and understudied role in how the category and knowledge products of 'population' are produced and stabilised: they are the invisible technicians who collect demographic 'raw data' (Shapin 1989). Postcolonial science and technology studies (STS) (Anderson 2009) concerns itself with excavating forms of knowing made invisible by dominant (Western) science (e.g., Harding 2009) and with focusing on the hybrid and partial products of colonial science (Harding 2009, p. 394), challenging simplistic narratives of biocolonialism that 'position scientists in the global North against subjects in the Global South' (Kowal et al. 2013, p. 471; see also van den Bersselaar 2006; TallBear 2013).[3] Scholars focus on the 'asymmetries of science in empire' as they manifest in projects including tropical health, ornithology, and anthropology (Jacobs 2016, p. 18; Schumaker 2001; Tilley 2011). Consequently, in contemporary projects sited in the Global South, scholars have begun to pay closer attention to middlemen and minor actors, including fieldworkers, community health workers, nurses, and other scientific workers (Nading 2013; Swartz 2013; Maes 2017; McKay 2018; Biruk 2018; Sariola and Simpson 2019).

The 'field', often conceived of as an expedient site of data extraction, is, in reality, a place dense with work routines, complex moral economies, exploitation, and normalising 'rituals of knowledge-making' (Halfon 2006, p. 794). People, things, and writing practices must be standardised in line with demographers' epistemic investments in high-quality data that can describe and provide a snapshot of a population (Knorr Cetina 1999). Recent work has begun to explore the precarious labour conditions, affects, ingenuities, and embodied knowledge practices of fieldworkers such as those with whom I spent time (see Nading 2012; Geissler 2013; Molyneux et al. 2013; Tichenor 2016; Swidler and Watkins 2017; Kingori and Gerrets 2019a). It was in fact the ad hoc and improvised embodied tactics and technologies employed by fieldworkers— often rooted in deviation from or tinkering with the standards and scripts to which they were meant to adhere—that resulted in the high-quality data demographers sought out. Others have shown how embodied skills and the care and labour put into scientific work by minor actors, including technical staff or field assistants, are 'tricks' that act as surplus labour. This is often invisibilised by the formal guidelines or written protocols that govern and regulate scientific practices across spaces such as laboratories, fields, epidemiological studies, or insectaries (Kelly and Lezaun 2017, p. 385; Raj 2007; Lorimer 2008; Coopmans and Button 2014; Kalender and Holmberg 2019). Elsewhere, I have shown how fieldwork entails learning to 'see like a research project' (Biruk 2012). This seeing relies on and requires tools and technologies such as maps, clipboards, questionnaires, photos, GPS devices, SUVs, and field attire, central props in structuring ways of seeing, gestures, and other forms of body-work enacted by fieldworkers (Boyer 2005; Vertesi 2012). Ethnographers and science studies scholars, then, refuse to take numbers and data at face value; nor do they regard them as free-floating and abstract entities untrammelled by the social and political residues they accumulate in their contexts of production.

Seeing the Sample: Embodied Counting

For fieldworkers, the field contained nested categories of spatialised difference set off from a larger background of 'noise'. They used hand-drawn maps and notes from past fieldwork teams, along with photos of individual respondents, to seek out the household where they were meant to carry out an interview. In general, the array of tools that fieldworkers used to 'see' and find a household—to make it visible against a larger background of village life and sociality—were very effective. Yet finding the right person to interview was, in the context of a longitudinal panel survey where the same person must be interviewed each field season to ensure high-quality data, a difficult task. Fieldworkers often came across imposters who would pretend to be the respondent a fieldworker sought or asked after by name, posing as members of the sample because they assumed they might receive benefits or incentives in the present or future. On the ground, the sample—an epistemological tool that demographers use to look into a population—morphed into a shape-shifting political community rife with leakages (Adams and Kasanoff 2004). For fieldworkers, the sample (which manifested as a set of individual respondents interviewed the prior year whom they had to locate with certainty) had to be treated in a careful way to ensure standardised and orderly collection of data. This labour included introductions to district commissioners, traditional authorities, and local police, meanwhile keeping up good relations between project staff members and sample communities. Fieldworkers attended funerals in villages where data were being collected, joined in initiation celebrations, purchased honey or chickens from local people, gave sick people rides to the hospital, and so on. These interactions elongated relationships between quantifying projects and the people they were counting, and were crucial—if invisibilised—tactics in ensuring effective data collection. Field-based population data are materialised through informal, improvised, and tactical social relations oriented towards ensuring sample 'purity' and completeness.

FIELD SCIENCES

The field has long played a starring role as the core unit of knowledge production in population science in Africa.[4] It is a key site in which demographers learn about the experiences and understandings people have of demographic phenomena of interest, such as birth, death, and reproduction. The field is where population scientists mobilise and reproduce categories and determinants associated with fertility, mortality, disease, and reproductive health, and it is in this space that population science comes into contact with the people from whom it seeks to coax out internalised knowledge, attitudes, and practice. Following Timothy Mitchell (1988, pp. 44–45), the field acts as an enframing technology, whereby messy space is made into an abstract and neutral vector nesting other conceptual containers that facilitate the isolation, enumeration, and comparison of items across households. Knowledge and material practices in the field, specifically practices of categorising and counting, assemble knowledge.

Anthropologists and STS scholars have examined the production of scientific knowledge as a cultural practice, rather than a value-free or neutral endeavour. Latour and Woolgar's (1979, p. 18) famous anthropological study of a laboratory served as a primer for future efforts to 'penetrate the mystique of science'. Focusing on the routine work carried out in a laboratory, Latour and Woolgar provincialised science, utilising ethnography to shed light on how the mundane and ritualised everyday activities of bench scientists lead to what they call the 'construction of facts' (p. 40), setting the foundation for scholarly work on cultures of science and technology that centres the laboratory as a nodal site in which natural and social orders are reconstituted and recombined (Woolgar 1982; Knorr Cetina 1995; Fischer 2007; Doing 2008). In Malawi, I paid close attention to the entangled components of sociotechnical networks that comprised technologies, practices, people, and non- or more-than-human actors as conjugated, impure, and mutually influential (Brives 2013). I found inspiration in Susan Leigh Star's (1999) call for an ethnography of infrastructure, wherein anthropologists attend to the 'background' against which scientists or others imagine themselves working, a 'background' that is actually hopelessly entangled with and co-productive of them and their projects. (Such approaches trouble the 'implied fantasy of a masterful, separate actor' by 'highlight[ing]...the activity of all the associated actors involved' [Mol 2010, p. 256].) Population data comes into existence through multiple tactics including designing questionnaires, encounters between research participants and respondents, paperwork, and so on (Mol 2002). Close study of the imbrication of material infrastructure, technologies, and human organisation is central to understanding the production of population as a category of knowledge. As Halfon (2006, p. 789) suggests, consensus among population scientists requires the 'construction of common frames of understanding, the production of institutional spaces for negotiation, the creation of languages that can bridge differences, the negotiation of expertise, and the building of facilitating technologies', even if population discourse is also always a site of ambiguity and conflict (Richey 1999). The field is an ideal site for examining how heterogeneous objects (people, organisations, machines, findings) fit into it and produce sociotechnical orders (Callon and Law 1997; Law 2009; Graboyes 2015). The entities that constitute this order, such as researchers, research subjects, field vehicles, databases, and policy, are not pre-formed but emergent (Law and Lien 2012; Fearnley 2015). Importantly, the practices that result from and hold together fieldwork are material-discursive; in other words, 'matter [such as questionnaires] and meaning [such as demographers' investment in clean data] are mutually articulated' (Barad 2007, p. 152).

Science studies scholarship has long focused on the laboratory as a canonical site in which science as cultural phenomenon can be observed, but scholars later came to recognise the out-of-doors field as an important site for understanding the social production and practices of science. First, the ideal type of a sterile, neutral, and standardised space for the production of scientific findings falls short even as an imaginary for the most well-resourced laboratories and containment facilities. Scientific knowledge production is entangled in material infrastructures that limit or enable capacity and ritualisation, and make science more of an improvised art than a scripted thing, caught up in the multiple and competing projects of actors who comprise such sites (Livingston 2012; Street 2014; Tousignant 2018). The field is a mental and social construct that makes fieldwork manageable and doable, one that is rigorously invested in, and maintained in thought and actions that include rituals, clothing, and rules, all of which aim to protect the purity of science from external influence symbolised by the 'outdoors' where research is unfolding (Kuklick and Kohler 1996). Practices concerned with policing and performing boundaries are especially important amid threats to purity of data, scientific space, and standardisation (i.e., geography and weather, reluctant research participants, or scarce resources) (see Tantchou 2014). Whereas the field gained meaning in everyday thought and practice among my interlocutors through its separation and difference from the 'office', recent work has troubled the strict divide between laboratory and field (or insides and outsides), showing how tropes of messy or 'outside' work (often amplified by the intertext of Africa as a 'white man's grave', see Curtin 1961) as juxtaposed to the sterile space inside the laboratory fail to capture how scientific actors, objects, and binaries themselves are reworked, fuzzy, and instable in their mutual entanglements and modifications (Candea 2010; Heggie 2016; Kelly and Lezaun 2017).

The Field as a Stage: Performing Difference

How do we dress for the field? We put on *chitenje*. We can't wear what we wear in the city. You have to suit the environment. (Malawian field supervisor, training for novice fieldworkers 2008)

[Fieldwork] camps were sited near enough to the village for the investigator to be able to see what was going on without being close enough to give rise to a feeling of intrusion. (Guidelines for the Housing of Staff for the Nyasaland Nutrition Survey 1938)

In these snippets, drawn from a training session for novice Malawian fieldworkers employed by an American survey project in 2008 and a set of guidelines for fieldwork in Malawi (then Nyasaland) in 1938, respectively, the field surfaces as a particular kind of thing and imaginary. The field for the demographic researchers and fieldworkers and the research team heading up an ambitious field-based colonial nutrition survey is a unit of knowledge production, a container from which information is meant to be collected in an orderly and expedient fashion. The field is imagined as distinct and distant from the office: fieldworkers must alter their sartorial choices upon entering it (e.g., putting on *chitenje*, a wrap skirt for women made of local colourful fabric), and investigators risk being seen as intruders. A prominent demographer told me in 2008, 'I'm used to sitting in my office crunching numbers and having the categories be anonymous, not personified...', pointing to a division between the 'real world' of the field and the place of knowledge-making referred to as the office. The head of the Nyasaland Nutrition Survey, Dr B.S. Platt, meanwhile suggested that the huts and office which would house members of the research unit would serve as an 'occasional retreat for writing up and working out results' (Berry and Petty 1992, p. 21). For those involved in population science, then, the field carries similar connotations and resonances as anthropologists' own 'field': a place for 'roughing it', a messy and unpredictable place for collecting 'raw data' that will be analysed and written up in the office, and a reservoir of cultural and other difference (Gupta and Ferguson 1997).

Training sessions for Malawian fieldworkers were important sites in which the field was brought into being as both a spatial unit and a category that was imagined to demarcate relevant slices of social reality. These sessions entailed about two weeks of intensive training in the ins and outs of being a good fieldworker, which involved imagining and bringing to life an entity called the field: fieldworkers were taught to transform villages into 'the field', conversations into 'data', and rural people into 'respondents'. The purpose of these trainings was to familiarise fieldworkers with the questionnaire or other instruments to be utilised in data collection, to standardise and harmonise data collection procedures, and to determine which fieldworkers should be let go. They also sought to initiate new fieldworkers into research culture, which necessitated their seeing themselves as different from the rural Malawians they would be interviewing. Material practices—such as learning to record information on the pages of a questionnaire, wearing less modern clothing than usual, or carrying a clipboard or canvas bag bearing the insignia of the foreign university heading up the project—operated to create and uphold boundaries and forms of social difference. Pre-fieldwork trainings initiate new fieldworkers into professional identities and are a site where social and spatiotemporal boundaries that undergird data collection are performed. In this way, the field was not a real place 'out there' that data collection teams entered, but a thing-concept materialised through everyday labour, boundary work, and rituals. These practices relied on and reproduced pre-existing divisions and social demarcations that characterised social life and imaginaries in Malawi (rural/urban, ethnic divisions, educated/uneducated, modern/traditional, and rational/irrational, village/city).

CONCLUSION

Bowker (2005) shows how databases and archives do not merely store facts, but hold the potential for birthing new categories or orders, enabling the possibility of reassembly into something else or otherwise. This is very much the case for population as knowledge object; the palimpsest of paperwork (or digital data) that piles up through successive years of longitudinal surveys like the ones discussed here becomes an archive of the continual revival of population narratives and discourses through media, development interventions, and policy advocacy (Sasser 2018, p. 48). Notably, ethnography, too, through its critical orientation towards practices of counting and quantification, stabilises certain versions of population: as imperial project, partial truth, reductionist endeavour, sociotechnical network, scientific fact or fiction, and racialised concept. Indeed, Scheper-Hughes (1997) called for a demography without numbers; Hartmann (2016) wishes population could be dropped from the development lexicon (p. 287); and Michelle Murphy (2017), writing against population, calls for 'better concepts for naming aggregate life' (p. 137). Yet, in the meantime, ethnographies of counting and classifying can reveal that the imperative to count produces social worlds and relations far beyond those represented in widely circulating quantitative data: *research cultures* are as deserving of study by anthropologists as the more canonical kinds of 'culture' (in the form of, say, traditional beliefs or rituals) they claim population scientists overlook, simplify, or ignore.

Theories and methods drawn from anthropological approaches to science and technology provide a toolkit for close examination of the material practices and technologies that stabilise—in different times and places—population(s) and populationisms (Bhatia et al. 2019). Anthropologists have been central to exposing the shortcomings of numbers, prompting them to call for the 'unmaking and remaking of demography' (Greenhalgh 1996, p. 62). Yet, travelling to the field(s) where population science has taken up temporary residence and decided what and whom 'counts' reveals the ways in which overlooked minor actors and mundane material practices directly involved in making and stabilising quantitative data have long unmade and remade imperial and top-down projects. Population is a concept stabilised through and within sociotechnical networks that entangle people, things, histories, and politics: anthropological attention to these practices illuminates how population is an unfinished project that births worlds and relations that far exceed those inscribed onto question-naires or archived in immortal databases.

Acknowledgements Many thanks to the editors of this volume for their leadership and direction, and to the anonymous reviewers who provided generous feedback that helped fine-tune this chapter. Thanks also to Lyndsey Beutin for helpful suggestions. Finally, I am grateful to the authors who have produced the fine scholarship I engage here.

NOTES

1. Booklet accessed in the Malawi National Archives ('The British Empire Exhibit').
2. Even as audiences were made to feel part of something larger ('mak[ing] the peoples of empire better known to one another'), the displays were rooted in representations of fundamental cultural difference that upheld racialised parti-tions between developed and undeveloped populations. Displays were 'calculated to arouse public interest in all efforts to conquer disease and unhealthy conditions of existence', for example ('The British Empire Exhibit'). In this sense, the exhibit produced population in two senses of the word: imperial totality *and* (other) people boxed together as distanced object in need of intervention (Murphy 2017, p. 135).
3. Greenhalgh (1996, p. 29) points out that an overemphasis on the racism of demographic science, in particular, produces 'demographic exceptionalism'.
4. In addition to the field-based enumeration projects described in this chapter, demographers also draw on vital statistics registries as data sources; as Jerven (2013) argues, statistical capacity and state infrastructures for making reliable and timely numbers are generally weak in Africa, making statistics registries an absent or poor source of data on the continent (see also Zuberi et al. 2003).

References

Adams, V. (2016). *Metrics: What Counts in Global Health*. Durham, NC: Duke University Press.

Adams, J. W., and Kasanoff, A. B. (2004). Spillovers, subdivisions and flows: Questioning the usefulness of 'bounded container' as the dominant spatial metaphor in demogra-phy. In S. Szreter, H. Sholkamy, and A. Dharmalingam (Eds.), *Categories and Contexts: Anthropological and Historical Studies in Demography*. Oxford, UK: Oxford University Press.

Allman, J. (1994). Making mothers: Missionaries, medical officers, and women's work in colonial Asante, 1924–1945. *History Workshop, 38*, 23–47.

Anand, N. (2011). Pressure: The politechnics of water supply in Mumbai. *Cultural Anthropology, 26*(4), 542–564.

Anderson, W. (2009). From subjugated knowledge to conjugated subjects: Science and globalisation, or postcolonial studies of science? *Postcolonial Studies, 12*(4), 389–400.

Angus, I., and Butler, S. (2011). *Too Many People?: Population, Immigration, and the Environmental Crisis*. Chicago, IL: Haymarket Books.

Appadurai, A. (1993). Number in the colonial imagination. In C. A. Breckenridge and P. van der Veer (Eds.), *Orientalism and the Postcolonial Predicament: Perspectives on South Asia* (pp. 314–340). Philadelphia, PA: University of Pennsylvania Press.

Barad, K. (2003). Posthumanist performativity: Toward an understanding of how matter comes to matter. *Signs, 28*(3), 801–831.

Barad, K. (2007). *Meeting the Universe Halfway: Quantum Physics and the Entanglement of Matter and Meaning.* Durham, NC: Duke University Press.

Belcher, E. (1923). The dominion and colonial sections of the British empire exhibition. *Journal of the Royal Society of Arts, 71*(3674), 388–396.

Benton, A., and Sangaramoorthy, T. (2012). Enumeration, identity, health. *Medical Anthropology, 31*(4), 287–291.

Berry, V., and Petty, C. (1992). *The Nyasaland Survey Papers, 1938–1943.* London: Academy.

Bhatia, R., Sasser, J. S., Ojeda, D., Hendrixson, A., Nadimpally, S., and Foley, E. E. (2019). A feminist exploration of 'populationism:' Engaging contemporary forms of population control. *Gender, Place and Culture, 27*(3), 333–350.

Biruk, C. (2012). Seeing like a research project: Producing 'high quality data' in AIDS research in Malawi. *Medical Anthropology, 31*(4), 347–366.

Biruk, C. (2018). *Cooking Data: Culture and Politics in an African Research World.* Durham, NC: Duke University Press.

Biruk, C. (2019). The MSM category as bureaucratic technology: Reflections on paperwork and project time in performance-based aid economies. *Medicine Anthropology Theory, 6*(4), 187–214.

Bledsoe, C. (2002). *Contingent Lives; Fertility, Time, and Aging in West Africa.* Chicago, IL: University of Chicago Press.

Bohon, S. A. (2018). Demography in the big data revolution: Changing the culture to forge new frontiers. *Population Research and Policy Review, 37*, 323–341.

Bonneuil, C. (2000). Development as experiment: Science and state building in late colonial and postcolonial Africa, 1930–1970. *Osiris, 15*, 258–281.

Bowker, G. (2005). *Memory Practices in the Sciences.* Cambridge, MA: The MIT Press.

Bowker, G., and Leigh Star, S. (1999). *Sorting Things Out: Classification and its Consequences.* Cambridge, MA: The MIT Press.

Boyer, D. (2005). The corporeality of expertise. *Ethnos, 70*(2), 243–266.

Brives, C. (2013). Identifying ontologies in a clinical trial. *Social Studies of Science, 43*(3), 397–414.

Brown, B. B. (1987). Facing the 'black peril': The politics of population control in South Africa. *Journal of Southern African Studies, 13*(2), 256–273.

Callon, M. (2002). Writing and (re) writing devices as tools for managing complexity. In J. Law and A. Mol (Eds.), *Complexities: Social Studies of Knowledge Practices* (pp. 191–217). Durham, NC: Duke University Press.

Callon, M., and Law, J. (1997). After the individual in society: Lessons on collectivity from science, technology and society. *The Canadian Journal of Sociology, 22*(2), 165–182.

Candea, M. (2010). I fell in love with Carlos the meerkat: Engagement and detachment in human-animal relations. *American Ethnologist, 37*(2), 241–258.

Cavanagh, J. R. (2016). Documenting subjects: Performativity and audit culture in food production in northern Italy. *American Ethnologist, 43*(4), 691–703.

Cohn, B. S. (1998). The census, social structure, and objectification in South Asia. In *An Anthropologist Among the Historians and Other Essays.* Oxford: Oxford University Press.

Constantine, S. (1984). *The Making of British Colonial Development Policy, 1914–1940.* Totowa, NJ: Frank Cass.

Cooper, M., and Waldby, C. (2014). *Clinical Labor: Tissue Donors and Research Subjects in the Global Bioeconomy.* Durham, NC: Duke University Press.

Coopmans, C., and Button, G. (2014). Eyeballing expertise. *Social Studies of Science, 44*(5), 758–785.

Cruz, T. M. (2016). The making of a population: Challenges, implications, and consequences of the quantification of social difference. *Social Science & Medicine, 174,* 79–85.

Curtin, P. D. (1961). The white man's grave: Image and reality, 1780–1850. *Journal of British Studies, 1*(1), 94–110.

Dixey, F. (1928). The distribution of population in Nyasaland. *Geographical Review, 18*(2), 274–290.

Doing, P. (2008). Give me a laboratory and I will raise the discipline: The past, present, and future politics of laboratory studies in STS. In E. J. Hackett, O. Amsterdamska, M. E. Lynch, and J. Wacjman (Eds.), *The Handbook of Science and Technology Studies* (pp. 279–295). Cambridge, MA: The MIT Press.

Erikson, S. (2019a). Global health futures? Reckoning with a pandemic bond. *Medicine Anthropology Theory, 6*(3), 77–108.

Erikson, S. (2019b). Faking global health. *Critical Public Health, 29*(4), 508–516.

Escobar, A. (1994). *Encountering Development: The Making and Unmaking of the Third World.* Princeton, NJ: Princeton University Press.

Farrell, M. (2019). Witch hunts and census conflicts: Becoming a population in colonial Massachusetts. *American Quarterly, 71*(3), 653–674.

Fearnley, L. (2015). Wild goose chase: The displacement of influenza research in the fields of Poyang Lake, China. *Cultural Anthropology, 30*(1), 12–35.

Fischer, M. J. (2007). Four geneaologies for a recombinant anthropology of science and technology. *Cultural Anthropology, 22*(4), 539–615.

Foucault, M. (2008). *The Birth of Biopolitics: Lectures at the Collège de France, 1978–1979.* London: Palgrave Macmillan.

Frankfurter, R. (2019). Conjuring biosecurity in the post-Ebola Kissi Triangle: The magic of paperwork in a frontier clinic. *Medical Anthropology Quarterly, 33*(4), 517–538.

Gammeltoft, T. M. (2008). Figures of transversality: State power and prenatal screening in contemporary Vietnam. *American Ethnologist, 35*(4), 570–587.

Geissler, P. W. (2013). Public secrets in public health: Knowing not to know while making scientific knowledge. *American Ethnologist, 40*(1), 13–34.

Geissler, P. W., Lachenal, G., Manton, J., and Tousignant, N. (Eds.) (2016). *Traces of the Future: An Archaeology of Medical Science in Africa.* Chicago, IL: University of Chicago Press.

Graboyes, M. (2015). *The Experiment must Continue: Medical Research and Ethics in East Africa, 1940–2014.* Columbus, OH: Ohio University Press.

Greenhalgh, S. (Ed.) (1995). *Situating Fertility: Anthropology and Demographic Inquiry.* New York City, NY: Cambridge University Press.

Greenhalgh, S. (1996). The social construction of population science: An intellectual, institutional, and political history of twentieth-century demography. *Comparative Studies in Society and History, 38*(1), 26–66.

Gupta, A., and Ferguson, J. (1997). Discipline and practice: the 'field' as site, method, and location in anthropology. In *Anthropological Locations: Boundaries and Grounds of a Field Science* (pp. 1–46). Berkeley, CA: University of California Press.

Halfon, S. (2006). The disunity of consensus: International population policy coordination as socio-technical practice. *Social Studies of Science, 36*(5), 783–807.

Harding, S. (2009). Postcolonial and feminist philosophies of science and technology: Convergences and dissonances. *Postcolonial Studies, 12*(4), 401–421.

Harkavy, O. (1995). *Curbing Population Growth: An Insider's Perspective on the Population Movement.* Berlin, Germany: Springer-Verlag.

Hartmann, B. (2016). *Reproductive Rights and Wrongs: The Global Politics of Population Control.* Chicago, IL: Haymarket Books.

Heggie, V. (2016). Higher and colder: The success and failure of boundaries in high altitude and Antarctic research stations. *Social Studies of Science, 46*(6), 809–832.

Hoeyer, K. (2019). Data as promise: Reconfiguring Danish public health through personalized medicine. *Social Studies of Science, 49*(4), 531–555.

Hull, M. (2012). Documents and bureaucracy. *Annual Review of Anthropology, 41*, 251–267.

Irani, L. (2019). *Chasing Innovation: Making Entrepreneurial Citizens in Modern India.* Princeton, NJ: Princeton University Press.

Ittman, K. (2010). Where nature dominates man: Demographic ideas and policy in British colonial Africa, 1890–1970. In D. D. Cordell, K. Ittman, and G. H. Maddox (Eds.), *The Demographics of Empire: The Colonial Order and the Creation of Knowledge* (pp. 59–88). Athens, OH: Ohio University Press.

Jacobs, N. (2016). *Birders of Africa: History of a Network.* New Haven, CT: Yale University Press.

Jerven, M. (2013). *Poor Numbers: How We Are Misled by African Development Statistics and What to Do About It.* Ithaca, NY: Cornell University Press.

Johnson-Hanks, J. (2007). Natural intentions: Fertility decline in the African Demographic and Health Surveys. *American Journal of Sociology, 112*(4), 1008–1043.

Kalender, U., and Holmberg, C. (2019). Courtesy work: Care practices for quality assurance in a cohort study. *Social Studies of Science, 49*(4), 583–604.

Kelly, A. H., and Lezaun, J. (2017). The wild indoors: Room-spaces of scientific inquiry. *Cultural Anthropology, 32*(3), 367–398.

Kingori, P., and Gerrets, R. (2016). Morals, morale and motivations in data fabrication: Medical research fieldworkers views and practices in two sub-Saharan African contexts. *Social Science and Medicine, 166*, 150–159.

Kingori, P., and Gerrets, R. (2019a). The masking and making of fieldworkers and data in postcolonial Global Health research contexts. *Critical Public Health, 29*(4), 494–507.

Kingori, P., and Gerrets, R. (2019b). Why the pseudo matters to global health. *Critical Public Health, 29*(4), 379–389.

Knorr Cetina, K. (1995). Laboratory studies: The cultural approach to the study of science. In S. Jasanoff, G. E. Markle, J. C. Peterson, and T. Pinch (Eds.), *Handbook of Science and Technology Studies* (pp. 140–167). Thousand Oaks, CA: Sage Publications.

Knorr Cetina, K. (1999). *Epistemic Cultures: How the Sciences Make Knowledge.* Cambridge, MA: Harvard University Press.

Kowal, E., Radin, J., and Reardon, J. (2013). Indigenous body parts, mutating temporalities, and the half-lives of postcolonial technoscience. *Social Studies of Science, 43*(4), 465–483.

Kuklick, H., and Kohler, R.E. (1996). Science in the field: Introduction. *Osiris, 11*, 1–14.

Lambek, M. (1993). *Knowledge and Practice in Mayotte: Local Discourses of Islam, Sorcery, and Spirit Possession*. Toronto, Canada: University of Toronto Press.

Latour, B., and Woolgar, S. (1979). *Laboratory Life*. Thousand Oaks, CA: Sage.

Law, J. (2009). Seeing like a survey. *Cultural Sociology, 3*(2), 239–256.

Law, J., and Lien M. E. (2012). Slippery: Field notes in empirical ontology. *Social Studies of Science, 43*(3), 363–378.

Livingston, J. (2012). *Improvising Medicine: An African Oncology Ward in an Emerging Cancer Epidemic*. Durham, NC: Duke University Press.

Lorimer, J. (2008). Counting corncrakes: The affective science of the UK corncrake census. *Social Studies of Science, 38*(3), 377–405.

Maes, K. (2017). *The Lives of Community Health Workers: Local Labor and Global Health in Urban Ethiopia*. New York City, NY: Routledge.

Mamdani, M. (2012). *Define and Rule: Native as Political Identity*. Cambridge, MA: Harvard University Press.

Mason, K. A. (2018). Quantitative care: Caring for the aggregate in US academic population health sciences. *American Ethnologist, 45*(2), 201–213.

McKay, R. (2018). *Medicine in the Meantime: The Work of Care in Mozambique*. Durham, NC.: Duke University Press.

Medina-Doménach, R. (2009). Scientific technologies of national identity as colonial legacies: Extracting the Spanish nation from Equatorial Guinea. *Social Studies of Science, 39*(1), 81–112.

Merry, S. E. (2011). Measuring the world: Indicators, human rights, and global governance. *Current Anthropology, 52*(S3), S83–S95.

Mitchell, T. (1988). *Colonising Egypt*. Berkeley, CA: University of California Press.

Mol, A. (2002). *The Body Multiple: Ontology in Medical Practice*. Durham, NC: Duke University Press.

Mol, A. (2010). Actor-Network Theory: Sensitive terms and enduring tensions. Kölner Zeitschrift für Soziologie und Sozialphyschologie. Sonderheft, *50*, 253–269.

Molyneux, S., Kamuya, D., Madiega, P.A., Chantler, T., Angwenyi, V., and Geissler, P.W. (2013). Fieldworkers at the interface. *Developing World Bioethics, 13*(1), ii–iv.

Mulwafu, W. O. (2011). *Conservation Song: A History of Peasant-State Relations and the Environment in Malawi, 1860–2000*. Winwick, UK: White Horse Press.

Murphy, M. (2012). *Seizing the Means of Reproduction: Entanglements of Feminism, Health, and Technoscience*. Durham, NC: Duke University Press.

Murphy, M. (2017). *The Economization of Life*. Durham, NC: Duke University Press.

Nading, A. M. (2012). Dengue mosquitos are single mothers: Biopolitics meets ecological aesthetics in Nicaraguan community health work. *Cultural Anthropology, 27*(4), 572–596.

Nading, A. M. (2013). Love isn't there in your stomach: A moral economy of medical citizenship among Nicaraguan community health workers. *Medical Anthropology Quarterly, 27*(1), 84–102.

Oudshoorn, N. (1997). From population control politics to chemicals: The WHO as an intermediary organization in contraceptive development. *Social Studies of Science, 27*, 41–72.

Petryna, A. (2009). *When Experiments Travel: Clinical Trials and the Global Search for Human Subjects*. Princeton, NJ: Princeton University Press.

Prince, R. J. (2020). From Russia with love: Medical modernities, development dreams, and Cold War legacies in Kenya, 1969 and 2015. *Africa, 90*(1), 51–76.

Raj, K. (2007). *Relocating Modern Science: Circulation and the Construction of Knowledge in South Asia and Europe, 1650–1900.* London: Palgrave Macmillan.

Rajan, K.S. (2017). *Pharmocracy: Value, Politics, and Knowledge in Global Biomedicine.* Durham, NC: Duke University Press.

Randall, S., Coast, E., and Leone, T. (2011). Cultural constructions of the concept of household in sample surveys. *Population Studies, 65*(2), 217–229.

Redfield, P. (2012). Bioexpectations: Life technologies as humanitarian goods. *Public Culture, 24*(1(66)), 157–184.

Richey, L. (1999). Family planning and the politics of population in Tanzania: International to local discourse. *The Journal of Modern African Studies, 37*(3), 457–487.

Riles, A. (2006). *Documents: Artifacts of Modern Knowledge.* Ann Arbor, MI: University of Michigan Press.

Rizzo, L. (2014). Visual impersonation: Population registration, reference books and identification in the Eastern Cape, 1950s–1960s. *History in Africa, 41*, 221–248.

Rodney, W. (1972). *How Europe Underdeveloped Africa.* London, UK: Bogle-L'Overture Publications.

Sariola, S., and Simpson, R. (2019). *Research as Development: Biomedical Research, Ethics, and Collaboration in Sri Lanka.* Ithaca, NY: Cornell University Press.

Sasser, J. (2018). *On Infertile Ground: Population Control and Women's Rights in the Era of Climate Change.* New York City, NY: NYU Press.

Scheper-Hughes, N. (1997). Demography without numbers. In D. I. Kertzer and T. Fricke (Eds.), *Anthropological Demography: Toward a New Synthesis* (pp. 201–222). Chicago, IL: University of Chicago Press.

Schumaker, L. (2001). *Africanizing Anthropology: Fieldwork, Networks, and the Making of Cultural Knowledge in Central Africa.* Durham, NC: Duke University Press.

Shapin, S. (1989). The invisible technician. *American Scientist, 77*(6), 554–563.

Sharpless, J. (1995). World population growth, family planning, and American foreign policy. *Journal of Policy History, 7*(1), 72–102.

Star, S. L. (1999). The ethnography of infrastructure. *American Behavioral Scientist, 43*(3), 377–391.

Stoler, A. L., and Cooper, F. (1997). Between metropole and colony: Rethinking a research agenda. In *Tensions of Empire: Colonial Cultures in a Bourgeois World* (pp. 1–58). Berkeley, CA: University of California Press.

Street, A. (2014). *Biomedicine in an Unstable Place: Infrastructure and Personhood in a Papua New Guinea Hospital.* Durham, NC: Duke University Press.

Summers, C. (1991). Intimate colonialism: The imperial production of reproduction in Uganda, 1907–1925. *Signs, 16*(4), 787–807.

Swartz, A. (2013). Legacy, legitimacy and possibility: An exploration of community health worker experience across the generations in Khayelitsha, South Africa. *Medical Anthropology Quarterly, 27*(2), 139–154.

Swidler, A., and Watkins, S. C. (2017). *A Fraught Embrace: The Romance and Reality of AIDS Altruism in Africa.* Princeton, NJ: Princeton University Press.

Szreter, S. (1993). The idea of demographic transition and the study of fertility change: A critical intellectual history. *Population and Development Review, 19*(4), 659–701.

TallBear, K. (2013). *Native American DNA: Tribal Belonging and the False Promise of Genetic Science.* Minneapolis, MN: University of Minnesota Press.

Tantchou, J. C. (2014). Blurring boundaries: Structural constraints, space, tools, and agency in an operating theater. *Science, Technology, & Human Values, 39*(3), 336–373.

Tichenor, M. (2016). The power of data: Global health citizenship and the Senegalese data retention strike. In V. Adams (Ed.), *Metrics: What Counts in Global Health* (pp. 105–124). Durham, NC: Duke University Press.

Tichenor, M. (2017). Data performativity, performing health work: Malaria and Labor in Senegal. *Medical Anthropology, 36*(5), 436–448.

Tilley, H. (2011). *Africa as a Living Laboratory: Empire, Development, and the Problem of Scientific Knowledge, 1870–1950.* Chicago, IL: University of Chicago Press.

Tousignant, N. (2018). *Edges of Exposure: Toxicology and the Problem of Capacity in Postcolonial Senegal.* Durham, NC: Duke University Press.

True, G., Alexander, L. B., and Richman, K. A. (2011). Misbehaviors of frontline research personnel and the integrity of community-based research. *Journal of Empirical Research on Human Research Ethics, 6*(2), 3–12.

van den Bersselaar, D. (2006). Acknowledging knowledge: Dissemination and reception of expertise in colonial Africa. *History in Africa, 33*, 389–393.

Vaughan, M. (1991). *Curing Their Ills: Colonial Power and African Illness.* Palo Alto, CA: Stanford University Press.

Venkat, B. J. (2019). A vital mediation: The sanitorium, before and after antibiotics. *Technology and Culture, 60*(4), 979–1003.

Vertesi, J. (2012). Seeing like a rover: Visualization, embodiment, and interaction on the Mars exploration rover mission. *Social Studies of Science, 42*(3), 393–414.

Woolgar, S. (1982). Laboratory studies: A comment on the state of the art. *Social Studies of Science, 12*(4), 481–498.

Zuberi, T., Sibanda, A., Bawah, A., and Noumbissi, A. (2003). Population and African society. *Annual Review of Sociology, 29*, 465–486.

CHAPTER 17

Peopled By Data: Statistical Knowledge Practices, Population-Making, and the State Registry

Alison Cool

On the surface, population statistics can seem like straightforward descriptions. Birth rates, for example, seem to represent phenomena—swells and ebbs in populations—that would occur with or without statistical confirmation. Population data, then, is about people. But how does that work—people turning into data, forming populations? What does it mean to say that data or statistics are 'about' something or someone? Questions like these have long guided anthropological studies of statistical knowledge practices. Ethnographers, historians, and science studies scholars working in a wide range of geographical and institutional contexts have detailed the effort that goes into making populations and the contingency of populations as sociotechnical achievements. From this perspective, populations are not born, but made—assembled out of data, numbers, and ideas about who counts. Statistics—referring at once to a discipline, method, and the forms of knowledge it produces—does the assembly work of population-making and holds the edifice together, but describes what it has built as if it had always been there. However, as anthropologists have argued, the modesty of statistics belies the scale and force of its accomplishments.

This chapter takes up the question of how populations come to be built and known through data and statistics. I offer a perspective on key insights that

A. Cool (✉)
University of Colorado, Boulder, CO, USA
e-mail: alison.cool@colorado.edu

M. H. Bruun et al. (eds.), *The Palgrave Handbook of the Anthropology of Technology*, https://doi.org/10.1007/978-981-16-7084-8_17

anthropological study of statistical technologies and population knowledge-making has yielded, highlighting productive theoretical directions. Drawing on ethnographic research in Sweden, I also offer a case study of how scientists work with and transform data to build populations—in this case, a population of Swedish twins. Following the data to the researchers who make use of it, the case study illustrates the labour-intensive and eminently social processes of creation and abstraction that allow data and statistics to be 'about' people or populations. Nevertheless, when some researchers offer accounts of population-making, they invoke a vernacular anthropology of 'registry culture' in which research participation is a valued tradition, the motivation for, rather than the outcome of national and scientific data collection. Throughout the chapter, I discuss how research into how populations are put together has helped to develop a nuanced reading of population statistics, attentive to the claims that are made as well as what is left unspoken.

Ethnographic and Statistical Representation

In anthropology, statistics can be polarising. Where some see a useful measurement device, others see a mechanism of distance and a technique for thin description. It can be difficult to run statistical tests on ethnographic data, as samples are often small, variables are connected in complex ways, and population parameters can be unclear (Chibnik 1985). However, for many cultural anthropologists, the methodological complexity of statistics is less salient than its relevance for ethnographic objectives. The long-standing tradition of immersive ethnographic fieldwork has contributed to a powerful identification of qualitative research with anthropological identity. From this perspective, cultural anthropology is explicitly defined by what it does not do: anthropologists are those who do not quantify. Statisticians, wielding formulas and numbers, cannot contribute to an anthropological project defined 'not [as] an experimental science in search of law but an interpretive one in search of meaning'— in other words, a humanistic pursuit (Geertz 1973, p. 5). For many anthropologists, however, the choice between law and meaning is false. After all, as philosophers remind us, science itself is a set of methods for finding meaning.

Still, identity is a stubborn problem and it can be easier to define groups through exclusion than common purpose. If we can no longer say exactly what ethnography is, we can invoke our common enemy: statistics. Even as ethnography has expanded beyond long-term immersion in a single location, statistical methods have often served as a foil to ethnographic methods, appearing at moments of heightened methodological anxiety. Early proponents of multi-sited ethnography, for example, cast global systems as worthwhile subjects of anthropological investigation while carefully distinguishing between grounded ethnographic efforts and statistical approaches. 'The idea that ethnography might expand from its committed localism to represent a system much better apprehended by abstract models and aggregate statistics seems antithetical to its very nature and thus beyond its limits. Although multi-sited ethnography is an exercise in mapping terrain, its goal is not holistic representation' (Marcus 1995, p. 99). Thus, one anthropological response to quantitative methods has been to point out that the processes of selection that allow human lives to be represented numerically are inevitably (though variably) reductive.

Other anthropologists have explored differences between ethnographic and statistical modes of representation less for what they reveal about anthropology than for insight into modern political power. Statistics, in this view, is best understood in light of the interventions it enables (Ferguson 1990; Scott 1998). From a governance perspective, what statistics has offered is 'not merely a mode of understanding and representing populations but an instrument for regulating and transforming them' (Asad 1994, p. 76). This is not to say that anthropological research has been politically neutral but that, in comparison with statistical accounts, ethnographic descriptions have been less effective tools of power. If statistical reasoning, more than ethnographic rendering, has been successfully deployed in 'projects aimed at determining the values and practices—the souls and bodies—of entire populations', then statistics emerge as social actors amenable to anthropological investigation (Asad 1994, p. 77). For political anthropologists, in particular, statistics became of interest—not as a method, but as a worthy subject for ethnographic investigation (Alonso and Starr 1987; Ballestero 2012; Bledsoe 2010; Erikson 2012; Lampland 2010; Urla 1993).

Making Populations with Statistics

The question, then, is not whether statistics represent populations accurately, but how statistical practices create and act upon populations they seem only to represent. Historical research has suggested that statistical methods accrued the ability to represent and intervene only gradually. Before the nineteenth century, people were counted and authorities kept records, but without an anchoring in the mathematics of probability and in the absence of an impersonal notion of objectivity, statistics was merely a name for a set of administrative procedures (Daston 1988; Desrosières 2002; Hacking 1990).

The descriptive approach to statistical knowledge-making was popular in Northern Europe. In Germany, Prussia, Belgium, the Netherlands, and the Nordic countries, statistical representation did not always require numbers— the ambition was to document the totality of activity within the nation's borders (Wilke 2004). People, along with flora and fauna, were considered national resources; statistical techniques offered a way to measure the state's power and identify unrealised potential. In England, the Plague inspired morbid attention to births and deaths; these mortality numbers supplied material for the seventeenth-century calculations that became known as political arithmetic (Westergaard 1932). The English technique of 'political arithmetic', with its emphasis on pragmatic, systematic measurement in the service of the state, was an important forerunner to the political and administrative capacities of modern statistical practices (Desrosières 2002; Glass 1978).

The development of statistical 'styles of reasoning' in the eighteenth and nineteenth centuries in Europe built on political traditions of counting and classifying people that varied from place to place (Hacking 1990). If the passionate pursuit of quantification was a widely shared administrative ambition, as states sought to describe themselves and their populations, they imposed methods after their own interests such that local 'measurement regimes' reflected local fears and desires (Porter 1996). National measurement regimes relied on material technologies—paper and ink, columns and rows—as they produced new abstractions.

One of the most powerful abstractions was the idea of the population—an entity composed of people but irreducible to its human elements. Populations came together through specific 'material procedures of objectification': the recording of births and deaths, the centralised assembly of records in life tables, and finally, the comparison and interpretation of numbers that the tables allowed (Desrosières 2002, p. 21). Each procedure required selections: which lives were worth recording? To what end? Because there is more than one way to answer these questions, each measurement regime produces a unique population. For scholars building on this approach, statistics came into focus as a form of politics in its own right—a way of 'governing by numbers' (Rose 1991).

GOVERNING BY NUMBERS

Statistical practices have been useful for making 'programs of government' work (Miller 2001, p. 379; Rose 1991). The power of numbers is enhanced by their apolitical appearance, their modest refusal to take credit for their accomplishments. Subjective descriptions depend on the reliability of their narrators, raising questions: Who should we trust? How do we know that what you say is true? Numbers, by contrast, seemed to offer objectivity, a truth equally true everywhere (Daston 1992; Kalthoff 2005; Longino 1989; Poovey 1998; Porter 1992). Statistics was an appealing proposition: objective representation—just the facts, plainly spoken. Opinions divided subjects, forced choices between right and wrong, toppled regimes. Statistical objectivity looked like a path to rational governance.

What could statistics describe? Anything, it seemed. A national citizenry or the labour force, migrants and schizophrenics. Statistical accounts of populations not only describe entities, but stabilise them by establishing the commonality of individuals within populations and their difference from those outside their parameters (Bunton and Peterson 2005; Davis et al. 2012; Krieger 2012; Reardon 2005). In other words, statistics is a way of drawing things together and holding them apart. The former can be thought of as commensuration and the latter as comparison, although the two are interdependent. Differences are elided while others are highlighted; commensuration, 'is notable for how rigorously it simplifies information and how thoroughly it decontextualizes knowledge' (Espeland and Sauder 2007, p. 17). Comparison invites competition, commensuration supplies standard measures by which competitors are made comparable. First place, second, or third—numbers as ordinals become rankings, quantitative reports belie the ambivalence of assessing differences in quality (Barker 2019).

Numbers point and index; they do all kinds of political work. Indicators, for example, answer policy questions—this intervention worked, these numbers moved (Rottenburg & Merry 2015, p. 2). Indicators are performative; they enact the state and produce publics (Biruk 2012; MacKenzie et al. 2008; Silverstein 2018; Verran 2010), tying together empowered individuals and state services, thus connecting a normative vision of society with an expert assessment of its well-being (Ruppert, 2015; Davies, 2015).

STATISTICAL SUBJECTS

Feminist anthropologists and anthropologists of science and medicine have described how statistical practices and quantitative imaginaries can both create and constrain particular forms of subjectivity. Taking inspiration from Foucault's notion of biopower, scholars have explored how techniques of classification, analysis, categorisation, and quantification take shape as forms of 'power-knowledge-pleasure' that simultaneously act on the body of the individual and the population (Braun 2007; Foucault 1990; Hinterberger 2012; Petersen and Bunton 1997; Rabinow 1992; Raman and Tutton 2010; Reardon 2007). In this approach, key questions include how statistical averages transform into social norms; how individuals are normalised, or recast as 'types'; and how people reorganise their behaviour in accordance with moral norms, recognising and constituting themselves as particular types of subjects (Igo 2008; Miller and Rose 2008; Sadre-Orafai 2020).

Reproduction—as a site of biopolitical intervention at the level of the individual and of the population—has been an important focus of this research (Andaya 2014; Franklin 1997; Konrad 1998; E. Martin 2001a; Rapp 2001, 2019). The calculation and management of national reproductive numbers like fertility rates, maternal mortality indices, or birth rates connect the citizen's body to the body politic (Brunson and Suh 2019; Chapman 2003; Greenhalgh 1995, 2003; Howes-Mischel 2017; Rivkin-Fish 2003; Scheper-Hughes and Lock 1987; Storeng and Béhague 2014). From eugenics movements to pronatalist policies, in regimes of 'reproductive governance', women's bodies and behaviours are often primary targets of public health surveillance, while interventions in reproduction have long been stratified along lines of race, class, and ethnicity (Braff 2013; D.-A. Davis 2019; Ginsburg and Rapp 1995; Krause 2001; Morgan and Roberts 2012).

The statistical estimation of risk and the surveillance of its distribution within and across populations have been central in reproductive interventions and large-scale public health projects (Aarden 2018; Bunton and Peterson 2005; Lee 2013; P. Martin 2001b; Mozersky 2012). However, the probabilistic language of risk, assessed at the population level, can be difficult to translate into the terms of individual experience. When communicated to publics as part of interventions aimed at individual behaviour, statistical assessments of risk are intended to interpellate 'members of populations deemed to be "at risk" such that they interpret the discourse as being about them' (Briggs 2003, p. 291). Of course, such messages routinely misfire, failing to resonate with the audiences they ostensibly address, who are nonetheless deemed responsible for 'managing' the risk they are said to represent. As statistical populations are collapsed into national publics, the management of risk emerges as a political problem. In contemporary approaches to the politics of evidence, however, risk has shifted from a problem of communication to both the means and the ends of interventions (Hoeyer 2019). The scale and temporality of probabilistic interventions in populations are in flux as 'bigger' data pinpoints 'smaller' deviations, enticing authorities with the allure of real-time responsibilisation (Taussig and Gibbon 2013; Zuiderent-Jerak 2010).

From personalised medicine to predictive policing, quantitative assessments of potential outcomes motivate pre-emptive action, while the sources of data and styles of calculations that form the basis for interventions are often obscured (Amelang and Bauer 2019; Armstrong 2017; Green et al. 2019; Gregory and Bowker 2016; Holmberg et al. 2013). As scholars have documented, new regimes of algorithmic governance fracture along established fault lines, encoding inequity by reproducing gendered and racialised biases latent in historical data (Benjamin 2019; Browne 2015; Noble 2018). If today's 'weapons of math destruction' have raised crucial questions about the fit between technology and democracy, it is important to situate current debates about data, security, surveillance, and the state within longer histories of quantification and its varied discontents (den Boer and van Buuren 2012; Cakici 2013; Larson 2017; Lupton 2016; Masco 2017; O'Neil 2016). Just as governments have pursued different answers to the historical question of what should be measured, citizens have questioned the authority and legitimacy of local measurement regimes at different times and for a variety of reasons (Árnason 2013; Ballestero 2015; Petryna 2002; Taussig 2009). However, at the same time that resistance to or refusal of government documentation and data collection emerged as important political objectives for some, others fought to be counted, recognising identification and registration as powerful forms of state acknowledgement (Abarca and Coutin 2018; McGranahan 2018; Prasse-Freeman 2020; Simpson 2014). The strategic mobilisation and contestation of data and statistics are anthropologically interesting for what they reveal about how particular populations have been made and unmade and what it has meant for people to know and to be known through data and numbers.

A POPULATION OF SWEDISH TWINS

Sweden, where I have done intermittent ethnographic research with scientists, statisticians, and other data experts over many years, has an extensive system of national population registers used in administration, official statistics, and research. Unusually comprehensive administrative databases can be found throughout Scandinavia, contributing to the development of a style of registry-based epidemiology throughout the region (Bauer 2014). In recent years, along with Nordic data storage and digital infrastructure, registers have been increasingly positioned as undervalued assets ripe for investment in a booming global data economy (Johnson 2019; Tupasela et al. 2020). Sweden, which has the largest economy and population of the Nordic countries, has been variously described by international observers as an 'El Dorado of data' (Craver 1991) and a 'model surveillance state' (Flaherty 1992).

I visited Sweden for the first time in 2006 as an American graduate student interested in studying women's experiences with twin and multiple pregnancies and new reproductive technologies. Through this preliminary work, I learned about the Swedish Twin Registry, which was described to me as the world's largest register of twins for scientific and medical research. It might also be described as a population-wide database of information about twins in Sweden. The Swedish Twin Registry (STR) and the researchers who maintain and use its twin data became the main focus of my graduate research, based on fieldwork in 2009–2011, which developed into a broader study, primarily based on fieldwork in 2017, of the ongoing scientific, legal, and political work that goes into producing Swedish data infrastructure and creating, circulating, and protecting Swedish data.

Many of the characteristics that have made the Swedish Twin Registry a compelling '(inter)national resource' (Pedersen 1996)—coverage that encompasses almost the total population, detailed longitudinal data, the possibility of record linkage through a widely used personal identification number—could describe any number of Swedish databases, from the Cancer Register to the Cause of Death Register. Each register within the national system of population registers can potentially be linked to all the others, a vast network of data in which each part leads back to the whole. 'Sweden has a number of well known international databases', noted an external reviewer in a 2000 report about the STR, 'and the twin registry maintains a solid place within this family of databases' (Lundberg et al. 2000, p. 119). If a family resemblance can be noted among Swedish population registers, the STR is the only one whose population is composed entirely of twins. As an identical twin, I was curious to learn more about this world-class collection of twins, a scientific 'gold mine' whose existence both disturbed and fascinated me (Cool 2014).

From the beginning, many of my interlocutors in Sweden—politely, but firmly—told me that neither Sweden nor twin research were particularly fascinating. 'There's nothing magical here', explained one senior researcher at the STR, when I first met her in 2006. In 2009, her colleague loaned me a thesis written by a sociologist who had interviewed him and other researchers in the department as an example of how the topic had already been studied as well as the methodological and theoretical shortcomings of an approach, like mine, employing qualitative interviewing and thematic analysis. Still, they and many of their colleagues and collaborators humoured me with interviews, answering my questions—usually, anyway; sometimes they told me a question was irrelevant or unscientifically leading, or spontaneously revised and improved my question before responding, 'If *that's* what you were asking'. They gave me access to their digital archives and trusted me with copies of hard-to-find reports and documents that I photographed and took care to return promptly.

The Swedish Twin Registry (STR) and the scientists and research subjects in its orbit offer a compelling microcosm, a case study that encapsulates many of the concerns and tensions of population-data-making and statistical knowledge production in Sweden. I draw on ethnographic examples from the STR and other members of its database family to illustrate how population data and knowledge are built on what initially appears to be a series of contradictions— born of national specificity and scientific universality, material yet intangible, burdened by history but relentlessly modern, magically fascinating and super boring.

TWINS, PEAS, AND BERRIES

'Are you and your twin as alike as two berries'?[1] This is one question that the Swedish Twin Registry uses to assess twins' zygosity, that is, to determine whether a pair of twins should be classified as what is commonly referred to as 'identical' or 'fraternal'. Variations on this question, which refers to 'two peas in a pod' in the English version, are commonly used in twin research around the world.[2] Classifying twins is essential, as the classic twin study method relies on a comparison of identical (monozygotic) twins, who share 100% of their inherited DNA, with fraternal (dizygotic) twins, who, like other biological siblings, share about 50% of their inherited DNA. The basic assumption behind the comparison is that a twin is exposed to approximately the same 'nurture' as his or her twin sibling—raised by the same parents, attending the same schools, privileged (or not) in similar ways—regardless of whether the twins are identical or fraternal. Against the backdrop of this assumed environmental sameness, the role of heredity should become discernible. Identical twins, described to me by one researcher as, 'two genotypes living side by side' should closely resemble one another for any attribute (eye colour, for example) whose expression owes more to genetic inheritance than environmental influence.[3] The logo for the Swedish Twin Registry—a perfectly matched pair of cherries linked by their stems—is a reference to the berry question, and recalls the fact that peas, berries, and twins all have long histories as subjects of research about heredity.

Twins came to occupy their special position in science with the rise of eugenics, which brought a new approach to heredity together with statistical and political methods linking individuals and populations in novel ways (Chase

1911; Danforth 1953; Paul 1995). At the end of the nineteenth century, English researcher Francis Galton drew these strands together when he was the first to propose the use of twins to study the relative effects of what he termed 'nature and nurture' (Galton 1876). Galton's previous work on the heritability of intelligence relied on statistical analysis of data from published histories of 'eminent families', in which he saw evidence that mental ability was both innate and heritable (Galton 1869). The results of his research aligned with his conviction that reproductive interventions to shore up the quality of the population were needed. Galton proposed the term 'eugenics' to describe such efforts to 'improve' the population (Bulmer 1999; Burbridge 2001; Galton 1904).

However, Galton's earlier studies had met with methodological critiques, undermining their power as legitimising evidence in support of eugenic policies. As he wrote, paraphrasing his critics' objections to statistical evidence of inheritance:

> It is to trifling accidental circumstances that the bent of [a man's] disposition and his success are mainly due, and these you leave wholly out of account—in fact, they do not admit of being tabulated, and therefore your statistics, however plausible at first sight, are really of very little use. (Galton 1876, p. 391)

After searching for a method that could withstand such a critique, 'by which it would be possible to weigh in just scales the respective effects of nature and nurture and to ascertain their several shares in framing the disposition and intellectual ability of men', he concluded that the 'life history of twins supplies what I wanted' (Galton 1876, p. 391). Galton's statistical approach to heredity led him to focus on measurable characteristics of individuals and their distribution within populations; twins suggested a way that environment and biology might be teased apart and tabulated (Cowan 1972).

After Galton, twin studies were further developed, incorporating changing understandings of hereditary transmission and the biology of twinning and applying innovations in statistical modelling. By the 1920s, the 'classic twin method' had acquired its basic form: 'One compares statistically the mono- and dizygotic pairs in respect of their "concordance" for the trait or disease in question' (Dahlberg 1926; Essen-Möller 1963, p. 65). Like pedigrees, family histories, and other eugenic research methods, twin studies made use of available population data to analyse frequencies and distributions of twin births and other life events. Given the rarity of twinning, researchers who had access to more comprehensive population records were more likely to find information about twins. For this reason, many early studies of twins use data from Northern Europe, where official statistics and meticulous parish records have long fuelled the fires of the mathematical imagination.

As twin studies proliferated in the 1920s and 1930s, researchers began to complain about the difficulties of finding twins, particularly in North America and the United Kingdom. 'Obtaining twin material', as one English psychiatrist wrote, 'is one of the main problems in this research' (Lewis 1931, p. 125).

Eugenicists appealed to various authorities for information about twins, as in a letter published in the *British Medical Journal* in 1935, directed to physicians: 'All that is required is that after attending the birth of twins, or triplets, the doctor should make a note of the details of the case and file it away for reference' (Thomson 1935). In the US, researchers had largely depended on school districts to supply the names and addresses of twins on request (Thorndike 1905; Wilson and Jones 1931). However, in the late 1930s, the new phenomena of twin conventions—social gatherings where twins came together to meet other twins and participate in events like parades and beauty contests—provided a convenient opportunity for researchers to test and gather samples from the twin attendees (Bacon 1936; Brooks 1963; Lavelda and Rowe 1976; Rife 1938).[4]

However, these piecemeal efforts were time-consuming; twins who were successfully assembled for one study were not easily tracked down for the next. As the quest for statistical power fed the desire for ever larger samples of twins, scientists began to see the utility of a more centralised approach to data collection. 'The ideal would be a complete register of all twin births with some account of their subsequent history ... and [for] twins and their parents [to] realize how much they can do by co-operating in research to help the advance of knowledge and so to perform a real public service' (Roberts 1935, p. 32).

Efforts to cultivate twin research subjects and compile more twin data in the 1940s and 1950s were often positioned as moves towards greater statistical rigour. However, researchers' post-war attempts to shore up the scientific legitimacy of twin studies can also be interpreted as moves to distance the method from its eugenic origins and genocidal associations. As scholars have noted, this chapter in the history of twin studies concluded in silence, as geneticists generally omitted rather than disavowed this part of their past (Ash 1998; Teo and Ball 2009). Nevertheless, the link that was forged between twins and heredity during this period proved durable.

TRACING THE TWINS

As scientists resumed pre-war discussions of twin records and registries, it seemed that the special significance of twins for genetic research they had once argued for could now be taken as an established premise. And if twins and their families recognised 'how much they could do' for science, they might be appealed to on that basis. At a conference in Maryland in 1953, an American geneticist who had recently returned 'from a tour de force through European twin research centers and conventions' reported favourably on the methodological developments and pursuit of statistically representative twin data he had observed among his scientific hosts (Kallmann 1954, p. 160). Furthermore, as he noted, there was some indication that twins might be aware that their responses to questionnaires were useful for scientists. 'In the investigation of traits requiring close personal contact with research subjects from various segments of the population, the twin-study method provides an innocuous approach to families who might not otherwise be willing to give information about their private lives' (Kallmann 1954, p. 160).

The responsiveness of twins to scientific inquiries was essential for creating representative samples. But before a questionnaire could be mailed or an interviewer sent to collect data, twins had to be located. Even if birth records made it possible to identify names and birthplace of twins, connecting names to current mailing addresses was difficult. In the US, one reason that twin veterans were used to form an early twin register was their military files made them easier to find: 'The population of the United States, particularly young adult males, is so highly mobile that it is almost impossible to maintain the integrity of a large list of persons without such aids' (Jablon et al. 1967, p. 157). By contrast, Nordic twin researchers often remarked on their success locating twins: 'It has proved possible to renew contact with all of them as the result of the excellent system of registration in Sweden' (Juel-Nielsen et al. 1958, p. 269). The process of assembling data for a twin register was still laborious, but the correct address made all the difference.

The scientists involved in creating the Swedish Twin Registry, initially compiled between 1959 and 1961, gave credit to the population registries that enabled their work, but made it clear that this was only the beginning of the complex informational choreography required. 'This system made it possible for us to follow-up any individual from his place of birth to his next place of living, and so on, until we found his current address or had to discard him as deceased. We started, in that way, with about 41 000 multiple birth records, hand screened from about 3 ½ million birth records from all Sweden during the period in question...' (Cederlöf et al. 1970, p. 351).

In Denmark, where the first population-based twin registry was established, work began in 1954. Researchers and assistants followed a winding path from local parishes, where official birth registers were maintained, to municipalities, where migration information was kept, to towns and cities, which held their own annual censuses as a supplement to the national censuses every fifth year, and concluded their search at the archives of local probate courts, where migration overlooked on the municipal level might be uncovered. 'As soon as they were traced', twins were sent questionnaires, and if they replied, the search was taken up again for medical records and information about family members (Hauge et al. 1968, pp. 316–317).

What did twins make of all this? Despite the abundance of data in the Nordic twin registries, this particular question is hard to answer. Decades before the STR was founded, thousands of Swedish twins had already been measured, fingerprinted, and photographed—a process referred to, at the time, as collecting twin material (Dahlberg 1926; Essen-Möller 1941).[5] When the Swedish Twin Registry began mailing questionnaires in 1961, most twins replied; many provided blood samples and submitted to physical examinations (Cederlöf 1964, 1966, 1968). Published twin studies sometimes include researchers' brief assessments of twin research subjects, referring, for example, to the 'excellent compliance of adult twins in the Finnish Twin Cohort' (Kaprio et al. 1987, p. 80).

Tests and experiments occasionally offer opportunities for researchers to interact with or observe their twin research subjects. These ambiguous encounters can prompt researchers to reflect on what might motivate twins to show up. Rhea, a psychologist conducting research with the registry, told me that it was 'really a wonderful thing to see [twins] come here, that they are happy to contribute to research … that they feel that they participate in something'. Rhea had previously worked with patients. She explained that her clinical background helped her design a twin study of psychotic disorders because she understood the clinical realities represented by diagnostic categories, how register variables corresponded—or not—to the severity of the hundreds of cases she had encountered in the past. For her collaborators, experts in biostatistics and molecular genetics, a variable was a variable. But for Rhea, data was about the patients she had cared for, the relatives she had talked to over the years. 'They are really flesh and blood for me, not register or single-study persons.'

Theo described a memorable economic experiment. 'I had a pair of identical twins who showed up—they were dressed identically, and they were both seven months pregnant. It was an absurd sight.' He had been surprised by how many twins participated but told me he thought 'a lot of twins just feel like it's their civic duty to help out if they can'. In general, though, he felt that 'Swedes are very cooperative and easy to deal with'.

Despite Rhea and Theo's experiences, many—perhaps even most—twin researchers in Sweden never come into contact with registered twins, relying on data collected by others. Some researchers explained that their true interest was in the data; the twins were a means to end. For example, Erik, an epidemiology PhD student, told me about a well-documented sample within the twin registry that he was using in a project. 'It's unique. It's the only sample of that sort in the world—nobody else has that kind of data.' Erik also said that when he started working with the STR, 'It wasn't really the twins that got me interested. It was more like—what kind of information did we have here and what kind of things could we do with the information?'

Erik gestured towards a national history of registration as a partial explanation of his access to valuable information. Expanding on this, he ventured that national record-keeping practices might have left a mark on those whose lives have been documented. 'Maybe that's an explanation as well—that there is some sort of registry culture here in Sweden that makes people want to contribute to scientific studies, in general. And I think that [because] twins actually find themselves quite special in Sweden, [it] makes it a good place to do these kinds of studies.' Thus, registration becomes more than a detail in the annals of administrative history; it re-emerges in the guise of registry culture, now an attribute of the Swedish population that manifests in individuals as a desire to participate in research. If the Swedish population in general are thought to exhibit a cultural propensity for data-driven science, Swedish twins—one highly studied population nested within another—would seem to be the standard-bearers of this particular form of cultural heritage.

THE MOST REPRESENTATIVE POPULATION IN THE WORLD

I might dismiss Erik's reference to a registry culture as a joke, a sly reference to an earlier anthropological era of national cultures and personalities. And yet, the idea is suggestive—not because it captures the essence of Swedish identity, but in its playful invocation of an imagined registry society, an overdetermined world of registry traditions and registry values. The registry world invites us to invert silly and serious—to see science as art and statistics as poetry—registry symbols and registry languages. Twins are boring and data is fascinating, patients are dull and variables are lively. Registry culture is a carnivalesque commentary on the absurdity and artistry of registration. Anthropologists arrive to study the numbers.

Erik's joke came back to me when I was visiting friends in Lund, a university town in southern Sweden. Students in Lund have an impressive roster of celebrations from boat races to black-tie dinners and a carnival held every four years. The highlight of the Lund Carnival is a parade with themed floats and costumed students. I watched the 2010 parade with my friend Emilia, a political science student from Göteborg. The carnival was rife with puns and arcane traditions, bringing out Emilia's enthusiasm for teaching me about Sweden in her half-joking, half-serious way.

The theme of one parade float, clad in blue and yellow bunting, was Sweden. The students waving from the float and dancing around it were dressed as stereotypical figures, some familiar—a blond Viking, Björn Borg—and some less so. A dancing white-and-green box of milk smiled at me as he passed. Even though I recognised his homemade costume as the inexpensive Swedish brand of low-fat milk found in all grocery stores and most people's fridges, I didn't understand why he was dressed up as milk. Emilia pointed out that the Swedish word for low-fat milk—*mellanmjölk*—literally meant 'in-between milk'. Avoiding the excessive indulgence of whole milk on the one hand and the deprivation of skim milk on the other, she explained, most people reached in the middle, and took the good-enough choice—low-fat milk. 'So that's what we say about ourselves', Emilia concluded, 'we are the land of low-fat milk. Kind of average and in the middle. Not too much, not too little, but just right'.

Although presented in a different register and context, the low-fat milk joke resonated with what I had heard from scientists working with twin data. Their descriptions of the Swedish population—as represented in the twin registry and other national databases—drew on similar ideas of the distinctively average, the in-between, and just right. Evald, for example, one of the younger professors at the STR, had told me, 'We're very similar to most other populations, so we're not outliers. We are very—at least, I think so, but I'm a Swede'. He smiled, and continued. 'Often we are like, we take a middle stand on everything, so maybe we are the most representative population in the world, I don't know!' After Evald said that, we sat there for a moment, my voice recorder flickering with red dots that moved in time with our laughter.

In interactions like this, Evald and his colleagues assured me from time to time that Swedish twins and the Swedish population in general were absolutely unremarkable. If pressed, someone might concede that there could be something exceptional, perhaps, about a population that was uniquely universal, so extraordinarily ordinary. But what was there to say? Everyone drank low-fat milk in the registry world.

CONCLUSION

If there's a deeper meaning in my twin researcher material, it might be found in these simultaneous disavowals and assertions of Swedish distinction. Faced with shifting and often contradictory demands of population-making and statistical knowledge production, researchers get caught between a Scandinavian exceptionalism and an ideal of universal truth, and something like a registry culture offers an appealing explanatory device. Registry culture, along with vernacular anthropological analyses of its particulars (Tilley 2010), can be read as critique, a message that says: anthropology is annoying—if not for its imperial underpinnings, then for the arrogance of a field that dispatches students around the world to ask about the obvious. In response, the vernacular anthropologist delivers culture ready-made, together with all the theory you need. After all, says the vernacular anthropologist, what you're interested in is what everyone around here calls common sense (Forsythe 1999). Twin research isn't magical, and anthropology isn't scientific. So what can you tell us that we don't already know?

I am here to tell you that we are as alike as two berries, two peas in a pod. When ethnography looks in the mirror, statistics stares back. Statistics blinks and ethnography winks. If *mellanmjölk* is so ordinary, why the parade? There is nothing to be said, but after 6890 words we are only getting started. You look at me and I look at you, and we agree that this is all data. The literature warns anthropologists about actors' categories, tells us to hold emic and etic apart, to distinguish between cultures and culturalisms (Chemla and Keller 2017). But here in the peapod, it gets tricky. Categories and cultures keep rolling around. Liturgical, vulgar, classical, or vernacular—they are as identical as drops of water. As you already know.

Nordic twin registries—like Noah's ark—were populated two by two, as researchers assembled all the twin material they could find. Scandinavian parish records, population registers, and systems of national identification that affixed a number to each citizen proved useful to those who wished to study twins. The availability of Nordic data is part of the complicated legacy of twin research, inextricable from the eugenic thinking and statistical reasoning that first suggested twins to Galton. The vision of twins as method of division, the perfect tool to sever nature from nurture, inspired demographic detective work around the world, but Nordic scientists were the most successful in tracking down twins.

Why does Sweden have the largest twin registry in the world? Well, why not? Registry culture spins the story around: there is nothing inherently interesting about twins, but the data in the registry is of great interest. Ordinary twins become special by giving samples and answering questions, enabling their representation in a data registry made all the more extraordinary with each additional response. This is the sense in which Swedish twins are sometimes celebrated as 'the true heroes of research' (Sjöberg 2005). Researchers step back and clap modestly as the twins parade by. But I would like to recognise them—the scientists—as the true heroes of the research, the true ethnographers of registry culture.

Acknowledgements I am grateful for the vastly generous, endlessly patient, and wise editorial guidance of Klaus Hoeyer and Brit Ross Winthereik and the insightful feedback from two anonymous reviewers. This chapter benefitted from conversations and suggestions from Georgia Cool, Donna Goldstein, Arne Höcker, and Carla Jones.

NOTES

1. The full question, from the STR's 1961 questionnaire, asks, 'During childhood, were you and your twin "as alike as two berries" or were you "no more similar to one another than siblings in general?"' ('*Var Ni och Er tvillingpartner under uppväxtåren "lika som bär" eller var ni "inte mera lika varandra än syskon i allmänhet?"*'). 'As alike as two berries', like 'two peas in a pod', is a colloquial expression that refers to two people or things that look very alike.
2. Norwegian twins are asked if they are as alike as 'two drops of water' (*to dråper vann*) (Kringlen 1999)
3. Technically, it would be more accurate to say that the assumption is that the twin study method yields an estimate of the relative weight of genetic factors (genotype) and non-genetic contributions to the variation of expression of a trait or disease (phenotype) within a population. The number produced through the comparison is known as a heritability estimate.
4. Twin conventions may have been, in part, a reaction to the explosion of media and popular interest in the identical Dionne quintuplets, born in 1934 in Canada. The Dionne quintuplets were subject to intense scientific and public surveillance. As babies, they were made wards of the province of Ontario, and raised by nurses in a private hospital built for the purpose of facilitating full-time psychological research on the quintuplets. The hospital was also a popular tourist attraction known as 'Quintland', where visitors could observe the children as they played outside. See (McKay 1994; Wright 2016)
5. The most ambitious early twin 'collections' were those of Gunnar Dahlberg at the State Institute for Race Biology in Uppsala (Dahlberg 1923, 1926) and Erik Essen-Möller at the Department of Psychiatry at Lund University (Essen-Möller 1963, 1970; Essen-Möller 1941).

REFERENCES

Aarden, E. (2018). Repositioning biological citizenship: State, population, and individual risk in the Framingham Heart Study. *BioSocieties*, *13*(2), 494–512. doi:https://doi.org/10.1057/s41292-017-0081-0.

Abarca, G. A., & Coutin, S. B. (2018). Sovereign intimacies: The lives of documents within US state-noncitizen relationships. *American Ethnologist*, *45*(1), 7–19. doi:https://doi.org/10.1111/amet.12595.

Alonso, W., & Starr, P. (Eds.) (1987). *The Politics of Numbers*. New York, NY: Russell Sage Foundation.

Amelang, K., & Bauer, S. (2019). Following the algorithm: How epidemiological risk-scores do accountability. *Social Studies of Science*, *49*(4), 476–502.

Andaya, E. (2014). *Conceiving Cuba: Reproduction, Women, and the State in the Post-Soviet Era*. New Brunswick, NJ: Rutgers University Press.

Armstrong, D. (2017). Clinical prediction and the idea of a population. *Social Studies of Science*, *47*(2), 288–299.

Árnason, V. (2013). Scientific citizenship in a democratic society. *Public Understanding of Science*, *22*(8), 927–940.

Asad, T. (1994). Ethnographic representation, statistics and modern power. *Social Research*, 55–88.

Ash, M. (1998). 'From "Positive Eugenics" to Behavioral Genetics: Psychological Twin Research Under Nazism and Since.' *Historia Pedagogica-International Journal of the History of Education*, 1 335–358.

Bacon, R. M. (1936, August 23). The Big Parade to "Twindiana". *The Sun*, 73.

Ballestero, A. (2012). Transparency Short-Circuited: Laughter and Numbers in Costa Rican Water Politics. *PoLAR: Political and Legal Anthropology Review*, *35*(2), 223–241. doi:https://doi.org/10.1111/j.1555-2934.2012.01200.x.

Ballestero, A. (2015). The ethics of a formula: Calculating a financial–humanitarian price for water. *American Ethnologist*, *42*(2), 262–278.

Barker, M. (2019). Dancing Dolls: Animating Childhood in a Contemporary Kazakhstani Institution. *Anthropological Quarterly*, *92*(2), 311–343.

Bauer, S. (2014). From Administrative Infrastructure to Biomedical Resource: Danish Population Registries, the "Scandinavian Laboratory," and the "Epidemiologist's Dream." *Science in Context*, *27*(2), 187–213. doi:https://doi.org/10.1017/S0269889714000040.

Benjamin, R. (2019). *Race After Technology: Abolitionist Tools for the New Jim Code*. Hoboken, NJ.: John Wiley & Sons.

Biruk, C. (2012). Seeing Like a Research Project: Producing "High-Quality Data" in AIDS Research in Malawi. *Medical Anthropology*, *31*(4), 347–366. doi:https://doi.org/10.1080/01459740.2011.631960.

Bledsoe, C. H. (2010). Sociocultural anthropology's encounters with large public data sets. *Anthropological Theory*, *10*(1–2), 103–111. doi:https://doi.org/10.1177/1463499610365376.

den Boer, M., & van Buuren, J. (2012). Security Clouds: Towards an ethical governance of surveillance in Europe. *Journal of Cultural Economy*, *5*(1), 85–103. doi:https://doi.org/10.1080/17530350.2012.640558.

Braff, L. (2013). Somos Muchos (We Are So Many) Population Politics and "Reproductive Othering" in Mexican Fertility Clinics. *Medical Anthropology Quarterly*, *27*(1), 121–138.

Braun, B. (2007). Biopolitics and the molecularization of life. *Cultural Geographies, 14*(1), 6.

Briggs, C. L. (2003). Why Nation-States and Journalists Can't Teach People to Be Healthy: Power and Pragmatic Miscalculation in Public Discourses on Health. *Medical Anthropology Quarterly, 17*(3), 287–321. doi:https://doi.org/10.1525/maq.2003.17.3.287.

Brooks, M. (1963). *Parental-daughter relationships as factors of non-marriage studied in identical twins.* Ph.D. Thesis. Ohio State University.

Browne, S. (2015). *Dark Matters: On the Surveillance of Blackness.* Durham, NC.: Duke University Press.

Brunson, J., & Suh, S. (2019). Behind the measures of maternal and reproductive health: Ethnographic accounts of inventory and intervention. *Social Science & Medicine,* 112730. doi:https://doi.org/10.1016/j.socscimed.2019.112730.

Bulmer, M. (1999). The development of Francis Galton's ideas on the mechanism of heredity. *Journal of the History of Biology, 32*(2), 263–292.

Bunton, R., & Peterson, A. (2005). *Genetic governance: Health, risk, and ethics in the biotech era.* Abingdon, U.K.: Routledge.

Burbridge, D. (2001). Francis Galton on twins, heredity and social class. *The British Journal for the History of Science, 34*(03), 323–340.

Cakici, B. (2013). *The Informed Gaze: On the Implications of ICT-Based Surveillance* [Doctoral Dissertation, Stockholm University]. http://urn.kb.se/resolve?urn=urn:nbn:se:su:diva-92956.

Cederlöf, R. (1964). Tvillingregistret. preliminaert meddelande. *Nordisk Hygienisk Tidskrift, 45,* 63–70.

Cederlöf, R. (1966). Urban factor and prevalence of respiratory symptoms and "angina ectoris". A study on 9,168 twin pairs with the aid of mailed questionnaires. *Archives of Environmental Health, 13*(6), 743.

Cederlöf, R. (1968). Tobaksrökning och hälsa: Resultat från epidemiologiska tvillingundersökningar. *Läkartidningen, 65,* 2727–2734.

Cederlöf, R., Floderus, B., & Friberg, L. (1970). The Swedish twin registry–past and future use. *Acta Geneticae Medicae et Gemellologiae, 19*(1), 351.

Chapman, R. R. (2003). Endangering safe motherhood in Mozambique: Prenatal care as pregnancy risk. *Social Science & Medicine, 57*(2), 355–374. https://doi.org/16/S0277-9536(02)00363-5.

Chase, J. H. (1911). Twins, Heredity, Eugenics. *Journal of Heredity, 2*(4), 287.

Chemla, K., & Keller, E. F. (2017). *Cultures without Culturalism: The Making of Scientific Knowledge.* Durham, NC.: Duke University Press.

Chibnik, M. (1985). The use of statistics in sociocultural anthropology. *Annual Review of Anthropology, 14*(1), 135–157.

Cool, A. (2014). Twins, nature and nurture. *BioSocieties, 9*(2), 225–227.

Cowan, R. S. (1972). Francis Galton's contribution to genetics. *Journal of the History of Biology, 5*(2), 389–412.

Craver, E. (1991). Gösta Bagge, the Rockefeller Foundation, and Empirical Social Science Research in Sweden, 1924-1940. In L. Jonung (Ed.), *The Stockholm School of Economics Revisited.* Cambridge, U.K.: Cambridge University Press.

Dahlberg, G. (1923). Twins and Heredity. *Hereditas, 4*(1–2), 27–32.

Dahlberg, G. (1926). *Twin births and twins from a hereditary point of view.* Stockholm, Sweden: Tidens.

Danforth, C. H. (1953). Eugenics, Galton and After. *American Journal of Human Genetics, 5*(1), 96–97.

Daston, L. (1988). *Classical Probability in the Enlightenment.* Princeton, NJ.: Princeton University Press.

Daston, L. (1992). Objectivity and the escape from perspective. *Social Studies of Science, 22*(4), 597–618.

Davis, D.-A. (2019). *Reproductive Injustice: Racism, Pregnancy, and Premature Birth.* New York, NY,: NYU Press.

Davis, K. E., Kingsbury, B., & Merry, S. E. (2012). Indicators as a technology of global governance. *Law & Society Review, 46*(1), 71–104.

Desrosières, A. (2002). *The Politics of Large Numbers: A History of Statistical Reasoning.* Cambridge, MA.: Harvard University Press.

Erikson, S. L. (2012). Global Health Business: The Production and Performativity of Statistics in Sierra Leone and Germany. *Medical Anthropology, 31*(4), 367–384. doi:https://doi.org/10.1080/01459740.2011.621908.

Espeland, W. N., & Sauder, M. (2007). Rankings and Reactivity: How Public Measures Recreate Social Worlds 1. *American Journal of Sociology, 113*(1), 1–40.

Essen-Möller, E. (1941). Empirische Ähnlichkeitsdiagnose bei Zwillingen. *Hereditas, 27*(1–2), 1–50. doi:https://doi.org/10.1111/j.1601-5223.1941.tb03250.x.

Essen-Möller, E. (1963). Twin research and psychiatry. *Acta Psychiatrica Scandinavica, 39*(1), 65–77.

Essen-Möller, E. (1970). The twin register of Lund. *Acta Geneticae Medicae et Gemellologiae, 19*(1), 355. doi:https://doi.org/10.1017/s1120962300025907.

Ferguson, J. (1990). *The anti-politics machine: 'development', depoliticization and bureaucratic power in Lesotho.* Cambridge, U.K.: Cambridge University Press.

Flaherty, D. H. (1992). *Protecting Privacy in Surveillance Societies: The Federal Republic of Germany, Sweden, France, Canada, and the United States.* Chapel Hill, NC.: University of North Carolina Press.

Forsythe, D. E. (1999). "It's Just a Matter of Common Sense": Ethnography as Invisible Work. *Computer Supported Cooperative Work, 8*(1–2), 127–145. doi:https://doi.org/10.1023/A:1008692231284.

Foucault, M. (1990). *The history of sexuality, Vol. 1: An introduction.* New York, NY.: Random House.

Franklin, S. (1997). *Embodied progress: a cultural account of assisted reproduction.* Abingdon, U.K.: Routledge.

Galton, F. (1869). *Hereditary Genius.* New York, NY.: Macmillan.

Galton, F. (1876). The History of Twins, as a Criterion of the Relative Powers of Nature and Nurture. *Journal of the Anthropological Institute of Great Britain and Ireland, 5*, 391–406. doi:https://doi.org/10.2307/2840900

Galton, F. (1904). Eugenics: Its Definition, Scope, and Aims. *American Journal of Sociology, 10*(1), 1.

Geertz, C. (1973). *The Interpretation of Cultures.* New York, NY.: Basic Books.

Ginsburg, F., & Rapp, R. (1995). *Conceiving the New World Order: The Global Politics of Reproduction.* Berkeley, CA.: University of California Press.

Glass, D. V. (1978). *Numbering the people: The eighteenth-century population controversy and the development of census and vital statistics in Britain.* New York, NY.: Gordon & Cremonesi.

Green, S., Carusi, A., & Hoeyer, K. (2019). Plastic diagnostics: The remaking of disease and evidence in personalized medicine. *Social Science & Medicine*, 112318. doi:https://doi.org/10.1016/j.socscimed.2019.05.023

Greenhalgh, S. (1995). *Situating Fertility: Anthropology and Demographic Inquiry*. Cambridge, UK: Cambridge University Press.

Greenhalgh, S. (2003). Planned births, unplanned persons: "Population" in the making of Chinese modernity. *American Ethnologist*, *30*(2), 196–215.

Gregory, J., & Bowker, G. C. (2016). The Data Citizen, the Quantified Self, and Personal Genomics. In D. Nafus (Ed.), *Quantified: Biosensing Technologies in Everyday Life*. Cambridge, MA.: The MIT Press.

Hacking, I. (1990). *The Taming of Chance*. Cambridge, U.K.: Cambridge University Press.

Hauge, M., Harvald, B., Fischer, M., Gotlieb-Jensen, K., Juel-Nielsen, N., Raebild, I., Shapiro, R., & Videbech, T. (1968). The Danish Twin Register. *Acta Geneticae Medicae et Gemellologiae*, *17*(2), 315–332. doi:https://doi.org/10.1017/S1120962300012749

Hinterberger, A. (2012). Publics and Populations: The Politics of Ancestry and Exchange in Genome Science. *Science as Culture*, *21*(4), 528–549. doi:https://doi.org/10.1080/09505431.2012.705272

Hoeyer, K. (2019). Data as promise: Reconfiguring Danish public health through personalized medicine. *Social Studies of Science*, *49*(4), 531–555. doi:https://doi.org/10.1177/0306312719858697

Holmberg, C., Bischof, C., & Bauer, S. (2013). Making Predictions: Computing Populations. *Science, Technology & Human Values*, *38*(3), 398–420. doi:https://doi.org/10.1177/0162243912439610

Howes-Mischel, R. (2017). Humanizing Big Numbers: Representational Strategies in Institutional Films about Global Maternal Mortality. *Visual Anthropology Review*, *33*(2), 164–176.

Igo, S. E. (2008). *The Averaged American: Surveys, Citizens, and the Making of a Mass Public*. Cambridge, MA.: Harvard University Press.

Jablon, S., Neel, J. V., Gershowitz, H., & Atkinson, G. F. (1967). The NAS-NRC twin panel: Methods of construction of the panel, zygosity diagnosis, and proposed use. *American Journal of Human Genetics*, *19*(2), 133–161.

Johnson, A. (2019). Data centers as infrastructural in-betweens: Expanding connections and enduring marginalities in Iceland. *American Ethnologist*, *46*(1), 75–88.

Juel-Nielsen, N., Nielsen, A., & Hauge, M. (1958). On the Diagnosis of Zygosity in Twins and the Value of Blood Groups. *Acta Genetica et Statistica Medica*, *8*(3/4), 256–273.

Kallmann, F. J. (1954). Twin data in the analysis of mechanisms of inheritance. *American Journal of Human Genetics*, *6*(1), 157–174.

Kalthoff, H. (2005). Practices of Calculation. *Theory, Culture & Society*, *22*(2), 69–97. doi:https://doi.org/10.1177/0263276405051666

Kaprio, J., Rose, R. J., Sarna, S., Langinvainio, H., Koskenvuo, M., Rita, H., & Heikkilä, K. (1987). Design and Sampling Considerations, Response Rates, and Representativeness in a Finnish Twin Family Study. *Acta Geneticae Medicae et Gemellologiae: Twin Research*, *36*(1), 79–93. doi:https://doi.org/10.1017/S000156600000461X

Konrad, M. (1998). Ova Donation and Symbols of Substance: Some Variations on the Theme of Sex, Gender and the Partible Body. *Journal of the Royal Anthropological Institute*, 4(4), 643–645.

Krause, E. L. (2001). "Empty cradles" and the quiet revolution: Demographic discourse and cultural struggles of gender, race, and class in Italy. *Cultural Anthropology*, 16(4), 576–611.

Krieger, N. (2012). Who and what is a "population"? Historical debates, current controversies, and implications for understanding "population health" and rectifying health inequities. *Milbank Quarterly*, 90(4), 634–681.

Kringlen, E. (1999). Tvillingstudier i psykiatrien. *Tidsskrift-norske laegeforening*, 119, 3322–3328.

Lampland, M. (2010). False numbers as formalizing practices. *Social Studies of Science, 40(3), 377-404.* doi:https://doi.org/10.1177/0306312709359963

Larson, J. L. (2017). Wild Eavesdropping: Observations on Surveillance, Conspiracy, and Truth in East Central Europe. *PoLAR: Political and Legal Anthropology Review*, 40(2), 342–349. doi:https://doi.org/10.1111/plar.12224

Lavelda, R, & Rowe, L. (1976). The History of the International Twins Association (I.T.A.). *Acta Geneticae Medicae et Gemellologiae*, 25(1), 387–388. doi:https://doi.org/10.1017/S0001566000014483

Lee, S. S.-J. (2013). Race, Risk, and Recreation in Personal Genomics: The Limits of Play. *Medical Anthropology Quarterly*, 27(4), 550–569. doi:https://doi.org/10.1111/maq.12059

Lewis, A. J. (1931). Genetic problems in psychiatry. *The Eugenics Review*, 23(2), 119–125.

Longino, H. (1989). *Science as social knowledge: Values and objectivity in scientific inquiry*. Princeton, NJ.: Princeton University Press.

Lundberg, I., Smedby, B., & Sørensen, T. (2000). *Scientific evaluation of the Swedish Twin Registry*. Forskningsrådsnämnden.

Lupton, D. (2016). The diverse domains of quantified selves: Self-tracking modes and dataveillance. *Economy and Society*, 45(1), 101–122. doi:https://doi.org/10.1080/03085147.2016.1143726

MacKenzie, D., Muniesa, F., & Siu, L. (2008). *Do Economists Make Markets?: On the Performativity of Economics*. Princeton, NJ.: Princeton University Press.

Marcus, G. E. (1995). Ethnography in/of the World System: The Emergence of Multi-Sited Ethnography. *Annual Review of Anthropology*, 24, 95–117.

Martin, E. (2001a). *The woman in the body: A cultural analysis of reproduction*. Boston, MA.: Beacon Press.

Martin, P. (2001b). Genetic governance: The risks, oversight and regulation of genetic databases in the UK. *New Genetics and Society*, 20(2), 157–183. doi:https://doi.org/10.1080/14636770123633.

Masco, J. (2017). 'Boundless informant': Insecurity in the age of ubiquitous surveillance. *Anthropological Theory*, 17(3), 382–403. doi:https://doi.org/10.1177/1463499617731178.

McGranahan, C. (2018). Refusal as political practice: Citizenship, sovereignty, and Tibetan refugee status. *American Ethnologist*, 45(3), 367–379. doi:https://doi.org/10.1111/amet.12671.

McKay, I. (1994). Why Tell This Parable? *Journal of Canadian Studies/Revue d'Études Canadiennes*, 29(4), 144–152.

Miller, P. (2001). Governing by Numbers: Why Calculative Practices Matter. *Social Research*, 68(2), 179–189.

Miller, P., & Rose, N. S. (2008). *Governing the Present: Administering Economic, Social and Personal Life*. Oxford, U.K.: Polity.

Morgan, L. M., & Roberts, E. F. S. (2012). Reproductive governance in Latin America. *Anthropology & Medicine, 19*(2), 241–254. doi:https://doi.org/10.1080/1364847 0.2012.675046.

Mozersky, J. (2012). *Risky Genes: Genetics, Breast Cancer and Jewish Identity*. Abingdon, U.K.: Routledge.

Noble, S. U. (2018). *Algorithms of Oppression: How Search Engines Reinforce Racism*, New York NY.: NYU Press.

O'Neil, C. (2016). *Weapons of Math Destruction: How Big Data Increases Inequality and Threatens Democracy*. New York, NY.: Crown.

Paul, D. (1995). *Controlling Human heredity, 1865 to the Present*. Atlantic Highlands, NJ.: Humanities Press.

Pedersen, N. (1996). En (Inter)national resurs. Svenskt tvillingregister ger upplysning om miljons och arvets betydelse vid sjukdom—Det svenska tvillingregistret—Storst i varlden—Anvands for att studera betydelsen. *Läkartidningen., 93*(12), 1127.

Petersen, A. R., & Bunton, R. (1997). *Foucault, Health and Medicine*. Abingdon, U.K.: Routledge.

Petryna, A. (2002). *Life exposed: Biological citizens after Chernobyl*. Princeton, NJ.: Princeton University Press.

Poovey, M. (1998). *A history of the modern fact: Problems of knowledge in the sciences of wealth and society*. Chicago, IL.: University of Chicago Press.

Porter, T. M. (1992). Quantification and the Accounting Ideal in Science. *Social Studies of Science, 22*(4), 633.

Porter, T. M. (1996). *Trust in numbers: The pursuit of objectivity in science and public life*. Princeton, NJ.: Princeton University Press.

Prasse-Freeman, E. (2020). Data Subjectivity in What State? *Harvard International Law Journal Frontiers, 61*. https://harvardilj.org/2020/03/data-subjectivity-in-what-state/. Accessed 8 July 2021.

Rabinow, P. (1992). Artificiality and enlightenment: From sociobiology to biosociality. *Anthropologies of Modernity: Foucault, Governmentality, and Life Politics*, 179–193.

Raman, S., & Tutton, R. (2010). Life, Science, and Biopower. *Science, Technology & Human Values, 35*(5), 711–734. https://doi.org/10.1177/0162243909345838.

Rapp, R. (2001). Gender, body, biomedicine: How some feminist concerns dragged reproduction to the center of social theory. *Medical Anthropology Quarterly, 15*(4), 466–477.

Rapp, R. (2019). Race & Reproduction: An Enduring Conversation. *Medical Anthropology, 38*(8), 725–732. doi:https://doi.org/10.1080/0145974 0.2019.1671838.

Reardon, J. (2005). *Race to the finish: Identity and governance in an age of genomics*. Princeton, NJ.: Princeton University Press.

Reardon, J. (2007). Democratic Mis-Haps: The Problem of Democratization in a Time of Biopolitics. *Biosocieties, 2*, 239–256.

Rife, D. C. (1938). Contributions of the 1937 national twins' convention to research. *Journal of Heredity, 29*(3), 83-09.

Rivkin-Fish, M. (2003). Anthropology, Demography, and the Search for a Critical Analysis of Fertility: Insights from Russia. *American Anthropologist, 105*(2), 289–301. doi:https://doi.org/10.1525/aa.2003.105.2.289.

Roberts, J. A. F. (1935). Twins. *Eugenics Review, 27*(1), 25–32.

Rose, N. (1991). Governing by numbers: Figuring out democracy. *Accounting, Organizations and Society, 16*(7), 673–692. doi:https://doi.org/10.1016/0361-3682(91)90019-B.

Sadre-Orafai, S. (2020). Typologies, Typifications, and Types. *Annual Review of Anthropology, 49,* 193-208.

Scheper-Hughes, N., & Lock, M. M. (1987). The mindful body: A prolegomenon to future work in medical anthropology. *Medical Anthropology Quarterly, 1*(1), 6–41.

Scott, J. C. (1998). *Seeing Like a State: How Certain Schemes to Improve the Human Condition Have Failed.* New Haven, CT.: Yale University Press.

Silverstein, B. (2018). Commensuration, performativity, and the reform of statistics in Turkey. *American Ethnologist, 45*(3), 330–340. doi:https://doi.org/10.1111/amet.12668.

Simpson, A. (2014). *Mohawk Interruptus: Political Life Across the Borders of Settler States.* Durham, NC.: Duke University Press.

Sjöberg, F. (2005, October 30). Svenska tvillingar forskningens hjältar. *Svenska Dagbladet.*

Storeng, K. T., & Béhague, D. P. (2014). "Playing the Numbers Game": Evidence-based Advocacy and the Technocratic Narrowing of the Safe Motherhood Initiative. *Medical Anthropology Quarterly, 28*(2), 260–279. doi:https://doi.org/10.1111/maq.12072.

Taussig, K.-S. (2009). *Ordinary Genomes: Science, Citizenship, and Genetic Identities.* Durham, NC.: Duke University Press.

Taussig, K.-S., & Gibbon, S. E. (2013). Introduction: Public Health Genomics— Anthropological Interventions in the Quest for Molecular Medicine. *Medical Anthropology Quarterly, 27*(4), 471–488. doi:https://doi.org/10.1111/maq.12055.

Teo, T., & Ball, L. C. (2009). Twin research, revisionism and metahistory. *History of the Human Sciences, 22*(5), 1.

Thomson, W. A. R. (1935). Needed: Information on Twins. *British Medical Journal, 1*(3865), 231.

Thorndike, E. L. (1905). Measurement of Twins. *Journal of Philosophy, Psychology and Scientific Methods, 2*(20), 547-553.

Tilley, H. (2010). Global Histories, Vernacular Science, and African Genealogies; or, Is the History of Science Ready for the World? *Isis, 101*(1), 110–119. doi:https://doi.org/10.1086/652692.

Tupasela, A., Snell, K., & Tarkkala, H. (2020). The Nordic data imaginary. *Big Data & Society, 7*(1), 2053951720907107. doi:https://doi.org/10.1177/2053951720907107.

Urla, J. (1993). Cultural politics in an age of statistics: Numbers, nations, and the making of Basque identity. *American Ethnologist, 20*(4), 818–843.

Verran, H. (2010). Number as an inventive frontier in knowing and working Australia's water resources. *Anthropological Theory, 10*(1–2), 171–178. doi:https://doi.org/10.1177/1463499610365383.

Westergaard, H. (1932). *Contributions to the History of Statistics.* London, U.K.: P.S. King.

Wilke, J. (2004). From parish register to the "historical table": The Prussian population statistics in the 17th and 18th centuries. *History of the Family, 9*(1), 63–79. doi:https://doi.org/10.1016/j.hisfam.2003.10.002.

Wilson, P. T., & Jones, H. E. (1931). A study of like-sexed twins: I. the vital statistics and familial data of the sample. *Human Biology*, *3*(1), 107–132.

Wright, C. (2016). They Were Five: The Dionne Quintuplets Revisited. *Journal of Canadian Studies*. doi:10.3138/jcs.29.4.5.

Zuiderent-Jerak, T. (2010). Embodied Interventions—Interventions on Bodies: Experiments in Practices of Science and Technology Studies and Hemophilia Care. *Science, Technology, & Human Values*, *35*(5), 677–710. doi:https://doi.org/10.1177/0162243909337119.

CHAPTER 18

Data Practices and Sustainable Development Goals: Organising Knowledge for Sustainable Futures

Anne Beaulieu

[I]mproving data is a development agenda in its own right.
—*A World that Counts,* Report of the UN's Secretary-General's
Independent Expert Advisory Group on a Data Revolution for
Sustainable Development 2014

A good indicator of a region's poverty or underdevelopment is a lack of
poverty or development data.
—Letouze (2015)

In May of 2019, the Intergovernmental Science-Policy Platform on Biodiversity and Ecosystem Services (IPBES) published a Global Assessment Report, which stated that one million species are at risk of extinction in the coming years (IPBES 2019). One of the prominent reactions to the report on the part of policy-makers, researchers, and other stakeholders, was to question how the IPBES could possibly know this. Other global assessments, whether about the state of ecosystems, energy reserves, climate change or GDP measures, and level of development, have also been the object of debate about whether we can act on the basis of these technical reports. Strikingly, the global scale and urgency in these debates is increasingly articulated around the knowledge

A. Beaulieu (✉)
Department of Knowledge Infrastructures, Campus Fryslân, University of Groningen, Groningen, Netherlands
e-mail: j.a.beaulieu@rug.nl

M. H. Bruun et al. (eds.), *The Palgrave Handbook of the Anthropology of Technology*, https://doi.org/10.1007/978-981-16-7084-8_18

355

infrastructures that yield the data needed to formulate, address, and monitor progress on global environmental problems and the alleviation of human hardship. Prominent examples of global objects are the average rise in temperature, the number of people living in poverty, or the amount of renewable energy produced worldwide. Knowledge infrastructures and the digital data flows they foster are therefore important loci of analysis, since they solidify how problems are formulated, orient to possible solutions, and legitimise and support specific actors while excluding others. In this chapter, anthropology of technology, in combination with science and technology studies and development studies, is used to foster a rich understanding of digital data practices and associated technologies. These include the accountability and inequality that are constituted by knowledge infrastructures.

The emerging technologies considered in this chapter—while generally falling under the label of 'digital'—range from the very small, portable, and even intimate (a mobile phone in the Global North) to the highly distributed and remote (satellite data, internet infrastructure). Importantly, these technologies are also largely configured as individual, corporate, global, and ongoing ('real-time'). They are furthermore deployed and valued in contrast to another complex set of technologies of public bureaucracy for state knowledge, usually based in national statistics offices (NSOs). The technologies used by NSOs are document-based, ordered according to temporal cycles for data gathering, review, and release (annually or five-year census cycle), and aligned to nation states. These different logics of evidence and their associated technologies merge, clash, and compete in the project of knowing about global objects. In both cases, the technologies are best understood as assemblages, suites of technologies articulated as knowledge infrastructures with a particular evidence-gathering logic (de Rijcke and Beaulieu 2014), rather than as separate or stand-alone 'tools'.

In this chapter, I focus on the knowledge practices enacted around a specific set of global objects, the Sustainable Development Goals (SDGs), to better characterise recent changes in the relationship between digital technologies of measurement and accountability mechanisms. The aim is to use anthropology of technology to provide insights into the data-intensive practices around knowledge infrastructures, and to problematise the novel uncertainties and inequalities that result from these changes.

DATAFICATION AND PROLIFERATION OF DATA

In the creation of global objects, the foregrounding of data is an important trend. This is overwhelmingly presented in public discourse as simply taking advantage of the data that is now available (Mayer-Schönberger and Cukier 2013). But this 'simple' use of 'existing' data is supported by a complex process of datafication (Dijck et al. 2018). The extension of automation, with the proliferation of digital technologies, the willing production of massive amounts of data, and the combination and circulation of data sets are all crucial components of datafication (Rieder and Simon 2016; Dijck et al. 2018; Beaulieu and Leonelli 2021). Datafication 'turns into data' many aspects of the world and of our behaviour that had not been formalised before, and renders activities quantifiable traces in which patterns can be discovered and future behaviour predicted. Datafication is best understood according to a layered model that puts neither data nor technology at its centre. It links at least four essential elements: the community that engages with data, forms of care, capacities to handle data, and data itself in its many forms (Beaulieu and Leonelli 2021). Datafication intersects with many core concepts of anthropological analysis, revealing the importance of understanding its dynamic in conjunction with commodification (Dalton and Thatcher 2015), identity (Beduschi et al. 2017; Zwitter et al. 2020), post-colonial relations (Cinnamon 2019; Couldry and Mejias 2019), remittance (Rodima-Taylor and Grimes 2019), and surveillance and control (Taylor 2016). To warrant this seemingly self-evident use of available data, data had to become part of socio-cultural practices (Rieder and Simon 2016) and integrated into our social epistemology (Jasanoff 2003)—socially supported and accepted ways of knowing.

SITUATED MEANINGS OF DATA TECHNOLOGIES AND DATA WORK

In this context of datafication, individuals create data in daily life through their interactions with networked and mobile data devices. This data is used to produce global objects. The meanings of data technologies and of their uses are situated and multiple, as scholarship in anthropology of technology reveals. A device like a mobile phone can be an intimate possession, used to quantify the self, and to integrate and manage ongoing intimate relationships. It can also be a common possession that is casually shared. In the first case, the connection of the technology with an individual self will be a valid assumption. In the second case, it will not, as Erikson's analysis of mobile phone use in Sierra Leone powerfully demonstrates (Erikson 2018).

Furthermore, anthropology of technology approaches is also essential to maintaining a critical stance towards technology use and to keep questioning the filters through which Global North actors see the relation to technology of Global South actors. For example, in studies of the Global South users, 'their new media practices are predominantly framed as instrumental and utilitarian, partly because development agendas drive this research with a strong historical bias towards socioeconomic impacts' (Rangaswamy and Arora 2013). The result is a greater emphasis being placed on farmers checking crop prices online than watching pornography on their mobile devices (Arora 2016). This body of work contains important exemplars to help understand meaning as situated and to avoid making universalising assumptions about data-producing technologies.

An anthropological approach also keeps the researcher alert to the role of data, beyond seeing it as an empirical representation of the world. This can help us understand why data is generated, even when the production and compilation of data are already known to be incomplete and uncertain, or to form an undue burden (Sullivan 2017). Data can constitute a strategic resource when fulfilling requests from aid agencies for compliance or preparedness, or may signal accountability and transparency (Sullivan 2017). Such data works for symbolic purposes can divert energies to 'performing' data, at the expense of primary care and the development of a health system on the ground (Erikson 2019). In addition, in the face of discussions of global data where large-scale and centralised systems dominate, ethnography can help draw attention to local work and to how the 'local level' is not merely a recipient of data services, but also an active participant (Baker and Karasti 2018). Finally, where data literacy approaches frame digital inequalities as being about insufficient access to technology or lack of skills, an anthropology of technology approach helps address the emerging inequalities of data-intensive societies, questioning not only access to the digital, but the very constitution of the digital itself (Cinnamon 2019).

Infrastructure and Data for Policy

When decision-makers use digital data to make decisions about global objects, they enact different lines of accountability. If they call for new sources of data and ways of knowing—for example, 'Big Data for Development'—then new actors may enter the stage or existing actors take on different roles. The current situation, in which data plays a compelling role in guiding international policy and enhancing trust in the policy-makers and their decisions, is the result of complex historical processes (Shapin 1994; Porter 1995). Increased formalisation, quantification, and automation accompany the use of data as evidence (Beaulieu 2001, 2004), at the expense of expert interpretation and deliberation. In the second half of the twentieth century, global objects have emerged in relation to the growing importance of international negotiations and global political organisations such as the United Nations (Miller 2004). As these objects were articulated through data infrastructures on the planetary scale (Beck et al. 2016), the corresponding mechanisms of accountability were also realigned. Anthropological and historical work has shown how a focus on data practices can serve to challenge consensus, nourish controversy, and politicise issues (Oreskes and Conway 2011), or support obfuscation in order to delay action (Proctor 1995). An ethnographic approach shows how transforming data practices can contribute to contestation or confirmation of engagements with what is known (Gabrys 2016), or not known, in a way that is not innocent (Guston 1999).

Data as Evidence and Technologies of Accountability

When policy-makers favour particular kinds of evidence, they also tend towards particular kinds of solutions. This means that risk and vulnerability also change, depending on which kind of evidence is selected. Work in anthropology of health and in development studies has thoroughly examined the focus on atomistic evidence for global health, and the damaging side effects of measurements, metrics, and data infrastructures (Adams 2016). A focus on measurable interventions, using the tools of statistics and an emphasis on metrics, leads to counting single variables and is best suited to evaluating interventions that address a single target (Adams et al. 2014). This ignores the messiness of local situations and tends to focus on solutions and innovations that take on discrete forms, such as products or drugs—in contrast to systemic change, new practices, or relationship-based interventions. Hypothesis-driven research also imposes quantitative metrics that have a logic of anticipation, since it excludes any other types of data that might arise as it does not fit the pre-ordained design (Adams et al. 2014). This is why it is so important to analyse practices of data production, sharing, aggregation, and circulation. They show the networks of power, and reveal that classifying the world and providing evidence for 'what works' (Pigg et al. 2018) are complex accomplishments.

A recurring theme in this body of work is the valuation that accompanies the production of documentation as evidence and the associated entwinement of technology and accountability. This can result in an audit culture (Strathern 2000). Such a culture includes a combination of physical, institutional, and conceptual aspects that value 'productive' activities, requiring productivity and self-description that are limiting and come at the cost of activities that do not fit into auditable returns (Strathern 2000). This growing trend (Rieder and Simon 2016) has been labelled a corporatisation of governance (Merry 2011) or the rise of the technocratic (Turnhout et al. 2019), all dynamics tied to 'high-modernism' (Turnhout et al. 2016). Policymakers increasingly face demands for a demonstrably auditable basis. The phrase 'evidence-based policy' abounds in documents on global objects, including the SDGs, to which we will now turn. While this phrase can seem innocuous or even undisputable (who will argue in favour of evidence-free policy?!), this language does point to the foregrounding of technical expertise and the backgrounding of political debate in policy-making. If policy-makers require evidence to act, and if digital data on a global scale is considered the best way to provide evidence, it follows that much attention and funding goes into developing the specific types of knowledge infrastructures that rely on datafication. I examine how this relationship develops around the SDGs in the rest of this chapter.

Data Promises for the Sustainable Development Goals

A prominent instance of the intersection of global knowledge questions and datafication is found in the Sustainable Development Goals (SDGs) formulated by the United Nations in 2015 in the declaration *Transforming our World: the 2030 Agenda for Sustainable Development*. The declaration elaborated on the Millennium Development Goals set in 2000, a global anti-poverty effort, generally considered in development and governmental circles to have been largely successful. With the aim of guiding policy for the following fifteen years, the *2030 Agenda* formulated seventeen SDGs. The underlying reports, and subsequent communications, are full of formulations that stress the interrelated and global nature of the issues targeted by the goals. The declaration speaks of 'global Sustainable Development Goals' and of 'universal and transformative Goals and targets' (United Nations 2015), while the latest annual report insists that these are 'global problems that require global solutions' (United Nations 2019). UN documents widely call for evidence-based policy and tie this appeal to the powers of a 'data revolution' (United Nations 2018).

In what follows, I analyse the various emerging assemblages that various agencies develop in order to provide the knowledge needed for the SDGs, while also problematising this need. These assemblages are born out of aspirations for better data and are often framed in terms of remedying the shortcomings of current knowledge infrastructures. The present chapter arises from line of work being developed at Campus Fryslân, University of Groningen, the Netherlands, to contribute critically to better knowledge infrastructures for sustainability. As such, it is a mapping exercise to situate dynamics around knowledge infrastructures and to identify possible sites of interventions and experimentation. This case is an analysis of the knowledge base for the SDGs, as articulated by the UN-focused international community leading SDG efforts. It covers the two years prior to the launch of the SDGs and the first five years of their operation (2015–2019). To understand the assemblages called for and set in place for the SDGs, I analysed reports, presentations, interventions, design meetings, recommendations, and critiques that address the knowledge needed for the SDGs and how it is to be generated. Methodologically, this chapter is based on fieldwork in the context of SDGs, in which data, infrastructures (Wouters and Beaulieu 2006; de Rijcke and Beaulieu 2014), and documents (Riles 2006) are seen as actions as well as things, and where social ends and the material organisation of processes intersect (Riles 2006; Pigg et al. 2018). I treat databases and data flows for the SDGs ethnographically, and consider how reporting and monitoring practices are sites of negotiation and shaping that do not simply 'reflect' phenomena, but can also have a symbolic and material function. Through close reading of infrastructures, policies, guidelines for data gathering, descriptions of standards for data, and data sharing, the boring details add up to a technical but no less normative view of what constitutes action, progress, and sustainability.

The rest of the chapter explores the site of negotiation and competition between ways of knowing, and shows how different dynamics are played out that connect the high-level pronouncements of policy-makers and their instantiation in data practices on the ground, with resulting shifts in the dynamics of accountability. In the following sections, I analyse five dominant dynamics in the maintenance, reinforcement expansion, and innovation of data infrastructures in relation to the SDGs.

Dynamic 1: Developing Global Data as Evidence

If the practices and institutions that enact the modernist ideals of data for development of the UN are further developed, then global data becomes available as evidence. This means gathering data on the national level using traditional instruments such as surveys and demographic data that are administered by National Statistics Offices (NSOs). These NSOs are themselves embedded in a rich culture of national statistics production that includes participation in federations, negotiations around standardisation, and agreements on best data practices, documentation, and audits. This data flows to international organisations that are custodians of particular SDG targets, and to data repositories, a dynamic that largely follows the well-known path of quantification discussed earlier, with important variations to shape data in relation to indicators (Ruppert and Isin 2019; Beck and Mahony 2018; Turnhout and Boonman-Berson 2011). This dynamic was already visible in the late 1980s (Fortun 2004) and is now well-established and powerful in policy circles. It stresses rationality, consistency, and predictability in knowledge infrastructures, and its epistemic move is to create a neutral, controlled background against which the object of interest can become manifest. The calls for further development in this vein unsurprisingly focus on capacity-building and better funding of NSOs. An important step for this dynamic is, first, to implement the most traditional apparatus used to know populations and to establish basic administrative data systems. Such systems align institutions, data, and aid, thereby supporting those included while making those excluded even more vulnerable. Civil registration systems are therefore not only useful for producing statistics—they are also the institutions that extend identity and citizenship to people (Melamed n.d.). Those not included in these registries tend to come from the most vulnerable groups in the world's poorest countries—refugees, victims of human trafficking, and those living in remote regions or living a nomadic life. This vulnerability is compounded by preferences on the part of funders and donor agencies to work with countries that can demonstrate 'evidence-based need' and are able to measure impact (Cinnamon 2019). The result is that the established ability to produce evidence becomes a prerequisite for receiving aid. Data is itself a terrain where inequalities exist, with data rich and data poor countries. (Unidas 2014)

The first annual report on SDGs articulated high ambitions with regard to data:

> The data requirements for the global indicators are almost as unprecedented as the SDGs themselves and constitute a tremendous challenge to all countries. Nevertheless, fulfilling these requirements through building national statistical capacity is an essential step in establishing where we are now, charting a way forward and bringing our collective vision closer to reality. (United Nations 2016a, p. 3)

Data for SDGs produced through NSOs conforms to standardised categories (such as age, ethnicity, income). Such categories make combination and comparison possible (Rottenburg and Merry 2015; Porter 1995), whether across nations or over time. Comparison across countries is essential to maintain the isomorphism between data generated and the governance structures of the UN—nation-level data, for an organisation whose members are nations. Exchange and sharing of data are deemed necessary for the full implementation and review of SDGs. This is manifest in the concerted efforts to develop and share national reporting platforms, the development of a standard called statistical data metadata exchange (SDMX) as a common language to support the data flows for SDGs, a federated Information System for the SDGs (Open SDG Data Hub), and the use of APIs. Clearly, datafication of evidence for the SDGs is well underway.

Besides the global scale of production and sharing of data, another important feature is the association of goals with particular indicators. Indicators already played a prominent role in the Millennium Development Goals, with forty-eight indicators used to monitor progress towards the eight goals. The 17 SDGs have been articulated, first in relation to 169 targets, then in the shape of 234 indicators. In the first five years of the SDGs, indicators have become increasingly prominent, as both signs and objects of a growing technocratic reporting apparatus on a global scale. There is a pyramid-like construction in which data on specific indicators flows from mandated official national statistics offices, to international 'custodian agencies' like the WHO or World Bank. These in turn report on the progress made towards meeting the targets associated with the SDGs.

But, as noted above, indicators can only function in a stabilised field. The UN's institutional apparatus therefore produces not only definitions and guidelines for indicators, but also reports on the level of standardisation of indicators, the level of agreement on this standardisation, and the ability of national statistics offices to deliver on these indicators on the basis of various criteria. The road to knowing about the SDGs is therefore paved with indicators. The strength of the indicator discourse is such that even critiques of the bureaucratisation of development have tended to focus their attention on the appropriateness of indicators, arguing that the number of targets and indicators is out of proportion to the capacity for reporting on them (Roca and Letouzé 2016).

The dynamics around data as evidence for the SDGs is driven by the alignment of data production, data flows, and repositories, by reliance on quantification and standardisation, and further reinforcement of the nation state as key producer of data. The role of data in relation to the SDGs therefore varies from supporting policy to monitoring progress on them. It shapes what counts as progress towards diminishing inequalities and how comparisons are made across the world.

Dynamic 2: Disaggregation from Populations to Groups

A second dynamic links data to policy by innovating the relationship of data to knowing and acting. Typical of UN documents, the Sustainable Development Goals Report 2018 states:

> Without evidence of where we stand now we cannot confidently chart our path forward in realising the Sustainable Development Goals. To that end, this report also reflects on the challenges faced in the collection, processing, analysis and dissemination of reliable, timely, accessible and sufficiently disaggregated data, and calls for better evidence-based policymaking. Today's technology makes it possible to collate the data we need to keep the promise to leave no one behind. But, we need political leadership, resources and commitment to use the tools now available. (United Nations 2018, p. 3)

Note that not only the SDGs are challenging, but *data* in the service of policy also poses challenges: data needs to be reliable, timely, accessible, and sufficiently disaggregated. The first three attributes are classic issues in data gathering for UN purposes. Disaggregation is a somewhat more novel requirement, especially when posited as essential to the successful implementation of the SDGs. In tandem with the phrase 'evidence-based policy', the commitment to 'leave no one behind' is a staple of reports and communications about the SDGs, and a driver for data disaggregation. The UN initiatives link this goal to the existence of data and indicators that address specific groups within a population (United Nations 2016b). This link politicises data and indicators as means to reach an emancipatory end. If no one is to be left behind, then the data on progress towards the SDGs must be created and communicated in a way that avoids making some invisible (United Nations 2018, 2019).

While nation-level reporting has been entrenched in UN practices, variation within a country is repeatedly and increasingly stressed across the Sustainable Development Goals Reports issued between 2016 and 2019. An important element is the call to consider 'target populations' or 'groups', which are not well represented by population-level indicators (United Nations 2016a). This is a non-trivial aspiration that strongly contrasts with the foundational approach of NSOs, which focus on national populations. Given this departure from established definitions and instruments, the sparsity of data is not surprising. Current data gathering stands in the way, and groups such as.

> Children living outside of family care, persons with disabilities and older persons ... have largely fallen off the statistical 'map'. While innovative approaches for bringing these hidden populations into focus have begun to emerge, more resources and capacity-building efforts are needed to ensure that vulnerable groups receive their long-overdue place in the development agenda. (United Nations 2017)

Without disaggregation, these groups remain invisible and are therefore not served by development programmes. This line of reasoning links the availability of data and the possibility of action.

Disaggregation challenges 'populations' as the unit of data gathering, and warrants the use of new data sources and technologies, including partners beyond NSOs (civil society, the private sector, and academia) (United Nations 2019). Parallel organisations are emerging at the global level, such as DataPop and Global Pulse, and they are charged with the exploration of these dynamics for the UN. In addition, the newly created United Nations World Data Forum aims to serve as a platform to bring data producers and users together and to work on capacity development, disaggregation, and 'synergies across data ecosystems'. There are also changes underway in the work of NSOs, and of civil registration and vital statistics organisations, to make disaggregation possible, through efforts to insert additional features of groups in population-based systems.

We know that the creation and processing of population data is a major achievement (Ruppert 2012). The alignment of civil registration systems with national statistics offices and with the UN and its agencies requires mutual adjustments that can span decades before data flow is considered robust. Careful attention to such alignments reveals how new ones might be emerging, reshaping the existing relations between governance and evidence. In our data-fied world, as Hoeyer et al. (2019) have noted, visibility and counting merge. The kind of disaggregation being implemented will shape who those 'left behind' might be, as well as who will be able to speak on their behalf. What is produced are categories that create and perpetuate social differences, with implications for access to services, representation, education, and healthcare. As Cinnamon has noted, these processes tend to be 'opaque and under-regulated', bringing risks for 'the propagation of errors if these data are aggregated for use as proxy national development statistics (Taylor & Broeders, 2015)' (Cinnamon 2019, p. 12). The resulting assemblage creates particular vulnerabilities (Arora 2016), but the actors responsible are identifiable and accountable.

What we are seeing in the wake of the SDGs' efforts is a different assemblage of technologies, with a murkier chain of responsibility and accountability. In a context of population-level statistics, national governments are the relevant actors, whereas with global data, international organisations are the correspondent actors. But who is the relevant actor when we speak of 'no one' being left behind? Who is the actor for whom disaggregated data would be usable, and how does this kind of data shape the possibility for action? Too little attention has gone into asking whether the mobilisation of disaggregated data might also have the unintended effect of disempowering or stigmatising groups, making them even more vulnerable. The related issues of the empowerment of private corporations as gatekeepers of social knowledge and the disempowerment of the traditional actors such as NSOs have also been largely ignored.

Dynamic 3: Localisation of Data

A third set of calls for innovation in SDG data have to do with the localisation of data. In the context of data for SDGs, there is a mixed picture with regard to the foregrounding of geographical information. On the one hand, the UN paradigm of nation-level reporting remains dominant, with all UN platforms for the SDGs maintaining the nation state as the reporting unit for its members; on the other, reports and policy documents continue to call for increased localisation of the SDGs and their data. In line with the policy aims discussed in the previous section, the reasoning is that as long as variation within the space of a country is not known, the ability to leave no one behind remains limited since national averages hide intra-national disparities. The connection between having data and the possibility of acting is once again emphasised. In this case, however, it is articulated on the basis of the requirement for more granularity in terms of geographical location:

> National statistics can be acted upon when the data is broken down to focus on specific categories of interest or locality. While data is usually disaggregated across people-centric variables—such as gender, age, income, ...—the global indicator framework has specified that it is equally important to be able to analyse data across different geographic locations. (Working Group on Geospatial Information 2018)

To address this 'gap' between knowing and acting, the working group recommends combining geo-spatial information with SDG data.

The increasing prominence of geo-location is related to the increasing availability of positioning information (satellite data). This data is combined with signals from trackers (for animals, goods (IoT), etc.), or with data from mobile phones or internet-connected devices, to produce an approximation of location. The growing role of cities and regions as actors[1] in SDGs and in the areas of housing and transport (Hajer et al. 2015) also fuels demand for data that is more granular than at national level; actors seek data that corresponds to their sphere of influence.

Efforts to localise data reveal the obduracy of established data pipelines (de Rijcke and Beaulieu 2014). It is not a case of 'add geographical information and stir'. Official statistics and Earth observation data have developed separately, using different techniques in different institutions, and the multiple challenges of combining these types of data are not likely to be overcome in the short term (UN Environment 2019). Concretely, toolkits and platforms to localise SDG data are emerging, but they tend to come from organisations working in parallel to NSOs. At this institutional level, countries most in need of localised data may be those least able to generate it (Patole 2018). Just like the requirement for disaggregation, localisation goes beyond the current capacities of NSOs and developing this capacity requires additional investments.

Obtaining geo-located data raises major issues of access, ownership, and openness. Geo-located data often relies either on satellite data, which may be public or private, or on proxies such as triangulation of mobile phone signal or IP addresses of internet-connected devices. The network operators that collect and control this latter data are overwhelmingly private companies. The language of Article 76, of the United Nations document on the Sustainable Agenda indicates great optimism that this can be addressed through 'appropriate public-private cooperation to exploit the contribution to be made by a wide range of data, including Earth observation and geospatial information, while ensuring ownership in supporting and tracking progress' (United Nations 2016b). But given the extent to which public values clash with those of corporate platforms (Dijck et al. 2018; Zuboff 2019), such statements—five years later at the time of writing—already seem overconfident, bordering on naïve. Besides issues of entwined interests and ownership, the disaggregation and geo-location of data create new vulnerabilities. If being invisible means someone can be left behind, it also carries with it the possibility of being sought out (Letouzé and Vinck 2015). If disaggregation increases the risks of identifiability and stigmatisation, then localisation increases the risks of being physically found and targeted for intervention.

Dynamic 4: Diversification of Data Sources

The motifs of a 'data revolution' and of 'harnessing the power of Big Data' to enrich the range of data used have been part of the SDG discourse since about 2014. The UN World Data Forum meetings (2017 in Capetown, 2018 in Dubai, and Bern [online] 2020) further strengthen the calls for the use of 'Big Data' to leave no one behind (United Nations 2017). In the guide *Data Innovation for Development*, the promise is that

> alternative sources of data can and should play a role in pursuing development outcomes, and, as such, hold great promise for fulfilling the Sustainable Development Goals—both from the perspective of pursuing the outcomes as well as enabling (close to) real-time monitoring and evaluation. (Global Pulse 2016, p. 4)

The dominant discourse is that Big Data methodologies developed in business will replace current ones (UN Global Pulse 2016). For example, rather than relying on traditional household surveys, the use of night-time satellite imagery is proposed to measure consumption of energy and as a proxy indicator of poverty and growth (Jean et al. 2016; Henderson et al. 2012).

Typical of such Big Data projects is the exploration in the form of pilot projects of what these sources can mean as a complement to existing data; they are usually used as Tier III indicators for SDGs, for which no agreed-upon methods or standards exist. This makes them less comparable and more closely tied to their context of production, often outside NSOs. Thus, they may be '[c]ountry-specific indicators developed either by government through the national statistical system or by non-official data producers such as civil society, research institutions or the private sector' (United Nations Development Programme 2017). Projects to explore new indicators can include the scraping of content on social media platforms, such as using Twitter data to measure public sentiment on corruption (Tunisia, DIFD 2016); or the use of comments on official governmental Facebook pages in Botswana to measure satisfaction with government services (Celli and Stock n.d.); or combining public health data with data from private mobile phone network operators to track population movements in India to monitor the spread of TB (GSMA n.d.).

But even though the data may be big, it is also limited, although these limitations can be difficult to document (van der Vlist 2016; Kitchin 2016). The number of tweets or posts that can be retrieved, the access policies with regard to retrieval by users versus bots, and the algorithmic ordering and prominence of contents are all important conditions that can only partially be known by researchers. Even to corporate insiders, these elements often remain undocumented and undisclosed, in line with the proprietary nature of this data and with processes of commodification on these platforms (Dijck et al. 2018; Beaulieu and Leonelli 2021). Many of the conditions that shape data are, furthermore, subject to change, based on corporate strategy—to say nothing of ever-changing demographics of users and levels of access to these platforms over time. All this means that, even if the relevance and validity of this data can be established, the lack of baselines and the 'baseless data' of Big Data (Knox 2018) mean that comparing data over time or in different settings to monitor progress on the SDGs will be far from straightforward. Can we imagine development indicators based on a logic of 'now trending' or 'virality', rather than on the current constructs of external validity inspired by social science?

There are also differences between the statistical relationships of validity and causality valued by NSOs and development agencies and those fostered in corporate settings where predictive models dominate (Schutt and O'Neil 2013; UN Global Pulse 2016). In addition, corporate settings favour an iterative approach to models and welcome the constant growth of data. In contrast, most development work uses a framework shaped by more traditional social science research in which higher standards of inference are demanded and where the 'experimental set up' is the gold standard.

Calls for the use of more types of data may seem like a step towards creating a richer picture of development. But data comes with epistemological, political, and ethical strings attached. These new practices seem to be developing with a minimum of scrutiny of what it means for corporations to act as gatekeepers (Cinnamon 2019). Enthusiastically welcoming 'data philanthropy' (Kirkpatrick and Vacarelu 2019) means that maintaining warm relationships with corporations becomes essential, if access to data is dependent on corporate goodwill. Yet philanthropy cannot always be assumed.[2] This risk too tends to be backgrounded by the UN in favour of pleas for the development of international shared standards for data sharing and privacy-protection, (Kirkpatrick and

Vacarelu 2019). Other issues are sometimes noted, like the degree of penetration of technology needed for crowd-sourcing to be effective (Kirkpatrick and Vacarelu 2019). Such faith in the promises of Big Data, assumptions about the desirability of philanthropy, and a focus on individualised risks like personal privacy breaches leave systemic issues around diversification of data unaddressed.

Dynamic 5: Meaningful Accountability

In an effort to show progress across countries and across the different goals, the SDG Index orders countries according to their performance. This performance is based on indicators fed by complex data flows, and countries are ranked according to their performance across all seventeen goals (see Table 2.1 here: https://s3.amazonaws.com/sustainabledevelopment. report/2021/2021-sustainable-development-report.pdf). All this material forms the basis of the annual SDG Reports and of the data releases that can be explored via the dashboards, according to SDGs, region, country, or over time (Sachs et al. 2020).

The SDG Index is the apex of the data aggregation pyramid, and the ultimate distillation of quantified data produced by state bureaucracy according to global standards. It summarises a country's performance across the SDGs with single figures. The meaningfulness of such highly abstracted data has been critiqued, and a recent audit warns that differences between countries should not be given too much weight (Papadimitriou et al. 2019).

These critiques of metrics and indicators arise in tandem with calls for more meaningful assessments closer to the actual activities pursued (also heard in other fields, see de Rijcke et al. 2016, 2019). A more distributed, grounded approach to data is seen as an opportunity not only for more granular, more timely data, but also for meaningful accountability. What is interesting to note is that there is also an accompanying epistemological shift in relation to data and knowing: if the gold standard of the experimental form dominated as the hard-to-reach ideal for knowing about development initiatives, a different approach is emerging (Jensen and Winthereik 2012). In this discourse, a phrase that often recurs is that monitoring of development should aim 'to improve rather than (only) prove'. The specificity and rigidity of indicator data are at times argued to be in tension with learning and meaningful progress.

In this spirit, many organisations seek alternatives to what they consider to be overly narrow indicators. The Sustainable Development Goals Tool is a web-based tool developed by the Cambridge Conservation Initiative (CCI) (2018a). It provides practitioners with a simple interface to review systematically how their projects could be linked to the SDGs at the level of *targets*. Recall that the 17 goals are articulated through 169 targets, which are in turn linked to 234 agreed-upon indicators. CCI's tool allows conservation professionals to explore how their biodiversity projects can contribute to SDG targets, beyond the goals specifically formulated on biodiversity (Life Below Water [14]; Life on Land [15]). A wizard takes the user through a series of questions about what the project does, whom it involves, the kinds of activities pursued, and its expected impact, then suggests links between these answers and SDG targets. The user can add notes, modulate the level of importance (major/minor) and keep track of the relevant targets digitally. The outcome of the wizard is a list of targets to which a project contributes that can be exported and annotated, or used for interactive presentations and as an infographic.

The makers of the SDG Tool motivate their choice of the target level as a more meaningful anchoring point, arguing that a focus on indicators may miss many important project contributions. Indicators are critiqued as being in danger of becoming their own goal, pursued for their own sake—a well-known feedback loop in metrification (Beer 2015; Merry 2011; Rottenburg and Merry 2015). Targets are also preferred over goals, since goals are said to represent 'siloes' (hunger, poverty) whereas the target level does more justice to the 'integrated agenda [of the SDGs], incorporating the interlinkages between the social, economic, and environmental dimensions of sustainable development' (Cambridge Conservation Initiative 2018b). A similar point is also made by Bewley-Taylor, who argues that SDG targets help create awareness of the intersection of issues, such as drug control with food security or health, resulting in better action (2017).

If we contrast the SDG Tool of the conservationists with the scope of the SDG Index and global data assemblages of the UN agencies as predicated on their relationships to the NSOs, it seems a case of David versus Goliath. The UN's data on SDGs relies on a huge apparatus and makes use of highly standardised tools, methods, and institutions so that mediated data practices produce 'techno-metricized accountabilities' (Hoeyer et al. 2019). In contrast, the SDG Tool's gentle exploration—in dialogue with an embodied expert committed to a project—shows that digital technology *can* be modulated to yield a different kind of accountability. It remains a massive challenge to make such alternatives viable, as earlier efforts to implement information and monitoring systems that have a more situated logic have shown (Fortun 2004). The example of the SDG Tool illustrates that the sensitivity to variations in the uses and meanings of technology fostered by anthropology of technology is an important asset when approaching local reactions to global paradigms like the SDG Index.

CONCLUDING DISCUSSION

The five dynamics signal a number of shifts in how the SDGs are constituted as global objects. They are challenging for the UN, its agencies and NSOs (UNECE Steering Group 2019) in terms of 'sovereignty over data regimes' (Bigo et al. 2019, p. 6). They affect for whom SDGs are relevant, as well as who is enabled by and responsible for acting on them. We may not only be seeing a realignment of existing 'lines of accountability' (Guston 1999), but also a shift from the kind of accountability that dominated by the end of the twentieth century, based on system-level relations and access to data on public service delivery (Hoeyer et al. 2019). The use of Big Data from corporate actors does not align with the categories and techniques of modernist accountability that are dominant in the global and national statistical institutions.[3] To take but one example, we need to consider what reliance on data philanthropy means for the impetus to 'leave no one behind'. The shift in categories of citizens to consumer is a weighty one; does it also redirect the development agenda from an aspiration to extending universal rights to striving for total market penetration? These big questions need to be raised by anthropology of technology because the knowledge infrastructures we maintain and assemble contribute to their answers. The opacity of corporate data production, the accountabilities of corporations to their shareholders and customers rather than to citizens and governments, and the deep epistemic differences in statistical operations cannot be underestimated. What is at stake should not be reduced to technical questions of measurement, criteria, and accessibility (Merry 2011) or to cautionary notes on complying with privacy and security (Kirkpatrick and Vacarelu 2019).

The dynamics analysed are also generative of new possibilities, especially with regard to the temporality and spatiality of global objects. With regard to the temporal dimension, the stability of organisations and networks contributes to the creation of long-term data that has enabled us to track environmental change (Edwards 2019). 'Timeliness' is a feature of Big Data that has been enthusiastically embraced. The (near) real-time or short-term delivery of data is seen as an opportunity to develop 'early warning' practices (UN Global Pulse 2016). This temporal characteristic matters because it can shift knowledge infrastructures from a focus on monitoring progress accomplished, towards predictive policy-making. This may be an effective way to create a sense of urgency, but it can also limit the extent to which formulations of sustainable development, such as those of the Bruntland Report involving future generations, remain relevant because of clashing temporalities.

The scale of global objects is also called into question by these dynamics. While national institutions coordinated into global networks have dominated in recent decades (Edwards 2013; Beck et al. 2016), their work may cut us off from how we know climate or biodiversity in a more local sense. While the erasure of geography is part of what makes knowledge global, it also removes the possibilities for apprehending difference, heterogeneity, and complexity in the interactions between societies and natures (Turnhout et al. 2014; Turnhout et al. 2016). It makes invisible the relative responsibility for the creation of global problems and their differentiated impact in various parts of the world, an issue that has been especially closely analysed in the case of climate change and emissions (Beck et al. 2016; Latour et al. 2018). Indicators such as average global temperature obscure other potential signs of climate change that might mobilise actors (Turnhout et al. 2016). Calls to do data differently could even be seen as a kind of de-globalisation or re-localisation of data. Current attempts to disaggregate, localise, and diversify sources of knowledge and to articulate them in relation to the SDG targets might be a path towards reidentifying with issues meaningfully.

If the data flows of NSOs based on household surveys and socio-demographic, state-based data tend towards the global, many of the Big Data pilot projects so far tend towards the local and the specific. On a hopeful note, in several of the pilot projects, the context of data creation has been detailed, precisely because of the perceived lack of standards and mechanisms of stabilisation for this kind of data. There has, therefore, been more attention paid to the elements that create the 'baselessness' of Big Data (Knox 2018), its iterative nature, and the ever-changing condition of production. This may open up a gap in the business as usual of abstracting data and serve as a breeding ground for a more contextual approaches to data. This, in turn, might help us depart from linear notions of progress (Tsing 2015) and create different accounts of development. The scenario to avoid is that we end up with the worst of both worlds: stately, remote, aggregated data from NSOs and unaccountable and unverifiable data snapshots from Big Data obtained on the fragile basis of corporate goodwill. While some analysts see a gradual mixing rather than an abrupt shift to a new data regime (Ruppert and Isin 2019), this easing into a new configuration demands careful scrutiny. The sensibilities and tools of anthropology of technology equip us to keep asking not only whether privacy regulations are being respected but also, more fundamentally, how these dynamics around new sources of data change the science-policy relationship, and which new kinds of knowledge are being acted on, by whom, and on whose behalf.

Acknowledgements With thanks to the members of the Data Research Centre and Sabina Leonelli for ongoing conversations on these topics, and to Malcolm Campbell-Verduyn, the editors, and two anonymous reviewers for insightful comments on an earlier draft.

NOTES

1. See networks such as United Cities and Local Governments (UCLG), Global Covenant of Mayors for Climate & Energy) and USA-Sustainable Cities Initiative (USA-SCI).
2. A notable case, where telephone data in Sierra Leone, Liberia, and Guinea was *not* used to help face the Ebola epidemic in West Africa (McDonald 2016).
3. Edwards (2019) shows what happens to climate knowledge infrastructures when chains of evidence are destabilised through funding cuts, privatisation, fragilising of input, emerging types of review/audit that challenge established modes of expertise.

References

Adams, V. (2016). *Metrics: What Counts in Global Health* (Reprint edition). Duke University Press Books.

Adams, V., Burke, N. J., & Whitmarsh, I. (2014). Slow Research: Thoughts for a Movement in Global Health. *Medical Anthropology, 33*(3), 179–197.

Arora, P. (2016). Bottom of the Data Pyramid: Big Data and the Global South. *International Journal of Communication, 10*(0), 19.

Beaulieu, A., & S. Leonelli (2021). *Data and Society: A Critical Introduction*. SAGE Publications Ltd.

Baker, K. S., & Karasti, H. (2018). Data Care and Its Politics: Designing for Local Collective Data Management as a Neglected Thing. *Proceedings of the 15th Participatory Design Conference: Full Papers—Volume 1*, 10:1–10:12.

Beaulieu, A. (2001). Voxels in the brain: Neuroscience, informatics and changing notions of objectivity. *Social Studies of Science, 31*(5), 635–680.

Beaulieu, A. (2004). From brainbank to database: The informational turn in the study of the brain. *Studies in History and Philosophy of Science Part C: Studies in History and Philosophy of Biological and Biomedical Sciences, 35*(2), 367–390.

Beck, S., Forsyth, T., Kohler, P. M., Lahsen, M., & Mahony, M. (2016). The Making of Global Environmental Science and Politics. In U. Felt, R. Fouché, C. A. Miller, & L. Smith-Doerr (Eds.), *The Handbook of Science and Technology Studies* (pp. 1059–1086). Cambridge, MA: The MIT Press.

Beck, S., & Mahony, M. (2018). The IPCC and the new map of science and politics. *Wiley Interdisciplinary Reviews: Climate Change, 9*(6), e547.

Beduschi, A., Cinnamon, J., Langford, J., Luo, C., & Owen, D. (2017). *Building Digital Identities: The Challenges, Risks and Opportunities of Collecting Behavioural Attributes for new Digital Identity Systems*. [Report]. University of Exeter and Coelition.

Beer, D. (2015). Productive measures: Culture and measurement in the context of everyday neoliberalism. *Big Data & Society, 2*(1).

Bewley-Taylor, D. (2017). Refocusing metrics: Can the sustainable development goals help break the 'metrics trap' and modernise international drug control policy? *Drugs and Alcohol Today, 17*(2).

Bigo, D., Isin, E., & Ruppert, E. (2019). Data Politics. In D. Bigo, E. Isin, & E. Ruppert (Eds.), *Data Politics: Worlds, Subjects, Rights* (pp. 1–17). Routledge.

Cambridge Conservation Initiative. (2018a). *SDG Tool*. https://sdgtool.com/. Accessed 26 April 2020.

Cambridge Conservation Initiative. (2018b). *SDG Tool FAQ*. https://sdgtool.com/faq. Accessed 26 April 2020.

Celli, F., & Stock, M. (n.d.). *Measuring the Unmeasured—SDG Tier III Indicators A PILOT FOR THE GOVERNMENT OF BOTSWANA Final Report* (p. 11). Data-Pop Alliance and UNDP. https://datapopalliance.org/measuring-the-unmeasured/. Accessed 26 April 2020.

Cinnamon, J. (2019). Data inequalities and why they matter for development. *Information Technology for Development, 0*(0), 1–20.

Couldry, N., & Mejias, U. A. (2019). *The Costs of Connection: How Data Is Colonizing Human Life and Appropriating It for Capitalism* (1st edition). Stanford University Press.

Dalton, C. M., & Thatcher, J. (2015). Inflated granularity: Spatial "Big Data" and geodemographics. *Big Data & Society, 2*(2), 1–15.

de Rijcke, S. & Beaulieu, A. (2014). Networked neuroscience: Brain scans and visual knowing at the intersection of atlases and databases. In C. Coopmans, S. Woolgar, J. Vertesi, & M. Lynch (Eds.), *Representation in Scientific Practice Revisited.* Cambridge, MA: The MIT Press.

de Rijcke, S., Wouters, P. F., Rushforth, A. D., Franssen, T. P., & Hammarfelt, B. (2016). Evaluation practices and effects of indicator use—A literature review. *Research Evaluation, 25*(2), 161–169.

de Rijcke, S., Holtrop, T., Kaltenbrunner, W., Zuijderwijk, J., Beaulieu, A., Franssen, T., van Leeuwen, T., Mongeon, P., Tatum, C., Valkenburg, G., & Wouters, P. (2019). Evaluative Inquiry: Engaging Research Evaluation Analytically and Strategically. *Fteval Journal for Research and Technology Policy Evaluation,* 176–182.

Dijck, J. van, Poell, T., & Waal, M. de. (2018). *The Platform Society: Public Values in a Connective World.* Oxford University Press.

Edwards, P. N. (2013). *A Vast Machine: Computer Models, Climate Data, and the Politics of Global Warming.* MIT Press.

Edwards, P. N. (2019). Data Infrastructures under Siege: Climate as Memory, Truce and Target. In D. Bigo, E. Isin, & E. Ruppert (Eds.), *Data Politics: Worlds, Subjects, Rights* (pp. 21–42). Routledge.

Erikson, S. L. (2018). Cell Phones ≠ Self and Other Problems with Big Data Detection and Containment during Epidemics. *Medical Anthropology Quarterly, 32*(3), 315–39. https://doi.org/10.1111/maq.12440.

Erikson, S. (2019). Faking global health. *Critical Public Health, 29*(4), 508–516.

Fortun, K. (2004). From Bhopal to the Informating of Environmentalism: Risk Communication in Historical Perspective. *Osiris, 19,* 283–296.

Gabrys, J. (2016). Practicing, Materialising and Contesting Environmental Data. *Big Data & Society, 3*(2). https://doi.org/10.1177/2053951716673391.

Global Pulse (2016). A Guide to Data Innovation for Development—From Idea to Proof-of-Concept. Global Pulse, UNDP. https://www.oecd-opsi.org/toolkits/a-guide-to-data-innovation-for-development-from-idea-to-proof-of-concept/.

GSMA. (n.d.). *Helping End Tuberculosis in India by 2025.* https://www.gsma.com/betterfuture/wp-content/uploads/2018/12/Helping_end_Tuberculosis_in_India_by_2025.pdf

Guston, D. H. (1999). Stabilizing the Boundary between US Politics and Science: The Role of the Office of Technology Transfer as a Boundary Organization. *Social Studies of Science, 29*(1), 87–111.

Hajer, M., Nilsson, M., Raworth, K., Berkhout, F., Boer, Y. de, Rockström, J., Ludwig, K., & Kok, M. (2015). Beyond cockpit-ism: Four insights to enhance the transformative potential of the sustainable development goals. *Sustainability, 7*(2).

Henderson, J. V., Storeygard, A., & Weil, D. N. (2012). Measuring Economic Growth from Outer Space. *American Economic Review, 102*(2), 994–1028.

Hoeyer, K., Bauer, S., & Pickersgill, M. (2019). Datafication and accountability in public health: Introduction to a special issue. *Social Studies of Science, 49*(4), 459–475.

IPBES. (2019). *Summary for policymakers of the global assessment report on biodiversity and ecosystem services of the Intergovernmental Science-Policy Platform on Biodiversity and Ecosystem Services.* J. Shin, I. J. Visseren-Hamakers, K. J. Willis, & C. N. Zayas (Eds.). IPBES Secretariat.

Jasanoff, S. (2003). Technologies of Humility: Citizen Participation in Governing Science. *Minerva*, *41*(3), 223–244.

Jean, N., Burke, M., Xie, M., Davis, W. M., Lobell, D. B., & Ermon, S. (2016). Combining satellite imagery and machine learning to predict poverty. *Science*, *353*(6301), 790–794.

Jensen, C. B., & Winthereik, B. R. (2012). Recursive partnerships in global development aid. In S. Venkatesan & T. Yarrow (Eds.), *Differentiating Development*. Berghahn Books.

Kirkpatrick, R., & Vacarelu, F. (2019). A decade of leveraging big data for sustainable development. *UN Chronicle*, *55*(4), 26–31.

Kitchin, R. (2016). Thinking critically about and researching algorithms. *Information, Communication & Society*, *20*(1), 14–29.

Knox, H. (2018). Baseless data? Modelling, ethnography and the challenge of the Anthropocene. In H. Knox & D. Nafus (Eds.), *Ethnography for a data-saturated world* (pp. 128–150). Manchester University Press.

Latour, B., Stengers, I., Tsing, A., & Bubandt, N. (2018). Anthropologists Are Talking—About Capitalism, Ecology, and Apocalypse. *Ethnos*, *83*(3), 587–606.

Letouze, E. (2015). *Big Data & Development: An overview* [Data Pop Alliance White Paper Series]. Data-Pop Alliance, World Bank group, Harvard Humanitarian Initiative.

Letouzé, E., & Vinck, P. (2015). *The Law, Politics and Ethics of Cell Phone Data Analytics* [Data-Pop Alliance White Paper Series]. Data-Pop Alliance, World Bank Group, Harvard Humanitarian Initiative, MIT Media Lab and Overseas Development Institute.

Mayer-Schönberger, V., & Cukier, K. (2013). *Big Data: A Revolution that Will Transform how We Live, Work, and Think*. Houghton Mifflin Harcourt.

McDonald, S. (2016). *Sean McDonald—Ebola: A Big Data Disaster—The Centre for Internet and Society*. The Centre for Internet and Society. https://cis-india.org/papers/ebola-a-big-data-disaster. Accessed 8 July 2021.

Melamed, C. (n.d.). *The Race to Innovate for Development Should Not Leave Foundational Data Systems Behind*. United Nations; United Nations. Retrieved 4 July 2020, from https://www.un.org/en/chronicle/article/race-innovate-development-should-not-leave-foundational-data-systems-behind.

Merry, S. E. (2011). Measuring the World: Indicators, Human Rights, and Global Governance: with CA comment by John M. Conley. *Current Anthropology*, *52*(S3), S83–S95. https://doi.org/10.1086/657241.

Miller, C. A. (2004). Climate science and the making of a global political order. In S. Jasanoff (Ed.), *States of Knowledge*. Routledge.

Oreskes, N., & Conway, E. M. (2011). *Merchants of Doubt: How a Handful of Scientists Obscured the Truth on Issues from Tobacco Smoke to Global Warming* (Reprint edition). Bloomsbury Publishing.

Papadimitriou, E., Neves, A. R., Becker, W., European Commission, & Joint Research Centre. (2019). *JRC statistical audit of the Sustainable Development Goals index and dashboards*. http://publications.europa.eu/publication/manifestation_identifier/PUB_KJ1A29776ENN.

Patole, M. (2018). Localization of SDGs through Disaggregation of KPIs. *Economies*, *6*(1), 15.

Pigg, S. L., Erikson, S. L., & Inglis, K. (2018). Introduction: Document/ation: Power, Interests, Accountabilities. *Anthropologica*.

Porter, T. M. (1995). *Trust in numbers: The pursuit of objectivity in science and public life*. Princeton Univ. Press.

Proctor, R. N. (1995). *The Cancer Wars: How Politics Shapes What We Know And Don't Know About Cancer* (1st edition). Basic Books.

Rangaswamy, N., & Arora, P. (2013). Digital Leisure for Development: Reframing New Media Practice in the Global South. *Media, Culture & Society, 35*(7), 898–905. https://doi.org/10.1177/0163443713495508.

Rieder, G., & Simon, J. (2016). Datatrust: Or, the political quest for numerical evidence and the epistemologies of Big Data. *Big Data & Society, 3*(1).

Riles, A. (2006). *Documents: Artifacts of Modern Knowledge*. University of Michigan Press.

Roca, T., & Letouzé, E. (2016). La révolution des données est-elle en marche ? *Afrique contemporaine, 258*(2), 95–111.

Rodima-Taylor, D., & Grimes, W. W. (2019). International remittance rails as infrastructures: Embeddedness, innovation and financial access in developing economies. *Review of International Political Economy, 26*(5), 839–862.

Rottenburg, R., & Merry, S. E. (2015). A world of indicators: The making of governmental knowledge through quantification. In R. Rottenburg, S. E. Merry, S.-J. Park, & J. Mugler (Eds.), *The World of Indicators: The Making of Governmental Knowledge through Quantification* (pp. 1–33). Cambridge University Press.

Ruppert, E. (2012). The Governmental Topologies of Database Devices. *Theory, Culture & Society*, 116–136.

Ruppert, E., & Isin, E. (2019). Data's empire: Postcolonial data politics. In D. Bigo, E. Isin, & E. Ruppert (Eds.), *Data Politics: Worlds, Subjects, Rights* (pp. 207–227). Routledge.

Sachs, J. Schmidt-Traub, G., Kroll, C., Lafortune, G., Fuller, G., & Woelm, F. (2020). *The Sustainable Development Goals and Covid-19. Sustainable Development Report 2020*. Cambridge: Cambridge University Press. https://dashboards.sdgindex.org/rankings. Accessed 5 May 2021.

Strathern, M. (Ed.) (2000). *Audit Cultures: Anthropological Studies in Accountability, Ethics and the Academy*. (1st edition). Routledge.

Schutt, R., & O'Neil, C. (2013). *Doing Data Science*. O'Reilly & Associates.

Sustainable Development Goals Report 2019. (2019). Retrieved 22 August 2019, from https://www.un.org/sustainabledevelopment/progress-report/.

Shapin, S. (1994). *Social History of Truth: Civility and Science in Seventeenth-Century England*. University of Chicago Press.

Sullivan, N. (2017). Multiple accountabilities: Development cooperation, transparency, and the politics of unknowing in Tanzania's health sector. *Critical Public Health, 27*(2), 193–204.

Taylor, L. (2016). No Place to Hide? The Ethics and Analytics of Tracking Mobility Using Mobile Phone Data. *Environment and Planning D: Society and Space, 34*(2), 319–336. https://doi.org/10.1177/0263775815608851.

Tsing, A. (2015). *The Mushroom at the End of the World: On the Possibility of Life in Capitalist Ruins*. Princeton University Press.

Turnhout, E., & Boonman-Berson, S. (2011). Databases, Scaling Practices, and the Globalization of Biodiversity. *Ecology and Society, 16*(1). https://doi.org/10.5751/ES-03981-160135.

Turnhout, E., Neves, K., & de Lijster, E. (2014). 'Measurementality' in Biodiversity Governance: Knowledge, Transparency, and the Intergovernmental Science-Policy Platform on Biodiversity and Ecosystem Services (Ipbes). *Environment and Planning A: Economy and Space, 46*(3), 581–597.

Turnhout, E., Dewulf, A., & Hulme, M. (2016). What does policy-relevant global environmental knowledge do? The cases of climate and biodiversity. *Current Opinion in Environmental Sustainability, 18*, 65–72.

Turnhout, E., Tuinstra, W., & Halffman, W. (2019). *Environmental Expertise.* Cambridge University Press.

UN Environment (2019). *Global Environment Outlook 6.*

UN Global Pulse (2016). *Integrating Big Data into the Monitoring and Evaluation of Development Programmes.*

UNECE Steering Group (2019). *RESULTS OF THE UNECE 2018 PILOT STUDY OF DATA FLOWS FROM COUNTRIES TO CUSTODIAN AGENCIES RESPONSIBLE FOR SDG INDICATORS.* Task Team on Data Flows of the UNECE Steering Group on Statistics for Sustainable Development Goals. https://statswiki.unece.org/display/SFSDG/Statistics+for+SDGs+Home?preview=/127666441/255493371/2018%20Data%20Flows%20Pilot%20-%20Final%20Report.pdf.

Unidas, Grupo Asesor de Expertos Independientes sobre la Revolución de los Datos para el Desarrollo Sostenible del Secretario General de las Naciones. (2014). *A World That Counts: Mobilising the Data Revolution for Sustainable Development.* November. https://repositorio.cepal.org//handle/11362/40319.

United Nations (2014). *A World that Counts: Mobilising the Data Revolution for Sustainable Development.* Independent Expert Advisory Group on a Data Revolution for Sustainable Development. https://repositorio.cepal.org//handle/11362/40319.

United Nations (2015). *Transforming our world: The 2030 Agenda for Sustainable Development.* Sustainable Development Knowledge Platform. https://sustainabledevelopment.un.org/post2015/transformingourworld.

United Nations (2016a). *Sustainable Development Goals Report 2016.*

United Nations (2016b). *UN agency and Google collaborate on satellite data tools to manage natural resources.* United Nations. UN agency and Google collaborate on satellite data tools to manage natural resources, https://news.un.org/en/story/2016/04/526802-un-agency-and-google-collaborate-satellite-data-tools-manage-natural-resources.

United Nations (2017). *Sustainable Development Goals Report 2017.*

United Nations (2018). *Sustainable Development Goals Report 2018.*

United Nations (2019). *Sustainable Development Goals Report 2019.*

United Nations Development Programme (2017). *MONITORING TO IMPLEMENT PEACEFUL, JUST AND INCLUSIVE SOCIETIES: PILOT INITIATIVE ON NATIONAL-LEVEL MONITORING OF SDG16.*

van der Vlist, F. N. (2016). Accounting for the social: Investigating commensuration and Big Data practices at Facebook. *Big Data & Society, 3*(1), 1–16.

Working Group on Geospatial Information. (2018). *Work Plan 2018–19*. United Nations Secretariat. Global Geospatial Information Management. http://ggim. un.org/documents/Work-Plan_2018-2019.pdf. Accessed 8 July 2021.

Wouters, P., & Beaulieu, A. (2006). Imagining e-science beyond computation. In C. Hine (Ed.), *New Infrastructures for Knowledge Production: Understanding E-Science* (pp. 46–70). Idea Group.

Zuboff, S. (2019). *The Age of Surveillance Capitalism: The Fight for a Human Future at the New Frontier of Power* (1st edition). Public Affairs.

Zwitter, A. J., Gstrein, O. J., & Yap, E. (2020). Digital Identity and the Blockchain: Universal Identity Management and the Concept of the "Self-Sovereign" Individual. *Frontiers in Blockchain, 3.* https://doi.org/10.3389/fbloc.2020.00026.

PART III

Communities, Collectives, and Categories

CHAPTER 19

Communities, Collectives, and Categories

Introduction

Maja Hojer Bruun and Cathrine Hasse

Technologies are collective accomplishments, and they make collective life possible. The development of today's modern technologies is enabled through the collective and collaborative work of large teams of engineers and other professionals. Much more fundamentally, however, without social organisation, knowledge, skills, and learning processes, we would not be able to develop and use tools and technological artefacts, and they would make no sense to us either. In some way or another, anthropological studies of technology are always oriented towards human life, human experience, and agency, and the role of technology in forging human relations, sociality, and power structures. Technologies are located in human bodies, and these bodies belong to the social realm (Mauss 2007[1935]). This section of the handbook is dedicated to the diversity of communities, collectivities, and social categories that emerge together with technologies. All the contributing chapters, focusing on *race*, *class*, *gender*, *kinship*, *activism*, and *organisation*, explore the ways in which collectives, communities, and social categories are shaping and shaped by technologies. Before we go on to a fuller presentation of the chapters, we discuss how the concepts of community, collective, and category emerge across the contributions and in anthropological debates, especially those relating to technology, and finally we conclude how and why anthropologies of technology can make a difference in how we come to understand these key anthropological concepts.

M. H. Bruun (✉) • C. Hasse
Department of Educational Anthropology, Aarhus University, Aarhus, Denmark
e-mail: mhbruun@edu.au.dk; caha@edu.au.dk

M. H. Bruun et al. (eds.), *The Palgrave Handbook of the Anthropology of Technology*, https://doi.org/10.1007/978-981-16-7084-8_19

From its very origins, anthropology has studied how different technologically mediated forms of subsistence occasioned different forms of social organisation, such as the relocation of dwellings and following of seasonal cycles to hunt seals and caribou among Inuit (Boas 1964[1888]), the formation of collectives to irrigate rice fields in China (Fei et al. 1992[1947]), and kin and clan centred gardening among the Trobrianders (Malinowski 1935). Anthropologists, however, focus not only on forms of organisation but also on how human collectives understand themselves and their cosmologies through different technologies and technological practices, and how participation in these practices provide ways to experience and achieve the recognition of belonging. One classic example of this is the anthropological interest in house-building, houses, and the interrelation of the sociality and materiality of houses that goes back to Morgan (1881) and continued in the work of Levi-Strauss (1983) and Carsten and Hugh-Jones (1995) on 'house societies'. Studies of land tenure and gardening practices and their connection to myths of origin, village, kinship, and clan organisation are another example, dating back to Malinowski's work on the Trobrianders (1935) and continued by many others (e.g. Lemonnier 1992, 2012; Coupaye 2013). Bryan Pfaffenberger (2001) takes up Trobrianders' gardening practices and storehouse building as both technical and symbolic activities that communicate and cement the (belonging to the) group and embody the chief's power, while Annette Weiner (1976) explores the sex-gender system structuring garden formation, kinship networks, and modes of power.

On the other hand, social organisation and sociality *underpin* technological use, technological change, and technological relations. Thus, social groups and collectives have affected which technologies are adopted or developed at all. Contrary to the modernist 'standard view of technology' (cf. Pfaffenberger 1992), there has been no unilineal progression of technology from simple tools to complex machines; rather technologies spread, develop, and gain a foothold in unpredictable ways depending on the social relations in which they are embedded and societies' 'technological choices' (Lemonnier 1992, 1993). Sociologists and historians of technology behind the SCOT approach (the Social Construction of Technological Systems, Bijker et al. 1987), analysing the different variations and multidirectional developments of modern technologies, show how different social groups conceptualise and address different 'problems' in regard to different technology variations—whether bicycles, bakelites, or lightbulbs (Bijker 1995)—and how technological 'solutions' depend more on closing such controversies than producing technical breakthroughs. In anthropology, Pierre Lemonnier (1992, 1993) developed the concept of 'technological choices' to express why different societies seize, adopt, or develop some technical artefacts, features, or actions, while rejecting others. The driving forward, organising, and ordering of the technical always depends on, and goes in tandem with, social classifications and social meanings.

According to the division of labour in the modern sciences, anthropology specialised in small-scale communities, kinship, and unorthodox kinds of relatedness, and anthropologists continued to draw on these traditions when they turned their attention to modern states, societies, and technology. This includes a cautious approach to taking modern concepts such as 'society', 'the nation state', 'modern technology', and other abstractions at face value; instead, they explore how, and with what effects, such abstractions are produced and represented in local contexts. In this way, anthropologists have contributed to the aim of social studies of science and technology to break down the divide, and dichotomy, between Technology and Society—two powerful reifications of modernity and modern science—and to explore the deeply social and cultural nature of technology, in all its forms and manifestations. Correspondingly, the social also includes the technical and the biological.

Contemporary technologies, especially, but not limited to, information and communication technologies, have created new kinds of communities, challenging how anthropologists do fieldwork: How to participate, where, how, and with whom? How to grasp those fleeting moments where technologies give rise to collective action, collective sense making, and perhaps a sense of community? How to grasp how social categories are formed, negotiated, and disrupted by technology? The discussions in this section give rise to still further questions. Just as the imagined communities of modern nations were unthinkable without print technology (cf. Anderson 1983), what new collectivities, imagined communities, sociotechnical imaginaries, and other images of the social are presently emerging along with new communication technologies? What happens with the disputed anthropological concept of community when communities are studied through the lens of different technologies? What are the epistemological implications for anthropology's longstanding tradition of studying sociality, communities, and collectives? And does technology get fundamentally unstable, ambiguous, and unpredictable when seen through the social relationships and forms of organisation that underpin it and continuously change its meanings, uses, and beings?

COMMUNITIES AND TECHNOLOGIES IN ANTHROPOLOGICAL DEBATES

Of the terms community, collective, and social category, community seems to be the concept that has engaged general debates in anthropology the most (e.g. Cohen 1985; Amit and Rapport 2002, 2012; Creed 2006). Among all the different kinds of collectivities and figures of the social (e.g. 'society', 'the people', 'the public', 'the crowd', see also Kelty 2012), the formation and meanings of different kinds of *communities*, constituted by people, things and animals, humans, and non-humans, stand out as the most recurring theme in anthropological studies of technology. It is no surprise then that most of the contributors to this section refer to some kind of community in their chapters, for example, when 'the Turkish community' is claimed to be one collective as in Van Oorschot and M'charek's chapter or when national communities are imagined through technologies as in Robertson's and Bruun and Krause-Jensen' chapters.

Community as a certain category through which to understand social relations has changed its valence several times during the history of anthropology and cognate disciplines. At its best, the concept of community serves to interrogate the relationship between different social formations, and ideas of social formations, social solidarities, and identifications. It is compelling to begin our discussion of the concept of community with Benedict Anderson's (1983) landmark book, *Imagined Communities*. Dissociating the sense of being connected to a community from face-to-face interaction, Anderson demonstrated that *technology*, specifically mass printing and the rise of print capitalism, exercised a crucial role in building communities that cut across different geographical regions and demographics. Anderson's work (Anderson 1983) bridged the gap between Ferdinand Tönnies' (Tönnies 1963 [1887]) conceptual divide between *Gemeinschaft*—togetherness in confined, localised groups—and *Gesellschaft*—the impersonal connections between people in modern, urbanised societies—that had dominated the social sciences' understanding of small-scale 'communities' versus large-scale 'societies' in the twentieth century. Anderson pointed out how a sense of commonality and mutual identification evolved together with the spread of books, newspapers, and literacy—a sense of shared identity that later developed into nationalism. 'Sociotechnical imaginaries' (Jasanoff and Kim 2009) later developed as a concept in science and technology studies to show how technologies and imaginaries continue to play a crucial role in building new communities and cementing existing ones. 'The Blue Marble' image of the Earth taken by the Apollo 17 crew in 1972, shared on television screens all over the world, for instance, is one the most iconic images of all time and was a powerful catalyst for the birth of the environmental movement. Today, climate science and technology are leading to new imaginaries of the Anthropocene that mobilise new kinds of social movements (Callison 2014).

Imagined Communities attracted renewed scholarly attention to the concept of community. Anthropologists revisited their long tradition of studying communities; even in the 1930s Robert Redfield and Alfonso Villa Rojas (Redfield 1930; Redfield and Rojas 1934) showed that villages did not exist in isolation but were closely connected to the state. Urban ethnographers since the time of the Chicago school (e.g. Thrasher 1963[1927]; Wirth 1956[1928]; Whyte 1943) have critiqued the idea of urbanisation as tantamount to anonymity and social disorganisation, and pointed to the different communities, groups, and social institutions that formed in different sectors of modern cities and modern societies. Similar conclusions were repeated in anthropological studies of globalisation (e.g. Appadurai 1996) that showed how, for instance, transnational migrant and diasporic communities, and cultural differences among these communities, are maintained across national and other boundaries. Moreover, among ethnographers influenced by the Chicago School, and later the Manchester School and the Rhodes-Livingstone Institute, network analysis and new notions of social networks and connectedness were devised to trace the social relationships and forms of community among urbanites and migrants across boundaries of households (Bott 1971[1957]) and rural-urban divides (Mitchell 1969).

More recently, anthropologists have employed the concept of community to interrogate the relationship between modernity, social solidarity, and group identity as communication and production technologies move people across sites and (re)connect them in new ways (Amit and Rapport 2002, 2012). The flows of information, mobility, and other technologies—'technoscapes' (Appadurai 1996)—continue to challenge physical and biological boundaries today, exemplified by the existence of sociality in online places and worlds that exist independent of geography (Boellstorff 2010) and the rejection of sex-gender identities assigned at birth by medical doctors (Karkazis 2008), that effectively destabilise given communities and social categories. Today's information technologies continue to challenge limits of physical space and speed up time (Duclos et al. 2017; Duclos 2017). Networking tools such as news media and interest groups' websites and discussion fora, Facebook, Twitter, and online computer games allow a person to get in touch with many different groups and to shift between many different forms of interaction during a day. This raises and repeats important questions concerning the extension and limits of the notion of 'community' itself: namely, when something can be said to be a community and to what extent communities need common experiences and understandings to cohere as communities. The mere existence of global electronic communication networks through which people can get in touch with each other does not mean that they experience a sense of community, develop meaningful and mobilising collectivities, or engage in collective social action. On the other hand, the sense of belonging to a community may not persist over time, and community spirit, or 'communitas' (Turner 1969), may exist only in fleeting moments (e.g. Jensen and Winthereik 2015).

'Community' has come to reflect primarily positive emotions and an *idea* of belonging to a community, often thought of as a community of equals, rather than actual modes of social interaction[1] or forms of social and economic organisation with accompanying power struggles and inequalities. 'Community' has become a 'warmly persuasive word' (Williams 1976 cited in Creed 2006, p. 66), or a 'hurray'-word (Rapport and Overing 2000, p. 65), that rarely seems to be used unfavourably, unlike other terms of social organisation and collectivity such as state, society, or crowd (cf. Kelty 2012). The concept of 'community' can, for instance, be instrumentalised and claimed as a sales slogan or used for PR as when customers and users are presented by companies as 'brand communities' or 'user communities' even though there is little contact among them and they have no influence on how they are presented to the public or the market.

By comparison, the concept of technology can also have more negative connotations than that of community, and it may be exactly these latter connotations that technology companies wish to counteract by appropriating conceptions of community. When 'technology' is invoked in public debates, it often divides commentators into techno-pessimists and techno-optimists espousing dystopian or utopian visions (cf. Wyatt 2008). Negative judgements of technology can be linked to the general critique of industrialisation, commercialisation, and other estrangements and alienating characteristics of modern society and modern life, most clearly expressed by critical philosophers of technology like Martin Heidegger (1977 [1953]) and Karl Jaspers (2010 [1931]). Technology is often opposed to community, and even attributed with facilitating the corrosion of communities: Technologies such as mobility devices and capitalist modes of production can scatter labourers and families alike across countries and continents (Sennett 1998), and television and the Internet can contribute to social isolation by individualising users' leisure time (Putnam 2000). More recently, Turkle (2011) has argued that while social media appears to connect people it can actually work to estrange friends, lovers, and family members. Just as with other totalising proclamations, however, anthropologists have sought to disprove the universal scope of such claims through ethnographic studies of how modern technologies come to play active, meaningful, and socialising parts in everyday life and how they affect different people in very different ways. These include differences in the role and effects of technologies *within* communities where the benefits or detriments and experiences of technologies can be very different. This is shown by Sims (this volume), with digital learning and media technologies reinforcing divisions at school along the lines of entrenched social inequities of gender and racialised social class.

Moreover, 'community' usually connotes a solidary and binding quality of relatedness, and the notion of community is often scaled, that is, different levels of community are nested into each other to create unity or solidarity, as in images of a national community produced by the nation state that make references to families (Robertson, this volume) or the idea of paying one's 'debt to society' by doing 'community service' (Creed 2006, p. 17). In this respect the focus on technology may remind us that 'community' as both a claim, a feeling of belonging and a form of organisation is also a technology of government, and that communities can also be oppressive and coercive, as is reflected in several chapters in this section (e.g. Robertson and Dunbar-Hester).

Collectives and Technologies in Anthropological Debates

As with community, the authors in this section often refer to how different collectives and collectivities are formed around, or mediated through, technologies—from collectives deriving from practices of hacking (Dunbar-Hester), to technology companies and the different kinds of organising implied in them (Bruun & Krause-Jensen), to collectives as large as Mao-era China set in motion by new plans for how technology could transform not just women's labour but also their collective consciousness (Bray). Collectives may even be articulated or enacted in instances when the promise of the technologies is to *individualise* and offer individual treatment, as in Van Oorschot and M'charek's chapter where forensic technologies are supposed to single out suspects, and at the same time group people together as collectives.

Many anthropological studies of technology are devoted to the mobilisation of collective action, political activism, and social movements in relation to technology. Sometimes, the uses and/or misuses of certain technologies lead to unequal access to them, and can spur political organisation for or against their harnessing. Fortun (2001) focused on the aftermath of the 1984 explosion of the Union Carbide chemical plant in Bhopal, India as a case study of the dynamics and paradoxes of advocacy in competing power domains. Similarly, other anthropologists have engaged with anti-nuclear movements (Downey 1986; Gusterson 1996; Masco 2013), movements opposing genetically modified food (Harper 2004), and even with groups of anti-census activists (Hannah 2010). Dunbar-Hester (this volume) explores how hacker collectives deploy technologies for overtly political purposes.

Collectives can also be organised in opposition to or resistance against technologies, as investigated by anthropologists conducting fieldwork in off-grid communities (Vannini and Taggart 2015; Cross 2017), Amish or Mennonite communities (Cañás Bottos 2008), and in marginalised groups, often stereotyped as unfamiliar with technology, who have learned how to make and harness new technologies as platforms for advocacy and empowerment (e.g. Rapp and Ginsburg 2001). Social movements and activist groups are also often organised in response to technological breakdowns and disasters (e.g. Fortun 2001) and in conjunction with protests against the unequal distribution of technologies and unequal access to them.

In anthropological writing, collective action is often linked to collective understandings of the world, to symbols, norms, and values, and to perhaps the most controversial and widely used concept: 'culture'. Human experience, agency, and power are located in individuals and in collectives. Materials and artefacts, especially in anthropological analysis of rituals, have long played some role in keeping a collective together, as when memories in a group can be shared because a collective is embedded in bodily movements and artefacts (Connerton 1989). Until recently, however, technology has rarely played a major role in the analysis of the formation of such cultural collectives. This has changed with the emergence of anthropological analyses of social media (Burrell 2012; Costa 2016; Costa et al. 2016; Ruckenstein, this volume), internet-based gaming communities (Boellstorff 2010; Nardi 2009), and social movements using social media tools (Juris 2012). These studies evince that place, people, identity, and culture do not converge, as established by Gupta and Ferguson (1992) in their critique of modernist understandings of culture and community. As noted already in the 1960s by Fredrik Barth in *Ethnic Groups and Boundaries* (Barth 1969), social groups are not defined by their shared biological or cultural 'content' or shared locality, livelihood, or values, but by their ability to communicate boundaries. These 'communications' exist between small groups or large collectives, and they often involve technology, as when nation states communicate boundaries through arms races (e.g. Gusterson 2008) or when their communication is influenced by the development of technology, the so-called Techplomacy (Baugh 2017).

Collectives and their boundaries may be communicated faster and more easily and broadly today. Juris (2012) recounts how the alter-globalisation movement in the late 1990s began to employ Internet-based listservs, websites, and cell phones, and how Twitter and Facebook have completely transformed the way social movements have organised since the early 2010s. Think, for example, of the #FridaysforFuture movement that unites students all over the world to take action against climate change. Another prominent example is the democratic protests and uprisings across the Arab world, the so-called Arab Spring, that some even called the Twitter Revolution. With reference to the Occupy Movement in 2011-2012, Juris points out that physical meetings and the use of online technologies often went together, for example, following the hashtags #Occupy and staying at New York's Zuccotti Park; however, congregations of individuals in public squares do not necessarily make or represent a bona fide social movement. Thus, Juris (2012) points out that if there is no sustained collaboration over time, the protesters may not be able to learn the necessary political and organisational practices that come from sustained collaborations. As exemplified by the insurrection led by pro-Trump supporters at the United States Capitol on 6 January 2021, anti-government militias, and far-right conspiracy theorists such as QAnon, the Internet does not only mobilise progressive, open, and pro-democratic movements but also functions as an 'echo chamber' for segregated Internet publics and illiberal, even fascist, political collectives and actions (Boyer 2021). Furthermore, datafication can produce collectives of which the people involved are not even aware, much less informed. People can be grouped and 'profiled' on the basis of data tracks that they do not even know they have left behind, and these profiles can be used for advertising and for much more crucial economic activities, such as credit ratings (e.g. Zarsky 2016) and health assessments for insurance companies (Hogle 2016). New forms of Internet-based interaction may also give rise to new fantasies of the social and society as unmediated transactions between citizens, for example, what Nelms et al. (2017), in their analysis of business models using Bitcoin and the so-called sharing economy, call the social fantasy of 'Just Us'. When new disruptive economic systems are built with the help of digital technologies, such as the cryptographic protocols of blockchain transactions (see also Bruun et al. 2020) or the dispatch algorithms of Uber or Deliveroo, the social imaginary is not to build new collectives but to have interactions between individuals without any intermediating entities, whether states, companies, or any other collective institutions. The social is reduced to snapshot interactions, and social institutions are forsworn, but may at the same time rise anew under disguise, the irony being that the digital platforms come to function as intermediary institutions, and often charge fees for their services. References to social collectives as 'crowds' (cf. Kelty 2012), for instance, as in crowdsourcing, crowd computing, or the wisdom of crowds, are not just innocent descriptions of social realities but also powerful performative images that may form people's understanding of themselves and each other.

Studying collectives and collectivities through the lens of technology makes it apparent that they may be fleetingly formed through technological *materials* that may anchor what is commonly shared even momentarily, but that may have long-lasting effects as a result of the knowledge gained by learning what makes shared materials meaningful. As newcomers learn from old-timers in organisations (cf. Lave and Wenger 1991), technology together with other materials shape shared material-conceptual understandings which not only mediate but also anchor collectivities (Hasse 2020). What we have learned stays with us—even beyond our physical encounters—and takes part in shaping future learning in new organisations. An example of such learning processes could be 'digital detox' summer camps (Sutton 2020) or the artistic Burning Man festival (Turner 2009) that have developed into destinations for Silicon Valley elites and create a sense of collectivity beyond the actual events and organisations where these elites work.

CATEGORIES AND TECHNOLOGIES IN ANTHROPOLOGICAL DEBATES

In the processes of forming communities and collectivities through and with technologies, social categories are also formed and/or affected. The chapters in this section explore how categories, not least social categories, are shaped by technology and vice versa: from the level of kinship, the family, peer groups, and workplace organisations, via activist groups and movements, to the nation and beyond. Several chapters discuss how technological practices enact categories such as race, class, and gender (Oorschot & M'charek; Sims; Robertson; Bray), and are gendered, racialised, and classed in particular ways.[2]

In her discussion of the concept of community, Amit (2002) points to the important distinction between *group* and *category*. A person or entity can be assigned to many different social categories, but this does not tell us which categories will actually be drawn on for the mobilisation of social actions, the formation of meaningful communities, and self-identification. Amit refers to the example of the social category of 'Black' that became extremely important for political mobilisation against racism in Britain in the 1970s for certain groups, but was rejected by others (Amit 2002, p. 19). Social studies of technologies display many examples of how different kinds of technologies have created accentuated or distorted social categories, and how some technological artefacts, material arrangements, or designs create certain forms of order and social categories, such as urban planner Robert Moses' overpasses, famously described by Langdon Winner (1980), that reproduced class and racial segregation.

Some technologies come to represent 'objective' descriptions of 'the social world'. Modern statistics are a powerful example of how populations, and populations' different categories, are created by particular technologies and knowledge practices (see Cool, this volume), and feminist and critical race studies have documented how gendered and racialised biases are reproduced (e.g. Benjamin 2019). Studies of forensic technologies and genetics offer another example (Oorschot & M'charek). Categories can clash, as when young people are believed to be 'digital natives' and socially connected through electronic communication media and yet have been hit harder than any others by loneliness and social isolation during the COVID-19 lockdowns across Europe (Varga et al. 2021). Imposed social groupings and categories can be extremely powerful even though the subjects they are meant to describe reject them. How people's association with different categories is experienced, and whether people accept their ascribed status, form groups, or mobilise against this, are questions that anthropological studies of technology have taken up too. One important example is the concept of biosociality (Rabinow 1996), exemplified by the solidarity formed around cancer risk and cancer support groups that is catalysed by the rise of testing and screening (e.g. Svendsen 2006; Gibbon and Novas 2008).

THE CHAPTERS

All six chapters are examples of how technologies and technological activities create powerful social categories, communities, and collectives as well as being themselves (re)created by more or less powerful humans. The first three chapters consider how social categories such as *race, class,* and *gender* are enacted through technological practices, and the following three focus on different communities and collectives shaped by technology *kinship, activism,* and *organisation.*

Race is a dominant topic in the contribution by Irene van Oorschot and Amade M'charek that demonstrates how different forensic and legal practices employed in a famous Dutch murder case are active in producing and naturalising race as a category. In their practice-oriented, or praxiographic (Mol 2002), approach, technologies as entanglements of humans and non-humans in the making of facts and production of knowledge are active co-producers of reality, including the understanding of collectives. As the Milica van Doorn murder case unfolds over the course of seventeen years, several collectives are enacted through witness reports, databases, DNA analysis, and other criminological, forensic, and legal technologies that were intended for individualising and singling out suspects. Oorschot and M'charek make it clear that there is no unified 'Turkish community' reflecting the categorisations made during the police investigations, and the different collectives that are enacted at different times do not map onto each other.

Class as well as race and gender issues are debated in Christo Sims' chapter about a school in New York that was founded with the explicit goal of evening out differences of race, gender, and class through the use of digital learning and media technologies. The school, which emphasises a pedagogy of playfulness, games, and creativity, nevertheless inadvertently reproduces existing racial tropes, stereotypes, and inherited social divisions and hierarchies. The Euro-American (white) and Asian-American boys, who are most in line with the technology designers' and educators' ideas of 'geeking out', form dominant cliques, in contrast with less-privileged African-American (Black) and Latinx students who display their creativity and improvisation in ways that are not seen by teachers as 'legitimately unconventional'. Another irony that Sims pries apart is located in the school's philosophy, which can be traced back to the Institute for Research on Learning (IRL) in the 1980s and 1990s where anthropologists and others developed critiques of the then-dominant modernist, cognitivist, and individualist notions of learning (Lave and Wenger 1991). Their critique and shared concepts of 'communities of practice' have, however, become appropriated and instrumentalised.

Francesca Bray focuses on *gender* and stresses that 'the most important work that technologies do is to produce people'. In Bray's material cultural approach, specific technological cultures epitomise the embodiment and key medium of the given societies' struggles over social order. Technological cultures are, however, never homogeneous or stable over time, which is evident from Bray's analysis of how technology and gender are connected in different ways at different times in the history of the People's Republic of China, depending on its changing need for productive and reproductive labour. During the Maoist era, the Iron Girls and Professional Women's Brigades, who performed hard and dangerous physical work, became icons of gender equality, but once Maoist ideology was superseded by the so-called Reform Era the new production rationality required a different kind of labour force, and the Brigades were condemned as unfeminine. Today, in the Post-Reform era, women have acquired yet a new role and relationship to technology, in which women are judged mainly by their fertility and ability to raise 'good quality' children. In Bray's chapter, technology plays an important role in how nation states present themselves to their citizens and other nations.

This is also evident in Jennifer Robertson's chapter on *kinship* and the relationship between technology and various levels of community, from the family to the nation. It is part of the Japanese government's ideology and sociotechnical imaginary that the country is a 'robot superpower' and global leader in technology. As elsewhere (e.g. Carsten 2004), idealised images of kinship relations and the model family are evoked in relation to building the nation; in Japan, the state has invented the three-generation Inobe family with a humanoid household robot relieving the wife-mother of her household chores so that she can focus on her career via teleworking. Kinship systems are sociotechnical arrangements that produce certain kinds of social order and ontologies, and Robertson introduces different kinds of 'neo-kinship' and kinship practices that involve objects and non-human agents, consistent with Donna Haraway's thinking about cyborgs and kinship (Haraway 1991, 2016). Robertson's point is that the idealised robotic families of Abe's government campaigns do not offer progressive and liberating relationships, in line with Haraway's conceptions of a feminist cyborg, but rather reinforce retro-visionary and chauvinist models of kinship, the family, and the nation, including conventional and binarist gender roles. Robertson coins the term 'imagineerism' in reference to the convergence of imagination and engineering in the form of the backward-looking and techno-nationalist deployments of advanced technology.

In her chapter on *activism*, Christina Dunbar-Hester shows that technology is 'a unique domain for the discharge of political energies' and for the mobilisation of collective action, locating her discussion in the field of hacking and FLOSS (Free/Libre Open Source Software). Hackers share the conviction that their communities are open and innovative, and that they use their 'hacks' to question established truths, institutions, and world orders. Yet Dunbar-Hester's feminist hackers experience that some of their hacking activities are not deemed appropriate for a hackerspace event. In this way, the feminist hacking collectives that Dunbar-Hester describes expose tensions and inequalities at the core of these hacking communities. An important point is that, although many hacking communities can be described through their political affinities, ethnographers of activist technical communities have found that people's participation in these communities is often driven by political aims more than by an overt desire for community, sociability, or leisure-time recreation (see also Davies 2017; Coleman 2010).

Organisation and the cultures and sociotechnical imaginaries of engineering and engineering companies are the focus of Maja Hojer Bruun and Jakob Krause-Jensen's chapter in which they argue that corporate organisations are a key context when it comes to understanding the development and use of technologies. Drawing their data from two ethnographic examples—digitalisation in Danish shipping and a German robot company—they argue that digital technologies form the backbone of epochalist imaginaries of disruptions and solutions. The solutions, however, are very much tied to the way the problems are understood and formulated, which in practice leads to new problems. As in Robertson's and Bray's chapters, the focus here is on the national and corporate ideologies and imaginaries tied to technologies, with the further emphasis that digital technologies influence organisational realities. Thus, their chapter takes an intermediary position between the contributions, emphasising that technological agency is dominated by national and other collectives' ideologies and norms, and that technologies possess the agency to form collectives.

Conclusion: An Anthropological Commitment to Studying Sociality and Social Relatedness Through Technologies

Through the lens of technology, we become aware of new dimensions of perennial concepts of importance for anthropology, like community, collective, and social category. Technologies challenge us to explore openly what the human and the social is and what it might be, because the social and the technological are always imbricated, as the chapters in this section demonstrate. Technical actions, from shovelling mud to hacking, always also imply social relations and social meanings premised on or involving race, class, and gender. These relationships are continuously renegotiated and boundaries moved. New technologies can generate hopes for freer, equal, and more inclusive social communities. The hopes surrounding the development of the internet and digital technologies are a case in point; however, the language of openness, creativity, and trust can also eclipse the hierarchies, inequalities, and social injustices that still exist or are reinforced and reinvented in new forms.

Moreover, the chapters show that although new technologies, like robots and digital technologies, give rise to new imaginaries and fantasies about the social, 'society', or different kinds of 'community', we are reminded that these imaginaries and fantasies are not necessarily progressive, liberating, or utopian. Instead, they may reflect and reify existing categories and hierarchies and add fuel to nostalgic and backward-looking images of the social. Whenever we study and discuss technologies with an eye to communities, collectives, and social categories, we learn that the role of technology is neither neutral nor innocent and, furthermore, that we must remain alert to its powerful effects on human life. The challenge for anthropologists is to study and show how technologies connect people who share certain interests across sites, and how these interests are communicated. We also need to address the kind of new boundaries that are created over the course of this communication, and to explore how technological interactions can disrupt as well as reinvent communities, collectives, and social categories.

Acknowledgements We would like to thank the chapter authors, reviewers and our Handbook co-editors for comments and suggestions that have greatly improved this introduction.

Notes

1. It must be noted here that technologies disturb and extend our conceptions of what 'actual social interaction' is, both in respect to what is 'actual', what is 'social', and what is 'interaction'.
2. This Handbook section could also have included other categories like age (e.g. Lock 1993), sexuality (e.g. Ginsburg and Rapp 1995; Karkazis 2008) or 'disability/disabledness' (Moser 2006; Galis 2011; Ginsburg and Rapp 2019) and how they are shaped by technology and vice versa. What we present with race, class, gender, kinship, activists, and organisations are just examples.

References

Amit, V. (2002). Anthropology and Community: Some Opening Notes. In V. Amit & N. Rapport (Eds.), *The Trouble with Community. Anthropological Reflections on Movement, Identity and Collectivity*. London: Pluto Press.

Amit, V., & N. Rapport. (2002). *The Trouble with Community*. London: Pluto Press

Amit, V., & N. Rapport. (2012). *Community, cosmopolitanism and the problem of human commonality*. London: Pluto Press

Anderson, B. R. (1983). *Imagined Communities: Reflections on the Origin and Spread of Nationalism*. London: Verso.

Appadurai, A. (1996). *Modernity at large. Cultural dimensions of globalization*. University of Minnesota Press.

Barth, F. (1969). Introduction. In F. Barth (Ed.), *Ethnic Groups and Boundaries. The Social Organization of Cultural Difference*. Long Grove, Ill.: Waveland Press.

Baugh, P. (2017, July 20). 'Techplomacy': Denmark's ambassador to Silicon Valley. *Politico*. https://www.politico.eu/article/denmark-silicon-valley-tech-ambassador-casper-klynge/. Accessed 14 June 2021.

Benjamin, R. (2019). *Race after technology: abolitionist tools for the new Jim code*. Cambridge, England: Polity Press.

Bijker, W. E. (1995). *Of Bicycles, Bakelites, and Bulbs. Toward a Theory of Sociotechnical Change*. Cambridge, MA.: The MIT Press.

Bijker, W. E., Hughes, T. P., & Pinch, T. J. (Eds.) (1987). *The Social Construction of Technological Systems. New directions in the sociology and history of technology*. Cambridge, MA.: The MIT Press.

Boas, F. (1964[1888]). *The Central Eskimo* (Reprint. ed.). Lincoln: University of Nebraska Press.

Boellstorff, T. (2010). *Coming of Age in Second Life: An Anthropologist Explores the Virtually Human*: Princeton University Press.

Bott, E. (1971[1957]). *Family and social network. Roles, norms, and external relationships in ordinary urban families. Second edition. Preface by Max Gluckman*. London: Tavistock Publications.

Boyer, D. (2021, April 15). Digital Fascism. *Hot Spots, Fieldsights*. https://culanth.org/fieldsights/digital-fascism. Accessed 14 June 2021.

Bruun, M. H., Andersen, A. O., & Mannov, A. (2020). Infrastructures of trust and distrust: The politics and ethics of emerging cryptographic technologies. *Anthropology Today, 36*(2), 13-17.

Burrell, J. (2012). *Invisible users: youth in the Internet cafes of urban Ghana*. Cambridge, MA.: The MIT Press.

Callison, C. (2014). *How Climate Change Comes to Matter: The Communal Life of Facts*. North Carolina: Duke University Press.

Cañás Bottos, L. (2008). *Old Colony Mennonites in Argentina and Bolivia: nation making, religious conflict and imagination of the future*. Leiden: Brill.

Carsten, J. (2004). *After Kinship*. Cambridge: Cambridge University Press.

Carsten, J., & Hugh-Jones, S. (1995). Introduction. In J. Carsten & S. Hugh-Jones (Eds.), *About the house: Lévi-Strauss and beyond*. Cambridge: Cambridge University Press.

Cohen, A. P. (1985). *The Symbolic Construction of Community*. London: Tavistock Publications.

Coleman, G. (2010). The Hacker Conference: A Ritual Condensation and Celebration of a Lifeworld. *Anthropological Quarterly, 83*(1), 47-72. doi:https://doi.org/10.2307/20638699.

Connerton, P. (1989). *How societies remember.* Cambridge: Cambridge University Press.

Costa, E. (2016). *Social Media in Southeast Turkey.* London: UCL Press

Costa, E. et al., (2016). *How the World Changed Social Media.* London: UCL Press

Coupaye, L. (2013). *Growing artefacts, displaying relationships: yams, art and technology amongst the Nyamikum Abelam of Papua New Guinea.* New York: Berghahn Books.

Creed, G. W. (Ed.) (2006). *The Seductions of Community: Emancipations, Oppressions, Quandaries.* Santa Fe: School of American Research Press.

Cross, J. (2017). Off the Grid. Infrastructure and energy beyond the mains. In P. Harvey, C. B. Jensen, & A. Morita (Eds.), *Infrastructures and social complexity: A companion.* Abingdon, Oxon: Routledge.

Davies, S. R. (2017). *Hackerspaces: making the maker movement.* Cambridge, England: Polity.

Downey, G. L. (1986). Risk in Culture: The American Conflict over Nuclear Power. *Cultural Anthropology, 1*(4), 388-412. doi:https://doi.org/10.1525/can.1986.1.4.02a00020.

Duclos, V. (2017). Inhabiting Media: An Anthropology of Life in Digital Speed. *Cultural Anthropology, 32*(1), 21-27. https://doi.org/10.14506/ca32.1.03.

Duclos, V., Criado, T. S., & Nguyen, V.-K. (2017). Speed: An Introduction. *Cultural Anthropology, 32*(1), 1-11.

Fei, X., Hamilton, G. G., & Wang, Z. (1992 [1947]). *From the soil, the foundations of Chinese society: a translation of Fei's Xiangtu Zhongguo, with an introduction and epilogue.* Berkeley: University of California Press.

Fortun, K. (2001). *Advocacy after Bhopal: Environmentalism, disaster, new global orders.* Chicago: University of Chicago Press.

Galis, V. (2011). Enacting disability: how can science and technology studies inform disability studies? *Disability & society, 26*(7), 825-838. doi:https://doi.org/10.1080/09687599.2011.618737.

Gibbon, S., & Novas, C. (2008). *Biosocialities, genetics and the social sciences: making biologies and identities.* London: Routledge.

Ginsburg, F. D., & Rapp, R. (1995). *Conceiving the new world order: the global politics of reproduction.* Berkeley: University of California Press.

Ginsburg, F., & Rapp, R. (2019). "Not Dead Yet": Changing Disability Imaginaries in the Twenty-First Century. In V. Das (Ed.), *Living and Dying in the Contemporary World* (pp. 525-541). Berkeley: University of California Press.

Gupta, A., & Ferguson, J. (1992). Beyond "Culture": Space, Identity, and the Politics of Difference. *Cultural Anthropology, 7*(1), 6-23.

Gusterson, H. (1996). *Nuclear Rites: A Weapons Laboratory at the End of the Cold War.* Berkeley: University of California Press.

Gusterson, H. (2008). Nuclear futures: anticipatory knowledge, expert judgment, and the lack that cannot be filled. *Science and Public Policy, 35*(8), 551–560.

Hannah, M. G. (2010). *Dark territory in the information age: learning from the West German census controversies of the 1980s.* Farnham, Surrey: Ashgate.

Haraway, D. (1991). *A Cyborg Manifesto.* New York: Routledge.

Haraway, D. (2016). *Staying with the Trouble. Making Kin in the Chthulucene.* Durham & London: Duke University Press.

Harper, K. (2004). The genius of a nation versus the gene-tech of a nation: Science, identity, and genetically modified food in Hungary. *Science as culture, 13*(4), 471-492.

Hasse, C. (2020). *Posthumanist learning: What robots and cyborgs teach us about being ultra-social*. London: Routledge.

Heidegger, M. (1977[1953]). The question concerning technology (trans: Lovitt, W.). In *The Question Concerning Technology and Other Essays* (pp. 3-35). New York: Harper Torchbooks.

Hogle, L. F. (2016). Data-intensive resourcing in healthcare. *BioSocieties, 11*(3), 372-393.

Jasanoff, S., & Kim, S.-H. (2009). Containing the Atom: Sociotechnical Imaginaries and Nuclear Power in the United States and South Korea. *Minerva, 47*(2), 119-146.

Jaspers, K. (2010[1931]). *Man in the modern age*. Abingdon, Oxon: Routledge.

Jensen, C. B., & Winthereik, B. R. (2015). Test sites: attachments and detachments in community-based ecotourism. In M. Candea, J. Cook, C. Trundle, & T. Yarrow (Eds.), *Detachment: Essays on the Limits of Relational Thinking* (pp. 197-218). Manchester: Manchester University Press.

Juris, J. S. (2012). Reflections on #Occupy Everywhere: Social media, public space, and emerging logics of aggregation. *American Ethnologist, 39*(2), 259-279.

Karkazis, K. (2008). *Fixing Sex: Intersex, Medical Authority, and Lived Experience*. North Carolina: Duke University Press.

Kelty, C. (2012). Preface: Clouds and Crowds. *Limn* (2), 4-7.

Lave, J., & Wenger, E. (1991). *Situated learning: legitimate peripheral participation*. Cambridge: Cambridge University.

Lemonnier, P. (1992). *Elements for an Anthropology of Technology*. Ann Arbor: University of Michigan, Museum of Anthropology.

Lemonnier, P. (1993). *Technological Choices: Transformation in Material Cultures since the Neolithic*. London: Routledge.

Lemonnier, P. (2012). *Mundane objects: materiality and non-verbal communication*. Walnut Creek, CA.: Left Coast Press.

Levi-Strauss, C. (1983). *The Way of the Masks*. London: Jonathan Cape.

Lock, M. M. (1993). *Encounters with aging: mythologies of menopause in Japan and North America*. London: University of California Press.

Malinowski, B. (1935). *Coral gardens and their magic. A study of the methods of tilling the soil and of agricultural rites in the Trobriand Islands*. New York: American Book Company.

Masco, J. (2013). *The Nuclear Borderlands: The Manhattan Project in Post-Cold War New Mexico* (Course Book ed.). Princeton, NJ.: Princeton University Press.

Mauss, M. (2007 [1935]). Techniques of the body. In M. Lock & J. Farquhar (Eds.), *Beyond the Body Proper. Reading the Anthropology of Material Life* (pp. 50-68). Durham: Duke University Press.

Mitchell, J. C. (Ed.) (1969). *Social networks in urban situations: Analyses of personal relationships in Central African towns*. Manchester: Manchester University Press.

Mol, A. (2002). *The Body Multiple. Ontology in Medical Practice*. Durham: Duke University Press.

Morgan, L. H. (1881). Houses and House-Life of the American Aborigines. *Contributions to North American Ethnology, IV*(Washington).

Moser, I. (2006). Disability and the promises of technology: Technology, subjectivity and embodiment within an order of the normal. *Information, communication & society, 9*(3), 373-395.

Nardi, B. A. (2009). *My Life as a Night Elf Priest. An Anthropological Account of World of Warcraft*. Ann Arbor: University of Michigan Pres.

Nelms, T. C., Maurer, B., Swartz, L., & Mainwaring, S. (2017). Social Payments: Innovation, Trust, Bitcoin, and the Sharing Economy. *Theory, Culture & Society, 35*(3), 13-33.

Pfaffenberger, B. (1992). Social Anthropology of Technology. *Annual Review of Anthropology, 21*, 491-516.

Pfaffenberger, B. (2001). Symbols Do Not Create Meanings – Activities Do: Or Why Symbolic Anthropology Needs the Anthropology of Technology. In M. B. Schiffer (Ed.), *Toward an Anthropology of Technology*. Albuquerque: University of New Mexico Press.

Putnam, R. (2000). *Bowling Alone: The Collapse and Revival of American Community*. New York: Simon and Schuster.

Rabinow, P. (1996). *Essays on the anthropology of reason*. Princeton, NJ.: Princeton University Press.

Rapp, R., & Ginsburg, F. (2001). Enabling Disability: Rewriting Kinship, Reimagining Citizenship. *Public culture, 13*(3), 533-556. doi:https://doi.org/10.121 5/08992363-13-3-533.

Rapport, N., & Overing, J. (2000). Social and cultural anthropology. The key concepts. London & New York: Routledge.

Redfield, R. (1930). *Tepoztlan, a Mexican village: a study of folk life* (Reprint. ed.). Chicago: University of Chicago Press.

Redfield, R., & Rojas, A. V. (1934). *Chan Kom. A Maya village*. Washington: Carnegie Institution of Washington.

Sennett, R. (1998). *The corrosion of character: the personal consequences of work in the new capitalism*. New York: W. W. Norton.

Svendsen, M. N. (2006). The Social Life of Genetic Knowledge: A Case-Study of Choices and Dilemmas in Cancer Genetic Counselling in Denmark. *Medical Anthropology, 25*(2), 139-170.

Sutton, T. (2020). Digital harm and addiction: An anthropological view. *Anthropology Today, 36*(1), 17-22.

Thrasher, F. M. (1963 [1927]). *The gang: a study of 1313 gangs in Chicago*. Chicago: University of Chicago Press.

Tönnies, F. (1963 [1887]). *Community and Society*. New York: Harper & Row.

Turkle, S. (2011). *Alone together: why we expect more from technology and less from each other*. New York: Basic Books.

Turner, F. (2009) Burning Man at Google: a cultural infrastructure for new media production. *New Media & Society, 11*(1-2), 73-94.

Turner, V. W. (1969). *The ritual process: Structure and antistructure*. London: Routledge and Kegan Paul.

Vannini, P., & Taggart, J. (2015). *Off the Grid: Re-Assembling Domestic Life*. London: Routledge.

Varga, T. V., Bu, F., Dissing, A. S., Elsenburg, L. K., Bustamante, J. J. H., Matta, J., et al. (2021). Loneliness, worries, anxiety, and precautionary behaviours in response to the COVID-19 pandemic: A longitudinal analysis of 200,000 Western and Northern Europeans. *The Lancet Regional Health - Europe, 2*.

Weiner, A. B. (1976). *Women of value, men of renown: new perspectives in Trobriand exchange*. Austin: University of Texas Press.

Whyte, W. F. (1943). *Street corner society: the social structure of an Italian slum*. Chicago: University of Chicago Press.

Winner, L. (1980). Do Artifacts Have Politics? *Daedalus, 109*(1), 121-136.

Wirth, L. (1956 [1928]). *The ghetto* (4th edition). Chicago: University of Chicago Press.

Wyatt, S. (2008). Technological Determinism is Dead: Long Live Technological Determinism. In E. J. Hackett, O. Amsterdamska, M. Lynch, & J. Wajcman (Eds.), *The Handbook of Science and Technology Studies* (pp. 165-180). Cambridge, MA.: The MIT Press

Zarsky, T. (2016). The Trouble with Algorithmic Decisions: An Analytic Road Map to Examine Efficiency and Fairness in Automated and Opaque Decision Making. *Science, Technology, & Human Values, 41*(1), 118-132.

CHAPTER 20

Un/Doing Race: On Technology, Individuals, and Collectives in Forensic Practice

Race

Irene van Oorschot and Amade M'charek

The public benches of the courtroom are packed: today, 19 November 2019, is the day Hüseyin A. will finally appear before the court for the alleged rape and murder of 19-year-old Milica van Doorn in 1992. Twenty-seven long years have gone by between the discovery of her lifeless body in Zaandam and today's trial. That we are here today at all, we learn from the public prosecutor's convoluted account of the criminal investigation, is something of a technological and legal victory. While there were a few clues in the early stages of the investigation—one witness spoke of a 'singing man with a Turkish appearance' seen in the vicinity of the crime—the slow and tortuous search picked up speed only in 2017 when 133 men of Turkish descent living in the area of the crime in 1992 were asked to cooperate with familial DNA testing. These men were selected based on previous analysis of the DNA found on Milica's body, an analysis aimed at identifying the biogeographic ancestry of the unknown suspect. While the suspect, Hüseyin A., did not participate in the familial DNA testing, his brother did, leading the police straight to his door. A year later, Hüseyin A. is brought into the court by way of a side entrance.

I. van Oorschot (✉)
Life Science and Society Lab, KU Leuven, Belgium, Leuven
e-mail: irene.vanoorschot@kuleuven.be

A. M'charek
University of Amsterdam, Amsterdam, Netherlands
e-mail: a.a.mcharek@uva.nl

M. H. Bruun et al. (eds.), *The Palgrave Handbook of the Anthropology of Technology*, https://doi.org/10.1007/978-981-16-7084-8_20

The atmosphere in court is tense. Many of those in the audience are extended family, here to support Milica's closest family members: her father, her sister, her brother. Her mother is too frail to attend. Many of them have also been profoundly affected by the rape and murder of their cousin, or second cousin, as well as the slow and sometimes hopeless investigation process. Things will never be the same for them, her aunt tells us over coffee. 'Trusting people is more difficult. Especially men like him. I don't trust them anymore, Turkish men.' Checking twitter later, we see that she is not the only one foregrounding Hüseyin A.'s ethnicity. '#Milica was young to share in the joys of #diversity', one twitter commentator states. Another twitter user accuses a second of 'cuddling Muslims' when the second raises doubts as to Hüseyin A.'s guilt. The Milica van Doorn case, then, had struck a chord. Not only was it a victory of contemporary forensic investigation, combining biogeographic DNA research with familial DNA research; it also spoke to a set of anxieties regarding Turkish others, as well as the character and putative 'failure' of 'multicultural society'.

In this chapter, we wish to think with the Milica van Doorn case in order to shed light on the different ways Hüseyin A.'s 'Turkishness' was enacted as a result of different technologies. To our mind, it offers a particularly illustrative example of how technologies enact differences between people, and is especially evocative of the entanglement of DNA research with individuals and collectives, processes in which racial classifications play an important role. On the one hand, the Milica van Doorn case represents a concerted effort to find and judge an individual suspect, yet, on the other, the search mobilised collectives of different kinds: those with genetic ancestry in Turkey, for instance, or the 'Turkish community' in a Dutch town that was asked to participate in the investigation. Analysing these versions of collectives and their mobilisation in this case, this study zooms in on the multiplicity of difference, challenging the reader to disentangle (racial) classifications in specific practices in order to hold on to their never-quite-settled, never-quite-singular character.

To situate the discussion, we first sketch the outline of two histories of anthropological research: the discipline's engagement with questions of material culture, technology, and materiality; and its engagement (and discomfort) with the object of race. The chapter builds on both these histories, drawing from within the discipline as well as from outside sources, especially science and technology studies and feminist studies of technoscience.

Paying Attention to Technologies

The Milica van Doorn case raises a set of important questions about the way forensic technologies contribute to making differences in the affective and convoluted practices of crime and crime-solving. In that capacity, it requires attention—but of what sort? Of course, anthropology has a specific and unique mode of paying attention: that of ethnography, the writing of human collectives. While a detailed discussion is beyond the scope of this chapter, the debates of the 1980s on the various genres and poetics of ethnographic writing (see

Clifford and Marcus 1986) show that anthropology is a discipline with a very specific and reflexive relationship with regard to its own technologies of memory and transmission: from the object of the notepad to the poetics and politics of genre. It is especially aware of the performative dimensions of writing, in that it takes seriously the way the genre of the monograph—particularly when focused on one assumedly singular culture, such as 'the Nuer'—*performatively produces* certain cultures as internally homogenous and distinct from other cultures, hence running the risk of reifying culture (Abu-Lughod 1991).

However, this reflexivity with regard to the performative role of the technology of writing has not always been extended to an attention to the role of technologies and materialities of objects encountered 'in the field'. Pfaffenberger (1992) notes, for instance, that while anthropology has a long history of attending to materialities and technologies of various kinds, this history was treated with embarrassment and discomfort throughout much of the twentieth century. Associated with 'armchair anthropology' and '"fieldwork" undertaken by amateurs on collecting holidays' (Pfaffenberger 1992, p. 491), the study of material culture made way for the study of meanings, symbols, and rituals, perceived to be the *real* objects of anthropology, often conceived of as culture. As Kroeber and Kluckhohn argued, 'what is culture is the idea *behind* the artifact' (1952, p. 65 quoted in Pfaffenberger 1992, p. 492). It is only in the 1990s, Pfaffenberger suggests, that the study of materialities and technologies as actors in their own right seemed to make a comeback. It must be emphasised, however, that this comeback is rooted in the study of scientific knowledge practices in which instruments, technologies, and documents were demonstrated to play an active role in the production of knowledge, for instance, in Latour and Woolgar's (1979) ethnography of the making of scientific facts. Drawing on the 'principle of symmetry', Latour and Woolgar distribute the 'making of facts' among a variety of human and non-human actors. This emphasis on the entanglements of humans and non-humans in the practice of making facts and producing knowledge significantly rearticulates the more traditional understanding of anthropology as the study of human collectives; instead, *practices*, populated by both humans and non-humans, come into view as an object of study. Secondly, the turn to scientific practices also underscores the necessity to think of materialities and technologies not as simple reflections of 'culture', but rather as crucial *mediators* and actors in the making of worlds.

To underscore this key turn to practice, Annemarie Mol has, more recently, introduced the notion of *praxiography* (2002). In *The Body Multiple*, Mol praxiographically attends to the body and what the body is made to be in practice, analysing the specific case of atherosclerosis and the ways it is made known in the practices of different medical professionals. Crucial here is her emphasis not on this or that professional group (of doctors or nurses, for instance), but on the practices themselves, which involve both human and non-human actors: both patients and doctors, but also instruments of measurement, test protocols, and so on. She contrasts this emphasis on practices with the more traditional emphasis on human collectives—the *ethnoi*—in anthropology, and argues in favour of accounts that can take these non-human actors seriously. In so doing she incorporates measurement and diagnostic instruments and test protocols into her account of the way the disease atherosclerosis comes about, that is, is *enacted into being*. Indeed, she understands the technologies by which the disease atherosclerosis is known not as neutral entities that simply tap into or probe a pre-existing reality, but rather as active in the *enactment of realities* (see also Haraway 1988; Law 2004).

Moving from the study of human collectives and their cultures to practices, then, is also a move away from seeing technologies as simple reflections of culture to understanding them as active co-producers of the realities we inhabit. Technologies, in this view, need not be narrowly defined; rather, they are simply those non-human actors (or assemblages thereof) that mediate between observer and world. This understanding of technologies, then, is relational: it always seeks to situate and understand technologies as they are used in practice. But it is also agnostic with regard to their specific character or shape; a microscope may be a technology in a given setting, but so may legal or administrative forms, as well as case files (Hull 2012; van Oorschot 2014a, 2014b, 2018, 2021). In that capacity praxiography is less a stable research method (it has that in common with ethnography!), and more a way of paying attention not simply to human actors and their intentions, behaviours, and frames of reference, but to the *material texture* of these practices in which objects do things and make certain worlds possible.

Bringing these sensitivities to bear on the Milica van Doorn case, we suggest, requires that attention be paid not only to human actors, but also to the specific agency of non-human actors such as DNA samples, sequencing techniques, databases against which profiles may be compared, legal procedures, and witness reports. In this chapter, we are especially interested in the way this praxiographic focus on the making of truths can be taken to bear on a very specific and fraught 'natural' reality: that of *race* (M'charek 2005, 2013). The following section elaborates on anthropology's troubled relations with race.

DIFFERENCE IN THE MAKING: LEARNING WITH GENETICS

Uncomfortable Objects: Genetic Research in a Post-Racial Age?

From Kant's racial anthropology (Eze 1997) to the physical anthropology of the nineteenth and early twentieth century, anthropology has been an important participant in the biologisation and essentialisation of human difference (Stocking 1982): that is, it has been crucial in the production of knowledge about race. Physical anthropology played a critical role in connecting phenotypical variation—skin colour, skull size, hair texture—and behavioural variations, understanding them as constitutive of different types and as rooted in evolutionary, adaptive processes (Caspari 2003; MacEachern 2012). As a result, race was understood not solely as a biological entity; it included ideas about shared sentiments and temperaments, as well as inheritance and ancestry (Caspari 2003; MacEachern 2012; Stocking 1982).

Around World War II, however, anthropologists played an important role in reshaping the discipline's commitment to the study of human diversity (Selcer 2012). Not only did the American Anthropological Association denounce Nazi racism in 1938 (Visweswaran 1998), anthropologists also contributed to the famous UNESCO Statement on Race in 1950, which protested the biologisation, that is, racialisation, of difference. Pointing out that 'race' is not a biological fact but rather a 'social myth', this statement implicitly drew a sharp distinction between nature—we are all one race—and culture—the sphere of human difference. As a result of this shift, culture became a substitute for race as a catch-all for human difference: 'culture became everything race was not, and race was seen to be what culture was not: given, unchangeable, biology' (Visweswaran 1998, p. 72). Meanwhile, race was associated with the biological and with nature, thus falling entirely outside the purview of cultural anthropology. From an ontological foundation on which to build a discipline, race turned into a social reality to be studied by paying careful attention to the way 'bodies and bloodlines' become instrumental in the way people perceive themselves and the world (Fassin 2011).

It is against this background of anthropological anxiety with regard to its own fraught, colonial history that more recent advances in the biology of human difference, and especially genetic research, raise unique conceptual problems. In many ways, the late 1990s witnessed a *return of race*, both societally and academically. Societally, the publication of *The Bell Curve* (Hernnstein and Murray 1994), a book written by a psychologist (Hernnstein) and a political scientist (Murray), provoked intense discussions on the uses and abuses of the race concept. It is against this background that the ambitions of the Human Genome Project of the early 1990s are cast in striking relief. Yet, whereas the Human Genome Project was concerned with mapping the universal genome—suggesting that we all belong to one human family and that there is only one race, the human race—another international initiative, the Human Genome *Diversity* Project, became controversial overnight because it was not so much interested in what makes us the *same*, but rather paid special attention to *difference*. The latter project would focus on mapping genetic differences across different populations (see M'charek 2005; Reardon 2005).

Informing medical and forensic practices, these developments made the distinction between 'biology as matter for biologists' and 'culture as matter for anthropologists' particularly untenable. Not only is the distinction regularly transgressed by (popularised) genetic sciences, connecting genes to 'social' behaviours such as aggression, deviance, and crime (Raine 2008), the developments also resonated with a growing understanding of the nature-culture divide as a historically specific, and therefore not ontologically stable, part of Western cosmologies (see e.g. Descola and Palsson 1996; Hastrup 2014; Holbraad and Pedersen 2017). Hence, the question became: what can anthropologists know and say about the production of genetic differences? What is going on in these practices? Do they entail a return to nineteenth-century raciological classifications? Is the genetic 'population' simply race by another name?

Here, the move away from the study of human cultures and towards (scientific) practices captured in the notion of praxiography has been especially productive. Sensitised to the performative dimension of methods and technologies as they are used in scientific practices, various anthropologists have addressed these practices, asking the question: where and how is 'race' *done*, biologised, naturalised? In so doing, they have been able to demonstrate, for instance, that genetic research is the location of novel ways of inscribing and articulating biological differences (M'charek 2000; Goodman et al. 2012; Fullwiley 2007; Koenig et al. 2008; El-Haj 2007). The notion of *molecularisation* (Fullwiley 2007), in particular, has drawn attention to the way differences, in these practices, are enacted as located deep in the body. There, these differences are seen to hold the promise of individualisation: for example, the individualisation of medical treatment or, within forensics, where they function as a 'truth-machine' in the identification of suspects (Lynch et al. 2008).

At the same time, however, yet others have pointed out that the individualisation promised by the genetic sciences depends on and mobilises different *collectives*, such as genetic collectives grouped together due to a shared geographical location or shared ancestry (M'charek 2008, 2020; Koenig et al. 2008). Produced within these practices is not a single 'biological' population, but, depending on methods and databases used, multiple and not necessarily commensurable *collectives* (M'charek 2000). Of course, genetic research is also a collective enterprise that puts into motion contemporary constructions of who 'we' are—for instance, in attempts to construct a 'molecular portrait of Brazil' (Santos and Maio 2004), or Britain (Fortier 2012); in attempts to construct the original inhabitant of a Dutch village, the so-called Ur-Vlaardinger, based on DNA and ancestry research (de Rooij et al. 2014)—meanwhile shifting and reconfiguring conceptions of community, indigeneity, and descendance (Watt and Kowal 2019; Tallbear 2013). Furthermore, these technologies and their products are 'taken up' in settings already saturated with vernacular ways of making differences and envisioning collectives (Santos and Maio 2004), so that the questions facing us are many indeed. Precisely how does genetic research enact sameness and difference, individuals, and collectives? And where and how do these genetic modes of making individuals and collectives resonate or contrast with other ways of doing sameness and difference?

In the following, the praxiographic approach to the making of collectives is brought to bear on the Milica van Doorn case, with particular emphasis on the various identification practices by means of which police actors aimed to find their unknown suspect. Concretely, we have spoken with a key actor in the police investigation, followed and retrieved media coverage of the case, had conversations and corresponded with forensic geneticists on state-of-the-art developments in the field, delved into the literature on familial DNA testing, and reconstructed the case on the basis of the extensively argued legal verdict (available online through the website of the Dutch judiciary).[1]

Disentangling the Milica van Doorn Murder Case: Collectives in the Making

Let us first outline what this praxiographic understanding of technologies means for the approach to the case taken in this chapter. Understanding technologies in the loose sense as material-semiotic ways of acting, that is, of making differences, we zoom in on the different collectives that are articulated, and 'haunt' the proceedings, in court. In tracing the case from beginning to end, we want to highlight how various collectives were brought into being, showing how the suspect was, from quite early in the investigation, thought of as 'Turkish', but that 'being Turkish' was articulated in different ways, in relation to variously articulated collectives.

1992: A 'Singing Turkish Man on a Bike'

In the early period of the investigation, clues were few and far between. However, right after the homicide a witness came forward and told the police that she had seen a singing Turkish man on a bicycle in the vicinity of the crime scene. This piece of information initially offered hope for the criminal investigation: on the one hand, because it located a likely suspect in the vicinity of the crime and because the fact that the suspect was seen cycling suggested that he lived near the crime scene; on the other, the fact that the woman spoke of a man with a *Turkish* appearance was also suggestive. Both mode of transportation and the suspect's supposed 'Turkish appearance' would enable police actors to narrow down their focus. Hence, this witness report became a centrepiece in the criminal investigation.

It is important here to pause with this description and to see how it mobilises collectives, and the specific collectives it invokes. Indeed, if 'inscription devices' (Latour and Woolgar 1979) populate the labs of genetic scientists and have drawn attention there, then the crucial and transformative role of the *legal document* cannot be underestimated in the study of forensic settings (see also Vismann 2008; Hull 2012; van Oorschot 2021). By making information available about the there-and-then in the here and now of investigation (van Oorschot 2014b), legal documents such as this witness description enact realities and bring them into being (van Oorschot and Schinkel 2015). In this case, the witness report enacted a specific form of difference, one of Turkishness as something legible on the surface of the body. Included in this specific way of enacting difference is a specific visual regime that understands racial difference to be legible and interpretable at a glance. Turkishness here is not simply a national identity; precisely because it encompasses the suspect's body and appearance, it becomes race. Gilroy (1998) warns, however, that this mode of seeing and recognising the difference is historically situated; seeing 'race', he suggests, takes a specifically trained human 'sensorium' attuned to the recognition of racial types and kinds. This understanding of difference is not uncommon in investigatory settings; indeed, a large number of identification practices, from witness reports to facial composite sketches, rely on laypeople's assumed 'visual expertise' in drawing distinctions between different ethnicities or nationalities (see van Oorschot 2020; Bleumink et al. 2018). Yet, while the witness report produced the suspect as a non-Dutch other, it also spoke of 'riding a bike', which is suggestive of a rather specific collective: that is, one that includes labour migrants who came to the Netherlands throughout the 1960s and 1970s and their descendants. As such, this witness description itself becomes a technology of articulating and mobilising a collective of Dutch-Turkish men.

The witness description, however, did not (and could not) point to a specific person; after all, the eyewitness account sketches the contours of a collective, not an individual. Furthermore, the police had few other sources of information to go on; the DNA material found on Milica's body did not, in 1992, yield a match within the database as it existed then. However, it was conserved for possible later use, to be folded into the case the prosecutor was eventually able to make.

2002–2008: DNA Dragnets and Delineating Populations of Interest

The DNA from the unknown suspect would be mobilised in the years following the murder in order to exclude likely suspects. There were various attempts to gather DNA from a widening circle of people. From 2002 to 2004, people in Milica's immediate vicinity had been asked for samples as the population of interest was defined in line with vernacular police knowledge suggesting that the unknown suspect would have known Milica, either intimately (family) or in a looser sense (friends and acquaintances). Based on autosomal DNA these attempts did not yield a match, and investigators had to start taking more seriously the scenario that the suspect was not from Milica's 'circle'. However, as it is ethically and practically impossible to set up a DNA dragnet that includes everyone, police investigators turned to the unknown suspect's DNA materials. Could these help them delineate a target population?

The materials were sent to the lab of a Dutch expert on biogeographic ancestry, as it was hoped that the suspect's DNA would point to a specific geographical region, information which could help the police define and delineate a new collective of interest. The techniques used to construct the suspect's biogeographic ancestry were, at that time, quite new, but had been used once before. In an earlier case—the Marianne Vaatstra case—the suspect's biogeographic ancestry suggested that the perpetrator was probably of Northern European descent, contradicting popular suspicions which had focused on a nearby centre for asylum seekers (see Jong and M'charek 2018; de Knijff 2006). In the Milica van Doorn case, the analysis focused on two types of Y-chromosomal markers: short tandem repeats (STRs) and single nucleotide polymorphisms (SNPs). In tracing the likely geographical origin of the unknown offender, the geneticists drew on two databases: one built at the University of Leiden Medical Center (which included about 60,000 SNP profiles in 2007), the other the YHRD, or Y-chromosomal STR Haplotype Reference Database, a large public database of about 42,000 profiles (curated in the Charité, Berlin). These markers, located on the male sex chromosome, are interesting to forensic geneticists because they are known to be distributed unevenly over the human population and to occur more frequently in certain geographical areas. They reveal genetic variations that have arisen at a certain moment in time, which makes them acutely informative as all DNA can be dated back to that specific mutation, after which the genetic 'tree' branches out. While the exact haplotype that was found in this specific case is, with good reason, confidential information, we want to illustrate the technology used here by way of an example. Take for instance the following figure (Fig. 20.1), a so-called isofrequency map of a specific haplogroup, J2a.

This image, taken from the Wikimedia Commons, visually represents the relative frequency of this specific haplogroup as it is distributed geographically. Red areas correspond to higher frequencies within the population. From this map, we learn that this haplogroup is most often found in the area of contemporary Turkey and Armenia, with decreasing frequency the farther west and east one goes. We also learn, however, that is much rarer in Western Europe,

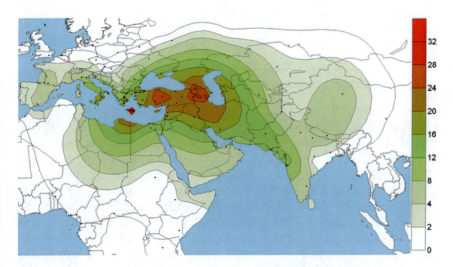

Fig. 20.1 A so-called "Isofrequency map of the Y-DNA J2a-M410 Haplogroup distribution" detailing the relative prevalence of a specific DNA haplogroup within the human population in a given territory. Source: Wikimedia Commons, retrieved 15 June 2020 through https://commons.wikimedia.org/wiki/File:The_spatial_distribution_of_M410(J2a)_clade_in_worldwide_populations.png

which would make this haplogroup and others like it especially informative and suggestive of non-Dutch descent.

Back to the Milica van Doorn case. While the exact haplogroups mobilised in identifying the unknown suspect's biogeographical ancestry are confidential, we learn from the verdict that the information pointed to a Turkish or perhaps North-African suspect. This information was then used, in 2008, to set up another DNA dragnet. In this case, men of Turkish and North-African descent living in the vicinity of the crime were asked, on a voluntary basis, for a DNA sample. Importantly, Hüseyin A. was among these men but was one of the few who declined to participate. Again, the police were no further forward in apprehending him.

Thus, it should be emphasised that the collective mobilised here is not only the result of the *spatial* mapping of geography and phenotype; at stake, too, is a *temporal* folding (Cf. M'charek 2014; M'charek and van Oorschot 2019). Figure 20.1, for instance, reflects patterns of migration that accompanied the spread of the Ottoman Empire, but the information on the suspect's likely biogeographical ancestry is also suggestive of more recent migration histories, such as the previously mentioned labour migration patterns of the 1960s and 1970s. The suspect's likely biogeographical ancestry is, in this case, informative and usable precisely because it is suggestive of a collective that was not 'originally' from 'here', but 'came here' during the latter half of the twentieth century. This indicates that while DNA may well function as 'a truth machine' (Lynch et al. 2008), it is also a *time machine*, drawing on both the longue durée of biological hereditary processes as well as social histories of labour migration from Turkey to Western Europe.

2017: Familial DNA and the Elusive 'Turkish Community'

In 2017, the criminal investigators decided that they needed to explore a last option: familial DNA searching. In the Dutch context, familial DNA research has the status of an *ultimum remedium*, only available to criminal investigators once all other options have been exhausted. As such its use is weighed against the criteria of proportionality and of subsidiarity: not only should a (limited) DNA dragnet be in proportion to the severity of the crime, but its inclusion and exclusion criteria should also be formulated in relation to the 'practical chance of success'. Given the fact that the suspect here was likely of Turkish descent, police actors thought it prudent to be very careful in their strategy. The Turkish community, in police perceptions, was already vulnerable to discrimination and marginalisation, and they did not want to risk criminalising entire families within it (see for a more in-depth discussion of the care police investigators took to avoid stigmatising the community, van Oorschot and M'charek 2021). Also important to the police was the fact that the technology was new and that this case was only the second in which it would be used (the previous being the aforementioned Marianna Vaatstra case, see Jong and M'charek 2018; M'charek et al. 2020). While this meant that there was little experience in using it, it was perceived as a promising technology, likely to be drawn on in future cases.

Importantly, police actors also took into account the tense political and diplomatic relations between Turkey and the Netherlands at the time. In March 2017, Dutch authorities had refused the Turkish Minister of Foreign Affairs, Cavosoglu, permission to land his aeroplane in Rotterdam and expelled the Turkish Minister of Family and Social Policy, Sayan Kaya. The Minister had wanted to speak to the Turkish community in the Netherlands on the upcoming Turkish referendum: a controversial topic, as this referendum would significantly strengthen the governing parties in the wake of the failed military coup in Turkey of 2016. Not only, then, did the police want to calibrate their strategy in relation to the spectre of discrimination very carefully, they also wanted to avoid offending Turkish sensibilities and harming diplomatic relations. Given these circumstances, the police investigation took place at a precarious moment in time in which what was perceived as the 'Turkish community' had to be approached with caution.

Thus, the investigators had to position their investigation of these 133 men strategically and, in order to do so, they instigated several steps. In the months before the start of the official inquiry, members of the 'police working group' got in touch with several key members of the 'Turkish community', notifying them of their plans and asking them for their support should hesitation or irritation arise among the members of the community. This proved no easy feat, however; indeed, the working group almost instantaneously ran up against several cleavages within the Turkish community, leading one of its members to describe it as 'the community that is no community'. Not only were there religious differences, the recent coup against Erdogan in 2016—which he had accused Gülen supporters of perpetrating—had also led to sharp divisions (NOS, 16 July 2016). Consequently, 'Turkishness' as a quality presumably shared by all community members proved particularly elusive—a realisation echoing, of course, anthropological suspicion regarding the uses (and misuses) of the notion of ethnicity or culture, which tend to elide differences within cultures and magnify differences between them (Abu-Lughod 1991; Kuper 1999). A highly individualised strategy, then, of going door to door and talking to people, enabling them to participate right then and there through a simple swab, was adopted and proved particularly effective. While it was feared that the 'community that is no community' would hesitate to participate in the DNA research, police officials found that all the men who were approached, except for the suspect himself, readily agreed.

The collectives mobilised and enacted through this technology are not the genetic, probabilistic collectives of Y-chromosomal testing encountered earlier. Instead, the police were dealing with a 'community that was no community', a community consisting of different families with roots in Turkey, meanwhile going door to door, explaining to these people the purpose of the DNA research and taking saliva samples in people's homes. Genetically at stake were also more granular hereditary similarities between the unknown suspect's DNA and the DNA of the men who participated. On 5 December 2017, Arnoud Kal, DNA specialist at the Dutch Forensic Institute (NFI), realised that one of the DNA profiles of the 132 men who were swabbed bore a marked similarity to that of the unknown suspect and concluded that 'the suspect must be his brother!' (de Volkskrant, 12 December 2018). As Hüseyin A. was the only member of his family who had not volunteered to participate (for the second time, it must be added) he was left as a likely suspect. He was apprehended on his way home from work, and, given the fact that there was now reasonable suspicion to justify it, a sample of his DNA was taken. This sample proved to match that of the traces on Milica's body.

A year later, a two-day trial is held. His lawyer, prior to the court hearing, tells us that 'the DNA is pretty definitive. Your only chance is offering a different story about how it got there'. In court, he will try to make the case that Hüseyin A. and Milica had a secret, sexual relationship, a line of argumentation brushed aside as the prosecutor emphasises that Milica van Doorn was a 'decent girl' [een proper meisje], would have told her friends about this relationship, and that there would have been virtually no time in her reconstructed, busy schedule in the days leading up to the offence for her and Hüseyin A. to have such relations. The prosecutor, similarly, treats the DNA as fairly definitive and, almost in passing, invokes the witness description of 1992 to further buttress her case that Hüseyin A. was, that night, seen near the vicinity of the crime. On 11 December 2018, Hüseyin A. is found guilty of the rape and murder of Milica van Doorn and sentenced to 20 years in prison. He has appealed the verdict.

'TURKISHNESS' AS A MATTER OF MULTIPLE TECHNOLOGIES AND COLLECTIVES

The discussion in this chapter has shown that this case—perhaps *any* case—is a complex entanglement of various knowledges (criminological, genetic, forensic), practices (gathering evidence, developing strategies, convincing individuals to participate in DNA research), objects (a body, DNA, but also 'the Turkish community'), documents (witness statements, police reports), and regulations (the 2012 law, the provision that familial DNA research is an *ultimum remedium*). What we tend to understand as a linear progression from crime, to evidence gathering, to the apprehension of a suspect, and to a conviction is actually a much more labyrinthine affair that only in retrospect can be understood as a progressive movement. Over the course of such investigations, multiple technologies make their appearance, each used in relation to specific purposes and goals—and each with their limitations and affordances. From documents pointing to an unknown suspect and enacting a specific, racially inflected visual regime, to DNA samples and specific analyses and techniques, both 'the individual' at stake and the collective of which he is supposed to be a member are produced in specific ways.

In this piece, we have zoomed in on the various ways the unknown suspect's 'Turkishness' was enacted, demonstrating that this 'Turkishness' was established by means of various technologies. A pragmatic understanding of technologies as material-semiotic assemblages that act has made it clear that they enact differences: 1988 from the very shaping of the 'human sensorium' (Gilroy 1998) to the complex analytical techniques used in DNA research. Methodologically, attention has been drawn to the way race is produced in practices of seeing, witnessing, and knowing, drawing especially on a praxiographic sensibility with regard to this specific case. The analysis has also demonstrated that, as it is dependent on the specific technologies used and practices within which it is mobilised, Turkishness itself is not a singular category or quality. Rather, it takes on various shapes as something on the surface of the body (in the witness description), as something in the body's depths (in DNA research into its geographical origins), or as something of culture and community. Hence, the collectives haunting the court were manifold: the collective of interpellated witnesses, experienced in seeing epidermal differences; the collective of men sharing genetic ancestry in a specific region in Turkey; and a collective, overlapping the previous one, of young men living in the vicinity of the crime in 1992. The men of the latter two groups are taken to be part of a wider Turkish community, yet one which turns out to be elusive, for it is as much defined by internal cleavages and distinctions as it is by the common denominators of religion or ethnicity. Finally, of course, there is the familial DNA, which evokes a collective order along the lines of genetics and kinship.

As Mol (2002) suggests, multiple realities are not necessarily a problem to actors working with them; often, there is no need for realities to be subsumed or made commensurable. At the same time, such realities may be brought into *relation* with each other, for instance, in the final court case in which the witness' description of the Turkish man singing on a bicycle was used to buttress the prosecutor's case. The criminal case offers an illustration, then, of the way multiple realities can be brought into relation with each other: a phenotype with genetic difference, genetic difference with socio-cultural realities and communities, and genetic affinities once again (see for specific strategies of bringing these collectives into relation with each other—or keeping them apart—van Oorschot and M'charek 2021). These insights resonate with the way M'charek (2000) has shown that human difference is not a singular reality: there are different ways to enact differences between collectives and populations within the practices of forensic genetics, and these differences are further rearticulated in various practices.

The relations made between these collectives may, in retrospect, suggest that it is easy to map biological and cultural collectives onto each other, or that the 'natural' reality of biogeographical ancestry is simply manifested on the surface of the body, in the suspect's phenotype. But a closer look complicates such understandings of the way collectives play a role in this case. Defining and delineating collectives involves various kinds of knowledges and technologies (criminological, cultural, forensic), takes multiple technologies (of writing, of memory, of seeing bodies, of isolating DNA, and of analysing it in relation to existing, every-evolving databases), and takes a lot of *work*. Nor do collectives easily map on to each other, even though that is the prosecutor's suggestion when he draws on the witness report to further buttress the case that it was indeed Turkish Hüseyin A. who was seen near the vicinity of the crime. It is also important to notice the fact that the collectives made and mobilised over the course of this investigation were, at times deliberately, *disconnected* from each other: according to the strategies adopted by the police, the fact that the suspect was likely of Turkish descent was treated with a lot of caution, as it could inflame already existing tensions. Precisely where and how these collectives are brought into (partial) relation with each other, and where they are not, are important sites for further anthropological study.

Acknowledgements We would like to thank the European Research Council (ERC) for supporting this research through an ERC-Consolidator Grant (fp7–617451-RaceFaceID-Race Matter: On the Absent Presence of Race in Forensic Identification). (RaceFaceID, PI: Prof. A. M'charek).

NOTE

1. Because the Milica van Doorn case is currently on appeal, some crucial actors involved in the case—particularly judges and prosecutors—could not be expected at this time to talk about the specifics of the case. However, as the court 'speaks through its verdicts', the research team made extensive use of the verdict as it was published on the website of the Dutch judiciary.

REFERENCES

Abu-Lughod, L. (1991). Writing Against Culture. In R. G. Fox (Ed.), *Recapturing. Anthropology: Working in the Present*. Santa Fe: School of American Research Press.

Bleumink, R., Jong, L., & Plajas, I. (2018). *Composite Method: Experimenting with the Absent Presence in Film and Facial Composite Drawing*. Amsterdam: Ir/Relevancies of Race Lecture Series.

Caspari, R. (2003). From Types to Populations: A Century of Race, Physical Anthropology, and the American Anthropological Association. *American Anthropologist, 105*, 65–76.

Clifford, J., & Marcus, G. (1986). *Writing Culture: the Poetics and Politics of Ethnography*. Berkeley & Los Angeles: University of California University Press.

Descola, P., & Palsson, G. (1996). *Nature and Society*. London & New York: Routledge.

de Knijff, P. (2006). Meehuilen met de Wolven? Inaugural lecture, *Leiden University*.

de Rooij, M., M'charek, A., & R. van Reekum. (2014). Tijdspraktijken: DNA en de On/Onderbroken Stad. *Sociologie, 10*(3), 319–337.

de Volkskrant. (2018, December 12). Hoe de politie na 25 jaar alsnog de moord of Milica van Doorn kon oplossen. E Stoker. https://www.volkskrant.nl/nieuws-achtergrond/hoe-de-politie-na-25-jaar-de-zaak-milica-van-doorn-alsnog-kon-oplossen~b2a42503/. Accessed 8 August 2019.

El-Haj, N. (2007). The Genetic Reinscription of Race. *Annual Review of Anthropology*, *36*, 283–300.

Eze, E. C. (1997). The Color of Reason: the Idea of 'Race' in Kant's Anthropology. In E. C. Eze (Ed.), *Postcolonial African Philosophy: a Critical Reader*. Hoboken, NJ.: Blackwell Publishing.

Fassin, D. (2011). Racialization. In F. E. Mascia-Lees (Ed.), *A Companion to the Anthropology of the Body and Embodiment*. Hoboken, NJ.: Blackwell Publishing.

Goodman, A. H., Moses, Y. T., & Jones, J. L. (2012). *Race: Are we so different?* Chichester, West Sussex, U.K.: Wiley-Blackwell.

Fortier, A. M. (2012). Genetic Indigenisation in 'The People of the British Isles'. *Science as Culture, 21*(2), 153–175.

Fullwiley, D. (2007). The Molecularization of Race: Institutionalizing Human Difference in Pharmacogenetics Practice. *Science as Culture, 16*(1), 1–30.

Gilroy, P. (1998). Race ends Here. *Ethnic and Racial Studies, 21*(5), 838–847.

Haraway, D. (1988). Situated Knowledges: The Science Question in Feminism and the Privilege of Partial Perspective. *Feminist Studies, 14*(3), 575–599.

Hastrup, K. (2014). *Anthropology and Nature*. London & New York: Routledge.

Herrnstein, R. J., & Murray, C. A. (1994). *The Bell Curve: Intelligence and Class Structure in American Life*. New York: Simon & Schuster.

Holbraad, M., & Pedersen, M. A. (2017). *The Ontological Turn: An Anthropological Exposition*. Cambridge: Cambridge University Press.

Hull, M. (2012). *Government of Paper: the Materiality of Bureaucracy in Urban Pakistan*. Berkeley: University of California Press.

Jong, L., & M'charek, A. (2018). The high-profile case as 'fire object': Following the Marianne Vaatstra murder case through the media. *Crime, Media, Culture, 14*(3), 347–363.

Koenig, B. A., Lee, S. S.-J., & Richardson, S. S. (2008). *Revisiting race in a genomic age*. New Brunswick, NJ: Rutgers University Press.

Kroeber, A. L., & Kluckhohn, C. (1952). *Culture: A critical review of concepts and definitions*. Cambridge, Mass: The Museum.

Kuper, A. (1999). *Culture: An Anthropologist's Account*. Harvard: Harvard University Press.

Latour, B., & Woolgar, S. (1979). *Laboratory Life: the Construction of Scientific Facts*. Princeton: Princeton University Press.

Law, J. (2004). *After Method: Mess in Social Science Research*. London: Routledge.

Lynch, M., Cole, S. A., McNally, R., & Jordan, K. (2008). *Truth Machine: The Contentious History of DNA Fingerprinting*. Chicago: University of Chicago Press.

MacEachern, S. (2012). The Concept of Race in Contemporary Anthropology. In R. Scupin (Ed.), *Race and Ethnicity: An Anthropological Focus on the United States and the World*. Upper Saddle River NJ.: Prentice Hall.

M'charek, A. (2000). Technologies of population: forensic DNA testing practices and the making of differences and similarities. *Configurations, 8*(1), 121–159.

M'charek, A. (2005). *The Human Genome Diversity Project: An Ethnography of Scientific Practice*. Cambridge, U.K.: Cambridge University Press.

M'charek, A. (2008). Silent Witness, Articulate Collectives: DNA Evidence and the Inference of Visible Traits. *Bioethics, 22*(9), 519–28.

M'charek, A. (2013). Beyond Fact or Fiction: On the Materiality of Race in Practice. *Cultural Anthropology, 28*(3), 420–442.

M'charek, A. (2014). Race, time, and folded objects: The HeLa error. *Theory, Culture and Society, 31*(6), 29–56.

M'charek, A. (2020). Tentacular Faces: Race and the Return of the Phenotype in Forensic Identification. *American Anthropologist.*

M'charek, A., & van Oorschot, I. (2019). What about Race? In A. Blok, I. Farias, & C. Roberts (Eds.), *Routledge Companion to Actor Network-Theory.* London: Routledge.

M'charek, A., Toom, V., & Jong, L. (2020). The Trouble with Race in Forensic Identification. *Science, Technology and Human Values.*

Mol, A. (2002). *The Body Multiple: Ontology in Medical Practice.* Durham: Duke University Press.

NOS. (2016, July 16). Gulen-beweging achter Turkse Coup? 'Zeer onwaarschijnlijk'. https://nos.nl/artikel/2118021-gulen-beweging-achter-turkse-coup-zeer-onwaarschijnlijk.html. Accessed 8 August 2019.

Pfaffenberger, B. (1992). Social Anthropology of Technology. *Annual Review of Anthropology 21, 491–516.*

Raine, A. (2008). From Genes to Brain to Antisocial Behavior. *Current Directions in Psychological Science, 17*(5), 323–328.

Reardon, J. (2005). *Race to the Finish: Identity and Governance in an Age of Genomics.* Princeton: Princeton University Press.

Santos, R. V., & Maio, M. C. (2004). Race, Genomics, Identities and Politics in Contemporary Brazil. *Critique of Anthropology, 24*(4), 347–378.

Selcer, P. (2012). Beyond the Cephalic Index. *Current Anthropology, 53*(5), 173–S184.

Stocking, G. W. ([1968] 1982). *Race, Culture and Evolution: Essays in the History of Anthropology.* Chicago & London: University of Chicago Press.

Tallbear, K. (2013). Genomic Articulations of Indigeneity. *Social Studies of Science, 43*(4), 509–533.

van Oorschot, I. (2014a). Seeing the Case Clearly: File-Work, Material Mediation, and Visualizing Practices in a Dutch Criminal Court. *Symbolic Interaction,* 37, 439–457.

van Oorschot, I. (2014b). Vouw- and Ontvouwpraktijken in Juridische Waarheidsvinding: Het Dossier-in-Actie. *Sociologie, 10*(3), 301–318.

van Oorschot, I. (2018). *Ways of Case-Making.* Dissertation. Rotterdam: Erasmus University.

van Oorschot, I. (2020). Culture, Milieu, Phenotype: Articulating Race in Judicial Sense-Making Practices. *Social and Legal Studies,* 9(6), 790–811.

van Oorschot, I. (2021). *The Law Multiple: Judgement and Knowledge in Practice.* Cambridge: Cambridge University Press.

van Oorschot, I., & Schinkel, W. (2015). The Legal Case File as Border Object: On Self-Reference and Other-Reference in Criminal Law. *Journal of Law and Society,* 42, 499–527.

van Oorschot, I., & M'charek, A. (2021). Keeping Race at Bay: Familial DNA Research, the 'Turkish Community', and the Pragmatics of Multiple Collectives in Investigative Practice. *Biosocieties, 16,* 553–573

Vismann, C. (2008). Files: *Law and Media Technology.* Stanford University Press.

Visweswaran, K. (1998). Race and the Culture of Anthropology. *American Anthropologist, 100*(1), 70–83.

Watt, E., & Kowal, E. (2019). What's at Stake? Determining Indigeneity in the Era of DIY DNA. *New Genetics and Society, 38*(2), 142–164.

CHAPTER 21

Learning, Technology, and the Instrumentalisation of Critique

Class

Christo Sims

This chapter explores the facility with which anthropological critiques of dominant theories of learning and technology are absorbed and instrumentalised by the hegemonic projects they target. It investigates these themes by tracing how anthropological critiques of mainstream cognitive theory and artificial intelligence research during the 1980s and early 1990s were adapted and deployed in the early 2000s as part of a philanthropic initiative that aimed to reinvent educational institutions for the digital age. In particular, the chapter traces how Lave and Wenger's (1991) notions of 'situated learning' and 'communities of practice' were adapted for a digitally networked era through the formulation of concepts such as 'networked publics' (Ito et al. 2009), 'affinity groups' (Gee 2003), and 'connected learning' (Ito et al. 2013). The chapter then turns to an ethnographic case study of an ambitious attempt to design a new model of schooling that was informed by and organised around these more technocratic adaptations of the earlier anthropological critiques. By focusing on how different student peer cultures at the school responded to the new model, the chapter illustrates how the reformers' adaptation and deployment of anthropological critiques ended up remaking, albeit unintentionally, many instrumentalist practices and entrenched social inequities, notably of gender and racialised social class. The chapter argues that this absorption and instrumentalisation of

C. Sims (✉)
University of California, San Diego, La Jolla, CA, USA
e-mail: chsims@ucsd.edu

anthropological critique occurred in large part through a gradual process of perspectival inversion: a steady move away from the concerns, understandings, and practices of learners and towards those of reformers, philanthropists, technology designers, educators, parents, and other adults charged with caring for and educating the young. At the same time, ritualised performances of the school's affinity with the earlier anthropological critiques and, more generally, counter-hegemonic struggles—a phenomenon that I refer to as *sanctioned counterpractices*—occluded not only the process of perspectival inversion but also many of the ways in which the school was contributing to the remaking of structural inequities.

ANTHROPOLOGICAL CRITIQUES OF MAINSTREAM COGNITIVE THEORY

In the second half of the twentieth century, cognitive psychology played an especially privileged role in shaping how many policymakers, experts, and members of the public understood relations between knowledge, learning, and computing technologies. At the risk of oversimplifying, mainstream cognitive theorising during the 1970s and 1980s tended to portray persons as minds, knowledge and culture as symbolic information, learning as the internalisation of that information, and cognition as a process in which individual (professional) minds manipulate symbols in order to solve problems and direct (rational) behaviour (Lave 1988, pp. 76–93). Successful learning, from this perspective, referred to a situation in which learners could accurately reproduce the validated forms of knowledge and information they had internalised. The learner was passive, and pedagogy was rote and instrumental.

Not coincidentally, similar assumptions underlay dominant understandings of computing technologies. Cognitivist theories of learning gained stature and influence alongside the rapid expansion of both the personal computing industry and artificial intelligence research during the 1970s and 1980s. Mainstream cognitive theory and AI research both relied on functionalist assumptions that not only allowed human minds and computers to be mapped onto each other, but also allowed computers to be imagined as an unproblematic extension of or replacement for human cognition. The theory of mind that was being developed in mainstream cognitive science and amongst artificial intelligence researchers during the 1970s and 1980s had strong parallels with the architecture of the computer, and as some critics noted at the time, the features of the latter appeared to be shaping theorising about the former (Dreyfus 1972; Dreyfus and Dreyfus 1986; Searle 1980; Suchman 1987). Just as programmers inscribed electronic bits into a computer's memory, so did societies or cultures inscribe information and knowledge into the minds of learners. And just as computers instrumentally ran algorithms on those bits of information in order to solve problems effectively and efficiently, so did human minds instrumentally process information in order to make plans, solve problems, and act rationally. Many of these assumptions and aspirations remain influential today.

It was against this backdrop that a number of anthropologists developed influential critiques of mainstream cognitive theorising and artificial intelligence research as they proposed alternative theories of knowledge, learning, and cognition. Working in parallel and sometimes in dialogue with scholars in Science and Technology Studies (e.g. Latour and Woolgar 1979; Knorr-Cetina and Mulkay 1983; Haraway 1988; Traweek 1988), anthropologists such as Jean Lave (1988), Lucy Suchman (1987), and Edwin Hutchins (1995) developed ethnographically informed critiques of the central premises of mainstream cognitive theory more generally, and its instrumental application in fields such as education, artificial intelligence, technology design, and scientific management, in particular.

While each scholar drew on different problematics—Lave on historical-materialist practice theories, Suchman on ethnomethodology, and Hutchins on Vygotsky-inspired activity theories—all argued for inverting conventional studies of cognition, which tended to prioritise the perspectives of experts, institutionally sanctioned forms of knowledge, and idealised notions of rational decision making.[1] They did so by conducting ethnographic studies of how people engaged in cognition and used technologies as part of their everyday situated activities. In doing so, they argued that cognition, knowledge, and learning were not features of individual minds but, rather, distributed accomplishments of ongoing social activities that took place in concrete environments. Importantly, by drawing attention to the *situated* character of knowledge, cognition, and learning, each anthropologist also drew attention to how seemingly mental phenomena were actually co-constituted with pragmatic engagement with technologies, tools, equipment, and artefacts, and often in ways that exceeded or escaped the purposes and uses that designers had ascribed to them. While Suchman, Lave, and Hutchins formulated key terms such as 'situated' and 'context' differently, each critiqued the abstract, mentalist, and decontextualised notions of information, knowledge, and skill that characterised mainstream cognitive theory and artificial intelligence research.[2] Each also challenged and aimed to supersede the entrenched dualisms they found in mainstream cognitive theorising, including those between subjects and objects, persons and worlds, minds and bodies, and humans and non-humans, the latter including artefacts, tools, and technologies.[3]

The influence of these anthropological critiques has been considerable and, in many ways, commendable. Suchman's and Hutchins's critiques are now canonical not just in cognitive science but also in fields that specialise in designing the human and social aspects of computer systems. Likewise, Lave's critiques have become canonical in fields as diverse as education, cognitive science, technology design, the learning sciences, and organisational studies.[4]

While the reach of these anthropological theories is laudable, the authors themselves acknowledge that many politically incisive aspects have been stripped away as their works spread. In some cases, the critiques have even been deployed in the service of the sorts of hegemonic projects that the anthropologists were challenging (cf. Vann and Bowker 2001; Duguid 2008; Lave 2008). Lave (2019) acknowledged this in a recent reflection on the uptake of her influential book, *Situated Learning: Legitimate Peripheral Participation* (1991), which she co-authored with the computer scientist Étienne Wenger:

> [T]he book is often cited as the source of two concepts, 'situated learning as legitimate peripheral participation' and 'communities of practice.' But when excised as simply things in themselves, as if they are not constituted as part of more comprehensive theoretical relations, concepts like 'situated learning' easily travel as mere slogans, plugged into common sense, uncritical theoretical and analytical contexts. (Lave 2019, pp. 134–135)

The remainder of this chapter sketches how the institutional locations from which these anthropological critiques were generated, adapted, and deployed appear to have contributed to their widespread circulation while also making them susceptible to adaptation, absorption, and instrumentalisation by dominant institutions and actors, a process that I refer to in this chapter as perspectival inversion. I begin by examining the unique institutional loci from which these critiques were generated, before focusing on influential attempts to update and apply Lave and Wenger's (1991) theory of situated learning to the digital age (cf. Gee 2003; Ito et al. 2009). In doing so, I trace a shift away from the concerns, understandings, and practices of the persons that anthropologists studied and towards those of persons charged with designing and managing sites central to the construction and exercise of hegemonic power.

INSTITUTIONAL LOCI OF ANTHROPOLOGICAL CRITIQUE

The widespread propagation, adaptation, and, at times, absorption and instrumentalisation of anthropological critiques of cognitive theory from the 1980s and 1990s can partly be attributed to the fairly distinct institutional loci in which these critiques were produced. Each of the anthropological texts introduced above were produced in what, at the time, were fairly unconventional locations for conducting anthropological research. Hutchins's theories of distributed cognition were developed at the University of California, San Diego, which hosted the founding meeting of the Cognitive Science Society in 1979 and is home to the first cognitive science department in the world. While trained as an anthropologist, Hutchins shared an appointment in the Cognitive Science Department at UCSD, and this institutional location contributed not only to the formulation of his theories but also to their spread in cognitive science and adjacent fields such as Human-Computer Interaction (HCI) and Computer Supported Collaborative Work (CSCW).

Similarly, both Suchman's *Plans and Situated Actions* and Lave and Wenger's *Situated Learning* were produced in multidisciplinary settings that, on the one hand, afforded them opportunities to conduct research and develop theory that crossed disciplinary silos but, on the other, were connected to and financially dependent on large technology corporations and actors with hegemonic agendas. *Plans and Situated Actions* is based on a study of computer scientists who worked at Xerox's famed Palo Alto Research Center (PARC), and Suchman worked as a researcher at PARC during and after publishing *Plans and Situated Actions*. Similarly, Lave and Wenger wrote *Situated Learning* while working at the Institute for Research on Learning (IRL), a multidisciplinary think tank and PARC spinoff. Both PARC and IRL were located in Silicon Valley, both rejected established disciplinary orthodoxies, yet both were also deeply connected to the cultures and interests of the technology industry. These connections likely aided what Lave acknowledges was an undertheorisation of political-economic and institutional relations in the original formulations of situated learning theory (Lave 2019, p. 134).[5] A similar critique could be made of Suchman's ethnomethodological analysis in *Plans and Situated Actions* and of Hutchins's theories of distributed cognition. While the uniqueness of the institutional settings in which these works were produced facilitated the development of highly original critiques of dominant lines of cognitive theorising, it also made them especially susceptible to absorption and instrumentalisation by more dominant actors and groups, such as technology corporations, management consultants, and philanthropic educational reformers.

To demonstrate this last claim, the remainder of the chapter focuses on one example where anthropological critique became absorbed and instrumentalised by dominant actors and agendas, examining how the institutional location in which *Situated Learning* was produced, IRL, appears to have shaped the dissemination and at times instrumentalisation of Lave and Wenger's ideas through a process of perspectival inversion. In particular, the sections trace the influence of IRL on one especially influential adaptation, absorption, and ultimate instrumentalisation of situated learning theory during the 2000s: the John D. and Catherine T. MacArthur Foundation's attempt to create a new field of expertise centred on Digital Media and Learning (DML). To illustrate the argument, I reflect on my own participation in the DML initiative and draw on my ethnographic study of a new school that attempted to implement concepts and principles that were being developed by beneficiaries of the DML initiative.

From Situated Learning to Digital Media and Learning

IRL was co-founded in the mid-1980s by John Seely Brown, a well-connected and influential computer scientist and organisational scholar. Brown was the director of PARC when he helped launch IRL as a spinoff. From the beginning, IRL aimed to challenge the dominant lines of cognitive theorising that were sketched earlier in this chapter. It did so by bringing together a highly interdisciplinary group of scholars—including anthropologists, developmental psychologists, computer scientists, management theorists, and linguists—in order to develop theories of cognition and learning that took both social contexts and tools, potentially including computing technologies, as constitutive features. In part due to its location in Silicon Valley and connections to the technology industry, theoretical concepts developed at IRL—including 'communities of practice' and 'situated learning'—quickly became influential, not only in fields such as anthropology and education but also in management consulting, organisational studies, computer science, technology design, and engineering (cf. Brown et al. 1989; Brown and Duguid 1991).[6]

In addition to providing institutional support for the creation of original and transdisciplinary critiques of mainstream cognitive theorising, IRL played a prominent role in forging a distribution network and discourse community around the works its members produced. For example, Brown and other members of IRL helped to found the *Learning in Doing* book series at Cambridge University Press, which published Suchman's *Plans and Situated Actions*, Lave and Wenger's *Situated Learning*, Wenger's *Communities of Practice*, and many other influential works that challenged dominant theories of the relations between learning, sociality, technology, and media. IRL was also instrumental in the formation of a new disciplinary field, the Learning Sciences, which adopted *Situated Learning* and other works produced at IRL as canonical texts.

My own forays into the legacy of IRL began not long after I started graduate school in the mid-2000s when I got involved in a collaborative research project that one of my professors was codirecting. Known as the Digital Youth Project, the initiative consisted of a team of over 20 scholars who ethnographically studied how young people in the United States were incorporating digital media into their everyday lives. The Digital Youth Project was at the vanguard of one of the MacArthur Foundation's major new philanthropic priorities, which aimed to explore the unprecedented opportunities for learning that networked digital media appeared to be making possible. The Foundation had grown disillusioned with its previous educational grant making, which focused on school reform in the city of Chicago, and John Seely Brown, who was now on the MacArthur Foundation's Board of Directors, championed and guided the new Digital Media and Learning initiative for the Foundation. The MacArthur Foundation supported the Digital Youth Project with a US$3 million grant and went on to spend over US$240 million on the broader initiative over the next 14 years.[7] In the process, they created a new field of expertise, known as Digital Media and Learning (DML).

While I did not realise it when I first got involved, the DML initiative was in many ways a direct descendent of the IRL's work in the late 1980s and 1990s. Not only did John Seely Brown champion and guide both initiatives, but several scholars who had been involved with IRL during the 1990s became central players in the new DML initiative.[8] This legacy also shaped the perspectives and goals of the Digital Youth Project as one of our stated aims was to update Lave and Wenger's theory of situated learning for an era in which networked computing and enhanced media engagement were becoming pervasive (Ito et al. 2009, pp. 13–14).

These legacies also had a direct impact on the book we produced at the end of the Digital Youth Project—titled *Hanging Out, Messing Around, and Geeking Out* or HOMAGO, for short (Ito et al. 2009)—which became foundational in the new field of Digital Media and Learning. For example, instead of Lave and Wenger's notion of 'communities of practice', which rested on an idea of co-participation in collocated activities, we developed the notion of 'networked publics' (Ito 2008; Ito et al. 2009, pp. 18–21), which was meant to extend the geographical loci of communities of practice towards digitally enabled forms of distributed sociality.[9] Like our intellectual predecessors at IRL, our formulation of networked publics was influenced by developments and discourses that were currently fashionable in the technology industry and amongst scholars of digital media technologies. In making a move away from artefact-mediated activity in local contexts and towards computer-facilitated forms of networked sociability, our ideas were shaped by influential work in media studies, such as Henry Jenkins's theory of 'participatory cultures' (Jenkins 1992; Jenkins et al. 2006), as well as more popular accounts of internet culture like the notion of the 'long tail', which had been developed and propagated by Chris Anderson (2004), then the editor-in-chief of *Wired* magazine. Similarly, we adapted Lave and Wenger's (1991) formulation of learning as a process of 'legitimate peripheral participation' and gave it a more tech-focused figuration with our notion of 'genres of participation' and a taxonomy of three such genres by which young people appeared to be learning through engagements with media and technology: 'hanging out', 'messing around', and 'geeking out' (Ito et al. 2009, pp. 14–18, 35–75).

With hindsight, the HOMAGO book and the interventions it helped inspire and justify illustrate how anthropological critiques of mainstream cognitive theorising from the 1980s and early 1990s can spread in ways that tend towards what I am calling perspectival inversion. While we presented HOMAGO as a mostly descriptive account of US young people's practices with digital media, a close reading evinces a proclivity to be in congruence with our funder's aspiration to transform educational institutions and processes for the digital age. For example, our notion of 'geeking out' was not just a descriptive category of how some, but not most, young people described their engagement with digital media technologies; it was also a normative target that could be deployed by designers of educational interventions and technologies. Implicitly in HOMAGO and explicitly in subsequent applications of the concept, 'geeking out' tended to be figured as a mode of digital media engagement that educational programmes and technology designers should attempt to cultivate in young people. Similarly, young people could be evaluated and compared against each other based on the degree to which they 'geeked out' with media technologies. This comparative measure, in turn, allowed for problematisations that legitimated educational interventions that were being developed by other scholars in the DML community. For example, the notion of the 'participation gap' (Jenkins et al. 2006), which can be read in part as a measure of who is and is not 'geeking out' with digital media technologies, legitimates philanthropic interventions and educational reform initiatives that attempt to close that gap. The MacArthur Foundation sponsored several such design interventions that took up our concepts in these ways, and through my work on the Digital Youth Project, I was able to gain access to study one of them ethnographically: an attempt to redesign the public school for the digital age. It was through my work on that project that I became more sensitive to how even counter-hegemonic anthropological theorising can aid, if often unintentionally, in processes of perspectival inversion and, thus, in remaking the structures and processes that the original theory critiques. The remaining sections sketch these dynamics.[10]

A School for the Digital Age

In the late 2000s I began a multi-year ethnographic study of an ambitious and well-intentioned reform project that had been sponsored as part of the Digital Media and Learning initiative: an attempt to 'reimagine' the public school for the digital age. The school, which I refer to as the Downtown School, was launched in New York City with considerable support from several philanthropic foundations, including the MacArthur Foundation, the city government, local universities, and transnational media and technology corporations.[11] Not long after it opened, the school also received prominent positive attention from local, national, and international news media. All these parties seemed to agree that the Downtown School was an especially innovative and promising attempt to transform schooling for a new digital era and economy.

In crafting designs for a new type of school, the project's founders and backers drew heavily on the anthropological critiques of mainstream cognitive theory discussed earlier in this chapter, as well as on concepts that were being developed by the Digital Youth Project and other members of the DML community, such as Henry Jenkins and James Paul Gee. According to the school's founders and backers, conventional schooling was badly out of touch with 'a digital, information rich, globally complex era prizing creativity, innovation, and resourcefulness'.[12] Drawing on *Situated Learning* and other critical assessments of conventional approaches to school-based learning, the school's founders and backers critiqued conventional schools for being overly bureaucratic, hierarchical, formulaic, and restrictive. Echoing anthropological challenges to mainstream cognitivist theorising, they contended that conventional schools prioritised the perspectives of experts and adults while neglecting the perspectives, interests, and practices of learners and young people. The school's designers added that conventional schooling focused on standardised forms of instruction and assessment, thereby rewarding passive behaviour and obsequiousness in students at a historical moment when creativity and innovation were prized. Rigid pedagogic scripts and strict hierarchies of authority, the school's designers and backers claimed, did not cultivate in students the agency, creativity, technical savvy, and unconventional thinking that the twenty-first century demanded. Additionally, the school's designers and backers argued that their proposed transformation would address the entrenched inequities of canonical schooling. Conventional schooling was no longer in touch with the realities of the contemporary world, they contended, so it was no wonder that so many students, particularly students from non-dominant backgrounds, were bored at school and not succeeding.

As an alternative, the school's founders designed the Downtown School to be organised like a game and sought to weave digital media throughout the curriculum. Both of these design decisions were made in an attempt to appeal to what the school's designers presumed were the interests and perspectives of young people, whom they figured as members of a 'digital generation'. The primary intellectual inspiration and justification for their vision of 'game-like' schooling came from the sociolinguist James Paul Gee and his colleague David Williamson Shaffer, both of whom had written influential books on the educational potential of video games (Gee 2003; Shaffer 2006). Gee and Shaffer also drew heavily on Lave and Wenger's theory of situated learning, transposing it to the digital realm, much as we had attempted to do in HOMAGO, and Gee was one of the main figureheads in MacArthur's DML initiative. In this 'game-like' model, students would be active and creative participants in the production of knowledge, rather than passive recipients. In a nod towards Lave and Wenger's notion of communities of practice, the fictive worlds of games were thought to furnish students with the necessary social context for learning. Students, in this view, would collectively and willingly 'take on' the roles of scientists, designers, coders, and other knowledge workers as they actively tried to solve problems in fictional game worlds that the school's designers had created. What is more, and in a gesture towards our valorisation of 'geeking out' in HOMAGO, students at the Downtown School would learn to hack, remix, and produce media and technology.

Similarly, the clear hierarchies of authority between educators and students that are common at conventional schools would be redrawn. Teachers at the Downtown School would act more like mentors and coaches than disciplinarians. Relatedly, students would be networked to each other and to various online communities, allowing them to learn by way of participating in 'networked publics', as we had theorised them in HOMAGO. This would allow them to connect their school lives to other situations in their lives where learning took place, a system which DML scholars were in the process of formulating as a prescriptive educational model they called 'connected learning' (Ito et al. 2013). Finally, the school would welcome students from any background, thus closing the 'participation gap' (Jenkins et al. 2006) and equitably preparing a new generation for the unprecedented opportunities and challenges of the twenty-first century.

On this last point, the Downtown School was admirably distinct from most public schools in New York City. The school opened with a single class of 75 6th graders (ages 11 and 12) and added a class each year until the first class reached 12th grade. I followed the school's first class of students from the school's founding until that class graduated from eighth grade. In the school's first year, approximately half of the students came from middle and upper-middle class households. The parents of these comparatively privileged students tended to have graduate degrees and successful careers in the culture industries, including academia, media production, design, publishing, and art. Nearly all of these more privileged students identified as White or Asian-American on Department of Education (DOE) surveys. Contrasting sharply with these students were students from significantly less-privileged social backgrounds. Approximately 40 per cent of the school's first class of students qualified for free or reduced-price lunch, a common proxy for lower socioeconomic status amongst education researchers in the United States, and nearly all of these lower-income students identified as Black or Latino/a on DOE forms. Finally, the school attracted boys to girls at an approximately three-to-two ratio, an early indicator that the school's innovative new model might entail unexamined cultural biases.

SANCTIONED AND UNSANCTIONED COUNTERPRACTICES

When I began fieldwork at the Downtown School, I was interested in developing an understanding of the various peer collectives, or cliques, that students formed in the course of attending the Downtown School. My attention to the students' peer collectives had been informed by my reading of Lave and Wenger (1991), which stressed the importance of focusing on the perspectives and experiences of learners over pedagogues, as well as classic ethnographies of schooling that also privileged student experiences, such as Paul Willis's *Learning to Labor* (1977), Penelope Eckert's *Jocks and Burnouts* (1989), and Bradley Levinson, Douglas Foley, and Dorothy Holland's edited volume *The Cultural Production of the Educated Person* (1996). All of these works argued, convincingly in my opinion, that broader processes of social and cultural reproduction and change were mediated by the partially autonomous practices of youth peer cultures. According to these ethnographers, institutionalised schooling did play a pivotal role in legitimating the sorting of new generations into the highly unequal positions of the adult division of labour, as more structural analyses of schooling (cf. Althusser 1971; Bourdieu and Passeron 1977; Foucault 1977) claimed. However, these ethnographers also argued that such processes were far from determined and that young people were hardly the cultural dopes (Hall 1981) or docile subjects implied by more structural analyses. Instead, Willis (1977), Eckert (1989), and Levinson et al. (1996) argued that the cultural practices that young people created and improvised with each other as they tried to give meaning to and forge identities within schools and other adult-controlled spaces mediated broader political and economic processes. Through negotiations over legitimate participation in these peer cultural practices, young people tended to assemble into different informal collectives or cliques that, in turn, mediated processes of learning, subjectivation, and, ultimately, social reproduction.

As Eckert (1995) observed, these informal peer collectives have much in common with the communities of practice theorised by Lave and Wenger (1991). They also appear to have much in common with the informal groups that many workers form as they attempt to navigate and give meaning to capitalist workplaces (van Maanen and Barley 1984; Orr 1996). Through ongoing negotiations over legitimate participation in these peer collectives, young people learn about the salient social divisions of adult society as they learn what it means to be a 'good' participant in the collective's practices. Importantly, the legitimacy and value of participation in these collectives is negotiated to a significant degree by members of the collective; legitimate participation in peer collectives is not determined by teachers or managers, although these authorities do play a role in shaping the conditions in which peer collectives assemble.

I was curious to see if and how these processes might play out differently in an organisation that, echoing both anthropological critiques of mainstream cognitive theory and popular discourses emanating from the tech industry, aspired to upend bureaucratic hierarchies and cultivate the agency, creativity, and autonomy of subordinates. As such, I spent much of my initial time in the field hanging out with the students as they went about their daily school routines. Within a few months of the school's opening, four dominant peer collectives, or cliques, had emerged. While some students moved between these collectives, some students left the school, and others arrived, and the overall divisions between the cliques remained fairly stable for the remainder of my time in the field, despite having to be regularly rebuilt.

From a sociological perspective, these divisions articulated two enduring axes of inequality: gender and racialised social class. All of the cliques were overwhelmingly organised around either a masculine or feminine orientation, and as such, they offered their participants different ways of doing masculinity and femininity (Sims 2014). While some students occasionally perforated the gendered boundaries of these groups, by and large students clustered in groups where all of the participants identified as either boys or girls. These masculinised and feminised groups were further divided by racialised social class, with a clique of predominantly privileged girls, a clique of predominantly privileged boys, a clique of predominantly less-privileged girls, and a clique that entirely comprised less-privileged boys. As noted earlier, these class divisions also mapped onto institutional markers of race and ethnicity.

And yet, despite these divisions, the practices that each collective generated were quite similar. In all cases, the peer groups debated, rewarded, and disciplined what they considered to be legitimate, good, and meaningful activity amongst members. Appropriate and valued uses of technological artefacts, and material culture more generally, were often the subjects of these deliberations, much as Lave and Wenger (1991), Suchman (1987), and Hutchins (1995) had theorised. And all of the groups celebrated creativity and improvisation in ways that exceeded the formal expectations of school authorities, as had the authors of HOMAGO (Ito et al. 2009) and the designers and philanthropic backers of the school.

However, it also became apparent that many of the practices that these peer collectives produced were not in keeping with what many adults who were affiliated with the reform project—including the school's designers, some of its administrators and teachers, and, especially, many of the highly involved parents, most of whom where White or Asian-American and economically privileged—had imagined as legitimate unconventionality in a school context. From the moment the school opened, the hope to create a 'game-like' model of schooling in which an adult-designed game world would stand in for communities of practice was assailed from multiple directions: many students were not especially taken by, and some mocked, the school's innovative pedagogic model, teachers expressed frustration about students not following directives, factions of privileged parents circulated rumours and then warned school officials about what they believed was threatening conduct by the cliques of predominantly Black and Latinx students, and members of the administration and design team worried about an embarrassing collapse of their much publicised experiment.

By winter of the school's first year, matters reached a breaking point after a sizable faction of privileged parents threatened to leave the school unless officials instituted strict zero tolerance policies. As I detail in my book, these parents were particularly anxious about some of the less-privileged students at the school, and their anxieties appear to have been moulded by unexamined racial tropes and stereotypes (Sims 2017, pp. 149–158). For example, at a PTA meeting, one parent, a professor, pressed school officials to discipline what she perceived to be dangerous and inappropriate behaviour by some of the less-privileged Black and Latinx students, stating, 'How do you deal with the infectious tendency of this behaviour, that spreads horizontally and infects others? It's transmitted from generation to generation and from person to person'. This last remark deserves comment not only because of its invocation of an enduring racist trope—the 'other' as an infectious pollutant—but also because it figures horizontality not as an ideal to uphold, as it is in the anthropologically derived theories that had influenced the school's designers, but, rather, as a threat to the moral and social order.

In response to these parents' threats to leave the school, officials finally capitulated and instituted a slew of strict management techniques that are familiar in conventional schools and disciplinary institutions more generally. In Tayloristic fashion, school authorities crafted detailed scripts that precisely specified what students should be doing at nearly all points of the day: the movement of students was tightly restricted, educators increased their surveillance of the cliques of predominantly less-privileged Black and Latinx students, transgressions of adult authority were quickly reprimanded, and several of the most influential members of the collectives of less-privileged students were suspended repeatedly. Many of the students subjected to the new disciplinary regime eventually left the school, whereas nearly all of their more privileged classmates remained. In short, despite drawing on counter-hegemonic anthropological accounts that celebrated the perspectives of learners, the Downtown School had become much like the urban public schools that it had been designed to replace, reinstating and reinforcing the very hierarchies of perspective and authority that it had critiqued. Put differently, the process of perspectival inversion had reached a culmination point.

Yet many of the adults who had designed and backed the project, as well as many of the parents who had called for zero tolerance policies, curiously continued to portray the Downtown School to each other, to the media, and to other educational reformers as substantively unorthodox and uniquely organised and equipped to foster young people's creativity, autonomy, agency, and ingenuity. The counter-hegemonic and technocentric imaginaries that had inspired and justified the experiment proved to be remarkably resilient in the face of events that thwarted their realisation in practice. How was this resiliency of idealism and hope accomplished?

In my book, I argue that fleeting and often ritualised moments when the school approximated its idealisation as an unconventional and subversive intervention—what I refer to in the book as *sanctioned counterpractices*—played an especially important role in sustaining and repairing many people's hopes for the experiment (Sims 2017, pp. 102–108). While much of the daily life at the Downtown School came to resemble life at a more conventional urban public school, and while the school was helping to remake many of the social divisions and hierarchies that the school's designers had hoped to bridge, there were moments when the adult-sanctioned practices at the school approximated designers' hopeful imaginings. For example, at the end of each trimester educators would diverge from strict school routines and institute a special week-long period in which students worked in groups on a single design challenge, such as building a Rube Goldberg machine. During these periods, reformers' hopeful imaginaries and the practices of students and educators converged: educator directives waned, unscripted responses by students were mostly accepted by adults, students had to figure out with each other what to do next, time pressures were eased, and so forth. These were moments of sanctioned counterpractice, and during these moments, the Downtown School did resemble the sociotechnical imaginaries and anthropologically derived theories that had inspired and legitimated the intervention.

While these moments of sanctioned counterpractice were fleeting compared to everyday school routines, and while sanctioned counterpractices were carefully bounded temporally and spatially by school authorities, they played an especially prominent role in shaping and sustaining hopeful ideas and feelings about the school, particularly for people who were spatially distal from daily life in the classrooms.[13] Representations and demonstrations of the school's sanctioned counterpractices were front and centre in the various ceremonies and festivals that school officials organised for parents and caregivers; they were highlighted in tours for prospective families, journalists, city officials, officers from funding agencies, and other invited guests; and they were regularly featured in representations of the school in the school's promotional materials; in media produced by the school's philanthropic sponsors; in academic reports produced by other members of the DML community; and in popular television, newspaper, magazine, book, and documentary media. Due to their prominence in these more public-facing rituals, demonstrations, and representations, sanctioned counterpractices appeared to help many people who were committed to the project in various ways to establish and maintain a sense that the Downtown School was an especially original and promising new model of schooling for the twenty-first century, one that cultivated creative, tech-savvy, contra-normative subjects. They also appeared to validate the effectiveness of an instrumentalised version of situated learning theory. That they did so even as daily life at the Downtown School became more conventional and conventionally problematic, testifies to how anthropological critiques can continue to act as counter-hegemonic icons even as they are subjected to processes of perspectival inversion that strip them of their more radical political significance.

CONCLUSION

The case of the Downtown School raises concerns about how counter-hegemonic critiques developed by anthropologists can be absorbed and instrumentalised as they enter sites of power and are subjected to processes of what I have been referring to as perspectival inversion. On the one hand, institutional appropriations of counter-hegemonic perspectives and theories are understandable: they appear to address many of the well-known and widely felt shortcomings of modern bureaucratic organisations; they promise to make an organisation more equitable, innovative, flexible, and competitive; they figure a more meaningful, connected, agentive, and creative future for subordinates who have little choice but to participate in modern institutions like schooling and corporations; and they espouse an ethic of horizontality and conviviality that contrasts sharply with the rigid hierarchies, social divisions, and inequities that characterise much of modern life. However, reformers who draw on counter-hegemonic perspectives and theories also tend to overlook and downplay the degree to which the institutions they aim to reform continue to rely on coercive and divisive modes of top-down governance. Luc Boltanski and Eve Chiapello make a similar observation:

> The rejection in the 1990s of hierarchy... is all the more striking in that the readership of the authors concerned basically consists of the *cadres* of large groups and multinationals, which, notwithstanding all their efforts, will have difficulty dispensing with hierarchy. (2005, p. 70, emphasis in original)

This chapter has examined one such difficulty in attempting to dispense with hierarchy. By tracing how anthropological critiques of mainstream cognitive theory and artificial intelligence research in the 1980s and early 1990s were gradually adapted and incorporated into a well-funded attempt to reimagine educational institutions for the digital age, the chapter has shown how counter-hegemonic theories and perspectives were subjected to a process of perspectival inversion that helped remake familiar forms of institutional practice, division, and hierarchy. Like many anthropologists, Lave, Suchman, and Hutchins fore-grounded the perspectives and experiences of learners, workers, and other 'just plain folks' (Lave 1988) in their efforts to challenge dominant common-sense theorising. The unusually multidisciplinary locations from which they formu-lated their critiques no doubt contributed to the works' originality and influ-ence, but it also made them particularly susceptible to appropriation by management consultants, designers, educational reformers, and other techno-cratic professionals who (re)design and manage institutions and technologies that are central to the exercise and reproduction of power relations. Such appropriations are not necessarily problematic, and indeed, it is laudable when anthropological theory travels beyond its usual academic networks and com-munities. However, the case of the Downtown School illustrates how such appropriations can end up privileging the interests, concerns, and obligations of reformers over those foregrounded in the original critiques, an inversion that generated tensions between reformers' ideals and acts. I have argued that these tensions were soothed, at least temporarily, through the orchestration, performance, celebration, and widespread publicising of what I call sanctioned counterpractices: fleeting and often ritualised moments when the organisa-tion's practices more closely resembled its espoused ideals. Yet, while these sanctioned counterpractices were quite effective at easing tensions and rejuve-nating morale, ultimately they helped obscure and legitimate the school's con-tributions to remaking many inherited social divisions, power relations, and hierarchies.

NOTES

1. For a more general review of these and other 'sociomaterial' approaches to edu-cation research, see Fenwick et al. (2011).
2. For a review of how different scholars approached the problem of 'situation' and 'context', see Chaiklin and Lave (1993); Lave (2019, pp. 27–50).
3. Tim Ingold mounted similar critiques in his advocacy for an ecological approach to theorising technical skill; see Ingold (1996, 1997).
4. These anthropological critiques extended far beyond the application of cogni-tive theory in educational settings, but they also complement and add ethno-graphic rigour to more sociological critiques of institutionalised schooling. For examples of the latter, see Apple (2012) and Selwyn (2011). Selwyn's work is relevant to the foci of this chapter in that it critiques mainstream discourses on education technology, many of which deploy concepts and assumptions from cognitive psychology. For an anthropological critique of educational institutions that draws on the works cited in this chapter, see Varenne and McDermott (1998).
5. Suchman's (2002) advocacy of 'located accountabilities' in technology produc-tion makes an analogous point. For an example of how to incorporate institu-tional analysis into theories of situated activity, see Dorothy Holland and Jean

Lave's edited volume, *History in Person* (2001), and, in particular, their discussion of the notion of 'local contentious practice'. In a related vein, Lave (2011) reflexively develops and applies her theory of learning to her own transformations as a scholar and theorist working in different institutional arrangements.

6. According to Vann and Bowker (2001, pp. 247–248), Etienne Wenger, Lave's co-author on *Situated Learning*, also played a prominent role in introducing anthropologically informed theories to management consultants when he published a follow-on volume to *Situated Learning*, titled *Communities of Practice* (Wenger 1998).

7. For an account of the formation of the Digital Youth Project, see Ito et al. (2019, p. xiii).

8. For example, Mizuko Ito, who worked at IRL and PARC in the 1990s, went on to run the Digital Youth Project before co-founding and acting as Research Director for the MacArthur-funded Digital Media and Learning Research Hub at the University of California, Irvine. I worked for the Ito and the Digital Media and Learning Research Hub for several years while I was a graduate student.

9. As we stated in the book, networked publics comprise 'the active participation of a distributed social network in the production and circulation of culture and knowledge' (Ito et al. 2009, p. 19).

10. For a fuller account, see: *Disruptive Fixation: School Reform and the Pitfalls of Techno-Idealism* (Sims 2017).

11. While I use a pseudonym for the school, I am aware that the school's uniqueness and notoriety make it impossible to anonymise the school's identity without effacing much of what makes the school theoretically and politically significant. As such, I use additional measures to protect the identity of research participants who shared information with me in confidence or whose actions I observed. I discuss the strategies I used to mitigate these risks in Sims (2017, pp. 182–183).

12. The quote comes from a report that the school's founders wrote about their planning processes.

13. In general, the people who remained most enthusiastic and hopeful about the Downtown School were people with little direct involvement in the classrooms. Given this spatial separation, their understandings and imaginings of the school appeared to be shaped primarily through representations and public rituals.

REFERENCES

Althusser, L. (1971). Ideology and Ideological State Apparatuses: Notes Toward an Investigation. In *Lenin and Philosophy and Other Essays* (pp. 127–188). New York: Monthly Review Press.

Anderson, C. (2004). The Long Tail. *Wired Magazine*, October 2004.

Apple, M. W. (2012). *Education and Power*. Second Edition. New York: Routledge.

Boltanski, L, & Chiapello, E. (2005). *The New Spirit of Capitalism*. New York: Verso.

Bourdieu, P., & Passeron, J. (1977). *Reproduction in Education, Society and Culture*. Beverly Hills, CA.: SAGE.

Brown, J. H., Collins, A., & Duguid, P. (1989). Situated Cognition and the Culture of Learning. *Educational Researcher, 18*(1), 32–42.

Brown, J. S., & Duguid, P. (1991). Organizational Learning and Communities-of-Practice: Toward a Unified View of Working, Learning, and Innovation. *Organization Science, 2*(1), 40–57.

Chaiklin, S., & Lave, J. (1993). *Understanding Practice: Perspectives on Activity and Context.* New York: Cambridge University Press.

Dreyfus, H. L. (1972). *What Computers Can't Do: A Critique of Artificial Intelligence.* New York: Harper & Row.

Dreyfus, H. L., & Dreyfus, S. E. (1986). *Mind Over Machine: The Power of Human Intuition and Expertise in the Era of the Computer.* New York: Free Press.

Duguid, P. (2008). Community of Practice Then and Now. In A. Amin & J. Roberts (Eds.), *Community, Economic Creativity, and Organization* (pp. 1–10). New York: Oxford University Press.

Eckert, P. (1989). *Jocks and Burnouts: Social Categories and Identity in the High School.* New York: Teachers College Press.

Eckert, P. (1995). Trajectory and Forms of Institutional Participation. In L. Crockett & A. Crouter (Eds.), *Pathways Through Adolescence: Individual Development in Relation to Social Contexts* (pp. 175–195). Hillsdale, NJ.: Lawrence Erlbaum.

Fenwick, et al. (2011). *Emerging Approaches to Educational Research: Tracing the Socio-Material.* New York: Routledge.

Foucault, M. (1977). *Discipline and Punish: The Birth of the Prison.* New York: Pantheon Books.

Gee, J. P. (2003). *What Video Games Have to Teach Us About Learning and Literacy.* New York: Palgrave Macmillan.

Hall, S. (1981). Notes on Deconstructing the Popular. In R. Samuel (Ed.), *People's History and Socialist Theory* (pp. 227–240). London: Routledge & Kegan Paul.

Haraway, D. (1988). Situated Knowledges: The Science Question in Feminism and the Privilege of Partial Perspective. *Feminist Studies*, 575–599.

Holland, D., & Lave, J. (2001). History in Person: An Introduction. In D. Holland & J. Lave (Eds.), *History in Person: Enduring Struggles, Contentious Practice, Intimate Identities* (pp. 3–33). Sante Fe: School of American Research Press.

Hutchins, E. (1995). *Cognition in the Wild.* Cambridge, MA.: The MIT Press.

Ingold, T. (1996). Situating Action V: The History and Evolution of Bodily Skills. *Ecological Psychology, 8*(2), 37–41.

Ingold, T. (1997). Eight Themes in the Anthropology of Technology. *Social Analysis: The International Journal of Social and Cultural Practice, 41*(1), 106–138.

Ito, M. (2008). Introduction. In K. Varnelis (Ed.), *Networked Publics* (pp. 1–14). Cambridge, MA.: The MIT Press.

Ito, M., Baumer, S., Bittanti, M., Boyd, D., Cody, R., Herr-Stephenson, B., Horst, H. A., Lange, P. G., Mahendran, D., Martinez, K. Z., Pascoe, C. J., Perkel, D., Robinson, L., Sims, C., & Tripp, L. (2009). *Hanging Out, Messing Around, and Geeking Out: Kids Living and Learning with New Media.* Cambridge, MA: The MIT Press.

Ito, M., Gutiérrez, K., Livingstone, S., Penuel, B., Rhodes, J., Salen, K., Schor, J., Sefton-Green, J., & Watkins, C. (2013). *Connected Learning: An Agenda for Research and Design.* Irvine, CA: Digital Media and Learning Research Hub.

Ito, M., Baumer, S., Bittanti, M., Boyd, D., Cody, R., Herr-Stephenson, B., Horst, H. A., Lange P. G., Mahendran, D., Martinez, K. Z., Pascoe, C. J., Perkel, D., Robinson, L., Sims, C., & Tripp, L. (2019). *Hanging Out, Messing Around, and Geeking Out: Kids Living and Learning with New Media—10th Anniversary Edition.* Cambridge, MA.: The MIT Press.

Jenkins, H. (1992). *Textual Poachers: Television Fans & Participatory Culture.* New York: Routledge.

Jenkins, H., Clinton, K., Purushotma, R., Robinson, A. J., & Weigel, M. (2006). *Confronting the Challenges of Participatory Culture: Media Education for the 21st Century*. Chicago, IL.: The John D. and Catherine T. MacArthur Foundation.

Knorr-Cetina, K., & Mulkay, M. (1983). *Science Observed: Perspectives on the Social Study of Science*. Thousand Oaks, CA.: Sage Publications.

Latour, B., & Woolgar, S. (1979). *Laboratory Life: The Construction of Scientific Facts*. Beverly Hills, CA.: Sage Publications.

Lave, J. (1988). *Cognition in Practice: Mind, Mathematics and Culture in Everyday Life*. New York: Cambridge University Press.

Lave, J. (2008). Epilogue: Situated Learning and Changing Practice. In A. Amin & J. Roberts (Eds.), *Community, Economic Creativity, and Organization* (pp. 283–294). New York: Oxford University Press.

Lave, J. (2011). *Apprenticeship in Critical Ethnographic Practice*. Chicago: University of Chicago Press.

Lave, J. (2019). *Learning and Everyday Life: Access, Participation, and Changing Practice*. Cambridge, U.K.: Cambridge University Press.

Lave, J., & Wenger, E. (1991). *Situated Learning: Legitimate Peripheral Participation*. Cambridge, U.K.: Cambridge University Press.

Levinson, B., Foley, D., & Holland, D. (1996). *The Cultural Production of the Educated Person*. Albany NY.: State University of New York Press.

Orr, J. E. (1996). *Talking About Machines: An Ethnography of a Modern Job*. Ithaca, NY.: Cornell University Press.

Searle, J. R. (1980). Minds, Brains, and Programs. *The Behavioral and Brain Sciences, 3*, 417–457.

Selwyn, N. (2011). *Schools and Schooling in the Digital Age: A Critical Analysis*. New York: Routledge.

Shaffer, D. W. (2006). *How Computer Games Help Children Learn*. New York: Palgrave Macmillan.

Sims, C. (2014). Video Game Culture, Contentious Masculinities, and Reproducing Racialized Social Class Divisions in Middle School. *Signs: Journal of Women in Culture and Society, 39*(4), 848–857.

Sims, C. (2017). *Disruptive Fixation: School Reform and the Pitfalls of Techno-Idealism*. Princeton, NJ.: Princeton University Press.

Suchman, L. (1987). *Plans and Situated Actions: The Problem of Human-Machine Communication*. Cambridge, U.K.: Cambridge University Press.

Suchman, L. (2002). Located Accountabilities in Technology Production. *Scandinavian Journal of Information Systems, 14*, 91–106.

Traweek, S. (1988). *Beamtimes and Lifetimes: The World of High Energy Physics*. Cambridge: Harvard University Press.

van Maanen, J., & Barley, S. R. (1984). Occupational Communities: Culture and Control in Organizations. *Research in Organizational Behavior, 6*, 287–365.

Vann, K., & Bowker, G. (2001). Instrumentalizing the Truth of Practice. *Social Epistemology, 15*(3), 247–262.

Varenne, H., & McDermott, R. (1998). *Successful Failure: The School America Builds*. New York: Westview Press.

Wenger, E. (1998). *Communities of Practice: Learning, Meaning, and Identity*. New York: Cambridge University Press.

Willis, P. (1977). *Learning to Labor: How Working Class Kids Get Working Class Jobs*. New York: Columbia University Press.

CHAPTER 22

Technology, Gender, and Nation: Building Modern Citizens in Maoist China

Gender

Francesca Bray

A technology is a material practice exercised in social context. The context imparts meaning both to the objects produced through technical action and to the persons producing them. From this perspective technologies are specific to a society, embodiments of its visions of the world, and its struggles over social order. In this sense the most important work that technologies do is to produce people: the makers are shaped by the making, and the users by the using. In particular, technology is one key medium through which gender identities are marked and gender regimes are defined (Bray 2007).

To anthropologists, the variations in how technologies are linked with female and male identities and capacities, within or between societies and over time, offer precious insights not only into the material constitution of gender regimes, but into subjectivity and governmentality more generally: they are particularly effective in showing how concrete technological practices weave the personal into the political (Bray 1997).

Technology has a lot to tell us about how gender works. Conversely, looking at technology through the lens of gender also prompts us to challenge many widespread modern assumptions about technology by asking deeper questions about its workings and ontologies. Specific genderings and definitions of technology are embedded in, and constitutive of, evolving *technological cultures*,

F. Bray (✉)
University of Edinburgh, Edinburgh, UK
e-mail: francesca.bray@ed.ac.uk

M. H. Bruun et al. (eds.), *The Palgrave Handbook of the Anthropology of Technology*, https://doi.org/10.1007/978-981-16-7084-8_22

that is, the characteristic ideas which societies hold about the forces mobilised by technological activities of various kinds; about how, whether, and to what ends they should or should not be used; the nature of their effects; and their political, moral, or metaphysical significance (Bijker 2007; Bray 2019). Technological cultures are never homogeneous or stable: they are continually being challenged and renegotiated. The destabilisation of categories and values by advances in *reproductive* technologies, discussed below, is a case in point. This chapter, however, focuses on an example of disruption in the technological culture of *production*. It presents the case of the Iron Girls of Maoist China, where an official re-coding of female technological capacities represented not simply a dramatic (if brief) reversal of the technocratic culture of socialist state-building, but a revolutionary re-casting of technological action as a form of moral becoming. But we begin with a brief survey of the field.

TECHNOLOGY AND GENDER IN ANTHROPOLOGY

It was not until the 1980s that anthropology started to address issues around technology and gender. By the 1960s and 1970s anthropologists no longer restricted their studies to 'simple' societies but had begun to anthropologise 'at home' as well, treating all societies as integral to the fabric of the modern, industrialised, global world. In the late 1980s, drawing inspiration from the rise of STS (science and technology studies), anthropologists took a further heretical step, accepting that science and technology were not modern creations—so rational and neutral that they existed beyond culture—but, rather, culture-laden, politics-saturated institutions crying out for critical analysis (Franklin 1995; Nader 1996). This coincided with the rise of feminist scholarship and gender theory, including a radical critique of science and technology as instruments of domination. Together with Foucault's arguments about bodies, discipline, and power, couched in terms of *biopower*, these new critical visions contributed the analytical tools for a vibrant new field, the anthropology of science and technology, which incorporated gender analysis as a core explanatory factor for how material practices, subjectivities, and governance connect in any specific context.

The late 1980s were also a time when technological innovations, including amniocentesis, foetal scanning, and in-vitro fertilisation, threw assumptions about the nature of biological reproduction, and human power to control it, into complete confusion. Since then, an ever-expanding panoply of reproductive technologies has repeatedly destabilised 'natural' gender roles and kinship relations, generating new ethical and legal quandaries about biology and kinship, life, death, and property rights, and the inequalities of gender, class, ethnicity, or nationality that underpin many of the technical operations involved. This has generated passionate debates around the world about the legitimate boundaries of technological innovation, shaking up the technological cultures of states and publics, and prompting the formation of new collectivities sharing values or goals related to reproduction: whether pro-lifers opposing the abortion of foetuses diagnosed with abnormalities or lesbian couples seeking ways to have biological offspring in hostile legal environments.

Anthropologists, long the professional experts on kinship systems, promptly seized the opportunities of this conjunction of technological, social, and theoretical ferment to examine biopower in action. They built a powerful and influential anthropological field examining how the new reproductive technologies influenced the ontologies, experiences, and possibilities of reproduction (Edwards et al. 1993; Franklin 1997). This body of work was both philosophically revelatory and, equally important (in the spirit of second-wave feminism and feminist manifestos such as *Our Bodies, Our Selves*[1]), politically engaged, taking on the mechanisms of patriarchy in family, society, and state, and the social inequalities as well as cultural differences of class, race, gender, and disability that affect reproductive decisions and access to technological intervention (Edwards 2000; Franklin and Ragoné 1998; Lock and Kaufert 1998; Markens et al. 2003; Rapp 1999). Anthropology's comparative perspective took such analysis well beyond the limits of common-sense Western assumptions, as in Marilyn Strathern's path-breaking collection of essays, *Reproducing the Future* (Strathern 1992). Prompted by the 1990 passage of the Bill for Human Fertilization and Embryology Act, Strathern famously brought insights from Melanesia, including the notion of parental 'dividuality', to bear on the possibilities opened up by the new procreative technologies under debate in the UK.

Initially anthropologists focused primarily on how reproductive technologies reshaped gender roles, disciplined gendered bodies, and imposed gendered social responsibilities in the Global North, where the technological innovations were pioneered. Soon attention turned to the Global South, where the moral and social challenges, and the demographic impact, were often even more dramatic (Inhorn 2007; Inhorn and Birenbaum-Carmeli 2008). To give an example connected to the case of the Iron Girls, China's leaders introduced the One-Child Family Policy (OCFP) in 1979. Simultaneously with the market reforms that disbanded collectives and encouraged household-level entrepreneurial activity, the OCFP was a classic example of biopower in action, a dramatically effective demographic intervention designed to discipline Chinese families as responsible citizens who would embrace the 'modern' attitudes towards reproduction necessary to make the nation a great economic power (Greenhalgh 2008).

The social urgency and philosophical richness of the challenges raised by reproductive technologies have only intensified over the decades as their use has spread around the world. Flows of genetic material have gone transnational, with all the inequalities that entails,[2] and technological innovation has moved from pills and amniocentesis into the ontologically charged realms of gene editing and cloning. So it is not surprising that the anthropological interest in reproductive technologies, which first took shape in the late 1980s, still has enormous stamina today (Edwards and Salazar 2009; Franklin 2007; Wahlberg and Gammeltoft 2018), nor that when most anthropologists think of technology and gender, it is reproductive technologies that immediately spring to mind.

In STS, sociology, and the history of technology, however, production and consumption figure as prominently as reproduction. While the main focus of studies of reproductive technologies has been on what we might call the reception of technology rather than its making—looking at the human impact of largely black-boxed technological interventions[3]—the perspectives of production and consumption shift attention to technical action as fashioning and self-fashioning. This approach looks at designers, makers, and users of specific technologies, or their use in work and leisure, communication, or education, as key sites where *action with or through technology* forms gendered subjectivities.[4] These themes are not absent from anthropology, but they are much less frequent and influential than studies of reproductive technologies and gender, and they often require reading between the lines. Given how important technological competence and sophistication are in modern societies as signifiers both of individual worth and of national status and potential, it is surprising not to find more. Looking at gender and technology in the world of work, for example, allows us to consider such themes as the performance of gender through technical action; the often complex relations of gender divisions of labour to regimes of power; how gendered attributions of technical aptitude or creativity inform hierarchies and values not only within the workplace, but in the nation or the global order; and last but certainly not least, what meanings or efficacy are attributed to technology in different contexts.

Anthropological studies of performing masculinity through technology range from a focus on scientists in the hyper-elite fields of high-energy physics and nuclear weapon design (Cohn 1987; Gusterson 1996; Traweek 1992), through car-mechanics for whom oil is the life-blood of masculinity and male bonding (Mellström 2004), to factory-floor workers, deprived of negotiating power by ruthless global competition, yet whose skilled intimacy with tools and machines nevertheless 'made it possible for a young man to express and confirm his ability to act' (Cross 2012, p. 140).

In contrast, as Cross notes, anthropological studies of women in factories tend to emphasise how the labour process, with its typically repetitive technical routines and gendered chains of command, alienates and disciplines women. In most such studies female agency, in the form of resistance or transgression, is exercised by escaping the machine through sickness (Ngai 2005; Ong 1987), or by hijacking it from its designed purpose (Fang 2013; Freeman 2000), not—as in the studies of masculinity—by gaining fulfilment through technical performance. Despite its critical intentions, anthropology here seems to channel the gender biases of the modern world, in which technological aptitude and agency are coded male.

TECHNOLOGY, MODERNITY, AND GENDER

For two centuries, since the Industrial Revolution, technology has been identified as an instrument of innovation and human progress. Societies and social groups were—and still are—ranked according to their degree of technological achievement. Race, ethnicity, class, and gender typically intertwine in the elaboration of such rankings, and their embedded claims to superiority and dominance both reflect and reinforce ideologies of social order (Lerman et al. 2003; Mellström 2009).

As they vied to extend their colonies and empires overseas, nineteenth- and twentieth-century citizens of the Western industrialised nations took 'machines as the measure of men' to justify their claims to rule over populations deemed primitive because they lacked steam engines or telegraphs (Adas 1989). At home, meanwhile, technology was used to construe women, non-whites, and the poor as primitives (Lerman 1997). From the 1850s to the present, the filtering and ranking of technical skills and their rewards by gender, race, and class has been steadily consolidated across the industrialising world in trade schools, engineering departments, technical colleges, and development programmes for the colonial or post-colonial world—and in employment practices and pay structures.

In the industrial worldview, 'real' technology was not represented by simple, ubiquitous work tools like needles, handlooms, or shovels, but by the machines that drove the economy forward. Technological innovation became an obsession: it was a key vector of progress, increasing efficiency, raising profits, and improving the human condition. And because real technology was all about innovation and transformation, what counted as technology even among industrial products was a continuously advancing frontier. Public fascination with trains and telegraphs as the heralds of modernity gave way to automobiles and aeroplanes, then to nuclear weapons and space technology, with AI (artificial intelligence) and the Internet of Things as today's acknowledged cutting edge.

Technology in the modern world is firmly coded male, but for most people this gendering of technology is not seen as ideological. Rather, men are viewed as having a *natural* affinity with technology while women are supposed to fear or dislike it. From childhood, men are encouraged to engage actively with machines, making, using, tinkering with, and loving them. Women may have to use technology in the workplace or in the home, but they are not expected to love it nor seek to understand it; they are considered passive beneficiaries of the inventive flame (Cockburn and Ormrod 1993; Mellström 2004).

Not surprisingly, then, the heroic inventors, the engineers, and experts to whom the capacity to actively develop technological knowledge is assigned were and still are almost exclusively men (Carrigan 2018; Stanley 1998; WES 2018).[5] The power of stereotypes has meant that women and other subalterns have been largely excluded from the knowledge elite of innovation. As members of the industrial workforce they are 'hands', not 'heads'; as office staff or farmers they are seen as simply operating the technical artefacts that are their work tools. The multiple technical skills they exercise do not count as technological competence. Employing women in technically skilled jobs is an easy way to cut costs, while demoting the prestige of the work by coding it female (Hicks 2017; Sacks 1988). Such de-skilling of women's work by re-classification reinstates gender inequalities in practice, while reinforcing stereotypes about the gendering of technology (Rosser 2005). Global divisions of labour likewise reproduce or exacerbate gendered stereotypes, for instance when transnational electronics companies seek out locations in Asia or Latin America with labour pools of women considered docile, deft-fingered, and cheap: ideal 'hands' for producing high-tech components in a field of cut-throat, cost-cutting competition (Fang 2013; Ngai 2005; Ong 1987).

Given the intimate entanglement of technological expertise with modernity, power, and respect, it is not surprising that it is also considered a potent force for equality and emancipation. Engels argued that the emancipation of women was an essential component of socialist revolution and that gender equality required liberating women from the patriarchal seclusion of the domestic sphere to engage in socially recognised labour (Engels 1884). Consequently, as a sign of their commitment to social transformation, many left-leaning nations followed the pioneering example of the early Soviet Union, admitting high percentages of women into the ranks of technological experts, both at the level of engineers and at the level of industrial mechanics or tractor drivers. In addition to the laudable goal of raising the status of women and thus modernising society, such policies had the added advantage of making fuller use of the nation's labour resources, especially when war took men away to battle. The most famous example here is 'Rosie the Riveter', the poster girl for American women in WWII, 'patriotically taking up factory jobs previously reserved for men' (Rupp 2004, p. 53).

When the war was over, however, and the de-mobbed soldiers needed their jobs back, Rosie was quickly banished back into the kitchen to be a good American wife and mom, promoting the national economy not through production but through reproduction-oriented consumption as she saved up for the appurtenances of a 'Cold War Kitchen' (Oldenziel and Zachmann 2009). Emancipation through technology has often proved conditional for women: women may prove their equality with men, working as engineers or riveters, just as long as men do not need their skilled jobs, and the nation does not require more babies or carers for the elderly. This system of gender coding, in conjunction with assumptions about what is and what is not 'real' technology, permeates the technological culture of modern societies. In what follows, however, I introduce a rare and radical subversion of that culture's principles: the Iron Girls movement of Maoist China, which flourished during the Cultural Revolution between 1966 and 1978.

No research permits were issued to foreign social scientists at that time, while internally anthropology was condemned as a bourgeois discipline, so there are no conventional ethnographies of the Iron Girls. There is, however, ample contemporary media documentation, and in the last few years a number of studies, several by former Iron Girls, have appeared that include interviews and oral histories (Jin 2006; Lu 2010; Wang 2017). Despite the importance of technology in forming the identity of the Iron Girls, these works discuss this aspect only superficially (Zhang and Liu 2015), if at all. Here I analyse those dynamics in anthropological terms, as I did earlier for technology and gender in imperial China (Bray 1997), by reading the sources against the grain to explore how material, cultural, and political context shaped not only the gendering of technology, but the very understanding of what technology signified, the forms it took, the agency it imparted, and its powers for change.

WORK AND THE RE-GENDERING OF TECHNOLOGY: MAOIST CHINA'S IRON GIRLS

A photograph that circulated around the world shows two helmeted women engineers of the Wuchang Women's Live Line Work Brigade dangling precariously in the air high above the Yangzi Valley. They are securing live, high-tension cables carrying 220,000 volts to a procession of pylons, newly erected along the main artery of the Yangzi River to supply electricity to the proliferating industries of central China. Women's work teams played a key role in building China's industrial power grid and other pioneering technical and material infrastructure in the 1960s and 1970s. 'We have progressed to the technical peak in live line work', one woman overhead line engineer said in an interview given to China's main newspaper, the *People's Daily*, in 1971.[6] A British overhead line engineer recently called this dangerous, highly skilled technical job, 'big boys' stuff' (Keating 2007). In Maoist China women did 'big boy's stuff' too.

The most famous example was the Iron Girls Brigade of Dazhai. Beginning in 1953, just after the village of Dazhai had been organised as a collective, the inhabitants of this arid, desperately poor, and environmentally degraded corner of China put together a ten-year plan to transform the landscape using the only resource they had: their own labour. Under the leadership of their illiterate village headman, Chen Yonggui, they built terraces and irrigation channels, houses, and access roads, all without machines, cement, or visiting experts. In 1963 a devastating flood swept away their achievements. As the villagers scrambled to rebuild, a young woman, Guo Fenglian, decided to organise a team of young women to undertake the hardest tasks. Armed not with heavy plant or sophisticated machinery but with simple shovels, wheel-barrows, determination, and ingenuity, the team worked wonders, sculpting the steep hills of Dazhai into cascades of fertile terraces. The villagers admiringly named these indomitable workers 'Iron Girls'. In 1964 Dazhai Commune and its Iron Girls' Brigade were both declared national models. Around the country, in agriculture and industry, from the new oilfields of Central Asia to the ancient farmlands of the heartlands now being redeveloped for intensive cropping, women's brigades sprang up everywhere.

The thirty years between the establishment of the People's Republic of China (PRC) in 1949 and the beginning of the so-called Reform Era in 1979 were a heady period of emancipatory promise and practice for women. In 1968, in a country where respectable women had traditionally been confined to the inner quarters of the home and where men were considered categorically superior to women in every domain, Mao made a revolutionary declaration: 'Times have changed: men and women are the same, whatever men comrades can do, women comrades can do too'. Women were exhorted to win equality and build a new world by working alongside men in the new agricultural and industrial collectives, taking an active part in the 'technological revolution' that would transform a patriarchal, so-called feudal society into a modern, egalitarian socialist state (Zhang and Liu 2015). Technological skills were a key weapon in the fight for gender equality. Under the slogan, 'Women hold up half the sky', millions of Chinese women could be found driving trains, operating oil-drills, lathes, and cranes, and building bridges, canals, and agricultural terraces. Iron Girls' Brigades and Women's Professional Brigades[7] worked on equal terms with male work teams in the drive to build the new socialist society—in fact they regularly beat their male colleagues in the production competitions that leaders of the time loved to organise (Funari and Mees 2013).

Throughout the Maoist era, the technical prowess, initiative, and determination of these women workers were celebrated in the Chinese media. Many were appointed to local and some to national political leadership. Outstanding achievements were honoured by the country's highest leaders. The photograph of the Wuchang Women's Brigade electrical engineers made it from the national press to the international propaganda journal *China Reconstructs*, under the title, 'How Chinese women won equality'. Posters, photos, and films of women hard at work in mines, factories, and construction sites, wielding tools or poring over blueprints they themselves had drawn up, circulated at home and abroad as powerful emblems of the liberated women of New China. Millions of women enrolled in the brigades.

The photograph of the Wuchang women workers attaching high-voltage wires to huge ceramic transformers fits perfectly into our expectations of how women would win gender equality by joining the ranks of a nation's technological pioneers, its aristocracy of labour. But what are we to make of equivalent pictures of the Dazhai Iron Girls, grinning triumphantly as they rest on their shovels among great mounds of mud?[8] A shovel is a very simple tool which most people would not think of as 'real' technology, but the Dazhai girls were explicitly celebrated as technological pioneers. So the anthropologist must ask: under what conditions are mud-shovelling and electrification made technologically equivalent?

The Cultural Revolution brought a revolution in the nation's technological culture (Bray 2019). During the 1950s China was closely aligned with the Soviet Union, receiving aid and following the same technocratic model of socialist development and hierarchies of expertise. Although model women workers proliferated, it was still an intellectual elite of university-educated men that produced and disseminated technical knowledge; industry was considered the crucible of social progress, providing both inputs and model for modernising agriculture and educating ignorant peasants. But following the Sino-Soviet split at the end of the 1950s, China was thrown onto its own resources. It had no capital, little industry, poor infrastructure, and more than 80% of the population were still peasants. Mao seized the opportunity to turn the classic technocratic model on its head. Rural China would be the crucible of a true social revolution; new technical knowledge would be produced by the masses; theory would emerge from collective practice and experience. China's past would not be repudiated wholesale, but would be resurrected and revised to serve the present. Throughout the Great Proletarian Cultural Revolution (1966–76) engineering schools were opened up to peasants; including women, tens of millions of 'educated youth' from the cities were sent in work teams 'up to the mountains, down to the villages' to learn from peasants, now repositioned epistemologically as knowledge-creators, and even CCP cadres were expected to learn from the masses (Andreas 2009; Schmalzer 2016).

It was in this iconoclastic context that shovels became advanced technology.[9] The fledgling PRC desperately lacked infrastructure: not only roads, bridges, and power grids to modernise industrial production and transport, but also land reclamation and hydraulic systems to increase supplies of food and raw materials. In lieu of capital and advanced technology, the CCP mobilised labour and history as resources. China's imperial past offered innumerable examples of engineering marvels—flood-control projects, irrigation works, canals, and bridges—achieved by coordinating the labour of thousands of workers equipped with shovels, buckets, wheel-barrows, winches, and ropes.

Hitherto the people identified as the initiators and heroes of these projects had been the elite men in charge: real officials or legendary heroes who devised sophisticated plans for supplying and managing ambitious and innovative projects. During the Cultural Revolution technological agency and the credit for the determination, ingenuity, and discipline needed to carry through such initiatives were transferred to the workers of the past,[10] and to the work teams of the present. The agency of work teams was not mere Party window-dressing; many workers did truly feel empowered (Jin 2006; Wang 2017). They devised the plans for collective action that allowed them to solve local challenges triumphantly, learning through practice, undaunted by failure, trying again and again, persuading doubters, working day and night through physical exhaustion, pain, and danger to achieve their final goal.[11] In accounting for their success, neither the workers themselves nor the Party or the media gave priority to conventional technological criteria: spirit, sacrifice, self-reliance, and determination were the key elements of their narratives. For the new socialist worker, female or male, technical competence was a means to an end, not a goal in itself: the efficacy and value of technology lay as much in action, in the politically transformative process of collective labour, as in the material outcome.

In these terms a shovel is as powerful and sophisticated a technology as a tractor, for the most important products of socialist labour are the new socialist person and the new socialist landscape. The distinction between traditional and modern tools and knowledge formats is blurred as manual workers learn on the job, collectively devising technical plans and management strategies. In ten years the Women's Bridge Building Company constructed six steel bridges in harsh terrain. Although the women had received little or no formal training, each of the bridges overcame a different technical challenge, and all are still standing today. Yet, in interviews, the women put hauling sacks of cement and manhandling steel girders on a par with drawing up the blueprints (Lu 2010, pp. 174–179). Indeed, the majestic transformations wrought simply with shovels and baskets, the cascading terraces that replaced eroded hillsides, the reservoirs and canals that brought water to thirsty fields, were achievements as impressive as the new oil-rigs or bridges, and were equally crucial contributions to building the nation.

In Maoist China the Iron Girls and Professional Women's Brigades were icons of gender equality, proof that women could equal or surpass men in technical jobs and could therefore contribute as much if not more than men to building a new socialist world. Embodying 'strength, self-confidence, initiative and familiarity with new technology', the Iron Girls represented the Maoist culmination of a new socialist ideal of womanhood (Chen 2003, p. 274). They were emulated by numerous women yearning to break out of traditional family roles and lead useful lives. There was, however, an unfortunate side-effect of CCP policies to take women out of the home and into the labour force: domestic work and its associated technical skills, the technologies of social reproduction, were now condemned as 'stupid' and worthless, so women could no longer take pride in them or view them as a contribution to society (Eyferth 2012; Flitsch 2008).

By 1974 more than two million women belonged to 340,000 Iron Girls and Women's Professional Brigades (Lu 2010, p. 94). The CCP celebrated them as 'the representational trope of a revolutionary era', and the public admired them for playing a highly visible and honoured role in the material and social transformation of their nation. They enjoyed social prestige as a group, despite being women (Jin 2006, p. 630). As peasant and working-class Chinese women came out of the isolation of their homes into the social labour settings of the Iron Girls era, they acquired a collective consciousness of their own social position and power. The Iron Girls offered a vision of female agency and possibility, a taste of freedom despite the hardship, the loss of which many women quietly mourned in the post-Mao decades.

One criticism levied at the Iron Girls movement post-1978 was that it ignored the constraints of women's reproductive physiology. Certainly most Iron Girls were unmarried. Rural wives found it difficult to abandon family responsibilities to labour through the night on infrastructural projects. The Professional Women's Brigades did include numerous married women with children; as they were based in industrial units they could rely on communal child-care facilities, even if they felt obliged to spend as little time as possible on maternal tasks like breast-feeding (Lu 2010, pp. 170, 283). Ultimately, however, women putting work before family was difficult for most Chinese to accept in practice. Once Maoist ideology was superseded and communal care facilities fell by the wayside with de-collectivisation in the 1980s, it was easy to condemn the Iron Girls and Professional Women as completely unfeminine.

Even more insidiously from a feminist perspective, as conventional techno-cratic values and hierarchies were restored in the name of rapid economic development, modernist gendering conventions resumed. School curricula, hiring practices, and media messages all hammered home the revisionist mes-sage that technological competence came naturally to men, whereas women were mentally unsuited to technological or scientific activity. With the turn to capitalist rationality and the rapid expansion of industry, China's development required a flexible labour force. The gender coding of labour skills was a very effective way to reduce women to a reserve labour pool (Honig and Hershatter 1988, pp. 242–272). As the engineers rose again to positions of national lead-ership (Andreas 2009; Greenhalgh 2008), workers of both sexes were deprived of technological agency, becoming hands, not heads, and when demand for workers fluctuated, women were the first to be laid off, a situation that would not have surprised Rosie the Riveter.

What are we to make of the brief moment when communist China appeared to have successfully turned the 'gender coding of modernity' (Harding 2008, p. 199) inside out, assigning to women not only technological skills but also technical capacities for organisation, leadership, and innovation? Why was it an interlude, rather than a lasting social transformation, and why did shovels, like women, lose their status in post-Reforms technological culture?

Forty years after the movement ended, we can analyse the story of the Iron Girls from start to finish, locating it in a longer genealogy of Chinese techno-logical cultures and gender regimes, as well as transnational circuits of knowl-edge production and other resource flows. The Iron Girl case is particularly illuminating because it shows a national government operating a deliberate political strategy to mobilise subaltern groups through technological action in order to break down social hierarchies, reconstitute society, and build new socialist collectivities, subjectivities, and values. It clearly shows how any re-gendering of technology, deliberate or incidental, also engages cross-cutting hierarchies of generation, class, profession, and education, the urban-rural divide and cleavages between 'traditional' and 'modern', and 'reproductive' and 'productive' labour. It affirms that in the modern industrial age, socially recognised technological competence is empowering for women as individuals, and as members of social groups, but shows the fragility of such achievements.

Comparing the anti-technocratic ontologies of technology and expertise during the Cultural Revolution to the capitalist rationalities of the post-collectivisation Reform period reminds us not only that the relationship between gender and technology is continuously renegotiated, but that these mutually constitutive categories are both equally fluid. A woman's perceived contribution to society shifts from homebound dependent to pioneering engineer of the new socialist world, then to disposable, unskilled factory fodder or model mother running a technically well-equipped home. One day a shovel is beneath notice, the next it has become a technology of social revolution, and then it disappears from the annals of technology, replaced by space shuttles and nano-technology institutes as national icons, and by smart-phones and high-speed trains as fashioners of everyday identity.

Meanwhile, in the domestic sphere, under the One-Child Family Policy women became responsible not only for controlling their fertility but for raising 'good quality' children to build a modern, rich nation. To this end, the post-Reform era has required women to acquire skills in a portfolio of biological, educational, and life-style—as well as work-related—technologies (e.g. Gottschang 2018; Lim 2008; Fang 2013; Zhang 2017), which deserve but have not yet received attention as a cohesive set of gendered reproductive technologies.

To conclude reproductive technologies have captured the imagination of anthropologists not least because of the challenges, social and philosophical, that they pose by generating 'emergent forms of life' (Fischer 2005). By comparison, the technologies of factory or kitchen may appear to present little that is novel for our understanding of gender regimes. But the case of the Iron Girls shows how production practices can also raise challenging philosophical and existential questions about the very nature of technology as a human activity. Viewed from the perspective of the long term, it also confirms that if we seek a fuller anthropological understanding of technology and gender, it makes little sense to look separately at reproduction and production.

Acknowledgements I would like to thank the editors of the *Handbook*, and the two anonymous reviewers, for their most helpful and constructive suggestions. The chapter is greatly improved in consequence.

NOTES

1. Published in 1971 by the Boston Women's Collective, the radical feminist handbook *OBOS* (as it quickly became known) encouraged women to resist the repressive domination of the medical establishment and take control of their own health and sexuality; re-issued many times, *OBOS* has been immensely influential internationally (Boston Women's Collective 1971; Davis 2007).
2. Israel is a case that has attracted particular attention (Birenbaum-Carmeli 2010; Gooldin 2013; Kravel-Tovi 2012).
3. Black boxes are devices or practices 'that are opaque to outsiders, often because their contents are regarded as "technical"' (MacKenzie 2005, p. 555).
4. For just a taste of this vast literature and its scope, see (Bix 2014; Horowitz 2001; Laemmli 2015; Maines 2001; Oldenziel and Zachmann 2009).
5. In the domain of reproductive technologies we must mention Ian Wilmut, the 'inventor' of Dolly the cloned sheep, who performed a God-like act of gender-

bending to 'overturn in a blaze of microvoltage the masculinist legacy of the "passive" egg' (Franklin 2007, p. 42).

6. (Lu 2010, pp. 129, 124). A still from a very popular film made in 1972 (Lu 2010, p. 124), this photo featured as the front cover of China's international propaganda magazine *China Reconstructs* (issue XXIII, 3, March 1974).

7. The 'Women's Professional Brigades' included mostly married women and were typically employed in industrial tasks; the 'Iron Girls' were unmarried rural women working in their home district.

8. Lu (2010, p. 73); https://www.gettyimages.co.uk/detail/news-photo/learn-from-dazhai-in-agriculture-poster-news-photo/527191406.

9. There is a curious analogy here with Frederick Taylor's famous investigation, presented to the US Congress in 1911, of 'the science of shoveling' (Taylor 2004, pp. 50–55). Taylor's goal, however, was not to glorify the labourers but to optimise their efficiency.

10. Histories of science and technology, which burgeoned during the Cultural Revolution, represented the grand projects of Imperial China as mass science in action.

11. Naturally we hear little about projects that did not ultimately succeed.

References

Adas, M. (1989). *Machines as the measure of men: Science, technology, and ideologies of Western dominance.* Ithaca, NY: Cornell University Press.

Andreas, J. (2009). *Rise of the Red engineers: The Cultural Revolution and the origins of China's new class.* Stanford: Stanford University Press.

Bijker, W. E. (2007). American and Dutch coastal engineering: Differences in risk conception and differences in technological culture. *Social Studies of Science, 37*(1), 143–151.

Birenbaum-Carmeli, D. (2010). Genetic relatedness and family formation in Israel: Lay perceptions in the light of state policy. *New Genetics and Society, 29*(1), 73–85.

Bix, A. S. (2014). *Girls coming to tech!: A history of American engineering education for women.* Cambridge, MA: The MIT Press.

Boston Women's Collective. (1971). *Our bodies, ourselves.* Boston: New England Free Press.

Bray, F. (1997). *Technology and gender: Fabrics of power in late imperial China.* Berkeley: University of California Press.

Bray, F. (2007). Gender and technology. *Annual Review of Anthropology, 36,* 37–53.

Bray, F. (2019). Technology. In H. Chiang (Ed.), *The making of the human sciences in China: Historical and conceptual foundations* (pp. 29–51). Leiden: Brill.

Carrigan, C. (2018). 'Different isn't free': Gender @ work in a digital world. *Ethnography, 19*(3), 336–359.

Chen, T. M. (2003). Female icons, feminist iconography? Socialist rhetoric and women's agency in 1950s China. *Gender & History, 15*(2), 268–295.

Cockburn, C., & Ormrod, S. (1993). *Gender and technology in the making.* London: Sage.

Cohn, C. (1987). Sex and death in the rational world of defense intellectuals. *Signs: Journal of Women in Culture and Society, 12*(4), 687–718.

Cross, J. (2012). Technological intimacy: Re-engaging with gender and technology in the global factory. *Ethnography, 13*(2), 119–143.

Davis, K. (2007). *The making of our bodies, ourselves: How feminism travels across borders.* Durham: Duke University Press.

Edwards, J. (2000). *Born and bred: Idioms of kinship and new reproductive technologies in England.* Oxford: Oxford University Press.

Edwards, J., Franklin, S., Hirsch, E., Price, F., & Strathern, M. (1993). *Technologies of procreation: Kinship in the age of assisted conception.* Manchester: Manchester University Press.

Edwards, J., & Salazar, C. (Eds.) (2009). *European kinship in the age of biotechnology.* New York and Oxford: Berghahn Books.

Engels, F. (1884). *The origins of the family, private property and the state.* Zurich: Hottingen.

Eyferth, J. (2012). Women's work and the politics of homespun in socialist China, 1949–1980. *International Review of Social History, 57*(3), 365–391.

Fang, I. (2013). The girls who are keen to get married. In C. Stafford (Ed.), *Ordinary ethics in China* (pp. 66–79). London: A&C Black.

Fischer, M. M. J. (2005). Technoscientific infrastructures and emergent forms of life: A commentary. *American Anthropologist, 107*(1), 55–61.

Flitsch, M. (2008). Knowledge, embodiment, skill and risk: Anthropological perspectives on women's everyday technologies in rural northern China. *East Asian Science, Technology and Society, 2*(2), 265–288.

Franklin, S. (1995). Science as culture, cultures of science. *Annual Review of Anthropology, 24*(1), 163–184.

Franklin, S. (1997). *Embodied progress: A cultural account of assisted conception.* London and New York: Routledge.

Franklin, S. (2007). *Dolly mixtures: The remaking of genealogy.* Durham, NC and London: Duke University Press.

Franklin, S., & Ragoné, H. (Eds.) (1998). *Reproducing reproduction: Kinship, power, and technological innovation.* Philadelphia: University of Pennsylvania Press.

Freeman, C. (2000). *High tech and high heels in the global economy: Women, work, and pink-collar identities in the Caribbean.* Durham, NC and London: Duke University Press.

Funari, R., & Mees, B. (2013). Socialist emulation in China: Worker heroes yesterday and today. *Labor History, 54*(3), 240–255.

Gooldin, S. (2013). 'Emotional rights', moral reasoning, and Jewish–Arab alliances in the regulation of in-vitro-fertilization in Israel: Theorizing the unexpected consequences of assisted reproductive technologies. *Social Science & Medicine, 83*, 90–98.

Gottschang, S. (2018) *Formulas for motherhood in a Chinese hospital.* Ann Arbor: University of Michigan Press.

Greenhalgh, S. (2008). *Just one child: Science and policy in Deng's China.* Berkeley and London: University of California Press.

Gusterson, H. (1996). *Nuclear rites: A weapons laboratory at the end of the Cold War.* Berkeley, CA and London: University of California Press.

Harding, S. G. (2008). *Sciences from below: Feminisms, postcolonialities, and modernities.* Durham: Duke University Press.

Hicks, M. (2017). *Programmed inequality: How Britain discarded women technologists and lost its edge in computing.* Cambridge, MA: The MIT Press.

Honig, E., & Hershatter, G. (1988). *Personal voices: Chinese women in the 1980's.* Stanford, CA: Stanford University Press.

Horowitz, R. (Ed.) (2001). *Boys and their toys? Masculinity, class, and technology in America.* New York and London: Routledge.

Inhorn, M. C. (Ed.) (2007). *Reproductive disruptions: Gender, technology, and biopolitics in the new millennium.* New York: Berghahn Books.

Inhorn, M. C., & Birenbaum-Carmeli, D. (2008). Assisted reproductive technologies and culture change. *Annual Review of Anthropology, 37*(1), 177–196.

Jin, Y. (2006). Rethinking the 'Iron Girls': Gender and labour during the Chinese Cultural Revolution (trans: Manning, K. E., & Chu, L.). *Gender & History, 18*(3), 613–634.

Keating, M. (2007, October 6). A working life: The overhead line engineer. *The Guardian.* https://www.theguardian.com/money/2007/oct/06/work5.

Kravel-Tovi, M. (2012). 'National mission': Biopolitics, non-Jewish immigration and Jewish conversion policy in contemporary Israel. *Ethnic and Racial Studies, 35*(4), 737–756.

Laemmli, W. E. (2015). A case in pointe: Romance and regimentation at the New York City ballet. *Technology and Culture, 56*(1), 1–27.

Lerman, N. E. (1997). 'Preparing for the duties and practical business of life': Technological knowledge and social structure in mid-19th-century Philadelphia. *Technology and Culture, 38*(1), 31–59.

Lerman, N. E., Oldenziel, R., & Mohun, A. (Eds.) (2003). *Gender & technology: A reader.* Baltimore: Johns Hopkins University Press.

Lim, S. S. (2008). Technological domestication in the Asian homestead: Comparing the experiences of middle class families in China and South Korea. *East Asian Science, Technology and Society, 2*(2), 189–209.

Lock, M., & Kaufert, P. A. (Eds.) (1998). *Pragmatic women and body politics.* Cambridge and New York: Cambridge University Press.

Lu, C. X. (2010). *How the Iron Girls movement changed women in China—The power of discourse in constructing social norms* (Ph.D. Thesis, University of Hawai'i at Manoa).

MacKenzie, D. (2005). Opening the black boxes of global finance. *Review of International Political Economy, 12*(4), 555–576.

Maines, R. P. (2001). *The technology of orgasm: 'Hysteria,' the vibrator, and women's sexual satisfaction.* Baltimore and London: Johns Hopkins University Press.

Markens, S., Browner, C., & Preloran, H. (2003). 'I'm not the one they're sticking the needle into': Latino couples, fetal diagnosis, and the discourse of reproductive rights. *Gender & Society, 17*(3), 462–481.

Mellström, U. (2004). Machines and masculine subjectivity: Technology as an integral part of men's life experiences. *Men and Masculinities, 6*(4), 368–382.

Mellström, U. (2009). The intersection of gender, race and cultural boundaries, or why is computer science in Malaysia dominated by women? *Social Studies of Science, 39*(6), 885–907.

Nader, L. (Ed.) (1996). *Naked science: Anthropological inquiry into Boundaries, power and knowledge.* New York: Routledge.

Ngai, P. (2005). *Made in China: Women factory workers in a global workplace.* Durham, NC and London: Duke University Press.

Oldenziel, R., & Zachmann, K. (2009). *Cold War kitchen: Americanization, technology, and European users.* Cambridge, MA: The MIT Press.

Ong, A. (1987). *Spirits of resistance and capitalist discipline: Factory women in Malaysia*. Albany: State University of New York Press.

Rapp, R. R. (1999). *Testing women, testing the fetus: The social impact of amniocentesis in America*. New York and London: Routledge.

Rosser, S. V. (2005). Through the lenses of feminist theory: Focus on women and information technology. *Frontiers: A Journal of Women Studies, 26*(1), 1–23.

Rupp, L. J. (2004). From Rosie the Riveter to the global assembly line: American women on the world stage. *OAH Magazine of History, 18*(4), 53–57.

Sacks, K. B. (1988). *Caring by the hour: Women, work, and organizing at Duke Medical Center*. Champaign: University of Illinois Press.

Schmalzer, S. (2016). *Red Revolution, Green Revolution: Scientific farming in socialist China*. Chicago: University of Chicago Press.

Stanley, A. (1998). *Mothers and daughters of invention: Notes for a revised history of technology*. New Brunswick, NJ.: Rutgers University Press.

Strathern, M. (1992). *Reproducing the future: Essays on anthropology, kinship and the new reproductive technologies*. Manchester: Manchester University Press.

Taylor, F. W. (2004). *Scientific management*. London and New York: Routledge.

Traweek, S. (1992). *Beamtimes and lifetimes: The world of high energy physicists*. Cambridge, MA: Harvard University Press.

Wahlberg, A., & Gammeltoft, T. (Eds.) (2018). *Selective reproduction in the 21st century*. London and New York: Palgrave Macmillan.

Wang, Z. (2017). *Finding women in the state: A socialist Feminist Revolution in the People's Republic of China, 1949–1964*. Berkeley: University of California Press.

WES. (2018). *Statistics on women in engineering*. Retrieved from https://www.wes.org.uk/content/wesstatistics. Accessed 8 July 2021.

Zhang, J. (2017). (Extended) family car, filial consumer-citizens: Becoming properly middle class in post-socialist South China. *Modern China* 43(1), 36–65.

Zhang, M., & Liu, B. (2015). Technology and gender: A case study on "Iron Girls" in China (1950s–1970s). *Technology in Society, 43*, 86–94. https://doi.org/10.1016/j.techsoc.2015.04.005

CHAPTER 23

Imagineerism: Technology, Robots, Kinship. Perspectives from Japan

Kinship

Jennifer Robertson

Technology tends to be regarded as a domain of innovation and invention that is forward-looking and focused on the future. I draw from my ethnographic and archival research in Japan to show that advanced technology, in particular robotics, and progressive values should not be conflated; the two are not automatically congruent. Idioms of family and kinship have been deployed to imbue Japanese technologies (or engineered artefacts) with uniquely Japanese character, and even to frame them as nostalgic by-products of Japanese uniqueness.[1] Yet Japan is also regarded as the go-to site for futuristic discourses, images, and forecasts of human-robot relations. I argue that these images are actually outdated and these forecasts backward-looking. Japan serves as a case study of imagineerism, or of the consequences of techno-nationalism as a declinist narrative; that is, imagining a robotised society of the future involves the reimagining of past society as an ideal to resurrect.

KINSHIP TECHNOLOGY

Kinship practices are usefully understood as a technology that produces ontologies, or, as frameworks that describe, represent, and create human relationships. These relationships are produced on several levels, from the individual

J. Robertson (✉)
University of Michigan, Ann Arbor, MI, USA
e-mail: jennyrob@umich.edu

© The Author(s), under exclusive license to Springer Nature Singapore Pte Ltd. 2022
M. H. Bruun et al. (eds.), *The Palgrave Handbook of the Anthropology of Technology*, https://doi.org/10.1007/978-981-16-7084-8_23

and familial to the communal and the national. They are biological, as flesh-and-blood humans are the nominal subject, but they are not necessarily genetic (or genomic) in their relationality. Although a rhetoric of 'blood' ties, or bio-genetics, may inform the functional structuring of kinship systems, social and cultural considerations, including individual sexual and gender orientations, have considerable symbolic and semantic importance. David Schneider (1968) broke new ground in kinship studies by demonstrating that Euro-American kinship was a system of symbols and meanings, and not simply a network of biogenetically interrelated, heteronormative nuclear familial roles. Kath Weston (1997) further challenged the heterosexist and procreational basis of kinship presented as self-evident by many anthropologists. She showed that many Americans, including African-Americans, lesbians, and gay males, do not actu-ally hold to a strict biogenetic interpretation of kinship, and instead exercise agency in choosing their families and kin.[2] Not mentioned by Weston but within her ethnographic framework are objectùm-sexuals, individuals who forge intimate relationships with objects that might also become marriage part-ners and families of choice (Frizell 2015; Objectùm-Sexuality Internationale 2015). Additionally, although they did not openly critique the Eurocentric blinders of human exceptionalism, early ethnographers of non-Western societ-ies and cultures reported many examples of non-human referents in kinship systems and lineages (e.g. Evans-Pritchard 1950, p. 362). More recently, bio-artists have experimented with creating novel kinships between humans and non-human agents (Kac 2009 [2007]).

Kinship thus provides a framework for human-robot and human-object rela-tionships by activating and engaging a diverse range of affinities transacted among humans, animals, organic, and inorganic things without assuming a priori their inherent goodness or badness, naturalness or unnaturalness. The term 'neo-kinship' has been used to describe fluid and complex forms of kin-ship practices, such those between humans, wildlife, and objects, enabled by biotechnology and robotics that are incorporated into or replacing the nuclear family (Campbell 2010; Neo-Kinship 2017). However, the use of 'neo' is pre-sentist, as if the interface (or kinship) of human and non-human (whether organic or inorganic) were a very recent phenomenon made possible by com-panion bots and digital assistants. Likewise, the technology aspect of kinship is neither limited to nor monopolised by new assistive reproductive technologies like in vitro fertilisation (IVF). In her insightful work on IVF, Sarah Franklin (2013), shows how technology has created the ability to 'culture biology in vitro' and to enable the emergence of new biological relatives. At the same time, however, IVF, modelled on biogenetically based systems of family forma-tion, technologically reproduces dominant Euro-American kinship patterns. IVF's logic is recursive; it 'goes forward by going backward' (Mathiason 2015, pp. 221–222)—a trajectory that figures centrally in my association of advanced technology with a declinist narrative. To recognise kinship itself as a technol-ogy is to understand and appreciate how manifold relationships and affinities among diverse agents are forged and transacted. Kinship activates and engages a network of relatedness, bonding, and obligations that enables the transmission of property and knowledge across generations through a classification of different agents and actors. This conception of kinship and relatedness underscores that they are social and cultural constructs and, to reiterate, do not map directly onto biogenetic relationships.

In this chapter, I focus on Japan as a case study illustrating how the technology of kinship structures human-robot relationships. That kinship is deployed both metaphorically and materially to structure (gendered) personhood and communities alike is well understood in the social sciences. That kinship informs the actual development of newly engineered technologies, such as household robots, is less understood. The imagined uses of technology—and here I include kinship—can structure the political framing of technological research and influence the physical development of technologies, such as robots (Müller and Tworek 2016, p. 106). 'Imagined uses' augments Raymond Williams' oft-cited observation that specific institutional forms do not follow from the character of technology per se, but from the predominant political and economic institutions of different societies (Williams 1981, p. 236).

Imagineering Versus Imagineerism

Japan is often characterised in the global mass media and Japanese policy papers alike as a 'robot superpower' (*robotto taikoku*). The country is imagined as the go-to site for images and (mercantilist) discourses of post-industrial forecasts about techno-national futures in multiple senses of new markets, economic security, resource sustainability, and social stability. Techno-nationalism may focus primarily on the new fields of robotics, artificial intelligence and machine learning, quantum computing and information systems, energy storage, and semiconductors (Capri 2020, p. 6), but, as I argue in the case of Japan, the imagined futures they occupy are not forward but backward-looking. That is, the *imagining* of a robotised society of the future is informed by the *reimagining* of past social structures and relationships (Robertson 2018a, b). These structures and relationships centre on notions of kinship and the alleged uniqueness of the Japanese cultural character. The enthusiasm for and embrace of advanced technologies, like robotics, should not be conflated with progressive thinking on the part of political leaders or engineers (cf. Zaidi 2008, p. 64).

I coined the term 'imagineerism' to describe what I have observed as a dominant mode of the political framing that structures the imagined uses of technology, including the technology of kinship. As a cognitive process, imagination is not value free; rather, it is constrained by experience and learned orientations, such as those fostered by upbringing and kinship practices. Imagineerism is an ideology and doctrine that advocates, endorses, and sanctions a techno-nationalist agenda of 'future-as-idealised-past'. The political and socio-cultural framing of research on human-robot interaction is mostly, perhaps inevitably, conservative and anachronous. As an ideology, imagineerism is less about 'innovation' and more about 'renovation'; that is, it does not advocate *new* values but rather the *renewal* of old values (Robertson 2008, 2018b, p. 35). Imagineerism incentivises 'conceptual conservatism' by imagining future social institutions, such as the household, as technologically improved and idealised versions of past ones.

As defined by philosopher of science Moti Nissani (1994), conceptual conservatism is the human tendency to cling to strongly held beliefs long after these beliefs have been decisively discredited or refuted. Think of present-day subscribers to flat-earth theory. Such behaviour is not simply an expression of wilful ignorance or emotional instability but also a product of 'purely cognitive aspects' of 'the failure to accommodate new ideas', as Nissani enumerates (1994, pp. 307–308).[3] Thus, imagineerism, as I define it, is a doctrine of stodgy banality, far from the ingenuity and resourcefulness associated with words like 'innovation' and 'imagination'. Although nearly identical, imagineerism must not be confused with 'imagineers'—persons who imaginatively engineer new types of technology—or 'imagineering'.[4]

I began this chapter with a discussion of the technology of kinship. In the context of imagineerism as a backward-looking deployment of advanced technology, I will now broaden my definition and use of 'technology' before returning to kinship as a framework for techno-nationalist discourse as well as for human-robot relations and robo-ethics. Technology also refers to the technical means or tools, both imagined and actually created, that are applied to affect a community's or society's ability to shape and adapt to a variety of environmental forces. Thomas Hughes (2005), a historian of science, points out that the Indo-European root of 'technology' is *teks*, meaning to fabricate or weave; the Greek *tekhnē* referred to an art, craft, or skill. Both of these early meanings, he observes, 'suggest a process of making' and creating, thereby suggesting an overarching definition of technology that emphasises creativity and control. In Europe and the United States, the word 'technology' was mainstreamed in the late 1950s as a more inclusive term than 'engineering', which it subsumed. Today, the word is also often used anachronistically to name things that in the nineteenth century were simply called machines (Hughes 2005, pp. 3–4).

Hughes' definition of technology corresponds to one advanced by Kenkichi Satō, a Japanese historian of technology and ecoethics. Satō emphasises that, fundamentally, 'technology (*gijutsu*) is learning from doing' or, literally, 'experience-based embodied practices' (*keiken kara mi ni tsukeru*). Technology is, he further explains, the 'actualization of the process of a successful series of perfected skills' (*seikō shita waza no rensa ga sugureta tekiyōryoku sunawachi 'gijutsu' o jitsugen suru*) (Satō 2008, pp. 51–52). Combined, Hughes' and Satō's definition of technology can be summarised as both a process and product of imagineering, that is, imagination plus engineering.

In the 1990s, the word *monozukuri* (lit. thing-making) was coined to describe Japanese manufacturing technologies and is widely used in advertising within Japan to emphasise the 'unique' character of Japanese imagineered products (Monozukuri 2016; Pringle 2010; Robertson 2018b, pp. 57–58).

The Japanese expression, 'Galápagos Syndrome' (*garapagosuka*, lit. Galápagosisation), refers to *monozukuri* products, especially mobile phones and tiny cars, designed exclusively for the fickle Japanese market. Although these are not made by traditional methods, they are specially crafted for Japanese consumers. The iPhone may be the best-selling smart phone in Japan, but close to half of all cell phones purchased in Japan are specially designed Japanese-made flip phones redolent of an earlier era of telecommunications (Byford 2017; Kawabata 2019; Stockwin and Ampiah 2017, p. 130). These examples of *monozukuri* illustrate the ways major industries foster cultural nostalgia through made-in-Japan-for-Japanese products (Shoji 2020).[5] On its own, nostalgia-tinged imagineering is a benign exercise. It is when transposed as cultural chauvinism, however, that the rhetoric of mystified nostalgia is easily manipulated to promote a conservative, backward-looking social order. As I will elaborate below, techno-nationalism and imagineerism go hand in hand.

'Blood' and *Kizuna*

At this juncture, a review of the historical context for the formation of Japanese techno-nationalism is in order. In the late nineteenth century, when feudalism was supplanted by a modern constitutional monarchy established under the Meiji Constitution (1889), kinship was invoked and exploited as a cipher for the nation, or 'family state' (*kazoku kokka*), a conflation of ethno-nationalism and culture. The introduction of universal education, conscription, national newspapers, and a household registration system (*koseki seido*) unified the Japanese people as members of a national household. In the words of the *Imperial Rescript on Education* (1890) memorised by students, the Japanese people were unique in constituting a filial family sharing the same 'blood' and ethnicity, presided over by the patriarch-emperor and his unbroken Imperial lineage.

As imagined in the twinned contexts of modernisation and imperialism, the technology of kinship reinforced a chauvinist ideology that fuelled Japan's emergence as an imperial power. A post-war constitution, promulgated in 1947, abolished the peerage but retained the emperor as a cultural symbol, granted universal suffrage, included a bill of rights, and outlawed the right to declare war. Although individual sovereignty is encoded in the constitution, the *koseki* (household registry) system was never dismantled. The 'family state' was thereby effectively preserved although the imperialist term *kazoku kokka* has been replaced by the folksier term *kizuna* (kin-like ties and bonds). Voted the ideograph (*kanji*) of the year in 2011, *kizuna* was widely used in government campaigns to promote national solidarity in the wake of the devastating trifold disaster (earthquake, tsunami, nuclear reactor meltdown) of 11 March 2011 and more recently in public safety announcements during the Covid-19 pandemic. The *koseki* system sustains deeply entrenched definitions of Japanese nationality, ethnicity, gender roles, and family structure as intrinsically linked primarily through the primacy of 'blood' or descent.

Despite references to 'blood' in Japanese nationalist discourse, households may include individuals who are 'dominant ethnic' Japanese citizens but not genetically related to a given family. Pragmatism dictates that there is no premium on biogenetic membership per se. If a married couple is childless or if their adult children are not competent, then a successor can be adopted. The adoptee, usually male, then assumes the family's surname and is added to their *koseki*. These adopted members add depth and strength to the household, which, ultimately, is an economic, corporate entity that must be reproduced in perpetuity—the members are generational custodians.[6] The *koseki* has also been used to demonstrate 'kintimacy' between humans and robots, even those that are not humanoids. In November 2010, Paro, a harp seal robot that has seen international success as a therapy animaloid, was granted a household registry (*koseki*). The inventor was recorded as the seal-bot's father. Media coverage of Paro's *koseki* was favourable (Robertson 2018b, pp. 137–140).

On the surface, the conferral of Paro's *koseki* may seem benign and inconsequential—even gimmicky. Quite the contrary. The *koseki* conflates family, nationality, and citizenship based on *jus sanguinus*. It also 'legally and ideologically prioritises the *ie* (household) over the individual as the fundamental social unit in Japanese society' (Chapman 2011, p. 3). Paro's 'blood', a product of *monozukuri*, consisted of Japanese manufactured and manually assembled electronic parts and synthetic materials. These definitions and deployments of family and *kizuna* by conservative politicians and engineers, have framed robotics in a techno-nationalist light. They claim that 'robots will rescue' Japan from labour shortages by eliminating the need for immigrants and thus helping to preserve the country's alleged ethnic homogeneity. And, as I elaborate below, robots are also imagined to help to restore 'family values' and to secure the stability of the household as a microcosm of Japanese society.

INNOVATION AS RENOVATION

Shinzō Abe, who, for health reasons, resigned the prime ministership in August 2020, eight years into his second term (2012–2020), is a 'Meiji man'; that is, he is both a moderniser and traditionalist. Topping Abe's nationalist agenda has been the revision of the 1947 constitution along the lines of the imperial constitution of 1889. Halfway through his short first stint (2006–2007) as prime minister, Abe, an enthusiastic advocate of Japan's robotisation, introduced *Innovation 25*, an ambitious plan for fully robotised households and workplaces by 2025 (Government of Japan 2007). (The plan remains on the official website of the prime minister along with updated versions.) I describe *Innovation 25* as 'retro-visionary' because it imagines that robots and technology will restore the 'traditional' household (*ie*), a microcosm of the family state, as opposed to the post-war 'democratic state' (*minshu kokka*), recently (re)imagined in terms of *kizuna*. 'Born in Japan' robots are imagined in *Innovation 25* as playing a key role in the preservation and stabilisation of not just any family, but specifically the patriarchal extended family, or *ie*, which conservatives regard as the core of a stable society. Clearly, techno-nationalism is a declinist narrative; preservation and stabilisation are invoked as motives *because* ideologues claim that family values and *kizuna* have been eroded by individualistic desires and pursuits.[7]

What demographic trends prompted *Innovation 25*? The number of two-generation families is declining in Japan and three-generation households are increasingly rare. The population of 125.9 million is ageing rapidly and the birth-rate has fallen below the mortality rate, prompting worries among pundits of a demographic catastrophe within several decades. Presently, nearly 30 per cent of the population is over 65 years of age, and only 13 per cent under 15 years of age. (When Abe introduced *Innovation 25*, the population was nearly 128 million, 21 per cent of whom were over 65 years of age.) Similar demographic profiles are shared by Italy, Portugal, and Germany in particular, all countries with ageing populations, low birth-rates, and growing robotics sectors. However, in Japan, heteronormative marriage remains the *only* sanctioned context for childbirth, effectively precluding single-by-choice parents and 'out' lesbian and gay couples from having children. Fewer women and men are keen on marriage, and the number of married couples declined to 4.7 per 1000 persons in 2018. Moreover, the mean age of first marriage was 31.1 for grooms and 29.4 for brides that year (Statistics Bureau of Japan 2019).

Women are reluctant to lose their careers and financial independence; marriage would entail their dependence on and subordination to husbands. Even married couples are opting not to have children, and demographers can no longer take for granted that marriages produce children. As illustrated in *Innovation 25*, however, one alternative to this loss of career and concomitant financial independence is for robot maids to relieve women of household chores and responsibilities, ostensibly making them more willing to get married and to have more than 1.3 children.

Innovation 25 includes a fictional ethnographic portrait of a day in the life of the three-generation Inobe family, whose invented surname is an abbreviation of the loan word *inobēshon* (innovation). The household is micromanaged by Inobe-*kun*, a child-size, male-gendered humanoid robot connected to the internet. Inobe-*kun* liberates Mrs Inobe from housework and childcare even though she telecommutes from home; her husband commutes by mass transit to an office (Robertson 2007, 2018b, pp. 50–79). In 2008, the Toyota Motor Corporation made a prototype of a multi-tasking humanoid 'house-assistant robot' inspired by Inobe-*kun*, a gimmicky project that was quickly mothballed (Rosie the robot maid 2008).[8] This retro-visionary plan to secure national stability credits technology and robotics as the main agents of social change. *Innovation 25* does not promise gender and sexual equality, but rather a continuation of gender and sexual complementarity: husbands work outside the home for a salary, and wives remain at home, assisted by a robot helper. Mrs Inobe's telework earns her not a salary but 'pocket money' (*okozukai*) (Robertson 2018b, p. 58).

Without the inclusion of feminist perspectives there will be no gender and sexual equality in the Japanese homes and offices of tomorrow irrespective of the presence of robots. *Plus ça change, plus c'est la même chose*. Funded by the state and corporations, it goes without saying that robotics is not a neutral tool and reflects the values of those institutions and their mostly male executives—only 6.5 per cent of the top 100 companies in Japan have a female CEO. While continuing to support the development of household robots along with industrial robots, the Japanese government has also pursued a more lucrative avenue by joining robotics with the arms industry (Onozuka 2016; Pfanner 2014). Not surprisingly, *Innovation 25* and its successors promote a vision of Japan as mercantilist empire, liberating the developing nations—former colonies—in Asia by providing technological expertise that will ultimately benefit Japan.

Meanwhile, in Japan, automation over replacement migration was enshrined in post-WW2 domestic policy, and today a robotic labour force within Japan is imagined as eliminating the need for migrant labour and insuring 'cultural and ethnic homogeneity' (Robertson 2018b, pp. 128–129). The techno-nationalist rhetoric continues to crescendo despite the fact that there is an urgent need for guest workers: to clean up the damaged and polluted Fukushima Dai'ichi nuclear reactor site, reconstruct the tsunami ravaged north-eastern coastline, construct Olympic and Paralympic venues, and supplement the diminishing ranks of native nurses and caregivers. New legislation implemented in 2019 created two categories of medium-skilled foreign workers to be employed in 14 labour-shortage sectors.[9] One group is limited to a maximum stay of five years and prohibited from bringing family members. A second group, with higher skill levels, is allowed unlimited work-visa renewals and can bring spouses and children but no other family members. Theoretically, this second group should be eligible for permanent residency and even citizenship. However, only a fraction of the 350,000 workers approved has been hired, basically due to various disagreements among different parties about guest workers' rights and their equal treatment with Japanese workers (Milly 2020).

Society 5.0

A decade after the debut of *Innovation 25*, the retro-visionary proposal remains a pipedream and Abe advisedly dropped the '25' and added 'Japan'. Along with 'Innovation Japan', newer buzzwords include 'Robot Revolution' and 'Society 5.0', which is described as the society of the future that will succeed, teleologically, Societies 1.0 (hunting and gathering), 2.0 (agriculture), 3.0 (industrial), and 4.0 (information). It is defined, enigmatically, as '[a] human-centred society that balances economic advancement with the resolution of social problems by a system that highly integrates cyberspace and physical space' (Cabinet Office 2020). The illustrated English-language synopsis of Society 5.0 on the Cabinet website blends lofty ideals with images of traditional gendered social structures.

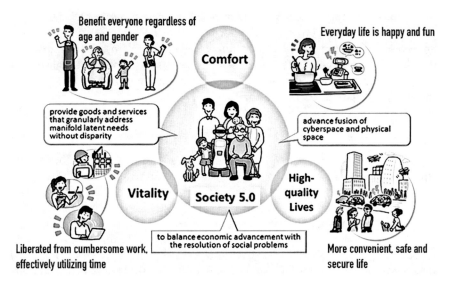

Fig. 23.1 Human-robot interaction and high-tech efficiency in Society 5.0. At the centre is the three-generation heteronormative family and their domestic robot and dog (Cabinet Office 2020). (The small, unbordered captions were redone by the author in a larger font for improved readability)

The explanatory cartoon (Fig. 23.1) accompanying this passage has four vignettes framing a light yellow circle in which is portrayed an apparently heteronormative multi-generational family (one set of grandparents, a married couple, their two children, one of which is a newborn), the household robot, and the family dog. In a vignette with the caption, 'everyday life is happy and fun', the housewife is in the kitchen 'chatting' with the robot as she stirs a pot on the stove. As in *Innovation 25*, Society 5.0 implies that a married woman who is freed from housekeeping and caretaking chores will be more able and willing to have (more) children. The traditional 'good wife, wise mother' and modern 'professional housewife' ideals for married women remain self-evident and dominant.

Promoted as a 'model future society', the addition of a maid robot in Society 5.0 only reinforces the present-day status quo. Outside of the home, in the 'human-centred' society of Society 5.0, there will be robot-run indoor farms, for robots will have replaced human farmers and factory workers (native and immigrant) to compensate for the ageing and shrinking labour force. Today, at least 50 per cent of the labour in automotive factories is already performed by robots. It has, however, proved to be far easier to robotise appliances themselves, from rice cookers to vacuum cleaners, than to build humanoid household assistants like Inobe-*kun* and the Toyota maid-bot. Thus, in 2018, Honda discontinued ASIMO, their male-gendered bipedal humanoid, and spun off several mobility and lumbar support devices based on the robot that are much more practical in everyday human society. ASIMO has proved to be more appropriate as a platform for other innovations but remains a brand ambassador for the auto company, which embodies both techno-nationalism and techno-globalism—Honda having a stake in domestic innovation and a share of the global market in manufacturing.

LIVING WITH ROBOTS

Stories about humans and robots in relationships and forming families are the stuff of Japanese *manga* (cartoons) and *animé* (animation films). Astro Boy (Tetsuwan Atomu) has a robot family and Doraemon, a blue and white bipedal robot cat, is adopted by a human family.[10] In 2016, the Japanese company SoftBank's website featured the fictional three-generation Asahi family and their robot Pepper smiling together at home. Osamu Tezuka's (1928–1989) ten laws of robotics were introduced at intervals in his *Astro Boy* comic book series during the early 1950s (*Mushi Purodakushon*, 1977). Unlike his contemporary, Isaac Azimov (1920–1992), who introduced three robot laws in 1942 and a fourth in 1985,[11] Tezuka's ten laws are not universal in scope and effectively integrate robots into human society where they share kinship bonds and perform familial roles. For example, Law Three stipulates that 'robots shall call the human who creates them "father"' (Robertson 2018b, pp. 1–2, pp. 129–131). Both Tezuka and Asimov presaged the integration of robots into the workplace and household long before actual human-robot interactions were possible.[12]

In large part, Tezuka's laws proceed from his easy familiarity with the Japanese family system. Moreover, situating robot laws within the context of the household, which is also a moral entity regulated by filial piety, obviates the need for a separate 'robo-ethics' (Robertson 2018a, p. 143). Note that in Japanese robotics today, 'ethics' is basically synonymous with 'safety', which is taken very seriously. The important point here is that familial order and filial obligations serve as a code of techno-ethics. The following examples illustrate the growing awareness outside of Japan of 'family' constituting both a safety zone and also a robo-ethics based on filial relationships. In January 2003, a Honda advertisement in *Smithsonian* featured ASIMO as part of a (white) American nuclear family (Robertson 2018a, p. 135). The ad was based on Honda's naïve assumption that, like the Japanese, mainstream Americans would also embrace the humanoid robot as part of the family. The majority of *Smithsonian* readers who blogged responses to the ad were not amused, and many complained that robots would take jobs away from humans! Honda quickly pulled the advertisement and began releasing commercials that integrated ASIMO into social situations with humans, but not as a member of a family. Fast forward to 2016. Early that year, the company Sen.se brought out Mother, a diminutive (16.5 cm, 0.5 kg) robot shaped like a *matryoshka* doll with a smiley face for use in the United States and Europe. Sen.se was formerly

Aldebaran Robotics (France) and is now incorporated into the multinational company, SoftBank, home of the robot Pepper. When activated by 'motion cookies'—linked to apps labelled walk, coffee, presence, teeth, door, medication, temperature, sleep, check, drink, and habits—Mother monitors multiple events and behaviours (Sen.se 2017). Like the stereotyped gender role after which she is named, the small but powerful Mother stays at home and keeps everyone and everything in order. Sen.se's Mother combines in one affective entity the characters of Yumiko Inobe and the robot Inobē-kun from *Innovation 25*, and the housewife in the Society 5.0 vignette.[13]

Japanese books such as *The Year 2025: A Day in the Life of the Inobe Family* (Eguchi and Fujii 2007), *Living with Robots* (Robo LDK Jikkō Iinkai 2007), and *A Society that Co-exists with Robots* (Sumida and Kudō 2018) are manuals for human-robot coexistence in the real world. *Living with Robots* emphasises that humans can obtain emotional comfort and care from robots, and can relate to them as familiar and reassuring interlocutors—something that some Japanese feel would not be possible with foreign caregivers (Robo LDK Jikkō Iinkai 2007, pp. 177–179). This issue is the subject of *Sayonara*, a recent play (2010) and film (2015), which stars Geminoid-F, an android created by roboticist Hiroshi Ishiguro, as the poetry- and platitudes-reciting caregiver of a woman with a terminal illness (who, perhaps ironically, is played by a 'white' actor who speaks in Japanese with the robot nurse). The playwright Oriza Hirata collaborated with Ishiguro to dramatise the possibility of employing androids as caregivers.

Five years earlier, in 2005, Mitsubishi engineer Junji Suzuki and his wife had 'adopted' a first-generation Wakamaru, anticipating by two years the attention to human-robot coexistence in *Innovation 25* and *Living with Robots*. Wakamaru, manufactured by Mitsubishi Heavy Industries from 2005 to 2009, is a yellow, male-gendered 'communication robot' initially advertised as a babysitter and personal butler. Named after a legendary samurai, its conical body includes two arms with mitten-like hands and a ball-and-socket type head with a curvy edge that gives the robot a cute, quizzical expression augmented by a synthesised child-like voice. Above Wakamaru's two large ovaloid eyes are infrared and ultrasonic 'eyebrow' sensors; the eyes further give the impression that the robot understands the emotions of the person looking at him (Mitsubishi Heavy Industries 2016; Robertson 2018b, p. 110). The meter-tall boy-bot sports wheels and carries its battery in a backpack shaped like those worn by elementary school students as part of their uniform.

For nearly a year and a half, the Mitsubishi engineer Suzuki kept a diary of interactions between the male-gendered robot and his family, including his two children, who right away treated Wakamaru like a playmate or younger sibling—pushing and pulling on him, and putting him in a chokehold. They perceived the robot as a weakling, and true enough, most sociable humanoids are quite fragile in their complexity and can be damaged if roughhoused. Wakamaru managed to survive these encounters without injury. Suzuki regarded the humanoid as the youngest of his children; he and his wife also made use of it as a house sitter. They linked their cell phones to the networked robot's internal camera, and were able to look in on the children and Suzuki's visiting elderly mother when they were out of the house. Suzuki notes that, like humans, robots develop personalities, and claims that Wakamaru's character was shaped through numerous interpersonal encounters with family and friends—and also from watching television (Robertson 2018b, p. 134; Suzuki 2007). As I explain below, the technology of kinship that frames human-robot relations is also an example of conceptual conservatism.

IMAGINEERISM REDUX

Technology (*qua* machinery and engineered devices) and robotics are infused with values that transcend their usefulness and convenience; they offer certain freedoms but can also be experienced as oppressive and dangerous. As I noted earlier, they are *not* neutral fields. State and corporate funding is crucial for robotics research and development. Thus, although many of these Japanese robots are cute (*kawaii*), they embody uncute political and economic ideologies and priorities. In the United States for example, robotics is heavily supported by the Department of Defence, and today in Japan, the robotics industry is increasingly incorporated into the lucrative weapons economy. The hardware and software that go into the production of cute humanoid and animaloid robots, many of which are one-off prototypes, are used in the manufacture of military equipment, although this techno-nationalist appropriation of robotics is not discussed much, if at all, in the Japanese mainstream media. As I have emphasised in this chapter, the *imagining* of a robotised society of the future is informed by a *reimagining* of the past. In other words, imagining the future can be a nostalgic activity, which, I argue, fosters a politics of conceptual conservatism.

'Imagineerism' describes how 'the future' becomes imagined as a technologically idealised version of 'the past'.[14] *Innovation 25* and its successor Society 5.0 highlight the operations and consequences of imagineerism; namely, a backward-looking technological nationalism. Similar juxtapositions of science and superstition, high-tech and low-tech, now and then, craft labour and industrial labour, are dramatically illustrated in the most recent Cabinet Office document on Society 5.0. The document focuses on generating *kizuna*, or kin-like ties, from ostensibly 'new values' through technologies like IoT (Internet of Things), or from the hyperconnectivity of things through the internet, and through AI (artificial intelligence). As explained on the Cabinet Office (2018) website, Society 5.0

> represents an effort to create a new social contract and economic model by fully incorporating the technological innovations of the fourth industrial revolution. It envisions embedding these innovations into every corner of its ageing society. … Japan wants to create…a 'super-smart' society, and one that will serve as a road map for the rest of the world.

Companion and household robots will provide 'living support', 'conversation', and 'caregiving'; '[r]eal-time automatic health checkups' will be possible through telemedicine (Cabinet Office 2018). A later report includes a graphic figure composed of four cartoon panels, each one representing a 'current society' scenario counterposed with its Society 5.0 version (Cabinet Office 2020). The 'social problems' vignette is illustrative:

> 'Current society' is illustrated by an image of an elderly man with a cane, circled by drops of sweat from exertion, standing in front of a thatched farmhouse. The caption reads: 'A variety of constraints exists with respect to social problems such as the aging society and regional depopulation making a sufficient response difficult'.

> 'Society 5.0' is illustrated by an image of an elderly man reaching for a package delivered by a drone. That he is excited is indicated by a halo of three exclamation point-like marks. The caption reads: 'Social issues *will be* overcome and humans *will be* liberated from various types of constraints' (my italics).

Innovation 25 and the new Society 5.0 proposal are both 'manifestos' simply declaring that new value *will be* born; social problems *will be* overcome; AI *will* free humans from the burdensome work of information analysis, and 'possibility open to humans *will* expand through the use of robots'. *How* exactly these changes *will be* achieved is not articulated. What is implied is that robotics and new technologies will ensure and secure Japan as, in effect, an ethno-national(istic) gated community. As imagined in *Innovation 25* and Society 5.0, robots will reinforce old values, such as the traditional, heteronormative, multigenerational household; the sexist division of labour; cultural and ethnic homogeneity; and corporate paternalism. Innovation is renovation, a product of imagineerism, an ideological Möbius Loop. Society 5.0 looks backward towards the future.

Epilogue

Culture is at the centre of nationalist projects, and like other nations, Japan is an 'imagined community' distinguished by 'cultural artifacts of a particular kind'—lexicological, for example (Anderson 1983, pp. 13–14, pp. 101–102). The *koseki* (household registry) sustains deeply entrenched definitions of Japanese nationality, ethnicity, gender roles, and family structure. Appeals to *kizuna* (kin-like ties) aim to foster communal mindedness and to override the uneven diffusion of material benefits in society. The widespread emphasis on the virtues of *kizuna* following the trifold disaster of 11 March 2011 and more recently, the Covid-19 pandemic, underscores the affective usefulness of familial slogans in narratives of national recovery.[15] These lexicons—*koseki* and *kizuna*, for example—are among the technologies of kinship that are used to engender relationships and transactions among humans, animals, and inorganic things. I have shown how human-robot interactions are framed and performed in familial terms and idioms of kinship. Techno-nationalism is a declinist narrative that redresses the perceived coming apart of a nation state and its social structures. Thus, as evidenced by scenarios illustrating *Innovation 25* and Society 5.0, 'born in Japan' robots are imagined to play key roles in the preservation and reinforcement of the traditional household and concomitant stabilisation of a historically continuous culture, the 'beautiful country' (*utsu-kushii kuni*) used by former PM Abe as a sobriquet for Japan.[16] Although Abe left as self-evident the meaning of 'beautiful', the adjective simultaneously describes an aestheticisation of politics (in the form of ethno-nationalism) and a politicisation of aesthetics (in the form of traditional values) (Robertson 2018b, pp. 33–34). We are reminded anew that techno-nationalist narratives can be scripted and enacted as updated and enhanced versions of a nostalgically idealised past way of life and living.

Acknowledgements Heartfelt thanks to Cathrine Hasse and Maja Hojer Bruun for inviting me to contribute a chapter on technology and kinship to this handbook. Thank you too to Celeste Brusati and Snait Gissis for commenting on an earlier draft. All translations from Japanese to English are my own unless otherwise indicated.

NOTES

1. Other especially useful national culture-focused 'case studies' of techno-nationalism that complement my analysis include Maurice Charland's (1986) study of Canadian railways and telecommunications, and S. Waqar H. Zaidi's (2008) interrogation of the conservative vision of British engineer-ideologues.

2. 'Families we choose' is not to be confused with 'fictive kin' which refers to people labelled by kinship terms (uncle, aunt, brother, sister) who are not related by biology or marriage.

3. I extend Nissani's thesis and posit that these strongly held beliefs include both longstanding rituals, cultural practices, and customs, *and* the decisive rebuttals/refutations discrediting them; that is, these beliefs and their refutations simultaneously exist in a dialectic as if they were mutually constitutive.

4. Imagineer(ing) is most often associated with the Walt Disney Imagineering Research and Development, Inc.

5. The kindling of nostalgia for a seemingly less complicated and simpler period has been stimulated by the Covid-19 pandemic and the accompanying lockdowns and travel restrictions (Shoji 2020).

6. The nation state and corporations have been characterised as types of extended families, paternalistic in design. In 2011 there were 81,000 adult adoptions that were transacted to secure the continuity of the same number of households (and the corporations associated with them). Most were adopted sons-in-law, who assumed the surname of their fathers-in-law (Mehrotra et al. 2013).

7. A very recent article in the English-language *Asahi Shimbun* reports that an online survey conducted by the Ministry of Health, Labour and Welfare in December 2019 but only released in October 2020, found that about 50 per

cent of adults 'do nothing to help out their neighbors or acquaintances' (Yamamoto 2020).

8. Japanese roboticists themselves have written books aimed at the general public that celebrate human-robot coexistence. Masahiro Mori's *The Buddha in the Robot* (2005 [1981]) was first published in Japanese under a different title in 1974. Between 2002 and 2007, roboticists at Waseda University published a seven-volume series of artsy cartoon-illustrated pamphlets that introduced readers to a future where human lives would be enhanced by 'helpful robots' (Waseda Daigaku Wabotto Hausu Kenkyūjo 2002–2007). Other relevant books are noted in this chapter.

9. These sectors are agriculture, aviation construction*, fisheries, food service industry, industrial machinery manufacturing, nursing care, automobile maintenance, building cleaning, electric and electronic information, food and beverage processing, lodging, material processing, and shipbuilding and ship-related sectors*. * indicates sectors approved for the second group (Milly 2020, p. 3).

10. Tetsuwan Atomu (Astro Boy) was created by Osamu Tezuka in 1951, and Doraemon, which ran as a cartoon from 1969–1996, was created by Fujiko Fujio, the joint pen name of two cartoonists, Hiroshi Fujimoto (1933–1996) and Motoo Abiko (b.1934).

11. Asimov's three laws were first elaborated in his 1942 short story, 'Runaround'; a fourth law, the zeroth law, was created much later in his novel, *Robots and Empire* (1985). The 'zeroeth' law continues the pattern where lower-numbered laws supersede the higher-numbered laws. (1) A robot may not injure a human being or, through inaction, allow a human being to come to harm; (2) A robot must obey the orders given to it by human beings, except where such orders would conflict with the First Law; (3) A robot must protect its own existence as long as such protection does not conflict with the First or Second Laws; (4/0.) A robot may not harm humanity, or, by inaction, allow humanity to come to harm. Tezuka's more sociological, family-based laws are: (1) Robots must serve humankind; (2) Robots shall never kill or injure humans; (3) Robots shall call the human who creates them 'father'; (4) Robots can make anything, except money; (5) Robots shall never go abroad without permission; (6) Male and female robots shall never switch [gender] roles; (7) Robots shall never change their appearance or assume another identity without permission; (8) Robots created as adults shall never act as children; (9) Robots shall not assemble other robots that have been discarded by humans; (10) Robots shall never damage human homes or tools.

12. Their laws have influenced the field of robot ethics although several roboticists in Europe, Japan, and the United States have proposed alternatives that address developments in AI and tangible robots (e.g. Murphy and Woods 2009).

13. For reasons not provided, the Sen.se website was taken down over the past year. Information on 'Mother' sales is not available. Most reviews of the robot date to 2014 when she debuted. What is important in the context of this essay is that SoftBank perceived that the Euro-American market would welcome household/family robots (see also Robertson 2018b, pp. 135–136).

14. Although I did not use the word 'imagineerism' at the time, I introduced the idea of advanced technology in the service of tradition and the status quo in my earliest articles on Japanese robotics (Robertson 2007, 2008).

15. *Kizuna* is invoked by Nikkei (persons of Japanese ancestry living outside of Japan) communities to promote solidarity during the Covid-19 pandemic as exemplified by community service websites in Japanese, English, Spanish, and Portuguese (Honda-Hasegawa 2020; Kizuna 2020).

16. Abe's book, a best seller, was published in 2006 and previewed *Innovation 25*. *Utsukushii kuni e* (Towards a Beautiful Country) bore the subtitle, *Jishin to hokori no moteru Nippon e* (Towards a Japan that possesses confidence and pride).

References

Abe, S. (2006). *Utsukushii kuni e. Jishin to hokori no moteru Nippon e* (Towards a Beautiful Country. Towards a Japan that Possesses Confidence and Pride). Tokyo: Bungei Shunjū.

Anderson, B. (1983). *Imagined Communities: Reflections on the Origin and Spread of Nationalism*. New York: Schocken Books.

Asimov, I. (1985). *Robots and Empire*. New York: Collins.

Asimov, I. (1991 [1942]). Runaround. In *Robot Visions*. New York: Penguin.

Byford, S. (2017, 29 June). How the iPhone won over Japan and gave the world emoji. *The Verge*. https://www.theverge.com/2017/6/29/15892640/iphone-anniversary-japan-success-emoji-history. Accessed 1 May 2020.

Cabinet Office (2018). Society 5.0. https://www.japan.go.jp/abenomics/_userdata/abenomics/pdf/society_5.0.pdf. Accessed 1 May 2019.

Cabinet Office (2020). Society 5.0. https://www8.cao.go.jp/cstp/english/society5_0/index.html. Accessed 15 March 2020.

Campbell, B. (2010). How biotechnology makes human kinship with wildlife visible. In M. Bolton & C. Degnen (Eds.), *Animals and Sciences: From Colonial Encounters to the Biotech Industry* (pp. 196–219). Newcastle upon Tyne, UK: Cambridge Scholars Publishing.

Capri, A. (2020, August). Techno-nationalism: The US-China tech innovation race. New challenges for markets, business and academia. *Hinrich Foundation Report*. Hong Kong: Hinrich Foundation.

Chapman, D. (2011). No more 'aliens': Managing the familiar and the unfamiliar in Japan. *The Asia Pacific Journal: Japan Focus, 9*(29), no. 2, 1–13.

Charland, M. (1986). Technological nationalism. *Canadian Journal of Political and Social Theory, 10*(1), 196–220.

Eguchi, K., & Fujii, R. (2007). *2025nen Inobe-ke no ichinichi* (The Year 2025: A Day in the Life of the Inobe Family). Tokyo: PHP Kenkyūjo.

Evans-Pritchard, E. E. (1950). Kinship and the local community among the Nuer. In C. D. Forde & A. R. Radcliffe-Brown (Eds.), *African Systems of Kinship and Marriage* (pp. 360–391). London and New York: Oxford University Press.

Franklin, S. (2013). *Biological Relatives: IVF, Stem Cells and the Future of Kinship*. Durham: Duke University Press.

Frizell, N. (2015, 13 January). Heartbreak is hard, even when your lover is the Eiffel Tower. *Vice*. https://www.vice.com/en/article/nnqpnm/breaking-up-with-the-eiffel-tower. Accessed 1 January 2016.

Government of Japan (2007). Innovation 25. Prime Minister of Japan and His Cabinet. http://japan.kanti.go.jp/innovation/interimbody_e.html. Accessed 1 May 2007.

Honda-Hasegawa, L. (2020). *Kizuna 2020: Nikkei no omoiyari to rentai—shingata koronauirusu no sekaiteki tairyū o ukete. Pandemikku no sanaka ni mita komyunitei no kizuna—sono hitotsu* (*Kizuna* 2020: Compassion and Solidarity among Nikkei in Response to the Global Coronavirus Pandemic. One Example of the *kizuna* Evident in the Midst of the Pandemic). *Discover Nikkei*. http://www.discovernikkei.org/en/journal/2020/7/21/pandemia-1/. Accessed 1 October 2020.

Hughes, T. (2005). *Human-Built World: How to Think about Technology and Culture.* Chicago: University of Chicago Press.

Kac, E. (2009 [2007]). *Signs of Life.* Cambridge, MA: The MIT Press.

Kawabata, S. (2019, 21 April). Flip phone popularity remains unbowed in smartphone era Japan. *The Mainichi.*

Kizuna (2020). https://www.gokizuna.org/. Accessed 1 October 2020.

Mathiason, J. L. (2015). Through the looking glass. Review of Sarah Franklin, *Biological relatives: IVF, stem cells, and the future of kinship. Cultural Critique, 91*(Fall), 220–233.

Mehrotra, V., Morck, R., Shim, J., & Wiwattanakantang, Y. (2013). Adoptive expectations: Rising sons in Japanese family firms. *Journal of Financial Economics, 108*, 840–854.

Milly, D. (2020, 20 February). Japan's labour migration reforms: Breaking with the past? MPI (Migration Policy Institute). https://www.migrationpolicy.org/print/16694#.X5R7BEKpE6A. Accessed 1 October 2020.

Mitsubishi Heavy Industries (MHI) (2016). https://www.mhi-global.com/products/detail/. Accessed 1 January 2016.

Monozukuri (2016). https://ja.wikipedia.org/wiki/ものづくり. Accessed 1 March 2016.

Mori, M. (1974). *Mori Masahiro no bukkyō nyūmon* (Mori Masahiro's Introduction to Buddhism). Tokyo: Kōsei Shuppansha.

Mori, M. (2005 [1981]). *The Buddha in the Robot.* (trans: Terry, C. S.). Tokyo: Kōsei Shuppansha.

Müller, S., & Tworek, H. (2016). Imagined use as a category of analysis: New approaches to the history of technology. *History and Technology, 32*(2), 105–119.

Murphy, R., & Woods, D. D. (2009). Beyond Asimov: The three laws of responsible robotics. *Intelligent Systems*, IEEE *24*, 12–20. https://www.computer.org/csdl/mags/ex/2009/04/mex2009040014.html. Accessed 1 January 2013.

Neo-Kinship (2017). https://www.sheridanandco.com/news/neo-kinship/. Accessed 1 October 2020.

Nissani, M. (1994). Conceptual conservatism: An understated variable in human affairs? *The Social Science Journal, 31*(3), 307–318.

Objectùm-Sexuality Internationale (2015). http://objectum-sexuality.org/. Accessed 1 January 2016.

Onozuka, T. (2016). *Sensō to heiwa to keizai: 2015nen no 'Nihon' o kangaeru* (War, peace and economy: A reflection on 'Japan' in 2015). *Kokusai buki iten* (*Global Arms Transfer*), *1*, 15–40.

Pfanner, E. (2014, 20 July). Japan Inc. now exporting weapons. *Wall Street Journal.* http://www.wsj.com/articles/japans-military-contractors-make-push-in-weapons-exports-1405879822. Accessed 1 February 2017.

Pringle, P. (2010). Monozukuri: Another look at a key Japanese principle. Japan Intercultural Consulting. http://www.japanintercultural.com/en/news/default.aspx?newsid=88. Accessed 1 March 2016.

Robertson, J. (2007). Robo Sapiens Japanicus: Humanoid robots and the posthuman family. *Critical Asian Studies, 39*(3), 369–398.

Robertson, J. (2008). Science fiction as public policy in Japan: Humanoid robots, post-humans, and *Innovation 25*. Woodrow Wilson International Centre for Scholars, Washington, D.C. *Asia Program Special Report, 140*, 29–34.

Robertson, J. (2018a, 18 July). Looking ahead by going back. The Sections Edition: Society for East Asian Anthropology. *Anthropology News*. www.anthropology-news.org.

Robertson, J. (2018b). *Robo Sapiens Japanicus: Robots, Gender, Family, and the Japanese Nation*. Berkeley: University of California Press.

Robo LDK Jikkō Iinkai (2007). *Robotto no iru kurashi* (Living with Robots). Tokyo: Nikkan Kōgyō Shinbunsha.

Rosie the robot maid, made by Toyota (2008, 27 October). *Impact Lab*. http://www.impactlab.net/2008/10/27/rosie-the-robot-maid-made-by-toyota/. Accessed 5 November 2008.

Satō, K. (2008). 'Gijutsu' ni tsuite no ikkōsatsu: gijutsu no teigi to sono imi (A consideration of 'gijutsu': Defining gijutsu and its meaning). *The Proceedings of the Technology and Society Conference*, 51–52.

Schneider, D. (1968). *American Kinship. A Cultural Account*. Englewoods Cliffs, NJ: Prentice-Hall.

Sen.se. (2017). Mother. https://sen.se/store/mother/. Accessed 1 February 2017.

Shoji, K. (2020, 25 April). Seeking solace from COVID-19 in Showa Era nostalgia. *The Japan Times*. https://www.japantimes.co.jp/news/2020/04/25/national/media-national/coronavirus-showa/. Accessed 1 October 2020.

Statistics Bureau of Japan (2019). *Statistical Handbook of Japan*. http://www.stat.go.jp/english/data/handbook/c0117.html. Accessed 1 January 2020.

Stockwin, A., & Ampiah, K. (2017). *Rethinking Japan: The Politics of Contested Nationalism (New Studies in Modern Japan)*. London: Lexington Books.

Sumida, M., & Kudō, S. (2018). *Robotto to ikiru shakai* (A Society That Co-exists With Robots). Tokyo: Kōbundō.

Suzuki, J. (2007). *Robotto no iru kurashi o kangaeru*, Part 2: 'Hito to hōmu robotto no kashikoi tsukiai kata'—Wakamaru *to sugoshita 500-nichi no kiroku* (Thinking about Living with Robots, Part 2: Intelligent Ways of Interacting with a Home Robot—A Chronicle of the 500 Days [We] Lived with Wakamaru). http://robonable.typepad.jp/trend/2007/09/wakamaru500_6173.html#tp. Accessed 1 January 2007.

Waseda Daigaku Wabotto Hausu Kenkyūjo (2002–2007). *Wabotto no hon (The Book of Wabot)*. 7 volumes. Tokyo: Chūō Kōronsha.

Weston, K. (1997). *Families We Choose: Lesbians, Gays, Kinship*. (Revised ed.). New York: Columbia University Press.

Williams, R. (1981). Communications technologies and social institutions. In R. Williams (Ed.), *Contact: Human Communication and Its History* (pp. 225–328). London: Thames and Hudson.

Yamamoto, K. (2020, 24 October). By and large, Japanese have lost their community spirit. *The Asahi Shimbun*. http://www.asahi.com/ajw/articles/13866655. Accessed 24 October 2020.

Zaidi, S. Waqar H. (2008). The Janus-face of techno-nationalism. *Technology and Culture, 49* (January), 62–88.

CHAPTER 24

Collectivities and Technological Activism: Feminist Hacking

Activism

Christina Dunbar-Hester

> *[I]t will be better if we can increase the numbers and proportion of people who can make/use tools to improve their own lives. Open tools are powerful— it's a good way to spend activist time.*
> —FLOSS activist, interview, New York City, July 2015

Collectivities can rally around technologies for political or affective reasons, or in manners that span both. This chapter explores activist collectivities that place technologies in a central role.[1] It then moves to review hacking, a narrower instance of this phenomenon, in order to set up a brief empirical case: affective and political affinities vis-à-vis the rise of feminist technopolitics in free/libre open source software (FLOSS)/hacking formations. Feminist hackers have exposed tensions at the core of these hacking communities, which are supposed to happily conjoin individual agency and pleasure with a sense of collective pursuit and belonging, but in practice have been exclusionary. Because technology tends to stand in for ideations and relations greater than artefacts unto themselves, FLOSS/hacking's failures to be inclusive were not perceived as pertaining to a marginal sphere of hobbyists tinkering with codes and hardware, but one that (would-be) participants understood as an extremely important political and affective domain. The chapter shows how interventions by

C. Dunbar-Hester (✉)
University of Southern California, Los Angeles, CA, USA
e-mail: dunbarhe@usc.edu

© The Author(s), under exclusive license to Springer Nature Singapore
Pte Ltd. 2022
M. H. Bruun et al. (eds.), *The Palgrave Handbook of the Anthropology of Technology*, https://doi.org/10.1007/978-981-16-7084-8_24

feminist FLOSS and hacking participants are meant to hack their communities, changing both their constitutions and what is 'produced' through hacking, including sociality as well as artefacts. It argues that as technologies function as 'ways for people to enact hopes and expectations more than realities' (in the words of Thomas Streeter 2017, p. 86), it is necessary for analysts to be highly sensitised to the ways in which collectivities come together to vest technologies with hope and longing.

Before assessing how *technology* is imagined and constructed within activist collectivities, it is worth taking the measure of the cultural import of the concept. 'Technology' is as much an ideologically charged domain as it is a mundane artefactual component of everyday life. According to historian of technology Leo Marx, in contemporary society, *technology* cannot help but *to stand in for things greater than artefacts*, and it is understood to have profound effects on social order. Conversations about technology are rarely about *artefacts in themselves* (although this phrasing may mislead us into thinking that a clear demarcation of technology from society, from power, and from social order is possible or even desirable). Many critics of technology and culture have observed that stories told about technology reveal as much about the tellers as about the artefacts (Sturken and Thomas 2004). For these reasons, technology is a special case for social analysis: it is no less a product of social relations than other domains of culture, but its stature is so great and its shadow so long that it is worth concerted attention.

TECHNOLOGY, ACTIVISM, AND COLLECTIVITIES

Technology is a unique domain for the discharge of political energies. In the collective imagination, it has been vested with the power to initiate change (even as this belief obscures the role of social and economic relations) (Marx 2010, p. 577). For these reasons, it is an attractive domain for activists, especially those already drawn to affective and political engagement with technology. In the 1960s and 1970s in the United States, members of the self-styled 'Appropriate Technology' (AT) movement identified this domain as one in which to enact their beliefs about how to live simpler, more harmonious, and pacific lives, at a scale that did not damage the environment, and could be repaired and renewed without reliance on mass industrialisation, long extractive supply chains, and the like. AT was not 'anti-technological' as it did advocate the adoption of community-scale and environmentally friendly technologies, but it opposed large, powerful technological systems including weapons technology, mechanised agriculture, and concentrated industrial energy generation (Pursell 1993; Turner 2006). It drew on older American transcendentalist tropes having to do with self-reliance and pride of work, attained through ownership of tools and cultivation of skills; echoes of the 'restrained republican gentleman' and independent producer ideals can be heard in AT's adherents' articulations of their attitudes towards technology (Pursell 1993, p. 636). These efforts contained political and affective, even spiritual dimensions; in the words of one person, 'Chopping wood or carrying water, done in the right spirit, are meditation…' (quoted in Turner 2006, p. 75). The AT movement's technologies of choice included bicycles, solar power, sustainable agriculture (including organic growing and composting practices etc.), low-head hydroelectric generation, and windmills (Pursell 1993, p. 629). Of especial importance for this chapter, communication technologies were also an object of focus, as AT left its imprint on numerous subsequent collectivities who applied its emphases on independent control and small-scale production to imagining communications infrastructure (e.g. Abbie Hoffman's 1970 countercultural classic, *Steal This Book*, contained a section on 'Free Communication').

Science and Technology Studies (STS) scholar David Hess has introduced what he calls 'technology- or product-oriented movements' (TPMs). He writes that 'TPMs are distinctive because their principle means of social change is the development of new or alternative forms of material culture, a means of change that is often associated with calls for significant institutional and policy changes as well' (Hess 2005, p. 517). Hess' emphasis is on social movements that ally with companies in order to design, produce, and distribute *products* that constitute material alternatives to existing technologies and products. Hess chronicles patterns of push-pull between groups who seek to have technologies fulfil political goals, and the firms with which they must align to connect to markets; he argues that there is 'a tendency over time for established industries to absorb the innovations of the TPMs, but in the process they also alter the design of the technologies and products to make them more consistent with existing technologies and with corporate profitability concerns' (Hess 2005, p. 516). He further notes that the ultimate aim of most TPMs is to support changes in 'consumption choices and lifestyle patterns' and that their goals are often 'embedded in a much more extensive agenda that is often linked to a broader social movement' (Hess 2005, p. 518). Thus, when firms bring material artefacts to life that satisfy some of the desires of the TPMs, there is still usually ample room for renewed and ongoing dynamic tension between social movement-based understandings of success and the more limited bases around which artefacts are built for market (Hess 2005, p. 532).

One of the groups that Hess addresses in his analysis is free/libre and open source software (FLOSS) developers, who reinterpret copyright law through the writing and distribution of software to which alternative licensing rules are applied. Sociologist Paul-Brian McInerney has studied how actors attempt to articulate connections between FLOSS and the non-profit sector. He attends to a social group that terms itself 'circuit riders', a progressive technology movement in the United States promoting information technology use among non-profit and grassroots organisations, suggesting that some technologies are inherently political, while others become politicised (McInerney 2009, p. 206). The circuit riders' case shows how actors have attempted to affix a particular politics to FLOSS, assigning relevance to FLOSS somewhat beyond that designated by many strong proponents within the phenomenon itself. According to the circuit riders, FLOSS was the correct technological choice for non-profit and grassroots actors, because there were equivalences between FLOSS and their worlds, centring on how FLOSS could support 'collaborative', 'cooperative', 'voluntary', and even 'anticapitalist' work (McInerney 2009, p. 215). (STS scholar Chris Kelty reminds us that free software creators were never wholly antimarket but also argues that the more radical antimarket stances within FLOSS were overtaken when 'open source' became ascendant [2008, p. x][2].)

McInerney's case delves into how relatively depoliticised[3] artefacts can come to have politics assigned to them by collectivities who seek to articulate technologies to their political beliefs and enrol other groups (non-profit sector organisations without a software/IT focus) to both adopt the artefact *and* shore up the association between artefact and politics. STS scholar Christina Dunbar-Hester (2014) has explored the related dynamic in her study of how low-power FM (LPFM) radio activists assign the artefact of low-power radio to their politics: they argue that LPFM is ideally suited to non-commercial, politically oriented, and local or community-scale use, which were all values they wished to promote in the media system. She uses the term *propagation* to refer to the interpretive work undertaken by the activists in combination with their hands-on work with radio technology (enacted in electronics tinkering and pedagogy). This distinguishes the radio activists from collectivities that form around technologies as *either* hands-on enthusiasts *or* advocates for the widespread adoption of these technologies; propagation represents the entwinement of hands-on technical work and evangelism directed towards other social groups. For the radio activists, the affective pleasure they take in tinkering with hardware and affirming a politics serves to strengthen the connection between these domains for them.

McInerney's and Dunbar-Hester's accounts both illustrate that, as widely diffused communication technologies assumed societal prominence, they were seized upon by activist collectivities seeking to hitch them to emancipatory, progressive politics. Anthropologists Todd Wolfson and Jeffrey Juris have also contributed to these discussions. In Juris' (2008) study of anti-corporate-globalisation mobilisations, he writes, 'activists increasingly express their utopian imaginaries directly through concrete organisational and technological practice' (p. 17). Wolfson and Dunbar-Hester's work highlights how the emphasis on technology within groups hoping to promote emancipatory politics can lead to the inadvertent centring of activist projects around those who are the most technologically capable and enthusiastic: often white, college-educated men. Wolfson (2012) further adds that the centrality of technology to the activist project (in his case, Indymedia) was a misinterpretation of the political beliefs of the Zapatistas, who had called for the use of new informational technologies—'a network of communication among all our struggles'—in twenty-first-century resistance (p. 150). Wolfson (2012, 2014) argues that Global North movements overestimated the centrality of these technologies to the activist project for the Zapatistas, with deleterious results for organising broad and deep movements.

These tensions over how 'apolitical' technologies may come to acquire politics, and whether widespread engagement with technologies has a politics, set up the discussions of hacking and feminist hacking that follow.

PLEASURES AND POLITICS OF HACKING

Hacking is not a single set of practices or cultural ethos. In fact, it is a contentious term and nebulous set of practices. Its cultural prominence can be mapped to the ascendance of computing, but 'hacking' can also apply to other non-computing artefacts: 'the hack as an unexpected and brilliant piece of technological detournement'.[4] This chapter takes an interest in hacking as it is pursued within FLOSS and hackerspace collectivities, defined by purposive engagement with technology in a shared (if not singular) political and technical imaginary, flowing from practices and ideologies in Euro-American networked computing communities.

Early networked computing provided a sense of community for its users, and also offered them the sense that the 'place' where they convened and communed had its own ethics, politics, and values (Jordan 2016, pp. 5–6). In parallel, computer programming itself emerged as a recognised skill with application in employment relations. The growth of this professional category witnessed the '[bifurcation] between free software and the programming proletariat', according to sociologist Tim Jordan (2016, p. 6). Although both pursuits were based on coding as a practice, different political valences of coding emerged as practitioners began to distinguish between coding in the service of collectively generated and community-owned projects versus coding for a corporate, for-profit employer or a government employer (in the national interest) (Jordan 2016, p. 6). All the while, Jordan argues, hacking was consistently tied to unequal social relations that not only uncritically adopted the masculinist biases of computing but amplified them, as the transgressive values and practices of hackers could shade into exaggerated misogyny (2016, p. 6). Hacking evolved into a self-conscious and increasingly socially prominent (or notorious) community of practice, which often emphasised breaking into (*cracking*) other computers on a network for the purposes of exploring and identifying vulnerabilities. Anthropologist Gabriella Coleman offers a rich description of the life-world of a budding hacker, arguing that his identity and commitments emerged through intersubjective experience: 'Many hackers did not awaken to a consciousness of their "hacker nature" in a moment of joyful epiphany but instead acquired it imperceptibly', through being thoroughly immersed in the cultural and technical facets of hacking alongside others engaged in the same activities (Coleman 2012a, p. 30).[5]

Even if not associated with 'joyful epiphany', hackers derive pleasure and communion from their activities. In the background lies an interpretation of networked computing as a means to experience collectivised consciousness, the history of which has been chronicled by Communication scholars Fred Turner and Thomas Streeter (Turner 2006; Streeter 2010). As noted above, FLOSS is a set of practices for the distributed collaborative creation of code that is made openly available through a reinterpretation of copyright law; it is also an ideologically charged mode of production and authorship that seeks to reorient power in light of participants' understandings of the moral and technical possibilities presented by the internet (Kelty 2008). 'Free' here means 'free as in speech, not free as in beer', an articulation which echoes the interpretive work that Turner argues the New Communalists undertook in the 1970s and 1980s. Hackerspaces are a cognate offline phenomenon, community workspaces where people with interest in computers, craft, and other types of fabrication come together to socialise and collaborate. This is not a mere pastime, as many practitioners are enthusiastic devotees.

Hacking is fruitfully understood by taking a genealogical approach, as suggested by sociologist Tim Jordan (2016), which includes taking notice of what is absent in social phenomena as well as what is present. This is particularly useful in understanding whether and how hacking has a relationship to politics and activism. Early threads of hacking, according to Jordan (2016), centred around altering technologies and manipulating information (p. 5). Hacking sensibilities also included the formation of communities, and the identification of coding as both a material practice and discursive resource. Free software played a special role, as programming 'bifurcated between free software and the programming proletariat. The activity of coding is the same for both and individuals may, and often do, occupy both positions but there are distinct roles as a coder for community owned and collectively generated program[s]. ... This is a broad distinction but it develops and begins to underpin many of the political aspects of coding' (Jordan 2016, p. 6). This distinction between material practice and discursive resource is important, as the latter allowed people engaged in coding to recognise themselves as members of a community and elevate writing code as a practice, thus elevating the social status of its practitioners. Though these developments may seem obvious from our present standpoint, Jordan reminds us they were contingent. Furthermore, their significance was not necessarily apparent in the moment, although it was at times crystallised through the circulation of texts like John Perry Barlow's 'Declaration of Independence in Cyberspace' and hacker The Mentor's 'The Conscience of a Hacker' (both of which are instantly recognisable as sacred texts that affectively bind community members) (Jordan 2016, p. 7). In other words, coding and circulating stories about coding became a means by which a community of coders showed themselves to themselves, to paraphrase anthropologist Barbara Myerhoff, and thus came into being as a community.[6]

Among hackers, there is *not*, in this genealogical telling, a commitment to political intervention, progressive or otherwise. In fact, hacker culture has displayed many politically regressive tendencies. As has been explored extensively, this includes a strong and exclusionary thread of masculinity (Jordan 2016; Jordan and Taylor 1998; Nafus 2012; Reagle 2013). Some high-profile proponents of open culture, such as Wikipedia founder Jimmy Wales, have even been heavily influenced by Ayn Rand and her so-called *objectivist philosophy*, which privileges individual power and entitlement (Rosenzweig 2006, p. 119). Lastly, the ethos of transgression favoured by many hackers contains a strong potential for retrograde political effects (Chen 2014; Coleman 2012b; Phillips 2015). This background is necessary to underscore that, although this chapter emphasises the mostly progressive intentions of diversity advocates in open-technology cultures, the political waters they swim in have a history of being populated by people and ideas ambivalent or even hostile towards these intentions.

A later development in hacking practice involved hacktivists who were invested in building tools that were meant to secure free and open (which also meant secure) exchange over the internet (Jordan 2016, p. 10; for antecedents, see Milan 2013, on radical techies). This animated some strands of hacking with a somewhat different political valence. Since the emergence of the global justice movement (also called the *anti-corporate globalisation movement*) of the late 1990s, many technology-oriented activists have focused their energies on building tools that remake the internet with the goal of supporting activism (Juris 2008; Milberry 2014). This includes FLOSS tools to enhance privacy in electronic communication, as well as activist-specific tools and software suites to permit activists to run email and other applications on independently built and maintained software (as well as hardware-like servers), pushing back on state and corporate surveillance and enclosure (Milberry 2014). Many scholars have noted that hacking can sound notes of revolt against commodification and alienated labour, more and less explicitly (Milberry 2014; Söderberg 2008). (Free software always contained but never fully realised antimarket/anticapitalist potentials, according to Kelty [2013].) Lastly, leaking and whistle-blowing are also political acts that may be tied to a hacker ethos ('information wants to be free'), as in the high-profile cases of Edward Snowden and Julian Assange,[7] among others (Coleman 2017).

Hacking also has a valence that has to do with diffuse production and every-day innovation that is essentially divorced from loftier politics, especially in North America. Rather, as STS scholar Sarah Davies shows, much hacking and making is driven by a desire for community and for participation in leisure pursuit that one finds personally meaningful.[8] This is related to claims that hacking can assume significance as unalienated labour, but Davies argues that a wider politics is actually circumscribed for many participants. She writes, 'Contrary to expectations of the maker movement as heralding social change, the benefits of hacking were viewed as personal rather than political, economic, or social; similarly, democratisation of technology was experienced as rather incidental to most hackers' and makers' experiences' (Davies 2017, p. 1). While this is not universal—hacking is certainly more politically valenced in other contexts—Davies' argument about hacking as 'mundane engagement' reveals a broader truth about the underspecified politics of hacking, which may have very little to do with social change. It is perhaps ironic that for all the ink that has been spilled trying to nail down what the politics of hacking might be, one contemporary iteration is in line with an older formulation of DIY in the United States, a project of suburban, post-war homeowners infusing a bit of 'autonomous production' into their consumption and leisure practices.[9] 'Customising and changing the world' can occur as a very domestic(ated) phenomenon (Davies 2017, p. 3). Delfanti and Söderberg (2018) write of 'hacking hacked' as the dialectic between hacking being recuperated 'from below' and the co-optation of (technological) critique by firms and capitalism.

What can be concluded about hacker politics? In the main, to generalise about hacker politics is fraught. Anthropologist Gabriella Coleman has written of hackers' 'political agnosticism' (2012a: conclusion),[10] but over time she has chronicled an evolving politicisation emerging as hackers have responded to perceived threats to their liberties and belief systems (2017). And yet, while it would be erroneous to conclude that hacker politics are monolithic, good or bad, neither are they neutral (to bastardise historian of technology Melvin Kranzberg's famous quote). Any formulation of *explicit* political stances occurs against the backdrop of general cultural assumptions, tending to emphasise altering and controlling technology, which has been related to a liberal—some would say libertarian—impulse that elevates the individual's exercise of freedom. Where this impulse leads is underdetermined, but not clearly in a progressive direction, nor necessarily tied to a notion of collective good. It is worthwhile for analysts of hacking to locate their cases and analyses within space and time, and to pick out the meaningful practices and components of belief that characterise each case carefully. Hacking as a practice is uniquely renewable, modifiable, and 'versionable'—this is what makes it hacking.

This chapter emphasises a genealogy of hacking within a Euro-American context, because this is relevant for the empirical case. But there is an important, rich, and growing vein of scholarship attuned to how the subjectivities and practices of hacking are taken up and modified to suit local conditions in contexts outside of Euro-American hacker lifeworlds. Hackathons and hacking subjectivities can be used to construct what postcolonial computing scholar Lilly Irani (2015) calls 'entrepreneurial citizenship', in which everyone is potentially an entrepreneur, producing not only economic but social value, legitimating investments in 'innovators', and subtly turning away from deliberative, democratic projects. Inarguably, although hacking subjectivities vary across contexts, and Irani's research is deeply sited in the politics of India as a nation, hacking subjectivities' aiding in negotiating neoliberal relations and modernities is a common feature as hacking travels the globe. Anthropologist Héctor Beltrán shows how Mexican hackers navigate their relationships with the state, private companies, and hacking communities, traversing hacking sites and communities ranging from radical leftist collectives to corporate sponsors: '"hacking" emerged as a way for young people to make sense of their futures in a precarious state and economy, as a way to let [their] "code work" intervene in narratives that have only delivered false hopes, and as a way to think alongside the system responsible for reinstating unequal opportunities' (Beltrán

2020, p. 12). While hacking in the Global North may be about breaking *out of* technological scripts that hackers find confining, for practitioners in Vietnam, it represented breaking *into* global technical cultures from which most people in Vietnam have been excluded, according to Information Studies scholar Lilly Nguyen (2016). Meanwhile STS scholar Anita Say Chan (2013) showed how in Peru, FLOSS activists were enthralled by the possibilities they imagined for upending historical dependencies experienced by their nation and region of the globe. Hacking outside the Global North is a topic deserving of its own review, which is outside the scope of this chapter.[11] Taken together these cases not only show empirical differences but yield an array of opportunities for critically theorising hacking, which is far from monolithic in how it unskeins as a locally situated global practice.

Hacking Communities: Feminist Hacking in FLOSS

The empirical case in this chapter, like the instances in the preceding paragraph, is one of nonhegemonic hacking. However, its milieu is hegemonic Euro-American FLOSS and open technology communities, where feminist hackers set about challenging the norms of their communities that had matured into an ethos of which they were critical. ('Open technology' simply designates porting the principles of FLOSS to hardware: 'open' is the key term.) This data is drawn from field and documentary research conducted from 2011–2016 across a host of online and offline sites mainly in North America (though representing some Europeans and traces of activities in Asia and Latin America), undertaken for a monograph on open technology collectivities orienting around 'diversity work'.

FLOSS' ethos has historically been characterised by a commitment to voluntarism and by an ambivalent relationship to formal structure, a tension between individualism and collectivity (Coleman 2012a, p. 44). Free software projects of the 1990s were 'experiments in coordination … [They were] exemplars of how "fun," "joy," or interest determine individual participation and how it is possible to maintain and encourage that participation and mutual aid instead of narrowing the focus or eliminating possible routes for participation' (Kelty 2008, p. 212). As FLOSS communities matured over time, some members began to agitate around the fact that FLOSS projects tended to be fairly homogenous in composition—a 2006 European Union policy report showed that FLOSS participation skewed heavily towards men, with women constituting less than 2% of contributors (Nafus et al. 2006; Lin 2005, 2006). FLOSS communities at the turn of the millennium had tolerated and even encouraged the pursuit of 'freedom' and transgression that many experienced as hostile environments (Nafus 2012; Reagle 2013). For example, Coleman (2012b) quotes a hacker in 2008 saying, 'Nowadays, it is claimed that the Chinese and even women are hacking things. Man, am I glad I got to experience "the scene" before it degenerated completely' (p. 100). Coleman and other have argued that these sorts of 'lulzy' trickster comments are not necessarily to be taken at face value. But nor should we accept that they do no harm. There was a manifest tension between the individualised routes to pleasure and agency that FLOSS had nurtured in its inception (Streeter 2010), versus longings for a collective and even progressive social project that is inclusive—open—towards many different kinds of people (Dunbar-Hester 2020). And exclusion in this realm was not merely exclusion from a marginal sphere of hobbyist tinkering, but one where customising and building new worlds was happening, as far as (would-be) participants were concerned.

As Coleman (2017) notes, as some strands of hacking experienced a heightened political orientation, they retained and expanded a tenacious commitment 'autonomous ways of thinking, being, and interacting' (p. S92). Feminist hackers have put forward a sharp critique of autonomy as (masculinist) independence and have instead emphasised autonomy as *deciding one's own dependencies*, rather than rugged individualism (Dunbar-Hester 2020, p. 114). In other words, they have taken up the precepts of hacking (autonomy and modifiability) and renewed and re-versioned them in a new direction.

Feminist hacking and feminist hackerspaces have arisen to iterate hacking itself. According to activist-scholar Sophie Toupin, 'Feminist hackerspaces can be understood as safer spaces where a set of common values is foregrounded by its members. Feminist hackerspaces are not an end in themselves, but rather a means to address some of the felt shortcomings of hacktivism and to possibly help create a stronger feminist hacker (counter)culture' (2015). If mainstream hacking contains an underarticulated politics centred on technological enthusiasms (and submerged regressive tendencies), feminist hacking redraws hacking towards more explicit politics and especially towards the centring of *sociality* as much as technology per se (Dunbar-Hester 2020; Toupin 2016). This is not just a tweak of norms. Feminist hacking's interventions take the hacking ethos of 'rough consensus and running code' that is used to solve technical problems or build new software artefacts (Kelty 2008). But feminist hackers are recoding their own communities. In other words, feminist hacking is a form of hacking that is congruent with how geeks solve technical problems: they are metaphorically adding code to their communities and debating how the new artefacts function (Kelty 2008). Thus an updated genealogy of hacking would include feminist hacking; it is hacking Taupin itself,[12] using hacker means.

Two categories of intervention include hacking sociality and hacking artefacts. A short empirical vignette of a hackerspace in Philadelphia, Pennsylvania (USA) illuminates both. In 2011 people left 'HackMake'[13] over fallout that occurred after disagreement over whether the space should host an event for hacking sex toys. Copy from the proposed event read, 'If you like hacking and you like sex toys, then this is the event for you. From DIY floggers to vibrators that vibrate in Morse code, the possibilities are endless.'[14] Proposed by two women, one of whom (Clara) was a board member of the space, other members opposed the event on several grounds, including that it might tarnish the space's public image, which they claimed was especially important as the group was in the process of pursuing tax status reserved for charitable non-profit organisations. Another member, Liam, wrote to the hackerspace's email list, saying, 'At the risk of coming off as a prude, I really don't like this idea. I don't think that it's appropriate to have this as an open house [event] … This isn't the sort of public face I was hoping all our new visitors … would be seeing.'

Quickly, though, the conversation escalated to a full-bore argument over the values of hacking, which in part turned on diversity and inclusion. These words, written before Clara's decision to leave, show her struggling with the fact that her workshop suggestion turned out to be contentious:

> So my concern here is that IT'S A HACKERSPACE. Initiative shouldn't be pun-ished, particularly initiative that shakes up old patterns. [HackMake] is really stratifying into hardware tinkering as the core interest, and white males as the demographic.
>
> I'm frustrated in the extreme right now. … And I definitely don't want to flounce off b/c I can't [host] a particular event, but you can see how this is a culmination of concerns that have been building for months.

Her statement that 'initiative shouldn't be punished, particularly initiative that shakes up old patterns' is at the heart of the matter. Many people conceive of hacking as expression of agency and even rewriting social order. It is therefore to be expected that, for some, the infusion of new kinds of people and new kinds of projects would be instantiations of this very agency. To be opposed by one's own community, in ways that seemed to uphold a social order of 'white males' as the primary agents of technology, was experienced as a stinging fail-ure and a moment of exclusion.

As noted in the opening to this chapter, those mounting intervention into FLOSS/hacking believe this realm to be a consequential one for the exercise of agency, making and customising worlds.[15] A New York City-based programmer and diversity advocate said in 2015, '[I]t will be better if we can increase the numbers and proportion of people who can make/use tools to improve their own lives. Open tools are powerful—it's a good way to spend activist time.' This underscores Marx's point that technology stands in for ideations and rela-tions greater than artefacts unto themselves. FLOSS/hacking communities' failures to be inclusive were excluding participants from making and remaking artefacts, but also keeping them from participating in an important realm of agency and potentiation. In other words, participation in hacking was a politics unto itself.

In the end, Clara's disgruntlement mounted to such a degree that she backed away from not only the event, but HackMake itself. She approached another hackerspace. And she was not alone; at least two other interlocutors also exited. The new space, which welcomed the sex toy hacking event, over time evolved into one that identified as a feminist hackerspace with an inclusive mission. It hosted electronics, sewing, crafts, arts, and other activities for adults and for children. Its members believed they were addressing 'felt shortcomings of hacktivism' and creating a stronger hacking culture, which conjoined craft, emancipatory politics, and sociality.

The details of this 'great toy hacking kerfuffle of 2011' (as it was colourfully characterised by Clara later) are idiosyncratic, not generalisable. A fallout over sex toy hacking is by no means the most common reason for 'forking' hacker-spaces. To an outsider, this episode borders on comic, possibly absurd, but it illustrates that much more than material goods are getting produced in open-technology communities. While eventually some electronic microcontrollers were attached to sex toys, this episode had other products: social relations, and a new infrastructure of care to guide relations. Not only did this episode increase investment in articulating the values of inclusivity at the second space, but Liam said HackMake reflected on its own practices as well.

Sociality hacks include a number of different activities: introducing codes of conduct for conferences and online spaces; backchannel communication to apprise community members of issues in their own or other projects or spaces (this can include praise for healthy projects, or warnings about 'unsafe' people or environments, representing a feminist politics of communicability) (Rentschler 2014, p. 68); and introducing community governance mechanisms meant to distribute power in more transparent and accountable ways (Dunbar-Hester 2020, Chapter 3). Artefacts can range from the material and mundane to the speculative, with much in between. A person at a feminist hacking event I visited in New York City in 2015 was working on coding a drop-down menu on a website to change it from exhibiting gender fields 'male' and 'female' to include trans and nonbinary options (Notes, 31 August 2015). More speculative artefacts included an artist's 2012 knitting project that used ethernet cables instead of yarn; she explained, 'I thought for myself, as I struggled to find an entry point into hardware that was interesting, what if I combined a craft that I already like (knitting) with hardware... Other people responded well to the piece, and I would be interested in pushing it further sometime in the future' (Dunbar-Hester 2020, p. 111). As she notes, this piece was a conversation starter (directed to the outside world) and a dialogue with herself over her own skill set and material practice. More speculative still was a 'cryptodance' which interpreted cryptographic public key exchange (based on the Diffie-Hellman model) in an experimental dance, conducted in the context of a feminist hacking convergence in Montréal in 2016 (Dunbar-Hester 2020, Chapter 4). This experimental event conjoined arts practice with pedagogy about cryptographic principles in computing. Dancers improvised moves and then moved across the space 'exchanging information' as the public key model functions.

Conclusions: Technologically Oriented Collectivity Formation as Social Relations

This survey of collectivities formed around technologies illustrates that people form affective and political affinities with technologies for a host of reasons. But for the analyst, a critical point is the degree to which collective engagement with technology is or is not meant to be about *technical artefacts per se*. This is harder to parse than it may seem but, in some ways, a clean separation is neither possible nor desirable. As cultural historian Thomas Streeter writes about the internet,

> The repeated discovery of culture inside what we have assumed to be the technological is not merely a cautionary tale about overgeneralising. Rather, it points to a general understanding of how what we call 'technologies' work. Technologies in the first instance perhaps work as ways for people to enact hopes and expectations more than realities; that is core to their social impact. (Streeter 2017, p. 86)

This points to the need for analytical engagement with technological collectivities to focus on the interpretations, cultural meanings, hopes, and expectations vested in technologies, distinct from the 'effects' of the technologies or even the 'effects' of the collectivities. Because technology draws political energies towards it, these energies are worthy of scrutiny in their own right as they tell stories that are as much about politics, affect, hopes, dreams, fears as they are about 'technology'.

Likewise, as some advocates of feminist hacking write, 'Feminist hacking/ making does not reify the creation of new artifacts but instead presents itself primarily as a method for encounter and engagement... This reorients the stakes of hacking/making beyond the creation or destruction of artifacts but towards the more difficult work of initiating encounters and social relationships' (S.S.L. Nagbot 2016).[16] A vaunted truism about social studies of technology put forth by historian David Noble is that 'behind the technology that affects social relations lie the very same social relations' (quoted in Wajcman 2015, p. 90). Technical artefacts and social relations—here, the longings, projections, and urgent searchings for better worlds—that affect them are imbricated. What do entanglements of collective hopes and material artefacts produce? Answering this question poses analytical challenges but yields significant rewards.

Notes

1. This chapter draws on literature that considers technologically oriented collectivities in situated contexts: mainly North American and European sites in the late twentieth and early twenty-first centuries.
2. Kelty (2013) writes that open source and free software possess different 'critical powers', with those of free software going largely unfulfilled.

3. Neither McInerney nor I would accept a characterisation of any technology as 'without politics'; he distinguishes between big *P* Politics and small *p* politics (2009, p. 209), which he claims is a paraphrase of Winner (1986).

4. Jordan (2016, p. 3) attributes this codification of 'the hack' to Steven Levy's famous 1984 book.

5. I use the masculine pronoun here because Coleman does throughout her chapter; she states, 'I use "he," because most hackers are male' (2012a, p. 25).

6. Myerhoff writes, 'One of the most persistent but elusive ways that people make sense of themselves is to show themselves to themselves ... by telling themselves stories... More than merely self-recognition, self-definition is made possible by means of such showings' (quoted in Orr 1990, p. 187).

7. Writing in the *New Yorker*, Raffi Khatchadourian stated that, 'For Assange, there is no real difference between a hack and a leak; in both instances, individuals are taking risks to expose the secrets of institutions' (2017).

8. Some practitioners and analysts differentiate more starkly between these terms; others view them as more synonymous. I might characterise hacking and making as distinct at the poles, but in my field sites, it is fair to say that one shades into the other gradually. See Maxigas (2012) for a fine-grained discussion of hackerspaces versus hacklabs, and an overview of the issues of categorisation.

9. Gelber (1997) points out how DIY was a practice of masculine identity construction, appealing to suburban homeowners who held white-collar jobs removed from a hands-on, rugged masculinity (Douglas 1987, chapter 6). While contemporary hacking expands DIY to include feminine craft/DIY practices, it often reinscribes (or wrestles with) (neo)traditionally gendered practices.

10. In a vein related to hackers' 'agnosticism', Sky Croeser has argued that members of the digital liberties movement attempt eschew political identification, in spite of participating in what Croeser calls 'profoundly political' activities (2012).

11. See also Ames et al. 2018; Lindtner 2015; Murillo 2020; Takhteyev 2012.

12. Fox et al. discuss 'hacking culture' which is related. They primarily examine how feminist hackerspaces challenge what counts as hacking, decentring masculine practices and particularly elevating feminine craft (2015).

13. A pseudonym; personal names are also pseudonyms.

14. Unless otherwise noted, all quotes in this vignette are from Dunbar-Hester 2020, Chapter 3.

15. This plural is a nod to Escobar's (2018) discussion of 'pluriverse'; like more radical feminist hackers, he also emphasises interdependences over individualist autonomy and a radical rethinking of power relations.

16. Also implicated here are analyses that centre care and repair (see for example, Puig de la Bellacasa 2011; Crooks 2019; Rosner 2018; Jackson 2014).

References

Ames, M., Lindtner, S., Bardell, S., Bardzell, J., Nguyen, L., Ahmed, S.I., Jahan, N., Jackson, S., & Dourish, P. (2018). Making Or Making Do? Challenging the Mythologies of Making and Hacking. *Journal of Peer Production, 12*. http://www.peerproduction.net/wp-content/uploads/2018/07/jopp_issue12_ames_etal.pdf. Accessed 8 July 2021.

Beltrán, H. (2020). Code Work: Thinking with the System in México. *American Anthropologist, 122*(3), 487–500. https://doi.org/10.1111/aman.13379.

Chan, A. (2013). *Networking Peripheries: Technological Futures and the Myth of Digital Universalism.* Cambridge, MA.: The MIT Press.

Chen, A. (2014, November 11). The Truth About Anonymous's Activism. *The Nation.*

Coleman, E. G. (2012a). *Coding Freedom.* Princeton, NJ.: Princeton University Press.

Coleman, E. G. (2012b). Phreakers, Hackers, Trolls: The Politics of Transgression and Spectacle. In M. Mandiberg (Ed.), *The Social Media Reader.* New York: New York University Press.

Coleman, E. G. (2017). From Internet Farming to Weapons of the Geek. *Current Anthropology, 58*(S15), S91–S102.

Croeser, S. (2012). Contested technologies: The emergence of the digital liberties movement. *First Monday, 17*(8). https://firstmonday.org/ojs/index.php/fm/article/view/4162.

Crooks, R. (2019). Times thirty: Access, maintenance, and justice. *Science, Technology & Human Values, 44,* 118–142.

Davies, S. (2017). Characterising Hacking: Mundane Engagement in US Hacker and Makerspaces. *Science, Technology, & Human Values, 43*(2), 171–197. https://doi.org/10.1177/0162243917703464.

Delfanti, A., & Söderberg, J. (2018). Repurposing the Hacker. Three Cycles of Recuperation in the Evolution of Hacking and Capitalism. *Ephemera: Theory & Politics in Organization, 18*(3), 457–476.

Douglas, S. (1987). *Inventing American Broadcasting.* Baltimore: Johns Hopkins University Press.

Dunbar-Hester, C. (2014). *Low Power to the People: Pirates, Protest, and Politics in FM Radio Activism.* Cambridge, MA.: The MIT Press.

Dunbar-Hester, C. (2020). *Hacking Diversity: The Politics of Inclusion in Open Technology Cultures.* Princeton, NJ.: Princeton University Press.

Escobar, A. (2018). *Designs for the Pluriverse: Radical Interdependence, Autonomy, and the Making of Worlds.* Durham, NC.: Duke University Press.

Fox, S., Ulgado, R., & Rosner, D. (2015). Hacking Culture, Not Devices: Access and Recognition in Feminist Hackerspaces. In *Proceedings of the 18th ACM Conference on Computer Supported Cooperative Work & Social Computing,* 56–68. ACM, Vancouver, BC.

Gelber, S. (1997). Do-it-yourself: Constructing, Repairing and Maintaining Domestic Masculinity. *American Quarterly, 49*(1), 66–112.

Hess, D. (2005). Technology- and Product-Oriented Movements: Approximating Social Movement Studies and Science and Technology Studies. *Science, Technology & Human Values, 30*(4), 515–535.

Irani, L. (2015). Hackathons and the Making of Entrepreneurial Citizenship. *Science, Technology, & Human Values, 40*(5), 799–824. https://doi.org/10.1177/0162243915578486.

Jackson, S. (2014). Rethinking Repair. In T. Gillespie, P. Boczkowski, & K. Foot (Eds.), *Media Technologies.* Cambridge, MA.: The MIT Press.

Khatchadourian, R. (2017, August 21) Julian Assange, A Man Without a Country. *New Yorker.* http://www.newyorker.com/magazine/2017/08/21/julian-assange-a-man-without-a-country.

Kelty, C. (2008). *Two Bits: The Cultural Significance of Free Software.* Durham, NC.: Duke University Press.

Kelty, C. (2013). There is No Free Software. *Journal of Peer Production, 3.* http://peerproduction.net/issues/issue-3-free-software-epistemics/debate/there-is-no-free-software/. Accessed 8 July 2021,

Jordan, T. (2016). A genealogy of hacking. *Convergence, 23*(5), 528–544. https://doi.org/10.1177/1354856516640710.

Jordan, T., & Taylor, P. (1998). A Sociology of Hackers. *The Sociological Review, 46*(4), 757–80.

Juris, J. (2008). *Networking Futures: The Movements against Corporate Globalisation.* Durham, NC.: Duke University Press.

Lin, Y. (2005). Gender Dimensions of FLOSS Development. *Mute, 2*(1), 38–42.

Lin, Y. (2006). Women in the Free/Libre Open Source Software Development. In *Encyclopedia of Gender and Information Technology.* Hershey, PA.: Idea Group.

Lindtner, S. (2015). Hacking with Chinese Characteristics: The Promises of the Maker Movement Against China's Manufacturing Culture. *Science, Technology, & Human Values 40*(5), 854–879.

Marx, L. (2010) Technology: The Emergence of a Hazardous Concept. *Technology and Culture 51*(3), 561–577.

Maxigas (2012). Hacklabs and hackerspaces – tracing two genealogies. *Journal of Peer Production, 2.* http://peerproduction.net/issues/issue-2/peer-reviewed-papers/hacklabs-and-hackerspaces/. Accessed 8 July 2021.

McInerney, P. (2009). Technology Movements and the Politics of Free/Open Source Software. *Science, Technology, & Human Values, 34*(2), 206–233.

Milan, S. (2013). *Social Movements and Their Technologies: Wiring Social Change.* New York: Palgrave Macmillan.

Milberry, K. (2014). (Re)making the Internet: Free Software and the Social Factory Hack. In M. Ratto & M. Boler (Eds.), *DIY Citizenship: Critical Making and Social Media.* Cambridge, MA.: The MIT Press.

Murillo, L. F. R. (2020). Hackerspace Network: Prefiguring Technopolitical Futures? *American Anthropologist, 122,* 207–221. https://doi.org/10.1111/aman.13318.

Nafus, D. (2012). 'Patches Don't Have Gender': What is Not Open in Open Source Software. *New Media & Society, 14*(4), 669–83.

Nafus, D., Leach, J., & Krieger, B. (2006). Free/Libre and Open Source Software: Policy Support (FLOSSPOLS), Gender: Integrated Report of Findings. University of Cambridge.

Nguyen, L. (2016). Infrastructural Action in Vietnam: Inverting the Techno-Politics of Hacking in the Global South. *New Media & Society, 18*(4), 637–652.

Orr, J. (1990). Sharing Knowledge, Celebrating Identity: Community Memory in a Service Culture. In D. Middleton & D. Edwards (Eds.), *Collective Remembering* (pp. 169–189). London: Sage.

Phillips, W. (2015). *This Is Why We Can't Have Nice Things: Mapping the Relationship between Online Trolling and Mainstream Culture.* Cambridge, MA.: The MIT Press.

Puig de la Bellacasa, M. (2011). Matters of Care in Technoscience: Assembling Neglected Things. *Social Studies of Science, 41*(1), 85–106.

Pursell, C. (1993). The Rise and Fall of the Appropriate Technology Movement in the United States, 1965–1985. *Technology and Culture, 34,* 629–637.

Reagle, J. (2013). "Free as in Sexist?": Free Culture and the Gender Gap. *First Monday, 18*(1). https://firstmonday.org/article/view/4291/3381.

Rentschler, C. (2014). Rape Culture and the Feminist Politics of Social Media. *Girlhood Studies, 7*(1), 65–82.

Rosner, D. (2018). *Critical Fabulations.* Cambridge, MA.: The MIT Press.

Rosenzweig, R. (2006). Can History Be Open Source? Wikipedia and the Future of the Past. *Journal of American History, 93*(1), 117–46.

S.S.L. Nagbot. (2016). Feminist Hacking/Making: Exploring New Gender Horizons of Possibility. *Journal of Peer Production, 8*, 1–10. http://peerproduction.net/issues/issue-8-feminism-and-unhacking/feminist-hackingmaking-exploring-new-gender-horizons-of-possibility/. Accessed 8 July 2021.

Söderberg, J. (2008). *Hacking Capitalism.* New York: Routledge.

Streeter, T. (2010). *The Net Effect: Technology, Romanticism, Capitalism.* New York: New York University Press.

Streeter, T. (2017). The Internet as a Structure of Feeling: 1992–1996. *Internet Histories 1*(1–2), 79–89.

Sturken, M., & Thomas, D. (2004). Introduction. In M. Sturken, D. Thomas, & S. Ball-Rokeach (Eds.), *Technological Visions: The Hopes and Fears That Shape New Technologies.* Philadelphia: Temple University Press.

Takhteyev, Y. (2012). *Coding Places: Software Practice in a South American City.* Cambridge, MA.: The MIT Press.

Toupin, S. (2015). Feminist Hackerspaces as Safer Spaces? *Feminist Journal of Art and Digital Culture, 27.* http://dpi.studioxx.org/en/feminist-hackerspaces-safer-spaces. Accessed 8 July 2021.

Turner, F. (2006). *From Counterculture to Cyberculture.* Chicago: University of Chicago Press.

Toupin, S. (2016). Feminist Hackerspaces: The Synthesis of Feminist and Hacker Cultures. *Journal of Peer Production, 5.* http://peerproduction.net/issues/issue-5-shared-machine-shops/peer-reviewed-articles/feminist-hackerspaces-the-synthesis-of-feminist-and-hacker-cultures/. Accessed 8 July 2021.

Wajcman, J. (2015). *Pressed for Time: The Acceleration of Life in Digital Capitalism.* Chicago: University of Chicago Press.

Winner, L (1986). Do Artifacts Have Politics? In *The Whale and the Reactor.* Chicago: University of Chicago Press.

Wolfson, T. (2012). From the Zapatistas to Indymedia: Dialectics and Orthodoxy in Contemporary Social Movements. *Communication, Culture & Critique, 5*(2), 149–70.

Wolfson, T. (2014). *Digital Rebellion: The Birth of the Cyber Left.* Urbana: University of Illinois Press.

CHAPTER 25

Inside Technology Organisations: Imaginaries of Digitalisation at Work

Organisation

Maja Hojer Bruun and Jakob Krause-Jensen

Just like all other technologies, digital technologies do not do anything in and of themselves. Rather, they are used in embodied practices by people with particular interests and passions, and in specific organisational and institutional contexts. The focus of this chapter lies on corporate work organisations and the way that digital technologies are produced and put to use with the intention to further the aims of such organisations, often with unanticipated outcomes. Organisations are good places to explore the social dependence and embeddedness of technology: they are important contexts for the production and use of technologies, which, in turn, profoundly impact life in them.

Organisations can broadly be defined as social units set up at particular moments in time to achieve certain aims: 'Organizations are many and various, but they all have explicit rules, a division of labour, and aims that involve acting on or changing everyday life' (Hirsch and Gellner 2001, p. 2). They are collective actors: more than the sum of their participants' interactions, they appear to the external world as one body, and, indeed, in many legal systems corporations are treated as 'legal persons'. Despite many organisational efforts, however, and as evidenced by the ethnographic studies reviewed and discussed in this chapter, organisations subsume divisions, ambiguous aims, and conflicting interests. There are, for instance, often significant differences between the

M. H. Bruun (✉) • J. Krause-Jensen
Department of Educational Anthropology, Aarhus University, Aarhus, Denmark
e-mail: mhbruun@edu.au.dk; jakj@edu.au.dk

© The Author(s), under exclusive license to Springer Nature Singapore Pte Ltd. 2022
M. H. Bruun et al. (eds.), *The Palgrave Handbook of the Anthropology of Technology*, https://doi.org/10.1007/978-981-16-7084-8_25

485

political and managerial aspirations and intentions of those who develop the technologies, those who make the decisions to implement them, and the practices and interests of those who use them in their everyday work life.

The classic objects of anthropological study were defined by social organising: in kinship systems, households, age sets, and so on, but not in 'organisations'. The corporate organisations we deal with in this chapter may seem solid and bounded from a distance but, as we argue, the boundaries are difficult to draw, and different kinds of organising, including those of states and international actors through policies and standardisation, are interlinked. This has become increasingly evident with the advent of computers, digital technologies and, in recent years, platform-based business configurations that render organisations opaque, boundaryless, invisible—and difficult to access for ethnographic scrutiny.

Digital technologies are developed by and implemented in different types of organisations: private firms, public institutions, and voluntary associations, not to forget scientific organisations that cut across the public-private categorisation.[1] Like organisations, technologies are tied to goal-oriented, purposive action (cf. Mauss 2006[1941/1948]). Thus, at a very general level technologies and organisations are similar in the sense that both are created to achieve particular goals. Along these lines, some even argue that organisations themselves are a kind of technology.[2] One consequence is that both organisations and technologies produce and thrive on hope and imaginaries (Appadurai 1996; Jasanoff and Kim 2009) that rest on strong positive ideas of what technologies might do to impact organisational performance.

Today, such imaginaries are often tied to information and communication technologies and are powerfully expressed in the ambition to 'digitalise' bureaucratic, industrial, and other operations. 'Digitalisation' is a broad term that covers the use of digital technology and digital data to change organisational processes and practices (Plesner and Husted 2020, p. 7). Actual processes and practices of digitalisation can be many different things, from the development and integration of nation-wide digital infrastructures for a health service system (Goffey 2016) to the utilisation of different digital technologies in everyday work practices—such as copying machines (Suchman 1987; Orr 1996), tracking devices (Bruun et al. 2015), and the use of online training and modelling software in engineering (Karsten 2020)—and new ways of organising and offering services through so-called digital platforms (Irani 2015).

The two ethnographic cases discussed in this chapter focus specifically on ethnographic studies in and of private companies where digital technologies are respectively produced and used by employed workers. In the chapter's first section we track anthropological studies of technology companies in the twentieth century, beginning with industrial technologies and technologies of modern engineering before the advent of computers and digital technologies. In the subsequent section, we explore digitalisation and how the hopes and fears connected to the 'digital' have brought technologies to the top of government and organisational agendas. Using two ethnographic examples from the robot industry in Germany (interconnected, sensor-equipped collaborative robots) and the shipping industry in Denmark (digital navigation tools), respectively, we demonstrate how powerful imaginaries of digital technological transformation and everyday work experiences with the development and use of digital technologies form the perceptions of decision makers and managers and transform the working lives of operators and navigators. In the final section we sum up our comparison of the two cases and take our discussion of digital technologies even further, arguing more generally that digital technologies, especially in the form of AI and algorithms, affect working life and organisations in ways that call into question our perception of what an organisation is.

ORGANISATIONAL ANTHROPOLOGY AND ETHNOGRAPHIES OF TECHNOLOGY COMPANIES

Anthropological research in companies and workplaces where modern engineering technologies are produced or employed has appeared under different auspices, from organisational anthropology or ethnography of organisations (Wright 1994; Bate 1997; Gellner and Hirsch 2001; Corsín Jiménez 2007; Ybema et al. 2009; Garsten and Nyqvist 2013) through industrial anthropology (Mollona et al. 2009) and the anthropology of work (Wallman 1979; Szymanski and Whalen 2011), to, more recently, design anthropology (Wasson 2000; Clarke 2011; Suchman 2011, 2021; Blomberg and Karasti 2013; Gunn et al. 2013; Smith et al. 2016, see also Pink et al., this volume), business anthropology (Jordan 2003; Moeran 2005; Baba 2006) and corporate anthropology (Cefkin 2009). We focus this review section on these organisational anthropological studies of technology companies, from shop floor ethnographies to the first anthropological studies of computerisation and digital infrastructures. Although these ethnographic organisational studies have taken place in technology companies, they have rarely made technology the explicit focus of their enquiries. The explicit interest and development of general theoretical models with which to examine the intertwining of humans and technology in organisations moved to the interdisciplinary field of science and technology studies, especially since the 1980s with the social construction of technological systems (SCOT) approach (Bijker et al. 1987), actor-network theory (Callon 1986; Latour 1996, 2005), and Wanda Orlikowski's structurational model of technology and sociomaterial practices (Orlikowski 1992, 2007). Instead, organisational anthropologists focused on social relations, culture, power, knowledge, and practice, and offered important insights into the meanings, identities, narratives, language, and practices of the people who develop and use technologies and the different organisational contexts in which technologies are used and adapted. We end the review section by pointing to a new generation of anthropological studies of digital and other infrastructures, computer programmers and data scientists, and AI and machine learning algorithms.

The first generation of American organisational anthropologists in the 1930s was part of the Human Relations Movement whose members defined themselves in opposition to Fredrick Taylor's technically inclined Scientific Management theory, which had turned questions of organisation and management into a modern, technical science close to engineering. Baba (2006) recounts how a generation of anthropologists (Warner, Arensberg, Chapple, Gardner, Richardson, Foote Whyte) conducted fieldwork in large corporations during the 1940s and 1950s, beginning with anthropologist William Lloyd Warner. Warner was a student of Alfred Radcliffe-Brown and had recently returned from doctoral fieldwork in Northern Australia when he joined the final phase of the Hawthorne project, the series of experiments between 1927 and 1932 aimed at increasing the productivity of the workers at the Western Electric Company's Hawthorne Works near Chicago under the leadership of organisational psychologist Elton Mayo (Schwartzman 1993; Wright 1994). In the 1950s and 1960s in the UK, under the influence of Max Gluckman at Manchester University, a group of anthropologists (Lupton, Cunnison, Wilson, Emmett, Morgan, and others) conducted a series of factory and shop floor studies. They adapted the Manchester School's focus on conflict in colonial societies and applied this attention to conflicts to understanding industrial relationships and tensions among management and workers, in contrast to Mayo's and Warner's more small-scale functionalist studies, which assumed shared interest among managers and workers (Wright 1994). Anthropologists and other ethnographers still retain an interest in industry, factory work, and shop floor studies (Mollona et al. 2009), both in the Western and non-Western worlds. These often focus on world systems and the negative social consequences of industrialisation and capitalist production (e.g. Nash 1979), on ethnicity, class, and gender inequalities (e.g. Ong 1987), and the organisation of unions and local forms of community and other resistance (e.g. Burawoy 1979).

In the 1980s and 1990s, the concept of culture was adopted by the larger interdisciplinary field of organisational and management studies (Schwartzman 1993; Wright 1994). The interest in organisational culture, although perceptions of it often differed from anthropology's more distributed and ambiguous notions of culture, opened the doors for a new generation of anthropological studies of corporate culture in hi-tech companies. A number of monographs in organisational anthropology have analysed how the notion of culture was used as part of corporate ideology and how messages of a common corporate identity have been developed, communicated, received, practised, and sometimes resisted by employees in different companies (Kunda 1992; Garsten 1994; Casey 1995; Ailon 2007; Krause-Jensen 2010).

Parallel to company studies conducted by university-based anthropologists, increasing numbers of anthropologists were hired in the private sector and began practising anthropology in industry and design. Challenging the psychologically oriented and individualist approaches to users and consumption in marketing studies and product development, they used fieldwork-oriented methods to describe context-dependent everyday interactions and practices instead of surveys and predetermined models of users. Collaborations with the participatory design movement became a particularly fruitful way to challenge positivist notions of 'human factors' and 'usability' in engineering and led to the establishment of design anthropology (Wasson 2000; Clarke 2011; Suchman 2011, 2021; Blomberg and Karasti 2013; Gunn et al. 2013; Smith et al. 2016, see also Pink et al., this volume).

At the same time, business anthropology (Jordan 2003; Moeran 2005; Moeran and Garsten 2012) and corporate anthropology (Cefkin 2009), together with anthropological approaches to consumer studies (Sunderland and Denny 2007), developed as subfields with their own journals and conferences where practicing and applied anthropologists meet (e.g. Ethnographic Praxis in Industry Conferences [EPIC], see Cefkin 2009; EASA's Applied Anthropology Network, see Podjed et al. 2021). The growth of the so-called experience economy and a new kind of 'soft capitalism' (Thrift 2005)—wherein services and not things are the main products and consumers are actively brought into capitalist cultural production through co-creation and user-driven innovation—reinforced the ways in which anthropology and ethnographic work has become valuable for industry, technology, and design (Marcus 1998; Löfgren and Willim 2005; Suchman 2013). Design anthropology, business anthropology, and corporate anthropology form a new generation of ethnographies that are both *of* technology companies and often conducted in collaboration *with* technology companies.

The first large corporation to hire a group of anthropologists and ethnographic researchers for technology development and design was Xerox's research lab, the Palo Alto Research Center (PARC) (Suchman 2013). Beginning in the late 1970s, anthropologists and computer scientists positioned in the interdisciplinary fields of computer-supported cooperative work (CSCW) and human-computer interaction (HCI) studied work practices in relation to technology and, in particular, the new work practices that accompanied the development of personal computers and networked computing. Among the core concepts that came out of this group's work were 'situated practice' (Suchman 1987; Orr 1996) and the visibility and invisibility of various technology-mediated work practices (Suchman 1995). In *Plans and Situated Actions*, Suchman (1987) traced the problem of human-machine communication to the notion of 'plans', and the conceptualisation of human action as the execution of plans, based on cognitive models. Computer designers programmed the computing machines with built-in artificial intelligence by breaking down interactions into sequences of plans and subgoals defined prior to the action itself. Suchman's analysis of video recordings of people's first encounter with this kind of computer-based instruction system, one attached to a large photocopier, showed a number of communicative breakdowns—the result of people making sense of the machine's instructions in *situated* and *contextualised* ways. Julian Orr's monograph *Talking about Machines* (Orr 1996) was based on fieldwork among copy machine repairmen. He points out that many ethnographic studies of work organisations have been curiously oblivious to technical practice—that is, the repairmen and their use of technology—and recommends careful examination of work as 'situated practice'. He describes how repairmen share stories as part of their work, narratives that are crucial to their endeavours and serve multiple purposes, helping to solve technical problems as well as building social identities and making organisations work.

Other concepts that have been groundbreaking in terms of understanding social practice in workplaces and practices involving the use of technology are the notions 'communities of practice' and 'legitimate peripheral participation', developed by anthropologist Jean Lave and computer scientist Etienne Wenger (1991) in the book *Situated Learning*, which challenged conventional, cognitivist theories of learning. Based on ethnographic research on craft apprenticeship among midwives, tailors, naval officers (drawing on the work of Hutchins 1993), and others, they developed the idea that learning is an integral dimension of *all* social practice and that apprentices and other newcomers learn through gradual (i.e. legitimate peripheral) participation in communities of practitioners, including all the conflicts and power relations that are involved in such learning processes.[3]

Suchman (1987), Star (1995), and Forsythe (2001) were among the first ethnographers to focus their research on computerisation and the development and expansion of the internet and digital infrastructures.[4] Although their work, and that of many other anthropologists (e.g. Dourish and Bell 2011), had significant impact in computer science and interdisciplinary fields—such as science and technology studies, human-computer interaction, medical informatics, and among practicing anthropologists—these debates have only been picked up in mainstream academic anthropology within the last decade as part of a rapprochement between anthropology, STS, and information studies, with increasing interdisciplinary collaborations between anthropology, computer science, and digital design. For instance, the ethnography of infrastructures has grown into a larger field of study in anthropology (see this handbook's section on infrastructure) that includes anthropological work on digital infrastructures (e.g. Bowker 2016; Goffey 2016; Knox 2016; Bruun et al. 2020). There is also a growing body of ethnographies of computer programmers and data scientists (e.g. Downey 1998; Helmreich 1998; Mackenzie 2006, 2017; Seaver 2017; Knox and Nafus 2018) and of the digitalisation of work practices, with a focus on organisations and organisational settings (Suchman 1995; Szymanski and Whalen 2011; Plesner et al. 2018; Karsten 2020).

Most recently, the attention of anthropological studies has been directed towards big data (e.g. Boellstorff and Maurer 2015), data and datafication (e.g. Ruckenstein and Schüll 2017; Douglas-Jones et al. 2021; see also Ruckenstein, Cool, Poirier, Biruk, and Beaulieu, this volume), and AI and machine learning algorithms (e.g. Seaver 2017, 2018). Much of what people do today leaves digital footprints and is recorded in the form of big data, the enormous and fast growing but often unstructured digital databases, incorporating data that is logged by digital devices, sensors, and website activities.

Datafication refers not only to the tendency that more and more aspects of our life are turned into digital data but also that data is seen as a new form of value. The all-pervasive collection and storage of data has enabled new forms of AI and machine-learning algorithms that open up new ways of organising industries, companies, workplaces, and work tasks—through digital transaction platforms like Amazon Turk, Airbnb, Uber, and Deliveroo, for example. In these digital platform companies, the relationships between the company, workers, and customers are structured in new ways: the productive organisation is stripped down to a minimum, as most workers are legally defined as private contractors and not as employees, and the work activity itself is fragmented into separate 'gigs' that are carried out by a multitude of people ('crowds') who are anonymous to the organisation and each other. Ethnographic studies of labour relations that are digitalised, partly automated, or organised through algorithms (e.g. Irani 2015; Schwennesen 2019; Ruckenstein and Turunen 2020) have, however, shown that, contrary to popularised images of a future where human workers have been rendered superfluous, AI algorithms and other automated systems require human assistance to do their work, even though this human labour is often eclipsed and rendered invisible.

As we argue in the following, there is a tendency that the power and revolutionising potential of new digital technologies are often overestimated. The concept of 'digitalisation' offers an apt illustration of a powerful imaginary of organisational change that deserves ethnographic attention and, as we suggest, should be historicised and studied ethnographically in its local projects and appearances, much as Tsing (2000) proposed concerning the concept and formation of globalisation.

DIGITALISATION, INNOVATION, AND DISRUPTION

Technological development influences and is influenced by organisations. A famous conceptualisation of the relationship between social organisation and technological development is one by Austrian economist and social theorist Joseph Schumpeter. Schumpeter describes innovation as a process of 'creative destruction' and points out that technological change always leads to organisational change, sometimes even a radical upheaval of social structures. Organisation theorist Clayton Christensen (1997) picked up on Schumpeter's ideas in his book *Innovator's Dilemma* and launched the notion of 'disruption' to argue that *digital technologies* accelerate and radicalise this process of sudden change. On the whole, Christensen's argument goes, digital technological evolution has a particular transformative and disruptive force because it happens at exponential rates. The stable reference for this argument is 'Moore's law', named after Intel's co-founder, Gordon Moore, who predicted in 1965 that the number of transistors on a microchip would double, and the cost of computers would halve about every two years (Moore 1965), so processing power would increase exponentially. Christensen's book had an enormous impact on the business world, partly because large investments were made in digital technologies, partly due to beliefs in, and fears of, 'disruptive innovation', that is, technological, often digital, innovations produced by entrepreneurs and start-ups rather than large market-leading companies that redefine existing markets and value networks.

If anything, digital technologies seem to have turbo-charged our fantasies, fears, and hopes. We find it useful, then, to think of 'digitalisation' with the help of the notion of 'imaginary'. As early as 1996 Arjun Appadurai urged us to focus on the new role of imagination in social life by '[bringing] together the old idea of images, especially mechanically produced images (in the Frankfurt School sense); the idea of the imagined community (in Anderson's sense); and the French idea of the imaginary (imaginaire) as a constructed landscape of collective aspirations ... now mediated through the complex prism of modern media' (Appadurai 1996, p. 31). Later, Jasanoff and Kim (2009) developed their notion of 'sociotechnical imaginaries' and similarly tied it to the nation state when they defined sociotechnical imaginaries as 'collectively imagined forms of social life and social order reflected in the design and fulfillment of nation-specific scientific and/or technological projects' (Jasanoff and Kim 2009, p. 120). As our cases demonstrate, such imaginaries are promoted at a national level, but they are also produced and kept alive by tech companies and industrial corporations.

With ideas of disruptive development looming in the background, the imaginary around digitalisation invokes ideas of rapid and epochal change driven by technology. Digitalisation comes to look like destiny, like an irresistible force that upsets business and work practices. 'Digitalisation' is thus a general call and an imprecise political programme with much the same properties and charismatic force as 'globalisation'. Like globalisation, digitalisation is often described as a thing or condition we cannot escape. Tsing (2000) has argued that instead of taking globalisation at face value and treating it as one single ideological system, anthropologists should study the many different and particular agendas and projects of globalisation, and the overlaps, alliances, collaborations, and complicities among them, in order to get a better grasp of these phenomena.

> I think we can discuss global projects, links and situations with a better frame: one that recognizes the making and unmaking of claims about the global, even as it examines the consequences of these claims in the world we know, and one that recognizes new and surprising developments without declaring, by fiat, the beginning of a new era. (Tsing 2000, pp. 333–334)

Following Tsing, it is important to acknowledge the influence of digital technologies on organisations and working lives without presuming that they affect us in uniform ways. Digitalisation as a claim and imaginary is often accompanied by ideas of 'disruption' that dispose us to exaggerate newness and rupture, disregard recalcitrant practices, ignore important continuities with the past, and overlook how digital technologies find their place in the existing social world. Organisations are some of the most important arenas where these socio-technical imaginaries are put into play—where the 'rubber meets the road' in Tsing's parlance (Tsing 2005, p. 6).

In the following, we describe two cases, from the robot industry in Germany and the shipping industry in Denmark, two key national industries, where digital technologies and imaginaries about digitalisation influence organisational realities, upset hierarchies, affect professional identities, and change work practices in multiple, unanticipated ways.

'Don't Trust a Video that You Haven't Faked Yourself'—Collaborative Robots and Engineered Imaginaries

In both Denmark and Germany, digitalisation is part of a larger national socio-technical imaginary of future progress and prosperity (cf. Jasanoff and Kim 2009). In Germany, the agenda that the country must keep its role as a leading industrial nation, with secure employment, safe workplaces, and employee participation, is propagated through a range of campaigns and policies under the headlines of Industrie 4.0 and The Fourth Industrial Revolution. This term is coined by engineer, economist, and founder of the World Economic Forum, Schwab (2017) and designates the idea that the interconnection of machines, devices, sensors, and people in the Internet of Things (IoT) constitutes a fourth industrial revolution, a sequel to the three revolutions of the steam engine, electrification, and computerisation. The idea underpinning Industrie 4.0's national technology strategy is that digitalisation, that is, the interconnection of industrial production with ICT, will bring further automation, lead to a highly flexible and customised production sector with skilled employees and gain back (some of) the workplaces lost during globalisation and the outsourcing of industrial production (Bundesministerium für Bildung und Forschung 2016).

In the industrial region of Stuttgart where we conducted fieldwork in 2017,[5] such future scenarios come into play in relation to the region's central industry: the automotive industry, which has long made use of industrial robots. A new type of interconnected and sensitive robotic arms called collaborative robots, or simply 'cobots', have become emblematic of Industrie 4.0, with their sensor systems and streaming of digital data into larger production systems. As one trade union leader stated, cobots must be seen as part of the symbolic 'staging' of Industrie 4.0 and of animating digitalisation, because digitalisation in itself is intangible, especially in comparison with the omnipresence, since the 1970s, of assembly line robots, the icons of automation. What distinguishes *digitalisation* from earlier generations of *automation*, is the integration of more and more computer-based information technology in all stages of production (cf. Zuboff 1988). Digitalisation not only extends opportunities for automation, it also adds streams of information to the automated processes because computer-based tools and microprocessor-based sensing devices *register* all the automated activities and make them visible, knowable, and shareable. This development started with the introduction of computers and implementation of enterprise resource systems in the 1990s that made it possible to collect, store, manage, and interpret data from different parts of production, increase the pace of clocked work, and enhance efficiency. Digitalisation thus adds a layer of reflexivity and opportunities for surveillance to automated processes. Furthermore, all the available digital data, often called big data, can be leveraged through artificial intelligence and machine learning, so that robots no longer just operate according to programs determined by humans; rather, the new generation of cobots can 'learn' by themselves and optimise their own operations.

When cobots are on display at industry fairs, in open labs, and in promotion videos on the internet, it is often in the form of funny gimmicks and friendly gestures: a cobot that opens a beer bottle and pours out a glass of beer in one seamless motion or one playing table tennis with a famous professional athlete. The state-of-the-art in robotics, however, is that it is still extremely arduous and time-consuming to make a cobot arm interact smoothly with the physical world. The human arm on which the cobot is modelled is far superior in sensoric and haptic intelligence, and each of the cobot's movements has to be carefully programmed and adapted to the item picked up, its shape and plasticity, so the cobot can get a grip of it without crushing it. Thus, it takes several days to make a perfect ten-second video performance. One roboticist dryly noted that both the control technology and battery life of robots today are unrecognisably far from the Hollywood versions of robots.

During fieldwork in one particular company that has specialised in the production of robots for the car industry since the 1970s it soon became clear that the figure and imagery of the cobot carried very different meanings in the company's different branches: the Research and Development Department, Product Development, the production halls, Sales, PR and Marketing, management, and a special Innovation Department. The Innovation Department was a unit close to the company's CEO, set up to accompany him to conferences and technology fairs and to conduct what the associates themselves called 'blue sky research', 'futurology', and 'the evangelism of robotics'. These self-proclaimed futurologists conjured up images of a general purpose service robot, referring to Jetsons' Rosie, the maid and housekeeping humanoid robot in the American animated television comedy 'The Jetsons' that was screened in the 1960s (for similar stereotyped gender roles of humanoid robots in Japan, see Robertson, this volume). Completely different images of collaborative robots, such as the promotion videos for the general public mentioned above, were produced by PR and Marketing Departments that managed the company's exhibitions and presentations at fairs and produced promotion videos as well as much drier, technical instructions for cobot buyers.

In the Research and Development Department, scientists and engineers worked on projects that were five to ten years from market ready, and they had very ambivalent attitudes towards the idealised imagery of collaborative robots. Some of them deliberated openly whether the new generation of interconnected robotics would lead to better workplaces—or just more unemployment. Many were impelled by their own technical fantasies of creating a robotic arm with the same performance as a human arm. This blend of technical fantasies and solid scientific ambition was linked to concrete scientific challenges and incremental improvements, closely tied to their specific scientific practices, thus resembling the techno-scientific imaginaries and visions that thrive among scientists and engineers and are often imbued with graphics and visualisations (Marcus 1995; cf. Haraway 1989; Fujimura 2003). When it came to the promotional videos and the futurologists' work in the Innovation Department, the attitudes of scientists and engineers ranged from ridicule to the pragmatic and cynical stance that overstated PR was necessary to calm the public's fear of technology and attract funding for new projects from funding bodies both within and outside the company. In this competition too it was clear that digitalisation was winning the race: software engineers, especially those with expertise in machine learning and AI, were hired in droves, at the expense of other areas of engineering. Commenting on the many fantastical promotional videos, one research leader remarked, 'Don't trust a video that you haven't faked yourself.' He pointed out several reasons why there is such a discrepancy between the promotional films found on YouTube and what robots can actually do: firstly, roboticists must make an impression on funders; and secondly, the films are selling robots to potential clients, politicians, and the public who often have no realistic idea what robots can and cannot do.

Thus, fieldwork made it evident that different images and imaginaries can be distributed and shared differently and serve different purposes in the different departments within a company. The visual representations of cobots, a national icon of Industrie 4.0, can stand for and animate hopes and fears of digitalisation, and blend with techno-scientific fantasies or concrete scientific ambitions, sometimes driven by commercial interests, of a future with service robots. The imagery never stands alone; rather, it is legible in many different ways, always enmeshed in and drawing on internal and external interests and power relations. Ethnographic fieldwork in technology companies and the larger business world, including industry organisations, policy makers and think tanks, labour unions and employers' organisations, permit contextualised readings of sociotechnical imaginaries as they interweave with work practices, cultural meanings, and power structures.

Ethnographic fieldwork, with its ambitions of understanding the development and use of technologies in practice, lends insight to many more aspects of organisations than merely the role of imaginaries. Another goal of doing ethnographic fieldwork in technology organisations is to capture everyday working life under the different technologies. As we have seen, even though digital technologies, and automation itself, have been in use for a long time, a new wave of political imaginaries and policies claim that digitalisation is brand-new and revolutionising. A major point in the following case of digital technologies onboard ships is to show, first, that digital technologies have been around for a long time and, second, that the implementation of new technologies is always time-consuming and is likely to disturb existing work routines and upset organisational orders and hierarchies in unanticipated ways.

'LIKE NURTURING SMALL PLANTS'—DIGITAL TECHNOLOGIES IN NAVIGATION

In the shipping industry, where we conducted fieldwork[6] in 2019 and 2020, the concept of 'organisation' can also be understood in multiple ways. To some degree a commercial ship represents a neatly demarcated social unit, much like the mythical image of Pacific Islands in anthropological enquiry. The ship's isolation, however, is an illusion too, since the ship is part of a larger shipping company that is, in turn, involved in maritime business organisations that lobby national and international governing bodies. 'Digitalisation' has a high priority in Denmark—in 2020 Denmark was top of the UN's E-Government Survey measuring the level of public digitalisation (United Nations 2020)—and together with the green transition, digitalisation is also currently a top strategic priority for the Danish shipping industry.

Danish shipping authorities and business organisations hope that digital technologies will make navigation safer, faster, and more fuel and cost efficient—and make the life of seafarers easier. This imaginary finds its ultimate expression in ideas and projects to create 'the autonomous ship' (Lloyd's et al. 2017), a vessel without navigators that is controlled by AI. Even if 'the autonomous ship' is a futuristic imaginary, the idea that digital technology and AI can alleviate human work is prevalent. There is an assumption that more and more digital technologies can be seamlessly integrated with existing work practices, ultimately leading towards complete automation. When we talked to developers of digital technologies for the shipping industry, they frequently emphasised that their products were 'plug and play', 'install and forget', or 'turnkey', a language that suggests that few costs and little time are required to learn how to use the new technologies, which almost run by themselves.

Shipping authorities and business organisations emphasised that digital technologies and digitalisation are not only about making well-known processes faster and more efficient; they also have the power to *disrupt* existing business models and organisational structures. When, for instance, we attended the Maritime Disrupters Academy, hosted by Danish Shipping, we were told that digital technologies build on 'interactive' forms of communication rather than 'broadcast' communication. Consequently, digital technologies were associated with new, more decentralised ways of organising at the Academy, taking the form of networks rather than hierarchies. This is, however, not how they were experienced on board the ships where we conducted fieldwork. On the contrary, when data about a ship's performance was made available to the shipping company through digital technologies and fast satellite internet connections, captains felt that this centralised power on land, thereby curtailing the navigators' (and ultimately the captain's) freedom to sail the ship according to his or her best judgement.

In the maritime world, characterised by most of its representatives as 'conservative'—that is, hierarchical and slow to change—digitalisation and the so-called smart technologies were often seen as a provocation and a burden. The line of command on board a ship is modelled on the military, with the captain at the top acting on behalf of the ship's owner and presiding over both the 'bridge' and the 'engine room', staffed by chief officer, second officer, third officer, and chief engineer, second engineer, third engineer, respectively. Organisations in the shipping industry in many ways epitomise the ideal-type bureaucracy of Max Weber (1947), originally drawn from the Prussian army. Yet 'bureaucracy' is vilified and demonised in the new ideas of disruptive innovation as a stifling and old-fashioned form of organisation ill-suited to adapting to rapid change. Fieldwork made it clear, however, that allegedly 'conservative' rule-following is not just a result of 'outdated mindsets'. Routines were seen as necessary and constructive because they create structure and predictability, two crucial elements on a ship, where the *safety* of the crew and cargo is a captain's first priority—and new digital technologies seemed to run against some time-worn 'best practices'.

Digital technologies are often created to assist navigators, but it is not always clear whether the technologies are offering advice or issuing commands. If it is not clear whether a new technology is intended to supply information to *support* the crew in *their* decision making, or whether the technology is issuing instructions that simply have to be obeyed, the captain is left facing a dilemma. Captains have ultimate responsibility for what happens on board, but should they obey orders issued by a machine with which they do not necessarily agree? Digital technologies sometimes upset the usual chain of command on board by giving the crew orders, telling them how to sail the ship and what route to choose.

Digitalisation is not only a future imaginary, however; in fact, digital technologies have been part of navigation for a long time. The ECDIS (Electronic Chart and Display and Information System) is a digital geographical information system running on satellite information, much like the GPS system. It was introduced 30 years ago and is now a legal requirement on board commercial vessels worldwide. The ECDIS and additional digital navigation tools (like AIS, ARPA, Automatic tracking aids, etc.) have supplanted former navigational technologies like the sextant and the paper chart, which for centuries had been 'the commonality of all ships' as one navigator told us. It has made navigation easier in the sense that previously it took two to three naval officers to sail a ship. Today only one officer and an assistant are required on the night watch. Experienced navigators agree, however, that the ECDIS does not mean that they have less to do, rather the contrary: their work tasks have changed and become more administrative.

It is often the case that the handling of new digital technologies is added onto established work routines that continue to be maintained (cf. Star and Strauss 1999; Star 2002). Despite the fact that ECDIS continuously logs and tracks the route of ships it is still legally required for naval officers to regularly note the direction and position of the vessel in an analogue logbook. Similarly, it is still a legal requirement to keep watch through the bridge windows with the same level of concentration as before the ECDIS was introduced. Thus, the new work practices connected to digital technologies are added as an extra layer of work on top of existing work practices.

Digital technologies are assumed to make life simpler and easier for naval officers, but seafarers often complain that they provide them with too much information. Life on the bridge is full of alarms: sounds that require the crew to *do* something. Alarms always sound terribly important, but often they are just updates of little or no consequence. Even so, they require the navigator's attention, because he or she has to acknowledge them to make them stop.

All new technologies require extra effort and work to function and deliver on their promise (Star 1991; Star and Strauss 1999), but, despite assurances of 'plug and play', digital technologies often require even more work than other kinds of technology because their interfaces continuously change: points on menus are added, moved, or taken away, and software gets updated, all of which lead to other changes and adaptations. Furthermore, digital technologies usually have to be integrated with other technologies on board, which calls for ceaseless calibrations. As one navigator told us, '[The new digital] technology must be cared for and nurtured like a small plant: You must continuously adjust, press buttons, download, transfer, and attune ... and technology on such screens ... it changes all the time.' Thus, one of the important differences between digital technologies like ECDIS and former navigation tools like the sextant and the paper chart is that the latter are relatively unchanging. The points on the navigational chart have to be updated, of course, but the technologies themselves are almost as immutable as the night sky. As a result of the ongoing changes in digital technologies, their users must continuously adapt and learn new skills.

The old pre-digital navigational technologies called for specific skills related to the maritime; navigation has been heralded as a prime example of an embodied skill acquired through situated practice, learning-by-doing. It has been an exemplary model of 'legitimate-peripheral' processes of learning, where the apprentice gradually moves into the centre of the 'community of practice' by slowly advancing up the hierarchies of accomplishment and responsibilities (Hutchins 1993). Many navigators emphasised that, core to the understanding of 'good seamanship', were critical judgement and the successful deployment of experience, which often depend on practitioners trusting their senses rather than relying on technology for support when making decisions. Navigators told us that they recognise the smell of smoke or hot metal and can detect the smallest change in vibration when a ship's engine is faulty or just a bit out of balance. According to them, such sensibilities are crucial when it comes to detecting safety hazards or preventing accidents. What sometimes troubles navigators, however, is that they are increasingly asked to *trust* digital technology. From their point of view, it is reckless to trust a technology that might fail or that they do not fully understand.

CONCLUSION

As our cases have demonstrated, digital technologies change the way organisations work, but they often do so in ways that are not anticipated in the imaginaries put forward by governments, business organisations, and tech companies. Thus, even though the movements and actions of technologies work towards the achievement of a goal (cf. Mauss 2006 [1941/1948]), the effects of, for instance, the development and implementation of new technologies in organisational contexts cannot be predicted or fully understood. In the business world, 'digitalisation' is often presented as a new historic moment of radical rupture embedded in narratives of exponential growth and disruption. The two cases have shown, however, that such imaginaries of digitalisation should be explored through careful engagement with particular organisational circumstances and work practices. First, digital technologies are not entirely 'new', but have a long history and have affected organisations in very different ways. In the case of the German automotive industry, digital technologies have been increasingly integrated with robots that have been part of the production process since the 1970s. In the maritime industry, digital navigation technologies (ECDIS) have also been around for decades. Second, digital technologies are often introduced on the assumption that they will make work-life easier. But the human environments in which they must find a place and the work routines to which they should be adapted are often overlooked and underestimated. Third, according to a common imaginary, digitalisation means the disruption of existing hierarchies and a decentralised way of organising. However, as was illustrated in the shipping case, digitalisation can mean that power is concentrated on land, establishing new hierarchies. In neither of the two cases were social relations and relations of power easily 'disrupted' by digitalisation and digital technologies, but we can certainly trace different continuities and dislocations of power. Anthropological studies of organisations must strike a fine balance between acknowledging the significance of the digital technologies on the one hand, and avoiding falling prey to eschatological pronouncements and epochalist description on the other.

The aim of this chapter has been to emphasise that organisations are important contexts for studying digital technologies, and draw attention to how they influence working life in organisations in many ways—to the point of changing what 'an organisation' might be. Organisations may appear transparent and clearly demarcated, with their explicit aims and payrolls defining who is in or out, but, as we have argued in this chapter, organisational boundaries are far from clear. This has become increasingly evident in recent decades with the advent of digital technological and platform-based business configurations that render organisations opaque, boundaryless, and invisible. From the perspective of organisational studies, making an algorithm or making a digital technology work can, in some instances, resemble making an organisation work. Digitalisation, datafication, and artificial intelligence open up new ways of organising industries, companies, workplaces, and work tasks, but these new forms cannot be predicted or inferred from the technologies. Here, ethnographic attention to classic concepts of culture, power, knowledge, and practice remains pertinent.

NOTES

1. Many important ethnographic studies have been conducted in, or in the vicinity of, scientific organisations and laboratories: Knorr-Cetina 1981; Lynch 1985; Latour and Woolgar 1986[1979]; Cohn 1987; Traweek 1988; Gusterson 1996; Rabinow 1996; Fujimura 1996; Helmreich 1998; Hasse 2000 to mention just a few.
2. In the work of Michel Foucault, the rationalities of government are often described as *technologies*, for example, 'technologies of government' and 'technologies of the self' (Foucault 1990[1976]), and Foucauldian understandings of government and power have been very influential in organisational studies and ethnographies of technology companies. These particular forms of rationality, discipline, and power have, however, rarely been linked directly to the material technologies involved through ethnographic studies.
3. For a critique of the instrumentalisation and absorption of the concepts of situated learning and communities of practice into the technology industry, see chapter by Sims, this volume.
4. Hakken and Andrews (1993) wrote an ethnography on computerisation and the transformation of class structures in the UK.
5. While based in the R&D department of one of Germany's leading producers of industrial robots, the fieldwork also expanded into many of the company's other departments and beyond the company to 'affected stakeholders' from labour unions, works councils, and industry organisations. A total number of 28 interviews were carried out. The study was part of a larger strategic research project on Responsible Ethical Learning With Robotics (REELER, https://reeler.eu) that traced 11 different robots in different sectors and different European countries.
6. The fieldwork was part of two research projects, 'The robot as a "colleague"' and 'Open Innovation in Blue Denmark—in spite of DNA and NDA', that took place in 2019–2020 and aimed to understand the role of technology in the shipping industry. The first project focused on navigation technologies and involved two to four-day field visits on board eight different ships, participation in business fairs in the maritime tech industry, seminars and conferences and 42 interviews with tech developers, maritime authorities, tech developers, and navigators (see https://projekter.au.dk/blaa-danmark/).

References

Ailon, G. (2007). *Global ambitions and local identities: an Israeli-American high tech merger*. New York, NY.: Berghahn Books.

Appadurai, A. (1996). *Modernity at large. Cultural dimensions of globalization*. University of Minnesota Press.

Baba, M. L. (2006). Anthropology and Business. In H. J. Birx (Ed.), *Encyclopedia of Anthropology* (pp. 84-117). Thousand Oaks, CA.: Sage Publications.

Bate, S. P. (1997). Whatever Happened to Organizational Anthropology? A Review of the Field of Organizational Ethnography and Anthropological Studies. *Human Relations, 50*(9), 1147-1175.

Bijker, W. E., Hughes, T. P., & Pinch, T. J. (Eds.) (1987). *The Social Construction of Technological Systems. New directions in the sociology and history of technology*. Cambridge, MA.: The MIT Press.

Blomberg, J., & Karasti, H. (2013). Ethnography: positioning Ethnography within Participatory Design. In J. Simonsen & T. Robertsen (Eds.), *Routledge International Handbook of Participatory Design* (pp. 86-116). New York & London: Routledge.

Boellstorff, T., & Maurer, B. (Eds.) (2015). *Data, Now Bigger and Better!* Chicago: Prickly Paradigm.

Bowker, G. C. (2016). How knowledge infrastructure learns. In P. Harvey, C. B. Jensen, & A. Morita (Eds.), *Infrastructures and social complexity: a companion* (pp. 391-403). Abingdon, Oxon: Routledge.

Bruun, M. H., Andersen, A. O., & Mannov, A. (2020). Infrastructures of trust and distrust: The politics and ethics of emerging cryptographic technologies. *Anthropology Today, 36*(2), 13-17. doi:https://doi.org/10.1111/1467-8322.12562.

Bruun, M. H., Krause-Jensen, J., & Saltofte, M. (2015). Tracking Porters: Learning the Craft of Techno-Anthropology in Health Informatics. In L. Botin, P. Bertelsen, & C. Nøhr (Eds.), *Techno-Anthropology in Health Informatics. Methodologies for improving human-technology relations* (pp. 67-79). Amsterdam: IOS Press.

Bundesministerium für Bildung und Forschung (2016). *Industrie 4.0. Innovationen im Zeitalter der Digitalisierung*. In Bonn: Bundesministerium für Bildung und Forschung (BMBF).

Burawoy, M. (1979). *Manufacturing consent: changes in the labor process under monopoly capitalism*. Chicago: University of Chicago Press.

Callon, M. (1986). Some Elements of a Sociology of Translation: Domestication of the Scallops and the Fishermen of St Brieuc Bay. In J. Law (Ed.), *Power, Action and Belief: A New Sociology of Knowledge* (pp. 196-223). London: Routledge and Kegan Paul.

Casey, C. (1995). *Work, Self and Society: After Industrialism*. London: Routledge.

Cefkin, M. (Ed.) (2009). *Ethnography and the Corporate Encounter. Reflections on Research in and of Corporations*. New York & Oxford: Berghahn.

Christensen, C. M. (1997). *The innovator's dilemma: when new technologies cause great firms to fail*. Boston, MA.: Harvard Business School Press.

Clarke, A. J. (2011). *Design anthropology: object culture in the 21st century*. Wien: Springer.

Cohn, C. (1987). Sex and Death in the Rational World of Defense Intellectuals. *Signs: Journal of Women in Culture and Society, 12*(4), 687-718.

Corsín Jiménez, A. (Ed.) (2007). *The Anthropology of Organisations*. Aldershot: Ashgate.

Douglas-Jones, R., Walford, A., & Seaver, N. (2021). Introduction: Towards an anthropology of data. *Journal of the Royal Anthropological Institute, 27*(S1), 9-25.

Dourish, P., & Bell, G. (2011). *Divining a digital future: mess and mythology in ubiquitous computing.* Cambridge, MA.: The MIT Press.

Downey, G. L. (1998). *The machine in me: an anthropologist sits among computer engineers.* New York: Routledge.

Forsythe, D. E. (2001). *Studying those who study us: an anthropologist in the world of artificial intelligence.* Stanford: Stanford University Press.

Foucault, M. (1990 [1976]). *The history of sexuality, Vol. 1.* New York: Vintage Books.

Fujimura, J. H. (1996). *Crafting science: a sociohistory of the quest for the genetics of cancer.* Cambridge, MA.: Harvard University Press.

Fujimura, J. (2003). Future Imaginaries: Genome Scientists as Socio-Cultural Entrepreneurs. In A. H. Goodman, D. Heath, & M. S. Lindee (Eds.), *Genetic Nature/Culture: Anthropology and Science Beyond the Two Culture Divide* (pp. 176-199). Berkeley: University of California Press.

Garsten, C., & Nyqvist, A. (Eds.) (2013). *Organisational anthropology: doing ethnography in and among complex organisations* London: Pluto Press.

Garsten, C. N. (1994). *Apple world: core and periphery in a transnational organizational culture.* Department of Social Anthropology, Stockholm University, Stockholm.

Gellner, D. N., & Hirsch, E. (Eds.) (2001). *Inside Organizations. Anthropologists at Work.* Oxford: Berg.

Goffey, A. (2016). Machinic operations. Data structuring, healthcare and governmentality. In P. Harvey, C. B. Jensen, & A. Morita (Eds.), *Infrastructures and social complexity: a companion* (pp. 366-378). Abingdon, Oxon: Routledge.

Gunn, W., Otto, T., & Smith, R. C. (2013). *Design Anthropology: Theory and Practice.* London & New York: Bloomsbury.

Gusterson, H. (1996). *Nuclear Rites: A Weapons Laboratory at the End of the Cold War.* Berkeley: University of California Press.

Hakken, D., & Andrews, B. (1993). *Computing myths, class realities: an ethnography of technology and working people in Sheffield, England.* Boulder: Westview Press.

Haraway, D. (1989). *Primate visions: gender, race and nature in the world of modern science.* New York: Routledge.

Hasse, C. (2000). Feedback-loop among physicists: Towards a theory of relational analysis in the field. *Anthropology in Action, 7*(3), 5-12.

Helmreich, S. (1998). *Silicon second nature: culturing artificial life in a digital world.* Berkeley, CA.: University of California Press.

Hirsch, E., & Gellner, D. N. (2001). Introduction: Ethnography of Organizations and Organizations of Ethnography. In D. N. Gellner & E. Hirsch (Eds.), *Inside Organizations. Anthropologists at Work.* Oxford, New York: Berg.

Hutchins, E. (1993). Learning to navigate. In J. Lave & S. Chaiklin (Eds.), *Understanding Practice: Perspectives on Activity and Context* (pp. 35-63). Cambridge: Cambridge University Press.

Irani, L. (2015). The cultural work of microwork. *New Media & Society, 17*(5), 720-739.

Jasanoff, S., & Kim, S.-H. (2009). Containing the Atom: Sociotechnical Imaginaries and Nuclear Power in the United States and South Korea. *Minerva, 47*(2), 119-146.

Jordan, A. T. (2003). *Business anthropology.* Illinois: Waveland Press.

Karsten, M. M. V. (2020). Dislocated dialogue: An anthropological investigation of digitisation among professionals in fire safety. *Organization (London, England).* doi:10.1177/1350508420961527.

Knorr-Cetina, K. D. (1981). *The manufacture of knowledge: an essay on the constructivist and contextual nature of science*. Oxford: Pergamon.

Knox, H. (2016). The problem of action. Infrastructure, planning and the informational environment. In P. Harvey, C. B. Jensen, & A. Morita (Eds.), *Infrastructures and social complexity: a companion* (pp. 362-365). Abingdon, Oxon: Routledge.

Knox, H., & Nafus, D. (Eds.) (2018). *Ethnography for a data-saturated world*. Manchester: Manchester University Press.

Krause-Jensen, J. (2010). *Flexible Firm. The Design of Culture at Bang & Olufsen*. New York: Berghahn Books.

Kunda, G. (1992). *Engineering Culture. Control and Commitment in a High-Tech Corporation*. Philadelphia: Temple University Press.

Latour, B. (1996). *Aramis, or The Love of Technology*. Cambridge, MA.: Harvard University Press.

Latour, B. (2005). *Reassembling the Social. An Introduction to Actor-Network-Theory*. Oxford: Oxford University Press.

Latour, B., & Woolgar, S. (1986[1979]). *Laboratory Life: the Social Construction of Scientific Facts*. Princeton, NJ.: Princeton University Press.

Lave, J., & Wenger, E. (1991). *Situated learning: legitimate peripheral participation*. Cambridge: Cambridge University.

Lloyd's Register Group, Qineti Q, & University of Southampton. (2017). *Global Marine Technology Trends 2030. Autonomous systems*. https://cdn.southampton.ac.uk/assets/imported/transforms/content-block/UsefulDownloads_Download/F9AFACCCB8B444559D4212E140D886AF/68481%20Global%20Marine%20Technology%20Trends%20Autonomous%20Systems_FINAL_SINGLE_PAGE.pdf. Accessed 8 July 2021.

Löfgren, O., & Willim, R. (Eds.) (2005). *Magic, culture and the new economy*. Oxford: Berg.

Lynch, M. (1985). *Art and artifact in laboratory science: a study of shop work and shop talk in a research laboratory*. London: Routledge.

Mackenzie, A. (2006). *Cutting Code: Software and Sociality*. New York: Peter Lang.

Mackenzie, A. (2017). *Machine learners: Archaeology of a data practice*. Cambridge, MA.: The MIT Press.

Marcus, G. E. (Ed.) (1995). *Technoscientific Imaginaries. Conversations, Profiles, and Memoirs*. Chicago & London: University of Chicago Press.

Marcus, G. E. (1998). *Corporate futures: the diffusion of the culturally sensitive corporate form*. Chicago: University of Chicago Press.

Mauss, M. (2006[1941/1948]). Techniques and Technology. In N. Schlanger (Ed.), *Techniques, technology and civilization* (pp. 147-153). New York & Oxford: Berghahn Books.

Moeran, B. (2005). *The business of ethnography: strategic exchanges, people and organizations*. Oxford: Berg.

Moeran, B., & Garsten, C. (2012). What's in a Name? Editors' Introduction to the Journal of Business Anthropology. *Journal of Business Anthropology, 1*(1), 1-19.

Mollona, M., Neve, G. d., & Parry, J. P. (Eds.) (2009). *Industrial work and life: an anthropological reader*. Oxford: Berg.

Moore, G. E. (1965). Cramming More Components onto Integrated Circuits. *Electronics, 38*(8), 114-117.

Nash, J. (1979). *We Eat the Mines and The Mines Eat Us: Dependency and Exploitation in Bolivian Tin Mines*. New York: Columbia University Press.

Ong, A. (1987). *Spirits of resistance and capitalist discipline: factory women in Malaysia.* Albany: State University of New York Press.

Orlikowski, W. J. (1992). The Duality of Technology: Rethinking the Concept of Technology in Organizations. *Organization science (Providence, R.I.), 3*(3), 398-427. doi:https://doi.org/10.1287/orsc.3.3.398.

Orlikowski, W. J. (2007). Sociomaterial Practices: Exploring Technology at Work. *Organization Studies, 28*(9), 1435-1448. doi:https://doi.org/10.1177/0170840607081138.

Orr, J. (1996). *Talking About Machines.* Ithaca & London: Cornell University Press.

Plesner, U., & Husted, E. (2020). *Digital organizing: revisiting themes in organization studies.* London: Red Globe Press.

Plesner, U., Justesen, L., & Glerup, C. (2018). The transformation of work in digitized public sector organizations. *Journal of Organizational Change Management, 31*(5), 1176-1190.

Podjed, D., Gorup, M., Borecký, P., & Montero, C. G. (Eds.) (2021). *Why the World Needs Anthropologists.* Abingdon & New York: Routledge.

Rabinow, P. (1996). *Making PCR: a story of biotechnology.* Chicago: University of Chicago Press.

Ruckenstein, M., & Schüll, N. D. (2017). The Datafication of Health. *Annual Review of Anthropology, 46*(1), 261-278. doi:https://doi.org/10.1146/annurev-anthro-102116-041244.

Ruckenstein, M., & Turunen, L. L. M. (2020). Re-humanizing the platform: Content moderators and the logic of care. *New Media & Society, 22*(6), 1026-1042. doi:https://doi.org/10.1177/1461444819875990.

Schwab, K. (2017). *The fourth industrial revolution.* London: Penguin Random House.

Schwartzman, H. B. (1993). *Ethnography in organizations.* London: Sage Publications.

Schwennesen, N. (2019). Algorithmic assemblages of care: imaginaries, epistemologies and repair work. *Sociology of Health & Illness, 41*(S1), 176-192. doi:https://doi.org/10.1111/1467-9566.12900.

Seaver, N. (2017). Algorithms as culture: Some tactics for the ethnography of algorithmic systems. *Big data & society, 4*(2). doi:https://doi.org/10.1177/2053951717738104.

Seaver, N. (2018). What Should an Anthropology of Algorithms Do? *Cultural Anthropology, 33*(3), 375-385. https://doi.org/10.14506/ca33.3.04.

Smith, R. C., Vangkilde, K. T., Kjærsgaard, M. G., Otto, T., Halse, J., & Binder, T. (Eds.) (2016). *Design anthropological futures.* London: Bloomsbury Academic.

Star, S. L. (1991). Invisible Work and Silenced Dialogues in Representing Knowledge. In I. Eriksson, B. A. Kitchenham, & K. G. Tijdens (Eds.), *Women, Work and Computerization: Understanding and Overcoming Bias in Work and Education* (pp. 81–92). Amsterdam: North Holland.

Star, S. L. (1995). *The Cultures of Computing.* Cambridge, MA.: Blackwell.

Star, S. L. (2002). Infrastructure and ethnographic practice. Working on the fringes. *Scandinavian Journal of Information Systems, 24*(2), 107–122.

Star, S. L., & Strauss, A. (1999). Layers of Silence, Arenas of Voice: The Ecology of Visible and Invisible Work. *Computer Supported Cooperative Work (CSCW), 8*(1-2), 9-30. doi:https://doi.org/10.1023/A:1008651105359.

Suchman, L. (1987). *Plans and Situated Actions. The problem of human-machine communication.* Cambridge: Cambridge University Press.

Suchman, L. (1995). Making Work Visible. *Communications of the ACM, 38*(9), 56-64. doi:https://doi.org/10.1145/223248.223263.

Suchman, L. (2011). Anthropological Relocations and the Limits of Design. *Annual Review of Anthropology, 40*, 1-18.

Suchman, L. (2013). Consuming Anthropology. In A. Barry & G. Born (Eds.), *Interdisciplinarity. Reconfigurations of the social and natural sciences* (pp. 141-160). London & New York: Routledge.

Suchman, L. (2021). Border Thinking about Anthropologies/Designs. In K. M. Murphy & E. Y. Wilf (Eds.), *Designs and Anthropologies. Frictions and Affinities.* Santa Fe: School for Advanced Research Press.

Sunderland, P. L., & Denny, R. M. (2007). *Doing Anthropology in Consumer Research.* Walnut Creek: Left Coast Press.

Szymanski, M. H., & Whalen, J. (Eds.) (2011). *Making Work Visible: Ethnographically Grounded Case Studies of Work Practice.* New York: Cambridge University Press.

Thrift, N. (2005). *Knowing Capitalism.* London: SAGE Publications.

Traweek, S. (1988). *Beamtimes and lifetimes: the world of high energy physicists.* Cambridge, MA.: Harvard University Press.

Tsing, A. (2000). The Global Situation. *Cultural Anthropology, 15*(3), 327-360.

Tsing, A. L. (2005). *Friction. An Ethnography of Global Connection.* Princeton & Oxford: Princeton University Press.

United Nations. (2020). *E-Government Survey 2020. Digital Government in the Decade of Action for Sustainable Development.* New York: United Nations Department of Economic and Social Affairs.

Wallman, S. (Ed.) (1979). *Social anthropology of work.* London: Academic Press.

Wasson, C. (2000). Ethnography in the Field of Design. *Human organization, 59*(4), 377-388. https://doi.org/10.17730/humo.59.4.h13326628n127516.

Weber, M. (1947). *The theory of social and economic organization.* London: The Free Press.

Wright, S. (1994). Culture in anthropology and organizational studies. In S. Wright (Ed.), *The Anthropology of Organizations* (pp. 1-31). London: Routledge.

Ybema, S., Yanow, D., Wels, H., & Kamsteeg, F. (Eds.) (2009). *Organizational Ethnography. Studying the Complexity of Everyday Life.* London: Sage.

Zuboff, S. (1988). *In the age of the smart machine: the future of work and power.* Oxford: Heinemann.

PART IV

Ethics, Values, and Morality

CHAPTER 26

Ethics, Values, and Morality

Introduction

Rachel Douglas-Jones, Maja Hojer Bruun,
and Dorthe Brogård Kristensen

Technologies generate questions: questions about how to live with them, make them, understand their implications, share their benefits, and limit their harms. Sometimes the questions are specific: what does a new way of doing something mean for those who reshape their lives around it? At other times, the questions are broader: should this technology exist at all? This section brings together the substantial contributions that anthropologists have made to discussing and analysing the disquiet and awe about technological advance, and the languages—ethics, values, and morality—with which it has been addressed. Across the chapters of this section, seven ethnographies explore sites and registries of contemporary contestations over technology. The technologies they discuss range from human enhancement through digital devices and energy, to lab-made food and stem cell technologies. What they share is a concern with how values become embodied in and contested through technological change, as people struggle to

R. Douglas-Jones (✉)
Department of Business IT, IT University of Copenhagen, Copenhagen, Denmark
e-mail: rdoj@itu.dk

M. H. Bruun
Department of Educational Anthropology, Aarhus University, Aarhus, Denmark
e-mail: mhbruun@edu.au.dk

D. B. Kristensen
Department of Business and Management, University of Southern Denmark,
Odense, Denmark
e-mail: dbk@sam.sdu.dk

© The Author(s), under exclusive license to Springer Nature Singapore
Pte Ltd. 2022
M. H. Bruun et al. (eds.), *The Palgrave Handbook of the Anthropology of Technology*, https://doi.org/10.1007/978-981-16-7084-8_26

settle normative questions about the form that human futures should take. Whether analysing how authenticity is mobilised or personhood negotiated, their shared focus on the empirical world allows the authors to engage in discussion of ethics, values, and morality from *inside* the practices under study (Pols 2018), moving beyond dichotomous notions of technology as either simply beneficial or harmful (Sharon 2013), and either eroding or supporting human agency.

When collecting ethics, values, and morality under one umbrella, however, it is necessary to acknowledge their distinct intellectual genealogies. Often used interchangeably in the field, the borderlines between our three concepts are neither set, nor are they settled. Over the twentieth century, ethnographers watched these terms shift in meaning, use, and theoretical explicitness within anthropology and across disciplines (Hoeyer 2020). At times, anthropologists summoned them to describe and frame debates they saw in the field; at other times they took them to be simply part of the ethnographic field and broader anthropological project.

In addressing the intersection of technologies with ethics, morality, and values, the chapters of this section tackle two subfields of the discipline described as 'under-studied'(Pfaffenberger 1992; Zigon 2008). While both *have* been integral to anthropological analyses, explicit or otherwise, the meeting point itself has seldom been synthesised. As the chapters collected here demonstrate, by closely following technological developments, ethnographers are uniquely positioned to document, analyse, and sometimes intervene in technological change, and are able to gain a 'conceptual handle on cultural assumptions that may not be overtly discussed' (Boellstorff 2008, p. 76, see also Albert 1956). They are well equipped to see, for example, the proximity of the religious and the technical, whether in the ways that multinational factories handle spirit visitations on the shopfloor (Ong 2010 [1987], 1988) or in the role of ritual in iron smelting (Barndon 2012). Whether they find themselves positioned alongside scientists, technology developers, device users, or within organisations, ethnographers often find practices connected with ethics, morality, and values, and sometimes these languages of description are ready to hand. As curiosities and anxieties about 'the social' are articulated—at times set apart from, at others woven through, the technological—they present ethnographers with routes into fieldwork. The chapters collected here demonstrate the breadth of approaches demanded by contemporary anthropologies of technology. In this section's Introduction, we contextualise anthropological approaches to ethics, morality, and values within a longer historical frame, outlining their conceptual histories and the ways anthropologists have worked with them in their studies of scientific and technological projects. We then introduce the chapters to come, situating ethnographic responses to technologies that promise to transform social, biological, and planetary life.

ANTHROPOLOGIES OF VALUES, ETHICS, AND MORALITY

In 2014, when Malaysia set out to foster its tech start-up culture, ethnographer Sarah Kelman observed that the role of the government in financing new companies created tensions with what her interlocutors felt constituted a 'true culture of entrepreneurship' (Kelman 2018, p. 65). At stake was the value of *failure*, which they regarded as an integral component of a 'true' start-up eco-system: state funding rendered it potentially unavailable, thus newly articulated as valuable (Kelman 2018). When geospatial technologies were brought in to digitally map neighbourhoods near Nairobi's 'Silicon Savannah' during Lisa Poggiali's fieldwork in Kenya, claims to the resulting knowledge (and power) of the maps were also articulated in value-laden language. Poggiali illustrates how GPS technologies were entangled with questions of expertise, legitimacy, and authority, the promise of an 'unmediated visual truth' (Poggiali 2016, p. 389) making 'notions of ethics, truth and prosperity' 'immanent to the digi-tal form' (Poggiali 2016, p. 395).

While many values are implicitly held (Keane 2016), technological change often prompts new explicitness or revelation. So, when anthropologists such as Kelman and Poggiali describe and discuss values today, they do so against a long-term historical backdrop. Concurrent with the mid-century, post-war interest in values, Raymond Firth (1953) remarked that the word 'value' was a 'hard worked one, and often used in a vague way' (p. 146). His contrast with philosophy's exactitude and its definitional deployment of 'values', to which we return later in this section, has remained an ongoing site of discussion. For Firth and scholars that followed, the study of values remained full of 'forbid-ding difficulties' (Dumont 2013 [1980]). In the United States, a key effort took the form of a push for mutual 'understanding' between cultures, a coun-terpart to the scientific world's division between facts and 'values' (Dumont 2013 [1980], p. 291; see also Read 1955; Brandt 1954) which took exemplary form in Clyde Kluckhohn's vast comparative study of values in five cultures (Kluckhohn 1951, 1956; Albert 1956; DuBois 1955; Powers 2000). Kluckhohn's study struggled with definitional work, settling for a time on val-ues as 'conceptions of the desirable' (cited in Graeber 2001, p. 3), but, aligned with the interests of the time, it was predominantly concerned with producing schemas, classifying, comparing, and measuring (Belshaw 1959). As Graeber notes, the will to theory—and to explicitness—in the project led to 'a sense of frustration' (2001, p. 4) and a project with 'no intellectual successors' (2001, p. 5).

Anthropologists of course continued to discuss, analyse, and point to values over the ensuing half century. Summarising past attempts to produce theories of value anthropological engagements with Marxism (Firth 1979), in 2001 David Graeber's synthetic analysis of value, values, and valuables in anthropol-ogy built primarily on the work of Marcel Mauss, Nancy Munn, and Melanesian exchange to formulate a theory of value that sought to reach beyond entrenched dualities between individual motivations and societal structure. Recognising the limits of pitting material objects against immaterial or philosophical 'val-ues', Graeber argued that valued objects are seen as *media* of value and 'pat-terns of action that in practice are called into being by the very fact that people value them' (2001, p. 259). Anthropologists studying projects of technological legitimation, then, including those they may be asked to participate in *in that role*, encounter regimes of valuation that sit in tension with how practitioners think about the making or use of contemporary technologies (Dussauge et al. 2015). Daniel Miller continued Graeber's line of thought in *The Uses of Value* (Miller 2008) wherein he aimed to bridge the divide between everyday notions of 'value' as price and priceless 'values', thereby offering a lens through which ethnographers could observe technologies translating between different forms of value (Lambek 2008), and theorise differences between what comes to count as a value in a given situation, practice, system, institution, or culture (see Svendsen et al., Hogle, Kristensen, all this volume).

Detailed ethnographic work with a comparative lens has followed technologies as they have been taken up in different places, helping illuminate the values the technologies carry, produce, reproduce, and engage. Margaret Lock's decades-long observations on organ transplants in North America and Japan (2001), for example, demonstrated how technologies 'reinvent death'; Karen-Sue Taussig (2009) illustrated how highly valued Dutch ideals of 'ordinariness' inform genetic categories and diagnosis, contrasting different national responses to genetic technologies (p. 85). Similarly, Ayo Wahlberg's (2018) long-term ethnography of sperm donation in China illustrates how the state's projects to improve the 'quality of the population' (p. 60) lead to the valuation of specific kinds of qualities in reproduction. Since Emily Martin's (1991) observation that sperm and eggs are *models*, heavily stereotyped ones at that, ethnographers of technology have been primed to pay closer attention to how both scientific knowledge and technologies are produced in contexts deeply informed by social and political values (Edwards et al. 2008). That capacity to see models of the world in technological objects (Dumit 2014; Haraway 1990) is a legacy evident in this section's readings of both the implicit and explicit values in technological formations.

Returning to the mid-twentieth century, as Kluckhohn's comparativist project gave way, anthropologists were invited in to the task of understanding technological development through the study of values. New directions opened up. In 1975, when funding bodies in the United States advertised in *Anthropology News*, the American Anthropological Association's newsletter, they did so under the heading 'Ethical and Human Value Implications of Science and Technology'. The call for research projects that engaged 'science/value' issues involving individual scientists, the impact of technological development on specific groups, or comparative approaches across cultures (Anthropology News 1975), foreshadowed what would in the 1990s crystallise as the formalised interdisciplinary scientific companion fields of ELSI (Ethical Legal and Social Issues) or ELSA (Ethical Legal and Social Aspects) in Europe (Hoeyer 2006), giving ethnographers both a new framing for their work, and a new set of theoretical engagements.

ETHICS

In its capacity to be both part of our research fields and our analytical language, ethics is a particularly multi-faceted concept (Hoeyer 2020; Stoczkowski 2008; Amoore 2020). The anthropology of ethics overall can today be regarded as a burgeoning field, even if, as Mattingly (2012) has pointed out, claims that the study of ethics is *novel* for anthropologists may be overstated. Foregrounding an ethics of the everyday (Laidlaw 2002, 2014; Zigon 2013), the 'ordinary' (Lambek 2010), the philosophical, and the religious (Robbins 2016), anthropologists have, in the last two decades, been drawn back to longstanding disciplinary interests in studies of social life of the politics inhering within what gets called 'the ethical'. Widespread interest is evident in the steady stream of volumes dedicated to its various dimensions (Heintz 2009; Sykes 2009), articles arguing for the need to give ethics a more central disciplinary place (Laidlaw 2002; Zigon 2007, 2009; Mattingly 2014; Fassin 2014), and books calling for closer attention to its empirical instantiations (Rydstrom 2003; Zigon 2008; Lambek 2010; Laidlaw 2014; Kapferer and Gold 2018). While Foucauldian approaches have deepened engagement with technologies of the self and virtue ethics as a meeting point with philosophy (Mattingly and Throop 2018), much of the discussion within the anthropological ethical turn has proceeded without particular engagement with technology, indeed, in parallel with the florescence of studies emerging since Western democracies foregrounded ethics as the language through which normative decisions about science and technology will be made.

As a result of the ELSI/ELSA programmes, the space of ethics is not left exclusively to the discipline of philosophy (Cribb et al. 2016); however, many have noted the uneasy relationship between social science and philosophy—both of which could be invited to speak about ethics and technology. Hoeyer (2006) identifies three forms of dissatisfaction amongst social scientists: that philosophy does not attend to context (a deficit model); that social scientists are better at studying ethics (a replacement model); and that bioethics itself wields and conceals relations of power (a dismissal model) (p. 204). There have been various responses. A stream of work within 'empirical ethics' has sought to offer a 'far richer account of morality than offered by bioethical principlism' (Parker 2009) by aiming to complicate and enlarge philosophical approaches to questions of ethics through ethnographic accounts. Elements of this tradition are present in this section, and scholars like Tamar Sharon (2013) have both used empirical work and examined philosophical and personal positions in the enhancement debate, interrogating notions of authenticity and autonomy in the field of self-tracking (Sharon 2016; see also Sanders 2017).

Of course, 'ethnographers … don't always ask the questions philosophers want answered' (Doris and Plakias 2008, p. 313). Tackling the formation and professionalisation of bioethics as a field and ambivalent companion to medical practice, ethnographers have studied how ethical norms are formalised, and contrasted the formation of bioethical regimes across countries (Fox and

Swazey 1984, 1992; Petersen 2011; Weisz 1990). They have sat in on ethics committee meetings (Stark 2011; Douglas-Jones 2015, see also this volume) and interrogated the role that bioethics has taken in furthering specific institutionalised and bureaucratic ideas of the good. Informed consent, for example, has been a particular site of contention for its ubiquity and politics (Hoeyer 2009; Hoeyer and Hogle 2014) and its prioritising of what can be documented over practices that centre the art of care (Mol 2010; Ladkin et al. 2016; Puig de la Bellacasa 2017; Trundle 2020; Manelin 2020). Reversing the relations of participation set up by informed consent, Ruha Benjamin suggests the notion of *informed refusal* as a way of demonstrating 'the limits of individual autonomy as one of the bedrocks of bioethics' (2016). Her analysis points to how a set of (Euro-American) values about the primacy of the singular subject ('individual') has become embedded in scientific mechanisms of assessing and governing technology and the knowledge it might produce. It opens onto questions of the moral as a way of thinking about technologies as part of wider cultural systems (Csordas 2013).

Morality

Like values and ethics, morality has moved in and out of ethnographic focus over the decades. An explicit concern for R. R. Marett (1931) at the start of the twentieth century, it has been sometimes 'taken for granted' (Edel 1962, p. 56), considered solved (Gellner et al. 2020), or assumed to be simply social convention and not a focus of study in its own right. Unsurprisingly, then, approaches vary and overlap (Csordas 2013). One approach, as Robbins has observed, is encompassing: 'given that anthropologists are interested in studying the ways people live together, those outside the discipline could be forgiven for expecting them to have been talking about morality all along' (Robbins 2012, n.p., see also Fortes 1987; Fassin 2012). Ethnographic accounts of religion, rituals, kinship, and law, from this perspective, can all be read as studies of morality in practice, especially if morality is broadly defined as 'a convenient term for socially approved habits' (Ruth Benedict in Zigon 2008, p. 1). Another approach is to attend to sites of moral conflict or 'breakdown' (Zigon 2009) and concomitantly to the choices that individuals face—their 'freedom' (Laidlaw 2002). This central theme in the anthropology of morality is often seen as a break with a collectivist Durkheimian paradigm of morality as shared social normativities (Durkheim 1974). For some, a distinction between ethics and morality should be clearly drawn (Zigon 2007), with the former a situation of reflexive consideration and the latter a more grounded disposition, a 'non-intentional' way of being (Zigon 2007, p. 135). This resulted in the anthropology of morality being critiqued from within for its limited engagement with '*creative* moral action' (Robbins 2012, np, emphasis added) as well as its absence of a 'common theoretical framework' (Beldo 2014).

By contrast with studies of the 'non-intentional', Signe Howell's edited collection (1997) formulated explicit methods for the study of 'local moral worlds'

(Kleinman 1999, 2006), the meeting of different 'moral orders' and moments of individual reflexivity, self-awareness, and 'moral knowing' (Parish 1994). Howell's processual thinking about morality supports analyses of technologies and their uses which are themselves in flux, and approaches such as those she recommends are evident in the chapters of this section. To borrow Mattingly's terminology (2014), the everyday emerges as a 'moral laboratory', where technological changes may permeate moral boundaries, produce anxiety, breakdown, or conflict. Studies of technology often operate in the borderlands of moral action. When Svendsen and her team, for example, study the use of pigs in neonatal research (Dam and Svendsen 2018; see also this volume), questions emerge that invoke these paradigms of moral anthropology: how is the human enacted, and how does its treatment differ from that of other non-human animals? (Svendsen, this volume) How is the 'normal' generated, sustained, and marked (Roberts 2013; Gammeltoft 2014)? Ethnographic research into how questions of morality emerge in settings of technological advance endlessly refracts the specifics of ongoing negotiation.

FUNDING, NORMATIVITY, AND ACTIVISM

When anthropologists are invited into spaces of technological development, they are often tasked with bringing 'society' into projects of science and technology (Ong and Collier 2005). In their capacity as translators of the social, their contributions can be far reaching: from interrogations of power relations, bureaucracies, and hierarchies to belief systems bound up in technocratic reasoning and labour (English-Lueck and Lueck Avery 2017; Graeber 2018). These conditions of entry matter for the topics studied and approaches taken; however, as Strathern cautioned, framing inquiry in this way often solidifies and reifies a 'social', missing the questions of *which* social will count, *who* will be heard (2005, p. 470). The process of finding out can often become the object of study for the handy 'social scientist'.

New funding regimes that foregrounded the ethical and societal dimensions of technological change (as discussed above) not only re-situated the discipline but provided the means by which a great deal of work took place in anthropological communities throughout the 1990s and 2000s. By the turn of the century, the burgeoning fields of new reproductive technologies and later, genomics, were hitting newspaper headlines around the world. These technological advances became arenas where novel societal questions reinvigorated classic anthropological questions, driven by technological advance. Whether deliberations were about selective reproduction, the moral economies of embryos, or the uneven globalisation of NRTs, ethnographers were following these new technologies on their travels (Birenbaum-Carmeli and Inhorn 2009; Gammeltoft and Wahlberg 2014; Hampshire and Simpson 2015; Ross and Moll 2020).

In short, technological change gave anthropologists new field settings. They became embedded in the hopes, stakes, and quandaries in IVF clinics, contributed to policy debates, and linked the new study of relations to existing disciplinary debates about kinship (Edwards 2000; Konrad 2005). The legacies of these new ethnographic sites—and many others—are evident in this Handbook section, with fieldworkers found in laboratories, policy worlds, and technologically mediated lives. Social scientists looking at technology today will now often be required to refashion themselves: ethics is itself a site of metonymy. While societal debate about technological transformation in diverse fields still emerges in the language of ethics (Corsín Jiménez 2008), in Europe, funding initiatives now direct researchers to reframe their critical enquiry in the languages of responsible research and innovation (RRI). Speaking to discourses and practices of participation and public engagement which social scientists have shaped over the past decade (Zwart et al. 2014; Hoeyer 2020) allows for a range of spaces of debate (although not necessarily transformation) of technological innovation projects (van Oudheusden 2014).

Regardless of the explicit framing, ethnographers continued to follow devices and their worlds on the move, generating nuanced pictures of technological emergence. Anthropology's engagement with the everyday means engagement with lives newly problematised through technologies (Lakoff and Collier 2004), although questions of normativity remain, with anthropological positions on the ethical, moral, and value-based positions of the discipline varying as much as they ever have (Scheper-Hughes 1995; Farmer 1999). In recent years, anthropological voices have engaged in debates around how current new technologies should be used, from the *Campaign Against Sex Robots* (Richardson 2016) to the *Campaign Against Killer Robots* (Sharkey and Suchman 2013), the planetary resources and human labour involved in Amazon Echo (Crawford and Joler 2018), and the *Environmental Data Governance Initiative* (EDGI) (Poirier, this volume). Whether explicitly enrolled in projects of change or redirection, ethnographic studies of technology that foreground questions of values, ethics, and morality are insightful for the dilemmas they make visible. How anthropologists narrate, give accounts of, and analyse these struggles is the work of critical analysis.

The Chapters

The chapters in this *Ethics, Values, and Morality* section, therefore, take up struggles over technology with a specific eye to where they arise. Together, the authors discuss *personhood, authenticity, beauty, enhancement, regimes, responsibility*, and *control*, which they show to be ethnographically at stake in the chapters' empirical cases. The contributions question normative frameworks foe technological futures, illustrate how debates about technological presents unfold, demonstrate ambiguity and certainty, and offer competing ideas of what it means to live with and through technology.

The authors of our first two chapters present the technological work of the life sciences in the settings of laboratories, where human categories, boundaries, and the concept of the human itself come under strain. Capturing the spirit of experiment and the challenge of observing negotiations around humanness, in the first chapter Svendsen, Dam, Navne, and Gjødsbøl, explore *personhood* as a sphere of complex moral work at the boundaries between human and non-human. Working comparatively, Svendsen et al. shift between two life science settings, first considering experimental work on neonatal research piglets and, subsequently, clinical research on genomic variations in children with rare diseases. The moral human person cannot be taken as the self-evident grounds for an anthropological study of technology, but must be turned into a question. Responding to this question, Svendsen et al. uncover the unpredictable ways in which the category of the human person and its moral obligations materialise and shape ideas of care, relatedness, responsibility, and worth.

Formative in thinking about category work, the critical scholarship of Donna Haraway has shaped anthropological thought about technologies and personhood for decades. From the *Companion Species Manifesto* (2003) to *When Species Meet* (2008), Haraway has inspired ethnographers to see how everyday work with technologies becomes a site of the moral imagination and boundary work accompanying the creation of profit or knowledge (2011). As Svendsen et al. describe, categories perform work in shaping ideas of care, 'responsibility', and value as much as innovation offers the relentless future. From participatory design to 'consultation', social practices connected with technology often contribute to the ways these categories themselves may be transformed. For Svendsen et al., geneticists working in the laboratories under study, 'liminal lives at the margins of established categories come to contain a potential for moral confusion as well as analytical innovation' (Svendsen et al., this volume).

Hogle's contribution deals with *authenticity*, its tie to power and economic relations, and its construction within changing sets of participants and conditions. Like Svendsen et al., she builds her analysis from a contrast of cases: organoids, miniature simplified organs, and cultured meat. Through these, Hogle analyses how such forms may disturb the social order or generate new ones and how they are tied to discussions of whether they are true to the original. What actually makes something 'real meat'? The important question for anthropologists is not whether the food—in this case cultured meat—is real but how the authentic is understood by various participants and how it matters within ethically constituted global bioeconomies (Weiss 2016; Hayden 2003). Hogle then explores the institutionalisation of authenticity and the classificatory systems through which cultured meat cells must pass. As anthropologists increasingly enter the spaces of technological innovation and deployment, we begin to see all that goes into their making and into their repurposing as their lives of use extend. How are policies aimed at facilitating technological solutions translated, and through whose hands? How are values and moral boundaries established and enacted?

With their shared focus on substitutability, Svendsen et al. and Hogle both analyse how relations are governed, and where lines of similarity and difference are drawn. Hogle's frame of the authentic illustrates how judgements of classification are already laden with value, while Svendsen and her colleagues show us both how piglets take on a 'plastic identity' (this volume), and how genomes in international databases become 'digital substitutes' for corporeal persons. Drawing on the anthropology of morality and ethics, our first two authors chart how the limits of life are both shaped and challenged by technological innovation, exposing and displacing anthropological ideas about originality.

With the next two chapters we move from laboratories into more explicitly interventionist settings and technologies mediated by consumption. While clinical ambitions for enhancing life remain somewhat at a distance in the opening chapters of laboratory studies, the chapters from Kristensen and Jarrín concern material technologies that have increasingly spread into matters of control and self-management of the human body, mediated by market-based solutions and technologies. Questions of ethics and morality here intersect with both the responsibilities of corporations (see Trnka, below) and experiences of the managed and surveilled life (Gregg 2018). Kristensen's contribution on *enhancement* repositions the human within technologies that promise better selves, through technologies that offer both a change in state (pharmaceutical) and those that offer a change in knowledge (self-tracking): those that affect a human body chemically and those which offer mechanical—or digital—optimisation. Based on empirical work on the use of pharmaceuticals and self-tracking Kristensen shows how enhancement technologies are inscribed in societal values of productivity, empowerment, and self-responsibilisation, but that the use of these technologies might ultimately challenge, resist, and creatively transform these values.

Optimisation is not only concerned with labour; it may address other objects. Plastic surgery, for example, is increasingly used as a means to produce and transform the body according to desired ideals (Gilman 1999; Blum 2003; Heyes 2007; Edmonds 2007; Kroløkke 2018; Ackerman 2010). In his contribution on the pursuit of *beauty* as an aesthetic ideal, Jarrín's chapter analyses the technology of plastic surgery, centring the knife itself as a technology deserving of ethical attention, making visible the complex moral and ethical considerations and 'visceral biopolitics' involved in beautification. Beauty norms consist of a multiplicity of systems of meaning, competing, clashing, and collaborating in the coproduction of the body beautiful. Thus, interrogating plastic surgery means interrogating how 'ideals' are generated and, crucially, materialised. Interventions on the body carry with them racialised normative regimes from which desires spring, with Jarrín's analysis finding that enhancement technologies promise more than physical transformation. Both Kristensen and Jarrín's work refuse the dichotomy of interventionist technology as either empowering or disempowering. Instead, they show the complex interweaving of bodies, norms, and hierarchies in local worlds, connections which lead to the transformation of the self as well as the emergence of new norms.

Our final cluster of chapters focuses more explicitly on formalisations of ethics within organisational and bureaucratic structures, and the oft revealing responses of people working within them (Venkatesan 2020). Moving between the 'ethicalisation' of corporate capitalism, the everyday moral experiences of digital teenagers, and ethics committee bureaucrats, the chapters illuminate what ethnographic attention brings to settings where terms and agreements, written guidelines, or policy are made. In her contribution, Mette High introduces the notion of competing *regimes* of ethics which employees of oil companies and industry actors negotiate. Drawing on fieldwork in the oil and gas industry, High notes that it is a sector 'steeped in moral language', full of corporate moral slogans, 'conjoining hydrocarbons with not only political and economic opportunities, but also explicit moral visions of the good'. Ethnographers working within corporations have followed with interest the meeting of business ethics and best practice guidelines (Chong 2018), and ethics as an integrated, sometimes anticipatory, component of technology development. Now recognisable amongst these strategies is the institutionalisation of corporate social responsibility, or 'CSR' (Taft 2021; Dolan and Rajak 2016; Welker 2009; Campoamor 2019), which sits alongside older mechanisms of social organisation such as professional codes of conduct and ethics charters. In High's analysis, CSR operates within and as part of business strategies—stories about and enactments of ethical ideals drawing on a 'powerful virtuous vocabulary of generosity and charity' and materialising 'moral visions of the good' (High, this volume).

It has become commonplace for newly emerging technologies to contain within their marketing strategies a general applicability 'for good'. Digital technologies in particular, given their claims for cross domain applicability, segment a part of their work as 'data for good' (Espinoza and Aronczyk 2021; Luca 2017). Whether addressing humanitarian projects, predicting natural disasters, increasing farming efficiency in countries feeling the brunt of the climate crisis or supporting social entrepreneurship or connected farm tractors, technology developers are at pains to demonstrate the potential for their products to 'do good'.

As High weaves together different registers and regimes of personal, professional, and corporate moral reasoning, so too does Susanna Trnka in her contribution on the stakes of *responsibility* for young peoples' use of digital health technologies. As she notes, the role of digital technologies in the health and wellbeing campaigns of the world's nation states is far from settled. As technologies are evaluated in policy, government, domestic, and personal spheres, ethnographic work shows the competing responsibilities (Trnka and Trundle 2017) to which they are subject. Two languages have come to the fore in advocating their use: personal responsibility and self-care. Trnka's work with young people (ages 14–24) in Aotearoa, New Zealand illustrates the stakes of *responsibility* when young people engage with digital health apps, making connections on behalf of themselves, family, friends, and strangers. Demonstrating her interlocutors' critical relationship to both the information they gain and the design features they encounter, Trnka argues that these technologies add new layers to the enactment of responsibility, 'refracting users' sense of where agency lies' (Trnka, this volume).

Trnka's questions about the role of global corporations lead anthropologists of technology to new sites and scales of analysis, following newly emerging regional norms around data, privacy, and the role of digital technologies in state-making, with ethnographic sites around the world. These moral and ethical questions about what it means to embed technologies deeply within our personal and inter-personal networks escape any easy national analysis, and require that we follow the technologies themselves. From models of Silicon Valley individualism to Europe's General Data Protection Regulation, we see these themes arising in scholarship on sharing (Nelms et al. 2017), and the ethical labour of cryptocurrency mining and extraction (Calvão 2019; Jutel 2021).

In the section's closing contribution, Douglas-Jones turns an ethnographic eye on ethics practitioners themselves. Working with committee members in the United States who have been overseeing research in one of the twentieth century's most controversial technologies—stem cells—her analysis asks how those working in emerging fields navigate their way through those undergoing transformation. Over the past 20 years, anthropologists have also come to study ethics as itself a legitimator of technologies, considering its role within public debates and the form given to deliberation over research and innovation futures (Edwards 1999; Hoeyer 2005; Franklin 2007; Hasse et al. 2018; Hoeyer and Tutton 2005). Their analyses have stretched from the variability of ethical norms when biomedical clinical trials travel (Petryna 2005, 2009) to the co-production of technology, economics, and politics (Rabinow 1999). Douglas-Jones is concerned with what will constitute ethical governance from the point of view of those central to administering it. Like Trnka, she is interested in how responsibilities are distributed between institutions and individual researchers, and re-distributed between committee members. The questions arising in regard to how stem cells are to be governed, as a particularly ethically charged area of technological change, apply beyond the biosciences. An anthropology of ethics must also grapple with limits. How should ethnographers respond to the corporate capture of ethics as a means of not dealing seriously (or at all) with societal concerns (Metcalfe et al. 2019)? Reading High's analysis of Corporate Social Responsibility alongside the reflections of ambivalent ethics committee members makes it evident that an anthropology of the ethics of technology takes seriously the space of the self-described ethical as itself an object of anthropological investigation.

Conclusion

Technological change gives rise to questions that anthropologists have sought to understand and sometimes reformulate. Ethnographic observations complicate simple normativities, showing the complexities of ethical, moral, and value-based relationships to technologies and technological change. We learn with and alongside those who tackle the new; we learn with those who become 'moral pioneers' (Rapp 1987). For decades, close observations emerging through ethnographic work have also been brought into broader conversations with scientists. Ethnographers have been invited to speak for social concerns through framework of ethics, value, and morality by governments and funding bodies, and by communities affected by technological change. If the ethical is a means through which the social becomes known to itself (Corsín Jiménez 2008), then is this an expansive or reductionist move?

As the chapters in this section show, working with technologies expands field research to sites full of contradiction, deliberation, and reflection. Taking the ethical and moral as a lens also points to the kinds of questions it is generative to ask of a wide range of technologies, particularly in the pervasive everyday of our digital worlds. How should new norms of attention be understood? Where can we see the refiguration of roles and responsibilities as technologies delegate tasks to citizens, patients, and carers? Ethnographic accounts rarely allow for a simple narrative of technological empowerment or of eroding agency; instead, the focus on changing relationships, priorities, and norms is shown to be contested, messy. While the anthropology of ethics has tended to focus work primarily on the individual, everyday, deliberative, the anthropology of technology shows the benefit of broadening attention in the field to the institutional, organisational, and societal roles of ethics discourses. In the chapters to come, authors' ethnographic accounts of technology are doors to further questions beyond the discipline. Whether enriching empirical ethics or expanding sites of attention for ethicists in other fields, the openness of anthropological question asking is a vehicle for querying the construction of emergent norms. This mode of enquiry could not be more necessary for contemporary anthropological research on technology.

References

Ackerman, S. L. (2010). Plastic Paradise: Transforming Bodies and Selves in Costa Rica's Cosmetic Surgery Tourism Industry. *Medical Anthropology, 29*(4), 403–423. https://doi.org/10.1080/01459740.2010.501316.

Albert, E. M. (1956). The Classification of Values: A Method and Illustration. *American Anthropologist,* 221–248.

Amoore, L. (2020). *Cloud Ethics: Algorithms and the attributes of ourselves and others.* Durham, NC: Duke University Press.

Anthropology News (1975). Ethical and Human Value Implications of Science and Technology Program. *Anthropology News, 16*(9), 14–15.

Barndon, R. (2012). Technology and Morality: Rituals in Iron Working among the Fipa and Pangwa Peoples in Southwest Tanzania. *Archaeological Papers of the American Anthropological Association 21*(1), 37–48.

Beldo, L. (2014). The unconditional 'ought': A theoretical model for the anthropology of morality. *Anthropological Theory, 14*(3), 263–279. https://doi.org/10.1177/1463499614534373.

Belshaw, C.S. (1959). The Identification of Values in Anthropology. *American Journal of Sociology, 64*(6), 555–562.

Benjamin, R. (2016). Informed Refusal: Toward a Justice-based Bioethics. *Science, Technology and Human Values, 41*(6), 967–990.

Birenbaum-Carmeli, D., & Inhorn, M. C. (2009). *Assisting Reproduction, Testing Genes: Global Encounters with the New Biotechnologies.* Oxford: Berghahn.

Blum, V. (2003) *Flesh Wounds: The Culture of Cosmetic Surgery.* Berkeley: University of California Press.

Boellstorff, T. (2008). *Coming of age in Second Life: An Anthropologist Explores the Virtually Human.* Princeton, NJ: Princeton University Press.

Brandt, R. (1954). *Hopi Ethics.* Chicago, IL: University of Chicago Press.

Calvão, F. (2019). Crypto-miners: Digital labor and the power of blockchain technology. *Economic Anthropology, 6*(1), 123–134.

Campoamor, L. M. (2019). There's an App for That: Telecom, Children's Rights and Conflicting Logics of Corporate Social Responsibility. *American Anthropologist, 121*(3), 667–679.

Chong, K. (2018). *Best Practice: Management Consulting and the Ethics of Financialization in China.* Durham, NC: Duke University Press.

Corsín Jiménez, A. (Ed.) (2008). *Culture and Well-Being: Anthropological Approaches to Freedom and Political Ethics.* London: Pluto Press.

Crawford, K., & Joler, V. (2018). Anatomy of an AI System. https://anatomyof.ai. Accessed 22 March 2021.

Cribb, A., Dunn, M., & Ives, J. (2016). *Empirical Bioethics: Theoretical and Practical Perspectives.* Cambridge: Cambridge University Press.

Csordas, T. J. (2013). Morality as a Cultural System? *Current Anthropology 54*(5), 523–546.

Dam, M. S., & Svendsen, M. N. (2018). Treating pigs: Balancing standardisation and individual treatments in translational neonatology research. *BioSocieties, 13,* 349–367.

Dolan, C., & Rajak D. (2016). *The Anthropology of Corporate Social Responsibility.* London: Berghahn.

Doris, J. M., & A. Plakias. (2008). How to Argue about Disagreement: Evaluative Diversity and Moral Realism. In W. Winnott-Armstrong (Ed.), *Moral Psychology: The Cognitive Science of Morality: Intuition and Diversity, Vol. 2* (pp. 303–331). Cambridge, MA: The MIT Press.

Douglas-Jones, R. (2015). A 'good' ethical review: ethics audit and professionalism in research ethics. *Social Anthropology, 23*(1), 53–67.

Dumit, J. (2014) Writing the Implosion: Teaching the World One Thing at a Time. *Cultural Anthropology, 29*(2), 344–362.

Dumont, L. (2013 [1980]). On Value: The Radcliffe-Brown Lecture in Social Anthropology, 1980. *Hau: Journal of Ethnographic Theory, 3*(1), 287–315.

Durkheim, E. (1974). *Sociology and philosophy.* New York: Free Press.

Dussauge, I., Helgesson, C. F., & Lee, F. (Eds.) (2015). *Value practices in the life sciences and medicine.* Oxford: Oxford University Press.

DuBois, C. (1955). The Dominant Value Profile of American Culture. *American Anthropologist, 57*(6), 1232–1239.

Edel, A. (1962). Anthropology and Ethics in Common Focus. *Journal of the Royal Anthropological Institute, 92*(1), 55–72.

Edmonds, A. (2007). The poor have the right to be beautiful: Cosmetic surgery in neoliberal Brazil. *Journal of the Royal Anthropological Institute, 13,* 363–381.

Edwards, J. (1999). Why dolly matters: Kinship, culture and cloning. *Ethnos, 64*(3–4), 301–324.

Edwards, J. (2000). *Born and Bred: Idioms of Kinship and New Reproductive Technologies*. Oxford: Oxford University Press.

Edwards, J., Harvey, P., & Wade, P. (2008). *Anthropology and Science: Epistemologies in Practice*. ASA Monographs 43. London: Bloomsbury.

English-Lueck, J. A., & Lueck Avery, M. (2017). Intensifying Work and Chasing Innovation: Incorporating Care in Silicon Valley. *Anthropology of Work Review, 38*(1), 40–49.

Espinoza, M. I., & Aronczyk, M. (2021). Big data for climate action or climate action for big data? *Big Data & Society*. https://doi.org/10.1177/2053951720982032.

Farmer, P. (1999). *Infections and Inequalities: The Modern Plagues*. Berkeley: University of California Press.

Fassin, D. (2012). *A Companion to Moral Anthropology*. Malden, MA: Wiley-Blackwell.

Fassin, D. (2014). The Ethical Turn in Anthropology: Promises and Uncertainties. *HAU: Journal of Ethnographic Theory, 4*(1), 429–35.

Franklin, S. (2007). *Dolly Mixtures: The Remaking of Genealogy*. Durham, NC: Duke University Press.

Firth, R. (1953). The study of values by social anthropologists. *Man, 231*, 146–153.

Firth, R. (1979). Work and Value: Reflections on Ideas of Karl Marx. In S. Wallman (Ed.), *Social Anthropology of Work* (pp. 177–206). London: Academic Press

Fortes, M. (1987). *Religion, Morality, and the Person: Essays on Tallensi Religion*. Cambridge: Cambridge University Press.

Fox, R. C., & Swazey, J. P. (1984) Medical morality is not bioethics: medical ethics in China and the United States. *Perspectives in Biology and Medicine, 27*, 336–60.

Fox, R. C., & Swazey, J. P. (1992). *Observing Bioethics*. Oxford: Oxford University Press.

Gammeltoft, T. (2014). *Haunting Images: A Cultural Account of Selective Reproduction in Vietnam*. Berkeley, CA: University of California Press.

Gammeltoft, T. M., & Wahlberg, A. (2014). Selective Reproductive Technologies. *Annual Review of Anthropology, 43*(1), 201–216.

Gellner, D. N., Curry, O.S., Cook, J., Alfano, M., & S. Venkatesen. (2020). Morality is fundamentally an evolved solution to problems of social co-operation. *Journal of the Royal Anthropological Institute, 26*(2), 415–417.

Gilman, S. (1999). *Making the Body Beautiful: A Cultural History of Aesthetic Surgery*. Princeton, NJ: Princeton University Press

Gregg, M. (2018). *Counterproductive: Time Management in the Knowledge Economy*. Durham NC: Duke University Press.

Graeber, D. (2001). *Toward an Anthropological Theory of Value*. New York: Palgrave.

Graeber, D. (2018). *Bullshit Jobs: A Theory*. New York: Simon and Schuster

Hasse, C., Trentemøller, S., & Sorensen, J. (2018). The use of ethnography to identify and address ethical, legal and societal (ELS) issues. *HRI' 18 Companion*, March 5–8, 2018, Chicago IL, USA.

Hampshire, K., & Simpson, B. (2015). *Assisted Reproductive Technologies in the Third Phase: Global Encounters and Emerging Moral Worlds*. Oxford: Berghahn.

Haraway, D. (1990). A Cyborg Manifesto: Science, Technology and Socialist-Feminism in the Late 20th Century, In D. Haraway (Ed.), *Simians, Cyborgs and Women: The Reinvention of Nature* (pp. 149–81). New York: Routledge.

Haraway, D. (2003). *The Companion Species Manifesto: Dogs, People and Significant Otherness*. Chicago, IL: Prickly Paradigm Press.

Haraway, D. (2008). *When Species Meet*. Minneapolis, MN: University of Minnesota Press.

Haraway, D. (2011). Speculative Fabulations for Technoculture's Generations: Taking care of unexpected country. *Australian Humanities Review, 50*, May 2011.

Hayden, C. (2003). *When Nature Goes Public: The Making and Unmaking of Bioprospecting in Mexico*. Princeton: Princeton University Press

Heintz, M. (Ed.) (2009). *The Anthropology of Moralities*. London: Berghahn

Heyes, C. J. (2007). *Self-Transformations: Foucault, Ethics, and Normalized Bodies*. Oxford & New York: Oxford University Press

Howell, S. (Ed.) (1997). *The Ethnography of Moralities*. London: Routledge.

Hoeyer, K. (2005). Studying Ethics as Policy. *Current Anthropology, 46*(5), S71–S90.

Hoeyer, K. (2006). "Ethics wars": Reflections on the Antagonism between Bioethicists and Social Science Observers of Biomedicine. *Human Studies, 29*, 203–227.

Hoeyer K. (2009). Informed Consent: the Making of a Ubiquitous Rule in Medical Practice. *Organization, 16*(2), 267–288.

Hoeyer, K. (2020). Ethics as a form of regulation in relation to data and bodily materials. In M.-A. Jacob & A. Kirkland (Eds.), *Research Handbook on Socio-Legal Studies of Medicine and Health* (pp. 333–348). Cheltenham, U.K.: Edward Elgar.

Hoeyer, K. & Tutton, R. (2005). "Ethics was here": studying the language-games of ethics in the case of UK Biobank. *Critical Public Health, 15*(4), 385–397. https://doi.org/10.1080/09581590500523533.

Hoeyer, K., & Hogle, L. F. (2014). Informed Consent: The Politics of Intent and Practice in Medical Research Ethics. *Annual Review of Anthropology, 43*, 347–362.

Jutel, O. (2021). Blockchain imperialism in the Pacific. *Big Data & Society*. https://doi.org/10.1177/2053951720985249.

Kapferer, B., & Gold, M. (2018). *Moral Anthropology: A Critique*. New York: Berghahn Books.

Keane, W. (2016). *Ethical life. Its Natural and Social Histories*. Princeton, NJ: Princeton University Press.

Kelman, S. (2018). The Bumipreneur dilemma and Malaysia's technology start-up ecosystem. *Economic Anthropology 5*(1): 59–70.

Kleinman, A. (1999). *Experience and its moral modes: culture, human conditions, and disorder*. The Tanner Lectures on Human Values. Salt Lake City: University of Utah Press.

Kleinman, A. (2006). *What really matters: living a moral life amidst uncertainty and danger*. Oxford: Oxford University Press.

Kluckhohn, C. (1951). Values and Value-Orientations in the Theory of Action: an Exploration in Definition and Classification. In T. Parsons & E. Shils (Eds.), *Towards a General Theory of Action* (pp. 388–433). Cambridge: Harvard University Press.

Kluckhohn, C. (1956). Towards a Comparison of Value-emphases in Different Cultures. In L. White (Ed.), *The State of the Social Sciences*. Chicago: Chicago University Press.

Konrad, M. (2005). *Nameless Relations: Anonymity, Melanesia and Reproductive Gift Exchange between British Ova Donors and Recipients*. Oxford: Berghahn.

Kroløkke, C. (2018). *Global Fluids: The cultural politics of Reproductive Waste and Value*. New York: Berghahn Books.

Ladkin, S., McKay, R., & Bojesen, E. (Eds.) (2016). *Against Value in the Arts and Education*. London: Rowman and Littlefield.

Lakoff, A., & Collier, S. (2004). Ethics and the anthropology of modern reason. *Anthropological Theory, 4*(4), 419–434.

Laidlaw, J. (2002). For an Anthropology of Ethics and Freedom. *The Journal of the Royal Anthropological Institute, 8*(2), 311–32.

Laidlaw, J. (2014). *The Subject of Virtue: An Anthropology of Ethics and Freedom*. New York: Cambridge University Press.

Lambek, M. (2008). Value and Virtue. *Anthropological Theory, 8*(2), 133–157.

Lambek, M. (Ed.) (2010). *Ordinary Ethics: Anthropology, Language and Action*. New York: Fordham University Press.

Lock, M. (2001). *Twice Dead: Organ Transplants and the Reinvention of Death*. Berkeley: University of California Press.

Luca. (2017). Whitepaper_ Data as a Force for Good. https://luca-d3.com/data-for-good#data-force-good-section. Accessed 22 June 2021.

Manelin, E. B. (2020). Health Care Quality Improvement and the Ambiguous Commodity of Care. *Medical Anthropology Quarterly, 34*(3), 361–377.

Marett, R. R. (1931). The beginnings of morals and culture: an introduction to social anthropology. In W. Rose (Ed.), *An Outline of Modern Knowledge* (pp. 395–430) New York: Putnam.

Martin, E. (1991). The Egg and the Sperm: How Science has Constructed a Romance Based on Stereotypical Male-Female Roles. *Signs, 16*(3), 485–501.

Mattingly, C. (2012). Two virtue ethics and the anthropology of morality. *Anthropological Theory, 12*(2), 161–184.

Mattingly, C. (2014). *Moral Laboratories. Family Peril and the Struggle for a Good Life*. University of California Press.

Mattingly, C., & Throop, J. (2018). The Anthropology of Ethics and Morality. *Annual Review of Anthropology, 47*(1), 475–492.

Metcalfe, J., Moss, E., & boyd, d. (2019). Owning Ethics: Corporate Logics, Silicon Valley and the Institutionalization of Ethics. *Social Research: An International Quarterly, 82*(2), 449–476.

Miller, D. (2008). The uses of value. *Geoforum, 39*(3), 1122–1132.

Mol, A. (2010). Care and its values. Good food in the nursing home. In A. Mol, I. Moser & J. Pols (Eds.), *Care in practice: On tinkering in clinics, homes and farms* (pp. 215–234), Bielefeld: Transcript Verlag.

Nelms, T. C., Maurer, B., Swartz, L. & Mainwaring, S. (2017). Social Payments: Innovation, Trust, Bitcoin, and the Sharing Economy. *Theory, Culture, and Society, 35*(3), 13–33.

Ong, A. (2010 [1987]). *Spirits of Resistance and Capitalist Discipline: Factory Women in Malaysia*. State University of New York.

Ong, A. (1988). The production of possession: spirits and the multinational corporation in Malaysia. *American Ethnologist, 15*(1), 28–42.

Ong, A., & Collier, S. (2005). *Global Assemblages: Technology, Politics and Ethics as Anthropological Problems*. Oxford: Blackwell Publishing.

Parker, M. H. (2009). Two concepts of empirical ethics. *Bioethics 23*(4), 202–213.

Parish, S. (1994). *Moral Knowing in a Hindu Sacred City*. New York: Columbia University Press.

Petersen, A. (2011). *The Politics of Bioethics*. London: Routledge.

Petryna, A. (2005). Ethical Variability: Drug Development and Globalizing Clinical Trials. *American Ethnologist, 32*(2), 183–197.

Petryna, A. (2009). *When Experiments Travel: Clinical Trials and the Global Search for Human Subjects*. Princeton, NJ: Princeton University Press.

Pfaffenberger, B. (1992). Social Anthropology of Technology. *Annual Review of Anthropology, 21*, 491–516.

Poggiali, L. (2016). Seeing (from) digital peripheries: Technology and Transparency in Kenya's Silicon Savannah. *Cultural Anthropology, 31*, 387–411. https://doi.org/10.14506/ca31.3.07.

Pols, J. (2018). Empirical ethics and the study of care. Web publication/site, Somatosphere. http://somatosphere.net/2018/11/a-readers-guide-to-the-anthropology-of-ethics-and-morality-part-iii.html. Accessed 8 July 2021.

Powers, W. R. (2000). The Harvard Study of Values: Mirror for Postwar Anthropology. *The History of the Behavioural Sciences, 36*(2), 15–29.

Puig de la Bellacasa, M. (2017). *Matters of Care*. Minneapolis, MI: University of Minnesota Press.

Rabinow, P. (1999). *French DNA: Trouble in Purgatory*. Chicago: University of Chicago Press.

Rapp, R. (1987). Moral pioneers: women, men and fetuses on a frontier of reproductive technology. *Women Health, 13*(1–2), 101–16.

Read, K. (1955). Morality and the Concept of the Person among the Gahuku-Gama. *Oceania, 25*(4), 233–282.

Richardson, K. (2016). The asymmetrical 'relationship': parallels between prostitution and the development of sex robots. *SIGCAS Comput. Soc., 45*(3), 290–293.

Robbins, J. (2012). On becoming ethical subjects: freedom, constraint and the anthropology of morality. *Anthropology of this Century, 5*.

Robbins, J. (2016). What is the matter with transcendence? On the place of religion in the new anthropology of ethics. *Journal of the Royal Anthropological Institute, 22*(4), 767–781.

Roberts, E. F. S. (2013). Assisted Existence: an ethnography of being in Ecuador. *Journal of the Royal Anthropological Institute, 19*, 562–580.

Ross, F. C., & Moll, T. (2020). Assisted Reproduction: Politics, Ethics and Anthropological Futures. *Medical Anthropology, 39*(6), 553–562. https://doi.org/10.1080/01459740.2019.1695130.

Rydstrom, H. (2003). *Embodying Morality: Growing Up in Rural Northern Vietnam*. Honolulu: University Hawai'i Press.

Sanders, R. (2017). Self-tracking in the digital era: Biopower, patriarchy, and the new biometric body projects. *Body & Society, 23*(1), 36–63.

Scheper-Hughes, N. (1995). The primacy of the ethical: Proposals for a Militant Anthropology. *Current Anthropology, 36*(3), 409–440.

Sharkey, N., & Suchman, L. (2013). Wishful Mnemonics and Autonomous Killing Machines. *AISB Quarterly, 136*, 14–22.

Sharon, T. (2013). *Human nature in an age of biotechnology: The case for mediated post-humanism, Vol. 14*. Springer Science & Business Media.

Sharon, T. (2016). Self-tracking for health and the quantified self: Re-articulating autonomy, solidarity, and authenticity in an age of personalized healthcare. *Philosophy & Technology, 30*(1), 93–121.

Stark, L. (2011). *Behind Closed Doors: IRBs and the Making of Ethical Research*. Chicago: University of Chicago Press.

Strathern, M. (2005). Robust Knowledge and Fragile Futures. In A. Ong & S. Collier (Eds.), *Global Assemblages: Technology, Politics, and Ethics as Anthropological Problems* (pp. 464–481). Blackwell Publishing Ltd.

Stoczkowski, W. (2008). The 'fourth aim' of anthropology: between knowledge and ethics. *Anthropological Theory, 8*(4), 345–356.

Sykes, K. (Ed.) (2009). *Ethnographies of Moral Reasoning*. New York: Palgrave Macmillan.

Taft, C. E. (2021). Performing Accountability and Corporate Social Responsibility. *Political and Legal Anthropology Review*. https://doi.org/10.1111/plar.12397.

Taussig, K-S. (2009). *Ordinary Genomes: Science, Citizenship and Genetic Identities*. Durham, NC: Duke University Press.

Trnka, S., & Trundle, C. (2017). *Competing Responsibilities*. Durham, NC.: Duke University Press.

Trundle, C. (2020). Tinkering Care, State Responsibility and Abandonment: Nuclear Test Veterans and The Mismatched Temporalities of Justice in Claims for Health Care. *Anthropology and Humanism, 45*(2), 202–211.

van Oudheusden, M. (2014). Where are the politics in responsible innovation? European governance, technology assessments, and beyond. *Journal of Responsible Innovation, 1*(1), 67–86.

Venkatesan, S. (2020). Afterword: Putting together the anthropology of tax and the anthropology of ethics. *Social Analysis, 64*(2), 141–154.

Wahlberg, A. (2018) *Good Quality: The Routinization of Sperm Banking in China*. Berkeley: University of California Press.

Weiss, B. (2016). *Real Pigs: Shifting Values in the Field of Local Pork*, Durham, NC: Duke University Press.

Weisz, G. (Ed.) (1990). *Social Science Perspectives on Biomedical Ethics*. Dortmund: Springer.

Welker, M. A. (2009). Corporate Security Begins in the Community: Mining, the Corporate Social Responsibility Industry, and Environmental Advocacy in Indonesia. *Cultural Anthropology, 24*(1), 142–179.

Zigon, J. (2007). Moral breakdown and the ethical demand: A theoretical framework for an anthropology of moralities. *Anthropological Theory, 7*(2), 131–150.

Zigon, J. (2008). *Morality: An Anthropological Perspective*. Oxford: Berg.

Zigon, J. (2009). Within a Range of Possibilities: Morality and Ethics in Social Life. *Ethnos, 74*(2), 251–276.

Zigon, J. (2013). On Love: Remaking Moral Subjectivity in Postrehabilitation Russia. *American Ethnologist, 40*(1), 201–215.

Zwart, H., Landeweerd, L. & van Rooij, A. (2014). Adapt or perish? Assessing the recent shift in the European research funding arena from 'ELSA' to 'RRI'. *Life Sciences, Society and Policy 10*(11). https://doi.org/10.1186/s40504-014-0011-x.

CHAPTER 27

Moral Ambiguities: Fleshy and Digital Substitutes in the Life Sciences

Personhood

Mette N. Svendsen, Mie S. Dam, Laura E. Navne, and Iben M. Gjødsbøl

Morality is a human capacity. In Western philosophy, what makes us human is our ability to have intentions and reflect upon and distinguish between right and wrong. This notion of the human is part of a division of labour between the natural and the human sciences. The natural sciences investigate the natural, non-speaking world; the human sciences investigate embodied mortal humans who can speak, reflect, build societies, and produce meaning from their interactions with each other and the natural world. The major claim of this chapter is that anthropological studies of morality in the life sciences derail this widespread notion of the human. The moral striving of humans caught up in the processes of producing scientific knowledge and biomedical technologies to save and prolong the life of mortal bodies takes us into ways of conceptualising the human which outgrow strict boundaries between person and thing, between human and animal, and between body and data.

Modern bioethics is the discipline of studying ethical issues related to technological advances in biology and medicine. Since the post-World War II period, a framework that ascribes moral status and basic rights to every human has undergirded bioethical practice and theory (Thompson 2013). In that respect,

M. N. Svendsen (✉) • M. S. Dam • L. E. Navne • I. M. Gjødsbøl
Department of Public Health, Centre for Medical Science and Technology Studies, University of Copenhagen, Copenhagen, Denmark
e-mail: mesv@sund.ku.dk; mda@sund.ku.dk; lana@vive.dk; ibgj@sund.ku.dk

M. H. Bruun et al. (eds.), *The Palgrave Handbook of the Anthropology of Technology*, https://doi.org/10.1007/978-981-16-7084-8_27

anthropology and bioethics are based on the same notion of the moral human as distinct from things or animals, yet the disciplines have very different intents. Whereas the typical bioethical approach is concerned with mapping different moral viewpoints in order to reach the right ethical position on an issue, anthropological studies of morality in the life sciences concern morality as a daily practice of seeking to answer the question of 'how or as what one ought to live?' (Laidlaw 2002, p. 324). An anthropological approach to morality explores how people strive for the good, experience incommensurable values, and make practical judgements (Lambek 2015; Mattingly 2014; Sharp 2019). In anthropology, morality is an empirical investigation of how people make themselves into certain kinds of persons within specific contexts and historical epochs (Laidlaw 2002). Anthropological studies of technology document how the making of knowledge and technology happens in a 'moral landscape' (Helgason and Pálsson 1997; Svendsen and Koch 2008) concomitantly shaped and reshaped through specific ways of creating, transforming, treating, working on, exchanging, and caring for new life forms. A central insight of these studies is that morality does not only enter the scene of action when technologies are packaged and ready for use in society. On the contrary, morality is integrated into the very processes of making medical knowledge and technology (Dumit 2012; Franklin 2007; Friese 2013a; Kaufman 2005, 2015; Morgan 2009; Sharp 2014, 2019; Strathern 1992). Morality shapes what can be known and what can be done.

In the first part of this chapter, we review the anthropological literature on morality in the life sciences by highlighting two analytical interests. First, we scrutinise anthropological studies on person and kinship in connection to the production of liminal lives. Then we discuss anthropological analyses of the biopolitical formations shaping moral practices in the context of technological innovations. In the second part of the chapter, we move to our ethnographic cases: an animal laboratory and a human genetics clinic in Denmark. We show how research piglets—modelled to stand in for humans in experimental neonatology—raise concerns about the boundary between human and animal, person and instrument. We then investigate how in clinical genetics, genomes are treated as potent representations of the human person, raising concerns about their future lives in data archives and contesting the boundary between person and data. Juxtaposing the literature and our empirical findings, we suggest that ethnographic studies on morality in the life sciences at one and the same time exemplify the meaning-making human being at the heart of the anthropological discipline and destabilise that very notion of the moral and mortal human.

Moral Experiences with Liminal Lives: Person and Kinship

In the 1990s, anthropologists entered the empirical sites of life science laboratories, biomedical clinics, regulatory institutions, biotech companies, and the homes of citizens and patients, encountering the possibilities and perils of new medical technologies and the conditions that produce them. As biotechnological developments initially took place in laboratories and clinics in Europe and the US, most anthropological studies were situated in that part of the world. Building on a long anthropological tradition for treating the boundary as a zone of potentiality, experiment, and cultural change (Douglas 1966; Turner 1969), a key interest of these studies has been moral experience in connection to the emergence of 'liminal lives' (Squier 2004). These liminal lives are reproductive substances and fetuses entering an increasingly uncertain terrain with the advent of advanced biotechnologies (Franklin 2013; Rapp 1999; Roberts 2011); cadaveric organ donors and comatose people in intensive care units (Bird-David and Israeli 2010; Jensen 2016; Lock 2002; Kaufman 2003); people with late stage dementia held in life through advanced care (Buch 2013; Gjødsbøl et al. 2017; Taylor 2008a); blood samples in biobanks (Hoeyer 2005); stem cell lines to be manipulated in the lab into future therapy (Franklin and Lock 2003; Hogle 2010); premature infants in incubators (Navne et al. 2017); and animals made to model humans in experimental science (Dam and Svendsen 2018; Sharp 2019). In following the social lives of these bodies and substances, ethnographic studies have directed attention to the ways in which liminal lives contest the distinction between person and thing in Western philosophy and give rise to moral ambiguities.

For example, transspecies embryos raise moral questions about what qualifies as a human embryo and how to differentiate between one hybrid embryo and another (Brown 2009; Thompson 2013). Other chimeric life forms—such as cells from a human inserted into a pig—elicit feelings of a boundary breach and elucidate moral and political efforts to maintain boundaries around the human, even at the level of cells and tissues (Hinterberger 2018). Lab animals are another site of this binary transgression, as they are at once valued for their role as human proxies while used precisely because their nonhuman status appears more morally palatable (Haraway 2008). Nevertheless, the daily care for animals in experimental spaces provokes moral ambiguities when they model humans and momentarily gain identities which blur their animality (Sharp 2019). While older anthropological studies of personhood treated the person as a universal category to be given different content in different empirical settings (Mauss 1985 [1938]; Fortes 1945), studies of the moral experiences related to caring for liminal lives track how people in labs and clinics come to question what a person is.

In connection to exploring the boundaries of the human person, anthropologists have devoted considerable analytical attention to the ways in which genetic and reproductive technologies promise, as well as threaten, configurations of kinship (Carroll 2016; Franklin and McKinnon 2001; Franklin 2013; Hird 2004; Klotz 2016). Marilyn Strathern's study of the regulatory and public debates about in vitro fertilisation (IVF) in the UK uncovered how the separation of the reproductive substances (egg and sperm) from the social categories of 'mother' and 'father' raised moral concerns about the relationship between biological and social ties. What used to be straightforward questions—'What is a parent?' or 'When does life begin?'—became morally challenging issues to be discussed in Parliament and decided in legal acts (Strathern 1992, 2011).

Monica Konrad's study of genetic testing illuminated how the mapping of genetic connections between people who are strangers to each other provoked questions about the social responsibilities which follow from biological connections (2005). Similarly, studies of genetic testing traced the ways in which identities and ethical obligations were crafted through genealogical knowledge (Nelson 2008; Klotz 2016; Rapp et al. 2001). Moreover, the pursuit of genetic knowledge in clinical practices provoked discussions around which forms of life get constituted as normal and abnormal, when, and why (Latimer 2015), and revealed processes of making the abnormal ordinary in family and society (Taussig 2009).

The moral controversies around IVF and the new genetics showed that biological facts are privileged in Euro-American kinship thinking, and part of anthropological theories which also considered the biological facts of reproduction as prior to social relations (Franklin 1997). In sum, studies on morality in connection to person and kinship spurred a theoretical interest in how exchange of bodily substances produces (or does not produce) a sense of relatedness between the involved parties. A central insight of these studies is that connections and mutuality may co-exist with difference and incommensurability.

EXTENDING THE FIELD OF MORAL ACTION: FROM BIOPOLITICS TO SYMBIOPOLITICS

Another key interest of anthropological studies of the life sciences is the biopolitical formations shaping moral practices. With inspiration from Michel Foucault, Nikolas Rose, and Paul Rabinow, studies of biopolitics have uncovered the intersection of state practices, market dynamics, and social experiences shaping the production and categorisation of life as well as ethical responsibilities. Anthropologists have explored the ways in which imaging techniques reify the fetus and transform it into a potent public and political image (Casper 1998; Rapp 1999; Taylor 2008b). Studies of prenatal diagnostics as a means of population surveillance have scrutinised the mechanisms of selection and the moral experiences of right and wrong which become part and parcel of this biopolitical governance (Gammeltoft 2014; Greenhalgh 2008; Schwennesen et al. 2010; Wahlberg 2018). At the other end of the life span, anthropologists have examined how possibilities for extending life through intensive care and transplant technologies de-naturalise death and create new forms of subjecthood such as the person with late-stage dementia, the comatose patient, and the cadaveric organ donor (Gjødsbøl et al. 2017; Lock 2002; Kaufman 2005; Sharp 2006). Sharon Kaufman has cracked open how '*the technical ability to intercede becomes the moral reason to proceed*' (2015, p. 164, emphasis in the original). By tracing the links between treatment protocols, clinical trials, insurance reimbursement policies, and the aspirations of health professionals and patients, her work uncovers an ethical field that expands what is considered 'treatable'. The drivers of this field relegate to the margins the moral quandary of drawing the line at when to prolong life and its consequences of poor living due to decline, dementia, disabilities, and suffering (Kaufman 2005, 2015).

The biopolitical framework has also been crucially important to anthropological investigations of the reconfiguration of body, person, and market when biology becomes available for use and exchange (Hoeyer 2013). In genetics, blood samples translated into bio-information and combined with health information from medical records and banked in large-scale databases hold the potential of 'biovalue' (Waldby 2002). Similarly, in reproductive medicine, oocytes, sperm, and embryos become transactable objects accessible to social circulation with the aim of producing families, health, and capital. Ethnographers have turned their attention to the sorts of 'moral promise' (Sharp 2014, p. 48) for health and wealth which emerge with new technological possibilities for manipulating life; the ways in which novel biological and genetic knowledge craft biosocialities (Gibbon and Novas 2008); how donation of tissue morally places donors in relation to larger communities (Cool 2016; Hoeyer 2003; Reardon 2017; Wahlberg 2018); and the 'ethical boundary work' (Wainwright et al. 2006) at the interface of lab and clinic.

With the circulation of biological material on a global market and the outsourcing of clinical trials, ethnographic studies have problematised how striving for the good (family, health, and wealth) in one part of the world draws upon global inequalities in other parts of the world. Michelle Murphy's historical study of the 'economization of life' (2017) illustrates how a 'spatialization of experiment' (p. 79) to villages in Bangladesh in the 1970s involved violent ways of devaluing the lives of poor women and families as part of creating economic value in the US. Experiments on populations through means of sterilisation and contraception were conducted by promising good lives for brown women. Based on present-day ethnography, anthropologists have raised awareness about exploitation and revealed how structural inequalities are invisibilised with notions of gift giving, commerce, or altruism (Cooper and Waldby 2014; Petryna 2009; Rajan 2008; Schepher-Hughes 2004). For example, transnational gestational surrogacy shifts reproduction into networks of social and economic inequality, where surrogates are reconceptualised as 'site(s) of potential productivity' through which to access this global market (Vora 2013, p. S100).

The biopolitical framework has predominantly been concerned with how biomedical regimes of power are produced by humans (Rees 2018, p. 47). With inspiration from a Latourian perspective on actor networks, life science ethnographers have extended the biopolitical framework to the nonhuman (Asdal et al. 2016; Friese 2013a; Kirk 2016) and suggested a shift from biopolitics to 'symbiopolitics' (Helmreich 2009). In Helmreich's work on oceanography, the concept of symbiopolitics allows for an investigation of the semiotic and material entanglements among human bodies, marine microbes, and bioinformatics. This extension of the anthropological perspective marks a shift from situating morality in relationships between human persons to approaching morality as produced and shaped in ecological relationships with diverse groups of actors across spaces and species (Haraway 2016; Helmreich 2009). Taking a pill or undergoing treatment in one part of the world places that individual in a chain of relationships to research animals, microbes, funding bodies, pharmaceutical companies, research subjects, and agricultural pharming across time and space. In the writings of Donna Haraway, this diverse group of actors become the individual's 'cyborg littermates' (2016, p. 104)—a kinship relationship which comes with new forms of moral responsibilities. In other words, these chains of connections have deepened and reshaped how anthropologists may imagine the human and the field of moral action.

Each of the ethnographic works we have summarized so far lays bare the driving moral ambition of the life sciences: to extend and enhance the life of the moral and mortal human. Paradoxically, maybe, ethnographic works about morality in the life sciences at one and the same time *confirm* that humans are moral beings (reflecting, striving, exercising judgement) and *displace* that very notion of the moral and mortal human by depicting the human as connected and vulnerable to other humans, animals, and environments. When entering the empirical field of the life sciences, anthropologists not only document the rich reflections of their interlocutors dealing with the liminal lives of genomes, foetuses, animals, tissue, and corpses, their ethnographies also come to unravel the unboundedness of the body and thus the global networks and conditions which enable and sustain it. This interconnectedness makes it increasingly difficult to determine where one body ends and another begins (Solomon 2016). In the words of Anna Tsing, 'if survival always involves others, it is also necessarily subject to the indeterminacy of self-other transformations' (2015, p. 29). Our journey through the ethnographic literature on morality in the life sciences demonstrates a shift from an empirical and analytical attention to *liminal lives* in labs and clinics to a concern with *precarious livelihoods* as a result of material and semiotic entanglements in more-than-human worlds.

In the next section, we turn to our ethnographic case study of moral experiences and practices in an animal laboratory and a human genetics clinic in Denmark. We were invited into these settings to study the ethics related to generating new biological knowledge and bringing this knowledge into the lives of clinics and patients. These invitations in themselves express the ways in which science and technology create moral uncertainty for people handling and caring for liminal lives. We begin in the animal laboratory where pigs model humans to create future health for premature infants; we then move to the genetics department, where genomes act as representations of humans in the effort to diagnose rare disease in children. We treat the everyday practices of one site as a prism for the other site and its practices (Svendsen et al. 2018). With this comparative methodology, we unravel the entanglement of morality, technology, and the notions of the human across dissimilar spaces in the life science field.

RESEARCH PIGLETS AS FLESHY SUBSTITUTES
IN EXPERIMENTAL SCIENCE

In an animal facility on a university campus in Copenhagen, a research group has specialised in using piglets as models of premature human infants at risk of devastating inflammation of the gut by necrotising enterocolitis (NEC). In the experiments, preterm piglets are taken by C-section and placed in individual incubators. Through a period of 5 to 26 days (depending on the experimental design), some of them develop NEC. On the last day of the experiment, the piglets are killed, cut up, and their organs turned into 70–80 tissue samples. By modelling NEC in the piglets, the researchers aim to study the possible preventive effects of different forms of nutrition and translate this knowledge into dietary regimes for premature infants in neonatal intensive care units (NICUs). The tissue samples provide the basis for their scientific analyses of how the gut matures and the best nutrition to prevent NEC and stimulate growth in infants. The medical condition of NEC is closely related to prematurity and it was only by exploring the possibilities of making preterm infants survive that the disease became clinically known. The imperative of saving infants and the technological advancements in neonatology thus condition the experimental practices in the pig laboratory. From a symbiopolitics perspective (Helmreich 2009), the lives of human infants in intensive care depend on and are intertwined with the life and death of research animals. Said differently, the governance of relations among entangled living beings is at the heart of developments of science and biomedical technology.

These symbiopolitical relations are based on treating research animals as biologically similar, yet morally different from humans. Thus, central to the modelling practice is an ambition to be true to the original, yet different, as Hogle's chapter on authenticity (this volume) explores in depth. In the Danish site, notions of the pig as sharing evolutionary kinship with humans, yet at the same time belonging to its own kind and different from the moral human, inform the instrumentality of the life, suffering, and death of the piglets on which the experiments are based. Such valuations of life—in this case ideas about the moral divide between humans and pigs—penetrate every laboratory practice and are closely connected to historically grounded practices and legislation; what have been termed the 'historical lineages' of laboratory work and clinical trials (Cooper and Waldby 2014, pp. 18–32; Sharp 2019, p. 20). For centuries, Denmark has claimed the pig as a resource for humans and become a world-leading, pork-producing country. The pig's moral status as an expendable does not mean, however, that its welfare is unimportant. In Europe, legislation on welfare for research animals expanded in the twentieth century. Starting in the 1960s, there has been an increasing understanding of animals as sentient beings and a stronger emphasis on the moral value of animals. This change in the moral landscape of animal experimentation is also reflected in guidelines which articulate research animals as holding 'intrinsic value which must be respected' (European Union 2010, paragraph 12). What moral ambiguities come to the fore in the experimental practices treating the pig as holding simultaneously instrumental and intrinsic value?

On the first day of the experiment,[1] when the piglets are transferred from the womb of the sow to the incubators, five scientists are busy preparing the piglets for the experiment. They weigh the animals, still anesthetised from the C-section, identify their sex, insert catheters through which they can be fed, check their respiration, and massage their lungs to 'get them up and running'. They provide each piglet with a letter and list all the letters in a spreadsheet. In these routines, the piglets appear as generic proxies (Sharp 2014, p. 46); that is, each piglet performs as common biology and stands in for every other piglet in the experiment. As a 'proxy', this common (pig) biology replaces the human due to its biological similarity to the infant. However, as we shall see, the lines between piglet and infant blur as the experiment unfolds.

Born prematurely and suffering from immature bowel and respiratory systems, the piglets are extraordinarily precarious lives, fully dependent on human care to stay alive. One or two graduate students are on watch day and night—feeding the piglets, checking on their condition, and providing individual care (regulating intake of food, expelling air from the abdomen, readjusting catheters, and carrying out cardiopulmonary resuscitation in acute situations). In these intimate care and feeding practices, the premature piglets not only resemble human infants in terms of their evolutionary kinship, their rosy snouts and pained grunts make the researchers respond as caring parents. Piglets and researchers form a kind of intimate interspecies kinship, which is essential to keep the compromised piglets alive during the experimental days (Dam et al. 2017). For some of the very weak piglets, which need intensive care, the spreadsheet—initially listing the piglets and providing information on their sex, birth weight, nutrition—comes to incorporate the researchers' daily notes on the wellbeing of each piglet. In these cases, the spreadsheet tells a full biography of the piglet—its appetite, skin colour, movements, pains, personality—similar to a medical record of a premature child in the NICU. Moreover, by consulting neonatologists about care practices in the clinic, as well as asking for advice regarding the condition of individual piglets, the researchers 'patientise' the piglets (Dam and Svendsen 2018) and hope to make the experiment more representative of the clinical situation.

In the laboratory practices, the piglets have a potential for being configured as *biological life* divested from social and moral relations and as qualified *biographical life* that is part of social and moral relations, with a past, present, and future, to be treated with different respect (Svendsen 2015). The two configurations should be seen as degrees rather than opposites. A continuum exists between one and the other and any being can come to contain amounts of both depending on the situation. For example, it is only by patientising the piglets and turning them into biographical lives that the researchers may succeed in keeping the piglets alive until the last day of the experiment and kill them as biological life. But treating and caring for piglets in pain create moral perils. As one senior researcher, Christian, explains to us, '[You need] to be conscious of the pain of the animal ... Your own feeling for the animal has to tell you if the pain is weak or strong ... How would you feel if your condition was like that [of the pig]?' In asking these questions, Christian is saying that the piglet's capacity to suffer equalises the relationship between piglet and researcher. Christian steps into the space of the piglet, and both researcher and piglet perform as sentient and responding beings. In this situation, morality is not only informed by the notion of the pig as biological life, but by a notion of the pig as a sentient biographical life. In another situation, a senior doctor involved in the pig studies says, 'We wish to do a lot with them and [this means that] we constantly challenge the ethics: how much [suffering] can they endure? When do we cross the border of good animal ethics?' The researchers' care practices expose the moral ambiguity at stake in, on the one hand, keeping suffering piglets alive to create the most promising samples and ensure good data and, on the other hand, wishing to end their suffering. The researchers' care practices and the involved moral negotiations are not isolated from the scientific work of feeding the animals, performing tests on them, and taking blood samples. Rather, care plays a constitutive role in the organisation of the experimental practice and the findings that result from them (Friese 2013b). The striving for 'the good' shapes model organisms, bioscientific knowledge production, and the extent to which animals can act as bridges between lab and clinic (Friese 2013b; Friese and Latimer 2019).

In reflecting upon how to relieve the pain of the piglets, a clinical neonatologist who also conducts research on piglets said that she finds the ethical decision to continue treatment or withdraw it and let the patient die to be similar in the pig laboratory and the human NICU. In both the clinic and the lab, she explained, the practice of taking care of a suffering body raises the question of how far to continue. In this conversation about suffering animals, the moral boundary between the human and the pig is permeable. It is not the case that only infants are treated as individual biographical lives, so are pigs. Nevertheless, the researchers never question the divergent destinies of precarious infants and piglets. Keeping the suffering piglet alive eventually ends with its death and transformation into samples, whereas keeping alive the suffering infant in the clinic bears the hope that it may survive and leave the NICU with its parents. In turning the piglets into a 'candidate for the human' (Bruns 2011, p. 45), the researchers expand the borders of humanity. In killing the piglets and turning them into samples, the researchers exclude the piglets from dying a 'human death' and thus move them back into the category of 'research animal'. In these situations, kindred relations come to entail not only closeness and mutuality, but difference and distance (Govindrajan 2018).

Nevertheless, working across these configurations of the piglets as biographical lives and as biological samples requires ethical boundary work (cf. Wainwright et al. 2006). In particular, the researchers' act of anaesthetising the animals and moving them from the incubators into the room for dissection creates a distinction between the sentient body (being cared for in the incubator) and the non-sentient body (ready to be killed at the table). At the same time, this distinction integrates their work by uniting good animal care and good science.

The symbiopolitical relations connecting the laboratory and clinic include the piglets in the making of the moral person (the infant) in the NICU. Moreover, the plastic identities of the piglets in the animal facility demonstrate that, at the same time as the experiment is based on the notion of the moral human hedged in from other creatures, the experimental practices outgrow and disturb that notion of the moral human. When piglets become near human, human preeminence cannot be upheld.

GENOMES AS DIGITAL SUBSTITUTES IN PRECISION MEDICINE

In a clinical genetics department 200 kilometres from the pig laboratory, a team of geneticists use the newest sequencing technologies to identify possible genetic causes of rare diseases in children. Many rare diseases are characterised by developmental delays and learning disabilities. In this setting, genomes—not smelling, warm, grunting (pig) bodies—are the liminal lives at the centre of the ambitions for enhancing life for children. The genome is the sum of an individual's DNA. The field of genetics developed from studies on the hereditary patterns of plants and animals (Müller-Wille and Rheinberger 2005), illustrating how—in this field as well—animals are part of the symbiopolitical relations shaping knowledge practices and their moral landscapes.

While the genome is invisible to the naked eye and fully dependent on high-tech machines and skilled experience to gain presence in the world (O'Riordan 2010), it is processed from a mundane blood or tissue sample. In the clinical genetics department, blood samples from the child and his/her parents provide the raw material for the analysis of the child's genome which, in combination with a clinical examination of the child's weight, height, head circumference, photos of the child (face, hands, feet, spine) and the parents' recollection of the child's early developmental history, may provide an explanation for his/her developmental delays. By comparing the child's genomic profile and clinical description with genomic profiles and medical descriptions from thousands of other children, the geneticists hope to identify a genetic cause of the child's problem (diagnosis) and concurrently use data from an international database as the empirical basis for scientific papers (research). Therefore, the parents are asked to consent to letting the child's tissue, photos, and clinical description enter the international database. As with the pig bodies and the data derived from them, taking the child's blood sample and data has the aim of improving public health (providing the child with a diagnosis) and advancing science (publishing scientific papers). What moral ambiguities are at stake in practices of collecting, storing, sharing, and using genomes? What notions of the human come to the fore?

In clinical consultations, the blood sample is talked about as a morally unproblematic biological thing only loosely connected to the person. In that sense, blood samples and genomic data resemble the dominant identity of the research piglet in the pig laboratory: biological life divested from social and moral relations. Nevertheless, there are moments when the genome gravitates towards biographical life. This is the case when the clinical geneticist introduces the child and his/her parents to the diagnostic process and passes on the results of the genetic analysis. Addressing a young teenager and his parents, the geneticist says, 'We found a spelling mistake in the recipe, and by that I mean that we all have a cookbook with recipes for how we are, and sometimes a spelling mistake sneaks into one of these recipes.' With the cookbook metaphor, the genome comes to tell the story about the current and future developmental and behavioural challenges the child may experience. In short, the genome comes to represent the biographical life of the individual person. This translation of biological life to biographical life parallels the interpretive work of people engaged in genealogical testing who experience that genetic facts open new questions about identity and origin (Klotz 2016; Nelson 2008).

That the genome represents a person is not new. From the early days of genomic science, the genome was depicted as 'the book of life' and treated as an object deserving extraordinary protection and respect (Nelkin and Lindee 2004). The genome had ethics (Hoeyer and Tutton 2005) in ways that other biological matter did not. Unlike the liminal lives of piglets and other research animals that have not attracted significant media attention in Denmark, human genomes continue to spur public discussions about the morally right way of collecting, storing, and using them. In 2017, the Danish government launched the establishment of a National Genome Center (NGC) as part of a national investment into precision medicine, referring to strategies for tailoring diagnosis, treatment, prevention, and research to the individual. In the Danish political vision, collected genomes are seen as transactable objects with a potential for generating biovalue (cf. Waldby 2002) by enhancing public health and attracting global investments to Denmark.

The establishment of the NGC provoked a heated public debate about how citizens' genomic data would be stored, what it might be used for when combined with other data about citizens, and who would gain access to the data. The debate exposed the biopolitical moral imperative to enhance population health by sourcing the data of the population and the equally strong imperative to protect the privacy and individuality of citizens by treating genomes as first and foremost personal property. In the public debate, everyone seemed to understand genomes as closely connected to the person and a source of potential future life. Genomes were not depicted as neutral or innocent entities, but conceived of as potent representations or extensions of individual citizens. They appeared as digital substitutes for human persons (Svendsen 2018). In the pig laboratory, piglets enter the scene of action as substitutes for humans, yet in daily practice they are able to gain the identity of the 'originals' they replace, that is, infants in the NICU. In the genetic clinic and in public debate, the genomes similarly represent embodied humans. Like the piglets, they have the potential to move from being inanimate instruments representing individuals to becoming animate persons gaining the identity of the 'original' mortal individuals they represent or acting as extensions of them. For a discussion of the ontological and epistemic ambiguities of substitutes of 'original' individuals, see Hogle's chapter on authenticity (this volume).

Back in the clinical genetics department, the geneticists see the sharing of data through international databases as a precondition for reaching health benefits. It is only by pooling data in big databases that the geneticists are able to create a diagnosis for the individual child in the clinic and advance their knowledge of the genetic causes of diseases. Moreover, in order to diagnose children with rare diseases, geneticists use international databases to establish connections between children who share the same genetic mutation, facial traits, and developmental histories. These children are strangers to each other and do not share descent, yet the diagnostic process (mediated by the international database) conditions an ethical self-formation in which they come to see themselves as connected through a rare genetic mutation.

In a conversation with the geneticists about their personal attitudes to having their own genomes stored in the NGC, they promptly responded, 'No thank you! Genomes contain the entire recipe [of the person].' This reaction to having their own data stored might seem contradictory to their daily practice of asking children and their parents to allow genomic data to be banked in international databases; however, instead of only mapping contradictions, anthropological studies of morality teach us to pursue what is at stake in moral perils, how people strive to realise morally worthy lives (Mattingly 2010, 2014), and how they experience struggles which may not have a resolution (Lambek 2015). The geneticists feared that their genomes might become the raw material of forms of health research which they did not wish to support. They particularly noted that psychiatric research may result in findings that are unbearable (i.e. a high risk of dementia or other psychiatric diseases in late life) or stigmatising. They worried that their digital substitutes might return to them or to insurance companies in the form of unwanted knowledge about their own or their children's risk of devastating disease. In other words, digital substitutes in state storage had the power to threaten their future quality of life and possibilities in life.

What also worried the geneticists was the scenario in which the genomes might connect with and generate biovalue for the wrong actors. Their moral peril contained a notion of the digital substitute set loose from the embodied 'original' and gaining the autonomy and agency associated with the moral human, and possibly threatening the moral human. The fear that attaches to the notion of the substitute is associated with losing control, being appropriated to another's end, and becoming unoriginal (Franklin 2007, p. 204). In a sense, the geneticists' opposition to having their data banked in the NGC expressed the fear of being devalued and reduced to a research tool (like the piglet) if it were to be used for research agendas they did not support. Unlike many North American life scientists, who have published their own genomic data as part of spearheading—and thus, controlling and extending—their science, the Danish geneticists did not expect their genomic data in the NGC to enhance their moral and scientific agency. In contrast, they see the international database they advocate for their patients as a way of strengthening the quality of life and moral agency of the individual. They hope that the database will not only help them provide a genetic explanation for the patient's challenges, but also provide the patient with more possibilities in life as a diagnosis gives access to special education and social benefits in adulthood.

The ambivalence about the substitute taking the place of the original reflects a notion of the human which is not contained in a mortal body, but may materialise in data and have eternal life. In their daily practice, the geneticists work hard to generate genetic knowledge from inanimate blood samples to improve the life of children and their families. That very endeavour, which aims at protecting and valuing the moral and mortal human, brings to life a conceptualisation of the human which is not bounded by a mortal body, but rather extended by and dependent on digital substitutes connecting him or her to other worlds, research agendas, commercial enterprises, and future lives.

CONCLUSION

In this chapter, we have explored how anthropological investigations of morality in the life sciences have been central to both the development of technology and social theory. Kinship expectations, biological potential, notions of species, and perceptions of self and other become exposed through tracking moral ambiguity. Our two case studies illuminate how animal researchers and geneticists seek to realise the moral imperative of prolonging and enhancing human life by modelling piglets as stand-ins for human infants and storing and interpreting DNA in international databases. These endeavours bring other species closer to the human in laboratory environments and treat DNA from human living bodies as not only connected with the life and livelihood of the 'original' source, but also as potentially connecting that very human to foreign research agendas, actors, and worlds in the future. The moral ambiguity, which arises when boundaries between human and animal, between person and thing, between body and data become blurred, outgrows the notion of the moral human at the heart of the anthropological discipline. It teaches us not to take the human as the self-evident ground for the anthropological study of technology, but to transform it into a question (cf. Rees 2018): What notions of the human and its moral obligations come to the fore in technological practices? With this question, we may begin to understand how technological practices contribute to shaping conditions for imagining and materialising the human.

By ethnographically following the exchange of biological material across laboratory and clinic, and across different parts of the world, anthropological scholarship on technology has treated morality as not only expressed in relationships between human actors, but shaped in assemblages of humans, animals, markets, and landscapes. In the global world of the life sciences, liminal lives at the margins of established categories come to contain a potential for moral confusion as well as analytical innovation. By uncovering the co-production of morality, technology, and society, anthropological scholarship has been pioneering in spurring theoretical discussions of person, body, kinship, politics—and the human.

NOTE

1. Some of the empirical examples below also appear in Svendsen et al. (2018) and Svendsen (2022).

REFERENCES

Asdal, K., Druglitrø, T., & Hinchliffe, S. (2016). *Humans, Animals and Biopolitics: The More-than-Human Condition*. London: Routledge.

Bird-David, N., & Israeli, T. (2010). A Moment Dead, a Moment Alive: How Situational Personhood Emerges in the Vegetative State in an Israeli Hospital Unit. *American Anthropologist, 112*(1), 54–65.

Brown, N. (2009). Beasting the Embryo: The Metrics of Humanness in the Transpecies Embryo Debate. *BioSocieties, 4*(2–3), 147–163.

Bruns, G. (2011). *On Ceasing to Be Human*. Stanford: Stanford University Press.

Buch, E. D. (2013). Senses of Care: Embodying Inequality and Sustaining Personhood in the Home Care of Older Adults in Chicago. *American Ethnologist, 40*(4), 637–50.

Carroll, K. (2016). The Milk of Human Kinship: Donated Breast Milk in Neonatal Intensive Care. In C. Krøløkke, L. Myong, S. W. Adrian, & T. Tjørnhøj-Thomsen (Eds.), *Critical Kinship Studies* (pp. 15–31). London: Rowman & Littlefield International.

Casper, M. J. (1998). *The Making of the Unborn Patient: A Social Anatomy of Fetal Surgery*. New Brunswick: Rutgers University Press.

Cool, A. (2016). Detaching Data from the State: Biobanking and Building Big Data in Sweden. *BioSocieties, 11*(3), 277–295.

Cooper, M., & Waldby, C. (2014). *Clinical Labor: Tissue Donors and Research Subjects in the Global Bioeconomy*. Durham: Duke University Press.

Dam, M. S., & Svendsen, M.N. (2018). Treating Pigs: Balancing Standardisation and Individual Treatments in Translational Neonatology Research. *BioSocieties, 13*(2), 349–367. https://doi.org/10.1057/s41292-017-0071-2.

Dam, M. S., Juhl, S. M., Sangild, P. T., & Svendsen, M. N. (2017). Feeding Premature Neonates: Kinship and Species in Translational Neonatology. *Social Science & Medicine, 179*, 129–136.

Douglas, M. (1966). *Purity and Danger: An Analysis of Concepts of Pollution and Taboo*. London: Routledge and Keegan Paul.

Dumit, J. (2012). *Drugs for Life: How Pharmaceutical Companies Define Our Health*. Durham: Duke University Press.

European Union. (2010). *Directive 2010/63/EU of the European Parliament and of the Council of 22 September 2010 on the Protection of Animals Used for Scientific Purposes*.

Fortes, M. (1945). *The Dynamics of Clanship among the Tallensi*. London: Oxford University Press.

Franklin, S. (1997). *Embodied Progress: A Cultural Account of Assisted Conception.* London: Routledge.

Franklin, S. (2007). *Dolly Mixtures: The Remaking of Genealogy.* Durham: Duke University Press.

Franklin, S. (2013). *Biological Relatives: IVF, Stem Cells, and the Future of Kinship.* Durham: Duke University Press.

Franklin, S., & Lock, M. (2003). *Remaking Life and Death: Toward an Anthropology of the Biosciences.* Santa Fe: School of American Research Press.

Franklin, S., & McKinnon, S. (2001). *Relative Values. Reconfiguring Kinship Studies.* Durham: Duke University Press.

Friese, C. (2013a). *Cloning Wild Life: Zoos, Captivity, and the Future of Endangered Animals.* New York: New York University Press.

Friese, C. (2013b). Realizing Potential in Translational Medicine: The Uncanny Emergence of Care as Science. *Current Anthropology, 54*(S7), S129–S38. https://doi.org/10.1086/670805.

Friese, C., & Latimer, J. (2019). Entanglements in Health and Well-being: Working with Model Organisms in Biomedicine and Bioscience. *Medical Anthropology Quarterly, 33*(1), 120–137.

Gammeltoft, T. M. (2014). *Haunting Images: A Cultural Account of Selective Reproduction in Vietnam.* Berkeley, Los Angeles, & London: University of California Press.

Gibbon, S., & Novas, C. (2008). *Biosocialities, Genetics and the Social Sciences.* London: Routledge.

Gjødsbøl, I. M., Koch, L., & Svendsen, M. N. (2017). Resisting Decay: Disposing (of) and (Re)valuing People with Late Stage Dementia in the Nursing Home. *Social Science and Medicine, 184*, 116–123.

Govindrajan, R. (2018). *Animal Intimacies. Interspecies Relatedness in India's Himalayas.* Chicago: Chicago University Press.

Greenhalgh, S. (2008). *Just One Child: Science and Policy in Deng's China.* Berkeley: University of California Press.

Haraway, D. J. (2008). *When Species Meet.* Minneapolis, MN: University of Minnesota Press.

Haraway, D. J. (2016). *Staying with the Trouble: Making Kin in the Chthulucene.* Durham: Duke University Press.

Helgason, A., & Pálsson, G. (1997). Contested Commodities: The Moral Landscape of Modernist Regimes. *The Journal of the Royal Anthropological Institute, 3*(3), 451–471.

Helmreich, S. (2009). *Alien Ocean: Anthropological Voyages in Microbial Seas.* Berkeley, Los Angeles, & London: University of California Press.

Hinterberger, A. (2018). Marked 'H' for Human: Chimeric Life and the Politics of the Human. *BioSocieties, 13*(2), 453–469.

Hird, M. J. (2004). Chimerism, Mosaicism and the Cultural Construction of Kinship. *Sexualities, 7*(2), 217–232. https://doi.org/10.1177/1363460704042165.

Hoeyer, K. L. (2003). 'Science Is Really Needed—That's All I Know': Informed Consent and the Non-Verbal Practices of Collecting Blood for Genetic Research in Northern Sweden. *New Genetics and Society, 22*(3), 229–244. https://doi.org/10.1080/1463677032000147199.

Hoeyer, K. L. (2005). The Role of Ethics in Commercial Genetic Research: Notes on the Notion of Commodification. *Medical Anthropology, 24*(1), 45–70.

Hoeyer, K. L. (2013). *Exchanging Human Bodily Material: Rethinking Bodies and Markets.* Dordrecht: Springer

Hoeyer, K. L., & Tutton, R. (2005). 'Ethics Was Here': Studying the Language-Games of Ethics in the Case of UK Biobank. *Critical Public Health, 15*(4), 385–397. https://doi.org/10.1080/09581590500523533.

Hogle, L. (2010). Characterizing Human Embryonic Stem Cells: Biological and Social Markers of Identity. *Medical Anthropology Quarterly, 24*(4), 433–450.

Jensen, A. M. B. (2016). Guardians of 'the Gift': the Emotional Challenges of Heart and Lung Transplant Professionals in Denmark. *Anthropology & Medicine, 24*(1), 111–126. https://doi.org/10.1080/13648470.2016.1193329.

Kaufman, S. (2003). Hidden Places, Uncommon Persons. *Social Science & Medicine, 56*(11), 2249–2261.

Kaufman, S. (2005). *And a Time to Die: How American Hospitals Shape the End of Life.* New York: Simon and Schuster.

Kaufman, S. (2015). *Ordinary Medicine: Extraordinary Treatments, Longer Lives, and Where to Draw the Line.* Durham: Duke University Press.

Kirk, R. (2016). Care in the Cage: Materializing Moral Economies of Animal Care in the Biomedical Sciences, c. 1945–. In K. Bjørkdahl & T. Druglitrø (Eds.), *Animal Housing and Human-Animals Relations: Politics, Practices and Infrastructures* (pp. 167–184). London: Routledge.

Klotz, M. (2016). Wayward Relations: Novel Searches of the Donor-Conceived for Genetic Kinship. *Medical Anthropology, 35*(1), 45–57.

Konrad, M. (2005). *Narrating the Predictive Genetics.* Cambridge: Cambridge University Press.

Laidlaw, J. (2002). For an Anthropology of Ethics and Freedom. *Journal of the Royal Anthropological Institute, 8*(2), 311–332.

Lambek, M. (2015). *The Ethical Condition: Essays on Action, Person, and Value.* Chicago: The University of Chicago Press.

Latimer, J. (2015). *The Gene, the Clinic, and the Family: Diagnosing Dysmorphology, Reviving Medical Dominance.* London: Routledge.

Lock, M. (2002). *Twice Dead: Organ Transplants and the Reinvention of Death.* Berkeley: University of California Press.

Mattingly, C. (2010). *The Paradox of Hope: Journeys through a Clinical Borderland.* Berkeley, Los Angeles, & London: University of California Press.

Mattingly, C. (2014). *Moral Laboratories: Family Peril and the Struggle for a Good Life.* Berkeley: University of California Press.

Mauss, M. (1985 [1938]). A Category of the Human Mind: The Notion of Person; the Notion of Self. In M. Carrithers, S. Collins, & S. Lukes (Eds.), *The Category of the Person: Anthropology, Philosophy, History* (pp. 1–25). Cambridge: Cambridge University Press.

Morgan, L. M. (2009). *Icons of Life: A Cultural History of Human Embryos.* Berkeley: University of California Press.

Müller-Wille, S., & Rheinberger, H.-J. (2005). Introduction. In S. Müller-Wille & H.-J. Rheinberger (Eds.), *A Cultural History of Heredity III: 19th and Early 20th Centuries* (pp. 3–7). Berlin: Max-Planck-Institute for the History of Science.

Murphy, M. (2017). *The Economization of Life.* Durham: Duke University Press.

Navne, L. E., Svendsen, M. N., & Gammeltoft, T. M. (2017). The Attachment Imperative. Parental Experiences of Relation-making in a Danish Neonatal Intensive Care Unit. *Medical Anthropology Quarterly, 32*(1), 120–137.

Nelkin, D., & Lindee, M. S. (2004). *The DNA Mystique: The Gene as a Cultural Icon.* Ann Arbor: University of Michigan Press.

Nelson, A. (2008). Bio Science: Genetic Genealogy Testing and the Pursuit of African Ancestry. *Social Studies of Science, 38*(5), 759–783.

O'Riordan, K. (2010). *The Genome Incorporated: Constructing Biodigital Identity.* London: Routledge.

Petryna, A. (2009). *When Experiments Travel. Clinical Trials and the Global Search for Human Subjects.* Princeton: Princeton University Press.

Rajan, K. S. (2008). Biocapital as an Emergent Form of Life: Speculations on the Figure of the Experimental Subject. In S. Gibbon & C. Novas (Eds.), *Biosocialities, Genetics and the Social Sciences,* (pp. 167–197). London: Routledge.

Rapp, R. (1999). *Testing Women, Testing the Fetus: The Social Impact of Amniocentesis in America.* New York: Routledge.

Rapp, R., Heath, D., & Taussig, K.-S. (2001). Genealogical Dis-ease: Where Hereditary Abnormality, Biomedical Explanation, and Family Responsibility Meet. In S. Franklin & S. McKinnon (Eds.), *Relative Values: Reconfiguring Kinship Studies* (pp. 384–412). Durham: Duke University Press.

Reardon, J. (2017). *The Postgenomic Condition: Ethics, Justice, and Knowledge After the Genome.* Chicago and London: University of Chicago Press.

Rees, T. (2018). *After Ethnos.* Durham: Duke University Press.

Roberts, E. F. S. (2011). Abandonment and Accumulation: Embryonic Futures in the United States and Ecuador. *Medical Anthropology Quarterly, 25*(2), 232–253. https://doi.org/10.1111/j.1548-1387.2011.01151.x.

Schepher-Hughes, N. (2004). Commodity Fetishism in Organs Trafficking. In N. Schepher-Hughes & L. Wacquant (Eds.), *Commodifying Bodies* (pp. 31–62). London: Sage.

Schwennesen, N., Svendsen, M. N., & Koch, L. (2010). Beyond Informed Choice: Prenatal Risk Assessment, Decision-Making and Trust. *Clinical Ethics, 5*(4), 207–216. https://doi.org/10.1258/ce.2010.010041.

Sharp, L. A. (2006). *Strange Harvest: Organ Transplants, Denatured Bodies, and the Transformed Self.* Berkeley, Los Angeles, and London: University of California Press.

Sharp, L. A. (2014). *The Transplant Imaginary: Mechanical Hearts, Animal Parts, and Moral Thinking in Highly Experimental Science.* Berkeley, Los Angeles, & London: University of California Press.

Sharp, L. A. (2019). *Animal Ethos: The Morality of Human-Animal Encounters in Experimental Lab Science.* Oakland: University of California Press.

Solomon, H. (2016). *Metabolic Living: Food, Fat, and the Absorption of Illness in India.* Durham: Duke University Press.

Squier, S. M. (2004). *Liminal Lives: Imagining the Human at the Frontiers of Biomedicine.* Durham: Duke University Press.

Strathern, M. (1992). *Reproducing the Future: Essays on Anthropology, Kinship and the New Reproductive Technologies.* Manchester: Manchester University Press.

Strathern, M. (2011). What Is a Parent? *HAU: Journal of Ethnographic Theory, 1*(1), 245–278. https://doi.org/10.14318/hau1.1.011.

Svendsen, M. N. (2015). Selective Reproduction: Social and Temporal Imaginaries for Negotiating the Value of Life in Human and Animal Neonates. *Medical Anthropology Quarterly, 29*(2), 178–195.

Svendsen, M. N. (2018). The "Me" in the "We": Anthropological Engagements with Personalized Medicine. *Encounters, 10*(5), 1–26.

Svendsen, M. N. (2022). *Near Human. Border Zones of Species, Life, and Belonging.* New Brunswick, NJ: Rutgers University Press.

Svendsen, M. N., & Koch, L. (2008). Unpacking the 'Spare Embryo': Facilitating Stem Cell Research in a Moral Landscape. *Social Studies of Science, 38*(1), 93–110.

Svendsen, M. N., Navne, L. E., Gjødsbøl, I. M., & Dam, M. S. (2018). A Life Worth Living: Temporality, Care and Personhood. *American Ethnologist, 45*(1), 20–33.

Taussig, K.-S. (2009). *Ordinary Genomes.* Durham: Duke University Press.

Taylor, J. S. (2008a). On Recognition, Caring, and Dementia. *Medical Anthropology Quarterly, 22*(4), 313–335.

Taylor, J.S. (2008b). *The Public Life of the Fetal Sonogram: Technology, Consumption, and the Politics of Reproduction.* New Brunswick & London: Rutgers University Press.

Thompson, C. (2013). *Good Science: The Ethical Choreography of Stem Cell Research.* Cambridge, MA: The MIT Press.

Tsing, A. L. (2015). *The Mushroom at the End of the World: On the Possibility of Life in Capitalist Ruins.* Princeton: Princeton University Press.

Turner, V. (1969). *The Ritual Process: Structure and Anti-Structure.* New Jersey: Transaction Publishers.

Vora, K. (2013). Potential, Risk, and Return in Transnational Indian Gestational Surrogacy. *Current Anthropology, 54*(S7), S97–S106. https://doi.org/10.1086/671018.

Wahlberg, A. (2018). *Good Quality: The Routinization of Sperm Banking in China.* Oakland: University of California Press.

Wainwright, S. P., Williams, C., Michael, M., Farsides, B., & Cribb, A. (2006). Ethical Boundary-Work in the Embryonic Stem Cell Laboratory. *Sociology of Health & Illness, 28*(6), 732–748. https://doi.org/10.1111/j.1467-9566.2006.00539.x.

Waldby, C. (2002). Stem Cells, Tissue Cultures and the Production of Biovalue. *Health, 6*(3), 305–323. https://doi.org/10.1177/136345930200600304.

CHAPTER 28

Enacting Authenticity: Changing Ontologies of Biological Entities

Authenticity

Linda F. Hogle

The proliferation of new engineered life forms has provided abundant opportunities for social scientists to analyse implications of increasingly integrated biological, machinic, and digital amalgams. Social scientists and ethicists have long brooded over interminglings of nature and artifice, human and technology, and the moral and practical dilemmas that arise. I suggest that what makes hybrid life forms troubling is not simply the extent to which they are natural, biological, or technological, but how true they are to the original. Moreover, more pressing than scrutinising the novelty of the material entities themselves is an analysis of how such forms disturb social orders or generate new ones. The lens of authenticity can inform such analyses, including revealing how the ethical is baked into scientific objects. The perspective of authenticity can be applied to other emerging themes in the anthropology of technology: in an era of 'alternative facts', deepfakes, and the increasing ease with which objects can be technologically counterfeited, the politics and ethics of authenticity are salient and timely.

Authenticity is defined as that which is factual, genuine, unadulterated, not counterfeited, but it can also mean a faithful rendition of an original, so as to reproduce essential features (Merriam-Webster n.d.). Authenticity as a perspective thus avoids the binaries of natural/technological or artificial/real. It also

L. F. Hogle (✉)
University of Wisconsin-Madison, Madison, WI, USA
e-mail: lfhogle@wisc.edu

M. H. Bruun et al. (eds.), *The Palgrave Handbook of the Anthropology of Technology*, https://doi.org/10.1007/978-981-16-7084-8_28

suggests an undisputed origin, implying trustworthiness or good faith. Things certified as authentic are endowed with legitimacy, which in turn determines value. There are moral overtones, then, begging scrutiny.

Authenticity is a core theme in anthropology, including ways that concepts of authenticity are contested and continually redefined across time, space, and political-economic ideologies (Clifford 1988; Fillitz and Saris 2012; Handler 1986; Hobsbawm and Ranger 1983; Lindholm 2002; Trilling 1972; Umbach and Humphrey 2018). My aim is not to redefine the boundaries of the authentic, but rather to show how things are made to matter as authentic entities, within a set of assumptions and valuations about what authenticity means.

Through the lens of authenticity, paradoxes inherent in using technologies to recreate an original are illuminated. While some emerging life forms have no counterpart in nature, others are biological analogues: functional duplicates made from an original. They are highly engineered fabrications, but to be successful as therapeutic or commercial entities, they must be received not so much as natural or technological but as 'the real thing'. In fact, scientists may delete or modify elements that would make them appear as they would in their 'natural' state. Such entities are understood as authentic-enough analogues through material and discursive practices in assemblages of expertise, governance regimes, economic and political interests, and presumed user expectations.

I illustrate with two examples: organoids and cultured meat. While they circulate in very different domains, both employ stem cells from a living human or animal to make analogues. Unlike prior technological substitutes that mimicked functions or structures, both coax nature to recreate itself—but in vitro and under human-directed conditions. Both are among a number of emerging technologies using what I call a techno-ethical imperative: a narrative of urgent need to create ethical futures through specific kinds of technologies. If it were only a matter of finding an ethical alternative to existing social problems, then any functioning substitute might do. Yet for biological analogues, tapping in to perceptions and values around a purified image of 'the real thing' is crucial to their justification. They depend on being enacted as authentic to establish their credibility and value as alternative ethical solutions to major problems of health and environmental and economic wellbeing, while generating value for consumers and inventors. Paradoxically, however, the two analogues I describe must distinguish themselves from the original. Importantly, it is their status as simultaneously authentic yet not original that creates ethical and practical tensions.

Choosing examples from very different spheres enables an anthropology of technology that moves beyond case-based novelty and a focus on the ontology of ambiguous entities, to observe phenomena across circumstances and assemblages. Examining authenticity-enacting practices themselves shows how they generate new knowledge objects, and new configurations of social relations and participants.

My data comes from interviews with scientists primarily in the US and UK, document analysis (research protocols, regulatory guidance), and secondary literature. The data derives from a broader project on authentication practices in cell and information technologies, in which I analyse material and discursive determinations as relations around trust and doubt (Hogle 2019, 2021).

I begin by briefly reprising relevant literature, showing how disparate works, ranging from concepts of nature and the authentic to theories of classification, to analysis of cultural practices around food, medicine, and the body, can be drawn together to widen anthropologists' ambit for analysing technologies and their entanglements with ethics. I then illustrate with organoids, followed by cultured meat.

Making Things Authentic: Lessons from Studies of Concepts of Nature, the Body, Food, and Their Classifications

Much has been written about concepts of nature and their central role in public policy and ethics debates. Scholars observe that concepts are historically and culturally situated; the mythos of nature as pristine, having intrinsic authenticity, and existing outside of human contexts is untenable (Douglas 1966; Escobar 1999; Keller 2008; Parry and Dupre 2010; Soper 2010). Nevertheless, nature has been used ideologically to assign value to things and to justify human rules, norms, hierarchies, and actions—what Daston and Vidal (2004) call the moral authority of nature.

Nature and culture, nature and artifice, human and technology have long been seen as oppositions. Disturbances of distinct oppositions have been seen as transgressions or threats, prompting endless scholarly preoccupation with the nature of 'nature' and 'what is the human?'. Landecker (2007) asks instead what it means to be *biological*, to provoke scrutiny of taken-for-granted biological 'facts' such as reproduction, genetic determinism, and cell fate. Franklin (2007, 2013) Parry and Dupre (2010), Rabinow (1999), Squier (2004), and others note that it is increasingly difficult to distinguish between the natural and technological. With the capability to alter genes, reverse cell development, and integrate biological-machinic-digital amalgams down to the molecular level, ontologies of the resulting entities are increasingly ambiguous. Cloning and chimeras, for example, raise questions about singularity and dignity (Franklin 2007; Hinterberger 2018; Svendsen et al., this volume).

Societies use category-making practices to manage uncertainty arising from ambiguous entities (Douglas 1966; Power 2007). For example, brain death, embryonic stem cells, and animal-human hybrids beg categories to sort and assign moral, legal, and economic status with which to direct how caregivers, lawyers, and regulators proceed. Bioethicists are preoccupied with such normative category-making based on ontologies, harmonising principles, and guidelines across technologies and locales. Yet this implies that there is a universal set of principles, disregarding differences in histories, cultures, and politics (Petersen 2011).

Social scientists, alternatively, contribute more nuanced understandings of hybridity, contingencies, and classifications (Epstein 2007; Hinterberger 2018). They attend to broader contexts, concepts, and histories including, for the topic at hand, animal husbandry (Franklin 2007; Ogle 2013), medical experimentation, and institutions of ethical oversight (Lederer 1995; Rothman 1990). They also point to moral implications of classifying new life forms, as Svendsen et al. (this volume) aptly illustrate. How they are created, defined, and cared for prescribes roles and relationships within care and legal-medical regimes. Categorisation practices are also related to the conditions in which entities have use-value and enter commercial circuits, as I have demonstrated with classifications of tissue-engineered products as devices or biologicals for regulatory and marketing purposes (Hogle 2009). When stem cells are named and classified according to their intended use, the goals and interests of those doing the classifying are reflected (Marks 2010). King and Lyall (2018) found that framing lab-cultured blood cells as natural or synthetic evoked broader meanings around blood donation, pharmaceutical treatments, and other familiar social practices.

Bowker and Star's classic work shows how classification systems become a taken-for-granted, powerful means of shaping life and actions (Bowker and Star 1999). The ways people and things are sorted have moral and legal ramifications for how they are treated, and whose voices are included or not in category-making. Boundaries, however, require work to maintain distinctions among kinds (Power 2007). Through empirical cases, Wahlberg and Bauer (Wahlberg and Bauer 2016) show how boundaries between categories are contested, maintained, and destabilised as novel life forms emerge. Boundaries are zones of potentiality, experiment, and cultural change (Svendsen et al., this volume).

Trying to hold categories of 'human' or 'natural' constant and separate, and assuming these are referents against which technologies can be understood, then, is problematic. It also risks missing important social phenomena. To describe the implosion of technical, organic, political, economic, and textual that characterise contemporary life, Haraway (Haraway 1991) uses the figure of the cyborg. She argues that we must take conditions arising from cyborg blurrings as our responsibility; the resulting politics of race, gender, social, and environmental inequities are all at stake. Franklin (2013) suggests that biology has become a relative condition: biology is embedded in new logics of social life, and these logics have become normalised as they are assimilated into everyday life.

Webster (2012) uses the term bio-object to talk about new biological artefacts causing new relations to life. Significantly, he asserts that it is more important to attend to the processes through which different life forms are created, rather than specific properties of bio-objects, especially since boundaries between species, life and non-life, human, and machine can be fluid. Understandings of an entity's ontology are shaped in interaction with broader sets of historical, political, and social experiences and meanings. Bennett (2010) and Barry (2001) further argue that entities' ontologies are always relational; that is, subject to change in interaction with assemblages. It follows that determining what is in a category or not is never static.

Feminist science and technology studies scholars argue that the knowledge and power processes embedded in such new logics inscribe and materialise the world in some forms rather than others. Strathern (Strathern 1992), for example, argues that in enterprise culture, natural entities are being designed specifically to meet anticipated consumer expectations and industrial production requirements. What she calls 'enterprising up' is a conflation of the essence of the original natural thing with features added specifically to create value and marketability, as in the use of biology-altering technologies to create uniformity in colour or size to match presumed consumer expectations of how the natural product should appear. Similarly, rather than adapting mechanical technologies to biology, plants and animals are being re-engineered to adapt to harvesting, processing, and transport equipment to facilitate supply chain requirements (Busch 2011; Kloppenberg 1988).

In such works, nature serves as the referent for artifice. Nature is also called on to order the world into 'natural kinds'. Similarly, authenticity is drawn upon to order and assign value to objects and experiences. Influential scholarship in this regard includes Benjamin's (1968) work on the aura of the original, and Baudrillard's (1981) work on simulacra and simulations. Both are commentaries on industrialisation and capitalism, emphasising the role of technologies in altering our experiences of the original. Baudrillard argues that we have become so reliant on models and simulations that it is difficult to distinguish them from reality. In his argument, based on art objects as examples, Benjamin argues that reproduction strips aesthetic authority from the original. However, for concepts of authenticity to work, there must be an assumption that there was a pristine, unadulterated 'real' original as a referent. Relevant to the topic at hand, Umbach and Humphrey (2018) note how authenticity is a dynamic political concept: 'Authenticity is constantly rearticulated and recoded as it is employed for new ideological purposes—or indeed to be criticized as a dangerous yet persistent "myth"' (p. 3; see also Fillitz and Saris 2012). Claims of authenticity are also directly linked to valuation, as objects are assessed and circulate in markets (Dussauge et al. 2015). Ownership and control over narratives about authenticity are thus consequential. This is particularly evidenced in narratives about food, to which I now turn.

Through food studies, anthropologists reflect on core issues of social relations, labour practices and inequities, identities, moral commitments, institutional infrastructures, and health and economic wellbeing or deprivation (Besky 2014; Klein and Watson 2016; Mintz 1985). Ethnographies of technologies such as genetic engineering, artificial insemination, cloning, pesticides, antibiotics, and automation show how they transform relations between producers and consumers, affect human and animal health, and co-construct political, economic, and ethical orders (Franklin 2007; Herring 2015; National Academy of Sciences 2017). Agribusiness technologies may make food more available and cheaper but distance consumers from food sources and producers. This affects trust in contemporary food systems, especially in light of food safety scares (Weiss 2016; West 2016). Consumers want assurance that food is what it is claimed to be.

More recent studies examine ways that people try to reconnect with food origins, not only for transparency and trust but to support sustainability and equitable relations among producers and consumers. Observers of the resulting alternative food movements (fair trade, buy-local, and artisanal foods) make sharp distinctions between industrialised and 'real' food: smaller-scale, minimally mediated production using craft-like traditional methods that evoke cultural heritage. Luetchford (2016), Galusky (2014), Weiss (2016), and others suggest that individuals express their values and constitute themselves as ethical beings through food choices. Connecting to the land, its seasonality and particularity, and to animals and plants as living entities, rather than industrial goods, formulates an ethos of food alternatives beyond normative food ethics. The linkage of 'heritagization' (West 2016), terroir (Paxson 2010, 2012; Trubek 2008), and minimal technical mediation creates an aura and mystique frequently referred to in food writings as authenticity (Grasseni and Paxson 2014; Umbach and Humphrey 2018; Weiss 2016).

However, it is not easy to make such clean distinctions. Eden-like images are countered by studies showing, for example, how fair-trade practices are undermined or misrepresented (Besky 2014; Luetchford 2016), and how very technological even small-scale agriculture is, with the use of sophisticated biochemistry, embedded RFID and biosensor chips, robotics, and data analytics (McGarity 2020; Paxson 2010).

Furthermore, authenticity can be a strategy. That is, producers may mobilise authenticity as rhetoric to increase sales or create brand distinction. While some producers may be disingenuous in representing products as authentic, for most others it is a matter of balancing contemporary marketing and scaled production techniques to sustain competitive pricing, with messaging that distances them from industrial commerce to attract customers by emphasising craft-like techniques (Beverland 2005; Grasseni and Paxson 2014; Paxson 2010; West 2016). Gilmore and Pine (2007), among many business pundits, argue that consumers want goods and services that engage them more personally and memorably. What the authors call the experience economy is about perceptions of authenticity: 'the *management of the customer perception of authenticity* becomes the primary new source of competitive advantage—the new business imperative' (p. 3, emphasis in the original).

Drawing these literatures together, readers can see that authenticity is tied to power and economic relations and is constructed within changing sets of participants and conditions. I next demonstrate how authenticity serves as a narrative to garner credibility, connote ethical innovation, and create value.

HUMAN ORGANOIDS

Organoids are aggregates of organ-specific cells cultured in vitro. To create them, adult stem cells are collected, reprogrammed to become the multiple cell types of the organ of interest, and co-cultured with cells specific to particular organs. Unlike conventional cell cultures, three-dimensional, more physiological systems are engineered to mimic the original body more closely. Cultures are modified in phases, to match the conditions of maturing tissue in nature. Cells then spatially and temporally self-assemble into small organ-like structures with physiological structures and functions resembling tissues in a developing human (Koo et al. 2019; Lancaster and Knoblich 2014). For example, gut organoids develop cavities with villus structures, secrete mucous-like substances, and absorb nutrients like an intestine. Given the right conditions, they can form structures from oral cavity, to stomach, to intestine and rectum. Retina organoids develop layers in the right order and position to transmit light signals. Lung organoids branch into airways with working cilia. Cerebral organoids can develop cortical layers, ventricles, and long axons that would ultimately connect to the rest of a body.

The 'liveliness' of such close analogues disrupts understandings of the relationship of the self and the body, but also opens new possibilities for tissue bioeconomies, as anthropologists of technology have noted (Hogle 2010; Kent et al. 2006; Sunder Rajan 2006; Waldby and Mitchell 2006; Webster 2012). Stem cells were a platform for organoid and other technologies, and organoids in turn are a platform for additional technologies. For example, vasculature made by 3D printing can be added to organoids or gene editing applied to determine if a disease could be 'cured' in vitro before trying in a patient.

While organoids might eventually be used for therapeutic transplantation, they are currently used to study disease and developmental biology, or to test for response to therapeutics or toxicities. For example, gut organoids are used to study intestine-microbe interactions in infections, and how diseases such as colon cancer or Crohn's disease develop and respond to drugs. Lung organoids are demonstrating how SARS2-CoV-2 ravages lungs, and which drugs work (Han et al. 2020; Salahudeen et al. 2020). Human organoids make good research tools because animal models cannot reproduce humans' physiology or life cycle, so findings frequently cannot be reproduced accurately.

Significantly, organoids are heralded as alternatives to pragmatic and ethical problems inherent in animal and human subjects experimentation. Chiefly, substituting organoids for living animals for preclinical studies or product safety tests decreases animal suffering, while producing more representative findings. Clinical trials in human subjects have been plagued with difficulties in recruiting eligible patients, high costs, and long completion times, leading to complaints about access, pricing, and timely introduction of new therapies. Early-stage trial costs might be diminished with less risk for human subjects. In addition to preventing side effects and suffering, researchers could test controversial, high-risk interventions before administering them to patients. Creating human organ analogues in vitro also provides more life-like, yet controlled conditions for research that would not be practically or ethically possible to do in humans. For example, brain organoids are being used to study developmental and neurodegenerative disorders such as Alzheimer's, and they provided the first direct evidence for a causal connection between the Zika virus and microcephaly. Also, for rare diseases, a patient's own cells can be used to research and potentially treat their disease, or to research genetic variants of a cancer. The ability to use induced pluripotent stem cells from specific patients offers the possibility of seeing how tissues of individuals or subpopulations might respond to drug treatments before trying them in living humans.

To become useful tools with value for producers, however, requires convincing scientists, clinicians, funders, and regulators that they are authentic enough to be surrogate human subjects and valid sources of evidence. Regulators look for the ability to form functional features and exhibit genetic and chemical markers of the organ of interest, plus additional critical quality attributes, to determine how closely they resemble real developing organs. Tests of such attributes act as authentication practices. Yet the process of selecting the attributes that verify organoids as 'real enough' says much about what counts as essential features of the original, and who has the authority to make such determinations.[1] Regulatory oversight enacts authenticity by approving certain representations of the original, while simultaneously shaping the form that the ultimate products will take. Authenticity and authority relations are thus tightly bound. For now, regulatory bodies (FDA in the US, EMA in Europe) accept organoid research as valid sources of preclinical and early phase trial data in lieu of some animal and human tests, especially when the number of available trial subjects is small. However, organoids must meet the same criteria as pharmaceuticals in Europe, speaking to the uncertainty around what kind of objects they are (Vives and Batlle-Morera 2020).

HUMAN SUBJECTS?

Organoids must also be enough like the real thing to be good models for research. That is, they must function as they do in a body and have the right genetic, anatomical, and physiological characteristics for the purpose at hand. The paradox is that while organoids are of interest because they recapitulate real tissue better than cell cultures, they are most valuable precisely because they exist outside of real, natural, environments in individual bodies and can be observed under controlled, highly engineered conditions. Additionally, if they are too authentic, they risk moral condemnation. Ethicists have long debated whether cells derived from humans—especially those with developmental potential—have special moral status or could count as human subjects. But it is organoids' Janus-faced status of real-but-not-original, natural-but-artificially-existing human matter that creates moral confusion and is the target of ethical critique (Boers et al. 2016; Koplin and Savulescu 2019; Lavazza and Massimini 2018).

This comes into sharp relief with brain organoids. Organoids are particularly useful for brain diseases, because animal models cannot demonstrate the kinds of complex interactions and cognitive sequelae of disease or treatments found in humans. Experimenting directly on living human subjects is ethically fraught because of the potential damage to cognitive, executive, motor, or sensory functions, and affected patients may lack cognitive capacity for informed consent. Yet creating 'mini-brains-in-a-dish' conjures worries that self-organising brain material might develop to a point where it could experience pain, or gain some sense of awareness. Scientists have been at pains to dispel fears that a working, sensing brain with possible consciousness is being created in the lab. They argue that cerebral organoids are small masses with no vasculature to get oxygen and nutrients to cells. One researcher showed that brain organoids lack the cell subtypes found in brains in vivo (Bhaduri et al. 2020). Others assert that they also lack the interconnectivity of human brains in bodies and do not develop cell signalling circuitry because they have no sensory input. This is key, since sensory stimulation shapes brain circuitry: human experiences affect brain development.[2] According to these scientists, cerebral organoids do not then develop and act the same way as native tissue in a host. These arguments are beginning to crumble, however, as other researchers are observing more highly developed features like a blood-brain barrier and have in fact recorded signalling somewhat similar to early developing humans (Cakir et al. 2019; Trujillo et al. 2019).

Brain organoids—like reproductive organoids—are particularly ethically sensitive entities. As such, they are accompanied by moral dilemmas about their source and use, but also exist in an uneasy set of social relations around their handling as research and regulatory entities. While they are not human subjects per se, they may be perceived as needing special protections or guidelines as though they are (Bredenoord et al. 2017; Chen et al. 2019; Lavazza and Massimini 2018).[3] Making things even more complicated, researchers sometimes liken brain organoids to brain tissue as it might appear in a second semester foetus. Currently, research on human embryos is not allowed in many countries after the neural tube begins to form, about 14 days after fertilisation. However, the point of creating a cerebral organoid is to study the very structures that might be forming well after 14 days without using a foetus.

Organoids' ambiguous status is thus both a source of ethical quandaries and their proposed solution. The ontological ambiguity is partly dealt with through material and discursive means, including devising nomenclature to distinguish between organoids (term reserved for those having markers, cell types, structure, and physiology of the target organ) from entities with physiologically relevant but incomplete components, or are grown in microfluidic or organ-on-a-chip systems. The challenge of settling definitions and terms reflects the difficulty in how authenticity is navigated, with significant implications for regulation and ethics.

Interestingly, researchers often told me in interviews that in practice, product sponsors cared less about whether organoid models were more *human* than that they were more *predictable*. Organoids under controlled, highly engineered conditions are more predictable than in a human subject's body, where other morbidities, diet, and behavioural patterns may affect cell function and interactions. More pragmatically, for diseases with multiple possible genetic mutations, developing many organoid variants is far more *efficient* than validating clinical trial protocols for so many variants. In developing commercial entities for testing, drug companies want a systematic, standardised way to predict failure of a candidate drug more quickly than a long, expensive clinical trial (Choudhury et al. 2020).

The emphasis on efficiency resurrects concerns about instrumentalisation of human material. Additional concerns include consent for donor cells and ownership of cells and their products, but focus primarily on the source and use of materials and what constitutes the human (Chen et al. 2019; Greely 2021; Koplin and Savulescu 2019; Vermeulen et al. 2017). Such critiques are common to a variety of human biological materials besides organoids. While valid, I argue that these endless debates risk missing other consequential issues. In the next section, I show how an anthropological lens broadens the view to illuminate how these new life forms encounter older social orders of scientific expertise, legal-regulatory authority, and ethical understandings while animating new ones.

AUTHENTICATION INFRASTRUCTURES

As models for humans, organoids are instruments for both material and conceptual changes. As Rheinberger (2010) has argued, different kinds of experimental systems create different kinds of epistemic objects, giving rise to new infrastructure systems in which forms of expertise, tools, economic forces, and sources of power may be reconfigured in consequential ways. Assumptions built into experimental models affect the kinds of questions asked (or not), and the way disease is understood. Assumptions that organoids are 'authentic enough' and 'ethical enough' to do the work of experimentation—and eventually, therapy—depend on material practices, as described above, while negotiating ethical concerns. Such processes are dynamic: as organoids encounter older legal-regulatory infrastructures, they disturb previously distinct regulatory categories of human-manufactured or procured native material, as well as notions of how best to govern them. Organoids, then, generate both new knowledge and social practices.

Organoids may well also disrupt the social relations of clinical trials. Existing research and clinical infrastructures are entrenched industries, with well-established procedures, oversight, and power relations. Globally, tens of billions in public and private funds are spent on clinical trials, with an additional $25 billion in economic impact for trial site communities (Battelle 2015). Organoids may allay costs for preclinical and early phase testing, but may clash with existing contract research organisations, worth $43 billion in 2019 (Frost and Sullivan 2020).

Social relations figure significantly in clinical research. As the Humbrecht organoid bank puts it, organoids are a way to bring the patient directly into the lab (huborganoids.nl). But which patients? And are patients' understandings, experiences with disease, or expectations of trials brought in as well? Some patients participate in trials as a way to access basic medical care, others as a way of experiencing control or directly engaging with their illness. Additionally, findings from organoid research are decontextualised not only from the whole interacting body, but from the living patient experiencing a disorder (Saha and Hurlbut 2011). That is, disease is not just a biological reality; rather, it emerges out of more complex interactions between disease, patients and physicians, and social organisation (Epstein 2007; Löwy 2000). Anthropologists of technology are well-positioned to analyse such questions of biosociality (cf. Rabinow 1999) arising from displaced subjectivity with organoids.

Turning from clinical research domains to the more publicly visible area of food, the next section discusses cultured meat. The assemblages differ, but the dynamics of enacting authenticity are similar.

CULTURED MEAT

Images of cattle grazing in pastures as modern-day cowboys watch over them and chickens pecking in an open yard while their farmers discuss their welfare, posted by livestock industry associations, convey a pastoral setting where food sources are carefully tended. Such representations contrast starkly with media depictions of animals crowded into warehouse-style indoor pens and fed unnatural diets. Less visible are the energy-intensive technologies, environmental degradation, and water over-use needed to turn animals into edible (and marketable) food. About a quarter of the earth's surface is used for livestock production, which is responsible for about 14.5% of greenhouse gas emissions (FAO 2017). Together with high energy costs of transport and preservation, human health effects of contaminants from fertilisers, manure and production of by-products, and questionable animal welfare practices, concerns about meat production are growing. Nevertheless, global demand for meat is estimated at 43.6 million tonnes in 2019 (FAO 2020; OECD 2020).[4] Reducing meat consumption is a logical response to these challenges, but converting enough meat eaters to vegetarianism is unlikely, and protein substitutes have not made a significant difference in consumption.

Cultured meat is posited as an alternative that addresses such problems, while making a more authentic, meat-like product than previous substitutes. Meat is among a number of products in the growing area of cellular agriculture, which combines cell culture technologies, genetic and tissue engineering, and in some cases, synthetic biology and 3-D printing, to make agricultural analogues. To make cultured meat (hereafter CM), cells are extracted from an animal's muscle and cultured in the lab, or early stem cells from other tissue (such as a feather) are reprogrammed to become muscle cells (iPSCs). Cells are co-cultured with all of the kinds of cells that would comprise muscle, including connective tissue cells, satellite cells, and fat cells, using culture media with specific growth factors, nutrients, and support or scaffold material on which cells can form tissue-like structures. Ingredients such as alginate are sometimes added to give the growing tissue support and firmness.[5]

While this may result in a consistency and texture resembling natural muscle tissue, turning the lab-grown structures into 'meat' requires recapitulating the sensory experience of eating, including appearance, taste, smell, and mouth-feel.[6] For example, animal muscle is part of a moving, eating body; how much its muscles are used and what it eats makes a difference in meat tenderness or toughness. To mimic physical conditions the cells would have in a pastured cow, mechanical, electrical, or magnetic forces are applied in bioreactors so muscle fibres will form as they would in nature. Some researchers add more fat cells or other materials on scaffold strings to reproduce marbling, a desirable trait in real meat. Interestingly, one researcher uses the fat ratio specific to Kobe beef, considered to be a luxury food.[7] For products such as hamburger or sausage, cells from various kinds of muscle could be combined (just like real hamburger), and the texture could be made loose and soft, but for something resembling a steak, the inner parts would need to be softer and the exterior firmer and able to brown like meat in cooking. Curiously, one company (Eat Just Inc.) makes chicken nuggets which are 70% CM and the rest is a plant-based material, to match the homogenised texture of existing fast-food nuggets. At the other end, French company Gourmey makes foie gras from duck egg cells, which they describe as 'ethical foie gras without force-feeding' (Gourmey.com).

Making CM taste and appear like the real thing is complicated, but making it too real may also evoke disgust (Manjoo 2012; Siegrist et al. 2018). Vegetal or chemical tastes from the culture process can be obscured by additives, but more than a thousand flavour compounds make up meat flavour and smell. Marketers recognise that the sensory experience of real meat—both raw and cooked—is key to success and must meet consumer expectations, if not reality. For example, consumers have expectations of appearance, which may not match butchered meat (cf. Berenstein 2018). Fresh animal meat typically is more purple, due to less oxidised myoglobin; reddish meat is oxidised and thus less fresh, yet consumers prefer it because they perceive it as fresher. Beet juice or heme pigments are added to give the appearance of the blood that would be in animal flesh.[8]

This raises intriguing questions about designing something to be faithful to the original. Material means of making CM into meat may reproduce the essence but not the reality of 'real' meat. CM is less exposed to bacteria—a good thing for food safety, but some bacteria affect flavour—in cheese for example, among other foods. Similarly, naturally occurring enzymes (cathepsins) that break down tissue in conventional meat production (leading to ageing and deterioration) actually tenderise meat and add flavour, especially on exposed surfaces. Should the effects of contamination or deterioration be replicated? Gene editing could improve nutritional characteristics or increase shelf life. Does it matter (if it does) that such interventions alter the original? After all, conventional meat is hardly natural or original, with additives and preservatives used to improve appearance and taste. I argue that what is interesting for anthropologists is less whether CM products are real because they contain original cells or because they duplicate the experience of the original but, rather, how the authentic is understood by various participants in the assemblage, and how it matters. I next examine discursive practices to illustrate.

What Does It Mean to Be Cow?

If social scientists and bioethicists are preoccupied with debates about what makes us human, participants in the assemblage around engineered meat are preoccupied with what it means to be cow. Mark Post (Mosa Meats), demonstrating the first cultured meat burger, famously argued that 'it's meat—just not in a cow'. Company literature states that the cells 'are doing what they would normally do inside the animal', and the company's mission is 'to produce *real meat* for the world's growing population that is delicious, healthier, better for the environment, and kind to animals' (mosameat.com, emphasis in the original). Just Meat advertises 'real meat without tearing down a forest or taking a life' (GOODmeat.co).

However, calling something 'real meat' is intensely political. There are lively disputes about whether cultured products can share the same name as the original animal source. Like the dairy industry's battle against anything being called milk that does not come from a lactating animal (nut or oat milk, etc.), the beef and poultry industries hotly contest the term being associated with products made in a lab. The US Cattlemen's Association lobbied to restrict the term to anything that has 'been born, raised, and harvested in the traditional manner' (National Cattlemen's Beef Association 2019). Others say that what is made in the lab is not meat per se; rather, it is only an ingredient with which to make a final product (Stephens et al. 2019; Tai 2020). Analysing legal histories of meat labelling, Tai (2020) notes that a number of US states are considering legislation to disallow the use of the term meat for lab-made products. Amendments to EU labelling requirements (2019) proposed restricting 'meat' to actual livestock-containing products. Member states' definitions vary, however; for example, the German Food Code Commission has a complex coding based on sensorial similarity of products to real meat.

Stephens, Sexton, and Driessen (2019) recount various terms used by participants, from 'in vitro' or 'lab-grown' meat to the more recent 'cultured' meat. These labels refer to the process and distinguish it from conventional production. Some participants instead promote the use of terms that evoke what the product is intended to do. The term 'clean' meat suggests that a lab-based process purifies not only the materials but also the morally contaminated conventional production methods (Stephens et al. 2019; Tai 2020). More provocative is 'slaughterhouse-free meat'. A survey of consumer responses to descriptions found that 'clean' or 'safe' meat scored best, especially regarding consumers' intent to buy.[9] Others insist on simply calling it meat, without adjectives.

Legal authorities struggle to address ontological ambiguities through classifications and definitions. In the US, animal products are traditionally overseen by the Department of Agriculture (USDA). However, food and cells (especially stem cells) are overseen by the Food and Drug Administration (FDA). In 2019, the USDA and FDA agreed to jointly oversee lab-grown products: the FDA will be responsible for premarket aspects of cell sourcing, banking, scaleup, and facility inspection, and the USDA will be responsible once cells are harvested and made into products, including labelling.[10] Both have statutory authority over food safety. At the EU level, CM products fall under a 'novel food' category (EU 2015/2283), requiring more stringent requirements than other foods. The Singapore Food Agency recently approved Eat Just's chicken nuggets as an 'alternative protein', but requires the use of 'mock' or 'cultured' in labelling.

Like organoids, classifications are thus part of the processes that enact meat as authentic or something else. There are more public ways that meat is also enacted as authentic. Stephens and Ruivenkamp (2016), for example, show how images and a high-profile cooking demonstration persuasively established CM as normal food, in contrast to depictions of CM in the lab. Companies merchandise their products by placing them in the meat section of stores, not with vegetarian meat substitutes.

A Post-Animal Techno-ethico-Economy?

The paradox is that to gain consumer acceptance, meet ethical expectations, and secure investments, CM must simultaneously be very much like the original in sensory experience and very unlike the original with its connotations of unsustainability and abuses. It must appear to be clean and controlled, but not artificial and industrially mass-produced, supporting consumers' values while supporting producers' capitalist values. The original-authentic is both slaughterhouse and imagined pastoral; the analogue is both controlled industrial product and animal-derived techno-ethical fix.

CM has been made to matter not just as a novel food alternative, but as an ethical pivot from existing food provisioning practices. CM providers position CM as real-but-more-ethical alternatives with which to create a new bioeconomy. Evoking major social problems of climate change, genetic engineering misuse, the destruction of wild forests, and colonialism in narratives about rebuilding the planet through one-health perspectives frame CM as the core solution (cf. GOODmeat.co).

Stephens (2013) situates the navigation of ethics and ontology within literatures of the sociology of expectations. That is, speculations about what CM can do for sustainability, environmental safety, food security, and animal rights are promissory narratives woven in to the very design of cultured meat. Luetchford (2016) might call this the marketisation of ethical consumption. As Stephens uncovered in interviews with animal welfare activists, however, ethical framings of CM are not homogenous and are sometimes counterintuitive (2013). In some activists' views, disaggregating the animal into bits does nothing towards the ethics of animal welfare. While whole animals are not slaughtered, animal donors are still used, sustaining an instrumentalist view of living creatures (Miller 2012). The core problem of animals as a food source is unresolved. In fact, CM narratives may serve to normalise continued meat consumption. Some critics argue that focusing ethical attention on ontology fails to confront more fundamental ethical issues of relations and responsibilities between humans and animals (Galusky 2014; Hopkins and Dacey 2008).

Furthermore, claims to sustainability are contradicted by data suggesting that there is potentially a bigger environmental footprint from alt-meat production than livestock in terms of energy costs and long-term climate impact (Lynch and Pierrehumbert 2019). Also, while it may be more sustainable than large-scale industrial agriculture, it does not address the more comprehensive global needs of food sovereignty, food insecurity, and maldistribution. Sexton (2019) further questions whether cultured food alternatives may ultimately amount to little more than Northern efforts to feed the global South with a 'protein fix' from corporate sources prioritising their own interests. Far from resolving ethical issues, CM may be just shifting them.

Like organoids, CM disrupts social orders and power hierarchies. To apprehend the entanglement of ethics and politics of authenticity in this domain fully, the prominent role of meat in societies must also be understood, including the deeply entrenched power relations of livestock-related industries.[11] Livestock advocacy groups strongly oppose CM, deploying ethical arguments to counter CM's claims to produce more ethical food systems. While the National Cattlemen's Beef Association (US) raises doubts about CM nutritional equivalency and safety and positions it as too ideologically leftist (2019), the European Livestock Voice (2021) casts CM as a spectre of big tech, urban, elitist, private enterprise and defends livestock's importance to economic welfare and nutrition for the world's poor. The formidable food industrial complex (processing, distribution, grocery and restaurant industries, and more) influences markets and legislation; their responses will be important to watch.

The ethics and politics of meat analogues are central to global debates about sustainability. Meat alternatives appear in the European Commission's 2030 Food Initiative as a way to achieve climate-smart and sustainable food systems, and in light of pandemic meat supply chain disruptions, CM is accelerating. Following the practices of regulating, certifying, and labelling, and the promotional strategies used to frame CM as authentic (or not) will shed light on how socio-ethical-technological assemblages are reconstituted around new biological forms.

Conclusions

I have shown a few of the material and discursive means by which biological analogues are fashioned as technologies, with embedded ethical regimes alloyed to authenticity. Authenticity is enacted not just because the analogues are crafted from original materials or because they conserve or essentialise original features but, rather, through various naming, promotional, legal, classificatory, and other ethico-technical techniques.

The ontological ambiguity of emerging bio-objects provides an opportunity to analyse how they are materialised through assemblages of practices, technologies, and theories that configure action. A constellation of technologies enable these entities to exist as authentic analogues, with particular values and ethical regimes baked in. They are also 'cultured up', to use Franklin (2013) term: they are shaped in interaction with broader sets of historical and social experiences and meanings around eating and human experimentation. CM and organoids challenge givens about what is food, what is a human subject, and who has the authority to judge. Importantly, ontologies are inseparable from what they enact in the world (Barry 2001; Bennett 2010). There is much at stake: to invoke authenticity is to claim legitimacy, and on this basis, establish value. Claiming authenticity, however, is highly political, as I have shown.

Finally, I argue that what is more important than whether emerging life forms such as biological analogues are real or authentic is the process by which they are enacted as such, or fail to be enacted. The fetishism of authenticity—including what it means to be human or animal—should not overshadow crucial questions about other important social phenomena. The examples I have described materialise the world in particular ways that may include or exclude certain participants, serve fewer, more elite individuals, and may or may not solve ethical problems they purport to address. Studying how such bio-objects come into being, and more importantly, animate politics and ethics in consequential ways is ripe for anthropological inquiry.

Acknowledgements I thank Dorthe Brogård Kristenson, Klaus Hoeyer, Mette Svendsen, and Ayo Wahlberg for helpful exchanges and anonymous reviewers for their comments. I am indebted to Phillip Schneider for research assistance and for creative insights.

Notes

1. I cover authentication practices for cells elsewhere (Hogle 2019, 2021).
2. This led some journalists to describe the organoids in terms suggesting human emotions: 'stressed out', 'confused', and 'disorganized' (Economist 2019; Weiler 2020).
3. Hinterberger (2018) and Svendsen et al. (this volume) discuss similar complexities with humanised animal models (chimeras), showing how the human is enacted through material practices in the lab.

4. Estimates are usually given in metric tonnes (1 mT = 1000 kg or 2205 lbs), based on carcass weight, not final product weight. Estimates vary, depending on whether fish or exotic meats are included. The OECD estimates global per capita consumption at 33.8 kg; however, meat consumption varies considerably based on country wealth (2020). Notably, previous estimates forecasted an increase in consumption; however, consumption has decreased by about 2.8% due to production disruptions connected with the pandemic and animal disease outbreaks (FAO 2020, p. 45). Consequently, recent forecasts estimate increased demand for meat alternatives.

5. For details, see Arshad et al. (2017). Embryonic stem cells may also be used.

6. There are fascinating cultural considerations in terms of flavour preferences and religious requirements (Kenigsberg and Zivotofsky 2020; Yaffe-Bellany 2020).

7. This raises interesting questions about heritage breeds and terroir, much debated in cuisine discourse. Berkshire pork is more acidic (due to diet and genetics), Wagyu beef is fattier and buttery, and Iberico pork raised on acorns has a prized flavour. I address this elsewhere as a further amplification of what is at stake with notions of the authentic; see also Weiss (2016).

8. The history of efforts to improve foodstuffs through preservatives, flavourings, additives, and genetics is relevant, as is the history of foods faked and adulterated to make them appear like the original, but too extensive to be covered here. See for example Berenstein (2018) and Blum (2018).

9. Survey results are found at https://www.gfi.org/the-naming-of-clean-meat. See also Stephens et al. (2019), and for consumer perceptions, Bryant and Barnett (2018), Marcu et al. (2015) and Verbeke et al. (2015).

10. The agreement is found at: https://www.fsis.usda.gov/wps/wcm/connect/0d2d644a-9a65-43c6-944f-ea598aacdec1/Formal-Agreement-FSIS-FDA.pdf?MOD=AJPERES. See also the National Academy of Sciences (2017).

11. Ogle (2013) chronicled how meat consumption links multiple histories of homesteading, the railroad and transportation industries, supply chain infrastructures, urbanism, and industrialism since the nineteenth century.

References

Arshad, M., Javed, M., Sohaib, M., Saeed, F., Imran, A., & Amjad, Z. (2017). Tissue engineering approaches to develop culture meat from cells: a mini review. *Cogent Food & Agriculture, 3*(1). doi:https://doi.org/10.1080/2331193 2.2017.1320814.

Barry, A. (2001). *Political machines: Governing a technological society.* London: Athlone Press.

Battelle Technology Partnership Practice (2015). Biopharmaceutical industry-sponsored clinical trials: impact on state economies. Technical Report. http://phrma-docs. phrma.org/sites/default/files/pdf/biopharmaceutical-industry-sponsored-clinical-trials-impact-on-state-economies.pdf. Accessed 18 June 2019.

Baudrillard, J. (1981). *Simulacra and simulations.* Ann Arbor: University of Michigan Press.

Benjamin, W. (1968). The work of art in the age of mechanical reproduction. In H. Arendt (Ed.), *Illuminations* (pp 217-252). New York: Schocken Books.

Bennett, J. (2010). *Vibrant matter: A political ecology of things*. Durham, NC.: Duke University Press.

Berenstein, N. (2018). *Flavor added: The science of flavor and the industrialization of taste in America*. Ph.D. Thesis. University of Pennsylvania. Philadelphia, Pennsylvania.

Besky, S. (2014). *The Darjeeling distinction: Labor and justice on fair-trade tea transplantations in India*. Berkeley: University of California Press.

Beverland, M. B. (2005). Crafting brand authenticity: the case of luxury wines. *Journal of Management Studies, 12*(5), 1003-1029.

Bhaduri A., Andrews M. G., Mancia L. W., Jung D., Shin D., Allen D., Jung D., Schmunk G., Haeussler M., Salma J., Pollen A. A., Nowakowski T. J., & Kriegstein A. R. (2020). Cell stress in cortical organoids impairs molecular subtype specification. *Nature, 578*(7793),142-148.

Blum, D. (2018). *The poisoner's handbook*. New York: Penguin Press.

Boers, S. N., van Delden, J. M., Clevers, H., & Bredenoord, A. (2016). Organoid biobanking: Identifying the ethics. *EMBO Reports, 17*(7), 938-941.

Bowker, G., & Star, S.L. (1999). *Sorting things out: Classification and Its consequences*. Cambridge, MA.: The MIT Press.

Bredenoord, A., Clevers, H., & Knoblich, J. (2017). Human tissues in a dish: The research and ethical implications of organoid technology. *Science, 355*(6322), eaaf9414. doi:https://doi.org/10.1126/science.aaf9414.

Bryant, C., & Barnett, J. (2018). Consumer acceptance of cultured meat: a systematic review. *Meat Science, 143*, 8-17.

Busch, L. (2011). *Standards: Recipes for reality*. Cambridge, MA.: The MIT Press.

Cakir, B., Xiang, Y., Tanaka, Y., Kural, M. et al. (2019). Engineering of human brain organoids with a functional vascular-like system. *Nature Methods, 16*, 1169–1175. doi:https://doi.org/10.1038/s41592-019-0586-5.

Chen, I., Wolf, J., Blue, R., Moreno, J., Ming, G-L., & Song, H. (2019). Transplantation of human brain organoids: Revisiting the science and ethics of brain chimeras. *Cell Stem Cell, 25*(4), 462-472.

Choudhury, D., Ashok, A., & Naing, M. (2020). Commercialization of organoids. *Trends in Molecular Medicine, 26*(3), 245-249.

Clifford, J. (1988). *The predicament of culture: 20th century ethnography, literature and art*. Cambridge, MA.: Harvard University Press.

Daston L., & Vidal F. (Eds.) (2004). *On the moral authority of nature*. Chicago: University Chicago Press.

Douglas, M. (1966). *Purity and danger*. London: Routledge.

Dussauge, I., Helgesson, C-F., & Lee, F. (2015). *Value practices in the life sciences & medicine*. New York: Oxford University Press.

Economist (2019, 29 August). What is a brain? Cerebral organoids are becoming more brainlike. https://www.economist.com/science-and-technology/2019/08/29/cerebral-organoids-are-becoming-more-brainlike. Accessed 5 September 2019.

Epstein, S. (2007). *Inclusion: The politics of difference in medical research*. Chicago: University of Chicago Press.L

Escobar, A. (1999). After nature: Steps toward an anti-essentialist political ecology. *Current Anthropology, 40*(1), 1-30.

European Livestock Voice (2021). Opinion: The European livestock sector's views on the recent push for synthetic meat. https://meatthefacts.eu/home/activity/latest-news/opinion-the-european-livestock-sectors-views-on-the-recent-push-for-synthetic-meat/. Accessed 14 July 2021.

Fillitz, T., & Saris, J. (2012). *Debating authenticity: Concepts of modernity in anthropological perspective.* Oxford: Berghahn Books.

Food and Agriculture Organization of the United Nations (FAO) (2017). *Land use and agricultural practices 1961–2017.* Fao.org/economic/ess/environment/data/land-use/vu. Accessed 8 February 2020.

Food and Agriculture Organization of the United Nations (FAO) (2020). *Food Outlook: Biannual Report on Global Food Markets.* Rome. doi:10.4060/ca9509en. Accessed 9 December 2020.

Franklin, S. (2007). *Dolly Mixtures: the remaking of genealogy.* Durham, NC.: Duke University Press.

Franklin, S. (2013). *Biological relatives: IVF, stem cells, and the future of kinship.* Durham, NC.: Duke University Press.

Frost & Sullivan (2020). *Hybridization of clinical trial designs reviving global CRO market post-pandemic; 2019–2024.* Santa Clara, CA.

Galusky, W. (2014). Technology as responsibility: failure, food animals, and lab-grown meat. *Journal of Agriculture and Environmental Ethics, 27,* 931-948.

Gilmore, J., & Pine, B.J. (2007). *Authenticity: What consumers really want.* Cambridge, MA.: Harvard Business School Press.

Grasseni, C., & Paxson, H. (2014). Introducing a special issue on the reinvention of food: connections and mediations. *Gastronomica, 14*(4), 1-6.

Greely, H. (2021). Human brain surrogates research: The onrushing ethical dilemma. *The American Journal of Bioethics, 21*(1), 34-45. doi:https://doi.org/10.1080/15265161.2020.1845853.

Han, Y., Duan, X., Yang, L. et al. (2020). Identification of SARS-CoV-2 inhibitors using lung and colonic organoids. *Nature, 589,* 270–275. doi:https://doi.org/10.1038/s41586-020-2901-9.

Haraway, D. (1991). *Simians, Cyborgs and Women.* New York: Free Press.

Herring, R. (Ed.) (2015). *Oxford Handbook of Food, Politics and Society.* Oxford: Oxford University Press.

Handler, R. (1986). Authenticity. *Anthropology Today, 2*(1), 2–4.

Hinterberger, A. (2018). Marked 'h' for human: Chimeric life and the politics of the human. *BioSocieties, 13*(2), 453–469.

Hobsbawm, E., & Ranger, T. (Eds.) (1983). *The invention of tradition.* Cambridge: Cambridge University Press.

Hogle, L. F. (2009). Pragmatic objectivity and the standardization of engineered tissues. *Social Studies of Science, 39*(5), 717–742.

Hogle, L. F. (2010). Characterizing embryonic stem cells: Biological and social markers of identity. *Medical Anthropology Quarterly, 24*(4), 433–450.

Hogle, L.F. (2019). Authentication: A prologue. Paper presented to the Society for the Social Study of Science, (New Orleans, 9 September).

Hogle, L.F. (2021). *Authenticating persons and things: Sociotechnical systems of trust in an era of artifice.* Unpublished ms.

Hopkins, P. D., & Dacey, A. (2008). Vegetarian meat: Could technology save animals and satisfy meateaters? *Journal of Agricultural and Environmental Ethics, 21*(6), 579–596.

Keller, E.F. (2008). Nature and the natural. *BioSocieties, 3,* 117–124.

Kent, J., Faulkner, A., Ingrid Geesink, I., & Fitzpatrick, D. (2006). Culturing cells, reproducing and regulating the self. *Body & Society, 12*(2), 1–23. doi:https://doi.org/10.1177/1357034X06064296.

Kenigsberg J. A., & Zivotofsky A. Z. (2020). A Jewish religious perspective on cellular agriculture. *Frontiers in Sustainable Food Systems, 3*, 128. doi:10.3389/fsufs.2019.00128.

King, E., & Lyall, C. (2018). What's in a name: are cultured red blood cells 'natural'? *Sociology of Health & Illness, 40*(4), 687-701.

Klein, J., & Watson, J. (Eds.) (2016). *The handbook of food and anthropology.* London: Bloomsbury.

Kloppenberg, J. (1988). *First the seed: the political-economy of plant biotechnology.* Madison: University of Wisconsin Press.

Koo, B., Choi, B., Park, H., & Yoon, K-J. (2019). Past, present, and future of brain organoid Technology. *Molecules and Cells, 42*(9), 617–627.

Koplin, J., & Savulescu, J. (2019). Moral limits of brain organoid research. *Journal of Law, Medicine & Ethics, 47*, 760-767.

Lancaster, M. A., & Knoblich, J. A. (2014). Organogenesis in a dish: modeling development and disease using organoid technologies. *Science, 345*(6194), eaam1247125. doi:https://doi.org/10.1126/science.1247125.

Landecker, H. (2007). *Culturing life: How cells became technologies.* Cambridge, MA.: Harvard University Press.

Lavazza A., & Massimini M. (2018). Cerebral organoids: ethical issues and consciousness assessment. *Journal of Medical Ethics, 44*(9), 606-610.

Lederer, S. (1995). *Subjected to science.* Baltimore, MD.: Johns Hopkins Press.

Lindholm C. (2002). Authenticity, anthropology and the sacred. *Anthropology Quarterly, 75*, 331-338.

Löwy, I. (2000). The experimental body. In R. Cooter & J. Pickstone (Eds.), *Companion to medicine in the 21st century* (pp. 435-449). New York: Routledge.

Luetchford, P. (2016). Ethical consumption: the moralities and politics of food. In J. Klein & J. L. Watson (Eds.), *The handbook of food and anthropology* (pp 387-405). New York: Bloomsbury Publishing.

Lynch, J., & Pierrehumbert, R. (2019). Climate impacts of cultured meat and beef cattle. *Frontiers in sustainable food systems.* doi:https://doi.org/10.3389/fsufs.2019.0005.

Manjoo, F. (2012, 26 July). Fake meat so good it will freak you out. *Slate.* https://slate.com/technology/2012/07/bedyond-meat-so-real-it-will-freak-you-out.html. Accessed 7 July 2019.

Marcu, A., Gaspar, R., Rutsaert, P., Seibt, B., Fletcher, D., Verbeke, W., & Barnett, J. (2015). Analogies, metaphors, and wondering about the future: Lay sense-making around synthetic meat. *Public Understanding of Science, 24*(5), 547–562.

Marks, N. J. (2010). Defining stem cells? Scientists and their classification of nature. *The Sociological Review, 58*(S1), S32-50.

McGarity, R. (2020). Code season. *MIT Technology Review.* 52-57.

Merriam-Webster. (n.d.) "Authentic." *Merriam-Webster.com Dictionary,* https://www.merriam-webster.com/dictionary/authentic. Accessed 29 October 2019.

Miller, J. (2012). In vitro meat: Power, authenticity and vegetarianism. *Journal of Critical Animal Studies, 10*(4), 41-63.

Mintz, S. (1985). *Sweetness and power: the place of sugar in modern history.* New York: Penguin Books.

National Academy of Sciences (2017). *Preparing for future products of biotechnology.* Washington, DC.: The National Academies Press. http://doi.org/10.17226/24605

National Cattlemen's Beef Association (2019). NCBA responds to Politico article on politics of meat. https://www.ncba.org/ourviews2.aspx?NewsID=6923.

Organization for Economic Coordination and Development (OECD) (2020). *Meat consumption.* doi:10.1787/fa290fd0-en. Accessed 12 December 2020.

Ogle, M. (2013). *In meat we trust: An unexpected history of carnivore America.* Boston, MA.: Houghton Mifflin Harcourt.

Parry, S., & Dupre, J. (2010). Introducing nature after the genome. *Sociological Review, 58*(S1), 3-16.

Paxson, H. (2010). Locating value in artisan cheese: reverse engineering terroir for new-world landscapes. *American Anthropologist, 112*(3), 444-457.

Paxson, H. (2012). *The life of cheese: Crafting food and value in America.* Berkeley: University of California Press.

Petersen, A. (2011). *The politics of bioethics.* New York: Routledge.

Power, M. (2007). *Organized uncertainty: Designing a world of risk management.* Oxford University Press.

Rabinow, P. (1999). Artificiality and enlightenment: from sociobiology to biosociality. In J. Crary & S. Kwinter (Eds.), *Zone 6 Incorporations* (pp. 181-193). New York: Zone Books.

Rheinberger, H-J. (2010). *An epistemology of the concrete: Twentieth-century histories of life.* Durham, NC.: Duke University Press.

Rothman D. J. (1990) Human experimentation and the origins of bioethics in the United States. In G. Weisz (Ed.), *Social science perspectives on medical ethics: culture, illness, and healing* (pp. 185-200). Dordrecht: Springer.

Saha, K., & Hurlbut, B. (2011). Disease modelling using pluripotent stem cells: making sense of disease from bench to bedside. *Swiss Medical Weekly, 141*:w13144. doi:10.4414/smw.2011.13144.

Salahudeen, A. A., Choi, S. S., Rustagi, A. et al. (2020). Progenitor identification and SARS-CoV-2 infection in human distal lung organoids. *Nature, 588*, 670–675. doi:https://doi.org/10.1038/s41586-020-3014-1.

Sexton, A. (2019). Framing the future of food: the contested promises of alternative proteins. *Environment and Planning E: Nature and Space, 2*, 47-72. doi:https://doi.org/10.1177/2514848619827009

Siegrist, M., Sütterlin, B., & Hartmann, C. (2018). Perceived naturalness and evoked disgust influence acceptance of cultured meat. *Meat Science, 139*, 213-219.

Soper, K. (2010). Unnatural times? The social imaginary and the future of Nature. *The Sociological Review, 57*(2), 222-235.

Squier, S. (2004). *Liminal Lives: Imagining the human at the frontiers of biomedicine.* Durham, NC.: Duke University Press.

Stephens, N. (2013). Growing meat in laboratories: the promise, ontology and ethical boundary-work of using muscle cells to make food. *Configurations, 21*(2), 159-181.

Stephens, N., & Ruivenkamp, M. (2016). Promise and ontological ambiguity in the in vitro meat imagescape: from laboratory myotubes to the cultured burger. *Science As Culture, 25*, 327-355.

Stephens, N., Sexton, A., & Driessen, C. (2019). Making sense of making meat: Key moments in the first 20 years of tissue engineering muscle to make food. *Frontiers in Sustainable Food Systems.* doi:https://doi.org/10.3389/fsufs.2019.00045.

Strathern, M. (1992). *Reproducing the future: Anthropology, kinship and the new reproductive technologies*. Manchester, U.K.: Manchester University Press.

Sunder Rajan, K. (2006). *Biocapital. The constitution of postgenomic life*. Durham, NC.: Duke University Press.

Tai, S. (2020). Legalizing the meaning of meat. *Loyola University Chicago Law Journal*, *51*, https://ssrn.com/abstract=3456241. Accessed 8 July 2021.

Trubek, A. (2008). *The taste of place: A cultural journey Into terroir*. Berkeley & Los Angeles: University of California Press.

Trilling, L. (1972). *Sincerity and authenticity*. Cambridge: Cambridge University Press.

Trujillo, C. A., Gao, R., Negres, P. D., Gu, J., Buchanan, J. et al. (2019). Complex oscillatory waves emerging from cortical organoids model early human brain network development. *Cell Stem Cell, 25*, 558-569.

Umbach, M., & Humphrey, M. (2018). *Authenticity: The cultural history of a political concept*. London: Palgrave Macmillan.

Verbeke, W., Marcu, A., Rutsaert, P., Gaspar, R., Seibt, B., Fletcher, D., & Barnett, J. (2015). 'Would you eat cultured meat?': Consumers' reactions and attitude formation in Belgium, Portugal and the United Kingdom. *Meat Science, 102*, 49–58.

Vermeulen, N., Haddow, G., Seymour, T., Faulkner-Jones A., & Shu, W. (2017). 3D bioprint me: a socioethical view of bioprinting human organs and tissues. *Journal of Medical Ethics, 43*, 618-624.

Vives, J., & Batlle-Morera, L. (2020). The challenge of developing human 3D organoids into medicines. *Stem Cell Research & Therapy, 11*(1), 72. doi:https://doi.org/10.1186/s13287-020-1586-1.

Wahlberg, A., & Bauer, S. (2016). *Contested categories: life sciences in society*. New York: Routledge.

Waldby, C., & Mitchell, R. (2006). *Tissue economies: blood, organs and cell lines in late capitalism*. Durham, NC.: Duke University Press.

Webster, A. (2012). Bio-objects. In N. Vermeulen, S. Tamminen, & A. Webster, (Eds.) *Bio-objects: Life in the twenty-first Century* (pp. 1-12). Surrey, UK: Ashgate.

Weiler, N. (2020). Not 'brains in a dish': Cerebral organoids flunk comparison to developing nervous system. *University of California San Francisco News*. https://www.ucsf.edu/news/2020/01/416526/not-brains-dish-cerebral-organoids-flunk-comparison-developing-nervous-system Accessed 14 July 2021.

Weiss, B. (2016). *Real pigs: shifting values in the field of local pork*. Durham, NC.: Duke University Press.

West, H. (2016). Artisanal Foods and cultural economy: Perspectives on craft, heritage, authenticity and reconnection. In J. Klein & J. L. Watson (Eds.), *The Handbook of Food and Anthropology* (pp. 406-433). New York: Bloomsbury Publishing.

Yaffe-Bellany, D. (2020, 7 January). Impossible dumplings and beyond buns: Will China buy fake meat? *New York Times*, https://www.nytimes.com/2020/01/07/fake-pork-china. Accessed 7 January 2020.

CHAPTER 29

Technologies of Beauty: The Materiality, Ethics, and Normativity of Cosmetic Citizenship

Beauty

Alvaro Jarrín

The technologies that beautify the body are sometimes characterised as simply skin-deep, but beauty can engender very visceral feelings for those who pursue it. Calling plastic surgery and other cosmetic enhancement technologies superficial, and thus less worthy of scholarly analysis, misses the very consequential ways in which biopower shapes beautification practices. Our dismissal of beautification as shallow betrays a certain Euro-American bias, and deriding those who consume plastic surgery as 'addicts' results in the reinforcement of inequalities inherent in the practice (Pitts-Taylor 2007). In countries like Brazil, plastic surgery has a much higher status within both popular and medical culture, with plastic surgeons ranking amongst the most esteemed doctors in the country. Beautifying technologies are also imagined as having a more consequential impact in a person's life in locations where they are more widely accepted—people believe that cosmetic technologies could potentially provide upward mobility and its effects are even tied to notions of citizenship (Jarrín 2017; Liebelt 2019; Pussetti 2019). Consequently, people become willing to undergo more radical procedures or a higher number of consecutive surgeries as plastic surgery becomes normalised and frequently more affordable. Cosmetic technologies that require placing an implant within the body, and

A. Jarrín (✉)
College of the Holy Cross, Millville, MA, USA
e-mail: ajarrin@holycross.edu

569

M. H. Bruun et al. (eds.), *The Palgrave Handbook of the Anthropology of Technology*, https://doi.org/10.1007/978-981-16-7084-8_29

which can have potential long-term health impacts for a patient, cannot be said to be simply skin-deep or superficial medical procedures.

Technologies of beauty, therefore, enact particular social norms on the body and have significant material effects and ethical implications that anthropologists should not ignore. Although there is a long history of anthropological analysis of ritual markings on the body, such as tattoos, scarification, and other bodily aesthetic adornments, anthropology was somewhat late to the scholarly analysis of medical cosmetic technologies, particularly in comparison to the extensive literature commenting on these technologies within feminist theory and cultural studies. Ritualistic or artistic markings such as tattoos also require technological expertise, but they differ from medical technologies because they do not depend on a biopolitical regime, backed by medical authority, that describes certain bodies as deviant and others as normative (Foucault 1990). It is this impulse towards normalising bodies that underlies most cosmetic procedures and that, therefore, complicates their analysis, because it means we need to account for the intersection of technology with biopower and examine the moral underpinnings of these technologies. Anthropologists like Lesley Sharp and Elizabeth Roberts have demonstrated that even though scientific or medical actors usually disavow any moral judgement in their pursuit of truth, moral judgements about bodily worth, in fact, permeate their thinking and inform all their decisions (Roberts 2012; Sharp 2014). This is particularly true for cosmetic surgeons, who claim to be applying universal standards of beauty but are instead utilising their own moral judgements to determine what is beautiful and applying their own ethical standards to determine which cosmetic technologies are worth pursuing and which technologies need to be abandoned (Jarrín 2017). Technologies are never morally or ethically neutral.

Nonetheless, consumers who submit their bodies to plastic surgery and other cosmetic enhancements are not simply passive recipients of these moral and ethical norms, but subjects who bring their own moral norms into play and actively engage with the multiple meanings of beautification. Ethnographic approaches are particularly useful in this regard and have contributed important insights about what drives consumers of plastic surgery to adhere to the practice, demonstrating that local hierarchies of gender, race, and class strongly influence what is considered beautiful and what makes cosmetic enhancement meaningful. Few of these ethnographic studies, however, are based on fieldwork carried out among the health providers themselves or have analysed the medical discourses that legitimise aesthetic procedures. In my view, the anthropology of beauty must be reframed as an anthropological study of technology and technological expertise to account for the assemblage of actors that enact beauty on the body. A Latourian (1987) approach to plastic surgery, for example, helps anthropologists trace how some beautification procedures gain popularity and scientific backing over others, providing a more complex picture of how these technologies become blackboxed as medical facts, how they develop over time, or how they capture new markets. As new body parts, such as genital organs, become the object of beautification (Jones 2017), feminist critique also becomes more urgent and needs to ask harder questions about ethical limits we should place on this global industry.

Understanding beauty through a Science, Technology and Society (STS) lens also helps us redefine what technology is and what it does in the social realm. Cosmetic procedures render the body pliable in a way that reveals our posthuman, cyborg condition, whereby technologies are no longer separate from the human body but are rather central to its becoming (Jarrín and Pussetti 2021). Beautification technologies provide many insights into the embodied aspects of technology and the ways it is viscerally experienced by those submitting their bodies to cosmetic enhancements. Even a simple cosmetic product available over the counter, such as a lip gloss that uses hyaluronic acid to cause the lips to swell and gain volume, can have significant impacts on the subjectivation of consumers and can be tied to racial forms of exoticism depending on the cultural context. In Brazil, the surgical correction of the 'negroid nose' cannot be separated from long-standing biopolitical designs that sought to whiten the population and is propelled by ongoing forms of antiblackness that affectively devalue Afro-Brazilian features in popular culture (Jarrín 2017). Among African immigrants to Portugal, skin-lightening products are perceived as producing a more European body and allowing individuals to fashion themselves as global cosmopolitan consumers (Pussetti 2019). In all these examples, the biopolitical and the visceral are irrevocably intertwined, as consumers submit their bodies to race, class, and gender norms that are larger than themselves and yet are felt intimately, providing meaning to their experience of embodiment. Additionally, all these beauty practices imply certain risks to one's health that remain underexamined, as market priorities push those concerns aside. As anthropologists, we need to be attuned to those new forms of embodiment and risks and analyse how cosmetic technologies are shaping the world we live in.

This chapter proposes the concept of 'visceral biopolitics' to tackle the way in which larger sociopolitical forces become intimately embodied through cosmetic technologies. I define 'visceral biopolitics' as the imbrication of biopower with affective forms of embodiment within technologies of beauty. Visceral biopolitics addresses the ways beauty is felt in relation to aesthetic hierarchies that exist within a particular society, and which map onto long-standing gender, race, and class hierarchies. Biopolitics and viscerality cannot be examined separately, because the medical and biopolitical discourses that reassert local hierarchies of gender, race, and class—as beauty norms usually do—always intersect with the complex but visceral perceptions of beauty and ugliness circulating among patients, which sometimes comply with, but sometimes resist, those beauty norms. There are a multiplicity of systems of meaning competing, clashing, and collaborating in the coproduction of the body beautiful. When the biopolitical and the visceral are at the forefront of an STS approach, some key questions that emerge for the anthropological analysis of beauty include the following: (1) How is knowledge about beauty produced, and on whose bodies is that form of biopower developed? (2) What kind of claims about the racialised, classed, and gendered body are made by plastic surgeons and other health professionals, and how do they relate to local embodied inequalities? (3) How do consumers negotiate the medical discourses, the technological innovations and, more importantly, the risks that the beauty industry presents them? (4) How do affective forms of embodiment enable how and why consumers consent to these beauty practices?

In the first part of this chapter, I review some of the literature within beauty studies and analyse the unique contributions that anthropology has made to this growing field. I make the case that ethnographic approaches are particularly well positioned to add Foucauldian, affective, and STS forms of analysis to the study of technologies of beauty. In the second part of this chapter, I focus on a case study arising from my own research: facial lipectomy or buccal fat excision, which has become particularly popular in Brazil despite the high risks associated with these procedures. I argue that the technological promise of radically transforming the body pushes health professionals to ignore the risks of these technologies, which are externalised onto patients. The profit-driven effort to market technologies of beauty encourages health providers to wash their hands of ethical concerns, given how easy it is to blame consumers for taking those risks within a neoliberal context: consumers within neoliberalism are thought of as rational individuals who are free to make choices, and not as subjects who are rendered vulnerable by larger power structures. Anthropologists should reject that neoliberal logic and explore the structural inequalities that complicate consent and hide the true risks of cosmetic procedures. The ethical concerns that arise from the expansion of beautification technologies across the world and across the geographies of our bodies demand an activist, feminist anthropology that insists upon accountability from the cosmetics companies and health professionals that drive the beauty industry.

A Short Overview of the Scholarship on Beauty

Technologies of Gender

The field of beauty studies has been shaped by an important early debate between Susan Bordo and Kathy Davis. Bordo (1993) understood beauty norms and the postmodern obsession with surface and appearance as a crucial new form of gender oppression and took issue with the more sympathetic view espoused by Davis. As a sociologist, Davis (1995) found that women who embraced plastic surgery experienced it as a form of agency and a way to take control of their own lives. In response to Bordo's critique, Davis (2003) made the point that feminists who portray plastic surgery patients as dupes are implying their own moral superiority, without accounting for that which makes plastic surgery desirable or pleasurable. This debate, in many ways, demonstrated how different methodological approaches affect how we understand beauty, since Bordo favoured a cultural studies critique that focused on social structure, and Davis preferred the intimacy of ethnographic research that let her pay more attention to individual agency. Many feminist scholars since then have negotiated this difficult balancing act between agency and structure when writing about beauty.

Cosmetic enhancement, nonetheless, began to be understood as another 'technology of gender' (De Lauretis 1987) that shapes and disciplines feminine subjectivities in particular ways. Focusing on the medical discourses of cosmetic surgeons, Anne Balsamo (1992) pointed out that this medical discipline was deeply invested in the gender binary and described it as the 'biotechnological reproduction of gender'. Other authors, on the other hand, began to explore how plastic surgery is portrayed in our wider culture. Virginia Blum (2003) examined how popular culture shapes our perceptions of plastic surgery as a way to achieve gendered beauty and made the case that celebrity culture was central to the American desire for beautification. Victoria Pitts-Taylor (2007), in turn, critiqued the ways in which we pathologise consumers of plastic surgery when we describe them as 'surgery junkies', which displaces ethical concerns away from the beauty industry and onto the subjectivity of patients. Interestingly, both Blum (2003) and Pitts-Taylor (2007) included autoethnographic details in their books, describing their own ambivalent experiences while undergoing rhinoplasties and providing unique insights into what makes plastic surgery desirable, but also detailing the painful recovery it entails. The main limits of this early feminist work was that it was very focused on Euro-American experiences with plastic surgery, and did not fully address how race intersects with cosmetic enhancement (Crenshaw 1990) or how it was experienced elsewhere. It was also work that solely focused on cisgender women, and only more recent scholarship has begun to tackle how transgender women experience gender norms through medical procedures such as facial feminisation surgery (Plemons 2017).

Race, Eugenics, and Biopolitics

Two cultural histories of cosmetic surgery, by Elizabeth Haiken and Sander Gilman, uncovered how central race had been to the rise of this medical discipline. Haiken (1997) argued that a certain appearance came to be associated with upward mobility in the United States, and this led immigrants and people of Jewish descent to embrace plastic surgery, particularly rhinoplasty, as a way to assimilate into mainstream society. Gilman (1999) added the insight that medical discourse in the early twentieth century exhibited a clear Neo-Lamarckian understanding of race, whereby it was assumed that acquired characteristics were inheritable and that racially improving an individual through surgery would benefit future generations as well. Thus, although cosmetic surgery is a highly gendered practice, it is also traversed by class and race inequalities, and it has always engaged in raciological thought. Virginia Kaw (1993) added one of the first anthropological interventions into the literature, by examining how Asian-American women embraced plastic surgery in order to avoid the racial stereotypes of dullness and passivity associated with their eyes, which particularly affected them in the job market. It would take another decade, however, for anthropology to really examine beautification as a technology of racialisation.

Marcia Ochoa's excellent ethnography on Venezuelan beauty pageants described how 'somatechnics' like plastic surgery and hormones were among the tools used by both cisgender women and *transformistas* to produce modern femininities. Ochoa (2014) argued that the racialised femininities associated with Venezuelan citizenship, which led to beauty pageant victories, were those that, at most, claimed a slight racial mixture within an otherwise white national norm. Alexander Edmonds (2010) similarly focused on how plastic surgery was associated with a modern and sexualised Brazilian femininity and argued that this effort to modernise is why the country offers plastic surgery to the poor. Edmonds noticed there was a tension between the claims made by plastic surgeons that their medical discipline celebrates racial miscegenation, and their efforts to medicalise and correct the 'negroid nose', but he rejected a Foucauldian analysis of the practice. This claim has been challenged by more recent work on plastic surgery in Latin America. Lauren Gulbas (2013) argued that plastic surgery works as a 'technology of whiteness' in Venezuela, reaffirming the stigma associated with black features. Elsa Muñiz (2013) claimed that ethnic plastic surgeries in Mexico resurrect eugenics for the multicultural era. Finally, in my own work (Jarrín 2017), I described the eugenic origins of the Brazilian medical discourses that portray plastic surgery as a form of racial uplift. I argued that the expansion of plastic surgery within the public health system was a sign of long-standing biopolitical and raciological aims to craft a more normative population and engage in practices of whitening through surgery.

Transnational Beauty and Its Effects/Affects

Recent literature has focused on beautification and the beauty industry as transnational practices, generating significant debate on the topic. Beauty pageants have long served as national and transnational stages where women perform the ideal embodiment of nationhood, beauty, and race (Banet-Weiser 1999; King-O'Riain 2006; Ochoa 2014). Nowadays, neoliberal forms of 'postfeminism'[1] that encourage personal empowerment through consumption and beautification are becoming globalised through forms of mass media like reality television (Banet-Weiser and Portwood-Stacer 2006) and through the digital surveillance enabled by social media (Elias and Gill 2018). In the worldview encouraged by 'postfeminism', women in the Global South are imagined as empowered only insofar as they are able to consume beauty and fashion (Dosekun 2015). Additionally, beauty can also intersect with biopower and empire-building when beauty schools in Afghanistan are thought of as part of the 'civilising process' taking place after the American invasion of that nation (Nguyen 2011).

Notions about beauty travel so easily from one context to the next, in my view, because global affective structures have inexorably tied beauty to hope and optimism, transforming it into a form of cultural capital that transcends the nation (Jarrín 2017). As Coleman and Moreno Figueroa (2010) have argued, there are very similar elements in how British and Mexican women experience both the temporality and the affective attachments associated with beauty. Nonetheless, we should remain sceptical of claims that global beauty ideals can be reduced to Western imperialism or global homogenisation (Jha 2015). For example, although skin lighteners are consumed around the world they are experienced very differently depending on the context: skin lighteners were tied to the racism of apartheid in South Africa (Thomas 2020); they allowed the Jamaican diaspora to pursue forms of 'browning' that can destabilise both black and white beauty standards (Tate 2012); and they are used by African immigrants in Portugal to Europeanise their features and stake an aesthetic claim to European citizenship (Pussetti 2019). Similarly, recent scholarship questions the idea that the desire for double-eyelid surgery in South Korea or in China is simply about Westernising one's appearance and demonstrates that there are much more complex negotiations between global and national beauty standards driving the high rates of that surgery among both men and women (Holliday and Elfving-Hwang 2012; Hua 2013).

Everywhere that anthropology turns its eye, it finds that local histories, mobility, and transnational inequalities shape how race, class, and gender become intertwined with beauty. Plastic surgery is seen as engendering mobility, for example, in the case of Colombian and Mexican women who get cosmetic surgery in the hope it will give them the bodily capital to marry American men they meet online (Schaeffer-Grabiel 2006). Travestis (transgender sex workers) from Argentina and Brazil understand plastic surgery as central not only to their embodied subjectivity, but also to their ability to migrate to Europe (Alvarez 2017; Vartabedian 2018). American and European tourists, on the other hand, use their mobility and relative wealth to acquire cosmetic surgery in Latin America (Ackerman 2010; Casanova and Sutton 2013) and gender reassignment surgery in Thailand (Aizura 2018), reasserting older racial and national imaginaries of these nations in the process. Ultimately, however, cosmetic surgery patients are portrayed as solely responsible for any risks that they take, absolving the beauty industry from answerability for making the practice possible in the first place (Casanova and Sutton 2013). In the following section, I examine more closely how the availability of experimental subjects is central to the development and sale of new aesthetic procedures that then become very profitable for the beauty industry.

The Vulnerability of Skin and Buccal Fat Excision in Brazil: A Case Study

Bichectomia, known in English as facial lipectomy or as buccal fat excision, is a relatively new surgery that has taken Brazil by storm. Plastic surgeons and dental surgeons who specialise in this procedure claim that by reducing the volume of one's cheeks, the surgery provides 'finer and more delicate facial features', heightening one's cheekbones and jawline.[2] They claim that famous celebrities, like Kim Kardashian, Madonna, and Angelina Jolie, have probably undergone this procedure, reversing the effects of ageing, and they also advertise the procedure as relatively uncomplicated, quick, and affordable. What is interesting about *bichectomia* is the speed with which it became adopted as a surgical technique in Brazil, and the underlying reasons it became so popular. Although buccal fat excision was first described in a medical article by an American plastic surgeon in 1991 (Matarasso 1991), it is not very popular in the United States, where plastic surgeons are very careful about permanent bodily alterations that are irreversible or risky and could lead to lawsuits. The fatty tissue of the cheeks, one American surgeon explained in a website called Healthline, is something that one loses naturally with age, thus removing one's buccal fat pads prematurely can actually lead to a very gaunt look, rather than an attractive one.[3] A peer-reviewed journal article by two American plastic surgeons similarly warned about the lack of studies on the long-term effects of this surgery and cautioned surgeons against it (Benjamin and Reish 2018).

In comparison, the medical literature on *bichectomia* in Brazil is incredibly optimistic about the procedure. One article describes it as 'safe' and as providing 'facial harmony' to patients (Faria et al. 2018), and another says it is relatively 'simple and fast' compared to other surgeries (Júnior et al. 2018). This enthusiastic embrace by medical professionals led to the growth of this surgery in Brazil, from 120 facial lipectomy procedures in 2014, to 500 procedures in 2015,[4] then to more than 7000 procedures in 2016.[5] The exponential growth became a self-fulfilling prophecy, since surgeons were able to market the procedure as fashionable and groundbreaking—one journalist described the growing desire for this new procedure as a 'fever' that confirmed Brazil's penchant for plastic surgery.[6] Another selling point of the surgery is that it can be carried out not only by plastic surgeons, but also by qualified dental surgeons (Almeida and Alvary 2018). My original fieldwork on plastic surgery in Brazil described how different medical disciplines negotiate the right to enact aesthetic procedures on the body—plastic surgeons sometimes collaborate and sometimes compete with dermatologists, obstetricians, and endocrinologists in efforts to develop new beautification techniques (Jarrín 2017). Although dental surgeons have long been invested in beautification through dental implants and craniofacial surgeries, their entrance into experimental facial procedures is relatively new and is driven by the huge profits of the beauty industry. Medical schools like the Velasco Institute, in São Paulo, teach dental surgeons how to carry out not only *bichectomias* but also collagen injections, botox injections, dermal fillers, and facelifts that use 'thread' implants to stretch the skin.[7] The Velasco Institute boasts that they teach these medical procedures to dental surgeons not only from Brazil but also from all over Latin America and Europe.[8]

Brazil became a global centre for knowledge production within disciplines like plastic surgery, dermatology, and dental surgery because it has the human capital and the deregulation necessary to develop those techniques. An American plastic surgeon once told me, 'Brazilian surgeons are pioneers. ... You know why? Because here they don't have the institutional and legal barriers to generate these new techniques. In the U.S. that is not the case: you always have the regulations, the FDA, on your back.' I highlight this comment not to portray the United States as better regulated or more advanced, but because the American surgeon was complaining about FDA regulations. I find this comment revealing because it demonstrates that Brazil is considered an ideal experimental setting, where surgical creativity is not stifled or curtailed, allowing the 'offshoring' of experimental procedures, in a similar way to how clinical trials are also offshored (Petryna 2009). For every medical school opened in Brazil, there are few rules on what is possible or ethical, and there are hundreds of patients willing to undergo these experimental procedures because they are offered at low cost or for free. In a video for the Velasco Institute, one of the chief dental surgeons claimed that nearly 2000 patients signed up for the chance to get a free *bichectomia* in exchange for becoming a 'model' within their teaching modules.[9]

Although I have not carried out interviews at the Velasco Institute, the working-class patients I interviewed at similar medical schools called themselves *cobaias*, or guinea pigs, and knew perfectly well they were running risks by opting for these experimental treatments. They always compare these risks, however, with their daily precarious situations, like living in dangerous neighbourhoods or being unable to trust the government. Patients measure medical risk, in other words, in relation to larger structural issues that render their bodies and choices vulnerable, and they frequently complain about how underfunded or understaffed the public health care system in Brazil is, despite health being considered a basic health right. In this context, plastic surgeons or other medical providers that offer beauty seem like a benevolent force that provides a form of bodily capital otherwise denied to them. The patients' ability to consent to these surgeries is complicated by the structural inequalities they experience every day and by the portrayal of plastic surgery as a miraculous equaliser, providing the promise of upward mobility and self-improvement. In that race to craft new bodily topographies as perfectible, however, these patients end up shouldering all the risks of these surgeries. In the neoliberal context, it is fairly easy for doctors to claim that patients are rational consumers who knew the risks involved when they signed the consent forms, and thus avoid any repercussions. Medical and legal responsibility in Brazil can be described as an assemblage that continuously externalises risks onto the bodies of patients, blaming them for making the wrong choice whenever a procedure goes awry, rather than pinning the blame on the medical professions that offer these surgeries in the first place (Jarrín 2017).

When a *bichectomia* goes awry, it is because the human skin resists these attempts at excision and transformation—it remains vulnerable and/or intractable, despite the surgical desire to make it pliable. Even the optimistic portrayals of *bichectomia* in Brazil admit that there are possible complications a knowledgeable surgeon must be aware of, including severe oedemas, tissue necrosis, and even the severing of important facial nerves, leading to different forms of facial paralysis (Klüppel et al. 2018). The skin, muscles, nerves, and fatty tissue of our face are interconnected forms of flesh and are dependent on each other for smooth operation, representing a complex anatomical structure that developed over millions of years of evolutionary adaptation. The buccal fat pads, more specifically, are a specialised form of fatty tissue that serve clear mechanical functions, including acting as gliding pads during mastication and cushioning important facial structures from any impact (Zhang et al. 2002). Nonetheless, the Brazilian medical literature on buccal fat pads portrays these parts of the human anatomy as superfluous and, indeed, as pathological—they are described in one article as fat deposits that do not respond to exercise and weight loss, and which, therefore, 'can give the face a rounded appearance, thereby creating a disharmonic facial contour' (Faria et al. 2018). There is a racialised tone to these pathologising statements, because in Brazil the very description of a 'round face' always reminds people of racial stereotypes imputed to poor north-eastern migrants, thought of as uglier and less cultured than their wealthier south-eastern counterparts. Another scholarly article openly describes buccal fat pads as more prominent among 'the obese, mestizos and orientals', while their removal can produce slender and younger faces (Olivares and Torres 2018). This medical discourse is clearly about reproducing a Eurocentric ideal, but such racial preferences are rarely expressed so openly.

The anthropologist Robin Sheriff (2001) has described the taboo that surrounds discussing race or racism in Brazil, because it seems un-Brazilian to bring up discrimination or racial hatred in a country that is still considered by many to be a racial democracy. Nonetheless, she also portrays the ways in which whiteness becomes a form of bodily capital that is subtly but constantly reinforced as more beautiful and desirable than non-whiteness. Elizabeth Hordge-Freeman (2015) demonstrates that beauty is one of the central ways by which racial hierarchies become reinforced in Brazil, creating 'aesthetic hierarchies' that affectively value or devalue body parts. I push this argument further by arguing that these aesthetic hierarchies become reified by medical discourses that naturalise the biopolitical desires to craft a more homogenous population through beauty. Most of the references to *bichectomia* describe it simply as a surgery that can produce 'finer features' or 'harmonise' the face, but these descriptions are haunted by very old racial typologies that equate finer features or harmonious shapes with whiteness. Beauty became associated with racial improvement as early as the 1920s, when Brazilian eugenicists pushed for the whitening of the nation through mass European immigration based on the idea that this would also beautify and perfect the nation as a whole (Jarrín 2017). A hundred years later, these eugenic desires resurface through aesthetic surgeries like *bichectomia*, based on deeply held, visceral assumptions that 'finer features' are more desirable than 'round faces' or 'wide noses'. Most of the surgeons I interviewed claimed that beauty could be objectively measured and was simply more abundant in the parts of the nation that had received a larger proportion of European immigrants. They portrayed blackness, on the other hand, as excessive and only desirable insofar as it provided Brazilian women with their sensual curves. Too much blackness or too much racial mixing needed to be tempered through surgery, particularly when it came to a patient's face.

The interpretations of what is beautiful in Brazil, therefore, are permeated by affective evaluations that are experienced as so visceral that they seem completely natural, despite being shaped by long bodily histories and persistent racial ideologies. What I call 'visceral biopolitics' attempts to explain the ways that biopower and affect intersect to create systems of meaning that shape both medical discourses regarding ideal bodies and engender the real desires of patients to transform their bodily or facial features. Viscerality, as Holland et al. (2014) argue, 'registers those systems of meaning that have lodged in the gut, signifying the incursions of violent intentionality into the rhythms of everyday life' (p. 395). The violence of the everyday is what patients need to navigate as they ponder whether an aesthetic procedure is worth the risk. In most cases, beauty is simply too imbricated with gendered forms of citizenship and hopes for upward mobility for working-class patients to deny themselves the opportunity of a free or low-cost surgery when it becomes available. Their ability to consent to these surgeries is complicated by structural inequalities that shape how beauty *feels* and the promises it holds. Similarly, the enthusiastic embrace that doctors give to aesthetic procedures like *bichectomia*, and its exponential growth after being marketed as an innovative and quick way to create thinner faces, demonstrates that doctors themselves are also swayed by their own promises. Buccal fat removal is in actuality not a very impressive surgery, the results are almost imperceptible in many cases and do not seem to justify the risks that patients are asked to undertake. Nonetheless, the medical discourse surrounding 'finer features' is so powerful because it has a visceral, affective tie to racial hierarchies that surgeons consciously or unconsciously seek to reaffirm. In that context, surgeons are also unwilling to deny themselves the opportunity to use a new technique that holds the biopolitical promise of transforming and uplifting the Brazilian population towards whiteness.

The concept of visceral biopolitics, however, allows me to focus on the materiality of the skin as well, and the ways in which it refuses to become a docile landscape of surgical intervention. The skin's vulnerability in relation to the scalpel—the ways it undergoes trauma, becomes scarred, becomes infected, and becomes severed from nerves and muscles as surgeons attempt to remove buccal fat from the tissue that surrounds it—demonstrates its visceral intractability no matter what power surgeons think they hold. As Tim Ingold (2011) argues, 'the skin is not an impermeable boundary but a permeable zone of intermingling and admixture' (p. 87), and we need to consider the ways the skin becomes an actant in its own right, interacting with the world in ways that cannot be always controlled and shaped by human desires. A person's skin has its own history and its own entanglement to the other tissues that surround it, refusing the simplicity of medical discourses that mark it as old, as superfluous, or as pathological. As the largest organ on the body, the skin matters, and it does not respond in passive ways to the surgical cuts to which our contemporary world subjects it. The skin is in many ways a testament to the violence of the scalpel and an indelible marker of our complicated social and racial history.

CONCLUSION

This chapter has argued that technologies of beauty are multi-layered social phenomena that require multiple theoretical approaches to capture their complexity. First, a feminist analysis is necessary, because cosmetic enhancement is very often deeply invested in the gender binary, even when it involves trans-identified bodies. Second, a critical race analysis reveals the ways in which technologies of beauty reassert racial ideologies and become imbricated within larger biopolitical projects. Third, a transnational analysis reveals how notions about beauty travel across the world, impelled by the beauty economy, by empire, by migration, and by tourism, blurring national boundaries but always operating in ways more complex than simple homogenisation. Finally, anthropological and STS approaches provide insight into how knowledge about beautification is produced, using certain bodies as experimental subjects and externalising medical risks onto these vulnerable bodies. Patients are frequently driven by strong affective attachments to beauty that complicate their ability to consent to these risks. Concepts such as 'visceral biopolitics' help to move us beyond the early structure/agency debates surrounding plastic surgery, to consider how cosmetic enhancement can be simultaneously empowering and disempowering. Anthropological approaches to technologies of beauty need to be methodologically innovative and theoretically expansive in order to account for the reasons why beauty remains such a powerful force in the world, and why people are willing to go to such lengths to beautify their bodies in different contexts.

NOTES

1. I do not believe we live in a postfeminist world (feminism is incredibly useful and urgent as an analytic), but the literature that analyses postfeminism uses the term to indicate neoliberal and individualistic approaches to women's rights that undo many feminist victories.
2. Website for Dr Leandro Camargo, 'one of those responsible for the dissemination and popularization of *bichectomia* in Brazil'. https://www.drleandrocamargo.com.br/. Accessed 23 April 2021.

3. '13 Beauty Procedures This Plastic Surgeon Says "No" To.' *Healthline*. https://www.healthline.com/health/beauty-skin-care/dangerous-plastic-surgery-procedures#cheek-fat-removal. Accessed 23 April 2021.
4. Section on *Bichectomia* in the website for the dental clinic Iarossi, located in Guarulhos, São Paulo, Brazil. https://www.iarossi.com.br/bichectomia/. Accessed 23 April 2021.
5. 'Know everything about bichectomy: from the objectives to the recovery.' Website for Orofacial Clinic TwoFace, located in Goiânia, Brazil. https://two-face.com.br/blog/saiba-tudo-sobre-bichectomia-dos-objetivos-a-recuperacao. Accessed 23 April 2021.
6. 'Cheek reduction becomes a fever in Brazil and reinforces the country's title as the one with most plastic surgeries in the world.' *R7*. https://meuestilo.r7.com/diminuicao-da-bochecha-vira-febre-no-brasil-e-reforca-o-titulo-de-pais-que-mais-faz-cirurgias-plasticas-no-mundo-24082019. Accessed 23 April 2021.
7. 'Practical Courses on Orofacial Harmonization.' Website for the Velasco Institute. https://www.institutovelasco.com.br/cursos-2/. Accessed 23 April 2021.
8. 'Who We Are.' Website for the Velasco Instituto. https://www.institutovelasco.com.br/quem-somos/. Accessed 23 April 2021.
9. 'I liked orofacial harmonization, where do I start?' Video on the official YouTube channel for the Velasco Institute. https://www.youtube.com/watch?v=biMFqfnAw5A. Accessed 23 April 2021.

REFERENCES

Ackerman, S. L. (2010). Plastic Paradise: Transforming Bodies and Selves in Costa Rica's Cosmetic Surgery Tourism Industry. *Medical Anthropology, 29*(4), 403–423. https://doi.org/10.1080/01459740.2010.501316.

Aizura, A. Z. (2018). *Mobile Subjects: Transnational Imaginaries of Gender Reassignment*. Durham: Duke University Press.

Almeida, A. V., & Alvary, P. H. G. (2018). A bichectomia como procedimento cirúrgico estético funcional. *Facit Business and Technology Journal, 1*(7), 3–14.

Alvarez, A. G. (2017). Cuerpos Transitantes: Para uma historia de las identidades travesti-trans em la Argentina. *Avá, 31*, 45–71.

Balsamo, A. (1992). On the Cutting Edge: Cosmetic Surgery and the Technological Production of the Gendered Body. *Camera Obscura, 10*(1), 206–237.

Banet-Weiser, S. (1999). *The most beautiful girl in the world: Beauty pageants and national identity*. Berkeley: University of California Press.

Banet-Weiser, S., & Portwood-Stacer, L. (2006). 'I just want to be me again!': Beauty pageants, reality television and post-feminism. *Feminist Theory, 7*(2), 255–272. https://doi.org/10.1177/1464700106064423.

Benjamin, M., & Reish, R. G. (2018). Buccal Fat Excision: Proceed With Caution. *Plastic and Reconstructive Surgery Global Open, 6*(10), e1970. https://doi.org/10.1097/gox.0000000000001970.

Bordo, S. (1993). *Unbearable Weight: Feminism, Western Culture and the Body*. Berkeley: University of California Press.

Blum, V. (2003). *Flesh Wounds: The Culture of Cosmetic Surgery*. Berkeley: University of California Press.

Casanova, E. M., & Sutton, B. (2013). Transnational Body Projects: Media Representations of Cosmetic Surgery Tourism in Argentina and the United States. *Journal of World-Systems Research, 19*(1), 57–81. https://doi.org/10.5195/jwsr.2013.509.

Coleman, R., & Moreno Figueroa, M. (2010). Past and Future Perfect? Beauty, Affect and Hope. *Journal for Cultural Research, 14*(4), 357–373. https://doi.org/10.1080/14797581003765317.

Crenshaw, K. (1990). Mapping the margins: Intersectionality, identity politics, and violence against women of color. *Stanford Law Review, 43*, 1241–1300. https://doi.org/10.2307/1229039.

Davis, K. (1995). *Reshaping the Female Body: The Dilemma of Cosmetic Surgery.* New York: Routledge.

Davis, K. (2003). *Dubious Equalities and Embodied Differences: Cultural Studies on Cosmetic Surgery.* Lanham, MD.: Rowman & Littlefield Publishers.

De Lauretis, T. (1987). *Technologies of Gender: Essays on Theory, Film and Fiction.* Bloomington: Indiana University Press.

Dosekun, S. (2015). For western girls only? Post-feminism as transnational culture. *Feminist Media Studies, 15*(6), 960–975. https://doi.org/10.1080/14680777.2015.1062991.

Edmonds, A. (2010). *Pretty Modern: Beauty, Sex, and Plastic Surgery in Brazil.* Durham: Duke University Press.

Elias, A. S., & Gill, R. (2018). Beauty surveillance: The digital self-monitoring cultures of neoliberalism. *European Journal of Cultural Studies, 21*(1), 59–77. https://doi.org/10.1177/1367549417705604.

Faria, C., Dias, R., Campos, A., Daher, J., Costa, R., & Barcelos, L. (2018). Bichectomy and its contribution to facial harmony. *Revista Brasileira de Cirurgia Plástica, 33*(4), 446–452. https://doi.org/10.5935/2177-1235.2018rbcp0164.

Foucault, M. (1990). *The History of Sexuality: An Introduction, Vol. 1.* (trans. Hurley, R.). New York: Vintage.

Gilman, S. (1999). *Making the Body Beautiful: A Cultural History of Aesthetic Surgery.* Princeton: Princeton University Press.

Gulbas, L. E. (2013). Embodying Racism: Race, Rhinoplasty and Self-Esteem in Venezuela. *Qualitative Health Research, 23*(3), 326–335. https://doi.org/10.1177/1049732312468335.

Haiken, E. (1997). *Venus Envy: A History of Cosmetic Surgery.* Baltimore: Johns Hopkins University Press.

Holland, S.P., Ochoa, M., & Tompkins, K.W. (2014). On the visceral. *GLQ: A Journal of Lesbian and Gay Studies, 20*(4), 391–406.

Holliday, R., & Elfving-Hwang, J. (2012). Gender, Globalization and Aesthetic Surgery in South Korea. *Body & Society, 18*(2), 58–81. https://doi.org/10.1177/1357034x12440828.

Hordge-Freeman, E. (2015). *The Color of Love: Racialization, Stigma, and Socialization in Black Brazilian Families.* Austin: University of Texas Press.

Hua, W. (2013). *Buying Beauty: Cosmetic Surgery in China.* Hong Kong: Hong Kong University Press.

Ingold, T. (2011). *Being Alive: Essays on Movement, Knowledge and Description.* London: Routledge.

Jarrín, A. (2017). *The Biopolitics of Beauty: Cosmetic Citizenship and Affective Capital in Brazil.* Berkeley: University of California Press.

Jarrín, A., & Pussetti, C. (2021). The Uncanny Aesthetics of Repairing, Reshaping and Replacing Human Bodies. In A. Jarrín & C. Pussetti (Eds.), *Remaking the Human: Cosmetic Technologies of Body Repair, Reshaping and Replacement*. London: Berghahn Books.

Jha, M. (2015). *The Global Beauty Industry: Colorism, Racism, and the National Body*. London: Routledge.

Jones, M. (2017). Expressive Surfaces: The Case of the Designer Vagina. *Theory, Culture & Society, 34*(7–8), 29–50. https://doi.org/10.1177/0263276417736592.

Júnior, R. M., Gontijo, G., Guerreiro, T. C., de Souza, N. L., & Moreira, R. (2018). Bichectomia, a simple and fast surgery: case report. *Revista Odontológica do Brasil Central, 27*(81), 98–100.

Kaw, E. (1993). Medicalization of Racial Features: Asian American Women and Cosmetic Surgery. *Medical Anthropology Quarterly, 7*(1), 74–89. https://doi.org/10.1525/maq.1993.7.1.02a00050.

King-O'Riain, R. C. (2006). *Pure Beauty: Judging Race in Japanese American Beauty Pageants*. Minneapolis: University of Minnesota Press.

Klüppel, L., Marcos, R. B., Shimizu, I. A., Silva, M. A. D. D., & Silva, R. D. D. (2018). Complications Associated with the Bichectomy Surgery. *RGO—Revista Gaúcha de Odontologia, 66*(3), 278–264. https://doi.org/10.1590/1981-863720180003000143488.

Latour, B. (1987). *Science in action: How to follow scientists and engineers through society*. Boston: Harvard University Press.

Liebelt, C. (2019). Aesthetic citizenship in Istanbul: on manufacturing beauty and negotiating belonging through the body in urban Turkey. *Citizenship Studies, 23*(7), 686–702. https://doi.org/10.1080/13621025.2019.1651088.

Matarasso, A. (1991). Buccal fat excision: aesthetic improvement of the midface. *Annals of Plastic Surgery, 26*(5), 413–418. https://doi.org/10.1097/00000637-199105000-00001.

Muñiz, E. (2013). Del mestizaje a la hibridación corporal: la etnocirugía como forma de racismo. *Nómadas, 38*, 81–97.

Nguyen, M. T. (2011). The Biopower of Beauty: Humanitarian Imperialisms and Global Feminisms in an Age of Terror. *Signs, 36*(2), 359–383. https://doi.org/10.1086/655914.

Ochoa, M. (2014). *Queen for a Day: Transformistas, Beauty Queens and the Performance of Femininity in Venezuela*. Durham: Duke University Press.

Olivares, J., & Torres, E. (2018). The Buccal Fat Pads (Preliminary Report). *Cosmetology and Oro Facial Surgery, 4*(1), 128.

Petryna, A. (2009). *When Experiments Travel: Clinical Trials and the Global Search for Human Subjects*. Princeton: Princeton University Press.

Pitts-Taylor, V. (2007). *Surgery Junkies: Wellness and Pathology in Cosmetic Culture*. New Brunswick: Rutgers University Press.

Plemons, E. (2017). *The Look of a Woman: Facial Feminization Surgery and the Aims of Trans-Surgery*. Durham: Duke University Press.

Pussetti, C. (2019). From Ebony to Ivory: 'Cosmetic' Investments in the Body. *Anthropological Journal of European Cultures, 28*(1), 64–72. https://doi.org/10.3167/ajec.2019.280107.

Roberts, E. (2012). *God's Laboratory: Assisted Reproduction in the Andes*. Berkeley: University of California Press.

Schaeffer-Grabiel, F. (2006). Flexible Technologies of Subjectivity and Mobility across the Americas. *American Quarterly, 58*(3), 897–914. https://doi.org/10.1353/aq.2006.0068.

Sharp, L. (2014). *The Transplant Imaginary: Mechanical Hearts, Animal Parts and Moral Thinking in Highly Experimental Science.* Berkeley: University of California Press.

Sheriff, R. (2001). *Dreaming Equality: Color, Race, and Racism in Urban Brazil.* New Brunswick: Rutgers University Press.

Tate, S. A. (2012). *Black beauty: aesthetics, stylization, politics.* London: Ashgate Publishing, Ltd.

Thomas, L. M. (2020). *Beneath the Surface: A Transnational History of Skin Lighteners.* Durham: Duke University Press.

Vartabedian, J. (2018). *Brazilian 'Travesti' Migrations: Gender, Sexualities and Embodiment Experiences.* New York: Palgrave Macmillan.

Zhang, H.M., Yan, Y.P., Qi, K.M., Wang, J.Q., & Liu, Z.F. (2002). Anatomical structure of the buccal fat pad and its clinical adaptations. *Plastic and Reconstructive Surgery, 109*(7), 2509–2518.

CHAPTER 30

The Optimised and Enhanced Self: Experiences of the Self and the Making of Societal Values

Enhancement

Dorthe Brogård Kristensen

> *'To choose to be better is to be human.'*
> —Savulescu et al. (2004, p. 670)

The desire to become better is at the heart of human existence. This is a claim that has been advocated, criticised, contested, and explored philosophically and empirically in studies of 'enhancement' and 'optimisation'—terms that refer to practices oriented towards the betterment of the self and interventions in the present to create a better future (Elliott 2003, 2011). Today they are not only associated with specialised disciplines but also with everyday practices where they reflect a moral imperative for the human being to strive continuously to become a better version of themselves (Rose 2007; Elliott 2003, 2011). Examples of technologies for bodily enhancement include plastic surgery, neural implants to alter memory or behaviour, psychopharmaceuticals used to modify emotions and cognition, and some genetic interventions. Assisted reproduction and embryo selection might also be seen as enhancing, by virtue of their ability to select for certain traits. Other technologies (tracking devices, apps, wearables) and practices (mindfulness, meditation, or psychedelic drugs)

D. B. Kristensen (✉)
Department of Business and Management, University of Southern Denmark, Odense, Denmark
e-mail: dbk@sam.sdu.dk

© The Author(s), under exclusive license to Springer Nature Singapore Pte Ltd. 2022
M. H. Bruun et al. (eds.), *The Palgrave Handbook of the Anthropology of Technology*, https://doi.org/10.1007/978-981-16-7084-8_30

that aim to alter wellbeing, moods, and general quality of life are arguably less about bodily enhancement than performance optimisation.

The purpose of this chapter is twofold: firstly, to present the two terms and map the different positions in the discussion, mainly based on the work of scholars within bioethics; secondly, drawing from a larger anthropological project on optimisation that included Margit Anne Petersen's study on pharmaceutical enhancement (Petersen et al. 2015a, 2015b; Petersen et al. 2019), and my own work on self-tracking (Kristensen and Ruckenstein 2018; Bode and Kristensen 2016), the chapter will show how anthropological and qualitative studies have nuanced the bioethical debate as well as given rise to new sets of questions. The concepts of enhancement and optimisation have overlapping use, but originate in two different but parallel streams of literature seemingly differentiated by the dichotomy of chemical versus mechanical and digital technologies. Described by one scholar as 'a process by which a given aim can be achieved to a maximum extent', optimisation—developed in disciplines such as mathematics, computer science, and physics—is often used in relation to the study of mechanical and organisational improvement as well as self-tracking technologies (Meißner 2016, p. 238). The concept has moved from the study of systems in physics and computers to the study of practices that facilitate improvement in human life. While the term optimisation has not been subject to the kind of debate enhancement has faced in the bioethical context, the use of the term in qualitative studies has given rise to discussions of bodily experiences and control.

Enhancement, on the other hand, has been intensely debated and defined as the 'use and regulation of substances and artifacts understood by some to improve the functioning of human bodies beyond that are associated with "normal" function' (Pickersgill and Hogle 2015, pp. 1–7). The enhancement literature mainly focuses on interventions that instigate biological and biochemical changes in human bodies and brains using pharmaceutical, surgical, or genetic techniques (Clarke et al. 2016; Juengst and Moseley 2016). Yet, if enhancement is about improving ourselves beyond what is considered normal, who decides what 'normal' is? If we can modify, transform, and improve the self, what, then, is the 'authentic' self? And do we even have the right to enhance ourselves as we wish via technology (Sharon 2013)? These questions have given rise to a range of dilemmas and intense ethical debates among bioethicists, medical humanities scholars, philosophers, and social scientists which are based on notions and concepts of authenticity, alienation, and human nature.

A crucial point for bioethicists has been the distinction between restorative therapies as treatments and interventions as improvements to the body and its functions (Juengst and Moseley 2016). Besides helping to determine what is morally permissible, there are pragmatic policy concerns about how to proceed in medical practice. Others, however, find that the distinction between therapy and enhancement is 'at best blurred and at worst non-existent' (Chan and Harris 2006, p. 362; Hogle 2005; Pickersgill and Hogle 2015). In a similar vein, Peter Conrad and Deborah Potter (2004) argue that the line between what is deemed necessary treatment and what is an enhancement can be blurred and may shift as definitions of disease might change; they, therefore, suggest using the term enhancement more broadly, understanding it as involving the 'improvement' of the mind, body, and performance (e.g. Conrad and Potter 2004; Coveney et al. 2011).

The debate on enhancement between the critical voices—the so-called bioconservatives—and the pro-enhancement views of so-called transhumanists is based on divergent and politicised notions of what a human being is, with technology either being considered a force that alienates a human being from itself, a neutral entity, or one that can 'empower' human beings (Sharon 2013). Between these polarised stances are more nuanced positions that call for approaches towards understanding technologies of betterment that are either more practice-based or more subtle theoretically (Sharon 2013; Pickersgill and Hogle 2015). While bioethicists' discussions of the past mostly addressed frontier technologies such as genetics and reproduction technologies, in recent years a number of anthropological and qualitative studies have focused on empirical studies of everyday practices of enhancement.

This chapter begins by presenting the scholarly and bioethicist debate and then moves onto empirical examples. It is shown that everyday experiences of enhancement and optimisation do not mirror the themes, optimism, and worries brought up by scholars in the bioethics debate; rather, other questions and perspectives emerge. I demonstrate that technologies facilitate a co-evolving of technology and the self to produce new experiences, emotions, and transformations of the self, thereby actively responding to and even resisting societal values of productivity and efficiency. Moreover the chapter demonstrates that different sets of questions emerge in regard to the two technologies: in the case of the pharmaceutical these relate to notions of agency, authenticity, and legitimacy; in the case of self-tracking to notions of values in human life and biomedical authority.

Theorising Optimisation and Enhancement

The question—'what is a human being?'—is central to current debates on enhancement and optimisation. As argued by Van Den Eede (2015), theorists from a range of different backgrounds have searched for the human being amid technology: a search that takes multiple forms as critique, defence, or a mixture of both. From a 'pre-postmodern' viewpoint, also referred to as instrumentalism, technology was viewed as a means to an end (Van Den Eede 2015, p. 151). Later, a critical perspective—the substantivist view—emerged wherein technology was no longer seen as a neutral object serving to enhance human purposes and this has, to a great extent, served as a background for scholarly work on both optimisation and enhancement.

An understanding of the term optimisation was initially proposed by Heidegger (Dreyfus 1997), who is regarded by interpreters as a representative of the substantivist view (Van Den Eede 2015). In his essay, 'The Question

Concerning Technology' (1977), Heidegger presented a very sceptical account of technology, one inspired by industrial growth and the horrors caused by weapons of mass destruction. To Heidegger, technology involves the disclosure of reality; thus, the essence of technology is a 'mode of revealing' as human beings bring themselves forth through the use of technology. Consequently, reality is understood in terms of what is available to, and what can be controlled by, human beings. Heidegger suggests that the essence of modern technology is to seek increasingly greater flexibility and efficiency *simply for its own sake*: 'expediting is always itself directed from the beginning ... towards driving on to the maximum yield at the minimum expense' (1977, p. 15). As a result, not only nature but also humanity becomes standing reserves of raw material, something that is available for production and manipulation. As we will see later in the chapter, this view of technologies' potential for dehumanising and alienation runs through the writings of sociology and the bioethicist debate on enhancement.

The term *technologies of optimisation* was introduced by the sociologist Nikolas Rose (2007) to designate medical technologies that, he argues, do not seek merely to cure diseases but also to control the vital processes of the body and mind. In his work Rose (2007) overlaps his use of the terms enhancement and optimisation and proposes a more nuanced view of technologies, indicating both their disciplining and empowering affordances. What is new is not so much the technology, but that human beings have entered the age of 'biological control' where they shoulder much greater responsibility in the realms of the biological (Rose 2007, p. 16). The key feature of technologies of optimisation is a forward-looking vision, as they seek to 'reshape the vital future by action in the vital present' (Rose 2007, p. 18). The new processes of the self can also be regarded as giving rise to an 'entrepreneurial self' (Sennett 1998) wherein the bodily self is perceived as a personal enterprise under the efficiency regime of managerialism. This goes hand in hand with developments in so-called neoliberal governance structures, whereby the responsibility for an optimised self (in terms of age, health, productivity, etc.) is increasingly transferred from collective systems to the individual (Lupton 1995). According to the sociologist Emily Martin, this is associated with the shrinking of social institutions, leading to the individual becoming a site for investment perceived as 'flexible collections of assets' (Martin 2000, p. 582). Hence, Martin argues, people increasingly come to speak of themselves as mini-corporations and as projects that must continually be invested in, nurtured, managed, and developed. Embedded in the urge to manage and improve the performance of the self is the administrative practice of performance reviews, from corporate organisations to educational and creative institutions, from managers and employees to individual entrepreneurs of their own selves.

While the concept of optimisation is mostly used in relation to computers, employing mechanical metaphors for improvement and efficiency or societal optimisation processes, enhancement technologies rest on 'the idea of using medicine, or surgery, or other kinds of medical technology not just to cure or control illnesses but rather to enhance, or improve, human capacities and characteristics' (Elliott 1998). According to the bioethicist Carl Elliott, who writes in an American context, the source of demand for enhancement lies in 'the pressure and fears of ordinary American life' (2003, p. 365). He continues, 'These enhancement technologies are often "enhancements" in name only. Their use is less a search for perfection than a search for social acceptance, less a desperate effort to win the race than to avoid finishing last.' Furthermore, he asks whether the result is an authentic self or one invented by altering biology through surgery, medicines, or devices, and imagined through media advertising, health advisory groups, and their images. The notion of enhancement is also linked to modern consumer culture as it is often provided by goods that can be bought and sold. The body becomes a project through which self-identity is constructed and its maintenance requires the consumption of goods, thereby linking desire, production, and consumption (Bordo 1998; Featherstone 1991). Consumers can purchase height, intelligence, beauty, and a pleasant personality on the market. As noted by Brey (2009), if demands are great and prices low, certain forms of enhancement can be normalised. Consequently, the norms of normality can be pushed and redefined, often homogenising according to Western notions of beauty.

Neoconservatism and Transhumanism/Libertarians and a Mediated Perspective

Over the last 20 years, bioethical and policy-oriented discussions have revolved around the appropriateness of enhancement for human beings and societies, with transhumanists such as Julian Savalescu and Nick Bostrom (2009) and Ray Kurzweil (2005) celebrating and embracing the possibilities offered by technologies on one side of the spectrum, and political philosophers and bioethicists like Francis Fukuyama (2003), Jürgen Habermas (2003), and Michael Sandel (2007), raising a much more critical and sceptical voice on the other.[1] Both proponents and critics of enhancement proceed from ideas of authenticity, autonomy, and fairness. In recent years, scholars have also sought to establish conceptual frameworks such as postphenomenology and posthumanism, in which humans and technology are perceived as mutually defined, a perspective that can give insights into the implications of emergent biotechnologies for notions such as subjectivity, nature, and human nature (Sharon 2013, p. 10; Van Den Eede 2015; Coeckelbergh 2013).

The position of bioconservatives is characterised by their insisting on a distinction between therapeutic applications of biotechnology and 'non-medical ends'. While medical/therapeutic use of technology 'does not desecrate nature but honors it' (Sandel 2004, p. 57), enhancement technologies are perceived as fundamentally changing human nature. Referring to Huxley's *Brave New World*, the political scientist Fukuyama argues that in a world where all human beings get what they want, they no longer retain the characteristics that give them human dignity. Their world has become unnatural as human nature has been altered, which is regarded as hubris. As phrased by Fukuyama:

> The most significant threat posed by contemporary biotechnology is the possibility that it will alter human nature and thereby move us into a 'posthuman' stage of history. ... [H]uman nature shapes and constrains the possible kinds of political regimes, so a technology powerful enough to reshape what we are will have possible malign consequences for liberal democracy and the nature of politics itself. (Fukuyama 2003, p. 7)

Critics of enhancement technologies also worry that they threaten our efforts to achieve authenticity and that they will separate us from what is our own. It is argued, furthermore, that enhancement technologies undermine human autonomy, exemplified by the case of parents making genetic choices for embryos, transforming their offspring into consumer products rather than individuals valued in their own right (Sandel 2007; Kass 2002). Moreover, the use of enhancement technologies leads to social inequality between those who can afford them and those who cannot.

The other position, that of pro-enhancement, is represented by so-called transhumanist and libertarian orientations (Savulescu et al. 2004; Bostrom 2005; Savulescu and Bostrom 2009; Kurzweil 2005; Harris 2010). One pro-enhancement argument is that human nature has already been changed by technology. Modern enhancements are merely based on extensions of existing ones, such as spectacles, binoculars, vaccination, and even writing (Harris 2010, p. xi), so the use of enhancement does not alter nature; on the contrary, it makes it possible to take control of evolution and to ameliorate genetic inequalities (Harris 2010; Savulescu et al. 2004). In *The Singularity is Near* (2005), Kurzweil suggests that we upload ourselves to a computer system and enjoy a nonbiological existence leading towards invulnerability and immortality and that we transcend our present bodily existence through the use of enhancement technologies. In a similarly optimistic vein, Harris writes:

> Enhancements will be enhancements properly so-called if they make us better at doing some of the things we want to do, better at experiencing the world through all of the senses, better at assimilating and processing what we experience, better at remembering and understanding things, stronger, more competent, more of everything we want to become. (Harris 2010, p. 2)

An alternative position, taking the perspective of mediated posthumanism, is proposed by Tamar Sharon (2013), who suggests replacing the concept of alienation with that of mediation. Through this lens, technologies are no longer seen as artefacts that alienate human beings from themselves and from nature, or from authentic ways of being; rather, they offer a possible engagement with the world (Sharon 2013, p. 92). With inspiration from postphenomenology, STS, cyborg studies, and French post-structuralism, Sharon further extends the notion of 'technological mediation' to regard technologies as active mediators in the relationship between human beings and their world (Sharon 2013, pp. 11–12). This approach recognises the heterogeneous and emergent nature of humans and views humans and technology, subjects and objects, nature and culture as interwoven. Hence human subjectivity is seen as a property which is constantly shaped and transformed through engagement with technologies.

Another approach to 'transformations of the self' is offered in Mark Coeckelbergh's book, *Human Being @ Risk* (2013), in which, in a similar vein as Sharon, he critically assesses the current enhancement debate, while proposing to take a point of departure in notions of risk and vulnerability. Using the term risk emphasises the object and the events—the things that might happen to us—while vulnerability emphasises the subject: the potential victim of risk. Vulnerability is not a property of the human, but a feature of the relation between us and the world (2013, p. 44). In this context human beings use technologies to compensate for risk and vulnerability; while technologies do not do away with vulnerability, they transform the experience and management of it. In the following section, I explore empirical examples of enhancement and optimisation which illustrate the point made by Sharon and Coeckelbergh, countering commonly understood views of striving towards being superhuman and, instead, presenting technologies as tools for the transformation of subjective experience. The chapter shows how technologies *invite* people to engage as they seek to optimise and improve their lives and to create themselves—and the transformations of their perceptions of themselves that ensue (Ihde 1990; Verbeek 2005).

THE EXAMPLE OF PHARMACEUTICAL COGNITIVE ENHANCEMENT

Pharmaceuticals are not only prescribed as treatments, but also increasingly used to enhance the mental capabilities of individuals who are not ill (Vrecko 2013, 2015; Elliott 2003). Pharmaceutical cognitive enhancement (PCE) refers to interventions to boost concentration, attention, and levels of comprehension (Steward and Pickersgill 2019; McCabe et al. 2014; Petersen et al. 2015a; Coveney 2012; Hupli et al. 2016; Vargo and Petróczi 2016) that have become increasingly common in many Western countries; indeed a survey of 119 US college students found that 6.9 per cent had used PCE (McCabe et al. 2005). This trend has given rise to number of social, ethical, and policymaking issues: for instance, whether it constitutes a form of cheating, whether the use of prescription drugs for non-therapeutic purposes should be legalised, and whether their use is a consequence of pressure.

The material quality of pharmaceuticals enables lay persons to reappropriate their use and effects (Van der Geest and Whyte 1989; Collin 2016), which means that the same pharmaceuticals can have different functions and effects depending on the contexts in which they are consumed (Collin 2016). Furthermore, the demand for these drugs may easily support lifestyle and personal choices, transforming such medication into a 'vehicle of self-improvement' (Conrad 2007 in Coveney et al. 2011, p. 383). This signals a conceptual shift within medicine, one in which the body is no longer thought of as stable and static but as an object that can be moulded, reconfigured, and transformed. It has, furthermore, been argued that drugs can serve as catalysts, as material objects around which identities and new socialities emerge (Collin 2016).

Most bioethical debates on the use of PCE discuss availability and the normative and moral boundaries between students who take part in such practices and those who do not (DeSantis et al. 2008). It has been claimed that we are entering an era in which enhancement drugs will be available as legal or illicit substances for those who wish to take them as so-called smart drugs designed to make us better humans or even better than human (Miller and Wilsdon 2006). It has been predicted that this will lead to widespread use that will change how we live our lives and generate new ways of enhancing and controlling the brain. Zohny (2015), on the other hand, argues that there is no evidence that PCEs augment cognitive abilities among users.

Another common point of departure for many bioethicist discussions is the notion of authenticity: what it might mean to live authentically, and whether regular pharmaceutical use may result in an 'inauthentic' life (Parens 2000, 2005; Hogle 2005; Pickersgill and Hogle 2015). While some scholars argue that drugs can reveal a more authentic self, as they can remove the barriers that prevent people from fashioning themselves as they wish to be (Kramer 1993; Elliott 2003), others argue that drugs 'alienate' people from themselves and the world (Fukuyama 2003). Another discussion revolves around the notion of risk, an argument that suggests that as long as PCEs are safe enough for healthy individuals to use from a health point of view, access should not be prohibited (Petersen and Petersen 2019). Indeed, libertarians like John Harris argue that the drugs should be freely available to all those who want them (Harris 2010), although more critical approaches to the phenomenon refer to notions of safety, social control, and fairness. Some of the critical arguments are that non-prescription use of pharmaceuticals, such as study drugs, is dangerous and should be countered (McCabe et al. 2005); that institutions create a need and desire for pharmaceutical control and the medicalisation of children's behaviour as part of an oppressive biopolitics (Horwitz 2002 in Singh 2013b); and that the use of PCE creates unequal opportunities for those who can and those who cannot afford it.

Until recently, what have been notably missing from bioethicist's discussions are empirical insights into the everyday use of cognitive enhancing pharmaceuticals (Vrecko 2013), a lacuna addressed by qualitative studies within the social sciences and humanities that have provided empirical insight into students' lived experiences, perceptions, and practices in connection with the use of drugs and PCE (Steward and Pickersgill 2019; Petersen et al. 2015a, 2015b). What emerges from these studies are new sets of questions that refer to notions of agency, authenticity, legitimisation, and experiences of the self.

Agency, Authenticity, and Legitimacy in the Usage of Enhancement Drugs

As noted above, the notions of agency and autonomy lie at the centre of bio-ethicist discussions of the use of stimulant drugs. The ethical questions raised concern for the notions of autonomy and freedom versus the pressure to enhance. Empirical studies, however, show that while the use of stimulants is often connected to a desire to attain maximum performance levels and control over body and health, thereby facilitating an instrumentalisation of the body (Collin 2016), it does not compromise a sense of autonomy; on the contrary, it supports the capacity for moral agency.

The theme of authenticity is linked to the question of whether a medication can in itself enhance this quality. Critical voices in this debate argue (Kureishi 2012; Fukuyama 2003) that children who are treated with Ritalin, for example, are passive victims of medicalisation, that they are 'stupefied' by the drug and turned into robots or obedient zombies (see Singh 2013a, 2013b for review). Empirical findings show, however, that self-perceived authenticity as such is not threatened by the use of PCE. Peter Kramer argued as early as 1993, in the book *Listening to Prozac*, that the experience of authenticity can be mediated by medication. Psychologist Ilina Singh (2013a, 2013b), researching drug treatment for attention deficit hyperactivity disorder, interviewed more than 150 school children with ADHD aged between 9 and 15 in the USA and UK about their experiences of using Ritalin. Her study shows that, while some children report threats to authenticity, drugs are generally not viewed as challenging or compromising it (Singh 2013a, 2013b). As one informant pointed out:

> INT: Who would you say is the real Justin? The Justin on medication, or the Justin off medication. Or, would you say actually, you know, I don't agree that I'm real one way, or not real the other way?
>
> Yeah, I don't agree with that. I'm just ... there's only a slight change in my personality, but I'm still the same person. (Justin, US, age 14). (Singh 2013a, p. 361)

Another informant expresses it in a similar way, observing that, 'With medication it's not that you're a different person; you're still the same person, but you just act a little better. Medication will help you control yourself. (Angie, US, age 11)' (Singh 2013a, p. 361). Singh consequently argues that, with stimulant medication, children feel that they have increased their decision-making power (Singh 2013b, p. 821).

The use of enhancement drugs is also connected to discussions of legitimacy, more specifically how students legitimise and account for their use of study drugs, and how the use is situated in a specific context. Students typically are unaware of the health risk associated with the use or they minimise the severity of it (DeSantis and Hane 2010). An example is provided by Steward and Pickersgill (2019) who studied UK students' use of modafinil, a drug orig-inally designed to treat narcolepsy that can also be used to eliminate the need for sleep. They interviewed 16 undergraduate students concerning their per-spectives on study drugs and the decision-making associated with their con-sumption and found that the materiality of modafinil as a pill had consequences for perceptions of efficacy and risk. As one said, 'I feel like because it comes packaged properly, it should do less damage, versus recreational drugs where you just get who-knows-what from who-knows-who' (Steward and Pickersgill 2019, p. 350). The prescription status of the drug meant that the students perceived it as a reliable means of determining dosage, thereby reinforcing perceptions of safety. Contrary to a study of students in the US by de Souza (2015) and DeSantis and Hane (2010), Steward and Pickersgill found that users were confident in their research and knowledge of the pharmaceuticals they used and reported that they would not consume drugs without what they considered adequate research. As one user observes:

> Building up to taking them … I did quite a lot of research, weighing up the pros and cons and the difference between all types of study drugs that were available to me, to decide which one would suit me best for my personal needs and wants. It wasn't a spontaneous decision at all. (Steward and Pickersgill 2019, p. 350)

Studies have also shown that situational pressure is linked with drug-taking practice (DeSantis and Hane 2010; Hupli et al. 2016; Steward and Pickersgill 2019). Study drugs had the positive effects of allowing the user to 'get things done' and complete tasks in a timely manner (de Souza 2015); the use of modafinil to effect wakefulness, for example, matched a demand for efficiency and increased productivity, which served as a means of legitimising its use. As Steward and Pickersgill (2019) argue, the assessment was flexible and changed with shifting circumstances; consequently an initial risk perception could be overridden by pressure. This is illustrated by one user's explanation: 'I was super against taking them at first … by 2nd year I was like, that's fucking stu-pid, I need to pass my classes' (p. 352).

Enhancing Productivity and Having Fun

While academic performance enhancement was the driver for the use of study drugs, in many cases the stimulant also affects users' emotions and feelings. Scott Vrecko's (2013) study argues that while the capacity of stimulants to improve performance was quite limited, emotional dynamics played an impor-tant role in university students' use of stimulant-based medications, something associated with attention quality but also pleasure and emotion. Vrecko there-fore questions the assumptions behind labelling these drugs primarily 'cogni-tive enhancers' (2013, p. 10).

These findings resonate with those of Margit Anne Petersen, who conducted a study on prescription stimulants in New York which included a total of 20 students aged 19–32 (Petersen et al. 2015a, 2015b; Petersen et al. 2019). The study showed that students think of pharmaceutical performance enhancers as something they actively choose rather than something they are pressured into using (Petersen and Petersen 2019). Students in this study regarded unproductive laziness as 'a mechanical problem' and saw Adderall as a missing ingredient: as something to 'jumpstart the motor' or a way to 'program' the self. Taking the pill was something that brought a sense of excitement, flow, and focus, as Debbie phrased it:

> I'll take the pill, and it's moderately like magic. My brain will like kick into gear, and be like 'Okay, you're going to write this cognitive neuroscience paper, it's got to be 30 pages long.' And I just go. I put on music, and it's just like those movie sequences where people fly through time (Debbie, MA student). (Petersen et al. 2019, p. 111)

The users argued that a good cause, such as overcoming procrastination in order to meet a deadline, justified the use of study drugs, thus serving to normalise and even legitimise such use in the context of study. It therefore legitimised the use of drugs more broadly, regardless of whether users had a condition like ADHD; it also legitimised getting them from a doctor by pretending to display the symptoms.

> It's a joke, I mean, he's a legitimate doctor … a psychiatrist … but it's a revolving door, and just people coming in for almost the same kind of stuff. … He has a little index card, he's got like ten questions on it but almost anybody would say yes to those questions, like 'have you ever misplaced your keys before', 'do you have trouble thinking about or focusing on what you're studying', 'do you ever have trouble sleeping'. If you answered yes to 4 or 5 of them then he says okay, you're a good candidate and that's it. (Petersen et al. 2015a, p. 203)

Most of the students in this study, however, saw a clear difference between recreational drug use and study drug use; as one phrases it, 'I want to be the best that I can be. So really, if there is anything to take out of this … if you are responsible if you educate yourself, if you don't abuse it, it can be a useful tool' (Petersen et al. 2015b, p. 179). Thus, they judged the drug based on the context in which it was used. The students indicated that they could manage without PCE but that it made things easier, faster, and more fun, as it affected the actual experience of working hard, transforming it into something enjoyable (Petersen et al. 2015b). In conversations, students also reflected on the mixing of work and play as a moral grey zone of which they were not entirely aware. At times they even doubted the effect of the drugs (Petersen et al. 2019, p. 117). Use was consequently embedded in reflection and questioning the effects, the nature of productiveness, whether quantitative enhancement also meant qualitative enhancement, and whether it was the self or the technology 'doing the work'.

We also see how the goals change; aiming for optimisation gives rise to questions about productivity and whether that is a goal to strive for. Through the use of PCE the students embrace the neoliberal ideology of aiming for increased productivity, but they also doubt, question, and even resist it (Petersen et al. 2015b). Moreover, in many cases students tap into laymen's discourses on health and risk, creating a 'counterpublic' as they self-manage and self-medicate in a way that contrasts with official health discourses by actively downplaying risks. Apparently the students manage to live up to societal demands by actively choosing to enhance themselves with drugs, thereby making life tolerable or in some cases even turning productivity into pleasure. Thus, their embrace of the neoliberal agenda of productivity concomitantly displays a declining trust in medical providers and their authority, and the increasing role of pharmaceuticals in everyday life, illustrating the complexity of drawing clear-cut lines between therapy and enhancement. This also demonstrates that pharmaceutical technologies are not neutral, but coded with ideologies about relationships, social lives, self-image, and the characteristics of their users (Coveney et al. 2011; Kramer 1993; Rose 2007). In the following section I turn to another empirical example, that of self-tracking, which builds on my own research from 2012 to 2018 among members of the Quantified Self community in Denmark.

Self-tracking and Optimisation

Terms like 'self-tracking' and 'the quantified self' have become part of public discourse since 2007 when Gary Wolf and Kevin Kelly, the editors of the lifestyle technology magazine *Wired*, introduced the terms via a website (quantifiedself.com), a number of articles, and blog entries. Today digital self-tracking refers to the measurement and collection of data through the use of commercial apps on smartphones, tablets, and computers, which provide the opportunity to monitor sleep, eating habits, weight, sports activities, calorie intake, and so on. The data can be connected to social media sites, where, for example, one's running route, speed, or diet are shared with other users. Digital self-tracking requires that the subjects themselves are engaged in their own personal data collection, which serves as a means for exploring, optimising, and improving their lives. This takes place in the context of a moral imperative and public discourse that encourages self-management and responsibility. Citizens are expected to stay informed, to make the right choices for themselves with regard to exercise, diet, rest, and sleep, based on government guidelines, and to evaluate health risks as a strategy of 'making the most of' and 'optimising' all aspects of life (Ruckenstein and Pantzar 2017; Lupton 2016).

In the scholarly literature self-tracking technologies have been framed in terms of empowerment, self-esteem enhancement (Swan 2009, 2012), and increased self-knowledge and discovery (Wolf 2010). Swan was one of the pioneers in advocating a vision of self-tracking as a tool of empowerment for the patient and a 'philosophical and cultural context for moving away from the fix-it-with-a-pill mentality to the empowered role of the biocitizen in achieving the personalised preventive medicine of the future' (Swan 2012, p. 113). This stands in sharp contrast to scholars who, inspired by Foucault, feminist analytics, and/or other traditions within critical sociology, advance a critical approach to self-tracking, which they see as tied up with issues of surveillance and control (Ajana 2017; Reigeluth 2014; French and Smith 2013). The literature has often examined optimisation from a negative perspective that resembles Heidegger's critique of our ongoing attempts to optimise ourselves technologically (Dreyfus 1997); this is exemplified by Boesel's (2013) equating self-tracking with 'big data, data mining, surveillance, loss of privacy, loss of agency, mindless fetishization of technology, even utter dehumanization' (in Meißner 2016, p. 23). Sanders (2017) argues that while self-tracking technologies might expand individuals' capacity for self-knowledge and self-care they also facilitate unprecedented levels of 'biometric surveillance, expand the regulatory mechanism of both public and fashion/beauty authorities and enable increasingly rigorous body projects'. In a similar vein, Ajana (2017) argues that self-tracking practices represent an instantiation of a 'biopolitics of the self'; Moore and Robinson (2016) and Moore (2017) argue that they risk subordinating workers' bodies to neoliberal, corporeal capitalism; while Till (2014) claims that self-tracking can be seen as a form of 'digital labour' that enables higher levels of activity and increased productivity among workers.

Self-tracking Technologies, Documentation, and Experiences of the Self

A number of studies within the social sciences and humanities have explored how people use self-tracking technologies in everyday life (Fotopoulou and O'Riordan 2016; Lomborg and Frandsen 2016; Lomborg et al. 2018; Lupton 2017, 2019; Ruckenstein 2014; Sharon and Zandbergen 2017; Kristensen and Ruckenstein 2018; Fors et al. 2019; Weiner et al. 2020). Rather than the achievement of the perfectly optimised, calculable, and controlling 'quantified self', these studies point to the dynamic and situational practices of the 'quantifying self' (Sharon and Zandbergen 2017), the mutual constitution and intertwining of data and the self (Sharon 2016; Kristensen and Ruckenstein 2018; Mopas and Huybregts 2020), experiences of flow (Lomborg et al. 2018), temporal aspects of the self (Schüll 2016), and the emergence of subjective feeling and sensory experiences (Ruckenstein 2014; Lupton 2017). In these examples optimisation sometimes appears as a theme and as part of practice; rather than positioning optimisation as either positive or negative, the studies pose new sets of questions in relation to bodily experience, values, power relations, and biomedical authority.

The term optimisation is also approached in a different way within the QS movement. One of the founders of QS, Gary Wolf (2016), presents self-tracking as an assemblage of technologies used by trackers 'to ensure that their medical practitioners don't miss the particulars of their condition', as a tool to track mental health in an attempt to 'find their own way to personal fulfilment amid the seductions of marketing and the errors of common opinion' or, by fitness trackers, as a means to understand their strengths and weaknesses. Wolf refers to this as reverse engineering, as the self-tracker might 'push back on theoretical assumptions' as well as engaging in 'personal, pragmatic conversations about first hand experiences tracking weight, exercise, food, sleep, symptoms of disease or other experiences and measures' (Wolf 2016, p. 67). Wolf's statement reflects his awareness that self-tracking is not just about optimisation but also discovery and that the optimisation lens is too narrow to provide profound understanding of why people self-track and what they aim to do.

Overall, members of the QS movement describe self-tracking as a dynamic, open-ended process, rather than activity with a fixed goal. The numbers, graphs, and visualisations make sense from an individual's viewpoint as data points for the perception of the self. They are also highly personal, as the specific methods and analytical procedures are profoundly influenced by personal interests and goal setting. This allows for self-diagnosis and self-medication; moreover, the lack of standardised procedures has sparked creativity on a personal level (Christiansen et al. 2018). The first part of the process is to select data points, which might concern the quality of sleep, stress, grief, sneezing, bodily pain, weight gain, happiness, heart beat rate, mood, the number of steps taken during a day or meals consumed and their content, and the correlation between food and bodily symptoms such as allergies. One participant in my own study, for example, tracked his time use, movements (through Google Maps), and intake of food (by registering calories, vitamins, and minerals). The acquired data offers a sense of having practices documented, while also assisting in identifying possible areas for improvement (Kristensen and Ruckenstein 2018). Furthermore, while the original goal might have been associated with the idea of optimisation, enhanced sensory and emotional experiences are often reported as side effects of self-tracking. This does not necessarily lead to users becoming more or less authentic, rather it reflects a mode of experimenting in order to reach awareness and knowledge of the self. As one self-tracker phrases it:

> Everything is relative ... to me it does not make sense to talk about looking for a kind of substance. Or getting to know myself. Because it changes all the time. But I do find it an entertaining task for about three months. It is all about saying, what happens if I adjust the context? Do I change? Or if I adjust the context, do I get where I want to be? Then I must try that. (Kristensen and Ruckenstein 2018, p. 8)

Thus, rather than a process with a fixed end or goal, the relationship between user and technology is dynamic, ongoing, a tension or negotiation that produces meaning (Sharon and Zandbergen 2017) and an embodied and technologically mediated sensing of the bodily self (Mopas and Huybregts 2020, p. 37). The internal dialogue serves to internalise the optimisation goal;

however, this also creates new experiences and surprises. As one participant in a QS meeting explained of tracking physical activity:

> [T]here is a communication between your subjective knowledge and your objective knowledge that you are creating. You always do this kind of cross-check. I feel like I get a lot of activity, but my data shows me I am not, then I have a conversation: 'what do I trust?' and 'how do I recalibrate?' So that I am starting to say, 'now what I feel aligns with my objective data and I trust my objective data more'. Or you say, 'I trust my subjective data more, my subjective feeling, intuition more, and I can now process that data in a way that aligns with the subjective feeling'. (Sharon and Zandbergen 2017, p. 6)

To other participants self-tracking serves to develop special sensory skills, even a sixth sense, as in learning to tell how many calories are in a portion and how much food weighs by looking at it or knowing intuitively when a target of 10,000 steps has been reached (Sharon and Zandbergen 2017; Kristensen and Ruckenstein 2018). Generally, self-tracking generates sensory feelings, but it can also generate a feeling of being self-responsible and taking control over one's life, as illustrated in a quote from Deborah Lupton's study on self-tracking among Australians.

> I guess I just wanted to be more independent and less reliant on people to support me. So that's medical people and health work. And gradually through tracking, it doesn't do away with the need for professionals, but it's helped me to become more independent and more balanced. My physical and mental health began to stabilise. (Lupton 2019, p. 74)

Self-tracking, therefore, often provides the feeling of betterment and control—in many cases associated with a lessening reliance on other people and health professionals—which very much reflects the notion of the self-responsible citizen (Lupton 2019). In the long run, however, the feeling of improvement and betterment may come to a dead end—an experience of 'hitting the wall'; in these cases the original enthusiasm shifts into a more negative or sceptical attitude, with self-tracking being experienced as burdensome and restrictive, and optimisation goals increasingly questioned (Kristensen and Ruckenstein 2018). This may also lead to the re-evaluation of norms and values, one example being that of a self-tracker who recorded his working hours to discover that a lower number of working hours resulted in higher output quality, leading him to reduce the number of hours he worked (Meißner 2016). Another case is that of the self-tracker who explored the correlation between productivity and happiness to discover that high productivity decreased the experience of happiness, while social life increased it; this led him to prioritise his social life to a greater degree (Christiansen et al. 2018).

Hence, the practice of self-tracking becomes inscribed, to some extent, in a discourse of optimisation, but the practice itself reflects a messier reality, one made up of tensions and contradiction. Similarly, while self-tracking resonates to a degree with a public discourse of autonomy and responsibilisation, in many cases it also challenges medical authority as self-trackers distance themselves from biomedical standards by relying on their own measurements. Overall, new sets of questions emerge—in my own study of Quantified Self (Kristensen and Ruckenstein 2018) and in the work of Sharon and Zandbergen (2017) and Lupton (2019)—that relate to how self-trackers experience their bodies through the use of self-tracking technologies and to the assemblage of technologies/practices and bodies as experienced and lived. They also lead to questions about the values of human life, with self-tracking comprising an indefinite process in which such questions become central, and to a questioning of medical authority, meanwhile highlighting and challenging power relations.

CONCLUSION: TECHNOLOGIES AS VEHICLES FOR SELF-TRANSFORMATION

This chapter has presented various scholarly positions on enhancement and optimisation. A departure point in the academic literature is that enhancement technologies reach beyond the normal, which builds on the problematic assumptions that there are fixed criteria of normality and that it is possible to make a clear-cut distinction between therapy and enhancement. One major challenge to this position is that values given to bodies and technologies are framed as external to technology itself, a view associated with fixed positive or negative evaluations of enhancement technology. By presenting two empirical cases of enhancement I have identified some of the nuances and complexities in its application. Pharmaceuticals and self-tracking used as means of enhancement and optimisation are never just chemical constituents or mechanical devices; rather, they can be catalysts for different types of practices and senses of identity that depend on the intention of use and context. In both cases the notion of agency is central, and in both cases autonomy is not perceived as being compromised. Thus, the worries expressed in philosophy (Heidegger 1977) and bioethics (Sandel 2007; Fukuyama 2003) about the dangers of technology in terms of dehumanisation and alienation are not mirrored in the empirical cases.

Secondly, we see the importance of materiality. Chemical enhancement versus mechanical/digital optimisation has generated discussions along distinctly different lines. If it is an ingested substance, discussion is rather likely to hinge on issues of authenticity, legitimacy, and risk, while optimisation through self-tracking technologies touches upon themes such as mechanical objectivity and control, where the goal is to reduce human interpretation by relying on machines, mechanical action, and—in this case digital—data when seeking evidence (Daston and Galison 2010; Kristensen and Ruckenstein 2018). Self-tracking technologies emerge as a means of gaining knowledge about oneself and living a healthy life; as such, they become a vehicle for personal learning and transformation. Both empirical examples indicate that technologies facilitate a co-evolving of technology and the self, to produce effects and new experiences, emotions, and transformations of the self.

Thirdly we see the differences in use in different contexts; in other words, the reasons for using an enhancement technology make a moral difference. Lastly it was shown that enhancement technologies are inscribed in societal values of productivity, empowerment, and self-responsibilisation, but they may also challenge, resist, and creatively transform these values. As also argued by Pickersgill and Hogle (2015), empirical examples like those provided in this chapter challenge the notion that the use of enhancement/optimisation is driven by rational decision-making, which underpins some of the bioethical discussions; they provide a much more nuanced and complex understanding of the actual users, as well as indicating moral dilemmas and shifting norms. The empirical examples also illustrate the complexities present in the pursuit of enhancement and the demands and pressures of modern society. While users might start with the intention of enhancing and optimising, they are often transformed by the process, ultimately transforming the experience of themselves; on the other hand, they also actively respond to and even resist societal values of productivity and efficiency.

Acknowledgements This work was financed by a grant from The Danish Research Council (DFF-6107-0021) for the project "The Self as Laboratory" in collaboration with Margit Anne Petersen and Aja Smith. Moreover I thank Linda Hogle, Minna Ruckenstein, Klaus Lindgaard Hoeyer, Stine Adrian, Agnieszka Krzeminska, Alev Kuruoglu, Maja Hojer Bruun, and two anonymous reviewers for their insightful comments and critiques.

Note

1. For a more detailed account of different positions within this spectrum, see Gyngell and Selgelid 2016.

References

Ajana, B. (2017). Digital health and the biopolitics of the Quantified Self. *Digital Health, 3*.

Boesel, W. E. (2013). What is the Quantified Self Now? http://thesocietypages.org/cyborgology/2013/05/22/what-is-the-quantified-self-now/#more-15717. Accessed 27 November 2014

Christiansen, T. B., Kristensen, D. B., & Larsen, J. E. (2018). The 1-person laboratory of the quantified self community. In *Metric Culture*. Emerald Publishing Limited.

Bode, M., & Kristensen, D. B. (2016). The digital doppelgänger within. A study on self-tracking and the quantified self movement. *Assembling consumption: Researching actors, networks and markets*, 119–135.

Bordo, S. (1998). Bringing body to theory. *Body and flesh: A philosophical reader*, 84–97.

Bostrom, N. (2005). In defense of posthuman dignity. *Bioethics, 19*(3), 202–214.

Brey, P. (2009). Human enhancement and personal identity. In *New waves in philosophy of technology* (pp. 169–185). London: Palgrave Macmillan.

Chan, S., & Harris, J. (2006). Cognitive regeneration or enhancement: the ethical issues. *Regen Med, 1*(3), 361–366.

Clarke, S., Savulescu, J., Coady, C. A. J., Giubilini, A., & Sanyal, S. (Eds.) (2016). *The ethics of human enhancement: understanding the debate.* Oxford University Press.

Coeckelbergh, M. (2013). *Human being@ risk: Enhancement, technology, and the evaluation of vulnerability transformations, Vol. 12.* Springer Science & Business Media.

Collin, J. (2016). On social plasticity: the transformative power of pharmaceuticals on health, nature and identity. *Sociology of Health & Illness, 38*(1), 73–89.

Conrad, P. (2007). *The medicalization of society: on the transformation of human condition into treatable disorders* (pp. 3–19). Baltimore: Johns Hopkins University Press.

Conrad, P., & Potter, D. (2004). Human growth hormone and the temptations of biomedical enhancement. *Sociology of Health & Illness, 26*(2), 184–215.

Coveney, C., Gabe, J., & Williams, S. (2011). The Sociology of cognitive enhancement: Medicalisation and beyond. *Health Sociology Review, 20*(4), 381–393.

Coveney, C. (2012). Cognitive Enhancement? Exploring Modafinil Use in Social Context. In M. Pickersgill & I. V. Keulen (Eds.), *Sociological Reflections on the Neurosciences* (Vol. Advances in Medical Sociology 13, pp. 203–228). Bingley: Emerald Group Publishing Limited.

Christiansen, T. B., Kristensen, D. B., & Larsen, J. E. (2018b). The 1-Person Laboratory of the Quantified Self Community. In B. Ajana (Ed.), *Metric Culture: Ontologies of Self-Tracking Practices* (pp. 97–115). Emerald Publishing Limited.

Daston, L., & Galison, P. (2010). *Objectivity.* New York: Zone Books.

DeSantis, A. D., Webb, E. M., & Noar, S. M. (2008). Illicit use of prescription ADHD medications on a college campus: a multimethodological approach. *Journal of American College Health, 57*(3), 315–324.

DeSantis, A. D., & Hane, A. C. (2010). "Adderall is definitely not a drug": justifications for the illegal use of ADHD stimulants. *Substance Use & Misuse, 45*(1–2), 31–46.

de Souza, R. (2015). "I've Thought About This, Trust Me": Understanding the Values and Assumptions Underlying Prescription Stimulant Misuse Among College Students. *International Journal of Communication, 9,* 19.

Dreyfus, H. L. (1997). Heidegger on gaining a free relation to technology. *Technology and Values,* 41–54.

Elliott, C. (1998). *What's wrong with enhancement technologies?* CHIPS Public Lecture, University of Minnesota.

Elliott, C. (2003). *Better than well: American medicine meets the American dream.* WW Norton & Company.

Elliott, C. (2011). Enhancement technologies and the modern self. *Journal of Medicine and Philosophy, 36*(4), 364–374.

Featherstone, M. (1991). The body in consumer culture. *The body: Social Process and Cultural Theory,* 170–196.

Fors, V., Pink, S., Berg, M., & O'Dell, T. (2019). *Imagining Personal Data: Experiences of Self-Tracking.* Bloomsbury Publishing.

Fotopoulou A., & O'Riordan K. (2016). Training to self-care: fitness tracking, biopedagogy and the healthy consumer. *Health Sociology Review, 26,* 54–68.

French, M., & Smith, G. (2013). 'Health' surveillance: New modes of monitoring bodies, populations, and polities. *Critical Public Health, 23*(4), 383–392.

Fukuyama, F. (2003). *Our Posthuman Future: Consequences of the Biotechnology Revolution*. Farrar, Straus and Giroux.

Gyngell, C., & Selgelid, M. J. (2016). Human Enhancement: Conceptual Clarity and Moral Significance. In S. Clarke, J. Savulescu, C. A. J. Coady, A. Giubilini, & S. Sanyal, (Eds.), *The ethics of human enhancement: understanding the debate* (pp. 111–126). Oxford University Press.

Habermas, J. (2003). *The future of human nature*. John Wiley & Sons.

Harris, J. (2010). *Enhancing evolution: The ethical case for making better people*. Princeton University Press.

Heidegger, M., (1977). *The question concerning technology, and other essays*. New York: Harper & Row.

Hogle, L. F. (2005). Enhancement technologies and the body. *Annual Review of Anthropology 34*, 695–716.

Horwitz, A. V. (2002). *Creating Mental Illness*. University of Chicago Press.

Hupli, A., Didžiokaitė, G., & Ydema, M. (2016). Toward the smarter use of smart drugs: Perceptions and experiences of university students in the Netherlands and Lithuania. *Contemporary Drug Problems, 43*(3), 242–257.

Ihde, D. (1990). *Technology and the lifeworld: From garden to earth* (No. 560). Indiana University Press.

Juengst, E., & Moseley, D. (2016). *Human Enhancement*. Stanford Encyclopedia of Philosophy.

Kass, L. (2002). *Life, liberty and the defense of dignity: the challenge for bioethics*. Encounter Books.

Kramer, P. (1993). Listening to prozac: a psychiatrist explores antidepressants drugs and the remaking of the self. *Nova York, Viking*.

Kristensen, D. B., & Ruckenstein, M. (2018). Co-evolving with self-tracking technologies. *New Media & Society, 20*(10), 3624–3640.

Kureishi, H. (2012, February 18). The art of distraction. *The New York Times*.

Kurzweil, R. (2005). *The singularity is near: When humans transcend biology*. Penguin.

Lomborg, S., & Frandsen, K. (2016). Self-tracking as communication. *Information, Communication & Society, 19*(7), 1015–1027.

Lomborg, S., Thylstrup, N. B., & Schwartz, J. (2018). The temporal flows of self-tracking: Checking in, moving on, staying hooked. *New Media & Society, 20*(12), 4590–4607.

Lupton, D. (1995). *The imperative of health: Public health and the regulated body*. Sage.

Lupton, D. (2016). The diverse domains of quantified selves: self-tracking modes and dataveillance. *Economy and Society, 45*(1), 101–122.

Lupton, D. (2017). Feeling your data: Touch and making sense of personal digital data. *New Media & Society, 19*(10), 1599–1614.

Lupton, D. (2019). 'It's made me a lot more aware': a new materialist analysis of health self-tracking. *Media International Australia, 171*(1), 66–79.

Martin, E. (2000). Mind-body problems. *American ethnologist, 27*(3), 569–590.

McCabe, S. E., Knight, J. R., Teter, C. J., & Wechsler, H. (2005). Non-medical use of prescription stimulants among US college students: Prevalence and correlates from a national survey. *Addiction, 100*(1), 96–106.

McCabe, S. E., West, B. T., Teter, C. J., & Boyd, C. J. (2014). Trends in medical use, diversion, and nonmedical use of prescription medications among college students from 2003 to 2013: Connecting the dots. *Addictive Behaviors, 39*(7), 1176–1182.

Meißner, S. (2016). Effects of Quantified Self Beyond Self-Optimization. In S. Selke (Ed.), *Lifelogging* (pp. 235–248). Springer.

Miller, P., & Wilsdon, J. (2006). Better humans. *The politics of human enhancement and life extension.* London: Demos.

Moore, P., & Robinson, A. (2016). The quantified self: What counts in the neoliberal workplace. *New Media & Society, 18*(11), 2774–2792.

Moore, P. V. (2017). *The quantified self in precarity: Work, technology and what counts.* Routledge.

Mopas, M., & Huybregts, E. (2020). Training by feel: wearable fitness-trackers, endurance athletes, and the sensing of data. *The Senses and Society, 15*(1), 25–40.

Parens, E. (Ed.) (2000). *Enhancing human traits: Ethical and social implications.* Georgetown University Press.

Parens, E. (2005). Authenticity and ambivalence: Toward understanding the enhancement debate. *Hastings Center Report, 35*(3), 34–41.

Petersen, M. A., Nørgaard, L. S., & Traulsen, J. M. (2015a). Going to the doctor with enhancement in mind–An ethnographic study of university students' use of prescription stimulants and their moral ambivalence. *Drugs: Education, Prevention and Policy, 22*(3), 201–207.

Petersen, M. A., Nørgaard, L. S., & Traulsen, J. M. (2015b). Pursuing pleasures of productivity: university students' use of prescription stimulants for enhancement and the moral uncertainty of making work fun. *Culture, Medicine, and Psychiatry, 39*(4), 665–679.

Petersen, M. A., Enghoff, O., & Demant, J. (2019). The uncertainties of enhancement: A mixed-methods study on the use of substances for cognitive enhancement and it's unintended consequences. *Performance Enhancement & Health, 6*(3–4), 111–120.

Petersen, M. A., & Petersen, T. S. (2019). Why prohibit study drugs? On attitudes and practices concerning prohibition and coercion to use pharmaceutical cognitive enhancement. *Drugs: Education, Prevention and Policy,* 1–9.

Pickersgill, M., & Hogle, L. (2015). Enhancement, ethics and society: towards an empirical research agenda for the medical humanities and social sciences. *Medical Humanities, 41*(2), 136–142.

Ruckenstein, M. (2014). Visualized and Interacted Life: Personal Analytics and Engagements with Data Doubles. *Societies, 4*(1), 68–84.

Ruckenstein, M., & Pantzar, M. (2017). Beyond the quantified self: Thematic exploration of a dataistic paradigm. *New Media & Society, 19*(3), 401–418.

Reigeluth, T. (2014). Why data is not enough: Digital traces as control of self and self-control. *Surveillance & Society, 12*(2), 243–254.

Rose, N. (2007). *The politics of life itself: Biomedicine, power, and subjectivities in the 21st century.* Princeton: Princeton University Press.

Sandel, M. J. (2007). *The case against perfection: Ethics in the age of genetic engineering.* Harvard University Press.

Sandel, M. (2004). The case against perfection. *The Atlantic Monthly* (April 2004), 51–62.

Sanders, R. (2017). Self-tracking in the digital era: Biopower, patriarchy, and the new biometric body projects. *Body & Society, 23*(1), 36–63.

Savulescu, J., Foddy, B., & Clayton, M. (2004). Why we should allow performance enhancing drugs in sport. *British Journal of Sports Medicine, 38*(6), 666–670.

Savulescu, J., & Bostrom, N. (Eds.) (2009). *Human enhancement.* OUP Oxford.

Schüll, N. D. (2016). Data for life: Wearable technology and the design of self-care. *BioSocieties, 11*(3), 317–333.

Sennett, R. (1998). *The corrosion of character: The personal consequences of work in the new capitalism*. WW Norton & Company.

Sharon, T. (2013). *Human nature in an age of biotechnology: The case for mediated post-humanism* (Vol. 14). Springer Science & Business Media.

Sharon, T. (2016). Self-tracking for health and the quantified self: Re-articulating autonomy, solidarity, and authenticity in an age of personalized healthcare. *Philosophy & Technology, 30*(1), 93–121.

Sharon, T., & Zandbergen, D. (2017). From data fetishism to quantifying selves: Self-tracking practices and the other values of data. *New Media & Society, 19*(11), 1695–1709.

Singh, I. (2013a). Not robots: children's perspectives on authenticity, moral agency and stimulant drug treatments. *Journal of Medical Ethics, 39*(6), 359–366.

Singh, I. (2013b). Brain talk: power and negotiation in children's discourse about self, brain and behaviour. *Sociology of Health & Illness, 35*(6), 813–827.

Steward, A., & Pickersgill, M. (2019). Developing expertise, customising sleep, enhancing study practices: exploring the legitimisation of modafinil use within the accounts of UK undergraduate students. *Drugs: Education, Prevention and Policy*, 1–9.

Swan, M. (2009). Emerging patient-driven health care models: An examination of health social networks, consumer personalized medicine and quantified self-tracking. *International Journal of Environmental Research and Public Health, 6*, 492–525.

Swan, M. (2012). Health 2050: The realization of personalized medicine through crowdsourcing, the quantified self, and the participatory biocitizen. *Journal of Personalized Medicine, 2*(3), 93–118

Till, C. (2014) Exercise as Labour: Quantified Self and the Transformation of Exercise into Labour. *Societies, 4*, 446–462.

Van Den Eede, Y. (2015). Where is the human? Beyond the enhancement debate. *Science, Technology and Human Values, 40*(1), 149–162.

Van der Geest, S., & Whyte, S. R. (1989). The charm of medicines: metaphors and metonyms. *Medical Anthropology Quarterly, 3*(4), 345–367.

Vargo, E. J., & Petróczi, A. (2016). "It was me on a good day": exploring the smart drug use phenomenon in England. *Frontiers in Psychology, 7*, 779.

Vrecko, S. (2013). Just how Cognitive is "Cognitive Enhancement"? On the Significance of Emotions in University Students' Experiences with Study Drugs. *AJOB Neuroscience, 4*(1), 4–12.

Vrecko, S. (2015). Everyday drug diversions: A qualitative study of the illicit exchange and non-medical use of prescription stimulants on a university campus. *Social Science & Medicine, 131*, 297–304.

Verbeek, P. P. (2005). *What things do: Philosophical reflections on technology, agency, and design*. Penn State Press.

Weiner, K., Will, C., Henwood, F., & Williams, R. (2020). Everyday curation? Attending to data, records and record keeping in the practices of self-monitoring. *Big Data & Society, 7*(1).

Wolf, G. (2010, April 28). The data-driven life. *The New York Times*.

Wolf, G. (2016). Quantified self: Reverse engineering. In D. Nafus (Ed.), *Quantified: Biosensing Technologies in Everyday Life* (pp. 67–72). Cambridge, MA: The MIT Press.

Zohny, H. (2015). The myth of cognitive enhancement drugs. *Neuroethics, 8*(3), 257–269.

CHAPTER 31

Articulations of Ethics: Energy Worlds and Moral Selves

Regimes

Mette M. High

Corporate capitalism today is marked by a striking concern with ethics. Business performance is commonly evaluated in relation to fair trade standards, corporate social responsibility (CSR) practices, and environmental sustainability frameworks. This performance is often rendered public through an audit culture of accreditation and certification, brandishing and promoting companies' ethical behaviour (Dolan 2010; Jaffe and Howard 2010; Muehlebach 2012). While the language of ethics has been strongly adopted by corporate actors, it has also long provided a cornerstone for disapproval, with critics pointing to corporate shortcomings if not outright failings, be it corporate greed, human rights violations, or detrimental environmental practices (Kirsch 2014; Sawyer 2004). Ethics has thus become a battleground where corporations and critics uphold the kind of flourishing that they believe should be brought into being.

Described by some as 'ethical capitalism' (Barry 2004), this ethicalisation of corporate capitalism does not necessarily imply that companies and their critics are now embracing deeper, more profound moral imperatives than they did in the past. Instead, it is a moment in capitalist practice where ethics are actively and concertedly demonstrated, with some practices being categorised and made visible as ethical, while others are not (Strathern 1996). In a 'risk society' where risks are perceived as not only natural and inevitable but also as

M. M. High (✉)
University of St Andrews, St Andrews, UK
e-mail: mmh20@st-andrews.ac.uk

© The Author(s) 2022
M. H. Bruun et al. (eds.), *The Palgrave Handbook of the Anthropology of Technology*, https://doi.org/10.1007/978-981-16-7084-8_31

anthropogenic and avoidable, corporations stand as key producers of, and contributors to, perceived risks (Beck 2006). This is intensified through neoliberal economic policies that have led many governments to retreat from their role in caring for the well-being of citizens and posited the market as the most efficient replacement and focus. With consumers and investors pushing for greater transparency and accountability, not from governments but from corporations, auditing has become a prime tool for assessment, demonstrating as well as condemning corporations' ethical behaviour. It has become a way for leveraging demands that corporations demonstrate responsibility, sustainability, and transparency. Applied across geographical regions, political regimes, and economic sectors, ethics is now an explicit public part of global corporate practice and central to the scrutiny advanced by critics, extending far beyond any single industry.

This ethicalisation of corporate capitalism is particularly evident in industries that are involved in the transformation of natural resources into market assets, such as the energy sector. Energy companies' direct engagements with the environment, its many inhabitants (human as well as non-human), and its desired riches (oil, gas, coal, uranium, wind, sun, water, peat, timber) bring everyone into close and tense relationships where there is much at stake for all parties and the production of risk becomes an immediate issue. These relationships are enacted across multiple sites and multiple scales as energy companies implicate others through technological infrastructures, institutions, and discourses, as well as through their powerful 'performances and re-enactments of future prosperity' (Lord and Rest 2021, p. 83; see also Weszkalnys 2016). It is an industry where sociotechnical imaginaries embrace individuals and collectivities, the immediate and the distant, the past and the future, paucity and prosperity, hope and despair. As has been well documented by scholars (see, e.g. Behrends et al. 2011; Strauss et al. 2013; Weszkalnys and Richardson 2014), in these multi-scalar encounters stakeholders are often highly unequally positioned and able to mobilise very different capacities, resources, and networks. Yet, as Suzana Sawyer (2004) notes in her work on oil production in the Ecuadorian Amazon, 'the power differentials we see across the globe are hardly inevitable. They emerge from the sticky webs of social relationality' (p. 16). She demonstrates with great nuance how an indigenous organisation fought against a US oil producer by subverting and redeploying the state's neoliberal proclamations of corporate care. Given the centrality of ethics in today's corporate capitalism, I suggest that we explore with similar attention and nuance the ways in which energy companies, as composite constellations, draw on and engage with ethics.

I will focus here on the sprawling oil and gas industry, which is 'vast on all counts' (Appel et al. 2015, p. 19) and steeped in moral language. From small independent companies to big multinationals, corporations present their purposes as not only being about finding and supplying hydrocarbons to meet global demand but also about improving people's lives. Nestled within modernist ideologies of technological development and progress, public-facing moral ambitions to be a 'force for good' in the world—'serving societies and communities' and having 'a positive impact'—reverberate through the industry, across countries and positions. Corporate brochures and websites promote catchy moral slogans, which are also emblazoned on corporate merchandise, such as mugs, caps, and golf polo shirts. These declarations of moral ambition (High 2019) appear as near-ubiquitous protagonists for the industry, ending up in potentially unexpected places, far away from rigs, field offices, and board rooms. As 'traveling technologies' (von Schnitzler 2013), they render tangible that this is an endeavour couched in moral terms, conjoining hydrocarbons with not only political and economic opportunities but also with explicit visions of what is deemed good and right. These ethical claims fly in the face of those who do not share the same or similar visions. As an industry that, for many, is associated with wealth accumulation, political inequalities, and environmental disasters, the vocal front-facing articulation between hydrocarbons and ethics begs the question of how the industry considers the production of oil and gas ethical projects. And how, in turn, do these resources come to be part of highly specific, as well as widely shared, forms of moral reasoning and practice? In what ways do these ethical projects also entail modes of working on the self as a certain kind of subject? That is, at a more fundamental level, how does the production of energy come to be ethical?

To begin exploring these questions, it is important to recognise that the public-facing moral proclamations are simultaneously assertive yet partial, demonstrative yet incomplete. They intersect with, form part of, and are challenged by what I propose to call 'regimes of ethics'. These regimes are sometimes formal yet fluid, distinctive yet rarely consistent (see also High 2018; Lambek 2018). Inspired by Andrew Lakoff and Stephen Collier's (2004) work on developing 'a broader understanding of contemporary configurations of ethical reflection and practice' (p. 420), I propose an analytical framework that is not limited to individuals' attempts to develop a virtuous character but also includes the more widely dynamic configurations in which ethical activities are articulated. As noted by Cheryl Mattingly and Jason Throop, the demarcation of 'moral selves' in the recent anthropological turn to neo-Aristotelian traditions of virtue ethics risks reproducing an individualism that is reminiscent of the Western humanist tradition (Mattingly and Throop 2018, p. 481; see also Mahmood 2003; Mattingly 2012; Wentzer and Mattingly 2018). This individualism 'animated our philosophies and our ethics for so long: the universal subject, stable, unified, totalized, individualized, interiorized' (Rose 1998, p. 169). Focusing on such individualisation of ethics would not only hark back to 'outworn and problematic metaphysical assumptions' (Wentzer and Mattingly 2018, p. 144); it would also hide from view how ethics is intrinsically entangled in, part of, and disrupting wider social processes. I contend that to understand how ethics conjoins with economic practices, such as in today's 'ethical capitalism', demands an appreciation of not just moral selves but also moral worlds.

The notion of regime brings attention to these broader ethical configurations, suggesting congeries of moral reasoning and practice. I use *regime* here to indicate not aspects of governmentality, such as in the work on 'carbon democracy' (Mitchell 2009), 'energopolitics' (Boyer 2014, p. 7), and 'petrocultures' (Szeman 2019), but rather to indicate a manner, method, or arrangement that reaches across individual instantiations and circumstances. As such, regimes of ethics are abstractions that are underpinned by specific values in specific instances and sites. Whilst this might seem to bear some semblance to Joel Robbins's (2013) structuralist value theory, the proposed analytic differs in important ways. Robbins draws on Dumont's *Homo hierarchicus* to suggest that societies have identifiable 'paramount values'. These values reign supreme by encompassing subordinate values or co-exist in configurations of value pluralism that can be more or less stable, with the possibility of giving rise to dramatic clashes of value conflict in order to reach a value resolution. In his work, the identified values mapped onto societies at large appear so abstracted as to emerge clear, coherent, and neat, fundamentally decoupled from, and uncontestable by, the messiness of life. Instead, in order to take this messiness seriously in analytical terms, I approach regimes as emerging dynamically and animatedly, acquiring a provisional distinctiveness and direction. As the regimes intersect and interrelate in varying ways, this analytic acknowledges that there are many potential responses to the question, 'how should one live?'

In this chapter, I focus on three differentiated regimes of ethics that are central to the ways in which oil and gas companies conjoin their pursuit of hydrocarbons with ethics. Firstly, I explore corporate social responsibility (CSR) frameworks that are central to the 'facialising' (Shever 2010) and 'enacting' (Welker 2014) of corporations. I will show how oil and gas companies draw on the language and practice of ethics to balance stakeholder demands with 'the ever present need to make a profit' (Jenkins 2004, p. 24). While much scholarship has focussed on CSR in terms of external stakeholder engagement, I suggest CSR activities can also be part of fostering industry pride and company-wide 'moral communities' (Allahyari 2000). Whereas the CSR regime of ethics is positioned as a deliberate and explicit corporate strategy, a second regime of ethics is grounded in the professional codes of employees, partners, and subcontractors. I explore here US engineering ethics, which highlight the range of possibilities that can be pursued by engineers in the oil and gas workforce. Practices such as whistleblowing and breaking ranks in situations of unsafe practices are valued, epitomising individual ethical action in the context of corporate employment (Johnson 2017; Mitcham 2015). Both corporate social responsibility frameworks and engineering ethics highlight normative definitions of what is worthy to pursue and what should direct moral action. While CSR centres on corporate ambition and purpose, engineering ethics emphasise individual professional decision-making. Co-existing with these two formal regimes of ethics are also industry actors' own moral sensibilities. This third regime of ethics draws on my ongoing ethnographic research carried out since 2013 among predominantly small-scale private oil and gas producers, service companies, financiers, and other industry participants in Colorado, USA. I introduce a rancher-turned-oilman who might appear to echo emphatically industry moral visions, yet presents a life of flourishing that unsettles and questions the industry of which he has become part. By discussing these various articulations of ethics, my aim is to take seriously formal rules and codes, as well as industry actors' personal, potentially idiosyncratic, ethical reflection, and practice. I suggest that, given the stakes involved in different energy visions, it is timely and urgent that we recognise these multiple and competing regimes of ethics. While the oil and gas industry's moral visions might appear monolithic, firm, and unchallengeable, regimes of ethics indicate the underdetermined nature of ethical life.

Corporate Responsibilities

The President of the Society for Petroleum Engineers Sami Alnuaim recently made a call for greater 'industry pride'. He noted how 'our industry's mission is not limited to providing energy to support the global economy, but also to improving human lives. I am very proud of being part of this industry. Are you?' (Alnuaim 2019, p. 11). In his appeal to members, he expressed sentiments that are shared by my interlocutors in Colorado when he grounded pride in how 'the use of our products has raised living standards for billions of people' (Alnuaim 2019, p. 10). While this sense of servitude, of providing energy to meet the demands of consumers, is a frequent motive elaborated in industry advertising and news reports, it is also central to how industry actors position themselves as moral actors (High 2019, p. 34; see also Smith 2019a). It foregrounds how their work brings to market the 'lifeblood of oil' (Huber 2013) on which industrial life today has come to depend so heavily, while it also serves to deflect criticism and distribute blame across both producers and consumers when industry actors are criticised for their actions (Smith 2019b). Pointing to specific products and tracing their components back to the oil patch is a gleeful exercise for many of my interlocutors. Yet the President of SPE invited his members to take pride in not only the specific material products of their labour, but also in how the industry conducts its business. With CSR becoming central to how oil and gas companies address 'stakeholder concerns' and 'manage risks' (Knudsen et al. 2020), he recounted numerous CSR initiatives across the industry and remarked, 'We are now realizing that practicing CSR needs to be a way of running a successful business' (Alnuaim 2019, p. 11). The potential twinning of 'doing business' and 'doing good' offered an important source of industry pride, which he felt could be better harnessed by the industry.

The concept of corporate social responsibility (CSR), and its associated practices of community development (CD), and environmental and social governance (ESG) form a broad, growing, and flexible set of discourses, accounting regimes, and practical initiatives through which companies attempt to position themselves as moral actors. In their recent review of CSR scholarship,

Ståle Knudsen et al. (2020) note how both advocates and critics of CSR have found CSR primarily a business strategy, while critical studies generally see CSR as associated with the global neoliberal shift in policies. Richard De George (1996) has described how CSR evolved as a concept in the business environment of the USA in the 1960s along with the rise of consumer, environmental, and social activist groups' critiques of 'big business'. At this time, 'groups that had vested interests clothed their demands on business in terms that gave their demands more respectability. By calling them socially interested demands, they disguised the fact that they were often demands not of society as a whole, but of particular groups with special interests' (1996, p. 19). In order to respond to these demands, businesses used the same language and

> clothed their answers in terms of social responsiveness or social responsibility. No one knew exactly what those terms meant, but that was unimportant. The terms indicated some concern for the social good, the general welfare, or society as a whole. The term 'social responsibility' took some of the sting out of the charge that big business was part of a military-industrial complex that acted for its own benefit or for the benefit of an elite, rather than for the good of society. (De George 1996 p. 19)

While for decades various definitions, models, and practices were debated, Heleed Jenkins (2004) has shown how companies continue to struggle in their relationships with local stakeholders, partly because of the difficulty of actually delimiting stakeholders in a way that makes sense for all parties involved. As noted by Francisco García-Rodríguez et al. (2013, p. 375), this difficulty is particularly acute for oil and gas companies as they extract highly profitable natural resources at the risk of causing serious environmental harm in countries and among populations about which they might know little. Ethnographic work in this field has thus demonstrated how CSR policies, practices, and standards have largely evolved out of corporate responses to critics' disapproval, yet have rarely been implemented effectively in dealings with local stakeholders.

In her pioneering study of CSR at the multinational mining company Anglo American, Dinah Rajak (2011a) shows how CSR enables corporations to lay claims to and demonstrate moral authority and extend, if not utilise, this in the places and communities where they operate. She found that CSR employees brought their own passionately held desires of 'doing good' to their work of 'empowering' and 'partnering' the participants of their programmes, celebrating publically the elusive win-win solution to political and economic inequalities. Yet, through the performance of CSR, employees ultimately re-inscribed unequal gift relationships that stirred dependence rather than empowerment. Despite virtuous discourses of partnership, equality, and sameness, the politics of the 'development gift' (Stirrat and Henkel 1997; see also Jenkins 2004) thus cemented unwanted power relations between giver and recipient that were predominantly in the interest of the giver. As other research reminds us, while such hierarchical relations of patronage might not be the intended outcomes of

CSR, they can facilitate the rebranding of companies. Elana Shever has shown in her work on Shell's CSR activities in Argentina how the investment in participatory community programmes gave the company a 'smiling face', reinforcing the image that Shell had 'good intentions and a friendly disposition' (Shever 2010, p. 28, see also Shever 2012). With its front of caring and compassionate corporate personhood, yet with limited obligations, the company deflected and diffused responsibility when confronted with accusations of poor practice. Perhaps indicative of a wider 'corporate ethic of detachment' (Cross 2011), Katy Gardner's (2015) study of Chevron's CSR activities in a Bangladeshi village near a large gas field also depicts a company's on-the-ground preference for distance and disconnection. Whereas villagers sought ongoing, open-ended relationships with Chevron in the hope of greater employment opportunities, infrastructural projects, and impending 'development', they experienced the oil and gas company as desiring a 'moral economy of disconnection' (Gardner 2015, p. 507; see also Gardner et al. 2012). Jobs were offered on-site but suddenly terminated, community programmes were initiated but implemented entirely by external subcontracted NGOs; many promises had been made but then abandoned without explanation. Advancing tropes of self-help and empowerment, the CEO of Chevron was clear that 'their motivation…was wholly profit-driven' (Gardner 2015, p. 506). Echoing Shell's insights from the Niger Delta where CSR activities were also presented as publicly and strategically advancing the interests of their business (Edoho 2008), Chevron's CEO concluded that 'CSR was "good business"' (Gardner 2015, p. 506; see also Anderson and Bieniaszewska 2005; Frynas 2005).

While these accounts demonstrate how CSR partakes in the (re)production of capitalist relations through the consolidation of hierarchical social relationships between corporations and critics, they can appear 'remarkably one sided and remarkably stable…the only happenings, meanings and consequences worth recording appear to be those that can be entered into a corporate balance sheet or appear as indices of profit' (Cross 2014, p. 126). In contrast, Jamie Cross argues that the labyrinthine ethical accounting regimes of CSR, with standardised ISO certifications, conventions, and policy forums (Rajak 2011b), can also be a means through which employees perform and create professional personhood. In his fieldwork in India where the CSR accounting regime was considered a key part of management training, the trainee managers found the performance of bureaucratic rituals, procedures, and practices that centred on countless ethical accounting documents creative and formative. They felt it was 'a task through which they could perform themselves as modern professionals' (Cross 2011, p. 42), capable of abstracting and decontextualising themselves from local relationships and becoming proficient in globally translatable forms of expertise.

Focusing on employees who are not directly involved in CSR as the unit of analysis has received relatively scant attention in the CSR literature, yet recent studies in this field indicate a striking influence of CSR on employees' own attitudes to their work and their employer. In a study of CSR activities in the oil and gas industry, Kenneth De Roeck and Nathalie Delobbe (2012) found that 'an organization with a poor reputation in the environmental realm can still strengthen its legitimacy in the eyes of internal stakeholders by engaging in concrete initiatives that preserve and promote the natural environment' (p. 408). In such instances, CSR helped reinforce employees' organisational identification and trust, strengthening their sense of loyalty and readiness to take responsibility for company operations. While many external stakeholders felt frustrated and disappointed, if not furious with CSR, many internal stakeholders felt a growing affinity for their company's values and mission (see also Fatma et al. 2018). Given the CSR activities, they were better able to support their company's efforts and tap into that source of 'industry pride' that the aforementioned President of SPE had identified.

In my ethnographic research in Colorado, CSR activities are also an important aspect of how individual employees come to embrace company values and mission, but also how they collectively come to form company-wide 'moral communities' (Allahyari 2000). In 2014, a medium-sized oil and gas producer was heavily involved in a drilling programme across the high plains of Weld County in the North-Eastern corner of the state. While landmen worked on the legal title work, reservoir engineers and geophysicists prepared the drilling activities, and others negotiated subcontractor and limited partner involvement. Spread out across multiple floors in the company building, frequent meetings brought people together in their small, focussed teams. Only rarely did they come together in larger groups, in which case it was for occasions such as management announcements, training sessions, or information gathering. However, CSR activities offered spaces where people collectively took pride in projects outside any single area of specialisation and focus. It also physically brought people together across all teams. With an explicit public-facing corporate emphasis on 'caring', the company encouraged its employees to donate their work time and volunteer in soup kitchens or women's shelters, if not helping to build a playground in a nearby community. The hours that were donated this way were then matched in dollar terms by the company to its outreach activities. Most of the employees took part in this, building friendships and networks that strengthened their usual teams while also reaching far beyond. As such, CSR offered this company a virtuous vocabulary and suite of actions that helped foster stronger teams which the company needed, as it was about to head into a commodity downturn.

When oil and gas companies draw on the language and practice of ethics in their CSR initiatives, their noticeable success is thus among their own employees. As oil and gas companies fund schools and hospitals, wildlife sanctuaries and playgrounds, microcredit schemes and participatory community development, poverty alleviation schemes and food banks, they turn their moral visions of the good into specific material corporate strategies that are likely to resonate strongly with their own employees, while also keeping a clear and strong focus on improving the bottom line. For oil and gas companies, CSR is thus a business strategy that, by operationalising international standards and conventions which draw on the powerful virtuous vocabulary of generosity and charity, offers them a win-win twinning of hydrocarbons and ethics, even if it is in ways that may not be intended.

ENGINEERING ETHICS

While CSR is part of the vocal front-facing articulation of moral ambition in the oil and gas industry, it co-exists with other regimes of ethics that present industry actors with different frameworks for ethical reasoning and practice. As an industry that encompasses a broad range of professions and skills, there has been a growing recognition that everyone carries special moral obligations. In today's 'risk society', this has partly been emphasised through the formalisation of workplace health, safety, and environment (HSE) policies. These aim to evaluate, manage, and improve safety culture among employees in the industry, as well as promote externally the standards they seek to uphold. As I have also experienced in my fieldwork, both on rigs and off-site, 'HSE culture is the number one priority in the oil and gas sector' (Makambura 2018). From her fieldwork in Equatorial Guinea's offshore oil and gas fields, Hannah Appel (2012) captures this sense of 'HSE culture' well when she notes how 'the offshore's saturation with practices, performances, media, and bureaucracies of risk avoidance and safety gave it the immediate feeling of an immersive, hermetic environment' (p. 695). While she considers how the HSE culture contributes to the prefabricated 'modularity' of a global capitalist project, such as an offshore rig, by attempting to disentangle it from the sociopolitical reality of Equatorial Guinea, I will here consider it as part of a broader regime of normative professional codes of ethics that require industry actors to recognise and evaluate their immediate and specific entanglements at the workplace.

In the USA, formalised HSE frameworks in extractive industries evolved around the turn of the previous century, amidst concerns about work hazards faced by miners. These frameworks soon branched into broader concerns about engineering practices across various industries. While official health and safety standards, specifically governing the oil and gas industry, only emerged in the 1980s, codes of engineering ethics, for example, emerged much earlier. As noted by Carl Mitcham (2015), this relatively early emergence of engineering ethics has been crucial for the particular ideals of ethical responsibility that are predominant in engineering today. In the USA, as a civilian profession, engineering arose out of the military and this 'military ethos of obedience to authority exercised a formative influence on engineering conceptions of responsibility' (p. 50). Initially engineers were trained in the military as regimented national corps with a duty to defend and an ethos of obedience to authority. While professional engineering schools were eventually established and specialisations emerged, 'engineers remained duty-bound to obey their employers, whether a non-military branch of government or a private corporation' (p. 51). They were thus subject to employers' ideas and standards of what was considered to be right and wrong. However, in the 1960s, when activist movements spurred the emergence of CSR frameworks, they also called attention to tensions between national and corporate interests on the one hand and public safety, health, and welfare on the other. The intense fears of atomic warfare at the time demonstrated and rendered plain the radically different interests of the nation, corporations, and the general public. This period inspired a new code of ethics, which in later versions lists as its first fundamental canon that 'engineers shall hold paramount the safety, health and welfare of the public' (p. 54). As such, an engineer's loyalty was no longer to an authority like the military or a corporation but rather to the general public, ensuring engineering practices serve the public good.

In recent decades, professional ethics for engineers has centred on 'preventive ethics' (Harris et al. 2013, p. 11), commonly expressed in rules oriented towards the prevention of professional malpractice, misconduct, and harm to the public. The rules are often phrased as prohibitions, using clear negative wording. For example, in the Code of Ethics of the National Society of Professional Engineers (NSPE), it states that 'engineers shall not reveal facts, data or information without the prior consent of the client or employer except as authorized by law or this Code'. This negative character of the code not only makes it easier to enforce, as it renders violations clear and specific, but also supports the notion that 'before engineers have an obligation to do good, they have an obligation to do no harm' (Harris et al. 2013, pp. 12–13). Scholars have noted how these negative obligations afford engineering ethics a markedly conservative and stultifying ethos that fails to encourage engineers 'to question or contest why engineering is being used to support particular ends' (Smith and Lucena 2021). It also marginalises and deprioritises 'what can be called "aspirational ethics", namely the use of professional knowledge to promote the human good' (Harris 2008, p. 154). Placing value on compliance and obedience, the rules present moral actors as individual decision-makers who are, first and foremost, rule-followers (Stovall 2011; Vanderburg 1995). To illustrate the implications of any negligence or misjudgement, case studies of accidents and disasters are used in the teaching of engineering ethics, such as the Deepwater Horizon tragedy in the Gulf of Mexico or, as I experienced during my fieldwork, a recent gas explosion in Firestone, Colorado. These case studies offer forceful evidence of what can happen if an engineer strays from what is deemed right and wrong.

These cases of accidents and disasters acquire trajectories that span and interconnect realms of engineers with government, corporations, and publics. They become important pedagogical tools for the industry as it seeks to learn from the past and improve practices for the future. Casting risk avoidance as a virtue, the combination of the codes of ethics with the detailed case studies highlights how the industry frames its operations in terms of ethical sensibilities. Yet, as noted by Deborah Johnson, 'engineers are not required to explain or justify their behavior to publics until something goes wrong or until engineers—in the act of whistleblowing—bring something to the attention of a public' (2017, p. 96). It is in these moments that accountability practices become public. When a disaster occurs, it is government agencies that are held accountable for what happened rather than engineers (Johnson 2017). Engineers are usually included in the teams that report to the government agency, but they are not considered responsible for the health, safety, and welfare of the public. However, when an engineer blows the whistle on a threat to the public, his commitment to the public becomes strikingly visible. It is in these situations that the engineer renders apparent that he recognises that he has a responsibility that goes beyond the demands of his employer or client and beyond his own interest. It is in these situations that he becomes celebrated for his courage and heroism. The stakes are high as 'engineers who blow the whistle are often seen as heroes [while] those who stay silent are rarely held to account' (Johnson 2017, p. 95). It is in whistleblowing that the individual engineer breaks ranks and publically affirms not just his obedience and loyalty to his profession but also the rightness in the codes of ethics. As such, the whistleblower emerges as a 'moral exemplar' (Humphrey 1997) of individual decision-making, affirming his loyalty and obedience to the normative regime of engineering ethics.

As a regime of ethics, these professional codes highlight the range of possibilities that can be pursued by individual employees when finding themselves entangled in difficult and challenging work situations. With its conservative ethos grounded in prohibitions and admonitions, it can assist engineers to be part of a 'modular' capitalism that benefits from a labour force's obedience and loyalty. In an industry where offshore drilling rigs, travelling through international waters, rely on multinational teams to come together at short notice and where onshore operations demand flexible and transient crews, the clear declarations of right and wrong in the formal rules and codes are conducive to advancing industry and worker interests. The implicit identification of the abstracted individual as an autonomous and isolated moral actor further supports a self-cultivation that is apt for this sprawling and constantly re-configuring sector. As a regime of ethics that undergirds the professional practices of many in the oil and gas industry, the narrow and circumscribed 'microethical' focus (Herkert 2005) can be seen to bolster the industry's corporate practices and visions of flourishing.

Corporate social responsibility frameworks and engineering ethics offer insights into some of the distinctive regimes of reasoning and practice that inform the conjoining of hydrocarbons with ethical sensibilities. However, if we attend only to these particular regimes of ethics characterised by their official codes and predefined aims, the emerging moral worlds can seem noticeably static and monolithic. Industry interests and corporate practices may appear unchallenged, perhaps even unchallengeable, across multiple scales ranging from individual to corporate action. In order to explore and recognise the more personal and potentially idiosyncratic ways in which industry actors make sense of their worlds and their unique contribution *as* moral actors, I suggest we also need to consider regimes of ethics that move beyond formal declarations of right and wrong.

Oil, God and Liberty

In my ethnographic research in Colorado, I have come to know rig hands, mud engineers, landmen, geo scientists, capital providers, investment bankers, executives, and many others. I have had a temporary office within a drilling company, which has afforded me opportunities to be part of daily company life, ranging from on-site drilling operations and investor presentations to industry events and barbeques. I have listened to countless unprompted and often emotional accounts of people's 'industry pride', to such a degree that I see these as amounting to a distinct regime of ethics that is shared, yet idiosyncratic, in its articulation of value. These accounts echo similar themes, transcending people's individual positions and specific company within the industry. While I had come to almost anticipate these unprompted accounts of 'oil as a force for good', I was still surprised when a rancher in 2019 in the heart of Colorado's 'oil country' voiced it too.

Norm, as I will refer to him, was a third-generation rancher who ran about 1000 cattle on the family ranch which had been founded by his grandfather in 1888. His grandfather started the ranch with 110 acres and Norm had been able to build it up to 38,000 acres. It extended as far as the eye could see, continuing to the horizon across the plateau in almost all directions. As we drove on the dirt roads across his property, he showed me places that held distinct memories from his childhood: an almost hidden ditch amidst the sagebrush bushes where he had fallen off his first horse and an elevated flat hill where his grandfather had built basic wind turbines on wooden frames. Describing just how attached he was to this place that anchored so many memories and so much knowledge built up over the years, he said, '131 years my family has been here. I'm not going to go anywhere. I'm 61 years old. My grandparents died here. My parents died here. I will die here'. With a piercing commitment to honour the promises he made to his father to continue the family ranch, he recounted some tough times: when hailstorms and blizzards cost cattle lives, when diseases and epidemics raged, and when meat prices dropped so low that it almost put an end to the ranch. He lamented what he saw as a lax work ethic among youth today, describing how difficult it was to get good workers and scoffing at their wishes for 'weekends off' and 'vacation time'. While he inspected some of the cattle, he reminisced, 'My dad just worked hard. I don't think they ever took a vacation. We worked from sunup to sundown. That was just how it was. That was what everybody had to do to survive. You had to work to live. It was never a job. It was a lifestyle'. The pressure to bring the cattle through the season was immense as, like other ranchers in the region, they worked on borrowed money. They borrowed in the spring and then paid back when they sold their cattle in the autumn. Sometimes they had good years, at other times bad. Ranching was demanding and fundamentally unpredictable, with pressing questions often centring on money. As we crested a hilltop, a drilling rig and some tank batteries appeared in the distance. Norm looked at me and said, 'Dad always thought it'd be nice to get some extra money. And then this started'.

Today Norm is deeply involved in the oil and gas industry. With more than 800 wells on his property and with new ones still being drilled, it has become one of the largest oil and gas operations in the state. In addition to receiving royalty payments on the produced hydrocarbons, he also saw it as an opportunity to partner with the industry and run all operations except for the actual drilling. This has turned into four major companies, owned and run by himself and his son. Employing more than 1200 people, these companies do everything from water hauling to road building, from well pad construction to waste disposal. The oil and gas business now dominates their lives, especially as they have become involved in operations across the USA. One day, as we sat chatting in their enormous barn, which has been turned into a luxurious private bar complete with neon signs, arcade machines, pool table, and vintage cars, Norm and his son both agreed that they had never envisioned being able to make this kind of money. Norm has now become a major charitable donor in the area, supporting initiatives from the local food bank to women's shelters. But rather than setting these up as formal CSR activities, Norm did not want the formalities and paperwork. 'I write a cheque and support causes that matter to me, causes that are being led by good people'. Having grown up with the uncertainties of ranching, this industry actor felt that oil and gas had not only safeguarded the ranch and its future but also enabled him to donate generously to causes he supported.

His gratitude for what the oil and gas industry had given him was deeply felt. He saw his riches as not merely a question of 'having done the right thing at the right time'; nor was it just about having been determined and hard working. For him, oil and gas were blessings bestowed by God. As I have detailed elsewhere (2019), many of my interlocutors held Christian-inspired outlooks. As I was once told by a seasoned drilling engineer, 'You either come *with* Christ or you come *to* Christ in this industry'. Given the broad geographic overlap of the so-called Bible belt with drilling sites, Christianity in its various forms was often a more or less explicit referent in daily life, both within and beyond company spaces. For Norm, hydrocarbons were gifts that brought life and prosperity to all of humankind. While it was clear that he himself had enjoyed immense prosperity from oil and gas, it was less clear how these resources had enriched the lives of others, beyond the recipients of his philanthropy, not just materially but also spiritually. In what ways were oil and gas gifts from God? Conversations about God were often woven seamlessly into conversations about 'energy independence', with Norm emphasising the importance of the USA becoming independent from other countries in its energy supply. As gifts from God, oil and gas were there to be developed to provide the electricity for houses and the fuel for trucks; they were there to relieve people of the cold in the winter and the heat in the summer. For Norm, developing US oil and gas meant that the country could ideally be self-reliant for its energy and have 'unfettered' foreign policy relations with nations such as Russia, Saudi Arabia, and others. Norm reasoned that by not fighting over oil and, instead, relying on domestic energy production, there would be less motivation for wars and many conflicts could be avoided. As a God-created purveyor of peace and prosperity, hydrocarbons were for Norm an unquestioned good.

While Norm saw oil and gas as a blessing, many people saw it differently. He had recently experienced a clash with a local politician. The encounter was for him striking and he would return to it, recounting it with what seemed like sharp clarity. It was a moment that constituted a confrontational situation in which the very terms of ethical activity were articulated and intensified. Rather than entailing a 'moral breakdown' (Zigon 2007; see also Robbins 2004) in which self-questioning, doubt, and struggle are part of the experience of 'moral torment' (Zigon 2007, p. 142), the situation rendered clear and explicit some of the values that Norm held. He recounted to me how he had given a statement in support of oil and gas production in the state. Once he had finished his statement, the politician had responded disapprovingly, 'You just want the money. You are greedy and just want to get as much money as you can. Because that's all you care about! Money!' According to Norm, he had then looked the politician in the eye and replied, 'Yes, you are so right! That's indeed all I care about. I couldn't care less about the environment, about the land, about the rivers, about the air. I just want money!' Along with many others present, the politician had apparently stared at him with an expression that conveyed seeming disbelief that this man really stood there, in front of an audience, admitting to his greed. But Norm had continued:

> Everybody wants a cleaner planet—we all do. Our kids live here, we live here. It's not like we live separately. Why do you think I run all these businesses? I saw an opportunity to make money, yes. But I also saw that running these businesses was the *only* way I could truly protect our environment. I care about this place so much more than anyone else. This ranch has been a really pristine ranch for a long time. We never overgrazed it. Always very careful in how we managed it. When the oil and gas came along, we wanted to make sure they didn't make a mess of it. We wouldn't let them make a mess here. Nobody takes care of your home like you do! This land means everything to me.

That this rancher-turned-oilman self-identified as a libertarian and had been awarded the Independence Institute's annual award in recognition of his charitable support for its activities underscores how he saw the conjoining of oil and gas with ranching through the prism of not only energy independence but also individual freedom.

Rather than offering blanket advocacy for the industry, however, he saw his own control over operations as paramount. Distancing himself from large corporations, top-down management, and executive greed, he valued liberty as a core principle, emphasising the necessity of freedom of choice and individual judgement. While, in his case, it led to his involvement in oil and gas operations, he was also horrified and deeply critical of so-called low-end operations. Indeed, for him, such poor practices reaffirmed the importance of individual control when engaging with this industry. As he commented, 'There are some low end companies out there that have made messes on ranchers and farmers. We have seen some farms they have just made a mess out of. If my Dad would have seen this on our place, he would have shot me! When the oil price was high, some people just got stupid!' While he felt he had been accused of 'getting stupid' in his presumed greed for money, he deflected the accusations back onto others, in particular the executives of these 'low-end' companies and the people leasing their land to them. For Norm, their reverence for the environment was eclipsed by their pursuit of profit, wanting to extract as much wealth as possible from the ground while leaving behind oil spills and open wastewater pits. When I highlighted how his substantial acreage gave him a much stronger negotiating position with the producers than others would experience, he just nodded and said, 'I have been fortunate'. It was this 'fortune' that had enabled him to exercise the individual control that he valued and that he regarded as fundamental to any involvement with the oil and gas industry. Through this, he had come to share and take part in promotion of the industry's moral vision that the production of oil and gas was 'a force for good' which 'improved people's lives'. It had enabled him to deliver on the promise to his father while making what he saw as a positive contribution to the lives of others. But he was never to be a 'company man'.

While Norm's ethical sensibilities firmed up and offered advocacy for industry practices, it also led to disruption and the emergence of new companies directed by different moral visions. He distanced himself from 'Big Oil' and rejoiced in local control. He lent support to those who were keen to pursue a similarly entrepreneurial path and would help with the eradication of 'low-end' companies. His 'industry pride' encouraged greater production of oil and gas, while also insisting on more local ways for this to happen.

Concluding Thoughts

While industry actors may share the same moral vision that is put forth so vocally by oil and gas companies, their regimes of ethics and underlying values can differ greatly. From the CSR ethical accounting regimes that materialise virtues of charity and generosity, through the professional codes of engineering ethics that enshrine individuals' obedience and loyalty, to an industry actor's emphasis on libertarian values, a moral vision that sees the production of oil and gas as 'a force for good' can thus emerge from radically different regimes of ethics. If focusing on moral visions without considering the regimes of ethics through which such visions are articulated, we risk overlooking the great commonalities and differences in ethical sensibilities, simplifying the reasoning and practices that flourish and sustain them.

When studying industries in general, and the oil and gas industry in particular, it is important to avoid such analytical simplification as it can lead to the industry's moral visions appearing monolithic, so solid and so uniform, as to overshadow any potential alternatives. It can create moral worlds that seem devoid of fragility and contestation, emerging as firm and inevitable features of 'ethical capitalism'. To do so would not only be to treat companies as black boxes of profit maximisation and employees as their mere mouthpieces, collectively superior at demonstrating their moral visions. It would also be to turn the politics of inequality, with which the oil and gas industry is so closely associated, into an epistemological truism: How could we ever come to know the world as any different? It would create conditions of knowledge in such a way that moral worlds cannot surprise and cannot be contested. While some might find comfort in 'the image of the world offered by social sciences...[as] one of misery, of suffering, of injustice' (Stoczkowski 2008, p. 348), we would fail to recognise what is demonstrated and rendered visible in each articulation of a moral vision. It is by attending to energy ethics as involving multiple co-existing regimes of ethics, and by being critical of our own moral presuppositions, that we can respect the epistemological grounds for our work and ensure its political potential to see new worlds.

Acknowledgements This project has received funding from the European Research Council (ERC) under the European Union's Horizon 2020 research and innovation programme under grant agreement no. 715146. I also gratefully acknowledge the funding I have received to carry out this research from the Leverhulme Trust (ECF-2013-177) and the British Academy (EN150010). Over the years of researching the oil and gas industry in Colorado, I have become indebted to many people. I would especially like to thank those of you who have opened doors, shared with me so generously, and invited me into your lives. I would also like to thank friends and colleagues, in particular my Energy Ethics research team and the larger Centre for Energy Ethics community at the University of St Andrews. All of you have inspired, supported, and challenged me along the way. Any shortcomings, however, remain entirely my own.

References

Allahyari, R. A. (2000). *Visions of charity: volunteer workers and moral community*. Berkeley: University of California Press.

Alnuaim, S. (2019). Corporate social responsibility: a source of industry pride. *Journal of Petroleum Technology*, July, 10–11.

Anderson, C. L., & Bieniaszewska, R. B. (2005). The role of corporate social responsibility in an oil company's expansion into new territories. *Corporate Social Responsibility and Environmental Management, 12*(1), 1–9.

Appel, H. (2012). Offshore work: oil, modularity, and the how of capitalism in Equatorial Guinea. *American Ethnologist, 39*(4), 692–709.

Appel, H., Mason, A., & Watts, M. (2015). Introduction: oil talk. In H. Appel, A. Mason, & M. Watts (Eds.), *Subterranean estates: life worlds of oil and gas* (pp. 1–26). Cornell University Press.

Barry, A. (2004). Ethical capitalism. In W. Larner & W. Waters (Eds.), *Global governmentality: Governing international spaces* (pp. 195–211). London: Routledge.

Beck, U. (2006). Risk society revisited: theory, politics and research programmes. In J. F. Cosgrave (Ed.), *The sociology of risk and gambling reader* (pp. 61–83). London: Taylor & Francis.

Behrends, A., Reyna, S., & Schlee G. (Eds.) (2011). *Crude domination: an anthropology of oil.* Oxford: Berghahn.

Boyer, D. (2014). Energopower: an introduction. *Anthropological Quarterly, 87*(2), 309–333.

Cross, J. (2011). Detachment as a corporate ethic: materializing CSR in the diamond supply chain. *Focaal, 60*, 34–46.

Cross, J. (2014). The coming of the corporate gift. *Theory, Culture & Society, 31*(2–3), 121–145.

De George, R. T. (1996). The myth of corporate social responsibility: Ethics and international business. In J. W. Houck & O. F. Williams (Eds.), *Is the good corporation dead?: social responsibility in a global economy* (pp. 17–36). London: Rowman & Littlefield.

De Roeck, K., & Delobbe, N. (2012). Do environmental CSR initiatives serve organizations' legitimacy in the oil industry? Exploring employees' reactions through organizational identification theory. *Journal of Business Ethics, 110*(4), 397–412.

Dolan, C. S. (2010). Virtual moralities: The mainstreaming of Fairtrade in Kenyan tea fields. *Geoforum, 41*(1), 33–43.

Edoho, F. M. (2008). Oil transnational corporations: corporate social responsibility and environmental sustainability. *Corporate Social Responsibility and Environmental Management, 15*(4), 210–222.

Fatma, M., Khan, I., & Rahman, Z. (2018). Striving for legitimacy through CSR: an exploration of employees responses in controversial industry sector. *Social Responsibility Journal* 15. https://doi.org/10.1108/SRJ-07-2017-0116.

Frynas, J. G. (2005). The false developmental promise of corporate social responsibility: evidence from multinational oil companies. *International Affairs, 81*(3), 581–598.

García-Rodríguez, F. J.,García-Rodríguez, J. L., Castilla-Gutiérrez, C., & Major, S. A. (2013). Corporate social responsibility of oil companies in developing countries: from altruism to business strategy. *Corporate Social Responsibility and Environmental Management, 20*(6), 371–384.

Gardner, K. (2015). Chevron's gift of CSR: moral economies of connection and disconnection in a transnational Bangladeshi village. *Economy and Society, 44*(4), 495–518.

Gardner, K., Ahmed, Z., Bashir, F., & Rana, M. (2012). Elusive partnerships: gas extraction and CSR in Bangladesh. *Resources Policy, 37*(2), 168–174.

Harris, C. E. (2008). The good engineer: Giving virtue its due in engineering ethics. *Science and Engineering Ethics, 14*, 153–164.

Harris, C. E., Pritchard, M. S., & Rabins, M. J. (2013). *Engineering ethics: concepts and cases.* Belmont, CA.: Cengage Learning.

Herkert, J. R. (2005). Ways of thinking about and teaching ethical problem solving: Microethics and macroethics in engineering. *Science and Engineering Ethics, 11*(3), 373–385.

High, M. M. (2018). A question of ethics: the creative orthodoxy of Buddhist monks in the Mongolian gold rush. *Ethnos, 83*(1), 80–99.

High, M. M. (2019). Projects of devotion: energy exploration and moral ambition in the cosmoeconomy of oil and gas in the Western United States. *Journal of the Royal Anthropological Institute, 25*(S1), 29–46.

Huber, M. T. (2013). *Lifeblood: oil, freedom, and the forces of capital*. Minneapolis: University of Minnesota Press.

Humphrey, C. (1997). Exemplars and rules. In S. Howell (Ed.), *The ethnography of moralities* (pp. 25–47). London: Taylor and Francis.

Jaffe, D., & Howard, P. H. (2010). Corporate cooptation of organic and fair trade standards. *Agriculture and Human Values, 27*(4), 387–399.

Jenkins, H. (2004). Corporate social responsibility and the mining industry: conflicts and constructs. *Corporate Social Responsibility and Environmental Management, 11*(1), 23–34.

Johnson, D. G. (2017). Rethinking the social responsibilities of engineers as a form of accountability. In D. P. Michelfelder, B. Newberry, & Q. Zhu (Eds.), *Philosophy and Engineering* (pp. 85–98). Cham, Switzerland: Springer.

Kirsch, S. (2014). *Mining capitalism: the relationship between corporations and their critics*. University of California Press.

Knudsen, S., Rajak, D., Lange, S., & Hugøy, I. (2020). Bringing the state back in. *Focaal, 88*(1), 1–21.

Lakoff, A., & Collier, S. J. (2004). Ethics and the anthropology of modern reason. *Anthropological Theory, 4*(4), 419–434.

Lambek, M. (2018). On the immanence of ethics. In C. Mattingly, R. Dyring, M. Louw, & T. S. Wentzer (Eds.), *Moral engines: exploring the ethical drives in human life* (pp. 137–54). Oxford: Berghahn.

Lord, A., & Rest, M. (2021). Nepal's water, the people's investment? Hydropolitical volumes and speculative refrains. In T. Loloum, S. Abram, & N. Ortar (Eds.), *Ethnographies of power: a political anthropology of energy* (pp. 81–108). Oxford: Berghanh.

Mahmood, S. (2003). Ethical formation and politics of individual autonomy in contemporary Egypt. *Social Research: An International Quarterly, 70*(3), 837–866.

Makambura, A. A. (2018). *Health safety and environment, HSE in the oil and gas industry*. Conference Proceedings from the International Conference on Petroleum Engineering, August 6–7, Dubai, USE.

Mattingly, C. (2012). Two virtue ethics and the anthropology of morality. *Anthropological Theory, 12*(2), 161–184.

Mattingly, C., & Throop, J. (2018). The anthropology of ethics and morality. *Annual Review of Anthropology, 47*, 475–492.

Mitcham, C. (2015). Ethics is not enough: from professionalism to the political philosophy of engineering. In S. S. Sundar (Ed.), *Contemporary ethical issues in engineering* (pp. 48–80). Hershey, PA: IGI Global.

Mitchell, T. (2009). Carbon democracy. *Economy and Society, 38*(3), 399–432.

Muehlebach, A. (2012). *The moral neoliberal: welfare and citizenship in Italy*. University of Chicago Press.

Rajak, D. (2011a). *In good company: an anatomy of corporate social responsibility*. Stanford University Press.

Rajak, D. (2011b). Theatres of virtue: Collaboration, consensus, and the social life of corporate social responsibility. *Focaal, 60*, 9–20.

Robbins, J. (2004). *Becoming sinners: Christianity and moral torment in a Papua New Guinea society*. University of California Press.

Robbins, J. (2013). Monism, pluralism, and the structure of value relations: A Dumontian contribution to the contemporary study of value. *HAU: Journal of Ethnographic Theory, 3*(1), 99–115.

Rose, N. (1998). *Inventing our selves: psychology, power and personhood*. Cambridge: Cambridge University Press.

Sawyer, S. (2004). *Crude chronicles: indigenous politics, multinational oil, and neoliberalism in Ecuador*. Duke University Press.

Shever, E. (2010). Engendering the company: corporate personhood and the "face" of an oil company in metropolitan Buenos Aires. *PoLAR: Political and Legal Anthropology Review, 33*(1), 26–46.

Shever, E. (2012). *Resources for reform: oil and neoliberalism in Argentina*. Stanford University Press.

Smith, J. M. (2019a). Boom to bust, ashes to (coal) dust: the contested ethics of energy exchanges in a declining US coal market. *Journal of the Royal Anthropological Institute, 25*(S1): 91–107.

Smith, J. M. (2019b). The ethics of material provisioning: insiders' views of work in the extractive industries. *The Extractive Industries and Society, 6*, 807–814.

Smith, J. M., & Lucena, J. C. (2021). Ch. 49: Socially responsible engineering. In D. Michelfelder & N. Doorn (Eds.), *Routledge Handbook of Philosophy of Engineering* (pp. 661–673). New York: Routledge.

Stirrat, R. L., & Henkel, H. (1997). The development gift: the problem of reciprocity in the NGO world. *The Annals of the American Academy of Political and Social Science, 554*(1), 66–80.

Stoczkowski, W. (2008). The 'fourth aim' of anthropology: Between knowledge and ethics. *Anthropological Theory, 8*(4), 345–356.

Stovall, P. (2011). Professional virtue and professional self-awareness: A case study in engineering ethics. *Science and engineering ethics, 17*(1), 109–132.

Strathern, M. (1996). From improvement to enhancement: an anthropological comment on the audit culture. *Cambridge Anthropology, 19*(3), 1–21.

Strauss, S., Rupp, S., & Love, T. (Eds.) (2013). *Cultures of energy: power, practices, technologies*. Left Coast Press.

Szeman, I. (2019). *On petrocultures: globalization, culture, and energy*. Morgantown: West Virginia University Press.

Vanderburg, W. H. (1995). Preventive engineering: strategy for dealing with negative social and environmental implications of technology. *Journal of Professional Issues in Engineering Education and Practice, 121*(3), 155–160.

von Schnitzler, A. (2013). Traveling technologies: infrastructure, ethical regimes, and the materiality of politics in South Africa. *Cultural Anthropology, 28*(4), 670–693.

Welker, M. (2014). *Enacting the corporation: an American mining firm in post-authoritarian Indonesia*. University of California Press.

Wentzer, T. S., & Mattingly, C. (2018). Toward a new humanism: An approach from philosophical anthropology. *HAU: Journal of Ethnographic Theory, 8*(1–2), 144–157.

Weszkalnys, G. (2016). A doubtful hope: resource affect in a future oil economy. *Journal of the Royal Anthropological Institute, 22*(S1), 127–146.

Weszkalnys, G., & Richardson, T. (2014). Resource materialities: new anthropological perspectives on natural resource environments: introduction. *Anthropological Quarterly, 87*(1), 5–30.

Zigon, J. (2007). Moral breakdown and the ethical demand: a theoretical framework for an anthropology of moralities. *Anthropological Theory, 7*(2), 131–150.

CHAPTER 32

Competing Responsibilities and the Ethics of Care in Young People's Engagements with Digital Mental Health

Responsibility

Susanna Trnka

In recent years, questions of how to effectively harness digital technologies for promoting mental and physical wellbeing have become a hotbed of governmental, corporate, and social debate. Across many nations, government health campaigns increasingly focus on encouraging the development of 'informed patients' who employ digital resources to engage in self-care. Australia, for example, now has a 'digital mental health gateway', directing users through a myriad of online counselling services. USAID has created 'global digital health trackers' to provide structure and organisation to ever-proliferating online health resources, while the European Commission invests in streamlining 'digital tools for citizen empowerment' by establishing a 'digital single market' (European Commission 2018).

Enhancing patients' capacities for personal responsibility and self-care is at the forefront of many digital health endeavours. Arguably, however, while 'self-care' often involves the promotion of self-responsibility, it simultaneously promotes other modes of ethical engagement, such as care for, or from, (known and unknown) others and concerns over states', societies', and corporations' responsibilities for ensuring mental wellbeing. Indeed, the broader literature

S. Trnka (✉)
University of Auckland, Auckland, New Zealand
e-mail: s.trnka@auckland.ac.nz

M. H. Bruun et al. (eds.), *The Palgrave Handbook of the Anthropology of Technology*, https://doi.org/10.1007/978-981-16-7084-8_32

on responsibility suggests that despite privileging personal responsibility, advanced liberal societies create a fertile and contested ground upon which multiple, 'competing responsibilities' flourish (Trnka and Trundle 2014; see also Cook 2016; Gobby et al. 2018). Digital technologies add additional layers to how responsibility is enacted, enabling new forms of seemingly continuous, person-person and person-technology relations and consequently refracting users' sense of where agency lies, be it within themselves, in their relations with (human) others, or in technologies themselves. Drawing on a case study of young New Zealanders' digital technology use, this chapter examines how a newly emerging ethics of care recasts understandings and enactment of responsibility for mental wellbeing.

RESPONSIBILISATION AND BEYOND

Contemporary analyses of responsibility, within anthropology and more broadly, largely focus on examining the role of increased self-responsibility within modern governmentality.[1] Scholars have documented the growing emphasis on personal responsibility across diverse geographic settings and social phenomena, including leisure, health, sports, education, and environmental activism (Bretherton et al. 2016; Fullagar 2007; Lupton and Smith 2018; Rawolle et al. 2017; Thörn and Svenberg 2016). As this literature attests, one of the key mechanisms of neoliberal or advanced liberal forms of governance is the divestiture of obligations from the state onto independent, self-managing, and self-empowered subjects, a process known as *responsibilisation*.

The term 'responsibilisation' was coined by Nikolas Rose (2006) and emerged from a broader project examining how the promotion of neoliberal ideals since the 1970s initiated the emergence of new kinds of state-citizen relations. According to Peter Miller and Rose (2008), the change that took place

> entailed the deployment of new technologies of governing from the center through powerful means of governing at a distance: these appear to enhance the autonomy of zones, persons, entities, but enwrapped them in new forms of regulation—audits, budgets, standards, risk management, targets ... It entailed a new conception of the subjects to be governed: that these would be autonomous and responsible individuals, freely choosing how to behave and act. We saw the emergence of novel strategies of activation and responsibilization ... We saw the birth of a new ethic of the ... responsible, autonomous individual obliged to be free. (p. 18)

One area where the constitution of responsibilised subjects is perhaps most visible is healthcare as patients are incentivised to engage in an increasing array of activities to maintain or improve their mental and physical wellbeing. Patient-led groups compose research agendas and youth and adults self-diagnose and investigate suspected illnesses online (Dumit 2012; Epstein 1998; Lupton 2019). New technological 'fixes' (Weinberg 1966) are central to these strategies: we are expected to become responsible patients by using technologies such as peak flow metres to check our respiratory levels (Trnka 2017), making decisions about whether to undergo genetic testing for diseases such as breast cancer (Gibbon 2006), or digitally monitoring our vital statistics (Lupton 2019). While societies' hopes of finding solutions to health problems embrace a range of technologies (DelVecchio Good 2001), there is particular emphasis on digital technologies for promoting self-responsibility; the 'will to app', as Albury et al. (2019) phrase it, often prevails in contexts where patient responsibilisation is a governmental, corporate, and patient-driven objective.

Responsibility, however, takes a multitude of forms and directionalities. The autonomous, responsibilised subject idealised by neoliberal rhetoric is engaged in a range of interdependencies that exist between friends or within families, at schools and workplaces, with respect to the environment, the state, companies, and local or global communities (Trnka and Trundle 2017, p. 10). Some of these forms of responsibility align with neoliberal ideals and may promote a sense of individual empowerment, while others involve obligations and needs that reinforce our inherent inter-relationality.

Numerous studies have evoked the multiplicity of responsibilities at play even when the forces of responsibilisation are at their strongest, such as when public health campaigns stressing 'responsible' contraception are renegotiated by women who consider pregnancy 'a valuable gift from God' (Fordyce 2012, p. 124), or principals facing school reforms promoting 'competitive performativity' insist instead on foregrounding 'the profession's long-standing responsibility for and commitment to equality and the public good' (Gobby et al. 2018, pp. 159–160). One analytical avenue for examining responsibilities' multiplicities is James Laidlaw's conceptualisation of responsibility as diffused across networks. Laidlaw (2010, p. 150) argues that even though responsibility is often *rhetorically* portrayed as individualised, in actual practice, even in contexts where 'there is a fairly explicit individualist ideology' such as British Common Law, responsibility is frequently recognised as 'distributed among persons and groups in various ways'. Inspired by Actor Network Theory (ANT), Laidlaw (2010) suggests that the various facets of attributing responsibility for an action—namely, interpretations of cause, intention, state of mind, and (sufficient or insufficient) response by the agents thought to be involved—'need not coincide within the same individual, or for that matter the same collectivity. They may be distributed among the entities involved in a network or a chain of events' (p. 150). Laidlaw gives various illustrative examples, from Azande attributions of witchcraft to Western insurance policies that redistribute obligation across collectivities, demonstrating how responsibility is not always viewed as vested entirely within a single actor.

As shown by these and other works, including a growing number focused specifically on digital technology use, responsibilities can reverberate and crisscross, both within actors and across collectivities and networks, creating intricate geographies of obligation, care, and inter-relationality (Akrich 1992; Mol et al. 2010; Oudshoorn 2011; Schwennesen 2017). Responsibility is, moreover, not only multiple and sometimes diffuse, but there are also differences in *kind*, such as personal versus institutional responsibility (my responsibility to my students is shaped by but also differs from that of the educational institution that employs me). In order better to grasp such differences in kind analytically, it is useful to consider personal, inter-personal, and state/corporate responsibilities in turn.

Catherine Trundle and I (Trnka and Trundle 2014, 2017) address both the multiplicity and variability in kinds through the three-faceted model of 'competing responsibilities' which locates personal responsibility as one of three types of responsibility, alongside inter-personal care for the Other and the collective responsibilities of states and corporations. The competing responsibilities model, moreover, highlights personal responsibility as including, but not entirely characterised by, responsibilisation, to indicate how personal responsibility itself may be variously configured.

While personal responsibility is a hallmark of advanced liberalism, an historical and cultural emphasis on 'the care of the self' clearly pre-dates contemporary governmentality (Foucault 1997; Reiser 1985). In his work on ancient Greek and Roman society, Foucault (1990) examined projects of self-realisation, in particular the 'arts of existence':

> those intentional and voluntary actions by which men not only set themselves rules of conduct, but also seek to transform themselves, to change themselves in their singular being, and to make their life into an oeuvre that carries certain aesthetic values and meets certain stylistic criteria. (pp. 10–11)

Other scholars note similar activities in other contexts, for example, the intensive self-cultivation and emphasis on personal responsibility integral to religious identity within Protestant Christianity, Thervāda Buddhism, and Russian Orthodoxy (Carrithers 1985; Zigon 2010).

One of the self-improvement activities Foucault (1997) examines in depth is self-reflective letter writing which involved an accounting of mundane daily practices, 'a whole set of meticulous notations on the body, health, physical sensations, regimen and feelings [that] shows the extreme vigilance of an attention that is intensely focused on oneself' (p. 220; also Foucault 1988). Well before the rise of advanced liberalism, letter writing was 'a question of both constituting oneself as an "inspector of oneself," and hence of gauging the common faults, and of activating the rules of behaviour that one must always bear in mind' (Foucault 1997, p. 220). Foucault, moreover, noted the concern citizens had with self-cultivation as a prerequisite for appropriate civic participation; here, honing self-responsibility was not a route towards individualism but towards increased inter-relationality. Personal responsibility can thus be multiple, that is, part of moves towards responsibilisation *and* something that stands outside or even counter to it (cf. Trnka 2017). Personal responsibility remains, however, only one facet of how responsibility is enacted and envisioned.

A second kind of responsibility is care for the Other or 'recognition and action motivated by one's commitment to the welfare of the Other' (Trnka and Trundle 2017, p. 11). Responsibility has long been envisioned to include not only agency and ownership of one's actions, but also responsiveness and answerability to others (cf. Kelty 2008; Laidlaw 2010). While there is no singular definition of what 'care' entails, it frequently involves being responsible for recognising and responding to another's needs (Gilligan 1982; Martin et al. 2015; Mol 2008). It is an active engagement that may involve negotiating power or even wresting away control from the Other as care relations are not always inherently equal but allow for varying degrees of dependence (Puig de la Bellacasa 2011; Mol 2008).

To different extents, one is not only a provider, but also a recipient of acts of care. While the rhetoric of advanced liberal responsibilisation downplays the importance of such inter-relations, to be a competent, self-cultivating subject is often predicated upon the activities undertaken on behalf of oneself by others (Trnka 2017; cf. Danholt and Langstrup 2012). Individualism arguably *requires* being supported by a nexus of inter-personal relationships, be they familial, pedagogical (i.e. mentor-student), or other intimate ties. This can be the case even when using digital (or other) technologies specifically designed to automate care and enhance personal responsibility, given the frequent need to adjust, side-line, or 'repair' systems and programmes (Schwennesen 2019) in ways that may in fact intensify inter-personal relations of care between medical professionals and patients (Langstrup and Winthereik 2008; Pols 2010) or among patients and family members (Mort et al. 2013; Weiner and Will 2018).

The third and final facet of competing responsibilities is larger, collective modes of obligation, often encapsulated in social contract ideologies. Ideas of 'responsible states' and 'responsible citizens' are underpinned by ideologies that highlight exchanges and reciprocities between different parties. Often deeply rooted, they are also historically malleable as understandings of the rights and obligations of citizens and states shift over time (McKeon 1957; also Kelty 2008). Such ideologies, moreover, involve not only citizen-state relations but also citizen-corporation relations, since corporations are increasingly held accountable not only for their profitability but also their morality, as reflected by the growth of corporate social responsibility (CSR) programmes promoting activities that ostensibly benefit the wider public (Smith 2017; Welker 2013). Through CSR, corporations take on responsibilities either divested or never carried out by the state, constituting themselves as a third participant in reciprocal exchanges with community groups (Smith 2017).

Not only is there a variety of kinds of responsibilities but there is also diversity in how people respond to calls to take up duties and obligations, be it through cultivating greater personal responsibility, inciting acts of 'irresponsibilisation' (Hunt 2003), engaging in other modes of reasoning (Sharon 2015), or recasting accountability and obligation onto others, such as the state, corporations, or other collectivities. Often they may find themselves pulled in various directions as a 'multiplicity of conceptions' of appropriate behaviour and 'the "competing modes of responsibility" [they entail] … produce affordances, tensions, paradoxes and counter-conducts in responses to being held responsible' (Gobby et al. 2018, p. 162). Examinations of responsibility, including personal responsibility, thus cannot restrict themselves to considering how inculcating self-responsibility acts as a facet of governing at a distance, no matter how prevalent this dynamic may be, as even the most direct attempts at fostering independent, self-empowered, responsibilised subjects incite a myriad of responses.

DIGITAL TECHNOLOGIES AND DEVELOPING ETHICS OF CARE

The desire to promote patient responsibility and self-care is often a key motivating factor in the creation of digital resources for improving mental wellbeing. Indeed, many (but not all) users of these resources are drawn to them for the same reason, at least initially. But there is a wide range of ways these resources end up being deployed, in part due to the (anticipated and unanticipated) possibilities inherent within them—what Ian Hutchby (2001) refers to as 'technological affordances'—and how users come to adapt and re-interpret them. While technologies are designed with envisioned uses and 'scripts' (Akrich 1992; Latour 1992), users often employ them differently, exploiting unforeseen opportunities (Pols 2010). Actual use then promotes the creation of new and different resources. The dynamic interchange—technology altering behaviour while behaviour alters technology—is a perfect example of Sheila Jasanoff's (2004) notion of 'co-production' or the ways that 'knowledge and its material embodiments are at once products of social work and constitutive of forms of social life' (p. 2). While one side of the relationship (the impact of technology on society) generally receives more social attention, Jasanoff's point is to highlight that this is in fact a two-way street. To adequately assess 'matters of care' with respect to networks that include technological actants (Puig de la Bellacasa 2011), we must, therefore, look beyond analyses of design or intent to examine both how responsibility and care are actually 'enacted in particular practices, … everyday activities, objects, and routines' (Pols 2010, p. 376) and how these practices reconfigure technology.

There is, by now, a growing genealogy of works from various disciplines analysing (or speculating about) digital technologies' effects on contemporary morality, personhood, and inter-relationality. Among the most prominent are some decidedly negative accounts. Zygmunt Bauman (2003), for example, uses the notion of 'liquid love' to denote how digital communication encourages intense but fleeting relationships, ostensibly stripping away longer-term inter-personal exchanges and responsibilities that lie at the heart of social life. In a similar vein, Sherry Turkle (2011) suggests that by fostering a different pace of exchange that seeds fear of spontaneity, digital technologies encourage loneliness.

Ethnographic examinations often address similar issues but from a different angle, focusing on how the practices digital technologies enable come to be imbued with moral meaning by those involved in them. Ilana Gershon (2010), for example, employs the concept of 'media ideologies' to examine how individuals and collectivities develop ideas about the appropriate use of digital platforms for ending intimate relationships, based on their perceived ethical implications—whether, for example, it is uncaring to end a relationship via text message or a change of Facebook status. Based on their 'media ideologies' or sense of what is right and wrong with respect to media use, groups such as friends or co-workers develop 'idioms of practice' or more or less standardised ways of communicating with one another (Gershon 2010). Mirca Madianou and Daniel Miller (2013), in turn, advocate a 'polymedia' approach that looks across the use of various platforms to examine how individuals and communities come to select specific media for particular purposes and the social dynamics, affective relations, and moral consequences that ensue. While Gershon focuses primarily on individuals' choices (predominantly among US college students), Madianou and Miller (2013, p. 182) highlight shared understandings within different cultural groups that encourage conformity around the selection of media for particular purposes. In both formulations, the ethical is transformed but—significantly—not determined by the technological affordances of new forms of communication.

With this in mind, I have been leading a team conducting research on how young people in New Zealand, aged 14–24, use digital technologies for health purposes.[2] From 2015 to 2020, we carried out semi-structured interviews with 120 young New Zealanders who answered our invitation to discuss 'young people's use of health apps'. More than half chose to speak about mental health (and some about spiritual and social health) in addition to physical health. Many diverged from the app-focused questions to describe their engagements with digital technologies more generally. We adopted a participant-focused, rather than platform-focused approach, attending to the broad range of platforms that participants employed, following Madianou and Miller's (2013) polymedia framework (see also Renniger 2015). As this was originally envisioned as a pilot project,[3] our approach was notably open-ended, and we encouraged interviewees to share whatever accounts of digital technology use they deemed relevant.

Inter-relationalities of Care

While one of the central tenets of digitally focused, patient-led care is that individuals should take responsibility for their *own* wellbeing, self-help endeavours are, in fact, often highly inter-personal, as young people use and produce digital mental health resources to engage in both self-care and care of others, such as family members, friends, or people encountered online. Young people's engagements with digital technologies must therefore be understood in light of not only their own self-care strategies, but also their engagements in collective endeavours to promote mental wellbeing. These practices, moreover, have profound implications for young people's understandings and enactments of personal and inter-personal responsibility and their relationships with, and perceptions of, the state, corporations, and society at large.

Our interviews revealed that the majority of our respondents had used digital resources to seek information and advice on mental health-related issues. Some fulfilled the iconic image of the 'empowered patient', avidly researching their own care. For example, Alex (16, NZ American), who was considering gender reassignment, sourced most of their information about it online. As with many young people, maintaining privacy was crucial to Alex and digital communication was deemed an ideal way to access information without exposing their activities to parents, friends, or medical professionals (cf. Gibson and Carthwright 2014). Alex also embraced the potential fluidity of online relations which enabled receiving support from others without having to commit themselves to a particular position as they explored different ideas about gender. As Alex explained:

> There's always the hesitancy to bare your deepest, darkest emotions to people, I mean, especially to close friends because … you might find yourself saying things that you know you don't really sort of stand by, but they'll remember you saying this thing. It's one of those things where … intimacy and closeness, it almost becomes a bad thing with friends.

Here the 'liquid' relations that Bauman critiques become part of a self-conscious strategy for seeking support for one's mental wellbeing while also protecting oneself from a possible longer-term backlash.

Alex's secrecy was neither unusual, nor emblematic, of young people's online activities. Many respondents used digital resources not only for their own mental health needs, but also on behalf of others for whom they felt responsible. Albert (18, NZ Chinese) described using information he found by looking up 'depression' on Wikipedia to 'give my mum counselling sessions', when she seemed to be struggling. Demonstrating both his desire to assist her and awareness of his limitations, he recounted, 'I'd tell her to talk her problems out—do what a counsellor does. If there's anything I can't help with her, I'd tell her she'd have to see an actual counsellor'.

Taking responsibility for others did not, however, always entail sharing things openly together. While some like Alex stressed the importance of privacy to protect themselves from judgement, others were motivated by the perceived need to protect those they care about from unnecessary distress. Simon (15, NZ European) recounted how online research allowed him to assess his mental wellbeing before disclosing any concerns to his mother and unnecessarily upsetting her:

> I wouldn't tell my mum 'I think I've got depression' or something because then she'd freak out. But if I search it up, I can just have a quick look, be like 'Oh yeah, do I have that or don't I?' If I did have it then I'd go and tell my mum, but if I didn't, then [I'd] just leave it.

In a similar way, Julie (17, NZ European) spoke about sharing her feelings on *Vent* (an app designed for emotional expression) when she did not want to distress her friends: 'If you don't want to tell your friends something, like it would be a burden on them, you don't want to bring them down, so you just go on *Vent*'. Taking responsibility for mental health was thus cast in terms of being attentive to the potential effects activities may have not only on the sufferer, but those close to them as well.

Young people also described using technology in tandem to share responsibility jointly for someone's mental wellbeing. This approach was enabled by the way that apps are shareable across multiple devices and/or log-ins. Several women spoke about using period trackers to track their emotional states. Some linked their period trackers with those of female friends or, in one case, a twin sister, in order to forewarn themselves of when the other person might be feeling emotionally down or vulnerable.

Siobhan (23, NZ European), who suffers from Attention-Deficit/Hyperactivity Disorder, went a step further, syncing together her period tracker and Google calendar to create a powerful tool for tracking her emotions and coordinating her daily activities that she shared with her boyfriend. She explained:

> When you log in [to the period tracker] and say your period started or whatever, it will update [that information] on the calendar too. ... If I can try and control [what I do on] a couple of those days, it benefits me. .... [I] have everything in different colours, so if I look at a week, I can see if I've got balance ... If work has just overloaded the week and I've got no social [activities], then I know it's not a good idea. ... I definitely use my calendar as some sort of mental health prediction and also [to monitor] 'am I doing okay'?

Her boyfriend used the calendar to see how Siobhan's week was shaping up and, if necessary, took steps to ensure she stayed in 'balance'.

Siobhan: [The calendar] would actually help him know where I was at during the week, or what was [going on with me]... and he would be able to see if I need to take a break, or ...

Interviewer: Did he ever comment, like 'I think this week you're working too much' or ...?

Siobhan: He wouldn't say it in words. He quite likes spontaneous things, so instead he would tell me that I'm busy during this period of time [so it is reserved] and he would then take me out for dinner or we'd just go to the beach or something. He would do something to make me have a break.

In addition to sharing or even taking over responsibility for another's mental wellbeing, young people spoke about engaging in reciprocal exchanges of support, for example, by responding to online posters' requests for advice. Some of these efforts were spurred by the immediate return of improving their own understandings of self-help strategies. For Alex, helping others online was a tangible way of providing self-care:

> Helping people out [online] is always something … where it's also like you can learn. Like, if you tell people, 'Just do this, and do that', and then you start thinking, 'Oh, maybe I should do that myself'.

For others, the reward came primarily from being recognised as knowledgeable and useful to others. Megan (18, NZ European) was 17 when she diagnosed herself as suffering from depression using a mental health chat site. Grateful for the help she received, she felt an ethical need to 'give back' to the community. She undertook a brief, 20-question training and became a registered 'listener', assisting people coping with a range of issues, including anxiety, depression, and homicidal impulses, which left her feeling both empowered and overwhelmed (see also Trnka 2016).

At first, Megan outlined her 'counselling sessions' as a fairly straightforward process of 'helping people figure out what they are feeling'. Her 'clients', as she called them, selected her from an array of 'listeners' profiled on the website and either texted or called her to relate their feelings. It soon became evident, however, that some counselling sessions were harder than others.

When asked what kind of assistance she received from the website moderators, she explained she has access to a 'suicide button' which, when clicked, forwards her conversation to a moderator who is a professional therapist. She described the one occasion she used it: speaking to a man who repeatedly threatened to kill his family, Megan felt both frightened and hesitant, not knowing whether to click the button as 'that button is for a suicide alert and he wasn't suicidal, but homicidal'. Finally realising she was out of her depth, she alerted the moderators. When I queried what sort of follow-up support occurred, she related how, after each call, she receives a form for notifying the moderators how the session went, 'but obviously, you don't want to complain too often about these things'. Rather than relying on the forum's formal mechanisms, she turned to her peers, setting up an email group with three other young women 'listeners' who have agreed to 'debrief' one another after tricky sessions, thus protecting their reputations as competent counsellors. Megan's account reflected her strong desire to take responsibility for others while also finding it occasionally overwhelming. Not wanting to be seen as irresponsible or inadequate, she creatively came up with her own coping strategy.

Other interviewees described retreating from requests for care, even if it meant feeling irresponsible. Janelle (24, NZ Latin American), who used a mood tracker, described being thrown off guard when someone she did not know began to message her continually about their emotional and psychological struggles:

> I was having a bad day and wrote something [into the app] along the lines of 'I'm feeling angry, why won't people do things the way I want them to'? Almost immediately I had three replies from other users, [one of whom stated], 'I know what you mean—my parents annoy me so much when they do things their way'!

I replied and after a few exchanges, my correspondent began writing more and more about her parents. She informed me that they were both alcoholics and that she was really struggling, at times wondering what was the point of it all. I became genuinely concerned ... [and] found myself suggesting she look into Al-Anon [a support group for relatives and friends of alcoholics], as leaving her alone in such despair felt like neglect.

The next morning I'd almost forgotten about the whole thing when I suddenly got another message from my 'new friend'. She wanted to know how I was doing and if I felt better. She also wanted to let me know she had been looking into Al-Anon and might be going to a meeting near her. I looked at my phone and a huge sense of regret filled me. Did I really want to establish constant communication with this person? But then again, what was the point of reaching out to others if I had no intention of holding more than one conversation with them? In the end, I didn't reply, as it felt inappropriate to carry on. My 'friend', however, carried on messaging me, asking me how I was feeling and expressing concern over my silence. ... A month later I deleted the app out of sheer exasperation: I didn't want to be constantly reminded of the guilt I felt for not replying.

For Janelle, this encounter raised profound questions about her ethical obligations to strangers keen to communicate on a more intimate level than she would like. Initially, she felt obligated to respond, but later felt unable to assist in the way that seemed to be desired. Reciprocity broke down and figuring out what might feel 'right' within a developing ethics of care seemed too heavy a burden. Even though severing communication felt irresponsible, it appeared the only way out, leaving her in an ethical conundrum that never quite dissipated, even after she deleted the app.

Emma (15, NZ South African) did not shy away from emotionally intense reciprocities of care but envisioned her online activities as much broader in scope, constituting a generalised gift of care to whoever might need it. Three years before our interview, at the age of 12 and coping with self-harm, anxiety, and depression, she set up her own YouTube mental health vlog because, she explained, 'I wanted to be able to relate to others and not feel so alone, as well as have other people not feel so alone'. Emma depicted her channel as a carefully constructed, informational forum intended as a counterpoint to the minefield of erroneous or dangerous online information. In addition to making and posting informational videos, she went to great lengths to provide individualised information:

> There are people who come to me [via my channel] who are suicidal and it's like
> obviously very difficult to have to deal with that, and I try search up like [crisis]
> lines that they can call in their country.

At times, she found the pressure overwhelming. 'I'm glad I have my family, so if it gets too difficult I just go to them. Or, you know, [to] my therapist', she explained, adding that she reminds herself that when it comes to other people's problems, 'It's not my responsibility. I can only do as much as I can, you know?'

Emma's ambivalence over the extent of her capabilities and responsibilities to others was compounded by the fact that such encounters are novel forms of engagement, not only for a 12-to-15-year-old, but also, given the relatively short history of health vlogs, for society in general. Moreover, while online interactions do indeed enable fleeting encounters between individuals, encouraging 'connection without constraint' (Wesch 2009, p. 27), in some cases, even casual readers of forums feel a sense of responsibility to respond to posters who express distress (Turkle 2011). This may be even more pronounced when someone has a recognised online presence, as having followers can elicit a strong sense of obligation (Reed 2005). The sense of obligation that Emma feels towards those who contact her is thus unsurprising, despite her assertion that she is not responsible for their wellbeing. As 'patient experts' who recast themselves as providers of care, both she and Megan drew on formal and informal support systems (parents, therapists, crisis buttons, peer-to-peer 'debriefings') to assist them in developing new understandings of ethical care in contexts where their own sense of what is and is not appropriate (cf. Gershon 2010), much less a more standardised, collective ethics of care (cf. Madianou and Miller 2013), have yet to be established.

State, Social, and Corporate Obligation

While much of young people's discussion with us focused on either self-care or inter-personal dynamics and the ethical obligations they entail, many used this occasion to comment on state and social obligations. Several asserted the need for more and better face-to-face, government-supported counselling services. Amongst them were those who expressed *no* desire to use digital technologies for mental health purposes, as they viewed help as predicated upon face-to-face interactions with counsellors or medical professionals who can tailor advice to individuals' specific needs. Asked if he would ever seek mental health advice online, Richard (15, NZ European) replied, 'No, not really. I really only trust a professional in the flesh. Because everyone's got a body, but no one's got the same mind, you know'. Tamati (16, Māori) recounted engaging in self-care strategies while also speaking to a counsellor, but asserted he would never seek help online given its unreliability:

I think I'd probably get heaps of like, 'Do you have Asperger's?' tests and the like ... but they'd be bullshit ones. Every time it would come up, 'No, you're completely fine with Asperger's.' Or it would be like, 'You're 100% autistic.'

Others, who had clear online strategies, nonetheless emphasised the value of health services (or, in the cases of high-school students, educational services) due to their professional responsibilities to provide face-to-face treatment. Some who had struggled with serious mental health issues furthermore highlighted the need for the ongoing accountability that healthcare professionals provide. Jenna (24, NZ European), who sometimes suffered from severe depression, noted the need for interventions that are not easily achievable online. She explained that unlike online posters,

> health professionals can [step in]. ... If you are having a bad week and you miss a doctor's appointment, your doctor is *gonna* ring up, especially with mental health stuff. ... If you have not been out of bed in three days, your doctor is going to remind you of that and is going to motivate you to get up and come out. Whereas with a website, you don't have to get out of bed to look at it, no one is *gonna* chase after you.

Young people also repeatedly invoked the state's responsibility to provide care that is reliable, responsive, and well-trained. Several criticised the government for not providing more accessible and affordable face-to-face care, while others pointed out that they searched for online solutions only because of the prohibitive cost of doctors' or counsellors' visits. None of them called upon the government to ensure more or safer online services.

Additionally, many respondents underscored social stigmatisation as one of the key hurdles for coping with mental health issues, again shifting focus away from individual self-care to the articulation of collective needs. Allison (24, NZ European) explained:

> I think it's... really hard for people even just to admit they've got mental health issues, and then to go to anyone else [about it] ... because we don't accept mental health. Like I don't think people could really like to go to employers and be like, 'Hey, I have a mental health condition.' That would, I think, be really frightening.

Michael (17, NZ European) expressed a similar, if more politically charged view:

> There's not enough—they don't teach us enough about it [in school]. 'Cause the government, I think before Labour [the Labour-led coalition government], [it] was kinda like, 'Nah, nah, let's just sweep it under the rug, doesn't exist. What, mental health? Shhh.'

These perspectives echo recent findings that Australian LGBTQI+ youth welcome the introduction of new mental health apps, but 'addressing stigma around mental health was seen as a greater priority for many, as was addressing the inadequate information and support available ... through schools and mainstream health services' (Byron 2019, p. 51). They also coincide with broader examinations of how 'normative expectations of "health citizenship"' may be simultaneously embraced and tempered by calls for the state to be more active in providing the structural necessities of healthy living (Spoel et al. 2014).

In contrast to state and social responsibilities, corporate responsibility received much less attention. While a few interviewees briefly expressed concern over data collection, most accepted this as an inevitable, negative facet of digital technology use, a finding that correlates with recent work noting users' general lack of interest in how corporations use and profit from their self-tracking data (e.g. Lomborg et al. 2018; Lupton 2017). Moreover, in no case did our interviews spark discussion of the social obligations of corporations. This is quite striking as the responsibilities of producers of platforms and programmes to their users have been the subject of both extensive scholarly critique (e.g. Lupton 2014; Shaw and McCosker 2019) and media attention. The interview period (2015–2020) furthermore coincided with both Facebook's expansion of intervention messages sent out to posters suspected of considering suicide or self-harm and the Facebook/Cambridge Analytica data scandal. This makes young people's focus on state and societal obligations even more significant.

Beyond Human Responsibility?

There emerged, however, yet another foci of responsibility that young people are concerned about: the platforms or programmes themselves. Sarah (24, NZ European) is a case in point. She had recently begun living on her own and described relying on apps and websites to take control of her healthcare needs. 'Google is my parents', she said, with respect to making sense of illness. But digital health also had its downside. Recounting her battle with an eating disorder, she described becoming 'almost addicted' to a calorie-counting app over the course of two years:

> You just get obsessed with numbers, worrying over three calories. ... I think it was just the numbers that you could see going up and down [on the app]. ... [It] became quite restrictive and overwhelming. ... I was like super restrictive and like unhealthily so, and lost a ton of weight but I was just losing my social life because I was like, 'Oh, I can't go out because I don't know what is in my food.'

Asked to clarify whether she thought the app *instigated* or *enabled* her compulsion, Sarah replied, 'The apps give you a means to fuel this obsession that I think most people, or maybe most girls, have with body image. It gives you a way to track it and focus... [and] really *achieve* something'.

She then, however, described the app's 'demands' on her whenever she took a break from it:

[Nowadays] I just turn off all the [apps'] notifications 'cause otherwise they can just pop up on your screen at certain times during the day. If you haven't been focusing on it, it is like, 'Ohhh, come back to me!' [Laughs] It [the app] would be like, 'You haven't logged your food this morning', or, 'You haven't logged your food in a couple of days, like a *we-miss-you* kind of thing.' Some other apps email you, being like, 'Oh, we miss you—you seem to be inactive for a while.' Like reaching out through other methods if notifications aren't working, which ... is just too much. ... But maybe that is just me, like I hate ... being told things from technology.

Wanting to ensure that she never again finds herself obsessing over calories, when Sarah bought a Fitbit, she carefully stuck coloured tape over the calorie-counter so it could not be read.

In Sarah's account, technology is depicted as having agency, communicating affect ('we miss you') and at least partly responsible for encouraging a destructive dieting regime. She expresses considerable ambivalence over whether technology's 'micronudges' (Schüll 2016) towards counting calories exacerbated her inclinations or helped constitute them. Is this merely a deflection from fully acknowledging her own responsibility for her eating disorder? Or a recognition of a more diffuse 'geography of responsibilities' (Akrich 1992; Schwennesen 2019) at play? As Natasha Dow Schüll and others (e.g. Lomborg et al. 2018) note, such ambivalence often mirrors the ambivalence inherent in the design itself: 'the nudge is a curious mechanism, for it both presupposes and pushes against freedom; it assumes a choosing subject, but one who is constitutionally ill equipped to make rational, healthy choices' (Schüll 2016, p. 328). But here it was a case of the user pushing back against apps which are viewed as acting 'unhealthily'.

One of the looming questions for an anthropology of technology is whether apps, programmes, or platforms may become responsible entities. If so, what forms will their responsibilities take? And how can they be held accountable? Everyday experience suggests people relate to certain technologies as imbued with responsibility, be it the car that came out of nowhere to sideswipe you on the drive home or the computer that malfunctions whenever a deadline looms (Laidlaw 2014, p. 183). On the one hand, in recounting their experiences with digital technologies, young people were merely reflecting this tendency, particularly perhaps in moments when acknowledging one's own responsibility might feel challenging. On the other hand, if responsibility is a matter of *recognition* and *response* (cf. Hage and Eckersley 2012; McCarthy 2007), just how far away *are* we from vesting it in platforms or programmes? If we consider responsibility to be multiple and often diffuse as well as diverse in kind, what will the consequences be—and for whom—if objects and programmes cannot be deemed to act irresponsibly?

In the digital sphere, the development of increasingly sophisticated AI warrants more attentiveness to just how responsibility is conceptualised and vested in law, public, or institutional policy and other social domains. We have long considered non-human entities such as corporations capable of being deemed responsible (or irresponsible), treating them, in some circumstances, as 'legal persons'. Although there are times when corporate irresponsibility is held against specific individuals (as, e.g. in the landmark 2019 laying of criminal charges for opioid distribution against specific pharmaceutical executives), often it is the obverse (Merle 2019). As Jessica Smith (2017) indicates in her analysis of mining companies' responses to environmental degradation, when it comes to assigning blame, who exactly constitutes the corporation can be 'infuriatingly intangible' (p. 126).

States and corporations aside, in general, as Ghassan Hage and Robyn Eckersley (2012) suggest, 'although we do speak of responsibility in relation to non-humans, such as "the faulty wires were responsible for the fire", faulty wires can only be *declared* responsible, they cannot be, in our culture, *held* responsible as humans are' (p. 1). What, however, would be lost or gained if entities that (for now, at least) cannot make moral judgements nor have affective responses (cf. Laidlaw 2014), such as feeling relief, shame, or guilt (or actually 'missing us'), are to be *held* accountable for their actions? Attributions of responsibility are, like all social forms, malleable, historically changing social facts. Given the dynamic interactionality, or co-production (Jasanoff 2004), of digital technologies and social forms, one of the key tasks of an anthropology of technology may well be to remain attentive to just what new forms of accountability, duty, and obligation lie ahead of us.

Acknowledgements Many thanks to both reviewers for their feedback and to Rachel Douglas-Jones for her care and enthusiasm in shepherding this chapter to completion. I am indebted to the young people who shared their stories and to the student research assistants who contributed to this project: Andrea Merino Ortiz, Claire Black, Mira Bi, Shyla Rose Kelly, Imogen Spray, Thibaut Bouttier-Esprit, Brodie Quinn, and Miriama Aoake. This research was supported by the University of Auckland's Faculty of Arts Summer Scholars Programme (2015–2020); the Faculty Research Development Fund; InternetNZ; and the Royal Society of New Zealand Marsden grant, '*Ka Hao te Rangatahi*: Fishing with a New Net? Rethinking Responsibility for Youth Mental Health in the Digital Age'.

Notes

1. Many of the ideas in this section originate from Trnka and Trundle (2014, 2017).
2. Interviews were conducted by the author and seven research assistants, following ethical approval from the University of Auckland Human Participants Ethics Committee.
3. What was anticipated to be a summer spent interviewing 10–20 participants developed into a much larger, five-year study.

References

Akrich, M. (1992). The de-scription of technical objects. In W. E. Bijker & J. Law (Eds.), *Shaping technology/building society: Studies in sociotechnical change* (pp. 205–224). Cambridge and London: The MIT Press.

Albury, K., Byron, P., & Shaw, F. (2019). Introduction: The will to app: digitising public health. *Media International Australia, 171*(1), 3–8.

Bauman, Z. (2003). *Liquid love: On the frailty of human bonds*. Malden, MA: Polity.

Bretherton, P., Piggin, J., & Bodet, G. (2016). Olympic sport and physical activity promotion: the rise and fall of the London 2012 pre-event pass participation 'legacy'. *International Journal of Sport Policy and Politics, 8*(4), 609–624.

Byron, P. (2019). 'Apps are cool but generally pretty pointless': LGBTIQ+ young people's mental health app ambivalence. *Media International Australia, 171*(1), 51–65.

Carrithers, M. (1985). An alternative social history of the self. In M. Carrithers, S. Collins, & S. Lukes (Eds.), *The category of the person: Anthropology, philosophy, history* (pp. 234–256). Cambridge: Cambridge University Press.

Cook, J. (2016). Mindful in Westminster: The politics of meditation and the limits of neoliberal critique. *Hau: Journal of Ethnographic Theory, 6*(1), 141–161.

Danholt, P., & Langstrup, H. (2012). Medication as infrastructure. *Culture Unbound, 4*, 513–532.

DelVecchio Good, M.J. (2001). The biotechnical embrace. *Culture, Medicine and Psychiatry, 25*(4), 395–410.

Dumit, J. (2012). *Drugs for life: How pharmaceutical companies define our health*. Durham, NC: Duke University Press.

Epstein, S. (1998). *Impure science: AIDS, activism, and the politics of knowledge*. Berkeley: University of California Press.

European Commission. (2018). Communication on enabling the digital transformation of health and care in the digital single market: empowering citizens and building a healthier society. https://ec.europa.eu/digital-single-market/en/news/communication-enabling-digital-transformation-health-and-care-digital-single-market-empowering.pdf. Accessed 14 August 2020.

Fordyce, L. (2012). Responsible choices: situating pregnancy intention among Haitians in south Florida. *Medical Anthropology Quarterly, 26*(1), 116–135.

Foucault, M. (1988). *The history of sexuality, Vol. 3: The care of the self* (trans: Hurley, R.). New York: Knopf Doubleday.

Foucault, M. (1990). *The history of sexuality, Vol. 2: The use of pleasure* (trans: Hurley, R.). New York: Vintage Books.

Foucault, M. (1997). *Ethics: Subjectivity and truth*. P. Rabinow (Ed.) (trans: Hurley, R. et al.). New York: New Press.

Fullagar, S. (2007). Governing healthy families: Leisure and the politics of risk. In M. Casado-Diaz, S. Everett, & J. Wilson (Eds.), *Social and cultural change: Making space(s) for leisure and tourism* (pp. 67–78). Bristol: Leisure Studies Association.

Gershon, I. (2010). *The break up 2.0: Disconnecting over new media*. Ithaca and London: Cornell University Press.

Gibbon, S. (2006). Nurturing women and the BRCA genes: gender, activism and the paradox of health awareness. *Anthropology & Medicine, 13*(2), 157–171.

Gibson, K., & Carthwright, C. (2014). Young people's experiences of mobile phone text counselling: balancing connection and control. *Children and Youth Services Review, 43*, 96–104.

Gilligan, C. (1982). *In a different voice*. Cambridge, MA: Harvard University Press.

Gobby, B., Keddie, A., & Blackmore, J. (2018). Professionalism and competing responsibilities: moderating competitive performativity in school autonomy reform. *Journal of Educational Administration and History, 50*(3), 159–173.

Hage, G., & Eckersley, R. (2012). Introduction. In G. Hage & R. Eckersley (Eds.), *Responsibility* (pp. 1–11). Melbourne: Melbourne University Press.

Hunt, A. (2003). Risk and moralization in everyday life. In R.V. Ericson & A. Doyle (Eds.), *Risk and morality* (pp. 165–192). London: University of Toronto Press.

Hutchby, I. (2001). Technologies, texts and affordances. *Sociology, 35*(2), 441–456.

Jasanoff, S. (Ed.) (2004). *States of knowledge: The co-production of science and social order*. New York: Routledge.

Kelty, C. M. (2008). Responsibility: McKeon and Ricoeur. *Anthropology of the Contemporary Research Collaboratory*. ARC Working Paper no. 12. http://hdl.handle.net/10524/1625. Accessed 20 September 2020.

Laidlaw, J. (2010). Agency and responsibility: Perhaps you can have too much of a good thing. In M. Lambek (Ed.), *Ordinary ethics: Anthropology, language, and action* (pp. 143–164). New York: Fordham University Press.

Laidlaw, J. (2014). *The subject of virtue: An anthropology of ethics and freedom*. Cambridge: Cambridge University Press.

Langstrup, H., & Winthereik, B.R. (2008). The making of self-monitoring asthma patients: mending a split reality with comparative ethnography. *Comparative Sociology, 7*, 362–386.

Latour, B. (1992). Where are the missing masses? The sociology of a few mundane artifacts. In W. E. Bijker & J. Law (Eds.), *Shaping technology/building society: Studies in sociotechnical change* (pp. 225–258). Cambridge and London: The MIT Press.

Lomborg, S., Thylstrup, N.B., & Schwartz, J. (2018). The temporal flows of self-tracking: checking in, moving on, staying hooked. *New Media & Society, 20*(12), 4950–4607.

Lupton, D. (2014). The commodification of patient opinion: the digital patient experience economy in the age of big data. *Sociology of Health & Illness, 36*(6), 856–869.

Lupton, D. (2017). Personal data practices in the age of lively data. In J. Daniels, K. Gregory, & T. McMillan Cottom (Eds.), *Digital sociologies* (pp. 339–352). Bristol: Policy Press.

Lupton, D. (2019). 'It's made me a lot more aware': a new materialist analysis of health self-tracking. *Media International Australia, 171*(1), 66–79.

Lupton, D., & Smith, G.J.D. (2018). 'A much better person': The agential capacities of self-tracking practices. In B. Ajana (Ed.), *Metric culture: Ontologies of self-tracking practices* (pp. 57–76). London: Emerald Publishing.

Madianou, M., & Miller, D. (2013). Polymedia: towards a new theory of digital media in interpersonal communication. *International Journal of Cultural Studies, 16*(2), 169–87.

Martin, A., Myers, N., & Viseu, A. (2015). The politics of care in technoscience. *Social Studies of Science, 45*(5), 625–641.

McCarthy, E. (2007). Land of saints and tigers: the transformation of responsibility in Ireland. *Journal of the Society for the Anthropology of Europe, 7*, 3–7.

McKeon, R. (1957). The development and significance of the concept of responsibility. *Revue International de Philosophie, 1*, 3–32.

Merle, R. (2019, April 4). Warren's plan to jail more CEOs would upend legal standards, critics say. *Washington Post*. https://www.washingtonpost.com/business/2019/04/04/problem-with-elizabeth-warrens-plan-jail-more-ceos/. Accessed 10 August 2020.

Miller, P., & Rose, N. (2008). *Governing the present: Administering economic, social and personal life*. Malden, MA: Polity.

Mol, A. (2008). *The logic of care: Health and the problem of patient choice*. London: Routledge.

Mol, A., Moser, I., & J. Pols, eds. (2010). *Care in practice: On tinkering in clinics, homes, and farms*. New York: Columbia University Press.

Mort, M., Roberts, C., Pols, J., Domenech, M., & Moser, I. (2013). Ethical implications of home telecare for older people: a framework derived from a multisited participative study. *Health Expectations, 18*, 438–449.

Oudshoorn, N. (2011). *Telecare technologies and the transformation of healthcare*. Basingstoke, Hampshire: Palgrave Macmillan.

Pols, J. (2010). The heart of the matter: about good nursing and telecare. *Health Care Analysis, 18*, 374–388.

Puig de la Bellacasa, M. (2011) Matters of care in technoscience: Assembling neglected things. *Social Studies of Science, 41*(1), 85–106.

Rawolle, S., Rowlands, J., & Blackmore, J. (2017). The implications of contractualism for the responsibilisation of higher education. *Discourse: Studies in the Cultural Politics of Education, 38*(1), 109–122.

Reed, A. (2005). 'My blog is me': texts and persons in UK online journal culture (and anthropology). *Ethnos, 70*(2), 220–242.

Reiser, S. J. (1985). Responsibility for personal health: a historical perspective. *Journal of Medicine and Philosophy, 10*, 7–17.

Renniger, B. J. (2015). 'Where I can be myself.' *New Media & Society, 17*(9), 1513–1529.

Rose, N. (2006). *The politics of life itself: Biomedicine, power and subjectivity in the twenty-first century*. Princeton, NJ: Princeton University Press.

Schüll, N. D. (2016). Data for life: wearable technology and the design of self-care. *BioSocieties, 11*, 317–333.

Schwennesen, N. (2017). When self-tracking enters physical rehabilitation: from 'pushed' self-tacking to ongoing affective encounters in arrangements of care. *Digital Health, 3*, 1–8.

Schwennesen, N. (2019). Algorithmic assemblages of care: imaginaries epistemologies and repair work. *Sociology of Health & Illness, 41*(S1), 176–192 10.1111/1467-9566.12900

Sharon, T. (2015). Healthy citizenship beyond autonomy and discipline: tactical engagements with genetic testing. *BioSocieties, 10*, 295–316.

Shaw, F., & McCosker, A. (2019). Mental health support apps and 'proper distance': relational ethics in mHealth. *Media International Australia, 171*(1), 9–22.

Smith, J. (2017). From corporate social responsibility to creating shared value: Contesting responsibilization and the mining industry. In S. Trnka & C. Trundle (Eds.), *Competing responsibilities: The ethics and politics of contemporary life* (pp. 118–132). Durham, NC: Duke University Press.

Spoel, P., Harris, R., & Henwood, F. (2014). Rhetorics of health citizenship: exploring vernacular critiques of government's role in supporting healthy living. *Journal of Medical Humanities, 35*, 131–147.

Thörn, H., & Svenberg, S. (2016). 'We feel the responsibility that you shirk': movement institutionalization, the politics of responsibility and the case of the Swedish environmental movement. *Social Movement Studies, 15*(6), 593–609.

Trnka, S. (2016). Digital care: agency and temporality in young people's use of health apps. *Engaging Science, Technology, and Society, 2,* 248–265.

Trnka, S. (2017). *One blue child: Asthma, responsibility and the global politics of health.* Palo Alto: Stanford University Press.

Trnka, S., & Trundle, C. (2014). Competing responsibilities: moving beyond neoliberal responsibilization. *Anthropological Forum, 24*(2), 136–153.

Trnka, S., & Trundle, C. (2017). Competing responsibilities: Reckoning personal responsibility, care for the other and the social contract in contemporary life. In S. Trnka & C. Trundle (Eds.), *Competing responsibilities: The ethics and politics of contemporary life* (pp. 1–24). Durham, NC: Duke University Press.

Turkle, S. (2011). *Alone together: Why we expect more from technology and less from each other.* New York: Basic Books.

Weinberg, A. M. (1966). Can technology replace social engineering? *Bulletin of the Atomic Scientists, 12*(10), 4–8.

Weiner, K., & Will, C. (2018). Thinking with care infrastructures: people, devices and the home in home blood pressure monitoring. *Sociology of Health & Illness, 40*(2), 270–282.

Welker, M. A. (2013). *Enacting the corporation: An American mining firm in post-authoritarian Indonesia.* Berkeley: University of California Press.

Wesch, M. (2009). YouTube and you: experiences of self-awareness in the context collapse of the recording webcam. *Explorations in Media Ecology, 8*(2), 19–34.

Zigon, J. (2010). *'HIV is god's blessing': Rehabilitating morality in neoliberal Russia.* Berkeley, CA: University of California Press.

CHAPTER 33

Committee Work: Stem Cell Governance in the United States

Control

Rachel Douglas-Jones

What stories can a cell tell? The cells of this chapter are stem cells, which, since their isolation in humans and growth in a laboratory two years before the turn of the millennium, have been objects of intense negotiation. Their status as biological objects and social entities has been discussed and acted upon across scientific, legal, and social worlds, leading to the declaration in the early 2000s that they are a 'spectacle ripe for anthropological analysis' (Hogle 2005, p. 24). In the two ensuing decades, anthropologists have indeed worked intensively on this 'spectacle', following scientific and social developments and efforts to put stem cells to work towards human and more-than-human ends. These efforts have come with significant debates, following cells into sites of science regulation, laboratory advance, medical advance, and moral unease.

I consider how a *cell* captures the attention of anthropologists of technology, both in its material form and specifically for how it has been subject to contrasting forms of governance. The initial terrain is familiar to scholars of reproduction and new reproductive technologies, since human biological material has increasingly become a matter of use, manipulation, and intervention. My own research tackles a specific instance and history of stem cell governance: the embryonic stem cell research oversight committee (ESCRO) in the United States. ESCROs were introduced in 2005 as a form of oversight of

R. Douglas-Jones (✉)
Department of Business IT, IT University of Copenhagen, Copenhagen, Denmark
e-mail: rdoj@itu.dk

© The Author(s), under exclusive license to Springer Nature Singapore Pte Ltd. 2022
M. H. Bruun et al. (eds.), *The Palgrave Handbook of the Anthropology of Technology*, https://doi.org/10.1007/978-981-16-7084-8_33

the use of embryo materials in basic research and development of therapeutic interventions (NAS 2005a, 2010). Their function was to provide a form of voluntary oversight for institutions receiving federal funds, and they were widely adopted as forms of local oversight, charged with considering appropriate access to cell lines, consent of donors, checking restrictions on cell line use, and creating a body of engagement for PIs undertaking novel work. A mere eight years later, an editorial in the *American Journal of Bioethics* was calling for ESCROs to be thanked and disbanded, obsolete in the face of advancing science and fading controversy. As the philosopher Hank Greely put it at the time, stem cell research was 'not rocket science any more' (2013, p. 44).

Considering both the shifting grounds of stem cell science and the fate of technologies of governance that out-live controversy, my focus on ESCROs (known also as SCROs in the wake of stem cells beyond E for embryonic) allows us to see how ethics committee work can stand alone as a site for anthropological analysis of new technologies. As condensers of meaning, loci of discussion, committees are a revelatory tool of governance in ethical struggles and their settlements. I suggest that in the context of exploring questions of ethics, value, and morality, we regard committees as venues for a bureaucratic form of ethics (Hoeyer and Tutton 2005; Jacob and Riles 2007; Murphy and Dingwall 2007; Hedgecoe 2012; Stark 2011). In contrast with an ethics of the lived everyday (Lambek 2010), they are attempts to set out a settlement of 'the good', socially authorised as a shared arena of discussion. They are also often a means of delegating societal questions about the implications of technological advance, illustrating how anthropologists studying technology need to draw on the burgeoning anthropology of bureaucracy (Heyman 2004; Hull 2012; Bear and Mathur 2015; Mathur 2015, 2020); the framings of risk-management in complex systems (Perrow 1992[1984]; Vaughan 1996); and scholarship on accountability (Power 1997; Strathern 2000) to make sense of the form ethics takes within committee worlds. Before discussing the perspectives I elicited from committee members on their work, and what happens to fields of governance that grow up around controversial technologies, I provide an overview of literature pertaining to stem cell research and use. Anthropologists have made extensive contributions in studying stem cells and their environs over the past few decades, and the work I review below offers a rich base of theory, built from ethnographic and comparative engagements, from which to understand the stakes of governing stem cells through committees.

Countless biomedical textbooks and articles offer definitions of stem cells, from the colloquial 'cellular putty' (Coghlan 2014) to cells that 'break all the rules' (Lovell-Badge 2001, p. 89). First isolated in the early 1980s by Evans and Kaufman (1981) and Martins (1981), who each derived pluripotent embryonic stem cells from the embryos of mice, stem cells have been pursued, as Franklin terms it, as 'multi-talented multipliers' (2005, p. 62). They and their properties are often described in the scientific and literary language of *potency*, an idea that captures anthropologists as much as it does biologists (Taussig et al. 2013; Geesink et al. 2008; Cooper 2003). Following these cells, their potency and potential, takes ethnographers into a range of sites, from laboratories to courts, hearings, and homes. In laboratory studies, stem cells are tightly bound up in technologies of biological advance. Devices, techniques, and skills are all required to work with stem cells, from culture methods to suspension technologies, dry ice and cryotubes, barcodes and freezers, molecular imaging, and computationally supported image reconstruction through algorithmic means. The cells themselves—by virtue of their fundamental character—are also regarded as a technology, a 'technology that can reprogram the cell in a way that transforms what were formerly thought of as its inherent one-way tendencies to decline into capacities for unlimited production' (Franklin 2005, p. 65; see also Franklin 2001; Landecker 2006; Waldby and Squier 2003).

As the skills to work with stem cells became more readily established in the scientific community at the start of the twenty-first century, Linda Hogle brought the stem cell to anthropological attention as a 'spectacle' (2005), raising as she did so a set of questions about evidence, interest groups, global scientific advance, and the negotiation of 'sets of cultural and religious values about protections of life … against equally sacred values associated with the pursuit of capital and concepts of a "good life"' (Hogle 2005, p. 24). Condensing these issues, stem cells have arguably played a role as a 'theory machine' for 'exploring ideas about life, knowledge, commerce, governance and ethics' (Bharadwaj 2012, p. 304). My summary of the anthropological literature that tackles their empirical and theoretical richness is organised around four key themes that broadly tell a chronological story: the thematic continuities and disjunctions with earlier work on new reproductive technologies, the invocation of ethical anxieties, accounts of contrasting governance, and the promissory world of the translation of stem cell science into regenerative cures.

KINSHIP AND GENEALOGY

Stem cells emerge in conversation with debates about human reproduction: their history is closely intertwined with in vitro fertilisation (IVF) technologies. As Franklin has observed, IVF became a 'platform' technology used beyond reproduction for livestock breeding, genetic diagnosis, cloning, and stem cell research (Franklin 2006b, 2013). Indeed, when James Thomson and his team at the University of Madison, Wisconsin, derived the first human embryonic stem cell line in the late 1990s (Thomson et al. 1998), the researchers worked with 36 embryos from patients who had been undergoing IVF and donated their embryos after completing the treatment (Eguizabal et al. 2019). For this reason, as scholars following the trajectories of cells across borders and jurisdictions have observed, '[h]uman embryonic stem cell lines can never be completely disentangled from reproduction' (Merleau-Ponty et al. 2018).

How stem cells become available for research is a matter of contrast across settings, and the means by which they become available for research during

IVF treatments have been closely analysed (Franklin 1999). Gottweis, Salter, and Waldby describe this becoming-available as 'disentanglement': a 'process of purification—donation to clinic and then to laboratory, disaggregation, immortalization, passage—transforms the embryo into a more properly anonymized, scientific object' (Gottweiss et al. 2009, p. 35). In Denmark, Svendsen and Koch (2008) track the making of 'spare' embryos earlier, arguing that they are 'not straightforward biological facts' and analysing how they are placed and re-placed within networks of research and kin in moments of donation (p. 93; see also Svendsen 2011; Ehrich et al. 2010). Drawing on ethnographic work in Ecuadorian IVF clinics, Roberts (2007, 2011) discusses how the possibility of freezing embryos is made sense of, working specifically with anxieties around their *accumulation*. Surveying Chinese donors and interviewing patients, Rosemann and Luo (2018) describe the specific value of IVF embryos, when some couples were 'literally (cryo-)banking on a change in China's [one-child] birth politics' (p. 457).

Across these examples, embryos and the stem cells that research can derive from them are placed by donors, technicians, and researchers within different regimes of value (Rosemann 2014; Saniei 2012). Many researchers have turned to the Foucauldian language of biopolitics to express these intersections (Lock 2001; Inhorn and Tremayne 2012; Thompson 2013): with life 'envisioned at the molecular level' (Marsland and Prince 2012, p. 455) come new initiatives to optimise it (see also Kristensen this volume). For Franklin, this means that 'cellular functionality has become a field of property speculation' (2005, p. 62), the potential turned into 'biovalue' (Waldby 2002), part of the 'promissory capital' (Sunder Rajan 2006) discussed more broadly beyond stem cell research (Brown et al. 2006; Brown and Kraft 2006) and through a feminist lens (Waldby and Cooper 2010).

To make something 'spare' is both to classify and to value, folding stem cells into tissue economies (Waldby and Mitchell 2006; Franklin 2006a; Cooper 2008) and commodity regimes (Hoeyer et al. 2009). Spare invokes both aversion to 'waste' (Waldby 2008) and novel futures that rest on what Ehrich et al. call 'informed uncertainty' (2011). Since banks for biological materials already existed, they were introduced for umbilical blood stem cells internationally, with ethnographic work from Taiwan (Sleeboom-Faulkner and Chang 2016; Chang 2016) and Spain considering the distinctions between public and private value within these economies (Santoro 2009). As Roberts observes for the language of 'life' (2013), values infuse the language used to discuss embryos that may be given for research, from the 'sacrifice' of unborn lives to the promise of lives saved, justified in the United States through what Charis Thompson (2013) has called a 'pro-curial' attitude. These 'twenty-first century biotechnological modes of being' are weighed, from sacrifice and destruction to life and hope (Bharadwaj and Inhorn 2016, p. 79; Benjamin 2013; Benjamin and Hinkson 2017).

CATEGORIES, ONTOLOGIES, AND ETHICS

Researchers have shown how definitions of stem cells, oocytes, and embryos are careful negotiations. Language matters. It is necessary to be specific, as the 'embryo' becomes a 'basket category' (Franklin 2006a, p. 168). Roberts notes that what will count as an embryo in Ecuador depends on institutional definitions and industry agreement (2011, p. 236), and numerous scholars have observed the political negotiations around the British creation of a category of 'pre-embryo', to designate the period prior to 14 days of development (Strathern 1991; Becker 2000; Ragoné and Twine 2000). Widespread pursuit of clarity about what stem cells 'actually are' has led scholars towards discussions of their ontology, and the ontological labour that goes into working with them. Charis Thompson's book-length account of making 'good science' describes this as 'ethical choreography' (Thompson 2013). For Sheila Jasanoff, the work that states do in regulating stem cells is a kind of 'ontological ordering' (2005, p. 147), allowing for these 'elusive, recalcitrant entities that resist characterization and standardization' (Hogle 2010, p. 433) to be separated and governed. As Hinterberger (2020) observes of debates over managing 'human-animal chimeras' in the United Kingdom and the United States, while such cellular entities are useful for science, they are a 'lightning rod of ethical, legal and regulatory anxieties in many countries' (p. 1067). In her work on chimeric lifeforms, Hinterberger (2018) counters their presumed character as 'liminal and monstrous' with an analysis that shows how elusive the human itself becomes when 'intertwined with chimeric life' (p. 453). Comparing how embryos have been managed in labs and across differing jurisdictions, Jasanoff describes this process of 'sorting out, classifying and reclassifying key elements of human reproduction in accordance with the felt rightness of a legal order' as a kind of ontological politics (Jasanoff and Metzler 2020, p. 6). Moments of 'surgery' carve out decisions on what something 'is', a settlement accomplished through committee and council work: 'resolv[ing] puzzles at the borderlines of ontological and moral specification' (Jasanoff 2011, p. 61) and rendering them 'knowable as legal, ethical, technical or economic entities' (Morrison 2020, p. 4; Stephens and Dimond 2015).

As products of experimentation with human tissues, stem cells have been a battleground of not only ontological but also ethical debate, a 'space of rancorous moral discord, rife with proclamations of salvation of apocalypse' (Ong and Collier 2005, p. 5) and '"revolutionary" potential' (Franklin 2005, p. 59). Countries diverge on policy, offering either government support and funding for research, partial restriction of funds and cell lines, or, at times, outright bans (Gottweis 2002; Bender et al. 2005; Hauskeller and Weber 2011; Sperling 2004, 2008; Metzler 2012). Some have created research environments according to self-proclaimed national values, criminalising some experiments and bureaucratising others (Hine 2017; Ho et al. 2010; Zhang 2011). The restrictions in the United States in particular, Ong and Collier observed near the time, 'invoked[d] a form of humanism that claims to be concerned not with a culture or a particular social group with but with human life as such' (2005, p. 5). Nonetheless, testing procedures and conventions 'are socially negotiated within particular sociopolitical-technical networks' (Hogle 2010, p. 434) and the settlement of these negotiations could, Ong and Collier concluded, 'only be made *effective* through specific political and technical arrangements (2005, p. 5, emphasis added). The framework of 'ethical, legal and social issues' (ELSI) of the 1990s struggled to contain these debates. As Friese reports, Charis Thompson approached the Asilomar stem cell gathering of 2006 with an argument that 'the politics of conducting stem cell science made it clear that ethics, law and society were not simply implicated in downstream applications of scientific research but rather in the conduct of science itself ... [necessitating] ethical, legal, social, political, economic, theological, and historical aspects' (Thompson 2006, cited in Friese 2013, p. S130). In other words, the questions that were vexing stem cell research were not simply about its outcomes and uses, but embedded in the premises of its conduct.

Governing Promissory Worlds

Ethnographic accounts of the emergence of stem cells research and its applications across different contexts have been particularly valuable in understanding cell stories (Bender et al. 2005; Franklin 2018). This is particularly evident in studies of international laboratories and clinics, with the translation of stem cell science into therapeutics closely followed by patients and ethnographers alike with hope, while becoming a central concept in discussions of treatments and cures (Ganchoff 2004; Petersen and Seear 2011). The landscape of regulation is uneven, national, and not harmonised (Gross 2001; Rosemann 2011; Rosemann and Chaisinthop 2016; Sleeboom-Faulkner et al. 2018), resulting in a plurality of standards and practices for stem cell treatment,[1] which have flourished throughout the first decades of the twenty-first century (Prainsack 2006; Prainsack and Gmeiner 2008). Following debates in China and India, Sleeboom-Faulkner et al. have commented that '[a] very large grey area exists between translational stem cell research and applications that comply with the ideals of randomised control trials and good laboratory and clinical practice, and what is often referred to as snake-oil trade' (2016, p. 240; see also Patra and Sleeboom-Faulkner 2009). Yet ethnographers have also questioned what will count as evidence, prioritising ethnographic accounts and stem cell treatments in a broader discussion of health and illness by suggesting that stem cell treatment narratives 'disturb several regimes of truth' (Prasad 2014, p. 151; Hogle and Das 2017). On the basis of his work in New Delhi clinics since 2002, Bharadwaj argues for expansive understandings of regenerative medicine (Bharadwaj 2013a, 2013b, 2015; Bharadwaj and Glasner 2008; see also Cooper 2004, 2006). Critical of analytical responses to Human Embryonic Stem Cell (hESC)-based therapies (often considered by patients as a 'last resort'), he has worked with doctors and patients receiving cultured embryonic stem cells during their 'Indian Odysseys' (Bharadwaj 2013a) to demonstrate the complex lives of 'cures' (Bharadwaj 2017; Hogle 2018). Thus, while some literature takes up the framework of medical tourism (Thompson 2008; Wahlberg and Streitfellner 2009), with patients travelling for care, Priscila Song (2010, 2011) suggests that a 'biotech pilgrimage' is a more appropriate framing. In her ethnography of the translational life of foetal cell therapies in China, she sees a form of faith intertwining with technology, travel, and political economy.

Today, stem cells also enter more-than-human conversations, as work on extinct and at-risk species turns to genetic continuity, technologies 'migrat[ing] from human biomedical contexts into the "feral" landscape of biodiversity conversation, carrying with them the imaginaries of potential to both literal and figuratively reproduce different futures' (Allen 2019, n.p.). As Allen writes, conservation biologists and geneticists working with resources at the Centre for Species Survival's Genome Resource Bank regard genomics as 'the real solution'; they just 'hope the tech gets there in time' (Allen 2019).[2] While contemporary with the more-than-human turn in anthropology, the use of stem cells in conservation biology dates back to James Thomson's early work with embryo technologies with primate species at risk in Sulawesi, central Indonesia (Gitschier 2008). The return, I suggest, re-frames earlier debates, where species categories have caused considerable tension around the concept of the human itself (Hinterberger 2018).

Stem cell science continues apace. In the 2010s, researchers shifted from their use of embryonic stem cells to a new kind of cell, human-*induced* pluripotent stem cells (hiPSC). These did not come from embryos but from mature human cells, reprogrammed, and have been called 'ethical stem cells' (Jha 2011), posited as alternatives to or even replacements for human embryonic stem cells (Morrison 2020; Milne 2016). Created first in mice in 2006 and in humans a year later, the cells are what ethnographer Minna Meskus calls 'a new biomedical research tool' (2018, p. 2), an 'artificially created living substance' (p. 5) into which many treatment-related aspirations have been channelled (Hauskeller and Weber 2011; Ravven 2017). As these new forms of stem cells are developed and standardised (Eriksson and Webster 2008, 2015; Webster and Eriksson 2008), they have challenged earlier anthropological analyses, making new demands on analysts. For her part, Meskus ethnographically foregrounds the *craft* of making iPS cell technology possible, the 'human labour that involves practical skills' (2018, p. 6). It is here that biology, she argues, becomes technology. From Morrison, we learn that re-programming technologies are 'widely available in kit form' (2020, p. 4), taking account of the technical and ontological transformations to produce novel 'bio-objects' (Vermeulen et al. 2012); these must travel with an entourage of 'tethers' (Hinterberger and Porter 2015) of enduring legal and bureaucratic connections between biologically derived material and data 'as a condition of their mobility' in economies of research (Morrison 2020, p. 14; Sheller and Urry 2006).

Anthropological work with stem cell researchers, scientists, and publics, then, has moved with the promises of stem cells, through their moments of controversy and their inseparability from key ethical debates (Mulkay 1997; Landecker 2000; Jiang and Rosemann 2018). In 2020, as the COVID-19 pandemic expanded across the world, the United States Federal Trade Commission, set up to protect and educate consumers, was required to send letters to hundreds of companies that were claiming their products could treat or cure the disease. Here, stem cells were aiming to travel, and turned into therapies, were listed alongisde IV infusions of vitamins, electromagnetic field blocking patches, essential oils, and ozone therapies (FTC 2020). These letters were a reminder that treatments 'come into existence through science and law' and an anthropological gaze attends to the 'kinds of definitions and practices [that] make them valued objects of contention in the first place' (Landecker 1999, p. 203). In what follows, I lay out one response to the technological capacities to work with stem cells, oversight committees, and trace the promises and concerns that have sedimented into ethics as a bureaucratic form.

Embryonic Stem Cell Research Oversight Committees

My own research into stem cell worlds began in early 2013, shortly prior to the *American Bioethics* special issue with which I opened. When the National Academies of Sciences in the United States first released their recommendations introducing ESCROs on 26 April 2005, the committee's co-chair, Jonathan D. Moreno, argued that 'heightened oversight is essential to assure the public that stem cell research is being carried out in an ethical manner' (NAS 2005b). From this setup, he acknowledged that the recommendation for oversight committees 'set a higher standard than required by existing law of regulations', but felt it justified 'given the novel and controversial nature of embryonic stem cell research' (NAS 2005b). In the ensuing years, a pair of amendments followed from the National Academies of Science (NAS 2007; NAS 2008a) to clarify stem cell lines acceptable for use in research (2007), to guide work on human stem cells derived from non-embryotic tissues (including hiPSC), and to advise on reimbursement of donations of eggs (NAS 2008a, 2008b). The NAS's final report (2010) agreed to maintain the committees and their position within research institutions, along with their composition: 'The committee should include representatives of the public and persons with expertise in developmental biology, stem cell research, molecular biology, assisted reproduction and ethical and legal issues in hES cell research' (NAS 2005a, p. 5). As noted above, while ESCROs were widely adopted across the United States in 2005, there has been no systematic overview of how many institutions established one, how closely the compositional guidelines were followed, or the kinds of cases they looked at through the years (for a partial survey see Brown and Hiskes 2007).[3]

The 2013 provocation from bioethicist Hank Greely seemed to mark an impasse, with respondents to his editorial asking where the committees should go from that point. Some offered evaluative accounts from their own universities (Chapman 2013; Ellison 2013), others sought to dissolve ESCROs

(Aultman 2013) while dealing with stem cell tourism (Master and Resnik 2013). The eight responses put forward their own questions: is the specific expertise of ESCROs still necessary? Could ESCROs give way to more long-standing bodies, like Institutional Review Boards (IRBs), the more heavily institutionalised (and legally mandated) bodies overseeing all human subjects research? Did what ESCROs discussed fit within the human subjects jurisdiction of the IRB? And what did it mean that some bioethicists—members of the self-appointed discussion discipline for matters of societal concern (Stark 2011; Wilson 2013; Garrett et al. 2013; Hurlbut 2017)—thought their work was done, while others argued that there was still 'value to be gained' (Lomax 2013)?

At the time of my fieldwork, there was a limited overview of the distribution and tasks of ESCROs, something which remains the case today. Interviews revealed a variety of interpretations of the NAS guidelines, and the creation of a range of institutionalised roles and relationships, particularly as ethical concerns have continued to arise in the post-embryonic stem cell era. Since the suggestion to remove ESCROs from the landscape was made with little reference to what committee *members* thought about their jobs, or how they themselves considered the work they did, I set out to ask them. Exploring the particularities of these committees—their period of history, national context, and the way they order different discursive, epistemic, and democratic representations such that decisions can be taken about new entities of the biosciences—I wanted to understand how ESCROs think: what reasoning takes place?

Given the 'end of an era' context set up by Greely (Greely 2013), I chose to pursue the question of the ESCROs' role with sitting members of committees themselves: how they regard the trajectory of their small groups and the potential obsolescence of their work. As none agreed to observation, in part due to confidentiality agreements with the researchers whose work they review, I spoke instead with committee members in interviews lasting between 1 and 2 hours. I gathered accounts from 18 committee members[4] across 3 committees in 3 different US states, and produced transcribed dialogue of over 22 hours, leading to a thematic overview as a starting point for analysis.[5] I began by asking members about their perception of their roles and their understanding of the scope of the committee, before exploring whether its jurisdiction had changed or been negotiated over time, and their thoughts about its future. I made visits to three sites in three different states.[6] Site 1 is a private research-intensive university on the East Coast,; Site 2 is a large mid-west university, and Site 3 a public university in the Southwest. These institutional structures have their own priorities, institutional setups, and modes of reasoning, as they build their versions of the 'right' relations between science and knowledge, as distinct from that which cleaved off as 'the political'.[7]

I have shaped my analysis using interview excerpts which not only lay out deeply contrasting futures for these committees but also reveal profoundly different perceptions of the present and original role that ESCROs had in the space of controversial US American science governance. They offer deliberately different takes on the past role of ESCROs, and further work with committee members, administrators, and stem cell scientists would deepen our under-standing of whether these concerns are shared beyond the three committees I studied. In the meantime, thematised across these contrasting interpreta-tions—given by committee members themselves—lies a distinct unease with how committee work has come to be practised and the kind of governance over stem cell research that it actually constitutes.

False Premises?

Having conducted research with members of closed committees in the past (Douglas-Jones 2015, 2017), I knew that participating in research provided members with both an opportunity to speak about the intricacies of their work—a pleasure not often afforded with colleagues, given commitments to confidentiality—and an opportunity to speak candidly. More than once, inter-viewees refused to be recorded, or asked that the recording device be turned off. In a world where few members' names are published (Hinterberger 2018), it mattered that they could share their thoughts anonymously, and no identify-ing information is shared. I have, however, aimed to contextualise the position from which interviewees speak, whether expert member, lay-member, legal representative, administrator, or bioethicist. Amongst them I encountered considerable reflection on the role of the committee and, overall, a sense of the value of 'serving' the research community through the role. Under conditions of anonymity, some interviewees voiced agreement with the view that the work of ESCROs was 'complete', and more than that, perhaps, has been done for quite some time. One, whom I will call James, articulated his position in the form of a story, almost a parable. We had been talking for about half an hour, reviewing how he had come to serve on the committee and going through my usual opening questions about the kinds of cases they had seen and the discus-sions to which he had contributed. After a pause of seeming frustration with these details, James asked me, 'Look, does it [the ESCRO] serve a function?' I did not know how to answer. Sighing, he asked again, 'Would something bad happen if it [the ESCRO meetings] weren't happening?' He explained with the following story:

> Do you know the story of the guy of on a park bench tearing his paper into tiny little bits and a woman passing by says to him, 'What are you doing?' 'I'm keep-ing the elephants away, he answers. And she says, 'You're crazy', and he says, 'You haven't seen any elephants, have you?'

James sits on the committee as a professional ethicist, alongside his scientific, legal, and layperson peers. His story appears as a discussion of faith or unthink-ing routine, in this telling and elsewhere. Legal scholar Schlegel (2003) uses the same analogy to describe 'a series of steps, once undertaken for a good reason, the purpose of which has been lost' (p. 967), making it evident that James is casting the ESCRO as an apotropaic entity. From the Greek 'to ward off'—a form of ritual superstition, designed to keep away unspecified 'bad things'—the basic assumption here is that the action itself is futile because faith in the efficacy of action is based on an error about the world. In the eyes of the man on the bench, the tearing of paper is a *necessary activity*, warding off elephants, but to the passer-by his action achieves nothing, because what it claims to act upon does not exist. Translating the analogy back to committee work, the bench where the tearing of paper is happening is not a park, but the sealed room of committee discussions, a site where neither publics nor researchers can observe proceedings. James's perspective turns the work of the committee, its convening, discussions, and deliberation, as well as the long-term relationships it has developed with local researchers, into an exercise based on a false premise: there was never, in James's view, anything to be afraid of; there was no ethical issue at the heart of stem cell technologies. The committees, he felt, had been set up with a false premise. He doubted the value of the committee then, and now, but in delineating between ethical efficacy and ritual efficacy, pointed to a division between content and appearance.

In 2005, the year ESCROs were introduced, Hogle argued that 'political ritual is substituting for policy making' (2005, p. 24). James's invocation of paper shredding suggests ritualistic elements, but the salient point is the continuity of the committee as a performance, whether or not it had an ongoing role for its members or those whose work it reviewed. I continue with this theme below.

Democratic Failures

If James thought that committee work was the performance of paper tearing—without meaning because no threat had ever existed—other committee members also criticised the premise of their own committees, but for very different reasons. Members argued that oversight—in this closed committee—was misplaced, and ultimately a form of self-regulation protective of research institutions rather than a forum dedicated to a thorough exploration of the issues.

When I interviewed Hilary, a legal expert, about his role on his local committee, he spoke from a number of years' experience in participating in its meetings and discussions. He commented that 'I think these things [committees] are created to make it *look* as if it somehow resembles regulation, and to me it is almost the opposite of regulation'. We had a short half hour scheduled in his busy timetable, and emails chimed in throughout the conversation, punctuating his speech. Hilary's answers were brief, precise, and to the point. But as he answered my questions about the scope and role of the committee's work, he explained that he did not think the embryonic stem cell research oversight committee and its specific set of expertise was the right place to discuss where stem cell research should go, as research developed. 'I think it should be policy makers, not scientists', he said, 'who are deciding, "Should we create chimeras who are really quite human in their attributes?" and if so, do we keep them in cages, do we then decide at some point they have human rights?' Extracting from a recent set of case discussions in their committee,[8] Hilary continues, 'Those are pretty profound social policy issues, and to me it is shocking that in our country we leave it all to our scientists, and the most we do in the way of regulation is—at least for many of these issues—to have these so called "self-regulatory" bodies'. For Hilary, the *existence* of the committees is not 'enough' to constitute oversight.

One committee member observed rather wryly, 'Universities are, I mean, we're largely pro-science. So, I am not sure we're the best watchdog for all things scientific.' This critique echoes precisely those levelled at ESCROs by researchers in Charis Thompson's study of (and participation in) the ESCRO committee at Berkeley. Reflecting on what it takes to make 'good science'—in multiple meanings of the word—Thompson describes the foremost concern amongst committee members as 'enabling research in an environment of ethical controversy, and not about ethical inquiry' (2013, p. 64).

In these critiques of 'self-regulation' we find not only critique of committee membership but also the model of the committee itself. Contrasting James's and Hilary's positions, one is drawn to a retrospective sense of a process that was always lacklustre, if one wishes—as they did—for ideals of participation and democratic values. The ESCRO has some form of falsity in both cases, but not for the same reasons. For James, meetings continue in a ritualised format, a form of action that only appears to prevent something which, from another perspective, would not happen even if the practice ceased. The retrospective assessment is that there were never any 'elephants' in the first place: this is governance of (to him) a non-issue, the creation of the committees a shield from the heat of public opinion. For Hilary, the committee's creation is smoke-screen, the *appearance* of thoughtful engagement with the possibilities of stem cell research, but conducted entirely without the presence of the kinds of voices she/he thinks should be present. For Hilary, the committees are thus the wrong tool for a real job.

Sufficiency and Sustainability

ESCROs have now been part of research environments for 15 years and, so far, the 2013 call from bioethicists to dissolve their function has prompted action. Let us then consider the interviewees for whom ESCROs were fulfilling 'sufficient' role. This perspective was prominent among those who spoke 'from the institution', as they were inclined to maintain the committee for the sense that it was useful for things *other than* the content of its expert deliberation. The ESCRO constituted a specific site of knowledge (there is a documentable body to which one can point) and provided the imagined 'interface' between the university researcher and the public. This quote from Beverley, one of the committee's administrators, sums it up:

Beverley: I think it's one of the primary reasons to have a ESCRO: to be that interface between the public and uni[versity] researchers. We do

RDJ:

Beverley:

the right thing, have everything documented; it's a place to give assurance to the public that we're open about this kind of research. And that's been very rewarding to know that that is what we're doing.

So, can you tell me some ways in which you do that?

Just by having a committee, and having the researchers on campus submit a protocol for approval, gives us a list of everyone on campus that is doing SC research. We know what SC lines they're using, are there any issues with them, have they been approved by NIH, any federal funding involved just collecting that information.

If for Hilary the existence of committees was a serious shortcoming for oversight, that same existence is valued by institutions. University relationships to funding bodies come with accountability and documentation responsibilities, and when Beverley describes what researchers on campus do, she is thinking about relationships more internal to the world of research as a set of practices organised around ethics as a bureaucratic practice. However, I also found committee members considering the committee as a means of anticipating future controversy, and providing protection against it through the mere existence of 'process'. Listen to Lesley, a scientific member of the committee Beverley administrates, argue for the relationship his committee has built with researchers at their institute. '[The committee] have said that almost explicitly: it's good for you guys to come back to us and for us to vet it because it helps you if you are attacked later, because you can say you went through a very deliberative process, the ESCRO committee looked at this several times and we felt [... trails off]. So, you have the language to respond to that.'

This form of pre-emption means there is a *future* control over narrative, an imagined audience, public, and newspaper headlines. The deliberation of the committee is good here not for *what* it deliberates, but *that* it is deliberative. The lingering doubt about there being anything *particularly* ethically concerning about the research that falls under the remit of the ESCRO (as James doubted) clashed with a retained conviction that there was something different about the committees themselves—their free remit and scope for consideration. One committee member described the ESCROs thus: 'We're the "worry committee", we're designated to worry about this, but we don't really know what you should be worried about.' In this shift—'we' don't know what 'you' should be worried about—the committee member is marking a gap between the worry work that they do, and what observers of the committee, upon whose behalf the worrying is being done, might want the committee to be thinking about. Often, charismatic topics capture attention, but in contrast with Hogle's characterisation of the stem cell spectacular (2005), the idea of research as *mundane* came up repeatedly during interviews. As one bioinformatician put it, 'Once you have a cell line that is anonymous and was obtained in an appropriate way and you're not putting human brains into rats, there is almost no serious ethical issue once you've passed those problems. So, what do you need a committee to review?'

Hinterberger cites Charis Thompson's extensive reflections on the ethical 'choreography' of stem cell research, noting particularly her comment that 'putting these regulations into action is first and foremost about enabling research in an environment of ethical controversy, and not about ethical inquiry' (2013, p. 64, cited in Hinterberger 2020, p. 1079). The reflections above belong to a world of calm enablement, adding only the sense of stem cell research as well established, an analytic of temporality from the perspective of science itself. As long as you are not doing anything out of the ordinary, not 'putting human brains into rats', there are no issues to discuss. In pointing to the pervasive worry of chimaeras, Hinterberger observes that what is striking about ESCROs is the 'ontological paper trail' they create, the centuries long workings through of explicit categories, human and animal long divided (Hinterberger 2020, p. 1079). The bioinformatician's phrasing classifies the stem cell research that passes the committee's desk as 'normal science', in need of no committee gaze, out of the scope of worry.

Expansionism

This question of scope, particularly in the face of apparently 'solved' concerns around the ESCROs' original objects of review as hiPSC cells became more widely used, caused delight in some interviewees. While they continued to meet and discuss the cases that came to them from active stem cell researchers in their institutes, the possibility that the committee might change or mature its scope was an idea of promise. In formulating ESCROs, the National Academies of Sciences drew on the public legitimacy, recognised features, and bureaucratic model of the Institutional Review Board. As such, ESCRO deliberation was considered to constitute an efficient and effective mode of assuring ethical discussions, potentially ripe for introduction to other fields. However, unlike IRBs, the scope was more open. With frontier thinking, for some committee members jurisdiction of the ESCRO extended beyond the original embryonic stem cell remit to 'all sorts'. For some, dropping the 'E' for embryonic was sufficient to indicate the expansion of scope resulting from the advances in stem cell science reviewed above. But for others, new fields outside of stem cell work opened up. Listen to this call from Sandra:

> I think that there's a role for these committees, but it's a much broader role than we currently have and the only way to get there would be to redefine the whole raison d'etre for the whole thing. 'Hey, this model has worked really well around some difficult questions related to innovative stem cell work but there's all sorts of other things that could benefit from this sort of reflective deliberation.' [...] The ESCRO has been a good standing committee, for that specific area. What we need to do is create a way of expanding that.

For Sandra, the committee was already there and should be used beyond the 'one little area' on which it currently focused. As we discussed, she imagined a forum that existed on a standing basis 'for people to reflect or deliberate or think about the value of the work, the risks of the work' when doing 'innovative research or research that raises challenging ethical questions that currently do not fall under IRB or IACUC [Animal Care and Use Committee] review'. Yet it is a vast span from the first story's implication that the deliberation of ESCROs is as worthless as tearing up paper to fend off (possibly imaginary) elephants, to the conviction on the part of this latter group of people that this type of deliberation is so worthwhile that the broader university research community could do with some form of it. This bears on the way in which committees are a default option for governing emerging forms of technological and scientific advancement, with surprisingly little reflexivity about what 'a committee' is, how it works, or why it is taken to be a legitimate form of decision-making. The underlying purpose of committee discussion remains contested, and further research is needed on the role that committees with this specific remit play for researchers, within universities, and across research communities both within the United States and beyond.

Conclusion

Since their introduction in 2005, ESCROs have been feeling their way forward as a procedural innovation, set up to address the national anxieties around embryonic stem cell research that arose in the United States in the early part of the twenty-first century. They drew heavily on twentieth-century models of human subjects' protection, but the entities that were designated as within their jurisdiction did not fall under human subjects' regulations. Indeed, quite what these entities *were* was part of the determining work of the committees, as they moved back and forth between knowing entities and deliberating upon them, working to decide precisely what it was they were dealing with in the first place (Jasanoff 2011).

Formulated as a recognisable ethics response at a specific moment, ESCROs were the product of guidelines composed primarily from within the scientific community, with a recommended composition of scientifically trained persons. In this way ESCROs have remained a primarily scientific imaginary of the role that ethics should play for science. Reflecting on the legacies of the Asilomar DNA modification conference (1975), Jasanoff, Hurlbut, and Saha comment that 'under the guise of responsible self-regulation, science steps in to shape the forms of governance that societies are allowed to consider' (2015, n.p.), confining larger normative questions to expert groups and fundamentally shaping the relationship between scientific work and democratic deliberation.

My work has shown how voices within the committees themselves pull the future of the ESCRO in multiple directions, shoring up their views with normative statements on whether there are even any ethical concerns for the committees to handle. It is in these knots of governance that the American philosophies of public and expert reason that take form in the committees find expression, organising and suspending one once red-hot thread of the social contract of research. And it is here, too, that ethnographers of the social life of ethics—as a form of bureaucratic management over moral and value disagreements—suggest that efforts to settle public disagreement about foundational biological research will find its resolution. Exploring the epistemic authority of ESCROs, as they waver on the edge of dissolution, is a good place to start.

Acknowledgements This work was supported by the *Biology and the Law* research grant, funded by the Faraday Institute and hosted at the Kennedy School of Government, Harvard University (PI, Sheila Jasanoff). I thank project collaborators Sheila Jasanoff, Ben Hurlburt, Kris Saha, and Amy Hinterberger for their support during the design and analysis of this fieldwork. I also extend my thanks to the two anonymous reviewers for this Handbook for their clarifying and perceptive comments.

NOTES

1. Organising research by nation state does not always give meaningful comparisons, however, as Thompson observes in her discussion of Singaporean and South Korean stem cell research environments. There, she finds that multinational teams and considerable mobility both of patients and of researchers produce 'radical differences in access, affordability and health outcomes' (2010, p. 147).
2. Marnia Johnston also made the multispecies leap with stem cells in 2010, creating 'Paranoia Bugs' for a multispecies salon in the AAA meetings, New Orleans. See Kirksey 2010.
3. Two surveys have been conducted on ESCRO prevalence and behaviour, one with 40 respondents in 2007 by Krysten Brown (a PhD student in the Department of Sociology at the University of Connecticut) and Anne Hiskes (the ESCRO chair there) and one with 30 respondents in 2011 by the Interstate Alliance on Stem Cell Research (IASCR 2011). This was an informal survey ahead of the 2011 World Stem Cell Summit. Notably, the survey covered 15 ESCROs in California, 3 in Massachusetts, 2 in Connecticut, and 1 in Maryland, Missouri, Florida, Pennsylvania, Oregon, Wisconsin, Washington, and New York, respectively.
4. Interviewees are anonymous. This is both by agreement with them and by request of the IRB that reviewed this study.
5. In addition I searched online for recommendations, transcripts, consultations, the NAS documents from 2005 to 2007 through which ESCROs were recommended, professional networks, blogs, newspaper releases, and any surveys.
6. Institutional structures make effectual the transition between allowable and disallowable—the institutions matter. However, details of the specific university cultures under study were beyond the scope of the pilot research.
7. Site 3, for example, does not have an ESCRO, and as part of exploring how maps of jurisdiction and concern are drawn, we thought it would be important to include it as a site in order to address the relationships between different committees and how they perceive the landscape of research. At Site 3 we talked to members of the IRB, the IACUC, and the Biosafety committee, where some interviews were conducted with Ben Hurlbut.

8. In her work on how chimaeras are thought and managed in the United States and the United Kingdom, Hinterberger observes a 'vigorous response from governing authorities to biological entities that do not easily fit into the established legal and political orders' (2020, p. 1073).

REFERENCES

Allen, A. v. (2019, May 19). Resurrecting Ferrets and Remaking Ecosystems. *Anthropology News*. https://anthropology-news.org/index.php/2019/05/16/resurrecting-ferrets-and-remaking-ecosystems/. Accessed 10 June 2021.

Aultman, J. (2013). Dissolution of ESCROs and evolution of a national ethics committee for scientific advancement. *American Journal of Bioethics, 13*(1), 61–2.

Bear, L., & Mathur, N. (2015). Remaking the Public Good: A New Anthropology of Bureaucracy. *The Cambridge Journal of Anthropology, 33*(1), 18–34.

Becker, G. (2000). *The Elusive Embryo: How Men and Women approach New Reproductive Technologies*. Berkeley, CA: University of California Press.

Bender, W., Hauskeller, C., & Manzei, A., (Eds.) (2005). *Crossing Borders: Cultural, Religious and Political Differences Concerning Stem Cell Research*. Munster: Agenda Verlag.

Benjamin, R. (2013). *People's Science: Bodies and Rights on the Stem Cell Frontier*. Stanford, CA: Stanford University Press.

Benjamin, R., & Hinkson, L. R. (2017). What do we owe each other? Moral debts and racial distrust in experimental stem cell science. In N. Ehlers & L. R. Hinkson (Eds.), *Subprime Health: Debt and Race in U.S. Medicine* (pp. 129–154). Minneapolis, MI: University of Minnesota Press.

Bharadwaj, A. (2012). Enculturating Cells: The Anthropology, Substance, and Science of Stem Cells. *Annual Review of Anthropology, 41*, 303–17.

Bharadwaj, A. (2013a). 'Subaltern Biology? Local Biologies, Indian Odysseys, and the Pursuit of Human Embryonic Stem Cell Therapies'. *Medical Anthropology, 32*(4), 359–73. https://doi.org/10.1080/01459740.2013.787533.

Bharadwaj, A. (2013b). 'Ethic of Consensibility, Subaltern Ethicality: The Clinical Application of Human Embryonic Stem Cells in India'. *Biosocieties, 8*, 25–40. https://doi.org/10.1057/biosoc.2012.41.

Bharadwaj, A. (2015). 'Badnam Science? The Spectre of the "Bad" Name and the Politics of Stem Cell Science in India'. *South Asia Multidisciplinary Academic Journal, 12*(online). https://doi.org/10.4000/samaj.3999.

Bharadwaj, A. (2017). Cultivated cure, regenerated affliction: Encounters with ALS and stem cell regeneration in India. *Medicine Anthropology Theory, 4*(3), 143–152.

Bharadwaj, A., & Glasner, P. (2008). *Local Cells, Global Science: The Rise of Embryonic Stem Cell Research in India*. Abingdon: Routledge.

Bharadwaj, A., & Inhorn, M.C. (2016). Conceiving Life and Death: Stem Cell Technologies and Assisted Conception in India and the Middle East. In V. Das & C. Han (Eds.), *Living and Dying in the Contemporary World* (pp. 67–82). Berkeley, CA: University of California Press.

Brown, N., Kraft, A., & Martin, P. (2006). The Promissory Pasts of Blood Stem Cells. *Biosocieties 1*(3), 329–48.

Brown, N., & Kraft, A. (2006). Blood ties: Banking the Stem Cell promise. *Technology Analysis & Strategic Management, 18*(3–4), 313–327.

Brown, A., & Hiskes, K. (2007). *A National survey of embryonic stem cell research oversight (ESCRO) committees*. University of Connecticut.

Chang, H-C. (2016). The multiple roles of cord blood banks in Taiwan: competition and collaboration. *New Genetics and Society, 35*(3), 246–266. https://doi.org/1 0.1080/14636778.2016.1209106.

Chapman, A.R. (2013). Evaluating ESCROs: perspectives from the University of Connecticut. *American Journal of Bioethics, 13*(1), 57–8. https://doi.org/10.108 0/15265161.2012.747026.

Coghlan, A. (2014, 30 January). Stem cell timeline: the history of a medical sensation. *New Scientist*. https://www.newscientist.com/article/dn24970-stem-cell-timeline-the-history-of-a-medical-sensation/. Accessed 10 June 2021.

Cooper, M. (2003). Rediscovering the immortal hydra: stem cells and the question of epigenesis. *Configurations, 11*, 1–26.

Cooper, M. (2004). Regenerative medicine: stem cells and the science of monstrosity. *Medical Humanities, 30*(1), 12–22.

Cooper, M. (2006) Resuscitations: Stem Cells and the crisis of old age. *Body & Society, 12*(1), 1–23.

Cooper, M. (2008). *Life as Surplus: Biotechnology and Capitalism in the Neoliberal Era*. Seattle, WA: Washington University Press.

Douglas-Jones, R. (2015). A 'good' ethical review: audit and professionalism in research ethics. *Social Anthropology, 23*(1), 53–67.

Douglas-Jones, R. (2017). Making Room for Ethics: Spaces, Surveys and Standards in the Asia-Pacific Region. *Science & Technology Studies, 30*(3), 13–34.

Eguizabal, C., Aran, B., Chuva de Sousa Lopes, S. M., Geens, M., Heindryckx, B., Panula, S., Popovic, M., Vassena, R., & Veiga, A. (2019). Two decades of embryonic stem cells: a historical overview. *Human Reproduction Open, 1*.

Ehrich, K., Williams, C., & Farsides, B. (2010). Fresh or frozen? Classifying "spare" embryos for donation to human embryonic stem cell research. *Social Science & Medicine, 71*(12), 2204–2211.

Ehrich, K., Williams, C., Farsides, B., & Scott, R. (2011). Embryo futures and stem cell research: the management of informed uncertainty. *Sociology of Health and Illness, 34*(1), 114–129.

Ellison, B. (2013). Making ESCRO committees work in New York. *American Journal of Bioethics, 13*(1), 63–64. https://doi.org/10.1080/15265161.2012.747023.

Eriksson L., & Webster, A. (2008). Standardizing the unknown: practicable pluripotency as doable futures. *Science as Culture, 17*(1), 57–69.

Eriksson, L., & Webster, A. (2015). Standardizing Work as a Recursive Process: Shaping the Embryonic Stem Cell Field. *New Genetics and Society, 34*(1), 72–88. https:// doi.org/10.1080/14636778.2014.998818.

Evans, M., & Kaufman, M. (1981). Establishment in culture of pluripotential cells from mouse embryos. *Nature, 292*, 154–156. https://doi.org/10.1038/292154a0.

Franklin, S. (1999). Dead Embryos: Feminism in Suspension. In L. Morgan & M. Michaels (Eds.), *Fetal Subjects, Feminist Positions*. (pp. 61–82). Philadelphia: University of Pennsylvania Press.

Franklin, S. (2001). Culturing Biology: Cell Lines for the Second Millennium. *Health, 5*(3), 335–354.

Franklin, S. (2005). Stem cells R us: emergent life forms and the global biological. In A. Ong & S. J. Collier (Eds.), *Global Assemblages: Technology, Politics and Ethics as Anthropological Problems*. (pp. 59–78). New York & London: Blackwell.

Franklin, S. (2006a). Embryonic Economies: The Double Reproductive Value of Stem Cells. *BioSocieties*, *1*(1), 71–90.

Franklin, S. (2006b). The Cyborg Embryo: Our Path to Transbiology. *Theory Culture and Society*, *23*(7–8), 167–187.

Franklin, S. (2013). *Biological Relatives: IVF, Stem Cells and the Future of Kinship*. Durham, NC: Duke University Press.

Franklin, S. (2018). Somewhere Over the Rainbow, Cells Do Fly. In A. Bharadwaj (Ed.), *Global Perspectives on Stem Cell Technologies*. (pp. 27–49). Palgrave Macmillan.

FTC. (2020, June 4). FTC Sends Letters Warning 35 Marketers to Stop Making Unsupported Claims That Their Products and Therapies Can Effectively Prevent or Treat COVID-19. https://www.ftc.gov/news-events/press-releases/2020/06/ftc-sends-letters-warning-35-more-marketers-stop-making. Accessed 10 June 2021.

Friese, C. (2013). Realising Potential in Translational Medicine: The-Uncanny Emergence of Care as Science. *Current Anthropology*, *54*(7), S129–S138.

Ganchoff, C. (2004). Regenerating Movements: Embryonic Stem Cells and the Politics of Potentiality. *Sociology of Health and Illness*, *26*(6), 757–774.

Garrett, J. R., Jotterand. F., & Ralston, C. (2013). *The Development of Bioethics in the United States*. Springer.

Gitschier, J. (2008) Sweating the Details: An Interview with Jamie Thomson. *PLoS Genet*, *4*(8). https://doi.org/10.1371/journal.pgen.1000182.

Geesink, I., Prainsack, B., & Franklin, S. (2008). Stem cell stories 1998–2008. *Science and Culture*, *17*(1), 1–11.

Gottweis, H. (2002). Stem Cell Policies in the United States and in Germany: Between Bioethics and Regulation. *Policy Studies Journal*, *30*, 444–469.

Gottweiss, H., Salter, B., & Waldby, C. (2009). *The Global Politics of Human Embryonic Stem Cell Science. Regenerative Medicine in Transition*. New York: Palgrave Macmillan.

Greely, H. (2013). Assessing ESCROs: Yesterday and Tomorrow. *American Journal of Bioethics*, *13*(1), 44–52.

Gross, M. (2001). Stem Cells Fuel Bitter Ethical Divisions. *Current Biology*, *11*(15), R581–R582. https://doi.org/10.1016/S0960-9822(01)00354-2.

Hauskeller, C., & Weber, S. (2011). Framing Pluripotency: iPS Cells and the Shaping of Stem Cell Science. *New Genetics and Society*, *30*(4), 415–431.

Hedgecoe, A. (2012) Trust and regulatory organisations: The role of local knowledge and facework in research ethics review. *Social Studies of Science*, *42*(5), 662–683

Hine, J. (2017). *Canada's Science: An Ethnography of Ethics and Expertise in Stem Cell Biology*. PhD Dissertation, Princeton University.

Hinterberger, A. (2018). Marked 'h' for human: Chimeric life and the politics of the human. *BioSocieties*, *13*, 453–469.

Hinterberger, A. (2020). Regulating Estrangement: Human-Animal Chimeras in Postgenomic Biology. *Science Technology and Human Values*, *45*(6), 1065–1086.

Hinterberger, A., & Porter, N. (2015). Genomic and Viral Sovereignty: Tethering the Materials of Global Biomedicine. *Public Culture*, *27*(2), 361–386.

Ho, W. C., Capps, B., & Voo, T.C. (2010). Stem Cell Science and Its Public: The Case of Singapore. *East Asian Science, Technology and Society: An International Journal*, *4*(1), 7–29.

Hogle, L. (2005, October). Stem Cell Policy as Spectacle Ripe for Anthropological Analysis. *Anthropology News*, 24–25.

Hogle, L. (2010). Characterizing Human Embryonic Stem Cells: Biological and Social Markers of Identity. *Medical Anthropology Quarterly, 24*(1), 433–450.

Hogle, L. (2018). Intersections of Technological and Regulatory Zones in Regenerative Medicine. In A. Bharadwaj (Ed.), *Global Perspectives on Stem Cell Technologies* (pp. 51–84). Palgrave Macmillan.

Hogle, L., & Das, A. (2017). The social production of evidence: regenerative medicine and the 21st Century Cures Act. *Regenerative Medicine, 12*(6), 581–586.

Hoeyer, K., & Tutton, R. (2005) "Ethics was here": studying the language-games of ethics in the case of UK Biobank. *Critical Public Health, 15*(4), 385–397.

Hoeyer, K., Nexoe, S., Hartlev, M., & Koch, L. (2009). Embryonic entitlements: stem cell patenting and the co-production of commodities and personhood. *Body and Society, 15*(1), 1–24.

Hull, M. S. (2012). *Government of Paper: The Materiality of Bureaucracy in Urban Pakistan.* Berkeley: University of California Press.

Hurlbut, B. J. (2017). *Experiments in Democracy: Human Embryo Research and the Politics of Bioethics.* New York: Columbia University Press.

Inhorn, M. C., & Tremayne, S. (Eds.) (2012). *Islam and Assisted Reproductive Technologies: Sunni and Shia Perspectives.* New York: Berghahn.

Jacob, M.-A., & Riles, A. (2007). The New Bureaucracies of Virtue: Introduction. *Political and Legal Anthropology Review, 30*(2), 181–191.

Jasanoff, S. (2005). In the democracies of DNA: Ontological uncertainty and political order in three states. *New Genetics and Society, 24*(2), 139–156.

Jasanoff, S. (2011). Making the facts of life. In S. Jasanoff (Ed.), *Reframing Rights: Bioconstitutionalism in the Genetic Age* (pp. 59–84). Cambridge, MA: The MIT Press.

Jasanoff, S., & Metzler, I. (2020). Borderlands of life: IVF embryos and the law in the United States, United Kingdom, and Germany. *Science, Technology, & Human Values, 45*(6), 1001–1037. https://doi.org/10.1177/0162243917753990.

Jasanoff, S., Hurlburt, B., & Saha, K. (2015). CRISPR Democracy Gene Editing and the Need for Inclusive Deliberation *Issues in Science and Technology* 32(1), 25–32

Jha, A. (2011, March 13). Look, No Embryos! The Future of Ethical Stem Cells. *The Guardian* (online edition). https://www.theguardian.com/science/2011/mar/13/ips-reprogrammed-stem-cells. Accessed 25 April 2021.

Jiang, L., & Rosemann, A. (2018). Human embryo gene editing in China: the uncertain legal status of the embryo. *Biosocieties.* https://doi.org/10.1057/s41292-018-0116-1.

Kirksey, E. (2010, October). Tactics of Swarming. *Anthropology News.*

Lambek, M. (Ed.) (2010). *Ordinary Ethics: Anthropology, Language and Action.* New York: Fordham University Press.

Landecker, H. (1999). Between Beneficence and Chattel: The Human Biological in Law and Science. *Science in Context, 12*(1), 203–225.

Landecker, H. (2000). Immortality, in vitro: a history of the HeLa cell line. In P. E. Brodwin (Ed.), *Biotechnology and Culture* (pp. 44–58). Bloomington: Indian University Press.

Landecker, H. (2006). *How Cells Become Technologies.* Cambridge, MA: Harvard University Press

Lock, M. (2001). The alienation of body tissue and the biopolitics of immortalized cell lines. *Body and Society, 7*(2–3), 63–91.

Lomax, G. (2013). The great ESCRO experiment: there is still value to be gained. *American Journal of Bioethics, 13*(1), 55–6.

Lovell-Badge, R. (2001, November 1). The future for stem cell research. *Nature, 414*, 88–91.

Marsland, R., & R. Prince. (2012). What is life worth? Exploring biomedical interventions, survival and the politics of life. *Medical Anthropology Quarterly, 26*(4), 453–69.

Martins, G. R. (1981). Isolation of a pluripotent cell line from early mouse embryos cultured in medium conditioned by teratocarcinoma stem cells. *PNAS, 78*(12), 7634–7638. https://doi.org/10.1073/pnas.78.12.7634.

Master, Z., & Resnik, D. B. (2013). Promoting public trust: ESCROs won't fix the problem of stem cell tourism. *American Journal of Bioethics, 13*(1), 53–5.

Mathur, N. (2015). *Paper Tiger: Law, Bureaucracy and the Developmental State in Himalayan India*. Cambridge: Cambridge University Press.

Mathur, N. (2020). Afterword: the utopianization of bureaucracy. *Social Anthropology, 28*(1), 112–120.

Heyman, J. M. (2004). The Anthropology of Power-Wielding Bureaucracies. *Human Organization, 63*(4), 487–500.

Meskus, M. (2018). *Craft in Biomedical Research: The iPS Cell Technology and the Future of Stem Cell Science*. Palgrave Macmillan.

Metzler, I. (2012). On Why States Still Matter: In Vitro Fertilization Embryos Between Laboratories and State Authorities in Italy. In N. S. Vermeulen, S. Tamminen & A. Webster (Eds.), *Bio-Objects: Life in the 21st Century* (pp. 151–170). London: Ashgate.

Milne, R. (2016). In Search of Lost Time: Age and the Promise of Induced Pluripotent Stem Cell Models of the Brain. *New Genetics and Society, 35*(4), 393–408.

Morrison, M. (2020). Making bio-objects mobile: behind the scenes of a translational stem cell banking consortium. *Biosocieties*. https://doi.org/10.1057/s41292-020-00207-3.

Mulkay, M. (1997). *The Embryo Research Debate: Science and the Politics of Reproduction*. Cambridge: Cambridge University Press.

Murphy, E., & Dingwall, R. (2007). Informed consent, anticipatory regulation and ethnographic practice. *Social Science & Medicine, 65*(11), 2223–2234.

NAS, National Academies of Science. (2005a). *Guidelines for Human Embryonic Stem Cell Research*.

NAS, National Academies of Science. (2005b, April 26). Press Release: Guidelines Released for Embryonic Stem Cell Research. *Office of News and Public Information*. https://www8.Nationalacademies.org/onpinews/newsitem.aspx?Record ID=11278. Accessed 10 June 2021.

NAS, National Academies of Science. (2007). *Report: 2007 Amendments to the National Academies' Guidelines for Human Embryonic Stem Cell Research*.

NAS, National Academies of Science. (2008a). *Report: Amendments to the National Academies' Guidelines for Human Embryonic Stem Cell Research*.

NAS, National Academies of Science. (2008b, September 5). Updated Guidelines for Stem Cell Research Released. https://www8.nationalacademies.org/onpinews/newsitem.aspx?RecordID=12260. Accessed 10 June 2021.

NAS, National Academies of Science. (2010). *Guidelines for Human Embryonic Stem Cell Research*.

Merleau-Ponty, N., Vertommen, S., & Pucéat, M. (2018). I6 passages: on the reproduction of a human embryonic stem cell line from Israel to France. *New Genetics and Society, 37*(4), 338–361, https://doi.org/10.1080/14636778.2018.1548269.

Ong, A., & Collier. S. J. (2005). Introduction. In A. Ong & S. J. Collier (Eds.), *Global Assemblages, Anthropological Problems*. Berg.

Patra P. K., & Sleeboom-Faulkner, M. (2009). Bionetworking: experimental stem cell therapy and patient recruitment in India. *Anthropology & Medicine, 16*(2), 147–163.

Perrow, C. (1992[1984]). *Normal Accidents: Living with High-Risk Technologies*. New York: Basic Books.

Petersen, A., & Seear, K (2011). Technologies of hope: Techniques of online advertising of stem cell treatments. *New Genetics and Society, 30*, 329–346.

Power, M. (1997). *The Audit Society*. Oxford: Oxford University Press.

Prainsack, B. (2006). Negotiating Life: The Regulation of Human Cloning and Embryonic Stem Cell Research in Israel. *Social Studies of Science, 36*(2), 173–205.

Prainsack, B., & Gmeiner R. (2008). Clean soil and common ground: the biopolitics of human embryonic stem cell research in Austria. *Science and Culture, 17*(4), 377–395.

Prasad, A. (2014). Ambivalent journeys of hope: Embryonic stem cell in a clinic in India. *Health, 19*(2), 137–153.

Ragoné, H., & Twine, F. W. (Eds.) (2000). *Ideologies and Technologies of Motherhood: Race, Class, Sexuality, Nationalism*. New York: Routledge.

Ravven, W. (2017, January 16). A Conversation with Shinya Yamanaka. *The New York Times* (online edition). https://www.nytimes.com/2017/01/16/science/shinya-yamanaka-stem-cells.html. Accessed 5 February 2021.

Roberts, E. F. S. (2007). Extra Embryos: Ethics, Cryopreservation and IVF in Ecuador and Elsewhere. *American Ethnologist, 34*(1), 188–199.

Roberts, E. F. S. (2011). Abandonment and Accumulation: Embryonic Futures in the United States and Ecuador. *Medical Anthropology Quarterly, 25*(2), 232–253.

Roberts, E. F. S. (2013). Assisted Existence: An Ethnography of Being. *Journal of the Royal Anthropological Institute, 19*, 562–580.

Rosemann, A. (2011). Modalities of Value, Exchange, Solidarity: Exploring the Social Life of Stem Cells in China, *New Genetics and Society, 30*(2), 181–192.

Rosemann, A. (2014). Standardization as situation-specific achievement: Regulatory diversity and the production of value in intercontinental collaborations in stem cell medicine. *Social Science & Medicine, 122*, 72–80.

Rosemann, A., & Luo, H.Y. (2018). Attitudes on the Donation of Human Embryos for Stem Cell Research among Chinese IVF Patients and Students. *Journal of Bioethical Inquiry*. https://doi.org/10.1007/s11673-018-9862-9.

Rosemann, A., & N. Chaisinthop. (2016). The pluralization of the international: networks of resistance and alter-standardization in regenerative stem cell medicine. *Social Studies of Science, 46*(1), 112–39.

Saniei, M. (2012). Human embryonic stem cell research in Iran: the significance of the Islamic context. In M. Inhorn & S. Tremayne (Eds.), *Islam and the Biotechnologies of Human Life* (pp. 194–219). Oxford: Berghahn.

Santoro, P. (2009). From (Public?) Waste to (Private?) Value: The Regulation of Private Cord Blood Banking in Spain. *Science Studies, 22*(1), 3–24.

Schlegel, J. H. (2003). Taking Schlag Seriously: Practices in the Legal Academy: But Pierre, If We can't think normatively, what are we to do? *University of Miami Law Review, 57*(3), 955–972.

Sheller, M., & Urry, J. (2006). The New Mobilities Paradigm. *Environment and Planning A, 38*, 207–226

Sleeboom-Faulkner, M., & Chang, C.H. (2016). The private, the public and the hybrid in umbilical cord blood banking – A global perspective, *New Genetics and Society*, *35*(3), 223–227. https://doi.org/10.1080/14636778.2016.1219227

Sleeboom-Faulkner, M., Chen, H.D. & Rosemann, A. (2018). Regulatory capacity building and the governance of clinical stem cell research in China. *Science and Public Policy*. https://doi.org/10.1093/scipol/scx077/4675127.

Sleeboom-Faulkner, M., Chekar, C.K., Faulkner, A., Heitmeyer, C., Marouda, M., Rosemann, A., Chaisinthop N., Chang, H.C., Ely, A., Kato, M., Patra, P.K., Su, Y, Sui, S., Suzuku, W., & Zhang, X. (2016). Comparing national home-keeping and the regulation of translational stem cell applications: an international perspective. *Social Science and Medicine, 153*, 240–249.

Song, P. (2010). Biotech Pilgrims and the Transnational Quest for Stem Cell Cures. *Medical Anthropology, 29*(4), 384–402. https://doi.org/10.1080/0145974 0.2010.501317.

Song, P. (2011). The proliferation of stem cell therapies in post-Mao China: problema- tizing ethical regulation. *New Genetics and Society, 30*(2), 141–153. https://doi. org/10.1080/14636778.2011.574375.

Sperling, S. (2004). From crisis to potentiality: managing potential selves: stem cells, immigrants and German identity. *Science Public Policy, 31*(2), 139–49

Sperling, S. (2008). Converting ethics into reason: German stem cell policy between science and the law. *Science and Culture, 17*(4), 363–75.

Strathern, M. (1991). Partners and Consumers: Making Relations Visible. *New Literary History, 22*(3), 581–601.

Strathern, M. (Ed) (2000). *Audit Cultures: Anthropological Studies in Accountability, Ethics and the Academy*. Routledge: London and New York.

Stark, L. (2011). *Behind Closed Doors: IRBS and the Making of Ethical Research*. Chicago: University of Chicago Press.

Stephens, N., & R. Dimond. (2015). Unexpected Tissue and the Biobank that Closed: An Exploration of Value and the Momentariness of bio-objectification Processes. *Life Sciences, Society and Policy*. https://doi.org/10.1186/s40504-015-0032-0.

Sunder Rajan, K. (2006). *Biocapital: The Constitution of Postgenomic Life*. Durham, NC: Duke University Press.

Svendsen, M. N. (2011). Articulating Potentiality: Notes on the Delineation of the Blank Figure in Human Embryonic Stem Cell Research. *Cultural Anthropology, 26*(3), 414–437.

Svendsen, M., & Koch, L. (2008). Unpacking the "Spare Embryo": Facilitating Stem Cell Research in a Moral Landscape. *Social Studies of Science, 38*(1), 93–110. https://doi.org//10.1177/0306312707082502.

Taussig, K. S., Hoeyer, K., & Helmreich, S. (2013). The Anthropology of Potentiality in Biomedicine. *Current Anthropology, 54*(7), S3–S14.

Thomson, J., Itzkovitz-Eldor, J., Shapiro, S. S., Waknitz, M. A., Swiergiel, J. J., Marshall, V.S., & Jones, J. M. (1998). Embryonic stem cell lines derived from human blastocysts. *Science, 282*(5391), 1145–1147. https://doi.org/10.1126/ science.282.5391.1145.

Thompson, C. (2006). *Ethical, legal, and social implications of stem cell research*. Paper presented at the Berkeley Stem Cell Center Retreat, Asilomar, CA.

Thompson, C. (2008). Medical tourism, stem cells, genomics: EASTS, transnational STS and the contemporary life sciences. *East Asian Science and Technology Society, 2*, 433–48.

Thompson, C. (2010). Asian regeneration? Nationalism and internationalism in stem cell research in South Korea and Singapore. In A. Ong, & N. N. Chen (Eds.), *Asian Biotech: Ethics and Communities of Fate* (pp. 95–117) Durham, NC: Duke University Press.

Thompson, C. (2013). *Good Science: The Ethical Choreography of Stem Cell Research.* Cambridge, MA: The MIT Press.

Vaughan, D. (1996). *The Challenger Launch Decision: Risky Technology, Culture and Deviance at NASA.* Chicago: University of Chicago Press.

Vermeulen, N., Tamminen, S., & Webster, A. (Eds.) (2012). *Bio-Objects: Life in the 21st Century.* London: Ashgate.

Waldby, C. (2002). Stem Cells, Tissue Cultures, and the Production of Biovalue. *Health, Illness and Medicine, 6,* 305–23.

Waldby, C. (2008). Oocyte markets: women's reproductive work in embryonic stem cell research. *New Genetics and Society, 27*(1), 19–31, https://doi.org/10.1080/14636770701843576.

Waldby, C., & Squier, S. (2003). Ontogeny, ontology and phylogeny: embryonic life and stem cell technologies. *Configurations, 11*(1), 27–46.

Waldby, C., & Mitchell, R. (2006). *Tissue Economies: Blood, Organs and Cell Lines in Late Capitalism.* Durham, NC: Duke University Press.

Waldby, C., & Cooper, M. (2010). From reproductive work to regenerative labour: The female body and the stem cell industries. *Feminist Theory, 11*(1), 3–22.

Wahlberg, A., & Streitfellner. T. (2009). Stem cell tourism, desperation and the governing of new therapies. In O. Döring (Ed.), *Life Sciences in Translation: A Sino-European Dialogue on Ethical Governance of the Life Sciences* (pp. 81–97). BIONET Textbook.

Webster, A., & Eriksson, L. (2008). Governance-by-Standards in the Field of Stem Cells: Managing Uncertainty in the World of 'Basic Innovation. *New Genetics and Society, 27*(2), 99–111. https://doi.org/10.1080/14636770802077009.

Wilson, D. (2013). What can history do for bioethics? *Bioethics, 27*(4), 215–223.

Zhang, J. Y. (2011). Scientific institutions and effective governance: a case study of Chinese stem cell research. *New Genetics and Society, 30*(2), 193–207.

PART V

Infrastructures, Linkages, and Livelihoods

CHAPTER 34

Infrastructures, Linkages, and Livelihoods

Introduction

Brit Ross Winthereik and Ayo Wahlberg

Social life is upheld through and shaped by material-symbolic constructions that embed values and afford human activity. This is true for contemporary societies as well as for past forms of social organising. In *The Central Eskimo* (1888), Franz Boas makes an ethnographic case for studying intimate interdependencies between people and their (built) environments if we are to understand their 'mode of life'. Having observed and stayed with the Inuit people he met during expeditions to Baffin Island in Northeastern America in the 1880s, Boas describes how 'the migrations or the accessibility of the game compel the natives to move their habitations from time to time, and hence the distribution of the villages depends, to a great extent, upon that of the animals which supply them with food' (1888, p. 419). In this way, Inuit habitations were not site-bound; rather, habitation was a dynamic social activity that took place over time and over wide expanses of land in ways that demonstrated inescapable connections between people, animals, material things, built structures, and the landscapes around them.

B. R. Winthereik (✉)
Department of Business IT, IT University of Copenhagen, Copenhagen, Denmark
e-mail: brwi@itu.dk

A. Wahlberg
Department of Anthropology, University of Copenhagen, Copenhagen, Denmark
e-mail: ayo.wahlberg@anthro.ku.dk

M. H. Bruun et al. (eds.), *The Palgrave Handbook of the Anthropology of Technology*, https://doi.org/10.1007/978-981-16-7084-8_34

A few decades later, Bronislaw Malinowski, in defence of a holistic approach, would likewise make a case for studying the webbed interconnections that upheld and shaped social life:

> [T]he modern Ethnographer ... with his tables of kinship terms, genealogies, maps, plans and diagrams, proves an extensive and big organisation, shows the constitution of the tribe, of the clan, of the family. ... [Conversely,] an Ethnographer who sets out to study only religion, or only technology, or only social organisation cuts out an artificial field for inquiry, and he will be seriously handicapped in his work. (Malinowski 1922, pp. 16–17)

In his work, Malinowski argued for an all-encompassing perspective on human society that includes multiple elements and phenomena.

In China, Fei Xiaotong argued that it was 'the soil' that was foundational for observable patterns of social life as 'people live together in the same place so that they can be close to their fields ... [and] where irrigation is required, people must work together as a group' (Fei 1992[1947], p. 40; Wittfogel 1957; see also Andersen this volume). From one perspective this can be read as material-ecological determinism: people become what they are as a consequence of their engagement with particular material structures. But we may want to consider them as early attempts to grasp the role of material matter in infrastructur*ing* social relations as a way of providing better accounts of life as it unfolds beyond a bounded locality, linking it to other times and places elsewhere.

What we are arguing is that the role of material matter in the formation and maintenance of linkages has been a concern since the very beginning of the anthropological discipline as physical structure, environment, spirits, and nature have been seen as key elements in organising relations between people. We see attention to this organising in what, in recent years, have come to be conceptualised as infrastructures, both within anthropology and in the neighbouring disciplines of sociology, human geography, and science and technology studies (STS). Indeed, we can say that early twentieth-century ethnographic efforts to describe and analyse 'the Kula system of trading' (Malinowski 1922, p. 25), *African Political Systems* (Fortes and Evans-Pritchard 1940), 'modes of association' (Fei 1992[1947], p. 63), or 'systems of kinship and marriage' (Radcliffe-Brown and Forde 1950), all sought to demonstrate how modes of life within human societies were always located within systems of interconnectedness and linkages that included material objects, subsistence practices, skills of transportation, distributions of dwellings, ritual forms, and/or ways of exercising authority which, together, constituted 'a vast complex of activities, interconnected, and playing into one another, so as to form one organic whole' (Malinowski 1922, p. 52).

And so, without always having granted them an exceptional role, anthropologists have, nonetheless, long seen technologies as integral to human life. This relative invisibility of technologies in anthropological studies would, however, change with the development of a specialised sub-field (see Bruun and Wahlberg this volume). Since its inception in the 1980s, the anthropology of technology has been rooted in a conceptualisation of socio-technical *systems* in terms of a 'distinctive technological activity that stems from the linkage of techniques and material culture to the social coordination of labor' (Pfaffenberger 1992, p. 497). While this initial conceptualising of the field did not mention infrastructures as such, implicit in the concern for linkages and modes of coordination was an interest in how social relations were upheld beyond a single site of study. At the same time, in STS, a more explicit conceptualisation of infrastructures was taking place, problematising taken-for-granted boundaries between technical and social realms (see Star and Ruhleder 1996; Bowker and Star 2000; Downey and Dumit 1997). It is only relatively recently that anthropologists have begun turning their analytical attention explicitly to infrastructures understood as the linkages, contingencies, solidifications, and circulations of people, ideas, and goods upholding our livelihood (see Larkin 2013; Anand et al. 2018; Harvey et al. 2016).

Our choice to focus on infrastructure and especially infrastructur*ing* in a handbook for the anthropology of technology pertains to the capacity of such physical instalments, webbed within infrastructures, to establish, uphold, and transform relations. In his *Annual Review of Anthropology* article on 'The Politics and Poetics of Infrastructure', Brian Larkin (2013) argues that 'infrastructures are matter that enable the movement of other matter. Their peculiar ontology lies in the facts that they are things and also the relation between things ... [i.e. they] are built networks that facilitate the flow of goods, people, or ideas and allow for their exchange over space' (pp. 329, 328). This observation that a material structure is what it is through its ability to make relations, both fixed and durable as well as dynamic and in flux, is specified by Penny Harvey, Casper Bruun Jensen, and Atsuro Morita in their introduction to *Infrastructures and Social Complexity: A Companion* (2016) in terms of a double relationality:

> Infrastructures ... are extended material assemblages that generate effects and structure social relations, either through engineered (i.e. planned and purposefully crafted) or non-engineered (i.e. unplanned and emergent) activities. Seen thus, infrastructures are doubly relational, due to their simultaneous internal multiplicity and their connective capacities *outwards*. (p. 5)

This double relationality, we believe, is an occasion for anthropologists to attend to infrastructures as both 'product' and process without necessarily having to do a study of an infrastructure. In contemporary social life, thinking in terms of infrastructur*ing* is exactly what allows ethnographers to study, for example, global interconnectedness across multiple scales, sites, and practices, including digitalisation practices and politics, the climate crisis, pandemic governance, multinational corporations, financial systems, deforestation, biodiversity, and much more, that happen on a more-than-human scale (Carse 2014).

ANTHROPOLOGICAL STUDIES OF INFRASTRUCTURES
AND INFRASTRUCTURING

While twentieth-century anthropology certainly offered insights into economic exchange and political and kinship systems that connected elements beyond a single locality, labelling such systems 'infrastructures' would of course be anachronistic. As already noted, it is only recently that 'systems' of various kinds have come to be conceptualised as infrastructures in anthropology. Studies of socially complex and wide-spanning material systems such as Inca roads and communication forms did exist (see Harvey et al. 2016), but it was phenomena such as networked, digital technologies, the emergence of global markets for consumer goods, and intensified migration that created a surge of interest among anthropologists in addressing those underlying structures head on, as objects of anthropological study.

Consequently, over the past few decades, anthropologists on all continents have begun ethnographically tracing movements of people, information, ideas, energy, goods, remittances, investments, biological materials, and more, beyond single sites of study (Marcus 1995; Ong and Collier 2005; Andersen et al. 2020; Wahlberg this volume). These studies of flow, movement, and displacement have brought with them a keen interest in how human lives and socialities are shaped materially as well as politically. Whereas early infrastructure studies in STS mainly focused on how information and communication systems were shaping scientific and organisational expertise, anthropology's empirical focus has been different from the start. Ethnographically attending to water distribution systems (Anand 2017; Morita 2016), transport networks (Harvey and Knox 2015), electricity grids (Özden-Schilling 2019), transnational gas pipelines (Barry 2013), environmental conflict (Richardson 2016), data centres' relations of exchange with nation states that produce green energy (Maguire and Winthereik 2019), or cross-continental, deep-sea fibre-optic cable webs (Starosielski 2015), anthropologists have often been interested in how material infrastructures underpin the consolidation of a global capitalist economy alongside mass-mediated imaginaries (Tsing 2004; Appadurai 1996).

Perhaps needless to say, infrastructure studies draw on the rich resources made available by both STS and anthropology in, for example, studies of gaming, climate modelling, data practices, recommendation systems, microbiology, and reproductive technologies (Boellstorff 2008; Walford 2012; Hoeyer 2019; Seaver 2017; Helmreich 2009; Inhorn 2015; Schüll 2014; Wahlberg 2018). These studies show a significant overlap in their interests in the effects of infrastructuring; for example, particular attention has been paid to the power relations built into infrastructures (Reeves 2016; Anand 2015). In this sense, they relate to research done by one of the founding figures of infrastructure studies in STS, Susan Leigh Star (Star 1989), whose interest lay in the sociological study of science and technology, in the invisibility of infrastructures (Star 1991), and in who and what they exclude (Star and Strauss 1999; Bruni 2005). Star and colleagues spoke of infrastructures' capacity to fade into the woodwork, only becoming visible—or partly visible—upon breakdown (Timmermans et al. 1998); hence, to address the empirical problem of locating infrastructures they suggested that ethnographers, rather than asking 'What is an infrastructure?', should ask 'When is infrastructure?', thereby placing emphasis on the constant work of maintenance and repair needed for infrastructuring (Velho and Ureta 2019).

Attending to their political and world-making effects, anthropologists have studied infrastructures' roles in nation-building and as 'harbingers of modernity', showing how, rather than forming a stage on which social and political forces are enacted, infrastructures are themselves material instalments that embed social, political, and symbolic dimensions (Anand 2017). Infrastructure studies problematise the very question of how some things are brought to hang together in the first place, and other things afforded to travel. Empirically approaching and analysing something *as an infrastructure* thus allows for a problematisation of how things come to be connected and made to move.

In anthropological studies of technology, one of the things that the notion of infrastructuring problematises is scale. Consider 'macroscopic' studies of political economies that tend to demonstrate a convergence in how airport terminals, shopping malls, global smartphone brands, skyscraper-lined financial districts, and subway systems appear as facsimiles regardless of continent, reflecting how 'world cities point to new economic capacities and infrastructures which construct, assemble, and channel flows of information, goods, and influences' (Simone 2001, p. 16). Attending to how—by what means, and to what effects—flows are made possible diffracts the narrative of globalisation as a homogenising force and directs the gaze to sites where the macro- and the microscopic assemble.

This is not to say that the grandeur of infrastructures cannot be attended to ethnographically, as size and scope play an important role in understanding them. The infrastructure-as-spectacle that demonstrates the capacities of the state is, for example, described in studies of electricity and energy where dams and power plants perform states and governments as mighty and in control (Jensen 2019; Kirshner and Power 2019; Loloum 2019). Attending both to the construction of a modern state, for example, and to local effects on a population or on the nature of specific infrastructural designs, ethnographers have insisted on describing the particularities that shape processes of infrastructuring—that is, 'the ongoing and continual processes of creating and enacting … infrastructures' (Karasti and Blomberg 2018)—in different localities. Whether in the daily operations of maintaining Mumbai's water supply (Anand 2017), the ambiguous uptake of cell phones in Jamaica (Horst 2006), or the anticipated hazards that arise in an 'interoceanic' highway-building project between the Andean highlands of Peru and Amazonian Brazil (Knox and Harvey 2011).

It is little wonder then that infrastructure has become a key concept within the anthropology of technology. As Penny Harvey and Hannah Knox (2015) argue in their monograph, *Roads: An Anthropology of Infrastructure and Expertise*, 'the opening up of anthropology to the study of infrastructures …

has had the effect of further unsettling the question of the project or purpose of anthropological description' (p. 2). If twentieth-century anthropology had holistically examined forms of social organisation with attention to material culture and ecology, by the end of the century, infrastructuring had become a contextualising move that would no longer consider legislation, nation-state politics, global economic systems, techno-science, or nature as residing 'outside' social organisation and cultural life. Previously understood as 'context', these elements now became part of the analysis in anthropology's 'infrastructural turn' (Keith and de Souza Santos 2021). Thus, studies of 'the micro', which is to say locality-based ethnographic explorations, are combined with reflections on infrastructuring as a scale-making practice in and by itself. While the socio-cultural problems that anthropologists have studied were always ethnographically and historically situated, the analytical take on locality changed to encompass multiple scales at once.

THE CHAPTERS IN THIS SECTION

Located within the large and evolving body of infrastructure studies within the anthropology of technology, in this section our focus is on infrastructures as material instalments and the processual aspects of infrastructures (i.e. infrastructuring) as empirically and analytically interesting. We have invited authors whose work concerns *energy*, *food production*, *water*, *electricity*, and *payment systems* as a way to elicit the value in attending to infrastructures and infrastructuring. While there are countless other empirical domains that could have been selected, these nevertheless represent some of the 'big' infrastructures that have shaped social worlds (and vice versa) in virtually all parts of the world. What is more, each of these infrastructures and their modes of infrastructuring have in recent times been implicated in some of the biggest global challenges the world is currently facing: from food security to pollution, digital divides, climate change, and social inequality.

In her chapter on energy, Gökçe Günel uses her recent ethnographic work on electricity production in Ghana to think more broadly about what she describes as the 'cumulative' manner in which *energy infrastructures* change at a time of 'energy transition'. She writes, 'As populations around the world imagine a departure from fossil fuels and a transition to renewable energy resources, they wonder what these new technologies will look like' (Günel this volume), insisting that anthropological studies of energy infrastructures and the processes of infrastructuring they entail are essential to any such processes of reimagination. By linking up 'leapfrogging' imaginaries, for example, with practical humanitarian uses of renewable energy through solar lamps or photo-electric lighting kits, anthropologists can show the gaps and discordances that emerge in the daily appropriation or rejection of new technologies.

In his chapter on *food infrastructures* in China, Mikkel Bunkenborg demonstrates how such infrastructures are about much more than 'merely' ensuring a reliable supply and distribution of food for a population of 1.4 billion people on a daily basis. Against a backdrop of a series of major food safety scandals that have led to sickness and death among consumers, sociologists in and scholars of China have come to describe 'post-Mao China as a society haunted by a lack of social trust' (Bunkenborg this volume). And, while state authorities and local government officials in Hebei province have been engaged in a series of initiatives to try to restore trust, through his ethnographic research in the village of Fanzhuang, Bunkenborg shows how 'bottom up' strategies of building trust involved personal relations—getting to *know* producers—rather than the kinds of verified (over)seeing of production that food safety regulations emphasised.

Alongside food supply, anthropologists have also studied how *water flows* have become crucial to the legitimacy and stability of nation states, as well as to the livelihoods and wellbeing of people (Anand 2017; Strang 2005; Andersen 2019; Paerregaard et al. 2016; Hastrup and Hastrup 2015). In her chapter on water infrastructuring, Astrid Oberborbeck Andersen argues that a certain ethnographic flexibility is required if we are to follow water in the field:

> When placing water at the centre of an anthropological analysis, what seems at first to be moving or flowing is water. By following water, the analytical perspective can swiftly shift from particular technological devices, such as the faucet, buckets, and meters, to pipes and infrastructural systems, watersheds, and international management regimes. (Andersen this volume)

Hence, we need ethnographic methods that allow us to link water relations to the waterworlds of which they are a part across the globe.

The *electrification* of a nation has long been considered a marker of progress within regimes of international development and by national governments who celebrate the inauguration of new power plants and the extension of national grids to 'remote' parts of their countries (Abram et al. 2019). In her chapter on electricity, Simone Abram shows how electrical infrastructures are both adaptable and resistant, as well as evident and invisible, as they come to shape daily life in different ways: for example, when electric meters are bypassed and electricity rerouted in shanty towns. With the ubiquity of electricity in a neon-lit, urbanised world, gaps and losses become all the more apparent in moments of 'black out', 'shortage', or 'surges'. As such, as she writes, 'technical and political constraints of different kinds reveal the political character of national-grid ambitions, and the limitations to even the most fully developed grids' (Abram this volume).

Finally, in her chapter on infrastructural perspectives on *digital payments*, Sunniva Sandbukt posits her ethnographic engagements with the use of digital wallets in Indonesia as an occasion to think about how the kinds of infrastructures that underpinned the standardisation of value into money forms are currently being reshaped in a time of increasing digitalisation of payments and related cashless transactions. Through her interactions with drivers who use various app-based services which give them access to customers who are looking for a ride, she traces the way digital payments accrue in a driver's 'digital wallet' only to be moved to a bank account in order to be extracted through an ATM. The smartphones, online banking services, and ATM machines that form the material backdrop of such digital payment infrastructures enable transactions, but they also create forms of exclusion (e.g. when driver ratings are used by an app's algorithms to privilege certain drivers at the cost of others) leading to creative efforts by drivers to 'game the system' as they came to know its logics.

Each of these chapters shows us how studying and analysing social practices when it comes to food, electricity, (digital) payments, water, and energy can benefit from the analytical notions of infrastructures and infrastructuring. As the contributors situate the unique lives and life situations of people within broader political economies that are materially afforded, they further develop key points made by Star and Ruhleder (1996): firstly, infrastructures are embedded within each other (Chalfin 2014; von Schnitzler 2008; Langstrup 2013). Secondly, infrastructures are often invisible, enabling certain kinds of work and relation-making, meaning that we are not always cognisant of the infrastructures that make social action possible. Thirdly, infrastructures are expansive, extending beyond single events or activities and, while in a sense they 'tie them together', how they do this work, again, is hard to understand when 'inside' the infrastructure. Fourthly, infrastructures are learned through communities of practice (Lave and Wenger 1991) or practice collectives (Wahlberg 2018) which form around given tasks. Fifthly, their reach and saliency are formed by and shape social conventions just as they rely on and produce technical standards (Jensen and Winthereik 2013). And lastly, infrastructures often surface during times of 'breakdown' (Bowker and Star 2000; Larkin 2016). To paraphrase Clifford Geertz's retelling of an Indian story heard during fieldwork, when it comes to infrastructuring we are dealing with relations all the way down (Geertz 1973, p. 28).

INFRASTRUCTURING METHODOLOGIES

Through the five chapters that make up this section of the Handbook of the Anthropology of Technology, we see how an anthropology of technology has come to be inextricably tied to empirical, analytical, and methodological concerns for infrastructures. Infrastructures are everywhere part of the ways in which humans organise, offering interesting vantage points from which to understand societies, power relations, stability and change, identity, meaning-making, future-making, and politics. They are empirically ubiquitous, urbanising forms of living based on mass transit, electricity, water pipes, industrial food production, sewage systems, information and communication technologies, financial systems, and more that can be found in all corners of the world.

Not only are infrastructures everywhere, they have also occasioned a rethinking and redesign of methodology within the anthropological discipline. Infrastructures are analytically interesting, as they span worlds to make new boundaries and compel researchers to question well-known entities and the divisions among them. As already noted, infrastructures are, at one and the same time, evolving and stable. They shape social worlds (Harvey and Knox 2012) and are simultaneously sites of ontological experimentation (Jensen and Morita 2015), just as they are technological through and through, as well as political, social, and cultural. As such, they are difficult to delimit, which is part of their attraction when we, as analysts, are required to make decisions about analytical angles. With infrastructures, not even boundaries between the empirical and the analytical are pregiven but are considered phenomena to be disassembled by the analyst. By so doing we may learn to account for how infrastructures inscribe social worlds and are themselves inscribed in them (Jensen 2014). Infrastructures thus challenge us methodologically, spanning the local/global, the short-term/long-term, and the large/small (Edwards 2003; Jensen and Winthereik 2013). We end this section introduction with a few examples of how engaging with infrastructures anthropologically has led to methodological experimentation.

First off, Morita (2017) has outlined 'infrastructural inversion' as a strategy to capture empirically the ways in which multispecies infrastructures are dynamically shaped, as a contrast to notions of techno-infrastructures that 'tame' a wild nature. Infrastructural inversion was originally developed by Geoffrey Bowker in his book *Memory Practices in the Sciences* (2005), where he suggested making a figure-ground reversal so as to avoid considering social and cultural practices as somehow existing 'on top of' a sub-stratum of material matter. 'Bringing the infrastructural "ground" up front in this way facilitated understanding of how complex chains of material relations reconfigure bodies, societies, and *also* knowledge and discourse in ways often unnoticed' (Harvey et al. 2016). Scholars such as Morita have taken up this approach as a way of accounting for the unseen yet structuring effects of material systems. It can be done by directing one's analytical gaze towards that which 'lies beneath' any social organisation but, as noted by Harvey and colleagues (2016), it can also be a strategy to attend to 'naturally occurring' infrastructural inversions or technological break-downs that become public scandals, like in leakage of personal data from systems owned by state authorities.

A second example comes from Winthereik and colleagues who developed the 'Energy Walk' as a way to shed light on ways in which the linking of material objects and physical landscape can 'infrastructure' people's imagination, in this case around future energy worlds (Winthereik et al. 2019; see also Maguire et al. 2021). Watts, Maguire, and Winthereik labelled the effect of conducting research through a design object—The Digital Walking Stick (2019)—to highlight the way in which such an object would facilitate the making of relations with existing or 'old' energy infrastructures present in the landscape. The walking stick would function by becoming part, and allowing the user of the stick to become part, of landscapes and infrastructures of energy that were partly technical, partly social, and partly political.

Thirdly, building on the work of, among others, James Ferguson (1990), Arturo Escobar (1995), Emily Martin (1994), Susan Greenhalgh (2008), and Joseph Dumit (2012), Wahlberg (this volume) has proposed 'assemblage ethnography' as a methodology to 'generate insight into the ways in which certain problems, or better yet problematisations, take form' where the object of study is not the lived experiences of informants as such. Rather, it is the historically and ethnographically situated ways in which a certain aggregate problem like 'over-population' comes to stabilise over time, as well as the ways in which a 'reproductive complex' has come to comprise 'a total set of laws, regulations, family planning institutions, quotas, information campaigns, experts, hospitals, clinics, pharmaceutical companies, premarital counselling sessions, prenatal screening services, and more' (Wahlberg 2018, pp. 10–11). Assemblage ethnography takes as its point of departure that, to grasp a single site in a world of global flows, the ethnographer needs to leave that site and trace the connections, institutions, technologies, and logics that shape this site across scales. In this perspective, ethnographic fieldwork is as much a question of assembling together a host of elements to make visible how the global is always in the local and vice versa, as well as making a case for how connections and specific entanglements come to matter.

Yet another example can be found in an exercise-based mode of approaching infrastructures. Developed by Andrea Ballestero and Brit Ross Winthereik (2021) this mode of conducting research works harmoniously with ethnographic field work of any kind (single site, multi-sited, or assemblage), extending the curiosity of field work into the sorting, ordering, and sense-making practices that characterise ethnographic analysis. Using the framing device of a protocol, it invites researchers to establish playful relations with the material and also with colleagues through step-by-step 'recipes'. Given the hard to bind nature of infrastructures and the ways in which they are doubly relational and hybrid, a collaborative, experimental approach helps by trying out and accounting for new ways of unpacking them. This form of analysis by protocol thus infrastructures the knowledge-making practices in which ethnographers engage by playing with constraints versus freedom.

Finally, digital methods, in all their different forms and shapes, have in recent decades offered an entry point into methodological innovation, as new digital forms have generated a host of novel ways to span multiple sites, scales, and temporalities through methodological experimentation. Digital methods such as netnography (Kozinets 2015), virtual ethnography (Boellstorff et al. 2012; Hine 2000), and trace ethnography (Geiger and Ribes 2011) have been complemented with offline studies of online practice (Horst and Miller 2012; Kingod 2020). What these new forms of ethnography have in common is a focus on how digitally mediated linkages, connections, and associations can coalesce in and around a certain empirical field which, at the same time, ties the digital to the social lives of people. In a situation where figure-ground relations are hard to establish—what is empirical, what is analytical, what is theoretical?—and where normativity is hard-wired into the systems and platforms used for research, lateral or sideways movement across a site is the norm rather than the exception. In a certain sense, the ethnographer's data-generating practices come to resemble the digital environment itself: networked, malleable, and thoroughly political, which is to say, non-neutral (see Munk and Winthereik this volume).

In conclusion, the infrastructural turn within anthropology generally, and the anthropology of technology more specifically, has inspired if not necessitated methodological innovation given that site-based participation, observation, and interviewing not only became multi-sited (Marcus 1995) but also multi-scalar. Anthropological studies of infrastructuring thereby broadened to include new forms of ethnographic data collection that have been archival and document-based while also at times involving multispecies observations and interactions.

There are, of course, numerous further forms of methodological experimentation currently taking place within the anthropology of infrastructures. What we collectively show in this section introduction and the chapters that follow is that ethnographically studying infrastructuring processes has led to new forms of ethnography which are enriching the discipline of anthropology in conversation with related disciplines of STS, sociology, and more. As we alluded to in the opening of this introduction, modern ethnography has from its outset, and in a rejection of nineteenth-century evolutionary, Victorian anthropology, insisted that all human societies are complex. In a similar way, the recent 'infrastructural turn' in anthropology has insisted that humans have indeed always been infrastructured in the ways that they organise and lead their daily lives. By paying close attention to effects of infrastructuring anthropologists will be better equipped to differentiate between both the infrastructures and their social consequences.

References

Abram, S., Winthereik, B. R., & Yarrow, T. (Eds.) (2019). *Electrifying anthropology: exploring electrical practices and infrastructures.* London: Bloomsbury Academic.

Anand, N. (2015). Leaky states: Water audits, ignorance, and the politics of infrastructure. *Public Culture, 27*(2(76)), 305–330.

Anand, N. (2017). *Hydraulic city: Water and the infrastructures of citizenship in Mumbai.* Duke University Press.

Anand, N., Gupta, A., & Appel, H. (Eds.) (2018). *The promise of infrastructure.* Duke University Press.

Andersen, A. O. (2019). Assembling Commons and Commodities: The Peruvian Water Law between Ideology and Materialisation. *Water Alternatives, 12*(2), 470–487.

Andersen, S. L., Andersen, O., Petersen, J., & Wahlberg, A. (2020). Traveling health-promoting infrastructures: A meta-ethnographic analysis. *Health, 24*(5), 606–622.

Appadurai, A. (1996). *Modernity at large: cultural dimensions of globalization.* University of Minnesota Press.

Ballestero, A., & Winthereik, B. R. (2021). *Experimenting with Ethnography: A companion to analysis.* Durham & London: Duke University Press.

Barry, A. (2013). *Material politics: Disputes along the pipeline.* John Wiley & Sons.

Boas, F. (1888). *The Central Eskimo.* Sixth Annual Report of the Bureau of Ethnology to the Secretary of the Smithsonian Institution, 1884–1885, Government Printing Office, Washington.

Boellstorff, T. (2008). *Coming of age in Second Life: An anthropologist explores the virtually human.* Princeton University Press.

Boellstorff, T., Nardi, B., Pearce, C., & Taylor, T. L. (2012). *Ethnography and virtual worlds: A handbook of method.* Princeton University Press.

Bowker, G. C. (2005). *Memory practices in the sciences.* Cambridge, MA: The MIT Press.

Bowker, G. C., & Star, S. L. (2000). *Sorting things out: Classification and its consequences.* Cambridge, MA: The MIT Press.

Bruni, A. (2005). Shadowing software and clinical records: On the ethnography of nonhumans and heterogeneous contexts. *Organization, 12*(3), 357–378.

Carse, A. (2014.) *Beyond the big ditch: politics, ecology, and infrastructure at the Panama Canal.* Cambridge, MA: The MIT Press.

Chalfin, B. (2014). Public things, excremental politics, and the infrastructure of bare life in Ghana's city of Tema. *American Ethnologist, 41*(1), 92–109.

Downey, G. L., & Dumit, J. (1997). *Cyborgs & citadels: anthropological interventions in emerging sciences and technologies.* Santa Fe: School of American Research Press: distributed by the University of Washington Press.

Dumit, J. (2012). *Drugs for life: how pharmaceutical companies define our health.* Durham: Duke University Press.

Edwards, P. N. (2003). Infrastructure and modernity: Force, time, and social organization in the history of sociotechnical systems. *Modernity and technology, 1*, 185–226.

Escobar, A. (1995) *Encountering Development.* Princeton: Princeton University Press.

Fei, X. (1992[1947]). From the Soil: The foundations of Chinese society (trans: Hamilton, G., & Zheng, W.). Berkley: University of California Press.

Ferguson, J. (1990). *The anti-politics machine: 'development', depoliticization and bureaucratic power in Lesotho.* Cambridge: Cambridge University Press.

Fortes, M., & Evans-Pritchard, E. E. (Eds.) (1940). *African Political Systems.* London: Oxford University Press.

Geertz, C. (1973). *The interpretation of cultures.* New York: Basic Books, Inc.

Geiger, R. S., & Ribes, D. (2011). Trace Ethnography: Following Coordination through Documentary Practices. *44th Hawaii International Conference on System Sciences*, 1–10. https://doi.org/10.1109/HICSS.2011.455.

Greenhalgh, S. (2008). *Just one child: Science and policy in Deng's China.* Berkley: University of California Press.

Harvey, P., & Knox, H. (2012). The enchantments of infrastructure. *Mobilities, 7*(4), 521–536.

Harvey, P., & Knox, H. (2015). *Roads: An anthropology of infrastructure and expertise.* Cornell University Press.

Harvey, P., Jensen, C. B., & Morita, A. (Eds.) (2016). *Infrastructures and social complexity: A companion.* Taylor & Francis.

Hastrup, K., & Hastrup, F. (Eds.) (2015). *Waterworlds: Anthropology in fluid environments.* Oxford: Berghahn Books.

Helmreich, S. (2009). *Alien ocean: Anthropological voyages in microbial seas.* Berkley: University of California Press.

Hine, C. (2000). *Virtual ethnography.* London: Sage.

Hoeyer, K. (2019). Data as promise: Reconfiguring Danish public health through personalized medicine. *Social studies of science, 49*(4), 531–555.

Horst, H. A. (2006). The blessings and burdens of communication: cell phones in Jamaican transnational social fields. *Global Networks, 6*(2), 143–159.

Horst, H. A., & Miller, D. (Eds.) (2012). *Digital anthropology*. London: Routledge.

Inhorn, M. C. (2015). *Cosmopolitan conceptions: IVF sojourns in global Dubai*. Duke University Press.

Jensen, C. B. (2014). Continuous Variations: The Conceptual and the Empirical in STS. *Science, Technology and Human Values, 39*(2), 192–213.

Jensen, C. B. (2019). Can the Mekong speak? On hydropower, models and 'thing-power.' In S. Abram, B. R. Winthereik, T. Yarrow & A. Sarkar (Eds.), *Electrifying anthropology: exploring electrical practices and infrastructures* (pp. 120–137). London: Bloomsbury Academic.

Jensen, C. B., & Winthereik, B. R. (2013). *Monitoring movements in development aid: recursive partnerships and infrastructures*. Cambridge, MA: The MIT Press.

Jensen, C. B., & Morita, A. (2015). Infrastructures as ontological experiments. *Engaging Science, Technology, and Society, 1*, 81–87.

Karasti, H., & Blomberg, J. (2018). Studying infrastructuring ethnographically. *Computer Supported Cooperative Work (CSCW), 27*(2), 233–265.

Keith, M., & de Souza Santos, A. A. (2021). *African cities and collaborative futures: Urban platforms and metropolitan logistics*. Manchester University Press.

Kingod, N. (2020). The tinkering m-patient: Co-constructing knowledge on how to live with type 1 diabetes through Facebook searching and sharing and offline tinkering with self-care. *Health, 24*(2), 152–168.

Kirshner, J. D., & Power, M. (2019). Electrification and the everyday spaces of state power in postcolonial Mozambique. In S. Abram, B. R. Winthereik, T. Yarrow & A. Sarkar (Eds.), *Electrifying Anthropology: Exploring Electrical Practices and Infrastructures* (pp. 139–159). London: Bloomsbury Academic.

Knox, H., & Harvey, P. (2011). Anticipating harm: regulation and irregularity on a road construction project in the Peruvian Andes. *Theory, Culture & Society, 28*(6), 142–163.

Kozinets, R. V. (2015). Netnography. *The international encyclopedia of digital communication and society*, 1–8. https://doi.org/10.1002/9781118767771.wbiedcs067.

Langstrup, H. (2013). Chronic care infrastructures and the home. *Sociology of Health & Illness, 35*(7), 1008–1022.

Larkin, B. (2013). The politics and poetics of infrastructure. *Annual Review of Anthropology, 42*, 327–343.

Larkin, B. (2016, November 15). Ambient Infrastructures: Generator Life in Nigeria. *Technosphere Magazine*.

Lave, J., & Wenger, E. (1991). *Situated learning: Legitimate peripheral participation*. Cambridge: Cambridge University Press.

Loloum, T. (2019). Touring the nuclear sublime: Power-plant tours as tools of government. In S. Abram, B. R. Winthereik, T. Yarrow & A. Sarkar. (Eds.). *Electrifying anthropology: exploring electrical practices and infrastructures* (pp. 180–199). London: Bloomsbury Academic.

Maguire, J., & Winthereik, B. R. (2019). Digitalizing the State: Data Centres and the Power of Exchange. *Ethnos*, 1–22.

Maguire, J., Watts, L., & Winthereik, B. R. (2021). Energy Worlds in Experiment. Manchester: Mattering Press.

Malinowski, B. (1922). *Argonauts of the Western Pacific: An account of native enterprise and adventure in the archipelagoes of Melanesian New Guinea*. London: Routledge & Kegan Paul Ltd.

Marcus, G. E. (1995). Ethnography in/of the world system: The emergence of multi-sited ethnography. *Annual Review of Anthropology, 24*(1), 95–117.

Martin, E. (1994). *Flexible bodies: Tracking immunity in American culture from the days of polio to the age of AIDS*. Beacon Press.

Morita, A. (2016). Infrastructuring amphibious space: The interplay of aquatic and terrestrial infrastructures in the Chao Phraya delta in Thailand. *Science as Culture, 25*(1), 117–140.

Morita, A. (2017). Multispecies infrastructure: Infrastructural inversion and involutionary entanglements in the Chao Phraya Delta, Thailand. *Ethnos, 82*(4), 738–757.

Ong, A., & Collier, S. (2005). *Global Assemblages: Technology, Politics, and Ethics as Anthropological Problems*. London: Blackwell

Özden-Schilling, C. (2019). Big grid: The computing beast that preceded big data. In S. Abram, B. R. Winthereik, T. Yarrow & A. Sarkar (Eds.). *Electrifying anthropology: exploring electrical practices and infrastructures* (pp. 160–179). London: Bloomsbury Academic.

Paerregaard, K., Stensrud, A. B., & Andersen, A. O. (2016). Water citizenship: Negotiating water rights and contesting water culture in the Peruvian Andes. *Latin American Research Review, 51*(1), 198–217.

Pfaffenberger, B. (1992). Social anthropology of technology. *Annual Review of Anthropology, 21*(1), 491–516.

Radcliffe-Brown, A. R. & Forde, D. (1950). *African Systems of Kinship and Marriage*. London: Oxford University Press.

Reeves, M. (2016). The black list: on infrastructural indeterminacy and its reverberations. In P. Harvey, C. B. Jensen, & A. Morita (Eds.), *Infrastructures and Social Complexity: A Companion* (pp. 296–308). London & New York: Routledge.

Richardson, T. (2016). Where the Water Sheds: Disputed Deposits at the Ends of the Danube. In M. Bozovic & M. D. Miller (Eds.), *Watersheds: Poetics and Politics of the Danube River* (pp. 307–336). Brighton, MA: Academic Studies Press.

Schüll, N. D. (2014). *Addiction by design: Machine gambling in Las Vegas*. Princeton University Press.

Seaver, N. (2017). Algorithms as culture: Some tactics for the ethnography of algorithmic systems. *Big Data & Society, 4*(2).

Simone, A. (2001). On the worlding of African cities. *African Studies Review, 44*(2), 15–41.

Star, S. L. (1989). *Regions of the mind: brain research and the quest for scientific certainty*. Stanford, CA: Stanford University Press.

Star, S. L. (1991). Power, Technologies and the Phenomenology of Standards: On Being Allergic to Onions. In J. Law (Ed.), *A Sociology of Monsters: Power, Technology and the Modern World* (pp. 27–57). Oxford: Basil Blackwell.

Star, S. L., & Strauss, A. (1999). Layers of Silence, Arenas of Voice: The Ecology of Visible and Invisible Work. *Computer Supported Cooperative Work, 8*, 9–30.

Star, S. L., & Ruhleder, K. (1996). Steps toward an ecology of infrastructure: Design and access for large information spaces. *Information systems research, 7*(1), 111–134.

Starosielski, N. (2015). *The undersea network*. Durham: Duke University Press.

Strang, V. (2005). Common senses: Water, sensory experience and the generation of meaning. *Journal of Material Culture, 10*(1), 92–120.

Timmermans, S., Bowker, G. C., & Star, S. L. (1998). The Architecture of Difference: visibility, control and comparability in building a nursing interventions classification. In A. Mol (Ed.), *Differences in medicine* (pp. 202–225). Durham & London: Duke University Press.

Tsing, A. L. (2004). *Friction: An ethnography of global connection.* Princeton University Press.

Velho, R., & Ureta, S. (2019). *Frail modernities: Latin American infrastructures between repair and ruination.* Taylor & Francis.

von Schnitzler, A. (2008). Citizenship prepaid: water, calculability, and techno-politics in South Africa. *Journal of South African Studies, 34*(4), 899–917.

Wahlberg, A. (2018). *Good quality: The routinization of sperm banking in China.* Berkley: University of California Press.

Walford, A. (2012). Data moves: taking Amazonian climate science seriously. *The Cambridge Journal of Anthropology, 30*(2), 101–117.

Winthereik, B. R., Watts, L., & Maguire, J. (2019). The Energy Walk: Infrastructuring the Imagination. In J. Versi, & D. Ribes (Eds.), *digitalSTS: A Field Guide for Science & Technology Studies* (1st edition) (pp. 349–364). Princeton University Press.

Wittfogel, K. A. (1957). *Oriental despotism: a comparative study of total power.* New Haven: Yale University Press.

CHAPTER 35

Accumulation: Exploring the Materiality of Energy Infrastructure

Energy

Gökçe Günel

It is common for contemporary accounts of energy transitions to portray a shift from fossil fuels to renewable energy sources, document how the politics of renewable energy vary in distinct social contexts, and investigate how governmental and corporate intervention impacts on energy technologies (Abram et al. 2019; Appel et al. 2015; Bakke 2016; Boyer 2019; Howe 2019; Love and Garwood 2011; Smil 2010). Many proponents of this shift imagine that energy transitions will take time and that they will occur in response to price incentives and profit motives (Malm 2016). Anthropologists have explored energy issues during various crises, exemplified by the literature from the World War II period, the 1970s oil crisis, and the contemporary climate emergency (Boyer 2014; Loloum et al. 2021; Smith and High 2017; Rogers 2015); thus, while the scholarship on energy in anthropology is not new, climate change–related environmental problems have driven anthropologists to formulate 'energy transitions' as a distinct focus.

Despite its extensive range, the scholarship on energy and climate change rarely acknowledges that humans have consistently added new energy sources to the mix rather than transitioning from one source to the next. Over the past two centuries consumption of energy from every source has grown extensively. Despite conventional narratives of 'energy transition' today, rarely are older sources of energy completely abandoned or replaced. Some scholars rightly

G. Günel (✉)
Rice University, Houston, TX, USA
e-mail: gg15@rice.edu

M. H. Bruun et al. (eds.), *The Palgrave Handbook of the Anthropology of Technology*, https://doi.org/10.1007/978-981-16-7084-8_35

argue that the energy transition narrative depoliticises and obscures a wide variety of social, political, and ethical transformations (Kuzemko 2016), and 'has narrowed the scope of how anthropologists understand and engage with the ethical dilemmas posed by energy' (High and Smith 2019, p. 11). Still, there is a general agreement in the literature that an anticipated transition from fossil fuels to renewable resources is and should be around the corner. In this piece and elsewhere in my work (Günel 2020), however, I suggest that energy infrastructures have in fact changed in what science and technology studies scholar Benjamin Sovacool (2016, p. 212) calls 'cumulative rather than fully substitutive' ways, and offer the term 'energy accumulation' as a more accurate descriptor of the transformations humans are experiencing.

Below I draw on my ethnographic work on electricity production in Ghana between 2016 and 2020 and seek to foreground the 'cumulative' manner in which energy infrastructures change. In doing this research, I have benefited from speaking to energy experts who work at Ghanaian institutions, including the Energy Commission, the Electricity Company of Ghana (ECG), and GridCo, as well as engineers who work with independent power producers, such as Sunon Asogli, Aksa, and Karpower, generating electricity for the Ghanaian grid. In some ways, the grid itself has offered me a map of the people who should be involved in the research, guiding me to spend time with electricity generators, distributors, and users. I have mainly asked how new energy infrastructures emerge and tracked the actors who make these emergent infrastructures possible. While much of the scholarship on new energy infrastructure looks at the Global North, prioritising European countries (see, for instance, Drackle and Krauss 2011; Henning 2008; Knight 2017; Krauss 2010), my inquiry focused principally on Turkish-built electricity-generation infrastructure in Ghana and spotlighted South-South collaboration between Turkish and Ghanaian engineers and policy-makers. At a time when the impacts of climate change are increasingly indubitable, the project studied how environmental transformations in Ghana shape infrastructural networks.

ENERGY ACCUMULATION

'If you're in trouble, you don't think straight', said Ibrahim, an electrical engineer with the Electricity Company of Ghana (ECG), to describe Ghana's power crises. In a meeting room on the fifth floor of the Electro Volta House building, our windows looked out on Accra's Black Star Square, a modernist public square built by the country's first president and pan-African statesman Kwame Nkrumah in 1961 in celebration of Ghana's independence from colonial rule. On the wall a monthly calendar featured newly completed electrical substations across the country. A promotional sign that hung from the ceiling celebrated the company's fiftieth anniversary, suggesting that it had been powering the socio-economic growth and development of Ghana for half a century. Like many of the other employees I met there in late 2019, Ibrahim wore a button-down shirt featuring the ECG logo, tailored for him from fabric printed in recognition of the company's fiftieth anniversary.

Until 1997, state-owned hydroelectric power plants produced all of Ghana's electricity (Awopone et al. 2017). In the words of historian Stephan Miescher (2014, p. 341), the opening of Ghana's Akosombo Dam in 1966 and the creation of Lake Volta—the world's largest human-made lake by surface area and the fourth-largest reservoir by volume—'produced different temporalities of an industrialized future that would transform the country's rural past and create new cities, factories, and infrastructures'. In the inauguration ceremony, Kwame Nkrumah announced, 'It is in this spirit of fruitful collaboration for a better world for all that I ... inaugurate the Volta River Project. Let us dedicate it to Africa's progress and prosperity. Only in this way will Africa play its full part in the achievement of world peace and for the advancement of the happiness of mankind' (Ayensu 2013, p. 19). Nkrumah was overthrown by a military coup a few months after this ceremony. 'The future envisioned by Nkrumah, in which each would give according to his ability and receive according to his needs,' literary scholar and cultural historian Saidiya Hartman (2007, p. 177) observed, 'had been eclipsed'.

Inadequate rainfall and rising temperatures associated with climate change have negatively impacted the hydroelectric power station at Lake Volta, at times completely incapacitating it (Silver 2015; Yarrow 2017). At a time when power demand was increasing across the country, the dams could no longer satisfy national electricity needs. Most of the new power producers that have started operating in Ghana since the early 2000s have been thermal stations that rely on natural gas, stockpile light crude oil, and burn heavy fuel oil. Unlike Nkrumah in his inauguration of the Akosombo Dam, these power producers have not offered teleological narratives about progress, but rather quick, stop-gap solutions that provide immediate relief to Ghanaian consumers, bridging electricity shortages until the renewable energy infrastructure starts producing electricity for the country.

Between 2012 and 2015, an electricity crisis resulted in unprecedented levels of load shedding throughout Ghana. Power for industries and homes was out for twenty-four hours at a time and turned back on only for twelve-hour periods. *Dumsor*, the name given to the crisis—meaning 'off and on' in Twi—was brought about by low water levels in hydroelectric dams due to climate change, disruptions to natural gas flows from Nigeria, and alleged mismanagement of the grid infrastructure. In response, Ghanaian decision-makers such as Ibrahim saw a further expansion and diversification of the country's energy portfolio as a possible solution to the crisis, shifting the nation's energy production portfolio further away from hydropower and towards fossil fuels.

In seeking to resolve *dumsor*, the Electricity Company of Ghana, the sole electricity distributor servicing the south of Ghana, signed forty-three power purchase agreements with different vendors.[1] 'Prices were so high during the emergency', Ibrahim said. 'And many of the contracts we signed stated that we would pay whatever we agreed, which was double or more what we would usually pay: say, for instance, pay 18 cents per kilowatt hour for energy that should cost perhaps 9 cents, for the next decade. After paying double for a decade you renegotiate.' In agreeing to these measures, decision-makers with the Electricity Company of Ghana, such as Ibrahim, found themselves participating in processes that extended the electricity crisis even further (see Mbembe and Roitman 1995, p. 325).

In 2020, private fossil fuel-powered thermal plants produced about two-thirds of Ghana's total electricity. Between 2015 and 2019, the country's electricity supply went from 2800 megawatts—which was sized to the demand placed on the grid—to over 5000 megawatts. 'A hungry man does not need a table full of rice', Joseph, a senior electrical engineer and executive from Ghana's grid company GridCo, said during an interview in his Tema office in December 2019. 'Why build 5,000 megawatts when you can't consume it?'

Many independent power producers entered the Ghanaian market on 'take-or-pay' contracts, whereby the Electricity Company of Ghana either bought electricity from them or paid them a penalty for electricity it did not use. For instance, the agreement Karpowership signed with ECG in 2017 indicated that its floating power plant would supply 470 megawatts of electricity to the Ghanaian grid for a full decade. As a result, the Ghanaian government paid over $500 million per year to different power producers for electricity it could not need or consume, instigating major financial strain on the country's economy. In 2019 and 2020, decision-makers across Ghanaian institutions looked for ways to monetise this electricity excess. Some proposed rural electrification campaigns that would improve irrigation across the country, thereby reducing flooding and safeguarding food security. An Energy Commission programme labelled Drive Electric Initiative promoted the use of electric vehicles in the greater Accra region and beyond. The new power plants triggered an excess of fossil fuel-powered electricity on the country's grid, instigating a new set of challenges.

In 2017, a news report revealed that the contract with the Emirati thermal power station AMERI had been overpriced by $150 million, eventually leading to the removal of the Energy Minister Boakye Agyarko from his position.[2] Another corruption scandal broke out in April 2020, when, according to the US Securities and Exchange Commission,

> Asante Berko, a former executive of a foreign-based subsidiary of a US bank holding company, arranged for his firm's client, a Turkish energy company, to funnel at least $2.5 million to a Ghana-based intermediary to pay illicit bribes to Ghanaian government officials in order to gain their approval of an electrical power plant project.[3]

Given the context of mistrust and corruption, decision-makers in the country called for a renegotiation of these contractual terms.[4] In the meantime, new energy sources and relations continued to be developed. Of the 5000-megawatt electricity production capacity on the grid, only 40 megawatts came from solar, produced by Chinese companies in Winneba. In early 2020, an additional 100-megawatt plant was under construction in Bui. A second strand of solar electricity generation took place through rooftop solar panels, which have emerged as viable options for individuals and institutions with access to upfront capital. Many industrial facilities have also built rooftop solar panels, cutting their reliance on the Electricity Company of Ghana by half.

In an insightful article, literary critic Jennifer Wenzel (n.d.) points out that two terms characterise contemporary understandings of energy: transition and impasse. For her, '[t]ransition refers to the social, cultural, economic, political, and technological processes involved in a society transitioning from one predominant fuel source to another—say, from wood and whale oil to coal and kerosene in centuries past; or from fossil fuels to renewables and greener energy sources today'. If certain fuels and infrastructures acquire social, political, and financial centrality at certain times, and yet do not always replace former fuels, the contemporary moment is one of transitioning from fossil fuels to renewable energies. Impasse, on the other hand, is 'the immobilizing sociopolitical predicaments of the present: that is, everything in petromodernity, the present form of collective life, that stands in the way of energy transition'.

Yet the transformation in energy infrastructure in Ghana followed neither of these trends. Instead, Ghana experienced an accretion of various kinds of energy infrastructure, with varying and changing degrees of importance to its economy. What has taken place in Ghana since the turn of the twenty-first century, accelerating as a result of the final episode of *dumsor*, is therefore best understood not as an energy transition or impasse but as energy accumulation.

Transitioning in Reverse

The linear, developmentalist, and progress-oriented logic of the term 'energy transition' placed Ghana in what historian Dipesh Chakrabarty (2000, p. 8) would call 'an imaginary waiting room of history', out of touch with contemporary trends and always playing catch-up. In this context, the new power producers, such as the powership, offered stop-gap solutions that relied on fossil fuels.

Paul, an energy specialist I met at the University of Ghana, recognised the linearity of the dominant energy transition narrative. 'Maybe we are transitioning in reverse', he said. And indeed, many of the natural gas and heavy fuel oil-powered generating plants in Ghana had previously been used in countries like China and Turkey, uprooted, broken down into pieces, and carried in cargo ships to serve the Ghanaian grid. For instance, the first and the largest independent power plant in the country, Sunon Asogli, had been in use in China between 1991 and 2007. The natural gas-fired plant started selling electricity to the Ghanaian grid in 2009, after its value had already depreciated. In some ways, Paul had accepted the linear narrative of a transition and expected a move from fossil fuels to renewable energy resources to take place in Ghana.[5]

Yet, given that the energy landscape he closely observed did not correspond to the expected timeline of energy transitions, Paul wondered if Ghana as a country was moving backwards, although presumably it had to move forward. By arguing that Ghana was transitioning in reverse, he made sense of his environment while keeping an attachment to the dominant terms of the energy debate.

But Paul's comment is not only a reflection on Ghana. It also offers an important corrective to the global debate on energy transitions, demonstrating how such apolitical, seamless, and unidirectional development is a reconstitution ex post facto of a messy process that rarely finds empirical footing. While the imaginary of a transition to renewable energy sources has been tempting, as it would allow humans to extend their lifestyles into the future while eliminating carbon emissions from fossil fuels, evidence suggests that renewable energy infrastructure only minimally displaces fossil fuels (Thombs 2018). As sociologists Richard York and Shannon Elizabeth Bell (2019, pp. 40–43) document, 'historically, no established energy source has undergone a sustained decline with the addition of a new energy source. Rather, consumption of all energy sources has typically grown, a trend that has been maintained for over two centuries.' York and Bell make a second important point, suggesting that 'adding new energy sources may, in some circumstances, actually accelerate consumption of other resources, even in areas outside the energy sector'. They use whales as an example, overturning a common narrative suggesting that the use of fossil fuels in the last decades of the nineteenth century might have helped whale populations.

> [T]he discovery of petroleum did not suppress whale oil consumption, helping to save the whales; rather, it actually spurred a dramatic increase in whaling. This increase occurred because fossil fuel-powered ships could catch more and larger whales more rapidly than could sail ships and rowboats, and new uses were developed for whale oil (e.g., for margarine after the development of hydrogenation).

In this context, new fuels, such as petroleum, contributed to the growth and development of former resources, such as whales, for new purposes. Others have echoed York and Bell's critique of the energy transition narrative, suggesting that the term transition should be re-evaluated given that 'the advent of new sources of energy does not lead to the abandonment of earlier sources' (Gellert and Ciccantell 2020, p. 216). Instead, energy accumulates, rendering the Ghanaian case emblematic of energy dynamics.

Why is energy transition such a popular notion? The literature on energy and climate change is laden with this perspective, and even features a recent subdiscipline called 'Transition Management'.[6] According to York and Bell (2019, p. 40), this labelling is mainly due to a 'common mistake made in analyses documenting so-called energy transitions', whereby scholars focus on 'the proportion of the energy supply that is generated from various sources'.[7] But beyond this issue of calculation, it is important to remember that a narrative of energy transitions mirrors modernisation theories in that progression through stages of national economic development should ensure technological innovation and overall social and political welfare. Perhaps the most well-known theory of modernisation, Walt Rostow's *Stages of Economic Development: A Non-Communist Manifesto* (1960) argued that economic development would also result in innovative energy systems. Theories of progress such as Rostow's *Stages* reproduced the assumption that innovation would stem from the Global North, and only slowly spread to the Global South, ensuring 'take-off' and 'high mass consumption' in these regions.[8] All in all, modernisation projects categorised people and places in terms of whether they belonged to the past or the future (Fabian 1983; also see Barnes and Mathews 2016). The authors of these theories investigated what the future should hold, and provided instructions on how to reach it. The narrative of energy transitions reproduced the common tropes of these theories, mainly relying on national-scale analyses, seeking technological breakthroughs in the Global North, and hoping they would be appropriately applied in the Global South.

Such evolutionary understandings of energy are not new to anthropology. One of the earliest and most significant figures in the literature on energy is Leslie White (1943), who attempted to revitalise evolutionary theory through his research on energy technologies in the 1940s, suggesting that a social group's energy use defined its standing in an evolutionary cycle (also see Adams 1978). Yet newer generations of anthropologists have challenged this evolutionary perspective. For instance, Laura Nader's work on energy physicists shed light on how these experts equated technological development with social progress. By studying up, Nader (1981, p. 99) was able to uncloak what energy physicists considered possible and impossible and display how they drew those boundaries. Taking this lead, scholars continued to work on how resources impact on governance and development and charted the international alliances and disputes that are formed through energy networks. Some important examples of this literature are Fernando Coronil's (1997) work on how Venezuela's oil industry facilitated development projects, conjuring them up like magic, and Suzana Sawyer's (2004) emphasis on indigenous communities' struggles with US-based oil companies and their transnational neoliberal logics in Ecuador. Such scholarship acted as correctives to the fact-driven, quantitative analyses of global energy markets that dominated the field in the post-energy crisis era and unpacked oil's very contextual politics (also see Apter 2005).

Recent work in anthropology explicitly attempts to disavow the teleological assumptions that accompany narratives on energy transitions, seeking to avoid explaining new energy projects in terms of the purposes they serve, or as functions of their ends, and instead attempting to examine the causes of their rise (Günel 2019; Limbert 2010; Weszkalnys 2015). One example is Mandana Limbert's (2010) analysis of oil depletion in Oman, which foregrounds a non-linear perception of time: when the oil runs out or becomes less valuable, Omanis might return to a pre-oil past, once again inhabiting palm-frond *barasti* huts rather than air-conditioned villas. While some see such cyclicality as preordained, coming to terms with the fact that fossil fuels will cease to be engines of economic growth for Oman, others seek to extend petrotopias in their present forms (LeMenager 2014). Drawing on research in offshore oil exploration in São Tomé and Príncipe, a former Portuguese colony in the African Atlantic, Gisa Weszkalnys (2015) explores how oil emerges as an ambiguous source of future wealth. While Limbert's work showcases how Omanis anticipate the end of the dreamtime of oil, Weszkalnys looks at a context where this dream remains emergent.

What can anthropologists learn from this literature as they navigate contemporary energy crises? Energy infrastructures, as Antina von Schnitzler (2016, p. 28) puts it in reference to pre-paid meters, are often 'harnessed to distinct ethical regimes and political projects'; in other words, the politics of renewable energy are not predetermined and will be shaped contextually (also see Smith and High 2017). As Dominic Boyer (2019) and Cymene Howe's (2019) work on wind power in Mexico confirms, the introduction of renewable energy could reinforce existing modes of political power rather than offering innovative forms of inclusivity. Specifically, Dominic Boyer's idea of 'energopolitics' links energetic power to political power, underlining how fuels are enablers for the production of specific regimes. In their timely duograph, they broadly ask, 'What future configuration of energopolitics—taking this term now in its broadest sense of "energy politics," aeolian and beyond—could guarantee the national health and wealth desired by government; the expanding profitscape desired by capital; the responsive, lossless infrastructure desired by the grid?' (Boyer 2019, p. 157). Expanding this perspective, research on wind and solar power stations focuses on the tensions that emerge between local and federal institutions, and demonstrates how renewable energy markets proliferate through negotiations between multinational corporations, nation-state level institutions, and local landscape practices—at times despite protest from local communities (Drackle and Krauss 2011; Jacobson 2007; Knight 2017; Krauss 2010; Love and Garwood 2011; McDermott Hughes 2021). While celebrating renewable energy infrastructures as agents of climate change mitigation, the literature pauses to probe whether and how these technologies might contribute to the production of just societies, and asks if this particular energy transition might generate opportunities for social change.

While theories of leapfrogging to renewables have been popular in imagining future energy regimes, scholars have not fully researched how transformations occur in places where such leaps are expected to arise (for exceptions see Akrich 1994; Cross 2013; Degani et al. 2020; Mains 2012; Winther 2008). One valuable strand of work focuses on the humanitarian uses of renewable energy in devices such as solar lamps and photoelectric lighting kits and begins to unpack the roles they play as the material and symbolic inklings of a future leap. Although these devices are not always adopted by communities (see Akrich 1994), and therefore might not reach their end goals, as Jamie Cross (2013, p. 369) argues, they 'successfully assemble a wide array of concerns and interests, politics, moralities and ethics'. It is increasingly important to describe and analyse the social, political, technological, and financial conditions under which corporations and governments deprived of ample resources invest in new energy infrastructures, how decision-makers and users envision their energy futures, what services they are able to afford under existing circumstances, and which infrastructure providers they are able to approach. By answering these questions from ethnographic perspectives, anthropologists will be better able to critique the emphasis on renewable energy transitions.

In a context where the energy transition narrative remained mainstream, some energy professionals in Ghana hoped the country would leapfrog to renewables, and imagined that new business models would support this leap. 'Have you seen the solar map of Ghana?' Raymond, a Harvard-educated, in-house legal advisor to GridCo, asked me enthusiastically during a meeting in July 2018. 'We are missing opportunities by not building solar here.' By invoking the idea of leapfrogging, Raymond attempted to challenge modernisation theory's basic assumptions, and argue against the notion that the countries of the Global South must fulfil specific stages of progress. Yet the prospect of leapfrogging maintained the teleological horizons of modernisation theory, offering those who were left behind the seeming opportunity to spring forward, while maintaining their roles as disadvantaged participants in a modernisation rat-race. The path of development remained unchanged by their forward spring. Inspired by novel paradigms of development, Raymond referred to the most commonly used examples of technological leapfrogging, suggesting that people in sub-Saharan Africa have adopted cell phones, mobile payment systems, and digital banking apps. Renewable energy infrastructures could perhaps constitute the next 'stage-skipping technology', allowing Ghana to avoid fossil fuels.[9] Raymond celebrated the green financing programmes recently started by some Ghanaian banks, which offered funding for domestic and institutional consumers bidding to build rooftop solar panels. 'Once you prove that your project is lowering emissions, your interest rates fall. There are incentives for building solar', representatives at Ghana's Cal Bank confirmed (see Günel 2021). Dressed in polo shirts advertising their green financing programmes, four Cal Bank men told me that they offer three- to five-year loans for rooftop solar projects, but have had trouble attracting individuals with stable enough jobs for these loans.

Regardless of popular narratives on energy transitions and leapfrogging, the future did not hold the promise of stable flows of electricity on the grid for energy professionals in Ghana. Instead, many energy professionals anticipated consistent power outages and looked for personal ways in which they could shape the inevitable. Joseph from GridCo told me that he lived very close to the headquarters of the grid company in Tema because he wanted to arrive at the control room as quickly as possible when a blackout occurred. He prioritised this proximity to the control room above all else. A devoted member of one of the most popular charismatic churches in West Africa, Joseph summarised his relationship to *dumsor* by using an analogy: 'Can you kill the devil? The world would be a very beautiful place if you could kill the devil. But you can't kill it. You have to stay away from its control.' According to Joseph, unstable flows and increasing electricity costs would continue to characterise the Ghanaian grid for the years to come. Despite their countless complications, Joseph hoped that energy accumulation would temporarily manage to keep the devil away.

CONCLUSION

A change in fuels demands and produces a change in associated technologies (see Sieferle 2001). As populations around the world imagine a departure from fossil fuels and a transition to renewable energy resources, they wonder what these new technologies will look like. What kind of batteries will people use to store renewables? How would a new electricity grid work? Will car companies be able to make electric cars more desirable? What will happen to the disused coal plants that populate landscapes globally? Will humans innovate their way out of fossil fuels, or will they have to do more work to maintain existing resources, rendering old tools anew? While these commonly asked energy questions might seem technical at first sight, they are fundamentally about how humans have historically modified and will reconfigure their social, political, and economic lives.

It is difficult to know fuels, energy, and energy infrastructures. Fuels appear in our social worlds in the form of oil, wood, animal labour, human labour, natural gas, or coal. The list goes on (see Pinkus 2016). But what does energy mean, exactly? Energy is not a physical object with given dimensions, such as mass and length. Rather, energy has to be understood in terms of its conversion, or the potential for conversion in the future, between different forms, such as heat and work. By measuring energy, scientists have created it as an object; in other words, measurement has created the object it measures (see Coopersmith 2010; Smith 1998; Daggett 2019). Since energy is so contingent, humans are led to think about it by looking at energy infrastructures, referring to power plants, the grid, car engines, or electric lights. But most do not have direct access to what energy might mean or do. Ultimately, energy is relational. Perhaps this is why it is so hard to know or grasp fully.

The mounting global pressures of environmental degradation and rising energy demand will require anthropologists to do research in a range of contexts, demonstrating how fuels impact on their constituents in unexpected ways. Anthropological research on political, economic, and social relations in the places where energy is harnessed, distributed, and used will allow scholars from all fields to address energy's centrality to human life. By studying energy infrastructures, anthropologists will generate multi-scalar analyses that challenge nation-state boundaries and foreground underrepresented narratives. Overall, anthropologists will have a critical role in repudiating the techno-optimist ideas that dominate contemporary understandings of energy futures.

Acknowledgements Wenner Gren Foundation, University of Arizona, Brandeis University Crown Center for Middle East Studies, and Rice University have provided support for fieldwork on electricity generation in Ghana.

Notes

1. Northern Electricity Distribution Company (NEDCo), the second electricity distribution company in Ghana, services the north. Because the northern part of the country has fewer industrial facilities, the power supply of NEDCo is significantly lower than ECG, rendering ECG the most significant actor in electricity distribution. Since the unbundling of the country's electricity sector in the early 2000s, these two companies only serve as distributors and have no power production capacity.

2. Exposed: John Mahama brings Ameri Group to Namibia https://www.vg.no/nyheter/utenriks/i/vEqJ4/exposed-john-mahama-brings-ameri-group-to-namibia. Accessed 20 November 2020.

3. For more information on the case, see: https://www.sec.gov/litigation/litreleases/2020/lr24794.htm Accessed 20 November 2020. For Berko's response, see: https://www.myjoyonline.com/news/national/asante-berko-rejects-bribery-allegations-by-u-s-securities-and-exchange-commission/. Accessed 20 November 2020.

4. See for instance: https://www.ghanabusinessnews.com/2019/07/30/government-to-renegotiate-take-or-pay-contracts-in-the-energy-sector/. Accessed 20 November 2020.

5. As sociologists Louise Seamster and Victor Ray argue, debates over progress often take three shapes: 'slow cumulative progress in knowledge and morality; cataclysmic social change attained through upheavals, violence, or innovational leaps; and regression (anxiety about society moving backward, coupled with the normative assumption society should move forward)'. Seamster, L. & Ray, V. (2018, p. 317).

6. See for instance: Loorbach, D. (2007). *Transition Management: New Mode of Governance for Sustainable Development.* Utrecht, Netherlands: International Books.

7. Although Bell and York's article is illuminating, the conclusions they offer, such as a cap and trade system, could leave countries of the Global South stranded with no access to electricity, while favouring the maintenance of existing patterns of consumption in the Global North.

8. While Rostow did not initially acknowledge the environmental footprint of such stages of development, in the 1990 preface to the third edition of his classic work, he pointed out the 'strains on the physical environment that global industrialization and urbanization may impose', suggesting how 'existing strains on the forests, arable land, and species as well as increasing pollution of air and bodies of water make it difficult to contemplate complacently a more than doubling of global population, with the increase overwhelmingly concentrated in countries likely to be experiencing dramatic increases in those technologies that now carry with them the greatest threats of pollution'. Perhaps not surprisingly, he concluded that 'corrective action [would] depend on forehanded domestic and international public policy' (Rostow 1990, pp. xix–xx).

9. For an example of this argument, see Batinge et al. (2017). Also see Günel (2021).

REFERENCES

Abram, S., Winthereik, B. R., & Yarrow, T. (2019). *Electrifying Anthropology: Exploring Electrical Practices and Infrastructures.* London: Bloomsbury.

Adams, R. N. (1978). Man, Energy, and Anthropology: I Can Feel the Heat, But Where's the Light?. *American Anthropologist, 80,* 297–309.

Akrich, M. (1994). The de-scription of technical objects. In W. E. Bijmer & J. Law (Eds.), *Shaping Technology/Building Society: Studies in Sociotechnical Change* (pp. 205–224). Cambridge, MA: The MIT Press.

Appel, H., Mason, A., & Watts, M. (Eds.) (2015). *Subterranean Estates: Life Worlds of Oil and Gas.* Ithaca: Cornell University Press.

Apter, A. (2005). *The Pan-African Nation: Oil and the Spectacle of Culture in Nigeria.* Chicago: University of Chicago Press.

Awopone, A. K., Zobaa, A. F., & Banuenumah, W. (2017). Assessment of optimal pathways for power generation system in Ghana, *Cogent Engineering, 4*(1): 1314065.

Ayensu, E. S. (2013). *Lake of Life: Celebrating 50 Years of Volta River Authority.* Accra: Volta River Authority.

Bakke, G. (2016). *The Grid: The Fraying Wires Between Americans and Our Energy Future.* New York: Bloomsbury

Barnes, J., & Mathews, A. (2016). Prognosis: Visions of Environmental Futures. *Journal of the Royal Anthropological Institute, 22*(S1), 9–26.

Batinge, B., Musango, J. K., & Brent, A. C. (2017). Leapfrogging to Renewable Energy: The Opportunity for Unmet Electricity Markets. *South African Journal of Industrial Engineering, 28*(4), 32–49.

Boyer, D. (2014). Energopower: An Introduction. *Anthropological Quarterly, 87*(2), 309–333.

Boyer, D. (2019). *Energopolitics.* Durham: Duke University Press.

Chakrabarty, D. (2000). *Provincializing Europe: Postcolonial Thought and Historical Difference.* Princeton: Princeton University Press.

Coopersmith, J. (2010). *Energy, the Subtle Concept: The Discovery of Feynman's Blocks from Leibniz to Einstein.* New York: Oxford University Press

Coronil, F. (1997). *The Magical State: Nature, money, and modernity in Venezuela.* Chicago: University of Chicago Press.

Cross, J. (2013). The 100th Object: Solar Lighting Technology and Humanitarian Goods. *Journal of Material Culture, 18*(4), 367–387.

Daggett, C. (2019). *The Birth of Energy: Fossil Fuels, Thermodynamics, and the Politics of Work.* Durham: Duke University Press.

Degani M., Chalfin, B., & Cross, J. (2020). Introduction: Fuelling Capture: Africa's Energy Frontiers. *The Cambridge Journal of Anthropology, 38*(2), 1–18.

Drackle, D., & Krauss, W. (2011). Ethnographies of Wind and Power. *Anthropology News, 52*(5), 9.

Fabian, J. (1983). *Time and the Other: How Anthropology Makes its Object.* New York: Columbia University Press.

Gellert, P. K., & Ciccantell, P. S. (2020). Coal's Persistence in the Capitalist World-Economy: Against Teleology in Energy "Transition" Narratives. *Sociology of Development, 6*(2), 194–221.

Günel, G. (2019). *Spaceship in the Desert: Energy, Climate Change, and Urban Design in Abu Dhabi.* Durham: Duke University Press.

Günel, G. (2020). Energy Accumulation. *e-flux.* https://www.e-flux.com/architecture/accumulation/339454/energy-accumulation/. Accessed 20 November 2020.

Günel, G. (2021). Leapfrogging to Solar. *South Atlantic Quarterly, 120*(1), 163–176.

Hartman, S. (2007). *Lose Your Mother: A Journey Along the Atlantic Slave Route.* New York: Farrar, Straus and Giroux.

Henning, A. (2008). Temporal Landscapes of Public Good: Negotiating solar collectors among ancient remains. *Social and Cultural Geography, 9*(1), 27–40.

High, M., & Smith, J. M. (2019). Introduction: The Ethical Constitution of Energy Dilemmas. *Journal of the Royal Anthropological Institute, 25,* 9–28.

Howe, C. (2019). *Ecologics.* Durham: Duke University Press.

Jacobson, A. 2007. Connective power: Solar electrification and social change in Kenya. *World Development, 35,* 144–162.

Knight, D. (2017). Energy talk, temporality, and belonging in austerity Greece. *Anthropological Quarterly, 90*(1), 167–191.

Krauss, W. (2010). The 'Dingpolitik' of wind energy in Northern German landscapes: an ethnographic case study. *Landscape Research, 35,* 195–208.

Kuzemko, C. (2016). Energy Depoliticization in the United Kingdom: Destroying Political Capacity. *British Journal of Politics and International Relations, 18*(1), 107–124.

LeMenager, S. (2014). *Living Oil: Petroleum Culture in the American Century.* New York: Oxford University Press.

Limbert, M. (2010). *In the Time of Oil.* Stanford: Stanford University Press.

Love, T., & Garwood, A. (2011). Wind, sun and water: Complexities of alternative energy development in rural northern Peru. *Rural Society, 20,* 294–307.

Loloum, T., Abram, S., & Ortar, N. (2021). Politicizing Energy Anthropology: an introduction. In T. Loloum, S. Abram, & N. Ortar (Eds.), *Ethnographies of Power: A Political Anthropology of Energy.* Berghahn (EASA Series).

Mains, D. (2012). Blackouts and Progress: Privatization, Infrastructure, and a Developmentalist State in Jimma. *Cultural Anthropology, 27*(1), 3–27.

Malm, A. (2016). *Fossil Capital: The Rise of Steam Power and the Roots of Global Warming.* New York: Verso.

McDermott Hughes, D. (2021). *Who Owns the Wind: Climate Crisis and the Hope of Renewable Energy.* New York: Verso.

Miescher, S. (2014). "Nkrumah's Baby": The Akosombo Dam and the dream of development in Ghana, 1952–1966. *Water History, 6,* 341–366.

Mbembe A., & Roitman, J. (1995). Figures of the Subject in Times of Crisis. *Public Culture, 7*(2), 323–352.

Nader, L. (1981). Barriers to Thinking New About Energy. *Physics Today, 34*(9), 99–104.

Pinkus, K. (2016). *Fuel: A Speculative Dictionary.* Minneapolis: University of Minnesota

Rogers, D. (2015). Oil and Anthropology. *Annual Review of Anthropology, 44,* 365–80.

Rostow, W. W. (1990 [1960]). *The Stages of Economic Growth: A Non-Communist Manifesto.* Cambridge: Cambridge University Press.

Sawyer, S. (2004). *Crude Chronicles: Indigenous Politics, Multinational Oil, and Neoliberalism in Ecuador.* Durham, NC: Duke University Press.

Schnitzler, A. (2016). *Democracy's Infrastructure: Techno-Politics and Protest after Apartheid.* Princeton: Princeton University Press.

Seamster, L., & Ray, V. (2018). Against Teleology in the Study of Race: Toward the Abolition of the Progress Paradigm. *Sociological Theory, 36*(4), 315–42.

Sieferle, R. P. (2001 [1982]). *Subterranean Forest: Energy Systems and the Industrial Revolution* (Trans. Osman, M.). Cambridge: The White Horse Press.

Silver, J. (2015). Disrupted infrastructures: An urban political ecology of interrupted electricity in Accra. *International Journal of Urban and Regional Research, 39*(5), 984–1003.

Smil, V. (2010). *Energy Transitions: History, Requirements, Prospects.* New York: Praeger.

Smith, J., & High, M. (2017). Exploring the anthropology of energy: Ethnography, energy and ethics. *Energy Research & Social Science, 30*, 1–6.

Smith, C. (1998). *The Science of Energy: A Cultural History of Energy Physics in Victorian Britain.* Chicago: The University of Chicago Press.

Sovacool, B. (2016). How long will it take? Conceptualizing the temporal dynamics of energy transitions. *Energy Research & Social Science, 13*, 202–215.

Thombs, R. P. (2018). Has the relationship between non-fossil fuel energy sources and CO_2 emissions changed over time? A cross-national study, 2000–2013. *Climatic Change 148*, 481–490.

Wenzel, J. (n.d.). *Forms of Life: Thinking Fossil Infrastructure and its Narrative Grammar.*

Weszkalnys, G. (2015). Geology, Potentiality, Speculation: On the Indeterminacy of First Oil. *Cultural Anthropology, 30*(4), 611–639.

White, Leslie. (1943). Energy and the evolution of culture. *American Anthropologist, 45*(3), 335–356.

Winther, T. (2008). *The Impact of Electricity: Development, Desires and Dilemmas.* Oxford: Berg.

Yarrow, T. (2017). Remains of The Future: Rethinking the Space and Time of Ruination through the Volta Resettlement Project, Ghana. *Cultural Anthropology, 32*(4), 566–591.

York, R., & Bell, S. E. (2019). Energy transitions or additions?: Why a transition from fossil fuels requires more than the growth of renewable energy. *Energy Research and Social Science, 51*, 40–43.

CHAPTER 36

Food Infrastructures and Technologies of Trust in Contemporary China

Food

Mikkel Bunkenborg

As societies urbanise and industrialise, the production of food is moved out of sight and the majority lose touch with the people, places, and procedures involved in producing their food. Complex and opaque infrastructures of production, control, and distribution emerge between producers and consumers, and the vast productive capacity of such industrialised food systems has a dark side, not only in the form of exploitative labour regimes, cruelty to animals, and environmental damage, but also in the form of foodstuffs that are unhealthy, contaminated, or even downright poisonous. Yet industrial food systems grow and cohere despite the fact that there is plenty of information to stimulate suspicion in the daily news, and ample documentation of actual malpractices, as well as suggestions for alternative ways of producing food in the social science literature. The vast geographic and social distances between producers and consumers that characterise contemporary food infrastructures mean that people increasingly rely on food produced by distant strangers, and as this disconnection provides a fertile ground for suspicion and distrust, it also establishes the necessity for procedures that allow people to establish some degree of trust in the products they ingest. The need to ascertain that one's food is safe is obviously universal but the issues of food and trust have been entangled in a particularly urgent manner in

M. Bunkenborg (✉)
China Studies, Department of Cross-Cultural and Regional Studies,
University of Copenhagen, Copenhagen, Denmark
e-mail: bunkenborg@hum.ku.dk

© The Author(s), under exclusive license to Springer Nature Singapore
Pte Ltd. 2022
M. H. Bruun et al. (eds.), *The Palgrave Handbook of the Anthropology of
Technology*, https://doi.org/10.1007/978-981-16-7084-8_36

contemporary China, and this chapter accordingly turns to China to explore some examples of what one might call technologies of trust.

Academic and popular debates in China have pointed to an absence of social trust as a salient feature of Chinese society since Mao and the problematisation of trust has encouraged governmental interventions that aim to establish a 'culture of integrity' (诚信文化). The recurrent food scandals that culminated in the 2008 exposure of milk tainted with melamine have played no small part in the erosion of social trust, and the provision of safe food has accordingly become a key concern in comprehensive government plans for surveillance and control. While strategies for establishing some degree of trust in the safety and quality of foodstuffs are rolled out from above, consumers and producers have their tactics to deal with the same issue from below. Drawing upon fieldwork in rural Hebei, the chapter outlines how multiple different technologies of trust operate simultaneously on different levels. While engaging in increasingly specialised forms of agricultural production, some local farmers still cultivate their own vegetables for home consumption, and like urban consumers, they employ a variety of methods to establish trust in foodstuffs and vendors. A traditional socialist technology for provision of special supplies is in evidence at a farm run by a unit of the People's Liberation Army to produce safe food for military personnel. And just across the road from the military farm, and its controlled production of 'special produce' (特供), cadres from the county bureau of agriculture are stepping up their efforts to monitor agricultural production, and hope that they will eventually contribute to realising an efficient system for universal surveillance and control of all the food produced and traded on the vast Chinese market. As the ethnographic description will show, all these individual, collective, and governmental schemes to get trustworthy food ran into difficulties but, despite their shortcomings, they serve here as examples of the technologies of trust that make food infrastructures cohere, despite the disconnection of producers and consumers.

INFRASTRUCTURING FOOD

Among the first to propagate the term 'food infrastructures', the authors of a special issue of the online journal *Limn* suggest that systems of food production, provision, and consumption can fruitfully be approached as forms of infrastructure. Whereas the concept of 'food systems' implicitly suggests that systemic coherence can be taken for granted, the concept of 'food infrastructures' stipulates that such coherence is achieved rather than given. Making contemporary forms of mass production and mass consumption of food cohere in predictable ways, the authors emphasise, is something that requires constant efforts of maintenance and creativity.

> Achieving that predictability requires many specific modes of organizing and creating the world: viable and authoritative standards, distribution models, labeling protocols, safety guidelines, business models marketing and end-users. Hence,

infrastructures are composed not only of physical artifacts and natural resources, but also human labor, forms of knowledge, laws and decrees, organizations and institutions, tastes and interests. (Jauho et al. 2014)

Approaching the complex links between food production and food consumption as forms of infrastructure entails attention to the contingent nature of these arrangements, to the constant socio-material tinkering required to make them work, and to the implicit political and ethical assumptions that are hard-wired into the way food is produced, distributed, and consumed. Coining the related term 'culinary infrastructures', Pilcher (2016) points out that the concept of food infrastructures gestures simultaneously at the physical, technical, and economic aspects of food systems, and at issues of culture and meaning that would usually be captured by a word like foodways. Yet the attempt to combine attention to the material and symbolic dimensions of food is exactly what characterises classical sociological and anthropological studies of food such as those by Goody (1982) and Mintz (1985), and while the recent infra-structuring of food takes a cue from science and technology studies, it also represents a continuation of decades of food studies that have critiqued indus-trialised production and consumption and documented alternative ways of dealing with food.

As processes of industrialisation and urbanisation remove people from settings where they can produce their own food, humans across the globe become increasingly dependent on complex systems of food production and distribution. The dire consequences of industrialised food production—in terms of environmental damage, mistreatment of animals, exploitative labour conditions, and adverse effects on consumer health—are the subject of an extensive literature that deals with multiple topics and places, ranging from slaughterhouses and poultry production in North America (Pachirat 2011; Striffler 2005; Stull and Broadway 2013) to labour conditions in tea plantations in India (Besky 2013; Chatterjee 2001), the politics of producing tomatoes and bananas in the Americas (Barndt 2002; Striffler and Moberg 2003), and the implications of eating cheap and fatty meat cuts in the Pacific Islands (Gewertz and Errington 2010). The long supply chains associated with industrial food production means that consumers are often unaware of the arrangements that provide their food, and critical descriptions of food production that expose pollution, cruelty, inhuman labour conditions, and unhealthy or contaminated products are quite shocking to the minority of consumers who read them.

While food studies reflect and affirm a deep scepticism towards industrial food production, they also document a variety of different responses that seek to give consumers a sense of control over the food they ingest. Growing one's own food while living organically in a dacha in Russia (Caldwell 2011) or moving to the countryside to establish independent organic farms in China (Cody 2019) are but two examples from an extensive literature on alternative practices. Among many other forms of food activism (Counihan and Siniscalchi 2014), people engage in the production of local food (Janssen 2017), in community-supported agriculture (Hansen 2020), or community gardening (Poulsen et al. 2014), and this goes hand in hand with the valorisation of traditional forms of craft production (West 2016). Taking an active role in its production is one way of ensuring the safety of one's food and combatting the inequities of industrial food production, but it remains a minority solution. Around the globe, consumers in urban and increasingly even in rural settings depend upon products from a globalised food industry for their daily sustenance, and many, if not most, have to live with a nagging suspicion of the food they consume and the opaque arrangements that made the products materialise in local stores and markets. Critical studies of industrial food production and descriptions of counter-movements among consumers give the impression of a disconnection between the production and consumption of food, a disconnection that results not only in sporadic attempts to reconnect with production in various ways but also in a general lack of trust in food (Kjærnes et al. 2007; Kneafsey et al. 2008). One might turn to theories about risk society and late modernity for explanations, but keeping the concept of infrastructure in mind, one could also explore how this evident disconnection is bridged in practical terms. What technologies and forms of work are invested in making mass production and consumption of food systemically coherent?

Ensuring trustworthy foodstuffs is obviously a universal problem. The appointment of cup-bearers and food tasters for noblemen in many parts of the world and the use of silver chopsticks to detect poisoned food in China are two historical examples of procedures to deal with the potential dangers of eating that predate industrial food production. But industrial food production and its inherent disconnection of producer and consumer exacerbate this problem and are perhaps necessarily accompanied by the proliferation of new procedures to produce trust. Describing how Vietnamese consumers build trust in food, Figuié et al. (2019) suggest that 'distanciation' makes food safety a major concern for consumers in late modernity. The specific technological apparatuses and combinations of consumer discernment, governmental control, auditing, and certification obviously differ from one place to another: being concerned with fake products in Bulgaria (Yuson 2016) is different from grappling with adulterated food in Mumbai (Solomon 2015). Yet the exchange of food does generally seem to call for a broad variety of socio-material interventions to establish the trustworthiness of foodstuffs, interventions that are here described as 'technologies of trust'. The term resembles what Wahlberg (2018, p. 136) has called a 'technology of assurance'—'a configuration of strategies and techniques within which certain persons, activities, and/or objects come to be vouched for over others'—but what is proposed here is a heuristic device rather than an analytical concept. As a first step towards fleshing out technologies of trust as a possible set of socio-material interventions concerned with the production of trust, this chapter makes the local imbrications and understandings of trust and food in contemporary China a point of departure.

TRUSTING FOOD IN CHINA

Lack of trust in the quality and safety of foodstuffs is a governance problem that has been given high priority in the People's Republic of China since the 2008 milk scandal; President Xi Jinping has even described unsafe food as something that could make the people question whether the Communist Party is fit to rule the country (Wu et al. 2017). In a bid to stop a seemingly unending series of food and drug scandals, the president has proposed to ensure 'tongue-tip safety' (舌尖安全) for the people of China by introducing the 'four strictest' (四个最严), implying that China will implement laws to ensure the strictest standards, the most stringent supervision, the most severe punishment, and the most serious accountability. At the highest political level, the provision of safe food to the masses is described as an indicator of governmental competence, and food is cast as a medium through which the masses can taste the competence of the ruling party at the tip of their tongues. The political stakes in food safety have become very high indeed, and a document issued by the Central Committee of the Communist Party of China and State Council (2019) gives a sense of the political urgency and the complexity of reforms required to assuage concerns about unsafe food. Ranging from soil pollution and excessive use of agrichemicals to unlabelled products and illegal factories, the document also outlines schemes to ensure the digital traceability of foodstuffs. Enterprises dealing with food, the document states, will have special files in the national information-sharing platform, thus incorporating the surveillance of food into the large-scale project of digital surveillance known as the *social credit system* (社会信用体系) (State Council 2014). As an evolving eco-system of partially integrated digital platforms for collecting, storing, and selectively publicising data concerning the trustworthiness of persons and enterprises, the social credit system is not so much concerned with credit as with trust. The word *xinyong* (信用) has both meanings—credit and trust—and, while the English term has associations with credit ratings, the system actually deals with social trust more broadly, addressing a pervasive concern with an absence of social trust that has been built up over decades in academic and journalistic representations of Chinese society.

Trust has been a hot topic among sociologists working on China and their insistence that trust is absolutely necessary for a modern society—and that there is too little of it in contemporary China—has had considerable political impact. Francis Fukuyama describes China as a country characterised by familism and a low level of social trust, observing, 'There is a very strong inclination on the part of the Chinese to trust only people related to them, and conversely to distrust people outside their family and kinship group' (Fukuyama 1995, p. 75). Chinese sociologists working on trust often invoke similar Weberian binaries that have been popularised through the work of Fei Xiaotong (费孝通) but, unlike Fukuyama, they tend to be rather more sceptical about the strength and value of family-based trust in contemporary China. In a study of the odd discrepancy between a vociferous public debate about a lack of trust and the findings of the World Value Survey, which actually ranks China as a society with a relatively high degree of general trust, Dominik Linggi (2011) explores the specificity of Chinese conceptions of trust through some of the Chinese sociological literature on the contemporary *Vertrauenskrise* (信任危机). The crisis of trust is described not simply as an absence of social trust but also as a weakening of trust based on friendship and kinship. Perhaps the most vocal contributor to the early debate on China's trust crisis was Zheng Yefu (郑也夫), professor of sociology and author of the monograph *On Trust* (信任论) (2001).[1] In this book, Zheng Yefu drew upon such luminaries as Giddens and Luhmann to develop a model of trust that included three major forms: trust in personal relations, trust in money, and trust in experts. The crisis of trust in contemporary China, Zheng Yefu claimed, was not just a lack of systemic forms of trust in money and experts, it was also a lack of trust among family and friends. Taking a point of departure in the expression *shashu* (杀熟) which means 'to exploit family and friends' or, more literally, 'killing familiars', he pointed out that it became a common term in the 1990s because it reflected common social practices such as direct marketing, where people exploited their social relations for personal gain. According to Zheng Yefu, China was facing not only a lack of systemic trust among strangers but also a diminishing trust among familiars, and taken together, this constituted a collapse of social trust (Zheng 2001, p. 222).

Food safety played a central role in this perceived collapse of social trust. In a seminal article on the long series of food scandals in post-Mao China, the anthropologist Yan Yunxiang examined the issue of food safety through the lens of risk theory and argued that food safety problems, particularly the deliberate production of poisonous food, were contributing to a rapid decline in social trust.

> The widespread production and distribution of contaminated and fake foods, as indicated above, has played an especially vicious role in further spreading distrust in strangers and social institutions. The most damaging risk that poisonous foods, together with other food-safety problems, present to Chinese society is therefore the risk of distrust. (Yan 2012, p. 719)

Outlining the changing moral landscape of China, Yan Yunxiang offers a sociological narrative of incomplete modernisation and suggests that the root cause behind ploys to make money on poisonous food is the continued existence of a traditional, particularistic morality with no regard for the lives of strangers (Yan 2011, 2014). The production/circulation of poisonous food plays a crucial role in this narrative as it is both an indication of a complete disregard for the health and safety of unknown others and the very stuff that threatens to further exacerbate the distrust of strangers. Numerous other scholars have written about an ongoing moral crisis in China (Ci 2014; Kleinman et al. 2011; Lee 2014), but it is particularly through the work of Yan Yunxiang that the recurrent food safety scandals have come to function as a significant argument in support of a broader narrative that describes post-Mao China as a society haunted by a lack of social trust and calls for its urgent promotion in contemporary Chinese society.

The cure for the crisis of trust, Zheng Yefu suggested in 2002, might take inspiration from Shanxi merchants who extended credit to each other on the basis of familiarity and reputation.

> In the present society of strangers, there needs to be a record that follows you always. In the past, the personal dossier was very exhaustive, but we used it in a one-sided way. I find that the personal dossier should serve all of society, the personal dossier should be public. … When there is a record, people will care about their reputation. (Zheng 2002)

Conflating trust and credit, and advocating the publication of 'personal dossiers' (档案)—the secret files with personal information kept by the work unit and the Public Security Bureau in China—Zheng Yefu's writings may well have inspired proponents of the social credit system, which also combines credit ratings with a variety of non-financial data points. As the idea that China suffered from a pervasive lack of social trust came to resemble an established fact after the turn of the millennium, the social credit system emerged as a technological fix that promised to produce social trust artificially through operations of surveillance and documentation that extend into most social domains. Inserted into this particular context, the term trust can no longer be understood as the opposite of control; instead of designating 'an important lubricant of a social system' (Lu et al. 2008, p. 22), a confidence that allows people to operate in the absence of control and certainty, trust is cast as something that grows from control.

Considering that food safety played no small role in generating the crisis of trust that the social credit system is set to remedy, it is not surprising that food production has become an object of surveillance. In an ethnographic study of a high-end restaurant in the city of Hangzhou, Caroline Merrifield (2020) contrasts approaches to food safety based on seeing and knowing. Governmental policies to improve food safety revolve around *seeing*. Pushing for transparency, the regulations in Zhejiang province require 'sunshine kitchens' (阳光厨房) fitted with glass walls and video cameras; making the preparation of food entirely transparent to the customers is supposed to prevent malpractices and inspire trust. In contrast to this obsessive concern with seeing, the restaurant owners emphasise the use of raw materials sourced from suppliers who have long-standing personal relations to a handful of procurement agents who work for the restaurant. The procurement agents visit the farmers in person, they recognise the value of high-quality produce, and food safety at the restaurant is accordingly built on *knowing* the producers and their products in an intimate way. Merrifield opens a window onto a regulatory drive for surveillance, transparency, and traceability that has a significant impact on the production and circulation of food in China; however, even as projects of universal surveillance are effectively reconfiguring the field, the strategies of seeing imposed upon producers and distributors by government agencies from above evidently strike consumers as being less convincing than the old-fashioned tactics of knowing, pursued from below. As Merrifield points out, seeing cannot definitively assuage the fear that things are not what they seem, and knowing may well remain a superior basis for trust.

Recurrent food scandals are a problem that weighs heavily on the Chinese party-state and it has become inextricably entangled with a perceived lack of social trust. Unsafe food is seen to reflect, and in turn exacerbate, an absence of social trust, and food has accordingly come to play a central role in governmental attempts to produce social trust. Partially integrated with the social credit system, governmental approaches to food are essentially panoptic, and the sunshine kitchens offer an apt illustration of the practical consequences of this insistence on transparency. As a contrast to governmental strategies of surveillance, Merrifield presents the cultivation of interpersonal relations and implicitly calls for an ethnographic exploration of alternative ways of ensuring trustworthy foodstuffs. In a context where relations between producers and consumers are rapidly changing, and where there is limited faith in governmental schemes of surveillance and control, what other technologies of trust can be mobilised to ensure safe food?

Changing Food Infrastructures in Rural Hebei

The growth of market-driven industrialised food production in post-Mao China has had profound effects on the Chinese countryside, where farmers engage in increasingly specialised forms of agriculture as producers and purchase much of their food at the end of long supply chains as consumers. In the Hebei township of Fanzhuang (范庄), for instance, agricultural production was decollectivised in 1983, and the farmers gradually stopped growing wheat and maize in order to plant pear trees on the small plots of land that were allotted to each household. In 2002, when I first visited, pears had already become the only real cash crop in the township but most farmers still had vegetable plots of varying sizes and many reared pigs and chickens in their courtyards. Industrially produced foods were available in a dozen small shops but most of the food consumed by the 5000 inhabitants was still produced in the vicinity. Much of this remaining familiarity with the people and processes involved in the production of one's food has disappeared over the past two decades. Those who farm have specialised even further in a form of pear production that relies on a broad array of agrichemicals, and while people offer very diverse estimates of the toxicity of the fertilisers, pesticides, herbicides, fungicides, and plant hormones used in pear production, hardly anyone would claim that all this chemistry is entirely harmless. Very little of the harvest is consumed in the township itself; but there is a market for the pears, and the farmers have mostly resigned themselves to a form of production that provides cash income. Engaging in various forms of wage labour has become common, and most households now find that they have little time for small-scale, side-line productions of food that are not financially viable. Increasingly, the consumption patterns in Fanzhuang have come to resemble those of urban China. Several large supermarkets supply the township with industrially produced food similar to that available in Chinese cities, and while one can still find some local produce at the market held every five days, most of the trade is conducted by professionals who source their goods from wholesalers in the county seat or further afield.

Subsistence agriculture is largely a thing of the past in China, and people in the countryside are just as suspicious about the products they buy and sell on the market as their urban peers. Lora-Wainwright (2013, p. 110) describes how farmers in Sichuan province see no alternative to using pesticides on their cash-crops but have a separate production of food for home consumption, and Oxfeld (2017, p. 187) notes that the reason why farmers in Southeast China continue to produce their own rice and vegetables is not because it's profitable, but because they doubt the safety of the wider food system. In Fanzhuang many families grow various gourds, string beans, groundnuts, tomatoes, chillies, and other vegetables for home consumption either in their courtyards or on small plots hidden away among the pear trees. Such home-grown greens are prized for their wholesomeness and superior taste, and they are often given as gifts to friends and members of the extended family. However, the specialisation in pear trees has progressed to a point where everyone is obliged to purchase at least some of their food from strangers, and this has produced a seemingly endless variety of techniques for ascertaining the quality of foodstuffs. Much like vendors everywhere in China use counterfeit detectors to check the quality of the money, buyers bring their own techniques of discernment to bear upon their purchases. The stem of a pear can reveal whether it was treated with hormones; the overly perfect exterior of a tomato may be read as a sign of forced growth; and the authenticity of a pack of cigarettes can be judged not just by the taste, but also by examining the paper, feeling the tightness of the tobacco, and taking it apart to see the build-up of the filter.

The ethnographic literature on responses to food safety issues in China provides many examples of the tactics employed by urban food consumers to acquire safe food for themselves and their children (Fihl 2020; Hanser and Li 2015; Klein 2013), and similar concerns are evident in the countryside. The food infrastructures of China have long since made transactions among strangers indispensable, even in rural economies, and rural consumers are not unlike their urban peers in their use of socio-material interventions and techniques of discernment to procure trustworthy food. What makes rural approaches really interesting, however, is the fact that people in the countryside have access to land. Despite the highly specialised forms of agricultural production that increasingly dominate farmers lives, some farmers still manage to grow their own vegetables or gain access to foodstuffs that are not intended for the market.

SPECIAL SUPPLY

Not so far from Fanzhuang, a military unit established its own farm to ensure the quality of the food served in its canteens. Having rented the land five years earlier, the unit set off 65 *mu* (one hectare equals 15 *mu*) for wheat and maize and invested an estimated RMB 4–5 million (one USD was around 6.5 RMB) in the establishment of a walled 100 *mu* farm with greenhouses, fish ponds, sheds for poultry, and stables for pigs. In the spring of 2017, the farm was run by an officer and five permanent employees who supervised different branches of production. The fields and greenhouses of the farm produced a great variety of crops ranging from potatoes, onions, tomatoes, squash, aubergines, garlic, celery, and okra to pears, apricots, haws, and grapes. In addition to pigs, fish, chicken, ducks, and geese, the farm could also boast of a pair of black swans that might one day grace the table of a general. Having consulted with the farm about the availability of different forms of produce, the canteens would order what they needed for the following day and the produce was then harvested in the morning and sent off. The meals of the permanent staff on the farm were prepared by a chef who obviously used produce from the farm, and from the many comments—on the colour of the eggs, the texture of the chicken, the fish that came straight out of the pond, and so on—it was evident that they enjoyed the quality of what they produced. The farm as such would hardly qualify as a socialist paradise; indeed, most of the manual labour was carried out by a few dozen day labourers hired from a nearby village. It was only women and elderly men, one of the supervisors told me, who were willing to accept the daily rate of RMB 40 for women and RMB 45 for men, and the day labourers had to take their meals at home. Yet, leaving the unfairness of the distribution aside, it was quite remarkable how the labourers, the permanent staff, the army personnel, and the outsiders who got a chance to sample the produce in one way or another seemed to agree that the products from the farm were tasty and safe.

The fact that certain privileged groups in China have access to specially produced goods, and thus avoid the risks associated with the market, is a public secret that people often comment upon with a mixture of resentment and envy. In an article that may be read as a political jab at the Communist Party, Tsai Wen-hsuan (2016) traces the outline of these systems and concludes that they serve to perpetuate a high degree of social inequality. Echoing Yan Yunxiang (2012, p. 723), Tsai suggests that the practice started in the 1950s to ensure ample supplies of food for high-ranking officials in the face of public food shortages but, in recent decades, the system, known as 'special supplies' (特供),[2] has been geared towards the provision of safe food. The public resentment of the inequality inherent in these systems of special supply is understandable, but it is worth remembering that even a perfectly transparent market does nothing to combat economic inequality and that systems of special supply continue to exist in China as a partially successful socio-material response to the problem of delivering safe food.

Despite the evident popularity of the food from the military farm, production was being closed down when I revisited the site half a year later. An administrative reform in the army had brought new leaders into power who were apprehensive about the legality of the lease agreement and the political implications of running their own farm to procure safe food. There was another 25 years left on the lease and the farm represented a substantial investment but it was decided to shut it down discreetly, and for a few days I participated in butchering most of the livestock. One evening after dinner, we captured some 400 roosting chickens and tied their legs. The following day, a team of day labourers was assembled to scald and pluck the chickens, and an elderly cook started slitting their throats, whispering to each of them, 'Don't blame me, blame the boss, it was he who gave the order'. Another team had started butchering the pigs, and a few days later they started on the fish. Amidst the confusion about the fate of the farm, the tropical species of fish in the ponds had begun to die as the weather got colder, but in the course of a few days, a ton of fish was caught with nets and butchered. Usually, the surplus production from the farm would have been distributed among army personnel as 'welfare' (福利) but the new leaders had discontinued this practice, so the farm was left with a surplus, some of which was sold to counterbalance budget cuts and some distributed informally among the workers and their friends. The following year there was only a skeleton crew manning the farm, but they did keep up a small production of eggs and vegetables so that friends and family members who visited the farm not only got to try their hand at catching the few surviving fish with fishing rods but also had a chance to sample the special supplies that were no longer produced in quantity. The production of special supply was grinding to a halt on the military farm but, just across the road, the county agricultural bureau was installing new equipment and gearing up for a new regime of transparency in agriculture.

Surveillance, Transparency, and Traceability

'The really dangerous agrichemicals (农药) aren't even produced any more', the head of a county agricultural bureau in Hebei explained during an interview in spring 2017. 'Peasants used to store these poisonous chemicals in their homes and thought little of the cumulative harm to human bodies, but now it's mostly a question of spraying too often, especially on the small farms, where farmers tend to do as they please.' The offices of the bureau looked somewhat sleepy and run-down but the leader insisted that they were making progress towards ensuring food safety and enthusiastically explained about the schemes for certification of 'safe' (无公害), 'green' (绿色), and 'organic' (有机) produce. On a visit to the facilities for agricultural inspection the following day, 4 million RMB worth of newly installed laboratory equipment, funded by higher administrative levels, suggested that food safety really had become a political priority. The equipment made it possible to run simple chromatography tests for residues of agrichemicals on 4000 samples a year, as well as more complicated tests to determine exactly which substance was used on a few hundred samples a year. The three technicians employed to run the tests were being trained elsewhere, the bureau head explained, but they were scheduled to start work in the early summer when the harvesting of vegetables in greenhouses and fields began. Testing the produce was part of concerted effort to monitor the use of agrichemicals at the site of production, and the bureau head felt that their efforts had some effect on improving food safety. Yet to be really efficient, the bureau head continued, the testing of samples would need to be integrated with new systems of traceability to allow identification of sources of contamination at any point of the commodity chain.

One of the problems singled out in food safety campaigns is the circulation of unmarked products on the market. Known as 'three nos' (三无), they carry no information about the manufacturer, the date of production, or the production licence. It is obviously extremely hard to monitor products that have been so thoroughly cut free from the social world in which they are produced and traded, so food safety policies are not just about ensuring that products are what they claim to be but also about producing the traces of documentation that will enable the authorities to hold people accountable. Writing about the Chinese dairy industry in the wake of the milk scandal, Megan Tracy (2016) describes how attempts to create transparency in milk production involves not only elaborate systems of testing and documentation to link individual farmers to samples and test results, but also the installation of video cameras that allow the dairy processing company to observe the milking. The pervasive distrust of food goes hand in hand with a distrust of the people involved in producing, processing, and trading food, and attempts to ensure the transparency of these processes thus result in new systems of documentation and surveillance. In his monograph on organic farming, for instance, Sacha Cody (2019) describes how a member of an NGO engaged in rural reconstruction spoke out at a meeting to emphasise that certification and periodic checks were not enough to convince consumers that the produce was truly organic.

> 'How can urban consumers be confident', she asked, 'that the items they purchase will really be organic?' She proposed a full-scale monitoring system, complete with video cameras placed throughout farms, to observe farmers' every behaviour and hold them accountable. (p. 40)

The 2019 document on food safety from the State Council envisions even more elaborate technological interventions by establishing a unified platform for the traceability of agricultural products and advocating the use of big data, artificial intelligence, and block-chain technology.

The head of the agricultural bureau foresaw a future where their efforts would be an integrated part of a functional system for testing and tracing foodstuffs in all of China, but he was also pretty confident that such a system would require a complete reorganisation of agricultural production. 'It's impossible to monitor all these small farmers', he claimed. 'They don't have a brand name they need to protect and they have little to lose if they are found out.' As the volume of food produced by small-scale producers was relatively less significant, the agricultural bureau focused on testing samples from larger farms established on plots rented from small-scale farmers. Even as the employees at the agricultural bureau were foreseeing an eventual reorganisation of agricultural production, they were not particularly optimistic about the positive effects of increased surveillance. One day, when some of them were taking me to a restaurant in the county seat, we began discussing the surveillance cameras that were set up next to all the traffic lights. Even the slightest mistake would result in a ticket, the driver said. If the camera caught you speeding or running a red light, you would be identified by your licence plate and get a ticket the following day. But then again, the driver continued, he was not particularly bothered by the cameras. One of the police officers who processed the tickets was an old friend of his, and the officers had a whole list of licence plates that belonged to friends whose infractions they chose to ignore. It turned out that the employees from the bureau were already on the list, and it seemed they had a rather realistic take on the way techno-optimistic attempts to produce transparency and trust by artificial means will quickly produce new areas of darkness and corruption.

Conclusion

Approaching industrial food production as a form of infrastructure draws attention not just to the socio-material assemblages that facilitate the movement of food across vast geographical distances but also to the remedial interventions introduced to compensate for the social disconnection that occurs when producers and consumers are worlds apart. According to Star and Bowker (2006), infrastructures tend to fade into the woodwork—unobtrusive, transparent, and taken for granted—as working infrastructures are normally invisible until they break down. Yet while the infrastructures that subtend industrial food production may at times have been perceived by some groups as unobtrusive and transparent, there is a growing critical literature that presents them as alienating and opaque systems that should be fixed or replaced by better alternatives. In China, it was primarily a series of scandals involving unsafe food that made food infrastructures painfully obtrusive to a wider public in the post-Mao decades, and discussions about the provision of food became inextricably entangled with debates about social trust. Unsafe food was read as something that expressed, and in turn exacerbated, a lack of trust, and thus attempts to fix the broken infrastructures of industrial food systems came to revolve about ways of producing trust. The social credit system may be seen as a national technology of trust, a grand fix that promises to solve the problem of trust, including trust in food, once and for all, through universal surveillance, but as people await the implementation of these plans, there are many other technologies of trust in play in China.

The ethnographic material presented in this chapter explores how people in rural Hebei engage with the problem of establishing trust in food. Despite the convenience of supermarket shopping, rural consumers have misgivings about the safety of products available there and, while they continuously develop new ways of ensuring the quality of foodstuffs on the market, they retain an evident preference for food produced by themselves or by people they know. Meanwhile, the employees in the agricultural bureau are not only stepping up surveillance but also foreseeing a reorganisation of agricultural production to conform to a new regime of visibility. Caroline Merrifield's distinction between trust based on knowing and on seeing is clearly relevant here but perhaps it is even more useful to think of the contrast as a polarity, as opposite ends of a whole spectrum of technologies of trust that range from knowing people and products so well that trust never arises as an issue, to seeing in such detail and with such certainty that trust is actually superfluous. Somewhere between the trust grounded in interpersonal relations and the trust derived from abstract systems of governmental quality control, there is the confidence that people had in the food produced at the military farm. A somewhat anachronistic set-up that was breaking up in the current political climate, the production of special supplies in a small enclave was nevertheless a technology of trust that seemed to work. Personal acquaintance between army personnel and people working the farm obviously played a role, but what seemed to make the military farm work as a technology of trust was the manageable scale of the social system involved in production and consumption. In this respect, the military farm was not entirely dissimilar from the model of community-supported agriculture that is currently gaining popularity in parts of China (Hansen 2020), and perhaps the creation of such smaller units of production and consumption may be a viable technology of trust in a context where producers and consumers become increasingly disconnected.

The social and geographic distances that industrial food production interposes between producers and consumers give rise to widespread and, not infrequently, well-founded suspicions about various aspects of the food available on the market. Accordingly, the systemic coherency of contemporary food infrastructures requires a constant effort from consumers, producers, and regulators to suspend their distrust of food produced by strangers and to establish at least a semblance of trust. In China, where the rapid transformation of food infrastructures in the post-Mao era has been accompanied by food scandals and public concern with the safety of the foodstuffs available on the market, the need for technologies of trust has been particularly acute. This is reflected in attempts to navigate and rectify the food market that range from micro-social techniques for cultivating relations to producers and discerning the qualities of their products, to grand governmental schemes that impose schemes of surveillance and certification upon all food production in the entire country. Studying such disparate socio-material interventions as different responses to a singular problem of establishing trust in food, and tracking them as they unfold in various social settings, is something that will require an anthropology of technology that is unafraid of jumping scales and conscious of the interoperability of social and technological solutions to human problems.

Acknowledgements The research project 'Moral Economies of Food in Contemporary China' was funded by the Independent Research Fund Denmark. The chapter has benefitted from discussions with colleagues in this research project, Anders Sybrandt Hansen and Ingrid Fihl and with the other contributors to a special issue of *Journal of Current Chinese Affairs* that grew out of the project: Caroline Merrifield, Ellen Oxfeld, Erika Kuever, Jakob Klein, and Jamie Coates. Thanks to Jia Meina, Judy Farquhar, Lai Lili, Yan Hairong, and Zhao Xudong for memorable conversations about food in China.

Notes

1. Professor Zheng Yefu is also the editor of a volume entitled *Trust in Chinese Society* 中国社会中的信任 (Zheng 2003) and the translator of the anthology on trust edited by Diego Gambetta (1988).
2. In terms of providing a genealogy for the term, it is hardly just an etymological coincidence that the character 供, composed of the characters for 'person' 人 and 'to share' 共, also means 'to offer as sacrifice or tribute'. Offering up sacrifices to deities is called 上供 and if the term 'special supplies' 特供 conjures up the logic of a redistributive economy, it is not exclusively associated with the socialist economy of Maoism, but also with imperial and religious logics of redistribution.

References

Barndt, D. (2002). *Tangled routes: women, work, and globalization on the tomato trail.* Lanham, MD: Rowman & Littlefield Pub.

Besky, S. (2013). *The Darjeeling distinction: labor and justice on fair-trade tea plantations in India.* Berkeley: University of California Press.

Caldwell, M. L. (2011). *Dacha idylls: living organically in Russia's countryside.* Berkeley: University of California Press.

Central Committee of the Communist Party of China and State Council 中共中央 国务院. (2019). 关于深化改革加强食品安全工作的意见. *(Opinions on Deepening the Reform and Strengthening of Food Safety Work).* http://www.gov.cn/zhengce/2019-05/20/content_5393212.htm. Accessed 10 May 2021.

Chatterjee, P. (2001). *A time for tea: women, labor, and post/colonial politics on an Indian plantation.* Durham, NC: Duke University Press.

Ci, J. (2014). *Moral China in the age of reform.* New York, NY: Cambridge University Press.

Cody, S. (2019). *Exemplary Agriculture: Independent Organic Farming in Contemporary China.* Singapore: Palgrave Macmillan.

Counihan, C., & Siniscalchi, V. (2014). *Food activism: agency, democracy and economy.* London: Bloomsbury.

Figuié, M., Moustier, P., Bricas, N., & Loc, N. T. T. (2019). Trust and Food Modernity in Vietnam. In J. Ehlert & N. K. Faltmann (Eds.), *Food Anxiety in Globalising Vietnam* (pp. 139–165). New York: Springer.

Fihl, I. (2020). Risky Eating: Shanghai Families' Strategies to Acquire Safe Food in Everyday Life. *Journal of Current Chinese Affairs, 48*(3), 262–280. https://doi.org/10.1177/1868102619898926.

Fukuyama, F. (1995). *Trust: the social virtues and the creation of prosperity.* New York: Free Press.

Gambetta, D. (1988). *Trust: making and breaking cooperative relations.* New York: B. Blackwell.

Gewertz, D. B., & Errington, F. K. (2010). *Cheap meat: flap food nations in the Pacific Islands.* Berkeley: University of California Press.

Goody, J. (1982). *Cooking, cuisine, and class: a study in comparative sociology.* Cambridge: Cambridge University Press.

Hansen, A. S. (2020). Subsistence Solidarity and the Extension of Trust: Moral Economies of Organic Farming in Northern China. *Journal of Current Chinese Affairs, 48*(3), 301–321. https://doi.org/10.1177/1868102620920506.

Hanser, A., & Li, J. C. (2015). Opting Out? Gated Consumption, Infant Formula and China's Affluent Urban Consumers. *The China Journal, 74,* 110–128. https://doi.org/10.1086/681662.

Janssen, B. (2017). *Making local food work: the challenges and opportunities of today's small farmers.* Iowa City: University of Iowa Press.

Jauho, M., Schleifer, D., Penders, B., & Frohlich, X. (2014). Preface. Food Infrastructures. *Limn* (4). https://limn.it/articles/preface-food-infrastructures/. Accessed 10 May 2021.

Kjærnes, U., Harvey, M., & Warde, A. (2007). *Trust in food: a comparative and institutional analysis.* Houndmills, U.K.: Palgrave Macmillan.

Klein, J. A. (2013). Everyday Approaches to Food Safety in Kunming. *The China Quarterly, 214,* 376–393. https://doi.org/10.1017/S0305741013000325.

Kleinman, A., Yunxiang, Y., Jun, J., Lee, S., Zhang, E., Tianshu, P., et al. (2011). *Deep China: the moral life of the person: what anthropology and psychiatry tell us about China today.* Berkeley: University of California Press.

Kneafsey, M., Cox, R., Holloway, L., Dowler, E., Venn, L., & Tuomainen, H. (2008). *Reconnecting consumers, producers, and food: exploring alternatives.* Oxford, UK: Berg.

Lee, H. (2014). *The stranger and the Chinese moral imagination.* Stanford, CA: Stanford University Press.

Linggi, D. (2011). *Vertrauen in China: Ein kritischer Beitrag zur kulturvergleichenden Sozialforschung.* Wiesbaden: VS Verlag für Sozialwissenschaften.

Lora-Wainwright, A. (2013). *Fighting for breath: living morally and dying of cancer in a Chinese village.* Honolulu: University of Hawai'i Press.

Lu, H., Feng, S., Trienekens, J. H., & Omta, S. W. F. (2008). Performance in vegetable supply chains: the role of Guanxi networks and buyer–seller relationships. *Agribusiness, 24*(2), 253–274. https://doi.org/10.1002/agr.20158.

Merrifield, C. (2020). Seeing and Knowing: Sourcing Safe Food in Zhejiang. *Journal of Contemporary China, 48*(3), 281–300. https://doi.org/10.1177/1868102620920124.

Mintz, S. W. (1985). *Sweetness and power: the place of sugar in modern history.* New York: Viking.

Oxfeld, E. (2017). *Bitter and sweet: food, meaning, and modernity in rural China.* Oakland, CA: University of California Press.

Pachirat, T. (2011). *Every twelve seconds: industrialized slaughter and the politics of sight.* New Haven: Yale University Press.

Pilcher, J. M. (2016). Culinary Infrastructure: How Facilities and Technologies Create Value and Meaning around Food. *Global Food History, 2*(2), 105–131. https://doi.org/10.1080/20549547.2016.1214896.

Poulsen, M. N., Hulland, K. R. S., Gulas, C. A., Pham, H., Dalglish, S. L., Wilkinson, R. K., & Winch, P. J. (2014). Growing an Urban Oasis: A Qualitative Study of the Perceived Benefits of Community Gardening in Baltimore, Maryland. *Culture, Agriculture, Food and Environment, 36*(2), 69–82. https://doi.org/10.1111/cuag.12035.

Solomon, H. (2015). Unreliable eating: Patterns of food adulteration in urban India. *Bio Societies, 10*(2), 177–193. https://doi.org/10.1057/biosoc.2015.10.

Star, S. L., & Bowker, G. C. (2006). How to infrastructure. In L. A. Lievrouw & S. Livingstone (Eds.), *Handbook of new media: Social shaping and social consequences of ICTs* (pp. 230–245). London: SAGE.

State Council 国务院. (2014). 社会信用体系建设规划纲要(2014-2020年) (*Outline Plan for the Establishment of the Social Credit System).* http://www.gov.cn/zhengce/content/2014-06/27/content_8913.htm. Accessed 8 July 2021.

Striffler, S. (2005). *Chicken: the dangerous transformation of America's favorite food.* New Haven: Yale University Press.

Striffler, S., & Moberg, M. (2003). *Banana wars: power, production, and history in the Americas.* Durham: Duke University Press.

Stull, D. D., & Broadway, M. J. (2013). *Slaughterhouse blues: the meat and poultry industry in North America* (2nd edition). Belmont, CA: Wadsworth Cengage Learning.

Tracy, M. (2016). Multimodality, Transparency, and Food Safety in China. *PoLAR: Political and Legal Anthropology Review, 39*(S1), 34–53. https://doi.org/10.1111/plar.12170.

Tsai, W.-H. (2016). Delicacies for a Privileged Class in a Risk Society: The Chinese Communist Party's Special Supplies Food System. *Issues and Studies, 52*(2), 1–29.

Wahlberg, A. (2018). *Good Quality: The Routinization of Sperm Banking in China* (1st edition). Berkeley, CA: University of California Press.

West, H. G. (2016). Artisanal Foods and the Cultural Economy: Perspectives on Craft, Heritage, Authenticity and Reconnection. In J. A. Klein & J. L. Watson (Eds.), *The Handbook of Food and Anthropology* (pp. 406–434). London, U.K.: Bloomsbury Publishing Plc.

Wu, X., Yang, D. L., & Chen, L. (2017). The Politics of Quality-of-Life Issues: Food Safety and Political Trust in China. *Journal of Contemporary China, 26*(106), 601–615. https://doi.org/10.1080/10670564.2017.1274827.

Yan, Y. (2011). The Changing Moral Landscape. In A. Kleinman, Y. Yunxiang, J. Jun, S. Lee, E. Zhang, P. Tianshu, W. Fei, & G. Jinhua (Eds.), *Deep China: The Moral Life of the Person: What Anthropology and Psychiatry Tell Us About China Today* (pp. 36–77). Berkeley, CA: University of California Press.

Yan, Y. (2012). Food Safety and Social Risk in Contemporary China. *The Journal of Asian Studies, 71*(3), 705–729.

Yan, Y. (2014). The Moral Implications of Immorality. *Journal of Religious Ethics, 42*(3), 460–493.

Yuson, J. (2016). Food Provisioning and Foodways in Postsocialist Societies: Food as Medium for Social Trust. In J. A. Klein & J. L. Watson (Eds.), *The Handbook of Food and Anthropology* (pp. 289–307). London, U.K.: Bloomsbury Publishing Plc.

Zheng, Y. 郑也夫. (2001). *信任论 (On Trust)*. 北京: 中国广播电视出版社.

Zheng, Y. 郑也夫. (2002). *中国的信任危机 (China's Trust Crisis)*. Paper presented at the Lecture April 13th 2002. http://www.aisixiang.com/data/1890-2.html. Accessed 10 May 2021.

Zheng, Y. 郑也夫. (Ed.) (2003). *中国社会中的信任 (Trust in Chinese Society)*. 北京: 中国城市出版社.

CHAPTER 37

Water Infrastructures: The Making and Maintenance of Material and Organisational Connections

Water

Astrid Oberborbeck Andersen

One early morning in June 2011, the inhabitants of Primero de Junio, an urban settlement on the outskirts of the city of Arequipa in Southern Peru, gathered in the neighbourhood square with shovels and other tools. The sun was announcing its arrival from behind the volcanoes and people were wearing warm clothes to keep out the morning chill. Six leakage points had been identified in the pipeline carrying water from a nearby reservoir to the *piletas* (public water taps) that supplied approximately 120 households with water. All households had been called on to participate in today's *faena* to fix the leaks, yet many were missing. Approximately 37 settlers had shown up and attendees were divided into six groups, each working to fix a leak. Holes were dug to reach the thin PVC pipes that transported the water, new pieces of PVC were used to repair the leaks, and the holes were closed again. Isabel, president of the local water committee, was walking from group to group, supervising the *faena*. At 8 o'clock the work was done, the pipes were covered, and *vecinos* (neighbours) queued up to have their participation registered. The sun was now fully out, burning through the dry air and dust that was periodically carried up by a gust under the blue sky.

A. O. Andersen (✉)
Aalborg University, Aalborg, Denmark
e-mail: aoan@hum.aau.dk

© The Author(s), under exclusive license to Springer Nature Singapore
Pte Ltd. 2022
M. H. Bruun et al. (eds.), *The Palgrave Handbook of the Anthropology of Technology*, https://doi.org/10.1007/978-981-16-7084-8_37

The word *faena* literally means work, or task to be done. In Primero de Junio, when talking about a *faena*, people are referring to an obligatory collective work session dealing with a common part of the neighbourhood. In autonomously built urban settlements in Peru, such as Primero de Junio, *faenas* are crucial events, through which the neighbourhood is constructed, both in material terms—neighbours physically engage in transforming the landscape around them—and in organisational and political terms. What is assembled and maintained in the *faena* is not just material infrastructure but also social and moral connection: a membership (of rights and responsibilities) to the local neighbourhood community.

Human use of, and engagement with, water has always been, and will continue to be, intrinsically linked with infrastructures and technologies of many kinds. Soon after an anthropologist directs attention to water in social and cultural settings, technologies such as wells, buckets, valves, and measuring devices, or infrastructures including canals, pipes, and dams, whirl into view and unavoidably become a part of the scene of study, or maybe even a part of the object of ethnographic attention. While it is true that studies of water bring with them technologies and infrastructure—because it takes technologies and infrastructures to control flows and make use of water—the reverse is also the case: water in itself can be seen as a social infrastructure or technology, since it channels and shapes social practices and relations. Water, in a sense, distributes particular forms of social organisation, labour, politics, and technological efforts, thus arranging and structuring activities around it.

The distribution, management, and use of different kinds of water bodies and flows afford particular and varying forms of sociality. It matters whether human life unfolds around a lake, a river, a stream, or a coast, in an arid region or in an environment in which precipitation and water abound. For this reason, anthropological studies of water have, in recent years, increasingly attended to the materiality and properties of water in different ecological, political, and geographical contexts (Strang 2016; Ballestero 2019b). A premise of this chapter is that water and society play mutually active roles in shaping each other (K. Hastrup 2013) and that this shaping happens through and with infrastructures and technologies. Human-water relations intrinsically take place in a human-technology-infrastructure-water nexus. How these relations are conceptualised, what is brought to the fore and what is placed as ground, depends on the particular empirical context being studied, as well as the analytical choices made by the anthropologist. Water does things (or waters do things): to the world, to sociality, to anthropology, and vice versa. This chapter presents anthropological insights on water, water technologies, and infrastructures, and it shows how water, as much as it shapes social, economic, and political life, also has the capacity to infrastructure anthropological theory and engagement.

Water is good to think with, metaphorically and materially (Chen et al. 2013). As it flows, freezes, or evaporates, it challenges binaries and boundaries like nature-culture and material-abstract (Ballestero 2019b). In the following, I describe and discuss multiple ways in which water has *infrastructured* anthropological scholarship over time. As convincingly stated by Stefan Helmreich (2011), based on his research on and with marine biologists: 'seawater has operated as a "theory machine" for generating insights about human cultural organization' (Helmreich 2011, p. 132). Although particular properties can of course be ascribed to oceans and seawater, I suggest that we stretch the claim to water in general: water operates as a theory machine in anthropology, and can, therefore, conceptually be seen as a technology in and of itself. The point here is that an anthropological theory of water can never be universal and general. Rather, through empirical and ethnographic studies of different and manifold water-human-technology configurations, different theories about human life with water emerge. What anthropology brings to the study of waterworlds, I suggest, are rich and nuanced analyses of the complexity and multiplicity of specific relations and lifeworlds, based on empirical research. The anthropology of water shows that water is never only one. Rather, the ways water and social life constitute each other are specific and dependent on context: the particular flows and volumes of water, the livelihoods that depend upon these flows, and the technologies and infrastructures at hand. Whether in the form of rivers (Rademacher 2011; Barnes 2014), oceans (Helmreich 2011), dams and canals (Stensrud 2016; Carse 2014), aquifers, wells (Vium 2016), lakes (Orlove 2002; Zee 2017), sea ice (K. Hastrup 2013), tsunamis (F. Hastrup 2011)—to list a representative range—anthropological studies of waterworlds are characterised by bringing to the fore material and technological practices, as well as political and infrastructural arrangements.

'Water' is thus a common denominator for many different material embodiments of particular substances—or beings—and chemical compositions, flows, water bodies, currents, and so on (Ballestero 2019b). The role that technologies and infrastructures play in shaping and giving direction to these many substances is crucial and never neutral. Technology and infrastructure offer themselves as sites where practices, values, conflicts, and interests are played out, and hence serve as entry-points to the exploration of human-water relations. Especially in times of abundant talk about 'the global water crisis', general and in the singular, anthropology points out how water, global, and crisis always unfold and take place in particular, distinct, relational, situated configurations and contexts (Paerregaard and Andersen 2019). Crucial questions follow from this: how to approach, analyse, and understand water-human relations in a tension between water as a global concern—that is, as generalisable, as equally necessary for all human and other life on earth—and at the same time as particular, as constituent of social and material worlds that are diverse? What methodological and analytical tools are available for anthropologists to deal with this tension? How do technologies and infrastructures help us pay attention to both particulars and generals? And what ontological, political, and ethical implications follow from the analyses made in this tension?

The chapter deals with these questions and is organised around the ways that properties of different water flows and socialities demand different kinds of anthropological attention (methods and theories), and how they, in turn, have infrastructured anthropological engagement and theory. First, I begin with a literature review that highlights key works in anthropological studies of water, infrastructures, and technologies. Second, we return to the Quilca-Chili river basin in Southern Peru, to follow water and technologies around in the urban watershed. Third, the case is discussed in relation to analytical challenges related to anthropological studies of water technologies: how to scale perspectives and how to make analytics travel from one context to another. Technologies and infrastructures as material (and more-than-material) practices play a central role as ethnographic fixing points.

Currents in the Anthropology of Water and Technology

Roughly put, anthropology of water can be divided into two types: studies in which water appears as part of the context, as a backdrop, or as part of the scene in which something else is being studied; and studies in which water is part of the empirical and analytical object of study—studies in which water and water technologies play a central role in shaping social relations and life, or in which the object being studied is the relationship between water and humans or society, including technologies and infrastructure. Of the first kind are studies of coastal communities living from fishing or navigation. In Malinowski's *Argonauts of the Western Pacific* (1922) the focus of the study is the Kula trading system among communities in the Trobriand Archipelago. Descriptions of canoes, their meaning and function, and how they are built and sailed contribute to the ethnography as a kind of contextual information, or background. Readers may extract that the maritime and island environment in which this life unfolds is crucial in shaping the technological and cultural practices that make the society of Trobrianders function. To Malinowski, the canoes were approached as 'items of material culture … made for a certain use, and with a definite purpose; it is a means to an end, and we, who study native life, must not reverse this relation, and make a fetish of the object itself' (Malinowski 1922, p. 105). In Malinowski's work, the ocean, as well as the technologies used to navigate it, is approached as material culture, and naturalised (even romanticised) as a part of the anthropological account. The canoe, its construction and use, its relation to the water, and its central importance in travel, fishing, and in magic, taboos, customs, and myths are richly and carefully described. Technologies and water, and their properties in terms of shaping social relations, were not of interest for Malinowski. Rather, through these careful descriptions, Malinowski sought to show how culture and the many artefacts and skills served to satisfy the needs of the Trobrianders.

Malinowski was not the first or the only anthropologist to engage with island communities and seafaring. Indeed, an extensive body of historical and contemporary anthropological literature describes seas and coastal communities, figuring technologies, and especially connections—more or less centrally as objects of empirical and analytical concern (Aswani 2020). Networks for trading and exchange (Ammarell 1999) or indigenous navigational knowledge (Genz 2011), which are the centre of attention of many studies, can in their own way be considered infrastructures and technologies, since they enabled the mobilisation of humans, as well as the anthropological theories coming out of their study. Much theorising of human-maritime interaction has thus resulted from anthropological engagement in Oceania and island communities world-wide, where oceans connect humans more than they separate them. Pauwelussen and Verschoor (2017), in a study of coral and human ontological multiplicities in Indonesia, take the land-sea distinction to the extreme, by introducing 'amphibiousness' as a concept that dissolves humans and corals in Bajau Indonesia as terrestrial and marine beings respectively, and rather describes both as moving and living between such states (pp. 295–296).

With amphibiousness, we are moving into the domain of the second kind of studies—those that centre water-technology relations empirically and analytically. During recent decades, anthropologists have increasingly turned their eyes and efforts towards 'waterworlds' in different contexts (Rasmussen and Orlove 2015). Waterworlds as a concept was coined by Kirsten Hastrup (2009) as the conceptual framing of a collaborative research project studying responses to water-related disasters in different locations, all impacted by climatic changes prompted by the melting of ice, sea-level rise, or the drying of lands accelerating desertification in Sahel and elsewhere (K. Hastrup 2009). As a concept, waterworlds enables the exploration of 'social worlds configured by water in one form or another' (Hastrup and Hastrup 2016, p. 1). The concept was further elaborated by Orlove and Caton (2010) as 'the totality of connections that water may have in a given society' (p. 403). The latter propose to study water as a 'total social fact', since it connects different domains of life and is 'integral, even essential, to many if not most domains or institutions of society' (Orlove and Caton 2010, p. 402). Although the focus in the work of these scholars is not infrastructures and technologies as such, approaching water as a *connector* ascribes infrastructural qualities to water in relation to social life.

The centring of water and technologies in social and anthropological scholarship has not happened outside of historical as well as theoretical contingencies. Human-water relations were central in the shaping of early anthropological theory. Irrigation systems played a central role in the development of diffusionist theories arguing that cultural and societal change was caused by the geographical spread of technologies. Invention and innovation were hence understood to take place in civilisational centres, and from there spread—through cultural contact and the adoption and adaptation of technologies—to more peripheral culture areas (see Harris 1968). Diffusionist theories affected not only how we (scholars and broader publics) understand water but also how we understand technology and infrastructure as central drivers for societal development and 'modernity'.

Adaptation is still on the research agenda within anthropology of water, yet in a different context. Global warming and the increase and intensification of climate-related disasters have been shown to have severe implications for the availability, management, and use of fresh water and have caused a heightened awareness in populations, in public debates, and in scholarship of the importance not only of water but of the wellbeing of environments and ecosystems, and of the tremendous consequences of their potential collapse. Floods, storms, sea-level rise, hurricanes, heat waves, droughts, and desertification all increase the pressure on water systems worldwide. Population growth and the intensification of agriculture, industry, and trade add to the list of phenomena that challenge the availability of fresh water and healthy ecosystems. Infrastructural and technological solutions are increasingly questioned as sole ideal responses to these challenges; modernity is no longer given as the obvious pathway to development, and thus also offers itself as object for critical inquiry. These occurrences have resulted in a growing body of anthropological scholarship attending to climate change through the socio-natural dynamics related to changing hydrological phenomena, such as monsoons (Bhat 2019), floods (Whatmore 2013; Jensen and Morita 2019), droughts (Zee 2017; Vium 2016), and anthropogenic impacts on different water bodies and ecologies (Whitington 2016; Vaughn 2017).

Theoretical currents within anthropology and the social and human sciences more broadly can be seen as responses to changing historical and global conditions. Scholarship, both within and beyond anthropology, has contributed to and enabled the material properties and qualities of water, infrastructure, and technologies to figure more prominently and as primary focus in inquiries and analyses in a range of fields: new materialism (e.g. Bennett 2010) and a turn to materiality more broadly (Harvey et al. 2013); an ontological turn (Henare et al. 2006) or opening (de la Cadena 2014); object-oriented ontology (Morton 2011); a turn to performativity (Abram and Lien 2011) and to multispecies relations (Tsing 2015); and, directly related to water, the coining of 'blue humanities' (Alaimo 2019). Common for these currents is a decentring of the human in the making of social worlds, that is, an emphasis on more-than-human agents and agencies in the making of sociality and environments. In contrast to the accounts of diffusionists and functionalists, these approaches do not naturalise and neutralise water, technology, and infrastructure, but rather place these as central in the analysis, as co-constituents of social worlds.

Water Infrastructuring Politics: Power, Governance, Control

Historian Karl August Wittfogel was among the first to connect water and infrastructure with power and forms of governance. In his influential work *Oriental Despotism: A Comparative Study of Total Power* (1957) he argued that despotic regimes and centralised state formations emerge and gain legitimacy through the building and management of large irrigation infrastructures (Wittfogel 1957; see also Strang 2016). Although many scholars have since discarded Wittfogel's theory for being deterministic and false, it has 'haunted' political and cultural analyses of water relations as a strong reference since its first publication (Ley and Krause 2019). Wittfogel's approach was Marxist, and the 'hydraulic empires' he compared were India and China (Wittfogel 1957). Studies that connect water, infrastructure, and power are still prevalent but the theoretical and empirical emphasis has shifted significantly from Wittfogel's universalistic and totalising claims towards the situated, partial, multiple, and open-ended qualities of the ways in which water, infrastructure, power, and society are constitutive of each other.

The book *Cultivating the Nile: The Everyday Politics of Water in Egypt* (2014) by Jessica Barnes is a good example. While also linking irrigation technologies and power, the focus is on how politics and power are made through the contingent practices of farmers, bureaucrats, politicians, and consultants. Irrigation water and power are both produced through networks of daily practices of irrigation, administration, and expert discussions; non-human actors, such as irrigation pumps, pipes, training manuals, regulatory frameworks, and policy documents, actively mediate the production and negotiation of water rights (Barnes 2014). In Barnes' analysis water availability and distribution do not determine politics and forms of governance; they rather mediate (or infrastructure) political relations and practices; water as a natural resource is not a given but is continuously produced as such. Barnes highlights the transformative capacities of water, and that its 'fluidity affects the forms of governance that evolve around it' (Barnes 2014, p. 35).

Nikhil Anand (2011, 2017) also studies how different 'technopolitical forms' take shape around water supply, yet in a different context: the urban water supply system in Mumbai, India. Anand highlights infrastructures as 'political structures and cultural forms' (Anand 2017, p. 14). This means that infrastructure and technologies do not only function to distribute water. Rather, by bringing together legislation, politicians, plumbing, pipes, and pumps they become productive of 'hydraulic citizenship': 'a form of belonging to the city enabled by social and material claims made to the city's water infrastructure' (Anand 2011, p. 545). In postcolonial Mumbai, social and physical differences and inequalities are thus produced and reproduced by connects and disconnects created by infrastructure as technopolitical forms.

The regulatory and bureaucratic forms that take shape around water flows, their infrastructures, and how their management and control lead to concentration of power are recurrent themes in the anthropology of water (Rademacher 2011; Rasmussen 2015). Legislative and institutional frameworks emerge around the management of water (Paerregaard et al. 2016; Andersen 2019). Veronica Strang has written extensively on different notions of ownership connected to water (Strang 2011) and the trend towards privatising and commercialising water services in different parts of the world (see also Hoag 2019). Strang has added a contemporary twist to Wittfogel's concept of 'despotic regimes', bending the concept to describe how transnational and privatised regimes of water governance and management increasingly promote water as a commodity (Strang 2016, p. 295).

Emerging markets for water services and public-private partnerships for the construction of large-scale water infrastructures, and the new roles that states take in such endeavours, can be seen as organisational infrastructures through which water relations are produced (Ullberg 2019). How large-scale water infrastructures impact ecosystems and local socio-cultural worlds (Carse 2014) and, in turn, how the socio-cultural (organisational) infrastructures channel access to water, or the lack of it (Andersen 2016), are phenomena that continuously need anthropological attention.

Water Infrastructuring Worlds: Meaning, Knowledge, and Beyond the Material

Whereas material practices, infrastructures, and technologies are visible, and thus offer themselves, concretely, for observation and explication through verbal communication and material manifestations, much of the knowledge and meaning that go into the distribution, management, and use of water and resource systems are invisible, tacit, and thus demand other sensitivities from anthropological researchers. Not only politics and power are shaped by different water flows; water flows through and shapes very different lifeworlds in which water exists (ontologically) as different beings.

Lansing's *Priests and Programmers: Technologies of Power in the Engineered Landscape of Bali* (2007 [1991]), as the title indicates, could well be placed in the above section. The study describes the many kinds of expertise that go into managing and governing water resources in Bali. Water temples, shrines, and ritual technologies are as crucial as the skills of engineers when it comes to exercising control over irrigation (Lansing 2007 [1991], p. 5). Lansing shows that too fixed a focus on material practices and technologies risks producing 'blindness' to crucial dimensions related to control and use of water in a given context.

Veronica Strang also stresses the invisible dimensions of watery relations in human societies. In *The Meaning of Water* (Strang 2004), her monograph about the River Stour in Dorset, England, she emphasises that 'water is experienced and embodied both physically and culturally' (Strang 2004, p. 4). Strang explores the sensory experiences of water interactions with the human body, the direct interactions of people with water as a material artefact, and how this interaction, the ever transformative quality of water, has generated metaphors and meanings that transcend the individual person (Strang 2004, p. 49). Strang addresses how these dimensions of water are both universal, in that humans in all parts of the world engage directly and bodily with water, and particular: sensory experiences are shaped in engagement with particular socio-cultural and physical contexts (Strang 2004, p. 50). Understanding the spiritual and non-material dimensions of water is as important as engineering expertise, especially when it comes to understanding the diverging ways in which water is valued, and the many conflicts that exist worldwide related to water.

Similar themes are elaborated by Stensrud (2016) as she explores how the tension between water as one and multiple unfolds in the Andean highlands of Southern Peru. Although encouraging an ethnographic attention to material practices in order to understand how water is used and managed in relational webs, she suggests that knowledge practices should be included in ethnographic studies of waterworlds to cast light on the multiple worlds and realities that emerge through the use and management of water. The kind of water that Stensrud examines originates in precipitation and glaciers that are increasingly melting due to climate change. The peasant communities in which she works engage with water and the environment through relations of reciprocity, affect, and materiality in the shape of ritual offerings. Mountain protectors (*Apus*) are attended to as authorities that provide water, as are state water authorities: 'Water can be both countable units of litres per second and a living substance offered by a mountain being. Moreover, different practices—including knowledge practices and material practices—give rise to diverse and entangled worlds' (Stensrud 2016, p. 78). Other-than-human beings, such as water and *apus*, are part of the relational webs of infrastructures and authorities that actively contribute to the flows of water. Ontological differences between 'modern water' (Linton 2010) and 'relational water' should be taken into account when seeking to understand how climate change challenges water availability and supply in different contexts.

I end this outline of literature on water-human-infrastructure relations with a view to the future and how future waterworlds come into being. *A Future History of Water* (Ballestero 2019a) traces how water access becomes a human right through continuous, mundane practices and technologies. These, in turn, enable the making of present and future realities. Ballestero's ethnography unfolds across Costa Rica and Brazil, among state officials, NGOs, politicians, and activists, following what she calls four 'technolegal devices' or technologies used in the mundane management of water for human consumption: formula (the economic regulators used to calculate the price of water), indices (consumption patterns statistics), lists (legal definitions of water), and pacts (political agreements). The otherwise invisible water relations that come into view in this ethnography are the different and changing ideologies of value upon which the tension between water as human right and water as an element that has a price (yet is not a commodity) rests. These technolegal devices are productive of 'technolegal metaphysics' through which water is performed and distributed (Ballestero 2019a, pp. 48–52).

Time and temporalities abound as analytical themes in anthropology of water and the technologies tied to it. Water flows are in themselves inherently temporal and no less significant are the temporal regimes imposed upon different waterworlds by the technologies used to control and distribute water in different contexts. These, but also the very geologies that shape water bodies and flows, push anthropologists to attend to time and temporality in new ways, not only as future but also as fenland deep time (Irvine 2020) or rivers as time events (Khan 2019).

This review section has shown that water-technology/infrastructure-society are entangled in myriad ways. They are, however, also entangled conceptually and theoretically within the histories and structures of anthropological analysis. This entanglement has effects not only in terms of how we as scholars understand water but also in terms of how we understand technology, infrastructure, and the distinction between the two.

MAKING WATER FLOW IN AN URBAN WATERSCAPE

In Primero de Junio, on the outskirts of Arequipa, neighbours—mainly women—gather every morning to fetch water from *piletas*, public taps. Eight buckets per household, the agreed-upon daily ration, are collected during the early hours. The *pileta* is a lively place: people chat, joke, or comment on current events; news of common interest is announced here, such as new connections or an upcoming *faena*. When the *pileta* runs dry, the space around it empties; some buckets may be left standing there, waiting to be picked up. It is always uncertain, however, how long water will flow, and with what pressure. On days with low pressure in the system, filling each bucket takes longer, the crowd waiting around the *pileta* gets bigger, and the mood becomes tense.

The *pileta* and its water are a focal point in the neighbourhood landscape, structuring everyday practices and rhythms and assembling social and material dynamics related to water as one.

When water pressure is low, pipes leak, or *piletas* break and no water is available, social dynamics change. When water is absent, the planned doings of the day have to be re-thought; basic problems and small conflicts arise, both needing solutions. Breakdowns in the system produce scarcity of water, or water flowing in the wrong direction, and demand that *vecinos* gather and take action. By ethnographically examining the dynamics of water scarcity and community responses to it we can gain insight into how water and the technologies that make it flow are constitutive of social and political life.

Arequipa, with one-million inhabitants, sits between the Pacific coast and the Andean highlands. Whereas the city centre is located at an altitude of 2400 metres above sea level (m.a.s.l.), Primero de Junio sits on the slopes of the volcano Chachani, at 2700 m.a.s.l. Arequipa's topography is marked by verticality; three volcanoes embrace the city, pointing towards the high Andean ridge. These geological and topographical conditions collaborate with climate and ecology to generate a particular hydrology for life in Arequipa, without which the area would be a desert, like its surroundings.

The water is said to be born (*nacer*) in the upper parts of the basin, which is where most precipitation occurs. Water reaches Arequipa via the Chili River, which belongs to the Quilca-Chili river basin. This basin extends over 13,817 km^2, from the Andean ridge, with altitudes up to 6288 m.a.s.l., to the coastal plains, where the waters gathered within the basin flow into the Pacific Ocean. This highly unequal (temporal and spatial) distribution of rainfall and surface water means that infrastructure and technologies for monitoring and management are pivotal to securing supply for all parts and activities in the river basin. Besides rainfall, water exists in the forms of atmospheric humidity, snow and ice stored in glaciers, and as surface runoff (TYPSA-TECNOMA-ENGECORPS 2013). Precipitation is captured in glaciers and *bofedales* (high-altitude peat bog wetland acting like giant natural sponges) in the highlands. Networks of soil, grass, Andean camelids, and other entities such as lakes, glaciers, and the verticality of mountains do the infrastructural work of storing water in rich black soils, which slowly filter and appear in springs downstream. Together, these make nature act as infrastructure (Carse 2012). The water that reaches the city, however, is stored in a human-controlled grand hydraulic system: seven dams, rivers, and canal connections in the highlands, from where water is regulated and released to reach its functional destinations in the city. This technological infrastructure makes the Quilca-Chili watershed one of Peru's most 'intervened-in'; without the dams, there would not be enough water to feed current and growing levels of human activities in Arequipa. Agriculture, industry, generation of hydropower, tourism, mining, and a growing urban population draw upon the same sources of water. These uses alter the quality and characteristics of water in a variety of ways before returning it to the river, and not all wastewaters are treated first. Farmers cultivating further downstream, who irrigate with water from the river, complain that their crops do not qualify for export due to high levels of contamination. Finally, water flows into the Pacific Ocean.

Like the people from Arequipa, two-thirds of Peru's population of 32.5 million live on the arid Pacific slope of the Andean ridge, which traditionally depended on runoff from Andean glaciers for water supply. During recent decades, Andean glaciers have melted rapidly, generating concern about future water availability (Oré et al. 2009; Mark et al. 2010). The rainy season, which is becoming more unstable, spans December to March. The rest of the year is sunny, warm, and dry. Water scarcity is always a potential peril in this landscape and must be counteracted by careful management. Canals are as common as roads, reservoirs and ponds frequently meet the eye, and mobile water tanks circulate constantly to provide the neighbourhoods not connected to the potable water system with water. All these features provide material evidence of the labour, resources, technology, and infrastructure required to distribute water.

To reach Primero de Junio, water is pumped uphill, defying gravity, from a treatment plant, via canals, reservoirs, control systems, and pipes before finally reaching public taps and faucets. On its way uphill the water is distributed to several urban neighbourhoods. Some receive it 24 hours a day, with direct household access, but further uphill, in neighbourhoods of more recent establishment, water pressure diminishes, and the water flow ends at public water taps.

Presión/*Pressure*

Among engineers in Arequipa *presión del agua* (water pressure) refers to the amount of physical force that is put on water to make it flow through a given infrastructure, or to the amount of force the water exerts when coming out of the pipe. Engineers also use the term to name the social tension that arises when a resource becomes scarce in relation to demand for it. Among residents in peripheral urban areas, such as Primero de Junio, *presión* qualifies and quantifies the volume of water that comes out of taps every morning, and it is decisive in terms of daily practices and wellbeing. The lower the pressure, the longer each bucket takes to fill, and the longer the wait at the *pileta*. *Presión* also describes the action and intentionality of mobilising and protesting—making their demands and claims heard and responded to—by political authorities. Pressure is thus an emic term used by engineers and residents to qualify and evaluate different kinds of bio-physical, technological, and socio-political forces. Such a term, empirically derived from the bio-physical qualities of water, can be used as an entry point for ethnographic examination of what water is for dwellers on the outskirts of the city and to analyse how physical processes are linked to social life and political intentionalities and practices.

Nikhil Anand (2011) has developed a concept of 'pressure' along similar lines in his studies of municipal water supply systems and the infrastructures of citizenship in Mumbai. Anand uses 'pressure' to unfold and analyse how political and technological processes are entangled in Mumbai. In order to make water flow to marginal parts of the city, settlers claim water by engaging what he calls 'varying repertoires of pressure' (Anand 2011, pp. 543–544). Anand's use of 'pressure' as an analytic resonates with the emic term '*presión*' used by people in Arequipa to refer to the physical property of water flow and the situational mobilisations and protests exercised to make claims on water. As in Mumbai, *vecinos* in Primero de Junio engage complex infrastructural articulations between technologies of politics and politics of technologies, to make claims and perform 'hydraulic citizenship' (Anand 2011). The two similar concepts, generated in different urban water contexts, make a case in point that facilitates discussion of the productive tension between the universal and the singular, and how well concepts travel. *Presión*, I suggest, is similar and comparable to Anand's *pressure*, but they are not the same concept. Both analytics describe and qualify how settlers access water in and from a marginal position in the city they inhabit. In at least two ways, however, *presión* in Arequipa is different from *pressure* in Mumbai. The first is the vertical topography of Arequipa, and the gravity pulling water downhill. This condition makes particular material arrangements necessary in order to generate the desired water pressure for the people around the *pileta*. Mumbai, in contrast, is rather flat. The second difference is the ways in which distinctly 'Peruvian' or 'Latin American' (as opposed to 'Indian' or 'South Asian') histories and contingencies shape the ways in which *presión* emerges and is experienced as an empirical fact, including the particular ways in which collectives mobilise to obtain essential services.

Primero de Junio was founded as a housing association in 1997 by a group of migrants from rural parts of the neighbouring highland departments seeking a better life in the city. Most of the work of obtaining and constructing basic services, such as digging ditches for pipes and placing them, has been carried out by the neighbours themselves, in *faenas*: collective work sessions similar to the one described in the opening of this chapter. For people on the margins of the city, urban life means the hard work of converting the dry mountain slope into liveable space, a process of accommodation that requires material reordering as well as engagement in neighbourhood organisations. Making water flow to a marginal settlement—including the physical work of maintenance and pipe-fitting—takes organisation. Neighbours and neighbourhoods form as collectives around lacking water services:

> [W]ater is essential for all, and to obtain our water we created a front with the neighbourhoods around us to apply jointly for service projects. When there is a massive claim, the authorities have to listen to it, because these people are really in need. We have obtained things through the state; but we have to keep the pressure constant to get what we ask for. Along the way we've had to organise many protests. (Interview, president of development front of Primero de Junio)

During fieldwork, I would often bump into the kind of protests mentioned by the president: a dense group of people marching through the city centre of Arequipa, making demands to the provincial, regional, and central state authorities, or protesting about a rise in tariffs. Such protests mostly took shape as peaceful marches through the streets, with banners, whistles, and shouted statements about a united people, dissatisfaction with the political authorities, and claims for basic services like water, sewers, or electricity for their neighbourhood. Although marginal urban settlers and their leaders are not included in the formal organs of water governance, this population—through its capacity to exercise socio-political pressure—does obtain influence in decisions made regarding water flows and planning of new infrastructure in the city. It takes physical pressure for the water to flow uphill, and it takes socio-political pressure on the political infrastructure to achieve basic services. As the leader of *Asociación de Urbanizaciones Populares de Arequipa* (AUPA), one of the largest organisations of urban dwellers in Arequipa, explained:

> We organise people of the marginal neighbourhoods, and coordinate protests to make claims to the authorities, and make them finance water and sewerage projects. There is a lot of internal fighting, but we have one common objective: to develop our neighbourhoods. If we don't push, it won't come out.

The physical pressure of the flow of water coming out of the tap every morning is a material manifestation of the social and political conditions of the people in

Primero de Junio. 'Pressure' as an analytic qualifies the way people insist on making themselves a space in which to exert influence over their own lives in the city. Water abundance and scarcity are not produced solely by infrastructure and technologies, but also by sociotechnical processes. In Primero de Junio, the *pileta*, the *faena*, and *pressure* are a part of the infrastructure—physical and material—with which people engage in order to make water flow their way. In Anand's words, these are 'repertoires of socio-technical pressure'. The specific forms that the Arequipan repertoire takes, the specific practices and forces at play, however, are different to those employed by settlers in Mumbai. *Presión* and *pressure* are concepts that enable us to compare Arequipa and Mumbai, but they are not the same.

Water Technologies as Material (and Beyond Material) Practices

In the above, I have attended to material practices around water technologies and infrastructure in the urban waterscape of Arequipa, and shown how the flow of, and access to, water is constitutive of social and political relations, as well as technological and infrastructural ones. Several ethnographic potentialities and challenges emerge from tightly connecting social, technical, biophysical, and political aspects in anthropological studies of waterworlds.

When placing water at the centre of an anthropological analysis, what seems at first to be moving or flowing is water. By following water, the analytical perspective can swiftly shift from particular technological devices, such as the faucet, buckets, and meters, to pipes and infrastructural systems, watersheds, and international management regimes. Once the analysis unfolds, it is clear that neither humans nor technologies are stable. The task of the ethnographer is to find entry-points: where to start the research; singling out something to look at, fixing it for a while, before letting it go; scaling; and zooming. What will be the figure and what will be ground in a given study? Water, technology, infrastructure? Where do connections and relations start and end? The materiality of water technologies and infrastructures, and the properties of different water flows and bodies offer a multiplicity of entry-points to the study of waterworlds. Yet the methodological and analytical challenges of delimitation are similar to those of other fields.

Concepts emerge from empirical encounters with social worlds; concept-phenomena that are descriptive of bio-physical functions, forces and practices of water, geology, and people. Using such concepts in a generative way, moving to an analytic exploration, emphasising that relations, processes, and practices are simultaneously material, discursive, and organisational can be one way of scaling the perspective. '*Presión*' is one such analytic, which in the case above serves to move the ethnography from an emic and bio-physical domain, through description, to an analytical domain, in which the concept is used to qualify sociotechnical relations connected to water supply in Arequipa. *Presión* resonates with *pressure*, proposed by Anand (2011) to describe technopolitics of water supply in Mumbai. A focus on waterworlds and their material practices enables an anthropology that is situated through its sensitivity to the particular yet comparative across different regions and contexts.

In the chapter I have outlined central themes relevant to the study of water. Water-society relations are always more than human and always imply the making, management, and distribution of technological and infrastructural practices. What anthropology brings to the understanding of waterworlds is its holistic and integral approach, which—specific for each context—enables more than technical understandings of how hydrological systems work and how these shape sociality.

Although there are aspects of infrastructures and technologies that make them appear functional, universal, and independent of social and cultural relations, neither technologies nor infrastructures exist or function outside of societies and social relations. One crucial role of anthropology in the study of water infrastructures and technologies is to show how particular technological constellations shape social relations in specific ways, never neutral, but connected with existing inequalities and power structures.

It is important to keep in mind that water flows through more than secular ecologies.

Materiality is often tied to more-than-material qualities of different kinds: religious practices, temples, ideologies, and more. Attending to materiality and delimiting it as such is premised on a binary between the material and the non-material, the physical and the meta-physical (religious, spiritual, intangible). Beyond-material forms are always present and active in the shaping of waterworlds, and deserve ethnographic attention.

Digital data and smart water technologies are new, seemingly immaterial forms influencing water supply systems in different parts of the world. New questions, challenges, and ethnographic fields demanding detailed inquiry emerge as water supply systems become inhabited by smart metres and as big data, algorithms, and artificial intelligence are increasingly envisioned and employed to control and optimise water flows. What happens when data infrastructures and water infrastructures entangle? What forms will water relations take when water infrastructures are datafied? So far, few anthropologists have started to look into such questions (see Hogan 2015).

Water breaks boundaries and rearranges empirical and analytical binaries: nature-culture and urban-rural are two of the dichotomies that are broken down when water is at the centre of anthropological analysis; such studies emphasise how environments and societies mutually shape each other. Future waterworlds with new assemblages of technologies and infrastructures will keep producing binaries and taken-for-granted categories. Anthropology will not run out of tasks in the study of sociotechnical waterworlds.

Acknowledgements Research for this chapter was funded by the Independent Research Fund Denmark. I am grateful to Karsten Pærregaard and Astrid B. Stensrud who were guiding colleagues throughout the project 'From Ice to Stone: Water Scarcity, Climate Change, and Conflict Resolution in the Andes of Southern Peru'. I owe thanks to *vecinos* in Primero de Junio and to engineers and others in Arequipa who accepted my fieldwork presence with patience and generosity. I acknowledge the participation of the River Chili and other water bodies in shaping my research. Thanks to Handbook editors, reviewers, and colleagues at Aalborg University for productive feedback on chapter drafts.

References

Abram, S., & Lien, M. E. (2011). Performing Nature at World's Ends. *Ethnos, 76*(1), 3–18. https://doi.org/10.1080/00141844.2010.544855.

Alaimo, S. (2019). Introduction: Science Studies and the Blue Humanities. *Configurations, 27*(4), 429–432. https://doi.org/10.1353/con.2019.0028.

Ammarell, G. (1999). *Bugis Navigation*. New Haven, CT: Yale University Southeast Asia Studies.

Anand, N. (2011). PRESSURE: The PoliTechnics of Water supply in Mumbai. *Cultural Anthropology, 26*(4), 542–564. https://doi.org/10.1111/j.1548-1360.2011.01111.x.

Anand, N. (2017). *Hydraulic City. Water and the infrastructures of citizenship in Mumbai*. Durham: Duke University Press.

Andersen, A. O. (2016). Infrastructures of progress and dispossession: Collective responses to shrinking water access among farmers in Arequipa, Peru. *Focaal, 74*, 28–41. https://doi.org/10.3167/fcl.2016.740103.

Andersen, A. O. (2019). Assembling Commons and Commodities: The Peruvian Water Law between Ideology and Materialisation. *Water Alternatives, 12*(2), 470–487.

Aswani, S. (2020). New Directions in Maritime and Fisheries Anthropology. *American anthropologist, 122*(3), 473–486. https://doi.org/10.1111/aman.13380.

Ballestero, A. (2019a). *A Future History of Water*. Durham: Duke University Press.

Ballestero, A. (2019b). The Anthropology of Water. *Annual Review of Anthropology, 48*, 405–21. https://doi.org/10.1146/annurev-anthro-102218-011428.

Barnes, J. (2014). *Cultivating the Nile: The Everyday Politics of Water in Egypt*. Durham: Duke University Press.

Bennett, J. (2010). *Vibrant Matter, A Political Ecology of Things*. Durham & London: Duke University Press.

Bhat, H. (2019, June 27). 'Malhar'. Theorizing the Contemporary. *Fieldsights*. https://culanth.org/fieldsights/malhar. Accessed 8 July 2021.

Carse, A. (2012). Nature as infrastructure: Making and managing the Panama Canal watershed. *Social Studies of Science, 42*(4), 539–563. https://doi.org/10.1177/0306312712440166

Carse, A. (2014). *Beyond the Big Ditch: Politics, Ecology, and Infrastructure at the Panama Canal*. Cambridge, MA: The MIT Press.

Chen, C., MacLeod, J., & Neimanis, A. (2013). Introduction: Toward a Hydrological Turn? In C. Chen, J. MacLeod, & A. Neimanis (Eds.), *Thinking With Water* (pp. 3–22). Montreal, Queþbec: McGill-Queen's University Press.

de la Cadena, M. (2014, January 13). The politics of modern politics meets ethnographies of excess through ontological openings. Theorizing the Contemporary, *Fieldsights*. https://culanth.org/fieldsights/the-politics-of-modern-politics-meets-ethnographies-of-excess-through-ontological-openings. Accessed 8 July 2021.

Genz, J. (2011). Navigating the Revival of Voyaging in the Marshall Islands: Predicaments of Preservation and Possibilities of Collaboration. *Contemporary Pacific, 23*(1), 1–34.

Harris, M. (1968). *The Rise of Anthropological Theory*. New York: Thomas Y. Crowell Company.

Harvey, P., Casella, E., Evans, G., Knox, H., Mclean, C., Silva, E., Thoburn, N., & Woodward, K. (2013). *Objects and Materials: A Routledge Companion*. London: Routledge.

Hastrup, F. (2011). *Weathering the World: Recovery in the Wake of the Tsunami in a Tamil Fishing Village*. New York: Berghahn Books.

Hastrup, K. (2009). Waterworlds: Framing the Question of Social Resilience. In K. Hastrup (Ed.), *The Question of Resilience. Social Responses to Climate Change* (pp. 11–30). Copenhagen: The Royal Danish Academy of Sciences and Letters.

Hastrup, K. (2013). Water and the Configuration of Social Worlds: An Anthropological Perspective. *Journal of Water Resource and Protection, 5*, 59–66. https://doi.org/10.4236/jwarp.2013.54A009.

Hastrup, K., & Hastrup, F. (2016). Introduction. Waterworlds At Large. In K. Hastrup & F. Hastrup (Eds.), *Waterworlds. Anthropology in Fluid Environments* (pp. 1–22). New York and Oxford: Berghahn.

Helmreich, S. (2011). Nature / Culture / Seawater. *American Anthropologist, 113*(1), 132–144. https://doi.org/10.1111/j.1548-1433.2010.01311.x.

Henare, A. J. M., Holbraad, M., & Wastell, S. (2006). *Thinking through Things: Theorising Artefacts Ethnographically*. London: Routledge.

Hoag, C. (2019). 'Water is a gift that destroys': Making a national natural resource in Lesotho. *Economic Anthropology, Economic Anthropology, 6*(2), 183–194. https://doi.org/10.1002/sea2.12149.

Hogan, M. (2015). Data Flows and Water Woes: The Utah Data Centre. *Big Data & Society, 2*(2), 1–12. https://doi.org/10.1177/2053951715592429.

Irvine, R. D. G. (2020). *An Anthropology of Deep Time. Geological Temporalities and Social Life*. Cambridge: Cambridge University Press.

Jensen, C. B., & Morita, A. (2019). Deltas in Crisis: From Systems to Sophisticated Conjunctions. *Sustainability, 12*(4), 1322. https://doi.org/10.3390/su12041322.

Khan, N. (2019). At Play with the Giants: Between the Patchy Anthropocene and Romantic Geology. *Current Anthropology, 60*(S20), S333-S341. https://doi.org/10.1086/702756.

Lansing, J. S. (2007[1991]). *Priests and programmers, technologies of power in the engineered landscape of Bali*. Princeton, NJ: Princeton University Press.

Ley, L., & Krause, F. (2019). Ethnographic conversations with Wittfogel's ghost: An introduction. *EPC: Politics and Space, 37*(7), 1151–1160. https://doi.org/10.1177/2399654419873677.

Linton, J. (2010). *What is water? The history of a modern abstraction*. Vancouver: UBC Press.

Malinowski, B. (1922). *Argonauts of the Western Pacific: An Account of Native Enterprise and Adventure in the Archipelagoes of Melanesian New Guinea*. London: N.p.

Mark, B. G., Bury, J., McKenzie, J. M., French, A., & Baraer, M. (2010). Climate Change and Tropical Andean Glacier Recession: Evaluating Hydrologic Changes and Livelihood Vulnerability in the Cordillera Blanca, Peru. *Annals of the Association of American Geographers, 100*(4), 794–805. https://doi.org/10.1080/0004560 8.2010.497369.

Morton, T. (2011). Here Comes Everything: The Promise of Object-Oriented Ontology. *Qui Parle: Critical Humanities and Social Sciences, 19*(2), 163–190. https://www.muse.jhu.edu/article/431001.

Oré, M. T., del Castillo, L., van Orsel, S., & Vos, J. (2009). *El Agua, ante nuevos desafíos. Actores e iniciativas en Ecuador, Perú y Bolivia.* Lima: Instituto de Estudios Peruanos.

Orlove, B. (2002). *Lines in the Water: Nature and Culture at Lake Titicaca.* Berkeley: University of California Press.

Orlove, B., & Caton, S. C. (2010). Water Sustainability: Anthropological Approaches and Prospects. *Annual Review of Anthropology, 39*(1), 401–415. https://doi. org/10.1146/annurev.anthro.012809.105045.

Paerregaard, K., Stensrud, A. B., & Andersen, A. O. (2016). Water Citizenship. Negotiating Water Rights and Contesting Water Culture in the Peruvian Andes. *Latin American Research Review, 51*(1), 198–217. https://doi.org/10.1353/ lar.2016.0012.

Paerregaard, K., & Andersen, A. O. (2019). Moving beyond the commons/commodity dichotomy: The socio-political complexity of Peru's water crisis. *Water Alternatives, 12*(2), 459–469.

Pauwelussen, A., & Verschoor, G. M. (2017). Amphibious Encounters: Coral and People in Conservation Outreach in Indonesia. *Engaging Science, Technology, and Society, 3*, 292–314. https://doi.org/10.17351/ests2017.59.

Rademacher, A. (2011). *Reigning the River Urban Ecologies and Political Transformation in Kathmandu.* Durham: Duke University Press.

Rasmussen, M. B. (2015). *Andean Waterways: Resource Politics in Highland Peru.* Seattle: University of Washington Press.

Rasmussen, M. B., & Orlove, B. (2015). Anthropologists Exploring Water in Social and Cultural Life: Introduction. *American Anthropologists, 119*(4). Virtual Issue: https://anthrosource.onlinelibrary.wiley.com/hub/journal/15481433/exploring-water. Accessed 8 July 2021.

Stensrud, A. B. (2016). Climate Change, Water Practices and Relational Worlds in the Andes. *Ethnos: Journal of Anthropology, 81*(1), 75–98. https://doi.org/10.108 0/00141844.2014.929597.

Strang, V. (2004). *The meaning of water.* London: Bloomsbury

Strang, V. (2011). Fluid Forms. Owning Water in Australia. In V. Strang & M. Busse (Eds.), *Ownership and appropriation* (pp. 171–195). Oxford: Berg.

Strang, V. (2016). Infrastructural relations: Water, political power and the rise of a new 'despotic regime'. *Water Alternatives, 9*(2), 292–318.

Tsing, A. L. (2015). *The Mushroom at the End of the World: On the Possibility of Life in Capitalist Ruins.* Princeton: Princeton University Press.

TYPSA-TECNOMA-ENGECORPS. (2013). Diagnóstico participativo consolidado. Cuenca Chili tomo 1. Aspectos generales, marco normativo e institucional y descripción de la Cuenca.

Ullberg, S. B. (2019). Making the megaproject: Water infrastructure and hydrocracy at the public-private interface in Peru. *Water Alternatives, 12*(2), 503–520.

Vaughn, S. E. (2017). Disappearing Mangroves: The Epistemic Politics of Climate Adaptation in Guyana. *Cultural Anthropology, 32*, 242–268. https://doi.org/10.14506/ca32.2.07

Vium, C. (2016). Water and Its Absence in the Islamic Republic of Mauritania. *Anthropologica, 58*(2), 243–249. https://doi.org/10.3138/anth.582.R01.

Whatmore, S. J. (2013). Earthly powers and affective environments: an ontological politics of flood risk. *Theory, Culture and Society, 30*(7–8), 33–50.

Whitington, J. (2016). Modernist Infrastructure and the Vital Systems Security of Water: Singapore's Pluripotent Climate Futures. *Public Culture, 28*(2), 415–441. https://doi.org/10.1215/08992363-3427511.

Wittfogel, K.G. (1957). *Oriental despotism. A comparative study of total power.* London: Vintage.

Zee, J. C. (2017). Holding patterns: Sand and Political Time at China's Desert Shores. *Cultural Anthropology, 32*(2), 215–241. https://doi.org/10.14506/ca32.2.06.

CHAPTER 38

Electricity as a Field for Anthropological Theorising and Research

Electricity

Simone Abram

Electricity has a number of characteristics that make it difficult to handle. Like other physical forces (such as gravity), it is only perceptible to humans through secondary effects. Electricity is one feature of the electromagnetic fields that characterise the earth's physical form and is intrinsic to the living world. It is thus a category of effects that include the functioning of the nervous system of animals, forces that are produced actively by some creatures, such as electric eels, and natural phenomena that can kill those struck by lightning, for example. Only since the nineteenth century has electricity been domesticated to any significant extent, generated at will, and operated over cables and networks, yet for some time already it has dominated contemporary life in many parts of the world. Even where there is no grid, there are mobile phone chargers using electricity to change everyday life. Its infrastructures surround us, and while for many people electrical infrastructures remain in the background, for those in less-privileged situations they can be an ever-present irritant. This chapter asks how these effects categorised as electricity can be revealed from different perspectives. How can they be understood, what can anthropology specifically offer to help, and what can this tell us about anthropology?

Anthropologists have certainly been interested in electricity since its introduction as a technology, with electrical imagery and metaphors adopted enthusiastically by anthropologists from the early nineteenth century onwards. As

S. Abram (✉)
Durham University, Durham, UK
e-mail: simone.abram@durham.ac.uk

© The Author(s), under exclusive license to Springer Nature Singapore Pte Ltd. 2022
M. H. Bruun et al. (eds.), *The Palgrave Handbook of the Anthropology of Technology*, https://doi.org/10.1007/978-981-16-7084-8_38

Coleman outlines, 'scholars and spiritualists alike in the late nineteenth century made comparisons between divine powers or spiritual forces and electricity' (2019, p. 43). Electrical forces provided generative metaphors for ideas about social forces linking persons and things, and for other invisible forces such as the power of religious experience or the way that magic connected thought, intent, and effect. Electrical circuits provide a wealth of relational connections, including short circuits, capacities, and potentials, that take on metaphorical significance in everyday life. But it has also been clearly accepted among scholars and practitioners that electrical circuits are never purely material. The more 'alternative' approaches to electrical provision that grew in the 1970s (many inspired by Schumacher 1973) explicitly acknowledged the social context and relations inherent to infrastructure development. Indeed, the relationality of electricity and its associated infrastructures is widely acknowledged and closely examined in STS studies (see Silvast and Virtanen 2014).

Electromagnetic metaphors and models related to networks, systems, grids, fields, and currents still provide ripe discursive fruit for contemporary theorists, and a little reflection reveals how far these metaphors have soaked into the language. Anthropological fields themselves have re-engaged recently with the worlds of technology and science so that anthropology has returned to face its electrically inflected origins. Theorists have urged anthropologists to take the material and technical world seriously, rather than subsume it under the social (e.g. Latour 2002). This has been done to varying degrees in anthropologies of energy, but a particular focus on electricity has been relatively slow in emerging. It is interesting to note that significant work by pioneers such as Laura Nader were more focused on energy governance or examined specific technologies (such as nuclear reactors: Brooks 2012) or quality of life (e.g. Nader and Beckerman 1978; Nader 1981; Nader and Milleron 1979), reflecting a widespread preference across the discipline for studies related to resources or regimes, rather than the more elusive phenomenon of electricity itself and its infrastructures.

Most anthropological studies of electricity have looked at the more tangible services that electricity provides. Hence, Wilhite et al.'s paper on cross-cultural energy use behaviour (1996) looks at the cultural specificity of electric lighting and heating, yet the electrical infrastructure is securely backgrounded. On the other hand, work such as Jane Summerton's (2004) that directly questions the electron and what it means to people (including elements of magic) is firmly located in STS debates about the construction of 'users' and 'scripts' rather than anthropology. Electricity starts to come into focus in anthropology with the publication of Tanja Winther's seminal *Impacts of Electricity* in 2008, in which Winther focuses primarily on the developmental consequences of grid electrification in Zanzibar, noting how the meanings and significances of electricity slowly stabilised as new technologies started to settle in (cf. Ferguson 1999, cited in Winther 2008). Similarly, although Howe and Boyer's work on 'aeolian politics' (2015) seems more directly related to electricity, focusing as it does on wind-turbine generators, this too is oriented towards the politics of energy generation, land rights, and environmental rights rather than reflecting on electricity as a phenomenon. Perhaps this is for good reason. After all, when do anthropologists enquire about other physical phenomena such as gravity or magnetism?

A short special issue of *Cultural Anthropology* in 2015 on 'Anthropology Electric' under the editorship of Dominic Boyer, followed soon after by a Wenner-Gren-funded workshop in 2016 on 'electrifying anthropology' (led by Simone Abram and Brit Ross Winthereik) started to bring electricity into the limelight. Boyer sees electricity 'as' infrastructure and therefore as material politics and state power (2015), with electropolitics as the primary vector for analysis. Inspired by Mitchell's work on carbon democracy, Boyer suggests an equivalent 'electrical democracy', parallel to his Foucauldian approach to the politics powers of energy that he calls 'energopower' (2014). Where electricity itself intrudes is through the specific materialities of energy, its physics, and the technologies it enables. Özden-Schilling (2015) comes up against questions of supply and demand, seeing the parallel with economic theories, yet soon learns that electricity is not the kind of commodity more routinely traded and theorised. It is electricity's stubborn phenomenology that frustrates efforts to tame it by market mechanisms; the aim of an electricity grid is to maintain a reliable level of voltage while users 'draw' current from it. If the amount of current drawn off is not in balance with the amount being generated, the voltage will go either up or down, eventually causing the grid to fail. This can be framed in terms of balancing supply and demand, much as your body would rapidly fail if the supply and demand for oxygen were not in reasonable proportion. This is one reason that the financial aspects of electricity markets (which can be out of balance without immediate consequence) are at least one step removed from the actual deployment of electrical power. Terminologies such as 'supply and demand' have a quite different significance in relation to electricity than they do in relation to other commodities, making this an excellent place to introduce anthropological thinking and to deploy electrical ideas for anthropological theory.

So far, much of the thinking around electricity in anthropology has been about infrastructure and politics, but a focus on the electricity itself opens up a wealth of intellectual creativity, as I begin to outline below.

Speaking of Electricity

Electricity has become deeply embedded in the everyday life of much of the world's population in a short time and with it has followed a flowering of narratives and explanations of its workings. These diverge quite significantly from the scientific or engineering discourse. It may be a distraction to posit a dichotomy between science/technology and lay knowledge in the way that Lennon does for energy (2017), but the endurance of such dichotomies raises interesting questions. How is it that knowledge on electricity is withheld within the boundaries of a specialism? How has a profession ensured that so many people feel first fear rather than mastery in relation to electrical systems, to the extent that many people fear even to change a plug or rewire something as simple as a lamp? This process has yet to be documented, but the extreme gendering of electrical skill and knowledge[1] (Gooday 2004) is reflected in its vocabulary too. The invention of electricity as a scientific object entailed the invention of new vocabulary of measurement (watts, volts, amperes, etc.) that enshrined the masculinist hierarchies and scientist-personality cults of the period (see Bell et al. 2020).

What is interesting in the development of electrical systems is the mixing of technical and non-technical metaphors and images between the two domains, as formal and colloquial language seem to inform one another. For example, in the English language (although certainly in others as well), we may hear people talk about electrons flowing down a cable, yet the physics of electricity suggest that it is the rapid oscillation of electrons that creates a charge that can be observed using electrical meters. 'Flow', therefore, is metaphorical rather than descriptive. Nonetheless, a vocabulary of flows has become the common language of electricity, perhaps because of the enthusiasm with which scientists and engineers have tried to promote their inventions and discoveries by describing them using colloquial language. In doing so they generated a shared vocabulary that goes beyond the technical into realms of enchantment, spectacle, or awe, used about natural electrical phenomena as much as technological achievements (Nye 1990; Hughes 1983). This close relation of technical, symbolic, and social phenomena has followed electricity from its discovery and industrialisation, to create a coherent notion of electricity, to embed its functions into everyday life, and to promote it as a public good (Hughes 1983). Yet lightning and plug sockets are recognisably (ontologically) distinct, offering different kinds of relational potential, so how do we manage to describe them with the same language? Or rather, why do we have so much difficulty in describing them at all?

Gretchen Bakke has argued that one reason it is so difficult to explain electricity colloquially, in English at least, is because all our sentences involve nouns (Bakke 2019). In order to talk about things, we have to have things to talk about, but since electricity can only be understood through metaphor, that poses a problem. In physics, sometimes contradictory visual and linguistic metaphors are used as models to think about things that are not things, such as light, which can be imagined as waves or as packets of energy (photons), so that physicists have to think with two metaphors simultaneously. Electricity is similarly translated into metaphor so that we can grasp its features, yet it is easy to forget that these are, indeed, metaphors, and take them for things. Instead, the politics of things is more appropriately addressed through 'dingpolitik', where the things associated with putting electricity to use—the machines, cables, instruction manuals, and so forth—can be followed and analysed (Krauss 2010). But this move simply puts us back in our linguistic comfort zone and hardly brings us closer to the non-thingness of electricity itself. It is the kind of move that Stoller (1994) criticised in his work on the senses, where he argued that we cannot understand something like spirit possession merely by reading it as a text (i.e. as if it were a thing), when the affective and sensory and performative aspects of rituals are what give them historical depth, power, and meaning. This is not to equate electricity with spirit possession, but to show that a noun-bound language seems to leave us grasping for metaphors to describe intangible forces like electricity, fear, or magic.

Electricity relies on relations between different electromagnetic elements (magnets, the earth's magnetic fields, copper cables, etc.) that afford imaginative abstract thought around questions of scale, connectedness, and interdependence. These have long attracted expert knowledge, seized primarily by engineering and physics, leaving the social sciences and humanities to contemplate their socialisation and expression. Yet there is no prohibition on anthropologists gaining knowledge of physics and technology, just as there is no reason that technologists should not appreciate the socio-technicality of electricity as a phenomenon. Anthropologists proposing ethnographic research on electrical systems will need to think carefully about the degree of linguistic and technical knowledge they need to acquire in order to interpret appropriately what is said to them during fieldwork. This is, of course, a general problem for ethnographic research, wherein the position of the anthropologist is always one of partial knowledge and partial representation, but it is a particular problem in fields where anthropologists might fail to recognise the need to learn a specialist language, quite possibly because they fail to recognise that a distinct language exists. It is worth noting that in this language, electrical charge is not often referred to as voltage, but as *potential difference*. This is significant because electrical current only occurs when two poles of different charge come into contact—the reason why birds can comfortably sit on a 'high tension' (i.e. high voltage) cable whereas someone standing on the ground and touching that cable would die a horrible death. But the term *potential difference* also reveals that charge is indeed not a thing but a relation. And these relations can also be differentiated.

Elementary physics tells us that a current requires a closed circuit for charge to flow (lightning connects the charged particles in a storm cloud with the opposite charge of the earth's ground, crackling when the difference in charge becomes so great that the air flashes over, burning the gases of the atmosphere in an explosion that we hear as thunder). But the electrical charge that you need to refuel the battery in your mobile phone also connects you, through the phone and its cable, to a network of people and materials that maintain a supply of charge that you can access. If you live in Brazil, your access to an electrical socket may depend on whether your dwelling is recognised by the state: does your house have an address which entitles you to join the network and receive a bill (see Oakley et al. 2017)? If you are in rural Kenya, you might walk to the nearest village that has a charging kiosk and pay to access electricity there. If you are at an 'off-grid' mountain cabin in Norway, you might need to rig up an inverter to your solar panel so that it can work as a charger. If you are in certain French central railway stations, you might plug your phone into a bicycle-charger and ride the stationary bike to run its dynamo until either your phone is ready or your train is due to depart.

However you connect an appliance to an electrical circuit, you connect not only multiple elements of a material network, but the institutional, commercial, and exchange relations that tie you into a broader circuit of political, economic, and social networks (Silvast and Virtanen 2014). Electricity connects centres of control with distant action and creates patterns of dependence and independence, reproducing relations of power, hierarchies, and inequalities as it follows the predominant structures in society: the very structures that are effectively embedded in or embodied by technological infrastructures (Bell et al. 2020). At the same time, in the shadow of electrical connection are the disconnections effectively created by the partiality of electrical networks. Relations are unequal; electrical relations empower and disempower unequally, reinforcing existing hierarchies and establishing new routes for domination (Lennon 2017), as I indicate below.

Embedded Categories

Electricity's public significance is closely tied to the services that can be electrified and accessed, and it spans levels of governance, realms of the public and private, and such an inordinately wide range of what are known as 'electrical services' that it can soon become relevant to ask what purpose 'electricity' might have as a unifying category. Anthropologists might well ask whether it is analytically or intellectually appropriate to adopt the taxonomies and discursive constructions of other disciplines (such as, in this case, engineering or physics), or whether these are merely conventional. The relatively recent history of electrical technologies means that historians such as Thomas Hughes or David Nye (1990, 1997) can tell us a great deal about how these divisions came into being, for combined reasons related to industrial exploitation and experimental design.

Industrial categorisations have enduring resonance, reflecting prevailing ideologies at the time when electrical services were being invented and the colonial context in which they were disseminated. Coleman (2017), for example, shows with alarming clarity how electrical installations were used to perform the might of the British Empire in coronation festivities in India, lighting up festival grounds and radiating the light of the monarchy, while being brought in and withdrawn according to notions of who might be morally qualified to have access to electrical infrastructures. This is also evident in the context of 'concessionary imperialism' in the Arab Levant of the early twentieth century (Pascoe 2019, p. 120). Using market creation and capture, the imperial powers gained control over electrical services (trams, lighting), delegating enormous power to companies to control everyday mobility—but this also left them open to resistance. In Damascus, boycotts of the electrical tramways mobilised mass resistance, while Pascoe points out that conflicts over control of electrical infrastructures also became a mechanism for geopolitical competition between the French and Belgian Empires, while simultaneously opening routes for solidarity between dispersed anti-imperial movements. By linking Gandhian non-violence campaigns to Lebanese independence struggles through personal connections between the Grand Mufti, the head of the Khilafat movement, and the future independent Lebanese prime minister, electrical infrastructures linked social and political movements too.

The organisation of electrical infrastructures today can be traced back to the division of generation, transmission, distribution, and supply, categories that cause problems because they each imagine a different 'public' as the market for their operations (see Özden-Schilling 2015; Gal and Woolard 2001). From science studies, we know that technologies imagine and then generate publics, just as political discourse generates cohorts out of imaginaries around identity, race, gender, and so on. Resulting power systems are saturated in power relations, with particular formulations and expectations dominating through institutions, practices, or manoeuvres.

Bell et al. (2020) highlight how renewable energies have been co-opted by extractive regimes, such as the way that the notion of African land as a resource for European consumption popped up again in proposals that the Sahara be populated with solar farms to supply European electrical grids. The depoliticised technological discourse that allows such a suggestion not only to be thought but to be circulated and taken seriously across the energy industries and intergovernmental organisations reminds us how deeply technologies continue to be embedded as mechanisms for colonising practices. First, the technological imaginary appears (the Sahara as a solar power plant!), concealing the complex political and practical implications, which subsequently emerge framed as problems to be solved. As problem solving is the primary approach in areas such as engineering, the fact that 'problems' are not the only way to formulate such situations is often underemphasised. Proposed solutions can end up exacerbating tensions and sparking geopolitical conflicts. Renewable energy can equally fall into the extractive models pursued by the oil and fossil fuel industrial complexes (see also Folch 2013).

The geopolitics embedded in electrical systems may also be hidden in plain sight. A National Grid presumes a national population with specific characteristics, needs, and wants, subject to a national state that operates through particular bureaucratic structures and priorities. Decisions about who to connect to a national grid become politically difficult at the point where geography and demographics intrude, such as when residential density affects the investment/operation cost ratio of installing equipment. In my own fieldwork in the mountainous region of central France in the early 1990s, there were many arguments over whether people living in areas distant from infrastructural grids should expect to be connected by right; that is, whether the costs of connecting the whole population should be collectivised, or whether 'remote' dwellers should be expected to contribute to the cost as a function of their 'choice' to live in that location. Connection to a national grid thus became a question of citizenship and of the extent of and limits to the welfare state (cf. Ortar 2021; Forde 2020).

The materialisation of citizenship is reflected in Jamie Cross's description of distinctions made between grid electricity and micro-grids or home systems in the Indian electrical system (2019). Cross describes a division in the highlands of Odisha between settlements and industrial sites that are connected to the national electricity grid, whose street lights shine out over the valley at night, and a non-connected housing colony of Parojas, among the poorest peoples in India. Solar home kits might provide the colony's houses with electric light, but they fail to connect the villagers with the national programme of electrification and speak of the deep-seated hierarchical divisions in Indian society. As Cross argues, 'far from satisfying unmet needs for energy among the rural poor, India's off-grid solar revolution is making "the grid" an ever more pressing matter of public concern' (Cross 2019, p. 80). Rather than seeing Poroja Adivasis as cargo cultists who repurpose redundant telegraph poles and hang cables throughout their village in anticipation of the grid connection to come, they might equally be understood to be adopting the strategies of imagined neoliberal citizens who take initiative and responsibility for facilitating the delivery of state services themselves. Rather than include these citizens among others in a connected state, the state chose instead to provide segregated infrastructures reflecting social hierarchies.

The status of the grid as a symbol of citizenship is grounded in its significance as a product of the twentieth century's political and economic history of industrial modernism. Throughout much of that century, and increasingly through the post-Second World War era, a commitment to massive industrial scale spread around the world. Early electrical gigantism can be seen in the growing scale of hydroelectric power stations in the USA in the early part of the century, with the Hoover dam opening in 1936, and the mammoth multi-dam Tennessee Valley Authority (TVA) instigated in 1933, setting the path for 26 large hydroelectric dams from the 1940s onwards (see Lilienthal 1944; Selznick 1949; Thurman 1983). These dams, with their associated transmission infrastructure, were explicitly promoted as state-led development projects in the modernist modus, even if TVA was presented with a narrative of community-level engagement and benefit. Mega projects, from the Aswan Dam to more recent and ever larger projects such as the Chinese Three Gorges Dam, to now numerous giganticist (one might literally say megalomaniac) plans around the globe such as on the Nile (Hodbod et al. 2019), are moving from being statist national projects to international capitalist projects, following the changing global political economy.

RESISTANCE

Resistance was there from the start, as in the Levant (Pascoe 2019). Local unrest also emerged in the TVA programme as hydroelectric projects were perceived as the imposition of state power on peripheral areas, or more simply as land-grabs (Selznick 1949). Norwegian state plans from 1968 to dam the Alta River in Finnmark for hydroelectric power sparked protests so wide and so enduring that they eventually led to the setting up of a Sami parliament and an apology from the Norwegian king for the historic colonisation and oppression of Sami people.[2] Another form of resistance has gradually come to light through ethnographies of 'off-gridders'. Forde's ethnography of off-gridders in Wales (2017) and Vannini and Taggart's off-grid project (2014; and see lifeoffgrid. ca) further reveal the association between electrical connection and socio-political forms of collectivity. In both cases, off-gridders explicitly aim to break their ties with organised modernity to various degrees. Electricity is only one of the grids from which they remove themselves, but the metaphor of 'grid' spreads from the national system of electrical generation and its supply to cover all sorts of connecting mechanisms, from roads to telephones, water mains and sewers, television signals, and so on, or what Vannini and Taggart refer to as 'the "grids" upon which society is pegged, the grids through which our social relations are entangled'.[3] So, whilst the Adivasi claim the rights to equality and respect that participation in the national grid appears to offer, off-gridders in the Global North are leaping away from that recognition in the apparent pursuit of a quieter, slower life. That so many of them choose to retain access to the internet, mobile phones, private road vehicles, and other comforts of contemporary technological life indicates just how partial a retreat off-grid-ism can be and reminds us that electricity is not one thing: electrical services are many and varied, electricity is not entirely fungible.

What does it mean to say that electricity is not fungible? Surely electricity is just electricity, wherever it is used? Are there really different kinds of electricity? On the one hand, yes, of course, there are different kinds of electric current—different national grids use direct current and alternating currents at different frequencies and voltages, as well as different phases of current in combinations. Consumers of electrical services may remain perfectly ignorant of the details, but may still distinguish between electrical services and the current employed for different purposes. Winther and Bell's (2018) work on in-home displays shows people disaggregating their electricity use and beginning to make new associations between the gross readings found in electricity bills and the everyday actions and activities that they represent. Strengers et al. (2014) also demonstrate how people distinguish between necessary and optional use of electricity and electrical services, evaluating the use of electrical power to keep pets comfortable at home, versus the need to reduce consumption for environmental or economic reasons. Electricity is intimately tied into domestic relations, shaping the home environment in culturally specific ways, with the materiality of electricity also resisting how far electrical services can be adapted. Electricity also resists, in other words.

Loss and Losses

A crucial part of the infrastructure of electricity lies in the creation and maintenance of narratives around what constitutes a satisfactory system, narratives that are constantly under pressure from social, political, and economic challenges, as well as from changes in technological possibilities and industrial innovations. Aside from constant debates about appropriate charging, business, and financial models, utility and supply companies continually balance narratives of security and danger. They need populations to believe that electricity is sufficiently safe to provide a service people will want to buy, but that is sufficiently dangerous that they should not attempt to 'tamper' with infrastructure themselves. Hence, with governmental backing, they regulate and accredit training for electricians and other electrical experts, who are obliged to pay for licences and accredited training on a regular basis (such as the annual renewal of wiring regulations required of electricians[4]), and ally this with quality frameworks for switches and other safety mechanisms.[5] Hence the dangers that can arise from electrical shocks are held at bay with an infrastructure of training and regulation that simultaneously disciplines a workforce and creates exclusive professional expertise. A tinkerer in Britain, for example, who has sufficient knowledge might choose to wire their own home, it is true, but if they were to sell the property, they would require an official safety certificate produced by an authorised expert, and if they were foolhardy enough to wire anyone else's property, they would be liable for any errors or injuries arising from faults. Electrical safety can be seen as entailing its own 'shadow concept' in electrical danger, a shadow that carries an imminent threat to undermine the idea of electricity as a domestic(ated) service and that must be constantly held in check if the concept is to be maintained.

Just as voltage is described by engineers as potential difference, electrical supply is a potential service, not actuated until required. Paying attention to the workings of electrical systems themselves raises questions about the common political and economic discourses that also have multiple meanings. A particular example is the concept of losses, which are so easily laden with moral inflection—loss as theft, loss as waste, and so forth. Electrical system losses are rarely what they might seem to the casual observer, but throw out subcategories of absence that are interesting to think through. Consumers pay in relation to the number of turns of a meter-dial (or the digits clocked up on a digital meter), but they also pay for the collective loss of electricity through what are described as commercial or 'non-technical' losses and technical losses. The euphemistically named non-technical losses are the equivalent of shoplifted commodities—electrical current diverted into services but not paid for by the customer. This is particularly common where the preponderance of overhead electrical cables makes it technically feasible to 'hook' a cable informally on to the electrical supply 'behind' the meter. These kinds of 'theft' are quite well documented (e.g. Golden and Min 2012; Winther 2012) and have been the focus of many national campaigns to coerce people into paying for metered electricity. Less public attention is given to so-called technical losses: all those so-called inefficiencies in an electrical grid system that see the power drop, including heat lost as the current warms long-distance cables and inductance that forms part of the electromagnetic field, as well as cable and equipment faults that may raise the field around faulty equipment, particularly underground.[6] Technical losses are an intrinsic part of the grid, but whereas these are morally normalised as a 'technical' part of the function of a grid, so-called nontechnical losses are often aggressively targeted as a problem of governance, even when the exact relation between technical and non-technical losses may be difficult to specify. This, too, is a function of the particular relations employed in squaring the supply–demand–finance triangle, rather than being an inevitable function of electrical systems. After all, a fully functioning electrical grid could be paid for collectively out of general taxation (examples of these exist), but the overwhelming majority of contemporary grids are constructed under an infrastructural model that adopts a consumer-pays principle. It is precisely this system that brings with it the inequalities of access to grid electricity that have been heavily criticised globally and that lead to the criminalisation of those who do not or cannot pay for basic electrical services (e.g. Walker and Day 2012; Bouzarovski and Petrova 2015; Boardman 1991).

The combination of insurance regimes, accreditation of knowledge and skills, regulation, and commercial exclusivity in relation to utilities keeps them out of the realm of everyday interference for all but a professionalised cohort of workmen and occasionally women. On this note, it is well recognised that the electrical industries are overly dominated by men in the UK (and many other countries), but recent research reveals niches where professional women have had historically important roles (e.g. Harrison Moore 2020). Katie Lloyd Thomas describes how women saw opportunities for emancipation in the 1930s through roles in the nascent electricity industries as electrical demonstrators, 'housecraft' educators, technicians, and product specialists (2017, p. 54). A moment of radical change provided an opening for enterprising women to carve a place out of the otherwise masculinised professions that could be co-opted by women for work and creativity, revealing yet another partial relationality engendered (literally) by electrical choices.

Similar to other infrastructural systems, electrical systems are always a work in progress, susceptible to breakdown, reinvention, adaptation, and cooptation. Assumptions around gender, ethnicity, identity, rights, and responsibility are literally built into the system through their design (Strengers 2014), yet the infrastructure is often in flux, blending a legacy of material objects ('assets') with material, political, and social elements that must be reproduced or replaced. At each moment of significant change or doubt, the system is thrown into question, and new concepts can be created and adopted, debated or discarded.

Conclusions

As deeply as electricity is embedded in everyday life, in political debates, and in social and technical infrastructure, it has so far been less deeply explored in anthropology than other infrastructures. While that is starting to be remedied, there are few ethnographies that really take electricity seriously in its own right as a facet of life in many parts of the globe. Radical changes appear to be on the horizon for electrical infrastructures. Electricity grids are being decarbonised at different rates in many countries of the Global North, and grids are being expanded in other countries, but the notion of infrastructural nationalism is also coming into question. Few countries now have electrical grids that entirely respect national borders; European countries are increasingly interconnected by cables, international electricity markets, and cross-national policies, while several African countries have grids that do not link different parts of the same country. At the same time, technical and political constraints of different kinds reveal the political character of national-grid ambitions, and the limitations to even the most fully developed grids. The rise in accessibility of renewable electricity technologies is changing the workings of grids, which need to be more responsive to distributed generation, threatening centralised grid-management patterns of the past. Interest in mini-grids and renewable micro-grids is growing, posing questions about who owns assets, who has the right to benefit from their products, and who owns the externalities of their production, installation, and disposal.

The narratives of electrical development must necessarily also change in character. Hero-narratives such as those that describe the work of Edison, Westinghouse, and Tesla will not suffice to explain the changing infrastructures of electricity across the globe. Anthropology is one of the few disciplines that can link the high politics of development with the everyday experience of those who experience its effects and is a discipline that is well equipped to speak truth to power, exposing the techno-politics buried in wires and grids. But first, we must learn to speak about power itself and to follow electrical powers through the transformers, transistors, and transformations that they charge.

Acknowledgements I would like to thank the editors and the anonymous reviewers for enormously helpful comments and suggestions.

Notes

1. The number of women taking electrical engineering degrees stubbornly remains far below those undertaking other kinds of engineering study.
2. See https://snl.no/Alta-saken and http://kultur.nve.no/utstillinger/kampen-om-alta. Accessed 27 October 2020.
3. http://lifeoffgrid.ca/off-grid-living-the-book/. Accessed 26 July 2019.
4. Electricians in the UK must have access to the annual edition of British Standard BS7671 Wiring Requirements for Electrical Installations, for which an annual subscription currently costs between £69 and £406 plus VAT: https://electrical.

theiet.org/resources/digital/digital-packages/. Accessed 29 July 2019. See also HSE 2015.

5. It is fascinating to note that the switch was invented sometime after domestic lighting. At Cragside, said to be one of the first houses in the world—if not the first—to be electrified using hydroelectric power, in 1878, the table lamps predate toggle or button switches. www.nationaltrust.org.uk/cragside. Accessed 8 July 2021.

6. See https://www.ukpowernetworks.co.uk/losses/. Accessed 8 July 2021.

References

Bakke, G. (2019). Electricity is Not a Noun. In S. Abram, B. R. Winthereik, & T. Yarrow (Eds.), *Electrifying Anthropology: Exploring electrical practices and infrastructures* (pp. 25–41). London: Bloomsbury.

Bell, S. E., Daggett, C., & Labuski, C. (2020). Toward feminist energy systems: Why adding women and solar panels is not enough. *Energy Research & Social Science, 68,* 1–13. https://doi.org/10.1016/j.erss.2020.101557.

Boardman, B. (1991). *Fuel Poverty: From Cold Homes to Affordable Warmth.* Pinter Pub Limited.

Bouzarovski, S., & Petrova, S. (2015). A global perspective on domestic energy deprivation: Overcoming the energy poverty–fuel poverty binary. *Energy Research & Social Science, 10,* 31–40.

Boyer, D. (2014). Energopower: An Introduction. *Anthropological Quarterly, 87*(2), 309–333. https://doi.org/10.1353/anq.2014.0020

Boyer, D. (2015). Anthropology Electric. *Cultural Anthropology, 30*(4), 531–539.

Brooks, A. (2012). Radiating Knowledge: The Public Anthropology of Nuclear Energy. *American Anthropologist, 114*(1), 137–140.

Coleman, L. (2017). *A Moral Technology: Electrification as Political Ritual in New Delhi.* Ithaca: Cornell University Press.

Coleman, L. (2019). Widened Reason and Deepened Optimism: Electricity and morality in Durkheim's anthropology and our own. In *Electrifying Anthropology: Exploring electrical practices and infrastructures* (pp. 43–64). London: Bloomsbury.

Cross, J. (2019). No current: electricity and disconnection in rural India. In S. Abram, B. R. Winthereik, & T. Yarrow (Eds.), *Electrifying Anthropology: Exploring electrical practices and infrastructures* (pp. 66–81). London: Bloomsbury.

Ferguson, J. (1999). *Expectations of modernity: myths and meanings of urban life on the Zambian copperbelt.* Berkeley & London: University of California Press.

Folch, C. (2013). Surveillance and State Violence in Stroessner's Paraguay: Itaipu Hydroelectric Dam, Archive of Terror. *American Anthropologist, 116*(1), 44–57.

Forde, E. (2017). The ethics of energy provisioning: Living off-grid in rural Wales. *Energy Research & Social Science, 30,* 82–93.

Forde, E. (2020). *Living Off Grid in Wales: Eco-villages in policy and practice.* Cardiff: University of Wales Press.

Gal, S., & Woolard, K. A. (2001). *Languages and publics: the making of authority.* Manchester: St. Jerome Pub.

Golden, M., & Min, B. (2012). *Theft and Loss of Electricity in an Indian State.* International Growth Centre working paper 12/0060.

Gooday, G. (2004). *The Morals of Measurement: Accuracy, Irony and Trust in Late Victorian Electrical Practice*. Cambridge: Cambridge University Press.

Harrison Moore, A. (2020). Switching from the Master to the Mistress: A Women's Guide to Powering Up the Home. In A. Harrison Moore & R. Sandwell (Eds.), "Women and Energy", *RCC Perspectives: Transformations in Environment and Society, 1*, 25–29.

Hodbod, J., Stevenson, E. G. J., Akall, G., et al. (2019). Social-ecological change in the Omo-Turkana basin: A synthesis of current developments. *Ambio, 48*(10), 1099–1115.

Howe, C., & Boyer, D. (2015). Aeolian Politics. *Distinktion: Scandinavian Journal of Social Theory*, 31–48. https://doi.org/10.1080/1600910X.2015.1022564.

Hughes, T. P. (1983). *Networks of Power: Electrification of Western Society, 1880–1930*. Johns Hopkins University Press.

HSE (Health and Safety Executive). (2015). *The Electricity at Work Regulations 1989*. © Crown copyright 2015.

Krauss, W. (2010). The 'Dingpolitik' of Wind Energy in Northern German Landscapes: An Ethnographic Case Study, *Landscape Research, 35*(2), 195–208.

Latour, B. (2002). Morality and Technology, The End of the Means (trans: Venn, C.) *Theory, Culture & Society, 19*(5/6), 247–260.

Lennon, M. (2017). Decolonizing energy: Black Lives Matter and technoscientific expertise amid solar transitions. *Energy Research & Social Science, 30*, 18–27

Lilienthal, D. E. (1944). *TVA: Democracy on the March*. New York City: Harper & Brothers.

Lloyd Thomas, K. (2017). The Architect as Shopper. In H. Frichot, C. Gabrielsson, & H. Runting (Eds.), *Architecture and Feminisms* (pp. 54–65). London: Routledge.

Nader, L. (1981). Barriers to thinking about Energy. *Physics Today, 34*(9).

Nader, L., & Beckerman, S. (1978). Energy as it Relates to the Quality and Style of Life. *Ann. Rev. Energy, 3*, 1–28.

Nader, L., & Milleron, N. (1979). Dimensions of the "people problem" in Energy research and the factual basis of dispersed energy futures. *Energy, 4*(5), pp. 953–967.

Nye, D. E. (1990). *Electrifying America: Social Meanings of a New Technology, 1880–1940*. Cambridge, MA: The MIT Press.

Nye, D. E. (1997). *Consuming Power: A Social History of American Energies*. Cambridge, MA: The MIT Press.

Oakley, E., Angelini, A., & DeVore, J. (2017, December 19). Our Electric Exchanges. *Theorizing the Contemporary, Fieldsights*. https://culanth.org/fieldsights/our-electric-exchanges.

Ortar, N. (2021). Power Legacies at the Core of Everyday Life: The case of wood-burning stoves in France. In T. Loloum, S. Abram, & N. Ortar (Eds.), *Ethnographies of Power: A political anthropology of energy*. Oxford & New York: Berghahn.

Özden-Schilling, C. (2015). Economy Electric. *Cultural Anthropology, 30*(4), 578–588.

Pascoe, S. (2019). A "Weapon of the Weak": Electric Boycotts in the Arab Levant and the Global Contours of Interwar Anti-Imperialism. *Radical History Review, 134*, 116–141.

Schumacher, E. F. (1973). *Small is beautiful. A study of economics as if people mattered*. London: Blond and Briggs.

Selznick, P. (1949). *TVA and the Grass Roots; A Study in the Sociology of Formal Organization*. Berkeley & Los Angeles: University of California Press.

Silvast, A., & Virtanen, M. J. (2014). Keeping Systems at Work: Electricity Infrastructure from Control Rooms to Household Practices. *Science & Technology Studies, 27*(2), 93–114.

Stoller, P. (1994). Embodying Colonial Memories. *American Anthropologist, 96*(3), 634–648.

Strengers, Y. (2014). Smart energy in everyday life: are you designing for resource man? *Interactions, 21*(4), 24–31.

Strengers, Y., Nicholls, L., & Maller, C. (2014). Curious energy consumers: Humans and nonhumans in assemblages of household practice. *Journal of Consumer Culture, 16*(3), 761–780.

Summerton, J. (2004). Do Electrons Have Politics? Constructing User Identities in Swedish Electricity. *Science, Technology, & Human Values, 29*(4), 486–511.

Thurman, S. (Ed.) (1983). *A history of the Tennessee Valley Authority.* Tennessee Valley Authority Information Office.

Vannini, P., & Taggart, J. (2014). *Off the Grid: Re-Assembling Domestic Life.* London: Routledge.

Walker, G., & Day, R. (2012). Fuel poverty as injustice: Integrating distribution, recognition and procedure in the struggle for affordable warmth. *Energy Policy, 49*, 69–75.

Wilhite, H., Nakagami, H., Masuda, T., & Yamaga, Y. (1996). A cross-cultural analysis of household energy use behaviour in Japan and Norway. *Energy Policy, 24*(9), 795–803.

Winther, T. (2008). *The Impact of Electricity: Development, desires and dilemmas.* New York & Oxford: Berghahn Books.

Winther, T. (2012). Electricity Theft as a Relational Issue: A Comparative Look at Zanzibar, Tanzania, and the Sunderban Islands, India. *Energy for Sustainable Development, 16*(1), 111–119.

Winther, T., & Bell, S. (2018). Domesticating In Home Displays in Selected British and Norwegian Households. *Science & Technology Studies, 31*(2), 19–38.

CHAPTER 39

Circuit Board Money: An Infrastructural Perspective on Digital Payments

Finance

Sunniva Sandbukt

In October 2019, I was loitering in a corridor on one of the last days of the annual Ethereum Developers Conference, DevCon5, in Osaka, Japan, a conference dedicated to discussing cryptocurrencies, blockchain, and digital payments. Saturated from days of dense talks and mingling, I was standing with fellow conference stragglers when a man approached us with a metal briefcase. Opening the case, he pulled out plastic satchels filled with money for us to examine. 'CRYPTO CASH FOR HUMANS', read an accompanying cardboard tag.

The money-like thing handed to me had the familiar shape of a banknote, was made of soft plastic, and very colourful. The next thing you notice is the tech-paraphernalia covering it: a chip in the bottom right corner, an entire side of golden strips looking like something from a circuit board, an area marked NFC, and small golden perforations, numerically labelled. The note itself was beautiful, the gold an attractive contrast to the deep blues and purples and replicated in the English and Chinese lettering. The note was marked '1 KONG', and was illustrated with a peculiar rendition of the Roman god Mercury and, on the other side, an abstract planet with a triangular incision revealing its layers. It resembled something freshly materialised from a sci-fi novel.

S. Sandbukt (✉)
IT University of Copenhagen, Copenhagen, Denmark
e-mail: suns@itu.dk

757

M. H. Bruun et al. (eds.), *The Palgrave Handbook of the Anthropology of Technology*, https://doi.org/10.1007/978-981-16-7084-8_39

Months later, when I showed the note to a dear colleague, she expressed surprise at finding the *digital* money firmly in her hand. Expecting a computer screen, the circuit-board-esque features of this crypto-cash were disrupting her expectations of what makes money, well, money.

Questions about what makes money work, what it is worth, and how it is used have long been studied within economic anthropology, although the emergence of its digital forms has catalysed a recent discussion about the nature and origin of money itself (Maurer 2012). Moreover, it has brought a renewed focus on the infrastructures of payments, as transactions are increasingly facilitated through payment terminals, credit cards, and apps. In recent years, scholars have shown how this digitalisation can also be understood as encouraging the privatisation of transactional records. As a result, growing critical scholarship is interrogating how increasing dependencies, but also new forms of inclusion and exclusion, occur when transactional infrastructures are owned by private payments companies, a distinct change from the public utility of cash (Dalinghaus 2019).

In the first part of this handbook chapter, I begin by presenting literature from economic anthropology that leads to a conceptualisation of money as an infrastructure for keeping account of individual and societal debt relations. I choose this framing because it can be productive to think of digital money forms, not as digitised cash but as new technologies for accounting. Following this, I focus on the growing scholarship which attends to the subsequent infrastructural implications for everyday transactions, and finish with literature that examines how this digital transition has affected exchange relationships and led to growing intermediation and control through proprietary infrastructures.

In the second half of the chapter, I explore these dynamics through the empirical case of so-called *digital wallets* in Indonesia, addressing how the underlying infrastructure imposes conditions for exchange and configures users on either side of the exchange relationship. Finally, I conclude by discussing the relevance of ethnographic studies of digital payments and argue that an infrastructural perspective can draw attention to those details of value circulation and debt relationships that we might otherwise neglect in our day-to-day transactions.

Money, Debt, and Cashless Transactions

The study of economies within anthropology dates as far back as the discipline itself, providing a wide range of contributions that describe and analyse economic life from an anthropological perspective (see Malinowski 2014[1922]; Mauss 2016[1925]). Today the field extends beyond special-purpose money in highly localised social contexts, to the abstract values traded rapidly on stock markets (see Ho 2009; Zaloom 2006) and even cryptocurrencies (see Brunton 2019; Maurer 2017). My interest here is in what Bill Maurer defines as the anthropology of money (see Maurer 2006), which engages with the social meanings of money and its function in exchanges and value circulation. I am particularly interested in how money as a transactional technology is affected by digitalisation.

One of the early defining debates that characterised the field of economic anthropology was between the formalists and the substantivists. The former argued for the application of so-called universal mainstream economic market theory to the foreign settings that were now being explored by anthropologists (see Burling 1962; Cook 1966; Schneider 1974). Meanwhile, the substantivists argued for the importance of more localised economic analysis, stemming from the context of its creation (see Bohannan and Bohannan 1968; Polanyi 2001[1944]). Although this encouraged a more pluralistic approach, it was also criticised for reproducing a simplistic, reductive, and even romanticised understanding of people living in so-called primitive economies (Hann and Hart 2011).

The distinction between the two factions gradually faded, and arguments were made that perhaps there was merit to a middle-ground approach (see Cancian 1966) in which one does not under- or over-interpret the importance of socialised conceptualisations of economic relations (see Granovetter 1985). This led to an increasing emphasis within economic anthropology on thinking about the economy in terms of embeddedness and performativity (see Callon 1998), as well as in terms of social reproduction (see Gibson-Graham 2006; Meillassoux 1981[1975]; Weiner 1980). Importantly, money came to be treated as more than the object itself and seen as a reflection of social relationships. Thus, much of the ethnographic work on money has emphasised its social entanglements and the everyday economic lives of its users (see Dodd 2014; Maurer et al. 2018; Zelizer 1995).

Building on all of this, one of the most important contributions of economic anthropology has been the substantiation of the *credit theory* of money, which suggests that monetary systems derive from debit and credit relationships, as opposed to originating in barter, as claimed in mainstream economic teachings (Graeber 2011). This also provides an important paradigm shift in the study of digital payments because it introduces the notion that money can be viewed as more than a material object, but also as an infrastructure: a social infrastructure which, like its asphalt road and PVC pipe counterparts, is concerned not with the production of things, but with their circulation, with constraining and directing flows (see Elyachar 2010; Simone 2015). Facilitating the flow of resources and making complex societal debt relations visible, even tangible, money can be considered both a thing, as well as a relation between things (Larkin 2013). Thus, I turn now to literature engaging specifically with three core functions of money: as a store of value, medium of exchange, and unit of account (Maurer 2006). These conceptualisations matter because they impact on how money is translated into a digital form.

The notion that money functions as a store of value may seem straightforward at first glance: a ten dollar bill will buy an equivalent value of products. Then again, how is that value determined, and what is value anyway? David Graeber worked to develop an anthropological theory of value (Graeber 2001,

2013) to get beyond the paradigms of orthodox economic theory in which value is simply conflated with price, in part by examining economic, political, social, and linguistic understandings of value. He points particularly to the work of Marilyn Strathern, who showed that objects are themselves valued because of how they make important social relationships visible. In her foundational essay on the qualified self, she writes, 'what people exchange is always a totality: one perspective for another; your view of my assets for my view of yours. Thus are persons and objects created' (Strathern 1992, p. 188). Perceptions of value contribute to defining the world in terms of what might be considered important or desirable. Thus, the value of a money-object derives from its social context.

By contrast, the standardisation of value into money forms such as a symbolic metal coin firmly separates the money form from its socially constructed value. Reduced to a 'wholly abstract token' (Maurer 2018, p. 8) value might be determined through monetary policy or market speculation. Jane I. Guyer (2012) shows the interconnectedness between what she calls 'hard' and 'soft' currencies. Hardness alludes to durability, meaning it can hold its form and later be liquidated into other forms, a quality well suited for something that should store value. By contrast, soft currencies might have fluctuating or rapidly depreciating value (or may literally deteriorate), making them more suited as mediums of exchange.

Standardised or not, the forms of money in circulation will typically comprise a plurality, and Guyer was particularly interested in those transactions that involved the exchange of things with seemingly unequal or incommensurable values. Her research in equatorial Africa thus drew attention to the subtle ways in which conversions of value take place, finding that people also operate with a plurality of value scales (Guyer 2004). This challenged the idea that currencies evolve from multiple special-purpose forms of money to a singular all-purpose money form. Instead, she posits that both store of value and exchange continue to happen across multiple currencies, while also emphasising the interconnectedness of these dominant features of money (Guyer 2012, p. 2216).

Thus, the wholly abstract token is not a given evolutionary outcome. Nevertheless, this understanding continues to be prevalent in orthodox economic theory through the barter theory of money whereby money originated to facilitate the barter of disparate products, a mediator with so-called objective value. I may not need wool in exchange for my clay pots, but if we can agree on a standardised value in the form of a price, materialised in these coins, then we can exchange goods with them instead. Thus, money allegedly resolves situations where there does not exist what is known as the 'double coincidence of wants' (Graeber 2011, p. 22).

In this evolutionary narrative, so-called primitive forms of value, such as shells or beads, evolved through coins and paper forms to credit cards and cryptocurrencies. This detaches value from specific material affordances or social entanglements, and pays limited attention to where this objective value comes from. Pervasive and compelling as the narrative is, Graeber draws on decades of ethnographic research to point out that there is simply no evidence to support this origin myth. Thus, according to him, the premise itself is flawed, 'no one ever traded arrowheads for slabs of meat. Economists simply ignored this information' (Graeber 2011, p. 29). In his extensive 5000-year historical review of debt, Graeber points out that credit systems existed long before the invention of coinage, suggesting that the common perception is not only wrong, but also back to front: money is a materialisation of existing credit and debt relationships.

The *state theory* of money suggests that money emerged when governments began to issue currency, a form of 'money-proper' (see Ingham 2000) in which the value of a token was assured through state authority. Here, money is representative of the relationship between the citizen and the state or, as credit theorists would argue, a form of state-issued IOU, which has long since lost its connection to any tangible asset such as gold stored in a vault. This paradigm shift away from gold-backed currency was not without controversy, and many adherents of cryptocurrency still ascribe to what has been called a form of digital metallism, in which it is believed that money must have a form of intrinsic value, as perceived with gold, emerging separately from social relations (see Brunton 2017; Swartz 2018).

To conclude, I want to point out that cashless transactions are neither a novelty nor something exclusively associated with digital forms of money. For instance, Maurer cites research by Denise Schmandt-Besserat (1992) who identified tokens of account dating from 8000 and 3200 BCE. These devices allowed transactions to take place without exchanging any physical object, providing instead a record of transactions and obligations owed (Maurer 2018). Thus, there is extensive scholarship that supports the credit theory of money and understands money as an instrument of accounting.

Payments, Debris, and the Metadata of Digitalisation

An aspect of money that has been somewhat neglected in the literature, and which has gained renewed attention as a result of digitalisation, is that of the enabling mechanisms that allow those economic and financial transactions to happen: the underlying infrastructures of payment (Maurer 2012). For the value in money to be exchangeable, it must be in an acceptable form and, especially when that form is digital, there is a role for intermediaries who can facilitate acceptance. Payments can also be said to be the infrastructure that allows money to move, by organising, legitimating, and materially facilitating transactions (Rea et al. 2016, p. 3). In this section, I present a selection of the scholarship that engages with the impacts of the digitalisation of payments, the enabling and underlying infrastructures, and the emergent meta-value of our transactions. I choose here to focus on the literature that provides a critical perspective onto how digitalisation may lead to privatisation and proprietary infrastructures as this is an often neglected aspect of digital payments and one that can benefit from ethnographic research.

In their edited volume, *Paid: Tales of Dongles, Checks and Other Money Stuff*, Maurer and Lana Swartz (2017) draw attention to what they call the 'debris' of cashless transactions—the multitude of payment artefacts allowing money transactions to take place—writing, 'Like many critical infrastructures, most users only notice them when they are broken' (Maurer and Swartz 2017, p. xvii). What they point out is that much of this underlying payments infrastructure is rendered invisible by design through its *frictionless aesthetics*, which presents practical challenges for ethnographic research. After all, how do you observe or engage with transactional behaviour that takes place between a person and their fingers moving across a screen? How do you make visible exchanges when money is a numerical record in a remote database? The volume provides a great source of inspiration for ethnographic research into the material traces of cashless electronic payments, ranging from ATMs and receipts to hardware such as payment dongles, or physical gestures such as swiping.

Examining the material aspects of cashless transactions provides a contact point for studying digital payments but does not tell us what is being transferred instead of cash. At its core, digital payment is just banks requesting other banks to change their record of accounts through third-party infrastructural providers such as VISA or Mastercard. One could turn the phrase on its head and argue that a cashless society could more accurately be called a bank-transfer society (Scott 2017). As described earlier, rather than seeing digital money as a natural evolution of cash, it would thus be more accurate to think of the digitalisation of payments as the development of accounting technology. Thus, the ethnographic study of digital payments involves more than simply changed (or unchanged) economic practices, it challenges us to examine the political questions of where, how, and by whom that accounting takes place (see Swartz 2020).

While money and digital payment networks have largely been the domain of governments, banks, and established corporate actors such as VISA, Rea et al. (2016) draw attention to a recent infrastructural shift. Over the past decade, mobile network operators and other *fintech* actors are leveraging the communications network infrastructure they have already developed, 'attempting to use the networks they have built to carry another kind of data—financial data' (Rea et al. 2016, p. 2). Often referred to as *peer-to-peer* (P2P) transactions, technologies like M-Pesa in Kenya allow users to transact, for example, by sending airtime intended for phone use to each other in place of cash, providing a cheaper, faster, and safer alternative to conventional cash or bank transfers. In their review of the literature from the past decade on *mobile money*, Rea and Nelms make some important observations about how the concept of P2P transactions has come to be a 'fundamental transactional form' (Rea and Nelms 2017, p. 8). While P2P is commonly understood to be a directional description of how money flows (FROM peer TO peer), Rea and Nelms suggest that the 2 might instead be considered a placeholder for the intermediary facilitating the exchange (FROM peer THROUGH intermediary TO peer). In doing so, they point to an important avenue for ethnographic research, one centring not only on the users of this technology but also on those who create, implement, and control it.

Rachel O'Dwyer does just this when she asks us to consider emerging questions of sociotechnical control 'when pipes become banks' (O'Dwyer 2015). She argues that the increasing role of ICT companies in providing critical infrastructure for payments will result in the algorithmic governance of transactions, as rules become automated and hardcoded into the platforms and systems themselves. Where law traditionally relies on interpretation and the flexibility of a case-by-case basis for arbitration, algorithmic governance rigidly controls the actions of its users as determined, critically, by the intermediaries providing the software. O'Dwyer paraphrases Donald Mackenzie (2008) to say that 'algorithms are "engines not cameras"' (O'Dwyer 2015, p. 3), pointing to how these apps do not simply model existing transactional patterns; rather, they play a significant role in configuring users and determining what money is, who it belongs to, and how it circulates.

Alluding to this algorithmic configuration of users, Keith Hart described back in 1986 how the digitalisation of money also results in the digitalisation of our personal identities. Specifically, merging our money with our transaction history and leaving computers to assess our creditworthiness risk reducing people to 'a formal abstraction of individual human beings, to a cipher in a universe of numbers' (Hart 1986, p. 642). Or, as O'Dwyer formulates it three decades later, 'In virtualising money, non-cash payments materialize previously latent informational traces of who transferred money to whom and in exchange for what' (O'Dwyer 2015, p. 5). For Hart, money could be conceptualised as a form of collective memory—a technology for keeping track of our extended societal debt relationships. The money tokens in my pocket, the receipts in my wallet, and the numbers on my monthly bills, all 'constitute a way of summarizing relationships with society at a given time' (Hart 2007, p. 16). Where cash itself is anonymous, usable by whoever is holding it, digital money becomes hyper-personalised.

Digitalisation does not just move this infrastructure from our wallets to digital databases; it has facilitated an unprecedented aggregation and personalisation of *transactional metadata*. Referencing the digital storage of data, O'Dwyer describes this as producing a *cache society* in which the memory traces of our extended social relationships form a novel type of value for the intermediaries of our transactions (O'Dwyer 2018). For intermediaries, the value in providing payments infrastructure shifted from imposing fees or rents to the value of the transactional metadata itself. Thus, for the intermediaries 'the dream is for a system where value enters a network and circulates endlessly, never leaving as material cash' (Maurer 2016, p. 214). As Brett Scott points out, not only is the cache society a valuable business model for the companies controlling the infrastructure, this system of bank-based transactions also 'forms a panopticon that enables—in theory—all transactions to be recorded, watched and analysed, good or bad' (Scott 2017). The concern at the heart of this argument lies in both the increasing privatisation of monetary systems and the increasing power of its proprietors: centralised institutions verifying transactions through private databases.

FINANCIAL IN/EXCLUSION IN A DIGITAL ECONOMY

The increasing prominence of digital payments thus calls for more analytical study of the intermediation and infrastructural control involved in the digital economy. Here, ethnography has a particularly important perspective to offer, in its ability to demonstrate the visceral experience and conditions of being participants in such an economy. Recently, there has been more concentrated attention in the literature on the global push from both industry and governments towards becoming cashless societies, even to the point of demonetisation as seen in India (Peebles 2020). We see in the literature how arguments about *financial inclusion* are mobilised to justify the transition (see Sen et al. 2020), but also how there has been a paradigm shift in the industry. Where earlier emphasis may have been on financial aid, financial inclusion recasts those who are poor, unbanked, or socio-economically marginalised as a new and untapped market (Elyachar 2012). The literature in this section thus focuses on digital payments in the context of financial inclusion and asks who the imagined participants of this cashless future are, and how they might experience this digitalisation.

Digital payments in the form of mobile money came to be a central component in the financial inclusion and poverty reduction agenda because more people are understood to have access to phones than to bank accounts (see Burrell 2018; Rea and Nelms 2017). Thus far, much of the literature on mobile money and financial inclusion has been produced by development professionals who, according to Sibel Kusimba (2018), make assumptions about the financial needs of the poor that they seek to help. In contrast, Kusimba's research shows how communities in Western Kenya leverage digital forms of money to mobilise other money forms within the context of socially important life-cycle rituals. Mobile money did not fundamentally change the purposes of economic practices; rather, it became incorporated within existing hierarchies of value formed by the specific socio-economic context.

While mobile payments may indeed make certain services more affordable, safe, or cheap, engaging people currently existing outside formal systems is arguably also a strategy for converting a large number of people into customers. Deborah James, in her work on debt in South Africa, refers to this process as a deepening of the financial sector (James 2015). Julia Elyachar points to how private industry and fintech actors within the so-called payments space actually benefit from 'uncovering, developing, and mobilizing existing forms of infrastructure created by the bottom of the pyramid, the world's poorest, and building on them to create new kinds of financial and information services for a profit' (Elyachar 2010, p. 458). The leveraging of this social infrastructure by corporate actors takes place under the guise of *economic empowerment*, in which access to financial services is seen as a mechanism for reducing poverty.

There are also examples of private retailers offering access to personal financing in the form of credit cards in contexts where people do not have bank accounts; empirical cases show how such credit cards and their associated debts circulate between people in a new form of financial practice in which the access to credit can be shared (see Kolling 2020; Ossandón et al. 2018). However, such measures to 'include' people in formal financial structures, particularly through cashless payments, can also lead to increased vulnerability and financial instability. This is due to the increasing social entanglements in which people become both debtors and creditors, as Marie Kolling demonstrates in her empirical work in Brazil, but also because digital financial infrastructures quickly come to dominate the socio-economic context, making it difficult to opt out. Writing about the rapid introduction of digital financial inclusion initiatives in China, Nicholas Loubere observes that 'integration into the formal financial and economic systems is not really voluntary' (Loubere 2017, p. 17). Instead, he argues, these initiatives may lead to destructive outcomes, and reproduce existing inequalities and exploitative relations.

While some people are forcefully included, others encounter new forms of exclusion (see Donovan 2018; Roy 2010, 2018). Camilla Ida Ravnbøll describes how the introduction of cashlessness at music festivals in Denmark impacts upon the Roma who depend upon income from bottle collection, forcing them to adapt and change working strategies. She makes the critical point, that 'digital payments are not only about technology but also about defining social relations and hierarchical positions' (Ravnbøl 2020, pp. 16–17). Indeed, when first introduced, credit cards also alluded to a form of aspirational modernity in the form of a cashless society. However, Lana Swartz points out that participation in that modernity remained heavily socially regulated, and black Americans in particular were likely to have their cards declined as a form of payment, even when the technical infrastructure was in place. The Diner's Club credit card 'could only provide a privatised version of modernity that reflected and reinforced existing social difference' (Swartz 2017, p. 86). Notably, ethnographic research here can show us how those who are precluded from access are excluded not only from particular payment infrastructures but also from the vision of the modern society that cashlessness represents.

Digital 'Wallets' in Indonesia: Peers and Intermediaries

I turn now to my research on digital wallets in Yogyakarta, Indonesia. Similar to the contexts described above, statistically it is more common for Indonesian people to have access to a mobile phone than it is to have access to a bank account, and only a minority have access to debit or credit cards which would allow them to make digital payments (Azali 2016). Although e-commerce has long been booming, many payments still take place in the form of cash-on-delivery services, or through payment codes, which can be activated at an ATM or minimarket within a given timeframe, and then paid with cash (Pangestu and Dewi 2017). In the past five years, and particularly since 2017, there has been a rapid uptake of app-based digital wallets allowing users to convert cash and store it in a digital form on their smartphones.

I will focus on two main examples of such wallets, namely Go-Pay and OVO.[1] Go-Pay is the wallet situated within an app called Gojek. Famously Indonesia's first tech unicorn, Gojek started as a ride-hailing app by formalising contact with existing *ojek* drivers who provided motorcycle-taxi services, but now includes a wide range of services ranging from Go-Massage to Go-Food (Nastiti 2017). OVO is a stand-alone wallet app but also collaborates with various e-commerce platforms to provide an integrated digital payment mechanism. One such platform is Grab, a Singaporean company that also provides ride-hailing services in Indonesia. As transport is a critical service for many people, the self-described *online drivers* using these platforms often become the first point of contact with these novel digital wallets. The extensive fleet of drivers can act as exchange agents and the companies provide financial incentives encouraging them to sell their own digital balance to customers in exchange for cash. This indicates that the apps are interested in more customers using the digital payments infrastructure, rather than their using cash to pay for trips booked in the app.

It is important to understand that once a customer's money has entered the system and been converted into digital credit, it cannot easily be extracted again except by spending it. Extracting it would require either that the user connect their app to a bank account, or that they upgrade their account using formal ID, thus unlocking additional features. The denomination indicated in the app may be in rupiah (IDR) but, in effect, it functions as a company-specific token that can only be used as payment within the designated app ecosystem of services, thus keeping as many transactions as possible within the system. Both OVO and Go-Pay can be described as peer-to-peer (P2P) payments to the extent that they allow users to connect and exchange value using an intermediary platform (Ford and Honan 2017). During the first weeks of my fieldwork in 2018, I assumed that drivers and passengers shared, if not the same, then at least a similar digital wallet infrastructure. After all, from my perspective, I was making digital payments with my Go-Pay wallet to their Go-Pay wallet. In an early interview, I came to realise that this was not the case, as a Grab driver walked me through the app as seen from his perspective. This became the starting point for investigating how the app was configuring our interactions through the platform.

When it comes to wallets, drivers have two, neither of which is the same as my Go-Pay wallet.[2] Instead, they have a 'cash' as well as a 'credit' wallet. When booking a trip through the app, the customer chooses whether to make the payment digitally or with cash. Notably, if the customer selects a digital payment, the app offers them a 20 per cent discount on the trip. Digital payments accrue in a driver's 'cash' wallet throughout the day, and can eventually be moved to a connected bank account, to be extracted as cash at an ATM. In the case of cash payment, the customer pays the full price, handing it to the driver at the end of the trip. The driver will earn the same 80 per cent of the fare because the company now extracts a 20 per cent cut from the 'credit' wallet, which the driver keeps 'topped-up' for this purpose throughout the day. Thus, the company not only forgoes their cut in the case of digital payment, but they also offer it as a price reduction to the customer. Once again, it is evident that the company has an interest in increasing the number of digital transactions, indicating that the real value of this P2P exchange is in the transactional meta-data rather than the fees earned on the transactions themselves.

It is important to note that P2P was originally a technical term used to describe a technological infrastructure where two computer systems connect and share files *without* requiring a central server. With the growing fintech industry, the term has come to be used to describe a wide range of economic exchanges ranging from remittances to microfinance, from blockchain to digital wallets in Indonesia. Not only does the term 'peer' have specific social connotations associated with socio-economic equality, but most of the contexts described above also, in fact, require a central intermediary to facilitate the transaction. This raises questions about what it means to be a peer in these contexts, and how the intermediary companies governing the platforms are configuring this alleged peerhood.

Let me describe a Gojek advertisement released in 2016.[3] A young girl is asking her mother if she will be home in time to break the fast for Ramadan that evening. Donning her distinctive green Gojek helmet, the mother gives the girl a small package, telling her to open it when she breaks the fast. We see multiple clips of the mother driving passengers to and fro. It is hot, she is tired, and all these customers are cranky and rude. Her final passenger is taking food to an orphanage for Ramadan, and as she watches all the happy children, the mother smiles despite everything. Meanwhile, her daughter opens the gift, a box of dates, alone. It contains a card from her mother, apologising because they cannot be together, and explaining that mom needs to make sure everyone else gets home in time to celebrate. Finally, alone on her scooter and having her first drink of water, the mother receives several messages, as customers send grateful thanks and positive ratings through the app.

Firstly, this advertisement presents the imagined participants in the exchange: the service provider and the service user. Secondly, besides the green helmet, the company itself is hardly present: their role as an intermediator of the exchange only becomes apparent towards the end, when the phone makes its first appearance. The advertisement emphasises that the users are social equals who are helping each other out in an important cultural and religious event. What it does not emphasise is the precarity of the seemingly single mother, who cannot be home since she must work long hours. Instead, it almost seems as if she is doing this work out of a sense of social responsibility towards her peers. Notably, money is never seen nor mentioned.

Interfaces, Incentives, and a System that 'Doesn't Wanna Know'

While we can view such advertisements as analytical clues, the apps themselves present relatively closed digital environments. As they come to dominate important social infrastructures such as storage and transaction of money, they present new challenges for ethnographic researchers, and it is important to develop ways to navigate their specific research affordances (Dieter et al. 2018). Light et al. (2018) suggest that by analysing the mechanisms, affordances, and culturally embedded references within the interfaces of an app, it is possible to interrogate its invisible infrastructures (see also Star 1999). During my field-work, informants would invariably turn to the app to illustrate their points, and I too found myself recording thousands of screenshots as a way of document-ing my encounters. It drew my attention to the specific dynamics that the app imposed between the service provider and service user, the supposed peers of the exchange.

One such example was the built-in, one-way rating mechanism. Passengers score drivers on a scale from 1 to 5 stars. As a passenger poises to swipe, the distance between one or five stars is a matter of millimetres, but for a driver, it could mean suspension or permanent exclusion. The consequence is that pas-sengers wield significant power over the drivers and can demand detours or additional services. The drivers I spoke with felt obliged to appease their cus-tomers out of fear of a negative rating. For drivers, features such as pre-defined routes and trip price, the seconds within which to decide to accept an order, and the serious repercussions of cancelling, all made it clear who was the real customer from the perspective of the company. The conditions for drivers are hardly transparent. For instance, in the passenger interface during a top-up transaction, it is possible to see the balance in the driver's account before requesting an exchange. What I, the passenger, cannot see, is that the driver does not have the option to decline the request: in effect, losing control of their digital balance while also relying on customers to honour the exchange by handing over the equivalent in cash money.

On 8 March 2019, the Gojek car drivers in Yogyakarta went on strike in response to the introduction of a new system for earning 'bonuses' (Lufityanti 2019; Susmayanti 2019). The bonus system allows drivers to accumulate points for completed trips, with the points accumulating towards three target tiers. Reaching each tier results in the driver earning a 'cash' bonus, which appears in their 'cash' wallet after midnight, and which comprises a significant proportion of their daily income. For many whom I spoke to, it is the 'bonus' that makes the work financially viable. In answer to my questions about daily working hours, drivers would tell me that they went home when they were able to *tupo*, short for *tutup poin*, or 'closing the points'. As one driver explained, if you can-not close the points, then the money disappears at midnight, when the system resets. The change that the drivers were protesting was the sudden introduc-tion of four different tier systems, known as *skema*. Without knowing why, some drivers found themselves with tiers that capped at half the number of points compared to others. Furthermore, the value of the bonuses for the highest tier now differed significantly from *skema* to *skema*. In practice, it meant that a driver with the worst *skema* could never earn as much as a driver with the best one, even if completing as many rides. The drivers shared many theories with me as to what determined which *skema* you would get, but a rough consensus seemed to indicate that the determining factor was how many trips a driver had completed in the past two weeks. Thus, the effect of not working for any period of time compounds, potentially reducing income for weeks afterwards.

Drivers also experienced inequalities in regard to which accounts were able to receive customer orders, distinguishing between accounts that are *gagu*, muted, and accounts that are *gacor*, short for *gampang cari orderan*, describing a state in which it is easy to find orders. One informant described calling Gojek customer service after spending several hours without a single order, only to be told that his account was active and that the system was working fine. *Sistem ngakk mau tahu!* drivers would frequently exclaim to me, 'the system doesn't wanna know'. In practice, where a driver's account falls on the scale of *gagu* to *gacor* is likely governed algorithmically, and drivers described multiple practices they would deploy to make sure their accounts ranked highly for order distribution.

In practice, drivers could be doing the same amount of work, in term of hours spent online and available to receive orders, and never have equal income opportunities. Not only does promotion of the notion of peerhood conceal embedded inequalities between the 'peers' on either side of the P2P acronym, it also does not convey the extent to which inequalities are induced and exacerbated within each 'peer group'. It also obfuscates the role of the intermediary in defining the terms of the relationship and how value is determined and circulated.

Conclusion

In this chapter, I have explored how anthropological conceptualisations of money as a social infrastructure for keeping account of debt relations can inform our study of digital payments by positioning digital forms of money as developments of accounting technology rather than evolutions on cash. With this conceptualisation, it becomes possible to draw ethnographic attention to the infrastructures that enable digital transactions to take place. Through my case study of digital wallets in Indonesia, I have examined how such infrastructures affect transactional behaviour and the social relations of those engaging through them. As economic transactions become increasingly screen-based, digital payments pose particular challenges for ethnographers. When the interaction is mediated through interfaces in an app or on a computer screen, it can be difficult to observe the subtle details that impact upon transactional decision making. Furthermore, central digital mechanisms that now govern the economic lives of respondents may change from one day to the next. As the infrastructure governing transactions can change with every update, this is a topic of study that feels like a perpetually moving and intangible target. Thus, as Lana Swartz and Bill Maurer (2017) encourage, we need to dig deeper to uncover the material traces of digital payments and examine the spaces in which the digital materialises.

To convey what is at stake in the digitalisation of payments, Brett Scott draws comparisons with the process of neighbourhood gentrification by wealthier population groups and corporate actors. Cash as a public, state-issued infrastructure is associated with a poorer population, often operating without receipts. 'Digital payment, however, is the domain of large-scale globalised financial corporations, and cannot be separated from them or taken out of their view. To use—or to be forced to use—digital payments is to enter their sphere of influence and power' (Scott 2019). As with neighbourhoods, this gentrification can lead to dispossession, particularly for those depending on cash to make a living. While the value represented by cash can change owner when cash changes hands, making a digital payment is to request that an intermediary change their record of accounts. Thus, taking an infrastructural perspective to digital payments foregrounds political questions of control: control of the accounts, but also of the terms for the circulation of value itself. It draws attention to the power that private actors hold in organising proprietary infrastructure to enable novel forms of wealth extraction, converting the user not just into a consumer but also into a commodity by monetising transactional metadata.

Here, ethnographic methods provide an access point through which we can examine aspects of this circulation of digital value and draw attention to the practical experiences of people living in the digital economy; whether they experience new forms of transactional hierarchy, of financial practice, or forms of exclusion or dispossession. It can explore how industry terminology obscures and obfuscates the power dynamics encoded in the payments infrastructure. In my case study, formerly self-organised *ojek* are gradually being pressured to participate in the platform economy, where they are mobilised as financially incentivised agents who bring even more people into this privatised digital credit system.

However, an ethnographic approach can also help us to look beyond the infrastructure itself to give us detailed and nuanced accounts of how people navigate the seemingly rigid technological parameters imposed with proprietary infrastructure: repurposing and appropriating systems beyond uses that its developers might have imagined. The online drivers of Yogyakarta deploy a variety of practices to navigate the infrastructure and use its affordances against itself—conspiring with customers, taking trips offline to avoid the company cut, making 'fake orders' to earn their daily points, and using third-party software to obscure their GPS data from the prying eyes of the platforms—thus enacting peerhood in ways that were simultaneously catalysed by the presence of the specific infrastructure, but which also subverted and rejected the premises posed by it.

NOTES

1. https://www.gojek.com/gopay/ and https://www.ovo.id/ respectively. Accessed 8 July 2021.
2. Both apps have since incorporated a third commercial wallet for drivers, allowing them to move their earnings directly into the wallet they would use as customers.
3. Viewable at: https://www.youtube.com/watch?v=_u_OHKHSq8s. Accessed 8 July 2021.

REFERENCES

Azali, K. (2016). Cashless in Indonesia: Gelling Mobile E-frictions? *Journal of Southeast Asian Economies, 33*, 364–386. https://doi.org/10.1355/ae33-3e.

Bohannan, L., & Bohannan, P. (1968). *Tiv Economy*. Evanston, IL: Northwestern University Press.

Brunton, F. (2017). Silver. In B. Maurer & L. Swartz (Eds.), *Paid: Tales of dongles, checks, and other money stuff* (pp. 246–258). Cambridge, MA: The MIT Press.

Brunton, F. (2019). *Digital cash: The unknown history of the anarchists, utopians, and technologists who created cryptocurrency*. Princeton, NJ: Princeton University Press.

Burling, R. (1962). Maximization theories and the study of economic anthropology. *American Anthropologist, 64*(4), 802–821. https://doi.org/10.1525/aa.1962.64.4.02a00090.

Burrell, J. (2018). Technology and Social Relations—Infrastructures of Digital Money. In *Money at the margins: Global perspectives on technology, financial inclusion, and design* (pp. 151–154). New York: Berghahn Books.

Callon, M. (1998). Introduction: The Embeddedness of Economic Markets in Economics. *The Sociological Review, 46*, 1–57. https://doi.org/10.1111/j.1467-954X.1998.tb03468.x.

Cancian, F. (1966). Maximization as Norm, Strategy, and Theory: A Comment on Programmatic Statements in Economic Anthropology. *American Anthropologist, 68*(2), 465–470. https://doi.org/10.1525/aa.1966.68.2.02a00110.

Cook, S. (1966). The obsolete "anti-market" mentality: A critique of the substantive approach to economic anthropology. *American Anthropologist, 68*(2), 323–345. https://doi.org/10.1525/aa.1966.68.2.02a00010.

Dalinghaus, U. (2019). *Virtually Irreplaceable: Cash as Public Infrastructure*. Irvine, CA: IMTFI. Retrieved from IMTFI website: https://www.cashmatters.org/documents/39/IMTFI_Whitepaper_A4_Download.pdf. Accessed 8 July 2021.

Dieter, M., Gerlitz, C., Helmond, A., Tkacz, N., van der Vlist, F., & Weltevrede, E. (2018). *Store, interface, package, connection: Methods and propositions for multi-situated app studies* (Working Paper No. 4). Universität Siegen: Collaborative Research Center Media of Cooperation.

Dodd, N. (2014). *The social life of money*. Princeton, NJ: Princeton University Press.

Donovan, K. P. (2018). "Financial Inclusion Means Your Money Isn't With You": Conflicts over Social Grants and Financial Services in South Africa. In B. Maurer,

S. Musaraj, & I. V. Small (Eds.), *Money at the margins: Global perspectives on technology, financial inclusion, and design* (pp. 155–178). New York: Berghahn Books.

Elyachar, J. (2010). Phatic labor, infrastructure, and the question of empowerment in Cairo. *American Ethnologist, 37*(3), 452–464. https://doi.org/10.1111/j.1548-1425.2010.01265.x

Elyachar, J. (2012). Next Practices: Knowledge, Infrastructure, and Public Goods at the Bottom of the Pyramid. *Public Culture, 24*(1), 109–129. https://doi.org/10.1215/08992363-1443583.

Ford, M., & Honan, V. (2017). The Go-Jek effect. In E. Jurriëns & R. Tapsell (Eds.), *Digital Indonesia: Connectivity and divergence* (pp. 275–288). Singapore: ISEAS-Yusof Ishak Institute.

Gibson-Graham, J. K. (2006). *The End of Capitalism (as we knew it): A feminist critique of political economy.* Minneapolis: University of Minnesota Press.

Graeber, D. (2001). *Toward an anthropological theory of value: The false coin of our own dreams.* New York: Palgrave.

Graeber, D. (2011). *Debt: The first 5000 years.* Brooklyn, NY: Melville House.

Graeber, D. (2013). It is value that brings universes into being. *HAU: Journal of Ethnographic Theory, 3*(2), 219–243. https://doi.org/10.14318/hau3.2.012.

Granovetter, M. (1985). Economic Action and Social Structure: The Problem of Embeddedness. *American Journal of Sociology, 91*(3), 481–510. https://doi.org/10.1086/228311.

Guyer, J. I. (2004). *Marginal gains: Monetary transactions in Atlantic Africa.* Chicago: University of Chicago Press.

Guyer, J. I. (2012). Soft currencies, cash economies, new monies: Past and present. *Proceedings of the National Academy of Sciences, 109*(7), 2214–2221. https://doi.org/10.1073/pnas.1118397109.

Hann, C. M., & Hart, K. (2011). *Economic anthropology: History, ethnography, critique.* Cambridge, UK and Malden, MA: Polity Press.

Hart, K. (1986). Heads or Tails? Two Sides of the Coin. *Man, 21*(4), 637–656. https://doi.org/10.2307/2802901.

Hart, K. (2007). Money is always personal and impersonal. *Anthropology Today, 23*(5), 12–16. https://doi.org/10.1111/j.1467-8322.2007.00536.x.

Ho, K. Z. (2009). *Liquidated: An ethnography of Wall Street.* Durham: Duke University Press.

Ingham, G. (2000). "Babylonian Madness": On the historical and sociological origins of money. In J. N. Smithin (Ed.), *What is money?* (pp. 16–41). London: Routledge.

James, D. (2015). *Money from nothing: Indebtedness and aspiration in South Africa.* Stanford, CA.: Stanford University Press.

Kolling, M. (2020). Debt and Dirty Names: Tracing Cashlessness and Urban Marginality in Brazil. In A. Sen, J. Lindquist & M. Kolling (Eds.), *Who's cashing in? Contemporary perspectives on new monies and global cashlessness* (pp. 19–31). New York: Berghahn Books.

Kusimba, S. (2018). Money, Mobile Money and Rituals in Western Kenya: The Contingency Fund and the Thirteenth Cow. *African Studies Review, 61*(2), 158–182. https://doi.org/10.1017/asr.2017.145.

Larkin, B. (2013). The Politics and Poetics of Infrastructure. *Annual Review of Anthropology, 42*(1), 327–343. https://doi.org/10.1146/annurev-anthro-092412-155522.

Light, B., Burgess, J., & Duguay, S. (2018). The walkthrough method: An approach to the study of apps. *New Media & Society, 20*(3), 881–900. https://doi.org/10.1177/1461444816675438.

Loubere, N. (2017). China's Internet Finance Boom and Tyrannies of Inclusion. *China Perspectives, 2017*(4), 9–18. https://doi.org/10.4000/chinaperspectives.7454.

Lufityanti, G. (2019, April 10). Mogok Makan Driver Ojek Online di Yogyakarta Masih Berlanjut. Retrieved November 12, 2020, from Tribun Jogja website: https://jogja.tribunnews.com/2019/04/10/mogok-makan-driver-ojek-online-di-yogyakarta-masih-berlanjut.

MacKenzie, D. (2008). *An engine, not a camera: How financial models shape markets.* Cambridge, MA: The MIT Press.

Malinowski, B. (2014[1922]). *Argonauts of the Western Pacific: An account of Native Enterprise and adventure in the Archipelagos of Melanesian New Guinea.* London: Routledge.

Maurer, B. (2006). The Anthropology of Money. *Annual Review of Anthropology, 35*(1), 15–36. https://doi.org/10.1146/annurev.anthro.35.081705.123127.

Maurer, B. (2012). Mobile Money: Communication, Consumption and Change in the Payments Space. *Journal of Development Studies, 48*(5), 589–604. https://doi.org/10.1080/00220388.2011.621944.

Maurer, B. (2016). Cashlessness, Ancient and Modern. In *The Archaeology of Money: Proceedings of the Workshop "Archaeology of Money", University of Tübingen, October 2013* (pp. 209–226). UC Irvine: School of Archaeology & Ancient History, University of Leicester. Retrieved from https://escholarship.org/uc/item/5f65n7cv. Accessed 8 July 2021.

Maurer, B. (2017). Money as Token and Money as Record in Distributed Accounts. In N. Enfield & P. Kockelman (Eds.), *Distributed Agency* (pp. 109–116). New York: Oxford University Press.

Maurer, B. (2018). Primitive and Nonmetallic Money. In S. Battilossi, Y. Cassis, & K. Yago (Eds.), *Handbook of the History of Money and Currency* (pp. 1–18). Singapore: Springer. https://doi.org/10.1007/978-981-10-0622-7_2-1.

Maurer, B., Musaraj, S., & Small, I. V. (Eds.) (2018). *Money at the margins: Global perspectives on technology, financial inclusion, and design.* New York: Berghahn Books.

Maurer, B., & Swartz, L. (Eds.) (2017). *Paid: Tales of dongles, checks, and other money stuff.* Cambridge, MA: The MIT Press.

Mauss, M. (2016[1925]). *The gift: Expanded edition* (trans: Guyer, J. I.). Chicago, IL: HAU Books.

Meillassoux, C. (1981[1975]). *Maidens, Meal and Money: Capitalism and the Domestic Community.* Cambridge: Cambridge University Press.

Nastiti, A. D. (2017). *Worker Unrest and Contentious Labor Practice of Ride-Hailing Services in Indonesia.* Presented at the Arryman Symposium, Buffet Institute, Northwestern University. http://www.isrsf.org/files/download/442. Accessed 8 July 2021.

O'Dwyer, R. (2015). *When Pipes Become Banks: Sociotechnical Control in the Infrastructure of Payments.* Presented at the International Society for Information Studies, Université du Québec à Montréal. https://www.academia.edu/13534431/When_Pipes_Become_Banks_Sociotechnical_Control_in_Virtual_Payments. Accessed 8 July 2021.

O'Dwyer, R. (2018). Cache society: Transactional records, electronic money, and cultural resistance. *Journal of Cultural Economy, 12*(2), 133–153. https://doi.org/1 0.1080/17530350.2018.1545243.

Ossandón, J., Ariztía, T., Barros, M., & Peralta, C. (2018). Accounting in the Margin: Financial Ecologies in between Big and Small data. In B. Maurer, S. Musaraj, & I. V. Small (Eds.), *Money at the margins: Global perspectives on technology, financial inclusion, and design* (pp. 200–219). New York: Berghahn Books.

Pangestu, M., & Dewi, G. (2017). Indonesia and the digital economy: Creative destruction, opportunities and challenges. In E. Jurriëns & R. Tapsell (Eds.), *Digital Indonesia: Connectivity and divergence* (pp. 227–255). Singapore: ISEAS-Yusof Ishak Institute.

Peebles, G. (2020). As Above, So Below: Reflections on the Democratisation of Demonetisation. In A. Sen, J. Lindquist, & M. Kolling (Eds.), *Who's cashing in? Contemporary perspectives on new monies and global cashlessness* (pp. 104–113). New York: Berghahn Books.

Polanyi, K. (2001[1944]). Chapter IV: Societies and Economic Systems. In *The Great Transformations*. Boston: Beacon Press. http://taodesigns.tripod.com/polyani/ polyani44IV.html. Accessed 8 July 2021.

Ravnbøl, C. I. (2020). Exclusively Simple: The Impact of Cashless Initiatives on Homeless Roma in Denmark. In A. Sen, J. Lindquist, & M. Kolling (Eds.), *Who's cashing in? Contemporary perspectives on new monies and global cashlessness* (pp. 3–18). New York: Berghahn Books.

Rea, S. C., Dalinghaus, U., Nelms, T. C., & Maurer, B. (2016). Riding the Rails of Mobile Payments—Financial Inclusion, Mobile Phones, and Infrastructure. In L. Hjorth, H. Horst, A. Galloway, & G. Bell (Eds.), *The Routledge companion to digital ethnography* (pp. 364–373). New York: Routledge, Taylor & Francis Group.

Rea, S. C., & Nelms, T. C. (2017). *Mobile Money: The First Decade* (pp. 1–35) [Working Paper]. California: IMTFI.

Roy, A. (2010). *Poverty capital: Microfinance and the making of development.* New York: Routledge.

Roy, A. (2018). In/Exclusion: The Question of Exclusion. In B. Maurer, S. Musaraj, & I. V. Small (Eds.), *Money at the margins: Global perspectives on technology, financial inclusion, and design* (pp. 19–21). New York: Berghahn Books.

Schmandt-Besserat, D. (1992). *Before writing, Vol. 1: From counting to cuneiform.* Austin: University of Texas Press.

Schneider, H. (1974). *Economic Man.* New York: Free Press.

Scott, B. (2017, March 1). In Praise of Cash. *Aeon.* https://aeon.co/essays/if-plastic-replaces-cash-much-that-is-good-will-be-lost. Accessed 26 April 2019.

Scott, B. (2019, January 15). Gentrification of Payments—Spreading the Digital Financial Net. *Longreads.* http://longreads.tni.org/state-of-power-2019/digital-payment-gentrification/. Accessed 22 May 2019.

Sen, A., Lindquist, J., & Kolling, M. (Eds.) (2020). *Who's cashing in? Contemporary perspectives on new monies and global cashlessness.* New York: Berghahn Books.

Simone, A. (2015). Passing things along: (In)completing infrastructure. *New Diversities, 17*(2), 151–162.

Star, S. L. (1999). The Ethnography of Infrastructure. *American Behavioural Scientist, 43*(3), 377–391. https://doi.org/10.1177/00027649921955326.

Strathern, M. (1992). Qualified value: The perspective of gift exchange. In C. Humphrey & S. Hugh-Jones (Eds.), *Barter, exchange, and value: An anthropological approach* (pp. 169–191). Cambridge: Cambridge University Press.

Susmayanti, H. (2019, April 12). Buntut Aksi Mogok Makan Pengemudi, Gojek Tutup Kantor Perwakilan Yogya. *Tribun Jogja*. https://jogja.tribunnews.com/2019/04/12/buntut-aksi-mogok-makan-pengemudi-gojek-tutup-kantor-perwakilan-yogya. Accessed 19 November 2021.

Swartz, L. (2017). Cards. In B. Maurer & L. Swartz (Eds.), *Paid: Tales of dongles, checks, and other money stuff* (pp. 84–97). Cambridge, MA: The MIT Press.

Swartz, L. (2018). What was Bitcoin, what will it be? The techno-economic imaginaries of a new money technology. *Cultural Studies, 32*(4), 623–650. https://doi.org/10.1080/09502386.2017.1416420.

Swartz, L. (2020). *New money: How payment became social media*. New Haven: Yale University Press.

Weiner, A. B. (1980). Reproduction: A replacement for reciprocity. *American Ethnologist, 7*(1), 71–85. https://doi.org/10.1525/ae.1980.7.1.02a00050.

Zaloom, C. (2006). *Out of the pits: Traders and technology from Chicago to London*. Chicago: University of Chicago Press.

Zelizer, V. A. R. (1995). *The social meaning of money*. New York, NY: Basic Books.

INDEX

Printed in the United States
by Baker & Taylor Publisher Services